TORTS

Commentary and Materials

Thomson Reuters (Professional) Australia Limited
100 Harris Street Pyrmont NSW 2009
Tel: (02) 8587 7000 Fax: (02) 8587 7100
LTA.Service@thomsonreuters.com
www.thomsonreuters.com.au
For all customer inquiries please ring 1300 304 195
(for calls within Australia only)

INTERNATIONAL AGENTS & DISTRIBUTORS

NORTH AMERICA
Thomson Reuters
Eagan
United States of America

ASIA PACIFIC
Thomson Reuters
Sydney
Australia

LATIN AMERICA
Thomson Reuters
São Paulo
Brazil

EUROPE
Thomson Reuters
London
United Kingdom

TORTS: COMMENTARY AND MATERIALS

CAROLYN SAPPIDEEN
Professor of Law
University of Western Sydney

PRUE VINES
Professor
University of New South Wales Faculty of Law

HELEN GRANT
Professor of Law
Elon University School of Law, North Carolina, USA

PENELOPE WATSON
Senior Lecturer
Macquarie University Division of Law

TENTH EDITION

LAWBOOK CO.2009

Published in Sydney by

Thomson Reuters (Professional) Australia Limited ABN 64 058 914 668

100 Harris Street, Pyrmont, NSW

First edition, WL Morison 1955

Second edition, WL Morison, N Morris, RL Sharwood ... 1962

2nd impression 1967

Third edition, WL Morison, RL Sharwood, CL Pannam... 1967

2nd impression 1971

3rd impression 1972

Fourth edition, WL Morison, RL Sharwood, CS Phegan . 1973

2nd impression 1975

3rd impression 1979

Fifth edition, WL Morison, CS Phegan, C Sappideen 1981

Sixth edition, WL Morison, CS Phegan, C Sappideen 1985

Seventh edition, WL Morison, C Sappideen 1989

Eighth edition, WL Morison, C Sappideen 1996

Ninth edition 2006

Tenth edition 2009

National Library of Australia
Cataloguing-in-Publication entry
Title: Torts: commentary and materials / Carolyn Sappideen ... [et al.].
Edition: 10th ed.

ISBN: 9780455226866 (pbk.)
Notes: Includes index.
Subjects: Torts--Australia--Cases. Torts--Cases.
Other Authors/Contributors:
Sappideen, C. (Carolyn)
Dewey Number: 346.9403

Editor: Lara Weeks
Product Developer: Sarah Hullah
Publisher: Robert Wilson
Printed by Ligare Pty Ltd, Riverwood, NSW

This book has been printed on paper certified by the Programme for the Endorsement of Forest Certification (PEFC). PEFC is committed to sustainable forest management through third party forest certification of responsibly managed forests. For more info: www.pefc.org

PREFACE

This tenth edition of the casebook provided the authors the opportunity to review the content and manageability of the ninth edition. The ninth edition incorporated the changes brought by the civil liability legislation in Australia. The three years following the ninth edition have seen the courts grapple with the key concepts of autonomy and responsibility underpinning the civil liability legislation. The principal authorities exploring the reach of the legislation and its impact on the common law are extracted in this edition. The civil liability legislation is replete with what are effectively new defences. The common lawyer would be surprised to find matters which would be considered breach of duty issues being regarded as matters of defence. For example, the professional standard of care, the statutory *Bolam* test, is a defence. Similarly matters related to what is an obvious risk, dangerous recreational activities, are statutory defences.

The authors have been mindful that a casebook needs to be manageable for students. Consequently the length of the casebook has been significantly reduced, many of the case extracts reduced in length and the previous separate chapters on Standard of Care and Breach of Duty combined into a single chapter, Chapter 12.

The authors wish to thank Lawbook Co. for its generous help and support and for the many staff that assisted us throughout, including Sarah Hullah, Lara Weeks and Robert Wilson.

CAROLYN SAPPIDEEN
PRUE VINES
HELEN GRANT
PENELOPE WATSON

July 2009

ACKNOWLEDGMENTS

Extracts have been reprinted in this text with the kind permission of the:

Attorney General's Department – Commonwealth Government of Australia (Commonwealth Copyright Administration, Copyright Law Branch): http://www.ag.gov.au

- Negligence Review Panel, Review of the Law of Negligence: Final Report (Commonwealth of Australia, Canberra 2002)

Attorney General's Department, Western Australia (Government of Western Australia): http://www.wa.gov.au

- Western Australian Reports (WAR)

Council of Law Reporting for New South Wales:

- New South Wales Law Reports. © Council of Law Reporting for New South Wales

Council of Law Reporting for Victoria (Consultative Council of Australian Law Reporting):

- Victorian Law Reports (VLR)
- Victorian Reports (VR)

Incorporated Council of Law Reporting for England & Wales: http://www.lawreports.co.uk

- Appeal Cases (AC)
- Chancery Reports
- King's Bench (KB)
- Queen's Bench (QB)
- Weekly Law Reports (WLR)

LexisNexis Butterworths Sydney: http://www.lexisnexis.com.au

- Australian Law Reports (ALR)

LexisNexis Butterworths London: http://www.lexisnexis.co.uk

- All England Reports (All ER)

The Honourable Chief Justice J Spigelman AC: http://www.lawlink.nsw.gov.au/sc

- The Honourable Chief Justice J Spigelman AC, The New Liability Structure in Australia. Address to the Swiss Re: Liability Conference (Sydney, 14 September 2004). © The Honourable Chief Justice J Spigelman AC

Thomson Reuters (Professional) Australia Limited: http://www.thomsonreuters.com.au

- Australian Criminal Reports (A Crim R)
- Australian Law Journal Reports (ALJR)
- Commonwealth Law Reports (CLR)
- Federal Court Reports (FCR)
- Federal Law Reports (FLR)

Thomson Reuters (Professional) Australia Limited, is grateful to the publishers, authors, and government departments, who have allowed us to reproduce extracts of their work in this book. While every effort has been taken to establish and acknowledge copyright, the publiser tenders its apology for any accidental infringement. The publisher would be pleased to come to a suitable agreement with the rightful owners in each case.

TABLE OF CONTENTS

TABLE OF CASES

A

B

C

D

E

F

G

H

I

J

K

L

M

N

O

Q

R

S

T

X

Y

Z

TABLE OF STATUTES

NEW SOUTH WALES

NORTHERN TERRITORY

SOUTH AUSTRALIA

UNITED STATES

UNITED KINGDOM

TREATIES AND CONVENTIONS

PART 1: INTRODUCTION

PART 1

CHAPTER 1

Introduction

INTRODUCTION

[1.05] It is usual for torts casebooks to begin by considering what is tort law? But definitions referring to torts as the law of civil wrongs have trouble in going beyond this, and then need to distinguish torts from contract (breach of which is clearly a civil wrong) and criminal law (which is clearly about wrongs, but is not civil law).

The following is a useful attempt at explaining what the law of torts is about:

> The law of torts concerns the obligations of persons living in a crowded society to respect the safety, property, and personality of their neighbours, both as an a priori matter [that is, a matter of cause and effect] and as a duty to compensate for wrongfully caused harm, ex post [after the fact]. Tort law, in other words, involves questions of how people should treat one another and the rules of proper behaviour that society imposes on each citizen for avoiding improper harm to others, and for determining when compensation for harm is due. (D Owen, "Why Philosophy Matters to Tort Law", in D Owen (ed), *Philosophical Foundations of Tort Law* (Clarendon Press, Oxford, 1995), p 7.)

This explanation suggests that tort law has a function. It seems more useful to explore that function and whether tort law is useful in achieving its goals than to continue fruitless searches for definitions.

One of the perennial arguments in this area of law turns on whether there is a unifying principle underlying it. Perhaps coincidentally, this is embodied in Australia in the names of the two major journals covering the topic – the *Torts Law Journal* and the *Tort Law Review*. Sir John Salmond, the great New Zealand torts lawyer, thought that torts was just a miscellaneous collection of causes of action, bound together by no more than historical accident. The name *Torts Law Journal* seems based on this premise. On the other hand Pollock (*Pollock on Torts* (14th ed, PA Landon, 1939)) and Winfield (Winfield, "The Foundation of Liability in Tort" (1927) 22 Col L Rev, 1-11) argued that there was an underlying principle or set of principles fundamental to the law of tort. They pointed, for example, to obligation imposed by law rather than the person, to duties owed to the world at large rather than an individual, and to a range of interests being protected (such as personal integrity, reputation and economic and property interests). The name *Tort Law Review* seems to reflect this attitude. The debate continues. In this book we use the terms "tort" and "torts" interchangeably without implying any view on the merits of either standpoint.

There are many causes of action in tort. The historical context out of which they arose is long, but may be fairly briefly stated. At the end of the 12th century, the writ of trespass was used to deal with direct and forcible interference with the person, land or goods. Trespass had a peacekeeping function, which is why it retains its link with the criminal law. For a trespass to lie, a direct act was required. The forms of action were so rigidly defined that many indirect or consequential injuries could not be dealt with. In the 13th century the action of trespass on the case, or trespass on the similar case, or merely "case", developed to deal with consequential or indirect injuries. This development is discussed in Chapter 2. The classic difference between direct and indirect harm is shown by the difference between a person hitting another person on the head with a stick (direct) as opposed to dropping the stick on the road so that the other person trips over it (indirect or consequential).

The dominant cause of action in tort today is the tort of negligence. Negligence arose out of the action on the case. So did a number of other torts such as nuisance, defamation, malicious prosecution, deceit and conversion. One of the most significant attributes of an action on the case is that it requires proof of damage. For example, it is impossible to prove a case of negligence unless one can prove that the plaintiff has suffered damage.

Another very large group of torts are those based on trespass: trespass to goods, trespass to property, and trespass to person. Trespass to the person includes the torts of assault, battery and wrongful imprisonment. These will be discussed in Chapter 3.

There are other areas of liability that originally derived from actions on the case but are still developing as fully-fledged torts, for example, the tort of *Wilkinson v Downton* [1897] 2 QB 57 or intentional infliction of nervous shock.

It appears that the many types of torts can be classified not only by their origins but also by what they protect. For example, torts which protect the physical integrity of the person include negligence, assault, battery and false imprisonment; other torts protect a person's property (for example, trespass to land), or their enjoyment of property (nuisance, negligence); still others protect a person's reputation (for example, defamation) or other rights (for example, misfeasance in public office, malicious prosecution) or economic interests (passing off, interference with contract, negligence, and deceit).

[1.10] **Notes&Questions**

1. Does the explanation above differentiate tort from contract or other areas of law such as equity? Should it? Could you recognise a tort from this explanation?
2. Peter Cane in *The Anatomy of Tort Law* (Hart Publishing, Oxford, 1997) at vii, says: "For me, tort law is an exercise in applied ethics". In his view tort law is about applied principles of morality. As you read this book you might consider whether you agree with him.
3. How is tort law to be distinguished from contract and criminal law? Consider this scenario: Joseph has agreed to buy a car from Michael and has paid him $1000 for it. When he arrives to buy the car, Michael says to him, "I am not going to give you the car", and tries to give the money back. Joseph is very angry about this and punches Michael in the head, knocking him down. The police arrive and take Joseph into

custody and Michael to hospital. Michael is quite badly injured and is unable to work for three months. What aspects of this scenario might give rise to contractual, criminal law or tort issues?

Further reading

M Tilbury, "Remedies and the Classification of Obligations" and A Robertson, ""On the Distinction Between Contract and Tort"", both in A Robertson (ed), *The Law of Obligations: Connections and Boundaries* (Cavendish Press, Coogee, 2004).

THE ROLE OF TORT LAW

[1.15] Many answers have been given to the question, "what is the role of tort law?" In this book many of these functions are reflected in judicial statements, statutes and in theoretical writing. They may work together or conflict with each other. These roles may operate effectively or not. The following discussion considers some of the possible purposes of tort law.

Compensatory function

[1.20] Stated simply, the function of tort law is seen by many to be compensation for people who are injured by a wrong. For example, damages may be awarded where a person has been injured by the negligence of another. The injury might be to their person (personal injury) or to their property. When the damages are awarded they are awarded on the basis that the person should be put back into the position he or she would have been in had the accident not happened, so far as money can achieve that. In this instance damages are given as compensation. How successful is tort law at doing this?

The use of the tort of negligence as a regulatory framework for compensation is clearly inadequate. Where the law is dealing with personal injury, we know, for example, that in cases of catastrophic loss, such as where a person becomes quadriplegic as a result of an accident, that, even large sums of damages have tended to run out because of the difficulty of predicting the future. In the 1970s it was impossible to predict the changes to wages of both nurses and carers and the fact that the life expectancy of quadriplegics would so dramatically increase into the 1990s and beyond. Many people who were given very large awards, even record-breaking awards at the time, found that they were simply inadequate to keep them in modest comfort for their lifetime. A well-known example is the case of Gillian Thurston, who received a record award of £69,000 in 1965 for the quadriplegia she suffered as a result of a car accident. Despite careful investment of the award, eight years later in 1973 the gross income was less than the cost of the nursing she required even with her mother nursing her for seven hours a day (see *Thurston v Todd* [1965] NSWR 1158, affirmed (1966) 84 WN (Pt 1) (NSW) 231).

Part of the reason for this is the common law rule that damages must be paid in a lump sum. As Lord Scarman said in *Lim Poh Choo v Camden and Islington Health Area Authority* [1980] AC 174 at 183:

> Knowledge of the future being denied to mankind, so much of the award as is to be attributed to future loss and suffering – in many cases the major part of the award- will almost surely be wrong. There is really only one certainty: the future will prove the award to be either too high or too low.

There are other problems with seeing tort law as having a compensatory function – tort law requires the injured person to be able to prove that someone else caused the harm. In the absence of fault no compensation will be available. Thus a person who falls off a ladder in their own home and is badly injured may have no compensation while a person who has the identical accident but can show it happened in his or her place of employment by the fault of somebody will receive compensation. Ison called this the "forensic lottery" (T Ison, *The Forensic Lottery: A Critique of Tort Liability as a System of Personal Injury Compensation* (Staple Press, London, 1967)). To illustrate the problem it is useful to consider the statistics about where accidents happen. Australian Hospital Statistics for 2006-2007 showed that of the 878,000 people hospitalised for personal injury, the percentage who were injured in particular places was as follows:

TABLE 1.1 Australian Hospital Statistics: 2006-2007

Location of Injury	%
Health service area (complications of medical and surgical care)	38.98
Home/Residential institution	20.91
Highway	6.31
At work (trade, service, industry and construction (including farm 0.52%)	3.16
Sporting events	2.61
School	0.92

Source: Australian Institute of Health and Welfare, Australian Hospital Statistics 2006-2007, Table 11.5 http://www.aihw.gov.au/publications/hse/ahs06-07 (accessed 7 May 2009).

The *Quality in Australian Health Care Study* of 1995 found that 16.6% of all admissions to hospital were caused by "adverse events" – that is, by medical care. Later studies seem to confirm this rate (see Wilson and Van der Weyden, "The Safety of Australian Healthcare: 10 Years after QAHS" (2005) 182(6) *Medical Journal of Australia* 260). Only a very small proportion of people take claiming action for medical negligence and an even smaller proportion win their cases – in the United States one study found that about 10% of the people injured by medical attention sue; of those, about 50% settle the case before the matter is filed in court, another 40% of those were settled before the case went to trial, and only 10% actually went to trial. The evidence in Australia also suggests that the vast majority of medical accidents are never litigated. (Indeed, the few studies that have been done show that the vast majority of people do not litigate even where they have a reasonable case, see D Harris, et al, *Compensation and Support for Illness and Injury* (Clarendon Press, Oxford, 1984).)

After complications of medical and surgical care, the most common place to have an accident was at home where it is unlikely that someone could be sued for damages. This has led some people to argue for no-fault compensation schemes. In Victoria, the Motor Accident compensation scheme is a no-fault scheme, and in New Zealand (since 1974) there has been a no-fault scheme which covers all accidents. Others criticise these schemes since although they cover a broader range of claimants, they usually give a lesser amount of compensation (a percentage of average weekly earnings for example) than the tort system gives each individual.

Tort law as a compensatory function is therefore problematic. Recognition of some of these problems has led distributive justice theorists (theorists who argue that the important issue is how goods and/or harms are distributed amongst people in society) to argue that other ways of spreading both the risk of harm and the liability to pay compensation would be more effective. We discuss some of these below at [1.45].

[1.25] **Notes&Questions**

1. In the 1990s many jurisdictions placed "caps" or restrictions on the amount of damages that could be paid in an attempt to stop damages awards "blowing out". The amounts were further limited in the tort reform legislation that was passed in all the jurisdictions from 2002. What effect would this have on people who were catastrophically injured, such as those with quadriplegia? In fact, the number of catastrophic injury claims is quite small. The Minister for Transport in New South Wales, Mr J Watson, in introducing the *Motor Accidents (Lifetime Care and Support) Act 2006* (which provides for no-fault compensation for such people) observed that only half of the catastrophically injured people (approximately 250 per year in New South Wales) were compensated for their injury through the tort system (Hansard, NSW Parliament, Legislative Assembly, 9th March, 2006, p 21400).
2. Small claims, for example damages for broken ribs in a car accident, make up a significant proportion of the damages paid altogether by the tort system. According to I Nadarajah and H Jones, *Public Liability Handbook* (Thomson CPD, Kew, 2002) at 44, the average personal injury claim was for $25,000, and the average property damage claim for $5000, in 2001-2002. Less than 1% of claims were settled for more than $500,000, but these claims added up to 20% of the total costs of claims. To what extent do you think that small claims should be restricted in order to ensure that larger claims can be met?
3. Should the aim to compensate be abandoned as an aim of tort law if it is not adequately fulfilled?
4. It is estimated that the cost of personal injury to the community in NSW for the year 1998-1999 was $3.5 billion:
   Mary Potter-Forbes and Chris Aisbett, *Injury Costs: A Valuation of the Burden of Injury in New South Wales* (NSW Injury Risk management Research Centre, UNSW, 2003). The highest number of deaths from injury in Australia in 2003-2004 were caused by suicide (22%), followed by road traffic accidents (17%), poisoning (11%) and falls (30%) (G Henley, K Kreisfeld and J Harrison *Injury Deaths Australia 2003-04*, Australian Institutes of Health and Welfare, 2007). This reflects the male pattern with suicide at the top. Females were less likely to commit suicide and road traffic accidents were more likely to cause their deaths. The number of injuries leading to attendance at hospital is very high. The figures for 2004-2007 give rise to the following table:

TABLE 1.2: Leading causes of injury and poisoning hospital separations in persons of all ages, by sex, NSW 2004-05 to 2006-07

Rank for persons	Cause	Persons number per year	Persons per cent	Males number per year	Males per cent	Females number per year	Females per cent
1	Fall	56,789	38.3	25,192	29.9	31,596	49.3
2	Motor vehicle transport	15,433	10.4	10,258	12.2	5,175	8.1
3	Exposure to unspecified factor	14,543	9.8	9,388	11.2	5,156	8.0
4	Other injury/ poisoning	14,130	9.5	9,234	11.0	4,896	7.6

Rank for persons	Cause	Persons number per year	Persons per cent	Males number per year	Males per cent	Females number per year	Females per cent
5	Self harm	9,125	6.2	3,560	4.2	5,564	8.7
6	Struck by/against (unintentional)	7,376	5.0	5,615	6.7	1,761	2.7
7	Interpersonal violence	7,061	4.8	5,451	6.5	1,610	2.5
8	Cut/Pierce (unintentional)	6,498	4.4	4,789	5.7	1,708	2.7
9	Poisoning (unintentional)	3,872	2.6	1,889	2.2	1,983	3.1
10	Natural/ environmental factors	3,872	2.6	2,244	2.7	1,628	2.5
11	Overexertion/ repetitive movement	3,185	2.1	2,022	2.4	1,163	1.8
12	Fire/Burns	1,957	1.3	1,199	1.4	758	1.2
13	Threats to breathing (unintentional)	1,902	1.3	1,113	1.3	789	1.2
14	Machinery	1,785	1.2	1,669	2.0	116	0.2
15	Water transport (excluding drowning)	278	0.2	207	0.2	72	0.1
16	Drowning	214	0.1	159	0.2	56	0.1
17	Air transport	76	0.1	70	0.1	6	0.0
18	Rail transport	59	0.0	31	0.0	27	0.0
19	Firearm (uninten-tional)	35	0.0	33	0.0	2	0.0

Source: NSW Admitted Patient Data Collection and ABS population estimates (HOIST). Centre for Epidemiology and Research, NSW Department of Health.

What conclusions can be drawn from this table?

Deterrent function, law and economics, and insurance

[1.30] At its simplest, deterrence theory argues that if the wrongdoer is punished or made to pay for an accident he or she will try to avoid such accidents in future. For example, the argument might be made that employers who have to pay compensation to an employee who is hurt at work will create systems to ensure that that does not happen again; similarly, that manufacturers who are sued for injuring a person through the negligent manufacture of an item, will work to ensure that they do not have to pay that cost again. There may be some evidence for this argument, in that manufacturing organisations may have planning processes that take such issues into account. However, does this apply equally to individuals? What of the driver of the motor vehicle? Does the law of negligence have a deterrent effect on the driver's decision to drive fast or poorly?

The authors submit that, in terms of legal remedies, the fear of criminal prosecution is more likely to deter a driver from speeding or drink driving than tort law. The evidence that tort law has a deterrent effect is not particularly strong.

In relation to medical injuries, the evidence is not that there is no deterrent effect, but that there may be an over-reaction leading to over-servicing by the medical profession in relation to the prospect of being sued. The Harvard Medical Practice Study Group (in their study, *Patients, Doctors and Lawyers: Medical Injury, Malpractice Litigation and Patient Compensation in New York* (Harvard University Press, Cambridge, 1990)) found no evidence that the number of medical accidents was reduced by higher rates of litigation. Presumably, if tort law is effective as a deterrent there would be more accidents where tort law does not apply, and this has not proved to be the case in New Zealand where the Accident Compensation Scheme removes fault-based liability.

The notion that finding a person liable for a wrong will deter them or others from doing the same action again is also frequently seen as a function of tort law. Some of the strongest proponents of this view of tort law are law and economics scholars such as Guido Calabresi (*The Cost of Accidents: A Legal and Economic Analysis* (Yale University Press, New Haven, 1970)) and Richard Posner (and W Landes, *The Economic Structure of Tort Law* (Harvard University Press, Cambridge, 1987)). Calabresi argues that the goal of accident law should be to reduce the cost of accidents, while taking into account that our systems do not require the protection of life at all costs and that the system must be fair. He acknowledges that the latter is a difficult matter to achieve. Calabresi argues that to reduce the cost of accidents, a range of deterrents must be used, including various forms of loss-spreading, for example, by the use of insurance, and loss-shifting by the use of a fault principle of some kind so that the person who is at fault must pay. His central insight is that not only accidents, but the prevention of accidents costs money. Posner argues differently, suggesting that there is an inherent economic structure in the common law that can be identified. In his view the body of case law is effectively the market and the market adjusts to create the most efficient outcome. That is, in Posner's view, the laws of negligence work to create the most efficient outcome. The criterion he uses to determine efficiency is "Pareto efficiency". This is achieved when a transaction makes a person better off without making any other person worse off. He accepts a version of this known as Kaldor-Hicks efficiency, which accepts that a transaction is efficient if it leads to an overall gain so that the winners *could* compensate the losers out of their winnings. Needless to say this is a controversial theory since it regards as efficient the situation where one person might get a massive gain if in theory they could give other people compensation out of that gain.

The economic analysis of law in many cases begins with the concept of transaction costs. Transaction costs are the costs associated with any transaction including legal transactions. For example, they may include court costs, lawyer's fees, the time taken to finish the court case. They might also include non-monetary costs. The Coase Theorem, for which Ronald Coase ("The Problem of Social Cost" (1960) *Journal of Law and Economics* 1) won the Nobel Prize for economics, is stated by Markesinis and Deakin in this way:

> The assignment of legal rights and liabilities has no implications for economic efficiency as long as the parties involved in a particular dispute can bargain costlessly, that is to say, with *zero transaction costs*, to resolve that dispute. (BS Markesinis and SF Deakin, *Tort Law* (4th ed, Oxford University Press, Oxford, 1999), p 25.)

On this view, what matters to the parties concerned is not just what their legal rights are, but what their rights cost them – if the legal right would be attributed to one person, but it is worth more to the second person, the second person will buy it from the first. If the cost of obtaining a legal right (the transaction costs, for example court costs, lost profits while pursuing the right, the cost of time etc) is too high, a person may forgo the legal right. So if transactions costs are high this will have a significant impact on the use of legal rules. For example, if John is injured in a car accident when Fred is driving and John is injured to an extent which would cost $15,000 to put right, then John may consider taking Fred to court and suing him for negligence. However, if taking Fred to court will cost John $15,000 in court filing fees and costs for lawyers he will probably not bother to take him to court.

Another issue related to both economics and deterrence is insurance. If one considers loss spreading as a means of deterrence this allows us to consider the impact of insurance on negligence law. It can be argued that insurance actually prevents deterrence because the person at fault does not pay for their wrong, but merely pays their premium. This depends on the kind of insurance being used. Sometimes insurance premiums are varied on the basis of the history of the insured. It should be remembered that insurance varies from public insurance, such as social security, to private insurance taken out entirely at the will of the insured. Insurance is either indemnity (the insurer has to compensate the insured for the loss) or non-indemnity (the insurer compensates on the occurrence of a specified event regardless of the loss, for example, the insurer has to pay on the death of the insured). The most important category of insurance for tort purposes is liability insurance, which is a form of indemnity insurance. Indemnity insurance is important because it allows the insurer to take control of the legal proceedings (described technically, it confers the equitable right of subrogation on the insurer), so that the insurer stands in the shoes of and can make decisions for the insured. Important categories of insurance to consider for tort law are:

- First party insurance: when an insurer contracts to pay the insured on the occurrence of a particular or event or to cover a specified loss. Life insurance relates to an event and house insurance indemnifies the insured against loss. In either case, the loss is paid for regardless of whether the tort system is involved or not.
- Third party insurance: where a person insures themselves against having to pay money to someone else. Liability insurance is the most significant of these for tort law. In Australia it is compulsory in most jurisdictions for drivers to have third party personal injury insurance so that if they are at fault and cause an accident and have to pay for another person's injury they are covered and the person will be able to get compensation without the first person having to pay it all from their own pocket. Medical indemnity insurance protects medical practitioners in the event of a claim against them. Occupier's liability insurance is similar. The insurer will pay the claim of damages for the insured after the tort system completes its machinations. Thus it protects both the insured from having to pay, and perhaps becoming bankrupt as a consequence, and the injured plaintiff from having a damages award that will not be paid.
- Public insurance: covers everyone (the public) by reason of government action, for example, social security in the form of disability pensions, unemployment benefits (etc) which cover individuals if they lose their job or become disabled. In Australia this is a fairly limited protection that is not adequate for the severely injured.
- Insurance also may include a system of variable premiums so that a person (or class of persons) likely to cause harm will have to pay higher premiums. This is the case, for example, with Workers' Compensation insurance. Where a business has a history of making claims their premiums will rise compared with other similar businesses. So deterrence might operate in the context of insurance in such a situation.

For many years tort law cases, and especially negligence cases, were decided while ignoring the existence of insurance. A very few cases have taken it into account in relation to liability (see *Lynch v Lynch* (1991) 25 NSWLR 411). However, it has been far more common for courts to deliberately ignore the existence of insurance in personal injury cases (*Davie v New Merton*

Board Mills Ltd [1959] AC 604; *Dobson v Dobson* [1999] 2 SCR 753). Evidence of insurance is not generally admissible in jury trials, although it has been argued by some that the fact (or assumption) of the availability of insurance allows judges or juries to set damages at a very high level.

Insurance is now a fundamental part of our society. Insurance risks are assessed on a statistical basis in populations and the individual insured is considered in terms of statistical data. By contrast, tort law focuses on the interaction between two individual parties, and in the common law systems it actually allows the two parties to control the process, with the judge acting more like "referee" than investigator. This focus on the individual parties means that it is difficult for the law to deal with areas of law or fact which depend on the evaluation of evidence about populations. One example is epidemiological evidence in medicine, another being the ramifications of insurance.

It is frequently argued that insurance prevents the deterrent function of tort law from operating by preventing the damages flowing from the wrongdoer. There is clearly some truth in this statement, but it ignores two things. One, is that any deterrent effect may also flow from the fact of being blamed and bad publicity associated with such blame; there is also the question of increased premiums which may operate as a more effective deterrent than blame does, simply because they reappear every year to remind the insured of the desired behaviour. The second is that insurance may actually operate to remediate one of the troubling aspects of the dominant tortious action, negligence: often a wrongful act seems relatively blameless and the reparation required disproportionate to the blameworthiness of the behaviour. For example, a moment's inattention in a motor vehicle may lead to a catastrophic loss (see J Waldron, "Moments of Carelessness and Massive Loss" in D Owen (ed), *Philosophical Foundations of Tort Law* (Clarendon Press, Oxford, 1995)). Negligence is not about intentional harm; it is about accidental harm. In such a case insurance may operate to equalise the level of proportionality between the wrongful act and the harm done, at least where premiums are affected by assessment of risk and the track record of the insured, while the injured party still gets needed compensation.

[1.35] **Notes&Questions**

1. When you are driving your car to go to a party, which matters are likely to be the greater deterrent to speeding:

   (1) The likelihood that you the driver might get a speeding fine?

   (2) The likelihood that you the driver might have to pay compensation to a person who gets injured?

   (3) The likelihood that someone may get hurt?

   What does your answer tell you about the importance of tort law as a deterrent? Would your answer be different if you were considering a situation where you were the manufacturer of a product? Negligence fundamentally relates to carelessness and carelessness is a state of inadvertence. Can a person be "deterred" from being inadvertent? We can say to drivers "be more careful" but what do you think is the function of the law of negligence if someone, inadvertently, was careless?

2. Should the courts ignore insurance when they are deciding a case? Why or why not?

Further reading

G Schwartz, "Reality in the Economic Analysis of Tort Law: Does Tort Law Really Deter?" (1994) 42 UCLA L Rev 377.

J Stapleton, "Tort, Insurance and Ideology" (1995) 58 *Modern Law Review* 820.

P Vines, "Tort Reform, Insurance and Responsibility" (2002) 25(3) UNSWLJ 842.

Corrective justice

[1.40] The view that negligence law (and indeed much of tort law) is in some sense about moral rights is one of the dominant theories in tort law today. "Corrective justice" is the collective name for a number of theories that suggest moral rights as the basis of torts like negligence and trespass. Theories like that of Weinrib (EJ Weinrib, et al, "The Special Morality of Tort Law" (1989) 34 McGill LJ 403; and EJ Weinrib, "Towards a Moral Theory of Negligence Law" (1983) 2 *Law and Philosophy* 37) are concerned with responsibility. They ask: when is a person who causes harm regarded as responsible to compensate for the harm caused, that is, to pay damages? These theories are theories about individuals. They argue that individuals have specific obligations that are directly connected to rights. In another version of corrective justice, Perry ("The Moral Foundation of Tort Law" (1992) 77 *Iowa Law Review* 449) argues that this individualised sense of fault should be put together with "outcome responsibility", which is the theory that those who cause harm are responsible for it even if they are not at fault or "blameworthy". The argument is that when a person can be seen as causally responsible it makes moral sense for the proportion of loss shifted from the plaintiff to the defendant to be correlated with the level of blameworthiness of the defendant compared with other causally responsible people (the retributive element). For a retributive account of the need for maintaining proportionality between the wrong and the damages, see A Honore, "The Morality of Tort Law" in Owen (ed), *Philosophical Foundations of Tort Law* (Clarendon Press, Oxford, 1995). See proportionate liability in Chapter 15, Concurrent Liability.

Implicit in this argument is the view that free human agency underlies responsibility – "an agent is responsible for all and only his intentional actions" (see JL Mackie, *Ethics: Inventing Right and Wrong* (Penguin, Harmondsworth, 1977), p 208). Here the word "intentional" is used in the general way, rather than in the legal sense. One way of putting this is that an agent is only responsible for actions that he or she could have avoided. It can be argued that this is one of the reasons for the power of the concept of foreseeability in the law of negligence. One can only avoid what one can foresee.

However, the question of what one should avoid can have different answers according to notions of personal responsibility. If fault and responsibility are regarded as being about social welfare, that is ensuring the community as a whole does well, the moral objectives differ and the language of personal responsibility will shift to the language of collective responsibility and risk-bearing. The idea of collective responsibility and risk-bearing refers to the notion that a community as a whole might be regarded as deciding on the level of a risk to be borne together and therefore recognise that when a person suffers the outcome of that risk they should be compensated by the community. See [1.45] below on distributive justice and risk allocation. There have been times when judges have appeared to lean this way, but in Australia in recent years the concept of personal responsibility has been firmly focused on the individual's responsibility to care for him or herself. This orientation has also been the source of some of the reforms to the law of tort which are discussed below.

Further reading
C Schroeder, "Corrective Justice and Liability for Increasing Risks" (1990) 37 UCLA Law Review 439.

P Vines, "Fault, Responsibility and Negligence in the High Court of Australia" (2000) 8(2) *Tort Law Review* 130.

E Weinrib, "Correlativity, Personality and the Emerging Consensus on Corrective Justice" (2001) 2 *Theoretical Inquiries in Law* 107.

Distributive justice and risk allocation

[1.45] Another way of thinking about justice and moral responsibility is to think about tort law as a way of distributing goods, risks and losses. For example, the decision by a court to allocate responsibility to one party or another affects the distribution of the loss – either it remains on the injured person or the cost of that is shifted to the tortfeasor. If a public authority such as a council is involved and they are held responsible, the risk and the loss may be distributed amongst the ratepayers; if insurers are used, the loss is distributed amongst the premium payers. Distributive justice also considers how risk is distributed. Consider vaccines such as the pertussis (whooping cough) vaccine. The benefit of the vaccine (immunity from a disease which used to kill many infants) is distributed amongst the entire population except for the 1 or 2 people who are injured by side effects of the vaccine. They thus bear the burden of the risk for society as a whole. It has been suggested that the tort system fails in dealing with these kinds of cases in its focus on an individual wrongdoer (*E v Australian Red Cross* (1991) 105 ALR 53; see particularly the judgment of Wilcox J at first instance) when the whole society should recognise and compensate the person who has suffered the harm so that they can be healthy. This view has led to Vaccine Damage legislation in some United States jurisdictions and in the United Kingdom: *Vaccine Damages Act 1979* (UK); *National Childhood Vaccine Injury Act 1986* (US) (42 USCA).

Another version of distributive justice focuses on the rule that compensation is intended to place the plaintiff back in the position they would have been in had the accident not happened to them. This rule creates a situation where richer people get more damages than poor people because it takes more money to put them back in the situation they were in before the accident. Some distributive justice theorists argue that damages should be assessed on the basis of need rather than of reinstating previous positions: for example, see R Abel, "A Critique of Torts" (1990) 37 UCLA L Rev 785-831.

Further reading
T Keren-Paz, *Torts, Egalitarianism and Distributive Justice* (Ashgate, London, 2007).

Feminist theory of tort law

[1.50] Many of the perspectives on tort law are drawn on by particular groups in particular ways. When tort law is considered from a minority group perspective, (including the "minority" women) the basic question being asked is, is it fair? This is not the place for setting out all the feminist theories of tort law. It is useful to note, however, that one of the questions to be asked about tort law is "From whose point of view has the law been made?" It is useful also to recognise that when a person is not part of the group from whose point of view the law has been made, then it is very likely that that law may not operate fairly on them. Feminist theory has opened up these sorts of questions in a way that can also be called on by race theorists and other minority groups. Thus feminist theory has gone beyond the needs of women to offer structures of thought and questioning that can benefit many groups.

There are many forms of feminism and many forms of feminist legal theory. Feminist legal theorists have been interested in examining law to see how it perpetuates patriarchy, or male domination. Male dominance has been indisputable in western culture (and many other cultures) for centuries. However, that dominance has not always been explicit. Feminist scholars have been interested in examining the mechanisms by which dominance is achieved in order to "awaken women and men to the insidious way in which patriarchy distorts all of our lives" (L Bender, "A Lawyer's Primer on Feminist Theory and Tort" (1988) 38 *Journal of Legal Education* 3-37.) In relation to tort law the critiques tend to turn around a number of key issues. These include the valuing of women's work for damages purposes, the nature of the reasonable person of negligence law and the recognised types of harm. Some critiques also turn on the nature of legal reasoning, and ideas about rationality.

An excellent overview of feminist theory in relation to tort law is J Conaghan, "Tort Law and the Feminist Critique of Reason" in A Bottomley (ed), *Feminist Perspectives on the Foundational Subjects of Law* (Cavendish Press, Oxford, 1996). An overview of the American feminist scholarship in tort law is offered by L Bender, "An Overview of Feminist Torts Scholarship" (1993) 78 *Cornell Law Review* 575. A more general consideration of feminist legal theory is offered by Graycar and Morgan, *The Hidden Gender of Law* (2nd ed, Federation Press, Sydney, 2002). See, also, C Pateman, *The Sexual Contract* (Stanford University Press, Stanford, 1998); C Smart, *Feminism and the Power of Law* (Routledge, London, 1989); C MacKinnon, "Feminism, Marxism, Method and the State: Toward Feminist Jurisprudence" (1983) 7 (3) *Signs* 635.

It is beyond the scope of this chapter to go into further detail, but it is hoped that the literature referred to may excite some students to go further.

TORT LAW REFORM: COMMON LAW AND STATUTE

[1.55] The law of torts covers an enormous area of life matters. Although the most commonly used torts – trespass, nuisance, negligence and defamation – were originally (and continue to be) judge-made, statute has made significant inroads into the common law status of tort law. This is largely a 20th century phenomenon, but it is important to note.

Areas of law which have been carved out of tort law or modified by statute include:

- Workers' Compensation Schemes.
- Motor Accident schemes.
- Occupational Health and Safety regimes, including *Factories Acts*. These Acts required Factories to ensure safety in the factory and workplace and made employers strictly liable for some unsafe practices. See Breach of Statutory Duty in Chapter 17.
- Dust Diseases schemes (to deal with asbestosis and silicosis etc).
- Drug compensation schemes in some places, eg United Kingdom.

TORT LAW REFORM AFTER 2002

[1.60] Recently in Australia there has been a concerted push to regulate the law of negligence in relation to personal injury. This has given rise to legislation in each jurisdiction, of which the major Acts are:*Civil Law (Wrongs) Act 2002* (ACT);*Civil Liability Act 2002* (NSW);*Personal*

Injuries (Liabilities and Damages) Act (NT);*Personal Injuries (Civil Claims) Act* (NT);*Civil Liability Act 2003* (Qld);*Personal Injuries Proceedings Act 2002* (Qld); *Civil Liability Act 1936* (SA);*Civil Liability Act 2002* (Tas); *Wrongs Act 1958* (Vic); and*Civil Liability Act 2002* (WA).

In this book, for simplicity, the following abbreviations are used. ACT: CLWA; NSW: CLA; NT: PICCA; Qld: CLA; SA: CLA; Tas: CLA; Vic: WrA; WA: CLA.

These Acts will be referred to collectively as "the civil liability acts" in this text. These changes arose out of an unprecedented level of concern about the price and availability of insurance as insurance became more expensive and harder to get in Australia. This applied particularly to public liability insurance (insurance for legal liability for personal injury).

On 27 March 2002 a meeting of Ministers, endorsed by the Council of Australian Governments on 5 April, put the process of dealing with the insurance crisis in the hands of the Heads of Treasury (the collective of all Australian government treasurers). The Heads of Treasury announced a review into the law of negligence in July 2002. A Panel was appointed, chaired by Justice David Ipp. The Ipp Committee produced two reports by 2 October of the same year and made 61 recommendations (see Negligence Review Panel, *Review of the Law of Negligence, Final Report* (Commonwealth of Australia, Canberra, 2002)).

It was assumed by the Heads of Treasury and by large sections of the media that the "crisis" was caused by an ever-increasing level of litigation producing ever-increasing damages awards, created by an extremely litigious society bent on not taking responsibility for an individuals' own actions. In fact, Trowbridge Consulting/Deloitte Touche Tohmatsu said in its report to the Australian Heads of Treasury on 30 May 2002, "[t]here is no evidence of an 'explosion of litigation' in recent years". One of the difficulties in determining this was that there was no consistent method of collecting statistics across the Australian court systems. Where there was evidence of an increase in litigation this appears to have been reported without regard to the increase in population or any other matters which might increase the number, such as a change in the jurisdiction of a court as happened in New South Wales in 1997 /1998 when the District Court's jurisdictional limits were dramatically increased and there was a consequent increase in the number of cases heard in that court.

It was further assumed that reducing litigation and limiting damages awards would in turn reduce insurance premiums and make insurance more readily available. There is some doubt whether that promise has been fulfilled.

The Chief Justice of the New South Wales Supreme Court, the Hon Justice J Spigelman has considered, extra judicially, the process of reform in response to these concerns.

New Liability Structure In Australia

[1.65] The Hon Justice J Spigelman AC, *The New Liability Structure in Australia*, Address to the Swiss Re Liability Conference (Sydney, 14 September 2004).

The District Court of New South Wales has jurisdiction to hear motor accident claims and work injury damages claims irrespective of the amount claimed and all other common law claims where the amount claimed does not exceed about $750,000. Its civil jurisdiction is, to a substantial degree, a personal injury jurisdiction. Filings in the District Court have fallen from about 20,000 in calendar year 2001, to 13,000 in 2002 and to 8,000 in 2003. The reduced rate of filings is continuing this year. It is reasonably clear that something dramatic has happened to civil litigation in New South Wales. Similar effects are seen in other states.

New Liability Structure In Australia cont.

What these figures reveal is a dramatic change in the practical operation of the law of negligence in Australia over a few years. This is the result of two factors. First, there has been a substantial shift in judicial attitudes at an appellate level, led by the High Court of Australia. Secondly, there have been major changes to the law of negligence implemented by statute. ...

The historical background

For well over a century judges were universally regarded, in all common law jurisdictions, so far as I am aware, as mean, conservative and much too defendant-oriented. This led parliaments to extend liability, commencing with *Lord Campbell's Act*, then the abolition of the doctrine of common employment, the abolition of the immunity of the Crown, the creation of workers' compensation and compulsory third party motor vehicle schemes and provision for apportionment in the case of contributory negligence.

In Australia, about twenty to twenty-five years ago, the process of legislative intervention changed its character. It proceeded on the basis that the judiciary had become too plaintiff-oriented.....

Throughout Australia, in different ways and at different times, new regimes were put in place from about the early 1980s, particularly for the high volume areas of litigation involving motor vehicle and industrial accidents.... In all states what had come to be regarded as common law rights were significantly modified by legislative intervention. When I say, "come to be regarded", many of the causes of action were only available because of the previous century of legislative change, to which I have referred, which overrode the common law.

...

Professor Atiyah referred to a long-term historical trend of expanding the scope of the tort of negligence and the damages recoverable for the tort, as "stretching the law". There was, however, an equivalent, parallel trend, perhaps of even greater practical significance, of "stretching the facts".

Contemporary judges generally reached intellectual maturity at the time that the welfare state was a widely accepted conventional wisdom. The "progressive" project for the law of that era was to expand the circumstances in which persons had a right to sue. We are now more conscious of limits – social, economic, ecological and those of human nature. Hobbes has triumphed over Rousseau, but not over Locke. For several decades now the economic limits on the scope of governmental intervention have received greater recognition. The law cannot remain isolated from such broader trends in social attitudes.

In particular there has been a significant change in expectations within Australian society, as elsewhere, about persons accepting responsibility for their own actions. The idea that any personal failing is not your fault, that everyone can be categorised as a victim, has receded. The task is to restore an appropriate balance between personal responsibility for one's own conduct and expectations of proper compensation and care....

The debate in Australia, leading to recent statutory changes, focused on particular cases and a range of circumstances in which persons recovered damages, sometimes substantial damages, when there could be little doubt that they were the author of their own misfortune. One case referred to frequently involved a young man diving from a cliff ledge into a swimming pool without checking the depth of the water. The idea that the authority which owned the land should have put up a warning sign advising against diving is no longer, with the changing times, regarded as a reasonable basis for liability.

There seems no doubt that the past attitude of judges, when finding liability and awarding compensation, was determined to a very substantial extent by the assumption, almost always correct, that a defendant is insured. The result was that the broad community of relevant defendants bore the

New Liability Structure In Australia cont.

burden of damages awarded to injured plaintiffs. Judges may have proven more reluctant to make findings of negligence, if they knew that the consequence was likely to be to bankrupt the defendant and deprive him or her of the family home. ...

Over the course of a number of decades the effect of judicial decision-making was, in substance, to transform the tort of negligence from a duty to take reasonable care into a duty to avoid any risk by reasonably affordable means. That, in my opinion, was the practical effect of a stream of judicial decision-making at appellate level, particularly for that vast body of decisions that never come before an appellate court and, indeed, the even larger proportion of claims that are settled out of court in the light of a practitioners' understanding of the likely outcome.

The Australian judiciary has now become more sensitive to the broader implications of individual decisions by reason of the cumulative effect of such decisions. The progressive paring back of the tort of negligence by statutory changes over the course of two plus decades has itself had an impact on judges....

I have expressed the view both in judgments and extra judicially, that the judiciary cannot be indifferent to the economic consequences of its decisions. Insurance premiums for liability policies can be regarded as, in substance, a form of taxation (sometimes compulsory but ubiquitous even when voluntary) imposed by the judiciary as an arm of the state. For many decades there was a seemingly inexorable increase in that form of taxation by judicial decision. In Australia that increase has stopped as a result of a change in judicial attitudes and is likely, subject, of course, to the vagaries of the insurance market, to be reversed, as a result of legislative intervention throughout Australia.

At least indirectly in the case of judges, and overtly in the case of the parliaments, the shift in attitude has been driven by the escalation of insurance premiums and, in recent years, by the unavailability of insurance in important areas on any reasonable terms or at all....

There has been a steady stream of cases in the appellate courts, particularly in the High Court, in which the outcomes would have been different if the process of stretching the law and of stretching the facts had not been arrested and reversed....

It is quite likely that many of these cases would have been decided differently only a few years ago. I do not wish to imply that the development has been all one way. There have been important cases in which liability has been established in circumstances where the issue was debatable. Nevertheless, the drift of judicial decision-making is plain at a senior appellate level. It is unquestionably having an effect on trial judge decision-making of a substantial character.

The most difficult area with which the law is still grappling in this regard is that of liability for psychiatric injury. Difficult issues of a philosophical and factual character remain to be resolved in this field. The application of legal tests, in a context where expert evidence has few, and often no, objectively verifiable elements, is particularly difficult. This is exacerbated by the fact that the relevant area of expertise is only to a limited extent based on scientific research and has a wide element of discretion....

In this area Australian law is now unlikely to develop in any principled way by reason of statutory intervention, to which I will presently refer.

The sense of crisis

Legislative change over the last year or two has been driven by a perceived crisis in the price and availability of insurance. In Australia this focused on public liability and medical negligence. However, similar pressures had been building up in all areas for a number of years, including the high volume areas of industrial accidents and traffic accidents.

Over 2002-2003 there were virtually daily reports about the social and economic effects of increased premiums: cancellation of charitable and social events such as dances, fetes, surfing carnivals and Christmas carols; the closure of children's playgrounds, horse riding schools, adventure tourist sites and even hospitals; the early retirement of doctors and their refusal to perform certain services, notably obstetrics; local councils were shutting swimming pools and removing lethal instruments such as seesaws and roundabouts from children's playgrounds; our Sydney tabloid proclaimed "The death of fun"; many professionals could not obtain cover for categories of risks, leading to withdrawal of their services; for example, engineers advising on cooling tower maintenance could not get cover for legionnaires disease, building consultants could not get cover for asbestos removal, agricultural consultants could not get cover for advice on salinity; midwives were unable to get cover at any price; many professionals were reported to have disposed of assets so as to be able to operate without adequate cover or even any insurance.

The issue became highly charged politically. The talk was of "crisis". The concern of governments was motivated in part by the liability of government directly as a major employer, property owner and provider of services, particularly in education, health and transport. This was, however, reinforced by the emergence, over recent years of a role for government as a backstop for private insurers, as the reinsurer of last resort. It took many years for the government role of "lender of last resort" to take the institutional form of the contemporary central bank. We are in the early stages of institutional development of the "reinsurer of last resort" function.

... Governments at both levels of our federal system became involved in protecting policyholders when a major general insurer, HIH Limited, went into liquidation. This is exactly what happened long ago in the case of banks.

It is quite clear that governments have a very real financial interest in the operations of the tort system.

Whether by way of increases in insurance premiums or by way of a call on tax payers' funds it became widely accepted at all levels of Australian government and in the general community that the existing tort system had become economically unsustainable. The particular focus was the sudden escalation of premiums. Insurance premiums are the result of a multiplicity of factors, however, the cost of claims sets the basic structural parameters within which other forces operate. Those costs have increased considerably over recent decades.

Although the practical operation of the law of torts must determine to a substantial degree the level of premiums for liability insurance, the suddenness and size of the increases and the expansion of policy exclusions reflected developments in the insurance market, 9/11, HIH, etc. The underlying cause of the problem must, however, be distinguished from the immediate cause of the crisis.

Legislative change

In New South Wales legislative changes had commenced in a number of areas prior to the events of 2002-2003. Those events, however, led to a national response in which many of the New South Wales proposals were adopted more widely and legislation went even further than had been considered appropriate until that time.

The Commonwealth and the states appointed an inquiry to review the law of negligence. The Panel was chaired by the Honourable David Ipp, a judge of the New South Wales Court of Appeal. By and large, the recommendations of this panel have been implemented, with some variation, in all states and territories, with complementary national legislation almost complete. The principal thrust of the changes is the limitation of circumstances in which damages can be recovered for personal injury and the restriction of the heads and quantum of damage that can be so recovered. The changes are wide ranging ...

[Spigelman CJ then set out an account of the changes]

... The earlier changes to the law over the course of some two decades had resulted in significant differences amongst the respective schemes for transport accidents, industrial accidents and medical

New Liability Structure In Australia cont.

negligence. These arose because different insurers and administrators were involved in each area of liability. They had a great influence on what changes were required to bring down claims and, therefore, premiums, in a context were government had often announced an objective of reducing premiums in a particular area of insurance by a specific amount. These disparate processes created inexplicable and unjustified variations in the rules which applied. Quite different compensation was available depending on whether injury occurred in a car or in a car park or at work or on an operating table or in a public swimming pool or in a supermarket. The sense of fairness which is essential to the effective operation of the system had been attenuated.

The result of the new regime is to avoid the sense of inequality as a ground for unfairness. It has, however, replaced that ground with others and the debate is actively continuing. In particular, the introduction of caps on recovery and thresholds before recovery – an underwriter driven, not a principled change – has led to considerable controversy. The introduction of a requirement that a person be subject to fifteen percent of whole of body impairment – that percentage is lower in some States – before being able to recover general damages has been the subject of controversy. It does mean that some people who are quite seriously injured are not able to sue at all. More than any other factor I envisage this restriction will be seen as much too restrictive.

The evidence suggested that in smaller claims, say up to about $100,000, about half of total damages awarded was in the form of general damages. The threshold has made these claims virtually uneconomic from the point of view of the legal profession. Perhaps more than any other single change, it is the threshold for general damages that has led to the dramatic fall in filings in the District Court. This has been reinforced by the cap on lawyers' fees.

Small claims raise very real issues about transaction costs. Nevertheless, there is likely to be a growing body of persons who have suffered injury which they believe to be significant and who resent their inability to receive compensation.

The effective abolition of what insurance companies regard as small claims, albeit the matters are not small from the perspective of the injured person, is expected to have a considerable impact on premiums. Insurers convinced the governments that this was an important aspect of the changes required. My own suspicion is that insurers simply find it easier to compute the effect of such a change than of changes in applicable legal principle. Underwriters do not believe that they are capable of predicting changes in judicial behaviour and who can blame them ...

Conclusion

The change in the law of negligence in Australia has been quite dramatic. The working out of the new statutory regime has commenced and will take some time. There remains a significant debate as to whether or not the reforms have gone too far. Australian lawyers are focussing attention on the considerable increase that has been reported in insurance company profits. Political pressure on premiums is increasing but, in the long term, the level of premiums will be determined by the renewed ability of Australia to attract insurance company capital, particularly, the capital of reinsurers and by a turn in the insurance market cycle which, sooner or later, is inevitable.

[1.70] **Notes&Questions**

1. At the same time as personal injury litigation appeared to be increasing, litigation for pure economic loss (for example, suing the auditor of a company for negligent auditing causing massive economic losses) appeared to also be increasing. Why do you think the Heads of Treasury did not ask for this to be investigated?

2. What differences does it make to the development of tort law if it is embodied in legislation rather than in case law? Should legislation be resisted? Why?

3. Spigelman CJ refers to the concept of "personal responsibility" several times in his speech. In negligence, the ideas of personal responsibility which underlie the law may swing from an emphasis on responsibility for the self to an emphasis on responsibility for others. In Australia in the 1980s and early 1990s negligence law went through a period when it seemed to emphasise collective responsibility more than it had done in the past. For example, in *Nagle v Rottnest Island Authority* (1993) 177 CLR 423 the majority of the High Court held that the Authority owed a duty of care to a man who dived into a swimming hole and became a quadriplegic. They held that a person who owes a duty to others must take account of the possibility that they may fail to take proper care of their own safety. However, five years later, in *Romeo v Conservation Commission of the Northern Territory* (1998) 192 CLR 431, when Ms Romeo was seriously injured when she fell while drunk from a cliff in a Reserve, the court, by majority, held that the danger was obvious and that defendants should not have to warn against obvious dangers: *Romeo v Conservation Commission of the Northern Territory* (1998) 192 CLR 431 at 447. That is, the plaintiff could have and should have protected herself. Since then the High Court has continued to emphasise the importance of individual responsibility, autonomy and choice in a number of cases. This appears to be linked to a sharp increase in decisions favouring defendants over plaintiffs (see H Luntz, "Torts Turnaround Downunder" (2001) *Oxford Commonwealth Law Journal* 95). The rhetoric of personal responsibility was also a very important part of the tort reform process to which Spigelman CJ refers.

4. Spigelman CJ refers to a "duty to take reasonable care" and "a duty to avoid any risk by reasonably affordable means". What is the difference and why is he discussing it?

5. The issue of propensity to sue was a fundamental one in the tort reform process. The argument was that Australia had become a "blaming" society in which rather than take personal responsibility for themselves, people preferred to blame others and rushed to litigation, and this was creating a huge rise in litigation rates. There was very little accurate data which could be drawn on to base these claims at the time, but nor was there data to disprove it. The various jurisdictions in Australia all held their data in different ways (for example, some had professional negligence lists separately from motor accidents etc while others had personal injury lists distinct from other kinds of damage) which made it difficult to compare them. To add to this some jurisdictions had changed their court processes or jurisdictional limits, which also added to the confusion (for example, New South Wales changed the jurisdictional limit for the District Court from $250,000 to $750,000 in 1997). It was thus difficult to compare like with like. Other data was simply not collected (see EW Wright, "National Trends in Personal Injury Litigation" (2006) 14 *Torts Law Journal* 233). However, in the last few years a significant investigation of these claims in Australia, the United Kingdom and the US has been done. In Australia and the UK in particular it has become clear that litigation rates had clearly stabilised between 1995 and 2000.

6. For a discussion of the disproportionate impact of tort reforms, for instance, caps on damages on particular groups of people such as the very young, the elderly and the poor, see PH Rubin and JM Shepherd "The Demographics of Tort Reform" (2008) 4(2) *Review of Law and Economics* 591.

Further reading

EW Wright, "National Trends in Personal Injury Litigation: Before and After "Ipp"" (2006) 14(3) *Torts Law Journal* 233.

TORT LAW AND HUMAN RIGHTS

[1.75] On 2 March 2004 the Australian Capital Territory became the first part of Australia with a modern Bill of Rights – the *Human Rights Act 2004* (ACT). Victoria passed the *Charter of Rights and Responsibility* in July 2006 and it came into force on 1 January 2007. Both these Acts are based on the model of the United Kingdom *Human Rights Act 1998*. Australia is the only western country that does not have a national Bill of Rights in some form. The United Kingdom, the United States of America, Canada, New Zealand and Europe all have rights protection for their citizens. In Australia, any rights of citizens outside the jurisdiction of the Australian Capital Territory and Victoria can only be protected by the common law. Torts is the vehicle of common law which is supposed to protect the integrity of the person, economic integrity, their property and their reputation. It seems like the best vehicle for the protection of human rights under the common law.

Ashby v White (1703) 1 Brown PC 62; 1 ER 417 was decided in 1703. In that case the plaintiffs were voters whose votes had been wrongly disallowed by the defendants who were the returning officers. At trial the voters failed, but the dissenting judgment of Holt CJ argued strongly that they should succeed on the basis that Parliament had given the electors a right which carried a corresponding obligation on the part of the returning officers. On appeal the House of Lords agreed with Holt CJ.

This would seem like a good start for law supporting civil if not human rights, but English law failed to continue this process. When we define tort law we often say that tort law protects the individual's bodily integrity, property and reputation. What relationship does this sort of protection have with human rights?

> The salient feature that distinguishes human rights theories from "general" rights theories (or serves to qualify them) is that of their apparent necessary connection with the human condition. ... the assertion that human rights apply universally to all human beings flows directly from the notion that as a human being one is automatically entitled to respect for one's human dignity. On this basis the object of preserving and promoting the dignity of individual human beings constitutes the central concern of human rights (D Kinley, "The Legal Dimension of Human Rights" in D Kinley (ed), *Human Rights in Australian Law* (Federation Press, Sydney, 1998), p 4.)

As municipal law (law within a country) tort law raises issues of human rights, and in particular it raises the issues of protection of individual citizens against violation of their rights by government officials (see Sir Anthony Mason, "Human Rights and the Law of Torts" in P Cane and J Stapleton (eds), *Essays in Celebration of John Fleming* (Oxford University Press, Melbourne, 1998)). This can be done, for example, in the tort of negligence where public authorities are the defendant; and in torts such as misfeasance in public office, false imprisonment and assault and battery. For a long time crown immunity prevented many actions being brought against the government, but that is no longer the case. It is now possible to sue the government and therefore to vindicate certain rights by the use of common law rights. In a country with a bill of rights, these might be treated as human rights under the Bill, while in international law they would be regarded as human rights.

As previously mentioned, countries with a Bill of Rights include the United States of America, the United Kingdom, New Zealand and Canada. These countries' tort law is also closely connected with that of Australia, particularly the latter three. One question to be asked is: what effect does a Bill of Rights have on the tort law of a country? In 1966 the United Kingdom accepted the jurisdiction of the European Court of Human Rights. The United Kingdom was thus affected by the European Convention on Human Rights and was the first state to ratify it. However, this merely meant that the United Kingdom was answerable to other states in international law if it breached these rights. It did not make it possible for individuals to sue within the United Kingdom when such rights were infringed. This was remedied when the *Human Rights Act 1998* (UK) was passed, which by *Human Rights Act 1998*s 6 makes it "unlawful for a public authority to act in a way which is incompatible with a [European] Convention [on Human Rights] right".

In the United Kingdom the existence of the *Human Rights Act 1998* and the European Convention on Human Rights have led to the protection of a number of rights in relation to tortious actions which otherwise might not have been protected. For example, in *Osman v United Kingdom* [1999] 1 FLR 193; (1999) 28 EHRR CD 65, the Court of Human Rights in Strasbourg held that the House of Lords, in *Hill v Chief Constable of West Yorkshire*, had created an exclusionary rule in favour of the police which breached the right of access to a court (although in *Z v United Kingdom* [2001] 2 FLR 612; 10 BHRC 384 the European Court of Human Rights appear to resile from *Osman*).

The Victorian *Charter of Rights and Responsibility*, as mentioned above, is modelled on the UK *Human Rights Act 1998*. The Act provides for legislation to be interpreted to comply with human rights. This may have some impact on the treatment of aspects of tort law such as breach of statutory duty and the civil liability acts, particularly when a public authority is involved, since public authorities are covered by the Charter.

Can human rights be said to be protected by tort law in the absence of a Bill of Rights? In New Zealand, whose Bill of Rights does not confer a right of privacy, the Court of Appeal has recognised the existence of a tort of invasion of privacy (see *Hoskings v Runting and Pacific Magazines NZ Ltd* [2004] NZCA 101/03).

Australia is a signatory to the *United Nations International Covenant on Civil and Political Rights*. What effect does this have on the law of torts if any? Strictly speaking, it has none.

However, it is clear that some aspects of human rights and rights rhetoric do affect the common law and may be imported into it. In Australia, it was traditional to say that there was no right to privacy in Australia on the authority of *Victoria Park Racing and Recreation Grounds Co Ltd v Taylor* (1937) 58 CLR 479. But the High Court held in *Australian Broadcasting Commission v Lenah Game Meats* (2001) 208 CLR 199 that *Victoria Park Racing* did not prevent the establishment of a right to privacy and this was taken up in the District Court of Queensland in *Grosse v Purvis* [2003] QDC 151. Whilst that was rather a surprise it seems that the protection of human rights remains a possible role for tort law, although it has not been explored very much in Australia.

Using tort law to protect human rights has been explored elsewhere. Some people have begun to consider dealing with torture under the transnational tort legislation of the United States and under international law in general using a tortious paradigm. The United States *Alien Torts Claims Act 1789* (US) grants jurisdiction over "any civil action by an alien for a tort only, committed in violation of the law of nations or a treaty of the United States". Although this has not been often used, in 2005 a United State Court upheld a damages award of $4 million against a Chilean Army officer who was held responsible for the torture and murder of a political prisoner.

As international law begins to break down the state-to-state paradigm for legal action, tortious actions become possible. Thus victims of torture in Chile who have European citizenship have applied to the European Court of Human Rights under the access to justice provisions. (The *Jaccard-Veloso* application (Applic 44191/98)). Acts of torture will almost inevitably be tortious battery. It may be possible for a person tortured in one country to sue in another using the public international law rules (A Byrnes, "Civil Remedies for Torture Committed Abroad: An Obligation Under the Convention Against Torture?" in C Scott (ed), *Torture as Tort; Comparative Perspectives on the Development of Transnational Human Rights Litigation* (Hart Publishing, Oxford, 2001)). Within our own country tort law might be used in situations where we might not otherwise consider it, to bring actions regarding children in detention, for example.

Rights at common law are different from human rights in their scope and in how they are vindicated, but it is worth considering the relationship between tort law and human rights and the possibility of using tort law as an instrument to achieve human rights as you consider the materials in this book.

[1.80] **Notes&Questions**

1. What is tort law protecting if it is not protecting human rights? Consider the concept of a human right. How is it different from a common law right? Does the difference matter?
2. How can we protect human rights using the law of torts if we do not have a Human Rights Act/Bill of Rights?

Further reading

J Wright, *Tort Law and Human Rights* (Hart Publishing, Oxford, 2001).

USING THIS CHAPTER

[1.85] We hope that the issues raised in this chapter will stay with you as you read the later chapters. To that end we suggest some questions you might ask yourself as you read the later chapters.

1. Does the law as it is represented in the relevant chapter demonstrate the effectiveness of tort law as a corrective justice/distributive justice/compensation/deterrent/economic system?
2. To what extent does the law considered in the chapter take account of insurance? To what extent is it affected by insurance?
3. Whose points of view are vindicated by the law considered in this chapter? Is the characterisation of the harm suffered one that might be damaging to certain classes of plaintiff such as women, Indigenous people, the poor?
4. Are the rights being considered here legal rights or human rights and does it matter?
5. For further reading on the issues raised in this chapter, see T Ison, *The Forensic Lottery: A Critique of Tort Liability as a System of Personal Injury Compensation*, (Staple Press,

London, 1967); I Englard, *The Philosophy of Tort Law*, (Dartmouth Publishing, Aldershot, 1993); J Coleman, *Risks and Wrongs*, (Oxford University Press, Oxford, 1992); D Harris, et al, *Compensation and Support for Illness and Injury Compensation and Support for Illness and Injury* (Clarendon Press, Oxford, 1984); J Stapleton, "Tort, Insurance and Ideology" (1995) 59 MLR 820.

PART 2: INTENTIONAL TORTS

PART 2

CHAPTER 2

Introduction to Intentional Torts

INTRODUCTION: THE DEVELOPMENT OF MODERN DAY TRESPASS AND CASE

Historical context

[2.05] The action of trespass was the starting point in the development of the law of torts. Consequently, it is the logical place to commence study of individual torts. A brief historical overview of the development of tort law is necessary to understand the action of trespass and the distinction between trespass and another closely related tort, action on the case.

Originally, whether a person could seek compensation for injury depended upon whether their action fell within one of the recognised forms of writ. A writ was a command on behalf of the King that a case be heard by the courts. The types of actions for which a writ could be issued were limited. Basically, there were two relevant kinds of writs: the writ of trespass; and the writ of trespass on the case, otherwise referred to as action on the case, or case. If the alleged action did not fall within one of the recognised writs, then no action could be instituted and the plaintiff was left without means of redress for the wrong. Additionally, the incorrect choice left the plaintiff without redress; their choice of writ being irrevocable.

The civil action of trespass originally evolved from the criminal action of trespass. Criminal trespass arose due to the necessity of keeping the King's peace. Over time, the criminal action of trespass became more and more a civil action. This meant that the wrongdoer came to be accountable directly to the victim, as distinct from a criminal action in which accountability is to the state (originally the King). Allowing individuals to seek compensation directly from the wrongdoer prevented the wronged person from taking the matter into their own hands. There were three broad varieties of trespass: trespass against the body of the plaintiff (assault, battery and false imprisonment); trespass to goods; and trespass to land.

There are two views regarding the historical evolution of action on the case. The first is that it evolved from trespass. The second is that it evolved from innominate actions that existed quite distinct from trespass. These came to be classified generally as "case" through the idea that the writs initiating them elaborated the "special case". The view that case evolved from innominate actions appears to accord better with the fact that "case" represented a broad number of actions rather than a set of general principles under which a particular claim could be subsumed. Many varieties of case did, however, come to have their own names, which are the names of modern torts, for example, nuisance and negligence, though others remained innominate.

Whilst trespass and case continue today as available actions, the procedure of issuing writs referred to above has not survived. Today it is irrelevant whether an individual is suing in case or trespass from a procedural point of view, the process for instituting proceedings being the same for both actions.

Further reading

FW Maitland, *Constitutional History of England* (Cambridge University Press, Cambridge, 1908).

CHS Fifoot, *History and Sources of the Common Law: Tort and Contract* (Stevens & Sons Limited, London, 1949).

THE TRESPASSORY ACT: CHOOSING BETWEEN TRESPASS AND CASE

[2.10] When a plaintiff suffers damage or interference with an interest, a decision must be made regarding what type of action or actions will be instituted to seek compensation. In the context of intentional torts, the possible actions are:

- trespass to the person,
- trespass to land,
- trespass to chattels,
- conversion (action for interference with chattels),
- detinue (action for interference with chattels); and
- action on the case.

The following is an examination of the elements that make trespass and case distinct actions. The existence or non-existence of these elements will determine whether it is appropriate to sue in one or the other.

Directness

[2.15] The concept of directness is the first element that distinguishes trespass from action on the case. Trespass requires a direct act or interference whereas, if the act or interference is consequential, the appropriate form of action is case.

Hutchins v Maughan

[2.20] *Hutchins v Maughan* [1947] VLR 131; [1947] ALR 201 Supreme Court of Victoria (footnotes omitted)

HERRING CJ: 132 The complainant is a drover and on Easter Saturday 1944 he was droving in the vicinity 2,000 ewes. On his way to some unfenced land north of land where the baits were picked up he met the defendant, and was told by him that the paddock north of the Sanctuary in the vicinity was poisoned. With regard to the land where the baits were picked up he was also warned that there were baits all along the creek. The complainant apparently thought the defendant was bluffing about the poison along the creek, and a day or so later rode down along the creek with his dogs. He saw no sign of baits and two days later moved his sheep in and brought his dogs with him. Shortly after the dogs picked up baits and died.

Hutchins v Maughan cont.

The complainant's claim was laid alternatively in negligence, nuisance or trespass. The police magistrate upheld the defences taken so far as negligence and nuisance were concerned, but gave judgment for the complainant on his trespass claim. Before me it was conceded that the police magistrate was right in his decision as to negligence and nuisance. And the only question argued before me was whether on the facts of the case the police magistrate could properly enter judgment as he did for the complainant on his trespass claim. The laying of the baits was admittedly an unlawful act, and consequently it was not disputed that the complainant had a cause of action for the injuries he suffered as a consequence thereof. But it was contended for the defendant that such cause of action sounded only in case and not in trespass, and that the complainant having failed in his claims in case, viz., those for nuisance and negligence, is now without remedy.

The basis of the defendant's contention was that the injury suffered by the complainant in the present case was not occasioned by but was merely consequential upon the defendant's act complained of, viz., the laying of the baits, and so was not a trespass. The principle was thus stated in 1725 in *Reynolds v Clarke* (1725) 93 ER 747:

> The distinction in law is, where the immediate act itself occasions a prejudice, or is an injury to the plaintiff's person, house, land, etc., and where the act itself is not an injury, but a consequence from that act is prejudicial to the plaintiff's person, house, land, etc. In the first case trespass *vi et armis* will lie; in the last it will not, but the plaintiff's proper remedy is by an action on the case.

In 1773 in the famous case of *Scott v Shepard* (1773) 96 ER 525, Blackstone J said he "took the settled distinction to be that where the injury is immediate, an action of trespass will lie; where it is only consequential, it must be an action on the case." And he cited the example of a man's throwing a log into the highway; an example later made use of by Le Blane J in 1803 in *Leame v Bray* (1803) 102 ER 724 where the learned Judge said:

> But in all the books the invariable principle to be collected is that where the injury is immediate on the act done, there trespass lies; but where it is not immediate on the act done, but consequential, there the remedy is in case. And the distinction is well instanced by the example put of a man's throwing a log into the highway; if at the time of its being thrown it hit any person, it is trespass; but if after it be thrown, any person going along the road receive an injury by falling over it as it lies there, it is case ... trespass is the proper remedy for an immediate injury done by one to another; but where the injury is only consequential from the act done, there it is case.

... Each case must, of course, be determined on its own facts and in the present case the question is whether on its facts the injury the complainant suffered in the loss of his dogs was immediate or consequential, that is to say, whether it was directly occasioned by the defendant's act in laying the baits or was merely consequential upon that act. Now the baits were laid by the defendant before the complainant took his dogs on to the land in question. They may even have been laid before he arrived in the vicinity. And had he not chosen to come into the vicinity and bring his dogs with him he would have suffered no injury from the defendant's act. Nor indeed would he have done so, had he not taken his dogs on to the land where the baits were laid. The doing of the act therefore of itself did him no mischief. Before he could suffer an injury, he had himself to intervene by coming to the land and bringing his dogs thereon.

In these circumstances the injury he suffered cannot, in my opinion, be said to have followed so immediately in point of causation upon the act of the defendant as to be termed part of the act. It should rather be regarded merely as consequential upon it and not as directly or immediately occasioned by it. And so trespass does not lie in respect of defendant's act in laying the baits. Had the baits been thrown by the defendant to the complainant's dogs, then no doubt the injury could properly have been regarded as directly occasioned by the act of the defendant, so that trespass would

Hutchins v Maughan cont.

lie. As it was, it was necessary for the complainant himself to bring his dogs with him to the baits in order that the injurious consequences, of which he complains, should result from the defendant's act. His position is like that of the man who, going along the road upon which a log has been thrown, receives an injury by falling over it. In such a case the man who threw the log upon the road has, of course, caused the mischief, but trespass does not lie, as the injury is consequential upon his act and not immediately or directly occasioned thereby. Had the man who fell over the log not passed that way, he would have suffered no injury from the other's act.

[2.25] **Notes&Questions**

1. Arguably the issue of directness could more aptly be described as an issue of time or immediacy of the resultant contact. A test suggested by Sir John Salmond (in *Law of Torts* (10th ed, Sweet and Maxwell, London, 1945), p 4), is "Did the impact follow so closely on the defendant's act that it might be considered part of that act?" For example, defendant throws a lit firecracker into a busy outdoor market and it lands on Y's stall. Y throws the firecracker and it lands on R's stall. R throws the firecracker and it hits the plaintiff in the face exploding and blinding him. Due to the short period of time between the defendant's act and the plaintiff's injury, the appropriate action is trespass: see *Scott v Shepherd* (1773) 96 ER 525, referred to in the principal case.
2. In the context of trespass to land, refer to *Southport Corp v Esso Petroleum Co Ltd* [1954] 2 QB 182. A tanker, belonging to the defendant company, became stranded in the Ribble estuary and to float her the master discharged fuel oil into the estuary. The oil became deposited on the plaintiff's foreshore and the plaintiffs sought to recover the cost of the clean up by suing in negligence, nuisance and trespass. As far as trespass was concerned Denning LJ stated (at 195-6), "This discharge of oil was not done directly on to their foreshore, but outside in the estuary. It was carried by the tide on to their land, but that was only consequential, not direct. Trespass, therefore does not lie."
3. More recently the definition of directness in *Hutchins v Maughan* [1947] VLR 131; [1947] ALR 201 was approved by the Tasmanian Supreme Court in *Pargiter v Alexander* (1995) 5 Tas R 158. The defendant was found liable for trespass to chattels for taking the plaintiff's yacht.
4. In a recent case, *Rural Export & Trading (WA) Pty Ltd v Hahnheuser* [2007] FCA 153, the defendants who were animal liberationists, mixed pig meat into the feed bins of sheep which were pending export to the middle east to make the sheep unsuitable for export to Muslim countries. The meat was added to the feed bins prior to the sheep being delivered to the holding pens. Was the adding of the pig meat to the feed which may have been subsequently consumed (there was no evidence the sheep had actually ingested the meat) by the sheep a direct interference with the chattels (sheep)? No.

Fault

[2.30] The next distinguishing feature between trespass and case is fault. In the context of trespass, fault on the part of the defendant may be established by intentional or negligent conduct. The definition of intention is wider then that which a layperson would hold in respect of this element. It includes not only a desire or purpose upon the part of the defendant to cause an interference, but also encompasses situations in which the defendant should have had knowledge to a degree of substantial certainty that the interference would occur as result of their act. It is important to stress that the defendant needs only to intend (that is desire or have knowledge to a substantial certainty) the interference which the trespass seeks to protect, and not any harm that may result from the interference. For example, tapping a person on the shoulder to gain their attention does not in the normal case result in injury, however this was an act done with the purpose of touching the plaintiff's body (the interference) and consequently meets the element of intention for battery. The act of the defendant must also have been voluntary for it to be regarded as intentional. Consequently if person X shoves person Y so hard that Y lands on Z's land, there is no trespass by Y as Y's act was not voluntary and therefore he or she could not have possessed the necessary intent to enter the land. X however will be liable for the trespass if it can be proven that his or her purpose was to cause Y to fall onto Z's land or if on the facts it was substantially certain that by shoving Y in the direction he or she did, that Y would fall onto Z's land.

In regards to negligence as part of a trespass action, it should be noted that, like an action for negligence, it requires assessment of whether the defendant failed to exercise reasonable care and as a result caused the interference. However, unlike negligence, the interference does not have to result in harm. It would also appear that there is no requirement to prove that a duty was owed by the defendant to the plaintiff, which is an integral part of an action for negligence.

For actions on the case for intentional injuries, fault will be established providing, "... the defendant's act was so plainly calculated to produce some effect of the kind that was produced that an intention to produce it ought to be imputed to the defendant" (see *Wilkinson v Downton* [1897] 2 QB 57 per Wright J at 59 (extracted [3.135]). See also the case of *Nationwide News v Naidu* (2007) Aust Torts Reports 81-928 (NSWCA) (extracted [3.145]) for a recent analysis of fault in action on the case). It is irrelevant that is was not the defendant's purpose to cause the harm which eventuated as a person is presumed to intend the natural consequences of his or her actions. A defendant, though, will not be at fault if the plaintiff's injury was "not a consequence which might reasonably have been anticipated or foreseen" (*Bunyan v Jordan* (1937) 57 CLR 1 per Dixon J at 17).

[2.35] **Notes&Questions**

1. Refer to B Richards, K Ludlow & A Gibson, *Torts Law in Principle* (5th ed, Thomson Reuters Lawbook Co, 2009), [4.15], for added explanation of the concepts of intent and negligence in a trespassory action.
2. For a more detailed discussion of intention and action on the case, see [3.130]-[3.150].

[2.40] There are circumstances in which a defendant will not be found to have been at fault, either intentionally or negligently. The classic example, illustrated by Professor Fleming, is that of inevitable accident; that is, an accident neither intended nor able to be avoided by the exercise of reasonable care and skill. However, accident must be distinguished from mistake:

> Inevitable accident, finally, refers to cases where the particular consequence was neither intended nor so probable as to make it negligent. By contrast, in cases of mistake the consequence is often intended and the error consists in thinking that such a result does not constitute an invasion of another's legally protected interests. ... To illustrate: one who cuts down a tree in the vicinity of his boundary in such a manner that it will in all probability fall on his own ground, commits but an accidental trespass, if it crashes onto a neighbour's land. The

unauthorised entry, which is the injurious effect of the person's activity, was neither intended nor reasonably to be anticipated, and he is consequently absolved now that such an accidental trespass is no longer actionable. On the other hand if the person had thought that he owned all the land on which the tree would possibly fall and intentionally cut it so that it would come down on land which turns out to be a neighbour's, he has committed intentional trespass under mistake. The actual result which has come to pass was intended under the erroneous notion that it would not violate another's rights.

Such a mistake, even if one which a reasonable person might have made, is not as a general rule admitted as an excuse to civil liability. A trespasser who honestly believes that he is the owner or has the owner's authority or merely mistakes the boundary is nonetheless guilty of unlawful entry (JG Fleming, *Law of Torts* (9th ed, LBC Information Services, Sydney, 1998), p 84).

[2.45] **Notes&Questions**

1. Cases in which inevitable accident has been successfully proven include *Public Transport Commission (NSW) v Perry* (1977) 137 CLR 107, in which the plaintiff suffered an epileptic fit while waiting on the platform of a railway station causing her to fall onto the railway tracks negating a cross-claim of trespass to land, and *Smith v Lord* [1962] SASR 88, in which the driver, as a result of cardiac problem, suffered a blackout whilst driving; he had no knowledge of his condition at the time of the accident.
2. Would a defendant be able to claim a defence of inevitable accident if he or she was driving and felt unwell but nevertheless continued to drive and as a result of the onset of the illness lost control of the car injuring the plaintiff pedestrian? Not on the facts of *Leahy v Beaumont* (1981) 27 SASR 290 where the court found that the moment that the defendant driver started his coughing fit he should have pulled over, but yes on the facts of *Scholz v Standish* [1961] SASR 123 where the defendant driver lost control after being unexpectedly and unavoidably stung by a bee.

Negligent trespass v negligence

[2.50] It is apparent from the above discussion that historically an action for trespass could be brought in respect of an act of the defendant that was either intentional or negligent. With the development of negligence as an action in its own right, the question has arisen as to whether it is still possible to institute an action in trespass if the defendant's act was negligent and not intentional – has negligence subsumed the action of negligent trespass? For example, if a person drives negligently and in doing so hits the plaintiff, a pedestrian, is the action instituted by the plaintiff in negligence or in negligent trespass or can an action be brought for both?

Williams v Milotin

[2.55] *Williams v Milotin* (1957) 97 CLR 465 High Court of Australia (footnotes omitted)

[The plaintiff was struck while riding his bicycle in the street by a motor truck which was driven by the defendant in a negligent manner. The date assigned by the statement of claim for the occurrence is 7th May 1952. The writ of summons in the action was issued on 19th July 1955, that is to say more than three years after the alleged cause of action arose but less than six years. Pursuant to s 36 of the *Limitation of Actions Act 1936-1948* (SA) all actions for assault trespass to the person menace battery wounding or imprisonment shall be commenced within three years next after the cause of such action accrued but not after, and the defendant therefore claimed that the plaintiff's action was statute barred as although it was for negligence it could also have been brought in trespass and therefore the

Williams v Milotin cont.

operative provision was s 36. The plaintiff, however, relied upon s 35 which provides that, (c) actions which formerly might have been brought in the form of actions called actions on the case and (k) actions for libel malicious prosecution arrest or seduction and any other actions which would formerly have been brought in the form of actions called trespass on the case: shall, save as otherwise provided in this Act, be commenced within six years next after the cause of such action accrued but not after.]

DIXON CJ, McTIERNAN, WILLIAMS, WEBB AND KITTO JJ: 469 [T]he defendant's starting point is that the action the plaintiff has brought could formerly have been properly framed as an action of trespass to the person.

The word "formerly" seems to mean prior to the passing of the *Supreme Court Act 1878* of South Australia, by which the "judicature system" was adopted: cf. definition in s 5 of the *Supreme Court Act 1935* (SA).

At that time the present action might have been framed as an action of trespass. For it seems that the facts which the plaintiff, by his next friend, intends to allege are that he was immediately or directly hit by the motor car driven by the defendant as a result of the negligence of the defendant himself. There is no suggestion that the defendant intended to strike him. If that had been the allegation the action could have been brought in trespass and not otherwise. But as only the negligence of the defendant is relied upon, while the cause of action might have been laid as trespass to the person, the action might also have been brought as an action on the case to recover special or particular damage caused by the defendant's negligence. Had the damage been caused indirectly or immediately by the defendant or by his servant (a state of things to be distinguished from violence immediately caused by the defendant's own act) the action must have been brought as an action on the case and not otherwise. ...

[O]n the same set of facts two causes of action arose to which different periods of limitation were respectively affixed. In saying that two causes of action arose no more is meant than that two traditional categories continue to exist in the contemplation of the material provisions of s 35(c) and (k) and s 36 and that there is no difficulty in distinguishing between the categories either notionally or historically.

Plainly enough the plaintiff relies on the category which we commonly call negligence but which the statute looks at as an action of the kind which once was brought for the recovery of special or particular damage caused by conduct on the part of the defendant making it actionable, in this instance negligence. Why should the plaintiff's action be limited by any other period of time than that appropriate to the cause of action on which he sues? The two causes of action are not the same now and they never were. When you speak of a cause of action you mean the essential ingredients in the title to the right which it is proposed to enforce. The essential ingredients in an action of negligence for personal injuries include the special or particular damage – it is the gist of the action – and the want of due care. Trespass to the person includes neither. But it does include direct violation of the protection which the law throws round the person. It is true that in the absence of intention of some kind or want of due care, a violation occurring in the course of traffic in a thoroughfare is not actionable as a trespass. It is unnecessary to inquire how that comes about. It is perhaps a modification of the general law of trespass to the person. But it does not mean that trespass is the same as actionable negligence occasioning injury. It happens in this case that the actual facts will or may fulfil the requirements of each cause of action. But that does not mean that within the provisions of the *Limitation of Actions Act 1936*, ss 35 and 36, only one "cause of action" is vested in the plaintiff. If he had chosen to discard negligence and special or particular damage as ingredients in his cause of action and rely instead on the elements amounting to trespass or assault, something might be said for the defendant's reliance on s 36. But not otherwise. Read together, the true meaning and effect of s 35 and s 36 is that six years shall be the period of limitation for an action of damages based on negligence which formerly might have been brought as an action on the case in which the damages formed the gist of the action and negligence giving rise to the damage formed the conduct by reason of which it became actionable.

In our opinion the decision of the Supreme Court is right and the appeal should be dismissed.

[2.60] **Notes&Questions**

1. The law in Australia still proceeds upon the basis that an action may be brought for both negligent and intentional acts in a trespass action. For more recent support as to the continuing view: see *Parson v Partridge* (1992) 111 ALR 257 (SC Norfolk Island), per Morling CJ at 259-260; *Wilson v Horne* (1999) Aust Torts Reports 81-504, per Cox CJ at 65-790-65-791. It is also the current approach in Canada: *Renco v Fitness Institute Ltd* (1995) 25 OR (3d) 88 at 91 (Ont Ct Gen Div); *Bernett v Vancouver (City)* [1997] 4 WWR 505 at 514 (BC Sup Ct); *Non-Marine Underwriters, Lloyd's of London v Scalera* [2000] 1 SCR 551 at 578 and 618-9 (obiter) (Sup Ct Canada). Compare this with the English Court of Appeal in *Letang v Cooper* [1965] 1 QB 232, in which it was concluded by Lord Denning at 239-240 that "the distinction between trespass and case is obsolete".

2. Importantly there are unusual rules with respect to pleading and proving fault in a trespass action. The general rule is that the onus of proving (or disproving) the element of fault in an action for trespass is born by the defendant: *McHale v Watson* (1964) 111 CLR 384, *Hackshaw v Shaw* (1984) 155 CLR 614 and more recently *Anton v White* (unreported, New South Wales Court of Appeal, 30 March 2001). *McHale v Watson* (1964) 111 CLR 384 is authority for onus of proof in a non-highway case. Curiously, special rules arose with respect to discharge of fault in highway cases, with the plaintiff in such a case bearing the onus of proof of fault: *Venning v Chin* (1974) 10 SASR 299; *Lord v Nominal Defendant* (1980) 24 SASR 458. A highway case is one which involves injury which occurs on the highway or to property adjoining the highway. One of the reasons for this historical difference is based upon public interest. That is, the public has a right to use the highway but in doing so they and any person who has property adjoining the highway must accept a risk and therefore should bear the onus of proof.

3. The Canadian courts have also endorsed that the onus of proving fault is on the defendant in all but highway cases when it is the plaintiff that bears the onus of proof: *Renco v The Fitness Institute Ltd* (1995) 25 OR (3d) 88 at 91 (Ont Ct Gen Div); *Bernett v Vancouver City* [1997] WWR 505 at 514. Compare with the approach in England. In *Fowler v Lanning* [1959] 1 QB 426, Diplock J held that the onus of proof for fault in all trespass actions is on the plaintiff. This was confirmed in *Letang v Cooper* [1965] 1 QB 232 and continues to be the approach in England.

Damage

[2.65] The final element to be discussed in the distinction between trespass and case is that trespass is actionable per se, that is without proof of damage, whereas a plaintiff in instituting an action for case must be able to establish that he or she has sustained damage.

The High Court explained the policy behind the no damage concept in respect of trespass to land in *Plenty v Dillon* (1991) 171 CLR 635. In this case, police officers, whilst seeking to serve a summons, remained upon the plaintiff's land after permission to be on the land had been revoked. Their Honours Gaudron and McHugh JJ concluded that, although there was no resultant damage to land by the trespass, substantial damages should be awarded:

> The action also serves the purpose of vindicating the plaintiff's right to the exclusive use and occupation of his or her land. ... If the courts of common law do not uphold the rights of individuals by granting effective remedies, they invite anarchy, for nothing breeds social disorder as quickly as the sense of injustice which is apt to be generated by the unlawful invasion of a person's rights, particularly when the invader is a government official. The appellant is entitled to have his right of property vindicated by a substantial award of damages. (*Plenty v Dillon* (1991) 171 CLR 635 at 654-5.)

Similarly in the case of trespass to the person, an individual's right to bodily integrity and to liberty are rights that advocate protection: see *Secretary Department of Health and Community Services v JWB* and *SMB [Marion's Case]* (1992) 175 CLR 218 per Mason CJ, Dawson, Toohey and Gaudron JJ at 233, 249, 254 (extracted at [6.50]). Whilst the individual may not suffer any physical injury by being touched or imprisoned, to permit individuals to commit this type of interference without any remedial action will invite, as the High Court stated, anarchy. Society values highly the right of a person to decide who will and who will not touch their person and equally the right to freedom of movement.

A question arises, however, with respect to whether an action may be instituted for trespass to chattels when there is no damage sustained. It has been suggested that the policy reasons behind protecting property interests and preventing interference with the person do not extend to the protection of chattels; that is the law does not regard the protection of chattels without damage as warranting protection (see JG Fleming, *Law of Torts* (9th ed, LBC Information Services, Sydney, 1998), p 59. This is the approach in the United States: *Koepnick v Sears Roebuck & Co* 762 P 2d 609 (Ct App Az 1988)). However, dicta of the High Court is to the opposite effect (see generally, *Penfolds Wines Pty Ltd v Elliott* (1946) 74 CLR 204. See also *Pargiter v Alexander* (1995) 5 Tas R 158 at 161 (Tas Sup Ct) in which the defendant was liable for trespass to chattels for taking the plaintiff's yacht. Zeeman J stated that if there had been no actual damage the plaintiff would still have been entitled to nominal damages.) There are important reasons for protecting a person's interest in goods even without damage being sustained, for example, to preserve peace and order, and to prevent infringement of civil liberties. This was not an issue though in *Wilson v Marshall* [1982] Tas R 287, in which the Full Court of the Supreme Court of Tasmania held that it was not a civil trespass for a policeman to unlock the door of a car with a piece of wire in order to hold communication with the driver, who was seeking to prevent communication by locking the door and winding up the windows. The Court was of the opinion that damage would have to be shown.

Authority in Australia supports that damage is not required for trespass to the person, trespass to land and the weight of authority supports this as the better view in relation to chattels. In comparison, proof of damage is a requirement to be able to sue in case.

[2.70] **Notes&Questions**

Compare *Wilson v Marshall* [1982] Tas R 287 with the approach of the High Court in *Plenty v Dillon* (1991) 171 CLR 635. Why is a citizen's right to exclusive use and occupation of land more important than that of his or her right to chattels? Arguably the issues of anarchy and social disorder and sense of injustice could equally arise by an interference with chattels.

Perhaps the court in *Wilson v Marshall* [1982] Tas R 287 was concerned with upholding lawful process and found this to be compelling enough to find that there had been no trespass to chattels.

CONCLUSION

[2.75] Whilst an understanding of direct act, fault and damage will importantly assist in determining whether to sue in trespass or in case, once this choice has been made these elements cannot be forgotten. These elements will need to be pleaded and proven to support the choice of action. For example, if the plaintiff claims that they were intentionally run down by a motorist, their choice of action will be battery, a form of trespass to the person. In proving the battery, the plaintiff will need to establish the elements of direct act, fault, positive act, and harmful or offensive interference with their person. Whilst the plaintiff may have suffered injury it is not a requirement that they prove damage to be successful, however the degree of damage suffered may be important in an assessment of monetary relief. The elements of direct act, fault and damage will therefore be revisited throughout the discussion of the intentional torts in Chapters 3-5.

CHAPTER 3

Intentional Interference with the Person

INTRODUCTION

[3.05] This Chapter deals with two forms of tort action, trespass to the person and action on the case. (The essential differences between the two actions are discussed in Chapter 2.) In the context of intentional torts, the action on the case for the intentional infliction of harm is the relevant action on the case.

Trespass to the person has an important role to play in the protection of civil rights; that is, the right to bodily integrity, the right to liberty and the right to privacy. In recent times trespass has been used by victims of crime, bullying, domestic violence and child abuse to seek civil compensation for the wrong and to gain some kind of vindication. Medical law, specifically the need to ensure that medical professionals respect patients' rights to bodily integrity, is also of growing importance in the law of trespass.

Whilst it is arguable that the action on the case for intentional infliction of harm has little to offer in comparison to trespass, there is clear evidence of its resurgence. "The modern kinds of harm to which the tort might be applied include sexual, workplace and other harassment, invasions of privacy, and infliction of mental distress falling short of physical injury" (P Watson, "Searching the Overfull and Cluttered Shelves: *Wilkinson v Downton* Rediscovered" (2004) 23(2) U Tas LR 267 at 267).

Both trespass and case have valuable contributions to make in a modern common law legal process.

TRESPASS TO THE PERSON

[3.10] Trespass to the person protects an individual's right to bodily integrity and liberty. It encompasses the torts of battery, assault and false imprisonment.

Battery

[3.15] Battery is the intentional contact with the body of another person without that person's consent. Assault, in comparison, is the apprehension on the part of the plaintiff of an imminent battery (see [3.45]). Assault and battery will usually occur in quick succession, the plaintiff apprehending the imminent contact and the imminent contact then occurring. However, assault has and does occur without battery and battery may occur without an individual apprehending the contact. Each element of battery is dealt with in turn.

A positive act

[3.20] A plaintiff in any trespass action must establish that the interference complained of has occurred as a result of a positive act; that is, a positive act as opposed to a failure to act (termed an omission). In most cases it will be clear that the interference is caused by either a positive act or an omission to act. However, sometimes what may appear to be an omission the law nevertheless regards as a positive act, for example, in the case of *Fagan v Metropolitan Police Commissioner* [1969] 1 QB 439. Fagan, at the request of a police officer, moved his car and in doing so accidentally drove onto the foot of the officer. The officer yelled for Fagan to move the car. He refused and turned off the engine for a few minutes before moving the car. Fagan appealed his assault conviction upon the ground that his failure to move the car was an omission. The majority reached the conclusion, that although he failed to comply with the request, the failure was nevertheless a positive act. His initial act of driving the car onto the officer's foot was positive (even if accidental) and his failure to then remove it was an omission which occurred during the positive act of driving. That is, both the driving of the car onto the officer's foot and the failure to remove it are part of one continuous positive act.

A direct and intentional or negligent act

[3.25] In bearing the onus of proof, a plaintiff in addition to establishing that the act of the defendant that resulted in the unauthorised contact was positive, must prove that the act was direct. The defendant (the onus lying on him or her) may negate the battery by establishing that his or her actions were neither intentional nor negligent. In a highway case, the onus is on the plaintiff – refer to Chapter 2 [2.60] Note 2 for further discussion.The elements of direct act and fault are common to all trespass actions and are discussed at [2.15] and [2.30] respectively.

Unlawful touching

[3.30] Unlawful touching is the element that distinguishes battery from other trespass actions. Traditionally it was thought that the touching had to be of a hostile nature: "the least touching of another in anger is a battery" (*Cole v Turner* (1704) 6 Mod 149; 87 ER 907). Whilst in cases of domestic violence, physical abuse and rape, the touching is clearly of a hostile nature, touching which is not hostile can equally ground an action in battery, for example, a doctor who performs medical treatment after being denied permission by the patient commits a battery even if the treatment was performed to save the patient's life. The following case explains the circumstances which dictate when touching another's person is or is not a lawful touching.

Brian Rixon v Star City

[3.35] *Brian Rixon v Star City Pty Ltd (formerly Sydney Harbour Casino Pty Ltd)* (2001) 53 NSWLR 98 Court of Appeal of the Supreme Court of New South Wales

The appellant sued the respondent to recover damages for unlawful arrest, assault and false imprisonment. In June 1996, the appellant had been made the subject of an exclusion order issued under s 79 of the *Casino Control Act 1992*. On 25 November 1996, an employee of the respondent approached the appellant in the casino and informed him that, as an excluded person, he was required to follow him to an interview room. The appellant was held in this room for approximately an hour and a half before police arrived, during which time he claimed he suffered stress and anxiety. ...

The trial Judge found that the employee's actions could not amount to an assault because he lacked the requisite intention, or to a battery because he lacked the requisite hostile attitude. The actions for false imprisonment and unlawful arrest failed as the respondent acted within the scope of its legislatively conferred power in detaining the appellant.

SHELLER JA:

51 The placing of the hand on the shoulder could be a battery. As Holt CJ said in *Cole v Turner* (1704) 6 Mod 149; 87 ER 907 "the least touching of another in anger is a battery". On the other hand, as the Chief Justice said, "if two or more meet in a narrow passage, and without any violence or design of harm, the one touches the other gently, it will be no battery".

52 However the absence of anger or hostile attitude by the person touching another is not a satisfactory basis for concluding that the touching was not a battery. In *In re F (Mental Patient: Sterilisation)* [1990] 2 AC 1 at 73 Lord Goff of Chieveley said:

> In the old days it used to be said that, for a touching of another's person to amount to a battery, it had to be a touching "in anger" (see *Cole v Turner* per Holt CJ); and it has recently been said that the touching must be "hostile" to have that effect (see *Wilson v Pringle* [1987] QB 237, 253). I respectfully doubt whether that is correct. A prank that gets out of hand; an over-friendly slap on the back; surgical treatment by a surgeon who mistakenly thinks that the patient has consented to it – all these things may transcend the bounds of lawfulness, without being characterised as hostile. Indeed the suggested qualification is difficult to reconcile with the principle that any touching of another's body is, in the absence of lawful excuse, capable of amounting to a battery and a trespass.

53 In *Collins v Wilcock* [1984] 1 WLR 1172 Lord Goff (then Robert Goff LJ) sitting in the Divisional Court, at 1177-8 referred to the fundamental principle, plain and incontestable, that every person's body is inviolate, and that any touching of another person, however slight may amount to a battery. His Lordship referred to *Cole v Turner* (1704) 6 Mod 149; 87 ER 907 and to *Blackstone's Commentaries*, 17th ed (1830) Vol 3, 120:

> the law cannot draw the line between different degrees of violence, and therefore totally prohibits the first and lowest stage of it; every man's person being sacred, and no other having a right to meddle with it, in any the slightest manner.

His Lordship continued:

> But so widely drawn a principle must inevitably be subject to exceptions. For example, children may be subjected to reasonable punishment; people may be subjected to the lawful exercise of the power of arrest; and reasonable force may be used in self-defence or for the prevention of crime. But, apart from these special instances where the control or constraint is lawful, a broader exception has been created to allow for the exigencies of everyday life. Generally speaking, consent is a defence to battery; and most of the physical contacts of ordinary life are not actionable because they are impliedly consented to by all who move in society and so expose themselves to the risk of bodily contact. So nobody can complain of the jostling which is inevitable from his presence in, for example, a supermarket, an

Brian Rixon v Star City cont.

underground station or a busy street; nor can a person who attends a party complain if his hand is seized in friendship, or even if his back is, within reason, slapped: see *Tuberville v Savage* (1669) 1 Mod 3. Although such cases are regarded as examples of implied consent, it is more common nowadays to treat them as falling within a general exception embracing all physical contact which is generally acceptable in the ordinary conduct of daily life. We observe that, although in the past it has sometimes been stated that a battery is only committed where the action is "angry, revengeful, rude, or insolent" (see Hawkins, Pleas of the Crown, 8th ed (1824), vol 1, c15, section 2), we think that nowadays it is more realistic, and indeed more accurate, to state the broad underlying principle, subject to the broad exception.

Among such forms of conduct, long held to be acceptable, is touching a person for the purpose of engaging his attention, though of course using no greater degree of physical contact than is reasonably necessary in the circumstances for that purpose. So, for example, it was held by the Court of Common Pleas in 1807 that a touch by a constable's staff on the shoulder of a man who had climbed on a gentleman's railing to gain a better view of a mad ox, the touch being only to engage the man's attention, did not amount to a battery: see *Wiffin v Kincard* (1807) 2 Box & Pul 471; for another example, see *Coward v Baddeley* (1859) 4 H & N 478. But a distinction is drawn between a touch to draw a man's attention, which is generally acceptable, and a physical restraint, which is not. So we find Parke B observing in *Rawlings v Till* (1837) 3 M & W 28, 29, with reference to *Wiffin v Kincard*, that "There the touch was merely to engage [a man's] attention, not to put a restraint upon his person".

54 This distinction is explained in *Clerk & Lindsell on Torts*, 17th ed, 12-06 where the question is posed whether the physical contact imposed on the plaintiff was in excess of that "generally acceptable in everyday life". It is pointed out in a footnote that acceptable conduct must be considered in the context of the incident in dispute.

For an adult to jump on another and snatch her shoulder bag is clearly unacceptable. Between 13-year-old schoolboys it might perhaps be seen as "as unremarkable as shaking hands".

55 No error has been demonstrated which would entitle this Court to interfere with the trial Judge's finding that the touching lacked "the requisite anger or hostile attitude". More accurately, and consistently with her Honour's findings, it could not be said that the conduct of Mr Sheldon in the circumstances found and clearly for the purpose of engaging Mr Rixon's attention, was generally acceptable in the ordinary conduct of daily life. ...

60 In my opinion, Acting Judge Balla correctly dismissed Mr Rixon's claims. Accordingly, the appeal should be dismissed with costs.

—— ꕥ ——

[3.40] **Notes&Questions**

1. The Court in the principal case recognizes that touching does not need to be hostile to be battery; rather any touching of another without consent is unlawful. This is based upon the principal of personal inviolability.
2. The High Court of Australia endorsed the principal of personal inviolability in *Secretary Department of Health and Community Services v JWB and SMB* (*Marion's Case*) (1992) 175 CLR 218 (extracted at [6.50]). In this case the Court considered the application for an order authorizing sterilization of a mentally retarded teenager, Marion, brought by her parents. In determining that it was not in the best interests of the child to perform this operation, the Court affirmed an individual's right to personal

inviolability, referencing the well-known words of Cardozo J in *Schloendorff v Society of New York Hospital* 211 NY 125, 105 NE 92 (1914):

> Every human being of adult years and sound mind has a right to determine what shall be done with his own body; and a surgeon who performs an operation without his patient's consent commits an assault.

3. The principal case also accepts that in modern society there needs to be "a general exception [to the principle of personal inviolability] embracing all physical contact which is generally acceptable in the ordinary conduct of daily life". Hence the touching of Mr Rixon on the shoulder to gain his attention was found not to be an unlawful touching.

   Obiter comments of the High Court in *Marions' Case* and in *Boughey v R* (1986) 161 CLR 10 per Mason, Wilson and Deane JJ at 24-5 similarly recognise that:

   > commonplace intentional but non-hostile acts such as patting another on the shoulder to attract attention or pushing between others to alight from a crowded bus ... are, if committed inoffensively, regarded by the common law as ordinary incidents of social intercourse which do not, without more, constitute battery.

   This is also the approach in Canada: see *Non-Marine Underwriters, Lloyd's of London v Scalera* [2000] 1 SCR 551 (a case of sexual battery).

4. Closely related to an individual's right to bodily integrity is the ability of a person to consent to being touched. If a person consents to being touched then it follows there can be no battery, the touching being authorised. It is generally considered that consent is a defence to an intentional tort, rather than an element of the tort itself and consent is therefore discussed in Chapter 6 Defences to the Intentional Torts.

5. Many torts are also crimes; that a criminal action is brought does not prevent the victim bringing a tort or other civil action for compensation. The criminal action is brought by the state on behalf of the public, to punish and to deter similar behaviour. In comparison, an action is brought in tort, for example battery, by the injured plaintiff to seek compensation for the interference with his or her right (for battery the right to bodily integrity). The standard of proof for each action differs: in the criminal action the standard is beyond a reasonable doubt, whereas in the civil action a lower standard applies, that of balance of probabilities. Different rules of evidence also apply in civil cases. The difference in the standards of proof and rules of evidence can lead to different outcomes, for example, the famous case of OJ Simpson. In 1994 the former American NFL player was charged with the murder of his wife Nicole Brown and her boyfriend Ron Goldman after they were found gunned down outside Brown's home. OJ failed to turn himself into police and was the subject of a high speed pursuit which was televised nationally by American TV networks. He was acquitted of the murders in 1995. The parents of Ron Goldman then instituted a civil action for the wrongful death and battery of Goldman and the battery of Brown. In 1997 a jury returned a unanimous verdict in respect of all claims and awarded damages of $33 500 000 (to date only a small fraction of these damages have been paid).

Assault

[3.45] Assault occurs when the defendant by some act creates in the plaintiff a reasonable apprehension of imminent harmful or offensive direct contact with his or her person. That is, the plaintiff apprehends that a battery is about to occur. It is not necessary, however, for the battery to follow for the plaintiff to be able to institute an action. As this is a trespass action, reference should be made to Chapter 2 for discussion of direct act and fault. For the element of positive act, refer to [3.20].

Reasonable apprehension of imminent contact

[3.50] Assault is distinguished from other forms of trespass by the requirement that the plaintiff must experience "a reasonable apprehension of imminent contact" by the defendant. Whether or not the apprehension is reasonable is determined objectively with regard to the circumstances which existed at the time of the alleged assault (*Barton v Armstrong* [1969] 2 NSWLR 451).

For a plaintiff to have a "reasonable apprehension", the defendant must have the present and apparent ability of carrying out the battery. So, in the case of *Bradey v Schatzel* ([1911] St R Qd 206, see also *McClelland v Symons* [1951] VLR 157 at 163-164), the appellant's actions of appearing to load the rifle she was holding and then aiming it at the respondent police officer was held sufficient to constitute assault even though it was later discovered that the rifle had never been loaded. Further, that the police officer was not scared was also considered irrelevant to establishing assault, given that a reasonable person in these circumstances would have been.

How readily or immediately though must the ability to carry out the threat be for a plaintiff's apprehension to be reasonable? If the defendant is unarmed and threatens to go home to collect his gun and come back and shoot the plaintiff, is this sufficient to create a reasonable apprehension, or must he or she have been in possession of the gun at the time of making the threat; or alternatively, if the threat to shoot the plaintiff is sent by email to the plaintiff or made during a telephone conversation, can the plaintiff's apprehension ever be considered to be reasonable? Consider the following case.

Zanker v Vartzokas

[3.55] *Zanker v Vartzokas* (1988) 34 A Crim R 11 Supreme Court of South Australia

(footnotes omitted)

WHITE J: 11 [A] young woman accepted a lift from the defendant who had been sitting on a bench nearby while she made a telephone call. She had just missed a lift from her sister who had driven by while she was in the telephone booth. He asked whether she needed a lift and she said she did. He indicated his white van nearby. She asked him to follow her sister's gold coloured car. They both got in the defendant's van and he drove off. She said in evidence that she was a little nervous about accepting the lift and had tested the door as she got in.

The defendant accelerated the van and soon after it was under way, he offered her money for sexual favours. She rejected his offer. He persisted. She demanded that he stop to allow her to get out but he drove on, accelerating as he went, albeit rather slowly as the van was loaded. She repeated her demand, threatening to jump out; and she opened the passenger's side door slightly. He accelerated faster so she allowed the door to close.

The appellant then said, as the van was gathering speed: "I am going to take you to my mate's house. He will really fix you up." By this time, the van was travelling at 60 km/h. The threat in the

Zanker v Vartzokas cont.

circumstances put her in such fear that she opened the door and leapt out on to the roadside. She suffered some bodily injuries, although not as serious as might be expected.

The appellant conceded that he was unlawfully imprisoning the young woman but he was not charged with that crime. His argument before the magistrate, and on the appeal, was that the wrong charge of assault had been laid. His conduct did not, he said, constitute an assault. He had not touched her or gestured towards her. He disputed the young woman's version of the conversation but the magistrate accepted her evidence.

The magistrate found that the defendant's words, in the context of the acceleration which confined her to the cabin of his van, induced in her mind apprehension of injury later on.

The magistrate said:

> (The young woman) was, no doubt, afraid that she would be detained by the defendant and that at some time in the future she would be subjected to an assault, probably a sexual assault. That fear was real. It was induced by the words and the actions of the defendant. It was the defendant's intention to induce it, but it was not, in my judgment, a fear of immediate violence.

The magistrate dismissed the complaint for that reason.

The magistrate was referred to most of the authorities. He was of the opinion that assault was not proved where the conduct of the defendant induced a present fear in the intended victim's mind that later on, in the indefinite future, she would be or could be subjected to the threatened violence. Generally speaking, the authorities refer to the immediacy or imminence of the feared physical violence.

It is convenient to start with the most recent decision of the Full Court in this State. In *MacPherson v Brown* (1975) 12 SASR 184, the Full Court was divided on the question on the following facts. During student unrest at Flinders University, some students, including the defendant, occupied the administration building at the University. One of the lecturers, Dr Gibbs, assisted other staff in ousting the students and reoccupying the building. Next morning, some ill-feeling was expressed between the defendant and Dr Gibbs. In the afternoon, Dr Gibbs came across a group of thirty students (including the defendant) as he was walking to the registry building. There was an interchange between the defendant and Dr Gibbs but the defendant's words were not threatening. Dr Gibbs' path was barred by the group. He asked to be allowed through. He put his hand forward to move the defendant aside whereupon the defendant commented that Dr Gibbs was assaulting him. Other members in the group took up that cry. Being unable to move, Dr Gibbs twice more asked to be allowed through. He said in evidence that he was in fear of physical danger from the group including the defendant. The confrontation lasted about fifteen minutes. Eventually the group dispersed and Dr Gibbs was allowed to move on.

Against that factual background, Bray CJ and Jacobs J directed an acquittal of the defendant on a charge of assault because the magistrate himself had expressed a doubt whether the facts were sufficient to establish the charge but nevertheless proceeded to convict. Zelling J, on the other hand, held that the defendant was guilty of unlawful imprisonment which, in the circumstances of that case, necessarily involved an assault also. He would have upheld the conviction.

All members of the court pointed out that unlawful imprisonment and assault were separate offences; that an unlawful imprisonment did not necessarily imply an assault; and that a person guilty of an unlawful imprisonment could also be guilty of assault only if all the elements of the crime of assault accompanied the unlawful imprisonment.

In the case presently before me there was undoubtedly an unlawful imprisonment. The question is whether there were present, in addition, all of the elements of the crime of assault.

Zanker v Vartzokas cont.

In *MacPherson v Brown* (1975) 12 SASR 184, the court was principally concerned with the factual issue whether the defendant had engaged in conduct which he knew or ought to have known did or might give cause for belief of imminent harm in the mind of Dr Gibbs. It was in the course of considering that issue that certain remarks were made by the members of the Full Court in *MacPherson's case* about the other aspect of the immediacy or imminence of the physical harm. The other issue which greatly concerned the members of the Full Court was the distinction between assault and false imprisonment. ...

Zelling J said (at 210):

> ... for some fifteen or twenty minutes (Dr Gibbs) was not allowed to get away. The appellant says that he wished the crowd to know his (that is Gibbs') answers ... (He) used the crowd to imprison Gibbs by the implied threat of force to keep him there until he answered the questions to the appellant's satisfaction. The appellant ... used this group as a means of falsely imprisoning Dr Gibbs by inducing fear in (him) that if he tried to get away, his progress would be impeded and if necessary restrained until this confrontation had taken place ... In my opinion this particular false imprisonment does encompass within it both the actus reus and the mens rea of an assault. ...

Zelling J concluded (at 211):

> He encouraged and procured what (the crowd) did for his own ends and did nothing in the fifteen or twenty minutes of the confrontation to urge them to disperse because that would have frustrated his purpose of arraigning Gibbs and preventing Gibbs getting away by putting him in fear of physical obstruction if he tried to do so. Either way the result is the same. The finding of guilty of assault should stand.

Implicit in Zelling J's reasoning is that the fear had to be a present fear of physical harm in due course within the parameters of the incident of unlawful imprisonment – but the feared physical harm did not have to be immediate. The threat could operate immediately on the victim's mind but in a continuing way so long as the unlawful imprisonment situation continued.

I think that the reasoning of Zelling J, although not finding favour with the majority on the facts, is relevant and applicable here where the facts are quite different. The young woman was in immediate and continuing fear so long as she was imprisoned by the defendant. Unlike the "threat" and fear in *MacPherson's case*, this defendant's threat of violence was explicit, namely, that when they arrived at "his mate's house", "he will really fix you up". The threat was, it is true, to be carried out in the future but there was no indication by the defendant whether the "mate's house" was around the next corner or several or more streets away in the suburban area. A present fear of relatively immediate imminent violence was instilled in her mind from the moment the words were uttered and that fear was kept alive in her mind, in the continuing present, by continuing progress, with her as prisoner, towards the house where the feared sexual violence was to occur. It seems to me that the fallacy in the defendant's argument is the assumption that the words had effect only at the time when they were uttered and heard whereas they were ringing presently in her ears as a continuing threat, without the necessity for repetition, second by second as they progressed towards the house. ...

In *Barton v Armstrong* [1969] 2 NSWR 451, a civil case to which the principles of assault apply equally, Taylor J held, in dismissing an application by the defendant to strike out the plaintiff's pleadings, that an assault could be committed in the following alleged circumstances. The plaintiff pleaded that the defendant, a person of authority of whom he was generally in fear, rang him and threatened him with serious violence. He feared this threat and alleged that it was an assault. Taylor J (at 455) held that threats uttered over a telephone in such circumstances are not "properly categorised as mere words". Much depended on the circumstances. He held that threats over a

Zanker v Vartzokas cont.

telephone could put a reasonable person in fear of later physical violence and that this can constitute an assault although the victim does not know exactly or even approximately when that physical violence may be applied.

Taylor J also held that an assault can occur where a defendant threatens physical harm to a plaintiff unless he does what the defendant requires him to do. The plaintiff pleaded that the defendant was in such a strong position of power and influence that the plaintiff genuinely feared that the threats would be carried out at some time unless he did what was required. Taylor J noted (at 454) that many of the older cases were decided before the telephone was available as an instrument for making threats of future violence. He continued:

> However, the earlier cases seem to establish that the gist of the offence of assault is putting a person into apprehension of impending physical contact. The effect on the victim's mind is the material factor, and not whether the defendant actually had the intention or the means to follow it up.

In answer to the contention of defendant's counsel that threats over the telephone could not in law be capable of constituting an assault, Taylor J said (at 455):

> I am not persuaded that threats uttered over the telephone are to be properly categorised as mere words. I think it is a matter of the circumstances.

He then gave instances of telephone calls early in the morning in which the defendant threatens to come to kill or injure the complainant and asked: "How immediate does the fear of physical violence have to be?"

With respect, I do not think that is the question. I think the question is "how immediate must the threatened physical violence be after the utterance of the threat which creates the fear?" Put in that way, it can readily be appreciated that the fear is a continuing fear in the mind of the victim, the utterance having as much effect in an hour or so as it has at the moment of utterance.

I do not have to decide this appeal upon facts like those on *Barton v Armstrong* [1969] 2 NSWLR 451; nor do I necessarily subscribe to everything said by Taylor J in that case as to a telephone call being capable of constituting an assault upon a person at liberty. The striking difference in the facts in the appeal before me is that the fearful victim of future physical harm was not at liberty but always at the mercy of the defendant. One analogy is that she was in the captive position of a mouse to which a playful cat poses a continuing threat of injury or death at a time to be decided by the cat. There was no escape, no reasonable possibility of a novus actus interveniens to break the causal link between the threat and the expected infliction of harm. A further analogy is the position of a victim of a sadist. He imprisons his victim and enjoys the prospect of inflicting pain and of watching the fearful reaction of the victim to the threat of pain to be inflicted at a later time to be decided by the sadist.

For completeness, I quote again from Taylor J (at 455) in the above case:

> In my opinion the answer (to the above question which he had posed) is – it depends on the circumstances. Some threats are not capable of arousing apprehension of violence in the mind of a reasonable person unless there is an immediate prospect of the threat being carried out. Others, I believe, can create the apprehension even if it is made clear that the violence may occur in the future, at times unspecified and uncertain. Being able to immediately carry out the threat is but one way of creating the fear of apprehension, but not the only way. There are other ways, more subtle and perhaps more effective.

Threats which put a reasonable person in fear of physical violence have always been abhorrent to the law as an interference with personal freedom and integrity, and the right of a person to be free from the fear of insult. "If the threat produces the fear or apprehension of physical violence then I am of opinion that the law is breached, although the victim does not know when that physical violence may be effected." ...

Zanker v Vartzokas cont.

The young woman here reasonably believed in the defendant's intention and power to inflict violence in due course with the help of his "mate". Instead of striking out like the acquitted defendant in *Bruce v Dyer* (1966) 58 DLR (2d) 211, she jumped out.

During the course of argument, some examples were canvassed. In a hypothetical example, I asked counsel to assume that the defendant was threatening the victim in a remote scrub area where he was stalking her and calling out threats to rape her if and when he caught her. I also asked counsel to assume that the defendant could catch her and carry out his threat at any time he wished and that both he and she knew this was so. While he was taking no immediate steps to carry out his threats he continued to pursue her because he enjoyed the prolongation of her fear. I expressed the opinion that his original words uttered in those circumstances constituted an assault, for the reasons already given, namely because her fear was a continuing fear induced by his original words in a situation where he remained in a position of dominance and in a position to carry out the threatened violence at some time not too remote, thus keeping the apprehension, the gist of assault, ever present in the victim's mind. The facts in the present appeal are closely analogous to the facts in the hypothetical situation.

Further, the facts in the present appeal indicate that the violence threatened was more immediate and likely than *Barton v Armstrong* [1969] 2 NSWLR 451. Whether or not a finding of assault in *Barton v Armstrong* [1969] 2 NSWLR 451 could be supported at the trial, the assault here was proved, in my opinion, and a conviction for assault occasioning actual bodily harm should have been recorded. Once the assault was proved, the bodily harm resulting from the escape was "occasioned" in fact whether or not the defendant foresaw that she would jump out and injure herself. …

Appeal allowed

[3.60] **Notes&Questions**

Acts, acts and words or words alone *may* constitute threats considered enough to create a reasonable apprehension of an imminent battery. As the principal case states, it will depend upon the circumstances of each perceived threat. Words alone were not sufficient in *R v Knight* (1988) 35 A Crim R 314: threatening telephone calls were made over a period of time to members of the police force, a magistrate and a judge. Whilst acknowledging that severe threats had been made, the conviction was overturned as the prosecution had failed to provide evidence as to the threat of immediate violence. Lee J, with whom the other members of the Court agreed, questioned Taylor J's remarks in *Barton v Armstrong* [1969] 2 NSWLR 451 (discussed in *Zanker v Vartzokas* (1988) 34 A Crim R 11) that all that was required was impending rather than immediate likelihood of battery. Compare this with the English Court of Appeal decision of *R v Ireland* [1997] 1 All ER 112. In this case the Appellant telephoned three women on a number of occasions and when the women answered the telephone he remained silent. On occasions these calls were repeated over a short period of time, for example, 14 calls in an hour. As a result of these telephone calls the women suffered psychological injury. The issues before the Court were: (1) could a telephone call constitute an act; and (2) if so, could that act create a reasonable apprehension of imminent harm? The Court concluded that: (1) the making of the telephone call was an act and it did not matter whether there was words or silence; and (2) based upon the dicta of *Barton v Armstrong* [1969] 2 NSWLR 451, it would depend upon the particular factual circumstances as to whether the act constituted assault. In the present circumstances the Court concluded that the repeated phone calls would have resulted in the women apprehending, reasonably given past experience, the answering of the telephone and the ensuing psychological damage (imminent harm) that may occur as a result of another bout of silence. Is this extension of immediate too great? Consider the fact that the harm feared here is psychological damage – how does this sit with the apprehension of an imminent "battery"?

Fault

[3.65] Whilst a general discussion of the law in respect of fault (intent) occurs at [2.30] to which the reader should refer, there is an additional issue with respect to intent and assault: a defendant argues that they had no intention to actually carry through with their threat, for example, they may raise their fist above the face of the plaintiff but do not intend to punch him or her, will there be a lack of intent?

Hall v Fonceca

[3.70] *Hall v Fonceca* [1983] WAR 309 Supreme Court of Western Australia

(footnotes omitted)

[In an action for battery, the defendant claimed that he acted in self-defence to an assault committed on him by the plaintiff. The defendant's defence was upheld by the trial judge. The plaintiff appealed on the ground that, although the judge found that during an argument accompanied by some pushing, the plaintiff shook his left hand in front of the defendant's face and was seen to be about to raise his right hand, the judge had not found the necessary intent in the plaintiff to make these actions an assault.]

SMITH AND KENNEDY JJ: 313 At common law, the weight of opinion clearly favours the view that there must be, on the part of the assailant, an intention either to use force or to create an apprehension of the use of force on the part of the person being assaulted. That has not been of recent development. It is unnecessary to consider whether recklessness, where the assailant adverts to the consequence of his conduct, suffices for this purpose, although there is strong support for the view that it does ...

Although the authorities are surprisingly sparse in this area, we accept that an intention on the part of the assailant either to use force or to create apprehension in the victim is an element in an assault. Macrossan SPJ apparently had no doubt that the relevant intention on the part of the assailant was necessary to constitute an assault under the Code: see *R v McIver* (1928) 22 QJPR 173; see also *Fogden v Wade* [1945] NZLR 724 at 728. ...

The fact that his Honour found that, when the appellant moved his right hand, he had not intended to punch the respondent, is not determinative of the present case. It would have been sufficient to constitute a threat if there had been an intention on the part of the appellant to cause apprehension to the respondent. His Honour expressed his finding in terms of the code definition, in which the requirement of the relevant intent is implicit in the word "threatens", and in doing so, he set out what constituted the threat, namely "a combination of actions and attitude" ... we have not been persuaded that his Honour misunderstood the meaning of the word "threatens" in the code definition.

[Appeal dismissed. The concurring judgment of Wallace J has been omitted.]

[3.75] **Notes&Questions**

1. According to Smith and Kennedy JJ, for a defendant to be liable for assault, he or she must actually intend, that is, turn their mind to using force against the plaintiff or

creating the apprehension of force in the mind of the plaintiff. The assumption is that there is no action for negligent assault in trespass. The definition of intention in *Hall v Fonceca* [1983] WAR 309 was confirmed in *Rixon v Star City Pty Ltd* (2001) 53 NSWLR 98 (see extract at [3.35]), the Court of Appeal concluding that the placement by an employee of his hand on the plaintiff's shoulder, without force and without causing injury, lacked "the necessary intention to create in Mr Rixon an apprehension of imminent harmful or offensive contact ..." (at para [59]).

2. Sometimes the assault includes a verbal threat, which is conditional, for example, Assailant X follows Y down a dark lane, shoves Y against a wall and holding a knife to Y's throat, yells, "Give me your wallet and I won't cut you!" The imminent battery is conditional upon non-compliance with the stated request. Whether a conditional threat is calculated to cause apprehension of battery will depend upon the surrounding circumstances and in the given example there can be no doubt there was intent to cause apprehension on the part of Assailant X. Compare, however, with *Tuberville v Savage* (1669) 1 Mod Rep 3; 86 ER 684, an old English case in which the plaintiff placed his hand on his sword and said "[i]f it were not assize-time, I would not take such words from you". This conditional statement and accompanying act were held not to be an assault because the declaration was that there would in fact be no battery because the judges were in town (and Gentlemen kept their word). However in *Rozsa v Samuels* [1969] SASR 205, the conditional threat and accompanying acts were an assault. The plaintiff and defendant were both taxi drivers. The plaintiff had approached the defendant who was sitting in his cab and threatened to punch him in the head; the defendant had driven his cab to the front of the taxi rank rather than waiting his turn and refused to move. In response to the plaintiff's threat the defendant produced a table knife from under the dash and stated "I will cut you to bits if you try it" and proceeded to get out of the cab.

False imprisonment

False imprisonment is a direct act by the defendant that intentionally deprives the plaintiff of his or her liberty without lawful justification. False imprisonment significance lies in its protection of the liberty of individuals from unlawful detention. (For the common trespass elements of direct act and fault refer to Chapter 2 and for Positive Act refer to [3.20].)

Acting under direction

Like all trespass actions, the defendant must cause the imprisonment. This may be by virtue of the defendant's own actions or by actively promoting others to carry out the imprisonment. In *Dickenson v Waters Ltd* (1931) 31 SR (NSW) 593, the plaintiff, who was shopping at the defendant store, was accused of shoplifting by the shop inspector and taken to the manager's office. A police officer was called and said to the defendant's manager, "Do you wish to proceed against this person?" and the manager said "Yes". The plaintiff was subsequently charged with larceny and acquitted. The defendant store, rather than the police officer, was liable for the false imprisonment as the police constable in the given situation would not have taken the plaintiff into custody but for the manager's reply to his question. It is otherwise when the police exercise their own independent discretion and make a decision to effect an arrest (see *Myer Stores v Soo* [1991] 2 VR 597 [3.185] and for further examples see: *Meering v Grahame-White Aviation Co Ltd* (1919) 122 LT 44; *Sadler v Madigan* (unreported, Supreme Court of Victoria Court of Appeals, 1 October 1998) at [28].) Similarly in the recent High

Court case of *Ruddock v Taylor* (2005) 79 ALJR 1534, per Gleeson, Gummow, Hayne & Heydon JJ at [112]-[118] and Kirby J at [149]-[156], the Minister for Immigration and Multicultural Affairs was found to be responsible for the false imprisonment of the respondent and not the immigration officers who had detained him. The Minister had erroneously cancelled the respondents visa, and pursuant to s 189 of the *Migration Act 1958* (Cth), the immigration officers were required by law to detain the appellant – there was no opportunity for the exercise of independent discretion. Where there are several officers or persons who are "active in promoting and causing the detention of the respondent" each will be jointly responsible for the imprisonment (*Myer Stores v Soo* [1991] 2 VR 597 [3.185] per O'Bryan J at 617 and see McDonald J at 629-630).

An action for false imprisonment, however, will not lie against "a person who brings about an arrest by merely setting in motion the formal process of law, as by making a complaint before a Justice of the Peace or applying for a warrant, ... if there is any liability, it is only for the misuse of legal process such as the procuring of an arrest for an improper purpose" (*Casley v Commonwealth* (1980) 30 ALR 38 (WA SC) Wickham J at 46).

The principle of acting under direction applies equally to the other intentional torts.

Total imprisonment

[3.90] The element that is peculiar to false imprisonment is that the imprisonment itself must be total. There must be detention that prevents free movement in all directions, not merely obstruction of movement in a particular direction. Thus, in *Bird v Jones* (1845) 7 QB 742; 115 ER 668, even though the plaintiff was prevented from moving along a footway over a bridge by two officials blocking his way of passage, he was not falsely imprisoned. The imprisonment was not total as he could have turned around and exited the footway and used the footway on the other side of the bridge to cross.

Whether there is total detention depends on whether there is a reasonable means of escape. In *Burton v Davies* [1953] QSR 26, it was held that the plaintiff had no reasonable means of escape from the defendant's moving car when her only means of doing so was to jump from it. Equally, there may be imprisonment on board an aircraft (*Louis v Commonwealth* (1987) 87 FLR 277) and on a steam launch, such as in *R v Macquarie* (1875) 13 SCR (NSW) 264, when escape would have involved diving overboard and swimming ashore. Likewise the means of escape will not be reasonable if a person is justified in believing that they are being lawfully detained (see, for example, *Symes v Mahon* [1922] SASR 447 discussed at [3.110]) or will be physically detained if they attempt to leave (*Bahner v Marwest Hotel Co Ltd* (1969) 6 DLR (3d) 222 Affirmed 12 DLR (3d) 646 (Can) discussed at [3.105] Note 2, and see also *Myer Stores v Soo* [1991] 2 VR 597 [3.185]).

Sometimes the question of reasonable means of escape becomes a question of whether the imprisonment is, in any case, against the plaintiff's will. An example of this might arise if the plaintiff willingly enters premises subject to some condition involving restriction of the plaintiff's freedom. For example, a sign posted at the entrance of a Department Store stating that entry is conditional upon bags being inspected. Would a customer's refusal to have their bags searched as they leave the store permit the store to restrain the customer against his or her will?

Balmain New Ferry v Robertson

[3.95] *Balmain New Ferry Co Ltd v Robertson* (1906) 4 CLR 379 High Court of Australia (footnotes omitted)

[Appellants ran a steam ferry from Sydney to Balmain. Fares were not collected on the ferry or on the Balmain side, but were all collected at turnstiles on the Sydney wharf. A notice board a few feet over the turnstiles read: "Notice. A fare of one penny must be paid on entering or leaving the wharf. No exception will be made to this rule, whether the passenger has travelled by the ferry or not". The respondent paid a penny and passed through the turnstile on to the wharf. Discovering that he had missed the ferry, he argued with the officers on the turnstile that he should be entitled to leave the wharf without paying a further penny. After some 20 minutes, during which the respondent continued to assert and the officers to deny his right to pass out through the turnstiles without payment, the respondent eventually, in spite of opposing force on the part of the officers, squeezed his way out between the exit turnstile and the bulkhead and gained access to the street. These facts constituted the assault and false imprisonment for which the respondent sued.

The High Court, Griffith CJ, Barton and O'Connor JJ, held that the suit failed.]

GRIFFITH CJ: [in the course of a judgment in which he said he agreed with O'Connor J] 386 It is clear that the invitation which the defendants offered to members of the public to come upon their premises was conditional, and it must be taken that members of the public, who availed themselves of the permission, agreed to be bound by the terms on which it was granted so far as they were acquainted with them. ... If the plaintiff was aware of these terms he must be held to have agreed to them when he obtained admission. If he had been a stranger who had never before been on the premises, it would have been sufficient for the defendants to prove that they had done what was reasonably sufficient to give the plaintiff notice of the conditions of admission. ... In this case, however, it appeared that the plaintiff had been on the premises before, and was aware of the existence of the turnstiles and of the purpose for which they were used. It was therefore established that he was aware of the terms on which he had obtained admittance, and it follows that he had agreed to be bound by them. ...

O'CONNOR J: 388 The abridgement of a man's liberty is not under all circumstances actionable. He may enter into a contract which necessarily involves the surrender of a portion of his liberty for a certain period, and if the act complained of is nothing more than a restraint in accordance with that surrender he cannot complain. Nor can he, without the assent of the other party, by electing to put an end to the contract, become entitled at once, unconditionally and irrespective of the other party's rights, to regain his liberty as if he had never surrendered it. ...

In my view, it is immaterial whether the company did what was reasonable to direct public attention to the notice, or whether the plaintiff ever read it until his attention was called to it by the officer at the turnstile. ... The company was lawfully entitled to impose the condition of a penny payment on all who used the turnstiles, whether they had travelled by the company's steamers or not, and they were under no obligation to make an exception in the plaintiff's favour. ...

[Barton J concurred with O'Connor J in a brief judgment.]

[This decision was upheld on appeal to the Privy Council]

Robinson [sic] v Balmain New Ferry

[3.100] *Robinson [sic] v Balmain New Ferry Co Ltd* [1910] AC 295 (Privy Council)

LORD LOREBURN LC: 299 The question whether the notice which was affixed to these premises was brought home to the knowledge of the plaintiff is immaterial, because the notice itself is

Robinson [sic] v Balmain New Ferry cont.

immaterial. ... The defendants were entitled to impose a reasonable condition before allowing him to pass through their turnstile from a place to which he had gone of his own free will. The payment of a penny was a quite fair condition, and if he did not choose to comply with it the defendants were not bound to let him through. He could proceed on the journey he had contracted for. ...

[3.105] **Notes&Questions**

1. This issue came before the House of Lords in *Herd v Weardale Steel* [1915] AC 67. The Appellant had been lowered into a coal mine at 9.30 am. He and some of his fellow workmen decided to strike, and requested to be drawn up from the mine at about 11 am. The shift on which they were engaged did not end until 4 pm, and for some hours permission was refused. Finally the men were drawn up at about 1.30 pm. Herd sued his employers for wrongful imprisonment. The trial judge found in his favour and awarded £1 damages. (The employers had earlier successfully sued Herd for breach of contract.) Their Lordships endorsed the approach taken in *Balmain Ferry*. Viscount Haldane LC concluded:

   > ... when a man goes down a mine, from which access to the surface does not exist in the absence of special facilities given on the part of the owner of the mine, he is only entitled to the use of these facilities (subject possibly to the exceptional circumstances ...) on the terms on which he has entered.

   The exceptional circumstances to which his Lordship was referring may include a duty imposed by statute or a situation of imminent danger.

2. Whilst these cases support that entry into a contract is sufficient to make lawful an imprisonment, they are questionable. Glanville Williams, in his article "Two Cases for False Imprisonment" in RHC Holland & G Schwarzenberger (eds), *Law, Justice and Equity* (London, Pitman, 1967), pp 47-55, observes that unless it is unreasonable to release a person for matters of public policy, the person must be released. For example, under a contract of carriage on a train and the passenger insists on being released in the middle of the journey, which would cause great inconvenience to other passengers, then a temporary restriction of liberty would be justified. Williams is of the view that the imprisonment in *Herd v Weardale Steel* [1915] AC 67 cannot be justified merely as a way of enforcing performance of a contract. There was no evidence of an agreement by the plaintiff that his consent to stay down the mine should be irrevocable for the purpose of the law of tort. Rather the consequence of breach of contract is liability in damages for that breach and not the right to deprive someone of their liberty. See similar arguments in KF Tan's article titled "A Misconceived Issue in the Tort of False Imprisonment" (1981) 44 MLR 166. This is also supported by *Bahner v Marwest Hotel Co Ltd* (1969) 6 DLR (3d) 222 Affirmed in 12 DLR (3d) 646 (Can), in which the plaintiff, who refused to pay for a bottle of wine he had ordered with dinner was found to be falsely imprisoned by the hotel when their security guard blocked his exit and also when he was subsequently arrested by the police. The Court determined that there "was no reasonable and probable cause for imprisonment in either case". The Court did not see that breach of contract

justified the imprisonment. Arguably, the approach in the early 1900's in *Balmain Ferry* and *Herd v Weardale Steel* [1915] AC 67 does not reflect the importance today of the right to liberty; a fundamental civil right valued by modern society. It is highly doubtful that a restaurant patron who forgets his or her wallet could be forced to wash the dishes.

3. The case of *Herd v Weardale Steel* [1915] AC 67 is also relevant to the element of "positive act" discussed at [3.20]. Whilst the House of Lords found that the terms of the contract permitted the plaintiff's imprisonment, it would upon the basis of this reasoning have been the case that if the defendant manager had failed to raise the miner from the shaft at the end of his shift, this would have been false imprisonment. The terms of the contract of employment would have imposed upon the manager a positive duty to act. Upon this basis failure to release prisoners at the end of the term of their imprisonment has also been found to constitute false imprisonment (see [3.120] Note 1).

[3.110] It is also possible that a plaintiff is totally imprisoned without physical boundaries. This may occur if the plaintiff believes that he or she has no choice but to accompany a person or remain where they are. That is, the individual has not consented but is coerced by the relationship of power and submits to the control of the defendant. For example, in *Symes v Mahon* [1922] SASR 447, a warrant had been issued for the arrest of a person other than the plaintiff. The defendant police constable mistakenly told the plaintiff he was the man identified in the warrant. The defendant repeatedly told the plaintiff he would "have" to go to town with him, and the plaintiff went away to tell his wife, agreeing to join the train with the defendant the next day. At the train the defendant repeated that plaintiff would "have" to come. The plaintiff preferred to buy his own ticket and he and his wife travelled in a different compartment from the defendant. Murray CJ held that the plaintiff was imprisoned from the time he was required to enter the train until his formal release. This meant not only the train journey, but the tram journey to the police watch-house during which the plaintiff was allowed to go to his hotel to deliver his luggage, and the time during which he was permitted to leave the watch-house pending the arrival of a witness. Upon arrival of the witness the issue of the plaintiff's mistaken identity was cleared up and he was permitted to leave. The Chief Justice held that there was complete submission of the plaintiff to the control of the defendant in the reasonable belief that he had no way of escape that he could reasonably take.

Can a person though be said to be totally imprisoned if they are, at the time of imprisonment, unaware of their confinement? For example, a baby who is kidnapped is unaware of their restraint, or a person who is locked in a room whilst they are asleep, or a prisoner who is unaware that the term of his sentence has been incorrectly calculated? Can they nevertheless bring an action for false imprisonment? Consider the following case.

Murray v Ministry of Defence

[3.115] *Murray v Ministry of Defence* [1988] 1 WLR 692 House of Lords (NI)

(footnotes omitted)

[The plaintiff had been detained on suspicion of involvement with the IRA. From 7 am on the day of the arrest the detention was for a period in the house where she lived. She was not at first told that she was under arrest, though a formal statement was made by the arresting officer to this effect before she was taken from the house. It was held in the Court of Appeal that plaintiff's knowledge of

Murray v Ministry of Defence cont.

imprisonment is essential to the action for false imprisonment and that the plaintiff was not imprisoned for the purposes of the action until she was told of it. The House of Lords, however, held that there was imprisonment at the house, though it was lawfully justified. All the other law lords agreed with the speech of Lord Griffiths.]

LORD GRIFFITHS: 701 Although on the facts of this case I am sure that the plaintiff was aware of the restraint on her liberty from 7.00am I cannot agree with the Court of Appeal that it is an essential element of the tort of false imprisonment that the victim should be aware of the fact of denial of liberty. The Court of Appeal relied upon *Herring v Boyle* (1834) 1 CM & R 377; 149 ER 1126 for this proposition which they preferred to the view of Atkin LJ to the opposite effect in *Meering v Grahame-White Aviation Co. Ltd* (1919) 122 LT 44. *Herring v Boyle* (1834) 1 CM & R 377; 149 ER 1126 is an extraordinary decision of the Court of Exchequer: a mother went to fetch her 10 year old son from school on 24 December 1833 to take him home for the Christmas holidays. The headmaster refused to allow her to take her son home because she had not paid the last term's fees, and he kept the boy at school over the holidays. An action for false imprisonment brought on behalf of the boy failed. In giving judgment, Bolland B said at 381:

> as far as we know, the boy may have been willing to stay; he does not appear to have been cognisant of any restraint, and there was no evidence of any act whatsoever done by the defendant in his presence. I think that we cannot condone the refusal to the mother in the boy's absence, and without his being cognisant of any restraint, to be imprisonment of him against his will.

I suppose it is possible that there are schoolboys who prefer to stay at school rather than go home for holidays but it is not an inference that I would draw, and I cannot believe that on the same facts the case would be similarly decided today. In *Meering v Grahame-White Aviation Co Ltd* (1919) 122 LT 44, the plaintiff's employers, who suspected him of theft, sent two of the works police to bring him in for questioning at the company's offices. He was taken to a waiting-room where he said that if he was not told why he was there he would leave. He was told he was wanted for the purpose of making inquiries about things that had been stolen and he was wanted to give evidence. Unknown to the plaintiff, the works police had been instructed not to let him leave the waiting-room until the Metropolitan Police arrived ... Atkin LJ said at 53-54:

> It appears to me that a person could be imprisoned without his knowing it. I think a person can be imprisoned while he is asleep, while he is in a state of drunkenness, while he is unconscious, and while he is a lunatic. Those are cases where it seems to me that the person might properly complain if he were imprisoned, though the imprisonment began and ceased while he was in that state. Of course, the damages might be diminished and would be affected by the question whether he was conscious of it or not. So a man might in fact, to my mind, be imprisoned by having the key of a door turned against him so that he is imprisoned in a room in fact although he does not know that the key has been turned. ... If a man can be imprisoned by having the key turned upon him without his knowledge, so he can be imprisoned if, instead of a lock and key or bolts and bars, he is prevented from, in fact exercising his liberty by guards and warders or policemen. They serve the same purpose.

I agree with this passage. In the first place, it is not difficult to envisage cases in which harm may result from unlawful imprisonment even though the victim is unaware of it ... *The Restatement of Torts* ... requires that the person confined is conscious of the confinement or is harmed by it ... *Restatement of the Law, Second, Torts 2d* (1965) section 35, p 52.

If a person is unaware that he has been falsely imprisoned and has suffered no harm, he can normally expect to recover no more than nominal damages, and it is tempting to redefine the tort in the terms of the present rule in the American *Restatement of Torts*. On reflection, however, I would not do so. The law attaches supreme importance to the liberty of the individual and if he suffers a wrongful interference with that liberty it should remain actionable even without proof of special damage. ...

———— ꕥ ————

[3.120] **Notes&Questions**

1. There have been a number of cases in recent times involving the incarceration by prison authorities of prisoners beyond the term of their sentence as a result of miscalculation of the term of imprisonment, for example, by failing to take into account time already served. In *R v Governor of Brockhill Prison* [2000] 4 All ER 15, the House of Lords referred with approval to the decision of *Cowell v Corrective Services Commission of New South Wales* (1988) 13 NSWLR 714 (Sup Crt NSW CA). It was concluded in both cases that false imprisonment is a tort of strict liability and even though the defendant acted under the reasonable belief, that is, upon a good faith interpretation of the law, this interpretation was incorrect and the incarceration after the correct term of imprisonment expired became unlawful. Further, it was irrelevant that the prisoner was unaware of this at the time of his unlawful imprisonment. See also *Tang Jia Xin v Minister for Immigration and Ethnic Affairs* (unreported, Federal Court of Australia, 11 April 1996), in which the plaintiffs, two boat people who applied for and were refused refugee status, were detained beyond the period permitted by the *Migration Act 1958* (Cth) again upon the basis of a miscalculation of time. Compare with the case of *Ruddock v Taylor* (2005) 79 ALJR 1534 in which the respondent was twice detained by immigration authorities after his visa was, upon both occasions, erroneously cancelled. Section 189(1) of the *Migration Act 1958* (Cth) required an officer to detain a person whom the officer knew or reasonably suspected to be an unlawful non-citizen. A majority of the High Court found that even though the respondent Taylor's visa had been cancelled based upon a mistake of law, the immigration officer was unaware of the error and therefore his belief was sufficient to meet the reasonable suspicion standard in the Act. The officer in detaining Taylor was therefore acting under authority of the law. This case differs from that of *Tang Jia Xin* where there was no legal authority to detain given that the detention was based upon an error in the calculation of time. Compare also with the United Kingdom case of *ID v The Home Office* [2006] 1 All ER 183 in which the Court of Appeal reinstated an action for false imprisonment brought by a family after being refused asylum. There was a genuine question to be tried as to whether the immigration officer had reasonable grounds to detain. For a good discussion of the various Australian and English decisions with respect to this issue refer to M Fordham, "False Imprisonment in Good Faith" (2000) Tort L Rev 53.

2. As far as the element of fault is concerned, the better view is that no action lies for a negligent false imprisonment, rather the action is brought in negligence and the plaintiff will be required to prove that their negligent detention resulted in actual injury. For example, in the case of *Sayers v Harlow UDC* [1958] 1 WLR 623 the plaintiff was locked in a public lavatory owing to a faulty lock which was caused by the defendant's negligence. The plaintiff was injured when she attempted to climb out of the cubicle and the toilet roll rolled under her foot. The plaintiff was successful in recovering

damages subject to a reduction for contributory negligence; however the case was brought in negligence and not false imprisonment. Policy would seem to dictate that an individual suffer injury and bring their action in negligence, if not the floodgates to spurious or trivial claims may well open. For further discussion see U Burnham, "Negligent False Imprisonment–Scope for Re-Emergence?" (1998) 61 *Modern Law Review* 573. It should also be understood that the cases in Note 1 above, of detention longer than the permitted period are not of negligent false imprisonment, but intentional. For example, in the case of *R v Governor of Brockhill Prison* [2000] 4 All ER 15, the prison authorities may have negligently calculated the term of the sentence, but nevertheless they intentionally detained the prisoner beyond his lawful term of imprisonment.

3. What is the difference between an action for false imprisonment and an action for malicious prosecution? False imprisonment is a restraint on liberty that is imposed directly by the defendant while malicious prosecution results from an independent discretion that is interposed between the act of the defendant and the restraint. For example, if the plaintiff is wrongfully arrested and taken before a magistrate who remands the plaintiff in custody, there is no action for false imprisonment in respect of the period of restraint following the remand. The action must be in respect of malicious proceedings. In *Little v Law Institute of Victoria (No 3)* [1990] VR 257, Kaye and Beach JJ said (at 262) that to establish a case of malicious prosecution the plaintiff must prove: that the proceedings complained of were instituted or continued by the defendant; that the defendant instituted or continued the proceedings maliciously; that the defendant acted without reasonable and probable cause; and that the proceedings were terminated in the plaintiff's favour. Further the damage must be to reputation, or done to the person, such as danger to life, limb or liberty, or damage to property, such as being forced to expend money in answering charges. *Brooke v Grimpel* (1987) Aust Torts Reports 80-108 (Qld Sup Ct) is an example of a successful action.

ACTION ON THE CASE FOR INTENTIONAL HARM

Indirect intentional infliction of personal injury

[3.125] Among the torts so far explored, those classed as trespass may generally be committed intentionally or negligently, as a result of some direct interference. What happens when an individual is injured and the interference is indirect, is the plaintiff left without redress? One answer is that the plaintiff may sue in negligence, it being irrelevant whether or not the act was direct or indirect. Part II of this book deals at length with negligence. Negligence will not usually provide redress for a plaintiff who has suffered harm as the result of an intentional indirect interference (though dependent upon how the case is framed, negligence may be an available action). The answer is an action on the case.

Actions on the case developed to provide a remedy where injury was suffered as an indirect result of the defendant's actions and could be instituted in respect of both negligent and intentional acts. With the development of modern day negligence, its significance waned. However, its importance in tort law is remerging and "modern kinds of harm to which the tort might be applied include sexual, workplace and other harassment, invasions of privacy, and infliction of mental distress falling short of physical injury" (see the article by P Watson at [3.05]).

Today, for a plaintiff to successfully argue an action for indirect infliction of personal injury based upon action on the case, he or she must prove that the act, whilst indirect, was nevertheless intentional (fault) and resulted in harm.

Fault

[3.130] Being an intentional tort, intention upon the part of the defendant must be established. An early example of an action on the case is *Bird v Holbrook* (1828) 4 Bing 628; 130 ER 911. The defendant in this case rented and occupied a walled garden in which he grew tulips and other valuable flowers. To protect his property from thieves, he set up a spring-gun, activated by trip-wires across the garden. No notice of the spring-gun was posted. The plaintiff, a youth of 19, climbed the wall and entered the garden to catch a straying pea-hen. He set off the spring-gun and was shot in the leg. Best CJ determined that it would be wrong if people could avoid the consequences of their actions simply because their action was indirect.

> I am, therefore, clearly of opinion that he who sets spring-guns, without giving notice, is guilty of an inhuman act, and that, if injurious consequence ensues, he is liable to yield redress to the sufferer … He intended … that the gun should be discharged, and that the contents should be lodged in the body of his victim, for he could not be caught in any other way.

In *Bird v Holbrook* (1828) 4 Bing 628; 130 ER 911, the defendant's intention, that is, his desire that the plaintiff be injured, was clear on the facts: "he could not be caught in any other way". Whilst intention provides little difficulty in the above case since there was a clear desire or purpose on the part of the defendant to inflict injury, the next two cases discuss what "intention" means in the context of an action on the case.

Wilkinson v Downton

[3.135] *Wilkinson v Downton* [1897] 2 QB 57 Court of Queen's Bench (footnotes omitted)

[The facts are explained in the judgment of Wright J.]

WRIGHT J: 58 In this case the defendant, in the execution of what he seems to have regarded as a practical joke, represented to the plaintiff that he was charged by her husband with a message to her to the effect that her husband was smashed up in an accident, and was lying at The Elms at Leytonstone with both legs broken, and that she was to go at once in a cab with two pillows to fetch him home. All this was false. The effect of the statement on the plaintiff was a violent shock to her nervous system, producing vomiting and other more serious and permanent physical consequences at one time threatening her reason, and entailing weeks of suffering and incapacity to her as well as expense to her husband for medical attendance. These consequences were not in any way the result of previous ill-health or weakness of constitution; nor was there any evidence of predisposition to nervous shock or any other idiosyncrasy.

In addition to these matters of substance there is a small claim for 1s 101/2d for the cost of railway fares of persons sent by the plaintiffs to Leytonstone in obedience to the pretended message. As to this 1s 101/2d expended in railway fares on the faith of the defendant's statement, I think the case is clearly within the decision in *Pasley v Freeman* (1789) 3 TR 51 [100 ER 450]. The statement was a misrepresentation intended to be acted on to the damage of the plaintiff.

The real question is as to the £100, the greatest part of which is given as compensation for the female plaintiff's illness and suffering. It was argued for her that she is entitled to recover this as being damage caused by fraud, and therefore within the doctrine established by *Pasley v Freeman* (1789) 3 TR 51 [100 ER 450] and *Langridge v Levy* (1837) 2 M &W 519 [150 ER 863]. I am not sure that this would not be an extension of that doctrine, the real ground of which appears to be that a person who

Wilkinson v Downton cont.

makes a false statement intended to be acted on must make good the damage naturally resulting from its being acted on. Here there is no injuria of that kind. I think, however, that the verdict may be supported upon another ground. The defendant has, as I assume for the moment, wilfully done an act calculated to cause physical harm to the plaintiff that is to say, to infringe her legal right to personal safety, and has in fact thereby caused physical harm to her. That proposition without more appears to me to state a good cause of action, there being no justification alleged for the act. This wilful injuria is in law malicious, although no malicious purpose to cause the harm which was caused nor any motive of spite is imputed to the defendant.

It remains to consider whether the assumptions involved in the proposition are made out. One question is whether the defendant's act was so plainly calculated to produce some effect of the kind which was produced that an intention to produce it ought to be imputed to the defendant, regard being had to the fact that the effect was produced on a person proved to be in an ordinary state of health and mind. I think that it was. It is difficult to imagine that such a statement, made suddenly and with apparent seriousness, could fail to produce grave effects under the circumstances upon any but an exceptionally indifferent person, and therefore an intention to produce such an effect must be imputed, and it is no answer in law to say that more harm was done than was anticipated, for that is commonly the case with all wrongs. The other question is whether the effect was, to use the ordinary phrase, too remote to be in law regarded as a consequence for which the defendant is answerable. Apart from authority, I should give the same answer and on the same ground as the last question, and say that it was not too remote. Whether, as the majority of the House of Lords thought in *Lynch v Knight* (1861) 9 HLC 577 at 592, 596 [11 ER 854 at 860, 862], the criterion is in asking what would be the natural effect on reasonable persons, or whether, as Lord Wensleydale thought (at 600 [863]), the possible infirmities of human nature ought to be recognised, it seems to me that the connection between the cause and the effect is sufficiently close and complete. ...

There must be judgment for the plaintiff for £100 1s 101/2d.

[3.140] The following case provides a more recent examination of the issue of what constitutes fault for action on the case for intentional harm.

Nationwide News v Naidu

[3.145] *Nationwide News Pty Ltd v Naidu* (2007) 71 NSWLR 471 Court of Appeal of the New South Wales Supreme Court

(footnotes omitted)

[The respondent, Naidu a Fijian by birth, was employed by a security firm to provide security services at Nationwide News. He was promoted and came under the direct supervision of Chaloner, an employee of the appellant. The trial court found that Chaloner subjected the respondent to bullying behaviour which was extreme. This bullying occurred over a period of years and both within and outside the workplace. The bullying included racial taunts, abusive and offensive language, sexually inappropriate comments about Naidu's wife, sexual harassment, threats of physical harm, intimidation and offensive requirements including that Naidu ask permission to go to the toilet, that he return to work after being in a car accident although not well enough, and that he work weekends on the construction of Chaloner's home for no pay. As a result of the bullying Naidu was diagnosed with major depression and post-traumatic stress disorder.]

SPIGELMAN CJ:

Nationwide News v Naidu cont.

The Intentional Tort

66 The respondent has sought to uphold his Honour's award of damages in tort on the basis of the intentional tort it pleaded. This was done by way of notice of contention rather than notice of appeal, so that it arises only if the Court allows the appeal on the finding of negligence which, for the reasons I have given above, should occur.

67 His Honour's findings of fact are that Mr Chaloner wilfully committed a series of acts calculated to cause Mr Naidu physical harm, being a recognised psychiatric injury. This could constitute an intentional tort of the character identified in *Wilkinson v Downton* [1897] 2 QB 57; 66 LJQB 493 affirmed in *Janvier v Sweeney* [1919] 2 KB 316 and accepted, albeit without affirmation, by the High Court in *Bunyan v Jordan* [1937] HCA 5; (1937) 57 CLR 1 and *Northern Territory v Mengel* (1995) 185 CLR 307 at 347.

68 His Honour made all of the findings of primary fact required to establish the tort but refrained from concluding that the cause of action had been made out. He said:

> [186] The acts of Mr Chaloner were, of course, not mere negligence. They were deliberate and intended to demean, offend and injure. Because no particular occasion could be said to have caused the plaintiff's ultimate psychological illness, the defendants argue that the line of reasoning expressed in *Janvier v Sweeney* [1919] 2 KB 316 does not apply. It strikes me as extraordinary that, the intention of Mr Chaloner being as I have characterised it, he would not be liable for the actual injury he inflicted on the plaintiff, though he had not actually thought that what he was doing might do more than cause temporary, though acute and painful distress. In fact, I consider that Mr Chaloner was indifferent to the consequences of his malice and was content to cause as much distress as his actions were capable of inflicting, subject, I suppose, to the desirability of the plaintiff being able to continue to work in subjection to him. In this sense, this case is markedly different from the situation under consideration in *Tame* [*Tame v State of New South Wales* (2002) 211 CLR 317]. If *Janvier v Sweeney* (supra) be rightly decided – and there is no reason, I think, to suppose otherwise – it appears to follow that the defendants are both liable for such of Mr Chaloner's misbehaviour as was inflicted in the course of his employment, a matter to which I come in due course. As it happens, however, it seems to me that the defendants are liable in negligence – and Group 4 in contract – for the plaintiff's psychological injury at Mr Chaloner's hands and I have not, therefore, found it necessary to consider further the application of this line of authority to the present case.

69 His Honour also held:

> [205] … I have no doubt that Mr Chaloner realised that his behaviour would have caused some injury to the plaintiff. If he turned his mind to the risk of inflicting serious injury to the plaintiff, he was, at least, indifferent to the risk.

70 A conclusion in a particular case that what was involved was the intentional infliction of personal injury is a matter of significance, eg for deciding whether to award exemplary damages and also for determining any question of contribution between joint tort feasors. Indeed, with respect to a range of matters, notably the availability of exemplary damages, the distinction between an intentional tort and negligence will be of growing significance by reason of the exemption of the intentional torts by s 3B of the *Civil Liability Act 2002* from the provisions of that Act, which modify the common law of negligence in a number of significant respects. (See eg *New South Wales v Ibbett* [2005] NSWCA 445; (2005) 64 NSWLR 168.) …

72 In Australia it has been suggested that the *Wilkinson v Downton* [1897] 2 QB 57 line of authority has been "subsumed under the unintentional tort of negligence". (See *Magill v Magill* [2006] HCA 51; (2006) 81 ALJR 254 at [117].) However, this Court should follow the acceptance by the High Court of the authority of *Wilkinson v Downton* [1897] 2 QB 57 in *Bunyan v Jordan* [1937] HCA 5; (1937) 57 CLR 1 and in the joint judgment in *Northern Territory v Mengel* supra.

Nationwide News v Naidu cont.

73 The position in Australia appears to be that identified by Gleeson CJ in *Magill v Magill* [2006] HCA 51; (2006) 81 ALJR 254 supra at [20]. His Honour referred to *Wilkinson v Downton* [1897] 2 QB 57 and *Janvier v Sweeney* [1919] 2 KB 316 as cases which "would probably now be explained either on the basis of negligence, or intentional infliction of personal injury". As in the case of negligence, the requirement of "personal injury" means the test does not extend to any form of psychological damage but requires a recognised psychiatric condition. (Cf *Hunter v Canary Wharf Ltd* [1997] UKHL 14; [1997] AC 655 at 707.)

74 Although in some respects an intentional tort is more difficult to establish than negligence, it is not confined by a test of foreseeability and does not involve an inquiry into reasonableness of response... .

76 One issue that arises is what is meant by the word "calculated" in the *Wilkinson v Downton* [1897] 2 QB 57 and *Janvier v Sweeney* [1919] 2 KB 316 formulation of the tort. For the reasons I have set out above, psychiatric injury was reasonably foreseeable on the test of conceivable foreseeability adopted for the law of negligence. Clearly something substantially more certain is required for the intentional tort.

77 The word "calculated" is notoriously ambiguous: it can either mean a subjective, actual, conscious desire to bring about a specific result or it can mean what is likely, perhaps overwhelmingly likely, to occur considered objectively.

78 As McPherson JA said in *Carrier v Bonham* [2001] QCA 234; [2002] 1 Qd R 474 at [25]:

> To my mind, however, the problem is that the expression "calculated" which is used in those passages is one of those weasel words that is capable of meaning either subjectively contemplated and intended, or objectively likely to happen. See, for example, *O'Sullivan v Lunnon* [1986] HCA 57; (1986) 163 CLR 545, 549. The implication I draw from the context in which the word appears in the passages quoted is that it was being used in the latter and not the former sense. That seems plain to be so in what was said by Latham CJ in *Bunyan v Jordan* [1937] HCA 5; (1937) 57 CLR 1, 11, where, reverting to *Wilkinson v Downton*, his Honour remarked that the words in that case were of such a character and spoken in such circumstances that "it was naturally to be expected that they might cause a very severe nervous shock". Certainly that seems to have been the view of Dixon J who, in contrasting the facts of *Bunyan v Jordan* with those of *Wilkinson v Downton*, concluded (57 CLR 1, 17) that the harm which was said in fact to have ensued in the case before the High Court, was "not a consequence which might reasonably have been anticipated or foreseen".

79 This issue has not been determined authoritatively. It does appear that an actual subjective intention is not required. Indeed, the formulation in *Wilkinson v Downton* [1897] 2 QB 57 at 59 refers to an "imputed intention". (See also the reference by Latham CJ to the result that was "naturally to be expected" in *Bunyan v Jordan* [1937] HCA 5; (1937) 57 CLR 1 supra at 11).

80 It is not necessary, in this case, to decide, as McMurdo P suggests in *Carrier v Bonham* [2001] QCA 234; [2002] 1 Qd R 474 at [12], that "calculated" means "likely to have that effect". It may be that it is sufficient if the result satisfied a test of "substantial certainty". (See Trindade et al supra at 40-41.) However, a test of reckless indifference to a result will, in this context, satisfy the requirement of intention. (See Trindade et al at 41-42, 48, 56.) In the present case, the findings of Adams J establish such reckless indifference and that is sufficient to establish intention, just as it is in the criminal law.

81 The High Court has authoritatively established the test for recovery of consequential loss in the case of an intentional tort in terms of asking whether the particular head of damage is a natural and probable result of conduct. (See *Palmer Bruyn & Parker Pty Ltd v Parsons* [2001] HCA 69; (2001) 208 CLR 388 esp at [13], [73], [114]. See also *TCN Channel Nine v Anning* [2002] NSWCA 82; (2002) 54 NSWLR 333 at [100].)

82 There is no finding that Mr Chaloner did actually intend to inflict psychiatric damage. However, the nature and scale of his conduct was such, as the expert evidence confirmed, as to constitute a recognised psychiatric injury as a natural and probable consequence of that course of conduct. The limitations of foresight and remoteness are not applicable. (See *Palmer Bruyn* at [13] and [78].)

83 If sued, Mr Chaloner would, in my opinion, have been liable to pay the damages awarded to Mr Naidu on the basis of the intentional infliction of psychiatric injury. ...

[3.150]

Notes&Questions

1. The Court in *Wilkinson v Downton* [1897] 2 QB 57 determined that intention equated with whether the defendant had "wilfully done an act *calculated* to cause physical harm to the plaintiff that is to say, to infringe her legal right to personal safety, and has in fact thereby caused physical harm to her" (emphasis added). Does this mean that the defendant must have consciously turned his or her mind to causing physical harm to the plaintiff? Not based upon the facts of *Wilkinson v Downton* [1897] 2 QB 57 in which it was clearly only the conscious intention of the defendant to play a practical joke and not to cause psychiatric illness. In *Nationwide News Pty Ltd v Naidu* (2007) 71 NSWLR 471, Spigelman CJ discusses the ambiguity of the word calculated – "'calculated' is notoriously ambiguous: it can either mean a subjective, actual, conscious desire to bring about a specific result or it can mean what is likely, perhaps overwhelmingly likely, to occur considered objectively". His Honor found it unnecessary to affirmatively decide the issue concluding though that it certainly would include "a reckless indifference to a result".

2. In the extracted case of *Naidu*, Spigelman CJ refers to Macpherson CJ's judgment in *Carrier v Bonham* [2002] 1 Qd R 474 noting that Macpherson CJ decided that intention for action on the case means "likely to have the effect" or naturally to be expected as a result of the defendant's words and/or actions and that this is objectively assessed. This approach has also been taken in the Victorian cases of *McFadzean v CFMEU* [2004] VSCA at [454] and *Walker v Hamm and State of Victoria* [2008] VSC 596 at [76].

   Early authority also supports the approach taken in *Carrier v Bonham* [2002] 1 Qd R 474 as to the meaning of "intention". In *Bunyan v Jordan* (1937) 57 CLR 1, the plaintiff, a 22 year old female employee of the defendant, suffered nervous illness. The defendant, in an alcoholic condition, had on his table in the plaintiff's presence a revolver and poison. He uttered words out of her presence, but which she overheard, suggesting he was about to commit suicide, his notion apparently being that the demonstration that followed would excite feelings of horror and pity in, particularly, his sons. For this purpose he fired a shot, also out of the plaintiff's presence, but overheard by her. Given that the words were uttered and the shot fired outside the presence of the plaintiff it could not be said that the acts of the defendant were "calculated" to cause harm, rather the harm was accidental (per Latham CJ at 11-12). See also *Janvier v Sweeney* [1919] 2 KB 316; 121 LT 179, in which the defendant private detective posed as a detective from Scotland Yard and informed the plaintiff that unless she procured certain documents from her employer he would allege that she was a German spy (this occurred during World War I and the plaintiff's boyfriend was German). The jury found that the statements or some of them were calculated to cause physical injury to the plaintiff, were made with the knowledge that they were likely to cause injury, and illness to the plaintiff resulted.

3. More recent examples of successful suits for action on the case also exist. In *Tucker v News Media Ownership Ltd* [1986] 2 NZLR 716, the plaintiff successfully sued for action on the case. The plaintiff was seeking to publicly raise funds for a heart transplant and a newspaper reporter threatened to publish details of the plaintiff's criminal history. In *Grosse v Purvis* [2003] QDC 151, the plaintiff successfully sued in respect to injuries that she suffered, including post traumatic stress disorder, as a result of a relationship with a work colleague that went sour. The defendant persistently harassed the plaintiff by loitering outside her residence and work, following her, illegally entering her home and yard, making offensive phone calls to her and behaving offensively to her friends and relatives. In Canada a number of workplace harassment and wrongful dismissal cases have succeeded upon the basis of action on the case: *Rahemtulla v Vanfed Credit Union* (1984) 29 CCLT 78; *Prinzo v Baycrest Centre for Geriatric Care* (2002) 60 OR (3d) 474. In recent times the tort of action on the case has re-emerged in common law countries. For a comprehensive discussion of this issue, including cases that have involve privacy and harassment, refer to the article by P Watson at [3.05].

4. It should also be noted that there is some argument that action on the case has been subsumed into the action of negligence, see, for example, MacPherson JA's comments in *Carrier v Bonham* [2002] 1 Qd R 474 at [26]-[27], Lord Hoffman's comments in *Wainwright v Home Office* [2003] 4 All ER 969 at 980-982, and *Magill v Magill* (2006)81 ALJR 254 per Gummow, Kirby and Crennan JJ at [117]. In the extracted case of *Naidu*, Spigelman CJ (at [76]) rightly points out the comments in these cases are not binding authority, stating, "[t]he position in Australia appears to be that identified by Gleeson CJ in *Magill v Magill* (2006)81 ALJR 254 supra at [20]. His Honour referred to *Wilkinson v Downton* [1897] 2 QB 57 and *Janvier v Sweeney* [1919] 2 KB 316; 121 LT 179 as cases which 'would probably now be explained either on the basis of negligence, or intentional infliction of personal injury'". The amount of recent case law (see Notes 2 and 3 above) in this area also questions this assertion (for further discussion of this issue, see the article by P Watson, at [3.05]).

Damage

[3.155] Unlike an action for trespass, a plaintiff cannot recover for action on the case without proof of damage. In the context of intentional torts a successful plaintiff will be able to recover "for harm that is intended or that is the natural and probable consequence of the tortious act" (*TCN Channel Nine Pty Ltd v Anning* [2002] NSWCA 82 per Spigelman CJ at [100]).

Even if the plaintiff is able to establish that the damage was intended or was the natural and probable consequence of the tortious act, the law will not award damages in respect of some types of injury. In line with standard authority, a plaintiff is able to readily recover for physical injury. The same cannot be said of fright and other forms of emotional affront. The weight of current authority is that the emotional injury must be a recognisable psychiatric condition before it will sound in damages.

[3.160] **Notes&Questions**

1. *Wilkinson v Downton* [1897] 2 QB 57 permitted a plaintiff to recover for any consequences that flowed from the defendant's actions provided that the injury was not too remote, that is "the connection between the cause and the effect is sufficiently close and complete" (at 59, a test which is applicable in cases of negligence). The High Court in *Palmer Bruyn & Parker Pty Ltd v Parsons* (2001) 76 ALJR 163, determined that tests based upon reasonable foreseeability, developed to limit liability in cases of negligence and nuisance, are not suitable for determining the damages for an intentional tort. Instead the High Court applied the "natural and probable consequences" test. *Palmer* involved an action for injurious falsehood, which is a form of action on the case, and consequently the better view is that this approach will also apply to action on the case for indirect intentional harm to the person. See also the case of *Channel Nine Pty Ltd v Anning* [2002] NSWCA 82 per Spigelman CJ at [100], in which the New South Wales Court of Appeal applied the *Palmer* test to trespass to land.
2. Recent cases in which the issue of recovery for emotional injury have arisen continue to express the view that recovery is limited to physical injury including a recognised psychiatric injury: *Grosse v Purvis* [2003] QDC 151 (see [3.150] Note 3) was a case of workplace harassment and stalking in which the plaintiff was able to recover as she had suffered post traumatic stress disorder; the UK Court of Appeal decision of *Wong v Parkside Health NHS Trust* [2003] 3 All ER 932, a claim for workplace harassment, in which the plaintiff suffered both physical harm and a recognised psychiatric illness (the plaintiff however was unable to prove intention) and *Giller v Procopets* [2008] VSCA 236, a claim for intentional infliction of emotional distress was brought as a result of distributing and threatening to distribute videotapes of a sexual nature of the plaintiff. Whilst the majority required a recognised psychiatric injury to have been suffered, Maxwell P, dissenting on this point, argued that given the advances of science it was anachronistic to continue to require recovery subject to physical injury and a labelling of the mental distress as a recognised psychiatric injury. Instead the courts' focus should be upon "the nature and extent of the mental distress actually suffered by the plaintiff as a consequence of the defendant's conduct" (at [31]).

Conclusion

[3.165] The discussion so far has centred on the elements that must be established to plead and prove a prima facie case of intentional interference with the person, whether it be an action for trespass or case. Once a plaintiff has established their prima facie case, the defendant has the opportunity to defend the claim and may do so by pleading and proving one or more defences. The defences that are available in respect of the intentional torts are discussed in Chapter 6. If a plaintiff is ultimately successful in their action for intentional interference with the person, then the next issue that confronts the court is what relief the plaintiff should be awarded.

RELIEF FOR INTENTIONAL INTERFERENCE WITH THE PERSON

Compensatory damages

[3.170] Several types of damages may be awarded for interference with the person: nominal, compensatory, aggravated and exemplary.

In the case of trespass (though not action on the case) proof of damage is not required to be able to successfully maintain an action. However, lack of damage may affect the quantum of damages awarded. Consequently, in the case of *Stephens v Myers* (1830) 172 ER 725, as the plaintiff did not suffer any injury he was only awarded nominal damages of one shilling.

Where damage is suffered, the measure of compensatory damages in a tortious action is: "that sum of money which will put the party who has been injured ... in the same position as he would have been in if he had not sustained the wrong for which he is now getting his compensation or reparation" (*Livingstone v Rawyards Coal Co* (1880) 5 App Cs 25 at 39). To determine what amount of money will place the plaintiff in the position he or she was before the tort occurred, the unsuccessful defendant must compensate the plaintiff for the probable and natural consequence of their interference, whether it be battery, assault, false imprisonment and arguably for action on the case (on the basis this principle applies equally to all the intentional torts) (*Palmer Bruyn & Parker Pty Ltd v Parsons* (2001) 76 ALJR 163 and see [3.160] Note 1 with respect to application of this principle to action on the case). Such an award will be damages to compensate for things such as lost earnings, medical expenses, pain and suffering, loss of enjoyment of life and loss of amenities of life. (Refer to Chapter 14 Quantum of Damages for a detailed discussion of compensatory damages.) In recent years legislation has been enacted in all jurisdictions seeking to limit the award of damages for personal injury. The issue that arises is whether or not these limitations apply equally to personal injury that results from intentional torts as opposed to negligence?

McCracken v Melbourne Storm Rugby League Football Club

[3.175] *McCracken v Melbourne Storm Rugby League Football Club* [2005] NSWSC 107 New South Wales Supreme Court

(footnotes omitted)

HULME J: [1] On 12 May 2000, the Plaintiff was playing rugby league football as a member of the Wests Tigers Rugby League Football Club Pty Limited first grade team against the corresponding team of the First Defendant. The Second and Third Defendants were members of the First Defendant's team and employed by the First Defendant. During the course of the game the Plaintiff, carrying the ball, was tackled by the Second and Third Defendants, struck the ground with his head and was injured. He has not played football since.

[2] The Plaintiff claims damages from the Defendants contending that in the tackle, the Second and Third Defendants lifted the Plaintiff to a dangerous position, causing him to fall head first to the ground.

[3] With an eye to the provisions of section 3B of the *Civil Liability Act 2002*, in the Statement of Claim the Plaintiff also asserted that the actions of the Second and Third Defendants were "intentional and done with intent to cause injury, in that the Second and Third Defendants intended, during the performance of the tackle, to lift the Plaintiff and, having completed doing so, to then drive the Plaintiff forcefully into contact with the ground causing the Plaintiff's body to suffer some physical trauma and temporary non-serious soft tissue injury".

...

McCracken v Melbourne Storm Rugby League Football Club cont.

[34] On behalf of the Defendants it was submitted that the movements of the three persons involved were but normal, and to an appreciable degree unavoidable, incidents of an event involving three heavy players. I do not agree. A consideration of the video demonstrates the contrary. Similarly I do not agree that what occurred was but a normal incident in the game of rugby league.

[35] In that connection there are at least three factors which stand out. One is the inherent dangerousness of a player being upside down particularly when lifted to that position. A Second is that the rules of the game both recognise the danger and prohibit the event described as a dangerous throw. A Third is that it is not necessary in preventing the forward movement of a player to deal with him as the Plaintiff was dealt with.

...

[37] ... I am further satisfied that the intent of both of the Defendants in the tackle was to injure the Plaintiff. I do not by that suggest that injury of the severity that occurred was intended, but the evidence of Mr Ryan and Mr Bai quoted above satisfies me that some injury was intended by each of the Second and Third Defendants. Consideration of the nature and circumstances of the tackle as depicted in the video leads to the same conclusion.

[38] The *Civil Liability Act 2002* imposes limits on civil liability. Section 3(B) however provides:

> (1) the provisions of this Act do not apply to (or in respect of civil liability and awards of damages in those proceedings) as follows:
>
> (a) civil liability in respect of an intentional act that is done with intention to cause injury or death or sexual assault or other sexual misconduct – the whole Act except Part 7 (Self Defence and recovery by criminals) in respect of civil liability in respect of an intentional act that is done with an intent to cause injury or death.

[39] It was submitted on behalf of the Defendants that a consideration of the Second Reading Speech of the Premier when introducing the Bill which led to the Act indicates that this exception was designed to apply to only criminal conduct or perhaps criminal conduct and sexual misconduct. It is the fact that in his speech the Premier said:

> Importantly, intentional acts done with intent to cause injury or death or acts involving sexual assault are excluded. This exclusion ensures that the compensation for injuries arising from serious criminal acts is not limited by the Bill.

[40] There is a vast difference between that exposition of section 3(B) and the terms of the section.

[41] It was suggested that I should adopt a purposive construction of the Act recognising that it was intended to impose limits on civil liability and thus should grant a narrower rather than a wider operation to section 3(B). However, the civil liability which is excepted from the general provisions of the Act by section 3(B) is defined by reference to "an intentional act that is done with intent to cause injury or death or that is sexual assault or other sexual misconduct." By no reasonable interpretation of those words can one regard them as limited to conduct which is criminal. I would add, although I do not need to rely on it, that the reference to sexual assault would have been unnecessary if criminal conduct was the type of conduct which was excepted. In my view the words of the section should be given their ordinary English meaning.

[42] A question arises: What is encompassed within the word "injury"? I do not for the purposes of this case need to decide how minor a hurt may be to come within the expression. I am satisfied, particularly from Mr Ryan's evidence and from my consideration of the video, that what was intended by the Second and Third Defendants was injury which was not so minor that it could be regarded as perhaps an inappropriate use of the term. (Again I emphasise I do not suggest, and it was not suggested on the part of the Plaintiff, that the Second and Third Defendants intended to cause injury of the seriousness which occurred.)

McCracken v Melbourne Storm Rugby League Football Club cont.

[43] It follows from the conclusions at which I have arrived that the Plaintiff is entitled to succeed against the Second and Third Defendants. The First Defendant was, as I have said, someone who employed the Second and Third Defendants and it was not suggested that in that situation if they were liable the First Defendant was not.

[44] Accordingly, the Plaintiff is entitled to succeed against the First Defendant also.

[45] I direct judgment for the Plaintiff against each of the Defendants with damages to be assessed.

[The issue of liability in this case was dealt with separately by Hume J, see *McCracken v Melbourne Storm Rugby League Football Club Ltd* [2006] NSWSC 1250. At that time it was determined that as McCracken's injury occurred in Victoria, the relevant law was that of Victoria, and not New South Wales (at [3]). As the amendments to the Victorian legislation which limited recovery for personal injury damages, the *Wrongs and Other Acts (Public Liability Insurance Reform) Act 2002* (Vic), did not become operative until after McCracken suffered his injury, his damages fell to be assessed in accordance with the common law. McCracken then appealed the award of damages to the New South Wales Court of Appeal, see *McCracken v Melbourne Storm Rugby League Football Club Ltd* [2007] NSWCA 353. The Court of Appeal agreed that the relevant law was that of Victoria, and observed that therefore the allegation concerning intent to injure was unnecessary and irrelevant.]

[3.180] Notes&Questions

1. *McCracken* first of all provides us with an example of trespass to the person which can occur in the context of sporting contests (see [6.65]-[6.70]). Secondly, it assists in determining whether or not the legislation, enacted in almost every state and territory with the purpose of imposing limitations upon the damages that may be awarded for personal injury claims, applies to the intentional torts. Promulgation of the Civil Liability Acts (CLA's) had, at least in part, been based upon what were perceived as excessive awards in negligence cases, however it is not necessarily the case that the CLA's apply only to personal injury claims arising from an action for negligence.

2. It is certainly correct to state that *generally* in the case of New South Wales as determined in *McCracken*, the *Civil Liability Act 2002* (NSW) (NSW: CLA) will not apply to the calculation of personal injury damages for intentional torts. Section 3B of the NSW: CLA states that the CLA is not to apply to an "intentional act that is done with intention to cause injury or death or sexual assault or other sexual misconduct". In the principal case the court concluded that the CLA did not apply as the acts of the defendants' were clearly intentional and the purpose in tackling the plaintiff in the way that they did was to cause injury. Since the principle case there have been numerous cases in which the New South Wales courts have assessed damages for intentional torts upon this basis (see, for example, the cases referred to later in this note and also *Whitehouse Properties Trading As Beach Road Motel v McInerney* [2005] NSWCA 436, *State of New South Wales v Bujdoso* [2007] NSWCA 44). In 2007 the New South Wales Court of Appeal affirmed that the CLA generally does not apply to intentional torts: *Zorom Enterprises Pty Ltd v Zabow* [2007] NSWCA 106 at [6] and [13] (per Basten J, McColl and Campbell JJA agreeing).

   While the NSW CLA generally does not apply to intentional torts, it is arguable that this is not always the case. In determining the application of the NSW: CLA, s 3B states that the act does not apply to an "*intentional act* that is done with *intention to cause* injury or death or sexual assault or other sexual misconduct" (emphasis added). At common law, intention in the context of trespass includes a desire or substantial certainty to cause the trespassory interference (refer to [2.30]) and does not require an actual intent to cause injury. In comparison it would seem under s 3B, that unless there was actual intent to cause injury, death, sexual assault or sexual misconduct, the CLA will apply. Arguably this is the approach currently taken in New South Wales. In the case of *Coyle v NSW* [2006] NSWCA 95, the Court of Appeal referred to the trial judge's decision to apply the provisions of the CLA and not the common law in assessing compensation for an assault upon the plaintiff by a police officer. The trial judge had determined that whilst the officer intended to push past the claimant, he did not intend to injure the claimant and "[t]hus the injuries the claimant suffered were ... an 'unintentional consequence of the wrongful arrest'" (at [43]). It should be noted that applicability of the CLA was not one of the grounds of appeal before the appellate court.

Another issue which has arisen is whether the "intention to cause injury" in s 3B is limited to physical injury: see for example *Houda v State of New South Wales* [2005] NSWSC 1053 and *State of NSW v Ibbett* (2005) 65 NSWLR 168. In the *State of NSW v Ibbett* [2005] NSWCA 445, the court determined that the term "injury" was not meant to be limited to "physical injury" but was wider. The plaintiff in this case had brought an action for assault and also for trespass to land against the State and two police officers, who without warrant and without justification, entered the plaintiff's garage in pursuit of her son, and then waived a gun in Mrs Ibbett's face. The trial judge found in the Plaintiff's favour in respect of both the action for trespass to land and that the pointing of the gun at the Plaintiff constituted an assault. Spigelman CJ (at [21]) concluded that the term "injury" in s 3B, whilst it would certainly include personal injury, was meant to be wider and would include:

> ... harm to reputation, deprivation of liberty, or to injured feelings such as outrage, humiliation, indignity and insult or to mental suffering, such as grief, anxiety and distress, not involving a recognised psychological condition. ... An award for the emotional harm involved in apprehension of personal violence would not generally be regarded as an award for "personal injury damages" (see also Basten J at [217]).

Therefore if a defendant undertakes an intentional act with intent to cause any of these types of injuries, the NSW CLA will not apply to the award of damages for personal injury suffered by the plaintiff.

3. Fault can also be established in a trespass action by proving "negligent trespass". In the case of a negligent trespass it is likely that the NSW CLA will apply to the calculation of damages. If fault is based upon negligence it cannot be said that the act of the defendant was an "intentional act with the intention of causing injury". This was the view of the court in *State of NSW v Ibbett* [2005] NSWCA 445; see also the comments of Basten J at [12] in *Zorom Enterprises Pty Ltd v Zabow* [2007] NSWCA 106.

4. In respect to action on the case it will be recalled that the definition of intent for action on the case includes injury that the plaintiff could have reasonably anticipated in the circumstances. The courts have not yet had occasion to decide whether or not this type of intent falls within the type of intentional acts which are excluded from the CLA.

5. As to whether the Civil Liability Acts of other jurisdictions apply to personal injury claims resulting from intentional torts depends upon the specific legislative provisions:

(a) Tas: CLA, s 3B(1)(a); Vic: WrA, s 28C(2)(a) have provisions which replicate the New South Wales provision and therefore it is arguable that the Acts will operate in the circumstances outlined in Notes 1-3.

(b) The Western Australian provision is extremely similar to the New South Wales provision, but excludes the operation of the WA: CLA for an "unlawful intentional act that is done with an intention to cause *personal* injury to a person and sexual assault or other sexual misconduct" (WA: CLAs 3A, Item 1) (emphasis added). Consequently if the intent is to cause injury other than personal injury, though the resultant effect of the intentional act is personal injury for which damages are being sought, the restrictions on damages imposed by the CLA will apply. The approach as outlined in Note 2 of *State of NSW v Ibbett* (2005) 65 NSWLR 168 will not apply in WA because of the difference in terminology.

(c) The South Australian act applies to personal injury awards arising from a motor accidents even if intentionally caused and will also apply to intentional tort claims which cause personal injury if that injury was also partly caused by negligence; or some other unintentional tort on the part of a person other than the injured person; or in part by a breach of a contractual duty of care; or where personal injury results in death. (SA: CLA, s 51). Otherwise the act will not apply to personal injury from an intentional tort.

(d) The ACT: CLWA, s 92; NT: *Personal Injuries (Liability and Damages) Act* (NT), s 4 and Qld: CLA, s 50 apply to restrict damages for personal injuries arising from all intentional torts.

Exemplary or aggravated damages

[3.185] In addition to compensatory damages it may also be possible for a plaintiff to recover aggravated and/or exemplary damages for an intentional tort. Aggravated damages are awarded for deliberate conduct of the defendant which has resulted in an affront to the plaintiff. The award is focused upon the effect on the plaintiff of the tort and accordingly is assessed from the plaintiff's point of view.

Myer Stores v Soo [1991] 2 VR 597 provides a good example. An employee of the defendant claimed that a person captured on a television camera stealing goods looked like the plaintiff. On his next visit to the store the plaintiff was required to go to an office and be interviewed for an hour. Further harassing investigations were pursued until it became clear that the thief was not the plaintiff. On appeal the sum of $5,000 awarded by the trial judge was increased to $10,000. Murphy J said (at 604):

> the persistence by Myer in its expressed suspicion (at the very least) was completely insupportable in the circumstances. ... There was no reasonable ground shown for it. ... No apology was forthcoming. No admission of any mistake was ever made by Myer. The [source] of the accusation (the salesman in the hi-fi department) remained unknown, unidentified save as a Myer employee ... In these circumstances the damages were, in my opinion, aggravated.

In comparison, exemplary damages are awarded "to punish the defendant, and presumably to serve one or more of the objects of punishment – moral retribution or deterrence" (*Uren v John Fairfax* (1966) 117 CLR 118 at 149). To justify an award of exemplary damages the defendant's conduct must be considered to be sufficiently outrageous. For this reason the High Court has described "the remedy ...[as] exceptional in the sense that it arises (chiefly, if not exclusively) in cases of conscious wrongdoing in contumelious disregard of the plaintiff's rights" (*Gray v Motor Accident Commission* (1998) 196 CLR 1 at 9). As the punishment factor is based upon the degree of outrageousness of the defendant's conduct, the focus of the award is not upon the effect the defendant's behaviour may have had on the plaintiff, but on the conduct of the defendant.

It may be the case that certain factors operate to exclude an award of exemplary damages even where the conduct of the defendant would seem to be sufficiently outrageous. In *Gray v Motor Accident Commission* (1998) 196 CLR 1, the High Court denied an appeal that the trial judge and the Full Court of the Supreme Court of South Australia erroneously denied an award of exemplary damages. The respondent had deliberately struck the appellant with his motor vehicle with intent to cause the appellant grievous bodily harm causing serious injury to the appellant. The facts seem to clearly justify an award of exemplary damages; however the respondent had also been criminally sentenced to seven years imprisonment for his assault of the appellant. The Court found that "the purposes for the awarding of exemplary damages ... [had] been wholly met if substantial punishment is exacted by the criminal law. The offender is punished; others are deterred" and "... considerations of double punishment would otherwise arise" (*Gray v Motor Accident Commission* (1998) 196 CLR 1 at 14).

Arguments that the object behind exemplary damages of punishment would not be met if an insurance company would ultimately pay the damages award have not been unsuccessful. The High Court dealt with this issue firstly in *Lamb v Cotogno* (1987) 164 CLR 1 and then again in *Gray v Motor Accident Commission* (1998) 196 CLR 1. In *Lamb v Cotogno* (1987) 164 CLR 1 the plaintiff had thrown himself across the bonnet of the defendant's car and held on to the windscreen guttering at a time when the defendant had begun to drive it away from the plaintiff's premises. The defendant drove at 35 to 40 km per hour, swerving to dislodge the plaintiff, and then braked sharply so that the plaintiff was propelled across the bonnet on to the road and injured while the defendant drove off. The trial judge included a sum of $5,000 by way of exemplary damages in the award. The High Court rejected the argument that the objective of punishment would not be met; rather that appeasement of the plaintiff remained one object of exemplary damages and served to mark the court's condemnation of the defendant's behaviour, so that its effect was not entirely to be discounted by the existence of compulsory insurance (at 9-10).

Provocation of the defendant can also lead to reduction in the quantum of both exemplary and aggravated damages. For example, in the case of *Fontin v Katopodis* (1962) 108 CLR 177 (extracted [6.145]) the plaintiff provoked the defendant's reprisal by picking up a wooden T-square and breaking it across the defendant's shoulder. The defendant retaliated picking up a piece of glass from his workbench and throwing it at the plaintiff causing serious injury. The Court upheld the trial judge's reduction of the exemplary damages from £2850 to £2000 by reason of the provocation. The High Court determined that provocation could be used to reduce or eliminate pecuniary or aggravated damages but was not relevant to the assessment of compensatory damages.

[3.190] **Notes&Questions**

1. In the recent decision of *New South Wales v Ibbett* (2006) 229 CLR 638 the High Court upheld in a trespass to land action, awards of aggravated and exemplary damages. Mrs Ibbett sued the State based upon the illegal entry of her home by two

police officers (further facts appear at [3.180] Note 2). Aggravated damages were awarded in respect of the affront to the rights of the plaintiff Mrs Ibbett of the treatment of her son by the police, as well as herself (at 647-648). Exemplary damages were also awarded against the State regarding the conduct of the police officers and to reflect the State's responsibility for the oversight, training and discipline of members of the police force (at 653-654). In the *Case of Varmedja v Varmedja* [2008] NSWCA 177, the New South Wales Court of Appeal upheld an award of aggravated damages in respect of the humiliation and insulting behaviour of the defendant, which went beyond "*ordinary human fallibility*" (at [162]). The plaintiff, then 48, immigrated to live with the defendant, who was then aged 75. Shortly thereafter the defendant started taking Viagra and began to repeatedly rape the plaintiff, and force her to have oral sex despite her repeated refusals. Her rejection of his sexual advances had been met with threats and violence including pointing a shotgun at her head, beating her, driving a car in which she was passenger into a tree and threatening to have her deported or killed.

2. In the case of *Gray v Motor Accident Commission* (1998) 196 CLR 1, the High Court observed that whilst it is not usual, exemplary damages may be awarded for contumelious disregard of the rights of the plaintiff in an action based upon negligence. This statement of the law must now be tempered by the impact of the Civil Liability Acts in a number of jurisdictions. The Northern Territory has abolished awards for aggravated damages or exemplary damages for personal injury whether arising out of an intentional or a negligent tort (*Personal Injuries (Liabilities and Damages) Act* (NT), s 19). New South Wales has abolished aggravated, exemplary and punitive damages in respect to personal injuries awards where the act or omission that caused the injury or death was negligence (NSW: CLA, s 21). Queensland has abolished awards for these damages for personal injuries unless the claim for personal injuries was the result of an unlawful intentional act done with intent to cause injury or an unlawful sexual assault or other unlawful sexual contact (Qld: CLA, s 52). The legislation of the remainder of Australian jurisdictions does not address this issue and therefore the common law continues to apply.

   The New South Wales provision has been the subject of litigation in the case of *State of NSW v Ibbett* [2005] NSWCA 445 (see [3.180] Note 2 for a brief description of the facts of this case). The State's argument that the assault by the police officer was a negligent trespass and therefore under NSW: CLA, s 21 exemplary and aggravated damages could not be awarded, was rejected. The Court found that it was clear that it was a case of intentional trespass, but refrained from determining that if it had been a negligent trespass, exemplary and aggravated damages would have been barred, although the court did indicate that this was possible (Spigelman CJ at [16], Ipp J at [126] - [129] and Basten J at [217]). This case was subsequently appealed to the High Court (see Note 1 above) however the applicability of the CLA was not a ground of appeal and the High Court dealt with the appeal upon the basis that exemplary and aggravated damages could be awarded in respect of an intentional tort.

3. For an even clearer case of both aggravated and exemplary damages, see *Henry v Thompson* (1989) Aust Torts Reports 80-265 (Qld Sup Ct (FC)) in which case the plaintiff was beaten after his arrest for using obscene language and one of the defendants urinated on him. In finding the officers liable for battery the Court made an

award that included $10,000 for aggravated damages and a further $10,000 for exemplary damages. The awards were upheld by the Full Court.

Injunctions

[3.195] It is possible to obtain a quia timet injunction (an injunction granted to prevent an anticipated tort) where the plaintiff fears that they will be the subject of a future assault or battery. In order to satisfy the court that the injunction should be granted it will almost always be the case that there must have been a previous assault and/or battery. As with all injunctions the plaintiff must establish a prima facie case and the court must consider whether the balance of convenience favours the grant of the injunction "[t]he mere making of a complaint is not sufficient" (*Fisher v Fisher* [1988] VR 1028, and for a more detailed discussion of injunctions see [4.50]). Most cases concerning injunctions to prevent future battery and assaults have revolved around domestic situations, for example, *Corvisy v Corvisy* [1982] 2 NSWLR 557; *Zimitat v Douglas* [1979] Qd R 454; and *Parry v Crooks* (1981) 27 SASR 1.

CHAPTER 4

Trespass to Land

INTRODUCTION

[4.05] Trespass to land occurs when there is direct interference with property in the possession of another without his or her consent. For example: entry into a private house by a gatecrasher, dumping rubbish on another's property, spraying graffiti on buildings or structures, car parking on private property without permission, refusing to leave a nightclub when requested to leave, buildings or structures such as cranes encroaching on, or swinging over, adjoining property. The action for trespass to land serves a variety of purposes: first, it is an action which allows recovery of damage to land caused by a trespasser; secondly, it is a means of preserving the peace – a person in possession, even a squatter in possession will act aggressively to protect that possession against trespassers; thirdly, the action protects property rights – the action may be used as a means of determining rights to the land and preventing acquisition of property rights by a trespasser. (A trespasser may acquire title to the land at common law by a long period of open and continuous user in which others including the true owner are excluded.)

The action for trespass to land can also protect dignitary interests which include the occupier's right to privacy and security. The occupier's interest in not being disturbed includes an interest in family members and others with whom the plaintiff has a continuing relationship not being disturbed (*State of NSW v Ibbett* (2006) 229 CLR 638). Any unauthorised entry into property in the plaintiff's possession is a trespass. The more egregious interferences with privacy and security may warrant the award of aggravated and exemplary damages. For example, where a defendant had planted a microphone beneath the plaintiffs' bed (*Grieg v Grieg* [1966] VR 376), where a private investigator broke into the plaintiff's home at midnight to get divorce evidence (*Johnstone v Stewart* [1968] SASR 142), or where police officers unlawfully entered the plaintiff's property and brandished a gun at the occupier and her son, (*State of NSW v Ibbett* (2006) 229 CLR 638). If the defendant trespasses upon the plaintiff's land in order to take photographs or television footage, the plaintiff may be entitled to substantial damages for the trespass including aggravated and exemplary damages in appropriate cases. But the plaintiff is not automatically entitled to an injunction restraining the publication or telecast of those images. Damages will frequently be an adequate remedy

(*Lincoln Hunt Australia Pty Ltd v Willesee* (1986) 4 NSWLR 457, see [4.50]). Consequently, the action for trespass to land is limited in its capacity to protect privacy. In *Australian Broadcasting Corporation v Lenah Game Meats Pty Ltd* (2001) 208 CLR 199, unknown persons planted surveillance devices in the plaintiff's facility which processed and supplied possum meat. The footage was given to the Animal Liberation organisation who in turn gave it to the ABC. Although the information was gained as a result of trespass, there was no basis for restraining the ABC from showing the film. The High Court did not find it necessary to decide whether the Courts should develop a separate tort of privacy at least in relation to individuals (See Gleeson CJ, (at 225-226), Gummow and Hayne JJ (Gaudron J agreeing) (at 256); Kirby J (at 277). Callinan J (at 328), see also *Giller v Procopets* [2008] VSCA 236). The Australian Law Reform Commission has recommended that legislation be introduced at the federal level to provide a statutory cause of action for a serious invasion of privacy (see Australian Law Reform Commission, *For your Information: Australian Privacy Law in Practice*, Report No 108 (May 2008) Vol 1, recommendation 74-1, 88).

In common with all trespass actions, the action for trespass to land is actionable without the need to prove damage (although there is some doubt about this in relation to goods); the defendant bears the onus of disproving fault (subject to the Highway case exception, see [2.60] Note 2). A person who involuntarily enters land may lack the requisite fault (see *Public Transport Commission of NSW v Perry* (1977) 137 CLR 107, epileptic fit causing plaintiff to fall on to railway tracks) and the plaintiff bears the onus of proving that there was a direct interference. Unlike the action for trespass to the person, in an action for trespass to land the plaintiff must have a "title to sue". This requires the plaintiff to prove exclusive possession of the land at the time of the wrong, see [4.15]. Mistake is no defence. So police officers who had obtained a court order permitting them to enter property and install a listening device were guilty of trespass because the statute under which the order was made did not authorise a trespass (*Coco v R* (1994) 179 CLR 427).

LAND

[4.10] The tort of trespass is concerned with direct interference with land. Land includes the soil, subsoil (see *Di Napoli v New Beach Apartments Pty Ltd* [2004] Aust Torts Reports 81-278, rock anchors intruding into the plaintiff's subsoil constituted a trespass) and fixtures such as a house, factory, equipment where it is permanently attached to become part of the land, crops before harvesting even airspace above the land to the extent it is capable of enjoyment. In an early fore-runner to Google Earth, Skyviews in England photographed many large estates from an aircraft. Baron Bernstein of Leigh took strong objection fearing that terrorists might use the photos. The photos were taken several hundred feet above the ground. No action was available for interference with privacy but was the intrusion into the airspace over the Baron's land a trespass to his land? Griffith J in *Bernstein of Leigh (Baron) v Skyviews & General Ltd* [1978] QB 479 held that it was not. The mere taking of a photograph is not a trespass. Nor was the intrusion of the aircraft in the airspace above the Baron's land. A balance must be struck between the rights of the public to the beneficial use of airspace and the rights of the occupier. The latter's rights are restricted to "such height as is necessary for the ordinary use and enjoyment of his land and the structures upon it ... above that height (the occupier) has no greater rights in the airspace than any other member of the public". Actionable intrusions into the plaintiff's airspace can include such things as overhanging signs, building work and swinging cranes. These intrusions can result in substantial damages where airspace is commercially exploitable and in suitable cases injunctions will be awarded to restrain a continuing trespass: see *PCH Melbourne Pty Ltd v Break Fast Investments Pty Ltd* [2007] VSCA 311; *Lang Parade Pty Ltd v Peluso & Ors* [2005] QSC 112; *LJP Investments v Howard Chia Investments Pty Ltd* (1989) 24 NSWLR 490. In New South Wales, Queensland, Tasmania and the Northern Territory, the problem may be obviated by the grant of statutory easements, see *Conveyancing Act 1919* (NSW) s 88K; *Property Law Act 1974* (Qld), s 180; *Law of Property Act* (NT), ss 163 – 164; *Conveyancing and Law of Property Act 1884* (Tas), s 84J. See also *Access to Neighbouring Land Act 2000* (NSW).

Actual damage to a person or property on the surface caused by an aircraft is covered by international convention and legislation at the Commonwealth and State levels: *Damage by Aircraft Act 1999* (Cth); *Damage by Aircraft Act 1952* (NSW); *Air Navigation Act 1937* (Qld), ss 12 – 17; SA: *Civil Liability Act 2002*, s 62; *Damage by Aircraft Act 1963* (Tas); Vic: WrA, s 30; and *Damage by Aircraft Act 1964* (WA). The Australian Capital Territory is covered by the Commonwealth Act: *Damage by Aircraft Act 1999* (Cth), s 9(3). The Northern Territory has not enacted equivalent legislation.

TITLE OF THE PLAINTIFF

[4.15] The plaintiff must have "possession" of the land at the time of the trespass. Pollock'explains why possession rather than ownership is protected:

> in a settled and industrial state some amount of genuine doubt as to ownership and title must unavoidably follow upon the complexity of men's affairs; that protection must in some measure be given to persons dealing in good faith on the strength of apparently lawful title and to those who may afterwards deal with and claim through such persons; and that protection cannot be given effectually to the innocent without also protecting some who are not innocent...the seeming anomaly will be found indispensable for the adequate protection of true ownership itself. Another element...is the interest of public peace and order. Men will defend that which they deem their own even if the law purports to forbid them; and the wholesale allowance of redress by private force, or exposure of wrongful possessors to dispossession by newcomers having no better right, could create more and greater evils than any that could be thus remedied or prevented. ...It is also said that possession is in a normal state of things the outward sign of ownership or title, and therefore the possessor is presumed to be or to represent the true owner.... (Pollock and Wright, *An Essay on Possession in the Common Law* (Clarendon Press, Oxford, 1888), pp 3-4)

This reasoning is less cogent in Australia where ownership and most interests in land can be readily ascertained under the Torrens system for registration of interests in land (there are still some small pockets of land that are not under the system and governed by old system title). Nevertheless, "possession" rather than ownership is required to bring an action for trespass to land. This is a consequence of the early history of the common law where new forms of action based on loss of possession came to prominence as a consequence of the limitations of the older actions which protected ownership; the latter were procedurally difficult with antiquated forms of proof. For example, the method of proof for the principal action, praecipe in capite, was trial by battle (see P Butt, *Land Law* (5th ed, Lawbook Co, 2006) at [506], [510]).

The practical outcome is that if you have a lease, you, as tenant and not the landlord, have possession which is sufficient title to sue a trespasser who breaks into your flat. Can a tenant sue the landlord for unauthorised entry? What if you are staying in your parents' house whilst they are overseas on holiday and someone breaks in – can you sue in trespass? What if you found a vacant lot of land next to your house and just started using it, can you keep the next door neighbour out? The issue of title to sue is taken up in the following extract.

Newington v Windeyer

[4.20] *Newington v Windeyer* (1985) 3 NSWLR 555 Court of Appeal of the Supreme Court of New South Wales

(footnotes omitted)

[The plaintiffs had property adjoining a vacant area of land containing rockeries and gardens known as the Grove. Over a period of 50 years they treated the Grove as their own. They maintained the gardens, utilised the area for functions and paid the rates. The defendant also lived next door to the Grove, which was originally separated from it by a high picket fence. She had recently reconstructed her fence, so as to open it to the Grove, and attempted to use the Grove. The trial judge held she had trespassed. One question before the Court of Appeal was whether the plaintiffs had sufficient title over the Grove to sue for trespass. They were not the registered owners of the land which was registered in the name of a deceased estate.]

MCHUGH JA: 296 ... The respondents are not the owners of the registered title of the Grove, but that fact does not prevent them maintaining an action of trespass against the appellant. The modern law of real property continues to invoke the medieval doctrine that possession is prima facie evidence of seisin in fee and that an estate gained by wrong is nevertheless an estate in fee simple: *Wheeler v Baldwin* (1934) 52 CLR 609 at 632; *Allen v Roughley* (1955) 94 CLR 98 at 108. Seisin gives ownership good against everyone except a person who has a better, because older, title: *Wheeler v Baldwin* (1934) 52 CLR 609 (at 632-633); *Perry v Clissold* [1907] AC 73 at 79. A person who is in possession of land adverse to the true owner has a legal interest in the land even though the 12 year limitation period has not expired (*Perry v Clissold* [1907] AC 73). As long as a person does not abandon his possession, possession for less than 12 years enables him to exclude from the land any person who does not have a better title: *Allen v Roughley* (1955) 94 CLR 98 at 109-110, 115, 131, 135, 143. The above cases and principles relate to Old System title. But in *Spark v Whale Three Minute Car Wash (Cremorne Junction) Pty Ltd* (1970) 92 WN (NSW) 1087, Slattery J held that those principles are equally applicable to land held under the provisions of the *Real Property Act 1900*. Counsel for the parties accepted that the common law principles concerning adverse possession apply to land under the Torrens System. In my opinion the agreement of counsel was correct. *Spark v Whale Three Minute Car Wash* was correctly decided. Indeed, since 1979 it has become possible for adverse possession of land for 12 years to bring about the extinguishment of the title of the registered proprietor: *Real Property Act 1900*, s 45D.

The learned trial judge held that the respondents were in possession of the land at the time when the appellant sought to sue it. Conduct which indicates the taking of possession of land varies with the type of land concerned: *Wuta Ofei v Danquah* [1961] 1 WLR 1238; [1961] 1 All ER 596. The evidence indicates that the owners of Nos 1-4 the Grove had engaged in many acts of ownership over a period of nearly 50 years ... employed a man to mow the lawn ... maintenance of the trees, garden and rockeries ... birthday parties and wedding receptions ... entertainment of Dental Congresses ... have been assessed and paid rates ... blocked off attempts by Dr Kelly and the appellant to use the Grove.

[Hope JA agreed with the above as did Kirby P except that he reserved the point about the effect of the *Real Property Act 1900*. Appeal dismissed.]

[4.25] **Notes&Questions**

1. To sue in trespass to land, exclusive possession rather than ownership of land is required. Consequently, a tenant in possession under a lease can sue for trespass rather

than the landlord (*Hines v Hines* [1999] QCA 149) and the tenant can sue the landlord for trespass if the landlord enters without authority: see *Gifford v Dent* [1926] WN 336 and *Kelsen v Imperial Tobacco Co (of Great Britain and Ireland) Ltd* [1957] 2 QB 334 (advertising signs projecting into tenant's airspace).

2. There must be a right to *exclusive* possession. This will not be satisfied if the plaintiff does not have the right to exclude others and the plaintiff's interest is a contractual right to occupy only. In *Georgeski v Owners Corporation Sp49833* [2004] NSWSC1096 (see also *Bropho v State of Western Australia* [2007] FCA 519 at [470]-[475]) the plaintiff was the holder of a crown licence to use land below the high water mark, including a jetty and slipway on the George's River. The licence specifically stated that it did not grant exclusive possession to the licensee and reserved a right of public access to the foreshore at all times. The plaintiff sought an injunction preventing neighbours from using the plaintiff's jetty and slipway. Barrett J held that the plaintiff did not have title to sue for trespass and an injunction should be refused. Barrett J refused to follow the English authority in *Manchester Airport plc v Dutton* [2000] 1 QB 133 which held that the plaintiff who held a licence to enter property to lop and fell trees but who had not yet entered into possession could sue trespassers for possession of the land.

3. In *Newington* the plaintiffs had clearly taken possession, demonstrated by exclusive usage over an extended period of time. Their conduct exhibited the two elements essential for possession – intention to exclude others (animus possidendi) and actual possession by the exercise of acts of ownership. If your parents go overseas for three months leaving you living in the family home, who could sue for trespass? Would your parents be regarded as surrendering possession whilst they were away? A temporary absence would not amount to a surrender of possession. Might it be different if your parents go overseas on a three-year contract returning from time to time for holidays and continuing to pay rates and maintenance costs? Would you be able to maintain an action for trespass if someone broke into the house?

4. What would be the position if in *Newington v Windeyer* (1985) 3 NSWLR 555 (extracted above), the registered owner of the land took over the Grove and excluded the plaintiff? Possession is not good title against the true owner but a long period of continuous possession that is "open, not secret; peaceful, not by force; and adverse, not by consent of the true owner" can give legal title to the squatter (*Mulcahy v Curramore Pty Ltd* [1974] 1 NSWLR 464 at 475, per Bowen CJ). Limitation of Actions legislation has the effect of extinguishing the owner's title to land if no proceedings are brought to recover possession by the owner within a defined period of time. There may be some variation in the time required in the various jurisdictions to extinguish title (12 or 15 years) and the processes required to be registered as owner of the property: see *Abbatangelo v Whittlesea City Council* [2007] VSC 529; *Shaw v Garbutt* [1996] NSWSC 400. Does this mean that if a tenant rents a property for the requisite limitation period the tenant will be granted the title of the property as against the landlord? As to whether the owner could use force to exclude the squatter or is required to apply to the Court for an order for possession, see Edgworth, Rossiter & Stone, *Sackville and Neave Property Law, Cases and Materials* (7th ed, LexisNexis, 2004), pp 148-52.

TRESPASSORY CONDUCT

[4.30] The most obvious trespass is entry upon the land in possession of the plaintiff without the plaintiff's consent. There will be a trespass if the defendant:

- walks (or drives) onto the plaintiff's land without consent: see *Lincoln Hunt Australia Pty Ltd v Willesee* (1986) 4 NSWLR 457. In this case the defendants entered the plaintiff's business premises to interview the plaintiff. Their entry and questions had nothing to do with the ordinary business being conducted and accordingly the Court found that there was trespass from the moment of entry, or,
- remains upon land after permission to remain, express or implied, has been withdrawn: *Cowell v Rosehill Racecourse Co Ltd* (1937) 56 CLR 605. The plaintiff was ejected from the defendant's racecourse after paying four shillings for entry. He argued that payment entitled him to stay until completion of the event but the Court rejected his argument upon the basis that consent may be revoked at anytime and once it has been revoked he must leave within a reasonable time period or he would become a trespasser. The Court noted that the plaintiff may have an action for breach of contract but this did not preclude revocation of the consent, or
- places or throws or leaves any object or animal upon the land: see *Rigby v Chief Constable of Northamptonshire* [1985] 1 WLR 1242. In this case a trespass to land was committed when the police fired gas canisters into a gun shop in the bid to detain an intruder psychopath who had been shooting inside and out of the premises. The combination of the gas and the flammable powder in the shop resulted in a fire severely damaging the premises. In relation to the defence of necessity, see [6.110]. In *Konskier v B Goodman Ltd* [1928] 1 KB 421, the defendant builder left rubbish on the property that he should have removed under the building contract. The rubbish blocked a gully and caused rainwater to flood the premises. This was found to constitute a continuing trespass until the debris was removed.
- Encroachments by adjoining buildings, swinging cranes, scaffolding or structures on the plaintiff's land constitute a trespass. This problem is resolved in some States by statutory provisions which allow courts to provide remedies where there are encroachments, see, for example, *Encroachment of Buildings Act 1922* (NSW) and provision for easements of access, see [4.10] above.

The first case extracted *Kuru v State of New South Wales* [2008] HCA 26 demonstrates the rights of ordinary citizens to protection from unjustified entry to their homes.

Kuru v State of New South Wales

[4.35] *Kuru v State of New South Wales* [2008] HCA 6; (2008) 82 ALJR 1021, High Court of Australia

(footnotes omitted)

GLEESON CJ, GUMMOW, KIRBY AND HAYNE JJ: In the early hours of 16 June 2001, police received a report of a male and female fighting in a flat in suburban Sydney. Police treated the report as a "violent domestic" requiring available officers to attend as quickly as possible. Six police officers went to the flat. Mr Murat Kuru (the appellant) and his then fiancée (now wife) who lived there had had a noisy argument, but, by the time police arrived, the fiancée had left the flat with the appellant's sister. When police arrived, the front door of the flat was open. The police officers went into the flat. Two friends of the appellant, who did not live in the flat, were in the living room and the appellant was taking a shower in the flat's bathroom.

Kuru v State of New South Wales cont.

When the appellant came out of the bathroom, he found that the police were in the flat. The police asked if they could "look around" and the appellant agreed. After the police had looked in the two bedrooms, they asked to see "the female that was here". The appellant said that she had gone to his sister's house. He asked the police to leave the flat. The police asked for the sister's address and telephone number. The appellant said he did not know the address but at some point he wrote a telephone number (presumably his sister's number) on a piece of paper. The appellant repeated his demand that the police leave. He did this several times, very bluntly and with evident anger. Still the police did not leave.

At some point the appellant jumped onto the kitchen bench. He was later to say that he did this to get the attention of everyone in the room. Whether he then jumped off the bench towards the police, or jumped off in the opposite direction, was disputed. That dispute need not be resolved. There is no dispute that having got down from the bench, the appellant moved towards the police, with his arms outstretched, and made contact with one of the officers. A violent struggle followed. The appellant was punched, sprayed with capsicum spray, and handcuffed. As he was led to a police vehicle, he twice fell down stairs leading from his flat to the ground floor. He was taken to a police station and lodged in a cell wearing nothing but his boxer shorts. He was released from custody some hours later.

The appellant brought proceedings against the State of New South Wales in the District Court of New South Wales claiming damages for trespass to land, trespass to the person, and false imprisonment. ...

At first instance the appellant succeeded... The State appealed to the Court of Appeal of New South Wales. It alleged that it was not liable ....The appeal to the Court of Appeal was conducted on the basis that if the State's appeal against the finding that it was liable for trespass to land failed, its appeal against liability in respect of trespass to the person would also fail, and conversely, that if the appeal against the finding of liability for trespass to land were to succeed, the appeal in respect of liability for trespass to the person would also succeed. The claim for false imprisonment was treated as standing or falling with the claim for trespass to the person. That is, the parties conducted the appeal to the Court of Appeal on the footing that the single determinative issue between them was whether the police officers were trespassing in the appellant's flat when the appellant first made physical contact with one of their number.

Evidence given at the trial may well have permitted framing the issues between the parties differently. There was evidence that might have been understood as permitting, even requiring, examination of whether the appellant's conduct went beyond taking reasonable steps for the removal of trespassers, and whether the conduct of the police went beyond the application of reasonable force to arrest a person impeding them in the execution of their duty. But the parties having chosen to litigate the appeal to the Court of Appeal on the conventional basis that has been identified, neither sought in this Court to submit that any issue about the use of excessive force either by the appellant, if his ejecting the police officers was otherwise lawful, or by the police officers, if their restraining the appellant was otherwise lawful, should now be considered by this Court.

The Court of Appeal (Mason P, Santow and Ipp JJA) held that the State's appeal should be allowed. All members of the Court of Appeal concluded that, despite the appellant's withdrawal of permission for police to remain in his flat, the police were not trespassers when the appellant first made physical contact with one of the officers. The judgment entered at trial was set aside and in its place judgment was entered for the State.

The principal reasons for the Court of Appeal were given by Santow JA and Ipp JA. Those reasons differed in some respects but it is not necessary to explore those differences. Immediately, it is sufficient to say that both Santow JA and Ipp JA held that the police had both statutory and common law justification for remaining on the appellant's premises, despite the appellant having withdrawn permission for them to remain in his flat.

Kuru v State of New South Wales cont.

By special leave the appellant appeals to this Court. The appeal to this Court should be allowed. There was neither statutory nor common law justification for the police remaining on the appellant's premises. …

[Their honours then referred to the relevant statutory provisions of the *Crimes Act 1900* (NSW), ss 357F, 375G, 375H and continued:]

We are mindful of the difficulties of police in responding to apparent complaints about domestic violence. Such difficulties obviously lay behind the conferral of police powers in terms of ss 357F, 357G and 357H. Properly, those difficulties, and the importance of effective police intervention in response to suspected cases of domestic violence, were referred to by the Court of Appeal. However, the powers there granted were not unlimited. They were granted, relevantly, subject to the provisions of the Act. Those provisions reserved the right to the occupier to withdraw an invitation to police to enter and remain on the premises. If, in the present case, the police considered that it was necessary to re-enter the premises, the remedy was in their hands. They could seek a warrant from a magistrate, and this could be sought and provided by telephone.

It follows that the police officers who entered the appellant's flat had no statutory justification for remaining on the premises after he asked them to leave. Was there common law justification?

Common law justification?

The common law has long recognised that any person may justify what would otherwise constitute a trespass to land in cases of necessity to preserve life or property. The actions of fire-fighters, police and ambulance officers will often invoke application of that principle. There being no evidence of danger to life or property, it was not suggested that this was such a case. …

As was pointed out in this Court's decision in *Plenty v Dillon* (1991) 171 CLR 635, it is necessary to approach questions of the kind now under consideration by recognising the importance of two related propositions. First, a person who enters the land of another must justify that entry by showing either that the entry was with the consent of the occupier or that the entrant had lawful authority to enter. Secondly, except in cases provided for by the common law and by statute, police officers have no special rights to enter land. And in the circumstances of this case it is also important to recognise a third proposition: that an authority to enter land may be revoked and that, if the authority is revoked, the entrant no longer has authority to remain on the land but must leave as soon as is reasonably practicable.

In the case of a police officer's entry upon land, this is not necessarily a great burden. As has already been pointed out, the police officer may then (or earlier) seek a warrant which may be granted in large terms. Such a warrant may be sought by telephone. It is granted by a Magistrate. Although the grant of a warrant is an administrative act, it is performed by an office-holder who is also a judicial officer enjoying independence from the Executive Government and hence from the police. This facility is thus an important protection, intended by Parliament, to safeguard the ordinary rights of the individual to the quiet enjoyment of residential premises. Where a case for entry can be made out to a Magistrate, the occupier's refusal or withdrawal of permission to enter or remain may be overridden. However, this is done by an officer who is not immediately involved in the circumstances of the case and who may thus be able to approach those circumstances with appropriate dispassion and attention to the competing principles at stake.

In *Halliday v Nevill* (1984) 155 CLR 1, this Court held that if the path or driveway leading to the entrance of a suburban dwelling-house is left unobstructed, with any entrance gate unlocked, and without indication by notice or otherwise that entry by visitors or some class of visitors is forbidden, the law will imply a licence in favour of *any* member of the public to go on that path or driveway for any *legitimate* purpose that in itself involves no interference with the occupier's possession or injury to

Kuru v State of New South Wales cont.

the person or property of the occupier, or the occupier's guests. But as Brennan J pointed out in his dissenting opinion in *Halliday*, there are cases in which it is necessary to recognise that when it is police officers who seek to enter the land of another there is "a contest between public authority and the security of private dwellings".

Argument in this Court about an asserted common law justification for the police officers remaining in the appellant's flat necessarily referred to general statements made in decided cases, about "preventing" a breach of the peace ...when it is said that a police officer may enter premises to "prevent" a breach of the peace, it is necessary to examine what is meant by "prevent" and what exactly is the power of entry that is contemplated. Is the power to enter one which permits forcible entry? Does preventing a breach of the peace extend beyond moral suasion to include arrest? Is the preventing of a breach of the peace that is contemplated directed ultimately to prevention by arrest?

Some of these questions have since been considered in English decisions. Those later decisions proceed from the premise stated by Lord Diplock in *Albert v Lavin* [1982] AC 546 that:

> [E]very citizen in whose presence a breach of the peace is being, or reasonably appears to be about to be, committed has the right to take reasonable steps to make the person who is breaking or threatening to break the peace refrain from doing so; and those reasonable steps in appropriate cases will include detaining him against his will.

As is evident, not only from the passage just cited but also from some of the later English decisions, working out the application of a premise so broadly stated is not free from difficulty, not least in deciding what constitutes an actual or threatened breach of the peace and what steps, short of arrest, may be taken in response.

And for the same reasons, the State's submission, set out earlier in these reasons, to the effect that police may enter premises if they apprehended on reasonable grounds that a breach of the peace has occurred and may recur, or that a breach of the peace is imminent, suffers the same difficulties. Further, the State's submission that police may enter for "preventative *and* investigative purposes" would, by its reference to "investigative purposes", extend the power much further than any description of common law power given in the English cases. There is no basis for making that extension. Whatever may be the ambit of the power of police (or of a member of the public) to enter premises to *prevent* a breach of the peace, that power of entry does not extend to entry for the purposes of investigating whether there has been a breach of the peace or determining whether one is threatened.

Both parties in the present case accepted that police officers in New South Wales are duty bound to "keep the peace". [The Court then referred to the statutory source of such a duty and continued:]

It is not necessary to decide whether it is these provisions that obliged police officers in New South Wales to keep the peace. It is sufficient for present purposes to accept, without deciding, that at the time of the events giving rise to this litigation New South Wales police officers were bound to "keep the peace". But in the present matter, by the time police went to the appellant's flat, there was no continuing breach of the peace and nothing in the evidence of what happened thereafter suggested that, but for the police officers not leaving the flat when asked to do so, any further breach of the peace was threatened or expected, let alone imminent. However broadly understood may be the notion of a duty or right to take reasonable steps to make a person who is breaching or threatening to breach the peace refrain from doing so, that duty or right was not engaged in this case. It was not engaged because, by the time police arrived at the appellant's flat there was no continuing or threatened breach of the peace. And no breach of the peace was later committed or threatened before the eruption of the violent struggle that culminated in the appellant's arrest.

Kuru v State of New South Wales cont.

It follows that the continued presence of police officers in the appellant's flat, after he had asked them to go and a reasonable time for them to leave had elapsed, could not be justified as directed to preventing a breach of the peace. No other form of common law justification for remaining in the appellant's flat was suggested.

[The judgment of Heydon J dissenting has been omitted].

[4.40] **Notes&Questions**

1. The facts of *Halliday v Nevill* (1984) 155 CLR 1, mentioned in the case extract above, were as follows. The police saw Halliday, a disqualified driver, backing out of an open, unfenced driveway. When Halliday saw the police he drove back into the driveway. The police entered the driveway and arrested Halliday. The High Court held that the police had an implied licence to enter the driveway:

   > The question which arises is whether ... the proper inference as a matter of law is that a member of the police force had an implied or tacit licence from the occupier to set foot on the driveway for the purpose of questioning or arresting a person whom he had observed committing an offence on a public street in the immediate vicinity of that driveway. The conclusion which we have reached is that common sense, reinforced by considerations of public policy, requires that that question be answered in the affirmative (at [7]).

   Does a police officer, who reasonably suspects that a person may have committed a traffic offence, have an implied licence to follow that person into the garage of his mother's home and roll under the closing garage door to arrest him? No, see *State of New South Wales v Ibbett* (2005) 65 NSWLR 168 (the appeal to the High Court was on different grounds, (2006) 229 CLR 638).

2. Would a sales person who knocks on the front door have an implied licence to enter? Would a child who climbs the neighbour's fence to get a ball have an implied licence? What would be the effect of a sign saying "Trespassers will be prosecuted"? Will there be an implied licence for emergency workers, such as fire fighters and paramedics, to enter privately owned land?

3. In relation to business premises, is there an implied invitation to television reporters and camera crews to enter premises, interview and film staff and the business operator for the purposes of running a story on the plaintiff's shoddy business practices? Does it make a difference that the entry is not for the purposes of conducting business with the occupier? In *Lincoln Hunt Australia Pty Ltd v Willesee* (1986) 4 NSWLR 457 it was argued that there was an implied licence to enter in those circumstances. It was held that "the implied invitation by the plaintiff for the public to visit its premises was limited to members of the public bona fide seeking information or business with it or to clients of the firm, but not to people, for instance, who wished to enter to hold up the premises and rob them or even to people whose motives were to go onto the premises with video cameras and associated equipment or a reporter to harass the inhabitants by asking questions which would be televised throughout the State". Even if the matters raised were in the public interest, this did not justify the entry. However, the mere

fact of trespass does not automatically mean that the plaintiff is entitled to an injunction to prevent the telecast of the television footage taken during the trespass. But a plaintiff in an action in trespass may be able to recover both aggravated and exemplary damages, see [4.45].

4. A person knocks on your door and is given permission to use the bathroom. If the person steals your wallet, has a trespass to land been committed? If yes, on what basis? See *Barker v The Queen* (1983) 153 CLR 338 answering in the affirmative. Although this was a criminal case, similar principles have been applied to both civil and criminal proceedings.
5. A sign on a mailbox says "No Junk Mail". Does placing junk mail in the box give rise to a trespass to land?

REMEDIES

Damages

[4.45] The measure of damages in tort is: "that sum of money which will put the party who has been injured ... in the same position as he would have been in if he had not sustained the wrong for which he is now getting his compensation or reparation" (*Livingstone v Rawyards Coal Co* (1880) 5 App Cs 25 at 39). As with all trespass actions, in determining what amount of money will place the plaintiff in the position he or she was before the tort occurred, the defendant will be liable for the probable and natural consequences of the trespass: see *Palmer Bruyn & Parker Pty Ltd v Parsons* (2001) 208 CLR 388.

Damages are assessed as either the reinstatement cost or the diminution in value of the property, according to what is appropriate in the circumstances of the case (*Evans v Balog* [1976] 1 NSWLR 36). It will usually be the case that the cost of repairing property will outweigh the diminution of value of the property. What is therefore the appropriate award for the court to make will depend upon what is regarded as "fair compensation" in the circumstances (*Evans v Balog* [1976] 1 NSWLR 36, Samuels J at 39; *Barbagallo v J & F Catelan Pty Ltd* [1986] 1 Qd R 245). In making this assessment,

> [t]he test which appears to be the appropriate one is the reasonableness of the plaintiff's desire to reinstate the property; this will be judged in part by the advantages to him of reinstatement in relation to the extra cost to the defendant in having to pay damages for reinstatement rather than damages calculated by the diminution in value of the land ... Hence, it is sometimes said that a plaintiff may have the cost of restoration provided that it is not disproportionate to the diminution in value. (*Evans v Balog* [1976] 1 NSWLR 36, Samuels J quoting from *McGregor on Damages* (13th ed, Sweet and Maxwell, London), p 713)

In the case of damage to the plaintiff's home, it is now the clear approach of the courts that full reinstatement is to be preferred (*Evans v Balog* [1976] 1 NSWLR 36; *Parramatta City Council v Lutz* (1988) 12 NSWLR 293).

How far will the action for trespass allow recovery of consequential injury or damage? Could a plaintiff, for example, recover damagers for psychiatric illness as a consequence of the trespass? In *TCN Channel Nine Pty Ltd v Anning* (2002) 54 NSWLR 333 Spigelman CJ, in relation to a trespass by a television news crew, said:

> Damages can be recovered for harm that is intended or that is the natural and probable consequence of the tortious act (...*Palmer Bruyn & Parker Pty Ltd v Parson* [2001] HCA 69, (2001) 208 CLR 388...). Damage that is the 'natural and probable consequence' of conduct is

> within the "presumed intent" of the actor... *Palmer Bruyn & Parker* establishes that reasonable foreseeability is not an element of the test of recoverable damages...
>
> It is possible to conceive of a trespass to land in which psychiatric harm is actually intended or is within the trespasser's 'presumed intent' under the 'natural and probable consequences' test. This may be the case if a trespass occurred by way of leaving a cobra snake in a bedroom. Similarly, in the case of a stalker who enters property (although in such cases, a cause of action based on *Wilkinson v Downton* [1897] 2 QB 57 and *Janvier v Sweeney* [1919] 2 KB 316 may be more appropriate).
>
> A video camera, however damaging it may prove on occasions, is not a cobra, although there may be circumstances in which the stalker analogy is apt. Humiliation, injured feelings and affront to indignity may be a natural and probable consequence of intrusion by the media on private property. Such damage is compensable as aggravated damages. Such damage is different in kind to mental trauma. In my opinion, mental trauma – or indeed any form of personal injury – does not flow "naturally" and "probably" from a trespass to land committed in the way the Appellant acted, in all of the circumstances of this case. I reach this conclusion even though the nature of the intrusion carried with it the implicit prospect of broadcast to the public at large of the recording made during the trespass....
>
> Filming on premises and attempting to conduct an interview, even with a view to broadcasting does not, in the normal course, result in personal injury of any kind, including mental trauma, in a person of normal fortitude.

Damage to chattels is recoverable if it is the natural and probable consequence of the trespass. In *Hogan v AG Wright Pty Ltd* [1963] Tas SR 44 the defendant was held liable for the loss of the plaintiff's horse following the defendant's breaking down the fence which allowed that the horse to escape and suffer injuries leading to it being put down. It may also be possible to recover for financial loss which flows from the damage to land, for example, the loss of rent or damage which disrupts the plaintiff's business: see *Rust v Victoria Graving Dock Co* (1997) 36 Ch D 113; *Dodd Properties (Kent) Ltd v Canterbury City Council* [1980] 1 WLR 433.

The tort of trespass does not require proof of damage, but a plaintiff who has not suffered any damage may still be entitled to recover substantial damages as a "vindication of the plaintiff's right to exclusive possession": *Plenty v Dillon* (1991) 171 CLR 635; *TCN Channel Nine Pty Ltd v Anning* (2002) 54 NSWLR 333 at [178] ($25,000); *TCN Channel Nine Pty Ltd v Ilvariy Pty Ltd* [2008] NSWCA 9 ($60,000). In *Plenty v Dillon* (1991) 171 CLR 635 the High Court held that the entry by the police against the wish of the occupier was unlawful, being neither authorised at common law or under statute and therefore a trespass. Gaudron and McHugh JJ In a joint judgment said, in reference to the trial judge's view that the trespass was trifling, at [24]:

> ...we would unhesitatingly reject the suggestion that this trespass was of a trifling nature. The [police] deliberately entered the appellant's land against his express wish. True it is that the entry itself caused no damage to the appellant's land. But the purpose of the action for trespass to land is not merely to compensate the plaintiff for damage to the land. That action also serves the purpose of vindicating the plaintiff's right to the exclusive use and occupation of his or her land. Although the [police] were acting honestly in the supposed execution of their duty, their entry was attended by circumstances of aggravation. They entered as police officers with all the power of the state behind them, knowing that their entry was against the wish of the appellant and in circumstances likely to cause him distress. It is not to the point that the appellant was unco-operative or even unreasonable... .

The general principles governing the award of aggravated and exemplary damages are referred to in Chapter 3 Intentional Interference with the Person at [3.185]-[3.190]. There are numerous examples of cases where courts have awarded aggravated and exemplary damages for conduct arising out of trespass to land. Typical cases involve media intrusion by film crews uncovering what are alleged to be "dastardly deeds": see *TCN Channel Nine Pty Ltd v Anning* (2002) 54 NSWLR 333 (award of aggravated but not exemplary damages); *TCN Channel Nine Pty Ltd v Ilvariy Pty Ltd* [2008] NSWCA 9 (deceit in gaining entry) or unlawful entry by police officers who followed the occupier's son onto the property and waved a gun at the occupier and her son, *New South Wales v Ibbett* (2006) 229 CLR 638.

Injunctions

[4.50] An injunction may be awarded as a remedy for trespass to land. It may be available to prevent a threatened trespass to land but only if it appears that the defendant is likely to carry out the threat and the plaintiff would suffer irreparable damage. Injunctions may also prevent a continuing trespass or require the removal of objects which constitute a trespass: *HB Holmes Pty Ltd v Beers* [1986] 2 Qd R 739. In *LJP Investments Pty Ltd v Howard Chia Investments Pty Ltd* (1989) Aust Torts Reports 80-269, Hodgson J held that a mandatory injunction might be granted to vindicate a plaintiff's rights even though no damage was being caused by an encroachment; it would be unusual for a court to order damages and not an injunction if the effect was to permit the defendant to acquire an easement over the plaintiff's property. See also, *PCH Melbourne Pty Ltd v Break Fast Investments Pty Ltd* [2007] VSC 87 and P Butt, "Injunction to Remove Encroaching Building Operation" (1992) 66 ALJ 40. The court may make an order imposing an easement over land if the easement is reasonably necessary for the effective use or development of other land that will have the benefit of the easement: see *Conveyancing Act 1919* (NSW), s 88K; *Law of Property Act* (NT), s 164; *Property Law Act 1974* (Qld), s 180; and the *Conveyancing and Law of Property Act 1884* (Tas), s 84J.

In a number of cases plaintiffs have sought injunctions against the publication of photographs and video footage taken by television news crews whilst trespassing. In *ABC v Lenah Game Meats Pty Ltd* [2001] HCA 63; 208 CLR 199, Gleeson CJ said (at [51]-[52]):

> There is judicial support for the proposition that the trespassers, if caught in time, could have been restrained from publishing the film. In *Lincoln Hunt Australia Pty Ltd v Willesee* some representatives of a producer of material for television entered commercial premises, with cameras rolling, and harassed people on the premises. Their conduct amounted to trespass. Young J had to consider whether to restrain publication of the film. Because of the effrontery of the conduct of the defendants, he concluded this was a case for large exemplary damages, and that damages were an adequate remedy. On that ground, he declined an injunction. In accordance with settled practice, and principle, however, the first question he asked himself was as to the plaintiff's equity. Because of the ground on which he declined relief, he did not need to decide that question which, he said, took him "into very deep waters". However, he expressed the following tentative opinion, which has been taken up in later cases. "... I would have thought that there is a lot to be said in the Australian community where a film is taken by a trespasser, made in circumstances as the present, upon private premises in respect of which there is some evidence that publication of the film would affect goodwill, that the case is one where an injunction should seriously be considered." If, in the present case, the appellant had been a party to the trespass, it would be necessary to reach a conclusion about the question which Young J thought should seriously be considered. I would give an affirmative answer to the question, based on breach of confidence, provided the activities filmed were private. I say nothing about copyright.... But the case was one against the trespassers. That was why exemplary damages were available, and constituted a sufficient remedy.

ABC v Lenah was followed in *Seven Network (Operations) Ltd v Australian Broadcasting Corporation* [2007] NSWSC 1289. This case involved a stunt by the Chaser comedy team with an interim injunction being granted against the ABC to protect the confidentiality and goodwill of Channel 7. See the critical commentary by G Taylor and D Wright, "Protecting Privacy, Property and Possums: Australian Broadcasting Corporation v Lenah Game Meats Pty Ltd" [2002] Fed L Rev 6.

Civil liability legislation

[4.55] Legislation will only apply to actions for trespass to land in the most exceptional cases. Usually the conduct will not involve negligence, although technically an action is still available for negligent trespass (see [2.55]). The civil liability legislation could apply to assessment of personal injury damages resulting from a trespass, see ([3.180]) and to defences, see ([6.135 Note 6]).

CONCLUSION

[4.60] The modern action for trespass to land retains its importance as an action which protects a plaintiff's possession of land and in so doing protects interests of privacy and security. The action for trespass provides only partial protection for privacy interests depending as it does on an unauthorised entry to land in the plaintiff's possession, see ([4.05]). Whilst English cases have been more expansive on the question of who has title to sue (see [4.25 Note 2]), the Australian courts have felt bound by history to limit claims to claimants in possession at the time of the trespass. This is understandable where issues of title to land are involved, however, it is less compelling when security and privacy interests are at stake, see ([4.05]).

Further reading

G Taylor and D Wright, "Protecting Privacy, Property and Possums: Australian Broadcasting Corporation v Lenah Game Meats Pty Ltd" [2002] Fed L Rev 6.

CHAPTER 5

Interference with Chattels

INTRODUCTION

[5.05] The principal actions for interference with chattels which are examined in this chapter are: trespass to chattels, conversion (originally known as trover) and detinue. (This chapter will not consider the action for replevin which allows interim restoration of the chattel to the plaintiff pending the outcome of litigation where there is a trespassory taking or illegal seizure through judicial process (for more on this subject, see J Fleming, *The Law of Torts* (9th ed LBC Information Services, Sydney, 1998), pp 81-82)). Frequently a plaintiff may be able to bring more than one of these actions simultaneously. So if a defendant stole goods from the plaintiff and refused to return them on proper demand, actions would be available for trespass, conversion and detinue. The explanation for the overlap of actions lies in the history of the development of causes of action for injuries to chattels. The action for trespass to goods reflected the older criminal actions dealing with robbery so that it lay for direct interferences with goods in the possession of the plaintiff. Its principal limitations were that it was not available for indirect interferences or where the plaintiff was not in possession of the goods at the time of the wrong. So a person lawfully in possession of the goods who wrongly sold the plaintiff's goods would not be liable in trespass. The action for detinue would only lie where there had been a proper demand for return of the plaintiff's goods and a refusal to comply. It also had serious procedural disadvantages as it was subject to proof by wager at law, whereby "oath makers" were prepared to swear on oath their belief in the "assertor's oath". In the early common law, the action for detinue was not available where the goods had been returned but were damaged. These limitations led to the development of the action on the case for trover, now the modern action for conversion, see [5.60]. Over a period of time, the action for conversion largely covered the field occupied by the actions for trespass to goods and detinue. But the older forms of action continue to rattle their chains and form the basis of modern actions for injuries to chattels. Throughout this chapter the reader will see that although the tort of conversion is frequently available where claims for trespass and detinue can be brought, there are still some situations where actions for trespass and detinue offer special advantages to the litigant. This chapter will explore the differences between these various actions and the relative advantages each may bring. The first question is what are goods or chattels for these purposes.

CHATTELS

[5.10] The word "chattel" is often used as another term for "goods" or "moveable property". If property is permanently attached to land, it is regarded as part of the land and is protected by the action for trespass to land. For example, a tree that is planted in the ground is regarded as land, whereas a potted plant that can be moved is usually a chattel; an air conditioning unit or manufacturing equipment permanently attached to a building is land. The common law actions of trespass, conversion and detinue have long protected rights to tangible goods. Should this protection be extended to provide remedies for wrongful interferences with non-tangible assets such as internet domain names, rights which are not evidenced in paper form such as electronic transfers, airline etickets and the like? The Australian and English courts have resisted the use of torts actions for injuries to chattels for these purposes preferring to leave the issue of protection to Parliament. Contrast the position in United States, see *Kremen v Cohen* 337 F3d 1024(9th Circ 2003); *Compuserve Inc v Cyber Promotions Inc* (1997) 962 F Supp 1015 (US) and see [5.60].

Another issue is whether human tissue, genetic data and body parts can be protected by actions for interference with goods. This would require body tissue, body parts and DNA to be capable of ownership. There is some authority that property rights might be acquired over a corpse where there has been an investment of time, effort and skill in its preservation (*Doodeward v Spence* (1908) 6 CLR 406; *R v Kelly* [1999] QB 621), so that an action might be available to a museum for the theft of an Egyptian mummy or theft from a laboratory of preserved samples. See also P Vines "The Sacred and the Profane: The Role of Property Concepts in Disputes about Post-mortem Examination" (2007) 29 Syd LR 235. The Australian Law Reform Commission considered whether genetic samples should be capable of ownership and concluded by recommending that proprietary rights in preserved samples should continue but that there should be no legislation to confer property rights on human genetic samples (Australian Law Reform Commission, *Essentially Yours: The Protection of Human Genetic Information in Australia*, Report 96, 2003, Recommendation 20-1).

TRESPASS TO CHATTELS

Introduction

[5.15] Trespass to chattels occurs where there is a direct interference with chattels in the plaintiff's possession at the time of the interference. As this action is another form of trespass, the elements discussed previously requiring direct interference and the requisite fault continue to apply (see [2.20]-[2.30]). It is, however, difficult to argue that as a matter of policy, the action for trespass should be available for a negligent trespass to goods which causes no damage, see [2.65]. Especially where road accidents are concerned, negligent interferences with goods should be the sole province of the tort of negligence. There is no advantage on onus of proof in highway cases where the plaintiff has the onus of proof.

Title to sue is of central importance to determining which action or actions, trespass, conversion or detinue, is preferable because the title to sue varies for each action.

Title to sue

[5.20] The action for trespass to chattels protects possession rather than directly protecting ownership. Only a person with possession at the time of the interference can sue for trespass to chattels. Pollock's explanation as to why possession rather than ownership is protected is that:

> in a settled and industrial state some amount of genuine doubt as to ownership and title must unavoidably follow upon the complexity of men's affairs; that protection must in some measure be given to persons dealing in good faith on the strength of apparently lawful title and to those who may afterwards deal with and claim through such persons; and that protection cannot be given effectually to the innocent without also protecting some who are not innocent...the seeming anomaly will be found indispensable for the adequate protection of true ownership itself. Another element...is the interest of public peace and order. Men will defend that which they deem their own even if the law purports to forbid them; and the wholesale allowance of redress by private force, or exposure of wrongful possessors to dispossession by newcomers having no better right, could create more and greater evils than any that could be thus remedied or prevented. ...It is also said that possession is in a normal state of things the outward sign of ownership or title, and therefore the possessor is presumed to be or to represent the true owner... (Pollock and Wright, *An Essay on Possession in the Common Law* (Clarendon Press, Oxford, 1888), pp 3-4)

Even in a modern world this is a common sense rule. Other than a registered vehicle, would ordinary householders be able to *prove* ownership of all goods in their possession? For example, in *Hoath v Connect Internet Services* [2006] NSWSC 158, it was alleged that the documents that would prove title had been stolen leaving the plaintiff to rely on its possessory title.

The seminal case illustrating title requirements is *Penfold Wines Pty Ltd v Elliott* (1946) 74 CLR 204 extracted below. Before turning to this case it is necessary to say something about bailments. If you (the bailor) lend your spare computer to a friend (the bailee) on the basis that your friend (the bailee) will return it when you ask for it, this would be a bailment at will. Alternatively if you (the bailor) lend the computer to your friend (the bailee) for six months this will be a bailment for a fixed term. You (the bailor) may lend your computer to your friend (the bailee) for a specific purpose, for example, to install a new accessory, the computer to be returned when the purpose has been completed; this is a bailment for a specific purpose. Your friend (the bailee) has actual possession of the computer whilst it is on loan. If a trespasser stole the computer from your friend, (the bailee) who could sue? Could you (the bailor) sue your friend for trespass if your friend (the bailee) threw the computer into the swimming pool in a fit of rage whilst doing a torts assignment? In the case extracted below, Dixon J refers to the position of the bailor (you) where there is a trespass to the bailee (your friend's) possession or where your friend (the bailee) destroys or alters the nature of the goods whilst on loan.

Dixon J also refers to situations where the bailee's conduct is so inconsistent with the bailment (repugnancy) that the bailment (even if for a fixed term or for a specific purpose) comes to an end. When the bailment comes to an end the bailor is at common law entitled to regain immediate possession of the chattel. So again assume that you (the bailor) lent your friend (the bailee) a computer for six months (bailment for a fixed term) and during that period your friend (the bailee) took the hard drive and all the cards out of the computer and put it in her own computer. This conduct would be sufficiently repugnant to the bailment to bring it to an end. Although you as the bailor would have an immediate right to regain possession of the computer because the bailment has ended, is a right to immediate possession sufficient title to sue your friend (the bailee) for trespass? Dixon J, in the extracted judgment answers this question.

Penfolds Wines v Elliott

[5.25] *Penfolds Wines Pty Ltd v Elliott* (1946) 74 CLR 204 High Court of Australia

(footnotes omitted)

[Penfolds Wines sold wine in bottles which were embossed with the words "This bottle is the property of Penfolds Wines Ltd". The sale was on the condition that the bottles were not damaged, parted with or used for any purposes other than sale, consumption or use of its contents. Elliott, an hotelier, sold bulk wine to customers who brought in their own bottles for refilling. Elliott was aware that Penfolds retained property in their bottles. Penfolds Wines alleged, but was unable to prove, that Elliot had systematically collected their bottles and used them to sell bulk wine to customers. Penfolds was only able to prove that Elliott's brother had given Elliott two branded bottles for filling with wine. Two bottles of wine had been sold to a Pure Foods Act inspector (also an employee of the Brands Protection Association) accompanied by a Customs officer. It was accepted that Elliott did not intend to sell the bottles (only the contents) to the inspector. Those sections of the judgement dealing with conversion are extracted [5.105].

DIXON J: 222

... The case against the respondent, therefore, amounts to no more than this. He supplied a few customers with wine which he poured into bottles brought by them and left with him for the purpose. Some of these bottles bore brands showing that they belonged to the sellers of wine, or of other liquor who retained ownership of the bottles. Among such bottles, on at least one occasion, were bottles of the appellants, that is, the two left by the respondent's brother. The bottles were returned to those who brought them, no confusion in the identity of the bottles being proved. On the occasion of the visit of the inspector and the customs officer, the respondent surrendered to them, as if in obedience to the law, two such bottles in exchange for the value of the wine.

What wrong to possession or property on the part of the respondent do these facts disclose? I know of none. It cannot be trespass because there is, on the part of the respondent, no infringement upon the possession of any one. It cannot be conversion, because, on his part, there is no act, and no intent, inconsistent with the appellants' right to possession and nothing to impair or destroy it. It cannot be an innominate injury to the appellants' right to possession for which the remedy would have been a

Penfolds Wines v Elliott cont.

special action on the case, because he did no damage to the appellants' goods, the bottles. Detinue is, of course, irrelevant and so too would have been replevin ...

I think that it is quite clear that trespass would not lie for anything which the foregoing facts disclose. Trespass is a wrong to possession. But, on the part of the respondent, there was never any invasion of possession. At the time he filled ... bottles his brother left with him, he himself was in possession of them. If the bottles had been out of his own possession and in the possession of some other person, then to lift the bottles up against the will of that person and to fill them with wine would have amounted to trespasses. The reason is that the movement of the bottles and the use of them as receptacles are invasions of the possession of the second person. But they are things which the man possessed of the bottles may do without committing trespass. The respondent came into possession of the bottles without trespass. For his brother delivered possession to him of the ... bottles specifically in question. In the same way, if any other customer ever left bottles of the appellant with him for wine to be poured into them, those customers must have similarly delivered possession of the bottles to the respondent. His possession of the appellants' bottles was, therefore, never trespassory. That his brother was in possession of the ... bottles specifically in question there can be no doubt. If, as his evidence suggests, the latter did obtain the ... bottles immediately from a retailer of the appellants' wine, it may be that he held the bottles upon a bailment in which the appellants were bailors and he was bailee. Such a bailment needs a privity between them. But the inference is perhaps warranted that, in the distribution of the appellants' wines, each successive merchant or trader, from the wholesaler to the retailer, had an implied authority from the appellants to create a bailment of the bottles from the appellants to the buyer to whom the merchant or trader sold the wine. There is, however, no importance in the question whether the possession of the respondent's brother, and of any customers in like case with him, is to be considered independent or as that of a bailee from the appellants upon a bailment determinable on demand. For it has been settled for centuries, to quote the language of the *Year Book* (1498), 16 H VII, p 3, Pl 7: "that where one comes to the goods by lawful means by delivery of the plaintiff immediately at the first, he shall not ever be punished as a trespasser but by writ of detinue; nor any more shall his donee, vendee or sub-bailee who comes to the plaintiff's goods by such means" (cited by the late Mr Justice R S Wright in *Pollock and Wright's Possession in the Common Law* (1st ed, 1888), 137). ...

Some misunderstanding appeared to arise during the hearing of the appeal about two matters, which, for that reason, should be mentioned. The first is the rule that, where there has been a trespass de bonis an action lies against the person committing the trespass not only at the suit of the person in possession, but also at the suit of a person immediately entitled to possession. Thus, suppose that after a purchaser of the appellants' wine from a retailer had consumed the contents of the bottle, a stranger were to take the bottle out of his possession against his will; in such a case an action of trespass could be maintained against the stranger not only by the purchaser whose possession had been violated, but by the appellants as the persons immediately entitled to possession. It is sometimes said, in stating the rule, that an immediate right to possession is enough to support an action of trespass, meaning when an invasion of possession has taken place. The statement, however, seems to have been misunderstood and treated as if it meant that an owner of a chattel personal out of possession but entitled immediately to resume it could complain in trespass of any use of the chattel which he had not authorised made by the person in possession or by anyone acting under the latter's authority. This is not so ... . It is submitted that the correct view is that the right to possession, as a title for maintaining trespass, is "merely a right in one person to sue for a trespass done to another's possession; that this right exists whenever the person whose actual possession was violated held as servant, agent, or bailee under a revocable bailment for or under or on behalf of the person having the right of possession" (Pollock and Wright, 145).

Penfolds Wines v Elliott cont.

The second matter about which there appeared to be some misunderstanding is the effect of acts repugnant to a bailment and consequently operating as a determination of the bailment. The determination of the bailment may enable the bailor to maintain an action of conversion, but not of trespass.

> Any act or disposition which is wholly repugnant to (*Donald v Suckling* (1866) LR 1 QB 585 at 615) or as it were an absolute disclaimer of (*Fenn v Bittleston* (1851) 7 Ex 152 at 159, 160; 155 ER 895 at 899 per Parke B; Cf *Cooper v Willomatt* (1845) 1 CB 672; 135 ER 706; *Bryant v Wardell* (1848) 2 Ex 479; 154 ER 580) the holding as bailee revests the bailor's right to possession, and therefore also his immediate right to maintain trover or detinue even where the bailment is for a term or otherwise not revocable at will, and so a fortiori in a bailment determinable at will. But in trespass and theft the wrong is not, as in trover, to the plaintiff's right to possession, and the bailment cannot be determined by any tortious act which does not destroy the very subject of the bailment; and the only extension which this doctrine ever received at common law was that a bailee of a package or bulk might by taking things out of the package or breaking the bulk so far alter the thing in point of law that it becomes no longer the same thing – the same package or bulk – which he received and thereupon his possession was held to become trespassory (*Pollock and Wright*, pp 132-133).

There is some authority for the view that complete destruction of the chattel by the bailee might, for the same reason, amount to trespass … .

There is a third matter which perhaps should be mentioned and that is the supposed distinction between the consequences of the delivery by a bailee of possession of a chattel to a stranger and of the stranger's taking it out of his possession by his licence. There is slender but ancient authority for the position that, in the latter case, the licence of the bailee can be treated as void, if it be wrongful as against the bailor, and since there is a taking, as distinguished from a delivery, there may be found in it a trespassory asportation. Whether this refinement would now be maintained as valid need not be considered … .

The plain fact in the present case is that the respondent never did any trespassory act and therefore there is no wrong of which the appellants can complain as a trespass.

[Starke, McTiernan and Williams JJ agreed with Dixon J that appellants could not sue in trespass. Latham CJ dissented]

[5.30] **Notes&Questions**

1. The usual requirement is that a plaintiff must have possession of the chattel at the time of the trespass in order to sue. But strict adherence to this rule is impractical where the plaintiff is entitled to regain possession on demand under a bailment at will or where the goods were held on the plaintiff's behalf by an employee or agent. These exceptions are referred to by Dixon J in his judgment. Later authority has held that a company officer or employee does not hold possession or have a right to immediate possession personally sufficient to bring actions for trespass or conversion, *Burnett v Randwick City Council* [2006] NSWCA 196.

   The majority view in *Penfolds Wines Pty Ltd v Eillott* (1946) 74 CLR 204 was that a bailee cannot commit trespass to the goods being held for the bailor; the bailee cannot interfere with his or her own possession. But Dixon J suggests an exception to that rule – that the bailor can sue the bailee for trespass to the bailor's possession where the bailee destroys the goods or completely changes the nature of the goods.

2. What types of interferences did Dixon J say will amount to trespass? What types of interferences does his Honour say will not amount to trespass?
3. In the extract of *Penfolds Wines v Elliott* Dixon J refers to an innominate action on the case. This may be available where the owner of goods has neither possession (no trespass) nor an immediate right to possession (no conversion) at the time of the wrong and the goods suffer permanent damage or destruction; see A Tettenborn "Reversionary Damage to Chattels" (1994) 53 Cambridge LJ 326.

In determining title to sue, does the finder of a chattel who has physical custody of a chattel have the requisite "possession" and title to sue? What if the goods are found upon another's land and the landowner is unaware of the existence of the goods? The following case considers these questions.

National Crime Authority v Flack

[5.35] *Chairman, National Crime Authority and Another v Flack* (1998) 86 FCR 16 Federal Court of Appeal (footnotes partially omitted)

[Mrs Flack was a tenant of premises. She lived alone although her son (Glen), daughter and a friend had keys to the house. Her son visited about twice a week. The police had a warrant to search the premises which was issued on the basis that there was evidence that Mrs Flack's son Glen was storing drugs in the house. At the back of an unlocked cupboard, obscured by bags in front of it, a large locked briefcase was found which contained a large amount of money. Mrs Flack said when asked that she had never seen it before and did not know whose it was. The police seized the briefcase and its contents. When three and a half years had passed and no action was taken by the National Crime Authority in relation to the money, Mrs Flack asked for the return of the briefcase and the money. Did she have title to sue for its return? An application for special leave to appeal to the High Court was refused on 14 May 1999.]

HEEREY J: 22 ...

Mrs Flack's case is that she manifested an intention to exercise control over any chattels on the Glebe premises, including chattels of whose existence she was unaware: JG Fleming, *The Law of Torts* (8th ed, 1993), p 69.

The question has to be considered as at a point in time immediately prior to the discovery of the briefcase containing the cash. The issue is whether the occupier manifests a sufficient intention to control all chattels, known and unknown, which are on the premises, subject only to any superior right. Therefore one does not ask: "What was Mrs Flack's intention in relation to the large amount of cash?" All the cases which were contests between occupiers and finders were dealt with on the basis that the occupier was not aware of the existence of the chattel until the finder found it.

Since Mrs Flack was the tenant of an ordinary residential house she had possession in law of those premises. In the circumstances, that fact was sufficient to establish the requisite manifestation of intention to possess all chattels on the premises.

In *Parker v British Airways Board* [1982] QB 1004 the English Court of Appeal had to consider the question of an occupier's intention in relation to the international executive lounge at Terminal One, Heathrow Airport. The plaintiff had found a gold bracelet lying on the floor of the lounge. Donaldson LJ said (at 1018) that, the bracelet not being a fixture, the defendants' claim must "... be based upon a manifest intention to exercise control over the lounge and all things which might be in it".

His Lordship concluded (at 1019):

> It was suggested in argument that in some circumstances the intention of the occupier to assert control over articles lost on his premises speaks for itself. I think that this is right. If a bank manager saw fit to show me round a vault containing safe deposits and I found a gold bracelet on the floor, I should have no doubt that the bank had a better title than I, and the reason is the manifest intention to exercise a very high degree of control. At the other extreme is the park to which the public has unrestricted access during daylight hours. During those hours there is no manifest intention to exercise any such control. In between these extremes are the forecourts of petrol filling stations, unfenced front gardens of private houses, the public parts of shops and supermarkets as part of an almost infinite variety of land, premises and circumstances.
>
> This lounge is in the middle band and in my judgment, on the evidence available, there was no sufficient manifestation of any intention to exercise control over lost property before it was found such as would give the defendants a right superior to that of the plaintiff or indeed any right over the bracelet. As the true owner has never come forward, it is a case of "finders keepers".

Eveleigh LJ said (at 1020):

> A person permitted upon the property of another must respect the lawful claims of the occupier as the terms upon which he is allowed to enter, but it is only right that those claims or terms should be made clear. What is necessary to do this must depend on the circumstances. Take the householder. He has a key to the front door. People do not enter at will. They come by very special invitation. They are not members of a large public group, even a restricted group of the public, as users of the executive lounge may be. I would be inclined to say that the occupier of a house will almost invariably possess any lost article on the premises. He may not have taken any positive steps to demonstrate his animus possidendi, but so firm is his control that the animus can be seen to attach to it. It is rather like the strong room of a bank, where I think it would be difficult indeed to suggest that a bracelet lying on the floor was not in the possession of the bank. The firmer the control, the less will be the need to demonstrate independently the animus possidendi.

Sir David Cairns said (at 1021):

> I agree with both Donaldson LJ and Eveleigh LJ, that, in a situation at all similar to that which we are considering, the occupier has a better claim than the finder only if he had possession of the article immediately before it was found and that this is only so (in the case of an article not in or attached to the land but only on it) when the occupier's intention to exercise control is manifest. I also agree that such an intention would probably be manifest in a private house or in a room to which access is very strictly controlled. Where the borderline should be drawn would be difficult to specify, but I am satisfied that this case falls on the wrong side of the borderline from the defendants' point of view.

Thus all members of the Court of Appeal would readily accept that the occupier of a private home will ordinarily manifest the necessary intention to control chattels therein. In my respectful opinion that accords with common sense. I do not see that any different conclusion should be reached in the present case because Mrs Flack's son and daughter and her good friend Mr Sinclair had keys. The inference to be drawn is that keys given or lent by an occupier in such circumstances are provided for the recipients' ease of access and not for the purpose of conferring possessory rights over everything on the premises – at any rate not to the exclusion of, or on an equal basis with, the occupier. It would, for example, be an everyday occurrence for householders to give, or lend, or make available, keys to children, even children of primary school age. Similarly, an occupier may provide a key to guests, or to a house cleaner or other tradespeople.

The fact that the briefcase fairly obviously was not lost or mislaid but deliberately placed in the cupboard by the owner or previous possessor is a circumstance which makes no difference. There may be doubt as to whether it was hidden or cached. The cupboard was not locked. It was a logical place to

National Crime Authority v Flack cont.

store, or look for, such bags, irrespective of whether Mrs Flack often used it. Also, whoever put the briefcase there would presumably know that persons other than Mrs Flack had access to the house. And this person need not necessarily have known Mrs Flack did not use the cupboard. But in any event the authorities do not deny a possessory right to an occupier where the article in question has been hidden or deliberately placed on the premises: *Johnson v Pickering* [1907] 2 KB 437 at 444-445; *Re Cohen* [1953] Ch 88.

If Mrs Flack manifested the necessary intention to control chattels on the premises, how do her rights compare or compete with those of the appellants? If the briefcase containing the cash had been found by a guest on the premises, or a thief, it could hardly be doubted that Mrs Flack would have a superior right. But as against the true owner, Mrs Flack would have to yield.

The police executing the warrant were clothed with statutory rights to seize and take away any property which satisfied [statutory requirements]...regardless of whether any other person had possession, or indeed ownership. But at common law an article seized under warrant cannot be kept for any longer than is reasonably necessary for police to complete their investigations or preserve it for evidence. As Lord Denning MR said in *Ghani v Jones* [1970] 1 QB 693 at 709: "As soon as the case is over, or it is decided not to go on with it, the article should be returned."...

Therefore the appellants' rights to retain the goods taken from Mrs Flack's home ceased once it was conceded that those goods were not required for the purposes of further investigation or prosecution. The power to enter on private property and seize goods is a substantial interference with ordinary liberties and should not be extended beyond limits which the law prescribes: see *Levine v O'Keefe* [1930] VLR 70 at 72; *Challenge Plastics Pty Ltd v Collector of Customs* (Vic) (1993) 42 FCR 397 at 402-409.

Neither at common law nor under statute is there a general power of the State to forfeit goods simply because they appear "suspicious". The presence of a large amount of cash in a private home is certainly unusual. However the explanation need not necessarily be criminal conduct on the part of the occupier. It could be an eccentric distrust of banks, or conduct that is unlawful or improper, but not criminal, such as concealment from the tax authorities or a spouse or creditor. Before the learned trial judge the appellants did not attempt to prove any connection between the money and Mrs Flack's son. At most there was the fact that, on some grounds not disclosed at the trial, there had at one stage been sufficient cause disclosed for a warrant to be issued. And, notwithstanding the finding of a large amount of cash in a house to which Mrs Flack's son had access, no proceedings were ever brought against him ...

The appeal should be dismissed with costs.

TAMBERLIN J: 29... [T]he relevant test to be applied in determining whether the respondent had possession of the briefcase and its contents is ...whether the respondent manifested an intention to exercise control over the goods? The relevant time for making this determination is at a point immediately before the discovery of the briefcase.

...[T]he starting point for the determination is the premise that a person with exclusive possession over a private home, for example, an owner or lessee, is presumed to exercise control over each and every part of that home and everything in it. In the present case, the circumstance that children of the respondent had keys and were permitted access to the house does not detract from her exclusive possession because such access is only with her permission. In legal terminology they are licensees of those parts of the premises which they are permitted to access or occupy and the exercise by them of this permission does not extinguish the possession vested in the person with the exclusive right to occupy and the associated control which such possession carries with it.

As Pollock and Wright point out in their classic *An Essay on Possession in the Common Law* (1990), p 39, when speaking of possession in the context of a private home:

National Crime Authority v Flack cont.

> ... though an occupier may have no conscious specific intention concerning all the chattels in his house, or on his land, it is certainly his general intention that unauthorized persons shall not meddle with them.

The learned authors say (p 41):

> But it seems preferable to say that the legal possession rests on a real de facto possession, constituted by the occupier's general power and intent to exclude unauthorized interference.

Later they observe (p 42):

> The Common Law pays more regard to the fact that an occupier's general power to exclude strangers from any part of that which he occupies is independent of his knowledge or ignorance as to the specific contents of that part. Possibly the traditional dignity of the freehold may have something to do with this view, but it would seem that a lessee for years would have had the same right as against a sub-lessee.

The underlying concept appears to be that of the protection of the family home and its contents in order to prevent unauthorised interference. This notion is reflected in English linguistic usage, to some extent, by the saying that "An Englishman's home is his castle": see *Semayne's case* (1604) 5 Co Rep 91a; 77 ER 194.

The notion of a person intending to exercise possession or control over an article of which he or she was at all relevant times unaware is somewhat artificial. In some respects it is analogous to a legal "fiction" in the sense that it is a statement which on its face is false but is recognised as having utility in the application of legal principles: see Lon L Fuller, *Legal Fictions* (1967), pp 9 and 12. However, its proper characterisation in my view, is rather that of a rebuttable presumption of fact. The presumed intention of a housekeeper to extend the protection of her home to everything in it, is a concept which has been applied in the authorities and serves a useful purpose in resolving disputes between claimants to possession where there might otherwise be an unexplained gap or vacancy in the possessory chain. The presumption is designed to assist in the development of a coherent doctrine of possession. In his text, Professor Fuller specifically refers to fictions of applied law, such as the fiction of "finding" in an action of trover. It provides assistance in dealing with the difficult questions which can arise in deciding which of two competing parties, if any, has the better claim to possession of an article.

The nature of the premises and the location of the goods in question will be of considerable importance in any particular case. For example, the fact that the goods are located in a private home is most significant. Emphasis is placed by Pollock and Wright on the fact that the goods remain under the protection or control of the occupier of the private home unless and until some other person exercises a more direct or effective control. They emphasise the assumed general intention that unauthorised persons will not be able to interfere with goods in that home. In the normal course of events it may reasonably be inferred that a homeowner intends to extend the protection of his home to everything contained therein. ...

In my opinion the appeal should be dismissed with costs.

[Foster CJ dissented]

[5.40] **Notes&Questions**

1. Mrs Flack did not sue for trespass as there was no wrongful interference; the police had a valid warrant to take the briefcase. When the police were no longer authorised to retain the briefcase and its contents, Mrs Flack was still unable to sue in trespass, why? She was able to successfully sue in conversion and could have also brought an action for detinue, see [5.85] Note 4 and [5.150].

2. In the case above, the police obviously thought that the cash in the briefcase was drug money but were unable to prove this. Assume that the police did not have a valid warrant to take the briefcase, so that there was a trespass to goods, would it matter that Mrs Flack was not the owner of the briefcase and its contents? Is it a defence that someone else had better title (the jus tertii) than the person who had possession? The action for trespass to goods protects possession and possession is good title against a trespasser. It is no defence to a claim in trespass that someone else (not the plaintiff) is the owner, (the defence of jus tertii -better title). See *Wilson v Lombank Ltd* [1963] 1 WLR 1294. The defence of jus tertii is available if the defendant acts on the authority of the owner. It cannot be raised by a bailee against the bailor except where the bailee is acting on behalf of (or through) the person with better title or has made satisfaction to the person with a better title, see *Edwards v Amos* (1945) 62 WN (NSW) 204 at 206; *Anderson Group Pty Ltd v Tynan Motors Pty Ltd* [2006] NSWCA 22 at [7],[90]-[101]; *Hoath v Connect Internet Services* [2006] NSWSC 158 at [151]. See further discussion of the defence of jus tertii where the plaintiff was not in possession at the time of the wrong at [5.85] Note 4.

3. Exclusive possession of *private* land will usually give possessory title to anything found on or in the land. A possessory title is good title against a stranger without title. So Mrs Flack as lessee of a house in which goods were found was held to have a possessory title to the briefcase and its contents even though she was unaware of its existence in her house. An occupier of *private* property will usually have superior rights to a finder of a chattel on that land based on the occupier's exclusive possession. In *Burnett v Randwick City Council* [2006] NSWCA 196, a Council who lawfully took possession of premises under a Court order also took possession of gymnasium equipment in the premises even though the Council had no rights of ownership to the equipment. The Council's possessory title was good against all but a person with better title.

4. In the case extracted Mrs Flack had superior rights to the finder of the money but where the occupier does not exercise the requisite control and intention to exclude, a finder may have rights superior to the occupier. A finder may have better title where the property is one to which a section of the public may have access, such as in an airport lounge and the item is not embedded or attached to the property as in *Parker v British Airways Board* [1982] 1 QB 1004 (gold bracelet on the floor of the lounge cited in the judgments). Where the public have a general right of access such as a public park, will a finder always have a superior right to the legal occupier? If a medieval brooch was found using a metal detector and required digging nine inches into the subsoil to retrieve it, the legal occupier would have sufficient control and therefore possession, *Waverley Borough Council v Fletcher* [1996] QB 334. In *Parker v British Airways Board* [1982] 1 QB 1004, Donaldson LJ was of the view that a finder acquires very limited rights over the chattel if the finder takes it into his or her care and control with dishonest intent or in the course of trespassing. Thus, in *Hibbert v McKiernan* [1948] 2 KB 142, a trespasser on a golf course who took a ball left on the links with the intention of stealing it was held to have no rights against the occupier. But, if the occupier makes no claim there is authority that even a wrongful finder acquires protection against appropriation by others to avoid a "free for all": *Bird v Fort Frances* [1949] 2 DLR 79 (Ontario HC). An employee who finds a chattel during the employment takes

possession on behalf of the employer, *Willey v Synan* (1937) 57 CLR 200, if there are no competing claims by a person in exclusive possession of the land.

Interferences constituting trespass

[5.45] Everyday examples of trespass to goods include unauthorised conduct such as: stealing a motor vehicle; cattle rustling; injecting drugs into a racehorse prior to a race, destroying or damaging equipment, moving goods from one place to another as in *Pargiter v Alexander* (1995) 5 Tas R 158 where the plaintiff's yacht was taken and sailed from Tasmania to Sydney. Using goods without permission can also amount to a trespass. Latham CJ in *Penfolds Wines v Elliott* said (at 214-215):

> A mere taking or asportation of a chattel may be a trespass without the infliction of any material damage. The handling of a chattel without authority is a trespass... Unauthorised use of goods is a trespass; unauthorised acts of riding a horse, driving a motor car, using a bottle, are all equally trespasses, even though the horse may be returned unharmed or the motor car unwrecked or the bottle unbroken. The normal use of a bottle is as a container, and the use of it for this purpose is a trespass if, as in this case, it is not authorised by a person in possession or entitled to immediate possession.

Must the chattels be damaged?

[5.50] The normal rule for trespass is that the plaintiff is not required to prove damage in order to make out the cause of action, see Chapter 2 [2.65]. This makes sense where dignitary interests are protected (trespass to the person) or where issues of security, privacy or proprietary rights may be involved (trespass to land). What other interests might be protected? If someone takes your car for a joyride and returns it unharmed and with a full tank of petrol or a museum sign says "Do not touch the display" – should a claim in trespass be available? Latham CJ in *Penfolds* thought that actual damage to the chattel is unnecessary for trespass to chattels. There is, however, minor authority holding otherwise (*Everitt v Martin* [1953] NZLR 298 (negligent touching of a car not a trespass); *Wilson v Marshall* [1982] Tas SR 287 (unlocking car door with a piece of wire not a trespass). Contra *Pargiter v Alexander* (1995) 5 Tas R 158 relying on *Kirk v Gregory* (1876) 1 Ex D 550). Could it be argued, that as a matter of commonsense, that, like the action for battery, (see [3.40] Note 2) there is an implied consent to unintended trivial contacts which do not cause damage, distress or harm?

Trespass to goods: conclusion

[5.55] A plaintiff can sue for trespass to chattels if the plaintiff can prove possession at the time of the wrong and a direct interference with the chattel by the defendant. The defendant will need to disprove fault (unless it is a Highway case in which the plaintiff would bear the onus of proof (see [2.60] Note 2)). Finally, the plaintiff might not be required to establish that the interference resulted in damage to the chattel. The success of any action will of course be subject to the defendant not being able to avoid liability by proving a relevant defence, see Chapter 6, Defences to Intentional Torts.

CONVERSION

Introduction

[5.60] Lord Nicholls in *Kuwait Airways Corp v Iraqi Airways Co (Nos 4 & 5)* [2002] 2 AC 883 (HL) at [39] (the majority of the House of Lords agreeing) said that the key elements of the tort of conversion are:

> First, the defendant's conduct was inconsistent with the rights of the owner (or other person entitled to possession). Second, the conduct was deliberate, not accidental. Third, the conduct was so extensive an encroachment on the rights of the owner as to exclude him from use and possession of the goods. The contrast is with lesser acts of interference. If these cause damage they may give rise to claims for trespass or in negligence but they do not constitute conversion.

Professor Fleming similarly describes conversion as

> an intentional exercise of control over a chattel which so seriously interferes with the right of another to control it that the intermeddler may justly be required to pay its full value. (JG Fleming, *The Law of Torts* (9th ed, LBC Information Services, Sydney, 1998), pp 60-61)

The special feature of the action for conversion is that the remedy is a forced sale of the chattel to the defendant at the chattel's full value.

Conversion has its origins in the old action of trover, an action on the case, whereby a finder of lost goods, used, sold or otherwise disposed of the goods. In a claim based on trover, the plaintiff complained that certain goods were in the plaintiff's possession, they were lost, the defendant found them but did not return them but instead converted them to the plaintiff's own use. Over time the allegation that the goods were lost and then found became a fiction and the plaintiff was only required to prove a right to the goods (possession or an immediate right to possession at the time of the conversion) and acts of conversion by the defendant. The action for conversion provided an alternative claim for a wrongful taking or destruction where the plaintiff had possession at the time of the wrong. But there were also important differences to the claim in trespass which continue to apply:

- Title to sue: In trespass the plaintiff must have possession at the time of the interference, in conversion a plaintiff need not show possession at the time of the wrong; it is sufficient if the plaintiff had a right to immediate possession at that time.
- Conduct: (a) trespass requires a direct interference; there is no similar requirement for conversion; (b) trespass is available for minor interferences with goods in the plaintiff's possession whereas conversion requires a serious interference with the plaintiff's rights to the goods; (c) trespass, unlike conversion, does not require an assertion of dominion over the chattels contrary to the rights of the person entitled to possession;
- Fault: trespass might lie for a negligent interference (see [2.60] Note 1) but conversion does not.
- Remedies: The action for conversion results in a forced sale to the defendant so that the defendant becomes the owner whereas in trespass, the plaintiff remains the owner of the chattel but receives damages for loss or damage sustained.
- Defences: Where a plaintiff has possession at the time of the wrong, both in trespass and conversion, the better title of a stranger is not a defence (see [5.40] Note 2, [5.85] Note 4). In conversion where the plaintiff relies on a right to immediate possession the defendant can argue that the plaintiff has no *right* to possession (see [5.85] Note 4).

An action for conversion is available for the wrongful dealing with physical goods and chattels but can it be used to protect intangible rights? The tort of conversion is available where there has been a wrongful dealing with a document such as a title deed or a document which evidences a debt or obligation, such as a cheque or share certificate. A cheque that has been misappropriated can be the basis of an action for conversion; it is treated as a conversion of the money it represents (*MBF Australia Limited v Malouf* [2008] NSWCA 214; *Hunter BNZ Finance Ltd v ANZ Banking Group Ltd* [1990] VR 41). But the action is only available in relation to tangible chattels and goods. So, for example, the right to the credit balance held in a bank account (a chose in action) cannot be the subject of an action in conversion but the misappropriation of a cheque can (*Hoath v Connect Internet Services* [2006] NSWSC 158 citing *Ferguson v Eakin* (1997) NSWCA, 27 Aug 1997, unreported BC9703869, and see also *Foxeden v IOOF Building Society Limited* [2003] VSC 356). Does this give undue weight to a piece of paper when in both cases the issue is the loss of funds especially now that many transactions are electronic rather than paper based? What if someone used your eticket for an airline flight without your authority? Should this be a conversion? Lord Hoffman in the House of Lords in *OBG Ltd v Allan* [2008] 1 AC 1 at [99]-[106] described the claim for conversion in relation to a document as an anomaly which should not be extended particularly because conversion is a tort of strict liability (see [5.90]), and the imposition of strict liability would be inconsistent with the limitations on recovery of negligently inflicted economic loss (see Chapter 10). In the *OBG case* there was an invalid appointment of receivers. The receivers were not aware that the appointment was invalid. They took over OBG's business and assets and sold all assets. They also dealt with outstanding contracts and debts held by OBG. There was a clear conversion of tangible assets as the receivers were not lawfully entitled to deal with them. But in relation to OBG's contractual rights, the House of Lords, by majority, reaffirmed the orthodox rule that there can be no conversion of intangible goods. (The tort of negligence has limited capacity to give a remedy against interference with contractual rights, see Negligence: Economic Loss [Chapter 10].) Current Australian authority also supports this approach. Consequently, valuable internet rights are not protected by the action for conversion; an improper dealing with an internet domain name (and associated IP addresses and AS numbers) cannot be a conversion (*Hoath v Connect Internet Services* [2006] NSWSC 158 at [119]-[139] refusing to follow US authority to the contrary). However, an action for conversion or detention is, by statute, available for breach of copyright, *Copyright Act 1968* (Cth), s 116.

Conversion: title to sue

[5.65] The title required by the plaintiff to sue for conversion is either:

- possession when the wrongful act was done; or
- the right to immediate possession at that time.

Conversion may allow a plaintiff who is out of possession to sue, provided there is an immediate right to possession. In comparison the action for trespass requires actual possession at the time of the interference, (see [5.20]-[5.40]).

Right to possession: proprietary interest

[5.70] If a person hires construction equipment for six months but instead of returning it at the end of the six month period sells it to another in breach of the hiring agreement, the hire company has a right to immediate possession of the equipment and can sue in conversion. The hire company did not have actual possession at the time of the conversion (the sale and delivery of possession), but is entitled to get possession immediately and as the owner of goods has a legal right to the equipment. This illustrates the key elements of a "right to immediate possession". It is a right to regain possession immediately as well as some form of *legal* right to the goods (proprietary title). Beneficiaries under a trust have equitable rights and cannot sue without joining the trustee holding legal title, *Proceeds Inc v Lehman Bros International (Europe)* [1998] 4 All ER 675).

Sometimes a contract may give the plaintiff a contractual right to immediate possession of goods but not a proprietary right to those goods. This issue can arise where an unpaid vendor sells (transfers ownership) and delivers goods to a purchaser with a contractual right to take the goods back if payment is not made. In *Chinery v Viall* (1860) 5 H & N 288; 157 ER 1192 the ownership of sheep sold under contract passed to the purchaser prior to delivery, here the purchaser could sue the vendor for conversion for selling the sheep to a third party. The usual rule is that where "there is an unconditional contract for the sale of specific goods in a deliverable state, the property in the goods passes to the buyer when the contract is made, and it is immaterial whether the time of payment or the time of delivery, or both be postponed" (see *Sale of Goods Act 1923* (NSW), s 23 rule 1; *Goods Act 1958* (Vic), s 23 rule 1). Where property in the goods has passed to the purchaser – if the purchaser becomes bankrupt and creditors claim that they are entitled to the goods, the unpaid seller has no proprietary right to immediate possession to the goods as against the purchaser or in priority to the purchaser's creditors, *Jarvis v Williams* [1955] 1 All ER 108 (see also, *Islamic Republic of Iran v Barakat Galleries Ltd* [2008] 1 All ER 1177 at [30], following illegal plundering of Iranian antiquities, the contractual right to possession is sufficient title to sue if the plaintiff is owner once possession is obtained).

It has become common for commercial contracts to contain reservation of title clauses (Romalpa clauses) which provide that title to goods sold on credit will not pass until full payment is made. Note also that State Sale of Goods legislation reserves rights to the seller in conditional sales, see for example, *Sale of Goods Act 1923* (NSW), s 24(1), *Goods Act 1958* (Vic), s 24(1)). Where these clauses are effective, the vendor will have sufficient proprietary interest to maintain an action for conversion where there is an immediate right to regain possession. It should be noted that there are difficulties maintaining an action for conversion where the goods are incorporated into manufactured product, or into construction, see *Associated Alloys Pty Ltd v ACN001 452 106 Pty Ltd (in liq)* (2000) 202 CLR 588 and *Esanda Finance Corp Ltd v Gibbons* [1999] NSWSC 1094. Security interests in chattels are affected by state legislation, see [5.100] and *Southbank Traders Pty Ltd v General Motors Acceptance Corporation Australia & Anor* [2006] VSCA 102 and the proposed *Personal Property Securities Bill 2008* (Cth).

In addition to owners, certain classes of persons who have "special property" in the chattel have a sufficient interest to sue in respect of the chattel's conversion; common examples are bailees and holders of security interests in chattels such as pledges and liens. An example of a bailee having "special property" in the chattel is examined in *The Winkfield* [1902] P 42. Here, a plaintiff bailee in possession of the chattel is entitled to the full value of the chattel in a claim against a stranger not just the value of the plaintiff's interest; the bailee has a duty to account to the bailor for the reversionary value. As a general rule company officers or employees do not hold possession or have a right to immediate possession personally even if they are sole directors and shareholders, *Burnett v Randwick City Council* [2006] NSWCA 196.

At the time of the conversion

[5.75] The plaintiff must have an immediate right to possession at the time the conversion occurred. If an office leases a commercial photocopier under a three year lease and maintenance arrangement, whilst the lease (bailment) continues, the bailee has possession (and a right to immediate possession). The leasing company (bailor) does not have a right to immediate possession until the lease comes to an end, or is validly terminated by the leasing company (bailor) or terminated at common law. What is the position if the photocopier is sold by the user contrary to the terms of the lease (bailment) which entitles the leasing company (the bailor) to terminate the lease after giving notice? Does the leasing company have a right to immediate possession even if notice has not been given at the time of the wrongful sale? The following case explores this question.

Union Transport Finance v British Car Auctions

[5.80] *Union Transport Finance Ltd v British Car Auctions Ltd* [1978] 2 All ER 385 Court of Appeal (footnotes partially omitted)

[The plaintiffs claimed damages from the defendant auctioneers for the sale and conversion of a motor car given to them to sell by Smith. Smith was the bailee of the car from the plaintiffs under a hire-purchase agreement. Under a hire purchase agreement the title to the vehicle does not pass until all payments have been made. The agreement provided that selling the goods should be a breach of the agreement, and that if it occurred, the hiring could be declared terminated by the owner by forwarding a notice of default to the hirer's last known address and taking action immediately to repossess the vehicle. The plaintiffs succeeded at first instance. On appeal:]

ROSKILL LJ: 390 ...[T]he position at common law is this: if the bailee acts in a way which... destroys the basis of the contract of bailment, the bailor becomes entitled at once to bring that contract to an end, and thus at once acquires the right to immediate possession of the article bailed. ...

...[T]he only question that remains for consideration is whether the provisions of the present contract affect the basic common law position. Counsel for the defendants ..contends that because there is this express contractual right to bring this contract to an end only after notice of termination, there is no room for the survival ...of the basic common law rule.... I think...this argument is misconceived.... [T]hese clauses ...give a modicum of protection to the hirer but they also give certain specific contractual rights to the bailor in the happening of certain events. They give him the right to bring the contract to an end and to retake possession in the event of certain things happening. But they do not expressly deprive the bailor of any other rights that he may have at common law; and still less, in my view, do these clauses, either expressly or impliedly, confer any right, possessory or otherwise, on the bailee which would lead to a conclusion different from that which would follow at common law if the bailee deliberately, as happened here, tears up the contract of bailment by fraudulently selling the car through an auctioneer, to an innocent third party. Therefore, it seems to me, following the reasoning in *North Central Wagon & Finance Co Ltd v Graham* [1950] 2 KB 7, that even if there be room in principle for the existence of a contract which may contract out of the basic common law rule, it would require very clear language to deprive the bailor of his common law rights in circumstances such as these. In the case of the present contract the language used is nothing like strong enough to achieve that result.

Union Transport Finance v British Car Auctions cont.

[Roskill LJ then rejected the argument that the right to immediate possession remained in the bailee and continued:] During the argument Cairns LJ referred to the well-known Latin tag "nemo dat quod non habet" which may be translated into English as: "You cannot give what you have not got." In the present case, it seems plain that Mr Smith had nothing beyond a possessory title which he acquired when the agreement was entered into and he took delivery of the car, but which he lost the moment he destroyed the agreement by acting dishonestly, and that, therefore, he could not convey any title possessory or otherwise either to the auctioneer or to the innocent purchaser.

...I would dismiss the appeal.

BRIDGE LJ: I agree. I take as a safe starting point the classic statement of principle from *Pollock and Wright's Possession in the Common Law* (p 132):

> Any act or disposition which is wholly repugnant to or as it were an absolute disclaimer of the holding as bailee revests the bailor's right to possession, and therefore also his immediate right to maintain trover or detinue ...even where the bailment is for a term or is otherwise not revocable at will.

[I]t seems to me that it would make no difference to this statement of principle if [the concluding words] were altered to read "even where the bailment is otherwise only terminable by notice". Of course I accept, as does Roskill LJ, that in theory it would be perfectly possible to introduce into a contract of bailment a term expressly limiting the manner in which the bailee's right to possession as against the bailor could be terminated; in other words, an express term excluding the application of the principle of law cited. It seems to me that it would require the clearest express terms to have that effect. A clause which merely gives a right to terminate by notice for any breach of the contract of bailment could not possibly, in my judgment, be construed as having that effect. Its purpose is to enhance the rights of the bailor and not to curtail them. It gives him a right to terminate on any breach by the bailee of the contract of bailment, whether the breach by the bailee is a repudiation or not, for example, for a non-repudiatory breach by default in making punctual payment of hire. But it cannot possibly be construed as restricting his right to terminate the bailment without notice on the happening of a breach which is a repudiation....

I agree that the appeal should be dismissed.

[Cairns LJ agreed with the judgments of Roskill and Bridge LJJ and dismissed the appeal.]

[5.85] **Notes&Questions**

1. The bailee's conduct may give the bailor an immediate right to possession under the contract of bailment and also a right to immediate possession at common law. Usually the common law right will be in addition to contractual rights to terminate the bailment. A contractual requirement that notice be given would not usually exclude the common law rule. More elaborate mechanisms to trigger termination might. The common law rule was not excluded where a clause provided that the bailment could be terminated by the finance company serving a notice of default requiring the default to be remedied within a specific period: *Anderson Group Pty Ltd v Tynan Motors Pty Ltd* [2006] NSWCA 22 per Young CJ In Eq, (Santow JA agreeing) at [70]. This means that a bailment may be at an end at common law because of conduct totally inconsistent (repugnant) with the bailment but the contract upon which the bailment is based has not been terminated: *Hill v Reglon Pty Ltd* [2007] NSWCA 295 at [73], [85] (leave to appeal to the High Court refused).

2. At common law, conduct repugnant to the continuance of the bailment, will bring the bailment to an end and entitle the bailor to immediate possession of the chattel. This is sufficient title to sue for conversion or detinue but not trespass, see *Penfolds Wines Pty Ltd v Elliott* (1946) 74 CLR 204 (extracted at [5.25] and [5.105]). What conduct will suffice for these purposes? In *Anderson Group Pty Ltd v Tynan Motors Pty Ltd* [2006] NSWCA 22 the Anderson Group (bailee) was purchasing a Mercedes Benz under a hire purchase agreement from Esanda Ltd. The vehicle was delivered on behalf of Anderson to Tynan Motors (the defendant) for sale on consignment. Whilst it was at the defendant's premises it was stolen. Under the hire purchase agreement (bailment), the purchaser under the agreement was under an obligation to insure the vehicle and not to part with possession without prior written consent. The plaintiff had previously contacted Esanda to find out the final pay out figure so the car could be paid off and could be sold. The question before the Court was whether the bailee (Anderson Group) had any interest which would allow it to sue Tynan motors for the loss of the motor vehicle. One of the issues was whether the bailment continued or whether the failure to insure or the transfer of possession to Tynan Motors with the intention of selling the vehicle was so repugnant to the bailment that it came to an end. It was held neither was sufficient to bring the bailment to an end. There was no attempt to defraud Esanda as there was an intention to pay the money owed.

3. A bailment at will can be ended at anytime by the bailor who generally retains the right to immediate possession (subject to any argument whether conditions such as notice need to be first complied with).

4. In *Chairman, National Crime Authority v Flack* (1998) 156 ALR 501 (see [5.35]) Mrs Flack did not have possession of the money at the time of conversion, which was the failure to return the goods on demand. Why was she allowed to recover when she was not the owner of the money? Why couldn't the National Crime Authority argue that although it was no longer entitled to retain the money, someone else was the owner and had better title than Mrs Flack, the jus tertii defence? Where a plaintiff relies on a *right* to immediate possession as the basis for a claim in conversion, a defendant can argue that the plaintiff has no "*right*" or title to the property at all. What was Mrs Flack's *right* to possession? A plaintiff will have a "right" to possession if the plaintiff is entitled to regain possession as the owner, or where the plaintiff has some special property in the goods such as a security interest over the chattels, or has a prior possessory title based on actual possession. This possessory title, unless transferred, surrendered or forfeited, continues even if the plaintiff has lost possession and this possessory title is good title against a defendant who has no claim of right. This view is not universally accepted, see D Fox, "Relativity of Title at Law and in Equity" (2006) Camb LJ 330,338.

   So in *Chairman, National Crime Authority v Flack* (1998) 156 ALR 501 (see [5.35]) Mrs Flack could rely on her prior possessory title against the National Crime Authority as the basis of her *right* to immediate possession. What if the true owner of the money turned up later when Mrs Flack had no assets and there was no point in suing her to recover the money? Would the true owner be able to sue the National Crime Authority for conversion? Mrs Flack had a possessory title but what is the position if a plaintiff never had possession and consequently no possessory title. Clerk and Lindsell argue that in a (supposed) claim for jus tertii the defendant is saying "you have proved no title of any sort, and therefore you must fail"; it is *not* that a third party X has a better title. The "jus tertii" just forces the plaintiff to prove that the plaintiff has a "right" to possession (see *Clerk and Lindsell on Torts* (18th ed, Sweet & Maxwell, London, 2000) at [14-87]. Note this is not technically a "defence" as such but puts the plaintiff's title in issue (a traverse)). It is a *defence* to conversion that the defendant claims with the authority of a person with better title. This might be the case, for example, where the defendant is a bailee and the bailor's title is superior to the plaintiff's title. The claim that someone else has better title is not available to a bailee against his or her bailor, see ([5.40] Note 2. Nor is it available where the plaintiff has possession at the time of the conversion; this rule applies both to trespass to chattels and conversion where the plaintiff has actual possession at the time of the wrong, see [5.40] Note 2.

5. In *Chairman, National Crime Authority v Flack* (1998) 156 ALR 501 (see [5.35]) the police thought that the money found in Mrs Flack's house was drug money but could not prove it, so Mrs Flack was entitled to get the money back. Would it be a defence to a claim in conversion that the plaintiff intended to use the goods for an illegal purpose? In *Gollan v Nugent* (1988) 166 CLR 18, the High Court held, by majority, that it was not a defence to an action in conversion against the police that the plaintiff intended to use the goods seized to commit offences under the *Indecent Articles and Classified Publications Act 1975* (NSW) (at 43). But leave was granted to plead the defence that the articles were of an obscene or indecent nature so that on grounds of public policy a remedy should be refused. Note: legislation relating to confiscation of profits from illegal activities (if proven) may result in forfeiture to the Crown, see also *Anu v Keelty* [2007] FCA 77.

Conversion and fault

[5.90] In conversion, the plaintiff must prove that the defendant's conduct was intentional. Unlike the traditional rule for trespass, (see [5.15]) for conversion the defendant's conduct cannot be negligent. The relevant intention is an intention to deal with the chattel. For example, an auctioneer sells and delivers possession of a stolen painting in good faith to a purchaser. Even if the auctioneer is under the mistaken belief that the true owner has authorised the sale, the auctioneer will be liable for conversion of the painting having intentionally dealt with it (*Union Transport Finance v British Car Auctions* [1978] 2 All ER 385, extracted at [5.80]). A purchaser for value of the painting (without notice that it was stolen) who has taken possession is liable for conversion to the true owner for the painting's full value. A suggested rationale for retaining the strict liability rule is that any other rule would promote dishonesty. Tettenborn points out that as the law currently stands, no distinction is drawn between the innocent purchaser of a stolen painting and the dishonest thief selling it (see the arguments for reform by A Tettenborn "Damages in Conversion – The Exception or the Anomaly" (1993) Cambridge LJ 128). Both the innocent purchaser and the thief are theoretically liable for the full value of the chattel although the likelihood is that the thief will have disappeared leaving the innocent purchaser to be saddled with the cost. Lord Nicholls in *Kuwait Airways Corporation v Iraqi Airways* [2002] 2 WLR 1353 at [104] suggests that the distinction could be relevant in applying the remoteness of damage test, see [5.200]. Tettenborn also points out that the innocent purchaser cannot reduce the amount to be paid by arguing that the owner was contributorily negligent by failing to properly secure the chattel against theft. Moreover, an innocent purchaser can be liable even if the purchaser is only one in a succession of converters and not the original person who deprived the plaintiff of possession.

Dealings that constitute conversion

[5.95] A conversion can be committed in a variety of ways. This chapter considers the more common conduct that constitutes conversion. It is not intended to be exhaustive.

Sale

[5.100] In considering what conduct will constitute a conversion, one question to consider is whether a purported assertion of dominion that does not transfer title or affect possession can constitute a conversion, see [5.140]. Preliminary to this discussion, it should be noted that a wrongful sale of goods rarely gives good title to the goods to the purchaser so that a purported sale does not change the title to goods. This is because of the rule that the seller cannot give better title than the seller possesses (nemo dat quod non habet). So a thief cannot give good title to a bona fide purchaser of goods for value without notice of the owner's rights. This common law rule has been statutorily adopted in State sale of goods legislation: For example, the *Sale of Goods Act 1923* (NSW), s 26(1) provides: "Subject to the provisions of this Act, where goods are sold by a person who is not the owner thereof and who does not sell them under the authority or with the consent of the owner, the buyer acquires no better title to the goods than the seller had, unless the owner of the goods is by the owner's conduct precluded from denying the seller's authority to sell".

However, in some exceptional circumstances a wrongful sale by a person can give good title to a bona fide purchaser for value without notice. For example, in relation to uncollected goods, a purchaser may gain good title (*Uncollected Goods Act 1995* (NSW), s 34). There are other very limited exceptions under Sale of Goods legislation, see *Sale of Goods Act 1923* (NSW), ss 26(2), 28; *Goods Act 1958* (Vic), ss 30, 31, Pts 11, 111.

Where a wrongful sale does give good title to the purchaser, this is a conversion. The usual rule is, however, that a purported but ineffective sale which does not pass title to the goods is not a conversion unless coupled with delivery of possession to the purchaser, see [5.130].

Frequently issues arise where goods are purchased under a financing arrangement whereby the finance company has rights over the chattel until full payment is made. There is a special statutory regime dealing with the ranking and priority of security interests in chattels. Consideration of these issues are best left to later courses on commercial law save for noting special provisions relating to cars and boats. In relation to motor vehicles, the risk may be reduced by search inquiries such as in New South Wales, the register of encumbered vehicles (REVs) which is linked to the National Exchange of Vehicle and Driver Information (NEVDIS) recording stolen vehicles, Vic, The Vehicle Information Package (VIP).

A purchaser may take free of a security interest in relation to prescribed goods such as motor vehicles or boats under the Registration of Interest in Goods legislation: *Registration of Interest in Goods Act 1986* (NSW) and see *Registration of Interests in Goods Regulation 2004* (NSW), regs 24 – 29; *Security Interests in Goods Act 2005* (NSW); *Motor Vehicles and Boats Securities Act 1986* (Qld); *Chattel Securities Act 1987* (Vic) and see proposed federal legislation *Personal Property Securities Bill 2008* (Cth) and *Personal Property Securities Bill 2008*, Commentary May 2008 paras 2.10-2.14. The current legislation dealing with security interests does not appear to protect a purchaser of a stolen vehicle against a claim in conversion by the owner, see *Registration of Interest in Goods Act 1986* (NSW), s 9(2), *Motor Vehicles and Boats Securities Act 1986* (Qld), s 26.

Use

Penfolds Wines v Elliott

[5.105] *Penfolds Wines Pty Ltd v Elliott* (1946) 74 CLR 204 High Court of Australia (footnotes omitted)

[An earlier extract from this case, which includes a statement of the facts, appears at [5.25].]

LATHAM CJ: 218 Upon the assumption that the defendant's brother was lawfully in possession of the bottles as a sub-bailee, and upon the basis of the fact that the defendant came into possession of the bottles with the consent of his brother, it is still the case that the original bailment was determined when the defendant's brother delivered the bottles to the defendant to use for purposes absolutely inconsistent with the terms of the bailment, upon which alone he held them. The defendant then used them without any regard to the plaintiff's rights. A taking of the bottles without any intention to exercise permanent or temporary dominion over them, though it might be a trespass, would not be a conversion; but the actual use of the bottles for the benefit of the defendant and his brother was a conversion: see *Fouldes v Willoughby* (1841) 8 M & W 540 at 546; 151 ER 1153 at 1155, 1156 per Lord Abinger CB. The defendant in the present case handled and used the plaintiff's bottles for the purpose of exercising what he regarded as his right to use them for containing any liquid that he chose to put into them and to keep them for that purpose until he delivered them, with their contents, to his customers – his brother or other persons who brought branded bottles to him: See *Pollock on Torts* (14th ed, 1939), 286: "The grievance [in conversion] is the unauthorised assumption of the powers of the true owner. Actually dealing with another's goods as owner, for however short a time and however limited a purpose, is therefore a conversion." The defendant dealt with the bottles on the basis that he was entitled to hold them when brought to him by his brother or other customers and to use them for the purposes of his trade. In *Burroughes v Bayne* (1860) 5 H & N 296 at 305, 306; 157 ER 1196 at 1200, quoted by Sir William Holdsworth in *History of English Law*, Vol 7, p 415, Channell B said:

> Every asportation is not a conversion; and therefore it seems to me that every detention cannot be a conversion. If it were, the mere removal of a chattel, independently of any claim over it in favour of the party himself, or anyone else whatever, would be a conversion. The asportation of a chattel for the use of the defendant or third persons, amounts to a conversion, and for this reason, whatever act is done inconsistent with the dominion of the owner of a chattel, at all times and places over that chattel, is a conversion.

In the present case there was not, in my opinion, a mere removal of the bottles received from the defendant's brother independently of any claim over them in favour of the defendant or anyone else. There was a handling of the bottles, an actual user of them, for the purposes of the defendant's trade – for containing and disposing of the defendant's wine and for the use of the defendant's customer, his brother. Such dealing with the bottles, under a claim of right so to deal with them (a claim in which the defendant still persists) was inconsistent with the dominion of the owner of the bottles and was a conversion ...

STARKE J: 221 [His honour referred to the statements by Dixon J concerning the distinction between trespass, detinue and conversion and continued:] ...That statement accords, I think, with the common law and also with informed opinion upon the subject. And with that statement I desire to associate myself ... . In this case, however, I am content to assume in favour of the appellant that the evidence supports a conversion of two at least of the appellant's bottles. But to adopt the language of the learned Chief Justice of the Supreme Court the evidence does not establish that the respondent was in any systematic way or to any substantial extent dealing with the appellant's bottles in a manner inconsistent with its ownership, or that the respondent was handling the bottles of the appellant

Penfolds Wines v Elliott cont.

except rarely and casually. In the circumstances, said the Chief Justice, this is not a proper case for an injunction and the plaintiff should be left to any remedies which may be available to it at common law … .

DIXON J: 228 Conversion appears to me to be equally out of the question. …[N]othing in the course pursued by the respondent in receiving and filling bottles and returning them could possibly amount to the tort of conversion. The essence of conversion is a dealing with a chattel in a manner repugnant to the immediate right of possession of the person who has the property or special property in the chattel. It may take the form of a disposal of the goods by way of sale, or pledge or other intended transfer of an interest followed by delivery, of the destruction or change of the nature or character of the thing, as for example, pouring water into wine or cutting the seals from a deed, or of an appropriation evidenced by refusal to deliver or other denial of title. But damage to the chattel is not conversion, nor is use, nor is a transfer of possession otherwise than for the purpose of affecting the immediate right to possession, nor is it always conversion to lose the goods beyond hope of recovery. An intent to do that which would deprive "the true owner" of his immediate right to possession or impair it may be said to form the essential ground of the tort. There is nothing in the course followed by the respondent in supplying wine to his customers who brought bottles to receive it involving any deprival or impairment of property in the bottles, that is of the immediate right to possession. The redelivery of the bottles to the persons who left them could not amount to a conversion: *Union Credit Bank Ltd v Mersey Docks & Harbour Board* [1899] 2 QB 205 at 215, 216 per Bingham J. The redelivery could not amount to a conversion because, though involving a transfer of possession, its purpose was not to confer any right over the property in the bottles, but merely to return or restore them to the person who had left them there to be filled. Indeed if they had been withheld from that person, he could have complained, at least theoretically, of an actionable wrong, that is unless it were done as a result of the intervention of the true owners and upon their demand.

To fill the bottles with wine at the request of the person who brought them could not in itself be a conversion. It was not a use of the bottles involving any exercise of dominion over them, however transitory. There was, of course, no asportation and the older cases to the effect that an asportation of chattels for the use of the person taking them, or of a third person, may amount to a conversion can have no application. In any event, an intention cannot be imputed to the respondent of taking to himself the property in the bottles or of depriving the appellants thereof or of asserting any title therein or of denying that of the appellants. It was not an act derogating from the proprietary right of the appellant. There was no user on the footing that the respondent was owner or that the appellants had no title, in short no act of ownership. The essential elements of liability in trover are lacking.

Even if it had positively appeared that at times the wrong bottle was returned to the person who left one for filling, it may be doubted whether that would amount to conversion, considering the purpose and nature of the transaction and the absence of any intent to affect the ownership, particularly the ownership of branded bottles …

[After holding that Penfolds had no action in case, as to which see [5.25], [5.30] Note 3], his Honour continued:]

In point of policy there is no reason why the law should make it a civil wrong to put a chattel to some temporary and harmless use at the request and for the benefit of a person possessed of the chattel. …

In my opinion there is no foundation for the injunction and other equitable relief sought by the appellants and their appeal should be dismissed.

McTIERNAN J: 235 This use of these bottles was inconsistent with the dominion and right of property of the appellant in the bottles; the respondent used them in his business as receptacles for the wine ordered by his brother … the respondent took and used those bottles for the purposes of his own business and for his brother's purposes.

Penfolds Wines v Elliott cont.

There is no evidence that the respondent infringed the appellant's rights in any other way than by a conversion of two, or at the most three, of the appellant's bottles. I cannot see any evidence of a threatened further infringement to a material extent, or at all, of the appellant's rights … .

In my opinion both courts below were right in holding that this is not a proper case for an injunction. The appellant should be left to pursue any remedies it may have at common law.

WILLIAMS J: 242 The crucial question is therefore whether there was a conversion or threatened conversion of the bottles by the defendant.

I am satisfied that when the defendant filled and corked the two bottles, he must have seen the brands and known that he was using bottles which were not the property of his brother but of the plaintiff. Alternatively, I am satisfied that the plaintiff gave the defendant sufficient notice that the bottles were its property. In *Caxton Publishing Co Ltd v Sutherland Publishing Co* [1939] AC 178 at 202, Lord Porter said: "Conversion consists in an act intentionally done inconsistent with the owner's right, though the doer may not know of or intend to challenge the property or possession of the true owner." One form of conversion referred to in *Chitty on Pleading* (7th ed, 1844), Vol 1, p 172, …is "illegally using, or misusing goods; … a user as if the defendant or someone other than the plaintiff were the owner". "The loss or deprivation of possession suffered by the plaintiff need not be permanent. The duration of the dispossession is relevant with respect to the measure of damages, but makes no difference in the nature of the wrong": *Salmond on Torts* (10th ed, 1945), 289. "Any other wrongful disposition of goods, if it has the effect of depriving the owner of the use of them permanently or for a substantial time, is conversion; thus, if a person … hands them over to someone other than the true owner … such person is guilty of conversion": *Halsbury's Laws of England* (2nd ed), Vol 33, p 53. In *Powell v Hoyland* (1851) 6 Ex 67; 155 ER 456, the defendant obtained possession of certain property of the plaintiff. Subsequently, with knowledge of the plaintiff's title, he handed it over to his employers. It was held that he was guilty of conversion. In *Singer Manufacturing Co v Clark* (1879) 5 Ex D 37, the plaintiff had bailed his goods. Either the bailee or some other person pawned them with the defendant. The plaintiff demanded delivery, but the defendant refused to deliver the goods to the plaintiff and delivered them to the pawner. It was held that he was guilty of conversion.

The importance of rights attached to ownership vary according to the nature of the particular property. Bottles are meant to be filled so that to fill the bottle of another person is to deprive him of the use of his property. In the present case the brother purported to place the defendant in possession of the bottles as a bailee for him. If they had been "clean bottles", although in fact the property of the plaintiff, the defendant might not have been guilty of conversion in filling and returning them to the person from whom he got them, unless the plaintiff had made a claim that they were its bottles and had demanded their return: *Union Credit Bank Ltd v Mersey Docks & Harbour Board* [1899] 2 QB 205. But the indorsement on the bottles proclaimed that they were the property of the plaintiff. In *Hollins v Fowler* (1875) LR 7 HL 757 at 766, Blackburn J said: "In considering whether the act is excused against the true owner it often becomes important to know whether the person, doing what is charged as a conversion, had notice of the plaintiff's title. There are some acts which from their nature are necessarily a conversion, whether there was notice of the plaintiff's title or not. There are others which if done in a bona fide ignorance of the plaintiff's title are excused, though if done in disregard of a title of which there was notice they would be a conversion." The use which the defendant made of the bottles with knowledge of the plaintiff's title was, in the words of Blackburn J on the same page, "an interference with the property which would not, as against the true owner, be justified, or at least excused, in one who came lawfully into possession of the goods". He was, in the words of Brett J. (1875) LR 7 HL 784, "using the goods with the intent to exercise an act of ownership on his own behalf, or of someone (that is, his brother) other than the plaintiff".

For these reasons, I would allow the appeal and grant an injunction substantially in the limited form now claimed.

———— ꟷ ————

[5.110] **Notes&Questions**

1. Why was the defendant's use of the bottles sufficient to constitute conversion? Why did Dixon J (dissenting on this issue) consider that there was no conversion? Penfolds sought an injunction to prevent the defendant from continuing to deal with their bottles in the future. Whilst a majority found that there was conversion, the majority refused to grant the injunction as there was no likelihood of repetition.
2. In *Model Dairy Ltd v White* (1935) 41 Argus LR 423, the defendant deliberately and systematically collected the plaintiff's branded bottles and used them to sell the defendant's milk. The Victorian Supreme Court held that this was a conversion, awarded damages of 1s (10c) and granted an injunction. Compare this with the New Zealand High Court decision of *New Zealand Industrial Gases Ltd v Oxyman* (1992) 24 IPR 161, in which the Court determined that the defendant's act of filling the plaintiff's cylinders with gas was not conversion. Relying upon the approach of Dixon J in *Penfolds Wines v Elliott*, the Court concluded, "All that the evidence establishes is that the defendant inserted gas into a cylinder belonging to the plaintiff. I do not presently understand how that would impede the plaintiff's exercise of its right to possession of the chattel".
3. A person subscribes to a pay TV broadband news and entertainment service under a two year contract. The agreement provides that the equipment provided for this purpose is to remain the property of the provider and that the user is not permitted to use it for purposes other than under the agreement. A number of students rent a property with one of them subscribing to a limited pay TV service. The original subscriber has left the property. The service did not include the sports channels so X, an IT student, tampers with the equipment, and inserts a fake smartcard allowing access to all channels. Under the agreement, there are additional monthly fees payable for additional channels. Is an action for conversion available to the pay TV company against X?

Taking or receiving possession

[5.115] Generally, where a defendant wrongfully takes a chattel out of the plaintiff's possession with the intention of keeping it, the defendant will have exercised dominion or control over the chattel contrary to the rights of the owner and will be liable for conversion. So the theft of a chattel or even a taking of a chattel from the owner under the mistaken impression that it belongs to the taker would constitute a conversion. But an intention to retain the goods permanently is not necessary. Taking a car for a joy ride, even if there is an intention to return the car, constitutes a conversion: *Aitken Agencies Ltd v Richardson* [1967] NSWLR 65. See also *Triffit v Dare and Bowater Tutt Industries Pty Ltd* [1993] TASSC 158. But a very minor interference of short duration might not be sufficiently serious to warrant a forced sale (see *Schemell v Pomeroy* (1989) 50 SASR 450, where a joyride constituted a trespass, but conversion required a sufficiently serious interference to warrant a forced sale; damage to the vehicle satisfied this requirement).

[5.120] Wrongful taking of a chattel out of the plaintiff's possession will usually be both a trespass and a conversion. But not every trespass is necessarily a conversion. There are cases where the owner has lost possession as a consequence of the defendant's conduct but there is no conversion because there has been no intention to exercise dominion over the plaintiff's goods. In *Fouldes v Willoughby* (1841) 8 M & W 540, the plaintiff and his horses were on the defendant's steam ferry. In response to the plaintiff "misconducting" himself, the defendant put the horses on the shore. This was done for the purpose of inducing the plaintiff to leave the ferry. But the plaintiff remained on the ferry and the horses passed into the hands of third parties. The third parties refused to redeliver the horses to the plaintiff unless the plaintiff paid for the cost of their upkeep. The plaintiff refused. Was the ferry owner guilty of a conversion? The interference was not for the purposes of exercising some dominion over the horses and it was held that there was no conversion. Would an action for trespass to chattels have been available? Lord Nicholls in *Kuwait Airways Corp v Iraqi Airways Co (Nos 4 & 5)* [2002] 2 AC 883 at [41] said in reference to the case: "Whether the owner is excluded from possession may sometimes depend upon whether the wrongdoer exercised dominion over the goods. Then the intention with which acts were done may be material. The ferryman who turned the plaintiff's horses off the....ferry was guilty of conversion if he intended to exercise dominion over them, but not otherwise". If you park your car illegally on private property and the owner of the property unlocks the car using a coat hanger, releases the handbrake and pushes your car out onto the street and it is then stolen, can you sue the property owner for conversion?

[5.125] It is not necessary for conversion that the defendant take the chattel out of the possession of the person entitled to immediate possession. If you have purchased antiques through ebay for their market value from a person you later find out to have stolen the goods, can you be liable for conversion to the true owner? The purchase and taking possession of the goods is a conversion even if the purchaser acts in good faith and pays full value; it is an assertion of dominion or control over the goods contrary to the rights of the true owner (*Safari 4 X 4 Engineering Pty Ltd v Doncaster Motors Pty Ltd* [2006] VSC 460; *Johnson Matthey (Aust) Pty Ltd v Dascorp Pty Ltd* [2003] VSC 291 at [211]-[212]). Conversion is a tort of strict liability and the purchaser's good faith is not a defence. Subject to statutory exceptions (see [5.100]), a wrongful sale does not give title to the goods and the purchaser obtains no better title than the seller.

Delivery

[5.130] Wrongful delivery of a chattel can constitute conversion (*Tozer Kennsley & Millbourn (A'Asia) Pty Ltd v Colliers Interstate Transport Service Ltd* (1956) 94 CLR 384). It is no defence that there was a reasonable though mistaken belief by the defendant that it was entitled to deliver the chattel to the third party; liability is strict. So a storage facility that delivers goods to an impostor pretending to be the true owner or to someone else by mistake is liable for conversion. For example, in the case of *Union Transport Finance v British Car Auctions* [1978] 2 All ER 385 (extracted at [5.80]) the auctioneer sold a car in the mistaken belief that the vendor was entitled to sell the vehicle. The auctioneer was nevertheless liable for conversion.

But what of intermediaries who facilitate delivery. Are they also liable? Would ebay be liable in conversion for an online auction where it was found that the seller was not entitled to sell the article? In *Hollins v Fowler* (1875) LR 7 HL 757, Blackburn J said that a defendant would not be liable in conversion if the defendant's conduct was of a "mere ministerial nature". A dealing will not be "ministerial" if the defendant's conduct purports to affect the title to the goods (at 757, 766-767):

> One who deals with goods at the request of the person who has the actual custody of them, in the bona fide belief that the custodier (sic) is the true owner, or has the authority of the true owner, should be excused for what he does if the act is of such a nature as would be excused if done by the authority of the person in possession...Thus a warehouseman with whom goods have been deposited is guilty of no conversion by keeping them, or restoring them to the person who deposited them with him, though that person turns out to have had no authority from the true owner...And the same principle would apply to.. persons' acting in a subsidiary character, like that of a person who has the goods of a person employing him to carry them, or a caretaker, such as a wharfinger.

An auctioneer is not a mere intermediary for these purposes. An auctioneer purports to deal with title and takes an active role in selling the chattels and transferring possession to the purchaser, see *Union Transport Finance v British Car Auctions* [1978] 2 All ER 385 (see [5.80]). Would an auctioneer be liable in conversion if a stolen painting was given to the auction house to sell, it was not sold and was returned to the vendor without notice that it had been stolen? In *Marcq v Christie Manson & Woods Ltd* [2004] QB 286, the Court held in that situation that there was no conversion. Similarly, delivery on the order of the bailor by the bailee would not be a conversion (*In re Samuel* [1945] Ch 408).

Detention of goods

[5.135] The action for conversion, although originally limited to misfeasance was eventually held to also apply where there had been wrongful detention of goods, thus covering much of the ground of the older action for detinue, see [5.150]. An action in conversion may be brought if a plaintiff with an immediate right to possession demands the return of the chattel and the defendant wrongfully refuses the demand. The refusal amounts to an assertion of dominion contrary to the rights of the person entitled to possession. The defendant may be able to escape liability if refusal to return the chattel upon proper demand is not unreasonable. For example, there would be no conversion if the reason for the refusal was to enable inquiry as to whether the plaintiff was entitled to the chattel. But not if there is no uncertainty about the plaintiff's entitlement (*Flowfill Packaging Machines Pty Ltd v Fytore Pty Ltd* (1993) Aust Torts Reports 81-244) or if the reason for non return was the risk of industrial action by employees. (*Howard E Perry & Co Ltd v British Railways Board* [1980] 1 WLR 1375). But in conversion, unlike detinue (see [5.160]), there can still be a conversion even if there is no demand:

> The cases show that the mere detention by A of B's goods will not necessarily amount to conversion nor will the mere handling of them. But once the degree of user amounts to employing the goods as if they were one's own then a conversion is established. (Young J in *Flowfill Packaging Machines Pty Ltd v Fytore Pty Ltd* (1993) Aust Torts Reports 81-244 at 62,520.)

In *Kuwait Airways Corporation v Iraqi Airways* [2002] 2 AC 883, Iraq invaded Kuwait in 1990 and seized aircraft owed by Kuwait Airways Corp (KAC). The aircraft came into the possession of the Iraqi Airways who, in relation to the aircraft, had applied for certificates of airworthiness and registration for some of the aircraft, repainted the aircraft with the Iraqi Airways colours and used some of them for an occasional flight within Iraq. Was this sufficient for conversion? The House of Lords held that it could constitute conversion under English law. Lord Nicholls said (at [40]-[41]):

> "depriving" the owner of possession...is not to be understood as meaning that the wrongdoer must himself actually take the goods from the possession of the owner. This will often be the case...It is not so in the case of successive conversions. For the purposes of this tort an owner is equally deprived of possession when he is excluded from possession or possession is withheld from him by the wrongdoer.
>
> Whether the owner is excluded from possession may sometimes depend upon whether the wrongdoer exercised dominion over the goods. Then the intention with which acts were done may be material. The ferryman who turned the plaintiff's horses off the....ferry was guilty of conversion if he intended to exercise dominion over them, but not otherwise: see *Fouldes v Willoughby* (1841) 8 M & W 540; 151 ER 1153.
>
> Similarly, mere unauthorised retention of another's goods is not conversion of them. Mere possession of another's goods without title is not necessarily inconsistent with the rights of the owner. To constitute conversion detention must be adverse to the owner, excluding him from the goods. It must be accompanied by an intention to keep the goods... A demand and refusal to deliver up the goods are the usual way of proving an intention to keep goods adverse to the owner, but it is not the only way.

Denial of title

[5.140] Conversion normally requires dealing with possession or an effective dealing with title to the goods, Dixon J in *Penfolds Wines Pty Ltd v Elliott* (1946) 74 CLR 204 at 229 (see [5.105]) In exceptional cases a wrongful sale passes good title to a purchaser, see [5.100].But every assertion of title by a person in possession does not necessarily give rise to a conversion. So a claim that goods are owned by someone other than the true owner without effecting a change in possession may not be sufficient.

The previous illustrations have involved a defendant in possession, dealing with possession or wrongfully transferring title contrary to the rights of the person with a right to immediate possession. Sometimes a defendant might be treated as having constructive possession, see *Douglas Valley Finance Co Ltd v S Hughes (Hirers) Ltd* [1969] 1 QB 738 (paper transfer of lorries for the purpose of exploiting valuable licences relating to the vehicles). Can a defendant never in possession of the goods who neither deals with possession nor wrongfully transfers title to the goods be guilty of conversion? There is inconsistent Australian authority on this question with two authorities holding that there was no conversion: *Short v City Bank of Sydney* (1912) 15 CLR 148, 158 per Isaacs J; *Perpetual Trustees & National Executors of Tasmania Ltd v Perkins* (1989) Aust Torts Reports 80-295; and opposing dicta in *Motor Dealers Credit Corporation Ltd v Overland* (1931) 31 SR NSW 516, 519 (dicta yes).

A threat by the defendant's agent to sell the plaintiff's vehicle without any further conduct was held insufficient, (*Crowther v Australian Guarantee Corp Ltd* (1985) Aust Torts Reports 80-709).

It is clear that an assertion of dominion by a purported but ineffective sale without delivery of possession is not conversion (*Lancashire Waggon Co v Fitzhugh* (1861) 6 H & N 502; 158 ER 206). It might be sufficient for conversion if a defendant not in possession of the chattels prevents the plaintiff gaining access to his or her goods. This was the finding in *Oakley v Lyster* [1931] 1 KB 148 where the defendant claimed as his own the plaintiff's road making material. The defendant also used some of it and refused to allow the plaintiff access to the material on the defendant's land. The plaintiff was entitled as a tenant to leave the material on the land. This tenancy predated the defendant's purchase of freehold of the land.

In *Kitano v Commonwealth* (1974) 129 CLR 151 (at [55],[56] per Mason J) customs clearance was given for a yacht to leave port. Whilst the custom clearance allowed the ship to be sailed away, customs were not in possession of the yacht, nor did customs deal with, or transfer possession of it so there was no conversion. For similar reason if an auctioneer attends an "on site" auction of goods and merely purports to sell, leaving those who have possession to deliver the goods to the buyers, there can be no conversion as was the case in *Public Trustee v Jones* (1925) 25 SR (NSW) 526. Would it be conversion for a motor registry office to register a motor vehicle in the name of a person who was not the owner without knowledge that it had been stolen?

Conversion: conclusion

[5.145] The action for conversion remains the predominant tort available for non-negligent interferences with chattels. It has been particularly important where goods were being purchased on credit with the credit provider retaining rights to the goods, and the purchaser purports to wrongfully sell or otherwise deal with possession of the goods, see [5.80]. Its role in these types of cases is now less important with the introduction of legislation dealing with security interests in chattels and the more readily available means of checking security interests particularly in relation to motor vehicles, see [5.100]. The action for conversion has largely not met the challenge of the electronic age by providing protection where personal property is not reduced to documentary form, see [5.60]. It is likely that the action for conversion will become increasingly less important when information concerning ownership and security interests are readily available through online databases and the like. Its key elements remain that a plaintiff in an action for conversion will need to prove: the requisite title to sue – possession or an immediate right to possession – at the time of the conversion and intentional conduct amounting to a dealing with the chattels contrary to the rights of the plaintiff.

DETINUE

Introduction

[5.150] The action in detinue is available for the wrongful detention of goods where a person with the right to possession demands the return of the chattel and the defendant wrongfully fails to deliver the goods as requested. The defendant may or may not have come into possession of the goods lawfully.

Actions for detinue and conversion may lie in similar circumstances where the plaintiff demands return of the chattel and the defendant refuses to return it. The relevant title to sue in both actions includes a right to immediate possession at the time of the demand and refusal. The action for detinue has, however, some special features which differentiate it from a claim for conversion.

- Specific demand and refusal: the action for detinue, unlike the claim for conversion, (see [5.135]) requires a specific demand and refusal as the basis of the claim.
- Intention: conversion will not lie where the interference is a consequence of the defendant's negligence which results in the loss or destruction of a chattel; detinue may be available where a bailee breaches its duty of care owed to the bailor so causing the chattel to be lost or destroyed, see [5.175].

- Return of the chattel: the action in detinue theoretically permits the Court to order the return of the particular chattel to the plaintiff. So if the defendant refused to return to the plaintiff a very rare and irreplaceable vintage car, a court could make an order for specific restitution of the chattel to the plaintiff. This is not available for an action in conversion where satisfaction of the judgment vests title in the vehicle in the defendant, see [5.210] Note 1. There also may be provision in criminal legislation for restitution of stolen property, see for example, *Sentencing Act 1991* (Vic), s 84.
- Assessment of damages: the prima facie rule for conversion is that the chattel's value is assessed at the date of the conversion whereas in detinue the value of the chattel is assessed at the date of judgment, see [5.215].

Title to sue

[5.155] The plaintiff must have a right to immediate possession of the goods at the time of the demand and refusal; ownership is not a requirement and a possessory interest will suffice. In *Bolwell Fiberglass Pty Ltd v Foley* [1984] VR 97, Young CJ determined that it was unnecessary to determine ownership of the yacht as all that is required to sue in detinue is an immediate right to possession. A sub-bailee has sufficient title to sue for detinue, *Followmont Transport P/L v Premier Group P/L* [1999] QCA 232.

Demand and refusal

[5.160] The essence of this tort is said to be demand and refusal. The plaintiff must prove that:

(1) the plaintiff demanded the return of the chattel to which he or she is entitled; and

(2) the defendant has refused the demand.

In *John F Goulding Pty Ltd v Victorian Railway Commissioners* (1932) 48 CLR 157, the plaintiff delivered goods to the defendant to be carried by rail and when it reached its destination, to be delivered as ordered by the plaintiff. The plaintiff gave a direction as to delivery but the goods were never received. The defendants had mistakenly delivered the goods to persons who were not entitled to them and were unable to deliver upon the plaintiff's demand. The defendant was held liable in detinue for failure to deliver up the goods upon demand.

The demand

[5.165] The demand for return of the goods, which may be written or oral (*Egan v State Transport Authority* (1982) 31 SASR 481 at 520-521), must provide adequate and clear instructions concerning delivery of the goods, otherwise the demand will be insufficient to ground an action in detinue. This does not necessarily require the defendant to incur costs to deliver, it is sufficient if the goods are made available for the plaintiff to collect, *Hall v Hall* [2004] QDC 183 at [44]. In *Lloyd v Osborne* (1899) 20 LR (NSW) 190, the letter sent by the plaintiff's solicitor was found to be insufficient to constitute an effective demand. The letter stated that the defendant "at once deliver to her [the plaintiff] or to her agent all sheep branded X or FG (tar brand) which you unlawfully withheld from her". The demand did not identify an address to which the sheep should be delivered nor who was the agent of the plaintiff.

It also important that the demand unequivocally convey that the letter is a demand for return of the goods and that any existing consent to possession of the goods is revoked. A letter giving the defendant a variety of options, one of which is the return of the chattels, will not suffice (*Brambles Australia Limited t/as CHEP Australia v Tatale Pty Ltd & Venasti Pty Ltd* [2004] NSWCA 232). The one situation in which it may be permissible for the plaintiff not to make a demand is "where the defence of defendant shows clearly that if a demand had been made on him for possession of the property, he would have refused delivery" (*Baud Corporation NV v Brook* (1970) 40 DLR (3d) 418 at 423). Australian authority suggests a similar response, *Crowther v Australian Guarantee Corporation Ltd* (1985) Aust Torts Reports 80-709 (SC SA) Bollen J at 69,102; *Brambles Australia Limited t/as CHEP Australia v Tatale Pty Ltd and Venasti Pty Ltd* [2004] NSWCA 232 at [40]; *Egan v Sate Transport Authority* (1982) 31 SASR 481.

The refusal

[5.170] As a general rule there must be an express refusal to deliver the chattels before an action in detinue can arise. In *Lloyd v Osborne* (1899) 20 LR (NSW) 190 at 194, the New South Wales Supreme Court held that if the demand is sufficient, failure to take notice of it will be regarded as a refusal to deliver (contra *Nelson v Nelson* [1923] St R Qd 37 at 40). If it were otherwise a defendant could simply refuse to respond to the demand. But rarely will a plaintiff be driven to rely on detinue in these circumstances as the tort of conversion does not formally require a refusal to deliver, see [5.135].

The defendant may not be liable if refusal to return the chattel is reasonable. For example, the delay was occasioned by the defendant's inquires to ascertain whether the plaintiff was entitled to the goods (*Clayton v LeRoy* [1911] 2 KB 1031; *McCurdy v PMG* [1959] NZLR 553).

To whom can the demand be made?

[5.175] The demand is normally made to the person in possession of the goods. But a defendant no longer in possession may still be liable in detinue if the defendant has lost possession due to the defendant's wrongful conduct or negligence. The most common examples of this are:

1. if the defendant converts the goods, for example sells them to another without authority then the defendant is liable in detinue (upon demand and refusal to deliver) even though the defendant is no longer is in a position to deliver up the goods.
2. if a defendant negligently destroys or parts with the goods and is thereby unable to deliver them upon demand, the defendant is liable in detinue (*John F Goulding Pty Ltd v Victorian Railway Commissioners* (1932) 48 CLR 157, see [5.160]).
3. if the defendant fails to comply with the terms of the bailment and in doing so the goods are lost or destroyed. This will apply even though the defendant cannot be shown to have intentionally or negligently lost or destroyed the goods. For example if the bailee does not store the goods in the warehouse as instructed by the bailor, but another warehouse and that other warehouse is burnt down resulting in destruction of the goods (see *Lilley v Doubleday* (1881) 7 QBD 510).

[5.180] **Notes&Questions**

1. An action in detinue is complete once there has been a proper demand and refusal to deliver the chattel. In contrast in conversion, the action is complete when the defendant

deals with the goods contrary to the plaintiff's right to possession. If a valuable painting was stolen in 1985 and immediately sold to an innocent purchaser (P1). In 2007 the purchaser sells the painting at auction again to an innocent purchaser (P2). Could the original owner demand the painting from the second innocent purchaser (P2) and bring a claim in detinue when the purchaser refuses to return it? Identify the conduct that could constitute a conversion? If the relevant limitation period is six years from the date upon which the cause of action is complete (accrues), should a dispossessed owner have an indefinite period to bring proceedings in relation to the chattel? The limitation period will run from the date "when the *first cause of action* first accrues to the plaintiff", (emphasis inserted) see the *Limitation Act 1985* (ACT), s 18; *Limitation Act 1969* (NSW), s 21; *Limitation Act* (NT), s 19; *Limitation of Actions Act 1974* (Qld), s 12; *Limitation Act 1974* (Tas), s 6; *Limitation of Actions Act 1958* (Vic), s 6. The jurisdictions of South Australia and Western Australia do not impose such a limitation.

2. A bailor need prove only that goods were in the bailee's possession and were not re-delivered on demand, *Tozer Kemsley & Millbourne (Australasia) Pty Ltd v Collier's Interstate Transport Service Pty Ltd* (1956) 94 CLR 384. The onus is then on the bailee to show that reasonable care was taken with the goods. In *Westpac Banking Corporation v Royal Tongan Airlines* [1996] Aust Torts Reports 63,650 (81-403) (SC NSW) currency valued at $250,000 (approx) was sent by post from Nuku'alofa to Sydney, but did not reach Westpac. Qantas as a carrier of the post, among others, was sued as a sub-bailee of the currency and was found liable. Qantas was unable to show that they had not been negligent in the handling of the currency. Security procedures which were normally adopted for dealing with registered mail were not employed by Qantas in order to fast track the mail over the Christmas period. There was consequently a lack of supervision of the unloading and lack of documentation of the handling of the registered mail and registered mail was left in unsecured areas overnight. Qantas was therefore unable to show that it had not acted negligently in the loss of the $250,000.

Detinue: conclusion

[5.185] It will be an exceptional case where the action of detinue is available and the action for conversion is not. But there are some situations where the action for detinue provides some special advantages for litigants: it allows recovery of damages for negligent loss or destruction by a bailee, the bailee having the onus of disproof of breach of duty (note, in conversion, the plaintiff has to prove the conversion and in the tort of negligence, the plaintiff would have to prove the negligence); the opportunity to regain the chattel itself where the chattel has a unique or special character (see [5.215]), and potentially some advantages when it comes to assessment of damages ([5.215]). In the United Kingdom, the action for detinue has been abolished by statute which now provides that the action of conversion also lies for loss or destruction of goods where the bailee is in breach of its duty to the bailor (*Torts (Interference with Goods) Act 1977* (UK), s 2). In Australia, the action for detinue remains available with the plaintiff being required to prove the requisite title to sue ([5.155]) and a specific demand for return of the chattel and refusal to return the chattel ([5.160]). Where the plaintiff proves non-delivery, the onus is on the defendant to show no breach of duty.

REMEDIES

[5.190] A plaintiff's choice of action may be influenced by the available remedies and damages available. Save in a very exceptional situation involving negligence, Civil Liability legislation would not apply.

Trespass to chattels

[5.195] The principal remedy for trespass to chattels is damages. If the plaintiff has been totally deprived of the goods or the goods are destroyed, the plaintiff will be awarded an amount equal to its value; where the goods are damaged, the plaintiff will be entitled to the diminution in value of the chattel. The plaintiff is also entitled to recover consequential losses flowing from the trespass. In an appropriate case exemplary and aggravated damages may be awarded, see (3.185], [3.190]). See as examples, *Healing (Sales) Pty Ltd v Inglis Electrix Pty Ltd* (1968) 121 CLR 584 (unlawful seizure of electrical goods, award of exemplary damages); *Makryllos v George Laurens (NT) Pty Ltd* (1992) 111 FLR 204 (illegal seizure of caravans, aggravated damages awarded).

Conversion

[5.200] Special issues of causation arise in actions for conversion where there have been successive acts of conversion. If the first act of conversion deprived the plaintiff of possession of the goods, later acts of conversion do not worsen the plaintiff's position. How then can it be said that later acts of conversion have caused the plaintiff's loss? Lord Nicholls in *Kuwait Airways Corp v Iraqi Airways Co (Nos 4 & 5)* [2002] 2 AC 883 (HL) responded at [82]: "By definition, each person in a series of conversions wrongfully excludes the owner from possession of his goods. This is the basis upon which each is liable to the owner.... The wrongful acts of a previous possessor do not therefore diminish the plaintiff's claim in respect of the wrongful acts of a later possessor". In the *Kuwait Airways Corp case* 10 Kuwaiti aircraft had been seized by Iraq during the invasion of Kuwait. Six of the Kuwaiti aircraft were flown to Iran for safe keeping. The other four aircraft had been destroyed in the bombing of Mosul. Iran refused to return the six aircraft to Kuwait unless "a ransom" of $20m (US) was paid for the cost, upkeep and maintenance of the aircraft. One of the questions was whether Iraqi Airways was liable for this cost? The House of Lords held that it was. Lord Nicholls delivering the principal judgment in the House of Lords said (at [92]): "A person who misappropriates another's goods does so at his own risk. That is the nature of the wrong. He takes upon himself the risk of being unable to return the goods to their rightful owner. It matters not that he may be prevented from returning the goods due to unforeseen circumstances beyond his control." Lord Hoffman said at [129] "the person who takes (the chattel) is treated as being under a continuing strict duty to restore the chattel to its owner" with the consequence that it was irrelevant that if Iraqi Airways had not taken possession of the aircraft someone else would have; it was also irrelevant that Iraqi Airways would have been prevented by the Iraqi regime or by the conduct of Iran from returning the aircraft even if it wished to do so. Kuwaiti Airlines were also entitled to recover consequential losses such as the cost of repairing the aircraft, hiring substitute aircraft and loss of profits during the period Kuwaiti Airlines was deprived of possession.

Lord Nicholls in the *Kuwait Airlines case* also discussed the extent of liability for consequential losses (remoteness of damage rules). Lord Nicholls (Lord Hope of Craigend and

Lord Hoffman agreeing at [125], [169]) suggested that in an action for conversion where the defendant has acted dishonestly, the relevant rule for remoteness of damage should be whether the damage was a direct and natural consequence of the defendant's wrongdoing. But a more lenient rule of reasonable foreseeability should be applied to an innocent wrongdoer (at [103], [104]). The Victorian Court of Appeal in *National Australia Bank v Nemur Varity Pty Ltd* [2002] VSCA 18, [2002] 4 VR 252 rejected foreseeability as the relevant remoteness of damage test for conversion noting that more stringent tests should be applied. The preference was to adopt a test similar to contractual tests of remoteness rather than the tests applied for intentional wrongdoing (see [4.45]). Applying those tests, business losses would only be recoverable as consequential losses resulting from the conversion of cheques if the defendant had express notice or special knowledge (see Batt JA at [62]-[65], [71], Calloway JA at [9], Philips JA at [4]).

In an action for conversion, damages are the principal form for relief although in an appropriate case an injunction could prevent continuing conversions, see *Penfolds Wines v Elliott* [5.105]. In assessing damages for conversion, the court asks what damages will place the plaintiff in the position the plaintiff would have been if the tort had not been committed.

Sinclair v Haynes

[5.205] *Sinclair v Haynes* Supreme Court of New South Wales [2000] NSWSC 642 Supreme Court of New South Wales (footnotes omitted)

HAMILTON J: [1] Before me is a stated case in an action for conversion in the Local Court. The item converted was a horse float or trailer fitted out for use by a horse dentist. The plaintiff's family had been in horse dentistry for some hundred years and reference was made in the evidence to at least two other horse dentists in Australia. There is no dispute before me that the trailer was converted by the defendant. The point brought to this Court relates solely to the assessment of damages. Those damages were assessed on 20 February 1998 by Magistrate Crews at $12,000. ...

[2] [Hamilton J then referred to the issues raised in the case stated: whether the Magistrate had committed an error in law by holding that the trailer converted by the defendant was valued at $12,000 and whether there was proper evidence that the trailer was valued at $12,000. Hamilton J continued:]

[3] The appellant's point was ...that the appropriate damages in conversion are the value of the goods at the date of conversion; that prima facie the measure of those damages where there is a market in the goods is the price at which replacement goods can be bought in that market; and that it is only where it is established that there was no such market that the plaintiff can go to some other method of establishing value, for example, the price at which a manufacturer would manufacture and supply replacement goods: see *J & E Hall Ltd v Barclay* [1937] 3 All ER 620; *Gaba Formwork Contractors Pty Ltd v Turner Corporation Ltd* (1991) 32 NSWLR 175; *Furness v Adrium Industries Pty Ltd* (1993) Aust Tort Reports 81-245... Mr Hodgson submitted that it would have been easy for the plaintiff to establish whether or not there was a market in which trailers of the type converted could be bought and that the plaintiff, having failed to prove that there was no such market, she was unable to, and the Magistrate ought not to, resort to evidence of "value" which was in reality evidence of a manufacturing cost rather than of the price at which a replacement chattel could be bought in the market.

[4] The evidence, in my view, shows that ...$12,000 represented a replacement manufacturing cost rather than a purchase price in a market. The evidence was [that the trailer was] "a unique trailer in that it is purpose built." [His honour referred to the evidence given that at the date of the conversion, $12,500 represented the manufacturer's replacement price].

Sinclair v Haynes cont.

[5] However, for the appellant to succeed upon this stated case, she must succeed in persuading me that there was no evidentiary basis on which the learned Magistrate could have taken the manufacturer's price at the time of conversion as representing the value of the trailer for the purpose of assessing damages. ... Whilst no one spoke specifically of the existence or non existence of a market, it was plain that this was a one off item specially manufactured. ...The subject trailer [the plaintiff] had originally acquired by having it built in the sense that he bought an ordinary horse trailer for some $6,000 and then spent some $6,000 in having it converted. This involved some strengthening, the fitting of a crush, the fitting of an instrument chest, and various other specialised additions to allow for the fact that it had to contain horses which were undergoing the pain or discomfort of dentistry and might become "wild". ....

[6] While the existence of a market was not specifically asserted or denied in the evidence and not discussed expressly by her Worship in her judgment, I am of the view that it was entirely open to her Worship to come to the conclusion on the evidence that there was no market in floats of this type and that the appropriate course to ascertain the value of the converted float was to go to the cost of having a replacement float manufactured. In those circumstances it cannot be said that her Worship was in error in holding that the trailer converted by the defendant was valued at $12,000 and it is not correct to say that there was no appropriate or proper evidence of the value of the trailer to enable her Worship to find that the trailer was valued at $12,000.

[7] .... The result of my conclusion is that the question in the stated case is answered, No. I affirm the determination in respect of which the case was stated. I order that the appellant pay the respondent's costs of the stated case.

[5.210] **Notes&Questions**

1. The general rule for conversion is that the value of the chattel is assessed at the date of the conversion. This applies also to goods that were received by the defendant in altered form. In *Johnson Matthey (Aust) Ltd v Dascorp Pty Ltd* (2003) 9 VR 171, the plaintiff's employee stole gold from the plaintiff and mixed it with other metals, thereby reducing its value, and then sold the changed product to the defendant; the defendant was liable for the value of the mixed metals not the original gold. This rule is based upon the premise that the conversion is complete at the time of the conversion and satisfaction of judgment for conversion vests ownership in the converter from that date. What is the position if the chattel has increased in value between the date of conversion and the date of judgment? Courts have held that the plaintiff will be entitled to recover the increased value at the date of judgment provided that the plaintiff has not delayed commencing proceedings. So, for example, in *Egan v State Transport Authority* (1982) 31 SASR 481, the defendant converted the plaintiff contractor's machinery in 1966 and judgment was not until 1982. The plaintiff was entitled to the value of the machinery, which had increased due to inflation at the date of judgment. But a plaintiff should not be permitted to delay so as to increase the quantum of damages payable on a rising market. Ordinarily, in a case of fluctuating values, fairness requires that the increased value will not be recoverable once the plaintiff should reasonably have known of the conversion.
2. Generally, the plaintiff is entitled to the full value of the chattel at the date of the conversion. This is on the assumption that the full value represents the plaintiff's loss.

But if the plaintiff's loss is less than full value, the plaintiff will only be entitled to actual losses. (Note a plaintiff with a possessory title deprived of possession is entitled to full value, see [5.70].) In *Butler v Egg & Egg Pulp Marketing Board* (1966) 114 CLR 185, the Board was, by statute, owner of the eggs as soon as they were produced. The defendant producer had a statutory right to participate in the proceeds of sale of the eggs by the Board after certain deductions. The Board therefore had a right to immediate possession as soon as the eggs came into existence. The defendant sold the eggs instead of supplying them to the Board. The Board sued for conversion. The High Court held that the measure of damages was not the full value of the eggs at the date of the conversion. Rather it was the difference between the price the Board would have sold the eggs and the amount which it would have been bound to pay the producer. Taylor and Owen JJ, in a joint judgment, said (at 190-191) that if the full value were recovered the Board would be in a better position financially than if the defendant had complied with the Act and this would not accord with the general principles on which compensatory damages are assessed in contract and tort. Would a plaintiff be entitled to the full value of a set of photographs which the defendant converted by giving them away when the plaintiff intended that the photographs be given as a gift to a museum or art gallery? In *Myer Stores Ltd v Jovanovic* [2004] VSC 478, it was held that the plaintiff was not entitled to full value as there was no way to assess the value of prestige that might flow from gallery display. Might it be relevant that the plaintiff could have been entitled to a tax deduction for the gift as demonstrating some loss from the conversion?

3. Consistent with the principle that the plaintiff is only entitled to recover what the plaintiff has lost rather than profit from the conversion, where the defendant has some interest in the chattel, this is offset against the damages the plaintiff is entitled to recover, see *City Motors Pty Ltd v Southern Aerial Super Service Pty Ltd* (1961) 106 CLR 477. Similarly, the plaintiff's damages must take into account the value of improvements made to the chattel by the defendant as well as the costs the plaintiff would have necessarily incurred in relation to the goods: *McKeown v Cavalier Yachts Pty Ltd* (1988) 13 NSWLR 303, 308; *Venus Adult Shops Pty Ltd v Fraserside Holdings Ltd* [2006] FCAFC 188 at [27], *Coastal Recycled Cooking Oils Pty Ltd v Innovative Business Action and Strategies Pty Ltd* [2007] NSWSC 831 (costs of cartage and refining to be taken into account in assessing value of oil converted); *Bennnett v Goodwin* [2005] NSWSC 93) (plaintiff was entitled to the market value at the time of conversion, inclusive of GST, but less the depreciated value of improvements and without deduction for commission for sale).

4. Where the goods have been returned to the plaintiff, the plaintiff would be entitled to damages for the reasonable costs of any necessary repairs to the chattel and where the defendant has benefited from the use of the goods, damages for that use, *Kuwait Airways Corp v Iraqi Airways Co (Nos 4 & 5)* [2002] 2 AC 883 at [87]. Lord Nicholls in that case (at [88]) gave the following illustration from the decision in *Solloway v McLaughlin* [1937] 4 All ER 328: the plaintiff would be entitled to damages where the defendant wrongfully sells the plaintiff's shares at a high price and then replaces the equivalent shares when the market drops.

5. In addition to the market value of the goods, damages may also be claimed for consequential loss that the plaintiff has suffered as a result of the conversion. This could include loss of profits of a profit earning chattel (*Meredith v Eggins* [2006] QDC 164) subject to a duty to take reasonable steps to mitigate the loss (*Egan v State Transport Authority* (1982) 31 SASR 481).
6. As with trespass to chattels, it is possible that aggravated and exemplary damages may be awarded for conversion (*Healing v Inglis Electrix* (1968) 121 CLR 584).

Detinue

[5.215] A successful claim for detinue theoretically permits the return of the chattel itself. In contrast to the action for conversion (value assessed at the date of conversion), damages in detinue are assessed at the date of judgment. Where the plaintiff succeeds in an action based on detinue, the relevant Rules of Court permit the Court to make any of three forms of order: see *Civil Procedure Act 2005* (NSW), s 93; *Supreme Court Act 1995* (Qld), ss 24, 25; *Supreme Court (General Civil Procedure) Rules 2005* (Vic), r 21.03. The nature and purpose of these alternatives are discussed in the following extract.

General & Finance Facilities v Cooks Cars (Romford)

[5.220] *General & Finance Facilities Ltd v Cooks Cars (Romford) Ltd* [1963] 1 WLR 644 Court of Appeal (footnotes omitted)

DIPLOCK LJ: 648 This appeal raises a neat point as to the remedies available to a plaintiff who sues for the wrongful detention of goods. The plaintiffs by a specially indorsed writ claimed "the return of a mobile crane Index No OMF 347 or its value and damages for detaining the same". They pleaded their title to the crane and relied upon a demand for its delivery up dated 8 May 1961. The prayer included an alternative claim for damages for conversion.

There are important distinctions between a cause of action in conversion and a cause of action in detinue. The former is a single wrongful act and the cause of action accrues at the date of the conversion; the latter is a continuing cause of action which accrues at the date of the wrongful refusal to deliver up the goods and continues until delivery up of the goods or judgment in the action for detinue … .

The action in conversion is a purely personal action and results in a judgment for pecuniary damages only. The judgment is for a single sum of which the measure is generally the value of the chattel at the date of the conversion together with any consequential damage flowing from the conversion and not too remote to be recoverable in law. … this is not necessarily the same as the measure of damages for detinue where the same act constitutes detinue as well as conversion, although in many cases this will be so. …The law is in my view correctly stated in *Salmond on Torts* (13th ed), pp 287, 288. Notwithstanding that judgment for damages for conversion does not, until satisfied, divest the plaintiff of property in the chattel… (see the analysis of the cases in *Ellis v John Stenning & Son* [1932] 2 Ch 81) it does not entitle the plaintiff to the assistance of the court or the executive, videlicet the sheriff, in recovering possession of the chattel.

On the other hand the action in detinue partakes of the nature of an action in rem in which the plaintiff seeks specific restitution of his chattel. At common law it resulted in a judgment for delivery up of the chattel or payment of its value as assessed, and for payment of damages for its detention. This, in effect gave the defendant an option whether to return the chattel or to pay its value, and if the plaintiff wished to insist on specific restitution of the chattel he had to have recourse to Chancery: see *Re Scarth* (1874) 10 Ch App 234 at 235 per Mellish LJ. The *Common Law Procedure Act 1854*, s 78, gave

General & Finance Facilities v Cooks Cars (Romford) cont.

the court power to order delivery up of the chattel by the defendant without giving him the option to pay its value as assessed. Such an order was enforceable by execution, and if the chattel could not be found distraint could be had upon the defendant's lands and goods until he delivered up the specific chattel, or at the option of the plaintiff distraint could be had of the defendant's goods for the assessed value of the chattel. This, in effect, where the court thought fit to make such an order, gave the plaintiff an option to insist upon specific restitution of his chattel if the defendant did not deliver it up voluntarily; but this remedy was not available unless and until the value of the chattel had been assessed: see *Chilton v Carrington* (1855) 15 CB 730 [139 ER 612]. This remedy continues to exist under the modern law, but if the plaintiff does not wish to exercise his option to recover the assessed value of the chattel the assessment of its value is no longer a condition precedent to an order for specific restitution: see *Hymas v Ogden* [1905] 1 KB 246; RSC, O 48 r 1. In addition to an order for specific restitution of the chattel or for payment of its value as assessed, the plaintiff was always entitled to damages for wrongful detention of the chattel.

In the result an action in detinue today may result in a judgment in one of three different forms: (1) for the value of the chattel as assessed and damages for its detention; or (2) for return of the chattel or recovery of its value as assessed and damages for its detention; or (3) for return of the chattel and damages for its detention.

A judgment in the first form is appropriate where the chattel is an ordinary article in commerce, for the court will not normally order specific restitution in such a case, where damages are an adequate remedy: see *Whiteley Ltd v Hilt* [1918] 2 KB 808 at 819, 824. A judgment in this form deprives the defendant of the option which he had under the old common law form of judgment of returning the chattel; but if he has failed to do so by the time of the judgment the plaintiff, if he so elects, is entitled to a judgment in this form as of right: cf RSC, O 13 r 6. In substance this is the same as the remedy in conversion, although the sum recoverable, as I have indicated, may not be the same as damages for conversion, for the cause of action in detinue is a continuing one up to the date of judgment and the value of the chattel is assessed as at that date: see *Rosenthal v Alderton & Sons Ltd* [1946] 1 KB 374. A final judgment in such a form is for a single sum of money.

A judgment in the second form gives to the defendant the option of returning the chattel, but it also gives to the plaintiff the right to apply to the court to enforce specific restitution of the chattel by writ of delivery, or attachment or sequestration as well as recovering damages for its detention by writ of fieri facias: RSC, O 42 r 6. This is an important right and it is essential to its exercise that the judgment should specify separate amounts for the assessed value of the chattel and for the damages for its detention, for if the plaintiff wishes to proceed by writ of delivery for which he can apply ex parte (RSC, O 48 r 1) he has the option of distraining for the assessed value of the chattel if the chattel itself is not recovered by the sheriff. He would be deprived of this option if the value of the chattel were not separately assessed.

A judgment in the third form is unusual, but can be given: see *Hymas v Ogden* [1905] 1 KB 246. Under it the only pecuniary sum recoverable is damages for detention of the chattel. Its value need not be assessed and the plaintiff can only obtain specific restitution of the chattel by writ of delivery, attachment or sequestration. He has no option under the writ of delivery to distrain for the value of the chattel.

[Diplock LJ then went on to hold that a judgment in the second form (return of the chattel or recovery of its value as assessed and damages for its detention) required a separate assessment of the value of the crane and damages for detention. The assessment by the Master of a single sum representing the value of the chattel and damages for detention was not consistent with a judgment in the second form and the case should be remitted back to the Master for separate assessment of the value of the chattel and damages for detention.]

[Pearson LJ delivered judgment to the same effect.]

[5.225] **Notes&Questions**

1. If "the tort of detinue is not complete until the defendant fails to deliver up the chattels at the time of judgment" (*Egan v State Transport Authority* (1982) 31 SASR 481 at 529), what is the appropriate time for determining the market value of a chattel for purposes of the tort of detinue? How is this different to conversion? ([5.210] Note 1) Would a plaintiff be better off suing in detinue or conversion if there was a rising market or a falling market on each of those tests? Given the numerous exceptions to the general rule in a case of conversion (see [5.210]), this difference is less significant.
2. In special cases the court will make an order that the defendant return the chattel to the plaintiff. For example, the following have been held sufficiently special for an order for specific restitution: a yacht (*McKeown v Cavalier Yachts Pty Ltd* (1988) 13 NSWLR 303), a winning race horse (*Fitz-Alan v Felton* [2004] NSWSC 11) and a mortgage document (*Patroni v Conlan* [2004] WASC 1). Is there any scope for arguing that chattels which cannot be individually identified (fungibles) should be specifically recoverable? In *BIS Cleanaway (trading as CHEP) v Tatale & Anor; Brambles (trading as CHEP) v Tatale* [2007] NSWSC 378, McDougall J accepted the argument (at [124]-[127]) that damages would not be an adequate remedy where the defendant refused to return CHEP packing pallets. Although the pallets could not be called unique (in fact the reverse), there was a black market in the pallets and financial losses from loss of hire and costs of re-instating pallets when returned in the future would be difficult to accurately assess. McDougall J said that although an order for specific restitution usually required a chattel with special or unique qualities, the jurisdiction was not limited to these cases: "The question is one of the adequacy (or otherwise) of damages. The character of the chattel is but one of the matters to take into consideration" (at [125]). This approach is consistent with the approach in equity when considering whether a Court should award specific performance.
3. Consistently with the general principles applying to assessment of damages, the plaintiff is entitled to recover what has been lost, see [5.210]; damages may also be awarded for consequential losses flowing from the detention. This could include the costs of hiring a substitute chattel; in relation to a profit earning chattel, loss of profits that would have been earned and in relation to a non profit earning chattel, damages for loss of use during the detention, *Gallagher Panel Beating v Palmer* [2007] NSWSC 627 at [27]. In an appropriate case exemplary damages may be awarded, see *Egan v State Transport Authority* (1982) 31 SASR 481.

CONCLUSION

[5.230] It is remarkable that the common law of torts did not produce a single action to protect against the wrongful interference with property rights in chattels. A number of separate causes of actions developed. The principal actions, trespass to chattels, detinue and conversion have inconsistent and overlapping rules which do not protect the full range of property rights in a chattel. The tort of negligence may be available for negligent interferences with chattels. Where an owner of goods had neither possession nor a right to possession at the time of the wrong, the only action that would be available if the goods were permanently damaged or destroyed was the undeveloped innominate action on the case. A mere contractual right, as distinct from a proprietary right, in a chattel is not protected by conversion or detinue, see [5.70]. The Parliament of the United Kingdom did not take the opportunity to create a single tort covering all interests in a chattel when it enacted the *Torts (Interference with Goods) Act 1977* (UK). It did, however, abolish the old tort of detinue leaving conversion to cover this field with the addition of an action in conversion for loss or destruction of goods where a bailee was in breach of its duty to the bailor, s 2. Section 8 of the UK Act also made available the defence of jus tertii even in the case where a plaintiff was deprived of possession (see [5.40] Note 2) but only where the person with the better title can be actually named. So if the circumstances of *Chairman, National Crime Authority v Flack* (1998) 156 ALR 501 [5.35] occurred in United Kingdom, Mrs Flack would still be entitled to the money found in her cupboard as the police could not name the owner. The UK provision reduces the risk that an innocent purchaser might pay twice for a chattel, once in purchasing the chattel from a wrongdoer and again in an action in conversion by the dispossessed owner. Although Queensland considered the introduction of similar provisions in the 1990s, no Australian jurisdiction has followed the lead of the United Kingdom. The UK legislation overcomes the problems of the inconsistencies and the overlap between conversion and detinue and provides a basis for reform in Australia.

CHAPTER 6

Defences to Intentional Torts

INTRODUCTION

[6.05] In this Chapter we discuss the more prominent defences to the intentional torts: consent, necessity, self-defence and provocation. Reference is also made to statute law that may provide an effective defence.

CONSENT

[6.10] Consent is one of the most utilised of the defences to an intentional tort. Generally, if an individual gives their consent to an interference he or she cannot then complain when that interference occurs; permission has been given. Consent can be given in respect of both bodily and property interferences and therefore can provide a defence to battery, assault, false imprisonment, trespass to land and interference with chattels.

An element or a defence?

[6.15] Consent has been treated both as an element of the trespass action and as a defence. Therefore before examining the law of consent, some consideration is required as to which of these options is the better view. The important difference lies in who bears the onus of proof. Take battery as an example. If consent is a defence, the plaintiff need only plead and prove the positive direct touching of their person by the defendant. The defendant, in arguing consent as a defence, will be required to plead and prove the existence of the consent. Alternatively, if consent is treated as an element of trespass, then the plaintiff will be required to disprove that they consented to the defendant's interference.

At [3.40] Note 3, we noted that treating consent as a defence is generally considered to be the better view. An explanation of this is found in the comments of Justice McHugh in *Marion's Case* (1992) 175 CLR 218 at 310-311, extracted at [6.50]:

> In England, the onus is on the plaintiff to prove lack of consent. That view has the support of some academic writers in Australia, but it is opposed by other academic writers in Australia. It is opposed by Canadian authority. It is also opposed by Australian authority. Notwithstanding the English view, I think that the onus is on the defendant to prove consent. Consent is a claim of "leave and licence". Such a claim must be pleaded and proved by the defendant in an action for trespass to land. It must be pleaded in a defamation action when the defendant claims that the plaintiff consented to the publication. ... However, those who contend that the plaintiff must negative consent in an action for trespass to the person deny that consent is a matter of leave and licence. They contend that lack of consent is an essential element of the action for trespass to a person. I do not accept that this is so. The essential element of the tort is an intentional or reckless, direct act of the defendant which makes or has the effect of causing contact with the body of the plaintiff. Consent may make the act lawful, but, if there is no evidence on the issue, the tort is made out. The contrary view is inconsistent with a person's right of bodily integrity.

[6.20] **Notes&Questions**

1. Compare the English case of *Freeman v Home Office (No 2)* [1984] QB 524 in which McCowan J pointed out (at 537) that, if the onus was on the defendant, a statement of claim would need only to assert that the defendant, a doctor of medicine, had injected the defendant. If the defence admitted the injection, but pleaded consent, as it would have to do, and the defendant then died before the hearing of the action so that the defence was unable to call him, the plaintiff would be entitled to judgment without calling any evidence at all. This is also the position in New Zealand: *S v G* [1995] 3 NZLR 681 at 687; *H v R* [1996] 1 NZLR 299 at 305. AKN Blay, in his article "Onus of Proof of Consent in an Action for Trespass to the Person" (1987) 61 ALJ 25, also argues that the seriousness of being held guilty of battery for a defendant supports an approach of placing the onus upon the plaintiff.
2. The weight of Australian authority favours placing the onus on the defendant to prove consent: *Sibley v Milutinovic* (1990) Aust Torts Reports 81-013 (ACT Sup Ct) Miles CJ, and *McNamara v Duncan* (1979) 26 ALR 584 (extracted at [6.65]). More recently the New South Wales Court of Appeal expressed this view relying upon the approach of McHugh J in *Marion's Case*: *Cusack v Stayt* (2000) 31 MVR 517 at 520. The Supreme Court of Canada, in *Non-Marine Underwriters, Lloyd's of London v Scalera* [2000] 1 SCR 551 (at 565-7), also supports McHugh J's argument that the defendant should bear the onus of disproof:

    > The tort of battery is aimed at protecting the personal autonomy of the individual. Its purpose is to recognize the right of each person to control his or her body and who touches it, and to permit damages where this right is violated. The compensation stems from violation of the right to autonomy, not fault. When a person interferes with the body of another, a *prima facie* case of violation of the plaintiff's autonomy is made out.

> The law may then fairly call upon the person thus implicated to explain, if he can. If he can show that he acted with consent, the *prima facie* violation is negated and the plaintiff's claim will fail.

A similar argument can clearly be made in respect of other intentional torts, for example, a plaintiff has the right to liberty, and to the use and enjoyment of their land and chattels.

3. Although the defendant bears the onus of proving consent, this does not prevent a plaintiff providing evidence to the court to prove lack of consent.

Types of consent

[6.25] Consent may be either express or implied. A classic example of express consent would be the signing of a consent form to perform surgery or verbally agreeing to a physical examination. Consent may also be implied from the circumstances. For example, a boxer who enters the ring for a fight impliedly consents to being hit by his opponent. Implied consent also arises in many day-to-day activities, as Mason CJ, Dawson, Toohey and Gaudron JJ acknowledged in *Marion's Case* (1992) 175 CLR 218 at 310-311 at 233 citing *Collins v Wilcock* [1984] 3 All ER 374. *Marion's Case* is extracted at [6.50]:

> in respect of physical contact arising from the exigencies of everyday life – jostling in a street, social contact at parties and the like – there is an implied consent "by all who move in society and so expose themselves to the risk of bodily contact", or that such encounters fall "within a general exception embracing all physical contact which is generally acceptable in the ordinary conduct of daily life".

Additionally, consent may be provided by virtue of statutory provision or, as is discussed at [6.55] Note 4, it may be provided by way of court order.

The defendant, however, must not only establish that one of the types of consent was given, but also that consent when given was "effective". What, then, is effective consent?

Real and freely given

[6.30] For consent to be effective it must be "real" consent and it must be "freely given". Real consent refers to the individual having knowledge sufficient to enable them to understand the interference to which they are consenting. A disputed issue in this area of the law is the extent of the information that must be provided to ensure that the plaintiff has sufficient knowledge and understanding of the interference. This has been of particular importance in medical cases.

The current state of the law is that, in an action for trespass (as distinct from an action for negligence), consent will be real if the individual is informed in broad terms of the nature of the resultant contact. This is summed up by Bristow J in *Chatterton v Gerson* [1981] QB 432 per Bristow J at 443:

> once the patient is informed in broad terms of the nature of the procedure which is intended, and gives her consent, that consent is real, and the cause of action on which to base a claim for failure to go into risks and implications is negligence, not trespass. Of course if information is withheld in bad faith, the consent will be vitiated by fraud. Of course if by some accident, as in a case in the 1940s in the Salford Hundred Court where a boy was admitted to hospital for tonsillectomy and due to administrative error was circumcised instead, trespass would be the appropriate cause of action against the doctor.

[6.35] **Notes&Questions**

1. Authority in Australia clearly supports the view that the plaintiff need only be advised in broad terms of the nature of the interference for consent to be effective. See *Rogers v Whitaker* (1992) 175 CLR 479 at 490; *Ellis v Wallsend District Hospital* (1989) Aust Torts Reports 80-259 (NSW Sup Ct); and more recently the obiter comments of Gleeson CJ in *Rosenberg v Percival* (2000) 178 ALR 577 at 580 (HCA). This is also the common law in Canada: *Reibl v Hughes* [1980] 2 SCR 880 at 890-892; and the United Kingdom: *Sidaway v Bethlem Royal Hospital* [1985] AC 871 at 883 and 894.
2. Bristow's dictum in *Chatterson v Gerson* [1981] QB 432 refers to the fact that "fraud" vitiates consent. Some courts have narrowly interpreted what will constitute fraud. Provided that the defendant' s act is not essentially different in nature and character from that which was carried out, fraud will not be established. For example, in the Victorian case of *R v Mobilio* [1991] 1 VR 339, a radiographer, for his own sexual gratification and unrelated to the required procedure, obtained consent from a number of female patients to insert a transducer into their vaginas. The patients had consented to the bodily invasion for the purposes of medical treatment. The Court found that the consent was valid as the women had consented to insertion of the transducer into their vaginas and this is what had occurred.

   In comparison, a broad interpretation of fraud is found in the case of *Appleton v Garrett* [1997] 8 Med LR 75 (Queens Bench Division of the High Court). The Court held that consent was vitiated by a dentist performing unnecessary treatment on eight patients after he informed the patients the procedure was medically necessary. Would a plaintiff be able to sue in trespass where the plaintiff had unprotected consensual sex with the defendant who did not inform the plaintiff that he was HIV positive? Would a patient be able to sue the doctor who took blood for testing but did not tell the patient that It would be tested for HIV status or some genetic disorder? See *R v Cuerrier* [1988] 2 SCR 371 at 424-425 (Can Sup Ct).

[6.40] Consent will also be ineffective if it is not freely given. This is the case where a plaintiff consents under duress. For example, in *Aldridge v Booth* (1988) 80 ALR 1 the plaintiff consented to sexual intercourse with her employer in order to retain her job and in *Norberg v Wynrib* [1992] 2 SCR 226 (Can) a patient addicted to prescription drugs agreed to have sex with her Doctor in return for a continuing supply of drugs. In both cases there was a clear power imbalance between the defendant and the plaintiff, which resulted in consent being ineffectual.

Capacity to consent

[6.45] For consent to be effective the individual must also have legal capacity to consent. The following case considers the approach to be taken in respect of children and persons with a mental disability and their capacity to provide effective consent.

Marion's Case

[6.50] *Secretary Department of Health and Community Services v JWB and SMB [Marion's Case]* (1992) 175 CLR 218 High Court of Australia

(footnotes omitted)

MASON CJ, DAWSON, TOOHEY AND GAUDRON JJ: 234 [Their Honours' outline of the facts is extracted at [3.35], the case was on appeal from the Northern Territory.]

Assault, consent, medical treatment

... Sterilization comes within the category of medical treatment to which a legally competent person can consent. That is to say, Denning LJ's minority view in *Bravery v Bravery* [1954] 3 All ER 59 that sterilization was in itself an unlawful act to which consent gave no defence has not been followed. But what of medical treatment of those who, because of incapacity, cannot consent? What, besides personal consent, can render surgical intervention lawful?

The reasons for, and circumstances of, incapacity differ greatly. An adult who is normally of full mental capacity may be temporarily unable to consent due to, for example, an accident resulting in unconsciousness. Or a child's parents may be temporarily unavailable to give or withhold consent to emergency medical treatment of their child. In the case of medical treatment of those who cannot consent because of incapacity due to minority, the automatic reference point is the minor's parent or other guardian. Parental consent, when effective, is itself an exception to the need for personal consent to medical treatment ...

The scope of parental power

The two major issues referred to at the beginning of this judgment arise more specifically at this point in an examination of parental consent as an exception to the need for personal consent to medical treatment. As noted earlier, the first issue relates to the important threshold question of consent: whether a minor with an intellectual disability is or will ever be capable of giving or refusing informed consent to sterilization on his or her own behalf. Where the answer to that question is negative the second question arises. Is sterilization, in any case, in a special category which falls outside the scope of a parent to consent to treatment? Is such a procedure a kind of intervention which is, as a general rule, excluded from the scope of parental power?

By virtue of legislation, the age of majority in all States and Territories of Australia is eighteen years. Every person below that age is, therefore, a minor and under the *Family Law Act 1975* the powers of a guardian, generally speaking, cease at that age (s 63F). In some States a minor's capacity to give informed consent to medical treatment is regulated by statute but in the Northern Territory the common law still applies. The common law in Australia has been uncertain as to whether minors under sixteen can consent to medical treatment in any circumstances. However, the recent House of Lords decision in *Gillick v West Norfolk AHA* [1986] AC 112 is of persuasive authority. The proposition endorsed by the majority in that case was that parental power to consent to medical treatment on behalf of a child diminishes gradually as the child's capacities and maturity grow and that this rate of development depends on the individual child. Lord Scarman said:

> Parental rights ... do not wholly disappear until the age of majority ... But the common law has never treated such rights as sovereign or beyond review and control. Nor has our law ever treated the child as other than a person with capacities and rights recognised by law. The principle of the law ... is that parental rights are derived from parental duty and exist only so long as they are needed for the protection of the person and property of the child.

A minor is, according to this principle, capable of giving informed consent when he or she "achieves a sufficient understanding and intelligence to enable him or her to understand fully what is proposed".

This approach, though lacking the certainty of a fixed age rule, accords with experience and with psychology. It should be followed in this country as part of the common law.

Marion's Case cont.

Of course, the fact that a child suffers an intellectual disability makes consideration of the capacity to consent a different matter. The age at which intellectually disabled children can consent will be higher than for children within the normal range of abilities. However, terms such as "mental disability", "intellectual handicap" or "retardation" lack precision. There is no essential cause of disability; those who come within these categories form a heterogeneous group. And since most intellectually disabled people are borderline to mildly disabled, there is no reason to assume that all disabled children are incapable of giving consent to treatment.

To conclude this aspect, it is important to stress that it cannot be presumed that an intellectually disabled child is, by virtue of his or her disability, incapable of giving consent to treatment. The capacity of a child to give informed consent to medical treatment depends on the rate of development of each individual. And if *Gillick* is taken to reflect the common law in Australia, as we think it now does, these propositions are true as a matter of law in the Northern Territory.

Is sterilization a special case?

If it is clear, as it is in the present case, that the particular child is intellectually disabled to such an extent as to be incapable of giving valid informed consent to medical treatment, the second question arises; namely, whether there are kinds of intervention which are, as a general rule, excluded from the scope of parental power to consent to; specifically, whether sterilization is such a kind of intervention. Thus the question concerns the limits of parental power other than limits arising from the child's capacity to give personal consent.

Where their child is incapable of giving valid consent to medical treatment, parents, as guardians, may in a wide range of circumstances consent to medical treatment of their child who is a minor. This is clear in the common law and, by implication, in the *Emergency Medical Operations Act* (NT) which creates an exception to the need for parental consent in the case of emergency treatment. It is also implicit in the duty to provide the necessaries of life imposed by ss 149 and 183 of the Code. Where this parental power exists, two principles are involved. First, the subjective consent of a parent, in the sense of a parent speaking for the child, is, ordinarily, indispensable. That authority emanates from a caring relationship. Secondly, the overriding criterion to be applied in the exercise of parental authority on behalf of a child is the welfare of the child objectively assessed. That these two principles become, for all practical purposes, one is a recognition that ordinarily a parent of a child who is not capable of giving informed consent is in the best position to act in the best interests of the child. Implicit in parental consent is understood to be the determination of what is best for the welfare of the child.

In arguing that there are kinds of intervention which are excluded from the scope of parental power, the Commonwealth submitted that the power does not extend to, for example, the right to have a child's foot cut off so that he or she could earn money begging, and it is clear that a parent has no right to take the life of a child. But these examples may be met with the proposition that such things are forbidden because it is inconceivable that they are in the best interests of the child. Even if, theoretically, begging could constitute a financially rewarding occupation, there is a presumption that other interests of the child must prevail. Thus, the overriding criterion of the child's best interests is itself a limit on parental power. None of the parties argued, however, that sterilization could never be said to be in the best interests of a child with the result that it could never be authorised. On the contrary, the question whether parental power is limited only arises because the procedure may be authorised. But, the question whether it is in the best interests of the child and, thus, should be authorised is not susceptible of easy answer as in the case of an amputation on other than medical grounds. And the circumstances in which it arises may result from or involve an imperfect understanding of the issues or an incorrect assessment of the situation.

Marion's Case cont.

It is useful, at this point, to look at how sterilization has been treated in this regard in relevant cases. That is to say whether, and on what bases, sterilization has been treated as a special case, outside the ordinary scope of parental power to consent to medical treatment.

[Their Honours then discuss existing case law that has arisen in Australia, New Zealand, England and the United States].

Summary of earlier decisions

...Australian authority prior to the present case is evenly divided on the question whether court authorization is a mandatory requirement....

In the cases reviewed, the bases which emerge for isolating the decision to sterilize a child as a special case requiring authorization from a source other than the child's parents appear to be: first, the concept of a fundamental right to procreate; secondly, in some cases, a similarly fundamental right to bodily inviolability or its equivalent; thirdly, the gravity of the procedure and its ethical, social and personal consequences, though these consequences are not examined in any detail.

Can parents, as guardians, consent to sterilization? Conclusion

There are, in our opinion, features of a sterilization procedure or, more accurately, factors involved in a decision to authorize sterilization of another person which indicate that, in order to ensure the best protection of the interests of a child, such a decision should not come within the ordinary scope of parental power to consent to medical treatment. Court authorization is necessary and is, in essence, a procedural safeguard.... But first it is necessary to make clear that, in speaking of sterilization in this context, we are not referring to sterilization which is a by-product of surgery appropriately carried out to treat some malfunction or disease. We hesitate to use the expressions "therapeutic" and "non-therapeutic", because of their uncertainty. But it is necessary to make the distinction, however unclear the dividing line may be.

As a starting point, sterilization requires invasive, irreversible and major surgery. But so do, for example, an appendectomy and some cosmetic surgery, both of which, in our opinion, come within the ordinary scope of a parent to consent to. However, other factors exist which have the combined effect of marking out the decision to authorize sterilization as a special case. Court authorization is required, first, because of the significant risk of making the wrong decision, either as to a child's present or future capacity to consent or about what are the best interests of a child who cannot consent, and secondly, because the consequences of a wrong decision are particularly grave.

The factors which contribute to the significant risk of a wrong decision being made are:

(i) The complexity of the question of consent. Although there are some cases, of which the facts in Re X are an example, in which the parents can give an informed consent to an operation of sterilization on an intellectually disabled child and in which that operation is clearly for the benefit of the child, there is no unproblematic view of what constitutes informed consent. And, even given a settled psychological or legal rule, its application in many cases is fraught with difficulty. The fact that a child is disabled does not of itself mean that he or she cannot give informed consent or, indeed, make a meaningful refusal. And there is no reason to assume that those attempting to determine the capacity of an intellectually disabled child, including doctors, may not be affected by commonly held misconceptions about the abilities of those with intellectual disabilities. There is no doubt that some sterilization operations have been performed too readily and that the capacity of a child to give consent (and, later, to care for a child) has been wrongly assessed both here and overseas, historically and at the present time.

(ii) The medical profession very often plays a central role in the decision to sterilize as well as in the procedure itself. Indeed the question has been "medicalized" to a great degree. Two concerns emerge from this. It is hard to share the view of Cook J in *Re a Teenager* (1988) 94 FLR 181 that

Marion's Case cont.

absolute faith in the integrity of all medical practitioners is warranted. We agree with Nicholson CJ in *Re Jane* (1988) 94 FLR 1 that, as with all professions, there are those who act with impropriety as well as those who act bona fide but within a limited frame of reference. And the situation with which they are concerned is one in which incorrect assessments may be made. The second concern is that the decision to sterilize, at least where it is to be carried out for contraceptive purposes, and especially now when technology and expertise make the procedure relatively safe, is not merely a medical issue. This is also reflected in the concern raised in several of the cases reviewed, that the consequences of sterilization are not merely biological but also social and psychological. The requirement of a court authorization ensures a hearing from those experienced in different ways in the care of those with intellectual disability and from those with experience of the long term social and psychological effects of sterilization.

(iii) The decision by a parent that an intellectually disabled child be sterilized may involve not only the interests of the child, but also the independent and possibly conflicting (though legitimate) interests of the parents and other family members. There is no doubt that caring for a seriously handicapped child adds a significant burden to the ordinarily demanding task of caring for children. Subject to the overriding criterion of the child's welfare, the interests of other family members, particularly primary care-givers, are relevant to a court's decision whether to authorize sterilization. However, court involvement ensures, in the case of conflict, that the child's interests prevail.

The gravity of the consequences of wrongly authorizing a sterilization flows both from the resulting inability to reproduce and from the fact of being acted upon contrary to one's wishes or best interests. The fact of violation is likely to have social and psychological implications concerning the person's sense of identity, social place and self-esteem. As the Court said in *In re Grady* (1981) 426 A 2d 467, a decision to sterilize involves serious questions of a person's "social and biological identity". As with anyone, reactions to sterilization vary among those with intellectual disabilities but it has been said that "sterilized mentally retarded persons tend to perceive sterilization as a symbol of reduced or degraded status". Another study found that:

> Existential anxieties commonly associated with mental retardation are likely to be seriously reinforced by coercive sterilization of those who have had no children. Common sources of these anxieties include low self-esteem, feelings of helplessness, and need to avoid failure, loneliness, concern over body integrity and the threat of death.

The far-reaching consequences of a general rule of law allowing guardians to consent to all kinds of medical treatment, as well as the consequences of a wrong decision in any particular case, are also relevant. As Nicholson CJ pointed out in *Re Jane* (1988) 94 FLR 1 in the passage quoted earlier, such a rule may be used to justify other procedures such as a clitoridectomy or the removal of a healthy organ for transplant to another child.

For the above reasons, which look to the risks involved in the decision, particularly in relation to the threshold question of competence and in relation to the consequences of a wrong assessment, our conclusion is that the decision to sterilize a minor in circumstances such as the present falls outside the ordinary scope of parental powers and therefore outside the scope of the powers, rights and duties of a guardian under s 63E(1) of the *Family Law Act 1975*. This is not a case where sterilization is an incidental result of surgery performed to cure a disease or correct some malfunction. Court authorization in the present case is required. Where profound permanent incapacity is indisputable, where all psychological and social implications have in fact been canvassed by a variety of care-givers and where the child's guardians are, in fact, only considering the interests of the child or where their own interests do not conflict with those of the child, court authorization will ordinarily reproduce the

Marion's Case cont.

wishes of the guardian. But it is not possible to formulate a rule which distinguishes these cases. Given the widely varying circumstances, it is impossible to apply a single rule to determine what are, in the respondents' words, the "clear cases".

...

———— ꧁꧂ ————

[6.55] **Notes&Questions**

1. When does an adult have capacity and the right to consent or refuse consent to an interference with their own body? Refer back to [3.40] Note 2, and their honours Mason CJ, Dawson, Toohey, and Gaudron JJ's endorsement in *Marion's case* of the principal that "[e]very human being of adult years and sound mind has a right to determine what shall be done with his own body; and a surgeon who performs an operation without his patient's consent commits an assault" (per Cardozo J in *Schloendorff v Society of New York Hospital* 211 NY 125, 105 NE 92 (1914)).
   For an example of when an adult's refusal of treatment is not valid see *In re T (Adult: Refusal of Treatment)* [1993] Fam 95 (CA), in which T refused a blood transfusion. Whilst the Court recognised the right to bodily integrity of every adult, it held that the doctor must be satisfied that the illness or medication has not diminished their capacity, and that their capacity has not been overborne by another. Compare this with *Malette v Shulman* (1990) 67 DLR (4th) 321 (Can) (at [19]) where refusal of a blood transfusion by an adult for religious reasons was valid, the court importantly noting "[a] competent adult is generally entitled to reject a specific treatment or all treatment, or to select an alternate form of treatment, even if the decision may entail risks as serious as death and may appear mistaken in the eyes of the medical profession or the community."
2. *Marion's Case* also recognises that children in certain circumstances can possess the capacity to consent, adopting the approach in the United Kingdom of *Gillick* competency, "a minor is capable of giving informed consent when he or she achieves a sufficient understanding and intelligence to enable him or her to understand fully what is proposed".
   However, under *Gillick* competency does a child have a corresponding capacity to refuse therapeutic medical treatment? In *Re P (Medical Treatment)* [2004] Fam Law 716 the Court granted an order for a blood transfusion despite the objections of the nearly 17 year old child, who the court acknowledged refused the transfusion upon the basis of strongly held religious convictions which demanded respect. Nevertheless the best interests of the child required that the order be granted.
   There have been Australian Supreme Court decisions in which the refusal of medical treatment by a child has been overridden. In *Director General, New South Wales Department of Community Services v Y* (unreported, Austin J, Supreme Court of New South Wales, 7 July 1999) Austin J exercised the Court's parens patriae jurisdiction to override the wishes of a 15 year old child to refuse medical treatment for anorexia nervosa. His Honour referred to the approach taken by the English Courts and determined that the Court is able to exercise its inherent jurisdiction to countermand the wishes of the child if necessary. However, his ultimate decision was premised on the basis that the child was not competent due to her illness. More recently the Supreme

Court of Western Australia in *Minister for Health v AS and LS* (2004) 33 Fam LR 223 overrode the refusal of a 15 year old to blood transfusions which were necessary to combat the side effects of chemotherapy. The child's refusal was based upon his religious faith. Pullin J (at [19]) stated that the child being *Gillick* competent (which the court recognised was the case here) "while relevant and important did not prevent the court from authorising medical treatment where the best interest of the child require." See similar reasoning expressed by Gzell J in *Royal Alexandra Hospital v Joseph* [2005] NSWC 422 when overriding the refusal of a blood transfusion by a 16 year old boy based upon his religious convictions. For further discussion see See A Morris, "Gillick 20 Years On: Arrested Development or Growing Pains?" PN 2005, 21(3), 158-175.

3. Parental consent on behalf of children is clearly recognised as being valid, at least until the child is *Gillick* competent. However, as the majority judgment in *Marion's Case* suggests, there are limitations upon parental capacity to consent: see for example *Re Paul* [2008] NSWSC 960. In this case the 1 year old child was suffering from a form of cancer for which the appropriate treatment is chemotherapy. A side of effect of the chemotherapy could require the administration of blood transfusions. For religious reasons the parents refused consent to the transfusions. Based upon the best interests of the child the court overrode the parental refusal.

4. In cases where it is unclear whether the individual/patient has the requisite capacity to consent or refuse consent, the better course is to obtain a court ordered consent: *Marion's Case* at 249 and 250; *P v P* (1994) 181 CLR 583 at 597-8 (application for consent to sterilise a 16 year old girl who was intellectually disabled); *T v T* [1988] Fam 52 at 68 (application for consent to terminate the pregnancy of a 19 year old woman who was intellectually disabled). This was reiterated in the case of *Re Alex* (2004) 180 FLR 89, where court approval was sought for treatment of 13 year old that would begin a sex change process. The initial treatment was reversible, but later treatment would be irreversible. The Court of Appeal of the Family Court concluded that in these circumstances it would be prudent to seek court approval at the outset of the process.

   The ability to seek court ordered consent arises in the case of state courts pursuant to the inherent parens patriae jurisdiction (the court's power to take care of those who are not able to take care of themselves) and in the case of the Family Court pursuant to the "welfare" jurisdiction in s 64 of the *Family Law Act 1975* (Cth) (similar to the parens patriae jurisdiction except that it lacks the capacity to make the child a ward of the court).

   In *P v P* (1994) 181 CLR 583, the High Court determined that any State legislation concerning medical treatment is invalid to the extent it is inconsistent with the *Family Law Act 1975* and therefore the "best interests" test (pursuant to s 109 of the Commonwealth Constitution). It would follow that the inconsistency argument would also arise with respect to State legislation which permits medical treatment unless that treatment conforms with the best interests test and the circumstances in which court ordered consent must be gained. State Legislation which exists in respect of minors and consent to medical treatment includes: *Minors (Property and Contracts) Act 1970* (NSW) (consent of a minor over 14 or of a parent if the child is under 16, absolves a medical practitioner of liability for assault or battery (s 49)); *Children and Young Persons Act 1998* (NSW) (consent of the Supreme Court must be obtained before certain treatment is carried out on children under 16 years, for example sterilisation and long term injectable hormonal substances for contraception or menstruation regulation (s 175)), *Consent to Medical treatment and Palliative Care Act 1995* (SA)) (medical practitioner with the supporting written opinion of at least one other practitioner who has personally examined the child, can perform medical treatment with a minor's consent if they are of the opinion that the minor is capable of understanding the nature and consequences and risks of the procedure and the procedure is in the best interests of the health and well-being of the minor (s 12)).

All States have passed legislation concerning the donation by children of regenerative and non-regenerative tissue: *Transplantation and Anatomy Act 1978* (ACT), ss 11 – 16; *Human Tissue Act 1983* (NSW), Pt 2 Div 3; *Human Tissue & Transplantation Act* (NT), s 14; *Transplantation and Anatomy Act 1979* (Qld), ss 12B, 12C, 12D; *Transplantation & Anatomy Act 1983* (SA), ss 12, 13; *Human Tissues Act 1985* (Tas), s 12; *Human Tissue Act 1982* (Vic), ss 14, 15; *Human Tissue & Transplant Act 1982* (WA), ss 12, 13. Most states permit the removal of regenerative tissue for transplant to an immediate family member (ACT, Tas and WA extends to include relatives and SA any living person specified in the consent) conditional upon parental and child consent (subject to capacity) and certification by a medical practitioner or committee (Vic does not require certification). Only the Australian Capital Territory permits the removal of specified non-regenerative tissue and this is limited to immediate family members who would die without the transplant and it is conditional upon both parental and child consent (must have capacity to consent), certification by a medical practitioner and committee review. The Northern Territory prohibits the removal of regenerative and non-regenerative tissue other than blood from children. Despite legislative provision, *P v P* (1994) 181 CLR 583 is authority that the removal of tissue is subject to the best interests test and may well be the type of situation for which court authorisation is required, see for example the case of *In The Marriage of GWW and CMW* (1997) 21 Fam LR 612 in which consent was granted to harvest bone marrow of a child, with child's consent, to assist treatment of his Aunt.

5. A particularly contentious example of court ordered consent has been in respect to surgery authorising the separation of conjoined twins, which may and has led to the death of one of the children: see *Re A (children) (conjoined twins: surgical separation)* [2000] 4 All ER 961 and *Queensland v Nolan (An infant, By her Litigation Guardian Nolan)* [2002] 1 Qd R 454. For further discussion of these cases see the Defence of Necessity at [6.105] Note 6.

6. What of the rights of a fetus and the role of the court under its parens patriae jurisdiction? Does the court have the right to override the wishes of a pregnant woman to refuse treatment if the life of the unborn child is in danger? This issue is yet to be the subject of litigation in Australia. It is however the view of the Canadian and English Courts that the right of the mother to bodily integrity is paramount, a child in utero possessing no legal rights until born alive (*Winnipeg Child and Family Services (Northwest Area) v DFG* [1997] SCR 925; *St George's Healthcare NHS Trust v S* [1999] Fam 26 ([1998] 3 WLR 936; [1998] 3 All ER 673) overruling earlier authority to the contrary see *In re S (Adult: Refusal of Treatment)* [1993] Fam 123).

   Similarly, the common law in Australia, does not recognise an unborn child as a human being until it is born and born alive (*Attorney-General (Qld) (Ex Rel Kerr) v T* (1983) 46 ALR 275, Gibbs CJ at 286; *Watt v Rama* [1972] VR 353 (FC), Winneke CJ, Pape J at 360-1; *Harriton v Stephens* (2006) 226 CLR 52, Kirby J at 74). Recent dicta of members of the High Court that a decision to terminate or not terminate a pregnancy falls within the autonomy of the mother, supports the argument that the right of the mother to bodily integrity is paramount, see *Harriton v Stephens* (2006) 226 CLR 52, Kirby J at 92 and Crennan J at 124-5 and 134.

Consent must not be exceeded

[6.60] When an individual provides consent it has limits. When a defendant exceeds the limits of the consent that they have been given, the consent is ineffective. The following case considers how one assesses when a defendant's action is or is not outside the bounds of the given consent.

McNamara v Duncan

[6.65] *McNamara v Duncan* (1979) 45 FLR 152 Supreme Court of Australian Capital Territory (footnotes omitted)

[The defendant deliberately struck the plaintiff during a game of Australian Rules Football. The plaintiff had just kicked the ball, but the defendant continued to run towards him and hit him on the head, fracturing his skull. This was an infringement of the rules. Defendant's counsel argued that the plaintiff must be taken to have accepted the risk of this and that a little bit of foul play is a common, if not invariable concomitant of a game of football (or at least of Australian Rules Football).]

FOX J: 156 ...

I do not think it can reasonably be held that the plaintiff consented to receiving a blow such as he received in the present case. It was contrary to the rules and it was deliberate. Forcible bodily contact is of course part of Australian Rules Football, as it is with some other codes of football, but such contact finds justification in the rules and usages of the game. Winfield on Torts (8th ed) says (p 748) in relation to a non-prize fight: "a boxer may consent to accidental fouls, but not to deliberate ones." Street on Torts (4th ed), p 75 deals with the presumed ambit of consent in cases of accidental injury: "A footballer consents to those tackles which the rules permit, and, it is thought, to those tackles contravening the rules where the rule infringed is framed to maintain the skill of the game; but otherwise if his opponent gouges out an eye or perhaps even tackles against the rules and dangerously ..."

... As the present case is concerned with deliberate injury, it is not necessary to inquire whether there are any qualifications to this proposition where the injury is not deliberate. In my view, there is none where the injury was deliberately inflicted ... no evidence has been called to show that injuries from prohibited acts, or acts not within the rules and usages of the game, are more or less common ... even if the act were not deliberate there would be scant basis for holding that the plaintiff should be taken as having consented to receive a blow such as he received.

I am therefore of opinion that the plaintiff is entitled to succeed ...

[6.70] Notes&Questions

1. The judgment of Fox J in *McNamara v Duncan* (1979) 26 ALR 584 has been quoted with approval in subsequent cases. In *Sibley v Milutinovic* (1990) Aust Torts Reports 81-013 (ACT Sup Ct), the plaintiff was injured while playing in a training match for his soccer team. The defendant tackled the plaintiff twice in a way that observers described

as over-enthusiastic and then felled the plaintiff with a blow to the jaw. Miles CJ held the defendant's action was outside the scope of the rules and any consent, and held further that the plaintiff's action was outside what was to be expected in a friendly training match. The same approach was adopted in *Giumelli v Johnston* (1991) Aust Torts Reports 81-085 (Sup Ct FC SA) (Australian Rules Football), *Re Lenfield* (1993) 114 FLR 195 (Rugby), and *Insurance Exchange v Dooley* (unreported, NSWCA, 16 August 2000) at [57] (Baseball); see also the article by S Yeo, "Determining Consent in Body Contact Sports" (1998) 6 Tort L Rev 199.

2. Compare *Hilton v Wallace* (1989) Aust Torts Reports 68,448 (Qld Sup Ct), in which the defendant attempted to push members of the opposing rugby league team out of the way so a player on his own side underneath them could play the ball. The plaintiff was one of the players pushed and suffered permanent loss of vision when the defendant unintentionally put his finger in the plaintiff's eye while pushing. The evidence was that pushing a player not in possession of the ball was strictly against the rules, but that a referee would ordinarily condone it since it was in the interest of the side in possession to play the ball quickly and in the interest of the side not in possession to delay it. Should the defendant be held liable? No, as whilst strictly outside the rules of the game, accidental poking was nevertheless within the spirit and intendment of the rules, and something the plaintiff should have expected as incidental to the game. See also *Pallante v Stadiums Pty Ltd (No1)* [1976] VR 331 at 339 where the defendant punching the plaintiff on the nose during a boxing match was found to be "ordinarily and reasonably to be contemplated as incidental to the sport in question."

3. For an example of the application of this rule in a more informal setting, see *Blake v Galloway* [2004] 1 WLR 2844 (CA). The plaintiff and defendant, both 15 years were taking a break from music practice and became involved in "high-spirited and good natured horseplay". The game they created involved throwing pieces of bark chipping at each other. During the game, the defendant with no intention to inflict harm threw a piece of chipping and struck the plaintiff in the eye and he suffered significant injury. The Court of Appeal said that by participating in the game he "must be taken to have impliedly consented to the risk of a blow on any part of his body, provided that the offending missile was thrown more or less in accordance with the tacit understanding or conventions of the game" and nothing indicated "that the claimant's consent was restricted to the risk of being struck by objects being thrown at the lower part of his body" (at 2853).

4. Just as implied consent may be exceeded so can express consent. See, for example, *Murray v McMurchy* [1949] 2 DLR 442 (Can), in which the plaintiff patient consented to a caesarean operation. The Doctor performed the caesarean operation and also a tubal ligation for medical reasons, though there was no imminent threat to life. The Court found that the patient's consent was exceeded (see further [6.105] Note 2). See also *Walker v Bradley* (unreported, NSW District Court, 22 December 1993), in which a gynaecologist was found to have exceeded his consent when he performed a hysterectomy upon the plaintiff. The plaintiff made it clear that she would not consent to a hysterectomy in the absence of cancer. The gynaecologist found an ovarian cyst, but no cancer and nevertheless removed the patient's uterus.

5. Public policy issues may also place limits upon what may or may not be consented to. Does touching which may amount to a criminal offence, for example, entering a brawl, assisted euthanasia or sadomasochistic practices, fall within the realm of matters to which an individual has the capacity to consent? The common law has proceeded upon the basis that no person may consent to any touching which constitutes grievous bodily harm without good reason: *Attorney-General's Reference No 6 of 1980* [1981] 1 QB 715 at 719; *Marion's Case* (1992) 175 CLR 218 per Mason CJ, Dawson, Toohey and Gaudron JJ at 233. The rationale being if a person is able to consent to what amounts to a criminal offence, it will result in a state of lawlessness. Whilst some case law exists (*Bain v Altoft* [1967] Qd R 32 (Qld FC Sup Crt); *Murphy v Culhane* [1977] QB 94 (CA)) that the public interest issue only pertains to invalidity of consent under the criminal law, in view of the High Court's approach in *Marion's Case*, this is doubted.

NECESSITY

[6.75] The defence of necessity is closely related to consent. A defendant unable to gain the consent of the plaintiff might nevertheless act upon the basis that it is necessary for them to do so. For this defence to be successfully established the defendant will need to prove (1) their actions were necessary to prevent imminent harm to person or property, and (2) their actions were reasonable in the circumstances that existed, and proportionate to the risk posed.

Necessity and the protection of property

[6.80] The defence may be asserted by a person who commits an intentional tort out of the necessity of protecting property. The defence may be argued equally by the owner of the property or stranger as the Supreme Court of South Australia stated in *Produman v Allen* [1954] SASR 336:

> In principle, there seems no reason why the common law should not recognise an exemption from liability to pay damages for trespass to goods of "volunteers" or strangers who, from no other motive than the same desire to save the property of others from damage or destruction as they would feel if it were their own property which was in jeopardy, take reasonable steps on an occasion of urgent necessity to remove that property out of the way of danger or safeguard it by some other means. It would seem that in principle the present respondent should not be absolutely liable for damage caused by his interference with the property of another when he acted in the reasonable belief that his interference was justified by the necessity of the situation and was intended to benefit the owner. …
>
> It is so stated in *Clerk & Lindsell on Torts* (10th ed, 1947), 32, and the cases there cited in support of the statement are *Kirk v Gregory* (1876) 1 Ex D 55 and *Cope v Sharpe (No 2)* [1912] 1 KB 496. The law is stated in substantially the same terms in *Pollock on Torts* (15th ed, 1951), pp 121-122, as follows: "A class of exceptions as to which there is not much authority, but which certainly exists in every system of law, is that of acts done of necessity to avoid greater harm and on that ground justified". The learned author then considers such illustrations as pulling down houses to stop a fire, and continues: "There are also circumstances in which a man's property or person may have to be dealt with promptly for his own obvious good, but his consent, or the consent of anyone having lawful authority over him, cannot be obtained in time. Here it is evidently justifiable to do, in a proper and reasonable manner, what needs to be done. It has never been supposed to be even technically a trespass if I throw water on my neighbour's goods to save them from fire, or seeing his house on fire, enter peaceably on his land to help in putting it out. … These works of charity and necessity must be lawful as well as right. The test of justification seems to be the actual presence of imminent danger and a reasonably apparent necessity of taking such action as was taken".

Whether a defendant's acts are reasonable will be judged on the facts of each case. Any alternatives that may be available are considered in evaluating the reasonableness of the defendant's actions. When reading the next case consider whether there were any alternatives open to the defendant squatters.

Southwark London Borough Council v Williams

[6.85] *Southwark London Borough Council v Williams* [1971] Ch 734 Court of Appeal

(footnotes omitted)

[Defendants were a homeless family, unable to obtain housing, who "squatted" in an empty house owned by the Borough of Southwark. The Borough applied to the court for an order for immediate possession. Defendants sought to justify or excuse their action on two grounds: (a) that it was the statutory duty of the Borough to provide temporary accommodation to those in need; (b) necessity. As to (a), the court held that even if the Borough were in breach of their statutory duty, defendants were restricted to their remedies under the Act. As to (b):]

LORD DENNING MR: 743 I will next consider the defence of "necessity". There is authority for saying that in case of great and imminent danger, in order to preserve life, the law will permit of an encroachment on private property. That is shown by *Mouse's case* (1608) 12 Co Rep 63 [77 ER 1341], where the ferryman at Gravesend took 47 passengers into his barge to carry them to London. A great tempest arose and all were in danger. Mr Mouse was one of the passengers. He threw a casket belonging to the plaintiff overboard so as to lighten the ship. Other passengers threw other things. It was proved that, if they had not done so, the passengers would have been drowned. It was held by the whole court that "in any case of necessity, for the safety of the lives of the passengers" it was lawful for Mr Mouse to cast the casket out of the barge. The court said it was like the pulling down of a house, in time of fire, to stop it spreading; which has always been held justified pro bono publico.

The doctrine so enunciated must, however, be carefully circumscribed. Else necessity would open the door to many an excuse. It was for this reason that it was not admitted in *R v Dudley and Stephens* (1884) 14 QBD 273, where the three shipwrecked sailors, in extreme despair, killed the cabin-boy and ate him to save their own lives. They were held guilty of murder. The killing was not justified by necessity. Similarly, when a man who is starving enters a house and takes food in order to keep himself alive. Our English law does not admit the defence of necessity. It holds him guilty of larceny. Lord Hale said (*Pleas of the Crown*, i, 54) that: "if a person, being under necessity for want of victuals or clothes, shall upon that account clandestinely, and animus furandi, steal another man's food, it is felony." The reason is because, if hunger were once allowed to be an excuse for stealing, it would open a way through which all kinds of disorder and lawlessness would pass. So here, if homelessness were once admitted as a defence to trespass, no one's house could be safe. Necessity would open a door which no man could shut. It would not only be those in extreme need who would enter. There would be others who would imagine that they were in need, or would invent a need, so as to gain entry. Each man would say his need was greater than the next man's. The plea would be an excuse for all sorts of wrongdoing. So the courts must, for the sake of law and order, take a firm stand. They must refuse to admit the plea of necessity to the hungry and the homeless; and trust that their distress will be relieved by the charitable and the good. Applying these principles, it seems to me the circumstances of these squatters are not such as to afford any justification or excuse in law for their entry into these houses. ...

EDMUND DAVIES LJ: 746 As far as my reading goes, it appears that all the cases where a plea of necessity has succeeded are cases which deal with an urgent situation of imminent peril, eg the forcible feeding for an obdurate suffragette, as in *Leigh v Gladstone* (1909) 26 TLR 139 where Lord Alverstone CJ spoke of preserving the health and lives of the prisoners who were in the custody of the Crown; or performing an abortion to avert a grave threat to the life, or, at least, to the health of a pregnant young girl who had been ravished in circumstances of great brutality, as in *R v Bourne* [1939]

Southwark London Borough Council v Williams cont.

1 KB 687 in 1939; or as in the case tried in 1500 where it was said in argument that a person may escape from a burning gaol notwithstanding a statute making prison-breach a felony, "for he is not to be hanged because he would not stay to be burnt": see Glanville Williams, *Criminal Law, The General Part* (2nd ed), 725, 726. Such cases illustrate the very narrow limits with which the plea of necessity may be invoked. Sad though the circumstances disclosed by these appeals undoubtedly are, they do not in my judgment constitute the sort of emergency to which the plea applies ...

Finally, even if necessity could be invoked in such circumstances as the present, it could surely at most justify merely an initial entry into premises in such circumstances as those to which I have referred. I do not see how it could possibly be permitted to extend to and authorise continuing in occupation for an indefinite period of time, which was the understandable aim of the defendants when entering these premises. I therefore have to concur with Lord Denning MR in holding that the public weal demands that these appeals be dismissed. ...

[Megaw LJ delivered a concurring judgment.]

[6.90] **Notes&Questions**

1. In considering whether the acts of the defendant are reasonable in the circumstances, the court is asked to determine if the interference was outweighed by the imminent danger that existed. This may require consideration of issues of public policy, for example can necessity justify interferences that would be regarded as criminal in nature? The Court in *London Borough of Southwark v Williams* [1971] Ch 734 said no. Consider what would be the effect of a decision that the action of the squatters was founded upon necessity.

2. Australian Courts endorse the view that the defence of necessity must be "carefully circumscribed". This is evident in the dicta of Gleeson CJ, with whom Clarke JA and Ireland J agreed, in *R v Rogers* (1996) 86 A Crim R 542 at 546:

> The corollary of the notion that the defence of necessity exists to meet cases where the circumstances overwhelmingly impel disobedience to the law is that the law cannot leave people free to choose for themselves which laws they will obey, or to construct and apply their own set of values inconsistent with those implicit in the law.

3. Must there be a high degree of danger before the defence of necessity is available? In *Dehn v Attorney General* [1988] NZLR 564 the police relied on the defence of necessity to justify their trespassory entry upon the plaintiff's property. A relative had informed police that the plaintiff might be ill. The defence failed. Tipping J said (at 580) that

> a person may enter the land or building of another in circumstances which would otherwise amount to a trespass if he believes in good faith and upon grounds which are objectively reasonable that it is necessary to do so in order (1) to preserve human life, or (2) to prevent serious physical harm arising to the person of another or (3) to render assistance to another after that other has suffered serious physical harm. What the law's approach ought to be in cases involving apprehended danger to property is not immediately before me. If anything in that field the criteria should be stricter.

Could a defendant argue necessity to squeeze through a police road block nearly hitting police officers in order to get home to protect her property from bushfires? No, see *Dunjey v Ross* (2002) 36 MVR 170 (SC WA). In a criminal case involving speeding, necessity was upheld in the case of a medical emergency, see *Re Appeal of White* (1987) 9 NSWLR 427 at 448. Note also the following extract on the question of whether an emergency is required.

Necessity and protection of the person

[6.95] The defence of necessity also raises issues of particular importance to trespass to the person. The next case considers the issue of necessity in the medical context: in what circumstances, if any, may a medical practitioner rely upon necessity and how does this correlate with a patient's right to personal autonomy?

In re F (Mental Patient Sterilisation)

[6.100] *In re F (Mental Patient: Sterilisation)* [1990] 2 AC 1 House of Lords

(footnotes omitted)

LORD GOFF: [After quoting Cardozo J in *Schloendorff v Society of New York Hospital* 211 NY 125, 105 NE 92 (1914) (see [3.40] Note 2), Lord Goff continued.]

73 It is against this background that I turn to consider the question whether, and if so when, medical treatment or care of a mentally disordered person who is, by reason of his incapacity, incapable of giving his consent can be regarded as lawful. As is recognised in Cardozo J's statement of principle, and elsewhere (see eg *Sidaway v Bethlem Royal Hospital Governors* [1985] 1 All ER 643, [1985] AC 871 at 649 (All ER), 882 (AC) per Lord Scarman), some relaxation of the law is required to accommodate persons of unsound mind. In *Wilson v Pringle* [[1986] 2 All ER 440] the Court of Appeal considered that treatment or care of such persons may be regarded as lawful, as falling within the exception relating to physical contact which is generally acceptable in the ordinary conduct of everyday life. Again, I am with respect unable to agree. That exception is concerned with the ordinary events of everyday life, jostling in public places and such like, and affects all persons, whether or not they are capable of giving their consent. Medical treatment, even treatment for minor ailments, does not fall within that category of events. The general rule is that consent is necessary to render such treatment lawful. If such treatment administered without consent is not to be unlawful, it has to be justified on some other principle.

On what principle can medical treatment be justified when given without consent? We are searching for a principle on which, in limited circumstances, recognition may be given to a need, in the interests of the patient, that treatment should be given to him in circumstances where he is (temporarily or permanently) disabled from consenting to it. It is this criterion of a need which points to the principle of necessity as providing justification.

That there exists in the common law a principle of necessity which may justify action which would otherwise be unlawful is not in doubt. But historically the principle has been seen to be restricted to two groups of cases, which have been called cases of public necessity and cases of private necessity. The former occurred when a man interfered with another man's property in the public interest, for example (in the days before we could dial 999 for the fire brigade) the destruction of another man's house to prevent the spread of a catastrophic fire, as indeed occurred in the Great Fire of London in 1666. The latter cases occurred when a man interfered with another's property to save his own person or property from imminent danger, for example when he entered on his neighbour's land without his consent in order to prevent the spread of fire onto his own land.

There is, however, a third group of cases, which is also properly described as founded on the principle of necessity and which is more pertinent to the resolution of the problem in the present case. These cases are concerned with action taken as a matter of necessity to assist another person without his consent. To give a simple example, a man who seizes another and forcibly drags him from the path of an oncoming vehicle, thereby saving him from injury or even death, commits no wrong.

But there are many emanations of this principle, to be found scattered through the books. These are concerned not only with the preservation of the life or health of the assisted person, but also with the preservation of his property (sometimes an animal, sometimes an ordinary chattel) and even to certain conduct on his behalf in the administration of his affairs. Where there is a pre-existing relationship between the parties, the intervener is usually said to act as an agent of necessity on behalf of the principal in whose interests he acts, and his action can often, with not too much artificiality, be referred to the pre-existing relationship between them. Whether the intervener may be entitled either to reimbursement or to remuneration raises separate questions which are not relevant to the present case.

We are concerned here with action taken to preserve the life, health or well-being of another who is unable to consent to it. Such action is sometimes said to be justified as arising from an emergency; in *Prosser and Keeton Torts* (5th edn, 1984) p 117 the action is said to be privileged by the emergency. Doubtless, in the case of a person of sound mind, there will ordinarily have to be an emergency before such action taken without consent can be lawful; for otherwise there would be an opportunity to communicate with the assisted person and to seek his consent. But this is not always so; and indeed the historical origins of the principle of necessity do not point to emergency as such as providing the criterion of lawful intervention without consent. The old Roman doctrine of negotiorum gestio presupposed not so much an emergency as a prolonged absence of the dominus from home as justifying intervention by the gestor to administer his affairs. The most ancient group of cases in the common law, concerned with action taken by the master of a ship in distant parts in the interests of the shipowner, likewise found its origin in the difficulty of communication with the owner over a prolonged period of time, a difficulty overcome today by modern means of communication. In those cases, it was said that there had to be an emergency before the master could act as agent of necessity; though the emergency could well be of some duration. But, when a person is rendered incapable of communication either permanently or over a considerable period of time (through illness or accident or mental disorder), it would be an unusual use of language to describe the case as one of "permanent emergency", if indeed such a state of affairs can properly be said to exist. In truth, the relevance of an emergency is that it may give rise to a necessity to act in the interests of the assisted person without first obtaining his consent. Emergency is however not the criterion or even a prerequisite; it is simply a frequent origin of the necessity which impels intervention. The principle is one of necessity, not of emergency.

…

[T]he basic requirements, applicable in these cases of necessity, that, to fall within the principle, not only (1) must there be a necessity to act when it is not practicable to communicate with the assisted person, but also (2) the action taken must be such as a reasonable person would in all the circumstances take, acting in the best interests of the assisted person.

On this statement of principle, I wish to observe that officious intervention cannot be justified by the principle of necessity. So intervention cannot be justified when another more appropriate person is available and willing to act; nor can it be justified when it is contrary to the known wishes of the assisted person, to the extent that he is capable of rationally forming such a wish. On the second limb of the principle, the introduction of the standard of a reasonable man should not in the present context be regarded as materially different from that of Sir Montague Smith's "wise and prudent man", because a reasonable man would, in the time available to him, proceed with wisdom and prudence before taking action in relation to another man's person or property without his consent. I shall have more to say on this point later. Subject to that, I hesitate at present to indulge in any greater refinement of the principle, being well aware of many problems which may arise in its application,

In re F (Mental Patient Sterilisation) cont.

problems which it is not necessary, for present purposes, to examine. But as a general rule, if the above criteria are fulfilled, interference with the assisted person's person or property (as the case may be) will not be unlawful. Take the example of a railway accident, in which injured passengers are trapped in the wreckage. It is this principle which may render lawful the actions of other citizens, railway staff, passengers or outsiders, who rush to give aid and comfort to the victims: the surgeon who amputates the limb of an unconscious passenger to free him from the wreckage the ambulance man who conveys him to hospital; the doctors and nurses who treat him and care for him while he is still unconscious. Take the example of an elderly person who suffers a stroke which renders him incapable of speech or movement. It is by virtue of this principle that the doctor who treats him, the nurse who cares for him, even the relative or friend or neighbour who comes in to look after him will commit no wrong when he or she touches his body.

The two examples I have given illustrate, in the one case, an emergency and, in the other, a permanent or semi-permanent state of affairs. Another example of the latter kind is that of a mentally disordered person who is disabled from giving consent. I can see no good reason why the principle of necessity should not be applicable in his case as it is in the case of the victim of a stroke. Furthermore, in the case of a mentally disordered person, as in the case of a stroke victim, the permanent state of affairs calls for a wider range of care than may be requisite in an emergency which arises from accidental injury. When the state of affairs is permanent, or semi-permanent, action properly taken to preserve the life, health or well-being of the assisted person may well transcend such measures as surgical operation or substantial medical treatment and may extend to include such humdrum matters as routine medical or dental treatment, even simple care such as dressing and undressing and putting to bed.

The distinction I have drawn between cases of emergency and cases where the state of affairs is (more or less) permanent is relevant in another respect. We are here concerned with medical treatment, and I limit myself to cases of that kind. Where, for example, a surgeon performs an operation without his consent on a patient temporarily rendered unconscious in an accident, he should do no more than is reasonably required, in the best interests of the patient, before he recovers consciousness. I can see no practical difficulty arising from this requirement, which derives from the fact that the patient is expected before long to regain consciousness and can then be consulted about longer term measures. The point has however arisen in a more acute form where a surgeon, in the course of an operation, discovers some other condition which, in his opinion, requires operative treatment for which he has not received the patient's consent. In what circumstances he should operate forthwith, and in what circumstances he should postpone the further treatment until he has received the patient's consent, is a difficult matter which has troubled the Canadian courts (see *Marshall v Curry* [1933] 3 DLR 260 and *Murray v McMurchy* [1949] 2 DLR 442), but which it is not necessary for your Lordships to consider in the present case.

But where the state of affairs is permanent or semi-permanent, as may be so in the case of a mentally disordered person, there is no point in waiting to obtain the patient's consent. The need to care for him is obvious; and the doctor must then act in the best interests of his patient, just as if he had received his patient's consent so to do. Were this not so, much useful treatment and care could, in theory at least, be denied to the unfortunate. It follows that, on this point, I am unable to accept the view expressed by Neill LJ in the Court of Appeal, that the treatment must be shown to have been necessary. Moreover, in such a case, as my noble and learned friend Lord Brandon has pointed out, a doctor who has assumed responsibility for the care of a patient may not only be treated as having the patient's consent to act, but also be under a duty so to act. I find myself to be respectfully in agreement with Lord Donaldson MR when he said:

> I see nothing incongruous in doctors and others who have a caring responsibility being required, when acting in relation to an adult who is incompetent, to exercise a right of choice

> in exactly the same way as would the court or reasonable parents in relation to a child, making due allowance, of course, for the fact that the patient is not a child, and I am satisfied that that is what the law does in fact require.

In these circumstances, it is natural to treat the deemed authority and the duty as inter-related. But I feel bound to express my opinion that, in principle, the lawfulness of the doctor's action is, at least in its origin, to be found in the principle of necessity. This can perhaps be seen most clearly in cases where there is no continuing relationship between doctor and patient. The "doctor in the house" who volunteers to assist a lady in the audience who, overcome by the drama or by the heat in the theatre, has fainted away is impelled to act by no greater duty than that imposed by his own Hippocratic oath. Furthermore, intervention can be justified in the case of a non-professional, as well as a professional, man or woman who has no pre-existing relationship with the assisted person, as in the case of a stranger who rushes to assist an injured man after an accident. In my opinion, it is the necessity itself which provides the justification for the intervention.

I have said that the doctor has to act in the best interests of the assisted person. In the case of routine treatment of mentally disordered persons, there should be little difficulty in applying this principle. In the case of more serious treatment, I recognise that its application may create problems for the medical profession; however, in making decisions about treatment, the doctor must act in accordance with a responsible and competent body of relevant professional opinion, on the principles set down in *Bolam v Friern Hospital Management Committee* [1957] 2 All ER 118, [1957] 1 WLR 582. No doubt, in practice, a decision may involve others besides the doctor. It must surely be good practice to consult relatives and others who are concerned with the care of the patient. Sometimes, of course, consultation with a specialist or specialists will be required; and in others, especially where the decision involves more than a purely medical opinion, an inter-disciplinary team will in practice participate in the decision. It is very difficult, and would be unwise, for a court to do more than to stress that, for those who are involved in these important and sometimes difficult decisions, the overriding consideration is that they should act in the best interests of the person who suffers from the misfortune of being prevented by incapacity from deciding for himself what should be done to his own body in his own best interests.

[6.105] **Notes&Questions**

1. The most common circumstance in which the medical profession will be able to claim necessity is where a patient is brought to the medical facility whilst unconscious. Obiter dicta comments of members of the High Court support this approach: see *Marion's Case* at 310 per McHugh J: "Consent is not necessary … where … medical treatment must be performed in an emergency and the patient does not have the capacity to consent and no legally authorised representative is available to give consent on his or her behalf". See also *Rogers v Whitaker* (1992) 175 CLR 479 Mason CJ and Brennan, Dawson, Toohey and McHugh JJ at 489; *Malette v Shulman* (1990) 67 DLR (4th) 321 (Can) at 328-329.
2. If a patient has consented to an operation and an emergency arises during the procedure that is not within the scope of the consent, can the surgeon perform the procedure? Yes, providing it is necessary and not simply convenient: *Murray v McMurchy* [1949] 2 DLR 442 ([6.70] Note 4).

3. Does the defence of necessity override a competent adult's refusal of medical treatment even if the refusal seems irrational? Lord Goff in the principal case said no. Can the defence override a competent adult's refusal to have a blood transfusion as contrary to their religion? No. If the patient were brought in to the hospital unconscious, would the doctors be required to honour an advance directive which stated that blood was not to be given? Yes, see *Malette v Shulman* (1990) 67 DLR (4th) 321 (Can) ([6.55] Note 1). Would it make any difference that the patient was no longer committed to their religious beliefs, for example, was about to convert to another religion and had expressed the wish that they did not want to die? Yes, see *HE v A Hospital NHS Trust* [2003] Fam Law 733.

   See also *Re B (adult: refusal of medical treatment)* [2002] 2 All ER 449, in which the Court granted the claimant's request for a declaration that she, as a mentally competent patient, had the right to refuse treatment the result of which would be her death. Due to a devastating illness the claimant had become a tetraplegic and was being kept artificially alive by the use of a ventilator. This was despite objection from the hospital that the treatment was necessary in order that she continue to live. United States authority is to the like effect, see for example, *Bouvia v Superior Court* 225 Cal Rptr 297 (1986) (US) in which the Californian Court of Appeal concluded that a competent adult "has the right to refuse *any* medical treatment, even that which may save or prolong her life". Bouvia was a 28 year old who suffered from severe cerebral palsy, was a quadriplegic and suffered from acute arthritis. She had full mental capacity and had graduated from college. Bouvia was physically deteriorating and felt her quality of life "has been diminished to the point of helplessness, uselessness, unenjoyability and frustration. ... If her right to choose may not be exercised because there remains to her, in the opinion of the court, a physician or some committee, a certain arbitrary number of years, months or days, her right will have lost its value and meaning" (at 304). Despite the court's order that she had the right to remove her feeding tube, the result of which would be death, Bouvia has not exercised her right and is still living (as at 11 May, 2008). It should be noted that in the US, self determination is based upon the common law right to bodily integrity and the 14th Amendment of the US Constitution.

   Whilst there is no Australian authority on point, given the width of the right of self-determination, as specified in cases such as *Rogers v Whitaker* (1992) 175 CLR 479 and more recently in *Rosenberg v Percival* (2001) 205 CLR 434, a like approach may be adopted; see the following comment of Kirby J in *Rosenberg v Percival* (2001) 205 CLR 434 (at 480) (in the context of a duty to warn at common law of the risks associated with treatment):

   > Fundamentally, the rule is a recognition of individual autonomy that is to be viewed in the wider context of an emerging appreciation of basic human rights and human dignity .... There is no reason to diminish the law's insistence, to the greatest extent possible, upon prior, informed agreement to invasive treatment, save for that which is required in an emergency or otherwise out of necessity.

4. If parents refuse consent on behalf of their child to essential medical treatment (presuming the child is not *Gillick* competent ([6.55] Note 2), will necessity permit members of the medical profession to nevertheless treat the child? Although the defence of necessity may be the last resort for hospitals and

physicians, the better course is to apply to the court for an order for treatment in these circumstances. See *Rolands v Rolands* (1983) 9 Fam LR 320 (SC NSW) (order granted for an 11 year old when parents refused to consent to life saving treatment). See also *Re R* [2000] 2 Qd R 328 (SC Qld) in which Justice Lee provided court ordered consent in circumstances in which the parents had consented to essential surgery but not the administering of blood transfusions to their child on the grounds of their religious beliefs. His Honour was of the view that if an emergency situation had arisen the physicians would have been entitled to rely upon necessity. This is affected by legislation in some States, see Note 7.

5. Can necessity be a valid defence for a doctor performing a caesarean operation upon a pregnant woman against her wishes to preserve the life of the unborn child? This issue was briefly discussed under the defence of consent at [6.55] Note 6. The better view is that the court cannot authorise the operation in place of the mother's refusal of consent. Would pro life protesters sued for trespass to land have a defence of necessity that they were acting to prevent terminations of pregnancy? No. *Wilcox v Police* [1994] 1 NZLR 243.

6. A more extraordinary case in which necessity has been relied upon is that of In *Re A (children) (conjoined twins: surgical separation)* [2000] 4 All ER 961. A Court ordered consent was sought for an operation to separate Siamese twins, the performance of which would result in the death of one of the twins, Mary. Two of the justices based their decision upon necessity. Brooke LJ found that the situation satisfied the three requirements of the defence: that the act was needed to avoid inevitable and irreparable evil (the death of both twins if the operation was not performed), that the separation was no more than what was reasonably necessary to prevent the irreparable evil (that is preserving the life of one twin) and that this was not disproportionate to the evil to be avoided (the death of both twins). In a Queensland case which involved similar factual circumstances, *Queensland v Nolan (An infant, By her Litigation Guardian Nolan)* [2002] 1 Qd R 454, Chesterman J referred to the defence of necessity and the judgment of Ward LJ in *Re A*, noting in particular the conflict of duty faced by the doctors, that is, the duty not to operate because it would kill one of the twins conflicting with the duty to operate because failure to do so would kill the other twin. Chesterman J concluded that the law must allow an escape by choosing the lesser of the two evils and consequently the performance of the separation by the doctors could not constitute in these circumstances an unlawful act. For further discussion of the lawfulness of the decision in *Re A (children) (conjoined twins: surgical separation)* [2000] 4 All ER 961, refer to G McGrath & N Kreleger, "Killing of Mary: Have We Crossed the Rubicon?" (2001) 8 JLM 322.

7. In some cases it will be unnecessary for members of the medical profession to rely upon the common law defence of necessity due to a statutory provision authorising the administration of medical treatment: example, *R v Bournewood Community and Mental Health NHS Trust, Ex p L* [1999] 1 AC 458.

   Legislation exists in a number of jurisdictions authorising the administration of blood transfusions in emergency/life threatening situations to children without consent: *Transplantation and Anatomy Act 1978* (ACT), s 23; *Transplantation and Anatomy Act 1979* (Qld), s 20; *Human Tissue Act 1985* (Tas), s 21; *Human Tissue Act 1982* (Vic), s 24, *Human Tissue and Transplant Act 1982* (WA), s 21. In New South Wales and South Australia, legislation permits treatment (including blood transfusions) to occur in an emergency situation: *Children and Young Persons (Care and Protection) Act 1998* (NSW), s 174 and *Consent Medical treatment and Palliative Care Act 1995* (ACT), s 13.

Related to this, legislation exists to ensure that individuals who have a mental illness and are unable to consent, may be treated for their illness: *Mental Health Act 1962* (ACT), *Mental Health (Treatment and Care) Act 1994* (ACT); *Mental Health Act 2007* (NSW); *Mental Health and Related Services Act* (NT); *Mental Health Act 2000* (Qld); *Mental Health Act 1993* (SA); *Mental Health Act 1996* (Tas); *Mental Health Act 1986* (Vic); *Mental Health Act 1996* (WA). The Mental Health Acts only authorise psychiatric medical treatment and no other types. However, legislation does exist in most States to provide for the medical treatment of persons with either a mental illness or an intellectual disability and who, as a result of their illness or disability, do not possess the capacity to consent: *Guardianship and Management of Property Act 1991* (ACT); *Guardianship Act 1987* (NSW); *Adult Guardianship Act* (NT); *Guardianship and Administration Act 2000* (Qld); *Guardianship and Administration Act 1993* (SA); *Consent to Medical Treatment and Palliative Care Act 1995* (SA); *Guardianship and Administration Act 1995* (Tas); *Guardianship and Administration Act 1986* (Vic); *Guardianship and Administration Act 1990* (WA).

8. The defence of necessity of course may be applied outside of medical treatment. In the case of *State of New South Wales v Riley* [2003] NSWCA 208, the police relied upon the defence of necessity in respect of battery, false imprisonment and trespass to land. The police had apprehended the respondent after being called by a neighbour who had heard gunshots. The police had prior knowledge of the respondent's disturbed behavior, and that there had been previous gunshots heard from his premises. On the night of the arrest, the police had heard the gunshots and there was evidence that Riley had talked about suicide. Necessity was asserted in respect of the battery and false imprisonment on the basis that Riley was armed and dangerous. Necessity was also relied upon as a defence to the search of the Riley's home without warrant immediately following the incident and again an hour later. The Court of Appeal concluded that whilst "[n]ecessity can be justification for arrest without informing the person arrested of the reason. ... necessity could not possibly justify the over-tight application of handcuffs ...." As far as trespass to land was concerned, the first quick search was justified by necessity but the second search, occurring an hour later, could not be said to fall within the defence of necessity, no threat at that time being posed by the respondent. There was by then time and opportunity for the police to obtain a warrant.

9. In the case of *London Borough of Southwark v Williams* [1971] Ch 734 (extracted at [6.85]), Edmund Davies LJ referred to the case of *Leigh v Gladstone* (1909) 26 TLR 139 in which the force-feeding of prisoners on a hunger strike was seen as necessary given the quasi-parental position of the prison authority. Should a person lose the control of their right to bodily integrity upon coming under the

control of government authorities? Federal legislation permits the force-feeding of asylum seekers who are in detention in Australia (*Migration Regulations 1994* (Cth), reg 5.35), upon the written advice of a medical practitioner that if the treatment is not administered there is a serious risk to the detainee's life or health. Whether the detainee is competent to refuse consent is not a consideration. The effect of the Regulation is to deprive an individual of their right to bodily integrity. This is an issue of State interests, taken altruistically, to preserve the life of detainees. It is notable that *Leigh v Gladstone* (1909) 26 TLR 139 no longer represents the approach in the United Kingdom where the courts have determined that a detainee's right to bodily integrity permits a detainee to undertake a hunger strike if he or she so decides, subject to competency: see *Secretary of State for the Home Department v Robb* [1995] 1 All ER 677 at 681. For further discussion of this issue see M Kenny, "Force-Feeding Asylum Seekers: Challenging the State's Authority to Direct Medical Treatment" (2002) 27 Alt L J 107.

Necessity and negligence of the defendant

[6.110] There is one situation in which a defendant, although able to satisfy the elements of the defence of necessity will nevertheless be precluded from asserting the defence; that is where the defendant's own actions negligently created or contributed to the necessity. This was argued by the plaintiff in *Rigby v Chief Constable of Northamptonshire* [1985] 1 WLR 1242 at 1253. In this case, a psychopath broke into the plaintiff's gunsmith's shop, spread combustible smokeless powder on the floor, and began shooting. The police fired CS gas canisters into the shop and the intruder was detained. Unfortunately the combination of the gas canisters with the gun powder caused a fire and significant damage to the plaintiff's premises. The plaintiff argued that the police were negligent in using gas canisters and not a device, the Ferret, which achieved the same effect as the gas but without the fire risk. The court, while acknowledging the principle that necessity is unavailable where the defendant has negligently contributed to the necessity, found that the police had not acted negligently in failing to use the Ferret.

CONTRIBUTORY NEGLIGENCE

[6.115] A plaintiff's contributory negligence, where it is available is a defence to the plaintiff's claim. This defence typically applies to negligence actions. Originally the defence was absolute, that is, if the defendant was able to prove that the plaintiff was contributorily negligent then the defendant was absolved of liability, even if the defendant had also acted tortiously. Given the harshness of this rule, today apportionment legislation permits a court to apportion responsibility between the plaintiff and defendant having regard to their respective degrees of culpability. See ACT: CLWA, Pt 7.3; *Law Reform (Miscellaneous Provisions) Act 1965* (NSW), Pt 3; *Law Reform (Miscellaneous Provisions Act) Act* (NT), Pt V; *Law Reform Act 1995* (Qld), Pt 3; *Law Reform (Contributory Negligence and Apportionment of Liability) Act 2001* (SA), s 7; *Wrongs Act 1954* (Tas), s 4; *Wrongs Act 1958* (Vic), Pt V; *Law Reform (Contributory Negligence and Tortfeasor's Contribution) Act 1947* (WA), s 4. Contributory negligence is now generally a partial rather than a complete defence. The question that arises is whether this is a defence only to a negligence action or whether it can is available as a partial defence to an intentional tort?

This issue was considered in the case of *Horkin v North Melbourne Football Club Social Club* [1993] VR 153. The plaintiff in this case was a patron on the defendant's premises and his right to be there was revoked by the club. He failed to leave as requested and was ejected with more force than necessary. He suffered an injured elbow for which he successfully sued in battery. The judge however found that the plaintiff was guilty of contributory negligence as he was intoxicated, failed to leave when given a reasonable opportunity to do so, was loud and argumentative and had shoved past employees. The Trial Judge determined that he was 30% responsible for his injuries. The Victorian Supreme Court overruled the finding of contributory negligence stating that from a policy perspective it would be unfair and unjust to reduce the liability of the defendant for what was an intentional battery, on the basis that the plaintiff's carelessness had contributed to his injury: "the difference is not merely in degree but in kind, and the social condemnation attached to the fault differs markedly" between the parties.

[6.120] Notes&Questions

1. Whilst contributory negligence is not a defence to an intentional tort, this may not be the case if the intentional tort is based on negligent conduct of the defendant. This may be the situation with a negligent trespass. In this case the fault of the plaintiff and the defendant would be of the same kind, and the social policy reasons referred to in *Horkin* would not be applicable.
2. Whilst the principle from *Horkin* would appear to be straightforward, consider whether the following case is a correct application of the relevant principles. In *State of New South Wales v Riley* [2003] NSWCA 208, Hodgson JA, with whom Sheller JA and Nicholas JA agreed, determined that although the police action in imprisoning the plaintiff by handcuffing him too tightly and placing him in the police wagon was intentional, as the fracture that he suffered to his wrist *was an unintended and an indirect consequence*, the defence of contributory negligence was still available. Focus upon the emphasised phrase and consider the following. *Horkin* rejected contributory negligence for intentional trespass. In concluding here that the damage was "unintended and an indirect consequence" of the battery and false imprisonment, have their honours focused upon the element of "fault" in determining whether contributory negligence should or should not apply? Clearly the court focused not upon the element of fault but the consequences that flowed from the intentional act. Fault in trespass does not require that the consequences be intended, only the interference; here the handcuffing (battery) and placing the plaintiff in the wagon (imprisonment) were purposely (intentionally) undertaken – the interferences were not negligently caused. *Elite Protective Personnel v Salmon* [2007] NSWCA 322 explains that *Riley* is authority for the proposition that contributory negligence is not available at common law to a claim for damages for an intentionally inflicted injury. This would imply that the decision in *Riley* is correct as there was no intent to inflict injury. However the terminology "intentionally inflicted *injury*" (emphasis added) is drawn from s 3B of the NSW: CLA and does not represent the common law. Fault at common law focuses upon intention to interfere, not intent to cause injury.
3. It has been argued that contributory negligence should apply in respect of an action for conversion. If a plaintiff has not taken reasonable care in respect of the custody or security of their goods, for example leaves their car unlocked, keys in the ignition and

motor running whilst they dash into a shop to purchase a carton of milk, and their car is stolen, should not the plaintiff's damages be reduced upon the basis of his or her own negligence? After all, if the plaintiff had taken reasonable care in respect of the security of their motor vehicle, the opportunity to steal the car would not have arisen. Authority is firmly to the effect that contributory negligence is not a defence to conversion, that carelessness on the part of the plaintiff does not justify another taking or harming the plaintiff's chattel to the extent that damages should be reduced: *Day v Bank of New South Wales* (1978) 18 SASR 163 (Sup Ct SA) (defendant bank unsuccessfully argued that the plaintiff's actions contributed to the ability of the plaintiff's agent to misappropriate his cheques); *Wilton v Commonwealth Trading Bank of Australia* [1973] 2 NSWLR 644, (solicitor's clerk stole cheques payable to his employer, solicitors negligence no defence); *Australian Guarantee Corporation Ltd v Commissioners of the State Bank of Victoria* [1989] VR 617 (contributory negligence was not a defence to an action for conversion of a cheque).

4. The Civil Liability Acts contain provisions which specifically apply to the defence of contributory negligence. In respect of intentional torts where the defendant's interference is intentional, the legislation is not triggered and the common law position continues to apply. However, in all jurisdictions the acts operate in respect of negligently inflicted personal injuries (for further discussion of this point see [3.180] Notes 2, 3 and 5) and this is likely to include personal injury caused by an intentional tort which resulted from a defendant's negligent interference. (For further discussion of the Civil Liability Act provisions which operate in respect of contributory negligence refer to [16.140].)
5. For a detailed discussion of the elements that must be proven to establish the defence of contributory negligence refer to Chapter 16 Defences to Torts of Negligence at [16.65].

SELF-DEFENCE

[6.125] A defendant may be able to argue self-defence in respect of an action for trespass to the person. This is a complete defence and will absolve the defendant of liability. For this defence to be successfully established the defendant will need to prove that (1) there is a reasonable apprehension of physical aggression, and (2) that the force the defendant used did not exceed what was reasonably necessary to beat off the attack.

What will qualify as a reasonable apprehension of physical aggression and how is the extent of force that the defendant is or is not entitled to use determined? The following case considers this.

Fontin v Katapodis

[6.130] *Fontin v Katapodis* (1962) 108 CLR 177 High Court of Australia
(footnotes omitted)

[Katapodis had purchased goods from a store where Fontin was an employee. Fontin had incorrectly asserted that Katapodis did not pay for the goods. After the manager apologised for the misunderstanding, Katapodis began an altercation with Fontin and made an insulting remark to him. Fontin replied to Katapodis in similar fashion. Fontin then picked up a wooden T-square from Katapodis's work bench and broke it on his shoulder. Katapodis raised the T square to hit Fontin again. Fontin, picked up an off-cut of glass and threw it at Katapodis' face. Katapodis dropped the T square

Fontin v Katapodis cont.

and raised one of his hands to fend off the missile. It cut the socket of the thumb and severed the ulna nerve. Serious and permanent injury was done to the hand.]

McTIERNAN J: 180 These appeals arise out of an action for assault and battery. ...

It is clear that Fontin had a right to defend himself against being beaten by Katapodis. The question is whether, in the circumstances, it was reasonably necessary for him to throw the piece of glass at Katapodis in order to protect his right of personal safety. The piece of glass which he threw at Katapodis was capable of causing him serious injury. Aimed at the face it is clearly a very dangerous weapon. Apparently, Fontin realized this because he attempted to pitch it so that none of its edges would strike Katapodis. Katapodis had done only trifling harm to Fontin by hitting with the T square. Perhaps, Katapodis may have struck more severe blows if Fontin had not prevented him. But to throw the piece of glass at Katapodis as a means of self-defence was out of all reasonable proportion to the emergency confronting Fontin. No other weapon was available to Fontin but instead of throwing the piece of glass at Katapodis he could easily have moved away from him and thus have avoided further blows from the T square. Fontin had no need to stand his ground and it was not reasonably necessary for him to throw at Katapodis the cruel and cutting missile which he did throw. It was somewhat of the nature of a deadly weapon. The conclusion of Bridge J that, in the circumstances, it was not reasonably necessary for Fontin to use it in self-defence, is right. ...

OWEN J: 185 ... The learned trial judge found that, in throwing the piece of glass at the plaintiff, Fontin had used more force than was reasonably necessary to protect himself and, for this reason, rejected the plea of self-defence. ... In my opinion, no good reason has been advanced for disturbing ... the findings of fact made by the learned trial judge. He considered that Fontin might have taken steps of a less drastic kind to avoid the plaintiff's attack, for example, by moving out from behind the bench to his left. It is true that the fact that a means of escape was open to a person who claims to have been defending himself against attack is not a decisive factor in considering whether he has acted reasonably (*R v Howe* (1958) 100 CLR 448) and the weight to be attached to such a circumstance will necessarily vary according to the circumstances. In the present case, his Honour thought that the fact that a means of escape was open was a very material matter and, in my opinion, he was right in taking that view. A further fact which, to my mind, is of importance in considering the issue of self-defence is that before the piece of glass was thrown, Fontin had called to Miles, who was, he said, "about a yard away", and that Miles was moving to his assistance when the glass was thrown.

...

[Dixon CJ agreed in essence with Owen J]

[6.135] **Notes&Questions**

1. If the defendant was affected by alcohol or drugs and mistakenly thought that he or she was at risk of harm, would the defendant be able to rely on self-defence? Criminal law proceeds on the basis that self-defence may be available. In *Zecevic v DPP* (1987) 162 CLR 645 at 661 Wilson, Dawson and Toohey JJ stated the question as "... whether the accused believed upon reasonable grounds that it was necessary in self-defence to do what he did". The test is "a mixture of the objective and the subjective; it was not completely objective, in the sense of what a reasonable person would have believed, but rather it was what the accused himself might reasonably have believed in all the circumstances in which he found himself". Under the criminal law the question is therefore whether for example, the intoxication of the accused affected their perception of the risk that was posed. There is authority that the test in *Zecevic* applies to civil law

claims: *Miller v Sotiropoulos* (unreported, Court of Appeal of the Supreme Court of New South Wales, 18 August 1997), and *Underhill v Sherwell* (unreported, Court of Appeal of the Supreme Court of New South Wales, 18 December 1997). Whether it should be used in the civil context is open to question, particularly in light of the recent House of Lords decision of *Ashley v Chief Constable of Sussex Police* [2008] 3 All ER 573. The Court considered whether self-defence could be asserted by a police officer who during a raid had fired and killed the suspect. The officer had entered a darkened bedroom, in which the deceased was standing and had fired a shot killing him. There was no evidence of a gun. The criminal trial had been dismissed, on the basis that the officer had a mistaken belief of imminent harm. The question before the House of Lords was whether this approach should be taken in a civil case for assault and battery. The Court determined that for self-defence to be available when a defendant had the mistaken belief that they were in imminent danger of being attacked, the mistaken belief must not only be honestly held but also reasonably held. Their Lordships were of the view that the goals of criminal and civil law differ, criminal being aimed at individual responsibility and tort at providing "a framework for compensation for wrongs which holds the balance fairly between the conflicting rights and interests of different people". Consequently the belief held must not only be honestly held but also reasonably. On the basis of *Ashley*, a defendant affected by alcohol or drugs who unreasonably thought they were at risk could not rely on self-defence.

2. In determining the extent of force that the defendant is or is not entitled to use, the principle case applies the following test: whether in the circumstances it was reasonably necessary for the plaintiff to use the force he or she did to protect himself or herself. Application of this test includes consideration of the degree of danger which was posed, the means by which the self-defence was effected, whether there were any reasonable alternative means by which the defendant could have protected himself or herself and the circumstances of any previous interaction between the plaintiff and defendant. Consider the facts that the judges in *Fontin v Katapodis* (1962) 108 CLR 177 assessed in concluding that the force was excessive.

   The case of *Miller v Sotiropoulos* (unreported, Court of Appeal of the Supreme Court of New South Wales, 18 August 1997), is an example of a school yard altercation which resulted in court action. The Respondent and a friend had approached the Appellant during lunch recess, after hearing of an earlier incident involving the Appellant. After an exchange of words, the friend had unsuccessfully attempted to karate kick the Appellant in the head and had been escorted away by a teacher. There was then an exchange of words between the Respondent and Appellant, which escalated with the Respondent pushing his shoulder into the Appellant forcing him to slightly loose his balance and then the Appellant had stepped forward and punched the Respondent in the mouth. The Appellant pleaded self-defence, arguing that to him the shove with the shoulder was the same as a punch; that it indicated a fight and he was protecting himself. Several issues arose in this case. First, who bears the onus of proof in respect of self-defence. The Court of Appeal concluded that "self-defence is a matter of justification which must be specially pleaded and the onus of establishing which lies on the person pleading it", the defendant. Secondly, the Court discussed the weight to be given to the existence of a means of escape. Whilst acknowledging that the existence of a means of escape will not automatically result in the actions of the defendant being regarded as unreasonable, the court nevertheless concluded that "... if there be a means of escape open to a defendant [and he or she does not use it], that is a material marker", citing the joint Judgment of Wilson, Dawson and Toohey JJ in *Zecevic v Director of Public Prosecutions (Victoria)* (1987) 162 CLR 645 at 662-663, and Owen J in *Fontin v Katopidis* (1962) 108 CLR 177. Thirdly, in respect of proportionality the Court concluded that what occurred between the Appellant and the Respondent was "no more than a minor tussle". As a result the Respondent's actions, in a situation when his temper must have been high as a result of the earlier encounter, exceeded what could be regarded as reasonable retaliation, or as Meagher JA put it, "[i]t seems to me that a minor push cannot possibly justify a lethal punch in reply".

3. With the understanding that you now have of "reasonable apprehension of physical harm" and "proportionality of the response", consider the following: Would a battered wife who claims "battered wife syndrome" and injures her partner while he is sleeping be able to successfully plead self-defence? The High Court in *Osland v The Queen* [1998] 197 CLR 316 determined that battered wife syndrome is a proper matter for expert evidence but the "issue is not simply whether the accused is a battered woman. Rather, the issue is usually whether she acted in self-defence and, if not, whether she acted under provocation. They are issues which arise in the factual context of the particular case" (per Gaudron and Gummow JJ at 338). What then of an intruder who enters the defendant's house, does the defendant have the right to protect his or her own person and property and shoot the intruder? The answer is dependent upon reasonable apprehension and proportionality.

4. Self-defence may also be pleaded in respect of the defence of others: *Pearce v Hallett* [1969] SASR 423 and *Goss v Nicholas* [1960] Tas SR 133. The same principles that apply in respect of the self-defence of oneself necessarily apply: *Goss v Nicholas* [1960] Tas SR 133, Crawford J at 144. What, however, is the case when the defendant misconceives the need for assistance. For example the defendant sees a child struggling with a man who is trying to force the screaming child into a car. The defendant seeking to protect the child hits the man from behind. It is subsequently ascertained that the man was the child's father. In these circumstances would the defendant be able to rely upon self-defence of another? Refer to *Gambriell v Caparelli* (1974) 54 DLR (3d) 661 (Can) and *Ashley v Chief Constable of Sussex Police* [2008] 3 All ER 573 (Note 1 above). What policy reason do you think may justify the defence being available even though based upon mistake? To encourage Good Samaritans?

5. Property may be defended against intrusion or dispossession on principles which are close to those of self-defence: *Norton v Hoare* (1913) 17 CLR 310 at 321-322. The privilege may be exercised on behalf of both land and chattels, but generally only by the possessor, and subject to statutory provision. The amount of force which may be used against the person must be proportional to the evil to be prevented (*Richardson v Rix* (1989) 12 MVR 522), and in the case of trespass to land, a request to leave must first be made and opportunity given to comply with it unless the trespass was committed with force. Where the trespasser is doing no harm only the mildest of force may be used and it is doubtful whether deadly force may be used even in the case of felonious entry in the absence of threat to life.

6. In New South Wales the CLA limits the damages that can be awarded in respect of personal injury or property damage caused as a result of the self-defence: CLA, s 52. These provisions extend to actions for intentional harm. Section 52 preserves the basic elements of self-defence requiring that a person must believe that their conduct is necessary and that their response is reasonable in the circumstances (see *Presidential Security Services of Australia Pty Ltd v Brilley* [2008] NSWCA 204). It specifically applies the defence to situations in which the person believes the conduct is necessary to defend themselves or another, to prevent or terminate unlawful deprivation of liberty of themselves or another, to protect property from unlawful taking, destruction, damage or interference or to prevent criminal trespass to land or premises or to remove a person committing the trespass. If the response is reasonable and the belief exists then s 52 is a complete defence. There are two potential exceptions to this. First, if the person pleading self-defence was seeking to protect property or prevent criminal trespass or remove a person committing criminal trespass and their actions are intentional or reckless and result in death, self defence will not be available (s 52(3)). The second exception will only apply in exceptional circumstances: if the actions were not a reasonable response, damages are still not payable unless the circumstances of the case are exceptional and failure to award damages would be harsh and unjust (s 53(1)) and if the Court does award damages no damages are to be awarded for non-economic loss (s 53(2)). The onus is upon the defendant to prove self-defence, see *Presidential Security Services of Australia Pty Ltd v Brilley* [2008] NSWCA 204). No other jurisdiction has a similar provision in their CLA.

PROVOCATION: A DEFENCE?

[6.140] At common law provocation is not a defence to battery and assault: *Fontin v Katapodis* (1962) 108 CLR 177 (extracted [6.130] and [6.145]). In the case of Queensland and Western Australia however, defences under the Criminal Code have been extended by the courts to civil actions, and therefore statutory provocation may be pleaded and proven as a defence to an action for common law battery and assault (see *White v Connolly* [1927] St R Qd 75; *Wenn v Evans* (1985) 2 SR (WA) 263).

Whilst common law provocation is not a defence to battery and assault in other jurisdictions, a defendant may nevertheless choose to plead it. Why? The next case considers how provocation is relevant in an action for assault and battery and why a defendant may choose to plead it.

Fontin v Katapodis

[6.145] *Fontin v Katapodis* (1962) 108 CLR 177 High Court of Australia

(footnotes omitted)

[The facts are outlined n the extract at [6.130].]

OWEN J: 186 There remains a question relating to damages. The learned trial judge found that, as a result of his injuries, the plaintiff had incurred expense for medical and hospital treatment amounting to 100 pounds. He assessed the damages for earnings lost up to the date of the trial and for reduced earning capacity in the future at 1,600 pounds and went on to say "in respect of his general pain and suffering and loss of amenities and enjoyment of life I find that a fair figure for compensatory damages would be a further 1,250 pounds". This, as his Honour said, would normally result in a verdict against

Fontin v Katapodis cont.

Fontin for 2,850 pounds. He was of opinion, however, that since Fontin's action in throwing the glass had been provoked by the plaintiff, that fact might be taken into account in mitigation of damages. Accordingly he reduced the amount which he otherwise would have awarded to 2,000 pounds. In this respect, I think his Honour fell into error. In an action for assault, as in many other cases of tort, the conduct and motives of the parties may be taken into account either to aggravate or mitigate damages. In a proper case the damages recoverable are not limited to compensation for the loss sustained but may include exemplary or punitive damages as, for example, where the defendant has acted in a high-handed fashion or with malice. But the rule by which the defendant in an action in which exemplary damages are recoverable is entitled to show that the plaintiff's own conduct was responsible for the commission of the tortious act and to use this fact to mitigate damages has no application to damages awarded by way of compensation. It operates only to prevent the award of exemplary damages or to reduce the amount of such damages which, but for the provocation, would have been awarded. ...

In my opinion, the appeal by the defendant Fontin should be dismissed and that of the plaintiff should be allowed to the extent of increasing the damages awarded to him to 2,850 pounds.

———— ꙮ ————

[6.150] **Notes&Questions**

1. In the case of *Plumb v Breen* (unreported, Young J, Supreme Court of New South Wales, 13 December 1990) Young J applied *Fontin v Katapodis* (1962) 108 CLR 177 and *Horkin v North Melbourne Football Club Social Club* [1993] VR 153 concluding that provocation is not a defence in New South Wales to a battery. However, his Honour did note that the position was probably different in Queensland, citing Trindade and Cane (*The Law of Torts in Australia*, Oxford University Press) at 222.
2. In the case *Downham v Bellette* (unreported, Underwood J, Supreme Court of Tasmania, 30 June 1986), Underwood J concluded that the principle in *Fontin v Katapodis* (1962) 108 CLR 177, that provocation could be taken into account in the reduction of exemplary damages, was also intended to extend to aggravated damages. The plaintiff had defecated on his neighbour's driveway as part of a long running feud. This had lead to the defendant battering and falsely imprisoning the plaintiff. Underwood J determined that the "plaintiff" is disentitled from recovering aggravated damages by reason of his "provocative and insulting conduct".

PART 3: NEGLIGENCE

PART 3

CHAPTER 7

General Duty of Care

INTRODUCTION

[7.05] To an Australian lawyer today, negligence denotes a defined tort with three clearly outlined elements comprising the cause of action: the defendant must have owed the plaintiff a duty of care, that duty must have been breached, and that breach must have caused damage to the plaintiff. As negligence is an action on the case, damage is the gist of the action, and without damage no cause of action can lie: see [2.10]. However, the 1928 edition of *Beven on Negligence* began like this:

> The investigation of *Negligence in Law*, the subject of the ensuing treatise, does not undertake the analysis of any particular class of legal relations. It has to do with legal duties generally, though in a special aspect; that is, with duties as they appear when the normal standard of performance is not attained; and is thus primarily occupied with considering defaults in conduct, and only in the second place with the adequate discharge of obligations. It deals with an aspect, not with a division of law. (WJ Byrne and AD Gibb, *Negligence in Law by Thomas Beven* (4th ed, Sweet and Maxwell, London, 1928), p 1)

To the authors of *Beven on Negligence*, negligence was not a distinct tort, but merely an element or "aspect" of various torts and other legal categories. Similarly, in 1927, in *Healing*

& Co Pty Ltd v Harris (1927) 39 CLR 560, the High Court held that negligence was merely a question of fact. This changed in 1932 when the case of *Donoghue v Stevenson* [1932] AC 562 was decided in the House of Lords.

Today, for the tort of negligence to be established, a duty of care must first be shown to exist. This chapter explores some of the general principles governing the existence of a duty of care in negligence. If the circumstances are of a standard kind and come commonly before the courts, the judge may use an established legal formula or rule. This established rule will lay down the requirements for the duty of care relating to the class of case into which the one before the judge falls; that is, a legal formula establishes the particular duty situation. For example, it is well-established that drivers of cars on the highway owe a duty of care to other users of the highway. There are many of these formulae and their number increases from time to time. As Lord Macmillan put it in *Donoghue v Stevenson*, at 619, the "categories of negligence" are never closed. When a novel situation comes before a court – one which does not fit into an established principle – a new rule for the new situation may be established by resort to a "general principle". The cases extracted in this chapter present various versions of this general principle that, while they are related to one another, are not necessarily identical in concept and allow for much flexibility in operation.

In this chapter we emphasise the common law framework of the duty of care which in turn outlines the scope of the tort of negligence. Although there has been massive legislative intervention into the tort of negligence in recent years, it remains true to say that the structure and framework of the tort remain outlined by the common law. It is thus essential to master this framework before turning to the legislative changes.

In 1932 a situation arose that, in the past had been held to be governed by the law of privity of contract, thus preventing a duty of care in negligence arising. The case that followed set the pattern for the law of negligence from then onwards.

Donoghue v Stevenson

[7.10] *M'Alister (or Donoghue) v Stevenson* [1932] AC 562 House of Lords

(footnotes omitted)

[The facts are taken from the headnote to the report:]

562 By an action brought in the Court of Session (in Scotland) the appellant sought to recover damages from the respondent, who was a manufacturer of aerated waters, for injuries she suffered as a result of consuming part of the contents of a bottle of ginger beer which had been manufactured by the respondent, and which contained the decomposed remains of a snail. The appellant by her condescendence averred that the bottle of ginger beer was purchased for the appellant by a friend in a café at Paisley, which was occupied by one Minghella; that the bottle was made of dark opaque glass and that the appellant had no reason to suspect that it contained anything but pure ginger beer; that the said Minghella poured some of the ginger beer out into a tumbler, and that the appellant drank some of the contents of the tumbler; that her friend was then proceeding to pour the remainder of the contents of the bottle into the tumbler when a snail, which was in a state of decomposition, floated out of the bottle; that as a result of the nauseating sight of the snail in such circumstances, and in consequence of the impurities in the ginger beer which she had already consumed, the appellant suffered from shock and severe gastro-enteritis. The appellant further averred that the ginger beer was manufactured by the respondent to be sold as a drink to the public (including the appellant); that it was bottled by the respondent and labelled by him with a label bearing his name; and that the bottles were thereafter sealed with a metal cap by the respondent. She further averred that it was the duty of

Donoghue v Stevenson cont.

the respondent to provide a system of working his business which would not allow snails to ginger beer bottles, and that it was also his duty to provide an efficient system of inspect bottles before the ginger beer was filled into them, and that he had failed in both these duties and had so caused the accident.

The respondent objected that these averments were irrelevant and insufficient to support the conclusions of the summons.

The Lord Ordinary held that the averments disclosed a good cause of action and allowed a proof.

The Second Division by a majority (the Lord Justice-Clerk, Lord Ormidale, and Lord Anderson; Lord Hunter dissenting) recalled the interlocutor of the Lord Ordinary and dismissed the action.

[The appellant is occasionally referred to as the pursuer.]

LORD ATKIN: 578 Mr Lords, the sole question for determination in this case is legal: Do the averments made by the pursuer in her pleading, if true, disclose a cause of action? … 579 The case has to be determined in accordance with Scots law; but it has been a matter of agreement between the experienced counsel who argued this case, and it appears to be the basis of the judgments of the learned judges of the Court of Session, that for the purposes of determining this problem the laws of Scotland and of England are the same. …

It is remarkable how difficult it is to find in the English authorities statements of general application defining the relations between parties that give rise to the duty. The courts are concerned with the particular relations which come before them in actual litigation, and it is sufficient to say whether the duty exists in those circumstances. The result is that the courts have been engaged upon an elaborate classification of duties as they exist in respect of property, whether real or personal, with further divisions as to ownership, occupation or control, and distinctions based on the particular relations of the one side or the other, whether manufacturer, salesman or landlord, customer, tenant, stranger, and so on. 580 In this way it can be ascertained at any time whether the law recognises a duty, but only where the case can be referred to some particular species which has been examined and classified. And yet the duty which is common to all the cases where liability is established must logically be based upon some element common to the cases where it is found to exist. To seek a complete logical definition of the general principle is probably to go beyond the function of the judge, for the more general the definition the more likely it is to omit essentials or to introduce non-essentials. The attempt was made by Brett MR in *Heaven v Pender* (1883) 11 QBD 503 at 509, in a definition to which I will later refer. As framed, it was demonstrably too wide, though it appears to me, if properly limited, to be capable of affording a valuable practical guide.

At present I content myself with pointing out that in English law there must be, and is, some general conception of relations giving rise to a duty of care, of which the particular cases found in the books are but instances. The liability for negligence, whether you style it such or treat it as in other systems as a species of culpa, is no doubt based upon a general public sentiment of moral wrongdoing for which the offender must pay. But acts or omissions which any moral code would censure cannot in a practical world be treated so as to give a right to every person injured by them to demand relief. In this way rules of law arise which limit the range of complainants and the extent of their remedy. The rule that you are to love your neighbour becomes in law, you must not injure your neighbour; and the lawyer's question – Who is my neighbour? – receives a restricted reply. You must take reasonable care to avoid acts or omissions which you can reasonably foresee would be likely to injure your neighbour. Who, then, in law is my neighbour? The answer seems to be – persons who are so closely and directly affected by my act that I ought reasonably to have them in contemplation as being so affected when I am directing my mind to the acts or omissions which are called in question. This appears to me to be the doctrine of *Heaven v Pender* (1883) 11 QBD 503, 581 as laid down by Lord Esher (then Brett MR) when it is limited by the notion of proximity introduced by Lord Esher himself and AL Smith LJ, in *Le*

Lievre v Gould [1893] 1 QB 491 at 497, 504. Lord Esher says: "That case established that, under certain circumstances, one man may owe a duty to another, even though there is no contract between them. If one man is near to another, or is near to the property of another, a duty lies upon him not to do that which may cause a personal injury to that other, or may injure his property." So AL Smith LJ: "The decision of *Heaven v Pender* was founded upon the principle, that a duty to take due care did arise when the person or property of one was in such proximity to the person or property of another that, if due care was not taken, damage might be done by the one to the other." I think that this sufficiently states the truth if proximity be not confined to mere physical proximity, but be used, as I think it was intended, to extend to such close and direct relations that the act complained of directly affects a person whom the person alleged to be bound to take care would know would be directly affected by his careless act. That this is the sense in which nearness or "proximity" was intended by Lord Esher is obvious from his own illustration in *Heaven v Pender* (1883) 11 QBD 503 (at 510) of the application of his doctrine to the sale of goods. "This" (that is, the rule he has just formulated) "includes the case of goods, etc., supplied to be used immediately by a particular person or persons, or one of a class of persons, where it would be obvious to the person supplying, if he thought, that the goods would in all probability be used at once by such persons before a reasonable opportunity for discovering any defect which might exist, and where the thing supplied would be of such a nature that a neglect of ordinary care of skill as to its condition or the manner of supplying it would probably cause danger to the person or property of the person for whose use it was supplied, and who was about to use it. It would exclude a case in which the goods are supplied under circumstances in which it would be a chance by whom they would be used 582 or whether they would be used or not, or whether they would be used before there would probably be means of observing any defect, or where the goods would be of such a nature that a want of care or skill as to their condition or the manner of supplying them would not probably produce danger of injury to person or property." I draw particular attention to the fact that Lord Esher emphasises the necessity of goods having to be "used immediately" and "used at once before a reasonable opportunity of inspection". This is obviously to exclude the possibility of goods having their condition altered by lapse of time, and to call attention to the proximate relationship, which may be too remote where inspection even of the person using, certainly of an intermediate person, may reasonably be interposed. With this necessary qualification of proximate relationship as explained in *Le Lievre v Gould* [1893] 1 QB 491, I think the judgment of Lord Esher expresses the law of England; without the qualification, I think the majority of the court in *Heaven v Pender* (1883) 11 QBD 503 were justified in thinking the principle was expressed in too general terms. There will no doubt arise cases where it will be difficult to determine whether the contemplated relationship is so close that the duty arises. But in the class of case now before the court I cannot conceive any difficulty to arise. A manufacturer puts up an article of food in a container which he knows will be opened by the actual consumer. There can be no inspection by any purchaser and no reasonable preliminary inspection by the consumer. Negligently, in the course of preparation, he allows the contents to be mixed with poison. It is said that the law of England and Scotland is that the poisoned consumer has no remedy against the negligent manufacturer. If this were the result of the authorities, I should consider the result a grave defect in the law, and so contrary to principle that I should hesitate long before following any decision to that effect which had not the authority of this House. I would point out that, in the assumed state of the authorities, not only would the consumer have no remedy against the 583 manufacturer, he would have none against anyone else, for in the circumstances alleged there would be no evidence of negligence against anyone other than the manufacturer; and, except in the case of a consumer who was also a purchaser, no contract and no warranty of fitness, and in the case of the purchase of a specific article under its patent or trade name, which might well be the case in the purchase of some articles of food or drink, no warranty protecting even the purchaser-consumer. There are other instances than of articles of food and drink where goods are sold intended to be used immediately by the consumer, such as many forms of goods sold for

Donoghue v Stevenson cont.

cleaning purposes, where the same liability must exist. The doctrine supported by the decision below would not only deny a remedy to the consumer who was injured by consuming bottled beer or chocolates poisoned by the negligence of the manufacturer, but also to the user of what should be a harmless proprietary medicine, an ointment, a soap, a cleaning fluid or cleaning powder. I confine myself to articles of common household use, where everyone, including the manufacturer, knows that the articles will be used by other persons than the actual ultimate purchaser namely, by members of his family and his servants, and in some cases his guests. I do not think so ill of our jurisprudence as to suppose that its principles are so remote from the ordinary needs of civilised society and the ordinary claims it makes upon its members as to deny a legal remedy where there is so obviously a social wrong. …

595 I do not find it necessary to discuss at length the cases dealing with duties where the thing is dangerous, or, in the narrower category, belongs to a class of things which are dangerous in themselves. I regard the distinction as an unnatural one so far as it is used to serve as a logical differentiation by which to distinguish the existence or non-existence of a legal right. In this respect I agree with what was said by Scrutton LJ in *Hodge & Sons v Anglo-American Oil Co* (1922) 12 Ll L Rep. 183 at 187, a case which was ultimately decided on a question of fact: "Personally, I do not understand the difference between a thing dangerous in itself, as poison, and a thing dangerous as a particular thing. The latter, if anything, seems the more dangerous of the two; it is a wolf in sheep's clothing instead of an obvious wolf." The nature of the thing may very well call for different degrees of care, and the person dealing with it may well contemplate persons as being within the sphere of his duty to take care who would not be sufficiently proximate with less dangerous goods; so that not only the degree of care but the range of persons to whom a duty is owed may be extended. But they all illustrate the general principle. … 597 I need only mention to distinguish two cases in this House. … In *Caledonian Railway Co v Mulholland or Warwick* [1898] AC 216, the appellant company were held not liable for injuries caused by a defective brake on a coal waggon conveyed by the railway company to a point in the transit where their contract ended, and where the waggons were taken over for haulage for the last part of the journey by a second railway company, on which part the accident happened. It was held that the first railway company were under no duty to the injured workmen to examine the waggon for defects at the end of their contractual haulage. There was ample opportunity for inspection by the second railway company. The relations were not proximate. In the second (*Cavalier v Pope* [1906] AC 428), the wife of the tenant of a house let unfurnished sought to recover from the landlord damages for personal injuries arising from the non-repair of the house, on the ground that the landlord had contracted with her husband to repair the house. It was held that the wife was not a party to the contract, and that the well-known absence of any duty in respect of letting an unfurnished house prevented her from relying on any cause of action for negligence. …

599 My Lords, if your Lordships accept the view that this pleading discloses a relevant cause of action you will be affirming the proposition that by Scots and English law alike a manufacturer of products, which he sells in such a form as to show that he intends them to reach the ultimate consumer in the form in which they left him with no reasonable possibility of intermediate examination, and with the knowledge that the absence of reasonable care in the preparation or putting up of the products will result in an injury to the consumer's life or property, owes a duty to the consumer to take that reasonable care. …

Donoghue v Stevenson cont.

[Lord Macmillan and Lord Thankerton delivered concurring judgments. Lord Buckmaster and Lord Tomlin dissented. The case was remitted for trial.]

[7.15] **Notes&Questions**

1. A note on the history of the above action thereafter appears in 71 LQR 472.
2. Before *Donoghue v Stevenson* was decided, the courts had held that where a duty arose under a contract there could be no separate duty to the plaintiff. For example, in *Winter-bottom v Wright* (1842) 152 ER 402 (Exch), Wright had a contract with the Post Master General to provide a coach in a fit and proper condition to move the mail. Atkinson had a contract with the Post Master General to convey the coach and supply the horses and men. One of Atkinson's men, Winterbottom, was injured when the coach broke down. Winterbottom was held to have no remedy. *Donoghue v Stevenson* broke this nexus with contract.
3. What is the ratio decidendi of *Donoghue v Stevenson*? There is a possible ratio concerning manufacturer's liability for defective products and there is the "neighbour principle" which refers to the reasonable foreseeability of harm. Note that the answer to this question has varied over time.
4. The neighbour test from *Donoghue v Stevenson* continues to be cited in current cases. The case is therefore not just of historical importance as the foundation of modern negligence law. The basic test for the duty of care continues to be derived from it, with the addition of other factors which are discussed as this book progresses.

Acts or omissions

[7.20] In *Donoghue v Stevenson*, Lord Atkin referred to both acts and omissions as being able to give rise to a duty of care in negligence. However, it is more difficult to establish that there is a duty to do something at all (that is that the defendant should not have omitted to do something), than it is to establish a duty to do a thing with reasonable care (that is that their act was carried out wrongfully). An extension of the view that it is more difficult to establish a duty in relation to an omission which often troubles people is the common law view that there is no duty to rescue a person. In *Donoghue v Stevenson* the wrongful matter was an act, namely the wrongful manufacture of the drink. In the following case the wrongful matter was the failure to completely put out a fire.

Hargrave v Goldman

[7.25] *Hargrave v Goldman* (1963) 110 CLR 40 High Court of Australia (footnotes omitted)

[The respondent owned a grazing property in Western Australia on which a very large tree was struck by lightning. This set the tree on fire at a point about 80 feet (approx 24 metres) above the ground. The tree was right in the middle of the property, some 200 metres from the neighbours. The respondent organised for the tree to be chopped down which caused another tree to fall and catch on fire. He cleared the area in the vicinity of combustible material and damped the fire down; however he left the area while the logs were still burning, apparently thinking it was safe to let them burn themselves out. The fire got out of control and created a large bushfire which burnt out hundreds of

Hargrave v Goldman cont.

acres of land and spread to the appellant's property. The appellant sued the respondent in nuisance, negligence, ignis suus (the ancient rule making a person strictly liable for escape of fire), *Rylands v Fletcher* (1866) LR 1 Ex 265; (1868) LR 3 HL 330, and under the *Bush Fires Act 1954*. The following extract concerns only the negligence claim.]

WINDEYER J: 62 ... (iv) Negligence: The distinction between nuisance and negligence is not altogether clear cut. Until the recognition in modern times of negligence as a tort in itself, many actions of case which we would to-day say were based on negligence were described as being for nuisances. At the present day, and for present purposes, it may, I think, be stated as follows.

In nuisance liability is founded upon a state of affairs, created, adopted or continued by one person (otherwise than in the reasonable and convenient use by him of his own land) which, to a substantial degree, harms another person (an owner or occupier of land) in his enjoyment of his land.

In negligence liability is founded upon the negligent conduct of one person causing, to any degree, foreseeable harm to the person or property of another person (not necessarily an owner or occupier of land) to whom a duty of care was owed.

(v) Duty of care: In the present case the learned trial judge found expressly that, had the respondent taken reasonable care, he could have put out the burning logs. I take it that his Honour meant by this that the respondent did not act as a reasonably careful man, who had a duty to extinguish the fires, would have acted in the circumstances. That, the appellants say, is a finding of negligence on which they are entitled to judgment, and again they refer to the illustration that Scrutton LJ gave, in the passage I have quoted above, of stamping out a fire. His Lordship there recognized that, although the case had been debated as one of the duty to abate a nuisance, his proposition made liability depend on negligence. And he said: "I appreciate that to get negligence you must have a duty to be careful, but I think on principle that a landowner has a duty to take reasonable care not to allow his land to remain a receptacle for a thing which may, if not rendered harmless, cause damage to his neighbours" (1924) 1 KB, at 358.

Counsel for the respondent challenged the validity of this proposition, or at least its application in this case. The respondent, he 63 urged, had no legal duty to the appellants to extinguish the burning logs or render them harmless... It may be that insistence upon a duty of care as a separate element in liability for negligence is, in theory, unnecessary; for it may be comprehended in the idea of negligence itself, an act or omission being careless only when a reasonable man would appreciate, if he thought about the matter, that it could have harmful consequences.... 65

This case is not one in which the obligation to use care and skill arises from an undertaking to do some work for the benefit of another. In a case of that kind an obligation to exercise due care and skill arises from the entering upon the work, whether for reward or gratuitously. But here what the respondent did in relation to the fire was not done pursuant to any undertaking to the appellants, nor was it done specifically for their benefit. It did not increase the danger of the fire spreading. Probably it diminished it. It seems to me impossible to say that, because the respondent did something to control the fire, he incurred a liability that he would not have incurred had he done nothing. If that were the law, a man might be reluctant to try to stop a bush fire lest, if he failed in his endeavours, he should incur a liability that he would not incur if he remained passive. The question comes to this: In a case such as this has the occupier of land a duty at common law - I put statutory obligations aside for the moment - to act at all? It was said that we must go to *Donoghue v Stevenson* [1931] UKHL 3; (1932) AC 562, and that the principle of proximity would supply the answer. Fullagar J wrote of *Donoghue v Stevenson* (in a paper published in the *Australian Law Journal* (1951) Vol 25 p 278): "It was not, of course, intended to make, and it does not make, everything nice and easy".

Lord Atkin's well-known generalization explains the scope of a duty of care, that is to say it states who can complain of a lack of care when an obligation of care exists. But I venture to think that it is a

Hargrave v Goldman cont.

mistake to treat it as providing always a complete and conclusive test of whether, in a given situation, one person has a legal duty either to act or to refrain from acting in the interests of others. The very allusion shows that it has not this universal 66 application. The priest and the Levite, when they saw the wounded man by the road, passed by on the other side. He obviously was a person whom they had in contemplation and who was closely and directly affected by their action. Yet the common law does not require a man to act as the Samaritan did. The lawyer's question must therefore be given a more restricted reply than is provided by asking simply who was, or ought to have been, in contemplation when something is done. The dictates of charity and of compassion do not constitute a duty of care. The law casts no duty upon a man to go to the aid of another who is in peril or distress, not caused by him. The call of common humanity may lead him to the rescue. This the law recognizes, for it gives the rescuer its protection when he answers that call. But it does not require that he do so. There is no general duty to help a neighbour whose house is on fire.

The question in this case, however, is not whether a man must aid another who is in distress or rescue him from a peril. It is whether he must try to forestall and prevent a peril. A man who, while travelling along a highway, sees a fire starting on the adjacent land is not, as far as I am aware, under any common law duty to stop and try to put it out or to warn those whom it may harm. He may pass on, if not with a quiet conscience at least without a fear of legal consequence. Has the occupier of land a legal duty to his neighbour in respect of a fire that he finds on his side of the boundary fence, but none in respect of a fire that he sees on his neighbour's land just across the boundary, assuming in each case that he realized what might be the consequences to his neighbour of his own inaction? If so, on what principle of the law of negligence does the distinction depend? I do not find such questions easy. The doctrine of proximity does not give the answer, because the question assumes both physical proximity and the metaphysical proximity of Lord Atkin's doctrine. But we may, I think, push such troublesome problems into the background. The trend of judicial development of the law of negligence has been, I think, to found a duty of care either in some task undertaken, or in the ownership, occupation, or use of land or chattels. The occupier of land has long been liable at common law, in one form of action or another, for consequences flowing from the state of his land and of happenings there, not only to neighbouring occupiers, but also to those persons who come upon his land and those who pass by. And, as I have remarked elsewhere, the tendency of the law in recent times has been to lessen the immunities and privileges of landowners and occupiers and to increase their responsibilities to 67 others for what happens upon their land. To hold that the respondent had a duty to his neighbours to take reasonable care to prevent the fire on his land spreading would be in accordance with modern concepts of a land occupier's obligations. If it be a new step in the march of the law - and I do not think that really it is – then it is not a step which we need hesitate to take if nothing stands in the way. New precedents must accord with old principles: but as Lord Abinger CB once said, of an action for which no precedent was adduced, "We are therefore to decide the question upon general principles, and in doing so we are at liberty to look at the consequences of a decision the one way or the other": *Priestley v Fowler* (1837) 3 M & W 1 at 5 (150 ER 1030, at 1032).

But this is not a case that is bare of all authority. The learned trial judge based his conclusion on certain earlier decisions. The one most directly in point is *Batchelor v Smith* (1879) 5 VLR (L) 176, a judgment of the Supreme Court of Victoria (Stawell CJ and Stephen J) allowing a demurrer to a declaration alleging damage by spread of fire from the defendant's land. The Chief Justice in giving his reasons said: "It is the duty of any person who originates or brings any matter, animate or inanimate, attended with danger, on his ground, to keep it within due bounds; but there is no authority for the proposition for which the plaintiff contends, that, not having brought it, he must remove it" (1879) 5 VLR (L) 176, at 178. Stephen J concurred, saying: "The foundation of the whole case is that no duty was cast on the defendant to extinguish the fire" (1879) 5 VLR (L) 176, at 179. But the declaration had

Hargrave v Goldman cont.

expressly alleged that the defendant, although aware of the danger to his neighbour, allowed the fire to remain burning on his land for the purpose and with the intention of burning and destroying certain stubble, reeds, sawdust, and refuse. In the face of that, it is hard to see why the demurrer was allowed or what answer there was to counsel's argument that the defendant had adopted the fire as his own, and become responsible for any injury resulting from it, just as if he had lighted it himself. The case seems to have been argued on the basis of *Rylands v Fletcher* (1866) LR 1 Ex 265; (1868) LR 3 HL 330 and strict liability, and the decision, when analysed, cannot be regarded as of much weight in the present case. But its dogmatic denial of a duty has not been without effect... 68

The learned trial judge, after a careful review of the cases ... considered that the correct rule was laid down in *Batchelor v Smith* (1879) 5 VLR (L) 176. He was influenced in this view because he said it "accords with the broader rule that a landowner is under no liability for anything which happens to, or spreads from, his land in the natural course of affairs if the land is used naturally" (1963) WAR, at 108. To that proposition I now turn.

(vi) Things naturally on land: His Honour's statement echoes, but adds some words to, what Lord Goddard CJ said in *Neath Rural District Council v Williams* (1951) 1 KB 115, at 122, where a miscellany of illustration appears. But, like all propositions of a general character, the difficulty is not in its statement but in its application. Is country land in Australia "used naturally" if the occupier, aware of the risk of a bush fire that may cause a disaster to himself and his neighbours, does not act as a reasonably prudent man would act with a view to preventing this? Speaking generally, it is no doubt true that the law does not impose a duty upon anyone to arrest the processes of nature. But we are not concerned with generalities, but with the question whether the occupier of land must take care in the interests of his neighbours to prevent, if by reasonable measures he can, a small fire upon his land spreading and becoming a bush fire. That an answer to that question, arising in Australia to-day, should be sought for in a case about thistledown in England would surely surprise anyone who was not a lawyer. Are we – by examining what courts have said in cases about thistles, prickly pear, the roots of trees and the branches of trees, trees deliberately planted and trees growing naturally, rolling rocks, rabbits, weeds in watercourses, silt in streams, seaweed, snow and surface water – to abstract some general principle, to add qualifications to it, and then to try to apply it to a fire which lightning lit? I do not think so. ...

In some of the cases concerning things naturally on land the plaintiff's claim was based on nuisance: in some on negligence: in some on the doctrine of *Rylands v Fletcher* (1866) LR 1 Ex 265; (1868) LR 3 HL 330. The foundation-stone of the doctrinal edifice appears to be *Giles v Walker* (1890) 24 QBD 656, the case of the thistles. The action was in negligence. Lord Coleridge CJ disposed of it by saying: "I never heard of such an action as this. There can be no duty as between adjoining occupiers to cut the thistles, which are the natural growth of the soil. The appeal must be allowed" (1890) 24 QBD 656, at 657. Lord Esher agreed. Recently the decision has come in for some criticism. The thistles, although no doubt a natural growth, had only grown on the defendant's land after he had turned it from forest into ploughed land. And in *Davey v Harrow Corporation* (1958) 1 QB 60, Lord Goddard CJ, in delivering the judgment of the Court of Appeal, quoted (1958) 1 QB 60, at 71 a remark that Lord Esher had made during the argument, as reported in the Law Times: "This damage is not caused by any act of the defendant. Can you show us any case which goes so far as to say that, if something comes 70 on a man's land for which he is in no way responsible, that he is bound to remove it, or else prevent its causing injury to any of his neighbours?" (1890) 62 LT 933, at 934: Lord Goddard's judgment, in which he acknowledged his indebtedness to an article by Doctor Goodhart ("Liability for Things Naturally on the Land" (1930) 4 *Cambridge Law Journal* 13), went on, quoting directly from that article: "Apparently counsel did not reply, but had he known of *Margate Pier and Harbour Proprietors v Margate Town Council* (1869) 20 LT 564, it would have been a complete answer" (1958) 1

Hargrave v Goldman cont.

QB 60, at 72. In that case seaweed had been cast ashore by the sea. Left to lie, it became a nuisance to the neighbourhood. It was held that the landowner on whose land it was could be compelled to remove it. ... 71

In the result no more, I think, emerges from the cases than one would have expected, namely that liability for negligence depends ultimately upon a concept of fault and that no man can be held at fault, morally or legally, simply for a happening not caused by any human agency: and that often the law does not hold a man at fault because he does not take any steps to arrest the consequences of such a happening, although he knows they may be harmful to other persons: but that sometimes it does.

(vii) Conclusions: In my opinion a man has a duty to exercise reasonable care when there is a fire upon his land (although not started or continued by him or for him), of which he knows or ought to know, if by the exercise of reasonable care it can be rendered harmless or its danger to his neighbours diminished. Of course, 72 if the fire were brought by him upon his land – in the sense of being started or intentionally kept alight there by him or anyone for whose acts he was responsible – his duty would not be merely to take reasonable care: it would be the strict duty of *Rylands v Fletcher* (1866) LR 1 Ex 265; (1868) LR 3 HL 330.

Strong support for the existence of a duty of care to prevent the spread of fire is to be found in the House of Lords' approval in *Sedleigh-Denfield's Case* [1940] UKHL 2; (1940) AC 880 of the judgment of Scrutton LJ in *Job Edwards' Case* (1924) 1 KB 341 .... The dangers of fire have, from the earliest days of the common law, given rise to special responsibilities; and not only in the common law. ... And that a negligent failure to prevent the spread of a fire of unknown origin creates liability seems to be the rule in Canada also: see *Des Brisay v Canadian Government Merchant Marine Ltd* (1941) 2 DLR 209; *Mainella v Wilding* (1946) 2 DLR 749. ... But I do not think that the liability arising from a negligent failure to extinguish or confine a fire is a liability only to neighbouring landowners or occupiers. Liability in negligence extends to other persons who may be harmed, that is to say, to those who are neighbours in the lawyer's sense as well as those who dwell in the neighbourhood. The grave and widespread consequences of a bush fire may make the liability of a 73 careless individual ruinous for him; but this only emphasizes the seriousness of the duty of care ...

I would allow the appeal.

[Taylor and Owen JJ, in a joint judgment agreed that the appeal should be allowed. In their view whether the claim was in nuisance or negligence was of no significance here.]

[7.30] Notes&Questions

In the judgment of Taylor and Owen JJ (at 52-53) they observed "[t]he claim of the appellants does not rest merely upon the allegation that there was on the part of the respondent a failure to take reasonable steps to extinguish or prevent the spread of the fire in its original location in the fork of the tree. The respondent, did, in fact, take some steps and these were initially taken as much for the preservation of his own property as of that of his neighbours... But when the tree in question here was cut down a hazard of a different character was created and it is beyond doubt that the respondent was under a duty to use reasonable care to prevent it causing damage to his neighbours in the countryside". Why is the difference between the fire being originally in the fork of the tree, and the fire after the tree was cut down so important? What is the legal difference between these two matters?

The importance of duty

[7.35] Over the years following the decision in *Donoghue v Stevenson*, there has been debate about the importance of the duty of care. The duty of care has been described as "the unnecessary fifth wheel on the coach" (see Buckland, "The Duty to Take Care" (1935) 51 LQR 637 at 639). This view was based partly on the idea that the most important thing to be decided in a negligence case was whether there had been a breach of duty, and indeed in most litigated cases, this is the issue to be decided. In *Voli v Inglewood Shire Council* (1963) 110 CLR 74, Windeyer J at 86, said that one should not treat the duty of care as if it were a statutory enactment. This statement echoed the view of Lord Reid in *Home Office v Dorset Yacht Co* [1970] AC 1004 at 1026. However, in Australia by the time of *Hargrave v Goldman* (1963) 110 CLR 40 in 1963 (see [7.25]), Windeyer J said (at 63):

> The concept of a duty of care, as a prerequisite of liability in negligence, is embedded in our law by compulsive pronouncements of the highest authority. And it may well be that it could not be otherwise, if the law of negligence is to have symmetry, consistency and defined bounds, and its application in particular cases is to be reasonably predictable.

It may be argued that the view that the duty of care was unnecessary made sense when juries decided breach of duty after a limited direction by a judge. In those cases the juries' deliberations were not susceptible of analysis, being secret, and there was no profit in an elaborate analysis of the duty of care if juries were not going to take any notice of it. However, in England and Australia in the latter half of the 20th and early 21st century, juries are relatively rare in civil trials, leaving the judge with far more power and the power of the judge has relatively increased.

The duty of care operates to define the scope and substance of negligence law. It addresses the major questions of what it is that we regard as behaviour for which a plaintiff should be compensated. Because the concepts making up the duty of care define the scope of negligence, the issues within the duty of care resonate through the whole cause of action. To some extent, breach and causation are pre-empted by the duty of care concepts in determining what is regarded as responsible and irresponsible behaviour. It is the duty of care that delineates the area, then allowing the question of breach to be a mere fitting of the facts to the template of legal responsibility (see *Cook v Cook* (1986) 162 CLR 376). The duty of care, then, is of paramount importance to considering the development and the scope of the law of negligence. It continues to be of paramount importance even after the enactment of the tort reform changes of 2002 and following.

THE EXPANSION OF THE DUTY OF CARE

[7.40] In the 1960s, courts began to expand the tort of negligence by expanding the duty of care. Negligence began to move into areas that traditionally had been closed, such as pure economic loss, liability for third parties and liability of governmental (or public) authorities.

Pure economic loss was one of these areas. Traditionally, pure economic loss had been regarded as the domain of contract, and there was said to be a "bright line rule" preventing the use of negligence for pure economic loss (*Cattle v Stockton Waterworks* (1875) LR 10 QB 453; *Law Societe Anonyme de Remorquage a Helice v Bennetts* [1911] 1 KB 243). This position was maintained into the 1960s, but then began to be eroded. The following case was one of the most important cases in the expansion of the duty of care at this time.

Hedley Byrne & Co v Heller & Partners

[7.45] *Hedley Byrne & Co Ltd v Heller & Partners Ltd* [1964] AC 465 House of Lords (footnotes omitted)

[The plaintiffs, Hedley Byrne & Co Ltd, who were advertising agents, had placed some small orders for advertising space on behalf of a customer, Easipower Ltd. On receiving a favourable trading report from the customer's bank the plaintiffs placed substantial orders for advertising time on television and space in newspapers on a credit basis so that the plaintiffs became personally liable for the orders.

The plaintiffs became uneasy about the financial position of Easipower Ltd and sought a banker's report through their own bank, the National Provincial Bank Ltd. Advice was obtained by telephone from the defendants, who were merchant bankers with whom Easipower had an account. The advice expressed to be given in confidence and without responsibility on the part of the defendants, indicated that the company was good for normal business relations and would not undertake commitments it was unable to fulfil. The advice was confirmed in writing. About two months later the plaintiffs again asked their bank to make an exhaustive inquiry into the financial structure and status of Easipower Ltd. The defendants were again approached and this time reference was made to a £100,000 per annum advertising contract. In their written reply to the National Provincial Bank which was marked "Confidential. For your private use and without responsibility on the part of this bank or its officials" the (defendants) made the following statement: "Respectably constituted company, considered good for ordinary business engagements. Your figures are larger than we are accustomed to see."

This advice was passed on in writing to the plaintiffs who relied on it and as a result lost £17,661/18/6 when Easipower Ltd went into liquidation. The plaintiffs claimed this amount from the defendants alleging that they were in breach of a duty in giving their replies negligently. McNair J found that the defendants had been negligent but owed no duty to the plaintiffs. The Court of Appeal also held that there was no duty of care. The plaintiffs appealed to the House of Lords.]

LORD REID: 482 Before coming to the main question of law, it may be well to dispose of an argument that there was no sufficiently close relationship between these parties to give rise to any duty. It is said that the respondents did not know the precise purpose of the inquiries and did not even know whether the National Provincial Bank wanted the information for its own use or for the use of a customer: they knew nothing of the appellants. I would reject that argument. They knew that the inquiry was in connection with an advertising contract, and it was at least probable that the information was wanted by the advertising contractors. ...

The appellants' first argument was based on *Donoghue v Stevenson* [1932] AC 562; 48 TLR 494 (HL). That is a very important decision, but I do not think that it has any direct bearing on this case. That decision may encourage us to develop existing lines of authority, but it cannot entitle us to disregard them. Apart altogether from authority, I would think that the law must treat negligent words differently from negligent acts. The law ought so far as possible to reflect the standards of the reasonable man, and that is what *Donoghue v Stevenson* [1932] AC 562; 48 TLR 494 sets out to do. The most obvious difference between negligent words and negligent acts is this. Quite careful people often express definite opinions on social or informal occasions even when they see that others are likely to be 483 influenced by them; and they often do that without taking that care which they would take if asked for their opinion professionally or in a business connection. The appellant agrees that there can be no duty of care on such occasions, and we were referred to American and South African authorities where that is recognised, although their law appears to have gone much further than ours has yet done. But it is at least unusual casually to put into circulation negligently made articles which are dangerous. A man might give a friend a negligently-prepared bottle of homemade wine and his friend's guests might drink it with dire results. But it is by no means clear that those guests would have no action against the negligent manufacturer.

Hedley Byrne & Co v Heller & Partners cont.

Another obvious difference is that a negligently made article will only cause one accident, and so it is not very difficult to find the necessary degree of proximity or neighbourhood between the negligent manufacturer and the person injured. But words can be broadcast with or without the consent or the foresight of the speaker or writer. It would be one thing to say that the speaker owes a duty to a limited class, but it would be going very far to say that he owes a duty to every ultimate "consumer" who acts on those words to his detriment. It would be no use to say that a speaker or writer owes a duty but can disclaim responsibility if he wants to. He, like the manufacturer, could make it part of a contract that he is not liable for his negligence: but that contract would not protect him in a question with a third party, at least if the third party was unaware of it.

So it seems to me that there is good sense behind our present law that in general an innocent but negligent misrepresentation gives no cause of action. There must be something more than the mere misstatement. I therefore turn to the authorities to see what more is required. The most natural requirement would be that expressly or by implication from the circumstances the speaker or writer has undertaken some responsibility, and that appears to me not to conflict with any authority which is binding on this House. Where there is a contract there is no difficulty as regards the contracting parties: the question is whether there is a warranty. The refusal of English law to recognise any jus quaesitum tertii causes some difficulties, but they are not relevant here. Then there are cases where a person does not merely make a statement but performs a gratuitous service. I do not intend to examine the cases about that, but at least they show that in some cases that person owes a duty of care apart from any contract, and to that extent they pave the way to holding that there 484 can be a duty of care in making a statement of fact or opinion which is independent of contract. ...

[His Lordship then referred to the older authorities and commented on a passage in Lord Haldane's judgment in *Robinson v National Bank of Scotland* [1916] SC 154 at 157. He continued:]

486 This passage makes it clear that Lord Haldane did not think that a duty to take care must be limited to cases of fiduciary relationship in the narrow sense of relationships which had been recognised by the Court of Chancery as being of a fiduciary character. He speaks of other special relationships, and I can see no logical stopping place short of all those relationships where it is plain that the party seeking information or advice was trusting the other to exercise such a degree of care as the circumstances required, where it was reasonable for him to do that, and where the other gave the information or advice when he knew or ought to have known that the inquirer was relying on him. I say "ought to have known" because in questions of negligence we now apply the objective standard of what the reasonable man would have done.

A reasonable man, knowing that he was being trusted or that his skill and judgment were being relied on, would, I think, have three courses open to him. He could keep silent or decline to give the information or advice sought: or he could give an answer with a clear qualification that he accepted no responsibility for it or that it was given without that reflection or inquiry which a careful answer would require: or he could simply answer without any such qualification. If he chooses to adopt the last course he must, I think, be held to have accepted some responsibility for his answer being given carefully, or to have accepted a relationship with the inquirer which requires him to exercise such care as the circumstances require. ...

489 Now I must try to apply these principles to the present case. What the appellants complain of is not negligence in the ordinary sense of carelessness, but rather misjudgment, in that Mr Heller, while honestly seeking to give a fair assessment, in fact made a statement which gave a false and misleading impression of his customer's credit. It appears that bankers now commonly give references with regard to their customers as part of their business. I do not know how far their customers generally permit them to disclose their affairs, but, even with permission, it cannot always be easy for a banker to reconcile his duty to his customer with his desire to give a fairly balanced reply to an inquiry. And inquirers can hardly expect a full and objective statement of opinion or accurate factual information

such as skilled men would be expected to give in reply to other kinds of inquiry. So it seems to me to be unusually difficult to determine just what duty beyond a duty to be honest a banker would be held to have undertaken if he gave a reply without an adequate disclaimer of responsibility or other warning. …

492 [H]ere the appellants' bank, who were their agents in making the inquiry, began by saying that "they wanted to know in confidence and without responsibility on our part", that is, on the part of the respondents. So I cannot see how the appellants can now be entitled to disregard that and maintain that the respondents did incur a responsibility to them ….

493 I am therefore of opinion that it is clear that the respondents never undertook any duty to exercise care in giving their replies. The appellants cannot succeed unless there was such a duty and therefore in my judgment this appeal must be dismissed.

LORD MORRIS OF BORTH-Y-GEST: 502 It should now be regarded as settled that if someone possessed of a special skill undertakes, quite irrespective of contract, to apply that skill for the assistance of another person who relies upon such skill, a duty of care will arise. The fact that the service is to be given by means of or by the instrumentality of words can make no difference. Furthermore, if in a sphere in which a person is so placed that others could reasonably rely upon his judgment or his skill or upon his ability to make careful inquiry, a person takes it upon himself to give information or advice to, or allows his information or advice to be passed on to, another person who, as he knows or should know, will place reliance upon it, then a duty of care will arise. …

504 There was in the present case no contemplation of receiving anything like a formal and detailed report such as might be given by some concern charged with the duty (probably for reward) of making all proper and relevant inquiries concerning the nature, scope and extent of a company's activities and of obtaining and marshalling all available evidence as to its credit, efficiency, standing and business reputation. There is much to be said, therefore, for the view that if a banker gives a reference in the form of a brief expression of opinion in regard to creditworthiness he does not accept, and there is not expected from him, any higher duty than that of giving an honest answer. I need not, however, seek to deal further with this aspect of the matter, which perhaps cannot be covered by any statement of general application, because, in my judgment, the bank in the present case, by the words which they employed, effectively disclaimed any assumption of a duty of care.

LORD HODSON: [After referring to the earlier cases, continued:] … 513 It was held in *Low v Bouverie* [1891] 3 Ch 82; 7 TLR 582 (CA) that if a trustee takes upon himself to answer the inquiries of a stranger about to deal with the cestui que trust, he is not under a legal obligation to do more than to give honest answers to the best of his actual knowledge and belief, he is not bound to make inquiries himself. I do not think a banker giving references in the ordinary exercise of business should be in any worse position than the trustee. I have already pointed out that a banker, like anyone else, may find himself involved in a special relationship involving liability, as in *Woods v Martins Bank Ltd* [1959] 1 QB 55 but there are no special features here which enable the appellants to succeed. …

514 I agree with [Lord Morris] that if in a sphere where a person is so placed that others could reasonably rely upon his judgment or his skill or upon his ability to make careful inquiry such person takes it upon himself to give information or advice to, or allows his information or advice to be passed on to another person who, as he knows, or should know, will place reliance upon it, then a duty of care will arise.

I would dismiss the appeal.

LORD DEVLIN: … 526 The respondents in this case cannot deny that they were performing a service. Their sheet anchor is that they were performing it gratuitously and therefore no liability for its performance can arise. My Lords, in my opinion this is not the law, a promise given without

Hedley Byrne & Co v Heller & Partners cont.

consideration to perform a service cannot be enforced as a contract by the promisee; but if the service is in fact performed and done negligently, the promisee can recover in an action in tort ....

528 My Lords, it is true that this principle of law has not yet been clearly applied to a case where the service which the defendant undertakes to perform is or includes the obtaining and imparting of information. But I cannot see why it should not be: and if it had not been thought erroneously that *Derry v Peek* (1889) 14 App Cas 337 negatived any liability for negligent statements, I think that by now it probably would have been. It cannot matter whether the information consists of fact or opinion or is a mixture of both, nor whether it was obtained as a result of special inquiries or comes direct from facts already in the defendant's possession or from his general store of professional knowledge. One cannot, as I have already endeavoured to show, distinguish in this respect between a duty to inquire and a duty to state.

I think, therefore, that there is ample authority to justify your Lordships in saying now that the categories of special relationships which may give rise to a duty to take care in word as well as in deed are not limited to contractual relationships or to relationships of 529 fiduciary duty, but include also relationships which in the words of Lord Shaw in *Nocton v Lord Ashburton* [1914] AC 932 at 972 are "equivalent to contract", that is, where there is an assumption of responsibility in circumstances in which, but for the absence of consideration, there would be a contract. Where there is an express undertaking, an express warranty as distinct from mere representation, there can be little difficulty. The difficulty arises in discerning those cases in which the undertaking is to be implied. In this respect the absence of consideration is not irrelevant. Payment for information or advice is very good evidence that it is being relied upon and that the informer or adviser knows that it is. Where there is no consideration, it will be necessary to exercise greater care in distinguishing between social and professional relationships and between those which are of a contractual character and those which are not. It may often be material to consider whether the adviser is acting purely out of good nature or whether he is getting his reward in some indirect form. The service that a bank performs in giving a reference is not done simply out of a desire to assist commerce. It would discourage the customers of the bank if their deals fell through because the bank had refused to testify to their credit when it was good. ...

530 I regard this proposition as an application of the general conception of proximity. Cases may arise in the future in which a new and wider proposition, quite independent of any notion of contract, will be needed. ... I have another reason for caution. Since the essence of the matter in the present case and in others of the same type is the acceptance of responsibility, I should like to guard against the imposition of restrictive terms notwithstanding that the essential condition is fulfilled. If a defendant says to a plaintiff – "Let me do this for you; do not waste your money in employing a professional, I will do it for nothing and you can rely on me" – I do not think he could escape liability simply because he belonged to no profession or calling, had no qualifications or special skill and did not hold himself out as having any. The relevance of these factors is to show the unlikelihood of a defendant in such circumstances assuming a legal responsibility, and as such they may often be decisive. But they are not theoretically conclusive and so cannot be the subject of definition. It would be unfortunate if they were. For it would mean that plaintiffs would seek to avoid the rigidity of the definition by bringing the action in contract as in *De La Bere v Pearson Ltd* [1908] 1 KB 280 and setting up something that would do for consideration. That, to my mind, would be an undesirable development in the law; and the best way of avoiding it is to settle the law so that the presence or absence of consideration makes no difference ...

[His Lordship agreed with the dismissal of the appeal on the basis of the existence of the disclaimer.]

Hedley Byrne & Co v Heller & Partners cont.

LORD EARCE ... 540 If both parties say expressly (in a case where neither is deliberately taking advantage of the other) that there shall be no liability, I do not find it possible to say that a liability was assumed.

[His Lordship agreed that the appeal should be dismissed.]

[7.50] **Notes&Questions**

1. *Hedley Byrne* is a case about negligent words causing pure economic loss. The category of cases concerning pure economic loss is discussed further in Chapter 10.
2. What are the different impacts of words as opposed to deeds or acts? Are the Law Lords correct in thinking that the difference matters?
3. The different judgments here all focus on "something more" than mere reasonable foreseeability of harm being needed in order for there to be a duty of care. The "something more" includes "equivalence to contract", "reasonable reliance", "assumption of responsibility" and "undertaking to use a special skill for a person who he or she knows will rely on it". The pattern of requiring reasonable foreseeability of harm plus something more to establish the duty of care in most cases beyond simple personal injury has continued into the present.

[7.55] Soon after *Hedley Byrne* another case was decided which also expanded the duty of care. In this case, there were several hurdles for the plaintiffs. First, they had to sue a public authority (the Home Office), secondly the plaintiffs' injury was not caused directly by the Home Office but by the voluntary actions of other human beings and thirdly, there was a long chain of events in between the control of the Home Office and the damage to the plaintiffs' yacht.

Home Office v Dorset Yacht

[7.60] *Home Office v Dorset Yacht Co Ltd* [1970] AC 1004 House of Lords

(footnotes omitted)

[The facts are stated in the judgment of Lord Reid.]

LORD REID: 1025 My Lords, on September 21, 1962, a party of Borstal trainees were working on Brownsea Island in Poole Harbour under the supervision and control of three Borstal officers. During that night seven of them escaped and went aboard a yacht which they found nearby. They set this yacht in motion and collided with the respondents' yacht which was moored in the vicinity. Then they boarded the respondents' yacht. Much damage was done to this yacht by the collision and some by the subsequent conduct of these trainees. The respondents sue the appellants, the Home Office, for the amount of this damage.

The case comes before your Lordships on a preliminary issue whether 1026 the Home Office or these Borstal officers owed any duty of care to the respondents capable of giving rise to a liability in damages. So it must be assumed that the respondents can prove all that they could prove on the pleadings if the case goes to trial. The question then is whether on that assumption the Home Office would be liable in damages. It is admitted that the Home Office would be vicariously liable if an action would lie against any of these Borstal officers.

Home Office v Dorset Yacht cont.

The facts which I think we must assume are that this party of trainees were in the lawful custody of the governor of the Portland Borstal institution and were sent by him to Brownsea Island on a training exercise in the custody and under the control of the three officers with instructions to keep them in custody and under control. But in breach of their instructions these officers simply went to bed leaving the trainees to their own devices. If they had obeyed their instructions they could and would have prevented these trainees from escaping. They would therefore be guilty of the disciplinary offences of contributing by carelessness or neglect to the escape of a prisoner and to the occurrence of loss, damage or injury to any person or property. All the escaping trainees had criminal records and five of them had a record of previous escapes from Borstal institutions. The three officers knew or ought to have known that these trainees would probably try to escape during the night, would take some vessel to make good their escape and would probably cause damage to it or some other vessel. There were numerous vessels moored in the harbour, and the trainees could readily board one of them. So it was a likely consequence of their neglect of duty that the respondents' yacht would suffer damage.

The case for the Home Office is that under no circumstances can Borstal officers owe any duty to any member of the public to take care to prevent trainees under their control or supervision from injuring him or his property. ... That case is based on three main arguments. First it is said that there is virtually no authority for imposing a duty of this kind. Secondly it is said that no person can be liable for a wrong done by another who is of full age and capacity and who is not the servant or acting on behalf of that person. And thirdly it is said that public policy (or the policy of the relevant legislation) requires that these officers should be immune from any such liability.

The first would at one time have been a strong argument. ...

In later years there has been a steady trend towards regarding the law of negligence as depending on principle so that, when a new point emerges, one should ask not whether it is covered by authority but whether recognised 1027 principles apply to it. *Donoghue v Stevenson* [1932] AC 562 may be regarded as a milestone, and the well-known passage in Lord Atkin's speech should I think be regarded as a statement of principle. It is not to be treated as if it were a statutory definition. It will require qualification in new circumstances. But I think that the time has come when we can and should say that it ought to apply unless there is some justification or valid explanation for its exclusion. ...

Even so, it is said that the respondents must fail because there is a general principle that no person can be responsible for the acts of another who is not his servant or acting on his behalf. But here the ground of liability is not responsibility for the acts of the escaping trainees; it is liability for damage caused by the carelessness of these officers in the knowledge that their carelessness would probably result in the trainees causing damage of this kind. So the question is really one of remoteness of damage. And I must consider to what extent the law regards the acts of another person as breaking the chain of causation between the defendant's carelessness and the damage to the plaintiff.

There is an obvious difference between a case where all the links between the carelessness and the damage are inanimate so that, looking back after the event, it can be seen that the damage was in fact the inevitable result of the careless act or omission and a case where one of the links is some human action. In the former case the damage was in fact caused by the careless conduct, however unforeseeable it might have been at the time that anything like that would happen. At one time the law was that unforeseeability was no defence: *In re Polemis and Furness, Withy & Co Ltd* [1921] 3 KB 560. But the law now is that there is no liability unless the damage was of a kind which was foreseeable: *Overseas Tankship (UK) Ltd v Morts Dock and Engineering Co Ltd (The Wagon Mound) (No 1))* [1961] AC 388.

On the other hand, if human action (other than an instinctive reaction) is one of the links in the chain it cannot be said that, looking back, the damage was the inevitable result of the careless conduct. No one in practice accepts the possible philosophic view that everything that happens was predetermined. Yet it has never been the law that the intervention 1028 of human action always prevents the ultimate damage from being regarded as having been caused by the original carelessness. The convenient phrase novus actus interveniens denotes those cases where such action is regarded as breaking the chain and preventing the damage from being held to be caused by the careless conduct. But every day there are many cases where, although one of the connecting links is deliberate human action, the law has no difficulty in holding that the defendant's conduct caused the plaintiff loss. …

In *Haynes v Harwood* [1935] 1 KB 146 Greer LJ said, at 156:

> If what is relied upon as novus actus interveniens is the very kind of thing which is likely to happen if the want of care which is alleged takes place, the principle embodied in the maxim is no defence. The whole question is whether or not, to use the words of the leading case, *Hadley v Baxendale* (1854) 9 Ex 341, the accident can be said to be "the natural and probable result" of the breach of duty.

….

1030 These cases show that, where human action forms one of the links between the original wrongdoing of the defendant and the loss suffered by the plaintiff, that action must at least have been something very likely to happen if it is not to be regarded as novus actus interveniens breaking the chain of causation. I do not think that a mere foreseeable possibility is or should be sufficient, for then the intervening human action can more properly be regarded as a new cause than as a consequence of the original wrongdoing. But if the intervening action was likely to happen I do not think that it can matter whether that action was innocent or tortious or criminal. Unfortunately, tortious or criminal action by a third party is often the "very kind of thing" which is likely to happen as a result of the wrongful or careless act of the defendant. And in the present case, on the facts which we must assume at this stage, I think that the taking of a boat by the escaping trainees and their unskilful navigation leading to damage to another vessel were the very kind of thing that these Borstal officers ought to have seen to be likely.

There was an attempt to draw a distinction between loss caused to the plaintiff by failure to control an adult of full capacity and loss caused by failure to control a child or mental defective. As regards causation, no doubt it is easier to infer novus actus interveniens in the case of an adult but that seems to me to be the only distinction. In the present case on the assumed facts there would in my view be no novus actus when the trainees damaged the respondents' property and I would therefore hold that damage to have been caused by the Borstal officers' negligence.

If the carelessness of the Borstal officers was the cause of the plaintiffs' loss, what justification is there for holding that they had no duty to take care? The first argument was that their right and power to control the trainees was purely statutory and that any duty to exercise that right and power was only a statutory duty owed to the Crown. I would agree, but there is very good authority for the proposition that if a person performs a statutory duty carelessly so that he causes damage to a member of the public which would not have happened if he had performed his duty properly he may be liable …

The reason for this is, I think, that Parliament deems it to be in the public interest that things otherwise unjustifiable should be done, and that those who do such things with due care should be immune from liability to persons who may suffer thereby. But Parliament cannot reasonably be supposed to have licensed those who do such things to act negligently in disregard of the interests of others so as to cause them needless damage.

1031 Where Parliament confers a discretion the position is not the same. Then there may, and almost certainly will, be errors of judgment in exercising such a discretion and Parliament cannot have intended that members of the public should be entitled to sue in respect of such errors. But there must

Home Office v Dorset Yacht cont.

come a stage when the discretion is exercised so carelessly or unreasonably that there has been no real exercise of the discretion which Parliament has conferred. The person purporting to exercise his discretion has acted in abuse or excess of his power. Parliament cannot be supposed to have granted immunity to persons who do that. The present case does not raise this issue because no discretion was given to these Borstal officers. They were given orders which they negligently failed to carry out. ...

1032 Finally I must deal with public policy. It is argued that it would be contrary to public policy to hold the Home Office or its officers liable to a member of the public for this carelessness – or, indeed, any failure of duty on their part. The basic question is: who shall bear the loss caused by that carelessness – the innocent respondents or the Home Office, who are vicariously liable for the conduct of their careless officers? I do not think that the argument for the Home Office can be put better than it was put by the Court of Appeals of New York in *Williams v State of New York* (1955) 127 NE 2d 545, 550:

> ... public policy also requires that the State be not held liable. To hold otherwise would impose a heavy responsibility upon the State, or dissuade the wardens and principal keepers of our prison system from continued experimentation with "minimum security" work details – which provide a means for encouraging better-risk prisoners to exercise their senses of responsibility and honor and so prepare themselves for their eventual return to society. Since 1917, the legislature has expressly provided for out-of-prison work, Correction Law, ss 182, and its intention should be respected without fostering the 1033 reluctance of prison officials to assign eligible men to minimum security work, lest they thereby give rise to costly claims against the State, or indeed inducing the State itself to terminate this "salutary procedure" looking toward rehabilitation.

It may be that public servants of the State of New York are so apprehensive, easily dissuaded from doing their duty and intent on preserving public funds from costly claims that they could be influenced in this way. But my experience leads me to believe that Her Majesty's servants are made of sterner stuff. So I have no hesitation in rejecting this argument. I can see no good ground in public policy for giving this immunity to a government department. I would dismiss this appeal.

LORD DIPLOCK: 1057 The specific question of law raised in this appeal may therefore be stated as: Is any duty of care to prevent the escape of a Borstal trainee from custody owed by the Home Office to persons whose property would be likely to be damaged by the tortious acts of the Borstal trainee if he escaped? ...

1061 In two cases, *Ellis v Home Office* [1953] 2 All ER 149, and *D'Arcy v Prison Commissioners, The Times*, November 17, 1955, it was assumed, in the absence of argument to the contrary, that the legal custodian of a prisoner detained in a prison owed to the plaintiff, another prisoner confined in the same prison, a duty of care to prevent the first prisoner from assaulting the plaintiff and causing him physical injuries. Unlike the present case, at the time of the tortious act of the prisoner for the consequences of which it was assumed that the custodian was liable the prisoner was in the actual custody of the defendant and the relationship between them gave to the defendant a continuing power of physical control over the acts of the prisoner. The relationship between the defendants and the plaintiffs in these two cases, too, bore no obvious analogy to that between the plaintiff and the defendant in the present case. In each of the cases the defendant in the exercise of a legal right and physical power of custody and control of the plaintiff had required him to be in a position in which 1062 the defendant ought reasonably and probably to have foreseen that he was likely to be injured by his fellow prisoner.

In my view, it is the combination of these two characteristics, one of the relationship between the defendant custodian and the person actually committing the wrong to the plaintiff and the other of the relationship between the defendant and the plaintiff, which supply the reason for the existence of the duty of care in these two cases ... The latter characteristic would be present also in the relationship

Home Office v Dorset Yacht cont.

between the defendant and any other person admitted to the prison who sustained similar damage from the tortious act of a prisoner, since the Home Office as occupiers and managers of the prison have the legal right to control the admission and the movements of a visitor while he is on the prison premises. A similar duty of care would thus be owed to him. But I do not think that, save as a deliberate policy decision, any proposition of law based on the decisions in these two cases would be wide enough to extend to a duty to take reasonable care to prevent the escape of a prisoner from actual physical custody and control owed to a person whose property is situated outside the prison premises and is damaged by the tortious act of the prisoner after his escape ... 1063 The result of the survey of previous authorities can be summarised in the words of Dixon J in *Smith v Leurs*, 70 CLR 256, 262:

> The general rule is that one man is under no duty of controlling another man to prevent his doing damage to a third. There are, however, special relations which are the source of a duty of this nature.

From the previous decisions of the English courts, in particular those in *Ellis v Home Office* [1953] 2 All ER 149 and *D'Arcy v Prison Commissioners*, *The Times*, November 17, 1955, which I accept as correct, it is possible to arrive by induction at an established proposition of law as respects one of those special relations, viz.:

> A is responsible for damage caused to the person or property of B by the tortious act of C (a person responsible in law for his own acts) where the relationship between A and C has the characteristics (1) that A has the legal right to detain C in penal custody and to control his acts while in custody; (2) that A is actually exercising his legal right of custody of C at the time of C's tortious act and (3) that A if he had taken reasonable care in the exercise of his right of custody could have prevented C from doing the tortious act which caused damage to the person or property of B; and where also the relationship between A and B has the characteristics (4) that at the time of C's tortious act A has the legal right to control the situation of B or his property as respects physical proximity to C and (5) that A can 1064 reasonably foresee that B is likely to sustain damage to his person or property if A does not take reasonable care to prevent C from doing tortious acts of the kind which he did.

Upon the facts which your Lordships are required to assume for the purposes of the present appeal the relationship between the defendant, A, and the Borstal trainee, C, did possess characteristics (1) and (3) but did not possess characteristic (2), while the relationship between the defendant, A, and the plaintiff, B, did possess characteristic (5) but did not possess characteristic (4).

What your Lordships have to decide as respects each of the relationships is whether the missing characteristic is essential to the existence of the duty or whether the facts assumed for the purposes of this appeal disclose some other characteristic which if substituted for that which is missing would produce a new proposition of law which ought to be true. ... Nevertheless, any new sub-category will form part of the English law of civil wrongs and must be consistent with its general principles.

Since the tortious act of the Borstal trainees took place after they had ceased to be in the actual custody of the Borstal officers, what your Lordships are concerned with in the relationship between the Home Office and Borstal trainees is the responsibility of the Home Office to detain them in custody. To detain them at all would be to commit a civil wrong to them unless the legal right to detain them were conferred upon the custodians by statute or at common law. In the case of Borstal trainees that right is conferred by statute, viz., section 13 of the *Prison Act, 1952*. This makes lawful their detention within the cartilage of the Borstal institution and outside its cartilage in the custody or under the control of a Borstal officer. This section does not impose upon the Borstal officers or upon the Home Office ... any responsibility to continue to keep trainees in custody. The statute from which the right to detain is derived thus only gives the broadest indication of the purpose of the detention and confers upon the Home Secretary very wide powers to determine by subordinate legislation the way in which the powers of custody and control of Borstal trainees should be exercised by the officers of the prison service. In exercising his rule-making power, at any rate, it would be inconsistent with what are now

Home Office v Dorset Yacht cont.

recognised principles of English law to suggest that he owed a duty of care capable of giving rise to any liability in civil law to avoid making a rule the observance of which was likely to result in damage to a private citizen. For a careless exercise of his rule-making power he is responsible to Parliament alone. The only limitation on this power which courts of law have jurisdiction to enforce depends not on the civil law concept of negligence, but on the public law concept of ultra vires. ...

1065 If these [statutory] instructions [to the officers] with their emphasis on co-operation rather than coërcion are to be followed in a working party outside the confines of a "closed" Borstal or in an "open" Borstal they must inevitably involve some risk of an individual trainee's escaping from custody and indulging again in the same kind of criminal activities that led to his sentence of Borstal training and which are likely to cause damage to the property of another person. To adopt a method of supervision of trainees still subject to detention which affords them any opportunity of escape is, as Lord Dilhorne has pointed out, an act or omission which it can be reasonably foreseen may have as its consequence some injury to another person. But the same is true of every decision made by the Home Office, through the appropriate officers of the Borstal service, in the exercise of the statutory power to release a Borstal trainee from detention in less than two years from the time of his being sentenced or to release him temporarily on parole.

... But the analogy between "negligence" at common law and the careless exercise of statutory powers breaks down where the act or omission complained of is not of a kind which would itself give rise to a cause of action at common law if it were not authorised by the statute. To relinquish intentionally or inadvertently the custody and control of a person responsible in law for his own acts is not an act or omission which, independently of any statute, would give rise to a cause of action at common law against the custodian on the part of another person who subsequently sustained tortious damage at the hands of the person released ... 1067 In the instant case, it is the interest of the Borstal trainee himself which is most directly affected by any decision to release him and by any system of relaxed control while he is still in custody that is intended to develop his sense of personal responsibility and so afford him an opportunity to escape. Directly affected also are the interests of other members of the community of trainees subject to the common system of control, and indirectly affected by the system of control while under detention and of release under supervision is the general public interest in the reformation of young offenders and the prevention of crime.

These interests, unlike those of a person who sustains damage to his property or person by the tortious act or omission of another, do not fall within any category of property or rights recognised in English law as entitled to protection by a civil action for damages.... If the reasonable man when directing his mind to the act or omission which has this consequence ought to have in contemplation persons in all the categories directly affected and also the general public interest in the reformation of young offenders, there is no criterion by which a court can assess where the balance lies between the weight to be given to one interest and that to be given to another....

It is not the function of the court. for which it would be ill-suited, to substitute its own view of the appropriate means for that of the department or authority by granting a remedy by way of a civil action at law to a private citizen 1068 adversely affected by the way in which the discretion has been exercised. Its function is confined in the first instance to deciding whether the act or omission complained of fell within the statutory limits imposed upon the department's or authority's discretion. Only if it did not would the court have jurisdiction to determine whether or not the act or omission, not being justified by the statute, constituted an actionable infringement of the plaintiff's rights in civil law.

These considerations lead me to the conclusion that neither the intentional release of a Borstal trainee under supervision, nor the unintended escape of a Borstal trainee still under detention which was the consequence of the application of a system of relaxed control intentionally adopted by the Home Office as conducive to the reformation of trainees, can have been intended by Parliament to

Home Office v Dorset Yacht cont.

give rise to any cause of action on the part of any private citizen unless the system adopted was so unrelated to any purpose of reformation that no reasonable person could have reached a bona fide conclusion that it was conducive to that purpose. Only then would the decision to adopt it be ultra vires in public law. …

But although the system of control, including the sub delegation of discretion to subordinate officers, may itself be intra vires, an act or omission of a subordinate officer employed in the administration of the system may nevertheless be ultra vires if it falls outside the limits of the discretion delegated to him – ie, if it is done contrary to instructions which he has received from the Home Office. …

Where the act or omission is done in pursuance of the officer's instructions, the court may have to form its own view as to what is in the interests of Borstal trainees, but only to the limited extent of determining whether or not any reasonable person could bona fide come to the conclusion that the trainee causing the damage or other trainees in the same custody could be benefited in any way by the act or omission … If on the other hand the officer's act or omission is done contrary to his instructions it is not protected by the public law doctrine of intra vires. Its actionability falls to be determined by the civil law principles of negligence … … A cause of action is capable of arising from failure by the custodian to take reasonable care to prevent the detainee from escaping, if his escape was the consequence of an act or omission of the custodian falling outside the limits of the discretion delegated to him under the statute.

The practical effect of this would be that [there would be] no liability for such an escape in the Home Office for "negligence" [by an officer whose job it was to classify trainees].. … But to say this does not dispose of the present appeal, for the allegations of negligence against the Borstal officers are consistent with their having acted outside any discretion delegated to them and having disregarded their instructions as to the precautions which they should take to prevent members of the working party of trainees from escaping from Brownsea Island. Whether they had or not could only be determined at the trial of the action.

But this is only a condition precedent to the existence of any liability.

1070 Even if the acts and omissions of the Borstal officers alleged in the particulars of negligence were done in breach of their instructions and so were ultra vires in public law it does not follow that they were also done in breach of any duty of care owed by the officers to the plaintiff in civil law. …

What distinguishes a Borstal trainee who has escaped from one who has been duly released from custody is his liability to recapture, and the distinctive added risk which is a reasonably foreseeable consequence of a failure to exercise due care in preventing him from escaping is the likelihood that in order to elude pursuit immediately upon the discovery of his absence the escaping trainee may steal or appropriate and damage property which is situated in the vicinity of the place of detention from which he has escaped.

So long as Parliament is content to leave the general risk of damage from criminal acts to lie where it falls without any remedy except against the criminal himself the courts would be exceeding their limited function in developing the common law to meet changing conditions if they were to recognise a duty of care to prevent criminals escaping from penal custody owed to a wider category of members of the public than those whose property was exposed to an exceptional added risk by the adoption of a custodial system for young offenders which increased the likelihood of their escape unless due care was taken by those responsible for their custody.

I should therefore hold that any duty of a Borstal officer to use reasonable care to prevent a Borstal trainee from escaping from his custody was owed only to persons whom he could reasonably foresee had property 1071 situate in the vicinity of the place of detention of the detainee which the detainee was likely to steal or to appropriate and damage in the course of eluding immediate pursuit and

Home Office v Dorset Yacht cont.

recapture. Whether or not any person fell within this category would depend upon the facts of the particular case including the previous criminal and escaping record of the individual trainee concerned and the nature of the place from which he escaped. ...

In the present appeal the place from which the trainees escaped was an island from which the only means of escape would presumably be a boat accessible from the shore of the island. There is thus material fit for consideration at the trial for holding that the plaintiff, as the owner of a boat moored off the island, fell within the category of persons to whom a duty of care to prevent the escape of the trainees was owed by the officers responsible for their custody ...

[Lord Morris of Borth-y-gest, and Lord Pearson agreed that the appeal should be dismissed. Viscount Dilhorne dissented.]

[7.65] **Notes&Questions**

1. In *Dorset Yacht*, the plaintiffs faced two major difficulties that made the case a "hard case". The first was that the defendant was a public authority, in this case, a government department (see Chapter 11). The second was that the damage done was done not directly by the defendant's officers, but by third parties, who were human beings and therefore would normally be regarded as responsible for themselves.
2. It is notable that Lord Reid's judgment about the duty of care turns on his treatment of causation. This is a good time to note that although in the study of torts we notionally divide negligence into three main elements – duty, breach and causation of harm – in practice the elements frequently run together. The reason for this is that the same kinds of issues of foreseeability arise in all the elements of the cause of action, and so sometimes the courts do not maintain the distinctions between the elements as strongly as textbooks normally do.

[7.70] The following case is the third in the line of profoundly important cases in the expansion of the duty of care. Here the plaintiffs also faced extra hurdles in that the damage suffered created a defective structure which might or might not be characterised as pure economic loss. A second hurdle was that the plaintiffs also were attempting to sue a public authority. Issues surrounding suing public authorities are considered in Chapter 11. Although the approach taken in the following case was profoundly influential in England, it was never entirely accepted in Australia. It is included here for largely historical purposes only.

Anns v Merton London Borough Council

[7.75] *Anns v Merton London Borough Council* [1978] AC 728 House of Lords

(footnotes omitted)

[Anns, the plaintiffs/respondents, were lessees on long leases of seven flats in a block. Some of the plaintiffs were original lessees; others had leases by assignment. The building was completed in 1962. Structural movement caused cracks in walls and sloping of floors which appeared in 1970. Plaintiffs brought an action against the builders for damages for breach of contract and against the council for damages in negligence alleging that the plans required foundations greater in width than three feet, but they were in fact two feet six inches, and that the council had omitted to inspect or failed to discover the inadequacy of the foundations on inspection. The council had a power in the statute to

Anns v Merton London Borough Council cont.

require changes to building plans and a power to inspect the foundations of buildings. In the trial the judge held the action was statute-barred because time began to run from the date of the purchase of each of the properties and that was six years before the writs had issued. The Court of Appeal allowed the appeal, holding that the cause of action did not accrue until the person who was capable of suing discovered the damage. The House of Lords held that because there was some physical damage to the property, this could be classified as property damage rather than pure economic loss, and that the action was not statute-barred because the cause of action only arose when the state of the building was such that there was present or imminent danger to the health or safety of the persons occupying it. They then went on to consider the test for the duty of care in such situations.]

LORD WILBERFORCE: 751 Through the trilogy of cases in this House – *Donoghue v Stevenson* [1932] AC 562, *Hedley Byrne & Co Ltd v Heller & Partners Ltd* [1964] AC 465, and *Dorset Yacht Co Ltd v Home Office* [1970] AC 1004, the position has now been reached that in order to establish that a duty of care arises in a particular situation, it is not necessary to bring the facts of that situation within those of previous situations in which a duty of care has been held to exist. Rather the question has to be approached in two stages. First, one has to ask whether, as between the alleged wrongdoer and the person who has suffered damage there is a sufficient relationship of proximity or neighbourhood such that, in the reasonable contemplation of the former, carelessness on his part may be likely to cause damage to the latter – in which case a prima facie duty of care arises. Secondly, if the first question is answered affirmatively, it is necessary to consider whether there are any considerations which ought to negative, or to reduce or limit the scope of the duty or the class of person to whom it is owed or the damages to which a breach of it may give rise: see *Dorset Yacht case* [1970] AC 1004 at 1027 per Lord Reid. Examples of this are *Hedley Byrne's case* [1964] AC 465 where the class of potential plaintiffs was reduced to those shown to have relied upon the correctness of statements made, and *Weller & Co v Foot & Mouth Disease Research Institute* [1966] 1 QB 569; and (I cite these merely as illustrations, without discussion) cases about "economic loss" where, a duty having been held to exist, the nature of the recoverable damages was limited: see *SCM (United Kingdom) Ltd v W J Whittall & Son Ltd* [1971] 1 QB 337 and *Spartan Steel & Alloys Ltd v Martin & Co (Contractors) Ltd* [1973] QB 27. ...

[Lord Wilberforce then went on to argue that a consideration which might negative a duty of care would be whether the council was immune from suit because its decision was either ultra vires or where the act or omission could be characterised as policy or operational in nature. If it were to be regarded as a policy decision then the public authority could not be sued. He held that here the act at issue was operational and a duty did arise to owners and occupiers of a building because a reasonable building inspector would realise that they might be injured. Lords Diplock, Russell and Simon agreed with Lord Wilberforce; Lord Salmon took a similar approach, but did not refer to the policy/operation distinction.]

[7.80] **Notes&Questions**

1. The approach to duty taken by Lord Wilberforce in the two-stage test in *Anns* was rejected by Mason J in *Sutherland Shire Council v Heyman* (1985) 157 CLR 424 (see [7.100]) and has never been accepted per se in Australia. However, *Anns* illustrates the then trend, which also existed in Australia, of treating the duty of care in an increasingly expansive and principled way. Some issues considered in *Anns* remain pertinent to Australia, including the treatment of statutory authorities generally (see Chapter 11).

2. In *Murphy v Brentwood* [1991] 1 AC 398, the House of Lords determined that it would not follow *Anns v Merton London Borough Council* [1978] AC 728. In so doing the House in *Murphy v Brentwood* [1991] 1 AC 398 considered it had the support of the High Court of Australia in *Sutherland Shire Council v Heyman* (1985) 157 CLR 424. In both *Murphy v Brentwood* [1991] 1 AC 398 and *Department of the Environment v Thomas Batey & Son Ltd* [1991] 1 AC 499, Lord Wilberforce's view that the damage in such cases as these is physical rather than economic was rejected.

Principle or category

[7.85] The law relating to the duty of care can be seen as the constant development along a line created by the tension between desire for a unifying principle underlying the tort of negligence and desire for certainty within particular categories of negligence. Cases such as *Anns v Merton Borough District Council* [1978] AC 728 are examples of the courts taking a highly principled approach to the duty of care. Cases that we discuss below include some that reject a "very" generalised principled approach and seek to confine the duty of care according to categories so that the doctrine of precedent binds at a lower level of abstraction. Both of these approaches are important. The following chapters in this book are labelled according to categories of negligence. Such categories are defined by the kind of harm suffered (personal injury, property damage, pure economic loss etc), by whether the wrong was an act, or omission or words, by whether the plaintiff or the defendant had particular characteristics (employer/employee, private individuals etc). So if we think of *Donoghue v Stevenson* [1932] AC 562 as the paradigm category, it is in the category of personal injury caused by an act between private individuals (who, in that case, were manufacturer and consumer). Usually, once a category becomes established it is easy to predict when a duty of care will arise within that category. However, the categories may be modified by the search for principle. Further modification may be made by legislation. The starkest example of this is the legislation arising in all the Australian jurisdictions following the insurance crisis of 2001 and 2002, some of which attempted to modify certain aspects of the duty of care (see [1.60] for a brief discussion of the reform process).

The approaches to the duty of care have differed amongst the jurisdictions that influence Australia. We have already seen some of the developments in the English jurisprudence. In the 1980s, the Australian High Court began to develop a distinctly Australian jurisprudence, which included an approach to negligence based on a formulation of proximity by Deane J and which was taken up by the majority of the High Court. This formulation was regarded as especially important when dealing with cases which would not traditionally have been regarded as giving rise to a duty of care; that is, cases which in some way were novel in that they seemed to call for expansion of the duty of care in existing categories or the creation of new categories. In the following case the problem for the plaintiff was that she was claiming for psychiatric harm she suffered because of negligence causing harm to a third person, her husband. Her situation was not one which would have been regarded as giving rise to a duty of care 20 years earlier. How was the High Court to deal with this situation now?

Jaensch v Coffey

[7.90] *Jaensch v Coffey* (1984) 155 CLR 549 High Court of Australia
(footnotes omitted)

[The plaintiff was the wife of a motor cyclist seriously injured by a vehicle negligently driven by the defendant. The plaintiff did not see or hear the accident or its aftermath at the scene of the collision. But she suffered well-founded fear and shock that her husband might die, partly by reason of what she saw of her husband at the hospital to which he was taken and partly by reason of what she was told by the hospital staff. Although her husband in fact survived, she developed a psychiatric illness. The plaintiff recovered damages against the defendant in the Supreme Court of South Australia, and this was upheld by the Full Court. The defendant then appealed to the High Court.]

DEANE J: 578 The closest that the common law has come to providing a general remedy in respect of injurious conduct is the modern law of negligence with its hypothetical "neighbour" and associated test of 579 "reasonable foreseeability". ... A "neighbour" was identified as being, in the view of the common law, a person who is "so closely and directly affected by my act that I ought reasonably to have [her or him] in contemplation as being so affected when I am directing my mind to the acts or omissions which are called in question": [1932] AC 562 at 580. The significance of the requirement contained in the words "so closely and directly affected ... that" is that they constitute a control test upon the test of reasonable foreseeability. ... The "neighbour" requirement ... was a substantive and independent one which was deliberately and expressly introduced to limit or control the test of reasonable foreseeability.

The more than 50 years which have passed since the decision in *Donoghue v Stevenson* [1932] AC 562 have been marked by an apparently general ascendancy of the test of reasonable foreseeability in the law of negligence, at least in cases involving physical damage to person or property. ... Overall, one cannot but be conscious of a common, although mistaken, tendency to see the test of reasonable foreseeability as a panacea and, what is of more importance for present purposes, to refer to it as if it were, from the viewpoint of principle, the sole determinant of the duty of care ... what can properly be deduced from Mason J's remarks [in *Wyong Shire Council v Shirt* (1980) 146 CLR 40 at 44] is that, to adopt and qualify words used by Lord Reid in the *Dorset Yacht Co case* [1970] AC 1004 at 1027, the time has come when an equation between reasonable foreseeability of injury and a duty of care under the law of negligence can be accepted in cases involving ordinary physical injury unless there be "some justification or valid explanation for its exclusion". That approach corresponds generally with that adopted by Lord Wilberforce in the oft-cited passage from his judgment in *Anns v Merton London Borough Council* [1978] AC 728 at 751-752. Upon analysis, it reflects an acceptance, rather than a denial, of the existence of overriding limitations upon the test of reasonable foreseeability. ...

583 Reasonable foreseeability on its own indicates no more than that such a duty will exist if, and to the extent that, it is not precluded or modified by some applicable overriding requirement or limitation. It is to do little more than to state a truism to say that the essential function of such requirements or limitations is to confine the existence of a duty to take reasonable care to avoid reasonably foreseeable injury in the circumstances or class of case in which it is the policy of the law to admit it. ... The outcome of the present appeal largely turns upon the extent to which that [the proximity] requirement operates to preclude a common law duty of care arising in cases involving injury in the form of nervous shock sustained by a person by reason of actual or apprehended physical injury to another. That question must be approached in the context of what is involved in the notion of a relationship of "proximity". ...

584 Lord Atkin did not seek to identify the precise content of the requirement of the relationship of "proximity" which he identified as a limitation upon the test of reasonable foreseeability. It was left as a broad and flexible touchstone of the circumstances in which the common law would admit the existence of a relevant duty. ... It is directed to the relationship between the parties so far as it is

Jaensch v Coffey cont.

relevant. ... It involves the notion of nearness or closeness and embraces physical proximity ... between the person or property of the plaintiff and the person or property of the defendant, circumstantial proximity such as an overriding relationship of employer and employee or of a professional man and his client and causal proximity in the sense of the closeness or directness of the relationship between the particular act or cause of action and the injury sustained. ... The identity and relative importance of the considerations relative to an issue of proximity will obviously vary in different classes of case. ...

585 This does not mean that there is scope ... for it to be treated as a question of fact to be resolved merely by reference to the particular relationship between a plaintiff and defendant in the circumstances of a particular case. The requirement of a "relationship of proximity" is a touchstone and control of the *categories* of case in which the common law will admit the existence of a duty of care ... a question of law to be resolved by the processes of legal reasoning by induction and deduction. The identification of the content of the criteria or rules which reflect that requirement in developing areas of the law should not, however, be either ostensibly or actually divorced from the considerations of public policy which underlie and enlighten it.

[His Honour then reviewed the history of duties in respect of nervous shock, particularly in relation to his thesis that the test of reasonable foreseeability of harm should be restricted by considerations of proximity and continued:]

604 The limitations upon the ordinary test of reasonable foreseeability in cases of mere psychiatric injury are conveniently stated in negative form. ... The first ... is that reasonable foreseeability will not suffice to give rise to a duty of care to avoid psychiatric injury unassociated with conventional physical injury: a duty of care will not arise unless risk of injury in that particular form was reasonably foreseeable. [A second is] that, on the present state of the law, such a duty of care will not exist unless the reasonably foreseeable psychiatric injury was sustained as a result of the death, injury or peril of someone other than the person whose carelessness is alleged to have caused the injury; there is no need to consider here whether this limitation should be more widely stated as excluding such a duty of care unless the carelessness was in any event wrongful in the sense that it involved a breach of duty of care owed to the person who suffered or was at risk of physical injury. ... Both are satisfied in the present case and it is unnecessary to determine whether either or each of them is properly to be seen as part of the requirement of proximity of relationship or as constituting some other and special controlling rule based on policy considerations. As at present advised, I am inclined to see them as necessary criteria of the existence of the requisite proximity relationship in the sense that, for policy reasons, the relationship will not be adjudged as being "so" close "as" to give rise to a duty of care unless they be satisfied. ...

[His Honour went on to a further discussion of the cases to determine whether there were further limitations in the area of nervous shock whereby proximity requirements limited the test of reasonable foreseeability and rejected the view that the plaintiff must be within the area of physical danger from an accident herself. He continued:]

606 On the other hand, it would seem reasonably clear that the requisite duty relationship will not, in the present state of the law, exist in a case where mere psychiatric injury results from subsequent contact, away from the scene of the accident and its aftermath, with a person suffering from the effects of the accident. An example of psychiatric injury suffered as a result of such post-accident contact is that which may result from the contact involved in the nursing or care of a close relative during a period subsequent to immediate post-accident treatment: see, for example, *Pratt* [*Pratt v Pratt* [1975] VR 378].

There are at least two possible rationales of the distinction. ... One such rationale lies in considerations of physical proximity, in the sense of space and time, between the accident and its

Jaensch v Coffey cont.

immediate aftermath on the one hand and the injury on the other. The other lies in 607 causal proximity in that in the one class of case the psychiatric injury results from the impact of matters which themselves formed part of the accident and its aftermath, such as the actual occurrence of death or injury in the course of it, whereas, in the other class of case, the psychiatric injury has resulted from contact with more remote consequences such as the subsequent effect of the accident upon an injured person. ... On balance, I have come to the conclusion that the second, which justifies the line of demarcation by reference to considerations of causal proximity, is to be preferred as being the less arbitrary and better attuned both to legal principle and considerations of public policy. ... It would, in my view, be both arbitrary and out of accord with common sense to draw the borderline between liability and no liability according to whether the plaintiff encountered the aftermath of the accident at the actual scene or at the hospital to which the injured person had been quickly taken. ... What, then, is the effect of the fact that her nervous shock was caused by what she was told, as well as what she observed, at the hospital? ...

609 [T]he authorities plainly indicate that the overriding limitation upon the test of reasonable foreseeability does not preclude recovery in a case, such as the present, where the psychiatric injury was sustained as a result of the combined effect of what a plaintiff himself or herself observed and what he or she was told while at the scene of the accident or its aftermath. ... Indeed, while the question was not raised in argument and it is unnecessary to express a concluded view upon it, the position would appear to be that provided that psychiatric injury resulted from what was seen or heard at the scene of the accident or its aftermath, the fact that the injury was subsequently, and reasonably foreseeably, aggravated as a result of being told of the deterioration or death of the person injured will neither preclude recovery nor require apportionment between different causes. ... It follows that neither the requirement of proximity of relationship nor any other control upon the test of reasonable foreseeability operated, in the circumstances of the case, to preclude the existence of a common law duty of care owed to Mrs Coffey in respect of the psychiatric injury which she sustained. ...

[Gibbs CJ, Murphy, Brennan, and Dawson JJ delivered concurring judgments. The appeal was dismissed.]

[7.95] **Notes&Questions**

In the above case Gibbs CJ followed the analysis of Lord Wilberforce in the *Anns case* to reach a conclusion concurring with that of Deane J. In a brief judgment, Murphy J said that persons causing damage by breach of duty should be liable for all loss unless there are acceptable reasons of public policy for limiting recovery (at 556). He was not satisfied that there were acceptable reasons of public policy for limiting recovery here (at 558). Brennan J, though concurring in the result, expressed the duty considerations in nervous shock cases in a manner which declined to recognise limitations by special reference to proximity upon the general rule that the governing consideration is reasonable foreseeability (especially at 572). He considered that those cases in which special limitations upon the "neighbour" principle might be required, which he equated with the test of reasonable foreseeability, were generally, though not exclusively, cases of economic loss (especially at 574-576). Dawson J said that the basic test of liability in negligence for nervous shock was whether injury of that kind was reasonably foreseeable in all the circumstances of the particular case, and whether there was some other limit upon the recovery remained a matter of controversy. It was not necessary to decide that controversy for the purposes of deciding the appeal (at 611-612). Obviously it was not, since Brennan J came to the same decision as Gibbs CJ and Deane J.

Deane J's formulation basing the duty on the notion of proximity became profoundly influential. In the following case he expanded his explanation of it. Brennan J rejected Deane J's judgment and, as you will read below, Brennan J's judgment became highly influential in its turn. In this case, the plaintiffs' difficulty was that they were trying to bring an action in negligence against a public authority (traditionally a difficult thing to do) and they were trying to bring an action for a kind of harm for which traditionally negligent actions could not lie-pure economic loss. Indeed the first question the court had to deal with was deciding whether this was pure economic loss.

Sutherland Shire Council v Heyman

[7.100] *Sutherland Shire Council v Heyman* (1985) 157 CLR 424 High Court of Australia

(footnotes omitted)

[The plaintiffs bought a house in 1975 which distorted so that it leaked badly within a year, which after review, was determined to be due to inadequate footings. A permit had been issued by the defendant for the construction of the house in 1968, and there was evidence that if a proper inspection of the footings had been made in relation to their adequacy as required by the permit, which the council had power to carry out, they would easily have been found to be inadequate. But whether a council inspection which had been made extended to the footings was unclear. The trial judge found the council not negligent in approving the footings but guilty of negligence in its inspections and awarded damages, an appeal to the Court of Appeal was dismissed, and the council appealed to the High Court:]

MASON J: 449 The respondents' case was that the appellant was negligent in two respects: (1) in approving plans for the erection of the house, the foundations of which were inadequate and unstable and did not comply with the Act and ordinances; and (2) in failing to ensure that the foundations were inspected properly or at all. ...

456 As the evidence does not support a finding that the footings were inspected and merely supports the finding that the appellant was careless either in failing to inspect or in inspecting, the respondents must establish that the appellant was liable in negligence whether it inspected or failed to inspect. The critical question then is whether the appellant is liable on either basis. The answer depends on the general principles of the common law regulating the liability of a public authority in negligence in respect of its act or omission in the course of performing its statutory responsibilities. The application of the law of negligence, itself in course of evolutionary development, to public authorities has presented special problems. These problems are referable mainly to the character of a public authority as a body entrusted by statute with functions to be performed in the public interest or for public purposes. Some adjustment therefore needs to be made to accommodate the application of the principles and concepts of negligence to the acts and omissions of such a body. In what circumstances, if at all, does a public authority come under a common law duty of care in relation to the performance or non-performance of its functions? Can a cause of action for breach of a common law duty of care co-exist with a cause of action for breach of statutory duty? In what circumstances, if at all, is a public authority liable in negligence for loss or damage suffered by another through the fault of a third party, when the authority fails to perform a statutory function which has as its object the prevention or mitigation of loss or damage of that kind? To what extent are these questions affected by the circumstance that a public authority exercises policy-making and discretionary functions? These are the major issues of principle which lie behind the present appeal. ...

Sutherland Shire Council v Heyman cont.

458 It is now well settled that a public authority may be subject to a common law duty of care when it exercises a statutory power or performs a statutory duty. The principle that when statutory powers are conferred they must be exercised with reasonable care, so that if those who exercise them could by reasonable precaution have prevented an injury which has been occasioned, and was likely to be occasioned, by their exercise, damages for negligence may be recovered (*Caledonian Collieries Ltd v Speirs* (1957) 97 CLR 202 at 219-20; *Benning v Wong* (1969) 122 CLR 249 at 307-8) has been applied mainly to private Acts. However, it has been frequently applied in Australia to public authorities, notably public utilities, exercising powers under public statutes: *Sermon v Commissioner of Railways* (1907) 5 CLR 239 at 245, 254; *Essendon Corporation v McSweeney* (1914) 17 CLR 524 at 530; *Metropolitan Gas Co v Melbourne Corporation* (1924) 35 CLR 186 at 193-4, 197; *South Australian Railways Commissioner v Barnes* (1927) 40 CLR 179; *Cox Bros (Australia) Ltd v Commissioner of Waterworks* (1933) 50 CLR 108; *South Australian Railways Commissioner v Riggs* (1951) 84 CLR 586 at 589-90; *Voli v Inglewood Shire Council* (1963) 110 CLR 74 at 88, 89, 100; *Birch v Central West County District Council* (1969) 119 CLR 652). While some early statements of the principle suggest that the power given by statute is conditioned upon it being exercised without negligence so that negligent exercise amounts to an excess of authority (*McSweeney* at 530; *Metropolitan Gas Co*, at 197), the better view has always been that the cause of action in negligence arises under the principle by virtue of a breach of a duty of care existing at common law (*Geddes v Bann Reservoir Proprietors* (1878) 3 App Cas 430 at 455-6 ... 459 And, at least since the decision in *Fisher v Ruislip-Northwood Urban District Council and Middlesex County Council* [1945] KB 584, esp at 592-3, 615, 619-20, it has been generally accepted that, unless the statute manifests a contrary intention, a public authority which enters upon an exercise of statutory power may place itself in a relationship to members of the public which imports a common law duty to take care. ...

Generally speaking, a public authority which is under no statutory obligation to exercise a power comes under no common law 460 duty of care to do so (see *Revesz v Commonwealth of Australia* (1951) 51 SR (NSW) 63). But an authority may by its conduct place itself in such a position that it attracts a duty of care which calls for exercise of the power. A common illustration is provided by the cases in which an authority in the exercise of its functions has created a danger, thereby subjecting itself to a duty of care for the safety of others which must be discharged by an exercise of its statutory powers or by giving a warning ... There are other situations in which an authority's occupation of premises (*Voli*) or its ownership or control of a structure in a highway or of a public place (*Buckle v Bayswater Road Road Board* (1936) 57 CLR 259 at 286-7; *Aiken v Kingborough Corporation* (1939) 62 CLR 179) attracts to it a duty of care. In these cases the statute facilitates the existence of a common law duty of care. ...

461 And then there are situations in which a public authority, not otherwise under a relevant duty, may place itself in such a position that others rely on it to take care for their safety so that the authority comes under a duty of care calling for positive action. ...

464 If this be accepted, as in my opinion it should be, there will be cases in which the plaintiff's reasonable reliance will arise out of a general dependence on an authority's performance of its function with due care, without the need for contributing conduct on the part of a defendant or action to his detriment on the part of a plaintiff. Reliance or dependence in this sense is in general the product of the grant (and exercise) of powers designed to prevent or minimize a risk of personal injury or disability, recognized by the legislature as being of such magnitude or complexity that individuals cannot, or may not, take adequate steps for their own protection. This situation generates on one side (the individual) a general expectation that the power will be exercised and on the other side (the authority) a realization that there is a general reliance or dependence on its exercise of power (see Shapo: *The Duty to Act* (1977) pp 95-96). The control of air traffic, the safety inspection of aircraft and the fighting of a fire in a building by a fire authority (but cf *Bennett & Wood Ltd v Orange City Council*

Sutherland Shire Council v Heyman cont.

(1967) 67 SR (NSW) 426) may well be examples of this type of function. Whether the inspection of motor vehicles for registration purposes could generate such a general reliance is a more complex question (cf *Rutherford v Attorney-General* [1976] 1 NZLR 403 at 408-14). Whether the Council in the present case owed a duty of care to the respondents on this footing is a matter which I leave for later consideration. ...

466 In this case it matters not whether the damage sustained by the respondents is characterized as being economic loss or physical damage. It is how the affair stands, viewed from the appellant's perspective, that is important in relation to a duty of care. The foreseeable consequences of a failure to inspect were physical damage to a particular building resulting from faulty foundations and the incurring of expenditure by a subsequent owner in rectifying the defects. To deny the existence of a duty of care solely by reason of the legal characterization of the respondents' loss as economic – because the structure was flawed before they acquired property in it – is to ignore the significance of other circumstances in which the loss was sustained, circumstances which the appellant could readily foresee. One of the circumstances is that the respondents' loss reflects expenditure which averts personal injury to those who occupy the building.

In saying this I am not suggesting that a duty of care arises here simply because the authority could foresee the possibility of economic loss ensuing as a result of its failure to inspect. If there is a firm foundation for a duty of care in this case, it is to be found in reliance or dependence rather than mere foreseeability of physical damage or economic loss. Inspection generally results in the issue of a certificate in which event the principles regulating liability for negligent misstatement apply. ... 467 Because liability in respect of a certificate depends not only on foreseeability but also on reliance it is a fortiori that liability in negligence for inspection or failure to inspect, not resulting in the issue of a certificate, depends on foreseeable and reasonable reliance or dependence. I have difficulty with the notion that liability for negligent inspection can be grounded on foreseeability alone unless negligent inspection causes damage to the plaintiff in the sense of increasing the damage he would otherwise have sustained. If the authority is under no liability for negligent failure to inspect, how can it expose itself to liability by embarking on a negligent exercise of its power to inspect, without causing damage in the sense already mentioned? ...

468 So, if it is otherwise legitimate to hold that a public authority is under a common law duty of care in relation to a statutory power to inspect buildings in course of erection, the statute having as its object the prevention of injury from dangers arising from faulty construction, the fact that breach of the duty takes the form of a negligent omission is no reason for denying the existence of the duty or that it is a cause which materially contributes to the injury that ensues ...

Anns decided that a duty of care cannot arise in relation to acts and omissions which reflect the policy-making and discretionary elements involved in the exercise of statutory discretions. ...

469 The distinction between policy and operational factors is not easy to formulate, but the dividing line between them will be observed if we recognize that a public authority is under no duty of care in relation to decisions which involve or are dictated by financial, economic, social or political factors or constraints. Thus budgetary allocations and the constraints which they entail in terms of allocation of resources cannot be made the subject of a duty of care. But it may be otherwise when the courts are called upon to apply a standard of care to action or inaction that is merely the product of administrative direction, expert or professional opinion, technical standards or general standards of reasonableness. ...

470 It is clear enough that this was not a case in which the respondents specifically relied on the appellant's exercise of its power. The respondents neither sought a certificate under s 317A nor made any inquiry of the appellant relating to the condition of the building or its compliance with the Act and the ordinances. For that matter the respondents did not give evidence that they relied on the appellant having satisfied itself of these matters or the stability of the foundations.

Sutherland Shire Council v Heyman cont.

Moreover, the respondents did not by evidence or argument at 471 any stage of the proceedings advance a case of general reliance or dependence stemming from the existence of the legislative regime of control contained in Pt XI of the Act....

I conclude therefore that the respondents have failed to establish that the appellant owed them a duty of care and I would allow the appeal. ...

BRENNAN J: 477 The test of foreseeability of injury never has been applied as an exhaustive test for determining whether there is a prima facie duty to act to prevent injury caused by the acts of another or by circumstances for which the alleged wrongdoer is not responsible. Lord Diplock reminds us in *Dorset Yacht* (at 1060):

> The branch of English law which deals with civil wrongs abounds with instances of acts and, more particularly, of omissions which give rise to no legal liability in the doer or omitter for loss or damage sustained by others as a consequence of the act or omission, however reasonably or probably that loss or damage might have been anticipated.

... 478 I can be liable only for an injury that I cause to my neighbour. If I do nothing to cause it, I am not liable for the injury he suffers except in those cases where I am under a duty to act to prevent the injury occurring. Indeed, he is not in law my neighbour unless he is foreseeably "affected" by my conduct. But he can be said to be "affected" by my omission to act to prevent injury being done to him only if I am bound to act and do not do so. He cannot be said to be affected by my omission to act if I am not under a duty to him to act. Lord Atkin's "neighbour" test involves us in hopeless circularity if my duty depends on foreseeability of injury being caused to my 479 neighbour by my omission and a person becomes my neighbour only if I am under a duty to act to prevent that injury to him. Foreseeability of an injury that another is likely to suffer is insufficient to place me under a duty to him to act to prevent that injury. Some broader foundation than mere forseeability must appear before a common law duty to act arises. There must also be either the undertaking of some task which leads another to rely on its being performed, or the ownership, occupation or use of land or chattels to found the duty: cf Windeyer J in *Hargrave v Goldman* (1963) 110 CLR 40, at 66.

Thus a duty to act to prevent foreseeable injury to another may arise when a transaction – which may be no more than a single act – has been undertaken by the alleged wrongdoer and that transaction – or act – has created or increased the risk of that injury occurring. Such a case falls literally within Lord Atkin's principle in *Donoghue v Stevenson* [1932] AC 562. Where a person, whether a public authority or not, and whether acting in exercise of a statutory power or not, does something which creates or increases the risk of injury to another, he brings himself into such a relationship with the other that he is bound to do what is reasonable to prevent the occurrence of that injury unless statute excludes the duty. An omission to do what is reasonable in such a case is negligent whether or not the person who makes the omission is liable for any damage caused by the antecedent act which created or increased the risk of injury ...

481 Of course, if foreseeability of injury to another were the exhaustive criterion of a prima facie duty to act to prevent the occurrence of that injury, it would be essential to introduce some kind of restrictive qualification – perhaps a qualification of the kind stated in the second stage of the general proposition in *Anns*. I am unable to accept that approach. It is preferable, in my view, that the law should develop novel categories of negligence incrementally and by analogy with established categories, rather than by a massive extension of a prima facie duty of care restrained only by indefinable "considerations which ought to negative, or to reduce or limit the scope of the duty or the class of person to whom it is owed". The proper role of the "second stage", as I attempted to explain in *Jaensch v Coffey* (1984) 155 CLR 549 (ALJR at 438; ALR at 437), embraces no more than "those further elements [in addition to the neighbour principle] which are appropriate to the particular category of negligence and which confine the duty of care within narrower limits than those which would be defined by an unqualified application of the neighbour principle".

Sutherland Shire Council v Heyman cont.

I turn to inquire, therefore, whether there are any grounds in addition to foreseeability of injury for holding that the Council was under a duty to the respondents to inspect the footings, to discover that they were constructed on unstable and insecure foundations, to tell the builder on what foundations the footings should be constructed, and to enforce the prohibition on occupation until the footings were constructed in a good and workmanlike manner. A duty to act to prevent the occurrence of damage of the kind complained of by the respondents might arise because Parliament impliedly imposed the duty when it conferred statutory powers on the Council or because the circumstances are such that a duty arises at common law from what the Council did in exercise of its powers.

Statutory power as the source of statutory duty

482 A statutory power is not the same thing as a statutory duty. Before the repository of a statutory power can be liable in negligence for a failure to exercise it, the statute must (either expressly or by implication) impose a duty to exercise the power and confer a private right of action in damages for a breach of the duty so imposed. The question whether Parliament has conferred a private right of action depends upon the interpretation of the statute.... ...

483 Section 317A is the only provision in Pt XI that imposes a duty (namely, a duty to furnish a certificate) that is for the benefit of future purchasers of buildings, *inter alios*, who apply for such a certificate. Although an intending purchaser of a building constructed since Pt XI came into force might assume that the Council had exercised its powers under Pt XI with reasonable care and that it was therefore likely that the building had been built in compliance with the Act, Ordinance, and approved plans and specifications, s 317A provides for the making of the only representation by the Council on which such a purchaser is entitled to rely. The Council is under a duty to intending purchasers to use reasonable care in furnishing the certificate, a duty that arises at common law (if it does not arise by statute) when the Council knows that reliance will be placed upon it: see *Shaddock & Associates Pty Ltd v Parramatta City Council [No 1]* (1981) 36 ALR 385; 150 CLR 225.

If the court ascertains from the Act and Ordinance that Parliament did not intend to impose on the Council any other duty to future purchasers of property, it is not open to the court to remedy a supposed deficiency by superimposing a general common law duty on the Council to prevent any damage that future purchasers of property might suffer in the event of a non-exercise or a careless exercise of their statutory powers. To superimpose such a general common law duty on a statutory power would be to "conjure up" the duty in order to give effect to judicial ideas of policy. The common law does not superimpose such a duty on a mere statutory power. ...

487 The damage of which the respondents complain is structural damage to the house. Unless the risk of that damage was created or increased by some act done by the Council, the Council was under no duty to inspect the foundations, or to discover that the footings were constructed on unstable and insecure foundations or to tell the builder on what foundations the footings should be constructed or to enforce the prohibition on occupation of the building. There was no statutory duty to do those things. The only antecedent act done by the Council was its approval of the plans and specifications. There was no reason why the Council should have refused to approve the plans and specifications. If the builder, in accordance with his obligations under the Act, had constructed the building in accordance with the plans and specifications and the requirements of the Ordinance ("in a good and workmanlike manner") the structural damage would not have occurred. There was a risk, no doubt, that the builder might not construct the building as he was bound to do, but that was not a risk which the approval of the plans either created or increased. There is no duty on, indeed no power in, the Council to refuse approval to plans merely because they do not *minimize* the risk of defective and unworkmanlike construction. As the approval of the plans did not *increase* that risk, the structural damage that resulted from the builder's negligence cannot be attributed to the Council.

The Council is not charged with the performance of the supervisory functions of an architect.... The Council is merely empowered to require that the Act, the Ordinance, the plans and the specifications

Sutherland Shire Council v Heyman cont.

be observed, but an architect is ordinarily under a duty to give directions ensuring that the contract work is done in a good and workmanlike manner. Because there is a difference in the duty, there may be a difference in liability. ... The Council's actions did nothing to minimize the risk of defective footings, but they did not create or increase that risk. The Council's omission to exercise its powers of inspection more rigorously do not make it liable for the consequences of the builder's negligence. ...

494 The Council would have been under a duty to provide the respondents with information about the house had an application for a certificate under s 317A been made. None was made. There is no other statutory duty requiring the Council to give information about houses in its area. Nor is there a common law duty on councils to provide prospective purchasers of houses in their area with information about the soundness of the building under consideration... The respondents had no cause of action against the Council. The Council ought to have succeeded in the District Court and in the Court of Appeal. I would allow the appeal accordingly.

DEANE J: 495 Reasonable forseeability of loss or injury to another is an indication and, in the more settled areas of the law of negligence involving ordinary physical injury or damage caused by the direct impact of positive act, commonly an adequate indication that the requirement of proximity is satisfied. Lord Atkin's notions of reasonable foreseeability and proximity were, however, distinct and the requirement of proximity remains as the touchstone and control of the categories of case in which the common law of negligence will admit the existence of a duty of care (see, generally, *Jaensch v Coffey* (1984) 58 ALJR 426; 54 ALR 417 at 427-8 and 439-42 (ALJR), 419-20, 439-46 (ALR); *Governors of the Peabody Fund v Sir Lindsay Parkinson & Co Ltd* [1984] 3 WLR 953; [1984] 3 All ER 529 at 959-60 (WLR), 533-4 (All ER)). It will subsequently be seen that the ultimate question in the present case is whether the relationship between the Council and the respondents possessed the requisite degree of proximity to give rise to a relevant duty of care on the part of the Council to the respondents. At this stage, it is convenient to indicate my understanding of what is involved in the notion of proximity. To some extent, that involves a repetition of views expressed in the course of my judgment in *Jaensch v Coffey* (1984) 155 CLR 549 (58 ALJR at 441-2; 54 ALR at 443-6). ...

496 [Lord Atkin's notion of proximity] differed in nature from the test of reasonable foreseeability in that it involved both an evaluation of the closeness of the relationship and a judgment of the legal consequences of that evaluation. While this distinction between the notions of "proximity" and "reasonable foreseeability" has been obscured in judgments in many subsequent cases, particularly in cases where the existence of a duty of care went without saying, it remains a fundamental one. Conceptually, it underlay Lord Devlin's exposition of the principles of the law of negligence in *Hedley Byrne & Co Ltd v Heller & Partners Ltd* [1964] AC 465 and the speeches of the Law Lords in *Dorset Yacht Co Ltd v Home Office* [1970] AC 1004, esp at 1037-8, 1054-5 and 1059ff. It has been recognized and applied in this court in developing areas of the law of negligence (see, eg per Stephen and Mason JJ, *Caltex Oil (Australia) Pty Ltd v The Dredge "Willemstad"* (1976) 11 ALR 227; 136 CLR 529 at 574-6 and 590-3 (CLR); and per Gibbs CJ, *Jaensch v Coffey*, (1984) 155 CLR 549 58 ALJR at 428; 54 ALR, 419-20). In the House of Lords, it has been again asserted in clear terms by Lord Keith of Kinkel (in a speech with which the four other members of the House agreed) in the recent case of *Peabody Fund v Parkinson* [1984] 3 WLR; [1984] 3 All ER. ...

497 The requirement of proximity is directed to the relationship between the parties in so far as it is relevant to the allegedly negligent act or omission of the defendant and the loss or injury sustained by the plaintiff. It involves the notion of nearness or closeness and embraces physical proximity (in the sense of space and time) between the person or property of the plaintiff and the person or property of the defendant, circumstantial proximity such as an overriding relationship of employer and employee or of a professional man and his client and what may (perhaps loosely) be referred to as causal proximity in the sense of the closeness or directness of the causal connection or relationship between the 498 particular act or course of conduct and the loss or injury sustained. It may reflect an

Sutherland Shire Council v Heyman cont.

assumption by one party of a responsibility to take care to avoid or prevent injury, loss or damage to the person or property of another or reliance by one party upon such care being taken by the other in circumstances where the other party knew or ought to have known of that reliance. Both the identity and the relative importance of the factors which are determinative of an issue of proximity are likely to vary in different categories of case. That does not mean that there is scope for decision by reference to idiosyncratic notions of justice or morality or that it is a proper approach to treat the requirement of proximity as a question of fact to be resolved merely by reference to the relationship between the plaintiff and the defendant in the particular circumstances. The requirement of a relationship of proximity serves as a touchstone and control of the *categories* of case in which the common law will adjudge that a duty of care is owed. Given the general circumstances of a case in a new or developing area of the law of negligence, the question what (if any) combination or combinations of factors will satisfy the requirement of proximity is a question of law to be resolved by the processes of legal reasoning, induction and deduction. On the other hand, the identification of the content of that requirement in such an area should not be either ostensibly or actually divorced from notions of what is "fair and reasonable" (cf per Lord Morris of Borth-y-Gest, *Dorset Yacht Co Ltd v Home Office*, supra, at 1038-9 and per Lord Keith of Kinkel, *Peabody Fund v Parkinson* [1984] 3 WLR; [1984] 3 All ER at p 960 (WLR), 534 (All ER)), or from the considerations of public policy which underlie and enlighten the existence and content of the requirement.

In the present case, the Council's active connection with the erection of the house was limited to the exercise of some of its statutory powers and functions with respect to buildings within its local government area. Those statutory powers and functions and their partial exercise provide the context and the essential content of the only relevant relationship between the Council and the respondents with respect to the house. They are to be found in the provisions of the *Local Government Act 1919* (NSW) (the Act) and of the Ordinances made thereunder which were in force at the time when the plans of the house were approved (subject to conditions) by the Council and when the building was erected ... 500 The existence of liability on the part of a public governmental body to private individuals under those principles will commonly, as a matter of assumed legislative intent, be precluded in cases where what is involved are actions taken in the exercise of policy-making powers and functions of a quasi-legislative character (see, generally, *Wellbridge Holdings Ltd v Metropolitan Corporation of Greater Winnipeg* (1970) 22 DLR (3d) 470 at 476ff; *Anns v Merton London Borough Council* [1978] AC 728 at 754ff; *Takaro Properties Ltd v Rowling* [1978] 2 NZLR 314 at 325ff and 333ff). No such legislative intent can be assumed however in a case, such as the present, where the relevant powers and functions are of a routine administrative or "operational" nature. In such a case, the mere fact that a public body or instrumentality is exercising statutory powers and functions does not mean that it enjoys immunity from liability to private individuals under the ordinary law beyond the extent that there can be actually discerned in the relevant legislation an express or implied intent that the private rights of individuals be displaced or subordinated. Nor does it mean that the existence of the statutory powers and functions, the assumption of responsibility which may be involved in their exercise, or any reliance which may be placed upon a presumption that they have been or are being properly exercised is to be ignored or discounted in determining whether there existed in the relationship between public body or instrumentality and private citizen a degree of proximity which was adequate to give rise to a duty of care under the principles of common law negligence. ...

501 Be that as it may, however, the clear trend of authority has been to accept the principles of common law negligence enunciated in cases such as *Donoghue v Stevenson* [1932] AC 562 as being of general application ... In my view, that trend should continue to be accepted in this court and those principles should be recognized as governing liability in negligence for omissions as well as for acts of commission. That does not mean that the distinction between mere omission and positive act can be ignored in identifying the considerations by reference to which the existence of a relationship of

proximity must be determined in a particular category of case. To the contrary, the distinction between a failure to act and positive action remains a fundamental one. The common law imposes no prima facie general duty to rescue, safeguard or warn another from or of reasonably foreseeable loss or injury or to take reasonable care to ensure that another does not sustain such loss or injury (cf per Windeyer J, *Hargrave v Goldman* (1963) 110 CLR 40 at 66). ...

509 One can discern in the relevant provisions of the Act and Ordinances a number of purposes for which a local council's powers and functions with regard to the erection of buildings within its area were conferred. Those purposes included the advancement and maintenance of the general amenity of the neighbourhood, protection of health and the prevention of injury to the person or property of those within the area. ... It is however, in my view, impossible to discern in the relevant provisions of the Act and Ordinances anything which would warrant the conclusion that there had been included among the purposes for which those powers and functions were conferred a general purpose of protecting owners of premises from sustaining economic loss by reason of defects in buildings which they or their builders might erect or which they might purchase after erection. ... There is nothing in the evidence to suggest that the Council made 511 any particular representation to the respondents or anyone else about the exercise of its statutory powers and functions in relation to the house. Nor is there anything in the evidence to suggest that the respondents or anyone else placed any reliance upon the actual or assumed exercise by the Council of those statutory powers or functions ... Each of the above additional factors tends to indicate an absence – rather than a presence – of physical, circumstantial or causal proximity. They do not, by reference to any acceptable process of legal reasoning, supplement the existence of reasonable foreseeability of economic loss in a way which would warrant a conclusion that there existed in the relationship between the Council and the respondents the element of proximity necessary to give rise to a duty on behalf of the Council to take reasonable care to ensure that the respondents did not sustain economic loss by reason of a defect in the foundations of the building which they were purchasing. It follows that the respondents' action against the Council should have been dismissed ...

[Gibbs CJ and Wilson J held that the respondent had failed to establish either duty or breach and therefore agreed that the appeal should be allowed]

[7.105] **Notes&Questions**

1. This case both illustrates the historical changes in how the duty of care in negligence developed and is also a seminal case for the treatment of public authorities in Australian negligence law (see Chapter 11). For the treatment of defective structures see Chapter 9 and for pure economic loss see Chapter 10.
2. Brennan J's judgment in *Sutherland Shire Council v Heyman* (1985) 157 CLR 424 became profoundly important for the development of negligence in Australia after the departure of Deane J and Mason CJ from the High Court. It was also influential in the development of negligence in the House of Lords in England.

Proximity as the determinant of the duty of care

[7.110] During the 1980s, proximity-as-principle, as formulated by Deane J in *Jaensch v Coffey* (1984) 155 CLR 549 and later cases (*Sutherland Shire Council v Heyman* (1985) 157 CLR 424, *San Sebastian Pty Ltd v Minister Administering the Environmental Planning and Assessment Act 1979* (1986) 162 CLR 340 and *Gala v Preston* (1991) 172 CLR 243, culminating in *Burnie Port Authority v General Jones* (1994) 179 CLR 520 (extracted at [15.20] and *Bryan v Maloney* (1995) 182 CLR 609), became the dominant approach to negligence in Australia. This approach used proximity as an underlying conceptual determinant of whether the relationship between the parties was such that it was legitimate to make one party legally responsible to the other. It should be emphasised here that the focus of this approach was to consider the concepts of relationships and responsibility first, and only later to consider which category of case was at issue. In order to use proximity this way, even when the category is clear, one would still proceed to look to those traditional requirements in the category that reflect human notions of relationships and responsibility. Such indicators included reliance, assumption of responsibility, control and vulnerability, and so on.

Proximity was used by Deane J to develop a general principle of negligence that could operate either inside or outside recognised categories of liability. The proximity principle was used to overcome or extend various categories of liability, including occupiers' liability (*Hackshaw v Shaw* (1984) 155 CLR 614; *Australian Safeway Stores Pty Ltd v Zaluzna* (1987) 162 CLR 479), pure economic loss and nervous shock. For example, occupiers' liability had previously been dependent on a series of rules based on particular categories of occupier and entrant onto property (see, among myriad examples *Indermauer v Dames* (1866) LR 1 CP 274 (duty to invitee), *Lipman v Clendinnen* (1932) 46 CLR 550 (duty to licensee)). Using this approach, the question had to be asked, for example, "Is the plaintiff an invitee or a licensee?" The scope of the duty required was determined by the answer to this very specific question. In *Australian Safeway Stores Pty Ltd v Zaluzna* (1987) 162 CLR 479 and *Hackshaw v Shaw* (1984) 155 CLR 614 at 662, proximity was used to soften the categories of occupiers' liability; they lost their determinative nature, and became merely illustrative.

Similarly, using proximity, negligence overcame the *Rylands v Fletcher* (1868) LR 3 HL 330 category of tort law in *Burnie Port Authority v General Jones Ltd* (1994) 179 CLR 520. In *Burnie Port Authority*, extracted at [16.110], General Jones had frozen vegetables in a building owned by the Port Authority. The Port Authority was extending its building and used independent contractors to install refrigeration which required welding. The Port Authority was aware that there was highly flammable expanded polystyrene very nearby where the welding was to be carried out. The welding led to a fire. The trial judge held the Authority liable on the basis of ordinary negligence and the old ignis suus rule, which made a person who allowed fire to escape strictly liable. On appeal the Full Court held the authority liable not on the basis of ignis suus but on the basis of *Rylands v Fletcher* (1868) LR 3 HL 330. Liability under *Rylands v Fletcher* (1868) LR 3 HL 330 requires the defendant, having control of land, to bring something onto the land which might be dangerous if it escapes, and which does in fact escape. The damage results from the non-natural use of the land. On appeal from this ruling, the High Court held that *Rylands v Fletcher* (1868) LR 3 HL 330 should be subsumed into the law of negligence, by the use of proximity. Mason CJ, Deane, Dawson, Toohey and Gaudron JJ said in *Burnie Port Authority v General Jones Ltd* (1994) 179 CLR 520 at 539.

> Increasingly *Rylands v Fletcher* has come to depend on all the circumstances surrounding the introduction, production, retention or accumulation of the relevant substance. That being so, the presence of reasonable care or the absence of negligence in the manner of dealing with a substance or carrying out an activity may intrude as a relevant factor in determining whether the use of land is a "special" and "not ordinary" one.

And they said of proximity-as-principle:

> [I]ts practical utility lies essentially in understanding and identifying the *categories* of case in which a duty of care arises under the common law of negligence, rather than as a test for determining whether the circumstances of a particular case bring it within such a category, either established or developing.

Implicit in the statement is that one understands and identifies any categories of case where a duty might exist by reference to human notions of responsibility and relationships, which include reliance, vulnerability and control. To say proximity is not a test for determining whether the case is within the category is simply another way of saying that within the category the doctrine of precedent will govern the category in the ordinary way. The major role for proximity-as-principle was therefore in examining new categories as these cases showed. Another example is the judgment of Mason CJ, Deane and Gaudron JJ in *Bryan v Maloney* (1995) 182 CLR 609, which expanded the duty of care into a new category. In that case the court held that a builder could owe a duty of care to a subsequent purchaser of a house. The court did that by use of proximity as a principle; that is, they looked to see if there were in the relationship elements resonating with moral ideas of responsibility, such as, assumptions of responsibility, reliance and vulnerability.

Incrementalism and current approaches

[7.115] Throughout this period, Brennan J continued to resist proximity (*Hawkins v Clayton* (1988) 164 CLR 539 at 555; *Gala v Preston* (1991) 172 CLR 243 at 259). His approach was incremental, using reasonable foreseeability and analogy as in the quotation referred to in *Sutherland Shire Council v Heyman* (1985) 157 CLR 424, extracted above (*Sutherland Shire Council* at 481). The House of Lords consistently preferred his approach (see *Caparo Industries Plc v Dickman* [1990] 2 AC 605; *Murphy v Brentwood District Council* [1991] 1 AC 398). In *Caparo Industries Plc v Dickman* [1990] 2 AC 605, members of the House of Lords held that the law, while not eschewing underlying general principles in negligence, had moved in the direction of attaching greater significance to the more traditional categorisation of duty situations. Lord Bridge (at 618) went so far as to say that the concepts of proximity and fairness are not capable of the precise definition necessary to give them utility as practical tests, and they amounted in effect to little more than convenient labels to attach to the relevant features of different situations. Lord Roskill (at 628) regarded resort to the traditional categorisations as infinitely preferable to wide generalisations. The test established in *Caparo* has three stages. The first stage asks whether the harm was reasonably foreseeable; the second stage tests for proximity of relationship and the third stage asks whether it is fair and reasonable to impose a duty in the circumstances. Insofar as the English courts resort to "wide generalisations", proximity is not treated as a comprehensive point of reference as it was in Australia. This may be contrasted with the approach of the Canadian Supreme Court, which continues to use a test derived from Lord Wilberforce's two-stage test in *Anns v Merton London Borough Council* [1978] AC 728 at 751 which is extracted above. New Zealand has also continued to use the two-stage test (see *South Pacific Manufacturing Co Ltd v New Zealand Security Consultants & Investigations Ltd* [1992] 2 NZLR 282; *Invercargill City Council v Hamlin* [1996] 2 WLR 367; *Scott Group v McFarlane* [1978] 1 NZLR 553; *First City Corporation Ltd v Downsview Nominees Ltd* [1990] 3 NZLR 265).

When Kirby J came to the High Court of Australia he proposed for some time that the test that should be used should be the *Caparo* test. In *Pyrenees Shire Council v Day* (1998) 192 CLR 330, he put it forward and it was only after the rest of the High Court finally rejected it that he put it aside in *Graham Barclay Oysters Pty Ltd v Ryan* (2002) 211 CLR 540.

The High Court of Australia, however, despite some reservations about incrementalism (*Crimmins v Stevedoring Industry Finance Committee* (1999) 200 CLR 1 per Gummow J at [160]; *Brodie v Singleton Shire Council* (2001) 206 CLR 512 per Callinan J at [316]) began using it to develop new approaches to the duty of care. As the High Court decided cases after the 1990s, it is possible to discern new approaches to policy concerns in the judgments. For example, how should negligence fit in with other areas of law? Should it be allowed to take over other areas of law and if not, why not? These concerns are played out in the context of deciding the duty of care in novel cases.

Sullivan v Moody: Thompson v Connon

[7.120] *Sullivan v Moody; Thompson v Connon* (2001) 207 CLR 562 High Court of Australia

(footnotes omitted)

[The plaintiffs in these cases, and a previous case, *Hillman v Black* (1996) 67 SASR 490, were parents who had been accused of child abuse after medical practitioners who worked in a sexual assault referral centre at a hospital run by the State examined the children. The plaintiffs alleged that the medical practitioners carelessly came to a conclusion about child abuse and communicated it to the Department of Community Services in such a way that the father seemed to be the obvious cause of the abuse. The plaintiffs suffered shock, psychiatric injury and financial distress.]

GLEESON CJ, GAUDRON, MCHUGH, HAYNE AND CALLINAN JJ: [2]... ... It is claimed that the employees of the Department owed the plaintiff a duty of care in the course of their employment. ...

"It is alleged that employees ... gathered and used information about possible sexual abuse of the children without making adequate inquiry as to those facts, without exercising proper care and without following appropriate procedures for such cases. ... It is alleged that the employees of the Department failed to establish appropriate protocols for the diagnosis of sexual abuse of children. It is alleged that they failed to establish proper procedures to validate diagnoses of sexual abuse ...."

The relevant legislation

[18] In all three cases the statutory background was the same. There was a difference of opinion in the Full Court in *Thompson* as to whether it was conclusive, but it is plainly relevant.

[19] The Department of Community Welfare functions pursuant to the *Community Welfare Act 1972* (SA) ("the Act"). Section 10 of the Act provides that the objectives of the Department, and of the Minister of Community Welfare, include promoting the welfare and dignity of the community, and of individuals, families and groups within the community, by providing services designed to assist, amongst others, children to overcome disadvantages suffered by them ... [Section 91 provided for reporting where child abuse is suspected on reasonable grounds].

The supposed duty of care

[42] The argument was conducted upon the basis that it was foreseeable that harm of the kind allegedly suffered by the appellants might result from want of care on the part of those who investigated the possibility that the children had been sexually abused. But the fact that it is foreseeable, in the sense of being a real and not far-fetched possibility, that a careless act or omission on the part of one person may cause harm to another does not mean that the first person is subject to a legal liability to compensate the second by way of damages for negligence if there is such carelessness, and harm results. If it were otherwise, at least two consequences would follow. First, the law would subject citizens to an intolerable burden of potential liability, and constrain their freedom of action in a gross manner. Secondly, the tort of negligence would subvert many other principles of law, and statutory provisions, which strike a balance of rights and obligations, duties and freedoms. A defendant will only be liable, in negligence, for failure to take reasonable care to prevent a certain kind

Sullivan v Moody: Thompson v Connon cont.

of foreseeable harm to a plaintiff, in circumstances where the law imposes a duty to take such care. ... [The court then discussed *Donoghue v Stevenson* [1932] AC 562 and some of the cases before and after it]

[47] The references to "relations" [in Lord Atkin's judgment in *Donoghue*], and to the problem of deciding which relations are sufficiently proximate to give rise to a duty of care, in part reflects the previous history of the law of negligence, the focus of attention often being particular categories of relationship. The search was for a unifying principle which informed the decisions in respect to those categories. The actual conclusion in *Donoghue v Stevenson* [1932] AC 562 was that, at least in certain circumstances, the manufacturer of a product intended for human consumption stood in a sufficiently proximate relation to an ultimate consumer of the product to attract a duty of care. But Lord Atkin, in his formulation of principle, was seeking to find "a valuable practical guide", and warned against "the danger of stating propositions of law in wider terms than is necessary". Consistently with his reasoning, he might also have warned against the danger of stating such propositions in more categorical terms than is appropriate.

[48] As Professor Fleming said, "no one has ever succeeded in capturing in any precise formula" a comprehensive test for determining whether there exists, between two parties, a relationship sufficiently proximate to give rise to a duty of care of the kind necessary for actionable negligence. The formula is not "proximity". Notwithstanding the centrality of that concept, for more than a century, in this area of discourse, and despite some later decisions in this Court which emphasised that centrality, it gives little practical guidance in determining whether a duty of care exists in cases that are not analogous to cases in which a duty has been established. It expresses the nature of what is in issue, and in that respect gives focus to the inquiry, but as an explanation of a process of reasoning leading to a conclusion its utility is limited. The present appeals provide an illustration of the problem. To ask whether there was a relationship of proximity between the medical practitioners who examined the children, and the fathers who were suspected of abusing the children, might be a convenient short-hand method of formulating the ultimate question in the case, but it provides no assistance in deciding how to answer the question. That is so, whether it is expressed as the ultimate test of a duty of care, or as one of a number of stages in an approach towards a conclusion on that issue.

[49] What has been described as the three-stage approach of Lord Bridge of Harwich in *Caparo Industries Plc v Dickman* [1990] 2 AC 605 does not represent the law in Australia. ... There are policies at work in the law which can be identified and applied to novel problems, but the law of tort develops by reference to principles, which must be capable of general application, not discretionary decision-making in individual cases.

[50] Different classes of case give rise to different problems in determining the existence and nature or scope, of a duty of care. Sometimes the problems may be bound up with the harm suffered by the plaintiff, as, for example, where its direct cause is the criminal conduct of some third party. Sometimes they may arise because the defendant is the repository of a statutory power or discretion. Sometimes they may reflect the difficulty of confining the class of persons to whom a duty may be owed within reasonable limits. Sometimes they may concern the need to preserve the coherence of other legal principles, or of a statutory scheme which governs certain conduct or relationships. The relevant problem will then become the focus of attention in a judicial evaluation of the factors which tend for or against a conclusion, to be arrived at as a matter of principle. In *Donoghue v Stevenson* [1932] AC 562, for example, Lord Buckmaster, in dissent, was concerned that, if the manufacturer in that case was liable, apart from contract or statute, to a consumer, then a person who negligently built a house might be liable, at any future time, to any person who suffered injury in consequence; a concern which later cases showed to have been far from fanciful. The problem which has caused so much difficulty in relation to the extent of tortious liability in respect of negligently constructed buildings was not only foreseeable, but foreseen, in the seminal case on the law of negligence.

Sullivan v Moody: Thompson v Connon cont.

[51] In *Dorset Yacht Co Ltd v Home Office* [1970] AC 1004, Lord Diplock said:

> [T]he judicial development of the law of negligence rightly proceeds by seeking first to identify the relevant characteristics that are common to the kinds of conduct and relationship between the parties which are involved in the case for decision and the kinds of conduct and relationships which have been held in previous decisions of the courts to give rise to a duty of care.

[52] Conversely, conduct and relationships may have been held not to give rise to a duty of care, and the reasons for that holding may provide an important guide to the solution of the problem in a new case.

[53] Developments in the law of negligence over the last 30 or more years reveal the difficulty of identifying unifying principles that would allow ready solution of novel problems. Nonetheless, that does not mean that novel cases are to be decided by reference only to some intuitive sense of what is "fair" or "unfair". There are cases, and this is one, where to find a duty of care would so cut across other legal principles as to impair their proper application and thus lead to the conclusion that there is no duty of care of the kind asserted.

[54] The present cases can be seen as focusing as much upon the communication of information by the respondents to the appellants and to third parties as upon the competence with which examinations or other procedures were conducted. The core of the complaint by each appellant is that he was injured as a result of what he, and others, were told. At once, then, it can be seen that there is an intersection with the law of defamation which resolves the competing interests of the parties through well-developed principles about privilege and the like. To apply the law of negligence in the present case would resolve that competition on an altogether different basis. It would allow recovery of damages for publishing statements to the discredit of a person where the law of defamation would not.

[55] More fundamentally, however, these cases present a question about coherence of the law. Considering whether the persons who reported their suspicions about each appellant owed that appellant a duty of care must begin from the recognition that those who made the report had other responsibilities. A duty of the kind alleged should not be found if that duty would not be compatible with other duties which the respondents owed.

[56] How may a duty of the kind for which the appellants contend rationally be related to the functions, powers and responsibilities of the various persons and authorities who are alleged to owe that duty? A similar problem has arisen in other cases. The response to the problem in those cases, although not determinative, is instructive.

[57] In *Hill v Chief Constable of West Yorkshire* [1989] AC 53, the House of Lords held that police officers did not owe a duty to individual members of the public who might suffer injury through their careless failure to apprehend a dangerous criminal. Lord Keith of Kinkel pointed out that the conduct of a police investigation involves a variety of decisions on matters of policy and discretion, including decisions as to priorities in the deployment of resources. To subject those decisions to a common law duty of care, and to the kind of judicial scrutiny involved in an action in tort, was inappropriate. ...

[60] The circumstance that a defendant owes a duty of care to a third party, or is subject to statutory obligations which constrain the manner in which powers or discretions may be exercised, does not of itself rule out the possibility that a duty of care is owed to a plaintiff. People may be subject to a number of duties, at least provided they are not irreconcilable. A medical practitioner who examines, and reports upon the condition of, an individual, might owe a duty of care to more than one person. But if a suggested duty of care would give rise to inconsistent obligations, that would ordinarily be a reason for denying that the duty exists. Similarly, when public authorities, or their officers, are charged with the responsibility of conducting investigations, or exercising powers, in the

public interest, or in the interests of a specified class of persons, the law would not ordinarily subject them to a duty to have regard to the interests of another class of persons where that would impose upon them conflicting claims or obligations.

[61] There is also a question as to the extent, and potential indeterminacy, of liability. In the case of a medical practitioner, the range of people who might foreseeably (in the sense earlier mentioned) suffer some kind of harm, as a consequence of careless diagnosis or treatment of a patient, is extensive.

[62] The statutory scheme that formed the background to the activities of the present respondents was, relevantly, a scheme for the protection of children. It required the respondents to treat the interests of the children as paramount. Their professional or statutory responsibilities involved investigating and reporting upon, allegations that the children had suffered, and were under threat of, serious harm. It would be inconsistent with the proper and effective discharge of those responsibilities that they should be subjected to a legal duty, breach of which would sound in damages, to take care to protect persons who were suspected of being the sources of that harm. The duty for which the appellants contend cannot be reconciled satisfactorily, either with the nature of the functions being exercised by the respondents, or with their statutory obligation to treat the interests of the children as paramount. As to the former, the functions of examination, and reporting, require, for their effective discharge, an investigation into the facts without apprehension as to possible adverse consequences for people in the position of the appellants or legal liability to such persons. As to the latter, the interests of the children, and those suspected of causing their harm, are diverse, and irreconcilable. That they are irreconcilable is evident when regard is had to the case in which examination of a child alleged to be a victim of abuse does not allow the examiner to form a definite opinion about whether the child has been abused, only a suspicion that it *may* have happened. The interests of the child, in such a case, would favour reporting that the suspicion of abuse has not been dispelled; the interests of a person suspected of the abuse would be to the opposite effect.

[63] Furthermore, the attempt by the appellants to avoid the problem of the extent of potential duty and liability is unconvincing. They sought to limit it to parents. But, if it exists, why should it be so limited? If the suspected child abuser were a relative other than a parent, or a schoolteacher, or a neighbour, or a total stranger, why should that person be in a position different from that of a parent? The logical consequence of the appellants' argument must be that a duty of care is owed to anyone who is, or who might become, a suspect.

[64] A final point should be noted. The appellants do not contend that any legal right was infringed. And, once one rejects the distinction between parents and everybody else, they can point to no relationship, association, or connection, between themselves and the respondents, other than that which arises from the fact that, if the children had been abused, the appellants were the prime suspects. But that is merely the particular circumstance that gave rise to the risk that carelessness on the part of the respondents might cause them harm. Ultimately, their case rests on foreseeability; and that is not sufficient.

Conclusion

[65] The duty of care for which the appellants contend does not exist.

[66] The appeals should be dismissed with costs.

——— ൠ ———

[7.125] The issue of how the law of negligence should deal with situations where the actual damage is caused by a third party rather than the defendant continues to raise difficulties. In cases like *Dorset Yacht* (see [7.60] above), the matter may be resolved on the basis that there was a duty to control the people who did the damage, but when there is no such duty to control, when should a person be owed a duty of care to a person hurt by another? In answering this question, the High Court again made an attempt at establishing how hard cases should be dealt with in negligence law.

Modbury Triangle Shopping Centre v Anzil

[7.130] *Modbury Triangle Shopping Centre Pty Ltd v Anzil* (2000) 205 CLR 254 High Court of Australia

(footnotes omitted)

[The appellant was the owner of a shopping centre. The respondent was employed by a video shop which leased premises in the centre. The video shop faced the large outdoor car park for the centre. The video shop closed at 10 pm. The carpark was lit by lights on towers which were on a timer which turned the lights off at 10 pm. At 10.30 pm on a Sunday the respondent closed the video shop and walked toward his car parked in the carpark. He was attacked by three unknown men, one of whom was armed with a baseball bat, and was badly injured. Under the lease, lighting of the common areas was provided at the discretion of the appellant, and the tenant paid a proportion of the cost. Two years before the practice had been to leave the lights on till 11 pm; then the co-manager of the video shop had requested the lights to stay on until after 10.15 pm but this had ceased and for some 12 months before the attack the lights had been timed to go off at 10 pm.]

GLEESON CJ:

The duty

[13] Most actions in tort which come before trial courts arise out of relationships in which the existence of a duty of care is well established, and the nature of the duty well understood. ... In other cases, of which the present is an example, there is a real issue as to the scope of legal responsibility. Such an issue cannot then be resolved by a detailed recitation of the facts, the repetition of the standard rubrics under which discussion of the tort of negligence is commonly organised, and an appeal to common sense. ... In some cases, where there is a problem as to the existence and measure of legal responsibility, it is useful to begin by identifying the nature of the harm suffered by a plaintiff, for which a defendant is said to be liable. ...

[17] That an occupier of land owes a duty of care to a person lawfully upon the land is not in doubt. It is clear that the appellant owed the first respondent a duty in relation to the physical state and condition of the car park. The point of debate concerns whether the appellant owed a duty of a kind relevant to the harm which befell the first respondent. That was variously described in argument as a question concerning the nature, or scope, or measure of the duty. The nature of the harm suffered was physical injury inflicted by a third party over whose actions the appellant had no control. Thus, any relevant duty must have been a duty related to the security of the first respondent. It must have been a duty, as occupier of land, to take reasonable care to protect people in the position of the first respondent from conduct, including criminal conduct, of third parties. People in the position of the first respondent would include employees of tenants of the shopping centre, visitors to the shopping centre, including customers of tenants, users of the automatic teller machines, and, perhaps, any member of the public using the car park at any time for any lawful purpose.

[18] The basis of the duty which, as occupier, the appellant owed in relation to the physical state or condition of the premises was control over, and knowledge of, the state of the premises [*Commissioner for Railways v McDermott* [1967] 1 AC 169].

[19] The appellant had no control over the behaviour of the men who attacked the first respondent, and no knowledge or forewarning of what they planned to do. In fact, nothing is known about them even now. For all that appears, they might have been desperate to obtain money, or interested only in

brutality. The inference that they would have been deterred by lighting in the car park is at least debatable. The men were not enticed to the car park by the appellant. They were strangers to the parties.

[20] In *Smith v Leurs* (1945) 70 CLR 256 at 262, Dixon J said:

> It is, however, exceptional to find in the law a duty to control another's actions to prevent harm to strangers. The general rule is that one man is under no duty of controlling another man to prevent his doing damage to a third. There are, however, special relations which are the source of a duty of this nature. It appears now to be recognized that it is incumbent upon a parent who maintains control over a young child to take reasonable care so to exercise that control as to avoid conduct on his part exposing the person or property of others to unreasonable danger.

[21] Control was the basis of liability in *Dorset Yacht Co v Home Office* [1970] AC 1004, where Lord Morris of Borth-y-Gest, after citing the above passage, said that the case was one of a special relationship involving a duty to control another's actions.

[22] Reliance is sometimes the basis of a duty of care. Here there was no relevant reliance. Why the video shop could not have been closed in sufficient time to enable employees of the shop to walk to their cars before the lights went off (assuming they went off at 10 pm) was not investigated at the trial. There was nothing to prevent the first respondent's employer from making such arrangements for the security of its employees as it saw fit. The lease did not give the appellant the exclusive right to take measures for the safety and security of employees and customers of tenants.

[23] The present is not relevantly a case of assumption of responsibility. The respondents submitted that the appellant assumed responsibility for the illumination of the car park. That submission confuses two different meanings of responsibility: capacity and obligation. The appellant owned and occupied the car park, controlled the lights in it, and decided when they would be on and when they would be off. But the relevant question is whether the appellant assumed an obligation to care for the security of persons in the position of the first respondent by protecting them from attack by third parties. ...

[25] The fact that, as occupier of the car park, the appellant had the capacity to decide when, and to what extent, it would be lit at night, does not mean that the appellant assumed a particular responsibility to protect anyone who might lawfully be in the car park against attack by criminals. The policy adopted by the appellant as to the hour at which the lights went off suggests that the purpose of the lights was to attract customers, rather than deter criminals. Whether or not that is so, there is nothing in the evidence to suggest that the appellant assumed a responsibility which, at least in the case of employees of tenants of the Centre, might ordinarily be expected to be a responsibility of their employers. It was the first respondent's employer which decided the hour at which the video shop would close, and what, if any, arrangements would be made for the after-hours security of employees. ...

[26] Leaving aside contractual obligations, there are circumstances where the relationship between two parties may mean that one has a duty to take reasonable care to protect the other from the criminal behaviour of third parties, random and unpredictable as such behaviour may be. Such relationships may include those between employer and employee, school and pupil, or bailor and bailee. But the general rule that there is no duty to prevent a third party from harming another is based in part upon a more fundamental principle, which is that the common law does not ordinarily impose liability for omissions. This was explained by Lord Goff of Chieveley in *Smith v Littlewoods Ltd* [1987] AC 241 at 270. His Lordship said, with reference to a general duty of an occupier to take reasonable care for the safety of neighbouring premises:

> Now if this proposition is understood as relating to a general duty to take reasonable care *not to cause damage* to premises in the neighbourhood ... then it is unexceptionable. But it must not be overlooked that a problem arises when the pursuer is seeking to hold the defender

Modbury Triangle Shopping Centre v Anzil cont.

> responsible for having failed to *prevent* a third party from causing damage to the pursuer or his property by the third party's own deliberate wrongdoing. In such a case, it is not possible to invoke a general duty of care; for it is well recognised that there is no *general* duty of care to prevent third parties from causing such damage.

(original emphasis)

[28] As Brennan J pointed out in *Sutherland Shire Council v Heyman* (1985) 157 CLR 424, the common law distinguishes between an act affecting another person, and an omission to prevent harm to another. If people were under a legal duty to prevent foreseeable harm to others, the burden imposed would be intolerable. ...

[29] The control and knowledge which form the basis of an occupier's liability in relation to the physical state or condition of land are absent when one considers the possibility of criminal behaviour on the land by a stranger. The principle involved cannot be ignored by pointing to the facts of the particular case and saying (or speculating) that the simple expedient of leaving the car park light on for an extra half hour would have prevented the attack on the first respondent. If the appellant had a duty to prevent criminal harm to people in the position of the first respondent, at the least it would have had to leave the lights on all night; and its responsibilities would have extended beyond that. Furthermore, the duty would extend beyond the particular kind of harm inflicted by the criminals in the present case. It would presumably include criminal damage to property. If the baseball bat had been used, not against the first respondent, but against his car window, or if the car had been stolen, the same principle would govern the case. The unpredictability of criminal behaviour is one of the reasons why, as a general rule, and in the absence of some special relationship, the law does not impose a duty to prevent harm to another from the criminal conduct of a third party, even if the risk of such harm is foreseeable.

[30] There may be circumstances in which, not only is there a foreseeable risk of harm from criminal conduct by a third party, but, in addition, the criminal conduct is attended by such a high degree of foreseeability, and predictability, that it is possible to argue that the case would be taken out of the operation of the general principle and the law may impose a duty to take reasonable steps to prevent it. The possibility that knowledge of previous, preventable, criminal conduct, or of threats of such conduct, could arguably give rise to an exceptional duty, appears to have been suggested in *Smith v Littlewoods Ltd* [1987] AC 241. It also appears to be the basis upon which United States decisions relating to the liability of occupiers have proceeded. A leading American textbook (Prosser and Keeton on *The Law of Torts*, 5th ed, 1984), states that:

> The duty to take precautions against the negligence of others ... involves merely the usual process of multiplying the probability that such negligence will occur by the magnitude of the harm likely to result if it does, and weighing the result against the burden upon the defendant of exercising such care. ... There is normally much less reason to anticipate acts on the part of others which are malicious and intentionally damaging than those which are merely negligent; and this is all the more true where, as is usually the case, such acts are criminal. Under all ordinary and normal circumstances, in the absence of any reason to expect the contrary, the actor may reasonably proceed upon the assumption that others will obey the criminal law.

[31] That does not represent an accurate statement of the common law in Australia.

[32] The factor most commonly taken into account in the United States in determining whether criminal activity was reasonably foreseeable is knowledge on the part of the occupier of land of previous incidents of criminality.

[33] It could not reasonably be argued that the present is such a case. There had been illegal behaviour in the area. A restaurant near the car park had been broken into. During a period of a year before the incident in question, there had been two attempts to break into an automatic teller

machine. About a year before the incident, the car window of an employee of the video shop had been smashed. This does not indicate a high level of recurrent, predictable criminal behaviour.

[34] It is unnecessary to express a concluded opinion as to whether foreseeability and predictability of criminal behaviour could ever exist in such a degree that, even in the absence of some special relationship, Australian law would impose a duty to take reasonable care to prevent harm to another from such behaviour. It suffices to say two things: first, as a matter of principle, such a result would be difficult to reconcile with the general rule that one person has no legal duty to rescue another; and secondly, as a matter of fact, the present case is nowhere near the situation postulated.

[35] The most that can be said of the present case is that the risk of harm of the kind suffered by the first respondent was foreseeable in the sense that it was real and not far-fetched. The existence of such a risk is not sufficient to impose upon an occupier of land a duty to take reasonable care to prevent harm, to somebody lawfully upon the land, from the criminal behaviour of a third party who comes onto the land. To impose such a burden upon occupiers of land, in the absence of contract or some special relationship of the kind earlier mentioned, would be contrary to principle; a principle which is based upon considerations of practicality and fairness. The principle cannot be negated by listing all the particular facts of the case and applying to the sum of them the question-begging characterisation that they are special. There was nothing special about the relationship between the appellant and the first respondent. There was nothing about the relationship which relevantly distinguished him from large numbers of members of the public who might have business at the Centre, or might otherwise lawfully use the car park. Most of the facts said to make the case special are, upon analysis, no more than evidence that the risk of harm to the first respondent was foreseeable.

[36] The appellant is entitled to succeed upon the ground that its duty as an occupier of land did not extend to taking reasonable care to prevent physical injury to the first respondent resulting from the criminal behaviour of third parties on that land.

Causation

[37] The case provides an illustration of the interrelationship that sometimes exists between questions of legal responsibility and causation. … [40] The finding on causation adverse to the appellant can only be justified on the basis of an erroneous view of the nature of the appellant's duties as occupier. On an accurate legal appreciation of those duties, the appellant's omission to leave the lights on might have facilitated the crime, as did its decision to provide a car park, and the first respondent's decision to park there. But it was not a cause of the first respondent's injuries.

Orders

[41] The appeal should be allowed with costs. The orders of the Full Court of the Supreme Court of South Australia should be set aside. In place of those orders, the appeal to that Court should be allowed with costs, the judgment of the trial judge should be set aside and the action should be dismissed with costs. …

KIRBY J: … [60] In the way in which the present case was litigated, the [issue of the duty of care] was not seriously in contest. According to the respondent, that issue was actually conceded by the appellant before the Full Court. In any case, the relationship of a landlord to the employees of a tenant, coming onto common property pursuant to, and within the scope of, a tenancy, involves an established duty relationship. Certainly, in the case of a landlord managing the operations and common property of a commercial shopping centre, all of the elements are present to create the relationship which Lord Atkin described in *Donoghue v Stevenson* [1932] AC 562 as being that of a "neighbour". There is reasonable foreseeability of injury. There is also geographical proximity. There is, moreover, circumstantial proximity. In the present case, there is also causal proximity, in the sense that the actions or omissions of the appellant were of the kind that would directly affect a person such as the tenant's employee.

Modbury Triangle Shopping Centre v Anzil cont.

[61] To say this is not to return to the failed notion of "proximity" as the universal indicium of the duty of care at common law. It is, however, to accept that, in its narrow and historical sense, as a measure of factors relevant to the degree of physical, circumstantial and causal closeness, proximity is the best notion yet devised by the law to delineate the relationship of "neighbour". There is no inconsistency between the use of proximity for this limited purpose (with the requirement of foreseeability and the restraints of policy) and my statement, in an earlier case, that "proximity's reign ... as a universal identifier of the existence of a duty of care at common law, has come to an end". Used in the way I suggest, proximity remains a consideration. Self-evidently, some notion must be invoked to control the ambit of the duty. A duty of care is not one owed to the world at large. It is owed to one's legal "neighbour". That idea does not connote only the adjoining householder. Nor does it connote unknowable strangers. The appellant's relationship with a person such as the respondent was clearly proximate. ... the appeal was ultimately narrowed to the first of the two questions stated at the outset of these reasons, namely whether, in the circumstances, the established duty of care owed by the appellant to the respondent (generally stated as being to avoid foreseeable risks of injury to the respondent) extended to a duty to provide lighting of the car park adjacent to the video store until the ordinary time of the departure of employees such as the respondent. If it did, there could be no disputing the evidence that the appellant was in breach of that duty. There would then arise the second contested question of whether the breach, so established, caused or materially contributed to the respondent's damage.

The scope of the duty to guard against criminal acts by a third party

[65] [Courts in the USA, Canada, England and Australia]... have not accepted a universal principle excusing the person sued simply because the damage suffered arose out of the criminal acts of a third party. On the contrary, in many instances where the acts were foreseeable and the relationship between the parties was legally close (to use a neutral word), legal liability has been imposed. ...

It is true that, in a number of such cases, the relationship between the parties to the proceedings was, like that in *Lillie v Thompson* 332 US 459 (1947), that of employer and employee. This Court has repeatedly pointed out that such a relationship imposes a heavy duty of care and affirmative responsibilities of accident prevention. To that extent, employer and employee decisions may be distinguishable from the present case. However, they do serve to rebut any universal principle that, in Australian law, parties sued in negligence can escape liability simply because the damage complained of was caused by the deliberate criminal act of a third party. No principle of public policy, no general doctrine of denying relief and no concept of causal interruption has so far succeeded in forbidding recovery in such cases where the general principles of negligence law would otherwise uphold recovery. ...

[77] This review of legal authority therefore demonstrates that neither in Australia nor in any other common law country examined have claims in negligence for damage consequent upon the criminal acts of a third party been excluded as a universal category or class. Such claims have been evaluated by the application to the facts of each case of the ordinary principles of negligence law. For this Court now to hold that no duty of care of a relevant scope requiring reasonable preventive measures can arise in respect of the criminal acts of a third party would amount to a departure from basic legal doctrine. Moreover, it would isolate the approach of the common law in Australia from that of other like countries.

[Kirby J then considered policy matters]

[83] A principled solution to such claims lies not in adopting a universal exemption for supposed reasons of legal policy. Still less does it lie in attempting to confine recovery to an unknown and unknowable category of "special cases" or cases of "special relationships" or "special vulnerability". It lies in the neutral application of the basic rules of the law of negligence to the evidence proved and the

inferences drawn from such evidence in the particular case. ... But such questions scarcely warrant rejection of the present claim once an exemption for the criminal acts of a third party is rejected as a universal proposition. Here, the provision of approximately 20 minutes of extra lighting in the car park would hardly diminish individual responsibility on the part of employees of a tenant, such as the respondent. The co-manager had acted responsibly in bringing complaints to the notice of the appellant. It was the appellant, once on notice, that acted without responsibility. If such indifference is not then sanctioned by a verdict in favour of the respondent, the legal deterrence against unrealistic neglect and unjustifiable omission to act is completely removed. The "neighbour" of Lord Atkin has truly crossed to the other side of the street and the law will be upholding wilful indifference to the safety of others. This is not my concept of Lord Atkin's neighbour principle.

A duty of care of a relevant scope existed

... [89] Having reserved and exercised sole control over the common areas in this way, and having asserted that control in relation to the car park (by altering the hours of illumination and denying requests for its adequate extension) the appellant can scarcely contend that it was not, in law, responsible for the injuries received by the respondent in the darkened car park ...

[90] In the present case, the evidence accepted at the trial, and the inferences drawn from that evidence by the trial judge and the Full Court, fully justified their conclusion that a duty relationship existed. Authority also supported an expression of that duty as one that required the appellant to take reasonable care to avoid foreseeable risks of injury to the respondent. The duty expressed in such terms extended to include, at least, those steps reasonably necessary to protect the respondent from the consequences of foreseeable criminal acts by third parties. One such step would have been to leave the car park illuminated until about 10.20 pm. The facilities for doing so were in place. Doing so involved no expensive structural change. It required no acquisition of costly equipment. It had been done previously. The additional costs would have been minimal. Under the lease, those costs could in any case have been passed on to the tenant concerned ... [91] The liability owed to other entrants would depend on all the circumstances. Other entrants were not so repeatedly exposed to danger. They had not made special complaints and requests. Their presence within the centre would not have been so closely bound up in the mutual economic interests of the appellant, its tenants and their employees ... Reprogramming a simple light switch in the face of numerous requests to do so was scarcely an onerous burden. I do not accept that the law of negligence in Australia sanctions such obdurate indifference to the safety of persons such as the respondent. This is not, I believe, the common law in the United States, England or Canada. Nor do I consider that it is the common law in Australia.

[Kirby J held that the breach caused the damage and that the appeal should be dismissed. Hayne, Gaudron and Callinan JJ agreed with Gleeson CJ that the appeal should be allowed]

[7.135] **Notes&Questions**

1. The extracted case was followed in *Ashrafi Persian Trading Co Pty Ltd v Ashrafina* [2002] Aust Torts Rep 81-636 (NSW Ct of Appeal). In that case the plaintiff was assaulted by an unknown person while she was asleep in the motel owned and operated by her family. The assailant hit her through a small gap in the sliding window which was prevented by a security device from opening further. Heydon J (with whom Mason P and Handley JA agreed) said that the occupiers' duty did not extend to the criminal behaviour of third parties on the land except in special circumstances. She did

not fall into either of the exceptional cases which included a "high degree of certainty that harm would follow" or the existence of a special relationship of control such as an employer-employee -relationship.

2. The extracted case was criticised in J Dietrich, "Liability in Negligence for Harm Resulting from Third Parties' Criminal Acts: *Modbury Triangle Shopping Centre v Anzil*" (2001) 9 TLJ 152.

THE MEANING OF REASONABLE FORESEEABILITY

[7.140] As we have seen, the question of reasonable foreseeability is a central one in the question of whether the duty of care is owed, but what does it mean?

Chapman v Hearse

[7.145] *Chapman v Hearse* (1961) 106 CLR 112 High Court of Australia

(footnotes omitted)

[A car driven by the appellant Chapman collided from behind with the near side of another vehicle which was about to make a right turn at an intersection near Adelaide. The front vehicle was overturned by the impact and Chapman was thrown out of his car onto the roadway where he lay unconscious. Almost immediately after the accident three cars pulled up and the drivers of two of the cars went to assist to extricate some of the occupants. The driver of the third vehicle, a Dr Cherry, went to the aid of Chapman. While he was attending the unconscious man he was struck by another car, driven by the respondent Hearse, and suffered injuries from which he died.

Proceedings were instituted by the executor of Dr Cherry's will against the respondent under the *Wrongs Act 1936-1956* (SA). The respondent alleged contributory negligence on the part of the doctor and joined the appellant as a third party claiming contribution from him.

The trial judge (the Chief Justice of the South Australian Supreme Court) found that Hearse had been negligent and also that Chapman was liable to make a contribution of one-fourth of the damages awarded to the executor on behalf of the widow and children of Dr Cherry. Chapman appealed against the order for contribution and his appeal was dismissed by the Full Court of the Supreme Court of South Australia. He then appealed to the High Court.]

THE COURT (DIXON CJ, KITTO, TAYLOR, MENZIES AND WINDEYER JJ): [Their Honours first considered the request contained in the respondent's cross-appeal that the finding of the trial judge, that there was no contributory negligence on the part of Dr Cherry, should be reversed. However, they were of the opinion that no grounds existed for disturbing this finding. They then went on to consider the principal question of whether Hearse was entitled to recover a contribution from Chapman.]

119 The answer to this question depends upon whether Chapman would have been liable for the "same damage" at the suit of Dr Cherry's executor: *Wrongs Act 1936-1956*, s 25(c). This inquiry, the appellant somewhat emphatically asserts, must be answered in the negative. First of all, it is said, Chapman owed no duty of care to Dr Cherry. Alternatively, it is asserted that, even if he did, Dr Cherry's death was caused solely by the negligent driving of Hearse and not at all by any breach of duty on Chapman's part and, finally, the contention is raised that, on any view of the matter, the death of Dr Cherry, considered as a consequence of Chapman's negligence, was too remote to fix him with responsibility.

In the unusual circumstances of the case the point which calls first for attention is the position which Dr Cherry occupied vis-à-vis Chapman. At the time when Dr Cherry was run down he was standing – or stooping – near the centre of the road. It was dark and wet and there seems no doubt that visibility was poor. As a consequence the task of attending to the injured man, with no one

Chapman v Hearse cont.

present to warn oncoming traffic, involved Dr Cherry in a situation of some danger. But, says the appellant, this was quite fortuitous and not 120 a situation reasonably foreseeable by Chapman at the time when, as the result of his negligence, his vehicle collided with that of Emery. Then to emphasise the contention that Chapman owed no duty of care to Dr Cherry the appellant enlarged upon the sequence of events which led to the final result. None of these events, it was said, was reasonably foreseeable. It was not reasonably foreseeable that Chapman would be precipitated onto the roadway, that Dr Cherry should at that moment be in the immediate vicinity, that he, as a doctor, should be first on the scene and proceed to render aid to Chapman with no other person present to warn oncoming traffic or, finally, that within a few minutes Dr Cherry should be run down by a negligent driver. But this argument assumes as the test of the existence of a duty of care with respect to Dr Cherry the reasonable foreseeability of the precise sequence of events which led to his death and it was rejected, and rightly rejected, by the Full Court. It is, we think, sufficient in the circumstances of this case to ask whether a consequence of the same general character as that which followed was reasonably foreseeable as one not unlikely to follow a collision between two vehicles on a dark wet night upon a busy highway. In pursuing this inquiry it is without significance that Dr Cherry was a medical practitioner or that Chapman was deposited on the roadway. What is important to consider is whether a reasonable man might foresee, as the consequence of such a collision, the attendance on the roadway, at some risk to themselves, of persons fulfilling a moral and social duty to render aid to those incapacitated or otherwise injured. As Greer LJ said in *Haynes v Harwood* [1935] 1 KB 146 at 156: "It is not necessary to show that this particular accident and this particular damage were probable; it is sufficient if the accident is of a class that might well be anticipated as one of the reasonable and probable results of the wrongful act": see also *Hyett v Great Western Railway Co* [1948] 1 KB 345; and *Carmarthenshire County Council v Lewis* [1955] AC 549. Whether characterisation after the event of its consequences as "reasonable and probable" precisely marks the full range of consequences which, before the event, were "reasonably foreseeable" may be, and no doubt will continue to be, the subject of much debate. But one thing is certain and that is that in order to establish the prior existence of a duty of care with respect to a plaintiff subsequently injured as the result of a sequence of events following a defendant's carelessness it is not necessary for the plaintiff to show that the precise manner in which his injuries were sustained was reasonably foreseeable; 121 it is sufficient if it appears that injury to a class of persons of which he was one might reasonably have been foreseen as a consequence ....

[Applying these considerations, the court held that the appellant's first contention must fail.]

[7.150] **Notes&Questions**

1. The role of reasonable foreseeability has varied over time since *Donoghue v Stevenson* [1932] AC 562. However, it remains the central element in the test for the duty of care. It has been argued that it is important because without being able to foresee a risk one cannot avoid it, and without being able to consider the level and significance (reasonableness) of the risk one cannot decide whether it should be avoided.
2. The meaning of reasonable foreseeability is one area that has had close attention in the recent reforms to tort law. In *Wyong Shire Council v Shirt* (1980) 146 CLR 40 a risk was said to be reasonably foreseeable if it was "not fanciful or farfetched" ((1980) 146 CLR 40 Mason J at 47. This case is extracted at [12.35]). This has been frequently criticised as too low a threshold, not least by Deane J in *Jaensch v Coffey* (1984) 155 CLR 549, extracted above. More recent cases have emphasised the role of

reasonableness, suggesting that the threshold for reasonable foreseeability shou raised. See *Romeo v Conservation Commission of the Northern Territory* (1998) CLR 431; *RTA v Dederer* (2007) 324 CLR 330 where Gummow J said "The RTA's duty of care was owed to all users of the bridge, whether or not they took ordinary care for their own safety...however, the extent of the obligation owed by the RTA was that of a roads authority exercising reasonable care to see that the road is safe 'for users exercising reasonable care for their own safety': *Brodie v Singleton Shire Council*" (at [47]). That is, the RTA did not have to foresee dangers which would arise because of people failing to take care of themselves.

The unforeseeable plaintiff

[7.155] One of the most famous cases regarding the unforeseeable plaintiff is *Palsgraf v Long Island R R Co* 248 NY 339 (1928) (US). The plaintiff was standing on a railway platform in New York when two men ran to catch a train which was just pulling out of the station. When guards tried to help the men, one of them dislodged a parcel held by one of them and it fell. The parcel contained fireworks that exploded and knocked down some scales, which hit the plaintiff and injured her. Although courts at first instance and on appeal allowed her claim, the decision of the highest New York state court was against her, holding that she was an unforeseeable plaintiff.

In *Bale v Seltsam Pty Ltd* [1996] QCA 288, the appellant's husband, Mr Bale, worked for the respondent company from 1962-1965. During that time he came home with asbestos dust on his person, on his work-clothes that Mrs Bale washed, and in his car that she cleaned and used. Mrs Bale developed malignant mesothelioma in 1995 due to her inhalation of asbestos dust. The trial judge was highly critical of the respondent company's failure to take care of its workers and to institute safe systems of work into their factory well after the risks were known, but she held, and the majority of the Court of Appeal agreed, that Mrs Bale was an unforeseeable plaintiff. In the Court of Appeal, Helman J observed that: "at the relevant time that consequence [injury to Mrs Bale] was, having regard to the state of scientific knowledge on the subject, not reasonably foreseeable." The risk to workers was well known at the time. Fitzgerald P dissented saying:

> the respondent ought to have known, at the latest by the end of 1963, that there was a risk that amongst the unidentified and unknown possible toxic effects of asbestos dust was injury or illness to those, such as wives, who were exposed to it by its introduction into their homes and lives by their husbands bringing it with them from their place of employment. Further, because of the known toxicity of asbestos dust, the known uncertainty with respect to its effects, and the knowledge that injury or illness might not emerge for many years, that risk could not be dismissed as "remote", "slight", "far-fetched" or "fanciful" or otherwise ignored so as to absolve the respondent of any duty of care towards the wives of its employees.

In 2009 a woman in Mrs Bale's position was awarded damages by the Dust Diseases Tribunal of NSW. ("Dawson v James Hardie", reported in *Daily Telegraph*, 13 April 2009). It remains to be seen whether the higher courts continue to regard such a plaintiff as unforeseeable.

In *Tame v New South Wales* (2002) 211 CLR 317 (the High Court heard Mrs Tame's case simultaneously with an application for special leave to appeal in the case of *Annetts v Australian Stations Pty Ltd* (2002) 211 CLR 317, which is found at the same citation. This is extracted at [8.125]), the plaintiff, Mrs Tame, was involved in a motor accident in January 1991 where the other driver was at fault. The police erroneously filled in the accident report as showing that the plaintiff had a blood-alcohol reading of 0.14. In fact, that reading applied to the other driver. The police corrected the error within two to three months on the original form, but not in time to prevent the mistake being passed on to the insurer. However, the insurer paid a substantial sum to Mrs Tame in August 1994, meeting her claim for leg and back injuries under the *Motor Accidents Act 1988*. Mrs Tame became extremely anxious about the insurer's delay in paying for physiotherapy and sought counselling. She spoke to her solicitor about this and at this stage (June 1992) the solicitor told her about the wrong blood alcohol reading. She was told immediately by the police that it was a mistake, and in early 1993 she received a formal assurance that the mistake had been rectified and an apology. There was also clear evidence that the insurer did not believe she had been drinking. However, Mrs Tame continued to think that the delay in paying physiotherapy bills was related to the mistake on the form, and that other people might be thinking that the accident was due to her drunkenness. This became an obsession, she felt irrationally guilty and ashamed, and in 1995 she was diagnosed as suffering from psychotic depression. Her psychiatrist's evidence was that her inability to accept that the mistake had been rectified was part of the illness. Mrs Tame won at first instance, but both the Court of Appeal and the High Court rejected her claim, on the basis that the link between a misstatement on a form and nervous shock was too remote to be regarded as reasonably foreseeable.

[7.160] **Notes&Questions**

1. Risk is a central issue in the law of negligence, because it is the risk which must reasonably foreseen. There is some interesting literature on risk: M Douglas and A Wildavsky, *Risk and Culture* (UCLA Press, Berkeley, 1982); P Bernstein, *Against the Gods: The Remarkable Story of Risk* (John Wiley & Sons, New York, 1996) and J Coleman, *Risks and Wrongs* (Oxford University Press, Oxford, 1992).
2. Regarding principles and categories, note that Brennan J's incrementalism emphasised categories while Deane J's proximity-as-principle, and *Anns*, emphasised principle; see P Vines, "The Needles in the Haystack: Principle in the Duty of Care in Negligence" (2000) 23(2) UNSWLJ 35. What are the advantages and disadvantages of each approach? What does the current approach to the duty of care emphasise – principle or category?

POLICY AND THE DUTY OF CARE

[7.165] To some extent, it is arguable that the whole concept of the duty of care turns on policy and that this is the reason why it is so difficult to find a formula which can be used as a "litmus test" for whether a duty of care should exist or not. As Professor Fleming remarked:

> No generalisation can solve the problem upon what basis the courts will hold that a duty of care exists. Everyone agrees that a duty must arise out of some "relation", some "proximity", between the parties, but what that relation is no one has ever succeeded in capturing in any precise formula ... [and later] The inclusion of "what is just (fair) and reasonable [in the *Caparo* formulation]" is a discreet acknowledgment at long last of what in academic and popular discourse is more forthrightly referred to as "policy". It admits "instrumentalist" goals beyond the equities between *this* plaintiff and *this* defendant. Looking beyond the parties, it considers the wider effects of a decision on society; the burden it would inflict no less than the benefit it would secure. (J Fleming, *The Law of Torts* (9th ed, Law Book Co, Sydney, 1998), pp 151 and 154)

There are various forms of policy, however. They range from policy which is legally recognised to policy which is really no more than an imposition of a particular judge's personal values. Legally recognised policy matters relevant to the duty of care include the policy that people should not profit from their illegal behaviour, and policies offering immunity from tortious suit to certain people or groups, such as, military personnel when at war, judges, witnesses and barristers (see *D'Orta-Ekenaike v Victoria Legal Aid* (2005) 79 ALJR 755; *Giannarelli v Wraith* (1988) 165 CLR 543 (see [11.95])) in court and so on. Another policy is that judges should be extremely cautious about interfering with policy decisions of governmental bodies (see Chapter 11). Here we briefly consider one policy issue, the question of illegality.

Gala v Preston

[7.170] *Gala v Preston* (1991) 172 CLR 243 High Court of Australia

(footnotes omitted)

[Some young men including the plaintiff spent the afternoon consuming extremely large quantities of alcohol. They then stole a motorcar which they planned to use to commit burglaries. The plaintiff drove the car for a while and then swapped with another driver and was asleep when the car hit a tree. One passenger was killed and the plaintiff was injured.]

MASON CJ, DEANE, GAUDRON and McHUGH JJ: 244 The question raised in this appeal is: what are the principles which govern the liability of the driver of a motor vehicle to a passenger in that vehicle who is injured as a result of the careless driving of the vehicle, in the course of a joint enterprise that involves the commission of a criminal offence, being the theft of the vehicle and its unlawful use ... ("the Code")? The question is one of fundamental importance and it calls for a consideration of a number of decisions of this Court ...

Illegality as a defence to an action in negligence

248 In *Henwood v Municipal Tramways Trust (SA)* (1938), this Court rejected unanimously the argument that a passenger in a tram had no action in negligence against the tramway authority because he put his head out of the window of the tram in breach of a by-law made by the authority as a safety measure. ... The proposition for which *Henwood* stands as authority is that "there is no rule denying to a person who is doing an unlawful thing the protection of the general law imposing upon others duties of care for his safety", to repeat the words of Dixon and McTiernan JJ.

Illegality as a defence in cases of joint illegal enterprise

249 However, *Henwood* was not a case in which the plaintiff sustained injury in the course of the commission by plaintiff and defendant of a joint illegal enterprise. Whether a plaintiff in that situation could recover damages for negligence was the question which arose for consideration in *Smith v Jenkins*. The facts were similar to those in the present case. The plaintiff and the defendant, having assaulted and robbed the owner of a motor vehicle, unlawfully took the vehicle without the owner's consent. The plaintiff, who was a passenger, was injured when the vehicle left the road and collided with a tree due to the defendant's careless driving. The Court held unanimously that the plaintiff could not recover. Although the ratio of the decision is not altogether clear, it is best treated as deciding that, in the circumstances, no relevant duty of care arose on the part of the defendant to the plaintiff by reason of their participation in a joint illegal enterprise ...

But it would be wrong to regard the case as authority for the proposition that in all circumstances the participation of plaintiff and defendant in a joint illegal enterprise will negate the existence of a duty of care on the part of the defendant to the plaintiff, even when the alleged breach of duty arises in the execution of the criminal act. To take one example. the fact that a joint enterprise is carried on illegally in breach of safety regulations requiring a particular precaution to be taken should not

Gala v Preston cont.

preclude the existence of a relevant common law duty of care on the part of one participant to another unless circumstances of the parties' relationship, including the nature and incidents of the enterprise, are such as to make it unreasonable to fix a participant with a duty of care. There is no a priori reason why the illegality of a particular enterprise or activity should automatically negate the existence of a duty of care which might otherwise arise from the relationship which subsists between the parties, especially if it be accepted that the decision in *Smith v Jenkins* does not rest on public policy ...

252 The majority reasoning in *Progress and Properties* and *Jackson v Harrison* is inconsistent with the proposition that a defendant is under no duty of care whenever he or she is engaged with a plaintiff in the commission of a joint illegal enterprise and the alleged breach of duty arises in the execution of the criminal act ... There are two strands to the majority reasoning. The first is that, in cases involving a joint illegal enterprise, it is necessary to examine the relation of the illegality to the negligence complained of with a view to ascertaining whether it is possible or feasible for the court to determine an appropriate standard of care. If it is impossible or not feasible to do so, no duty of care arises. The second is that, in cases of illegality arising from infringement of statutory provisions which are designed to promote safety, e.g., traffic laws and industrial safety regulations, there is no reason why illegality of that kind should negate the existence of a duty of care ...

Commencing with *Jaensch v Coffey* (1984) 155 CLR 549, this court, in a series of decisions, has accepted that a relevant duty of care will arise under the common law of negligence only where the requirement of a relationship of proximity between the plaintiff and the defendant has been satisfied ... the onus lies on the party who asserts that, by reason of special and exceptional facts, the ordinary relationship of a driver towards a passenger is transformed into one which lacks the requisite relationship of proximity to give rise to a duty of care ...

253 In determining whether the requirement is satisfied in a particular category of case in a developing area of the law of negligence, the relevant factors will include policy considerations ...

254 So, in the present case, it is a matter of examining the relationship between the respondent and the first appellant with a view to ascertaining whether there was a relationship of proximity such as to give rise to a relevant duty of care on the part of the first appellant as driver of the motor vehicle to the respondent as his passenger ...

When attention is given to the circumstances of the present case it is difficult to see how they can sustain a relationship of proximity which would generate a duty of care. The joint criminal activity involving the theft of the motor vehicle and its illegal use in the course of a spontaneously planned "joy ride" or adventure gave rise to the only relevant relationship between the parties and constituted the whole context of the accident. That criminal activity was, of its nature, fraught with serious risks. The consumption by the participants, including the first appellant, of massive amounts of alcohol for many hours prior to the accident would have affected adversely the capacity of a driver to handle the motor vehicle competently. Despite the surprising conclusion of the primary judge, each of the parties to the enterprise must be taken to have appreciated that he would be encountering serious risks in travelling in the stolen vehicle when it was being driven by persons who had been drinking heavily and when it could well be the subject of a report to the police leading possibly to their pursuit and/or their arrest. In the special and exceptional circumstances that prevailed, the participants could not have had any reasonable basis for expecting that a driver of the vehicle would drive it according to ordinary standards of competence and care.

In this situation the parties were not in a relationship of proximity to each other such that the first appellant, as the driver of the vehicle, had a relevant duty of care to the respondent, as a passenger in the vehicle. In the circumstances just outlined, it would not be possible or feasible for a court to determine what was an 255 appropriate standard of care to be expected of the first appellant as the driver of the vehicle. To conclude that he should have observed the ordinary standard of care to be expected of a competent driver would be to disregard the actual relationship between the parties as

Gala v Preston cont.

we have described it. To seek to define a more limited duty of care by reference to the exigencies of the particular case would involve a weighing and adjusting of the conflicting demands of the joint criminal activity and the safety of the participants in which it would be neither appropriate nor feasible for the courts to engage.

[Brennan, Dawson and Toohey JJ agreed that the appeal should be allowed. However, Brennan and Dawson JJ considered that the law will not condone the commission of a criminal offence by granting a civil remedy and, in that context, the notion of proximity is unhelpful.]

[7.175] This issue of illegal activities and how they relate to negligence has also been taken up in the new civil liability legislation. For example, consider the Queensland legislation extracted below. The same or similar provisions arise in the other jurisdictions: ACT: CLWA (no equivalent provision but s 38 excludes liability for terrorism-associated risks); NSW: CLA, s 54; NT: PICCA, s 10; SA: CLA, s 43 (higher standard of proof); Tas: CLA, s 5A; Vic: WrA, s 14G (only requires the court to consider whether plaintiff was engaged in an illegal activity); WA: CLA (no equivalent provision).

Personal Injuries Proceedings Act 2002 (Qld)

[7.180] *Personal Injuries Proceedings Act 2002* (Qld), s 45(1), (2)

45 Criminals not to be awarded damages

(1) A person does not incur civil liability if the court is satisfied on the balance of probabilities that –

(a) the breach of duty from which civil liability would arise, apart from this section, happened while the person who suffered harm was engaged in conduct that is an indictable offence; and

(b) the person's conduct contributed materially to the risk of the harm

(2) Despite subsection (1), the court may award damages in a particular case if satisfied that in the circumstances of the case, subsection (1) would operate harshly and unjustly ...

[7.185] This is an example of a policy being clearly stated in legislation so that courts must follow it. Policy is not always so overtly stated. The duty of care itself is often redolent of the attitudes of the judiciary, or the community, to issues like moral fault and personal responsibility. In Australia this has been quite easily discernible in the High Court's change to the treatment of the duty of care. Harold Luntz has observed that until 1995 the High Court's negligence decisions favoured plaintiffs in 75% of cases. Since then the position has been reversed, with some 75% of defendants being successful (see H Luntz, "Torts Turnaround Downunder" (2001) 1 *Oxford University Commonwealth Law Journal* 95. For a discussion of the policies underlying this turnaround, see P Vines, "Fault, Responsibility and Negligence in the High Court of Australia" (2000) 8(2) *Tort Law Review* 130-145). This policy shift has been signalled by the High Court emphasising the language of personal responsibility, which is similar to the overt policy statements made in many Second Reading speeches before the new Civil Liability Acts were passed, and indeed, in the name of one of the amending Acts: *Civil Liability Amendment (Personal Responsibility) Act 2003* (NSW). It should be remembered that common law tests, such as the second stage of the *Anns* test and the "fair just and reasonable" third stage of the *Caparo* test (see below at [7.190] Note 2), are attractive partially because they allow overt expression of policy which otherwise, it could be argued, are disguised. The decision that a duty of care is to be owed in a new category of case is always a policy decision, and it is arguable that policy should be articulated clearly rather than hidden away in order to achieve the most transparent and effective decisions.

[7.190] Notes&Questions

1. One of the concerns about judges using policy arguments is that it might encourage them to be "judicial activists". This concern implicitly assumes that judges simply find and declare the law, but the notion that judges do not make new law has now been firmly rejected. See Justice M McHugh, "The Law-making Function of the Judicial Process" (1988) 62 ALJ 15. When judges refer to public policy they generally mean taking into account wider considerations than purely those issues between the parties. Some public policy matters are widely accepted, for example, the idea underlying the *ex turpi causa* rule, that people should not benefit from their illegal activities. However, it remains true that one person's "public policy" may be another person's "prejudice" or "bias"; and there is some concern about judges using public policy which is either unarticulated in their judgment or not the product of extensive and even-handed research. Further, because the parties in a case control the evidence, matters which are of wide public interest but which do not affect the parties, might not come to light as evidence.
2. In *Caparo Industries Plc v Dickman* [1990] 2 AC 605, the test for the duty of care was said to be a three-stage test which explicitly incorporated policy elements, see [7.115]. This test was dominant in England for some time, but only Kirby J in Australia took it up and in *Sullivan v Moody*, extracted at [7.120], the majority of the High Court rejected it completely. *Sullivan v Moody* itself is, of course, strongly policy-based, since it pays so much attention to the question of whether negligence should be allowed to interfere in other areas of law including defamation and the criminal justice process.
3. Governmental policy may create a situation where a public authority is immune from a suit in negligence. This was discussed in *Sutherland Shire Council v Heyman* (1985) 157 CLR 424, extracted at [7.100], and is discussed further in Chapter 11.
4. In *Yuen Kun Yeu v Attorny-General of Hong Kong* [1988] AC 175, the Privy Council was at pains to reduce the times at which policy would be brought into the question of whether a duty of care was allowed. Lord Keith, for the Council, said:

   > The second stage of Lord Wilberforce's test in *Anns v Merton London Borough Council* ... is one which will rarely have to be applied. It can arise only in a limited category of cases where, notwithstanding that a case of negligence is made out on the proximity basis, public policy requires that there should be no liability.

5. Why would the Privy Council have been concerned about this? In that case the plaintiffs lost moneys which they had deposited with a company registered under the *Deposit-taking Companies Ordinance 1983* (Hong Kong), when the company went into liquidation. The plaintiffs sued the defendant, as representing the Commissioner administering the Ordinance, claiming that they had deposited the money in reliance on the registration of the company by the Commissioner and that he should have known that the company's business was being conducted in a

manner detrimental to depositors, and either should not have registered the company or revoked its registration. The appeal to the Privy Council was against an order of a judge of the High Court of Hong Kong, striking out the plaintiff's statement of claim as disclosing no reasonable cause of action. The Privy Council dismissed the appeal.

6. What about the police connection to illegal acts? Should one be able to sue the police for inadequately dealing with crime? In *Hill v Chief Constable of West Yorkshire* [1989] AC 53, a man known as the "Yorkshire Ripper" had committed a series of murders and attempted murders on young women in England. The last woman to be killed was Miss Jacqueline Hill, a student aged 20. Miss Hill's mother brought an action in negligence against the West Yorkshire Police. The House of Lords rejected the claim, first because of a lack of proximity between the police and Miss Hill, who was not in any special class of people other than young women who were identifiably at risk, but also on policy grounds: Police activities would be badly affected if they could be sued for negligence in carrying out their duties. This "immunity" was criticised in *Osman v United Kingdom* [1999] 1 FLR 193; (1999) EHRR CD 65 by the European Court of Justice as breaching art 6 of the *European Convention on Human Rights*. Article 6 concerns the right of access to the courts. Although the European Court has somewhat resiled from this position, in *Brooks v Commissioner of Police for the Metropolis & Ors* [2005] UKHL 24, Lord Steyn said while *Hill* would be decided the same way again, it would be best for the principle in *Hill* to be reformulated in terms of the absence of a duty of care rather than a blanket immunity (at [27]). The policy principle in *Hill* has continued to be accepted in Anglo-Australian jurisdictions: see *Cran v NSW* (2005) 62 NSWLR 95; *Van Colle v Chief Constable of Hertfordshire Police; Smith v Chief Constable of Sussex Police* [2008] UKHL 50.

7. *Hill* was distinguished in *Batchelor v Tasmania* [2005] TASSC 11 where it was alleged that the failure of the police to arrest a man whose wife had told the police her husband had left a note saying he intended to shoot her and himself. While she was at the Police station the husband arrived. The police informed him that they were going to his home to seize his firearms and went with the wife to the property where they noticed a firearm missing. The police were outside the residence while the wife was inside. The husband shot the wife through the kitchen window and then shot himself. Their son suffered psychiatric injury on learning of her death. There was evidence that the police policy at the time was to arrest a person in such circumstances in order to facilitate a restraining order. The court gave leave to file a statement of claim in respect of the alleged negligence of the police.

8. Policy plays a large role in many other cases as well. Judicial policy about the treatment of pure economic loss is a significant issue in the duty of care (see Chapter 10). Similarly policy issues about the treatment of unborn children can make cases that are legally fairly straightforward seem extremely controversial. See, for example, *Cattanach v Melchior* (2003) 215 CLR 1, extracted in Chapter 8.

9. The legislative provisions extracted in [7.180] are an example of a policy which has been legislatively inserted in many of the civil liability act provisions. The impact of the policy is discussed by GS Watson in "Civil Claims and Civil Death: "Offender Damages" and the Civil Liability Act 2002 (NSW)" 16(2) *Torts Law Journal* 81.

THE "PUBLIC LIABILITY CRISIS", TORT REFORM AND THE NEW REGIME

[7.195] As discussed in Chapter 1, in 2002-2004 all the Australian governments in response to the perceived "public liability crisis" passed legislation designed to emphasise personal responsibility in personal injury litigation and ultimately reduce damages payable for personal injury. Some jurisdictions passed new principal Acts, other passed legislation that amended existing Acts. The full names of the acts as passed (new or amending) are: *Civil Law (Wrongs) Amendment Act 2003* (ACT); *Civil Liability Act 2002* (NSW); *Personal Injury (Liability and Damages) Act* (NT); *Personal Injuries Proceedings Act 2002* (Qld); *Civil Liability Act 2003* (Qld); *Wrongs (Liability and Damages for Personal Injury) Amendment Act 2002* (SA); *Civil Liability Act 2002* (Tas); *Wrongs and Other Acts (Public Liability Insurance Reform) Act 2002* (Vic); *Civil Liability Act 2002* (WA). This legislation varies amongst the jurisdictions and in some areas merely appears to codify already existing elements of the duty of care, while in other areas it modifies the law. The main pieces of relevant legislation are outlined in [1.60].

The foundation of the tort of negligence has been set out here as it has developed at common law. All the Australian jurisdictions now have legislation which affects the law of torts, with particular emphasis on the law of negligence. It is important to keep in mind that, for the most part, this legislation assumes and builds on the existence of the common law. In some cases it abolishes a matter or an area, in other cases it modifies the common law, and in a very few cases it creates an entirely new regime. However, the legislation is frequently incomprehensible unless interpreted in the light of the common law background. We now turn to a more detailed examination of various categories of the duty of care in negligence as they operate in the new common law and statutory regime.

[7.200] **Notes&Questions**

1. For a discussion of a whole range of issues surrounding the process of tort reform in Australia see "Reform of the Law of Negligence: Balancing Costs and Community Expectations" (2002) 8 (2) UNSWLJ Forum (also available in 25(3) UNSWLJ 808).
2. An outline of the changes to the duty of care in negligence created by the Civil Liability Acts is to be found in J Dietrich, "Duty of Care under the Civil Liability Acts" (2005) 13(1) TLJ 17. See also B McDonald, "Legislative Intervention in the Law of Negligence: The Common Law, Statutory Interpretation and Tort Reform in Australia" (2005) 27(3) *Sydney Law Review* 443.

CONCLUSION

[7.205] This chapter has attempted to introduce you to some of the general forms of argument used to formulate the tests for the duty of care in negligence at common law. Many of the cases considered in this chapter were cases that opened up new categories of negligence.

The chapters following take particular categories of negligence and consider the detailed issues required to be addressed within those categories in order to determine whether or not a duty of care exists in the new mixed common law and statutory regime.

CHAPTER 8

Duty: Personal Injury

INTRODUCTION

[8.05] In Chapter 7 we discussed the general approaches to the duty of care. Here we begin to consider the various categories of case within the duty of care. The categories are created by matching up characteristics such as the types of harm suffered, whether the wrong is an act or omission or words, whether the defendant is a public or private individual, whether the defendant and plaintiff are in some special relationship such as occupier and tenant, employer and employee or manufacturer and consumer. The kind of harm is often the most significant characteristic, because, negligence being an action on the case, damage is the gist of the action and must be proved. In this chapter we consider personal injury and in the next chapter we consider pure economic loss. Since cases do not necessarily always fall neatly into the categories of our chapters, note that Chapter 11 Special Defendants also includes cases of personal injury where it is caused by some special defendant, such as a public authority. Personal injury is the major area in which the Civil Liability regime intervenes. It does so on the basis that the common law is its background and gives the law its structure and form. The tendency of this legislation is not to interfere with the duty of care in many places, but to intervene much more at the stage of breach, causation and damages. However, there are places where the Acts do prevent a duty from arising or change the circumstances where a duty arises compared with the common law. These areas include mental harm, aspects of liability of public authorities, protection of volunteers and Good Samaritans among other things. In this chapter we begin by considering the duty of care which arises in the context of physical harm.

PHYSICAL HARM

Physical harm caused by acts

Grant v Australian Knitting Mills

[8.10] *Grant v Australian Knitting Mills* [1936] AC 85 Privy Council

(footnotes omitted)

[Dr Grant, the appellant, bought underpants from a retailer who had purchased them from Australian Knitting Mills. He wore them for a day and began to get itchy. At the end of a week he changed them for another pair. He developed dermatitis so severe that he had to spend 17 weeks in hospital. The garments had been washed so there were some evidentiary problems about the presence of free sulphites in them. Dr Grant won at the trial but the High Court held that the evidence was not sufficient for a finding for Dr Grant to be safe. Dr Grant appealed to the Privy Council.]

LORD WRIGHT for the Privy Council: ...

In the first place, their Lordships are of opinion that the disease was of external origin ... But then it was said that the disease may have been contracted by the appellant from some external irritant the presence of which argued no imperfection in the garments, but which only did harm because of the appellant's peculiar susceptibility. Thus the disease might have been initiated by the mechanical irritation of the wool itself, or if it was due to some chemical ingredient in the garments, that might have been something in itself harmless, either because of its character or because of the actual quantity in which it was present, so that the mischief was attributable to the appellant's own physical defect and not to any defect in the garments; the respondents, it was said, could not be held responsible for anything in the garments which would not be harmful in normal use. Two issues were thus involved; one, was the appellant's skin normal? and the other, was there in the garments, or any part of them, a detrimental quantity of any mischievous chemical?

The Chief Justice held that the appellant's skin was normal. He had habitually up to the material time worn woollen undergarments without inconvenience; that he was not sensitive to the mechanical effects of wool seemed to be proved by an experiment of his doctors, who placed a piece of scoured wool on a clear area on his skin and found, after a sufficient interval, no trace of irritation being produced. It was said that he had suffered from tuberculosis some years before, and that the disease had merely been arrested, not eliminated, and it was then said that tuberculosis made the patient more susceptible to skin disease, because it weakens the resistance of the skin and lowers the patient's vitality. But this contention did not appear to be established. It was admitted that the appellant's skin had by reason of his illness become what is denominated "allergic," that is, unduly sensitized to the particular irritant from which he had suffered; but that could throw no light on the original skin condition. A point was made that a skin ordinarily normal might transiently and unexpectedly show a

Grant v Australian Knitting Mills cont.

peculiar sensitivity, but that remained a mere possibility which was not developed and may be ignored. In the result there does not seem any reason to differ from the Chief Justice's finding that the appellant's skin was normal.

What then caused this terrible outbreak of dermatitis? The place and time of the original infection would seem to point to the cause being something in the garments, and in particular to something in the ankle ends of the underpants, because the inflammation began at the front of the shins where the skin is drawn tight over the bone, and where the cuff of the pants presses tightly under the socks against the skin, and began about nine or ten hours after the pants were first put on. The subsequent virulence and extension of the disease may be explained by the toxins produced by the inflammation getting into the blood stream. But the coincidence, it was pointed out, was not sufficient proof in itself that the pants were the cause. The appellant then relied on the fact that it was admitted in the respondents' answers to interrogatories that the garments, when delivered to the retailer by the manufacturers, contained sulphur dioxide, and on the fact that the presence of sulphur dioxide indicated the presence of free sulphites in the garment. If there were in a garment worn continuously all day next the skin free sulphites in sufficient quantities, a powerful irritant would be set in operation. Sweat is being slowly and continuously secreted by the skin, and combines with the free sulphites to form successively sulphur dioxide, sulphurous acid and sulphuric acid: sulphuric acid is an irritant which would produce dermatitis in a normal skin if applied in garments under the conditions existing when the appellant wore the underpants. It is a fair deduction from the answers and from the evidence that free sulphites were present in quantities not to be described as small, but that still left the question whether they were present in quantities sufficient to account for the disease.

It is impossible now, and was impossible at any time after the garments were washed, to prove what quantities were present when the garments were sold …

… It is admitted, as has been said above, that some sulphites were present in the garments, and there is nothing to exclude the possibility of a quantity sufficient to do the harm. On the whole, there does not seem adequate reason to upset the judgment on the facts of the Chief Justice. No doubt this case depends in the last resort on inferences to be drawn from the evidence, though on much of the detailed evidence the trial judge had the advantage of seeing and hearing the witnesses. The plaintiff must prove his case, but there is an onus on a defendant who, on appeal, contends that a judgment should be upset: he has to show that it is wrong. Their Lordships are not satisfied in this case that the Chief Justice was wrong.

That conclusion means that the disease contracted, and the damage suffered by the appellant, were caused by the defective condition of the garments which the retailers sold to him, and which the manufacturers made and put forth for retail and indiscriminate sale. The Chief Justice gave judgment against both respondents, against the retailers on the contract of sale, and against the manufacturers in tort, on the basis of the decision in the House of Lords in *Donoghue v Stevenson* [1932] AC 562. …

The retailers, accordingly, in their Lordships' judgment are liable in contract: so far as they are concerned, no question of negligence is relevant to the liability in contract.

But when the position of the manufacturers is considered, different questions arise: there is no privity of contract between the appellant and the manufacturers: between them the liability, if any, must be in tort, and the gist of the cause of action is negligence. The facts set out in the foregoing show, in their Lordships' judgment, negligence in manufacture. According to the evidence, the method of manufacture was correct: the danger of excess sulphites being left was recognized and was guarded against: the process was intended to be fool proof. If excess sulphites were left in the garment, that could only be because some one was at fault. The appellant is not required to lay his finger on the exact person in all the chain who was responsible, or to specify what he did wrong.

Grant v Australian Knitting Mills cont.

Negligence is found as a matter of inference from the existence of the defects taken in connection with all the known circumstances: even if the manufacturers could by apt evidence have rebutted that inference they have not done so.

On this basis, the damage suffered by the appellant was caused in fact (because the interposition of the retailers may for this purpose in the circumstances of the case be disregarded) by the negligent or improper way in which the manufacturers made the garments. But this mere sequence of cause and effect is not enough in law to constitute a cause of action in negligence, which is a complex concept, involving a duty as between the parties to take care, as well as a breach of that duty and resulting damage. It might be said that here was no relationship between the parties at all: the manufacturers, it might be said, parted once and for all with the garments when they sold them to the retailers, and were therefore not concerned with their future history, except in so far as under their contract with the retailers they might come under some liability: at no time, it might be said, had they any knowledge of the existence of the appellant: the only peg on which it might be sought to support a relationship of duty was the fact that the appellant had actually worn the garments, but he had done so because he had acquired them by a purchase from the retailers, who were at that time the owners of the goods by a sale which had vested the property in the retailers and divested both property and control from the manufacturers. It was said there could be no legal relationships in the matter save those under the two contracts between the respective parties to those contracts, the one between the manufacturers and the retailers and the other between the retailers and the appellant. These contractual relationships (it might be said) covered the whole field and excluded any question of tort liability: there was no duty other than the contractual duties.

This argument was based on the contention that the present case fell outside the decision of the House of Lords in *Donoghue's case*. Their Lordships, like the judges in the Courts in Australia, will follow that decision, and the only question here can be what that authority decides and whether this case comes within its principles ...

Their Lordships think that the principle of the decision is summed up in the words of Lord Atkin:

> A manufacturer of products, which he sells in such a form as to show that he intends them to reach the ultimate consumer in the form in which they left him with no reasonable possibility of intermediate examination, and with the knowledge that the absence of reasonable care in the preparation or putting up of the products will result in an injury to the consumer's life or property, owes a duty to the consumer to take that reasonable care.a

This statement is in accord with the opinions expressed by Lord Thankerton and Lord Macmillan, who in principle agreed with Lord Atkin.

In order to ascertain whether the principle applies to the present case, it is necessary to define what the decision involves, and consider the points of distinction relied upon before their Lordships.

It is clear that the decision treats negligence, where there is a duty to take care, as a specific tort in itself, and not simply as an element in some more complex relationship or in some specialized breach of duty, and still less as having any dependence on contract. All that is necessary as a step to establish the tort of actionable negligence is to define the precise relationship from which the duty to take care is to be deduced. It is, however, essential in English law that the duty should be established: the mere fact that a man is injured by another's act gives in itself no cause of action: if the act is deliberate, the party injured will have no claim in law even though the injury is intentional, so long as the other party is merely exercising a legal right: if the act involves lack of due care, again no case of actionable negligence will arise unless the duty to be careful exists. In *Donoghue's case* the duty was deduced simply from the facts relied on – namely, that the injured party was one of a class for whose use, in the contemplation and intention of the makers, the article was issued to the world, and the article was used by that party in the state in which it was prepared and issued without it being changed in any way and without there being any warning of, or means of detecting, the hidden danger: there was, it

Grant v Australian Knitting Mills cont.

is true, no personal intercourse between the maker and the user; but though the duty is personal, because it is inter partes, it needs no interchange of words, spoken or written, or signs of offer or assent; it is thus different in character from any contractual relationship; no question of consideration between the parties is relevant: for these reasons the use of the word "privity" in this connection is apt to mislead, because of the suggestion of some overt relationship like that in contract, and the word "proximity" is open to the same objection; if the term "proximity" is to be applied at all, it can only be in the sense that the want of care and the injury are in essence directly and intimately connected; though there may be intervening transactions of sale and purchase, and intervening handling between these two events, the events are themselves unaffected by what happened between them: "proximity" can only properly be used to exclude any element of remoteness, or of some interfering complication between the want of care and the injury, and like "privity" may mislead by introducing alien ideas. Equally also may the word "control" embarrass, though it is conveniently used in the opinions in *Donoghue's case* case to emphasize the essential factor that the consumer must use the article exactly as it left the maker, that is in all material features, and use it as it was intended to be used. In that sense the maker may be said to control the thing until it is used. But that again is an artificial use, because, in the natural sense of the word, the makers parted with all control when they sold the article and divested themselves of possession and property. An argument used in the present case based on the word "control" will be noticed later.

It is obvious that the principles thus laid down involve a duty based on the simple facts detailed above, a duty quite unaffected by any contracts dealing with the thing, for instance, of sale by maker to retailer, and again by retailer to consumer or to the consumer's friend. ...

One further point may be noted. The principle of *Donoghue's case* can only be applied where the defect is hidden and unknown to the consumer, otherwise the directness of cause and effect is absent: the man who consumes or uses a thing which he knows to be noxious cannot complain in respect of whatever mischief follows, because it follows from his own conscious volition in choosing to incur the risk or certainty of mischance.

If the foregoing are the essential features of *Donoghue's case*, they are also to be found, in their Lordships' judgment, in the present case. The presence of the deleterious chemical in the pants, due to negligence in manufacture, was a hidden and latent defect, just as much as were the remains of the snail in the opaque bottle: it could not be detected by any examination that could reasonably be made. Nothing happened between the making of the garments and their being worn to change their condition. The garments were made by the manufacturers for the purpose of being worn exactly as they were worn in fact by the appellant: it was not contemplated that they should be first washed. It is immaterial that the appellant has a claim in contract against the retailers, because that is a quite independent cause of action, based on different considerations, even though the damage may be the same. Equally irrelevant is any question of liability between the retailers and the manufacturers on the contract of sale between them. The tort liability is independent of any question of contract.

It was argued, but not perhaps very strongly, that *Donoghue's case* was a case of food or drink to be consumed internally, whereas the pants here were to be worn externally. No distinction, however, can be logically drawn for this purpose between a noxious thing taken internally and a noxious thing applied externally: the garments were made to be worn next the skin: indeed Lord Atkin specifically puts as examples of what is covered by the principle he is enunciating things operating externally, such as "an ointment, a soap, a cleaning fluid or cleaning powder." Mr. Greene, however, sought to distinguish *Donoghue's case* from the present on the ground that in the former the makers of the ginger-beer had retained "control" over it in the sense that they had placed it in stoppered and sealed bottles, so that it would not be tampered with until it was opened to be drunk, whereas the garments in question were merely put into paper packets, each containing six sets, which in ordinary course would be taken down by the shopkeeper and opened, and the contents handled and disposed of separately, so that they would be exposed to the air. He contended that though there was no reason to think that the garments when sold to the appellant were in any other condition, least of all as regards sulphur contents, than when sold to the retailers by the manufacturers, still the mere possibility and not the fact of their condition having been changed was sufficient to distinguish *Donoghue's case*: there was no "control" because nothing was done by the manufacturers to exclude the possibility of any tampering while the goods were on their way to the user. Their Lordships do not accept that contention. The decision in *Donoghue's case* did not depend on the bottle being stoppered and sealed: the essential point in this regard was that the article should reach the consumer or user subject to the same defect as it had when it left the manufacturer. That this was true of the garment is in their Lordships' opinion beyond question. At most there might in other cases be a greater difficulty of proof of the fact.

... In their Lordships' opinion it is enough for them to decide this case on its actual facts.

No doubt many difficult problems will arise before the precise limits of the principle are defined: many qualifying conditions and many complications of fact may in the future come before the Courts for decision. It is enough now to say that their Lordships hold the present case to come within the principle of *Donoghue's case*, and they think that the judgment of the Chief Justice was right in the result and should be restored as against both respondents, and that the appeal should be allowed, with costs here and in the Courts below, and that the appellant's petition for leave to adduce further evidence should be dismissed, without costs.

They will humbly so advise his Majesty.

[8.15] **Notes&Questions**

1. Was Dr Grant an abnormal plaintiff or a foreseeable plaintiff? See [7.155] for discussion of the unforeseeable plaintiff.
2. *Grant v Australian Knitting Mills* [1936] AC 85 is a product liability case, as was *Donoghue v Stevenson* [1932] AC 562. They should be read, therefore, in the broader context discussed in Chapter 9.
3. The distinction between an act and an omission is not always obvious. For example, what went wrong in *Donoghue v Stevenson* [1932] AC 562 was characterised as an act–the act of negligent manufacture; but it could also have been described as a failure to inspect ginger beer barrels for snails (that is, an omission). Generally, in a case like *Donoghue v Stevenson* [1932] AC 562, because the wrong can be characterised as an act, it is not treated as an omission, even though it can also be characterised as an omission. An omission was at issue in *Hargrave v Goldman* (1963) 110 CLR 40, extracted at [7.25]. A pure omission will be one that cannot be characterised as an act, and generally will turn out to be a failure to warn or a failure to rescue. As noted below at [8.25] failure to rescue cannot create liability at common law. However, failures to warn can give rise to a duty of care. This is particularly significant in the area of medical negligence. See [8.50] below where we discuss the particular case of failure to warn of the risks in sterilisation giving rise to the birth of a child.

Physical harm caused by omission

[8.20] Where a person has suffered physical harm, whether the harm was caused by an act or omission, may alter what is required to establish a duty of care. The reason for this is that it is harder to prove a link between something that was not done (omission), than it is for something that was done (act).

Romeo v Conservation Commission of NT

[8.25] *Romeo v Conservation Commission of the Northern Territory* (1998) 192 CLR 431 High Court of Australia

(footnotes omitted)

[The plaintiff Nadia Romeo was nearly 16 when she fell $6\,^1/_2$ metres from the top of a cliff in suburban Darwin. She became a paraplegic as a consequence of her injuries. She and a friend arranged to meet other young people for a beach party at a Reserve managed by the Conservation Commission. The reserve extends over eight kilometres of coastline and is a very popular place for the public to go and view the sunset. The two girls arrived at about 10.15 pm and consumed about 150 ml of rum before the accident occurred. Nadia was not an experienced drinker and the trial judge found that she was affected by alcohol but could not say to what degree her judgment and concentration were impaired. The girls fell over the cliff after 11.45 pm, but neither girl remembered the fall and there was no other direct evidence. There was a low wooden post and log fence some distance from the cliff. In between there was some open space and along the cliff some low vegetation was growing. There was a gap in this vegetation and the appellant was found on the beach at the point below the gap. The trial judge held that the two girls did not realise the location of the cliff and simply walked off the cliff thinking the gap was a footpath. At trial her claim was dismissed. On appeal she also failed. She appealed to the High Court.]

TOOHEY AND GUMMOW JJ:

The duty of care

454 The appellant relied heavily upon the decision of this Court in *Nagle v Rottnest Island Authority* (1993) 177 CLR 423 in which a statutory authority was held liable to a person who was injured when diving into the water at a reserve managed by the Authority. The respondent argued that the decision was distinguishable from the present case. In the event that this submission was not accepted, the respondent sought leave to challenge the correctness of the decision …

Angel J correctly identified the source of the duty of care upon the respondent as its control of the Reserve. His Honour distinguished *Nagle* as involving the failure to warn of a hidden danger when a warning sign would have been an effective deterrent to the plaintiff diving where he did.

Angel J … was clearly influenced by the statement of Dixon J in *Aiken v Kingborough Corporation* (1939) 62 CLR 179 that:

> the public authority in control of … premises is under an obligation to take reasonable care to prevent injury to such a person through dangers arising from the state or condition of the premises which are not apparent and are not to be avoided by the exercise of ordinary care.

However, that statement must be read in light of the majority judgment in Nagle while that decision stands. As will appear, in light of the majority judgment, the appeal must fail…

…In *Nagle* Brennan J [said]

> The test expressed by Dixon J in *Aiken v Kingborough Corporation* focuses attention on the nature of the danger itself assessed prior to the event according to the obviousness of the danger and the care ordinarily exercised by the public. In determining in a particular case the

Romeo v Conservation Commission of NT cont.

> measure of the duty of a public authority having control and management of a large area of land used for public enjoyment, the better assessment is likely to be made by reference to the test expressed by Dixon J.

As can be seen from the passage quoted, Brennan J placed emphasis on the nature of the danger itself, assessed before the event according to its obviousness and the care ordinarily exercised by the public. This is not the test of "concealed danger" pleaded by the appellant or referred to in some earlier decisions. It is simply that the care to be expected of members of the public is related to the obviousness of the danger.

The point from which the appellant fell was not a viewing point except in the sense that visitors used the car park in order to watch sunsets from their cars. It was an obvious part of the cliff, even allowing for the vegetation in the area. And the evidence does not support a conclusion that there was an appearance of a path leading to the edge. If reasonable foreseeability is isolated from any other consideration, there may have been a "risk" of someone falling over the edge of the cliff in the sense used by Mason J in *Wyong Shire Council v Shirt* (1980) 146 CLR 40 [78]:

> A risk which is not far-fetched or fanciful is real and therefore foreseeable.

But in the present case the risk existed only in the case of someone ignoring the obvious.

In putting the matter in that way, there is a danger of drawing in the question of contributory negligence of the plaintiff to what is a consideration of the duty of care on the defendant. For that reason we think it is preferable to approach the matter on the footing that there was a duty of care on the respondent to take any steps that were reasonable to prevent the foreseeable risk becoming an actuality. But reasonable steps did not extend to fencing off or illuminating the edge of a cliff which was about two kilometres in length. The relationship of the car park to the rest of the Reserve did not call for special precautions at the cliff face nearby. A sign might serve as a warning to someone unfamiliar with the area. But to someone who was familiar, as the appellant was, a warning sign would serve no purpose....

The respondent was under a general duty of care to take reasonable steps to prevent persons entering the Reserve from suffering injury. But the taking of such steps did not extend to fencing off an area of natural beauty where the presence of a cliff was obvious. In other words, there was no breach of the respondent's duty of care in failing to erect a barrier at the cliff edge. ... We would dismiss the appeal.

KIRBY J: [Kirby J expressed his preference for the *Caparo* [See [7.115]] test, but recognised that it had been rejected. He continued.]...

The foundation for the Commission's duty of care to the appellant was the statutory power of management and control of the reserve. But the factual circumstances of the case went beyond mere power. This was not a case of unalienated Crown land, left entirely, or virtually entirely, in its natural state. The cliffs were part of a public reserve, which attracted up to half a million visitors a year. Although it would be quite wrong to describe the reserve (as the appellant did) as akin to a suburban park, it was certainly close to the outlying suburbs of Darwin. The cliffs, to the knowledge of the Commission, attracted a proportion of those visiting the reserve. The Commission did not create the ungraded road and carpark as an allurement to people to visit the cliff area, but rather as a means of controlling traffic and limiting damage to the environment. However, these improvements certainly facilitated access to the cliffs by visitors. The positioning of logs at the edge of the carpark was obviously designed to mark the limit of vehicular access in a way that still preserved the natural character of the site. It would have been foreseeable that the logs would have been used by visitors, sitting on them and watching the scenery. It was obvious that visitors would arrive at the reserve and the cliffs of different ages, different visual capacities, different states of sobriety and exhibiting different levels of advertence to their surroundings.

Romeo v Conservation Commission of NT cont.

Accordingly, the elements of foreseeability and proximity were satisfied in this case. Subject to any special considerations of legal policy deriving, for example, from the fact that the Commission is a public authority with limited resources committed to its discretion, the considerations necessary in law to give rise to a duty of care were all satisfied. But the question remains: what was the scope of that duty and was the Commission in breach of it?

Scope of the duty

It is one thing to hold that a person owes a duty of care of some kind to another. But the critical question is commonly the measure or scope of that duty. The failure to distinguish these concepts can only lead to confusion.

The ordinary formulation of the common law is that a body such as the Commission must take reasonable care to avoid foreseeable risks of injury to persons entering an area such as the reserve, including the cliffs, as of common right. However, that expression of the duty must be elaborated if it is to be of any practical guidance. The entrant is only entitled to expect the measure of care appropriate to the nature of the land or premises entered and to the relationship which exists between the entrant and the occupier. The measure of the care required will take into account the different ages, capacities, sobriety and advertance of the entrants. While account must be taken of the possibility of inadvertance or negligent conduct on the part of entrants, the occupier is generally entitled to assume that most entrants will take reasonable care for their own safety ... But where, as here, the statutory duties are stated in general and permissive terms, the scope of the duty of care imposed by the common law will be no more than that of reasonable care. Where a risk is obvious to a person exercising reasonable care for his or her own safety, the notion that the occupier must warn the entrant about that risk is neither reasonable nor just. In considering whether the scope of the duty extends, in a case such as the present, to the provision of fencing or a wire barrier, it is not sufficient to evaluate that claim by reference only to the area of the Dripstone Cliffs. An accident of the kind which occurred to the appellant might have occurred at any other elevated promontory in every similar reserve under the control of the Commission to which members of the public had access. The projected scope of the duty must therefore be tested, not solely with the hindsight gained from the happening of the accident to the particular plaintiff but by reference to what it was reasonable to have expected the Commission to have done to respond to foreseeable risks of injury to members of the public generally coming upon any part of the lands under its control which presented similar risks arising out of equivalent conduct. ...

[Kirby J held that there was no breach of duty.]

HAYNE J: It was not (and could not be) seriously suggested that the respondent in this case owed no duty of care to members of the public that might go to areas which it manages. The real subject for debate was what that duty required of it, for it is only when the content or scope of the duty is identified that questions of breach and causation of damage can be considered ....

In this case the Commission owed visitors who lawfully entered land which it managed, a duty to take reasonable care to avoid foreseeable risks of injury to them. But the bare fact that the risk of the injury which in fact occurred was reasonably foreseeable (in the sense of not far-fetched or fanciful) does not conclude the enquiry about the scope of the Commission's duty. The duty is a duty to take *reasonable care*, not a duty to prevent any and all reasonable foreseeable injuries.

[Gaudron J dissented. McHugh J agreed with Kirby J that the content of the duty should be determined according to the principles in *Nagle*, but held that the appeal should be allowed because in his view the duty was breached and caused the harm. Hayne J agreed that the appeal should be dismissed. Brennan J would also have dismissed the appeal, but he thought that the duty should be based in the action for breach of statutory duty].

[8.30]

Notes&Questions

1. *Romeo* demonstrates the difficulty of discussing the duty of care in isolation from the other elements of the tort of negligence. While it is traditional to separate the tort into the elements of duty, breach and causation of damage, the question of the scope of the duty seems to lie somewhere in between duty and breach. The question of the difference between the scope of the duty and the standard of care is a difficult one. In the past, the duty of care at a fairly high level of generality would have been discussed, followed by a more specific discussion as to the breach of duty for which the standard of care would have to be established. This separation seems less clear now.

2. In *Nagle v Rottnest Island Authority* (1993) 177 CLR 423 the majority of the High Court (Mason CJ, Deane, Dawson and Gaudron JJ) held that the Authority owed a duty of care to a man who dived into a pool, struck his head on a rock and became a quadriplegic. The Authority promoted the venue for swimming and had a statutory duty to manage it for the benefit of the public. The majority held that this, therefore, brought the Authority into a relationship of proximity with visitors such that it owed them a duty of care. They also held that a person who owes a duty to others must take account of the possibility that one or more of the class to whom a duty is owed may fail to take proper care of their own safety. They held that a warning notice should have been put up.

   By contrast, Brennan J, dissenting, suggested that the real question to be asked was whether the danger to the public was apparent and not to be avoided by the exercise of ordinary care. This test arose from *Aiken v Kingborough Corporation* (1939) 62 CLR 179 per Dixon J and *Schiller v Mulgrave Shire Council* (1972) 129 CLR 116.

3. This chapter is a chapter on requirements for the duty of care to be established before considering the question of breach (of that duty). However, it is not always so easy to determine one without the other. In *Woods v Multi-sport Holdings Pty Ltd* (2002) 186 ALR 145, extracted at [12.130] the appellant had suffered a serious eye injury while playing indoor cricket. No protective helmet was provided, nor was there a warning that there was a risk of eye injury. It was held that there was a general duty of care to prevent personal injury but that there was no duty to warn because the risk was obvious. This case illustrates how artificial the division between duty and breach can be. Gleeson CJ commented on a remark in *Romeo* made by Kirby J who said "where a risk is obvious to a person exercising reasonable care for his or her own safety, the notion that the occupier must warn the entrant about that risk is neither reasonable nor just". Gleeson CJ said (at [39]) that although reasonable foreseeability was taken to mean "only that a risk is not one that is far-fetched or fanciful ... ultimately the question of fact is what a reasonable person, in the position of the defendant, would do by way of response to the risk". In his view the risk here was obvious and the trial judge

was right to hold that there was no negligence–the duty owed had not been breached. Members of the High Court have been at pains to emphasise that "obviousness" of the risk is only one of a number of factors to be taken into account in determining the scope of the duty. In *Woods v Multi-Sport Holdings*, Gleeson CJ (at [45]) observed of Kirby J's statement above:

> It is right to describe that observation as a comment. It is not a proposition of law. What reasonableness requires by way of warning from an occupier to an entrant is a question of fact, not law, and depends on all the circumstances, of which the obviousness of a risk may be only one.

Kirby J agreed and added (at [128]) "The duty to warn depends on the circumstances of the case, not just a suggested lack of 'obviousness' of the risk." Kirby J referred to the question of obvious risk. Obvious risks are patent or clearly apparent risks, and there is a connotation in the use of the term that suggests such risks are avoidable. The High Court has been using the term "obvious" in this way since before *Romeo* was decided. For most purposes this is a matter of breach of duty or setting the standard of care so this will be discussed in Chapter 12 Breach of Duty.

4. Note also that the tort reforms in most Australian jurisdictions include a definition of obvious risk and many of them also provide that there is no duty to warn of an obvious risk: NSW: CLA, s 5H; Qld: CLA, s 15; SA: CLA, s 38; Tas: CLA, s 17; WA: CLA, s 50. Whether a risk is obvious may go to the question of foreseeability of the harm and thus the common law has always considered it in relation to both duty and breach. See below for a discussion of obvious risk in the context of sport and recreation and see also Chapter 12 Breach of Duty.

5. Where the duty of care is based on the failure or omission of the defendant to do something it is more difficult to establish a duty than when the defendant has acted. What reasons could justify the increased difficulty of establishing a duty of care in respect of an omission? Consider how the duty and its scope have to be described, the evidentiary requirements and proof of causation.

Omissions and the duty to rescue

[8.35] Any discussion of omissions raises the vexed question of whether there is a duty to rescue. The general rule in the law of negligence is that there is no duty to rescue. This is partly because it is harder to establish a duty in relation to an omission rather than an act. Generally, people will not be required to rescue another person unless they have created the risk or endangered the person by their own actions. This should be distinguished from the moral duty to rescue. Thus, legally, an adult who has done nothing to increase the risk can stand by a shallow pool and watch a toddler drown, but if the adult already had the duty to supervise the toddler, or had put the toddler near the pool or inside a pool fence, then the duty to rescue would arise. For discussion of the duty to rescue, see *Stovin v Wise* [1996] AC 923 per Lord Nicholls; *Jaensch v Coffey* (1984) 155 CLR 549 Deane J at 578; *Home Office v Dorset Yacht* [1970] AC 1004 Lord Reid at 1027.

The fact that there is no duty to rescue has been used as a focus for feminist analysis of tort law. The argument is that tort law traditionally emphasises "male" values of essential separateness of individuals from each other, while a more "female" view would recognise that interconnectedness of all persons and thus be more likely to recognise a duty to rescue. See for example, L Bender, "A Lawyer's Primer on Feminist Theory and Tort" (1988) 38 *Journal of Legal Education* 3 and L Finley, "A Break in the Silence: Including Women's Issues in a Torts Course" (1989) 1 *Yale Journal Law and Feminism* 41.

Omissions, duty to warn and medical negligence

[8.40] The duty owed by medical practitioners to their patients is discussed in Chapter 11, but at this stage it is worth noting that one category which is possibly more important for medical practitioners than others is the duty to warn a patient of risks before the patient goes ahead with treatment. This often leads to litigation where the allegation is made that the doctor failed to warn (that is, omitted to warn) the patient of a particular risk which in fact eventuated.

Duties to third parties–controlling the conduct of others

[8.45] The law frequently attributes the conduct of one person to another, so that the latter becomes responsible for the former. This is considered later under the heading of Concurrent Liability in Chapter 16. Here we are concerned with cases where the defendant is directly liable for their own failure, or their servants' or agents' failure, to exercise care over the conduct of persons who cause harm to the plaintiff. In Chapter 7 we saw two examples of this: *Home Office v Dorset Yacht Co Ltd* [1970] AC 1004 and *Modbury Triangle Shopping Centre v Anzil* (2000) 205 CLR 254. Those two cases involved criminal activity by a third party. Dixon J said in *Smith v Leurs* (1945) 70 CLR 256 at 261-262 that it is rare to find in the law a duty to control the conduct of third persons in the interest of the plaintiff and there has to be a special relationship to found the duty. This passage continues to be quoted, especially as the extent to which recognition of such duties has imposed burdens on public authorities, and private persons, becomes a matter of concern to some courts. Nevertheless, in *Smith v Leurs* (1945) 70 CLR 256 itself, the High Court recognised that one such a special relationship did exist between a parent and those to whom a child might inflict injury by conduct involving unreasonable risk of injury. This is not liability of the parent for wrongdoing of the child, but for the parent's failure to exercise care in controlling the child's actions. This will only occur where the child is not itself responsible because the child is so young.

[8.50] **Notes&Questions**

1. In *Smith v Leurs* (1945) 70 CLR 256, a 13-year old boy had fired a stone from a slingshot which hit the plaintiff in the eye, severely injuring him. The plaintiff sued the boy's parents for negligently failing to control their son. The High Court held that a duty of care did arise, but that it had not been breached because the parents had acted reasonably in telling their son not to use the slingshot outside the family home.
2. Non-delegable duty arises in situations where there is a relationship of special vulnerability. Examples include the duty of employers to provide a safe system of work for employees and the duty of hospitals to patients and the duty of schools to children at school. All these duties can create a situation where the defendant is required to control the activities of others as part of its duty to the plaintiff. See Chapter 15 Concurrent Liability.
3. Pt VIIIA of the *Law Reform (Miscellaneous Provisions) Act* (NT), inserted in 1991 makes a parent of a child jointly and severally liable with the child, for damage done

intentionally to property by the child up to an amount of $5,000. Other liabilities are not affected. See Chapter 15 Concurrent Liability.

4. In *L v Commonwealth* (1976) 10 ALR 269, the plaintiff was put in gaol on remand and placed in a cell occupied by two prisoners who were known to have a history of violence. The prisoners sexually assaulted the plaintiff and injured him. It was held that the defendant owed a duty of care to the plaintiff to keep remand prisoners separate from other prisoners. See also *Dixon v State of Western Australia* [1974] WAR 65.

5. The issue of the responsibility of a defendant for the actions of a third party will also arise in relation to causation, the question being whether the third party's action broke the chain of causation linking plaintiff and defendant. See Chapter 13 Causation.

Unborn plaintiffs

[8.55] Unborn children raise a particular difficulty, because until the child is born it is not regarded as capable of having a cause of action. The simplest example is the where a manufacturer makes baby food before the baby is born and the baby later is given the baby food which causes illness. Here, the fact that the tortious act happened while the child was unborn does not matter since the damage is sustained after the child is born.

Where a child is injured while in the womb, an action may be brought by the child for pre-natal injuries, provided the child is later born alive. The child does not need to stay alive, merely to have drawn its first breath, for the action to coalesce. Where the allegation is that if the defendant had not been negligent the child would not have been born, an action by the parents may lie against the defendant. Actions have been brought by parents where the mother would not have conceived if not for the negligence ("wrongful conception", see *F v R* (1982) 29 SASR 437) or the pregnancy would have been terminated but for the negligence ("wrongful birth", see *McKay v Essex Area Health Authority* [1982] QB 1166). These are often very controversial cases. Some jurisdictions also allow actions for "wrongful life", which are actions brought by the child on the basis that they should not have been allowed to live because of their handicap. These actions are even more controversial because they involve comparison between existence as a handicapped person and no existence at all. Such cases typically involve a great deal of policy argument.

One of the questions in the following case was whether the parents had suffered a personal injury or a pure economic loss. It is arguable that the case, though controversial, simply involves a straightforward application of ordinary negligence principles.

Cattanach v Melchior

[8.60] *Cattanach v Melchior* (2003) 215 CLR 1 High Court of Australia

(footnotes omitted)

[Mrs Melchior consulted Dr Cattanach about having a tubal ligation to prevent conception. She told Dr Cattanach that when she was 15 her right ovary and right fallopian tube had been removed. When he performed the operation what he saw appeared consistent with that history, so he attached a clip only to the left fallopian tube. Unfortunately, Mrs Melchior fell pregnant as, contrary to her belief, her right fallopian tube had not been removed. The trial judge found that Dr Cattanach had too readily accepted his patient's assertion without checking or having it specifically investigated and that he should have warned her that if she was wrong about it she might conceive.]

GLEESON CJ: [dissenting]

Cattanach v Melchior cont.

... The trial judge, Holmes J, had before her three distinct claims for damages. This appeal is concerned only with the third. The first was a claim by Mrs Melchior for damages relating to the pregnancy and birth. Those damages were assessed and allowed at $103,672.39 ... The second claim was by Mr Melchior for loss of consortium as a result of his wife's pregnancy and childbirth. This claim was allowed, and, like the first claim, it is not the subject of the present appeal. [The third claim was the claim by the parents for damages for the cost of raising the child.] ...

Actionable damage

In order to succeed in their claim, the respondents must show that they have jointly suffered damage (which is the gist of an action in negligence), and that the appellants owed them a duty of care to avoid causing damage of that kind.

... Medical negligence resulted in human reproduction and a parent-child relationship, from which flowed the obligations reflected in the damages that were awarded at trial. Attention is then concentrated upon some of the financial consequences of that relationship. ... For my part, I would regard as an integral aspect of the damage, said to be actionable damage, the parent-child relationship.

The parent-child relationship is the immediate cause of the anticipated expenditure which the respondents seek to recover by way of damages. If they have suffered actionable damage, it is because of the creation of that relationship and the responsibilities it entails ...

That the incurring of the financial costs the subject of the respondents' claim was a foreseeable consequence of the medical negligence found to have occurred is not in question. However, one thing is clear. There is no general rule that one person owes to another a duty to take care not to cause reasonably foreseeable financial harm, even assuming that what is here involved is properly so described. The reasons for that were discussed in *Perre v Apand Pty Ltd* (1999) 198 CLR 180. The burden that would be imposed upon citizens by such a rule would be intolerable ...

The claim under consideration displays all the features that have contributed to the law's reluctance to impose a duty of care to avoid causing economic loss. The liability sought to be imposed is indeterminate. It is difficult to relate coherently to other rules of common law and statute. It is based upon a concept of financial harm that is imprecise; an imprecision that cannot be concealed by an arbitrary limitation of a particular claim in subject matter or time. It is incapable of rational or fair assessment. Furthermore, it involves treating, as actionable damage, and as a matter to be regarded in exclusively financial terms, the creation of a human relationship that is socially fundamental. The accepted approach in this country is that "the law should develop novel categories of negligence incrementally and by analogy with established categories". The recognition of the present claim goes beyond that, and is unwarranted.

The appeal should be allowed ...

McHUGH AND GUMMOW JJ:

The appellants would be liable under ordinary principles for the foreseeable consequences of Dr Cattanach's negligence ...

The appellants' primary submission to this Court is that there can be no award in damages for the cost of rearing and maintaining a healthy child who would not have been born but for the negligent failure of a gynaecologist to give certain advice. Further, and in the alternative, it is submitted that any such award of damages should be limited in some way, in particular by treating the arrival of the healthy child as a benefit to be set off against the damages.

The appellants based these submissions upon the propositions that, as a matter of the policy of the law, the birth of a healthy child is not a legal harm for which damages may be recovered, and that this

Cattanach v Melchior cont.

result would follow whether action was brought in tort or contract. This policy of the law, the appellants submitted, reflects "an underlying value of society in relation to the value of human life" …

Merely to repeat those propositions upon which the appellants rely does not explain why the law should shield or immunise the appellants from what otherwise is a head of damages recoverable in negligence under general and unchallenged principles in respect of the breach of duty by Dr Cattanach. …

[The judges discussed a number of examples of public policy in action in the law.]

… It does not advance understanding greatly, … to describe the expenditure required to discharge that obligation as "economic loss"

Nor is it correct to say that the damage that the respondents suffered was the parent-child relationship or the coming into existence of the parent-child relationship. … In the law of negligence, damage is either physical injury to person or property or the suffering of a loss measurable in money terms or the incurring of expenditure as the result of the invasion of an interest recognised by the law. The parent-child relationship or its creation no more constitutes damage in this area of law than the employer-employee relationship constitutes damage in an action *per quod servitium amisit*…. Similarly, for the purpose of this appeal, the relevant damage suffered by the Melchiors is the expenditure that they have incurred or will incur in the future, not the creation or existence of the parent-child relationship….

The unplanned child is not the harm for which recompense is sought in this action; it is the burden of the legal and moral responsibilities which arise by reason of the birth of the child that is in contention. The expression "wrongful birth" used in various authorities to which the Court was referred is misleading and directs attention away from the appropriate frame of legal discourse. What was wrongful in this case was not the birth of a third child to Mr and Mrs Melchior but the negligence of Dr Cattanach. … the appellants seek the proscription of a particular head of recovery of damages. The ground advanced is that the policy of the law does not allow of any treatment as compensable harm of the third category of damages awarded by Holmes J.

In this Court, the respondents dispute the first proposition that what was involved in the third category of the award made by Holmes J was a novel head of damages. They refer to the statement of general principle by McHugh J in *Nominal Defendant v Gardikiotis* (1996) 186 CLR 49 at 54:

> When a defendant has negligently injured a plaintiff, the common law requires the defendant to pay a money sum to the plaintiff to compensate that person for any damage that is causally connected to the defendant's negligence and that ought to have been reasonably foreseen by the defendant when the negligence occurred. The sum of money to be paid to the plaintiff is that sum which will put the plaintiff, so far as is possible, "in the same position as he would have been in if he had not sustained the wrong for which he is now getting his compensation". Consequently, when a plaintiff asserts that, but for the defendant's negligence, he or she would not have incurred a particular expense, questions of causation and reasonable foreseeability arise. Is the particular expense causally connected to the defendant's negligence? If so, ought the defendant to have reasonably foreseen that an expense of that kind might be incurred?

Both questions, posed with respect to the third category of the award at trial in the present case, should be answered in the affirmative …

… What was put by Isaacs J in *Wilkinson* (1915) 21 CLR 89 may be adapted to the present case by posing two questions. First, are the underlying values respecting the importance of human life, the stability of the family unit and the nurture of infant children until their legal majority an essential aspect of the corporate welfare of the community? Secondly, if they are, can it be said there is a general recognition in the community that those values demand that there must be no award of

Cattanach v Melchior cont.

damages for the cost to the parents of rearing and maintaining a child who would not have been born were it not for the negligent failure of a gynaecologist in giving advice after performing a sterilisation procedure?

Allowing an affirmative answer to the first question, nevertheless the answer to the second must be that the courts can perceive no such general recognition that those in the position of Mr and Mrs Melchior should be denied the full remedies the common law of Australia otherwise affords them. It is a beguiling but misleading simplicity to invoke the broad values which few would deny and then glide to the conclusion that they operate to shield the appellants from the full consequences in law of Dr Cattanach's negligence ...

The reliance upon values respecting the importance of life is made implausible by the reference to the postulated child as "healthy". The differential treatment of the worth of the lives of those with ill health or disabilities has been a mark of the societies and political regimes we least admire... To suggest that the birth of a child is always a blessing, and that the benefits to be derived therefrom always outweigh the burdens, denies the first category of damages awarded in this case; it also denies the widespread use of contraception by persons such as the Melchiors to avoid just such an event. The perceived disruption to familial relationships by, for example, the Melchiors' third child later becoming aware of this litigation, is at best speculative. In the absence of any clear and accepted understanding of such matters, the common law should not justify preclusion of recovery on speculation as to possible psychological harm to children. ...

In assessing damages, it is impermissible in principle to balance the benefits to one legal interest against the loss occasioned to a separate legal interest. The benefits received from the birth of a child are not legally relevant to the head of damage that compensates for the cost of maintaining the child. ... But the head of damages that is relevant in the present case is the financial damage that the parents will suffer as the result of their legal responsibility to raise the child. The benefits to be enjoyed as a result of having the child are not related to that head of damage. The coal miner, forced to retire because of injury, does not get less damages for loss of earning capacity because he is now free to sit in the sun each day reading his favourite newspaper. Likewise, the award of damages to the parents for their future financial expenditure is not to be reduced by the enjoyment that they will or may obtain from the birth of the child.

...

KIRBY J: ... In substance, the issue for this Court is which [option] represents the solution that seems most harmonious with the applicable considerations of legal authority, principle and policy, as viewed in contemporary Australia.

Option 1: no damages

In substance, the foundation for the first option can normally be traced to religious, political or social views resting upon specific attitudes to the dignity of the human person. ...

The notion that in every case, and for all purposes, the birth of a child is a "blessing" represents a fiction which the law should not apply to a particular case without objective evidence that bears it out. In any event, it is not the birth of the child that constitutes the harm, injury or damage for which the parents sue. Instead, it is for the economic harm inflicted upon them by the injury they have suffered as a consequence of the negligence that they have proved. Contrary to the assumptions that appear to have been accepted by the courts below, the present was not a case of pure economic loss. It was, rather, an instance of direct injury to the parents, certainly to the mother who suffered profound and unwanted physical events (pregnancy and child-birth) involving her person, after receiving negligent advice about the risks of conception following sterilisation. Any economic loss was not pure, but consequential ...

Cattanach v Melchior cont.

To deny such recovery is to provide a zone of legal immunity to medical practitioners engaged in sterilisation procedures that is unprincipled and inconsistent with established legal doctrine.

This being the case, the parents were entitled to recover damages for the economic consequences of the established physical events caused by the negligence without having to satisfy the special tests adopted by the common law for so-called "pure" economic loss, applicable to cases where such physical events are absent ...

...

In the present case the negligence of the appellants was established. It was found that such negligence caused direct loss to the parents, including the physical and emotional impact on the mother. Those findings are not in issue in this appeal. They constitute the starting point for analysis of the scope and limits of the parents' recovery. Ordinary principles of tort liability would entitle the victims of the appellants' wrong to recover from the appellants all aspects of their harm that are reasonably foreseeable and not too remote....

[Kirby J thought the appeal should be allowed. Hayne and Heydon JJ also thought the type of injury was personal injury and thought the appeal should be allowed. Callinan J joined the majority in thinking the appeal should be dismissed. He characterised the loss as economic.]

[8.65] **Notes&Questions**

1. The question of whether the damage was pure economic loss or personal injury is central to what the court thought had to be proved to establish a duty of care. However, Gleeson CJ and Callinan J also thought the appeal should be allowed despite characterising the loss as economic.
2. In *CES v Superclinics (Australia) Pty Ltd* (1995) 38 NSWLR 47 (CA), a woman had repeatedly been misdiagnosed as not pregnant and claimed that this had prevented her from the chance of procuring an abortion early enough in the pregnancy to be lawful. There was disagreement amongst the judges on the correct policy in relation to the issue of whether damages should be allowed for wrongful birth. This ranged from Meagher JA's view that no damages could be recovered because such a claim was "utterly offensive", to Priestley JA's view that it was allowable, but that the parents could have chosen to have the child adopted and once they had made the choice not to have the child adopted, no further damages would flow. From then on the parents were responsible for the costs of rearing the child. On the view of Priestley JA the principle that Superclinics was responsible for the damage flowing from their negligent advice and misdiagnosis was not impeded by a policy argument about abortion. However, Kirby J observed in the extracted case above that the argument has not been accepted "that a plaintiff is disentitled to damages because she failed to procure a termination of her pregnancy or, upon birth of the child, failed to arrange for its adoption". To what extent does *Cattanach v Melchior* (2003) 215 CLR 1 resolve these policy issues?
3. What do you think of the solution which some United States and Canadian judges have preferred, which is to allow the parents of a child born after the failure of sterilisation to recover damages for the pregnancy and birth (the immediate consequences to the mother) but no more. What policy ideas underlie this solution?

Wrongful life

Harriton v Stephens

[8.70] *Harriton v Stephens* (2006) 226 CLR 52 High Court of Australia

(footnotes omitted)

[The appellant, Alexia Harriton, was born with a catastrophic disability after her mother suffered from rubella, which was not diagnosed by her doctor. It was argued that if the parents had known of the rubella they would have terminated the pregnancy. Studdert J at first instance held that, although the respondents owed the appellants a duty of care not to injure the appellant, there was no duty to provide the mother of the appellants with the necessary information to enable an informed choice to be made in regard to whether the pregnancy should be terminated. In the NSW Court of Appeal, the majority were of the view that no duty was owed in respect of this kind of loss, Spigelman CJ because this duty did not reflect values generally held in the community and Ipp JA because it was impossible to compare existence with non-existence. The dissenting judge, Mason P, took the view that the duty owed to a pregnant woman extends to her foetus and that there was no critical difference between the facts which enabled parents to sue and the child's claim that she should not have been born. He rejected the argument that it is impossible to compare existence with non-existence. In the High Court, the leading judgment was delivered by Crennan J, with whom Gleeson CJ, Gummow and Heydon JJ wholly agreed, and Hayne and Callinan JJ substantially agreed. The only dissenting judgment, that of Kirby J, is the first judgment extracted and used for comparison in the notes that follow.]

KIRBY J: 73 Alexia Harriton … suffered from catastrophic disabilities as a consequence of exposure to the rubella virus *in utero*. Her disabilities include blindness, deafness, mental retardation and spasticity. She will require constant supervision and care for the rest of her life. …

An established duty category exists: … [I]t is now established that health care providers owe a duty to an unborn child to take reasonable care to avoid conduct which might foreseeably cause pre-natal injury. Such a duty has been held to exist even before conception. Once the child is born, the damage accrues in law and the child is able to maintain an action for damages. Unless some disqualifying consideration operates, the present case falls within the duty owed by persons such as the respondent to take reasonable care to prevent pre-natal injuries to a person such as the appellant. …

Subject to what follows, therefore, the appellant's case on the duty issue is an unremarkable one in which she sues a medical practitioner for failure to observe proper standards of care when she was clearly within his contemplation as a foetus, *in utero* of a patient seeking his advice and care. She was thus in the standard duty relationship for such a case. She evidenced the important "salient feature" of vulnerability to harm (in the event great harm), should the respondent not observe proper standards of case with respect to her. Denying the existence of a duty amounts, in effect, to the provision of an exceptional immunity to health care providers. The common law resists such an immunity.

77 *Conflicting duties*: It is suggested that a significant impediment to recognising a duty of care in this case is that it would potentially conflict with the duty the respondent owed to the appellant's mother. The fact that a putative duty may conflict with an existing duty has been identified as a reason for not recognising the first-mentioned duty. However, while this concern may initially appear persuasive, closer analysis reveals that it is impossible to justify. There are at least three reasons why this is so.

First, it is strongly arguable that the fact that a defendant is under conflicting duties of care is a consideration more satisfactorily accommodated under the rubric of breach than duty …

Harriton v Stephens cont.

Secondly, this argument would logically apply to exclude the duty owed by medical practitioners to unborn children in respect of pre-natal injuries. Such a duty has the same potential in every case to conflict with the duty owed to the mother ... However, it is not suggested that the duty of care concerning pre-natal injuries should be abolished.

Thirdly, invoking suggested incompatibility between duties as a reason for refusing to recognise a new duty fails to explain why the suggested duty should yield to an existing duty. Reasons may exist in a particular case for favouring the propounded duty to the child over that already in existence to the mother.

78 *Conclusion*: In the result, the respondent owed the appellant a relevant duty of care. ...

Unquantifiability of damage? The principal argument of the respondent for rejecting this appeal was that it was impossible to quantify the appellant's loss according to the compensatory principle. [The principle that to compensate an injured party damages should be awarded which as far as possible put the person back in the position they would hav been in if the wrong had not happened] This, so it was said, was because one cannot compare existence with non-existence because no one has any experience with non-existence ... Accordingly, the respondent submitted that because damage is the gist of the tort of negligence, the appellant's action must fail ...

Professor John Fleming found this argument unconvincing:

> Objection [to wrongful life actions] is made on the supposedly value-free ground that it is legally and logically impossible to assess damages on a comparison between non-existence and life even in a flawed condition. Yet such comparison is not required with respect to added (medical) expenses, which are moreover recognised in parental claims. Also symbolic awards are regularly made for pain and suffering, even for loss of expectation of life.

...

[I]t has long been established that difficulties of quantification do not preclude relief where it is accepted that the plaintiff has suffered actionable damage. A judge faced with a paucity of evidence must simply do the best that he or she can to assess the extent of the plaintiff's loss. So much is clear law. There is no reason to conclude that it is otherwise in a wrongful life case.

...

82 *Comparing existence and non-existence*: The proposition that it is impossible to value non-existence is undermined by the fact that, for some time, the courts have been comparing existence with non-existence in other legal settings. Thus, courts have declared lawful the withdrawal of life-sustaining medical treatment from severely disabled newborns and adults and from the terminally ill ... Such cases are distinguishable from the present. Unlike the case at hand, they are not concerned with assigning a monetary figure to the difference between existence and non-existence. However, one cannot escape the fact that they entail a judicial comparison between existence and non-existence. Furthermore, some courts which have denied wrongful life actions have done so not because the damage cannot be quantified but because they consider that existence will always be preferable to non-existence. As Professor Harvey Teff points out, "[p]aradoxically, this very premise logically entails the measurability *in principle* of non-existence".

... The appellant has unarguably suffered, and continues to suffer, significant pain and discomfort which she would not have had to endure had the respondent acted with reasonable care. It would be wrong to deny compensation where resulting damage has occurred merely because logical problems purportedly render that damage insusceptible to precise or easy quantification ...

The judicial discourse in the State Supreme Court in the present case and in other like Australian and overseas cases has been permeated by a search for the appropriate "comparator" ... It has resulted in a conclusion that such a "comparator" does not exist because the pos ited "comparator" is a foetus whose life would have been terminated by a medical practitioner acting with due care. To this apparently logical argument the foregoing cases afford two answers that, for me, are applicable and compelling. First, the comparator contemplated in this case, non-existence, is purely hypothetical – a fiction, a creature of legal reasoning only. No one is now suggesting the actual death of the appellant. Indeed, it is her very existence that gives rise to the pain, suffering and expense for which she brings her action. And secondly, there are limits to the insistence on this fictitious comparator where doing so takes the law into other inconsistencies and to a conclusion that is offensive to justice and the proper purpose of the law of negligence. ...

84 *Can non-existence ever be preferable?...*

In order to recover damages, the compensatory principle requires a plaintiff to show he or she has lost something as a result of the defendant's tort. In other words, a plaintiff needs to establish that he or she is worse off in some respect than he or she would otherwise have been. In ordinary personal injury actions, it is not necessary for a plaintiff to establish that, all in all, his or her life is worse than it would have been but for the defendant's tort. A plaintiff who suffers an injury, which is not sufficiently severe to lead him or her to think that the quality of life is materially less than it would have been but for that injury, is still entitled to bring an action for, and recover damages in respect of, that injury. The compensatory principle does not put such a person out of court.

The position is somewhat different in the case of wrongful life actions. ... [T]he only way for a person who owes her existence to the respondent's negligence to establish a loss is to show that the alternative, non-existence, would have been preferable ... In extreme cases, it may be a valid contention ...

86 *Conclusion on damages*: For the foregoing reasons, subject to what follows, I would hold that, on the birth of the child in a case such as the present, general damages for proved pain and suffering and special damages for needs created by the negligence of a medical practitioner in respect of a foetus in utero are recoverable in an action brought by or for that child ...

CRENNAN J: 115

The issues

The main issue is whether the appellant/child who was born disabled has a cause of action in negligence against the respondent/doctor on the agreed facts which stated that the doctor failed to advise the child's mother during her pregnancy of circumstances which would have led the child's mother to obtain a lawful termination of that pregnancy. If such a cause of action exists, the next issue is whether the heads of damages are limited to, or different from, damages generally available in claims for personal injury.

Consideration of the nature of the damage in this case, and the principles relevant to assessment of damages, leads to the result that the appellant has no cause of action against Dr P R Stephens.

To have a cause of action in negligence the appellant needs to show damage suffered by her and a duty of care on Dr P R Stephens to avoid that damage ...

The question of what, if any, categories of compensatory damages are available only arises when actual damage or injury, together with breach of a duty of care and causation, are established. ...

The appellant's counsel eschewed labelling the appellant's claim a "wrongful life" claim and emphasised that what was wrongful was Dr P R Stephens's failures to diagnose rubella and to advise. It was those failures which were said to have caused or materially or effectively caused the damage, namely Alexia Harriton's "life with disabilities". However, such claims have come to be recognised internationally for some decades as "wrongful life" claims ...

While precise facts have differed, a comparative survey reveals that many courts have recognised the difficulty and novelty of the question of whether life with congenital defects can be recognised as

Harriton v Stephens cont.

damage, at the suit of a disabled person who would not exist in the absence of the alleged negligence. Speaking generally, such claims have been resisted in common law jurisdictions... A right of action and a duty of care are inseparable ...

The position elsewhere

119 In the United Kingdom, the English Court of Appeal in *McKay v Essex Area Health Authority* [1982] QB 1166 unanimously rejected such a claim by a child affected by rubella as disclosing no reasonable cause of action against her local health authority and her mother's doctor ... In finding neither defendant was under any duty to the child to give the child's mother an opportunity to terminate the child's life, Stephenson LJ said:

> That duty may be owed to the mother, but it cannot be owed to the child.
>
> To impose such a duty towards the child would, in my opinion, make a further inroad on the sanctity of human life which would be contrary to public policy. It would mean regarding the life of a handicapped child as not only less valuable than the life of a normal child, but so much less valuable that it was not worth preserving, and it would even mean that a doctor would be obliged to pay damages to a child infected with rubella before birth who was in fact born with some mercifully trivial abnormality.

He then went on to recognise that a court could not evaluate non-existence for the purpose of determining whether a disabled child had lost anything by being born ...

[She discussed cases in the United States, Canada, Israel and Europe where courts have both accepted and rejected wrongful life claims].

Duty of care

123 In the present appeal, particular significance attaches to the need to preserve the coherence of legal principles, as emphasised in *Sullivan v Moody* (2001) 74 ALJR 1580; 183 ALR 404. ... It was not Dr P R Stephens's fault that Alexia Harriton was injured by the rubella infection of her mother. Once she had been affected by the rubella infection of her mother it was not possible for her to enjoy a life free from disability. The agreed facts assert that Dr P R Stephens should have treated Mrs Harriton differently, in which case rubella would have been diagnosed. However, on the agreed facts, it was not possible for Dr P R Stephens to prevent the appellant's disabilities. Dr P R Stephens would have discharged his duty by diagnosing the rubella and advising Mrs Harriton about her circumstances, enabling her to decide whether to terminate her pregnancy; he could not require or compel Mrs Harriton to have an abortion.

It is important to an understanding of the right or interest which the appellant is seeking to protect, to maintain the distinction between suing the doctor for causing physical damage, being the disability, and suing the doctor for causing a "life with disabilities", as the case was put by the appellant in this Court. The former is immediately caused by rubella, whereas the latter is said to be immediately, or materially, or effectively caused by the doctor's failure to advise the mother such that her response would have been to obtain a lawful abortion ... This raises the difficult question of whether the common law could or should recognise a right of a foetus to be aborted, or an interest of a foetus in its own termination, which is distinct from the recognised right of a foetus not to be physically injured whilst *en ventre sa mère*, whether by a positive act or by an omission.

It is an important consideration in determining whether a duty of care as alleged exists that it is only Mrs Harriton who was entitled to terminate her pregnancy lawfully in New South Wales, by reference to her physical and mental health.

A court is not able to infer from a mother's decision to terminate a pregnancy that her decision is in the best interests of the foetus which she is carrying. The law does not require that considerations of the mother's physical and mental health, which may render an abortion lawful, should be co-incident with the interests of her foetus.

Harriton v Stephens cont.

Equally, a mother with an ethical, moral or religious objection to abortion is entitled to continue her pregnancy despite risks identified by her doctor to her physical and mental health or despite being advised by her doctor that rubella may have affected the foetus she carries. In the context of wrongful birth claims, the decision of parents not to have even a lawful abortion has been respected by the law. … The duty of care proposed to the foetus (when born) will be mediated through the mother. The damage alleged will be contingent on the free will, free choice and autonomy of the mother. These circumstances can be expected to make it difficult for a court to assume that a possible conflict between the interests of mother and child would be "exceptional" and to complicate the task of a court in formulating normative standards of conduct against which breach of such a duty of care could be assessed.

It is not to be doubted that a doctor has a duty to advise a mother of problems arising in her pregnancy, and that a doctor has a duty of care to a foetus which may be mediated through the mother. However, it must be mentioned that those duties are not determinative of the specific question here, namely whether the particular damage claimed in this case by the child engages a duty of care. To superimpose a further duty of care on a doctor to a foetus (when born) to advise the mother so that she can terminate a pregnancy in the interest of the foetus in not being born, which may or may not be compatible with the same doctor's duty of care to the mother in respect of her interests, has the capacity to introduce conflict, even incoherence, into the body of relevant legal principle.

A further consideration is that there would be no logical distinction to be made between a duty of care upon a doctor as proposed, and a correlative duty of care upon a mother or parents who decline to have an abortion and choose to continue a pregnancy despite being informed of the risk of disability to the child. Such conduct would then be the intervening immediate cause of the damage claimed. The appellant's answer to this difficulty was that the mother's current right to make a choice and to terminate the pregnancy lawfully or not could not be cut down by recognising the right of a child to sue in respect of a life with disability. But this answer exposes rather than resolves the possible lack of coherence in principle occasioned by the appellant's claim. The risk of a parent being sued by the child in these circumstances was recognised in the United Kingdom in *McKay* and in California in *Curlender v Bio-Science Laboratories* 165 Cal Rptr 477 (1980) …

Damage

126 Because damage constitutes the gist of an action in negligence, a plaintiff needs to prove actual damage or loss and a court must be able to apprehend and evaluate the damage, that is the loss, deprivation or detriment caused by the alleged breach of duty. Inherent in that principle is the requirement that a plaintiff is left worse off as a result of the negligence complained about, which can be established by the comparison of a plaintiff's damage or loss caused by the negligent conduct, with the plaintiff's circumstances absent the negligent conduct. …

A comparison between a life with disabilities and non-existence, for the purposes of proving actual damage and having a trier of fact apprehend the nature of the damage caused, is impossible. …

There is no present field of human learning or discourse, including philosophy and theology, which would allow a person experiential access to nonexistence … There is no practical possibility of a court (or jury) ever apprehending or evaluating, or receiving proof of, the actual loss or damage as claimed by the appellant. It cannot be determined in what sense Alexia Harriton's life with disabilities represents a loss, deprivation or detriment compared with non-existence …

The practical forensic difficulty is independent of arguments about the value (or sanctity) of human life and any repugnance evoked by the appellant's argument that her life with disabilities is actionable. This objection to the cause of action is in no way affected or diminished by shifts in any absolute value given to human life (if such shifts have occurred), occasioned by liberalised abortion laws or other

Harriton v Stephens cont.

developments in the law in respect of lawful discontinuation of medical treatment where the welfare of a suffering person is the main consideration. A duty of care cannot be stated in respect of damage which cannot be proved by persons alleging such a duty has been breached, and which cannot be apprehended by persons said to be subject to the duty, and which cannot be apprehended or evaluated by a court (or jury) …

Analogy to decisions in the *parens patriae* jurisdiction is not apt, chiefly because the wardship cases do not require a forensic establishment of damage by reference to non-existence. The comparisons generally called for (in a non-tortious context) are between continuing medical treatment prolonging life and discontinuing medical treatment which may hasten death, always determined by reference to the best interests of the child or person unable to decide for themselves. It is possible for a court to receive evidence allowing it to undertake a balancing exercise in respect of those two possible courses of action before making a decision. As accepted in *In re J (A Minor) (Wardship: Medical Treatment)* [1991] Fam 33, such comparisons involve matters of degree and lack the absolute quality of a comparison between a life with disability (or suffering) and death. The analogy between this case and the wardship cases is also inapt because of the clear distinction between death accelerated by non-intervention or the withholding of medical treatment and death by the intervention of lawful abortion, a difference recognised in *In re J*. …

In the present case, the damage claimed cannot be the subject of evidence or forensic analysis … Not every claim for damage is actionable. The principles of negligence are designed to set boundaries in respect of liability. The analytical tools therefor, such as duty of care, causation, breach of duty, foreseeability and remoteness, all depend for their employment on damage capable of being apprehended and evaluated.

The value of life

128 There is nothing in the majority's rejection of the "blessing" argument in *Cattanach v Melchior* (2003) 215 CLR 1 or in their disinclination to bar a wrongful birth claim because of the law's recognition of broad underlying values of the importance of life, which prevents the additional observation in this case that it is odious and repugnant to devalue the life of a disabled person by suggesting that such a person would have been better off not to have been born into a life with disabilities.

In the eyes of the common law of Australia all human beings are valuable in, and to, our community, irrespective of any disability or perceived imperfection.… While Alexia Harriton's disabilities are described in the agreed statement of facts, her disabilities are only one dimension of her humanity …

The Court knows very little about Alexia Harriton but it is possible for the Court to infer that Alexia Harriton is no different in this respect from fellow human beings, despite the fact that her grave disabilities include mental retardation. A seriously disabled person can find life rewarding and it was not contended to the contrary on behalf of the appellant. It was not contended as a fact that Alexia Harriton cannot experience pleasure. The Court was informed Alexia Harriton commanded the devotion of her parents. …

To allow a disabled person to claim his or her own existence as actionable damage, is not only inconsistent with statutes prohibiting differential treatment of the disabled, but it is also incompatible with the law's sanction of those who wrongfully take a life. No person guilty of manslaughter or murder is entitled to defend the accusation on the basis that the victim would have been better off, in any event, if he or she had never been born. All human lives are valued equally by the law when imposing sentences on those convicted of wrongfully depriving another of life.

The compensatory principle

130 The fundamental principle governing the assessment of compensatory damages is well settled. …

Harriton v Stephens cont.

Providing compensation if liability is established is the main function of tort law; compensation is "[t]he one principle that is absolutely firm, and which must control all else"; if the principle cannot be applied the damage claimed cannot be actionable …

It can be accepted that mere difficulty in the calculation of damages is not a bar to recognising a cause of action, especially when damages conventionally awarded in personal injuries can assist. However, it is not possible on the facts of this case to apply the compensatory principle … The comparison which is called for on the agreed facts is a comparison between her life with disabilities and the state of non-existence in which she would have been, absent the doctor's alleged carelessness in failing to advise her mother, which advice would have led her mother to obtain a lawful abortion. It is not that the comparison is difficult or problematic. It is impossible, for the reasons already explained.

To posit that the necessary comparison can be achieved by comparing Alexia Harriton's "notional life without disabilities" with her actual "life with disabilities" (the comparator used in *Zeitsov v Katz* (1986) 40(2) PD 85 …) depends on a legal fiction. So too does a comparison of her "life with disabilities" with the life of "someone otherwise comparable with her in all respects except for her suffering and her needs", the "fictional healthy person". …

The common law is hostile to the creation of new legal fictions and the use of legal fictions concealing unexpressed considerations of social policy has been deprecated. Employment of either of the legal fictions proposed would have the effect of excepting the appellant from the need to come within well-settled and well-understood principles of general application to the tort of negligence. Also, the heads of damages sought to be recovered reveal the conceptual difficulty of assessing damages in respect of the appellant's claim. The appellant relies on conventional awards of damages in personal injury. However, there cannot have been any damage to the appellant's earning capacity and none was claimed. In respect of the appellant's special pain and disabilities caused by rubella, it was suggested that a comparison could be made in the light of the ordinary range of usual experience of pain and disabilities. As to medical and care needs, on the actual comparator, nothing is recoverable.

A life without special pain and disabilities was never possible for the appellant, even before any failures by Dr P R Stephens. Approaching the task of assessing general and special damages, as suggested, has the effect of making Dr P R Stephens liable for the disabilities, which he did not cause …

Conclusion

134 In the present case the damage claimed is not amenable to being determined by a court by the application of legal method. A duty of care cannot be clearly stated in circumstances where the appellant can never prove (and the trier of fact can never apprehend) the actual damage claimed, the essential ingredient in the tort of negligence. The appellant cannot come within the compensatory principle for measuring damages without some awkward, unconvincing and unworkable legal fiction. To except the appellant from complying with well-established and well-known principles, integral to the body of doctrine concerning negligence applicable to all plaintiffs and defendants in actions in all other categories of negligence, would occasion serious incoherence in that body of doctrine and would ignore the limitations of legal method in respect of the appellant's claim.

The other considerations, the autonomy of a mother in respect of any decision to terminate or continue a pregnancy, the problematic nature of the right or interest being asserted, the uncertainty about the class of persons to whom the proposed duty would be owed and the incompatibility of the cause of action with values expressed generally in the common law and statute all support the conclusion that the appellant does not have a cause of action against the respondent on the agreed facts … Life with disabilities, like life, is not actionable.

Harriton v Stephens cont.

The decision of the majority of the Court of Appeal should be upheld. The appeal should be dismissed with costs.

Legislative intervention

[8.75] After *Cattanach v Melchior* (2003) 215 CLR 1 was decided in the High Court a number of jurisdictions introduced legislation limiting the possibility of bringing actions concerned with the costs of rearing and maintaining a child. The Australian Capital Territory, New South Wales, South Australia and Queensland produced legislation to deal with the problem raised in the case. Qld: CLA, ss 49A and 49B deal specifically with the problem of failed sterilisation or contraception and prohibits the awarding of damages in such situations. The South Australian provision, SA: CLA, s 67, is slightly broader, and the New South Wales is provision broadest of all. NSW: CLA, s 71 prevents the awarding of damages for economic loss for the costs associated with rearing or maintaining a child in any action involving a claim for the birth of a child. It does not prevent the recovery of additional costs associated with rearing a child who has a disability, nor does it prevent claims for personal injury incurred pre-natally. A Bill in the Australian Capital Territory, similar to the New South Wales legislation which was presented in 2005, was negatived in 2007.

[8.80] **Notes&Questions**

1. In the extracted case, Kirby J said [at 97] ff:

> The pitfalls of adopting an inflexible approach on this issue can be seen from another legal context where a supposedly impossible comparison was initially invoked to justify acceptance of a wrong without a remedy. Several cases in the United Kingdom raised the question whether a pregnant woman, who was dismissed from her employment by reason of her becoming pregnant, was entitled to relief under the *Sex Discrimination Act 1975* (UK) (the SDA). The statutory test for unlawful discrimination required a comparison of the claimant's treatment with the treatment which an employee of the other sex would have received in similar circumstances.

In *Turley v Allders Department Stores Ltd* [1980] ICR 66, it was held that claims for relief under the SDA by women who had been dismissed from their employment, allegedly on the grounds of their becoming pregnant, must fail because the comparison contemplated by the SDA was impossible as there is no masculine equivalent of a pregnant woman.

The issue subsequently arose in *Hayes v Malleable Working Men's Club and Institute* [1985] ILIR 367. In that case, Waite J declined to follow *Turley* on the ground that, on his reading of the SDA, a strict comparison was not required. His Lordship's approach was later confirmed by the English Court of Appeal in *Webb v EMO Air Cargo (UK) Ltd* [1992] 2 All ER 43. In that case, Glidewell LJ stated that, holding that the dismissal of a pregnant woman was not contrary to the SDA because of the impossibility of making a comparison, "would be so lacking in fairness and in what I regard as the proper balance to be struck in the relations between employer and employee that we should only [accede to that argument] if we are compelled by the wording of the [SDA] to do so".

Do you think this argument has force in the context of wrongful life cases?

2. In the NSW Court of Appeal judgment, *Harriton v Stephens* [2004] NSWCA 93, Ipp JA observed (at [335]):

> idiosyncratic attempts to extend liability in tort law by fundamentally changing established principles and rules, motivated as they are by sympathy for plaintiffs, come at an immeasurable cost to the community, and involve judicial legislation that will ultimately result in loss of respect for the law.

Could his remarks equally apply to attempts to confine liability in tort law by fundamentally changing established principles and rules?

3. In *Watt v Rama* [1972] VR 353, the plaintiff alleged that the defendant by negligent driving injured the plaintiff's mother, who was pregnant with and subsequently gave birth to the plaintiff with brain damage. This was alleged to be due to injury to the mother's capacity to carry and deliver the plaintiff, or injury to the foetus of the plaintiff, or both. The preliminary questions of law which the court answered in favour of the plaintiff were whether the defendant owed a duty of care not to cause injury to the plaintiff and whether in the circumstances the damage was too remote.

Winneke CJ and Pape J in their joint judgment said that in the common case, the duty attaches to the defendant and is breached when the act or neglect occurs. But where the injury does not occur contemporaneously with the act of neglect, the relationship will not crystallise to create the duty until the plaintiff becomes defined, and the contingent or potential duty ripens into a relationship imposing the duty. The defendant in the present case should reasonably have foreseen that his negligence might cause injury to a pregnant woman in the car with which his collided and should equally have foreseen injury to the child she was carrying on birth. The potential relationship, capable of imposing the duty, would have crystallised at birth as would the child's correlative right of action.

4. Manufacturer X Co makes a brand of baby food, which has a shelf-life of two years. Baby Betty was given this at the age of four weeks in January 2004 and suffered severe gastroenteritis caused by negligent bottling. The product was made in February 2002. Did the manufacturer owe the baby a duty of care?

5. For further reading on this area see LCH Hoyano, "Misconceptions about Wrongful Conception" (2002) 65 MLR 883; D Weybury and C Witting "Wrongful Conception Actions in Australia" (1995) 3 TLJ 53; B Golder, "From *McFarlane* to *Melchior* and Beyond: Love, Sex, Mondy and Commodification in the Anglo-Australian Law of Torts" (2004) 12 TLJ 128.

6. In the United Kingdom, the topic of pre-natal injuries (the most notorious of which were those caused by the drug thalidomide (see Chapter 9, Duty – Defective Property or Goods)) was the subject of a report by the Law Commission which published its findings in 1974 (Report on Injuries to Unborn Children (1974) Law Commission No 60, Cmnd 5709). This led to the passage of the *Congenital Disabilities (Civil Liability) Act 1976* (UK). The Pearson Committee in its report in 1978 further reviewed the legislation (Cmnd 7054 paras 163, 1482). The *Congenital Disabilities (Civil Liability) Act 1976* makes the mother

generally immune from suit except in the case of negligent driving (ss 1, 2). The Pearson Committee in 1978 considered that the immunity should be extended to the father (Cmnd 7054 paras 163, 1482). The general principles applicable to children in Australia are that they may not sue their parents for mere neglect of parental duty but may do so in respect of positive subjection to hazards. Compare *Hahn v Conley* (1971) 126 CLR 276; *Cameron v Commissioner for Railways* [1964] Qd R 480 with *Rogers v Rawlings* [1969] Qd R 262; see also *Darcy v Nominal Defendant* [1985] 2 MVR 447. These principles would presumably extend to actions in respect of injuries before birth when the child was born alive and able to sue, following the above authorities. So, in *Lynch v Lynch* (1991) 25 NSWLR 411, the mother was held liable to the child when the child was born alive for negligent driving that injured the child in the womb.

Sport and Recreation

[8.85] Sport and recreation, by their nature, often result in physical injury. This is therefore a fertile field for examining the duty of care in negligence. In *Rootes v Shelton* (1967) 116 CLR 383 at 387, in a case which confirmed that participants in sport owe a duty of care to each other, Kitto J said:

> I cannot think that there is anything new or mysterious about the application of the law of negligence to a sport or a game. Their kind is older than the common law itself.

Indeed, one of the most often quoted Australian negligence cases is a water-skiing case: *Wyong Shire Council v Shirt* (1980) 146 CLR 40 (see [12.35]). A great many issues in negligence relating to sport are issues relating to the standard of care or breach of duty, but the question of the duty of care is our concern here. In the area of sporting activities one needs to consider the duty owed to, and between, participants, spectators, coaches, sports administrators and occupiers. Thus a wide range of duties may arise at common law, some of which have been affected by the Civil Liability Acts. First, we examine the common law approach to the duty of care in this area. In most cases it is no different from other physical injury cases, but in the following case the argument was that there was a duty to create different rules for the game.

Agar v Hyde

[8.90] *Agar v Hyde; Agar v Worsley* (2000) 201 CLR 552 High Court of Australia

(footnotes omitted)

GLEESON CJ: 558 These appeals raise the question whether a member of the board of a voluntary sporting association, which has the capacity to make and alter the rules of a sporting contest, is under a legal duty of care to players in relation to the risk of injury.

The appellants were individual members of the Board ... of an international Union, formed in relation to the sport of rugby football. One of the functions of the International Rugby Football Board ("the Board" or "the IRFB") was to frame and interpret the rules of the sport, called the "Laws of the Game". The Board met once a year, usually, although not invariably, in London. The individual appellants attended annual Board meetings as representatives of national member unions.

The respondents are both men who, whilst playing the sport in local competitions in Australia, suffered serious injury. At the time of their injuries they were aged 19 and 18 respectively. ...

The respondents contend that the rules in force at the time they suffered their injuries were such that they were exposed to unnecessary risk. The particular deficiencies in the rules, of which complaint is made, are said to relate to the formation of scrums.

Agar v Hyde cont.

Fundamental to the claims made against the appellants is the contention that, by reason of the capacity of the Board to make and change the rules of the game of rugby football, each appellant owed a duty of care to all players of the sport, including the respondents. The content of that duty was formulated in oral argument as a duty to take reasonable care in monitoring the operation of the rules of the game to 559 avoid the risk of unnecessary harm to players. In the course of further argument, the reference to monitoring the operation of the rules was altered to taking reasonable care to ensure that the rules did not provide for circumstances where risks of serious injury were taken unnecessarily.

In the argument for the respondents, references to "injury" were often made as references to "serious injury". On any view, the injuries suffered by the respondents were serious. However, if there is a duty of care related to risk of injury, there is no reason in principle to limit it to serious injury, and there are practical difficulties in seeking to do so. Depending upon the circumstances, what might be a minor injury to one person might have serious consequences, physical or economic, for another. It may be that the risk of injury from playing rugby football is so obvious, and the occurrence of injury to players so common, that unqualified references to injury were regarded as forensically embarrassing. Whether a solution can be found in the concept of "unnecessary risk" is a matter that will be considered below.

The existence of the asserted duty of care forms the central issue in these appeals ...

The Court of Appeal disagreed with the conclusion of Grove J that no duty of care was owed. ... For the reasons which follow, I consider that Grove J was correct. The appellants did not owe the respondents a duty of care of the kind upon which the claims against them depend....

561 It will be necessary to return to the nature of the control which is here said to exist.... We are concerned with adults participating voluntarily in amateur sport. The concept of control requires closer analysis in a context such as the present.

Voluntary participation in a sporting activity does not imply an assumption of any risk which might be associated with the activity, so as to negate the existence of a duty of care in any other participant or in any person in any way involved in or connected with the activity. That, however, is not to deny the significance of voluntary participation in determining the existence and content, in a given case, or category of cases, of an asserted duty of care.

People who pursue recreational activities regarded as sports often do so in hazardous circumstances; the element of danger may add to the enjoyment of the activity. Accepting risk, sometimes to a high degree, is part of many sports. A great deal of public and private effort, and funding, is devoted to providing facilities for people to engage in individual or team sport. This reflects a view, not merely of the importance of individual autonomy, but also of the public benefit of sport. Sporting activities of a kind that sometimes result in physical injury are not only permitted; they are encouraged. Sport commonly involves competition, either between individuals or teams. A sporting contest might involve body contact where physical injury is an obvious risk, or the undertaking by individual competitors of efforts which test the limits of their capabilities in circumstances where failure is likely to result in physical harm. Rules are of the essence of sporting competition. Individuals, or teams, wishing to compete must agree, personally or through membership of some form of association, upon the rules which will govern their competition. In the case of rugby football, as in the case of many other sports, there are layers of 562 voluntary associations, from a local to an international level, which provide facilities for individuals who wish to enjoy the game to participate in contests, and which, as part of providing those facilities, make, amend, interpret and enforce the rules of the game. Making and changing the rules may require giving weight to many considerations, some conflicting. It is not in dispute that they may include considerations relating to the safety of participants in the sport. It is at this point, and in this context, that the question of a legal duty of care arises.

The Court of Appeal said that the IRFB is a law-giver, and controls the game.... No individual appellant could amend the rules. No individual appellant controlled the game internationally. No

Agar v Hyde cont.

individual appellant was a law-giver. The most that can be said is that each appellant was one of a number of participants in a process by which, from time to time, the rules of the sport at an international level could be made and changed. There were other participants in the same process who have not been sued, but that simply serves to emphasise that it is individual responsibility that is in question, even though it is said that the appellants had that responsibility as members of a group. To speak of persons who were sent once a year to London, as representatives of national unions, as controlling a game of football played in a Sydney suburb, or a country town, by reason of their collective capacity to alter the international rules, is to speak of a remote form of control.

The content of the suggested duty is elusive. Reasonableness is the ultimate test, but reasonableness can only be determined in a context. The obligation, it is argued, is to see that the rules of the game do not expose players to unnecessary risk of serious injury. The risk of young men having their necks broken is a matter to be taken seriously; but some would say the same about other, and lesser, risks associated with rugby football. The game is based on activities such as tackling, scrummaging, rucking and mauling which, by the standards of most members of the community, are obviously dangerous, and which regularly result in injuries which many people, even if not all footballers, would regard as serious. By reference to what standards are such risks to be classified as necessary or unnecessary? What is an unnecessary risk in an inherently dangerous sport? When an obviously risky activity is engaged in, voluntarily, for pleasure, by an adult, how does a court determine whether a certain level of risk is unnecessary?

The qualification, "unnecessary", is of critical importance to the respondents' argument. If it were removed, the contention would be manifestly implausible. But ideas of what is an unnecessary risk in 563 playing a sport vary widely. It is probably the case that most people in the community would not play rugby football, and would regard any possible pleasure associated with the game as being outweighed by the risk of injury. Even amongst enthusiasts, there would be differing views as to the degree of risk that is acceptable. Individuals playing in the one match might have different levels of risk they are personally willing to accept. There are sports, including some codes of football, which carry much less risk of injury to players than rugby football. There is no objective standard by reference to which it is possible to decide that a given level of risk involved in rugby is acceptable, but that beyond that level, it is "unnecessary". The high degree of subjectivity of an assessment as to what level of risk inherent in the sport, as played according to a certain set of rules, is unnecessary, is a factor which weighs against a conclusion that there is a legal duty which, in its practical application, depends upon such an assessment. Furthermore, the risks involved in playing a body-contact sport arise from various sources. A risk might be inherent to an individual player with a particular vulnerability. Or it might result from the vigour with which an opponent, or a team-mate, plays. It cannot be the case that all avoidable risks have to be eliminated. The only way to avoid risk of injury is not to play. No doubt the rules of the game could be altered in many respects to make it safer, but people who enjoy playing, or watching, rugby football have other priorities.

Although the Court of Appeal denied that this would be a case of indeterminate liability, the extent of the potential liability is confined only by the number of people who choose to play the sport anywhere in the world. According to the Bye-Laws of the IRFB, at the relevant time, the first of the stated purposes for which the Board existed was to determine and safeguard the principles relating to amateurism in rugby football. Such an amateur sport may be played in many countries, in widely different circumstances, ranging from organised competitions to casual games, by people of different ages, physical abilities, vulnerabilities, and degrees of skill, enthusiasm, recklessness and courage. It is said that there is a duty, in relation to the rules of the sport, to take reasonable care to protect them all against unnecessary risk of injury. For practical purposes, the liability is indeterminate.

It cannot be denied that, to paraphrase the words of Lord Atkin in *Donoghue v Stevenson* [1932] AC 562, players of rugby football are so closely and directly affected by what the IRFB does that members

Agar v Hyde cont.

of the Board ought to have them in contemplation as being so affected, but neighbourhood in that sense is not the issue in the present case. Of course, the rules of the game affect the players of the game. It is equally clear that the rules will expose the players to the risk of injury in the sense that they will lay down the conditions of a physical contest in which some people are likely to be hurt. In that respect, 564 harm is foreseeable. It does not follow that the members of the Board were under a legal duty of care to the players of the game of the kind presently alleged. No existing category of case in which a duty of care has been held, in this Court, to exist, covers the present. That is not determinative, but it is significant. The Australian cases in which a duty of care has been found to exist in a sporting context are distinguishable from the present, and no attempt is made to argue that they are directly in point.

… …

I am unable to accept that the circumstances of life in this community are such that the conception of legal responsibility should be applied to the relation which existed between the appellants and all people who played the game of rugby football and were, on that account, affected by their action or inaction in relation to the rules of the game. Undertaking the function of participating in a process of making and altering the rules according to which adult people, for their own enjoyment, may choose to engage in a hazardous sporting contest, does not, of itself, carry with it potential legal liability for injury sustained in such a contest.

I would allow the appeals with costs, set aside the orders of the Court of Appeal and order that the appeals to that Court be dismissed with costs.

GAUDRON, McHUGH, GUMMOW AND HAYNE JJ: 565

In these cases … we are persuaded that it is not arguable that the appellants in either case owed the respondent a duty of care …

678 If the appellants owed a duty to these respondents, they must have owed a similar duty to the many thousands, perhaps hundreds of thousands, of persons who played rugby union throughout the world under the laws of the game which the IRFB had made. To hold that each of the individual appellants owed a duty of care to each person who played rugby under those laws strikes us as so unreal as to border on the absurd.

Further, from the earliest times, the common law has drawn a distinction between a positive act causing damage and a failure to act which results in damage. The common law does not ordinarily impose a duty on a person to take action where no positive conduct of that person has created a risk of injury to another person.

Here the appellants were members of the IRFB, an institution which "saw itself as the law-giver for the sport of rugby". But they have done nothing that increased the risk of harm to either of the respondents. The complaint is that they failed to alter the status quo, failed to alter the rules under which the respondents voluntarily played the game. In our view, they no more owed a duty of care to each rugby player to alter the laws of rugby than parliamentarians owe a duty of care to factory workers to amend the factories legislation.

In our opinion, when an appellant attended meetings of the Board, the law of negligence did not require him to conclude that thousands, 579 perhaps hundreds of thousands, of rugby players were so closely and directly affected by his presence as a Board member that he ought to consider whether he should propose an amendment to the laws of the game to protect each player from injury. Unless it did, no duty of care to the respondents could arise …

Each respondent, then, asserts that the appellants failed to cause a change in the laws of the game and that this failure was a breach of duty which caused the respondent injury. This statement of the argument tends to obscure the fact that it is an argument which has several discrete steps in it. It is necessary to give close attention to each of those steps.

Agar v Hyde cont.

Changing the laws of the game

If the negligence of the appellants consisted in their failure to change the laws of the game, it is important to consider their power to change those laws. How were they to "cause a change in the laws of the game"? ... 580

[A]ny alteration to the laws of the game required both a proposal (of which notice was given) and assent to that proposal by at least three-fourths of those present at the relevant meeting. Only if those steps were taken could the Board have "caused a change to the laws of the game". And no individual member of the Board could bring about a change without the assent of others. The most that an individual appellant could do was make a proposal to a Member Union or a Committee of the Board and vote in favour of any proposal that was put to the Board. So the case against each member of the IRFB must be that he owed a duty of care to every person who played the game to propose an amendment that would protect that player from injury and, when such an amendment was proposed, to vote for it. Presumably, the IRFB member would have discharged his duty of care by voting for the amendment even though it was rejected by the majority of members. Moreover, if the members of the IRFB who are sued in this litigation owed a duty to the respondents, so did earlier members of the IRFB.

Further, the IRFB's bye-laws defined it as "the association of national Rugby Football Unions in membership therewith in accordance with these Bye-Laws and comprises Member Unions and Associate Member Unions as hereinafter defined". The appellants therefore attended IRFB meetings as representatives of their Member Unions, not in a personal capacity. They had no authority to propose changes to the laws of the game except in the ways earlier mentioned and, because they were representatives, even to make a proposal to a Committee of the Board may have required some prior approval by the Member Union they represented.

Not only did no individual member of the IRFB have the power to change the laws of the game, the IRFB itself did not have the power to ensure that the rules it promulgated were adopted. The participation of individuals in any particular match was regulated by whatever association organised the match. Whether that association chose to adopt, without modification, the laws of the game promulgated by the Board of the IRFB was for it to say, perhaps influenced (even very 581 probably influenced) by whatever affiliations that particular association had with state, national or international associations... The decisions about what rules would be adopted were, therefore, made at each level of this process (club, regional, state and national level) by groups of part-time volunteers, many of whom were doing nothing more than trying to give something back to a sport from which they believed they had derived benefit as youths and young men.

The laws of a game like rugby football differ from norms of conduct enforced by the courts. The application of the rules embodied in the laws of the game in any particular rugby match is, in very important respects, a matter for the skill and judgment of the particular officials who controlled the match. Often enough (and always if the bystander on the touch line is to be believed) those judgments turn on individual and qualitative assessments made by the officials which have to be made instantly, no matter what the speed of play. Should every infraction of the rules be penalised? When should advantage be allowed? Should the game be allowed to flow with as little interruption as possible? What is "*unduly*" rough play in a body contact sport? What is "*dangerous*" play? All these and many other judgments must be made by the officials.

It follows that in no relevant sense did the Board of the IRFB, or those who attended its meetings as delegates, control what happened in the matches in which the respondents were injured. The IRFB did not organise either of these matches. It did not decide whether the laws of the game which it promulgated would be adopted in these matches. The highest point to which the respondents' contentions could rise was to assert that the IRFB "influenced" the way in which rugby football would be played in Australia. But it is not arguable that the influence amounted to control over the sport: at least at the level at which the respondents played. In particular, they were not subject to any *legal*

Agar v Hyde cont.

control by the IRFB or the delegates to its meetings. Nor can it be argued that they were subject to control in any *practical* sense. There were too many intervening levels of decision-making between the promulgation by the IRFB of laws of the game and the conduct of the individual matches in which the respondents were injured. What happened depended to a greater or lesser extent upon the several decisions of the national union, the local union and the association which organised the competition and on the decisions of the referees who acted in those matches.

The respondents were not participating as employees, whether of the IRFB or any of its constituent bodies or of any more local club or association. They were not subject to any legally binding obligation to accept direction from anyone else about their participation.... The IRFB's lack of control over the matches in which the respondents were injured is important. The respondents contend that the appellants should have changed the laws of the game to reduce the risk of players being hurt by the conduct of other players. That is, they contend that the appellants should have acted to control, or at least influence, the conduct of third parties (the other players) which was the immediate cause of the injury to each respondent. The short answer to the contention is that the appellants did not have power to do so. There are, however, further aspects of the matters that require the conclusion that the appellants did not owe the respondents a duty of care.

A breach of existing laws?

582 ... In Mr Hyde's case it is clear that he alleges that he suffered his injury when, in breach of the law forbidding opposing packs of forwards to engage in a scrum by one charging the other, the forwards of the opposing team charged his pack.

That breach of the laws may be relevant to claims he makes against other parties, but what is it alleged that the law-makers should have done? Although not spelled out in Mr Hyde's pleading, it may be argued that the law-makers should have altered the laws by providing such severe penalties for conduct of the kind in which his opponents engaged as to deter its occurrence or made new rules governing the formation of scrums. But what is there to say that even then the changed law would have been obeyed?

The IRFB, as law-maker, did nothing which facilitated or encouraged the breach of the rules by Mr Hyde's opponents. The most that can be said is that it did not sufficiently deter its breach. To hold that the appellants owed a duty to propose and join in making a law of the game which would have better deterred breach of the existing rules 583 is to extend notions of duty of care too far. It would cast a positive duty to act on individuals who could not control the voluntary conduct of others (the opposing players) which was the immediate cause of harm to the respondent. It is not necessary to go so far as to decide that, as a general rule, a person owes no duty with respect to the acts of a third party. But to cast a positive duty on the appellants to change the laws of the game would provide for compensation of a person who was injured, not because of anything which the appellants did, but because of the wrongful act of other players. To impose such a duty would attribute to the appellants a capacity to control the conduct of the players which they did not have. It would deflect attention from those who were responsible and it would dilute the notion of individual responsibility which lies at the core of the law of negligence.

Autonomy and responsibility

Mr Worsley makes no allegation of any breach of the laws of the game. If there was no breach of the laws, Mr Worsley would have no claim against his opponents. Each participant in the match was adult and must be taken to have consented to the application of physical force in accordance with the laws of the game. And not only would there be no actionable trespass in the opposing team doing what it did, there is nothing which would suggest that any player conducted himself, in playing *within* the laws of the game, so as to have broken any duty of care which *he* owed to the respondent.

Agar v Hyde cont.

If that is so, why should the law-makers be liable when the player who inflicted the injury is not? If the laws of the game define the conduct to which an adult participant consents, the law-makers should not be liable because they could have made the activity that the participant chose to undertake less dangerous. The absurdity of this proposition is highlighted by the fact that, in many activities, the danger is part of the activity's attraction. The participant may therefore not have chosen to engage in the activity at all if it was less dangerous.

The decision to participate is made freely. That freedom, or autonomy, is not to be diminished. But with autonomy comes responsibility. To hold that the appellants owed a duty of care to Mr Worsley would diminish the autonomy of all who choose, for whatever reason, to engage voluntarily in this, or any other, physically dangerous pastime. It would do so because it would deter those who fulfil the kind of role played by the IRFB and the appellants in regulating that pastime from continuing to do so lest they be held 584 liable for the consequences of the individual's free choice. The choices available to all would thus be diminished.

Separate questions may arise about school age children whose decisions are made or affected by others but those questions need not be considered in this case.

We consider that it is not arguable that the appellants owed the respondents a duty of care.

The appeals to this Court should each be allowed with costs.

[Callinan J agreed that the appeals should be allowed.]

[8.95] **Notes&Questions**

1. New South Wales has a Sporting Injuries Compensation Scheme pursuant to the *Sporting Injuries Insurance Act 1978* (NSW). The other jurisdictions do not have equivalents to this scheme.
2. In *Woods v Multi-sport Holdings Pty Ltd* (2002) 186 ALR 145 (see [8.20] and [12.130]) the appellant had suffered a serious eye injury while playing indoor cricket. No protective helmet was provided, nor was there a warning that there was a risk of eye injury. It was held that there was a general duty of care to prevent personal injury but that there was no duty to warn because the risk was obvious. Obviousness of risk has been given serious attention in the Civil Liability Acts. See [8.115] and Chapter 12, Breach of Duty.
3. A referee owes a duty of care to players: see *Smoldon v Whitworth* (1997) 5 TLJ 17.
4. A duty of care is also owed by organisers to spectators at sporting events: *White v Blackmore* (1972) 2 QB 651; *Wilkinson v Joycoeman* (1985) 1 Qd R 567

Sport and recreation and the civil liability legislation

[8.100] The new Civil Liability Acts have important provisions relating to sport in two main areas – one is provisions directly relating to sport and recreation; the other is provisions relating to the voluntary assumption of risk. In this chapter we deal with sport and recreation. Chapter 17, Defences to Torts of Negligence, examines the legislative provisions pertaining to voluntary assumption of risk.

Sport and recreation has been an area where, except in the Northern Territory and Victoria, the new Civil Liability Acts have made extensive provisions reducing the possibility of liability as well as affecting damages payable. The fact that there are strong limitations on liability for recreational matters and on damages for negligence under the Civil Liability Acts has led to a new interest in bringing actions for sporting injury under intentional torts, which might therefore avoid the limitations of the Act. For example, in *McCracken v Melbourne Storm Rugby League Football Club* [2005] NSWSC 107 it was argued that where the defendants raised the plaintiff to a dangerous position in a rugby league match and caused him to fall head first to the ground that this action amounted to an intentional tort that s 3B of the *Civil Liability Act 2002* (NSW) excluded from the operation of the Act.

Definition of recreational activities

[8.105] "Recreational activities" is defined broadly in all the jurisdictions. The New South Wales provision is typical.

Civil Liability Act 2002 (NSW)

[8.110] *Civil Liability Act 2002* (NSW), s 5K

5K Dangerous recreational activity means a recreational activity that involves a significant risk of physical harm and recreational activity includes (a) any sport (whether or not the sport is an organised activity) and (b) any pursuit or activity engaged in for enjoyment, relaxation or leisure, and (c) any pursuit or activity engaged in at a place (such as a beach, park or other public open space) where people ordinarily engage in sport or in any pursuit or activity for enjoyment, relaxation or leisure.

The Western Australian, Queensland and Tasmanian definitions of recreational activity are the same, but Queensland does not define "recreational activities" (see Qld: CLA, s 18; Tas: CLA, s 19; WA: CLA, 5E). The *Recreational Services (Limitation of Liability) Act 2002* (SA) allows a recreational service provider to modify the duty of care owed to a user by contract.

Obvious risks arising from dangerous recreational activities

[8.115] New South Wales, Queensland, Tasmania and Western Australia provide that there can be no liability for harm suffered from obvious risks of dangerous recreational activities, whether or not the injured person was aware of the risk: NSW: CLA, s 5L; Qld: CLA, s 19; Tas: CLA, s 20; WA: CLA, s 5H, 5I. New South Wales and Western Australia also provide that there is no liability for recreational activities where there is a risk warning: NSW: CLA, s 5M; WA: CLA, s 5I. The risk warning is very broadly worded and can bind children. Note also that there is no proactive duty to warn of an obvious risk (see [8.120]).

The Australian Capital Territory confines its treatment of recreational services to equine activities: Sch 3 of the *Civil Law Wrongs Act 2002* (ACT) provides that an equine professional is not liable for injury or death of a participant in equine activities that result from an inherent risk of the activity in certain circumstances including where the required warning notice has been displayed.

There are real concerns that the civil liability regimes for recreational activities set up immunities from suit that interact with duty and breach of duty issues without any clarity as to how courts should proceed in those circumstances. Obvious risk, itself, is a category that at common law may be relevant at the duty, breach and defence stages of analysis. The following section considers some of the issues in the legislation which the courts have tried to grapple with. We see them again in Chapter 16, Defences.

In *Fallas v Mourlas* (2006) 65 NSWLR 418 the defendant Fallas accidentally shot the plaintiff Mourlas in the leg while they were hunting kangaroos by spotlight at night in a motor vehicle. Mr Fallas was driving. Mr Mourlas was holding the spotlight while the other men shot. All the men except Mr Mourlas got out of the vehicle. Mr Fallas came back to the vehicle with a handgun. Mr Mourlas asked him not to get into the vehicle with a loaded gun, but Mr Fallas did and gave reassurances that it was safe and that the gun was not loaded. He entered the vehicle and while attempting to unjam his gun it discharged resulting in Mr Mourlas being shot in the leg. At trial the judge found Mr Fallas had been negligent and was not satisfied that the harm had taken place as a result of the materialisation of an obvious risk of a dangerous recreational activity. The defendant appealed. In the Court of Appeal Ipp JA held that spotlighting was a dangerous recreational activity within the definition of s 5K of the *Civil Liability Act 2002* (NSW) in that there was a significant risk that someone might handle a loaded gun negligently and therefore that someone might get shot. "Significant", in his view, meant a standard somewhere between a trivial risk and a risk likely to materialise. Tobias JA accepted this view and that a dangerous recreational activity was involved. In determining whether the risk that materialised was an obvious risk of the dangerous recreational activity, Ipp JA held that because this was a case of gross negligence such a risk might not be obvious and therefore he held that there was not the materialisation of an obvious risk from the dangerous recreational activity. On the other hand Basten J thought that this was not a dangerous recreational activity, but that if it were, there was a materialisation of the obvious risk. The court treated these sections of the Act as a defence. See also *Jaber v Rockdale City Council* [2008] NSWCA 98 (see [16.60] Note 2).

The statutory provisions relating to obvious risks under the civil liability Acts are regarded as Defences. See Chapter 16.

No proactive duty to warn of obvious risk

[8.120] The Civil Liability Act in New South Wales (s 5H), Queensland (s 15), South Australia (s 38) Tasmania (s 17) and Western Australia (s 5O) provide that there is no proactive duty to warn of an obvious risk, unless the plaintiff has requested advice or information about the risk from the defendant or the defendant is required by a written law to warn the plaintiff or the defendant is a professional and the risk is a risk of death or personal injury arising from professional services given by the professional.

The *Wrongs Act 1958* (Vic) does not have an equivalent provision, relying only on the presumption that the plaintiff was aware of an obvious risk (s 54). This presumption also exists in South Australia (s 37), NSW (s 5G), Queensland (s 14), Tasmania (s 16) and Western Australia (s 5N). Again, this is a matter of defence. See Chapter 17.

PSYCHIATRIC HARM

The concept of psychiatric harm

[8.125] "Nervous shock" is the term traditionally used to refer to psychiatric harm in the legal domain. The legal use of the term reflects Windeyer J's remark in *Mt Isa Mines v Pusey* (1970) 125 CLR 383 at 395, that law was "marching behind medicine, and limping a little". A better term to use is mental injury or psychiatric harm. Plaintiffs have recovered compensation for psychiatric harm in situations where:

- the psychiatric harm followed an injury to the self (*Donoghue v Stevenson* [1932] AC 562 and many other cases);
- the psychiatric harm developed after exposure to a situation of danger creating fear for the self (*Victorian Railways Commissioner v Coultas* (1888) 13 App Cas 222; *Dulieu v White & Sons* [1901] 2 KB 669) or within the zone of physical risk (*Bourhill v Young, Victorian Railways Commissioner v Coultas* (1888) 13 App Cas 222);
- the psychiatric harm developed after exposure to a situation where the plaintiff was safe from physical harm but feared for relatives (*Rook v Stokes Bros* [1925] 1 KB 141 where a mother saw driverless truck coming down a hill and feared for her children who were out of sight; and *King v Phillips* [1953] 1 QB 429);
- the psychiatric harm followed a situation where a relative has been badly injured or killed and the plaintiff saw or heard the accident (*Hinz v Berry* [1970] 2 QB 40, where the plaintiff and her family were picnicking and she was across the road with one child, heard something and turned around to see that a car had run down the remainder of the family; and *Dillon v Legg* (1968) 441 P 2d 912; 69 Cal Rptr 72 (US)) or the aftermath of the accident (*Jaensch v Coffey* (1984) 155 CLR 549; *McLoughlin v O'Brian* [1983] 1 AC 410); and,
- a rescuer or workmate developed psychiatric injury after witnessing a horrific scene. (*Mt Isa Mines v Pusey* (1970) 125 CLR 383 (worker/rescuer); *Chadwick v British Railways Board* [1967] 1 WLR 912 (rescuer); *Dooley v Cammell, Laird & Co Ltd* [1951] 1 Lloyd's Rep 271 (worker)).]

When a person is severely injured they may later suffer some kind of psychiatric harm, such as post-traumatic stress disorder or anxiety, which impacts severely on their ordinary life. In the situation where a person has been physically injured, when they claim damages they may claim not only for the physical injury but for the consequential (or "parasitic") mental harm which followed. In such a case, the duty of care is really owed on the basis of the original physical injury.

However, in some situations a person who has not been physically injured may suffer from mental or psychiatric harm because of negligence. If this is the case, the duty of care arises because of a duty in respect of psychiatric harm. This is a "pure" case of "nervous shock" or psychiatric harm. Such cases typically arise because a person saw or heard some traumatic event, or observed the physical injury or death of a loved one.

In order to bring an action in negligence for "nervous shock" or pure psychiatric injury, the plaintiff must show that it was reasonably foreseeable that a person in the plaintiff's position would suffer psychiatric harm if the defendant carried out the act contemplated. The psychiatric harm must be a form of harm that is compensable. In Australia, such harm must be more than mere grief or sorrow (*Mt Isa Mines v Pusey* (1970) 125 CLR 383 Windeyer J at 394: "Sorrow does not sound in damages") and it must be a recognised form of psychiatric injury. This is a matter for expert evidence.

Duty to avoid inflicting psychiatric harm: "nervous shock"

[8.130] The duty to avoid inflicting mental harm or psychiatric harm to another is one duty category that has traditionally had particular rules to be satisfied. This has been so partly because historically there was suspicion that a claim of psychiatric harm could easily be faked and there was some idea that psychiatric harm was not quite "real" compared with physical injury. Over time psychiatry has become more sophisticated and the law has become more convinced that psychiatric harm is real. However these concerns meant that it was not easy to establish a duty of care in psychiatric harm and special rules such as the rule that one had to be frightened for oneself or to have been physically present at an accident where a person was hurt operated to reduce the likelihood of a duty of care being recognised. Many of these rules have been ameliorated over time, most recently in the following case. Prior to reading the extract below, the reader is encouraged to re-read the extract at [7.90] of *Jaensch v Coffey* (1984) 155 CLR 549, which is one of the seminal Australian cases on the rules surrounding "nervous shock".

Tame v NSW; Annetts v Australian Stations

[8.135] *Tame v New South Wales; Annetts v Australian Stations Pty Limited* (2002) 211 CLR 317 High Court of Australia

(footnotes omitted)

[Two separate cases were heard together because they both concerned psychiatric harm. In short, Mrs Tame sought damages relating to a psychotic depression that developed following a series of events commencing with a car accident in 1991 and involving the incorrect recording in Police files that Mrs Tame had been drunk at the time of the accident (see [7.155] for more information on Mrs Tame's claim). Mr and Mrs Annetts' son James was employed by the defendant on a cattle station in the Kimberley district of Western Australia. He was 16 and the defendant had agreed that he was to be fully supervised. However, after seven weeks, James was sent to work alone as a caretaker on another cattle station. After a month, on 6 December 1986, a police officer telephoned Mr Annetts and told him his son was missing and was believed to have run away with another boy. Mr Annetts then collapsed and his wife took over the telephone conversation. The Annetts then travelled from New South Wales to Western Australia and in January 1987 were shown some of their son's belongings including a blood-stained hat. They travelled to Western Australia some nine times until Mr Annetts was informed by telephone that their son's vehicle was found on 26 April 1987. Later that day Mr Annetts was told a set of remains had been found nearby and he then returned again to Halls Creek to identify a skeleton in a photograph as being that of James. The coroner found that James died of dehydration, exhaustion and hypothermia in the Gibson Desert on or about 4 December 1986. Mr and Mrs Annetts claimed damages for nervous shock.]

GLEESON CJ: 333 In neither of the cases presented before the Court does the outcome turn upon the application of what are sometimes described as the "control mechanisms" of "sudden shock" and "direct perception or immediate aftermath". In fact, to some extent both cases demonstrate that those concepts cannot serve as definitive tests of liability. Mrs Tame's illness did not result from any "event" which itself, or in its aftermath, might have caused her a "shock". It resulted from the communication to her by her solicitor of the information that, in the past, a police officer had made an error about her in an accident report, which was soon corrected. In the case of Mr and Mrs Annetts, they reacted to distressing news of the disappearance, and death, of their son, such news being conveyed to them at a distance, and over a period of time.

I agree with Gummow and Kirby JJ that the common law of Australia should not, and does not, limit liability for damages for psychiatric injury to cases where the injury is caused by a sudden shock, or to cases where a plaintiff has directly perceived a distressing phenomenon or its immediate aftermath. It does not follow, however, that such factual considerations are never relevant to the question whether it is reasonable to require one person to have in contemplation injury of the kind that has been suffered by another and to take reasonable care to guard against such injury. In particular, they may be relevant to the nature of the relationship between plaintiff and defendant, and to the making of a judgment as to whether the relationship is such as to import such a requirement.

Tame v NSW; Annetts v Australian Stations cont.

I would respectfully adopt the observation of Brennan J in *Jaensch v Coffey* (1984) 155 CLR 549 at 571:

> In my opinion, the exigencies of proof of the elements of the cause of action impose the appropriate limits upon the scope of the remedy. Those limits are likely to be at once more flexible and more stringent than limits imposed by legal rules which might be devised to give effect to a judicial policy of restraining the remedy within what are thought to be acceptable bounds.

I turn now to the individual cases. …

Tame v The State of New South Wales

… There are, in my view, two reasons why Acting Sergeant Beardsley was not under a duty of care to Mrs Tame which required him to take reasonable care to avoid causing her injury of the kind she suffered …

As to the first reason, the case seems to me to be governed by the same principles as resulted in the denial by this Court of the existence of a duty of care in *Sullivan v Moody* (2001) 74 ALJR 1580; 183 ALR 404.

In the performance of his duties, Acting Sergeant Beardsley was completing an official report into the circumstances of a motor traffic accident. In the ordinary course, the report would be used in making a decision as to whether charges should be laid against anybody involved in the accident … The primary duty of a police officer filling out such a report is to make available to his or her superiors, honestly and frankly, the results of the observations, inquiries and tests that were made. It would be inconsistent with such a duty to require the police officer to take care to protect from emotional disturbance and possible psychiatric illness a person whose conduct was the subject of investigation and report.

Furthermore, as in *Sullivan v Moody* (2001) 74 ALJR 1580; 183 ALR 404, this is a case where the appellant claims to have been injured in consequence of what others were told about her. There is the same intersection with the law of defamation, and the same need to preserve legal coherence. …

In any event, the Court of Appeal was right to conclude that the psychiatric injury suffered by Mrs Tame, to which the error of Acting Sergeant Beardsley made a material contribution, was not reasonably foreseeable. This conclusion does not depend upon the application, as an inflexible test of liability, of a standard of normal fortitude; but the particular susceptibility of Mrs Tame to psychiatric illness is a factor to be taken into account…. If the requirement of foreseeability were truly and generally as undemanding as is sometimes claimed, then it might take Mrs Tame some distance to say that, this result having occurred, any psychiatrist would say that it would have been foreseen. But that is not the question. The question concerns the reasonableness of requiring Acting Sergeant Beardsley to have this possibility in contemplation when he completed the report. He could not reasonably have been expected to foresee that his mistake carried a risk of harm to Mrs Tame of the kind that resulted. It was not reasonable to require him to have her mental health in contemplation when he recorded the results of the blood tests.

The appeal should be dismissed with costs.

Annetts v Australian Stations Pty Ltd

… It may be observed … that the (assumed) facts of the case demonstrate the danger in treating what are often factual indicators of the presence or absence of proximity of relationship (to use Deane J's expression) as inflexible and indispensable conditions of such a relationship. Categorisation is a useful means of formulating legal principle, and of giving necessary guidance to trial courts, but sooner or later a case is bound to arise that will expose the dangers of inflexibility, especially in an area of the law which has reasonableness as its central concept. Ultimately, reasonableness defies rigorous categorisation of its elements.

Tame v NSW; Annetts v Australian Stations cont.

The process by which the applicants became aware of their son's disappearance, and then his death, was agonizingly protracted, rather than sudden. And the death by exhaustion and starvation of someone lost in the desert is not an "event" or "phenomenon" likely to have many witnesses. But a rigid distinction between psychiatric injury suffered by parents in those circumstances, and similar injury suffered by parents who see their son being run down by a motor car, is indefensible.

Here there was a relationship between the applicants and the respondent sufficient, in combination with reasonable foreseeability of harm, to give rise to a duty of care, though the applicants did not directly witness their son's death, and suffer a sudden shock in consequence. The applicants, on the assumed facts, who themselves had responsibilities for the care of their son, only agreed to permit him to go to work for the respondent after having made inquiries of the respondent as to the arrangements that would be made for his safety and, in particular, after being assured that he would be under constant supervision. Contrary to those assurances, he was sent to work, alone, in a remote location. In those circumstances there was a relationship between the applicants and the respondent of such a nature that it was reasonable to require the respondent to have in contemplation the kind of injury to the applicants that they suffered.

The respondent's breach of duty consisted in failing properly to care for and supervise the applicants' son, by sending him to work alone, in a remote area. He left his post, became lost in the desert, and died. For reasons already mentioned, this may not have been likely to result in a sudden sensory perception of anything by the applicants. But it was clearly likely to result in mental anguish of a kind that could give rise to a recognised psychiatric illness.

Special leave to appeal should be granted and the appeal allowed. I agree with the orders proposed by Gummow and Kirby JJ.

GUMMOW AND KIRBY JJ: Advances in the capacity of medicine objectively to distinguish the genuine from the spurious, and renewed attention to the need to establish breach, causation and a recognisable psychiatric illness that is not too remote, indicate the need for re-accommodation of the competing interests which are in play in "nervous shock" cases. But that accommodation is better achieved by direct attention to, rather than attempts to ignore, the conflict of interests involved. This reflects the preferred approach to defining the limits of liability in negligence, which takes as its starting point, not merely the actions of the defendant, but the interests which are sufficient to attract the protection of the law in this field. The recognition of those interests and the preferred resolution of conflicts between them assist in the formulation of the appropriate duty of care ...

A fundamental objective of the law of negligence is the promotion of reasonable conduct that averts foreseeable harm. In part, this explains why a significant measure of control in the legal or practical sense over the relevant risk is important in identifying cases where a duty of care arises. Further, it is the assessment, necessarily fluid, respecting reasonableness of conduct that reconciles the plaintiff's interest in protection from harm with the defendant's interest in freedom of action. So it is that the plaintiff's integrity of person is denied protection if the defendant has acted reasonably. However, protection of that integrity expands commensurately with medical understanding of the threats to it. Protection of mental integrity from the unreasonable infliction of serious harm, unlike protection from transient distress, answers the "general public sentiment" underlying the tort of negligence that, in the particular case, there has been a wrongdoing for which, in justice, the offender must pay. Moreover, the assessment of reasonableness, which informs each element of the cause of action, is inherently adapted to the vindication of meritorious claims in a tort whose hallmark is flexibility of application. Artificial constrictions on the assessment of reasonableness tend, over time, to have the opposite effect.

Tame v NSW; Annetts v Australian Stations cont.

Control mechanisms

... This Court is presently concerned with three control mechanisms which influenced the intermediate appellate courts. They are (i) the requirement that liability for psychiatric harm be assessed by reference to a hypothetical person of "normal fortitude", (ii) the requirement that the psychiatric injury be caused by a "sudden shock", and (iii) the requirement that a plaintiff "directly perceive" a distressing phenomenon or its "immediate aftermath". It is an objection to the adoption of these rules that this would substitute for the consideration in the particular case of the general requirements of duty of care, reasonable foreseeability, causation and remoteness of damage, notions which would foreshorten inquiry into those matters by the imposition of absolutes with no necessary relation to basic principles....

It should be decided here that the three control mechanisms listed above are unsound. ...

None of the three control mechanisms has been accepted by this Court as a pre-condition to liability for negligently inflicted psychiatric harm. The first of the mechanisms, the standard of "normal fortitude", is not a free-standing criterion of liability, but a postulate which assists in the assessment, at the stage of breach, of the reasonable foreseeability of the risk of psychiatric harm. Further, for the reasons that follow, the common law of Australia recognises neither the second nor third, "sudden shock" and "direct perception", as pre-conditions to the recovery of damages for negligently inflicted psychiatric harm.

As will become apparent, the requirements of "sudden shock" and "direct perception" of a distressing phenomenon or its "immediate aftermath" have operated in an arbitrary and capricious manner. Unprincipled distinctions and artificial mechanisms of this type bring the law into disrepute ... Moreover, the emergence of a coherent body of case law is impeded, not assisted, by such a fixed system of categories. Rigid distinctions of the type required by the "direct perception" rule inevitably generate exceptions and new categories, like the "immediate aftermath" qualification, as the inadequacies of the recognised categories become apparent and "hard cases" are accommodated. The old rule that "nervous shock" sounded in damages only where it arose from a reasonable fear of immediate personal injury to oneself (*Dulieu v White & Sons* [1901] 2 KB 669), and its subsequent relaxation to permit recovery where the plaintiff feared for the safety of another (*Hambrook v Stokes Brothers* [1925] 1 KB 141), illustrates the point. As the categories and exceptions proliferate, the reasoning and outcomes in the cases become increasingly detached from the rationale supporting the cause of action.

Psychiatric harm

Before turning to consider each of the postulated control mechanisms, it is appropriate to identify the justification that is said to support them. At base, the justification lies in a perceived distinction between psychiatric and physical harm. Authorities have isolated four principal reasons said to warrant different treatment of the two categories of case. These are (i) that psychiatric harm is less objectively observable than physical injury and is therefore more likely to be trivial or fabricated and is more captive to shifting medical theories and conflicting expert evidence, (ii) that litigation in respect of purely psychiatric harm is likely to operate as an unconscious disincentive to rehabilitation, (iii) that permitting full recovery for purely psychiatric harm risks indeterminate liability and greatly increases the class of persons who may recover, and (iv) that liability for purely psychiatric harm may impose an unreasonable or disproportionate burden on defendants ...

Several points may be made here. First, the concerns underlying propositions (i), (ii) and (iv) apply, to varying degrees, in cases of purely physical injury, yet it is not suggested that they justify denying a duty of care in that category of case. Secondly, many of these concerns recede if full force is given to the distinction between emotional distress and a recognisable psychiatric illness. ... It has been noted earlier in these reasons that the common law in many United States jurisdictions has developed

Tame v NSW; Annetts v Australian Stations cont.

differently. In Australia, as in England, Canada and New Zealand, a plaintiff who is unable affirmatively to establish the existence of a recognisable psychiatric illness is not entitled to recover (*Alcock v chief Constable of South Yorkshire Police* [1992] 1 AC 310 at 416). Grief and sorrow are among the "ordinary and inevitable incidents of life"; the very universality of those emotions denies to them the character of compensable loss under the tort of negligence. Fright, distress or embarrassment, without more, will not ground an action in negligence. Emotional harm of that nature may be evanescent or trivial.

The apparent disregard of the distinction between emotional distress and a recognisable psychiatric illness in some United States jurisdictions is significant in appreciating the restrictive common law rules that have there applied. ... To permit recovery for recognisable psychiatric illnesses, but not for other forms of emotional disturbance, is to posit a distinction grounded in principle rather than pragmatism, and one that is illuminated by professional medical opinion rather than fixed purely by idiosyncratic judicial perception. Doubts as to adequacy of proof (which are particularly acute in jurisdictions where civil juries are retained) are to be answered not by the denial of a remedy in all cases of mental harm because some claims may be false, but by the insistence of appellate courts upon the observance at trial of principles and rules which control adjudication of disputed issues.

Thirdly, the law of negligence already supplies its own limiting devices ... [I]n requiring a plaintiff to establish fault, causation and a lack of remoteness of damage, the ordinary principles of negligence circumscribe recovery. Further, the tort of negligence requires no more than reasonable care to avert reasonably foreseeable risks. Breach will not be established if a reasonable person in the defendant's position would not have acted differently. The touchstone of liability remains reasonableness of conduct.

The asserted grounds for treating psychiatric harm as distinctly different from physical injury do not provide a cogent basis for the erection of exclusionary rules that operate in respect of the former but not the latter. To the extent that any of these concerns are not adequately met in particular categories of case by the operation of the ordinary principles of negligence, they may be accommodated ... by defining the scope of the duty of care with reference to values which the law protects.

Normal fortitude

The attention given to this notion by both the Court of Appeal in *Tame* and the Full Court in *Annetts* may suggest that a plaintiff has no action unless he or she be an individual of "normal fortitude". ... However, it does not follow that it is a pre-condition to recovery in any action for negligently inflicted psychiatric harm that the plaintiff be a person of "normal" emotional or psychological fortitude or, if peculiarly susceptible, that the defendant know or ought to have known of that susceptibility. The statement by Spigelman CJ in the Court of Appeal in *Tame* that a plaintiff "cannot recover for 'pure' psychiatric damage unless a person of 'normal fortitude' would suffer psychiatric damage by the negligent act or omission" should not be accepted. Windeyer J observed in *Pusey* [*Mount Isa Mines v Pusey* (1970) 125 CLR 383] that the notion of a "normal" emotional susceptibility, in a population of diverse susceptibilities, is imprecise and artificial. The imprecision in the concept renders it inappropriate as an absolute bar to recovery. Windeyer J also pointed out that the contrary view, with its attention to "normal fortitude" as a condition of liability, did not stand well with the so-called "egg-shell skull" rule in relation to the assessment of damages for physical harm.

Analysis by the courts may assist in assessing the reasonable foreseeability of the relevant risk. The criterion is one of *reasonable* foreseeability. Liability is imposed for consequences which the defendant, judged by the standard of the reasonable person, ought to have foreseen. ...

However, the concept of "normal fortitude" should not distract attention from the central inquiry, which is whether, in all the circumstances, the risk of the plaintiff sustaining a recognisable psychiatric illness was reasonably foreseeable, in the sense that the risk was not far-fetched or fanciful *Wyong Shire council v Shirt* (1980) 146 CLR 40 ... Nonetheless, questions of reasonable foreseeability are not purely factual. Expert evidence about the foreseeability of psychiatric harm is not decisive. Such evidence cannot usurp the judgment that is required of the decision-maker. Further, it is not necessary that the particular type of disorder that eventuated be reasonably foreseeable; it is sufficient that the class of injury, psychiatric illness, was foreseeable as a possible consequence of the defendant's conduct …

Sudden shock

… "Nervous shock" operates as a common lawyer's shorthand for the categories of psychiatric harm which are compensable under the tort of negligence. The content of those categories alters with the development of psychiatric knowledge. Terminology should not impede appreciation of the nature and scope of psychiatric harm which may be proved by appropriate evidence and against which the tort offers protection.

In *Jaensch v Coffey* (1984) 155 CLR 549, Brennan J stated that:

> [a] plaintiff may recover only if the psychiatric illness is the result of physical injury negligently inflicted on him by the defendant or if it is induced by "shock"

…

No other member of the Court in *Jaensch v Coffey* (1984) 155 CLR 549 expressly adopted the requirement of "sudden shock" … Subsequent authority in the House of Lords has identified "sudden shock" as a distinct and necessary element of liability. So too trial and intermediate appellate courts in Australia have treated the remarks of Brennan J as authoritative. However, in the absence of acceptance by a majority of this Court of the need to establish "sudden shock", it is not a settled requirement of the common law of Australia …

As a growing body of criticism has pointed out, individuals may sustain recognisable psychiatric illnesses without any particular "sudden shock". … The pragmatic justifications for the rule are unconvincing, for the reasons given earlier at [192] to [196]. The harsh and arbitrary operation of the rule has attracted judicial criticism in various jurisdictions …

Assuming that the other elements of the cause of action have been made out, liability in negligence, for which damage is the gist of the action, should turn on proof of a recognisable psychiatric disorder, not on the aetiology of that disorder. Yet, on the present state of authority in the English Court of Appeal, a parent who observed an adult child deteriorate over 14 days whilst being negligently treated in the defendant hospital, and then die, must be denied recovery in respect of the negligence of the hospital because the parent's psychiatric harm was not induced by "shock" and the death when it came was "expected" …

An indication of the unsatisfactory foundation of the supposed rule in legal principle is a qualification which may have emerged in favour of employees who sue in respect of the failure of their employer to take reasonable steps to provide a safe system of work. In England, and it has been said in Australia, they may recover for psychiatric injury caused by the accumulation over time of occupational stress, and without the need to establish exposure to isolated trauma sustained in the workplace.

Cases of protracted suffering, as opposed to "sudden shock", may raise difficult issues of causation and remoteness of damage. Difficulties of that kind are more appropriately analysed with reference to the principles of causation and remoteness, not through an absolute denial of duty …

The "sudden shock" rule has some affinity with the requirement in several United States jurisdictions that the psychiatric harm be accompanied by some physical "impact", that is, bodily contact with the plaintiff as a result of the defendant's conduct. This has produced a line of authority in which liability turns upon the artificial identification of some trivial impact on the plaintiff. To require proof of "sudden shock" is often to mandate a similarly contrived search for an identifiable "triggering event". This is because the distinction upon which the "sudden shock" rule pivots is often illusory. On

Tame v NSW; Annetts v Australian Stations cont.

one view, both Mrs Tame and Mr and Mrs Annetts sustained, or may have sustained, a "sudden shock" when they were told respectively of the erroneous Traffic Collision Report and the disappearance or death of their son …

The requirement to establish "sudden shock" should not be accepted as a pre?condition for recovery in cases of negligently inflicted psychiatric illness.

Direct perception and immediate aftermath

This related "requirement" has not been authoritatively adopted by this Court as an essential ingredient in an action for negligence for psychiatric harm.

In *Pusey*, Windeyer J said:

> I do not question decisions that nervous shock resulting simply from hearing distressing news does not sound in damages in the same way as does nervous shock from witnessing distressing events. If the sole cause of shock be what is told or read of some happening then I think it is correctly said that, unless there be an intention to cause a nervous shock, no action lies against either the bearer of the bad tidings or the person who caused the event of which they tell. There is no duty in law to break bad news gently or to do nothing which creates bad news.

It will be necessary to return to this passage later in these reasons under the heading "Bearers of bad tidings". As will appear, bearers of bad news may be shielded from liability in negligence without a rule that the direct witnessing of distressing events is a necessary precondition to recovery.

In *Jaensch v Coffey* (1984) 155 CLR 549, Brennan J expressed the view, referred to above, that perception "by seeing, hearing or touching" a sufficiently distressing person, thing or event is a pre?requisite to recovery for negligently inflicted psychiatric harm. His Honour said that a psychiatric illness induced by "mere knowledge of a distressing fact is not compensable; perception by the plaintiff of the distressing phenomenon is essential". On this question, Gibbs CJ expressly reserved his position. Murphy J appeared to be of the view that "learning of", rather than witnessing, a spouse's injuries or treatment would be sufficient to found liability. Deane J doubted the need for direct perception …

Dawson J did not conclusively accept that there can be no liability for "shock" brought about by third party communication rather than by the sight or sound of an accident or its consequences. Indeed, *Jaensch v Coffey* (1984) 155 CLR 549 did not directly raise the issue; it was accepted that Mrs Coffey directly perceived the aftermath of her husband's accident.

Nonetheless, intermediate appellate courts in Australia have denied liability in the absence of direct perception. In *Gifford v Strang Patrick Stevedoring Pty Ltd* (2001) 51 NSWLR 606 at 616-617, the New South Wales Court of Appeal followed the decision of the Full Court in *Annetts*. Yet this approach had attracted strong criticism by the courts of New South Wales, Queensland and South Australia. At least one plaintiff (that in *Petrie v Dowling* [1992] 1 Qd R 284) who was told of the death of a child, but did not witness the accident or its immediate aftermath, has recovered damages in negligence for psychiatric harm. In *Andrews v Williams* [1967] VR 831 and *Tsanaktsidis v Oulianoff* (1980) 24 SASR 500, the plaintiff who did not witness the death of one or more close relatives, by reason of the plaintiff's own injury or lack of consciousness caused by the same accident, nonetheless was entitled to recover upon learning of that death.

Direct perception of a distressing phenomenon or its immediate aftermath appears to be a settled requirement of English law …

[Here the judges discussed United States, United Kingdom and Canadian authorities.]

In some instances, the development of the common law may proceed by analogy with what legislatures have determined to be the appropriate balance between competing interests in a given field. It is significant that legislation in New South Wales, the Australian Capital Territory and the Northern Territory permits the spouse or parent (as defined) of a person killed, injured or imperilled by the defendant's wrongful act to recover damages for consequent mental or nervous shock, regardless of whether they saw or heard the relevant incident.

Distance in time and space from a distressing phenomenon, and means of communication or acquisition of knowledge concerning that phenomenon, may be relevant to assessing reasonable foreseeability, causation and remoteness of damage in a common law action for negligently inflicted psychiatric illness. But they are not themselves decisive of liability. To reason otherwise is to transform a factor that favours finding a duty of care in some cases into a general pre-requisite for a duty in all cases. This carries with it the risk of attribution of disproportionate significance to what may be no more than inconsequential circumstances.

Bearers of bad tidings

… The rejection earlier in these reasons of the criterion of "direct perception" makes it appropriate to identify some qualifications to the passage from the judgment of Windeyer J in *Pusey* which has been set out. His Honour expressed the view, albeit in passing, that, where "shock" is caused purely by the communication of some happening, in the absence of an intention to cause "nervous shock", no action lies against either the bearer of bad tidings or the person who caused the event of which they tell. His Honour remarked that "[t]here is no duty in law to break bad news gently or to do nothing which creates bad news." The first proposition may be accepted without acceding to the second …

The discharge of the responsibility to impart bad news fully and frankly would be inhibited by the imposition in those circumstances of a duty of care to avoid causing distress to the recipient of the news. There can be no legal duty to break bad news gently. This is so even if degrees of tact and diplomacy were capable of objective identification and assessment, which manifestly they are not. Neither carelessness nor insensitivity in presentation will found an action in negligence against the messenger …

The outcome in Tame v New South Wales

It is unlikely that an investigating police officer owes a duty of care to a person whose conduct is under investigation. Such a duty would appear to be inconsistent with the police officer's duty, ultimately based in the statutory framework and anterior common law by which the relevant police service is established and maintained, fully to investigate the conduct in question …

No case in negligence can be made out against the respondent in respect of the conduct of Acting Sergeant Beardsley. This is because a reasonable person in Acting Sergeant Beardsley's position would not have foreseen that his conduct in carelessly completing the Traffic Collision Report involved a risk of causing a recognisable psychiatric illness to the appellant. … But it was not reasonably foreseeable that a person in the position of Mrs Tame would sustain a recognisable psychiatric illness from a clerical error which she was told was a mistake that had been rectified and in respect of which she received a formal apology. The appellant's reaction was extreme and idiosyncratic. The risk of such a reaction was far-fetched or fanciful and, in the manner indicated in *Wyong Shire Council v Shirt* (1980) 146 CLR 40, was not one which the law of negligence required a reasonable person to avoid …

The question of reasonable foreseeability involves an assessment respecting the foresight of a reasonable person in the defendant's position; that foresight may differ from the foresight of qualified psychiatrists. The judgment belongs, ultimately, to a court, not to an expert witness. In making that judgment, a court will draw upon its reserves of common sense and reasonableness.

The appeal in *Tame* should be dismissed with costs.

Tame v NSW; Annetts v Australian Stations cont.

The outcome in Annetts v Australian Stations Pty Ltd

The Full Court erred in failing to apply the ordinary principles of the tort of negligence, unhindered by artificial constrictions based on the circumstance that the illness for which redress was sought was purely psychiatric. In particular, neither the lack of the applicants' direct perception of their son's death or its immediate aftermath, nor the circumstance that the applicants may not have sustained a "sudden shock", is fatal to the applicants' claims. In accordance with the ordinary principles of negligence applied to the assumed facts, the respondent owed the applicants a duty of care. The preliminary issue formulated by Heenan J should be resolved in the affirmative.

The connections between the parties indicate the existence of a duty of care. An antecedent relationship between the plaintiff and the defendant, especially where the latter has assumed some responsibility to the former to avoid exposing him or her to a risk of psychiatric harm, may supply the basis for importing a duty of care ... So too in Australia courts have been more willing to permit recovery for psychiatric harm where the plaintiff and defendant were in a pre-existing relationship of employer and employee.

In the present case, the applicants sought and obtained from the respondent assurances that James would be appropriately supervised. The respondent undertook specifically to act to minimise the risk of harm to James and, by inference, to minimise the risk of psychiatric injury to the applicants. In those circumstances, the recognition of a duty of care does not raise the prospect of an intolerably large or indeterminate class of potential plaintiffs.

The applicants had no way of protecting themselves against the risk of psychiatric harm that eventuated. ... The control over the risk of harm to James, and the risk of consequent psychiatric harm to the applicants, was held to a significant, perhaps exclusive, degree by the respondent. It controlled the conditions under which James worked.

Is there, to adapt what was put and rejected on the facts in *Bryan v Maloney* (1995) 182 CLR 609 at 623-624., any real question of inconsistency between the existence of a duty of care to the parents of James and the legitimate pursuit by the respondent of its business interests? The answer is in the negative. ...

The application for special leave in *Annetts* should be granted and the appeal allowed ...

[Gaudron, McHugh, Hayne and Callinan JJ also agreed that Mrs Tame's appeal should be dismissed and the Annetts' appeal should be allowed.]

[8.140] **Notes&Questions**

1. For further reading on this area see D Butler, "Identifying the Compensable Damage in "Nervous Shock"" (1997) 5 (1) *Torts Law Journal* 67.
2. Various limitations and controls on recovery for nervous shock in an action for negligence have been suggested by authority at different times but later rejected. Some of these are:
   (a) Nervous shock is not a kind of injury which the law recognises as flowing from negligence in the ordinary sense of things: *VRC v Coultas* (1888) 13 App Cas 222. This holding was soon departed from in England, for example, *Dulieu v White & Sons* [1901] 2 KB 669 at 671-672. It was rejected by the High Court of Australia in *Mount Isa Mines Ltd v Pusey* (1970) 125 CLR 383 and *Jaensch v Coffey* (1984) 155 CLR 549.

(b) A plaintiff could only recover in respect of nervous shock operating through the mind where it is caused by immediate fear of immediate physical injury to the plaintiff: Kennedy J in *Dulieu v White & Sons* [1901] 2 KB 669 at 671-672. This proposition cannot stand with either *Mount Isa Mines* or *Jaensch v Coffey* (1984) 155 CLR 549 or with numerous modern cases, including the extract above. At this stage it is open to a tribunal of fact to allow recovery for nervous shock where foreseeability of harm by fire to the plaintiff's property is shown along with the causation of the nervous shock thereby: *Attia v British Gas Plc* [1988] 1 WLR 307. However, it is still considered insufficiently proximate if the plaintiff's shock comes from the realisation that physical injury might have happened to herself through a past incident: *Wilks v Haines* (1991) Aust Torts Reports 81-078.

(c) Members of the family of the deceased may recover on the basis that fear of immediate injury to a member of one's family may be treated on the same footing as fear of immediate injury to oneself: *Hambrook v Stokes Bros* [1925] 1 KB 141. This basis of duty to members of the family became an untenable proposition once the courts came to accept that family members might recover damages for shock even if involved in the "aftermath" of an accident in which a relative was injured or killed. The "aftermath" was at first taken to include cases where the shocked relative foreseeably was brought to the actual scene of the accident as in *Storm v Geeves* [1965] Tas SR 252 followed in *Benson v Lee* [1972] VR 879 and approved in *Mount Isa Mines Ltd v Pusey* (1970) 125 CLR 383. Any suggestion that recovery might be limited to plaintiffs involved in the aftermath of the accident in the sense of those who were personally present at the accident scene was disposed of in Australia by *Jaensch v Coffey* (1984) 155 CLR 549 and in England by the House of Lords in *McLoughlin v O'Brian* [1983] 1 AC 410. In both of these cases (*Jaensch* and *McLoughlin*) the plaintiff was personally present only at the hospital to which the dead or injured were taken soon after the accident, and in both cases judgment for the plaintiff was upheld.

(d) That the plaintiff may only recover for nervous shock resulting from what was observed with the unaided senses by the plaintiff and not that resulting from what the plaintiff was told about the accident: *Mount Isa Mines Ltd v Pusey* (1970) 125 CLR 383 although in *Alcock v Chief Constable of South Yorkshire Police* [1992] 1 AC 310 it was held to be relevant to the relationship of proximity between plaintiff and defendant.

(e) Where the news conveyed is negligently false, there is authority for holding the conveyor of it liable: *Barnes v Commonwealth* (1937) 37 SR (NSW) 311; compare *Furniss v Fitchett* [1958] NZLR 396.

3. In *Mount Isa Mines Ltd v Pusey* (1970) 125 CLR 383, the plaintiff was employed by the defendant in its power house. Owing partly to the neglect of the defendant properly to instruct two employees in the testing of a switchboard, an electric arc was produced which horribly injured them. The plaintiff went to the scene on hearing the noise and assisted one of the burnt men to an ambulance. The man died nine days later. The trial judge found that the defendant should have anticipated that other employees who

might go to the rescue would suffer nervous shock and perhaps injuries from burning. While the trial judge did not find that the specific mental illness suffered by the plaintiff was foreseeable, he found it enough that some psychiatric injury could have been foreseen. His judgment for the plaintiff on these findings was upheld by the Full Court of the Supreme Court of Queensland and ultimately by the High Court.

4. The common law requirements of the duty of care for psychiatric harm were considered again in *Gifford v Strang Patrick Stevedoring Pty Ltd* (2003) 214 CLR 269. The facts of the case are discussed below at [8.145]. There, all members of the court except Callinan J confirmed that sudden shock and direct perception should be rejected as determinants of recovery. Gleeson CJ again stressed (as he had in *Tame* and *Annetts*) that reasonable foreseeability be really "reasonable". The requirement of an identifiable psychiatric illness was again reiterated. The court regarded psychiatric injury to the children of an employee injured at work as entirely foreseeable, and emphasised the control the employer had over the situation compared with the vulnerability of the children.

5. Consider this scenario: Mr and Mrs X and their child fled Iran and eventually made their way to Australia where they entered the country as asylum seekers. They were detained in Woomera detention centre for several years while a determination was made as to their status as refugees. After about 12 months Mr X began to exhibit signs of psychiatric disturbance. A psychiatrist recommended that he be treated but nothing was done. Mr X was treated as a troublesome inmate and was placed in solitary confinement several times. After his wife and child were moved out of detention he was denied any contact with them for up to two months at a time. He continued to get worse. After 18 months several outside psychiatrists warned the private organisation running the detention centre that he needed treatment and wrote to the Immigration Department under whose auspices the detention centre was run saying the same thing. After two years the Commissioner for Human Rights wrote to the Immigration Department declaring that the man was "a psychiatric emergency". Still nothing was done for him. He was moved to Baxter Detention Centre and beaten severely by guards during the move which added to his trauma. He was finally released from detention in 2005 but psychiatrists think he will never recover. Can he bring a nervous shock action against the Immigration Department, or against the private owners of the detention facility? See *Badraie v Commonwealth* [2005] NSWSC 1195. This citation is a judgment on evidentiary and procedural matters arising in the course of the initial hearing. It is not a full judgment deciding the final outcome of the matter. However, some preliminary comments on the law in this area are made.

Koehler v Cerebos

[8.145] *Koehler v Cerebos (Australia) Ltd* (2005) 214 ALR 355 High Court of Australia

(footnotes omitted)

[This case considers psychiatric harm in the employment context. The appellant was employed three days a week as a merchandising representative of Cerebos. She could not perform her duties to her own satisfaction and repeatedly complained to management (orally and in writing) that the work had to be changed or she should be given more time, or have help to do it. However no changes were made. All her complaints were about the work, not suggestions that it was affecting her health. After five months she developed a psychiatric illness of which her work was a cause. She argued that there was a breach of her employer's common law and contractual duty to provide a safe system of work, and a breach of the *Occupational Safety and Health Act 1984* (WA). At trial the Commissioner found that she had developed complex fibromyalgia syndrome and major depressive illness. He also found her workload excessive and that her injury was foreseeable and that therefore the employer had breached its duty to ensure that all reasonable steps were taken to provide a safe system of work. The Full Court of the Western Australian Supreme Court held on appeal that the employer could not reasonably have foreseen the injury.]

McHUGH, GUMMOW, HAYNE AND HEYDON JJ: [10] It is not necessary to describe the appellant's complaints to management in any detail. It is enough to say that she complained orally and in writing on many occasions that she had too big an area, too many stores and very little time. Her weekly written reports sometimes recorded that she was working more than eight hour days. But all her complaints were directed to whether the work could be done; none suggested that the difficulties she was experiencing were affecting her health. She told management that there were two ways to solve the problems she was encountering: to reduce the number of stores she was to visit, or to have her work a fourth day. She nominated the stores that should be removed from her list and identified the representatives to whom they could be given. The employer took neither of the steps the appellant suggested and took no other action to alter the work expected of the appellant.

The appellant did not contend that the employer's failure to take these steps was a breach of an express or implied contractual stipulation regulating the work expected of her. In particular, she did not contend that her exchanges with her supervisors, when first shown a territory listing, gave rise to some relevant term of the employment agreement. She contended that the failure to take the steps she identified was a breach of the employer's common law duty to provide a safe system of work, a breach of an implied term of the employment contract that the employer would provide a safe system of work, and a breach of a statutory duty owed under the *Occupational Safety and Health Act 1984* (WA) …

The proper starting point

Because the appellant's claim was framed in negligence, and because her claim was brought against her employer, it may be thought necessary to have regard only to the well-established proposition that an employer owes an employee a duty to take all reasonable steps to provide a safe system of work. From there it may be thought appropriate to proceed by discarding any asserted distinction between psychiatric and physical injury, and then focus only upon questions of breach of duty. Questions of breach of duty require examination of the foreseeability of the risk of injury and the reasonable response to that risk in the manner described in *Wyong Shire Council v Shirt* (1980) 146 CLR 40. But to begin the inquiry by focusing only upon questions of breach of duty invites error. It invites error because the assumption that is made about the content of the duty of care may fail to take fundamental aspects of the relationship between the parties into account.

These reasons later show that this case may be decided, as it was by the Full Court, at the level of breach of duty, on the basis that the risk of psychiatric injury to the appellant was not reasonably foreseeable. It is, however, important to point out the nature of at least some of the issues that arise in connection with the content of an employer's duty of care.

The content of an employer's duty of care

The content of the duty which an employer owes an employee to take reasonable care to avoid psychiatric injury cannot be considered without taking account of the obligations which the parties owe one another under the contract of employment, the obligations arising from that relationship which equity would enforce and, of course, any applicable statutory provisions. (This last class may

Koehler v Cerebos cont.

require particular reference not only to industrial instruments but also to statutes of general application such as anti-discrimination legislation.) Consideration of those obligations will reveal a number of questions that bear upon whether, as was the appellant's case here, an employer's duty of care to take reasonable care to avoid psychiatric injury requires the employer to modify the work to be performed by an employee. At least the following questions are raised by the contention that an employer's duty may require the employer to modify the employee's work. Is an employer bound to engage additional workers to help a distressed employee? If a contract of employment stipulates the work which an employee is to be paid to do, may the employee's pay be reduced if the employee's work is reduced in order to avoid the risk of psychiatric injury? What is the employer to do if the employee does not wish to vary the contract of employment? Do different questions arise in cases where an employee's duties are fixed in a contract of employment from those that arise where an employee's duties can be varied by mutual agreement or at the will of the employer? If an employee is known to be at risk of psychiatric injury, may the employer dismiss the employee rather than continue to run that risk? Would dismissing the employee contravene general anti-discrimination legislation?

No doubt other questions may arise. It is, however, neither necessary nor appropriate to attempt to identify all of the questions that could arise or to attempt to provide universal answers to them. What is important is that questions of the content of the duty of care, and what satisfaction of that duty may require, are not to be examined without considering the other obligations which exist between the parties.

A deal of reference was made in argument to the decision of the English Court of Appeal in the several appeals heard together and reported as *Hatton v Sutherland* [200] 2 All ER 1. The appellant submitted that, consistent with what was said in *Hatton*, this Court should hold that where an employee claims damages from an employer for negligently inflicted psychiatric injury, only one question need be considered, namely, whether this kind of harm to this particular employee was reasonably foreseeable. That proposition should be rejected.

No doubt, as was pointed out in *Hatton*, there will be a number of factors which are likely to be relevant to answering the particular question identified in that case. Those factors would include both the nature and extent of the work being done by the employee, and the signs from the employee concerned–whether in the form of express warnings or the implicit warning that may come from frequent or prolonged absences that are uncharacteristic. What other matters might make the risk of psychiatric injury reasonably foreseeable was a question not explored in argument. It is a question that may require much deeper knowledge of the causes of psychiatric injury than whatever may be identified as common general knowledge. But neither the particular issues identified in *Hatton* nor the question from which they stem (was this kind of harm to this particular employee reasonably foreseeable?) should be treated as a comprehensive statement of relevant and applicable considerations. As Lord Rodger of Earlsferry pointed out in his speech in the House of Lords in the appeal in one of the cases considered in *Hatton v Sutherland* [200] 2 All ER 1, *Barber v Somerset County Council* [2004] 1 WLR 1089, it is only when the contractual position between the parties (including the implied duty of trust and confidence between them) "is explored fully along with the relevant statutory framework" that it would be possible to give appropriate content to the duty of reasonable care upon which an employee claiming damages for negligent infliction of psychiatric injury at work would seek to rely.

Issues about the content of the duty of care were not examined in any detail in the courts below. It was assumed that the relevant duty of care was sufficiently stated as a duty to take all reasonable steps to provide a safe system of work without examining what limits there might be on the kinds of steps required of an employer. Rather, attention was directed only to questions of breach of duty framed without any limitations that might flow from an examination of the content of the duty of care. As earlier indicated, the question of reasonable foreseeability is determinative.

Koehler v Cerebos cont.

The present case

The Full Court was right to conclude that a reasonable person in the position of the employer would not have foreseen the risk of psychiatric injury to the appellant. Because the appellant did not prove that the employer ought reasonably to have foreseen that she was at risk of suffering psychiatric injury as a result of performing her duties at work, her claim in negligence should have failed at trial. The appellant's alternative claims, in breach of contract and breach of statutory duty, have been treated at all stages of this litigation as raising no different issues from those raised by her claim in negligence. As is implicit in what has already been said about determining the content of the employer's duty of care, consideration of a claim in contract (founded on the breach of an implied term requiring reasonable care) would invite close attention to the other terms of the contract of employment, as well as the relevant statutory framework. The claims in contract and breach of statutory duty having been treated as they were both in the courts below and in this Court, it is unnecessary to consider them further in these reasons.

There are two reasons why the Full Court was right to reach the conclusion it did. First, the appellant agreed to perform the duties which were a cause of her injury. Secondly, the employer had no reason to suspect that the appellant was at risk of psychiatric injury.

It is sufficient for the purposes of the present case to attribute only limited significance to the appellant's agreement to perform the duties which brought about her injuries. In this case it is enough to notice that her agreement to undertake the work runs contrary to the contention that the employer ought reasonably to have appreciated that the performance of those tasks posed a risk to the appellant's psychiatric health. It runs contrary to that contention because agreement to undertake the work not only evinced a willingness to try but also was not consistent with harbouring, let alone expressing, a fear of danger to health. That is why the protests the appellant made (that performance of the work within the time available seemed impossible) did not *at the time* bear the significance which hindsight may now attribute to them. What was said did not convey at *that* time any reason to suspect the possibility of future psychiatric injury.

Although, in this case, the agreement to perform the work has only the limited significance we have indicated, that is not to say that, in another case, an employee's agreement to perform duties whose performance is later found to be a cause of psychiatric injury may not have greater significance. An employer may not be liable for psychiatric injury to an employee brought about by the employee's performance of the duties originally stipulated in the contract of employment. In such a case, notions of "overwork", "excessive work", or the like, have meaning only if they appeal to some external standard. (The industry evidence adduced by the appellant was, no doubt, intended to provide the basis for such a comparison and, as noted earlier, the Commissioner drew a comparison of that kind by concluding that the appellant's workload was excessive.) Yet the parties have made a contract of employment that, by hypothesis, departs from that standard. Insistence upon performance of a contract cannot be in breach of a duty of care.

At first sight, it may appear to be easy to read an employee's obligations under a contract, and an employer's rights to performance of those obligations, as subject to some qualification to the effect that performance of the obligations is excused if performance would be beyond what is required by some external standard, or is or may be injurious to health, or both injurious and beyond an external standard. But further examination of the problem reveals that there are difficulties in resolving the issue in this way.

Giving content to what we have called an "external standard" by which work requirements would be judged may not be easy. Presumably, it would be some form of industry standard. Assuming, however, that content can be given to that concept, its application would invite attention to fundamental questions of legal coherence. Within the bounds set by applicable statutory regulation, parties are free to contract as they choose about the work one will do for the other. In particular, within

Koehler v Cerebos cont.

those bounds, parties are free to stipulate that an employee will do more work than may be the industry standard amount. Often the agreement to do that will attract greater rewards than the industry standard. Developing the common law of negligence in a way that inhibited the making of such agreements would be a large step to take.

Adopting a qualification that hinges upon whether psychiatric injury is or may be sustained from performance of the work would require consideration of questions that are closely related to issues of foreseeability and it is convenient to turn to those issues.

In *Tame v New South Wales; Annetts v Australian Stations Pty Ltd* (2002) 211 CLR 317, the Court held that "normal fortitude" was not a precondition to liability for negligently inflicting psychiatric injury. That concept is not now to be reintroduced into the field of liability as between employer and employee. The central inquiry remains whether, in all the circumstances, the risk of a plaintiff (in this case the appellant) sustaining a recognisable psychiatric illness was reasonably foreseeable, in the sense that the risk was not far fetched or fanciful.

It may be right to say that it is now a matter of general knowledge that some recognisable psychiatric illnesses may be triggered by stress. It is, however, a further and much larger step to take to say that all employers must now recognise that all employees are at risk of psychiatric injury from stress at work. Yet it is that proposition, or one very like it, which must lie behind the Commissioner's conclusion that it required no particular expertise to foresee the risk of psychiatric injury to the appellant.

The duty which an employer owes is owed to each employee. The relevant duty of care is engaged if psychiatric injury to the *particular* employee is reasonably foreseeable. That is why, in *Hatton*, the relevant question was rightly found to be whether this kind of harm to this particular employee was reasonably foreseeable. And, as pointed out in that case, that invites attention to the nature and extent of the work being done by the particular employee and signs given by the employee concerned.

Because the inquiry about reasonable foreseeability takes the form it does, seeking to read an employer's obligations under a contract as subject to a qualification which would excuse performance, if performance is or may be injurious to psychiatric health, encounters two difficulties. First, the employer engaging an employee to perform stated duties is entitled to assume, in the absence of evident signs warning of the possibility of psychiatric injury, that the employee considers that he or she is able to do the job. Implying some qualification upon what otherwise is expressly stipulated by the contract would contradict basic principle. Secondly, seeking to qualify the operation of the contract as a result of information the employer *later* acquires about the vulnerability of the employee to psychiatric harm would be no less contradictory of basic principle. The obligations of the parties are fixed at the time of the contract unless and until they are varied.

Two caveats should be entered. First, hitherto we have referred only to the employer's performance of duties *originally* stipulated in a contract of employment. It may be that different considerations could be said to intrude when an employer is entitled to vary the duties to be performed by an employee and does so. The exercise of powers under a contract of employment may more readily be understood as subject to a qualification on their exercise than would the insistence upon performance of the work for which the parties stipulated when making the contract of employment.

Secondly, we are not to be understood as foreclosing questions about construction of the contract of employment. Identifying the duties to be performed under a contract of employment and, in particular, identifying whether performance of those duties is subject to some implied qualification or limitation, necessarily requires that full exploration of the contractual position of which Lord Rodger spoke in *Barber v Somerset County Council* [2004] 1 WLR 1089, against the relevant statutory framework in which the contract was made.

Koehler v Cerebos cont.

In this case, it is not necessary to consider any issue that might be presented by variation of the duties for which parties originally stipulate in a contract of employment because, in this case, there was not said to have been any variation of the appellant's duties. The evidence revealed that the appellant was a very conscientious employee. She may well have done more than her contract of employment required of her but the employer did not vary her duties from those originally stipulated when she was re-engaged as a part-time merchandising representative. And, as the appellant's complaints to her employer revealed, it was the performance of those duties which she found to be more than she could cope with.

Nor is it necessary to decide this case on the basis that the appellant's agreement to perform the duties which were a cause of her injuries is conclusive against her claim. The identification of the duties for which the parties stipulated would require much closer attention to the content of the contractual relationship between them than was given in the evidence and argument in the courts below. For present purposes, it is sufficient to notice that her agreement to undertake the tasks stipulated (hesitant as that agreement was) runs contrary to the contention that the employer ought reasonably to have appreciated that the performance of those tasks posed risks to the appellant's psychiatric health.

The conclusion that the employer had no reason to suspect that the appellant was at risk of psychiatric injury is the reason upon which the Full Court's conclusion hinged. Here there was no indication (explicit or implicit) of any particular vulnerability of the appellant. As noted earlier, she made many complaints to her superiors but none of them suggested (either expressly or impliedly) that her attempts to perform the duties required of her were putting, or would put, her health at risk. She did not suggest at any time that she was vulnerable to psychiatric injury or that the work was putting her at risk of such an injury. None of her many complaints suggested such a possibility. As the Full Court said, her complaints may have been understood as suggesting an industrial relations problem. They did not suggest danger to her psychiatric health. When she did go off sick, she (and her doctor) thought that the illness was physical, not psychiatric. There was, therefore, in these circumstances, no reason for the employer to suspect risk to the appellant's psychiatric health.

The Full Court was right to conclude that the employer was not shown to have breached a duty of care. The appeal to this Court should be dismissed with costs.

[Callinan J agreed that the appeal should fail.]

[8.150] **Notes&Questions**

1. In *NSW v Fahy* (2007) 81 ALJR 1021, the High Court treated police as employees (technically they are not) and looked at the scope of the duty of care to provide a safe system of work, The courts below had held that such a safe system of work included protection of police officers from psychiatric harm because their work involved dealing with extremely stressful situations. However the High Court by majority held that the duty was not breached or did not exist because any such safe system had to be one which did not detract from police service functions. See the note on the case by Peter Handford in (2007) 15 Tort L Rev 131.
2. The plaintiff claimed that he suffered PTSD as a result of being threatened, physically abused, harassed and humiliated by the officer, who was his superior in the corporation. A complaint had been made to higher superiors in the company. The defendant argued that the risk to the plaintiff was not foreseeable on the basis of one

complaint and therefore there was no duty of care. This argument was rejected by the Court of Appeal who held there was a duty of care and it was breached: Nationwide *News PL v Naidu & Anor* [2007] NSWCA 377.

Mental harm and the civil liability legislation

[8.155] In *Gifford v Strang Patrick Stevedoring Co* (2003) 214 CLR 269, the High Court commented on the statutory provisions enacted in the 1940s to expand liability for nervous shock. In *Gifford* a man was crushed to death by a forklift vehicle while he was working for his employer, a stevedoring company. His children were 19, 17 and 14 at the time this happened. They did not witness the accident but were informed of it later on the same day. They claimed to have suffered psychiatric injury from learning what had happened to their father.

After the decision in *Annetts v Australian Stations* in 2002 (see [8.125] above]), it was clear that the fact that the plaintiff had not witnessed the accident was not a bar to their recovery at common law. However, in *Gifford*, the respondents argued that s 4(1)(b) of the *Law Reform (Miscellaneous Provisions) Act 1944* (NSW) (replaced by the *Civil Liability Act 2002* (NSW), s 30) also required that they be within sight or hearing of the accident to be able to be compensated, and that this provision exclusively defines the limits of nervous shock liability. The appellants argued that the *Workers Compensation Act 1987* (NSW), s 151P in turn displaced the operation of s 4(1)(b). The High Court had no difficulty in holding that neither of these propositions was correct. The common law governed the situation because of the wording of s 4(1)(b), which conferred rights, rather than abolishing them. It was in the following terms.

Law Reform (Miscellaneous Provisions) Act 1944 (NSW), s 4

[8.160] *Law Reform (Miscellaneous Provisions) Act 1944*(NSW), s 4

4(1) The liability of any person in respect of injury caused after the commencement of this Act by an act, neglect or default by which any other person is killed, injured or put in peril, shall extend to include liability for injury arising wholly or in part from mental or nervous shock sustained by–

(a) a parent or the husband or wife of the person so killed, injured or put in peril; or

(b) any other member of the family of the person so killed, injured or put in peril where such person was killed, injured or put in peril within the sight or hearing of such member of the family.

[8.165] **Notes&Questions**

1. Equivalents to s 4(1) were in force in *Law Reform (Miscellaneous Provisions) Act 1955* (ACT), s 24 and *Law Reform (Miscellaneous Provisions) Act* (NT), Pt VII, although they varied in detail. See *Stergiou v Stergiou* (1987) 4 MVR 435.
2. *The Wrongs Act 1958* (Vic), s 23 also provided:

> In any action for injury to the person the plaintiff shall not be debarred from recovering damages merely because the injury complained of arose wholly or in part from mental or nervous shock

Statutory equivalents to s 23 of the Victorian Act were found in *Law Reform (Miscellaneous Provisions) Act 1944* (NSW), s 3(1); *Wrongs Act 1936* (SA) s 28. The Australian Capital Territory equivalent has been retained as Australian Capital Territory: CLWA, s 33; The Northern Territory equivalent was in *Law Reform (Miscellaneous Provisions) Act*, s 24(1) and has also been retained. Queensland had no equivalent.

The Civil Liability Act regimes

[8.170] The new Civil Liability Acts provisions concerning mental harm are worded differently from the previous legislative provisions. There are significant differences between the new Acts, with the New South Wales provision being the most stringent.

Civil Liability Act 2002 (NSW)

[8.175] *Civil Liability Act 2002* (NSW), s 30

30 Limitation on recovery for pure mental harm arising from shock

(1) This section applies to the liability of a person (the defendant) for pure mental harm to a person (the plaintiff) arising wholly or partly from mental or nervous shock in connection with another person (the victim) being killed or put in peril by the act or omission of the defendant

(2) The plaintiff is not entitled to recover damages for pure mental harm unless:

(a) The plaintiff witnessed, at the scene, the victim being killed, injured or put in peril, or

(b) The plaintiff is a close member of the family of the victim …

Close member of the family of a victim means:

(a) a parent of the victim or other person with parental responsibility for the victim, or

(b) the spouse or partner of the victim, or

(c) a child or stepchild of the victim or any other person for whom the victim has parental responsibility, or

(d) a brother, sister, half-brother, half-sister, or stepbrother or stepsister of the victim.

Spouse or partner means:

(a) a husband or wife, or

(b) the other part to a de facto relationship within the meaning of the *Property (Relationships) Act 1984*,

but where more than one person would so qualify as a spouse or partner, means only the last person to so qualify.

The provisions in the other jurisdictions (except for Queensland and the Northern Territory, which have no equivalent provision) are more reflective of the common law after *Tame/Annetts*. The provision in *Civil Liability Act 2002* (WA), s 5S(1) is extracted below as an example. See also NSW: s 32; SA: CLA, s 33, ACT: CLWA, s 34 and Tas: CLA, s 34. The statutes of each jurisdiction should be consulted because of their differences.

Civil Liability Act 2002 (WA)

[8.180] *Civil Liability Act 2002* (WA), s 5S

(1) a person ("the defendant") does not owe a duty of care to another person (the "plaintiff") to take care not to cause the plaintiff mental harm unless the defendant ought to have foreseen that a person of normal fortitude, might, in the circumstances of the case, suffer a recognised psychiatric illness if reasonable care were not taken.

(2) For the purposes of the application of this section in respect of pure mental harm, the circumstances of the case include the following-

(a) whether or not the mental harm was suffered as the result of a sudden shock;

(b) whether the plaintiff witnessed, at the scene, a person being killed, injured or put in peril;

(c) the nature of the relationship between the plaintiff and any person killed, injured or put in peril;

(d) whether or not there was a pre-existing relationship between the plaintiff and the defendant

(3) For the purpose of the application of this section in respect of consequential mental harm, the circumstances of the case include the personal injury suffered by the plaintiff.

(4) This section does not require the court to disregard what the defendant knew or ought to have known about the fortitude of the plaintiff.

——— ꧁꧂ ———

[8.185] **Notes&Questions**

1. The New South Wales provision extracted above is clearly intended to reduce the ability of plaintiffs to recover in nervous shock cases. The wording of the provision suggests that the decision in *Gifford v Strang* (which, although handed down in 2003, was decided under the previous legislation) can no longer apply where there is such legislation. New South Wales also has s 32 which is equivalent to WA s 5S.

2. In some jurisdictions recovery in a court for nervous shock may be precluded in motor accident cases by the general supersession of tort litigation in respect of motor accidents by statutory schemes. Similarly, some Civil Liability Act regimes for nervous shock will not apply to employer-employee relationships. For example, in New South Wales the CLA does not apply to employer-employee claims: s 3B; and the *Workers Compensation Act 1987* (NSW) provides by s 151P: "No damages for psychological or psychiatric injury are to be awarded in respect of an injury except in favour of (a) the injured worker, or (b) a parent, spouse, brother, sister or child of the injured or deceased person who, as a consequence of the injury to the injured person or the death of the deceased person, has suffered a demonstrable psychological or psychiatric illness and not merely a normal emotional or cultural grief reaction".

3. Does the New South Wales provision limit actions for nervous shock so that the plaintiffs in *Annetts*, extracted above, would now fail in their action? Do the other Civil Liability Act provisions have a different effect?

4. Police officers were called to the scene of a rail accident. When they got there the accident had already happened. There were bodies strewn around, and people in the process of dying or at risk of dying. The police officers had to cover the bodies and help with restoring order. They subsequently developed post traumatic stress disorder. Are

they able to recover under the civil liability legislation in the relevant jurisdiction? See *Wicks v Railcorp; Sheehan v State Rail* [2007] NSWSC 1346 (The answer was they could not recover in NSW because they did not not witness people being hurt or put in peril).

Mental harm and feminist critique

[8.190] There is a significant body of feminist literature discussing the tortious infliction of psychiatric harm. Feminist concerns are raised in complex ways by this area. At one level, feminist concerns are raised by the prevalence of women in these cases–and of women as mothers and wives in particular. Men also make these claims, but the position of women in these cases, especially as some of the early cases involved pregnant women, piqued the interest of feminists. But this is not of interest to feminists only because of who the plaintiffs might be. Feminist critiques of the nature of legal reasoning and of the way in which law categorises harms are also relevant to this area. The claim that there is more to a feminist analysis of the tort than whether women win or lose, does not diminish the fact that a hierarchy that privileges physical injury over emotional harm is more likely to be disproportionately detrimental to women. The reluctance to compensate for emotional damage reflects the suspicion that it is not as real as physical pain. And in turn this polarisation reflects Western liberal philosophy's dualism which separates rational from irrational and body from mind. "Hysteria" (which, for a long time was a significant psychiatric diagnosis) carries connotations of overreaction to imagined horrors. In contrast, physical injury is seen as real and observable and seems harder to fake. What makes this particularly interesting to feminist theorists is the observable fact that where these polarised issues are raised they tend to be identified as masculine or feminine and the masculine is frequently privileged. That is men are seen as people who are strong and therefore only get physical injuries; women are seen as weak and therefore more likely to suffer from emotional harm. At the same time that emotional harm is seen as suspect and possibly fraudulent because it is irrational. These are tendencies rather than constant findings, but they are significant because of the impact consistent privileging can have on those who are on the wrong side of the privilege.

[8.195] **Notes&Questions**

1. Considering *Annetts*, to what extent do you think the treatment of the parents in *Annetts* reflects any view that emotional harm is unreal?
2. In *Koehler*, the plaintiff's case turned on the contractual arrangements for her employment. How would a feminist critique analyse this case? Consider the fact that contractual and employment arrangements are generally regarded as very much part of the public (traditionally masculine) domain; consider also the artificiality of the separation between her two contracts of employment. How would the case have been determined if there had been no new contract of employment but all the other facts had remained the same?

   For more information on feminist critiques see: M Chamallas and L Kerber, "Women, Mothers and the law of Fright; A History:" (1990) 88 Mich L Rev 814; E Handsley, "Mental Injury Occasioned by Harm to Another: A Feminist Critique" (1996) 14 *Law and Inequality: A Journal of Theory and Practice* 391; P Handford, *Mullany and*

Handford's Tort Liability for Psychiatric Damage (2nd ed, Lawbook Co, 2006); H Teff, *Causing Psychiatric and Emotional Harm* (Hart Publishing, Oxford, 2008).

WRONGFUL DEATH

[8.200] At common law, the death of a plaintiff or defendant ended an action (the action "abated"). Similarly, the death of the plaintiff prevented a cause of action arising. The rule was stated in the well-known remark by Lord Ellenborough in *Baker v Bolton* (1808) 1 Camp 493: "In a civil court, the death of a human being could not be complained of as an injury". Both these rules have been ameliorated by legislation in all of the Australian jurisdictions.

Survival of actions

[8.205] Under legislation, the cause of action is no longer extinguished by the death of either party. The estate of the deceased may have an action brought against it or may bring an action against someone else. The legislation differs across the jurisdictions (see *Law Reform (Miscellaneous Provisions) Act 1955* (ACT), Pt II; *Law Reform (Miscellaneous Provisions) Act 1944* (NSW); *Law Reform (Miscellaneous Provisions) Act* (NT), Pt II; *Succession Act 1981* (Qld), s 66; *Survival of Causes of Action Act 1940* (SA); *Administration and Probate Act* (Tas), s 27; *Administration and Probate Act 1958* (Vic), s 29; *Law Reform (Miscellaneous Provisions) Act* (WA), s 4). The legislation allows the estate to recover damages for lost earning capacity between date of injury and death, funeral expenses, and medical expenses. See Chapter 14 Damages.

The dependant's action

[8.210] All the jurisdictions have enacted legislation to ameliorate the effect of the rule in *Baker v Bolton* (1808) 1 Camp 493 on the dependants of the deceased (see *Compensation (Fatal Injuries) Act 1968* (ACT); *Compensation to Relatives Act 1897* (NSW); *Compensation (Fatal Injuries) Act* (NT); *Civil Liability Act 1936* (SA), Part 5; *Wrongs Act 1958* (Vic), Part III; *Fatal Accidents Act 1934* (Tas); *Fatal Accidents Act 1959* (WA)). These pieces of legislation are known as "Lord Campbell's Act" after the person who introduced the first *Fatal Accidents Act 1846* into the United Kingdom parliament. Under this legislation the plaintiff (the deceased's legal personal representative or the dependants of the deceased) must establish that:

- the defendant's conduct caused the death;
- the defendant's conduct was wrongful; and
- the deceased could have brought an action for the injury had they not died (the "condition precedent").

There is also a separate question of whether the death caused the dependant's loss. Only if it did can the action be maintained. In *Haber v Walker* [1963] VR 339, the deceased had been brain damaged in a car accident caused by the defendant. The brain damage led to severe depression and he committed suicide. The court held that his suicide was not a voluntary act such as to break the chain of causation between the accident and his death.

Where the wrongful act is negligence, the ordinary rules of negligence apply, except that it is not necessary for the death to be foreseeable. Only personal injury need be foreseeable. See, for example, *Chapman v Hearse* (1961) 106 CLR 112, extracted in [7.145].

The people who can recover under this legislation are the dependants of the deceased. This is usually the spouse, children, siblings and parents of the victim. The exact details vary across the jurisdictions so the relevant legislation should be consulted. See [14.290]ff for the damages issues raised by Lord Campbell's Act actions.

[8.215] **Notes&Questions**

1. Given that wrongful death claims apply the ordinary rules of negligence, what impact do the Civil Liability Acts have on wrongful death claims by dependants?
2. Why was it necessary to limit Lord Campbell's Act actions to dependants? Should this be changed?

CHAPTER 9

Duty: Defective Property or Goods

INTRODUCTION

[9.05] In this chapter we consider three different areas of the duty of care. Generally, all that is needed to establish a duty of care in respect of property damage (as with personal injury) is foreseeability of harm: *Smith v Littlewoods Organisation Ltd* [1987] AC 241. This is so unless there is some specific extra matter which requires something else–that might include some cases where a public authority or a third party was involved or there was some other issue of public policy which altered the general rule. The areas of the duty of care we consider in this chapter arise in situations where property is damaged, but include the situation where a person buys or leases personal or real property, which at first sight seems to be sound and good, but is later discovered to be defective, thereby producing economic loss or physical injury. Product liability arises in relation to the manufacture and sale of goods. Liability for defective structures arises in two main ways of interest to us: when a building is purchased which later turns out to be defective and the builder or architect or council can be liable; and when a building is leased to a tenant and turns out to be defective, when a landlord may be liable for personal injury caused by the defect.

PRODUCT LIABILITY – LIABILITY FOR DEFECTIVE GOODS

[9.10] The duty of care may arise in relation to the manufacture, distribution and consumption of goods. In the early 19th century it was established that an owner of a chattel which was "dangerous in itself" had a duty to take precautions for the safety of others to the extent of the case where the owner lets it get out of his or her hands. Thus in *Dixon v Bell* (1816) 5 M & S 198; 105 ER 1023, the owner of a loaded gun was held liable when he allowed it into the hands of a servant, not in the course of her ordinary employment, and the servant shot the plaintiff by accident. However, for a long time the view was that the owner was not under a duty in tort where the chattel was in the hands of some other person, unless it was dangerous in itself. So, in *Winterbottom v Wright* (1842) 10 M & W 109; 152 ER 402, the owner was held not liable to a person injured by a stagecoach where the defendant had hired it to the Postmaster-General, even though the defendant was under a contractual duty to the Postmaster-General to keep it in repair.

After *Donoghue v Stevenson* [1932] AC 562 (extracted at [7.10]), the category of "dangerous things" was no longer regarded as significant as a category, although it could be relevant to the question of breach of duty. The duty of care, then, will arise in relation to defective products by the simple application of the ordinary principles of negligence. *Donoghue v Stevenson* [1932] AC 562 and *Grant v Australian Knitting Mills* [1936] AC 85 (at [8.10]) are classic examples of what we call "product liability". When a person is injured by a product, a range of ways in which they may recover damages arises. They may be able to sue in negligence, they may be able to sue in contract for breach of warranty, or breach of implied term of the contract as to the fitness of the product (this will depend on them being within the rules of privity of contract or covered by the relevant Sale of Goods legislation. The Sale of Goods Acts are: *Sale of Goods Act 1923* (NSW), *Goods Act 1958* (Vic); *Sale of Goods Act 1954* (ACT); *Sale of Goods Act 1896* (Qld); *Sale of Goods Act* (NT); *Sale of Goods Act 1895* (SA); *Sale of Goods Act 1896* (Tas); *Sale of Goods Act 1895* (WA). See also *Trade Practices Act 1974* (Cth), Pt V Div 2A; *Manufacturers' Warranties Act 1974* (SA); *Consumer Affairs and Fair Trading Act* (NT); *Manufacturers Warranties Act 1974* (SA); *Law Reform (Manufacturers' Warranties) Act 1977* (ACT); *Fair Trading Act 1989* (Qld)), or they may be able to bring an action under the *Trade Practices Act 1974* (Cth) Pt V (Consumer Protection) or Pt VA (Liability of manufacturers and importers for injury or loss caused by defective goods). Negligence need not be proved under Pt VA. Where there is loss suffered as a result of injury or death caused by defective goods liability will arise. Section 75AK provides a number of defences to a claim including the defence of "state of the art" or "development risk". This latter defence allows the defendant to argue that when the goods were supplied it was not possible under the state of technical knowledge to know of the defect.

When the tort of negligence is being used for a product liability claim there are a range of ways in which the action can be conceived. The relevant defect may be defective manufacture (as in *Donoghue v Stevenson* [1932] AC 562 or *Grant v Australian Knitting Mills* [1936] AC 85), defective design (for example, *O'Dwyer v Leo Buring Pty Ltd* [1966] WAR 67 where a bottle stopper was held to be defectively designed in that it ejected spontaneously out of the bottle) or even defective marketing such as a failure to label properly.

The following case arose in relation to contaminated food and shows the interaction of the common law of negligence with the product liability sections of the *Trade Practices Act 1974* (Cth).

Graham Barclay Oysters v Ryan

[9.15] *Graham Barclay Oysters Pty Ltd v Ryan* (2000) 177 ALR 18 Full Federal Court of Australia (footnotes omitted)

[Mr Ryan was one of over 100 people who became ill with Hepatitis A ("HAV") after eating contaminated oysters from a lake in New South Wales. The grower of the oysters was Barclay Oysters. The distributor was Barclay Distributors, a separate company owned by the same person. The evidence was that the HAV came into the lake through faecal contamination from various outlets, caravan parks and sewerage and storm water drains after a severe storm. There was evidence that HAV survives well for a long time in the environment. The oyster industry used a process of "depuration" to disinfect oysters by putting them in clean water disinfected by ultra violet radiation which kills any virus it comes into contact with. The State had put in place a mandatory policy of depuration for 36 hours with which Barclay had complied. The expert evidence was that depuration would reduce viral load but could not remove it completely and that therefore monitoring of water quality was necessary. Further evidence suggested that as it was known that the water became contaminated after storms, that harvesting should be delayed until testing could confirm safety. Barclay had delayed harvesting

Graham Barclay Oysters v Ryan cont.

for two days after the end of the storm. The primary judge found that the State had not done a sanitary survey which the expert evidence suggested was necessary. Barclays had had random oysters tested for E-Coli and they were negative, but there was no way to test for the presence of HAV. When the HAV epidemic occurred Barclays recalled their oysters and did not harvest for the rest of the season. Testing showed widespread faecal contamination in the estuary waters. The trial judge held that the Barclay companies owed a duty of care to consumers and it had breached and therefore, caused harm. The Barclay Companies appealed.]

LINDGREN J: [with whom Lee J agreed in respect of the Trade Practices matters.] … [480]

My conclusions on the Barclay companies' appeal on liability except as to the claims under the TP Act

[485] Lee J and Kiefel J are of the view that the Barclay companies' appeal in relation to the learned primary judge's finding that they were liable in negligence should be dismissed. I conclude below that Barclay Oysters is liable to compensate Mr Ryan under the TP Act. For these reasons I will not state in as ample a form, as I might otherwise have done, my reasons for differing from the learned primary judge, Lee J and Kiefel J, in thinking that the Barclay companies were not shown to be liable in negligence …

[503] It seems to me that on the evidence of the lack of any previous outbreak of health problems arising from the consumption of oysters grown in the lake and the lack of knowledge otherwise of Mr Barclay of the existence of an actual problem as distinct from potential sources of faecal contamination of the lake, the Barclay companies' duty of care did not reasonably require them either to take the course that his Honour outlined or to suffer a closure of their business until somehow they could be completely assured that they were putting into the market a product that was free of defects. …

[506] For the above reasons, in my opinion the Barclay companies' appeal should succeed in so far as the Barclay companies were found liable to Mr Ryan in negligence. …

Section 74B

[510] Section 74B of the TP Act provided as follows:

(1) Where:

(a) a corporation, in trade or commerce, supplies goods manufactured by the corporation to another person who acquires the goods for re-supply;

(b) a person (whether or not the person who acquired the goods from the corporation) supplies the goods (otherwise than by way of sale by auction) to a consumer;

(c) the goods are acquired by the consumer for a particular purpose that was, expressly or by implication, made known to the corporation, either directly, or through the person from whom the consumer acquired the goods or a person by whom any antecedent negotiations in connexion with the acquisition of the goods were conducted;

(d) the goods are not reasonably fit for that purpose, whether or not that is a purpose for which such goods are commonly supplied; and

(e) the consumer or a person who acquires the goods from, or derives title to the goods through or under, the consumer suffers loss or damage by reason that the goods are not reasonably fit for that purpose;

the corporation is liable to compensate the consumer or that other person for the loss or damage and the consumer or that other person may recover the amount of the compensation by action against the corporation in a court of competent jurisdiction.

(2) Subsection (1) does not apply:

Graham Barclay Oysters v Ryan cont.

> ... (b) where the circumstances show that the consumer did not rely, or that it was unreasonable for the consumer to rely, on the skill or judgment of the corporation.

[emphasis added]

[512] The primary judge analysed how, he thought, s 74B applied in the circumstances of the case. His Honour recorded that the Barclay companies did not dispute his analysis and relied only on subs (2)(b). That paragraph has two limbs: "non-reliance" and "unreasonable reliance". Barclay Oysters did not plead non-reliance in its defence but argued it before his Honour nonetheless. Barclay Oysters' amended notice of appeal raises only the ground that his Honour erred in failing to find that it was unreasonable for Mr Ryan to have relied on the skill or judgment of Barclay Oysters. ...

[515] Reliance is not referred to in s 74B(1): it is not expressed as an element that Mr Ryan had to prove in order to establish that Barclay Oysters was "liable to compensate" him under that subsection. Rather, non-reliance goes to displace the operation of subs (1), that is, to render it inapplicable. In these circumstances, the burden of proving non-reliance rested on Barclay Oysters: cf *Cavalier Marketing (Aust) Pty Ltd v Rasell* (1990) 96 ALR 375 (*Cavalier Marketing*) (Qld/FC) at 392 per Cooper J.

[516] Mr Ryan testified that when he consumed the oysters, he assumed that they would not cause him illness and that if he had thought they would do so, he would not have eaten them. There was no cross-examination of Mr Ryan or of the buyers of the oysters, his father Thomas John Ryan or his brother David Ryan, directed to showing that they or any of them understood that there could be no assurance that the oysters were fit to eat. Both the father and the brother testified that they bought the oysters direct from Barclay Oysters in Forster (his Honour assumed that the purchase had in fact been from Barclay Distributors in view of the respective roles played by the two companies) and gave some to Mr Ryan. In the circumstances, I think that the learned primary judge was entitled to conclude, as he did, that non-reliance had not been proved, and also to infer, as he did, that Mr Ryan had in fact relied on the skill and judgment of Barclay Oysters.

[Lindgren J then considered the second limb of s 74B(2)(b) concerned with unreasonable reliance.]

[518] Barclay Oysters submits that the phrase "unreasonable for the consumer to rely on the skill or judgment of the corporation" imports an objective element so that one must hypothesise a consumer who knew all relevant facts, such as, what the manufacturer (grower) knew or should have known, the circumstances in which the manufacture (growing) took place, and the steps available and not available to be taken by the manufacturer (grower) to ensure that the goods were reasonably fit for the purpose made known to it. Barclay Oysters submits that it would have been unreasonable for a hypothetical consumer, possessed of all this knowledge, to rely on the skill or judgment of Barclay Oysters to guarantee a virus-free oyster.

[519] Mr Ryan, on the other hand, submits that reasonableness is to be measured by reference to the particular consumer with his or her actual knowledge or lack of knowledge.

[520] Certain matters are clear:

- The expression "the consumer" in subs (2)(b) refers to the particular actual consumer referred to in subs (1).
- The reliance to which subs (2)(b) refers is reliance on the skill or judgment of the manufacturer (here, Barclay Oysters) in supplying the goods in the face of its having been apprised of the particular purpose of that consumer, that is, on the skill or judgment of the manufacturer as to the fitness of the goods for the particular purpose of that consumer made known to it.
- The expression "unreasonable for the consumer to rely" is, in terms, directed to the reasonableness or unreasonableness of the particular consumer's reliance, not the reasonableness or unreasonableness of the method or course of manufacture followed.

[521] To apply a totally subjective test would enlarge or diminish the protection given by the section according to the idiosyncrasies of the particular consumer. It is possible, but perhaps unlikely, that

Graham Barclay Oysters v Ryan cont.

parliament intended the provision to operate in this way. On the other hand, according to Barclay Oysters' submissions, understood literally, the provision would operate to defeat a consumer even where a manufacturer put a product which it knew to be defective into the market place, since, being deemed to know what the particular manufacturer knew, the consumer would rely on the skill or judgment of the manufacturer, unreasonably.

[522] It is important to appreciate the roles of the two limbs of para (b). The consumer's actual knowledge is addressed in the first limb (non-reliance). If the particular consumer knew that the manufacturer could not reasonably be understood to be accepting responsibility for the fitness of the goods for the particular purpose made known to it, the consumer would not in fact have relied on its skill or judgment.

[523] The second limb (unreasonable reliance) must be construed against the background of earlier parts of s 74B. It assumes:

(a) that the consumer made known to the manufacturer, whether directly or through the person from whom the consumer acquired the goods, the particular purpose for which the consumer acquired them (subs (1)(c) – as noted earlier there is a concession by Barclay Oysters in this respect in the present case); and

(b) that the consumer did in fact rely on the manufacturer's skill or judgment as to the fitness of the goods for that particular purpose (first limb of subs (2)(b)).

[524] Against this background, in what circumstances, it may be asked, might the consumer's actual reliance on the skill or judgment of the manufacturer have been unreasonable? It might be if, for example, the manufacturer had notified the particular consumer that it could not guarantee the goods' fitness for the consumer's particular purpose or if the particular consumer's knowledge or means of knowledge was equal to or exceeded that of the manufacturer. Perhaps, in addition, for the purpose of the application of the provision, there should be imputed to the particular consumer the knowledge that "a reasonable consumer" would have. Perhaps the particular consumer should also be treated as having taken any steps for his or her own protection that "a reasonable consumer" would have taken, having regard to the nature of the goods and the circumstances of the case. Be this as it may, in my view, ordinarily, there should not be imputed to the consumer special technical knowledge touching the process of manufacture of the goods. Yet it is knowledge of that kind that Barclay Oysters contends should be imputed to Mr Ryan.

[525] The evidence before the learned primary judge did not establish circumstances as to Mr Ryan's knowledge or that of the consumers generally that might have provided a basis for a finding that it was in fact unreasonable for Mr Ryan or for a reasonable consumer placed as he was, in accepting that the oysters were fit to eat, to rely on the skill or judgment of Barclay Oysters.

[526] In my opinion, the construction of the unreasonable reliance limb of s 74B(2)(b) advanced by Barclay Oysters should not be accepted.

Section 74D

[527] Section 74D of the TP Act was relevantly as follows:

(1) Where:

(a) a corporation, in trade or commerce, supplies goods manufactured by the corporation to another person who acquires the goods for re-supply;

(b) a person (whether or not the person who acquired the goods from the corporation) supplies the goods (otherwise than by way of sale by auction) to a consumer;

(c) the goods are not of merchantable quality; and

(d) the consumer or a person who acquires the goods from, or derives title to the goods through or under, the consumer suffers loss or damage by reason that the goods are

Graham Barclay Oysters v Ryan cont.

not of merchantable quality;

the corporation is liable to compensate the consumer or that other person for the loss or damage and the consumer or that other person may recover the amount of the compensation by action against the corporation in a court of competent jurisdiction. ...

(3) Goods of any kind are of merchantable quality within the meaning of this section if they are as fit for the purpose or purposes for which goods of that kind are commonly bought as it is reasonable to expect having regard to:

(a) any description applied to the goods by the corporation;

(b) the price received by the corporation for the goods (if relevant); and

(c) all the other relevant circumstances.

[emphasis added]

[528] Barclay Oysters accepted his Honour's analysis of s 74D and it is necessary for me to address only the issue that was debated on the appeal. This concerned the effect of the words emphasised above. Barclay Oysters' amended notice of appeal is to the effect that his Honour should have found that the oysters consumed by Mr Ryan satisfied those words (Barclay Oysters had not pleaded this matter in its defence, although submissions were put to his Honour on it and he dealt with them).

[529] Barclay Oysters submits that "all the other relevant circumstances" referred to in para (c) set out above included:

(a) The practical impossibility of testing the oysters for the presence of viruses.

(b) The grower's inability to know that his oyster leases had been subjected to viral contamination.

(c) The grower's inability to control the environment in which the oysters grow – in particular the entry of contaminants from private land or council stormwater drains, etc into the estuary water.

[530] The learned primary judge stated:

> The error in this approach is similar to that in relation to s 74B. The issue posed by s 74D(3) is not whether it was possible for the grower to ensure the oysters were free of viruses, but whether a purchaser would act reasonably in expecting they were. Unlike s 74B(2)(b), which directs attention to the acts and omissions of the particular consumer, s 74D(3) imposes an objective standard ("as it is reasonable to expect"), though that standard must be applied having regard to all relevant circumstances. In the present case those circumstances include the absence of any warning by the Barclay companies of the possibility of a virus in the oysters. Of course, this would not matter if it was well known to members of the public that viruses can survive even proper processing and depuration, but the evidence does not suggest it was.
>
> The s 74D claim should be determined in the same way as that arising under s 74B: the applicant is entitled to succeed on his own behalf against Barclay Oysters, although not Barclay Distributors. His representative claim against Barclay Oysters should be reserved.

[531] With respect, I agree with his Honour's conclusion, and, in substance, with his reasons. ...

[533] The words "as it is reasonable to expect" suggests a question as to the identity of the person or persons, the reasonableness of whose expectation is in question and is to be determined by the court. Possible contenders are:

1. the consumer or other person who suffers loss or damage;
2. a reasonable consumer placed as that actual consumer or other person was;
3. a reasonable bystander (in effect, the court).

[534] In my opinion consistently with both the objective nature of the standard aimed for and the consumer protection purpose of the provision, it is the second or third category of person whose

Graham Barclay Oysters v Ryan cont.

reasonable expectation is called into service by the statute, and in my opinion a reasonable bystander would seek to put himself or herself in the position of a reasonable consumer placed as the actual consumer or other person was. Accordingly, it is right to inquire into the reasonable expectations of a category (2) person.

[535] In *Cavalier Marketing*, Cooper J also suggested (at 403) that the test to be applied was the reasonable expectation of a reasonable consumer placed as the actual consumer or other sufferer of loss or damage (the person described in class (2) above) was.

[536] As in the case of s 74B discussed above, the provision is to be construed as a consumer protection measure (cf *Cavalier Marketing* at 400) and it would be wrong to measure the reasonable expectations of the hypothetical reasonable consumer against the specialist technical knowledge of oyster growers that it is impossible to be sure that the oysters they put into the market for the one and only purpose of being eaten, are in fact safe for that purpose.

[537] I discussed at [516] above the evidence that was before his Honour as to Mr Ryan's assumption about the quality of oysters he ate. There was no evidence before his Honour that consumers of oysters understood that there could be no assurance that they did not harbour the HAV. Barclay Oysters issued no warning to accompany its oysters and Mr Ryan ate them without having been apprised of the risk involved in doing so. He assumed that they were safe to eat. The absence of any warning was a circumstance that would lead a reasonable consumer, placed as Mr Ryan was, to assume that those responsible, ie the growers, had satisfied themselves that this was so.

[538] I see nothing unreasonable in my construction of the provision. It is not unreasonable for the legislature to adopt a policy of requiring a manufacturer to meet the reasonable expectations of consumers as to the fitness of the manufacturer's goods for their purpose or purposes. Consistently with that policy, if the manufacturer knows that it cannot be sure to meet those expectations, it must cease manufacturing, or, if possible, ensure that the consumer has agreed to bear the risk (perhaps by an appropriate warning with the result that the consumer's otherwise reasonable expectations are made unreasonable).

Section 75AD (and s 75AK)

[539] Section 75AD appears in Pt VA of the TP Act which was inserted in 1992 to provide remedies against manufacturers and importers of defective goods. The section reads as follows:

> If:
>
> (a) a corporation, in trade or commerce, supplies goods manufactured by it; and
>
> (b) they have a defect; and
>
> (c) because of the defect, an individual suffers injuries;
>
> then:
>
> (d) the corporation is liable to compensate the individual for the amount of the individual's loss suffered as a result of the injuries; and
>
> (e) the individual may recover that amount by action against the corporation;

Section 75AK(1)(c) provides that it is a defence if it is established, relevantly, that:

> ... the state of scientific or technical knowledge at the time when [the goods] were supplied by their actual manufacturer was not such as to enable [the] defect to be discovered.

His Honour stated (at [377]):

> The term "manufactured" is defined in s 75AA, for the purposes of s 75AD, in the same terms as in s 74A. Section 75AC(1) explains that "goods have a defect if their safety is not such as persons generally are entitled to expect". Consistently with what I have already said, it seems to me the elements stipulated by s 75AD are satisfied in this case. However, s 75AK(1)(c)

Graham Barclay Oysters v Ryan cont.

provides a defence to an action under s 75AD (among other sections) "if it is established that … the state of scientific or technical knowledge at the time when they were supplied by their actual manufacturer was not such as to enable that defect to be discovered". The paragraph obviously intends the defence be unavailable if the goods were supplied notwithstanding the possibility of discovery of the defect. Conversely, the defence is available if the defect was not capable of discovery before supply. In the present case, discovery and supply were mutually exclusive; the only test that would reveal the defect would destroy the goods. Accordingly, it seems to me the defence applies and the s 75AD claim fails.

[540] Mr Ryan cross-appeals, complaining that his Honour erred in sustaining Barclay Oysters' defence under s 75AK(1)(c).

[541] His Honour treated "the goods" as referring to the individual oysters: if an individual oyster were tested, it would be destroyed in the process and so supply of it to an individual would have become an impossibility.

[542] In my opinion his Honour was entitled to find that Barclay Oysters had discharged the onus of establishing that in December 1996, when it supplied the oysters, the state of scientific or technical knowledge was not such as to enable the presence of the HAV in them to be discovered.

[543] His Honour's statement that discovery of the defect and supply were mutually exclusive and that the only test that would reveal the defect would destroy the goods, assumes two other findings which I think his Honour must also be taken to have made and for which there was ample evidence:

- that it is legitimate to extrapolate from the result of the sample test only where there is relevant homogeneity between the total population from which the sample is taken and that this cannot be assumed to be so in relation to HAV and oysters;
- PCR gives false negatives; that is, while it is appropriate to rely on a positive test result, a negative one does not establish the absence of the HAV virus and in fact establishes no more than that the test did not establish its presence in the oyster actually tested. (2000) 177 ALR 18 at 150

[544] Counsel for Mr Ryan suggested that his Honour erred by construing the expression "to be discovered" as referring to nothing except "a physical verification in each and every oyster". They suggested an analogy:

> Thus his Honour's approach was to give a meaning to the expression "to be discovered" which was too narrow and inconsistent with a purposive approach to the construction of s 75AK(1)(c). It did not mean physical verification in each and every oyster. That would have been impossible. None would have been supplied. One can test his Honour's construction of s 75AK(1)(c) by taking the example of a bag of sugar and stipulating a scenario where to test for a contaminant one needed to take several sugar grains, dissolve them and test the liquid, with a positive result demonstrating that the bag of sugar contained a defect. One would assume that the s 75AK(1)(c) defence could not be made out. But that example is no different to the present case. One has destroyed part of the goods (the several grains). Further, to be definitive one would need to dissolve all of the sugar. But that would destroy all sugar and none would be supplied. On his Honour's construction the s 75AK(1)(c) defence would be made out. But that would enable the sugar manufacturer to supply sugar which was defective with the ready scientific and technical knowledge to identify the defect and avoid supply.

[545] In my respectful opinion the sugar analogy is a false one. It assumes the possibility of extrapolating from the individual grains of sugar to all the grains in the bag. But his Honour found that extrapolation was impossible in the case of the oysters. If it were impossible to make the extrapolation from the grains of sugar tested to all other grains in the bag, it would be true to say in that instance also that the testing and supply were mutually exclusive.

[546]… There was expert evidence in support of the following propositions:

Graham Barclay Oysters v Ryan cont.

- PCR testing was a sophisticated research tool in its infancy in 1996, was available in few laboratories and was unsuitable as a test to be carried out by persons, such as oyster growers, who had not had considerable laboratory training and experience;
- PCR testing had to be performed under laboratory conditions by skilled personnel and cost between $50 and $200 per sample;
- there was no routine test for detecting the presence of viruses in shellfish used anywhere in the world;
- because PCR testing gave false negatives, negative results could not be relied on, even in 1998;
- because of the propensity of viruses to cluster together, there might be one contaminated oyster in a bed of otherwise uncontaminated ones, yet because of the tiny quantity of the virus needed to infect a consumer, that one contaminated oyster might do so;
- as at November 1996, PCR had no role to play in the routine monitoring of viral contamination of oysters;
- reliable testing of oysters for viruses was not available in 1996;
- E coli was not an effective indication of the presence of viruses in oysters.

[547] If scientific and technical knowledge had enabled the fact that an oyster being put into the market did or did not carry the HAV to be discovered without destruction of that oyster, the defence under s 75AK(1)(c) would not have been available to Barclay Oysters (subject to what I say below). But his Honour found otherwise on the evidence and was entitled to do so, in my view.

[548] For the above reasons, Mr Ryan's cross-appeal should be dismissed …

KIEFEL J: …

Negligence

[606] A finding of a duty of care on the part of an oyster grower in the area requires considerations of the closeness of the relationship between it and consumers, and of any measures open to the consumers to protect themselves, in addition to the grower's knowledge of the risk: *Perre v Apand* at 631, 659, 664. A duty not to expose consumers to the risk of virus is readily satisfied. The existence of a duty of care was conceded at trial. It was submitted on the appeal that this did not, however, spell out the content of the duty. In my view, the above statement of duty is self-explanatory and the means by which it was to be achieved clearly available. [Kiefel J held that the duty was breached.]

Trade Practices Act claims …

[610] His Honour found that ss 74B and 74D were further sources of liability in Barclay Oysters. Section 74B(1) provides that a corporation is liable to compensate a consumer who suffers loss as a result of goods manufactured (which may include produce grown) not being reasonably fit for their purpose, which purpose was made known to the corporation. The purpose here was of course human consumption, of which the grower was aware. Submissions on behalf of Barclay Oysters and some other growers focused upon s 74B(2)(b), which provides that subs (1) is not applicable to a circumstance where the consumer did not rely, or it was unreasonable for it to rely, on the skill or judgment of the corporation. In their submission, the question of reliance on the part of consumers cannot be assumed, as his Honour approached the matter.

[611] In my view, it is plain that a consumer will necessarily rely upon the judgment of an oyster grower that oysters are fit for consumption. In the case of oysters, more so than other foods, it may be considered even more likely that consumers will harbour concerns but expect that the goods would not be available for sale if there was a real risk that they were contaminated. It follows from my reasons relating to liability for negligence, that the judgment Barclay Oysters exercised was when to return to

harvesting. In my view, his Honour was correct in holding Barclay Oysters (but not Barclay Distributors) liable on this basis and under s 74D. That provision concerns the merchantable quality of goods and whether a purchaser would act reasonably in expecting that they met such standards.

[612] In my view, Barclay Oysters' appeal should be dismissed. So far as concerns the Barclay companies' cross-claim against the council, it should be determined by the primary judge. As Lindgren J points out, that appears to have been accepted by those parties on the appeal.

The cross-appeal against Barclay Oysters

[613] Section 75AD of the *Trade Practices Act 1974* provides a liability for compensation in a corporation which supplies defective goods manufactured by it and a person suffers injury as a result of the defect. Section 75AK(1)(c), however, provides that it is a defence to such a claim if it is established that the defect could not be discovered, having regard to the state of scientific or technical knowledge at the time of supply. His Honour held that the defence was available, since the only test capable of detecting the virus – flesh testing – would destroy the oyster. Discovery and supply were therefore mutually exclusive.

[614] I would respectfully agree with his Honour's conclusion that the defence was available. The evidence relating to flesh testing was that it was problematic; it often failed to detect a virus; it frequently gave false negatives; and it could only be undertaken by samples which, so far as concerned oysters, could not be assumed to be representative. It is in that latter sense that I understand his Honour to say that the only *effective* test was to destroy each oyster to be offered for sale. The test could not in any sense be regarded as a proper or sufficient means of detection. In my view, therefore, it could not be said that scientific knowledge was such as to enable the virus to be detected within the meaning of s 75AK.

[Kiefel and Lee JJ held that Barclay Oysters breached its duty of care to Ryan. The court held that Barclay Oysters had contravened ss 74AB and 74D of the *Trade Practices Act 1974* (Cth).]

The following part of the case in the High Court shows how duty and breach often intertwine so as to be almost indistinguishable. The question of the scope of the duty may be seen as part of the duty question or part of the breach question.

Graham Barclay Oysters v Ryan

[9.20] *Graham Barclay Oysters Pty Ltd v Ryan; Ryan v Great Lakes Council; State of New South Wales* (2002) 211 CLR 540 High Court of Australia

(footnotes omitted)

[The aspects of the case which concern public authorities are extracted in Chapter 11.]

GUMMOW AND HAYNE JJ:

C. The Barclay Companies

[187] The Barclay companies concede that they owed a duty of care to their consumers, including Mr Ryan, to take reasonable care to ensure that the oysters they harvested and supplied were safe for human consumption. The immediate issue before this Court is whether the companies breached that duty. This requires consideration of the circumstances disclosed by the evidence before the primary judge …

[190] The duty of the Barclay companies did not extend to ensuring the safety of oysters in all circumstances. In *Wyong Shire Council v Shirt* (1980) 146 CLR 40, Mason J (with whom Stephen J and Aickin J agreed) stated:

Graham Barclay Oysters v Ryan cont.

> In deciding whether there has been a breach of the duty of care the tribunal of fact must first ask itself whether a reasonable man in the defendant's position would have foreseen that his conduct involved a risk of injury to the plaintiff or to a class of persons including the plaintiff. If the answer be in the affirmative, it is then for the tribunal of fact to determine what a reasonable man would do by way of response to the risk. The perception of the reasonable man's response calls for a consideration of the magnitude of the risk and the degree of the probability of its occurrence, along with the expense, difficulty and inconvenience of taking alleviating action and any other conflicting responsibilities which the defendant may have.

Neither Lee J nor Kiefel J expressed themselves as approaching their task by the sequential reasoning process which *Wyong Shire Council* mandates.

[191] An analysis of the competing considerations referred to in Wyong Shire Council is impeded, not assisted, by formulating the relevant duty of care in terms of its breach, which was the approach that the majority in the Full Court appeared to adopt. ...

[192] A duty of care that is formulated retrospectively as an obligation purely to avoid the particular act or omission said to have caused loss, or to avert the particular harm that in fact eventuated, is of its nature likely to obscure the proper inquiry as to breach. That inquiry involves identifying, with some precision, what a reasonable person in the position of the defendant would do by way of response to the reasonably foreseeable risk. ... The trial judge and the majority of the Full Court in the present case failed to identify with the necessary precision, by reference to considerations of the nature of those indicated in *Wyong Shire Council*, the reasonable response to the risk of harm that existed. In so failing, their Honours fell into an error of law. There is no serious dispute as to the facts to which the law is to be applied. Thus, it is appropriate for this Court to resolve the matter. For the reasons that follow, the proper application of principle requires a conclusion different to that reached in the Federal Court.

[193] The risk of injury which eventuated in this case was not far-fetched or fanciful; it was real and was therefore foreseeable. The Barclay companies knew that viral contamination of oysters could result from human faecal pollution of the waters in which oysters are cultivated. The companies knew that depuration alone was an inadequate guarantee of oyster safety. They were aware that there existed, in the vicinity of Wallis Lake, septic tanks, stormwater drains and other facilities which, if defective, could cause faecal pollution of the waters. There was some dispute about whether or not the Barclay companies had actual knowledge that any of those facilities were defective, or actual knowledge about the existence of specific pollution problems. Nonetheless, it was reasonably foreseeable that the conduct of the business of the Barclay companies involved a risk of injury to oyster consumers.

[194] What was the reasonable response to this risk? ...

[197] Given the state of relevant scientific knowledge at November 1996, it was not possible (and apparently is still not possible) to eliminate entirely the risk of viral contamination of oysters grown at Wallis Lake. The possibility of viral contamination is ever present when oysters are grown in an area where humans live. Only oysters grown in pristine waters will be free from viral contamination. ...

[201] Therefore, in practical terms, the alternatives open to the Barclay companies were (i) to cease harvesting and selling oysters after the November 1996 rainfall event until a sanitary survey was conducted and testing revealed an acceptable risk; or (ii) to sell oysters with a warning as to their possible viral contamination; or (iii) to cease growing oysters at Wallis Lake entirely, and, perhaps, to establish operations in pristine waters elsewhere. Given the attitude of both the Council and the State, and the apparent similarity between the November 1996 rainfall and previous rainfall events, option (i) effectively would have required the cessation of harvesting for an unspecified, potentially indefinite, period following any such heavy rainfall. Option (ii) is likely to have had the same effect as ceasing to sell oysters altogether. Option (iii) was not explored in any detail during argument and would have required relocation to some unspecified waterway isolated from human beings. Each of the three courses of action would have been either entirely destructive of, or highly disruptive to, the business of

the Barclay companies. Each represents alleviating action of the most difficult, expensive and inconvenient type. According to the settled principles propounded in *Wyong Shire Council*, such alleviating action can only be required by the law of negligence if the magnitude of the risk and the degree of probability of its occurrence are great indeed.

[202] Although a risk of viral contamination was ever present, this was the first recorded outbreak of hepatitis A, or any other oyster-related disease, caused by Wallis Lake oysters in almost a century of oyster growing. ... Notwithstanding the significant magnitude of the risk of harm that eventuated in this case, the degree of probability of its occurrence cannot be said to justify the difficult, expensive and inconvenient alleviating action contended for by the consumers. ... [T]he general consistency of the Barclay companies' conduct with the local quality assurance programme, which was itself formulated in response to the 1997 hepatitis A outbreak, reinforces the conclusion that the companies took reasonable care to ensure that their oysters were safe for human consumption.

[204] The trial judge and the majority of the Full Court erred in holding that the Barclay companies had breached their duty of care to the oyster consumers. The appeal by Barclay Distributors should be allowed. However, Barclay Oysters is in a different position. Given the finding at trial and in the Full Court, not challenged in this Court, that Barclay Oysters had contravened s 74B and s 74D of the *Trade Practices Act 1974*, the judgment obtained by Mr Ryan against that company should not be disturbed.

[Gleeson CJ, Kirby and Callinan JJ held that Barclay Oysters and Barclay Distributors had breached their duty of care; Gaudron and McHugh JJ agreed with Gummow and Hayne JJ that the Barclay companies had not breached their duty of care.]

[9.25] **Notes&Questions**

1. Bringing an action in negligence for product liability requires proof of fault, whereas bringing an action under Pt VA of the *Trade Practices Act 1974* (Cth) does not, as it is a strict liability matter, although as happened in *Ryan's case*, there are defences available to manufacturers. The Pt VA regime is similar to the European product liability regime.
2. What amounts to a defect in a product under the *Trade Practices Act 1974*? Section 75AC(1) says the question is whether the goods' "safety is not such as persons generally are entitled to expect". In *Carey-Hazell v Getz Bros & Co (Aust) Pty Ltd* [2004] FCA 853, a mechanical heart valve carried a risk that some patients might be injured because of its presence. This risk could be expressly conveyed to the patient by his or her doctor. For this reason, Kiefel J refused to hold that the heart valve was defective. The risk, therefore, depends on whether the doctor automatically conveys that risk to the patient.
3. A phenomenon known as "mass torts" (sometimes also referred to a "toxic torts") can arise where many people are affected by a defect in a product. The case extracted above is an example as Ryan was one of 184 people in the class action. Famous examples of mass torts include the effects of thalidomide (a drug which caused defects in foetuses if taken during pregnancy), Agent Orange (a chemical sprayed in the Vietnam war which appeared to have affected servicemen and their later-born children) and Diethylstilboestrol (DES) (a drug which was used to prevent miscarriages but was later discovered to cause vaginal cancer in the children who were foetuses at the time the

drug was given). These cases raise both duty and causation issues in a complex way. See R Goldberg, *Causation and Risk in the Law of Torts: Scientific Evidence and Medicinal Product Liability* (Hart Publishing, 1999) and Chapter 14, Causation.

Australia has lagged behind the United States somewhat in developing procedures to deal with mass torts. Some Australian plaintiffs have joined United States class actions for this reason. In Australia, mass tort litigation is likely to be carried out as test cases, or as representative actions under the *Trade Practices Act 1974* (Cth). Some class actions are also available for instances like *Ryan's case*. See JG Fleming, "Mass Torts" (1994) 42 *American Journal of Comparative Law* 507.

4. Failure to warn is a significant issue in product liability. This was an issue in the extracted case above (although the judges were aware that a warning would have meant that no-one would purchase the oysters). A warning may discharge the manufacturer's duty. But it may not. This will depend on how great the danger is. For example, it is not clear that a warning about the dangers of cigarette smoking is sufficient to discharge the duty of a cigarette manufacturer: see *Scanlon v American Cigarette Company (Overseas) Pty Ltd* [1987] VR 281. Can such a warning affect the position of the passive smoker?

5. One area of product liability which raises difficult issues is vaccination. When a vaccination program is carried out, occasionally a rare side effect of the vaccine may cause damage. For example, the whooping cough (pertussis) vaccine, in rare cases causes encephalitis or brain damage. However, whooping cough is extremely dangerous for young babies and often kills them. If a parent decides not to vaccinate their child because they fear this risk, this will be a rational decision only if most other children are vaccinated, because it is only if most children are vaccinated that the one child who is not bears a lesser risk than the other children. If most children are not vaccinated then they all bear the higher risk of being killed by the disease itself. Where the company that created the vaccine has not been negligent, children who are injured by the vaccine cannot recover under the tort of negligence. However, in a real sense those children are bearing a risk for the rest of the community. What does this tell us about the aims and effect of tort law? See [1.45].

6. For further reading in this area, see: IR Malkin and EJ Wright, "Product Liability under the Trade Practices Act–Adequately Compensating for Personal Injury?" (1993) 1 *Torts Law Journal* 63; J Stapleton, "Restatement (Third) of Torts: Products Liability: An Anglo-Australian Perspective" (1999) 34 *Texas International Law Journal* 45; J Stapleton, *Product Liability* (London, 1994); P Huber, *Liability: The Legal Revolution and its Consequences* (New York, Basic Books) (not solely about product liability, but very relevant to it). There is a body of literature on the economic study of product liability. See, for example, R Cooter and T Ulen, *Law and Economics* (Scott Foresman, Glenview Ill, 1988); G Priest, "A Theory of the Consumer Product Warranty" (1987) 90 Yale LJ 1297; G Calabresi, "First Party, Third Party and Product Liability Systems" (1984) 69 Iowa LR 833.

DEFECTIVE STRUCTURES

[9.30] Sometimes a building is built with a defect. Where the defect is obvious usually the parties will deal with the matter through their contractual arrangements. However, sometimes the defect is latent. In this case it can become a problem which is dealt with through the law of tort. If the defect has injured or endangered people's physical health the courts have traditionally held that the builder or architect is liable to anyone injured, not just the owner of the building. For example, in *Voli v Inglewood Shire Council* (1963) 110 CLR 74 the stage of a local council building collapsed due to inadequacy of the joists to take the load of the stage and a large number of people standing on it. The architect had specified the size of the joists. This specification was less than that required by the Council's building by-laws or the Australian Standard Associations, although the Council's officers had passed the plans. It was held that the architect owed a duty of care to people lawfully using the hall to design it to make it safe for the burden which was likely to be placed upon it, and had breached that duty which caused personal injury to the plaintiff. The architect was not exonerated from this duty by the fact that the Council had passed the plans.

However, sometimes a defective building is not actually dangerous but merely diminished in value, in which case the loss is economic loss. We have already seen one example of this in *Sutherland Shire Council v Heyman* (1985) 157 CLR 424 (see [7.100]). The later case of *Bryan v Maloney* (1995) 182 CLR 609 held that a builder could owe a duty of care to a subsequent purchaser of a house which was defective. The status of *Bryan v Maloney* (1995) 182 CLR 609 was considered again in the following case.

Woolcock Street Investments v CDG

[9.35] *Woolcock Street Investments Pty Ltd v CDG Pty Ltd* (2004) 216 CLR 515 High Court of Australia (footnotes omitted)

[The first respondent CDG was a company which acted as consulting engineers. They employed the second respondent as engineers. In 1987 CDG contracted to design a non-residential complex. One of the two owners of the complex refused to pay for a geotechnical inspection to be carried out so the geotechnical inspection was not done. CDG did do routine civil structural supervision of the foundations. In 1992 Woolcock purchased the property from the original owners. They did get a pre-purchase report from Townsville City Council who inspected the property, but not for structural flaws. In 1994 the building settled causing structural distress. The appellants commenced proceedings for failure to properly design the structure and foundations of the building, failure to properly construct the building and failure to take account of the nature of the sub-soil. At first instance Atkinson J stated a case asking whether a cause of action was available on these facts. The Court of Appeal answered no, on the basis that *Bryan v Maloney* (1995) 182 CLR 609, which would otherwise cover the matter, was confined to dwellings. Woolcock appealed to the High Court.]

GLEESON CJ, GUMMOW, HAYNE AND HEYDON JJ:

The issue

What did Bryan v Maloney decide?

526 In *Bryan v Maloney* (1995) 182 CLR 609, the Court (Mason CJ, Deane, Toohey and Gaudron JJ, Brennan J dissenting) decided that the builder of a dwelling house owed a subsequent purchaser, Mrs Maloney, of the house a duty to take reasonable care to avoid the economic loss which the subsequent purchaser suffered as a result of the diminution in value of the house when the fabric of the building cracked because the footings were inadequate. Both Mason CJ, Deane and Gaudron JJ in their joint

Woolcock Street Investments v CDG cont.

reasons, and Toohey J in his separate reasons, noted that there was no direct relationship between the builder and the subsequent purchaser, but concluded that the necessary relationship of proximity existed to warrant finding that the builder had owed the subsequent purchaser a duty of care ...

It is evident, then, that the conclusion that the builder owed a subsequent owner a duty to take reasonable care to avoid the economic loss which that subsequent owner had suffered depended upon conclusions that were reached about the relationship between the first owner and the builder. In particular, the decision in the case depended upon the anterior step of concluding that the builder owed the first owner a duty of care to avoid economic loss of that kind.

Both this anterior step, and the conclusion drawn from it, were considered in the context of the facts of the particular case–in which the building in question was a dwelling house. The propositions about assumption of responsibility by the builder and known reliance by the building owner were said to be characteristics of "the *ordinary* relationship between a builder of a house and the first owner" (emphasis added). At least in terms, however, the principles that were said to be engaged in *Bryan v Maloney* (1995) 182 CLR 609 did not depend for their operation upon any distinction between particular kinds of, or uses for, buildings. They depended upon considerations of assumption of responsibility, reliance, and proximity. Most importantly, they depended upon equating the responsibilities which the builder owed to the first owner with those owed to a subsequent owner.

Criticisms of Bryan v Maloney

The decision in *Bryan v Maloney* (1995) 182 CLR 609 has not escaped criticism ...

First, for the reasons given earlier, it may be doubted that the decision in *Bryan v Maloney* (1995) 182 CLR 609 should be understood as depending upon drawing a bright line between cases concerning the construction of dwellings and cases concerning the construction of other buildings. If it were to be understood as attempting to draw such a line, it would turn out to be far from bright, straight, clearly defined, or even clearly definable. As has been pointed out subsequently, some buildings are used for mixed purposes: shop and dwelling; dwelling and commercial art gallery; general practitioner's surgery and residence. Some high-rise apartment blocks are built in ways not very different from high-rise office towers. The original owner of a high-rise apartment block may be a large commercial enterprise. The list of difficulties in distinguishing between dwellings and other buildings could be extended.

Secondly, the decision in *Bryan v Maloney* (1995) 182 CLR 609 depended upon [Deane J's proximity-as-principle view of the duty of care]. Decisions of the Court after *Bryan v Maloney* (1995) 182 CLR 609 reveal that proximity is no longer seen as the "conceptual determinant" in this area.

Economic loss

The damage for which the appellant seeks a remedy in this case is the economic loss it alleges it has suffered as a result of buying a building which is defective. Circumstances can be imagined in which, had the defects not been discovered, some damage to person or property might have resulted from those defects. But that is not what has happened. The defects have been identified. Steps can be taken to prevent damage to person or property.

A view was adopted for a time in England that, because there was *physical* damage to the building, a claim of the kind made by the appellant was not solely for economic loss. That view was questioned in *Sutherland Shire Council v Heyman* (1985) 157 CLR 424 and rejected in *Bryan v Maloney* (1995) 182 CLR 609. It was subsequently also rejected by the House of Lords in *Murphy v Brentwood District Council* [1991] 1 AC 398. There is no reason now to reopen that debate and neither side in the present matter sought to do so. The damage which the appellant alleges it has suffered is pure economic loss.

Claims for damages for pure economic loss present peculiar difficulty. Competition is the hallmark of most forms of commercial activity in Australia ...

Woolcock Street Investments v CDG cont.

That is why damages for pure economic loss are not recoverable if all that is shown is that the defendant's negligence was a cause of the loss and the loss was reasonably foreseeable.

In *Caltex Oil (Australia) Pty Ltd v The Dredge "Willemstad"* (1976) 11 ALR 227; 136 CLR 529, the Court held that there were circumstances in which damages for economic loss were recoverable. In *Caltex Oil*, cases for recovery of economic loss were seen as being exceptions to a general rule, said to have been established in *Cattle v Stockton Waterworks* (1875) LR 10 QB 453, that even if the loss was foreseeable, damages are not recoverable for economic loss which was not consequential upon injury to person or property. In *Caltex Oil*, Stephen J isolated a number of "salient features" which combined to constitute a sufficiently close relationship to give rise to a duty of care owed to Caltex for breach of which it might recover its purely economic loss. Chief among those features was the defendant's knowledge that to damage the pipeline which was damaged was inherently likely to produce economic loss.

Since *Caltex Oil*, and most notably in *Perre v Apand Pty Ltd* (1999) 198 CLR 180, the vulnerability of the plaintiff has emerged as an important requirement in cases where a duty of care to avoid economic loss has been held to have been owed. "Vulnerability", in this context, is not to be understood as meaning only that the plaintiff was likely to suffer damage if reasonable care was not taken. Rather, "vulnerability" is to be understood as a reference to the plaintiff's inability to protect itself from the consequences of a defendant's want of reasonable care, either entirely or at least in a way which would cast the consequences of loss on the defendant …

In other cases of pure economic loss (*Bryan v Maloney* (1995) 182 CLR 609 is an example) reference has been made to notions of assumption of responsibility and known reliance. The negligent misstatement cases like *Mutual Life & Citizens' Assurance Co Ltd v Evatt* (1968) 122 CLR 556 and *Shaddock & Associates Pty Ltd v Parramatta City Council [No 1]* (1981) 36 ALR 385; 150 CLR 225 can be seen as cases in which a central plank in the plaintiff's allegation that the defendant owed it a duty of care is the contention that the defendant knew that the plaintiff would rely on the accuracy of the information the defendant provided. And it may be, as Professor Stapleton has suggested, that these cases, too, can be explained by reference to notions of vulnerability. (The reference in *Caltex Oil* to economic loss being "inherently likely" can also be seen as consistent with the importance of notions of vulnerability.) It is not necessary in this case, however, to attempt to identify or articulate the breadth of any general proposition about the importance of vulnerability. This case can be decided without doing so.

The appellant's claim

On the facts set out in the Case Stated …despite the first respondent obtaining a quotation for geotechnical investigations, the original owner of the land, by its manager, refused to pay for such investigations. (The respondents go further in their pleadings and allege that the original owner directed the adoption of particular footing sizes.) The relationship between the respondents and the original owner of the land was, therefore, not one in which the owner entrusted the design of the building to a builder, or in this case the engineer, under a simple, "non-detailed" contract. It was a relationship in which the original owner asserted control over the investigations which the engineer undertook for the purposes of performing its work.

In its pleading the appellant did not allege that the relationship between the respondents and the original owner was characterised by that assumption of responsibility by the respondents, and known reliance by the original owner on the respondents, which is referred to in the joint reasons in *Bryan v Maloney* (1995) 182 CLR 609. Such further facts as are agreed, far from supporting any inference that this was the nature of the relationship between the respondents and the original owner, point firmly in

Woolcock Street Investments v CDG cont.

the opposite direction. There was not, therefore, what was referred to in *Bryan v Maloney* (1995) 182 CLR 609 as "an identified element of known reliance (or dependence)" or "the assumption of responsibility".

It follows that the appellant's contention that the respondents owed it a duty of care cannot be supported by the reasoning which was adopted in *Bryan v Maloney* (1995) 182 CLR 609....

The relevance of the contract with the original owner

In this case, as in *Bryan v Maloney* (1995) 182 CLR 609 it is not necessary to decide whether disconformity between the obligations owed to the original owner under the contract to build or design a building and the duty of care allegedly owed to a subsequent owner will necessarily deny the existence of that duty of care. ...

In *Bryan v Maloney* (1995) 182 CLR 609, it was found that there was no disconformity between the duty owed to the original owner and the duty owed to the subsequent owner. ... This case can be determined without deciding whether disconformity of the kind we have mentioned would always deny the existence of a duty of care to a subsequent owner. There are other reasons for concluding that the respondents owed no duty of care to prevent the economic loss of which the appellant complains.

No vulnerability

... [The] facts do not show that the appellant could not have protected itself against the economic loss it alleges it has suffered. It is agreed that no warranty of freedom from defect was included in the contract by which the appellant bought the land, and that there was no assignment to the appellant of any rights which the vendor may have had against third parties in respect of any claim for defects in the building. Those facts describe what did happen. They say nothing about what could have been done to cast on the respondents the burden of the economic consequences of any negligence by the respondents. The appellant's pleading and the facts set out in the Case Stated are silent about whether the appellant could have sought and obtained the benefit of terms of that kind in the contract.

It may be accepted that the appellant bought the building not knowing that the foundations were inadequate. It is not alleged or agreed, however, that the defects of which complaint now is made could not have been discovered. The Case Stated records that, before completing its purchase, the appellant sought and obtained from the relevant local authority a certificate that the building complied with the *Building Act 1975* (Qld) and some subordinate legislation. That the defects now alleged were not discovered by a local authority asked to certify whether the building was "a ruin or so far dilapidated as to be unfit for use or occupation or [was] ... in a structural condition prejudicial to the inhabitants of or to property in the neighbourhood" says nothing about what other investigations might have been undertaken or might have revealed.

Finally, if it is relevant to know, as was assumed to be the case in *Bryan v Maloney* (1995) 182 CLR 609, whether buying the building represented a very significant investment for the appellant, there is nothing in the Case Stated or the appellant's pleading which bears on that question. ...

The present case arises in a different factual context from that considered in *Bryan v Maloney* (1995) 182 CLR 609 and can be decided without determining whether doubt should now be cast upon the result at which the Court arrived in that case.... Neither the principles applied in *Bryan v Maloney* (1995) 182 CLR 609, nor those principles as developed in subsequent cases, support the appellant's contention that on the facts agreed in the Case Stated and alleged in its statement of claim the respondents owed it a duty of care to avoid the economic loss which it alleged it suffered.

The appeal should be dismissed with costs.

[McHugh and Callinan JJ agreed in the outcome proposed by the joint judgment but held that *Bryan v Maloney* (1995) 182 CLR 609 was confined to dwellings. McHugh, Kirby and Callinan JJ used the five determinants of duty set out by McHugh J in *Perre v Apand* to determine the duty of care, but only Kirby J thought vulnerability existed. Kirby J held that vulnerability did not refer only to economic enterprise but also could refer to insidious risk which he found did exist in this case. He therefore dissented, holding that a duty of care could arise in the circumstances.]

[9.40] **Notes&Questions**

1. The position of public authorities, where they bear some responsibility for defective structures, is considered in *Sutherland Shire Council v Heyman* (1985) 157 CLR 424 (see [7.100]) and in Chapter 11.
2. The damage to the building in this case resulted in pure economic loss for the plaintiff. Why is this damage regarded as pure economic loss rather than property damage? The answer is that the building turns out to have always been defective. Because that is so, the purchaser bought a building which was worth less than he or she paid for it and in turn will not be able to sell it for the same relative value. The "duty of care relating to pure economic loss" is discussed in Chapter 10.
3. In England, neither the builder or designer of a defective building, nor the local council which inspected the property, owes a duty of care to any later owners of that property: *D & F Estates Ltd v Church Commissioners for England* [1989] AC 177; *Murphy v Brentwood District council* [1991] 1 AC 398. Why do you think the position was different in Australia?

LANDLORDS AND DEFECTIVE STRUCTURES

[9.45] For a long time landlords were regarded as being in a special position in relation to defective structures which they had leased to tenants. The rule in *Cavalier v Pope* [1906] AC 428 was that a landlord did not owe a duty of care in tort in respect of defective premises either to the tenant (presumably because they could inspect before leasing) or to any other user of the premises (because they were not parties to the lease). In *Northern Sandblasting Pty Ltd v Harris* (1997) 188 CLR 313 the High Court of Australia held that this rule is no longer part of Australian law.

The issue next arose for the High Court in the following case.

Jones v Bartlett

[9.50] *Jones v Bartlett* (2000) 205 CLR 166 High Court of Australia

(footnotes omitted)

[The plaintiff was injured when he walked through a glass door of the house of which his parents were tenants. The glass door complied with the Australian Standard at the time the house was constructed, but did not comply with the standard that would have applied if the house was being constructed at the time the lease was entered into.

Evidence was given that the landlords did not know that the glass did not comply, nor could they tell by looking at it. The appellant was awarded damages at first instance on the basis that the respondents were negligent in failing to have the house inspected before the plaintiff's parents rented

Jones v Bartlett cont.

it. An appeal to the WA Supreme Court on the part of the respondents was successful, the Full Court holding that although a duty of care was owed by the landlord, it had not been breached. The appellant then appealed to the High Court.]

GUMMOW AND HAYNE JJ: 210 [T]he Commissioner concluded that the respondents "had a degree of control in respect of the premises such that they came within the meaning of 'occupier of premises' as defined in s 2 [of the *Occupiers' Liability Act*]".

That conclusion should not be accepted. As explained earlier in these reasons, the construction given by the Commissioner to the terms of the Lease was incomplete. In any event, the question in this case is whether, when the appellant sustained his injuries, the respondents had control associated with and arising from their presence in or use of or activity in the premises. A question may have arisen respecting the application of the statutory definition if, at the relevant time, the respondents had lawfully asserted an immediate right to enter and control the premises or part thereof. However, the respondents had not done so. ...

Northern Sandblasting and the rule in Cavalier v Pope

The appellant submitted that *Northern Sandblasting* rejected what has been called the rule in *Cavalier v Pope* [1906] AC 428. This is so...

No discussion respecting the tort of negligence as it is now understood is found in the speeches in the House of Lords. In *Donoghue v Stevenson* [1932] AC 562, Lord Atkin said of *Cavalier v Pope* [1906] AC 428 that:

> [i]t was held that the wife was not a party to the contract, and that the well known absence of any duty in respect of the letting [of] an unfurnished house prevented her from relying on any cause of action for negligence.

... The result is that in Australia it is no longer correct that a landlord never owes any duty in negligence to occupants in respect of the condition of residential premises. The rejection of the rule in *Cavalier v Pope* [1906] AC 428 does not, however, go so far as necessarily to impose a duty upon the landlord to any person who may be on the premises at any given time. In *Northern Sandblasting*, the existence of some duty to the child of the tenants was assumed by the concession of the landlord. On the pleadings in the present case, the existence of any such duty was denied by the respondents. However, in their written submissions to this Court, the respondents conceded that they owed a duty of care to the appellant, the issues being its content and the presence of a breach of duty in the circumstances of the case. In our view, this concession was properly made, but to find the content of the duty in the particular case requires consideration of the wider question left unanswered in *Northern Sandblasting*.

In doing so, it would be of no utility merely to conclude that the duty is to be expressed simply as one to take reasonable care to avoid a foreseeable risk of injury to a person in the situation of the appellant. That would be to leave unanswered the critical questions respecting the content of the term "reasonable" and hence the content of the duty of care, matters essential for the determination of this case, for without them the issue of breach cannot be decided.

The landlord's duty to the tenant

The starting point is to consider the relationship between the landlord and tenant. In *Northern Sandblasting*, in a passage with which Gummow J agreed, Dawson J said of the duty of care between the landlord and a guest lawfully upon the premises that it was:

> that which arises under the ordinary principles of the law of negligence, namely, a duty to take reasonable care to avoid foreseeable risk of injury to the respondent. The nature and extent of the duty in the particular instance depends upon the circumstances of the case.

Jones v Bartlett cont.

This statement also holds true of the duty between the landlord and tenant. However, it is only the beginning of the inquiry. The difficulty lies in determining the nature and extent of any duty that exists and that which constitutes a breach thereof. The "circumstances" to be considered may differ between landlord and tenant and landlord and other persons. There is no necessary correlation between the respective duties, although the latter is likely to be less stringent than the former. This case, like *Northern Sandblasting*, is concerned with a letting for residential purposes. What follows is to be understood with that in mind. That which is required in respect of premises let for commercial or educational or other purposes may well differ, but that is not for decision in this case.

The basis upon which a landlord's duty in respect of residential tenancies is to rest is a matter of debate. One candidate is the element of "control" the landlord exercises over the premises at the time the tenant moves into occupation, in particular, the opportunity this affords for inspection by an expert engaged by the landlord. With respect, we agree with the view of the learned editors of *Prosser and Keeton on The Law of Torts* that this is a fiction devised to meet the case and not a particularly helpful one. For example, it would not cover cases in which the landlord never had control, either de facto in the case of back-to-back tenancies, or de jure in the case where a landlord assumes ownership after the tenant has gone into possession. …

Lord Atkin in *Donoghue v Stevenson* [1932] AC 562 asked whether the relations between the parties in question was so "close and direct" that the act complained of directly affected the plaintiff as a person whom the defendant "would know would be directly affected by his careless act". The relationship between landlord and tenant is so close and direct that the landlord is obliged to take reasonable care that the tenant not suffer injury. In considering the degree of care which must be taken, and the means by which a tenant may be injured, it must be borne in mind, as already discussed, that ordinarily the landlord will surrender occupation of the premises to the tenant. Thus, the content of any duty is likely to be less than that owed by an owner-occupier who retains the ability to direct what is done upon, with and to the premises. Broadly, the content of the landlord's duty to the tenant will be conterminous with a requirement that the premises be reasonably fit for the purposes for which they are let, namely habitation as a domestic residence.

This does not exceed the content of statutory requirements in various Australian jurisdictions, many of which were enacted to overcome the perceived deficiencies of the rule in *Cavalier v Pope* [1906] AC 428 … In the present field, affecting the daily lives and transactions of a very large proportion of the population, the Court should be slow to hold that the content of a common law duty rises above that which has been imposed by statute in various Australian jurisdictions.

Premises will not be reasonably fit for the purposes for which they are let where the ordinary use of the premises for that purpose would, as a matter of reasonable foreseeability, cause injury. The duty requires a landlord not to let premises that suffer defects which the landlord knows or ought to know make the premises unsafe for the use to which they are to be put. The duty with respect to dangerous defects will be discharged if the landlord takes reasonable steps to ascertain the existence of any such defects and, once the landlord knows of any, if the landlord takes reasonable steps to remove them or to make the premises safe. This does not amount to a proposition that the ordinary use of the premises for the purpose for which they are let must not cause injury; it is that the landlord has acted in a manner reasonably to remove the risks.

What constitutes the taking of reasonable steps will, as Dawson J noted in *Northern Sandblasting*, depend on all the circumstances of the case. … [They went on to discuss breach of duty] … where the existence of a dangerous defect was merely a possibility (albeit one later realised when the plaintiff was injured), the steps a landlord was required to undertake were only those that would be taken in the course of "ordinary reasonable human conduct". The matter is not an exercise of hindsight. The identification of the requisite steps will depend, among other things, upon whether an ordinary

Jones v Bartlett cont.

person in the landlord's position would or should have known that there was any risk; whether that person would or should have known of steps that could be taken in response to that risk; and the reasonableness of taking such steps.

However, in another case, a defect may not be unknown or unsuspected; the landlord may have sufficient knowledge or suspicion to make it unreasonable to fail to act. Such action may be called for even if it requires the attendance of experts.

Legislatures may decide to impose higher standards upon landlords, including specific obligations respecting such matters as electrical wiring and gas connections, and to do so in respect of some classes of premises rather than others. But that is another matter ...

The content of the landlord's duty in a case such as the present is not one of strict liability, to ensure an absence of defects or that reasonable care is taken by another in respect of existing defects. It is not a duty to guarantee that the premises are safe as can reasonably be made.

It remains to consider whether a landlord owes to others upon residential premises a lesser duty than that owed to the tenants themselves.

Other occupiers and entrants

The general principle, consistently with *Australian Safeway Stores Pty Ltd v Zaluzna* (1987) 162 CLR 479, is that liability for injury suffered by an entrant upon residential premises primarily will rest with the occupier. A tenant in occupation, rather than the landlord, has possession and control with power to invite or to exclude, to welcome in or to expel. Those asserting a duty often will be the guests or invitees of the tenant or persons present on the tenant's business or for their business with the tenant. It will be the tenant who is best placed to inform such persons of any dangers or defects, and the tenant who "is more directly in touch with emerging repair needs than a landlord who has surrendered possession".

However, dangerous defects are unlikely to discriminate between tenants and those on the premises whether as an incident of a familial or other personal relationship... The landlord's duty to take reasonable care that the premises contained no dangerous defects, owed in the sense earlier described to the tenants, extends to those other entrants we have identified.

Nevertheless, the duty of the landlord owed to these third parties, in many cases, will be narrower than that owed to them by an occupier such as a tenant. An example of facts not involving the placing of a duty on the landlord is a slippery floor; an unsecured gate to a fenced swimming pool may be another. The duty of care of the landlord to the third party is only attracted by the presence of dangerous defects in the sense identified earlier in these reasons. These involve dangers arising not merely from occupation and possession of premises, but from the letting out of premises as safe for purposes for which they were not safe. What must be involved is a dangerous defect of which the landlord knew or ought to have known.

It is unnecessary here to pursue this aspect of the case further. This is because, as indicated above, in the present case treating the appellant as in as good a position as his parents, the tenants, there was no breach of duty by the respondents. The glass door was not a dangerous defect in the relevant sense ...

The appeal should be dismissed with costs.

KIRBY J: ... [A]fter *Northern Sandblasting*, I consider that: (1) a landlord owes a duty of care not solely under the contract of lease and not only to tenants but also to third parties (such as permitted occupants and visitors) injured as a result of a patent defect in the tenanted premises; (2) a landlord may discharge such duty of care by undertaking an inspection of the premises prior to each lease or renewal of a lease, by responding reasonably to defects drawn to notice, and by ensuring that any repairs are made which such inspection or notice discloses to be reasonably necessary; and (3) a

Jones v Bartlett cont.

landlord may ordinarily discharge its duty by delegating such inspection and repair to a competent person. However, these conclusions leave open other questions: (4) whether the common law in Australia has developed sufficiently to impose on a landlord an affirmative duty to conduct, or procure the conduct of, a detailed inspection of every possible source of danger in the premises; (5) whether such inspection must be by experts capable of detecting latent defects not reasonably apparent to an untrained eye; and, (6) if so, whether the failure to procure such experts will impose legal liability on the landlord where a tenant or associated third party is injured by reason of a defect of which the landlord personally remains reasonably unaware.

The landlord's liability: overseas developments

All of the common law countries inherited from English law principles which accorded to landlords a highly favoured position in respect of liability in negligence at common law for damage suffered by tenants. Judges of the twentieth century, stimulated by protective legislation, have been gradually eroding this position as anomalous and unreasonable ...

The arguments of the parties

The appellant's contentions: ...

The common law in Australia could certainly impose on landlords the kind of duty argued for by the appellant if this Court so decided. However, a decision to do so is by no means self-evident or incontrovertible. For a court to impose such obligations, involving duties of affirmative action, would be unusual. Necessarily, it would have a retrospective effect. In the great variety of tenancy arrangements that exist, it could work a serious injustice on particular landlords. Such landlords, until now, have been entitled to assume that their duty was limited to that of taking reasonable care to avoid foreseeable risk of injury from defects of which they were on notice or of which (by appropriate inspection) they would reasonably become aware because they were obvious to a reasonable landlord or its agent. When legislatures impose significantly extended liability, they normally do so with notice, after public consideration and following an opportunity for advice on the ramifications. Such notice permits those affected to make their own judgments and to procure appropriate insurance. None of these steps can be taken by a court. All of these points were made in *Northern Sandblasting*.

It follows that the appellant's claim in contract was properly dismissed at trial. His claims based on breach of statute and negligence at common law were rightly rejected by the Full Court. As that Court acknowledged, the respondents owed a duty of care to the appellant. But that duty was limited to one of taking reasonable care to avoid a foreseeable risk of injury to a person in the position of the appellant. It was not shown that the respondents breached the duty as so expressed. It is unnecessary to consider the other arguments (principally related to causation) which would only have arisen if a different conclusion had been reached on the foregoing issues.

The appeal should be dismissed with costs.

[Gleeson CJ, Gaudron, and Callinan JJ agreed that the appeal should be dismissed. McHugh J dissented.]

[9.55] **Notes&Questions**

1. What would be the effect on society of imposing a duty on the landlord to ensure that a rental property was fit for habitation?
2. Which parts of the subject-matter of this chapter are not covered in the new Civil Liability Act reforms? Why do you think this is so?

3. Why would the landlord's duty of care sometimes lead to a lesser standard of care than that owed by the tenant to a visitor to the premises? See Occupiers' Liability at [11.85] ff.

CHAPTER 10

Duty: Economic Loss

INTRODUCTION

[10.05] As we have seen in previous chapters, the type of harm suffered by the plaintiff is a significant issue in determining the tests for the duty of care. In this chapter we examine the effect on the duty of care of a determination that the damage is pure economic damage. Pure economic loss is to be distinguished from consequential (or "parasitic") economic loss. When a person is physically injured and the court has accepted that the injury arose from negligence, when they assess damages they will include the economic loss which is consequential on that physical harm, for example, the loss of income or the profit lost after the building in which a business was carried out was burnt down. However, if the economic loss occurs in the absence of physical or property damage (or before it), the harm is regarded as "pure economic loss".

The basic rule in common law is that one cannot recover damages for the negligent infliction of pure economic loss. Pure economic loss is seen as arising normally from interference with contractual rights and therefore being properly a matter for the law of contract rather than for torts. In *Cattle v Stockton Waterworks* (1875) LR 10 QB 453, a waterworks company negligently installed a new water main. Consequently, a contractor was not able to complete some work for which he had contracted with the owner of the land where the water main was installed. The plaintiff informed the defendant waterworks company of the problem, but they failed to do anything with the result that the contractor's contract with the landowner became much less profitable. The court held that there was no liability in the waterworks company. This case is regarded as setting down the basic rule that one cannot recover damages for the negligent infliction of pure economic loss.

In the New York Court of Appeals, Cardozo J famously stated that treating pure economic loss in the same way as physical injury might mean that "a thoughtless slip or blunder ... may expose [defendants] to a liability in an indeterminate amount for an indeterminate time to an indeterminate class" (*Ultramares Corporation v Touch, Niven & Co* 174 NE 441 (1931) (US) at 444). The rationale for this lay in the principles of competition in business. Taking market share from another business necessarily involves inflicting economic loss on that business, but that is how business works. Thus simple infliction of economic loss cannot give rise to liability unless other compelling reasons arise. Where a person intentionally makes a false statement of fact in order to induce another person to act, and they do so to their financial detriment, the inducer will be held liable for deceit (*Pasley v Freeman* (1789) 3 TR 51; 100 ER 450; *Derry v*

Peek (1889) 14 App Cas 337). However, negligently caused pure economic loss was regarded as something for which no liability could arise. This remained the case until 1964 when *Hedley Byrne & Co Ltd v Heller & Partners Ltd* [1964] AC 465 was decided by the House of Lords (extracted [7.45]). In that case the problem was that pure economic loss was caused by negligent words.

CHARACTERISING THE HARM

[10.10] We saw in Chapter 7 that the characterisation of the harm suffered by the plaintiff can make a difference to the test required to establish the duty of care. Characterising the harm as pure economic loss is not always as easy as it may seem. For example, when a person buys a house for $500,000 and two years later discovers that the house was defectively built has that person suffered property damage or pure economic loss? This issue arose in *Anns v Merton London Borough Council* [1978] AC 728 and in that case Lord Wilberforce held that the damage was pure economic loss. In *Sutherland Shire Council v Heyman* (1985) 157 CLR 424 ([7.100]) and in *Woolcock Street Investments Pty Ltd v CDG Pty Ltd* (2004) 216 CLR 515 ([9.35]), the High Court also held that such damage was pure economic loss. Other matters that have been characterised as pure economic loss include the loss of the opportunity to sell potatoes in an especially lucrative market (*Perre v Apand Pty Ltd* (1999) 198 CLR 180) and the need to make alternative arrangements to transport oil when a pipeline owned by someone else was damaged (*Caltex Oil (Australia) Pty Ltd v The Dredge "Willemstadt"* (1976) 136 CLR 529). These are all cases where it was held possible to recover in negligence for the loss, but before 1964 in *Hedley Byrne v Heller* such cases were regarded as properly the domain of contract. Suing someone for loss of profit caused by negligence seems wrong when it was quite proper for one business to compete strongly with another and for that competition to result in less profit for one or other business. Thus, at this time it was thought that a person should be able to sue only in contract for lost profits. *Hedley Byrne v Heller* created an exception to this general rule.

PURE ECONOMIC LOSS CAUSED BY NEGLIGENT WORDS

[10.15] In *Derry v Peek* (1889) 14 App Cas 337, the House of Lords decided that mere negligent misstatement was insufficient to support an action for deceit. This case involved statements made in a company prospectus by the defendant directors and addressed to prospective investors, of whom the plaintiff was one. To the courts of that era the case also appeared to decide that, in circumstances like those of *Derry v Peek* (1889) 14 App Cas 337 itself, there was no common law action for negligence. This much was said by the Court of Appeal in *Le Lievre v Gould* [1893] 1 QB 491 and a stream of other decisions. As long as the Court of Appeal's interpretation of *Derry v Peek* (1889) 14 App Cas 337 in this aspect was accepted, duties of care in this area could only be very limited, for it would be difficult to find a relationship between the parties more proximate than that between directors and those to whom the prospectus was addressed.

After 1964 there was a changed view of *Derry v Peek* (1889) 14 App Cas 337. This view, which remains today, is that *Derry v Peek* (1889) 14 App Cas 337 decided nothing with regard to negligence at all, but only in regard to deceit. This is the view taken by the House of Lords in *Hedley Byrne & Co Ltd v Heller & Partners Ltd* [1964] AC 465, Lord Devlin saying (at 518-519) that there was no plea of innocent or negligent misrepresentation in *Derry v Peek*

(1889) 14 App Cas 337 and although, if there had been, it is clear that the House would have rejected it, "what your Lordships may be taken to have thought, though it may exercise great influence upon those who thereafter have to form their own opinion on the subject, is not the law of England".

After *Hedley Byrne v Heller* was decided it was clear that there could be a duty to take care to prevent pure economic loss caused by negligent words. However, questions remained regarding what conditions had to be met to determine when liability would arise and when it would not. Possibilities included requiring that the relationship between the parties was close so that it was similar to contract, requiring that the defendant had assumed responsibility for the statement, or that the plaintiff had reasonably relied on the statement.

The following case considered what had to be proved to establish a duty of care where pure economic loss had allegedly been caused by the auditors of a company.

Esanda Finance v Peat Marwick Hungerfords

[10.20] *Esanda Finance Corporation Limited v Peat Marwick Hungerfords* (1997) 188 CLR 241 High Court of Australia

(footnotes omitted)

[Esanda entered into an arrangement with Excel whereby it lent money to companies associated with Excel. Esanda accepted a guarantee of payment from Excel and Excel indemnified Esanda for certain other debts. PMH were the auditors who had certified Excel's accounts before these transactions occurred and which Esanda alleged caused them to enter into the transactions. Esanda alleged that PMH were negligent. Esanda suffered economic loss after excel was placed into receivership.]

DAWSON J: 252 ... In its statement of claim Esanda alleged that PMH were guilty of negligence. PMH sought to strike out these paragraphs on the basis that Esanda's statement of claim did not disclose enough to establish a duty of care on the part of PMH. The primary judge allowed Esanda to amend its statement of claim to add allegations that the standards of the Institute of Chartered Accountants required them to consider those who are likely to be the prime users of financial statements and that Esanda was one of those, and was therefore a person whom PMH did or should have foreseen might reasonably rely on their statements. The Full Court allowed PMH's appeal and struck down the amendments. ...

Apart from the accounting standards, no facts are pleaded by Esanda as the basis for alleging a duty of care on the part of PMH towards it. Of course, without a duty of care, there can be no liability in negligence. The plea that Esanda was a member of a class of persons who might reasonably and relevantly rely on the Excel accounts and the auditors' report was no more than a plea that it was foreseeable that carelessness in making the report might cause harm to Esanda. However, mere foreseeability of harm does not, where the only harm is pure economic loss, give rise to a duty of care. The reason for this is that a duty of care imposed by reference to the mere foreseeability of harm in the form of financial loss would extend liability in negligence beyond acceptable bounds. Financial loss occurs as the result of legitimate commercial competition, and commercial activity would be stifled if the law were to impose a duty to take care to avoid that loss. Moreover, if the circumstances in which there was a duty of care to avoid causing purely financial loss were not confined, the extent of the liability imposed would in many cases be virtually without limits, both in terms of persons and amount. Thus, for a duty of care to arise in cases of pure economic loss, the law requires, in addition to the foreseeability of harm, a special relationship between the parties which is described as a relationship of proximity.

Esanda Finance v Peat Marwick Hungerfords cont.

[In cases of pure economic loss] ... [t]he relationship of proximity which is required before a duty of care can arise may be established in any number of ways, but authority serves to identify certain circumstances which, either alone or in combination, may be sufficient for that purpose.

Hedley Byrne & Co Ltd v Heller & Partners [1964] AC 465 established in England that there might be liability in tort for negligent misstatement in circumstances in which information or advice is sought from a person possessing some special skill or judgment where that person knows or ought to know that reliance is being placed upon the information or advice by the person seeking it. In this country liability for negligent misstatement was recognised in *Mutual Life & Citizens' Assurance Co Ltd v Evatt* (1970) 122 CLR 628 and, notwithstanding that the matter went to the Privy Council on appeal, the somewhat wider formulation by Barwick CJ of the circumstances in which liability would be imposed has been accepted in subsequent cases. It is useful, therefore, to begin with that formulation, which is that whenever a person gives information or advice to another upon a serious matter (not merely social intercourse) where that person realises, or ought to realise, that he is being trusted to give the best of his information or advice as a basis for action on the part of the other, and it is reasonable for that other to act on the information or advice, the person giving it is under a duty to exercise reasonable care in so doing. In putting it that way, Barwick CJ had in the forefront of his mind information or advice proffered in response to a request, although he recognised that there may be "relatively rare" occasions when information or advice which is volunteered might give rise to a cause of action.

This case is one in which no allegation is made that the statements made by the auditors, PMH, were made at the request of Esanda. And *San Sebastian Pty Ltd v The Minister* (1986) 162 CLR 340 was a case in which the misstatement relied upon was not made at the request of the plaintiffs. In that case the plaintiffs were developers who sued a municipal council and a planning authority for negligent misstatements contained in documents dealing with a planning scheme which were placed on public display. They failed in their action because they failed to establish the misstatements upon which they relied, but the Court considered what would have been necessary to establish a relationship of proximity between the council and authority on the one hand and the developers on the other.

The majority pointed out that there is no convincing reason for confining liability for negligent misstatement to cases where there is a request for information or advice. The existence of an antecedent request for information or advice may assist in demonstrating reasonable reliance on the part of the person making the request. However, a request is not a necessary prerequisite for reasonable reliance. The trust of which Barwick CJ spoke is nowadays more often referred to as reliance and reliance was said in *San Sebastian* to be "a cornerstone of liability for negligent misstatement". Of course, the person acting, or refraining from acting, on the information or advice must demonstrate reliance in order to prove that any loss which flows therefrom was caused by the negligent misstatement. But that reliance must also be reasonable in all the circumstances and this may be demonstrated in any number of ways. As the majority said in *San Sebastian*:

> The maker of a statement may come under a duty to take care through a combination of circumstances or in various ways, in the absence of a request by the recipient. The author, though volunteering information or advice, may be known to possess, or profess to possess, skill and competence in the area which is the subject of the communication. He may warrant the correctness of what he says or assume responsibility for its correctness. He may invite the recipient to act on the basis of the information or advice, or intend to induce the recipient to act in a particular way. He may actually have an interest in the recipient so acting.

The absence of any request, and the absence of an intention on the part of a firm of auditors to induce a financier to act upon the audited accounts of a company by making finance available to it, led

Esanda Finance v Peat Marwick Hungerfords cont.

Brooking J (with whom Gobbo and Tadgell JJ agreed) to hold in *R Lowe Lippman Figdor & Franck v AGC Ltd* [1992] 2 VR 671 that the auditors owed no duty of care to the financier. He concluded that *San Sebastian* required this conclusion, saying:

> In the whole of this discussion it is made clear that a duty of care cannot exist in such cases unless the statement was made by the defendant with the intention of inducing the plaintiff, or members of a class including him, to act or refrain from acting in a particular way in reliance on the statement.

But an intention to induce a person to whom information or advice is given to act in a particular way is merely one of the various means by which it may be shown that the reliance by that person upon the information or advice is reasonable so that, in combination with other relevant circumstances, it may serve to establish a relationship of proximity which will support a duty of care. It was in this sense, I think, that the majority in *San Sebastian* commented that in cases where the defendant intends the information or advice to operate as a direct inducement to action, the reasonableness of the reliance will not be a critical factor.

Brennan J pointed out in *San Sebastian* that it is always necessary in cases of negligent misstatement to establish that the statement in question operated as an inducement to the person to whom it was made to act upon it. As I have said, that is just another way of saying that it is necessary to prove reliance in order to show that any loss was caused by reason of the negligence of the maker of the statement and for that purpose it does not matter whether the inducement was intentional or not. And a person who gives information or advice to another intending to induce the other to a course of action does not necessarily undertake to be careful in the information he gives or the advice he offers. The occasion for the advice or information may be of a purely social nature inconsistent with the assumption of any responsibility. Circumstances of the kind identified by Barwick CJ in *Evatt* must otherwise exist, although an intention to induce a particular course of action may point to their existence. Thus in *San Sebastian* Brennan J rephrased the words of Barwick CJ for the purposes of that case as follows:

> Where a representor gives information or advice on a serious or business matter, intending thereby to induce the representee to act on it, the representor is under a duty of care in giving that advice or information if three conditions are satisfied. First (corresponding with the first condition expressed by Barwick CJ), if the representor realises or ought to realise that the representee will trust in his especial competence to give that information or advice; second (corresponding with the third condition), if it would be reasonable for the representee to accept and rely on that information or advice; and third (applying the underlying principle of the law of negligence), if it is reasonably foreseeable that the representee is likely to suffer loss should the information turn out to be incorrect or the advice turn out to be unsound.

The relevance of an intention on the part of a person giving information or advice to induce another to act in a particular way may be seen in the approach adopted by the House of Lords in *Caparo Plc v Dickman* [1990] 2 AC 605. There emphasis was placed upon the purpose for which the statement in question, which was an auditors' report, was made. It was held that the purpose of the report was, in accordance with the English statutory scheme, to provide information to the company and the shareholders so that they might exercise their rights in those respective capacities and not to provide information to those who might be minded to invest in the company. Informing potential investors in the company lay outside the purpose of the report and no duty of care was owed to them. There was the possibility that they might rely upon the report for the purpose of investing in the company but that was not the purpose for which the report was given and the possibility was insufficient to establish their reasonable reliance upon it. That is, of course, another way of saying that the report was not given with the intention of inducing potential investors to act upon it, which in turn pointed to lack of reasonableness in their placing reliance upon it for that purpose.

Esanda Finance v Peat Marwick Hungerfords cont.

The statutory scheme governing duties which are imposed upon auditors may well be relevant in concluding whether an auditor's report is made with the intention of inducing a particular person, or persons falling within a particular class, to act upon it in a particular way. Or, which is much the same thing, it may indicate the purpose for which the report is made. In the end, those things will have a bearing upon whether any reliance placed upon the report is reasonable. The statutory scheme in this country may or may not be different in relevant respects from that which was examined in *Caparo*. But in the absence of any reference to that regime in Esanda's pleadings, no useful purpose is to be served by making any comparison here. In particular, the pleadings place no reliance upon the statutory role of auditors, nor do they refer to the public availability of audited accounts. And it is accepted by both parties that the accounting standards referred to in the pleadings have not been approved for the purposes of the *Companies (South Australia) Code* or the Corporations Law.

In its statement of claim Esanda does not allege any circumstance which might serve to establish any relationship of proximity between it and PMH. Mere foreseeability of loss by reason of its reliance upon the audited accounts of Excel is not sufficient for that purpose and that, in effect, is all that Esanda pleaded.

For these reasons, I would dismiss the appeal.

[Brennan CJ, Toohey, Gaudron, McHugh and Gummow JJ agreed that the appeal should be dismissed]

[10.25] **Notes&Questions**

1. In *Mutual Life & Citizens' Assurance Co Ltd v Evatt* (1968) 122 CLR 556, Barwick CJ (at 572-573) formulated the duty of care in respect of negligent words in this way:

> [The duty will arise] whenever a person gives information or advice to another, whether that information is actively sought or merely accepted by that other upon a serious matter … and the relationship … arising out of the circumstances is such that on the one hand the speaker realizes or ought to realize that he is being trusted … to give the best of his information or advice as a basis for action on the part of the other party and it is reasonable in the circumstances for the other party to seek or accept and in either case to act upon that information and advice.

Although the decision was overturned in the Privy Council, Barwick CJ's formulation has been accepted and applied by many cases ever since, including *Shaddock & Associates Pty Ltd v Parramata City Council (No 1)* (1981) 150 CLR 225; *Esanda* (extracted above) and *Tepko Pty Ltd v Water Board* (2001) 178 ALR 634 at [43].

2. In *James McNaughton Paper Group Ltd v Hicks Anderson & Co* [1991] 2 QB 113, the English Court of Appeal declined to recognise a duty of the defendant company accountant to a takeover body in respect of a negligent misstatement in the company's accounts which had induced the completion of the takeover. O'Neill LJ (at 121) considered that there was generally no duty in this kind of situation and that if exceptionally a duty was to be held to exist five matters required attention: (1) the purpose for which the accounts were drawn; (2) why the result was communicated to the plaintiff "advisee" (3) the relation between the adviser and the advisee and any third party involved; (4) the size of the class of advisees and the state of knowledge of the adviser; and (5) the reliance by the

advisee. O'Neill LJ was here applying to the position of auditors the general statement of principle by Lord Oliver in *Caparo Industries Plc v Dickman* [1990] 2 AC 605 at 638:

> What can be deduced from the *Hedley Byrne case*, therefore, is that the necessary relationship between the maker of a statement or a giver of advice (the "adviser") and the recipient who acts in reliance upon it (the "advisee") may typically be held to exist where (1) the advice is required for a purpose, whether particularly specified or generally described, which is made known either actually or inferentially, to the adviser at the time the advice is given; (2) the adviser knows, either actually or inferentially, that his advice will be communicated to the advisee, either specifically or as a member of an ascertainable class, in order that it should be used by the advisee for that purpose; (3) it is known either actually or inferentially, that the advice so communicated is likely to be acted upon by the advisee for that purpose without independent inquiry and (4) it is so acted upon by the advisee to his detriment.

In *AGC (Advances) Ltd v R Lowe Lippman Figdor & Franck* (1991) Aust Torts Reports 81¶072, Vincent J held that the conditions were satisfied to enable the plaintiff provider of funds to succeed against the company auditors. However, on appeal, the Full Court of the Victorian Supreme Court held that that relationship, of itself, was insufficiently proximate to found a duty of care. What was needed was also an intention to induce the plaintiff to act in reliance on the report: *R Lowe Lippman Figdor & Franck v AGC (Advances) Ltd* [1992] 2 VR 671.

3. In Canada, the Supreme Court has also held that auditors should not be held liable in situations like that in *Esanda* where they could merely foresee that others could rely on the reports they made, see *Hercules Managements Ltd v Ernst & Young* [1997] SCR 165.

4. Suppose that a real estate agent made a statement to the prospective purchasers of a motel, that "the business is a goldmine and good all year round. It is a great opportunity at a bargain price". The purchasers went ahead with their purchase. Would the real estate agent owe a duty of care to the prospective purchasers of the motel if it turned out that the business in fact had no potential? See *Norris v Sibberas* [1990] VR 161.

5. In *Hedley Byrne v Heller*, extracted at [7.45], the defendant ultimately won because of a disclaimer or exclusion clause. Whether such clauses will protect a party from negligence claims is always a matter of construction. See *Darlington Futures Limited v Delco Australia Pty Ltd* (1986) 161 CLR 500 where the court held that exclusion clauses must be given their ordinary and natural meaning and may exclude negligence when read in their context.

6. A duty of care in relation to pure economic loss has been held to be owed by solicitors to the beneficiaries of wills in certain circumstances: see *Hawkins v Clayton Utz* (1988) 164 CLR 539; *Hill v van Erp* (1997) 188 CLR 159; 142 ALR 687; *Ross v Caunters* [1980] Ch 297; *Watts v Public Trustee* [1980] WAR 97. See Chapter 11 and Chapter 15 Concurrent Liability for a discussion of the ability to sue concurrently in tort and contract in these situations.

7. The duty of care in relation to pure economic loss caused by negligent advice is a significant issue for many professionals including accountants, auditors, bankers, brokers, financial adviser and lawyers. In most Australian jurisdictions,

Professional Standards Acts have been enacted to limit liability for the members of occupational associations in certain circumstances. New South Wales passed its legislation in 1994, Western Australia in 1997, Victoria in 2003 and Queensland, South Australia and Tasmania in 2004. These are also discussed in Chapter 12 Breach of Duty.

8. Economic loss has been affected by the civil liability regimes in that proportionate liability may apply there, whereas it does not apply to personal injury. Under proportionate liability where there are multiple defendants, each will be required to pay the proportion of damages for which they are causally responsible. This is to be distinguished from solidary liability which applies when each defendant is liable for all the damages owed to the plaintiff *as to the plaintiff*, and *as between each other* they can sue for the proportion each owes. The latter system is advantageous for the plaintiff because it ensure the plaintiff gets the damages owed. The former is more advantageous to the defendant but risks the plaintiff being denied their full damages, see Chapter 14.

STATUTORY LIABILITY FOR MISLEADING STATEMENTS

[10.30] The *Trade Practices Act 1974* (Cth), s 52 and its State equivalents prohibit "misleading or deceptive conduct" and provide for compensation on proof of the conduct and damage. The State equivalents are the *Fair Trading Act 1992* (ACT), s 12; *Fair Trading Act 1987* (NSW), s 42; *Consumer Protection and Fair Trading Act* (NT), s 42; *Fair Trading Act 1989* (Qld), s 52; *Fair Trading Act 1987* (SA), s 56; *Fair Trading Act 1990* (Tas), s 14; *Fair Trading Act 1985* (Vic), s 11; *Fair Trading Act 1987* (WA), s 10. All the provisions apply only to "trade or commerce" and the Commonwealth legislation is confined by the constitutional limits. The provisions can be used as an alternative to negligence, or indeed to other torts, notably passing off (s 52 and passing off can be pleaded together by traders: *Hornsby Building Information Centre Pty Ltd v Sydney Building Information Centre Ltd* (1978) 140 CLR 216. The tort of passing off is an action now usually considered as part of intellectual property law. It concerns the protection of the plaintiff's property in his or her business name and reputation and therefore the "goodwill" of the business).

Section 52(1) relevantly provides:

> A corporation shall not, in trade or commerce, engage in conduct that is misleading or deceptive or is likely to mislead or deceive.

One of the benefits of this legislation for the plaintiff is that it removes the necessity to establish a duty of care. The section applies to both conduct and words.

PURE ECONOMIC LOSS CAUSED BY AN ACT OR OMISSION

[10.35] The following cases discuss instances where the pure economic loss is caused not by negligent words but by a negligent act or omission. Although the courts were reluctant to allow a duty for pure economic loss caused by words, they were reluctant for even longer to allow recovery for this. This was probably because the area of acts/omissions made it much harder to consider limiting factors such as reliance. Clearly, in a capitalist environment where competition for profit is regarded as necessary, allowing simple recovery for lost profits is ridiculous. The courts thus chose to put extra limiting factors on the duty of care in such cases.

Caltex Oil v The Dredge "Willemstadt"

[10.40] *Caltex Oil (Australia) Pty Ltd v The Dredge "Willemstadt"* (1976) 136 CLR 529 High Court of Australia

(footnotes omitted)

[The dredge passed over a pipeline while dredging in Botany Bay. It knew the pipeline existed and intended to avoid it. The pipeline was damaged in the accident. The pipeline belonged to AOR and Caltex was using it to transfer oil. While the pipeline was damaged Caltex incurred expenses, because it had to make alternative arrangements for the transfer of the oil.]

GIBBS J: 555 In my opinion it is still right to say that as a general rule damages are not recoverable for economic loss which is not consequential upon injury to the plaintiff's person or property. The fact that the loss was foreseeable is not enough to make it recoverable. However, there are exceptional cases in which the defendant has knowledge or means of knowledge that the plaintiff individually, and not merely as a member of an unascertained class, will be likely to suffer economic loss as a consequence of his negligence, and owes the plaintiff a duty to take care not to cause him such damage by his negligent act. It is not necessary, and would not be wise, to attempt to formulate a principle that would cover all cases in which such a duty is owed... All the facts of the particular case will have to be considered. It will be material, but not in my opinion sufficient, that some property of the plaintiff was in physical proximity to the damaged property, or that the plaintiff, and the person whose property was injured, were engaged in a common adventure.

In the present case the persons interested in the dredge and the employees of Decca (in particular Mr Austin) knew that the pipeline led directly from the refinery to Caltex's terminal. They should have known that, whatever the contractual or other relationship between Caltex and AOR might have been, the pipeline was the physical means by which the products flowed from the refinery to the terminal. Moreover, the pipeline appeared to be designed to serve the terminal particularly (although no doubt it would have been possible for it to serve other persons as well) and was not like a water main or electric cable serving the public generally. In these circumstances the persons interested in the dredge, and Decca, should have had Caltex in contemplation as a person who would probably suffer economic loss if the pipes were broken. Further, the officers navigating the dredge had a particular obligation to take care to avoid damage to the pipeline, which was shown on the drawing supplied to them for the very purpose of enabling them to avoid it. Decca had a similar obligation to draw the lines on the track plotter chart, in such a way that the navigators would not sail the dredge over the pipeline. In all these circumstances the particular relationship between the dredge and Decca on the one hand, and Caltex on the other, was such that both the dredge and Decca owed a duty to Caltex to take reasonable care to avoid causing damage to the pipeline and thereby causing economic loss to Caltex. It should therefore in my opinion be concluded that Caltex is entitled to recover the economic loss resulting from the breach of that duty of care. The quantum of damages is, as I have said, admitted.

For these reasons I would allow Caltex's appeals.

STEPHEN J: 573 The need, in cases of purely economic loss, for some further control of liability apart from that offered by the concept of reasonable foreseeability arises in part because, in cases of physical injury to person or property, the concept has been given a very far-reaching operation, far more extensive than may be thought to have been conveyed by Lord Atkin's reference to that which one "can reasonably foresee would be likely to injure" a person in the relationship of neighbour: *Donoghue v Stevenson* [1932] AC 562 at 580. This is perhaps well enough so long as what is in question is only liability for injury to person or property, the duty of care being fixed by reference to the plaintiff whose person or property is injured, those indirectly affected by the repercussions of the negligent act having suffered no such injury. But if economic loss is to be compensated its inherent capacity to manifest itself at several removes from the direct detriment inflicted by the defendant's carelessness makes reasonable foreseeability an inadequate control mechanism.

The need is for some control mechanism based upon notions of proximity between tortious act and resultant detriment to take the place of the nexus provided by the suggested exclusory rule which I have rejected. ...

As the body of precedent accumulates some general area of demarcation between what is and is not a sufficient degree of proximity in any particular class of case of economic loss will no doubt emerge; but its emergence neither can be, nor should it be, other than as a reflection of the piecemeal conclusions arrived at in precedent cases. The present case contains a number of salient features which will no doubt ultimately be recognised as characteristic of one particular class of case among the generality of cases involving economic loss. This will be typical of the development of the common law ... The existence of these features leaves no doubt in my mind that there exists in this case sufficient proximity to entitle the plaintiff to recover its reasonably foreseeable economic loss.

These features comprise the following:

(1) the defendant's knowledge that the property damage, a set of pipelines, was of a kind inherently likely, when damaged, to be productive of consequential economic loss to those who rely directly upon its use. To damage an item of productive equipment or an item used in conveying goods or services, such as power or water, is inherently likely to cause to its users economic loss quite apart from the physical injury to the article itself. Moreover the nature of a pipeline, used in conveying refined products from a refinery to another's terminal, is such as to indicate very clearly the existence of something akin to Lord Roche's common adventure, the person to whom the petroleum products are being delivered through it having a very real interest in its continued operation as a means of conveyance, whether or not possessing a proprietary or possessory interest in the pipes themselves;

(2) the defendant's knowledge or means of knowledge, from certain charts then in use on the dredge, that the pipelines extended across Botany Bay from the AOR refinery to the plaintiff's Banksmeadow terminal leading to the quite obvious inference that their use was to convey refined products from refinery to terminal, the plaintiff being in this sense a user of the pipeline.

These two factors lead to the conclusion that Caltex was within the reasonable contemplation of the defendants as a person likely to suffer economic loss if the pipelines were cut. Now, because the facts referred to in (1) and (2) above were within the reasonable contemplation of the defendants, it should have been apparent to them that more than one party was likely to be exposed to loss should the pipelines be severed by the defendants' negligence; accordingly the tortious infliction of property damage on any one of these parties becomes relevant; hence the significance of the following factor:

(3) the infliction of damage by the defendant to the property of a third party, AOR, as a result of conduct in breach of a duty of care owed to that third party.

There are two other relevant factors:

(4) the nature of the detriment suffered by the plaintiff; that is to say its loss of use, in the above sense, of the pipeline;

(5) the nature of the damages claimed, which reflect that loss of use, representing not some loss of profits arising because collateral commercial arrangements are adversely affected but the quite direct consequence of the detriment suffered, namely the expense directly incurred in employing alternative modes of transport. ...

Only one aspect of the factors which I have set out calls for particular comment, that is the element of knowledge, actual or constructive, possessed by the defendant about the use of the pipeline to convey products to the plaintiff's terminal. In *Glanzer v Shepard* (1922) 23 ALR 1425 at 1428, a case of economic loss without physical damage, Cardozo J observed that "constantly the bounds of duty are enlarged by knowledge of a prospective use"; this same concept, the defendant's knowledge of a

Caltex Oil v The Dredge "Willemstadt" cont.

prospective use, was employed by Denning LJ in *Candler v Crane Christmas & Co* [1951] 2 KB 164 and also finds expression in *Hedley Byrne* [1964] AC 465, in *Mutual Life & Citizens' Assurance Co Ltd v Evatt* (1968) 122 CLR 556, in this court and before the Judicial Committee ((1970) 122 CLR 628; [1971] AC 793), and in *Dimond Manufacturing Co v Hamilton* [1968] NZLR 705. Not only does it form part of the concept of special relationship necessary to establish liability for negligent misstatement but it is also relevant in establishing the appropriate degree of proximity in cases of negligence by act, as is shown in the extensive reliance placed upon it in *Rivtow Marine* (1973) 40 DLR (3d) 530. In the present case it assumes significance because the defendants, when the dredging operations were in progress, must be taken to have known that carelessness in those operations, causing injury to the pipelines, would affect Caltex in precisely the way it did, by aborting the continued use of the pipelines for the delivery to it of petroleum products. ...

It is for these reasons that I would allow the appeals by Caltex....

...

[Jacobs, Murphy and Mason JJ agreed that a duty of care arose.]

Perre v Apand

[10.45] *Perre v Apand* (1999) 198 CLR 180 High Court of Australia

(footnotes omitted)

[The appellants, the Perre brothers, owned land in South Australia where they grew potatoes. They had a lucrative contract to export potatoes to Western Australia. Western Australia had a regulation prohibiting the importation of potatoes grown on land affected by the disease bacterial wilt, and also of potatoes grown on land within a certain distance of affected land. By supplying infected seed, the respondents, Apand Pty Ltd, negligently introduced bacterial wilt onto the Sparnon's land, which was within the relevant distance of the Perres' land. It thus became impossible for the Perres' land or equipment to be used for potatoes destined for the Western Australian market. They, therefore, sustained pure economic loss. The Perres' interests included: Warruga Farms, where they grew and processed potatoes, and which was 3 km from the Sparnon's site; Rangara, where potatoes were grown (2 km from Sparnon's); the Perres' vineyards which were let to Warruga for processing potatoes; and the Perres as natural persons. In the Full Federal Court, it was held that Apand owed a duty of care to the Sparnons, and this was not challenged in the High Court. The Full Federal Court, however, held that no duty of care was owed to the Perres by Apand. The Perres appealed to the High Court.]

McHUGH J: 204 In my opinion, the Federal Court erred in not finding that Apand had a duty to take reasonable care to protect the Perres from economic loss and in not finding that it breached that duty by supplying the seed, through a selling agent, to the Sparnons. The decision and the reasoning in *Caltex Oil (Australia) Pty Ltd v The Dredge "Willemstad"* (1976) 136 CLR 529 have been criticised, most notably by the Judicial Committee of the Privy Council in *Candlewood Navigation Corporation Ltd v Mitsui OSK Lines Ltd* (1985) 3 NSWLR 159. But in my opinion the decision in *Caltex* was correct. Although the facts of the present case are very different from those present in *Caltex*, the reasons (with some modification) that led this Court in that case to hold that the defendant owed a duty to the plaintiff to protect it from economic loss, apply here. The losses suffered by the Perres were a reasonably foreseeable consequence of Apand's conduct in supplying the diseased seed; the Perres were members of a class whose members, whether numerous or not, were ascertainable by Apand; the Perres' business was vulnerably exposed to Apand's conduct because the Perres were not in a position to protect themselves against the effects of Apand's negligence apart from insurance (which is not a

Perre v Apand cont.

relevant factor); imposing the duty on Apand does not expose it to indeterminate liability although its liability may be large; imposing the duty does not unreasonably interfere with Apand's commercial freedom because it was already under a duty to the Sparnons to take reasonable care; and Apand knew of the risk to potato growers and the consequences of that risk occurring. ...

Duty of care and proximity
208 *The demise of proximity as a unifying theme*

Where a defendant knows or ought reasonably to know that its conduct is likely to cause harm to the person or tangible property of the plaintiff unless it takes reasonable care to avoid that harm, the law will prima facie impose a duty on the defendant to take reasonable care to avoid the harm. Where the person or tangible property of the plaintiff is likely to be harmed by the conduct of the defendant, the common law has usually treated knowledge or reasonable foresight of harm as enough to impose a duty of care on the defendant. Where a person suffers pure economic loss, however, the law has not been so willing to impose a duty of care on the defendant. By pure economic loss, I mean loss which is not the result of injury to person or tangible property.

Until 1963, the so-called "exclusionary rule" prohibited the recovery of any damages for pure economic loss suffered as the result of the negligence of another. Yet even before then, courts recognised that the rigour of the rule, if it ever existed in a pristine form, often occasioned injustice to plaintiffs. To overcome those injustices, the courts allowed recovery in a number of exceptional situations. Denial of recovery for pure economic loss remains the rule, but, since *Hedley Byrne & Co Ltd v Heller & Partners Ltd* [1964] AC 465 was decided in 1963, many exceptions to the rule have been recognised. However, they have been developed in a haphazard and ad hoc fashion with no single principle underlying them ...

No doubt one important reason why courts have felt the necessity to distinguish between liability for harm resulting in pure economic loss and liability for harm to person or tangible property is that pure economic losses frequently result in mere transfers of wealth. The plaintiff's loss is the defendant's or a third party's gain. Harm to person or property, on the other hand, ordinarily involves a net loss to social wealth. Furthermore, the risk of sustaining economic loss is "a burden which is much more often and easily spread than the risk of physical damage." So even with the demise of the exclusionary rule, courts in most jurisdictions still require a plaintiff in a pure economic loss case to show some special reason why liability should be imposed on the defendant ...

For some years in this Court, the "something more" was "proximity" which Deane J suggested in *Jaensch v Coffey* (1984) 155 CLR 549 "involves the notion of nearness or closeness". However, this Court no longer sees proximity as the unifying criterion of duties of care. The reason that proximity can not be the touchstone of a duty of care is that it "is a category of indeterminate reference par excellence."

210 *The need for a new framework for determining the existence of a duty of care*

Although proximity may no longer be the talisman for determining a duty of care, neither this Court nor the English courts – which have also rejected proximity as the duty of care determinant – have entirely abandoned the use of proximity as a factor in determining duty....

[McHugh J also rejected Gaudron J's approach based on 'precise legal rights'.].

So if proximity is not the unifying test for negligence, if the two stage and three stage tests are defective, if the "precise legal right" formula is unacceptable and if the categories and incremental approach is not accepted favourably by the majority of judges, is there any solution to the problems posed by the development of a tort of negligent economic loss? Or must we now accept that *Hedley Byrne* was a glorious mistake and retreat to the exclusionary rule of the common law?

The exclusionary rule is often justified on the ground that it is certain – which it certainly is. But its certainty is obtained by rejecting claims that most people would agree ought to sound in damages. As

Perre v Apand cont.

will appear, it is not necessary, in my view, to use the exclusionary rule to obtain stability and predictability in the law of negligently inflicted pure economic loss. Furthermore, in *Caltex Oil (Australia) Pty Ltd v The Dredge "Willemstad"* (1976) 136 CLR 529, this Court rejected the exclusionary rule, and nearly 25 years later there should be no turning back. ...

The need for predictability

215 ...If negligence law is to serve its principal purpose as an instrument of corrective justice, the principles and rules which govern claims in negligence must be as clear and as easy of application as is possible. ... That does not mean, however, that the common law must adopt arbitrary "bright-line" rules for the sake of certainty at the expense of what most people including judges would regard as a desirable result ... While stare decisis is a sound policy because it promotes predictability of judicial decision and facilitates the giving of advice, it should not always trump the need for desirable change in the law. In developing the common law, judges must necessarily look to the present and to the future as well as to the past.

...Perhaps another unifying principle may emerge and gain widespread acceptance. Past experience suggests that, if it does, its fall from favour will not be long in coming. Until a unifying principle again emerges, however, the best solution is to proceed incrementally from the established cases and principles....

In my view, given the needs of practitioners and trial judges, the most helpful approach to the duty problem is first to ascertain whether the case comes within an established category. If the answer is in the negative, the next question is, was the harm which the plaintiff suffered a reasonably foreseeable result of the defendant's acts or omissions? A negative answer will result in a finding of no duty. But a positive answer invites further inquiry and an examination of analogous cases where the courts have held that a duty does or does not exist. The law should be developed incrementally by reference to the reasons why the material facts in analogous cases did or did not found a duty and by reference to the few principles of general application that can be found in the duty cases ...

The present case is not one falling within any categories of liability hitherto recognised ... The present case is therefore novel in terms of the categories. But that does not mean that no duty of care was owed to the Perres. "The categories of negligence", said Lord Macmillan, "are never closed." The issue of duty must be decided by reference to the few general principles that appear to govern all cases of pure economic loss.

The reasons for denying or imposing a duty of care in cases of pure economic loss

The reasons for denying or imposing a duty of care in cases of pure economic loss

218 ... In determining whether the defendant owed a duty of care to the plaintiff, the ultimate issue is always whether the defendant in pursuing a course of conduct that caused injury to the plaintiff, or failing to pursue a course of conduct which would have prevented injury to the plaintiff, should have had the interest or interests of the plaintiff in contemplation before he or she pursued or failed to pursue that course of conduct. That issue applies whether the damage suffered is injury to person or tangible property or pure economic loss. If the defendant should have had those interests in mind, the law will impose a duty of care. If not, the law will not impose a duty....

Until 1963, the almost universal rule was that, absent contract or fiduciary relationship, a person owed no duty to avoid causing economic loss to another person, and, although no longer a universal rule, no duty is the general rule. Judges and academic commentators have subjected this exclusionary rule to an intense scrutiny which has yielded a broad consensus on the rationale for the rule. They generally agree that the theoretical underpinnings of the exclusionary rule are the need to avoid imposing indeterminate liability and the need to avoid imposing unreasonable burdens on the freedom of individuals to protect or pursue their own legitimate social and business interests without the need to be concerned with other persons' interests …

Nevertheless, when a court is satisfied that the economic loss suffered by the plaintiff was reasonably foreseeable by the defendant, that no question of indeterminacy of liability arises and that the defendant was not legitimately protecting or pursuing his or her social or business interests, it will often accord with community standards and the goals of negligence law, as an instrument of corrective justice, to hold that the defendant should have had the plaintiff's interests in mind when engaging or refusing to engage in a particular course of conduct. However, the common law in its desire to give effect to the autonomy of each individual does not generally require a person to act as if he or she were "my brother's keeper". That is particularly so when the defendant would have to take affirmative action to save a person from suffering harm.

What is likely to be decisive, and always of relevance, in determining whether a duty of care is owed is the answer to the question, "How vulnerable was the plaintiff to incurring loss by reason of the defendant's conduct?" So also is the actual knowledge of the defendant concerning that risk and its magnitude. If no question of indeterminate liability is present and the defendant, having no legitimate interest to pursue, is aware that his or her conduct will cause economic loss to persons who are not easily able to protect themselves against that loss, it seems to accord with current community standards in most, if not all, cases to require the defendant to have the interests of those persons in mind before he or she embarks on that conduct.

The principles concerned with reasonable foreseeability of loss, indeterminacy of liability, autonomy of the individual, vulnerability to risk and the defendant's knowledge of the risk and its magnitude are, I think, relevant in determining whether a duty exists in all cases of liability for pure economic loss. In particular cases, other policies and principles may guide and even determine the outcome. But I do not think that a duty can be held to exist in any case of pure economic loss without considering the effect of the application of these general principles.

Indeterminacy

220 In *Bryan v Maloney* Mason CJ, Deane and Gaudron JJ pointed out that one reason why the law will often refuse to impose a duty to take reasonable care to protect another person from economic loss is its concern to avoid the imposition of liability "in an indeterminate amount for an indeterminate time to an indeterminate class." Concern about indeterminacy most frequently arises where the defendant could not determine how many claims might be brought against it or what the general nature of them might be. One feature that is more likely to be present in economic loss cases than physical damage cases is the "ripple effect" of careless conduct. Dr Jane Stapleton has pointed out that "economic loss can 'ripple' down a chain of parties; for example, the loss of profits which D causes P may in turn cause loss of profits to P's supplier and in turn to that supplier's suppliers, etc."

However, it is not the size or number of claims that is decisive in determining whether potential liability is so indeterminate that no duty of care is owed. Liability is indeterminate only when it cannot be realistically calculated. … The number of claims or their size, therefore, does not of itself raise any issue of indeterminacy. Indeterminacy depends upon what the defendant knew or ought to have known of the number of claimants and the nature of their likely claims, not the number or size of those claims …

The common thread that may be drawn from the judgments of Gibbs, Stephen and Mason JJ in *Caltex* is that more than reasonable foreseeability of harm to a person is required before the defendant comes under a duty of care. Knowledge of harm to the plaintiff is a minimum requirement. However, in my opinion, the indeterminacy issue does not require that the defendant's knowledge be limited to individual persons who are known to be in danger of suffering harm from the defendant's conduct. Its

Perre v Apand cont.

liability can be determinate even when the duty is owed to those members of a specific class whose identity could have been ascertained by the defendant.

The problem of the "ripple effect" means that the courts must be careful in using constructive knowledge to extend the class to whom a duty is owed. It would not be wise, or perhaps even possible, to set out exhaustively when it would be permissible to rely on constructive knowledge. Speaking generally, however, it may be necessary to draw a distinction between using constructive knowledge to identify those within a class who are primarily affected by the defendant's negligence (the first line victims) and using constructive knowledge to identify those who have suffered economic loss purely as the result of economic loss to the first line victims. That is, as a general rule, no duty will be owed to those who suffer loss as part of a ripple effect. Ordinarily, it will be an artificial exercise to conclude that, before acting or failing to act, the defendant should have contemplated the interests of those persons who suffer loss because of the ripple effect of economic loss on the first line victims. While the defendant might reasonably foresee that the first line victims might have contractual and similar relationships with others, it would usually be stretching the concept of determinacy to hold that the defendant could have realistically calculated its liability to second line victims.

... The only criticism that I have of the reasoning in *Caltex* is that it imposed too narrow a test for determining to whom a duty was owed.

Unreasonable burdens on the autonomy of individuals

223 One of the central tenets of the common law is that a person is legally responsible for his or her choices. It is a corollary of that responsibility that a person is entitled to make those choices for him or herself without unjustifiable interference from others. In other words, the common law regards individuals as autonomous beings entitled to make, but responsible for, their own choices. The legal doctrines of duress, undue influence and criminal liability are premised on that view of the common law. In any organised society, however, individuals cannot have complete autonomy, for the good government of a society is impossible unless the sovereign power in that society has power in various circumstances to coerce the citizen. Nevertheless, the common law has generally sought to interfere with the autonomy of individuals only to the extent necessary for the maintenance of society. In the law of liability for economic loss, we have a notable example of the common law's concern for the autonomy of individuals. ... As long as a person is legitimately protecting or pursuing his or her social or business interests, the common law will not require that person to be concerned with the effect of his or her conduct on the economic interests of other persons. And that is so even when that person knows that his or her actions will cause loss to a specific individual. Thus, a consumer owes no duty to a trader not to cause loss to that person by withdrawing custom. However, where other indicia of duty are present, the cloak of immunity cannot extend to conduct which cannot be fairly described as a legitimate pursuit or protection of a person's interests. What then is not a legitimate protection or pursuit of one's interests?

Competitive acts not prohibited by law are legitimate unless they fall within the ambit of one of the economic torts to which I referred in *Hill v Van Erp* (1997) 188 CLR 159; 142 ALR 687. Ordinary competitive conduct imposes no duty to protect others from economic loss. At the other end of the spectrum, conduct involving deceit, duress or intentional acts prohibited by law could seldom, if ever, be regarded as done in the legitimate protection or pursuit of one's interests. However, it does not follow that, other indicia of duty being present, a person will always lose the immunity given to protect the autonomy of the individual merely because his or her conduct has been done in breach of law. It would be curious if breach of s 52, or a provision of Pt IV, of the *Trade Practices Act 1974* (Cth) automatically meant that the defendant owed a common law duty of care to all those that he or she knew would be affected by the breach. Between the extremes are acts whose legitimacy will no doubt

Perre v Apand cont.

affect minds differently. They are likely to involve sharp or ruthless conduct. Perhaps no more can be said in the abstract than that the line of legitimacy will be passed only when the conduct is such that the community cannot tolerate it.

Because protection of the individual's autonomy is the reason for the immunity conferred by the legitimate protection or pursuit of interest doctrine, that doctrine can have little, if any, application in a case where the defendant already owes a duty of care to do or not to do something. Thus, in *Caltex*, Stephen J, correctly in my opinion, thought a significant factor in support of the conclusion that Caltex was owed a duty of care was "the infliction of damage by the defendant to the property of a third party ... as a result of conduct in breach of a duty of care owed to that third party."

Vulnerability

225 Cases where a plaintiff will fail to establish a duty of care in cases of pure economic loss are not limited to cases where imposing a duty of care would expose the defendant to indeterminate liability or interfere with its legitimate acts of trade. In many cases, there will be no sound reason for imposing a duty on the defendant to protect the plaintiff from economic loss where it was reasonably open to the plaintiff to take steps to protect itself. The vulnerability of the plaintiff to harm from the defendant's conduct is therefore ordinarily a prerequisite to imposing a duty. If the plaintiff has taken, or could have taken steps to protect itself from the defendant's conduct and was not induced by the defendant's conduct from taking such steps, there is no reason why the law should step in and impose a duty on the defendant to protect the plaintiff from the risk of pure economic loss.

In *Esanda Finance Corporation Ltd v Peat Marwick Hungerfords* (1997) 188 CLR 241, an important factor in denying a duty of care was that the plaintiffs were sophisticated investors well able in the circumstances to protect themselves. On the other hand, this Court found a duty in *Hill v Van Erp* (1997) 188 CLR 159; 142 ALR 687 and in *Pyrenees Shire Council v Day* (1998) 72 ALJR 152 partly because of the defendant's control (and knowledge) and relative inability of the plaintiffs to protect themselves.

The law of contract

226 In determining whether the plaintiff was vulnerable, an important consideration will be whether the plaintiff could easily have protected itself against the risk of loss by protective action, particularly by obtaining contractual warranties ... The economic efficiency of a society requires that the person best able to deal with or avoid the consequences of an economic risk from a cost view should be responsible for the risk and its consequences ... Where another body of law can effectively deal with economic loss, a court should be slow to use negligence law to impose a duty of care on a defendant. This is particularly important where to do so would interfere with a coherent body of law in another field.

In the twentieth century, many areas of economic activity are extensively regulated ... by legislation and regulations. The judgment of Brennan CJ in *Pyrenees* shows that the potential for interference with such a body of law is vitally important in determining whether a common law duty of care should be imposed on a defendant. In terms of pure economic loss generally, however, it is the relationship of negligence with contract that must ordinarily be considered ... Australian courts must be careful before holding that the existence of obligations under a contract automatically denies liability in tort for pure economic loss. That said, if we are to aspire to a coherent law of civil obligations, courts must keep the contractual background in mind in determining whether a duty of care should be imposed on the defendant in pure economic loss cases. Developments in negligence should occur in sympathy with the law of contract. In *Hill v Van Erp* (1997) 188 CLR 159; 142 ALR 687, Gummow J said:

> Bingham LJ has observed that, like equity, the law of torts may, in appropriate circumstances, fill what otherwise are perceived to be "gaps" in what should be one coherent system of law ...

Perre v Apand cont.

That, of course, is not to assert that the function of the law of tort, with respect to recovery of economic loss caused other than by reliance upon deceitful statements, is limited to the filling in of gaps left by the law of contract. But it is a starting point …

This Court has recognised that in certain circumstances concurrent duties in tort and contract can exist and that the law of contract and the law of negligence are informed by differing rationales. That difference supports the conclusion that the vulnerability of the plaintiff may often be a justifiable, but not sufficient, reason for imposing a duty of care in cases of negligence resulting in pure economic loss where the plaintiff could not have protected itself in contract. One of the assumptions of the law of contract, for example, is that the parties can bargain to protect their interests. A plaintiff who is vulnerable – for whatever reason – cannot do this in any meaningful way. In its quest for corrective justice, the law of negligence may be able to fill the gap which the law of contract has left.

Vulnerability will often include, but not be synonymous with, concepts of reliance and assumption of responsibility. The widely used concepts of "reasonable reliance" and "assumption of responsibility" have come under criticism. This Court has recognised that neither concept represents a necessary or a sufficient criterion for determination of a duty of care, saying that commonly, but not necessarily, a duty will arise in cases which "involve an identified element of known reliance (or dependence) or the assumption of responsibility or a combination of the two". This statement provides an insight into why both reliance and assumption of responsibility have been rejected as a unifying criterion in cases of pure economic loss. Like proximity, reliance and assumption of responsibility are neither necessary nor sufficient to found a duty of care.

In my view, reliance and assumption of responsibility are merely indicators of the plaintiff's vulnerability to harm from the defendant's conduct, and it is the concept of vulnerability rather than these evidentiary indicators which is the relevant criterion for determining whether a duty of care exists. The most explicit recognition of vulnerability as a possible common theme in cases of pure economic loss is found in the judgment of Toohey and Gaudron JJ in *Esanda Finance Corporation Ltd v Peat Marwick Hungerfords* (1997) 188 CLR 241.

… The case law indicates that vulnerability as a test of duty is not restricted to the category of negligent misstatements. Nor are reliance and assumption of responsibility its only indicators. Thus, in *Hill v Van Erp* (1997) 188 CLR 159; 142 ALR 68, a case of negligent performance of a service, which is closely analogous to negligent misstatement, neither reliance nor assumption of responsibility to the plaintiff was present. Justice Gaudron dismissed these criteria as indicators of duty and relied on the concept of control to found a duty. But that is simply another way of saying that the plaintiff is vulnerable to the defendant's conduct because the defendant controls the situation. In dissent in *Hill v Van Erp* (1997) 188 CLR 159; 142 ALR 68, I said that the plaintiff's inability to protect her own interest (ie vulnerability) was the single strongest factor pointing to the existence of a duty. Brennan CJ, Dawson J and Toohey J based their judgments, at least in part, on a variant of the assumption of responsibility criterion which is a powerful indicator of the plaintiff's vulnerability to harm from the defendant's acts or omissions. Moreover, Dawson J and Toohey J also relied on the doctrine of "general reliance", which even more than "specific reliance" may be reduced to vulnerability.

… The degree and the nature of vulnerability sufficient to found a duty of care will no doubt vary from category to category and from case to case. Although each category will have to formulate a particular standard, the ultimate question will be one of fact. The defendant's control of the plaintiff's right, interest or expectation will be an important test for vulnerability. That test was applied by Gummow J in *Pyrenees* where his Honour noted that like the situation in *Hill v Van Erp* (1997) 188 CLR 159; 142 ALR 68, there was no evidence of actual reliance.

Insurance

230 Whether the plaintiff has purchased, or is able to purchase, insurance is, however, generally *not* relevant to the issue of vulnerability. In *Esanda Finance Corporation Ltd v Peat Marwick Hungerfords*

Perre v Apand cont.

(1997) 188 CLR 241, I pointed out that courts often wrongly assume that insurance is readily obtainable and that the increased cost of an extension of liability can be spread among customers by adding the cost of premiums to the costs of services or goods. In *Caltex* Stephen J rejected the contention that the existence of insurance or the more general concept of "loss spreading" were valid considerations in determining whether a duty of care existed. I agree with his Honour. They do not assist but rather impede the relevant inquiry. Loss spreading is not synonymous with economic efficiency – which will sometimes be a relevant factor in determining duty. Australian courts, however, have not accepted that loss spreading is the guiding rationale for the law of negligence or that it should be.

Knowledge and reasonable foreseeability

The cases have recognised that knowledge, actual or constructive, of the defendant that its act will harm the plaintiff is virtually a prerequisite of a duty of care in cases of pure economic loss. Negligence at common law is still a fault based system. It would offend current community standards to impose liability on a defendant for acts or omissions which he or she could not apprehend would damage the interests of another….

Conversely, where the defendant is not legitimately protecting or pursuing its own interests, current community standards would also seem to require that the knowledge of a defendant that its actions are likely to harm the interests of an ascertainable class of persons is a factor weighing in favour of imposing a duty. Questions of knowledge, actual and constructive, are always relevant in determining whether the defendant has breached a duty of care. But as the negligent misstatement cases show, they can be relevant in determining whether the defendant owed a duty to prevent economic loss to the plaintiff. To intrude questions of constructive knowledge of the risk into the duty question in every case of pure economic loss would run the risk of reinstating reasonable foreseeability as the criterion of duty in many cases. But where the defendant has actual knowledge of the risk and its consequences for an ascertainable class and is not legitimately pursuing or protecting its interests, I see no reason why that actual knowledge should not be an important factor in deciding the duty issue. Furthermore, because fault remains the basis of negligence liability, I see no reason why recklessness or gross carelessness should not be a relevant factor in determining whether a duty of care was owed. In *Caltex*, Stephen J seems to have thought that "the grossness of the wrongdoer's want of care" was a relevant matter in determining whether a duty of care should be imposed.

Apand owed a duty of care

231 Upon the facts of this case, whether or not Apand owed a duty of care depends on the answers to the following questions:

1. Was the loss suffered by the Perres or members of the group reasonably foreseeable?
2. If yes to question 1, would the imposition of a duty of care impose indeterminate liability on Apand?
3. If no to question 2, would the imposition of a duty of care impose an unreasonable burden on the autonomy of Apand?
4. If no to question 3, were the Perres or some of them vulnerable to loss from the conduct of Apand?
5. Did Apand know that its conduct could cause harm to individuals such as the Perres?

I do not think that any other factors are relevant in determining whether Apand owed a duty of care to the Perres. For example, no question of economic efficiency arises.

Apand does not dispute that the loss suffered by the Perres was reasonably foreseeable, and I think the rest of these questions should be answered favourably to the Perres or, at all events, to some of them.

Perre v Apand cont.

Upon the facts of this case, therefore, Apand owed a duty of care to the Perres to protect them from the loss of sales to the Western Australian market and diminution in the value of their farming lands. That is to say, Apand owed the Perres a duty to protect them from pure economic loss. In this Court, counsel for the Perres argued that their potatoes had suffered physical damage in that they suffered partial economic immobility. This argument is totally devoid of merit. The physical attributes of the potatoes were not affected in any way whatever. The case is one of pure economic loss. ...

The class

223 The real issue on indeterminacy is whether the class was ascertainable or effectively indeterminate. It is clear from sub-reg (ii) that the ascertainable class includes growers exporting to Western Australia. The problem is sub-reg (iii) which states that no potatoes can be exported to Western Australia if they have been "harvested, cleaned, washed, graded or packed with equipment or in premises with or in which potatoes, grown within 20 kilometres of a known outbreak of the disease Bacterial Wilt detected within the last 5 years, have been handled". To allow liability for all parties falling within the scope of the second limb would be to allow liability to an indeterminate class. It would not have been easy for Apand to have ascertained the number of persons who might be affected by bacterial wilt on the Sparnons' land because they have businesses of harvesting, cleaning, washing, grading or packing within 20 kilometres of Sparnons. Moreover, the sub-regulation appears to include cleaners, washers, graders and packers of potatoes whose premises are outside the 20 kilometre area but who deal with potatoes grown within that area. It would be even more difficult for Apand to determine the nature of the claims that persons falling within sub-reg (iii) might make. That being so, a class of persons which included all those falling within sub-regs (ii) and (iii) should be regarded as giving rise to indeterminate liability. This is nevertheless not fatal to the Perre interests, or at least not to all of them.

For the purpose of this case, a more limited class is ascertainable and limited. That class should be defined as the owners of, and the growers of potatoes on, land within 20 kilometres of the Sparnons where potatoes grown on that land were exported to Western Australia. Whether or not Apand knew who were the members of the class is beside the point. They were easily identifiable, particularly by Apand. Indeed, it would be surprising if Apand did not know every member of the class. Moreover, the general nature of the likely claims of members of the class – loss of sales for at least 5 years and diminution in the value of land – was not so vague, particularly to a person in Apand's position, that Apand was at risk of an indeterminate liability in respect of an indeterminate amount.

However, I do not think that processors of potatoes (including any of the Perres) should be taken to be members of an ascertainable class. No doubt it was reasonably foreseeable that processors might be at risk because they were in a potato growing area and it was quite likely that some of them would process potatoes within the 20 kilometre sphere of risk. But some of them might easily be outside the area but process potatoes grown within the area. To include the processors within the class would be to engage in a very artificial process. It is logically impossible to include in the class those who processed potatoes produced within the 20 kilometre area or even those whose plant was within the area but to exclude from the class those who otherwise harvested, cleaned, washed, graded or packed potatoes with equipment or in premises within 20 kilometres of an infected property. That being so, the processors of potatoes were not members of an ascertainable class.

Applying the above definition of the class in this case, it is obvious that Warruga Farms is within it because it grew potatoes for export to Western Australia. However, I would exclude it in its capacity as a potato processor. That being so, its losses, in so far as they are attributable to its processing of potatoes, are not recoverable from Apand. Determining whether the other members of the Perre group are within the class is more difficult, but I am of the opinion that some of them are also within the class. Rangara Joint Venture sold its potatoes to Warruga. But it effectively grew potatoes for export to Western Australia. It should therefore be included in the class. Perre's Vineyards owned the

Perre v Apand cont.

processing facility but let it to Warruga. They are not within the class. As for the Perres themselves, in so far as they were growers or owners of land, they were within the class.

Unreasonable burdens on the autonomy of Apand

235 What Apand did in this case was obviously in trade or commerce. It conducted the experiment to further its commercial interests – the production of potatoes that would be more suitable for winter growing and for crisping. It carried out the experiment in the way it did for its own commercial reasons. The question then is whether pursuit of those commercial interests makes the case one where Apand was under no duty of care to the Perres because it was legitimately pursuing its own business interests. In my opinion, that principle does not protect Apand in this case.

As I have pointed out, the immunity principle is the consequence of the common law's concern to protect the autonomy of the defendant and its freedom of action. Where the defendant is already under a restraint by reason of a duty owed to another, the rationale of the immunity rule disappears *in respect of conduct within the ambit of that duty*. Here Apand was already under a duty to take steps to protect the Sparnons against the consequences of bacterial wilt. That being so, Apand's autonomy and freedom of action is not relevantly impaired if it were held to owe the same duty to the Perres. The case would be one of extending liability for the same activity, not one of creating a new liability of a different kind with respect to different conduct.

Rejecting the claim for immunity based on the autonomy principle and the claim that to impose a duty would make its liability indeterminate does not mean, however, that Apand owed a duty to the Perres. It would have owed a duty only if there was some reason or reasons that required it to *have had* the interest or interests of the Perres in contemplation before supplying seed to Virgara Brothers for the purpose of Sparnons using it. In this case, those reasons must depend on the extent to which the Perres could easily protect themselves against economic loss and the actual knowledge of Apand as to the risks involved in the experiment and the magnitude of that risk.

Vulnerability

236 At all times, Apand had control over the experiment and where it would occur. The relevant acts and omissions occurred outside the lands occupied by the Perres and without their knowledge. They were likely to suffer loss of great magnitude if the Sparnons' property was infected with bacterial wilt as a result of its negligence, as Apand well knew. It is indisputable that growers within the class, such as the Perres, were at great risk as the result of the supply of the seed. Ignorant of the danger developing at the Sparnons' property, the Perres were not in a position to do anything that could protect their economic interests. There were no contracts that they could enter into to protect themselves. No barriers or other protection could they erect to protect their land and crops. The future of their businesses depended on events some distance away of which they did not know and could not avoid even if they had known. The vulnerability of the Perres to a risk of such magnitude was very great.

But in addition Apand knew both the risks to the growers of potatoes and to the owners of land on which potatoes were grown and all the potential consequences for them in supplying uncertified seed to the Sparnons. It knew that "[t]he main way of spreading 'Bacterial Wilt' is by planting infected seed potatoes which, sometimes depending on the seasonal conditions or time of harvest, may not show obvious disease symptoms." It knew that "'Bacterial Wilt' is a potentially serious and pernicious disease which can cause heavy losses to growers" and that "[i]nfected paddocks take up to 4-5 years to clear". It knew that "[t]he economic impact on a grower who has the disease on his farm can be disastrous – he is unable to continue to grow potatoes in that part of the farm and unable to sell his infected farm" and that "[t]he major cause of spread is through growers buying non certified seed." It knew that the Saturna seed that the Sparnons were about to plant was uncertified.

In the light of its knowledge and the vulnerability of the Perres, the case for holding that Apand owed them a duty to take reasonable care to protect them from economic loss is overpowering. The

Perre v Apand cont.

law of negligence, as an instrument of corrective justice, would be in a sorry state if it did not require Apand to have regard to the interests of the Perres when it supplied the seed to Virgara Brothers for planting by the Sparnons ...

GUMMOW J: 240 ... As is indicated in more detail later in these reasons, the so-called "economic torts" provide the legal means for the resolution of a range of commercial disputes which are beyond the reach of contract law. ...

Moreover, the law of tort is concerned with more than the economically efficient allocation of risk and transfer of losses. In earlier times, strict liability in respect of invasion of the person or property of the plaintiff was the touchstone so that, as McHugh J put it, "the common law holds no prejudice against strict liability". However, the general trend in modern authority, expressed in *Northern Territory v Mengel* (1995) 129 ALR 1, is "to the effect that liability in tort depends on either the intentional or the negligent infliction of harm". In *Caltex Oil*, Stephen J identified, with reference to the speech of Lord Atkin in *Donoghue v Stevenson* [1932] AC 562, a broad principle underlying liability in negligence; the "general public sentiment" that, in the case at bar, there has been wrongdoing for which, in justice, the offender must pay. A similar point was made by McLachlin J in *Canadian National Railway Co v Norsk Pacific Steamship Co* (1992) 91 DLR (4th) 289 Her Ladyship said that the "contractual allocation of risk" argument overlooks:

> the historical centrality of personal fault to our concept of negligence or "delict" and the role this may have in curbing negligent conduct and thus limiting the harm done to innocent parties, not all of whom are large enterprises capable of maximizing their economic situation.

McLachlin J also pointed out in the same passage that, in assigning liability to the "least-cost risk avoider", the argument assumes that (a) all persons or business entities organise their affairs in accordance with the laws of economic efficiency, and (b) all parties to a transaction share an equality of bargaining power which will result in effective allocation of risk. Moreover, it cannot be assumed that either all persons or business entities have sufficient information to assess risk or that the transaction costs in obtaining such risk information are equally burdensome.

The decision of this Court in *Caltex Oil* is authority at least for the proposition that, in a case such as the present, one does not begin with an absolute rule that damages in negligence are irrecoverable in respect of economic loss which is not consequential upon injury to person or property. The same may be said of more recent decisions of this Court and the House of Lords, as well as of the Supreme Court of Canada and the New Zealand Court of Appeal. ...

Certainly, even at the time *Cattle* was decided, there was no general prohibition upon the recovery of economic loss in tort. First, patents, copyrights and other forms of intellectual property which confer a permitted form of monopoly and are no more than incorporeal in nature, had long been protected by injunction and by actions for damages tried at law and treated as tortious. Secondly, even with respect to other property, such as interests in land, actionable damage might be purely economic in nature; the old action of slander of title in which the plaintiff complained that the defendant had scared off prospective purchasers of the plaintiff's property illustrates the point ... [He referred to the torts of passing off and interference with contract].

Thus, what often are identified as the "economic torts" provide many examples to support the proposition that *Cattle* cannot be taken as establishing any rule against recovery in tort of economic or financial loss unless it be consequential upon damage to the person or property of the plaintiff...

Here, of course, the law is still taking shape. This makes the scrutiny of its antecedents all the more important, particularly when modern decisions such as *Candlewood Navigation Corporation* proceed upon assumptions as to what was settled a century ago.

Perre v Apand cont.

It may be that most of the cases to which I have referred in examining the state of affairs at the time of *Cattle* can, at least in part, be explained as turning upon the necessity for malice or some other significant mental element, such as persistence after knowledge or notice of a plaintiff's rights. ...

The determination of what, as an aspect of the economic organisation of society, is regarded as acceptable commercial dealing, is for the common law and statute. The debate in this area, in particular concerning the role of negligence, may turn upon an often unarticulated major premise that the common law values competitive conduct ...

The interests for which protection is sought

In *Caltex Oil*, Stephen J referred to the importance placed by the exclusionary rule as to economic loss upon the existence in the plaintiff of a proprietary or possessory interest in property. His Honour continued:

> In the light of the origin, in the action on the case, of the tort of negligence, an origin in the context of which notions of the infringement of proprietary or possessory interests in property were by no means always essential to the cause of action, damage suffered being the gist of liability, it is curious that in this field of the tort of negligence an interest in property should be thought always to be a condition precedent to the right to recover for economic loss.

It may be implicit in decisions such as *Candlewood Navigation Corporation* that whilst, as a general proposition, the integrity of person and property are *sufficient* interests for protection by tort law, they are *necessary* interests where "pure" economic loss is claimed and the defendant has not been fraudulent and otherwise lacks sufficient animus towards the plaintiff. ...

Further, there is much to be said for the point made by McPherson JA in *Christopher v The Motor Vessel "Fiji Gas"* (1993) Aust Torts Rep 81-202 as to the tendency of the common law, in attempting to define the limits of liability in negligence for economic loss, to concentrate first upon the actions of the defendant. Rather, there first should be identified those interests which are sufficient to attract the protection of the law in this field. Again, in *Hawkins v Clayton*, Gaudron J observed that:

> where the act or omission complained of amounts to an interference with or impairment of an existing right which is known or ought to be known to the person whose acts or omissions are called into question then the issue of proximity may be open to determination by reference to factors somewhat different from those applicable where economic loss is occasioned without infringement or impairment of an otherwise recognized right.

Her Honour added:

> In actions in negligence for economic loss it will almost always be necessary to identify the interest said to have been infringed to determine whether the risk of loss or injury to that interest was reasonably foreseeable and whether a sufficient relationship of proximity referable to that interest was present so as to establish a duty of care.

One therefore begins the determination of the issues arising on this appeal by looking to identify the interests for which the Perres seek protection. These are not divergent but to a degree they are diverse ...

No general formula

252 ... [T]he present may be a case of a "gap" in the common law and raise the issue of whether, consistently with principle, the tort of negligence may fill it.

Moreover, this case does not fall in a field where to allow recovery in negligence for economic loss would cut across a well developed body of doctrine which already applied, with its own checks and balances, to the situation in question. The wisdom of encouraging the further march of negligence across such fields remains a matter of debate ... The question in the present case is whether the salient

Perre v Apand cont.

features of the matter gave rise to a duty of care owed by Apand. In determining whether the relationship is so close that the duty of care arises, attention is to be paid to the particular connections between the parties. Hence what McHugh J has called the "inherent indeterminacy" of the law of negligence in relation to the recovery of damages for purely economic loss. There is no simple formula which can mask the necessity for examination of the particular facts.... The case law will advance from one precedent to the next. Yet the making of a new precedent will not be determined merely by seeking the comfort of an earlier decision of which the case at bar may be seen as an incremental development, with an analogy to an established category. Such a proposition, in terms used by McCarthy J in the Irish Supreme Court, "suffers from a temporal defect – that rights should be determined by the accident of birth".

The emergence of a coherent body of precedents will be impeded, not assisted, by the imposition of a fixed system of categories in which damages in negligence for economic loss may be recovered. In Canada, it appears that what is identified as "contractual relational economic loss" is recoverable only in special circumstances and these can be defined by reference to three categories. The first is whether the claimant has a possessory or proprietary interest in the damaged property; the second is the general average cases in shipping law; and the third comprises cases where the relationship between the claimant and the property owner constitutes a joint venture. However, it has been necessary to add that the categories are not closed ...

I prefer the approach taken by Stephen J in *Caltex Oil*. His Honour isolated a number of "salient features" which combined to constitute a sufficiently close relationship to give rise to a duty of care owed to Caltex for breach of which it might recover its purely economic loss. In *Hill v Van Erp* (1997) 188 CLR 159; 142 ALR 687 and *Pyrenees Shire Council v Day*, I favoured a similar approach, with allowance for the operation of appropriate "control mechanisms". In those two cases, the result was to sustain the existence of a duty of care. ...

The salient features of the present case

255 [Here Gummow J set out the facts in detail.]

The result is that, at the time of the supply of the seed to the Sparnons, Apand knew or ought to have known that Warruga grew commercial potato crops within the 20 kilometre buffer zone, and knew of the special requirements of the Western Australian law with respect to importation of potatoes grown in adjoining areas to those where there was an outbreak of the disease. Apand was aware not only of the threat that bacterial wilt represented to growers, but of the presence of the disease in the Koo Wee Rup area where Mr Tymensen's property was located. ...

The evidence was that, leaving aside the Saturna seed, the only potato seed which Apand sent into South Australia had been certified under the Certification Scheme. Apand appreciated that the major cause of the spread of bacterial wilt was through growers buying non-certified seed. As a practical matter, Apand was in control of the initiation and conduct of the experimental activities using the Sparnons' property. Apand both selected and supplied the seed and chose the location for the experiment.

The Perres had no way of appreciating the existence of the risk to which they were exposed by the conduct of the Apand experiment and no avenue to protect themselves against that risk. They thus stood in quite a different position from that of the financier in *Esanda Finance Corporation Ltd v Peat Marwick Hungerfords* (1997) 188 CLR 241 which had the power to deal from a position of strength in ordering its commercial relationship with the party to whom it provided financial accommodation. Here, the relevant risk to the commercial interests of the appellants was in the exclusive control of Apand. Its measure of control was at least as great as that of the Shire in *Pyrenees Shire Council v Day*.

The effect of the Western Australian legislation upon the export market from South Australia was such that, within the buffer zone, the economic loss would flow directly and inevitably and the possibility of its occurrence would not be speculative.

The characteristics of the present case to which I have referred combined, subject to what follows, to bring the Perres and Apand into such close and direct relations as to give rise to a duty of care owed by Apand for breach of which purely economic loss may be recovered. The commercial enterprise and undertaking of the Perres was conducted through the medium of a complex of business structures, some of which dealt only or substantially *inter se*. Earlier in these reasons I have referred to the various components of the Perres' commercial enterprise and undertaking. Individual members of the Perre family, in different combinations, owned the Warruga land and the Rangara land, and these individuals are among the appellants. Warruga processed potatoes grown on the Warruga land and potatoes grown on the Rangara land which it had purchased from the joint venture and, in 1992, exported about 80 per cent of the processed potatoes to Western Australia. As I have indicated earlier in these reasons, the duty of care which I have identified was owed to Warruga.

The next question is whether the same is true of Vineyards. It owned the processing facility. The commercial utility of the facility was largely stultified by the operation of the Western Australian legislation. That result obtained because of the part the facility played in the overall Perre business. This was largely directed to the projection of its produce into the export trade, but not exclusively so. The facility remained available for use in domestic production, although that was less profitable to Warruga. The same is true of the Warruga land and the Rangara land. There is a question whether the duty extended to the individuals who owned these lands and to the members of the joint venture which grew potatoes for sale to Warruga. Apand was aware, as the letter received 12 April 1990 had made clear to it, of the threat to crops posed by the use of infected seed by "growers" but, in respect of the 20 kilometre buffer zone, the threat was perceived as one to interstate and export sales.

Vineyards and each of the individual appellants had interests in or related to land, the value of which was to some measure attached to the availability of the crops grown or processed by those appellants for projection into the course of the export trade to Western Australia. The joint venture would seem to have been at risk of a decline in the value of potatoes grown for supply to Warruga.

I would treat Apand's duty of care as extending to all these components of the Perre business and, on that footing, allow the appeal as to all of them. However, there remains the need on their part to show damage before they are able to demonstrate the existence of accrued causes of action. In that respect, the pleadings in their present state leave something to be desired …

[McHugh and Hayne JJ held that Warruga Farms could be distinguished from the other interests and that the duty only arose in relation to Warruga Farms. The other judges (Gleeson CJ, Gaudron J, Gummow, Callinan and Kirby JJ) regarded all the Perre interests as inextricably interconnected and held the duty of care owed in relation to all the interests.]

[10.50] **Notes&Questions**

1. In *Hill v van Erp* (1997) 188 CLR 159, the defendant was a solicitor who prepared a will for her client. The will left property to the plaintiff. The solicitor asked the plaintiff's husband to sign the will as a witness. He did this, and the testatrix (will maker) later died. The husband's signing of the will activated the witness-beneficiary rule, which prevents witnesses or their spouses from taking gifts under a will, so the plaintiff lost her inheritance. The High Court dismissed the solicitor's appeal. Brennan J noted that the very purpose of engaging a solicitor is to ensure that the

beneficiary takes the gift. The benefit would have gone to the plaintiff but for the solicitor's negligence. Dawson J agreed with that view and added that the beneficiary was clearly identified, as the plaintiff was in *Caltex Oil*. What was important was the position of the solicitor as a professional person of specialised skill and knowledge and the reliance of the testatrix on that skill and knowledge. Toohey J agreed generally with Dawson J Gaudron and Gummow JJ would also have dismissed the appeal. McHugh J dissented.

2. A large gas explosion in Victoria caused property damage and economic loss to business users of gas, domestic users and workers who lost their employment as a result of the explosion. The Supreme Court of Victoria held that a duty of care was owed to business users who had suffered damage to property which led to economic loss, but not for pure economic loss. It was held that no duty of care was owed to the domestic users or the workers for their pure economic loss (see *Johnson Tiles Pty Ltd v Esso Australia Pty Ltd* [2003] VSC 27).

3. Pure economic loss has mostly been excluded from the operation of the new Civil Liability Acts. Can you think of any reasons why this is so?

4. The Professional Standards Acts discussed in [10.25] Note 7 are also relevant to pure economic loss caused by an act. Consider engineers, architects and builders and whether they are likely to avail themselves of these ways of limiting their civil liability. See Chapter 11 Special Defendants.

5. To what extent is the distinction between contracts and torts the important barrier preventing the expansion of liability for negligence for pure economic loss? Do you think the law of negligence has gone beyond that? Is the idea of commercial competition now more significant in this area than the idea that torts and contract should cover separate subject matter?

CHAPTER 11

Duty: Special Defendants

INTRODUCTION

[11.05] As we have seen throughout Part 3 of this book, the current approach to the duty of care involves consideration of all the salient factors which contribute to the question of whether a duty should be owed. One very significant factor is the identity of the defendant. The paradigm negligence case is one between two individuals where there is no pre-existing relationship and where an act causes some physical injury (personal injury or property damage). In that sort of situation reasonable foreseeability on its own may be sufficient to determine whether there is a duty of care. When we move away from that situation, other requirements will arise. These requirements can differ according to the type of defendant. For example, when the defendant is a public authority certain requirements for establishing a duty of care arise; when the defendant is a manufacturer or designer of goods other requirements may arise, as we saw in Chapter 9. Other special defendants include occupiers, landlords, barristers, people performing military operations, employers and so on. We have already discussed some of these in previous chapters. Here we focus on some of the most significant special defendants.

PUBLIC AUTHORITIES

[11.10] Public authorities (sometimes known as statutory authorities) are bodies set up by statute for a public purpose. As Mason J said in *Sutherland Shire Council v Heyman* (1985) 157 CLR 424 (extracted at [7.100]) at 456-7, public authorities are bodies "entrusted by statute with functions to be performed in the public interest or for public purposes".. That is, public authorities have to exercise their powers in the public interest, not just as they choose, and they may be liable as a matter of public law if they exercise their powers outside that public interest. Because they are public bodies, the first and most obvious remedy when a public authority seems to be doing something wrong is recourse to administrative law. However, it is also possible to sue public authorities in negligence for compensation in certain circumstances.

One critical issue in considering the liability of public authorities is the fact that the public authority frequently only exists by virtue of the legislation which both creates it and gives it powers and duties. If a public authority is given a duty then it will be reasonably clear if it has exercised it negligently, although there remains the question of whether the public nature of the authority means that it should not be sued in private law. Generally the basic rule in such cases is the rule of law idea that all should be subject to the law, and this includes public authorities. However, if the public authority has been given a power (or discretion) then the question of whether it *should* exercise that power has to be answered – that is, should the public authority have done something? (That is, is there a duty of affirmative action?) The common law and now the Civil Liability Act regimes have taken a number of approaches to these questions in determining whether a duty of care is owed by public authorities.

Until *Anns v Merton London Borough Council* [1978] AC 728 (extracted at [7.75] was decided in the UK, public authorities were generally regarded as immune from suit in negligence where their failure to exercise a power was concerned. A few years later, the High Court of Australia considered what is now the leading Australian case on liability of public authorities in negligence, *Sutherland Shire Council v Heyman* (1985) 157 CLR 424 (extracted at [7.100]). This case concerned pure economic loss (in the form of reduced value of a house) caused by a council's failure to inspect the foundations of a property. There the court considered the policy/operation distinction and the concepts of special and general reliance.

The policy/operation distinction was a way of separating matters where the court felt it could impose a duty of care from those it could not. If a decision, including a decision not to exercise a power were a matter of policy then the court would not interfere and there would be no duty owed. If the matter was operational – merely the carrying out of some policy, then the court might find it possible to impose a duty of care. This distinction also reflected a particular concern about public authorities, namely the limited resources they may have from the public purse, and often policy matters are taken to include budgetary allocation decisions.

Later Australian cases have followed *Sutherland Shire Council v Heyman* (1985) 157 CLR 424 (paying particular attention to the judgment of Mason J), and refined and expanded it. In the course of that case Mason J discussed the doctrine of general reliance as a possible indicator that a duty of care should be imposed (*Sutherland Shire Council v Heyman* (1985) 157 CLR 424 at 462 ff). General reliance was based on community expectations that a statutory authority would be protecting the public in some way. Mason J gave examples of aircraft traffic control and fire fighting as illustrations. He discussed the notion that general reliance would arise where the government has supplanted private responsibility. General reliance is reliance by the community at large, and was to be distinguished from specific reliance which would arise only when there was actual reliance by the plaintiff or, as it was put in *Blessing v United States* 447 F Supp 1169 (1978) (US), where the plaintiff chooses to look to the authority for safety. (For example, in *Parramatta City Council v Lutz* (1988) 12 NSWLR 293 the plaintiff had notified the Council that she was concerned about the fire risk to her premises from those next door to her, and by doing that showed them that she was relying on their power to protect her in a situation where she could not, since she had no power over the next door premises.)

In *Pyrenees Shire Council v Day* (1998) 192 CLR 330 special and general reliance were considered again. Tenants (Eskimo Amber) occupied premises A, which were destroyed by fire, along with the adjoining premises B. The fire was caused by a defect in the chimney of Premises A. A few years earlier the fire authority had advised the Council that the fireplace was unsafe to use, and a Council inspector told the then tenants of the danger. The tenants did not tell the owner of the premises nor did they do anything to repair the chimney. The council had power to notify the new tenants or the owners but did nothing further. The Days were tenants of premises B, a shop, and they and Eskimo Amber sued the Council. At trial Eskimo Amber failed but the Days succeeded. The Court of Appeal agreed with this decision. In the High Court the Council's appeal against the decision in favour of the Days was dismissed, but the appeal of Eskimo Amber was allowed by a majority who held that a duty of care was owed both to the owners of premises A and to the owners of the adjoining premises B. The minority, who used general reliance, held that there was a duty of care owed to the owners of premises B, but not to the original owners of premises A – because the latter were not in the same position of vulnerability. The majority emphasised the fictional nature and the breadth of operation of the doctrine of reliance. Gummow J rejected general reliance as having too much affinity with public law theories of procedural fairness, and emphasised the need for the duty of care to arise independently as a matter of private law through the consideration of reasonable foreseeability and the salient factors relevant to the situation. These could include vulnerability, control and knowledge. Brennan CJ preferred to use statutory intention rather than the doctrine of general reliance to found a duty of care.

With this background, in the following case the High Court considered whether a public authority could be liable for failing to protect a worker employed by organisations subsidiary to it. The facts were quite singular.

Crimmins v Stevedoring Industry Finance Committee

[11.15] *Crimmins (as executrix of estate of Crimmins dec'd) v Stevedoring Industry Finance Committee* (1999) 200 CLR 1 High Court of Australia

(footnotes omitted)

[Crimmins was employed as a waterside worker at Port Melbourne between 1961 and 1965. Stevedoring operations were then regulated by the Australian Stevedoring Industry Authority (the Authority) which was established by the *Stevedoring Industry Act 1956* (Cth). The *Stevedoring Industry Act 1956* set out the powers and responsibilities of the Authority in relation to the regulation of stevedoring operations. The Authority was later abolished and replaced by the respondent pursuant to the provisions of the *Stevedoring Industry Acts (Termination) Act 1977* (Cth) (the *Termination Act*) and the *Stevedoring Industry Finance Committee Act 1977* (Cth). Section 14(b) of the Termination Act provided that the respondent was to assume "all the liabilities and obligations of the Authority that existed" as at 26 February 1978. During his employment Crimmins, from time to time, unloaded asbestos cargoes and in 1997 he was diagnosed with mesothelioma, a desease caused by exposure to asbestos. He argued that the SIFC as the successor to the Authority owed him a duty of care which had been breached and caused his mesothelioma. In the High Court the questions were whether a duty of care was owed to Crimmins and whether the SIFC owed the duty as successor to the Authority. The High Court held that SIFC was the successor to the Authority.]

McHUGH J: 50 The appeal is brought against an order of the Court of Appeal of the Supreme Court of Victoria which set aside a verdict for the plaintiff in an action for damages for negligence. The court held that the statutory authority did not owe a duty of care to the plaintiff and that, if it did and had breached that duty, its liability to the plaintiff was not transmitted to the respondent. In my opinion, the Court of Appeal erred in ruling against the waterside worker on both questions ...

51 The statutory authority owed a duty of care to the worker because it directed him to places of work where there were risks of injury of which the authority was, or ought to have been, aware and in respect of which, the authority knew or ought to have known that the worker was specially vulnerable. The worker's vulnerability arose as a result of the casual nature of his employment and his obligation to obey the authority's directions as to where he worked. Nothing in the legislation governing the authority's powers and functions negatived the existence of a common law duty of care. Furthermore, the respondent was liable for any liability which the predecessor would have had to the plaintiff because the relevant statutory provision should be construed in accordance with the principle that, where legislation is open to a construction that will save existing or potential common law rights, it should not be construed as abolishing or reducing those rights. ...

56 During this period, about 5000 waterside workers were registered with the Authority. Registration was governed by the Act and depended, inter alia, upon a medical examination and the satisfaction of the Authority's "reasonable requirements ... as to ... age, physical fitness, competence and suitability". However, the workers were employed not by the Authority, but by the stevedores (and occasionally the owner or master of a ship), employment being on a job by job basis. But the Authority's role was more than supervisory. The Authority allocated the waterside workers for work in accordance with the needs of the various employers – the workers having no say in the allocation. The Authority was responsible for the payment of attendance moneys, sick pay, long service leave and for public holidays. It funded these payments by a statutory levy on the employers. The Authority also had certain powers of discipline over the workers including the power in certain circumstances to cancel or suspend the worker's registration (though an appeal lay to the Commonwealth Conciliation and Arbitration Commission). Once a worker had been assigned to a wharf, however, he was subject to the direction of the employer, who would supply any safety equipment required by the relevant award. The Authority was generally ignorant of the structure or size of the ships to which the workers were allocated, and the nature of the cargoes to be handled there ...

Working conditions and safety on the waterfront

...

60 Although the Authority had an overarching supervisory and regulatory role with respect to safety on the waterfront, it is clear that the primary responsibility fell upon the employers. The award placed a number of very specific safety responsibilities upon the employers (and not the Authority) including an obligation to provide safety equipment where it was needed.

The duty of care alleged by the plaintiff

61 Upon these facts, the question arises whether the Authority, as well as the individual employers, owed a common law duty of care to the plaintiff. In my opinion, it did. The correct approach in determining whether a statutory authority owes a duty of care is to commence by ascertaining whether the case comes within a factual category where duties of care have or have not been held to arise. Employer and employee, driver and passenger, carrier and consignee are a few examples of the

Crimmins v Stevedoring Industry Finance Committee cont.

many categories or relationships where, absent statute or contract to the contrary, the courts have held that one person always owes a duty of care to another. Frequently, a statutory authority will owe a duty of care because the facts of the case fall within one of these categories. The authority may, for example, be an employer or occupier of premises or be responsible for the acts of its employees, such as driving on a public street.

62 There is one settled category which I would have thought covered this case: it is the well-known category "that when statutory powers are conferred they must be exercised with reasonable care, so that if those who exercise them could by reasonable precaution have prevented an injury which has been occasioned, and was likely to be occasioned, by their exercise, damages for negligence may be recovered". Similarly, in *Sutherland Shire Council v Heyman* (1985) 157 CLR 424, Mason J, citing *Caledonian Collieries Ltd v Speirs* (1957) 97 CLR 202, said that "[i]t is now well settled that a public authority may be subject to a common law duty of care when it exercises a statutory power or performs a statutory duty". ...

The plaintiff's case must stand or fall as one concerned with an affirmative obligation on the part of the Authority to take reasonable steps to protect the plaintiff from injury. ...

Basic to that determination, as always, is the question: was the harm which the plaintiff suffered a reasonably foreseeable result of the defendant's acts or omissions? A negative answer will automatically result in a finding of no duty. But a positive answer then invites further inquiry and a close examination of any analogous cases where the courts have held that a duty does or does not exist. In determining whether the instant case is analogous to existing precedents, the reasons why the material facts in the precedent cases did or did not found a duty will ordinarily be controlling.

73 The policy of developing novel cases incrementally by reference to analogous cases acknowledges that there is no general test for determining whether a duty of care exists. But that does not mean that duties in novel cases are determined by simply looking for factual similarities in decided cases or that neither principle nor policy has any part to play in the development of the law in this area. On the contrary, the precedent cases have to be examined to reveal their bases in principle and policy. Only then, if appropriate, can they be applied to the instant case....

77... In my opinion, adherence to the incremental approach imposes a necessary discipline upon the examination of policy factors with the result that the decisions in new cases can be more confidently predicted, by reference to a limited number of principles capable of application throughout the category. In this case, the relevant principles are found in cases concerned with the common law liability of statutory authorities, the control of another person's liberty and the duty to take positive action ...

General principles concerning statutory authorities

79 Common law courts have long been cautious in imposing affirmative common law duties of care on statutory authorities. Public authorities are often charged with responsibility for a number of statutory objects and given an array of powers to accomplish them. Performing their functions with limited budgetary resources often requires the making of difficult policy choices and discretionary judgments. Negligence law is often an inapposite vehicle for examining those choices and judgments. Situations which might call for the imposition of a duty of care where a private individual was concerned may not call for one where a statutory authority is involved. This does not mean that statutory authorities are above the law. But it does mean that there may be special factors applicable to a statutory authority which negative a duty of care that a private individual would owe in apparently similar circumstances. In many cases involving routine events, the statutory authority will be in no different position from ordinary citizens. But where the authority is alleged to have failed to exercise a power or function, more difficult questions arise.

80 In Australia, the starting points for determining the common law liability of statutory authorities for breach of affirmative duties are the decisions of this court in *Sutherland Shire Council v Heyman* (1985) 157 CLR 424 and *Pyrenees Shire Council v Day* (1998) 192 CLR 330. In *Heyman*, Mason J, speaking with reference to a failure to exercise power, said:

> Generally speaking, a public authority which is under no statutory obligation to exercise a power comes under no common law duty of care to do so ... But an authority may by its conduct place itself in such a position that it attracts a duty of care which calls for exercise of the power. A common illustration is provided by the cases in which an authority in the exercise of its functions has created a danger, thereby subjecting itself to a duty of care for the safety of others which must be discharged by an exercise of its statutory powers or by giving a warning ...

Public law concepts and the policy/operational distinction

81 Common law courts have offered a number of different solutions to the problem of imposing an affirmative duty of care on a statutory authority. In *Stovin v Wise* [1996] AC 923. Lord Hoffmann (with whose speech Lord Goff of Chieveley and Lord Jauncey of Tullichettle agreed) said:

> In summary, therefore, I think that the minimum preconditions for basing a duty of care upon the existence of a statutory power, if it can be done at all, are, first, that it would in the circumstances have been irrational not to have exercised the power, so that there was in effect a public law duty to act, and secondly, that there are exceptional grounds for holding that the policy of the statute requires compensation to be paid to persons who suffer loss because the power was not exercised.

82 With great respect to the learned judges who have expressed these views, I am unable to accept that determination of a duty of care should depend on public law concepts. Public law concepts of duty and private law notions of duty are informed by differing rationales. On the current state of the authorities, the negligent exercise of a statutory power is not immune from liability simply because it was within power, nor is it actionable in negligence simply because it is ultra vires. In *Heyman*, Mason J rejected the view that mandamus could be "regarded as a foundation for imposing ... a duty of care on the public authority in relation to the exercise of [a] power. Mandamus will compel proper consideration by the authority of its discretion, but that is all."

83 The concerns regarding the decision-making and exercise of power by statutory authorities can be met otherwise than by directly incorporating public law tests into negligence. Mr John Doyle QC (as he then was) has argued, correctly in my opinion, that there "is no reason why a valid decision cannot be subject to a duty of care, and no reason why an invalid decision should more readily attract a duty of care".

84 Another way in which courts in many jurisdictions have attempted to accommodate the difficulties associated with public authorities is the "policy/operational distinction". Mason J referred to this distinction in *Heyman*:

> The distinction between policy and operational factors is not easy to formulate, but the dividing line between them will be observed if we recognise that a public authority is under no duty of care in relation to decisions which involve or are dictated by financial, economic, social or political factors or constraints. Thus budgetary allocations and the constraints which they entail in terms of allocation of resources cannot be made the subject of a duty of care. But it may be otherwise when the courts are called upon to apply a standard of care to action or inaction that is merely the product of administrative direction, expert or professional opinion, technical standards or general standards of reasonableness ... In *Pyrenees*, two justices of this court expressed the view that the distinction was unhelpful on the facts of that case.

87 Despite these criticisms, there is some support in this country for the distinction.... It may be that functions and powers which can be described as part of the "core area" of policy-making, or which are

Crimmins v Stevedoring Industry Finance Committee cont.

quasi-legislative or regulatory in nature, are not subject to a common law duty of care. Outside this narrowly defined policy exception, however, as Professor Todd has argued, it seems preferable to accommodate the distinction at the breach stage rather than the duty stage ...

The obligation of a statutory authority to take affirmative action

93 ... In my opinion, therefore, in a novel case where a plaintiff alleges that a statutory authority owed him or her a common law duty of care and breached that duty by failing to exercise a statutory power, the issue of duty should be determined by the following questions:

1. Was it reasonably foreseeable that an act or omission of the defendant, including a failure to exercise its statutory powers, would result in injury to the plaintiff or his or her interests? If no, then there is no duty.
2. By reason of the defendant's statutory or assumed obligations or control, did the defendant have the power to protect a specific class including the plaintiff (rather than the public at large) from a risk of harm? If no, then there is no duty.
3. Was the plaintiff or were the plaintiff's interests vulnerable in the sense that the plaintiff could not reasonably be expected to adequately safeguard himself or herself or those interests from harm? If no, then there is no duty.
4. Did the defendant know, or ought the defendant to have known, of the risk of harm to the specific class including the plaintiff if it did not exercise its powers? If no, then there is no duty.
5. Would such a duty impose liability with respect to the defendant's exercise of "core policy-making" or "quasi-legislative" functions? If yes, then there is no duty.
6. Are there any other supervening reasons in policy to deny the existence of a duty of care (for example, the imposition of a duty is inconsistent with the statutory scheme, or the case is concerned with pure economic loss and the application of principles in that field deny the existence of a duty)? If yes, then there is no duty.

94 If the first four questions are answered in the affirmative, and the last two in the negative, it would ordinarily be correct in principle to impose a duty of care on the statutory authority.

95 I have already discussed some aspects of the last two questions. But it may be helpful to say something about the second, third and fourth of these questions and their impact on the last two questions.

The grant of powers for the protection of a specific class of plaintiff

... [S]ome powers are conferred because the legislature expects that they will be exercised to protect the person or property of vulnerable individuals or specific classes of individuals. Where powers are given for the removal of risks to person or property, it will usually be difficult to exclude a duty on the ground that there is no specific class. The nature of the power will define the class – for example, an air traffic control authority is there to protect air travellers. Furthermore, a finding that the authority has powers of this type will often indicate that there is no supervening reason for refusing to impose a duty of care and that no core policy choice or truly quasi-legislative function is involved.

Vulnerability

100 Except in cases where a statutory authority has assumed responsibility, taken control of a situation or is under a statutory obligation to act, it seems an essential condition for imposing a duty of care on an authority that the plaintiff is vulnerable to harm unless the authority acts to avoid that harm. I use the term "vulnerable" in the sense that, as a practical matter, the plaintiff has no or little capacity to protect himself or herself. In earlier cases, it was common to refer to the concept of general reliance or dependence as a necessary condition for imposing a duty of care on a statutory authority. As I

remarked in *Perre v Apand Pty Ltd* (1999) 198 CLR 180, however, while the concept of general reliance has been criticised, properly understood, the concept was merely one way of testing for an important requirement in the determination of duty of care – how vulnerable is the plaintiff as the result of the defendant's acts or omissions. In the context of the common law liability of statutory authorities, general reliance is a combination of the requirements of the existence of powers in the statutory authority to ameliorate harm and the vulnerability of the plaintiff to that harm. In that sense it was an important element for all the justices in *Pyrenees*. …

Knowledge

101… The authority defendant's knowledge was considered an important, even essential, factor weighing in favour of a duty in *Pyrenees*.

102 In *Perre*, I also discussed the issue of constructive knowledge… In my opinion, however, one must be very careful about using constructive knowledge in this area. *Pyrenees*, for example, would have taken on a very different complexion if the shire council did not have actual knowledge of the risk. Speaking generally, I think it is unlikely that a plaintiff could succeed because of the authority's constructive knowledge of an area of risk, unless it can be said that the defendant authority had an obligation to seek out the requisite knowledge in all the circumstances, including cases where the defendant authority already possesses certain actual knowledge, but fails to look further. It would be a far-reaching step to impose affirmative obligations on a statutory authority merely because it could have or even ought to have known that the plaintiff was, or was a member of a class which was, likely to suffer harm of the relevant kind.

The authority owed a duty of care to the plaintiff

The risk of harm to the plaintiff was reasonably foreseeable

103 Safety on the waterfront was part of the Authority's general responsibilities. I do not understand the respondent to contend otherwise. Keeping in mind the generalised nature of the inquiry at the duty stage, it is clear that it was reasonably foreseeable that, if the Authority failed to perform its safety functions with reasonable care, then waterside workers would be liable to suffer injury, even if only because it was reasonably foreseeable that the employers might be derelict in performing their own duties.

The plaintiff was vulnerable as the result of the directions of the Authority

104 To my mind, the factor that points compellingly to the Authority owing an affirmative duty of care is that the Authority directed the waterside workers where they had to work and that the failure to obey such a direction could lead to disciplinary action and even deregistration as a waterside worker. That factor points so strongly to the existence of a duty of care that it should be negatived only if to impose the duty was inconsistent with the scheme of the Act. It can seldom be the case that a person, who controls or directs another person, does not owe that person a duty to take reasonable care to avoid risks of harm from that direction or the effect of that control… [105] Sometimes the duty which arises from direction or control may extend to controlling the actions of a third party. …

107 What is required to discharge a duty arising from a direction or the control of a person's freedom of action will depend on the circumstances, and, in some cases, it may be very little. But usually the very fact of the direction or control will itself be sufficient to found a duty. Where the person giving the direction or in control of another person's freedom of action knows that there is a real risk of harm unless the direction is given or the control is exercised with care, the case for imposing a duty is overwhelming. I find it impossible to accept, for example, that, if the Authority knew that it was sending waterside workers to a ship where there was a high risk of death or injury, it owed no duty of care to those workers.

Crimmins v Stevedoring Industry Finance Committee cont.

108 No doubt the vulnerability of waterside workers to injury arose primarily from their working conditions in respect of which the award and s 33 of the Act made the employers responsible. But certain features of the relationship between the workers and their employers made the workers especially vulnerable to harm unless the Authority took action. The Authority knew that the workers were being directed to work on ships where there could be a significant risk of injury to the workers from the use of equipment and machinery, the stowage of cargo and the hazardous nature of the materials which the workers had to handle. It also knew that it was directing the waterside workers to participate in transient, casual employment on the waterfront – a factor recognised in s 25(b) of the Act. In this context, the power of the Authority to direct the waterside workers as to when and where they must work placed them in a very real position of vulnerability. The casual nature of the employment, employment sometimes lasting only for a few hours, was likely to mean that employers did not have the same incentives to protect their employees from harm as do employers who must utilise the same work force day after day. Fear of deregistration as a stevedore was likely to have been the greater incentive to better safety practices on the part of employers than concern for maintaining a fit and available work force. However, the extent of such fear must inevitably have depended upon the extent to which the Authority was prepared to intervene in the conduct of stevedoring operations.

109 No doubt the vulnerability of the plaintiff was reduced to some extent by him belonging to a union. But membership of a union could not justify the Authority ignoring the risks of harm which might flow from its directions. The bare fact of union membership was not enough to eliminate the vulnerability of the plaintiff and his effective inability to protect himself in the circumstances....

112 Subject to the question of whether the imposition of a duty is forbidden or would be inconsistent with the scheme of the Act or involves "core policy" issues, the plaintiff has made good his pleaded allegation that "the Authority was under a continuing duty of care ... in the exercise of its statutory functions, duties and powers to take reasonable care to avoid foreseeable risks of injury to the health of the plaintiff"....

The legislative scheme–the functions and powers of the authority

114 No common law duty of care can be imposed on a statutory authority if to do so is either forbidden by the relevant Act or is inconsistent with the statutory scheme. To that question, I now turn ...

130 In my opinion, an examination of the scheme and purpose of the Act reveals that the Authority possessed the necessary powers and functions to protect the specific class of waterside workers by ensuring that certain minimum standards of safety were observed, either by direct action, or via its control and influence over employers. Furthermore, nothing in the Act forbade, or was inconsistent with the imposition of, a common law duty of care on the Authority.

"Core policy-making" and "quasi-legislative" functions

131 Section 20 of the Act declared that any orders made by the Authority had the "force of law". This section indicates that orders made by the Authority were part of the exercise of a "quasi-legislative" function and beyond the scope of any duty of care. This, however, does not exhaust the Authority's powers, even within s 18(1) itself. The Authority still retained sufficient powers to ameliorate the risk of injury to the waterside workers and those powers do not fall within the definition of "core policy-making". The "policy/operational" distinction has certain difficulties that attend it, but the nature of the other powers and functions exercised by the Authority with respect to safety clearly fall closer to the "operational" end of the spectrum. Although they involve considerations of convenience, discretion and budgetary allocation, they are matters appropriately considered as part of the breach question.

Other policy factors

132 There are no other reasons to deny a duty of care. ...

148 The appeal should be allowed and the matter remitted to the Court of Appeal for further hearing.

GUMMOW J:

149 I agree generally with the reasons for judgment of Hayne J. ...

159 To determine the manner of interaction between a particular statute and the common law of negligence, it is necessary to comprehend the legislative scheme. The starting point will commonly lie, as in the present appeal, in the terms of the statute and a determination of the scope of its operation. It obscures rather than illuminates the scheme established by the legislature to posit a common law duty of care and then determine whether the existence of that duty has been negatived by the statute, or other factors. Such reasoning may fail to clearly elucidate the interaction between the common law and statute.... ...

160 Where such distinct and particular statutory schemes have been enacted, it is particularly inapposite to develop the law by increments. Incrementalism suffers from a "temporal defect".... This suggests that the existence of a duty of care does not turn on rules for recognising whether an appropriate increment is apparent.... The proper approach in the present appeal is to give due accord to the distinct and particular statutory scheme which has been enacted, from which rules as to the ambit of the common law can be identified for future cases ...

HAYNE J:

The duty of care alleged

260 [T]he appellant ... said that the Authority owed "a general duty of care ... to take reasonable steps to ensure that there were safe working conditions for waterside workers" and, in particular, "a mandatory duty ... to provide waterside workers with articles and equipment 'designed for the protection of workers' in carrying out their work". The specific duty was said to be imposed by s 17(1)(o) of the Act which provided that:

(1) The functions of the Authority are: ...

(o) to encourage safe working in stevedoring operations and the use of articles and equipment, including clothing, designed for the protection of workers engaged in stevedoring operations and, where necessary, to provide waterside workers with articles and equipment designed for that purpose. ...

261 The appellant pointed to a number of matters which were said to support the conclusion that the Authority owed waterside workers the general duty of care that has been described. The most important of these was said to be the relationship between the Authority and waterside workers – a relationship which gave the Authority powers of a kind ordinarily exercisable only by employers. Four particular powers were mentioned: (a) the power to discipline; (b) the power to require medical examinations; (c) the power to direct workers to turn up for work; and (d) if work was available, the power to direct waterside workers where and when to work. Describing the Authority's powers in this summary way is not complete and, to that extent, may be inaccurate. It is as well, therefore, to refer to the relevant provisions of the Act.

The functions of the authority ...

264 Regard must also be had to the fact that the Act cast obligations on registered employers. In particular, s 33(1) required a registered employer to ensure that "as far as is practicable ... stevedoring operations for which he has engaged waterside workers are expeditiously, safely and efficiently performed" ...

267 For the purpose of the performance of its functions the Authority had power to make orders. ... Section 20(1) of the Act gave legislative force to such orders. It provided that they should not be

Crimmins v Stevedoring Industry Finance Committee cont.

deemed to be Statutory Rules but should "have the force of law". A person who contravened or failed to comply with a provision of an order made by the Authority committed an offence ... [I]t is right then to say (as the appellant submitted) that, if work was available, the Authority had power to direct waterside workers where and when to work. Whether or not the Authority knew what cargoes were being unloaded, it was the Authority's act of allotting workers to particular stevedoring operations which determined which workers unloaded cargoes of asbestos.

269 These being the relevant powers and functions of the Authority, did it owe the deceased worker a duty of care in their performance and exercise?

Statutory authorities and negligence

270 The fact that the Authority is a statutory body given statutory discretions does not prevent the application of ordinary principles of the law of negligence. But the courts have often found the task of identifying the duty of care that is owed by a statutory body to be difficult. To whom is the duty owed? What is the content of the duty?

...

273 As I have pointed out, the appellant alleged that the Authority owed the deceased worker a duty to take reasonable care in the exercise of its statutory functions, duties and powers. But the central complaint of the appellant appeared to be that the Authority could and should have taken steps which, if taken, would have prevented the deceased worker suffering the injuries he did.

274 It is convenient to consider at this point the analogy which it was sought to draw between the relationship of the Authority to the deceased worker and the relationship of an employer to an employee.

Was the authority in a position similar to an employer? ...

285 The analogy which the appellant sought to draw between the Authority and an employer is not exact. It breaks down at several points. The Authority did not have day to day control of the system of work used for unloading individual ships. It did not have day to day control of the safety of the individual workplaces where stevedoring operations were conducted. It did have power to prescribe rules having the force of law that would generally govern such matters. It could provide safety equipment but, short of making a general order, it could not enforce the use of that equipment by workers or employers. Deciding whether to provide safety equipment would be affected by what other obligations the Authority had to meet to fulfil its statutory obligations and, in the case of safety equipment, it would be affected by considering (among other things) whether it would be better if employers could and would provide it.

286 No doubt the differences that I have identified suggest that it may be unsafe to rely on the analogy with an employer that the appellant sought to draw. But the differences are more significant than that. They reveal why no common law duty of care of the kind alleged by the appellant should be held to have been owed to the deceased worker.

...

Duty to make an order?

288 As I have said, the Authority could have required the use of respirators only by making a general order under s 18. The Authority owed no common law duty of care to the deceased worker in deciding whether or not to exercise that quasi-legislative power. There are several reasons why that is so.

289 First, to hold that the Authority owed waterside workers a duty of care that would be broken if the Authority did not make general orders providing for a safe system of work and safe place of work for those members would be contrary to the express statutory limitation on the Authority's exercise of

Crimmins v Stevedoring Industry Finance Committee cont.

its function to regulate the performance of stevedoring operations. Section 17(2) provided that the power of the Authority to regulate the performance of stevedoring operations should be exercised only where it was "essential for the proper performance" of that function. To impose the alleged duty of care on the Authority would transform the nature of the relationship between the Authority and individual stevedores that was prescribed by the Act: from one in which the Authority would limit the control of stevedores over waterside workers (or their manner of performance of stevedoring operations) only where to do so was essential, to one in which the Authority would interfere in the day to day operations of the waterfront.

290 Of course if the Authority were under a duty to take reasonable care, observing that duty could be said to be "essential" to the proper performance of its functions. But the point I seek to make is not one that depends upon some difficulty of reconciling the imposition of a common law duty of care with individual words in s 17(2). It is that s 17(2) was intended to achieve a particular balance between the role of the Authority and the role of employers and that balance would be transformed if it were to be held that the Authority was liable in negligence if workers suffered injury as a result of the Authority failing to exercise the powers given to it by s 18.

291 Secondly, as has been identified in a number of authorities, there are other, more deep-seated reasons for rejecting the imposition of a duty of care that would require the performance of quasi-legislative functions by a body such as the Authority.

292 Put at its most general and abstract level, the fundamental reason for not imposing a duty in negligence in relation to the quasi-legislative functions of a public body is that the function is one that must have a public rather than a private or individual focus. To impose a private law duty will (or at least will often) distort that focus. This kind of distinction might be said to find reflection in the dichotomy that has been drawn between the operational and the policy decisions or functions of public bodies. And a quasi-legislative function can be seen as lying at or near the centre of policy functions if policy and operational functions are to be distinguished. But as more recent authority suggests, that distinction may not always be useful and I do not need to apply it in deciding the present matter....

294 An order [under s 18], when made, had the force of law. An order could not lawfully be directed to a particular person or to a particular stevedoring operation; it had to have more general application. No doubt the class of persons affected by an order could be identified and in many (perhaps all) cases the class of persons for whose benefit the order was made could also be determined. It might be said that if those affected by the order and those for whose benefit the order is made can be identified, imposing a duty on a public authority to take reasonable care not to injure those persons would not distort the proper performance of that quasi-legislative function. I do not accept that this is so. Important as the interests of those two classes may be in deciding what order should be made, there will often be other important considerations that affect that question. To give only one example, the Authority may well have had to consider maintaining industrial peace as part of its obligation of securing expeditious, safe and efficient performance of stevedoring operations.... [295] To impose a common law duty of care on the Authority would have affected the way in which the body went about its task. It would have shifted the Authority's attention from what the general good of the industry required (which, of course, included workplace safety but was not limited to that) to what should be done to avoid the Authority being held responsible for particular breaches of workplace safety by those having primary responsibility for the task – the employers of waterside labour. Whatever may have been the social benefits of having the Authority fulfil that kind of role (and they may now be thought to have been large) it is essential not to lose sight of the fact that this is not the role that the parliament gave it. That being so, the courts should not, indeed cannot, do so.

296 The present case is even clearer. The appellant's complaint is that the Authority made no order. It did not exercise its quasi-legislative power. If the appellant is to succeed then, it is necessary to show

Crimmins v Stevedoring Industry Finance Committee cont.

that the Authority, exercising reasonable care, was duty bound to exercise its power to make a general order and to exercise that power in a particular way. What I have called the distortion of focus is greater if a common law duty to exercise the power (as opposed to a common law duty affecting how the power is exercised) is found to exist. It is greater because the imposition on the Authority of a duty owed to individuals means that the Authority would have been bound to consider the position of those individuals and to do so regardless of what other subjects may have properly required its time and attention in performing the functions given to it by the Act.... (The distortion of focus would be no less if the duty were cast in terms of a duty to consider making an order, but the appellant did not contend for such a duty.)

297 The Authority did not owe the deceased worker a duty to make an order under s 18.

Duty to supply equipment or warn?

... 299 These arguments of the appellant are all founded in allegations that the Authority failed to exercise its powers, not that it exercised them carelessly. I do not, however, consider that the classification of the alleged breaches as non-feasances rather than misfeasances concludes whether the Authority owed the deceased worker a duty of care to exercise the powers in question. The distinction between non-feasance and misfeasance is often elusive and even if that were not so, adopting that distinction as an exclusive test for deciding whether a duty was owed may well be inconsistent with *Pyrenees*. The majority of the court held in that case that the council owed a duty to exercise its statutory powers and was liable for failing to do so.

300 In this case the question of duty to take the steps I have identified (warning of danger, or encouraging safe working practices, or supplying respirators) should be resolved against the appellant for other reasons.

301 The particular warning or encouragement which it is said that the Authority should have given, and the particular equipment which it is said it should have supplied, relate to the dangers if workers inhaled asbestos fibres ... Nevertheless, if the Authority owed a duty of care to warn workers against the risk of inhaling asbestos fibres, there seems no reason to think that it would not also have owed a duty to warn workers of the many other kinds of risk they ran on the waterfront and to encourage safe working practices in these respects as well. And if the Authority owed a common law duty to provide respirators for use by workers (or to provide them if employers did not) the Authority presumably owed a like duty to provide all other necessary safety equipment ...

303 It is necessary to recall that the hypothesis for this branch of the argument is that the Authority owed no duty to require employers to provide, or employees to use, a safe system of work. If the Authority owed no duty to take coercive measures, any warning or encouragement it gave, any equipment it supplied, would be done in a context where the employer, not the Authority, had control over the effect that was given to the warning or encouragement and control over whether the equipment was worn.

304 The absence of control is very significant in deciding whether to hold that the Authority owed a duty of care to warn, encourage or to supply equipment ... 305 An employer owes an employee the duty of care it does because the employer not only puts the employee in harm's way but also controls, and is responsible for, the place and system of work to which the employee is exposed. It is that control over the safety of the place and system of work that leads to the conclusion that the employer owes a duty of care to employees about those matters. It is the absence of that control which distinguishes the position of the Authority from that of an employer. If the duty asserted in this case were performed (whether the duty is to supply equipment or warn or encourage) it would be for others, not the party subject to the duty, to determine whether the steps taken by that party were given any effect or were given no, or only limited, effect.

306 The persons responsible for creating the risks to which the deceased worker was exposed, and for avoiding those risks, were the employers of waterside labour. … its conduct was causally insignificant in the deceased worker's sustaining injury. At its highest, the complaint now made against the Authority is that it did not control others – the employers. And for the reasons I have given earlier, I reject the contention that the Authority was duty bound to exercise its order-making power to require modification of the system of work which was used by stevedores. The other complaints made (failure to warn, failure to encourage, failure to supply but not require) are even less causally significant …

312 The Authority did not owe the deceased worker a common law duty to warn against dangers or encourage safe working practices, and it owed no common law duty to supply safety equipment.

313 The appeal should be dismissed with costs.

[Gleeson CJ agreed with the judgment of McHugh J. Gaudron and Callinan JJ also agreed that the approach to take to a question of a common law duty to exercise statutory power is to begin with the question of common law liability and to modify it if the statute so requires. Gummow and Kirby JJ thought that the better approach was to begin with the statute to determine the scope of the duty. Kirby J wished to use the *Caparo* test to determine the duty of care. Hayne J specifically rejected that approach. Gummow and Hayne JJ both held there was no duty for a reason peculiar to this case, namely that the authority could only act by quasi-legislative activity. In the result the appeal of the widow was allowed 5:2 with Gummow and Hayne JJ dissenting.]

[11.20] The following case had many dimensions, which is why other parts of it have been extracted elsewhere in this text (see [9.15]). Here the public authority defendants were a local government council and a State.

Graham Barclay Oysters v Ryan

[11.25] *Graham Barclay Oysters Pty Ltd v Ryan; Ryan v Great Lakes Council; New South Wales v Ryan* (2002) 211 CLR 540 High Court of Australia

(footnotes Australia)

[The facts are outlined at [9.15].]

GUMMOW AND HAYNE JJ:

The outline of the litigation

116 These three appeals are brought against a decision of the Full Court of the Federal Court. They involve the alleged liability in negligence of particular growers and distributors of oysters, and relevant local and State governments, for harm suffered by consumers of oysters….

117 At first instance, the Federal Court (Wilcox J) held that the Council, the State and the Barclay companies were each liable in negligence to Mr Ryan and (subject to proof of damage) to the other 184 representative group members. The Full Court of the Federal Court (Lee, Lindgren and Kiefel JJ), by differently constituted majorities, upheld an appeal by the Council, and dismissed appeals by the State and the Barclay companies. In this Court, Mr Ryan seeks to restore the initial finding of negligence against the Council, while the Barclay companies and the State seek to have the negligence findings against them overturned. The appeal by the State should be allowed and that by Mr Ryan against the Council should be dismissed. In the appeal by the Barclay companies, the appeal by Barclay Distributors should be allowed …

Graham Barclay Oysters v Ryan cont.

A The Council

The claims in the Federal Court against the Council

133 These have fluctuated in the course of the litigation. By their re-amended statement of claim dated 21 April 1998, Mr Ryan and the other applicants submitted that the Council owed them (i) a duty regularly to monitor and test the waters, sediment and sea grasses of the Wallis Lake region for contamination and to monitor the impact of private landholders and the Council's sewerage systems on the water quality; (ii) at least in and after late November 1996, a duty to warn oyster farmers, wholesalers and retailers and the general public of the likely contamination of Wallis Lake and the likely unsafety of oysters harvested therefrom; (iii) a duty to take steps, directly or indirectly, to cause oyster farmers in the Wallis Lake region to cease the harvesting or supply of oysters in and after November 1996; (iv) a duty to set up and supervise the Wallis Lake Estuary Management Committee to report on and implement steps in respect of the management of water quality in the Wallis Lake region; and (v) a duty not to contaminate Wallis Lake and to ensure that the lake's water quality was not compromised by the Council's systems for the management of sewage (including by ensuring the maintenance of sewerage facilities in a proper state of repair). As will appear, not all of these claims were ultimately pursued in this Court.

134 At trial, Wilcox J held that the Council owed a common law duty of care to oyster consumers to take those steps that were reasonably open to it to minimise human faecal contamination of the lake. His Honour held that the Council had breached this duty… 135 On appeal, a majority of the Full Court of the Federal Court (Lindgren J and Kiefel J, Lee J dissenting) held that the Council owed no relevant duty of care to the consumers. …

The statutory provisions

136 Before identifying the precise way in which the alleged duty was formulated by counsel for Mr Ryan in submissions to this Court, it is appropriate to describe the statutory provisions which empowered the Council to act in respect of the situation at Wallis Lake.

137 The Council is constituted as a body corporate under Ch 9 of the *Local Government Act 1993* (NSW) ("the LG Act"). At the time of the events giving rise to this litigation, s 7 of that statute provided that the purposes of the LG Act included to provide the legal framework for an "environmentally responsible" system of local government (para (a)) and to require councils "to have regard to the protection of the environment in carrying out their responsibilities" (para (e)). Chapter 7 (s 68 – 185) of the LG Act was headed "What are the regulatory functions of councils?". S 68 set out a wide range of activities which generally required prior council approval; these included broadly defined categories of conduct in respect of water supply, sewerage and stormwater drainage work and the management of waste. Failure to obtain a requisite approval, and the carrying out of an activity otherwise than in accordance with an approval, were rendered criminal offences by s 626 and s 627. Cl 45 of the *Local Government (Water, Sewerage and Drainage) Regulation 1993* (NSW), made under s 748 of the LG Act, relevantly directed the Council, in determining an application under s 68 of the LG Act for approval to carry out sewerage work, to have regard to, among other things, "the protection and promotion of public health" and "the protection of the environment"….

The submissions in this Court

142 Before this Court, counsel for Mr Ryan contended that the Council owed the oyster consumers a duty (i) to exercise the powers conferred by s 191 and s 192 of the LG Act to carry out a sanitary survey of Wallis Lake and its tributaries and (ii) after identifying sources of pollution, to exercise its powers under s 124 and s 678 of the LG Act or s 27 of the *Clean Waters Act 1970* to remedy those problems.

… [C]ounsel for the Barclay companies envisaged a duty of care, owed by the Council to oyster consumers, to take reasonable care to identify and to remedy sources of pollution at Wallis Lake and its

Graham Barclay Oysters v Ryan cont.

tributaries. Adopting and adapting the terms used in *Brodie*, the Barclay companies asserted a duty on the part of the Council to take reasonable care that the exercise of or failure to exercise its powers to carry out works and repairs on sewerage installations did not create a foreseeable risk of harm to a class of persons (consumers of produce from the lake, or, more narrowly, consumers of oysters) which included Mr Ryan and the other applicants in the Federal Court. Two factors in particular were said to justify a duty in these terms. These were that (i) the Council was the only party with actual knowledge of the progressive deterioration of the sewerage infrastructure which imperilled the purity of the waters of Wallis Lake, and (ii) the Council had extensive statutory powers to prevent or to redress that deterioration and to mitigate the effects of any pollution.

145 The accuracy of these two observations may be accepted. However, the co-existence of knowledge of a risk of harm and power to avert or to minimise that harm does not, without more, give rise to a duty of care at common law. The totality of the relationship between the parties, not merely the foresight and capacity to act on the part of one of them, is the proper basis upon which a duty of care may be recognised. Were it otherwise, any recipient of statutory powers to licence, supervise or compel conduct in a given field, would, upon gaining foresight of some relevant risk, owe a duty of care to those ultimately threatened by that risk to act to prevent or minimise it. As will appear, the common law should be particularly hesitant to recognise such a duty where the relevant authority is empowered to regulate conduct relating to or impacting on a risk-laden field of endeavour which is populated by self-interested commercial actors who themselves possess some power to avert those risks.

146 The existence or otherwise of a common law duty of care allegedly owed by a statutory authority turns on a close examination of the terms, scope and purpose of the relevant statutory regime. The question is whether that regime erects or facilitates a relationship between the authority and a class of persons that, in all the circumstances, displays sufficient characteristics answering the criteria for intervention by the tort of negligence.

147 Where the question posed above is answered in the affirmative, the common law imposes a duty in tort which operates alongside the rights, duties and liabilities created by statute. In some instances, a statutory regime may itself, in express terms or by necessary implication, exclude the concurrent operation of a duty at common law. An example is provided by *Sullivan v Moody* (2001) 207 CLR 562....

148 However, contrary to submissions put on behalf of the Attorney-General for Western Australia (as an intervener in this Court), the discernment of an affirmative legislative intent that a common law duty exists, is not, and has never been, a necessary pre-condition to the recognition of such a duty....

149 An evaluation of whether a relationship between a statutory authority and a class of persons imports a common law duty of care is necessarily a multi-faceted inquiry. Each of the salient features of the relationship must be considered. The focus of analysis is the relevant legislation and the positions occupied by the parties on the facts as found at trial. It ordinarily will be necessary to consider the degree and nature of control exercised by the authority over the risk of harm that eventuated; the degree of vulnerability of those who depend on the proper exercise by the authority of its powers; and the consistency or otherwise of the asserted duty of care with the terms, scope and purpose of the relevant statute. In particular categories of cases, some features will be of increased significance. For example, in cases of negligent misstatement, such as *Tepko Pty Ltd v Water Board* (2001) 178 ALR 634, reasonable reliance by the plaintiff on the defendant authority ordinarily will be a significant factor in ascertaining any relevant duty of care.

150 The factor of control is of fundamental importance in discerning a common law duty of care on the part of a public authority. It assumes particular significance in this appeal. This is because a form of control over the relevant risk of harm, which, as exemplified by *Agar v Hyde* 201 CLR 552, is remote, in a legal and practical sense, does not suffice to found a duty of care. ...

Graham Barclay Oysters v Ryan cont.

152 The Council in the present appeal, by contrast, exercised a much less significant degree of control over the risk of the harm that eventuated [than did the Council in *Pyrenees*].. At no stage did the Council exercise control, let alone significant or exclusive control, over the direct source of harm to consumers, that is, the oysters themselves. It may be that the predominantly land-based sources of pollution were all ultimately subject to Council control. That, however, is the start, not the end, of the inquiry. Control over some aspect of a relevant physical environment is unlikely to found a duty of care where the relevant harm results from the conduct of a third party beyond the defendant's control. *Modbury Triangle Shopping Centre Pty Ltd v Anzil* (2000) 205 CLR 254 illustrates the point. What is significant here is the extent of control which the Council had over the risk of contaminated oysters causing harm to the ultimate consumer; control in that sense is not established by noting the Council's powers in respect of some or most of the sources of faecal pollution.

153 As Lindgren J observed in the Full Court, the relationship between the Council and the oyster consumers is indirect; it is mediated by intervening conduct on the part of others. Between the Council on the one hand and the oyster consumers on the other, there stands, in the present case, an entire oyster-growing industry comprising numerous commercial enterprises, each of which, in pursuit of profit, engages in conduct that presents an inherent threat to public safety. That threat arises from the insusceptibility of oysters to effective and reliable tests to identify contamination of the type that eventuated here.

154 In broad terms, the Council's statutory powers enabled it to monitor and, where necessary, to intervene in order to protect, the physical environment of areas under its administration. However, the conferral on a local authority of statutory powers in respect of activities occurring within its boundaries does not itself establish in that authority control over all risks of harm which may eventuate from the conduct therein of independent commercial enterprises. As the course of this litigation itself indicates, control over the safety of the Wallis Lake oysters for human consumption has been fragmented. The conduct of the Council did not "so closely and directly [affect]" oyster consumers so as to warrant the imposition of a duty of care owed by the former to the latter. There were "too many intervening levels of decision-making" between the conduct of the Council and the harm suffered by the consumers. As the trial judge noted, the Council had no direct responsibility for the operation of the oyster industry or the quality or safety of Wallis Lake oysters. It did not control the process by which commercial oyster growers cultivated, harvested and supplied oysters, nor the times or locations at which they did so. The Council has not been given, by virtue of its statutory powers, such a significant and special measure of control over the risk of danger that ultimately injured the oyster consumers so as to impose upon it a duty of care the breach of which may sound in damages at the suit of any one or more of those consumers.

155 The Council owed no relevant duty of care to the consumers. Mr Ryan's appeal should be dismissed.

B. The State

The claims in the Federal Court against the State

156 … Mr Ryan and the other applicants contended that the State, in its various manifestations [Minister for Fisheries, Committees formed by the Minister, the Environmental Protection Authority, the Director-General of the Department of Health, and the Minister of Health], owed them a range of duties of care…

158 The trial judge concluded that the State owed a duty of care to oyster consumers to take those steps that reasonably were open to it to minimise the risk of consumers contracting a viral infection from the oysters. …

159 A majority of the Full Court (Lee J and Kiefel J, Lindgren J dissenting) dismissed the State's appeal …

Graham Barclay Oysters v Ryan cont.

162 In argument before this Court, the evolution of the case against the State continued. Counsel for Mr Ryan described the State's duty of care in the following terms. It was said that the State had relevantly embarked upon one limb of what was necessarily a two-limbed approach to oyster safety. That is, the State had instituted a system of compulsory 36-hour depuration of oysters prior to sale, but it had failed to require what it knew was a necessary precondition to the effectiveness of depuration, being the carrying out of sanitary surveys to detect and to remedy pollution in oyster growing areas. It was submitted that, having embarked upon the management of the oyster industry in the way that it had, the State came under a duty of care to carry out the sanitary surveys that it knew were necessary to effectuate the depuration process. Further, if, after having identified sources of pollution, the safety of a particular oyster growing area could not be assured, the State was said to come under a common law duty to close the relevant fishery until the problem could be remedied.

163 Thus, as the case for Mr Ryan ultimately was advanced in this Court, the State's duty to consumers to take reasonable care to protect them from reasonably foreseeable risks of injury as a result of the consumption of oysters involved two related elements. These were (i) an obligation to conduct one or more sanitary surveys to identify and to remedy pollution sources and (ii) an obligation to close oyster fisheries that presented an unacceptable risk to public safety. The State was said to have breached its duty by its failure (a) to conduct a sanitary survey of the Wallis Lake region at some unspecified time before November 1996 and (b) to require the Wallis Lake growers to cease harvesting and selling oysters after the heavy rainfall of that month. ...

Sanitary surveys

166 Through the medium of the EPA, the State has powers under the *Clean Waters Act 1970* to remove, disperse, destroy or mitigate pollution of waters (s 27), to direct the removal, dispersion, destruction or mitigation of water pollution (s 27A) and to carry out inspections and investigations of premises (s 29). ... Together, these provisions empowered the State itself to conduct regular sanitary surveys of oyster growing areas including those at Wallis Lake.

167 Further, the State could require oyster growers to cooperate in the carrying out of a sanitary survey, or could make oyster harvesting in a particular area conditional on the prior completion of a sanitary survey. This could be achieved either as a condition of an aquaculture lease or permit or as an element of a commercial aquaculture industry development plan.

[The judge went on to say that under the *Fisheries Management Act 1994* the Minister had power to lease public water areas with conditions including requiring a survey. It also prevents aquaculture without a permit (subject to conditions) which the Minister may cancel or suspend if conditions are breached. The Minister can also set up development plans (programmes) to ensure the quality of shellfish taken from estuarine waters.]

Aquaculture permit holders are required to comply with the local programme in respect of the area in which their farm is located (Management Regulationreg 12G).

174 Neither the State programme nor a local Wallis Lake programme had been produced by November 1996 [when the heavy rainfall occurred].

175 Lindgren J explained in his reasons for judgment that Div 4 of Pt 2 of the Management Regulation reflects a political decision by the State to enlist shellfish industry participants in a system of industry-funded self-regulation or co-regulation, rather than to impose on that industry a publicly funded regulatory regime. In particular, the State decided not to adopt the approach of some other Australian and foreign jurisdictions which require regular sanitary surveys of oyster growing regions pursuant to a classification structure based on water pollution levels. This decision was reached after much consideration and was based in part on budgetary concerns. In accordance with that decision by the Executive Government of New South Wales, which found partial expression in the Regulations referred to above, the State neither required regular sanitary surveys of oyster growing areas (whether

Graham Barclay Oysters v Ryan cont.

as a condition of aquaculture leases or permits or otherwise) nor undertook to conduct such surveys itself. A decision of that nature involves a fundamental governmental choice as to the nature and extent of regulation of a particular industry. It is in a different category to those public resource allocation decisions which, in the manner described in *Brodie v Singleton Shire Council* (2001) 206 CLR 512, may be considered in determining the existence and breach of a duty of care by a public authority.

176 Once the nature of the decision by the State is appreciated, its observance by agents of the State in respect of any particular region falls outside the scope of any common law duty of care that may otherwise arise. The evidence did not establish that the State was aware of any particular risk of contamination in respect of the Wallis Lake fisheries.... In those circumstances, the "failure" on the part of the State to conduct a sanitary survey of Wallis Lake reflected simply a continued adherence to a previously settled policy of general application. The scope of any common law duty that may arise in those circumstances necessarily accommodates itself to, and is controlled by, the insusceptibility of that decision by the State to curial review under the rubric of the tort of negligence. It follows that the State was under no common law duty to conduct sanitary surveys of Wallis Lake.

Fishing closure

177 Section 189 of the *Fisheries Management Act 1994* provides that the Minister may prohibit the taking of fish cultivated under an aquaculture permit if satisfied that such taking should be suspended or that such fish is likely to be unfit for human consumption. Such a notification is called a fishing closure.

... Where [the Minister is satisfied], the discretion to prohibit the taking of fish is enlivened and the Minister's decision thereunder becomes, by virtue of s 8, a "fishing closure" enforceable under Div 1 of Pt 2 of the *Fisheries Management Act 1994*.

... 180 At the time of the contamination at Wallis Lake, Pt 4 (s 44 – 56) of the *Food Act 1989* (NSW) ("the *Food Act*") was headed "Particular powers of the Director-General". S 45(1)(b) thereof conferred power on the Director-General of Health, by order, to "prohibit the cultivation, taking, harvesting or obtaining, from an area specified in the order, of any food or of any food of a class or description so specified". S 44 provided that any such order could "be made only when the Director-General has reasonable grounds to believe that the making of one or more such orders is necessary in order to prevent or mitigate a serious danger to public health". ...

182 ...[A] duty to close the Wallis Lake fishery under s 189 formed part of the duty held to exist by the primary judge and by Lee J in the Full Court. Further, the power to close the fishery appeared to comprise the entire content of the duty of care identified by Kiefel J in the Full Court.

183 In argument before this Court, however, counsel for Mr Ryan disavowed reliance upon the powers of closure conferred by s 189 of the *Fisheries Management Act 1994* and s 45 of the *Food Act 1989*. That stance is understandable. The existence of satisfaction by the Minister or the Director-General as to the state of affairs specified in the respective provisions would be a jurisdictional fact upon which the exercise of their statutory powers was conditioned. There was no case made that such a state of satisfaction had existed.... It follows that neither the discretion conferred by s 189 of the *Fisheries Management Act 1994* nor that conferred by s 45 of the *Food Act 1989* was at any relevant time engaged. In the absence of that engagement, the statutory provisions, in the circumstances of this case, supplied no relevant statutory power to which a common law duty of care could attach.

184 In argument, counsel for Mr Ryan submitted that the State, through its various officers and agencies, enjoyed a range of non-coercive powers beyond those which have explicit legislative force. In particular, it was put that the State may, through its involvement in the oyster industry, persuade oyster fisheries voluntarily to cease harvesting for specified periods in the interests of public safety. This apparently is what occurred when the Wallis Lake fisheries temporarily ceased harvesting shellfish from

14 February 1997. That cessation of harvesting was voluntarily undertaken by the relevant aquaculture permit holders at the initiative of the State ... This was an instance of effective State action falling short of the invocation of ministerial powers under the *Fisheries Management Act 1994*. However, the evidence did not establish that the State had assumed (even if it had the legal competence to do so) any day-to-day control of the commercial activities of any oyster growers in the Wallis Lake area or elsewhere.

185 It may readily be accepted that public authorities, armed with statutory powers to compel, prevent or punish conduct, frequently exercise informal and non-coercive influence or persuasion over those persons and organisations against whom they are empowered formally to act. So much follows from the existence of an organised system of sanctions beneath which there is interaction between public authorities and industry participants. But the exercise or potential exercise of powers of supervision or persuasion of this type provides an insecure basis for a duty of care enforceable by the common law. This is so particularly where the duty allegedly is owed not to industry participants but to the ultimate consumer. That the practical content of any such duty would be elusive supports the conclusion that it does not exist. As counsel for the State asked rhetorically during argument, is such a duty to be described as a duty to be persuasive, especially persuasive or successfully persuasive?

186 The State owed no relevant duty of care to the oyster consumers. Its appeal should be allowed ...

[Gleeson CJ and Kirby and Callinan JJ held that the Barclay companies had breached their duty of care but in other respects generally agreed in the approach of Gummow and Hayne JJ. McHugh J held that neither the State nor the Council owed a duty of care.]

[11.30] The following case draws together the principles to be deduced from the earlier cases.

Amaca v NSW

[11.35] *Amaca Pty Ltd (Formerly Known as James Hardie & Co Pty Ltd) v New South Wales* [2004] NSWCA 124 New South Wales Court of Appeal

(footnotes omitted)

[Mr Hay was employed by a firm constructing a power station for the Electricity Commission of NSW (now Pacific Power). In the course of his employment Mr Hay was exposed to asbestos and contracted mesothelioma, which was diagnosed in 1993. Under the *Scaffolding and Lifts Act 1912* the State had the power to inspect work sites and give directions to prevent accidents and ensure compliance with the regulations. It used the NSW Department of Labour and Industry to do this and its inspectors had constant and regular access to the power station to inspect it and in 1958 produced a report saying that only in one area of the site did asbestos levels exceed the recommended international standard. Mr Hay sued both his employer and Pacific Power. These claims were settled, but both defendants cross-claimed against James Hardie, the manufacturer of the asbestos products. James Hardie became liable for payment and in turn cross-claimed against the state of NSW.

James Hardie's cross-claim against the State was dismissed by the trial judge (Curtis J) on the ground that it was not just and equitable that the State should contribute to the liability of James Hardie. This order was upheld by the Court of Appeal. An appeal to the High Court was allowed, so that the matter is now remitted to the Court of Appeal for hearing and determination conformably with the reasons of the High Court.]

IPP JA: (Mason P and McColl J concurring)

Amaca v NSW cont.

The duty of care issue

18 The determination whether the State owed Mr Hay a duty of care as asserted by James Hardie depends upon a proper understanding (and the application) of the principles laid down in *Pyrenees Shire Council v Day* (1998) 192 CLR 330, *Crimmins v Stevedoring Industry Finance Committee* (1999) 200 CLR 1, *Graham Barclay Oysters Pty Limited v Ryan* (2002) 211 CLR 540 and other decisions dealing with the negligent performance of statutory duties.

19 A clear and universal test for determining whether a duty of care arises has not been laid down. Each case depends on its own circumstances and the totality of the circumstances must be weighed in the balance. Depending on the facts, different factors have different degrees of significance. Nevertheless, *Pyrenees*, *Crimmins* and *Graham Barclay Oysters* point to and delineate the path that is to be followed.

20 The statements of approach of the members of the High Court in these leading authorities have to be seen in the context of the issues in each. There were singular and distinctive aspects about all these cases. Thus, the reasoning of the various justices cannot properly be understood without regard to the different facts in each case....

21 It is appropriate to commence the discussion on this topic by repeating Mason J's remarks in *Sutherland Shire Council v Heyman* (1985) 157 CLR 424.These remarks were referred to on a number of occasions in *Pyrenees*, *Crimmins* and *Graham Barclay Oysters* and are an important part of the discussion of the duty of care issue in those cases. His Honour said (at 459-461):

> Generally speaking, a public authority which is under no statutory obligation to exercise a power comes under no common law duty of care to do so: see *Revesz v The Commonwealth* (1951) 51 SR (NSW) 63. But an authority may by its conduct place itself in such a position that it attracts a duty of care which calls for exercise of the power. A common illustration is provided by the cases in which an authority in the exercise of its functions has created a danger, thereby subjecting itself to a duty of care for the safety of others which must be discharged by an exercise of its statutory powers or by giving a warning ... That it is the conduct of the authority in creating the danger that attracts the duty of care is demonstrated by *Sheppard v Glossop Corporation* (1921) 3 KB 132. There the highway authority was under no duty of care with respect to lighting, though the danger was foreseeable, because it did not create the danger. Having statutory power to make provision for the lighting of streets, it placed a lamp at a dangerous point in a street, the danger not being of its making, but extinguished the lamp at 9.00 pm in accordance with a general resolution applying to all streets in the borough. The authority was held not liable on the footing that the statute imposed no obligation to light, that the Authority having begun to light was under no obligation to continue to do so, and that having done nothing to make the street dangerous, it was under no obligation to give warning of the danger. Atkin LJ (at 51) explained earlier cases in which under the same statute local authorities had been liable for not lighting by stating that the local authorities had created the dangers which were responsible for the plaintiffs' injuries.
>
> There are other situations in which an authority's occupation of premises ... or its ownership or control of a structure in a highway or of a public place ... attracts to it a duty of care. In these cases the statute facilitates the existence of a common law duty of care. In the words of Lord Denning MR in *Scott v Green & Sons* [(1969) 1 WLR 301 at 304]: "The statute does not *by itself* give rise to a civil action, but it forms the foundation on which the common law can build a cause of action." As [*Voli v Inglewood Shire Council* (1963) 110 CLR 74] demonstrates, the breach of the common law duty may arise from the failure of the authority's officers to ascertain that the statutory requirements are satisfied. There, the officers who examined the plans and specifications of the shire hall failed to ascertain that the authority's by-laws relating to public buildings had been infringed with the result that a stage

collapsed and injured the plaintiff. The authority and its architect were held liable. Liability of this kind extends to liability for damage which is attributable to the positive and wrongful act of another ...

And then there are situations in which a public authority, not otherwise under a relevant duty, may place itself in such a position that others rely on it to take care for their safety so that the authority comes under a duty of care calling for positive action. Such a relationship has been held to arise where a person, by practice or past conduct upon which other persons come to rely, creates a self-imposed duty to take positive action to protect the safety or interests of another or at least to warn him that he or his interests are at risk ...

22 Nothing in *Pyrenees*, *Crimmins* and *Graham Barclay Oysters* is materially inconsistent with Mason J's remarks. What is significant for the purposes of this appeal are the following propositions, drawn from *Sutherland Shire Council v Heyman* (1985) 157 CLR 424:

(a) Generally, a public authority, which is under no statutory obligation to exercise a power, owes no common law duty of care to do so.

(b) An authority may by its conduct, however, attract a duty of care that requires the exercise of the power.

(c) Three categories are identified in which the duty of care may so be attracted.
  (i) Where an authority, in the exercise of its functions, has created a danger.
  (ii) Where the particular circumstances of an authority's occupation of premises or its ownership or control of a structure attracts to it a duty of care. In these cases the statute facilitates the existence of a duty of care.
  (iii) Where a public authority acts so that others rely on it to take care for their safety.

23 Mason J did not suggest that the categories of circumstances in which an authority may attract a duty of care are closed. Later cases, which are in accord with the general propositions laid down in *Sutherland Shire Council v Heyman* (1985) 157 CLR 424, have extended the categories to situations where an authority has control over a particular situation that carries with it a risk of harm of which the authority knows or should know. That is to say, where an authority has such control, a duty of care may (not, I stress, must) be recognised.

24 I turn now to *Pyrenees*. [He set out the facts and the approach taken by the judges] ...

27 Two differing strands of reasoning, relevant to this appeal, can be identified in *Pyrenees*. The first is exemplified by the following remarks of McHugh J (at 372, [115]):

> Given the extensive powers of the Council, its entry into the field of inspection on this occasion, if not other occasions, its actual knowledge of the danger to the health and property of the occupiers of [the street] and, at the least, its imputed knowledge that residents of the shire generally relied on it to protect them from the dangers arising from the use or condition of premises, the Council owed a duty of care to Mr and Mrs Day.

McHugh J considered that the tenants of the premises where the fire occurred (70 Neill Street) were not in the position of vulnerability of Mr and Mrs Day (at 72 Neill Street) and it was not reasonable for them to rely on the Council to exercise its powers to protect them from defects in their own premises.

28 It is to be noted that in *Graham Barclay Oysters* McHugh J said (at 581-582, [94]):

> I do not regard *Pyrenees* as a "control" case. Rather it is a case where the Council came under a duty of care because it knew of the risk of harm to specific individuals, it had power to take steps to eliminate the risk and importantly, at an earlier stage, had given directions to eliminate the risk.

29 What is the relevance of the earlier giving of directions? If *Pyrenees* was not a "control" case, the giving of directions, on the *Sutherland Shire Council v Heyman* (1985) 157 CLR 424 analysis, could only attract a duty of care if they created a danger or gave rise to reliance.

Amaca v NSW cont.

30 The remarks of McHugh J in *Graham Barclay Oysters* cast light on what his Honour meant in *Pyrenees* when he referred to the importance to be attributed to the Council's actions in giving directions to eliminate the risk. His Honour said (at 580, [91]):

> The powers and functions of the government of a polity are generally invested for the benefit of the general public. In the absence of a statutory direction, the mere existence of such a power in that government imposes no duty to exercise it for the protection of others. In that respect, its situation is analogous to a private citizen who, absent special circumstances, has no duty to take affirmative action to protect another person from harm ... Nor does the bare fact that the Executive government has exercised its powers from time to time create any duty to exercise its powers. Such exercises of power do not constitute "control" of an activity in the sense that that expression is used in the law of torts. They are merely particular exercises of powers that were invested in the Executive government for the benefit of the general public to be exercised at the discretion of the Executive government. Unless a particular exercise of power has increased the risk of harm to an individual, the Executive government of a polity does not ordinarily owe any common law duty to take reasonable care as to when and how it exercises its powers. No doubt circumstances may arise where conduct of the government, short of increasing a risk of harm, creates a duty of care. But such cases are less likely to arise than in the case of other public authorities. In particular, knowledge of specific risks of harm or the exercise of powers in particular situations is less likely to be a factor in creating a duty than in the case of an ordinary public authority. This is because the powers and functions of the Executive government are conferred for the benefit of the public generally and not for the benefit of individuals.

Despite his Honour's view that, generally, no duty of care arises from the mere exercise of powers, McHugh J appears to recognise the possibility (albeit an unlikely one) of "conduct of the government, short of increasing a risk of harm, creat[ing] a duty of care".

31 In summary, the first strand of the reasoning in *Pyrenees* emphasises the sole and actual knowledge of the Council of the risk of serious harm to identifiable individuals, the power of the Council to intervene, and the prior (but inadequate) intervention by the Council to eliminate the risk.

32 The second strand in *Pyrenees* is exemplified by the following remarks of Gummow J (at 389, [168]):

> The Shire had statutory powers, exercisable from time to time, to pursue the prevention of fire at No 70 [Neill Street]. This statutory enablement of the Shire "facilitate[d] the existence of a common law duty of care" (*Sutherland Shire Council v Heyman* (1985) 157 CLR 424 at 460), but the touchstone of what I would hold to be its duty was the Shire's measure of control of the situation including its knowledge, not shared by [the tenants] or by the Days, that, if the situation were not remedied, the possibility of fire was great and damage to the whole row of shops might ensue (cf *Parramatta City Council v Lutz* (1988) 12 NSWLR 293 at 328). The Shire had a duty of care "to safeguard others from a grave danger of serious harm", in circumstances where it was "responsible for its continued existence and [was] aware of the likelihood of others coming into proximity of the danger and [had] the means of preventing it or of averting the danger or of bringing it to their knowledge" [citation omitted].

33 The reference by Gummow J to the passage in *Sutherland Shire Council v Heyman* (1985) 157 CLR 424 at 460 is important as it indicates how the "statutory enablement of the Shire" could facilitate the existence of a common law duty of care. ...

35 Gummow J repeated [his] emphasis [on the control factor in *Pyrenees*] in *Crimmins* where his Honour J said (at 61, [166]) that in some cases:

> the powers vested by statute in a public authority may give to it such a significant and special measure of control over the safety of the person or property of the plaintiff as to oblige it to

> exercise its powers to avert danger or to bring the danger to the knowledge of the plaintiff. The powers of the appellant with respect to fire prevention in *Pyrenees Shire Council v Day* … were in this category

36 As I understand his Honour's remarks, the measure of control exercisable by the Council in *Pyrenees* was "significant and special" because of the sole and actual knowledge that the Council had of the risk, coupled with the particular powers it had which, if exercised, would have prevented the materialisation of the risk. …

38 Thus, the second strand of the reasoning in *Pyrenees* based the recognition of a duty of care on the part of the Council on a significant and special measure of control, a degree of seriousness of the risk, and a vulnerability of the owners and occupiers of the premises.

39 The differences between the two strands are not of major significance and are basically matters of emphasis.

40 I turn now to *Crimmins* … [The judge set out the facts and holdings] …

47 Gaudron J based her finding (that a duty of care existed) on similar grounds. Her Honour emphasised the casual nature of Mr Crimmins' employment, the lack of incentive to his employers to take care for his safety, the hazardous nature of the work, the Authority's knowledge of the hazards of asbestos, the fact that the Authority was in a position to take various steps (short of making orders having the force of law) to control or minimise those risks, and the powerful degree of control the Authority could exercise over workers and employers, including the power to register employers, to apply to the Commonwealth Industrial Court for their de-registration and to institute proceedings against an employer for statutory offences.

48 There is one other aspect of her Honour's reasons to which I should draw attention. Her Honour said (at 20-21, [31]-[32]):

> Different considerations apply with respect to the Authority's power under s 18(1) of the [*Industry Act*] to make orders, although not its power to "do all such other things, as [the Authority thought] fit". The power to do all such other things as the Authority thought fit necessarily extended to doing those things that were essential for and, also, those things that were conducive to the performance of its functions … And unlike the power to make orders, the power to do those things was not confined by succeeding sub-sections requiring consultations with interested organisations. There is, thus, nothing in the [*Industry Act*] to exclude the common law in relation to the power to "do all such other things, as [the Authority thought] fit".
>
> The critical consideration in relation to the Authority's order-making power under s 18(1) of the [*Industry Act*] is that, if made, orders would have had the force of law (s 20(1)(c) of the [*Industry Act*]. It is, thus, appropriate to characterise the power to make orders as legislative in nature. There is considerable incongruity in the notion that the common law might impose a duty of care in relation to the exercise or non-exercise of a power that is legislative in nature … Indeed, so incongruous is that notion that I am of the view that, as a matter of necessary implication, s 18 is to be construed as excluding the operation of the common law in relation to the Authority's exercise or non-exercise of its power to make orders.

49 Hayne J was of a similar view …

50 I find it difficult to draw any material distinction between the powers of the Authority in *Crimmins* to make orders and the power of the State in the present case to give directions under s 15 of the *Scaffolding and Lifts Act 1912*. Counsel did not pay particular attention to this point, however, and as a decision on the issue is not essential to the final conclusion to which I have come, I shall say no more about it.

51 As I have mentioned, Gummow J (at 61, [166]) observed that "[In some cases] the powers vested by statute in a public authority may give to it such a significant and special measure of control

Amaca v NSW cont.

over the safety of the person or property of the plaintiff as to oblige it to exercise its powers to avert danger or to bring the danger to the knowledge of the plaintiff." ...

53 *Crimmins* has always been regarded as a "very special" case. There can be little doubt that it has to be regarded as a "control" case of a unique kind. Its uniqueness lies in the degree of control that the Authority had over the actual entering into of contracts of employment, the conditions of work, and the conduct of both workers and employers. The vulnerability of the workers has also to be regarded as "special". Their very employment in practical terms was in the hands of the Authority and they were only casual workers with relatively weak bargaining power.

54 Before going to *Graham Barclay Oysters* it is worth noting that in *Brodie v Singleton Shire Council* (2001) 206 CLR 512 (the next High Court decision dealing with the negligent exercise of statutory powers) Gaudron, McHugh and Gummow JJ, after referring to *Sutherland Shire Council v Heyman* (1985) 157 CLR 424, *Pyrenees*, and *Crimmins* adopted the test of a "significant and special measure of control" (the phrase used by Gummow J in *Crimmins* (at 61, [166])....

55 I now turn to *Graham Barclay Oysters* itself... The High Court held that neither the Council nor the State owed a duty of care to the plaintiffs. The members of the High Court (by reason of the facts of the case) drew virtually no distinction between the position of the Council and the State. Generally, the Court held, as the headnote states, that:

> Government decisions about the proper extent of regulation of private or commercial behaviour, or of a particular industry, are inappropriate for judicial review.

It is, however, helpful to refer to some of the other grounds on which their Honours based their decisions.

56 Gleeson CJ held that the statutory powers on which the plaintiffs relied for their case against the State [and the Council] were powers to protect the general public ...

57 McHugh J observed, generally (at 576, [81]):

> A public authority has no duty to take reasonable care to protect other persons merely because the legislature has invested it with a power whose exercise could prevent harm to those persons. Thus, in most cases, a public authority will not be in breach of a common law duty by failing to exercise a discretionary power that is vested in it for the benefit of the general public ... But if the authority has used its powers to intervene in a field of activity and increased the risk of harm to persons, it will ordinarily come under a duty of care ... So also, if it knows or ought to know that a member of the public relies on it to exercise its power to protect his or her interests, the common law may impose a duty of care on the authority (*Sutherland Shire Council v Heyman* at 461, per Mason J).

58 McHugh J also found that the powers of the State did not constitute control in the relevant sense (at 581, [93]). Of significance to the present appeal is his Honour's remark (at 582, [95]): "Knowledge or imputed knowledge that harm may result from a failure to take affirmative action is not itself sufficient to create an affirmative duty of care".

59 Gummow and Hayne JJ regarded two factors as being of vital importance (see at 596, [144]). First, the fact that the Council (like the Council in *Pyrenees*) was the only party with actual knowledge of the potential source of harm (namely, the progressive deterioration of the sewerage infrastructure which imperilled the purity of the waters of Wallis Lake). Secondly, the fact that the Council had extensive statutory powers to prevent or to redress that deterioration and to mitigate the effects of any pollution. Their Honours said (at 596, [145]):

> [T]he co-existence of knowledge of a risk of harm and power to avert or to minimise that harm does not, without more, give rise to a duty of care at common law. The totality of the relationship between the parties, not merely the foresight and capacity to act on the part of one of them, is the proper basis upon which a duty of care may be recognised. Were it

Amaca v NSW cont.

> otherwise, any recipient of statutory powers to licence, supervise or compel conduct in a given field, would, upon gaining foresight of some relevant risk, owe a duty of care to those ultimately threatened by that risk to act to prevent or minimise it.

I would pause to note that these comments apply squarely to the present case.

60 Their Honours emphasised the importance of the particular terms of the statutory regime applicable...

61 Their Honours then referred to the importance of the existence of third parties, particularly commercial enterprises, constituting a tier of potential liability between the injured plaintiff and the local authority. ...

...

64 ... A duty of care was recognised in *Pyrenees* and *Crimmins* because of the exceptional circumstances in each; not because a radically new principle was laid down.

65 In summary, the following propositions can be drawn from *Pyrenees*, *Crimmins* and *Graham Barclay Oysters*:

(a) The totality of the relationship between the parties is the proper basis for the determination of a duty of care.

(b) The category of control that may contribute to the existence of a duty of care to exercise statutory powers includes control, generally, of any situation that contains within it a risk of harm to others.

(c) A duty of care does not arise merely because an authority has statutory powers, the exercise of which might prevent harm to others.

(d) The existence of statutory powers and the mere prior exercise of those powers from time to time do not, without more, create a duty to exercise those powers in the future.

(e) Knowledge that harm may result from a failure to exercise statutory powers is not itself sufficient to create a duty of care ...

The importance of actual knowledge of the risk

137 I will assume, nevertheless, that the State, at all relevant times, had actual knowledge of the risk of serious harm from asbestos dust to the workers on the power station site. I would note, in passing, that, were the issue of knowledge to become determinative (and that might be the case were the matter to be remitted to the Dust Diseases Tribunal for further factual findings), it would be important for a decision to be made as to whether the State had actual knowledge or imputed knowledge (or, whether the State had no knowledge whatever). ...

Did the State owe Mr Hay a duty of care?

140 I start the inquiry from the standpoint that, generally, a public authority, which is under no statutory obligation to exercise a power, owes no common law duty of care to do so. A common law duty of care will, however, arise when an authority, by its conduct, acts in a manner that requires the exercise of the power. The totality of the relationship between the parties has to be taken into account in determining whether a duty of care is to be recognised. The mere fact that statutory powers are provided and the authority concerned knows that harm may result from a failure to take affirmative action is insufficient to create an affirmative duty of care.

141 None of the specific exceptional categories identified in *Sutherland Shire Council v Heyman* (1985) 157 CLR 424 are categories into which the circumstances of this case fall. James Hardie's argument, however, is that the State attracted a duty of care, as the circumstances of the case are analogous to those in *Pyrenees*, or in *Crimmins*.

Amaca v NSW cont.

142 There was, undoubtedly, a power on the part of the State to direct Mr Hay's employer, Rolls Royce, to take appropriate remedial steps to prevent the inhalation by Mr Hay of asbestos dust. But the power of the State in this respect and the degree of control exercised by it differed significantly from the control exercisable by the Council in *Pyrenees* and the Authority in *Crimmins*.

143 The State was not the sole entity with knowledge of the potential dangers of the asbestos dust on the power station site. Rolls Royce and James Hardie (and, presumably, Pacific Power) had no less knowledge than the State. This fundamentally distinguishes this case from *Pyrenees*.

144 The control exercised by the State in this case came nowhere near the extraordinary degree of control exercisable by the Authority in *Crimmins*. The two are not comparable. The State had no power to direct Mr Hay where to work, and did not direct Mr Hay to work in a transient and casual employment – factors regarded in *Crimmins* as being of great importance. Mr Hay was not working in an industry that was a "uniquely organised one" (per Callinan J in *Graham Barclay Oysters* at 663, [317]).

145 Moreover, in this case, the State was empowered to regulate conduct in a situation where, in the words of Gummow and Hayne JJ in *Graham Barclay Oysters* (at 596, [145]), the field of endeavour was "populated by self-interested commercial actors who themselves possess some power to avert those risks". Rolls Royce and James Hardie, themselves, had ample power to avert the risks. The position of Pacific Power must also be taken into account (bearing in mind that it, too, was held liable to Mr Hay).

146 There was a tier of commercial entities in whom primary control over the activities of Mr Hay (in the case of Rolls Royce) and the hazardous products with which he was required to work (in the case of Rolls Royce and James Hardie) was vested.

147 Rolls Royce as employer owed Mr Hay the ordinary duty to provide a safe system of work. This duty of care is fundamental to the employment relationship. Rolls Royce had day-to-day control over the workplace and intimate and direct knowledge of what was taking place on site. Rolls Royce controlled and directed the activities of Mr Hay himself. The State did not have that degree of power and control. The practical capacity of the State to prevent danger to Mr Hay was substantially less than that of Rolls Royce. James Hardie, as manufacturer and supplier of the asbestos product, also had greater practical capacity than the State to prevent harm to Mr Hay. So had Pacific Power, as owner and occupier of the power station site.

148 I come to the issue of prior intervention to eliminate the risk.

... [I]n *Pyrenees*, in addition to the inspection by the Council, there had been a positive exercise of its powers to compel affirmative action (an exercise that proved to be inadequate).

152 In the present case, Mr Douglas argued that the State had "embarked upon the exercise of their powers by going along and inspecting [the premises and] getting a report". By the "report" he was referring to the Jones report. He submitted that the Jones report was a "warning signal like the letter in *Pyrenees*".

153 The Jones report, however, was not akin to the letter to the Council in *Pyrenees*. Although it set out recommendations (that were not implemented), it was not a document that called for or was capable of compelling affirmative action on the part of Rolls Royce or anyone else. It was not a statutory direction to eliminate the risk (as the letter in *Pyrenees* was).

154 The acts of the State relied on by James Hardie did not increase the risk of harm to any person, and did not engender in any relevant person a sense of reliance on the State. In my view, they are not of particular significance in determining whether a duty of care arose.

155 There are other factors that militate against the recognition of a duty of care in this case.

156 As in *Graham Barclay Oysters*, this is a case "where the duty allegedly is owed not to industry participants but to the ultimate consumer" (see Gummow and Hayne JJ at 596, [144-145] and 610,

[185]). This is, in itself, a factor to be taken into account. The reality is that, practically speaking, the State can only be liable if the employer is liable. The claim by James Hardie is an attempt by the manufacturer and supplier, a party directly responsible (with others) for the injury suffered by Mr Hay, to redirect the cost to it of having to pay part of Mr Hay's damages ...

157 In *Woolcock Street Investments* Gleeson CJ, Gummow, Hayne and Heydon JJ said in regard to the vulnerability of a plaintiff in cases where a duty of care to avoid economic loss has been held to have been owed (at [23]): ...

> Plaintiffs in circumstances such as the present would be able to protect themselves from the consequences of the State's want of reasonable care by relying on and claiming from those primarily responsible for the loss, namely, their employers, the suppliers and the owners and occupiers of the property involved.

158 Recognition of a duty of care in the present case would render the State liable to a "massive obligation" (per Callinan J in *Graham Barclay Oysters* at 665, [324]). The massive obligation would flow from the State being seen as potentially liable for failure to exercise its statutory powers whenever it has or ought to have knowledge that a work site is hazardous to workers, or that workers are working in conditions that could cause them harm. In other words, on James Hardie's argument, liability might attach to the State every time a worker is injured in circumstances where the State knew or ought to have known of the dangers on the site to which the worker might be exposed. That is going far indeed, and a finding of a duty of care that would lead to the incurring of extensive obligations in a multitude of situations is, to paraphrase Callinan J in *Graham Barclay Oysters* (at 665, [324]), a relevant and important circumstance that, although not decisive, weighs in the balance....

159 A further factor is that the duty contended for is a duty to control the conduct of third persons. As was said in *Woolcock Street Investments* by Gleeson CJ, Gummow, Hayne and Heydon JJ (at [89]): "The common law has always been reluctant to impose a duty to control others."

160 In *Parramatta City Council v Lutz* (1988) 12 NSWLR 293 Kirby P referred (at 308) to the judgment of the Privy Council in *Rowling v Takaro Properties Limited* [1988] AC 473. In that case Lord Keith referred to the danger of imposing excessive burdens on public authorities....

A finding that there is a duty of care may lead to the giving of premature and unnecessary directions and would be an incentive to not inspect particular buildings where it is known that hazards to workers are not self-evident and may be hard to find.

162 In all the circumstances I do not think that a duty of care as contended for by James Hardie should be imposed (that is, even assuming actual knowledge of the State at all relevant times of the possibility that a brief exposure to asbestos might cause the workers serious harm).

[Mason P and McColl JA agreed with Ipp JA.]

[11.40] **Notes&Questions**

1. Although special and general reliance have been rejected as doctrines the facts that contributed to those doctrines remain very important in considering the existence of a duty of care in relation to a public authority. Similarly, although the policy/operation distinction appears to have been rejected, it is still clear that at the breach stage questions of allocation of resources remain important in considering how a "reasonable public authority" would behave. See Chapter 12 Breach of Duty.
2. In *Pyrenees Shire Council v Day* (1998) 192 CLR 330, a duty arose partly because the council had begun to Act (by notifying of the chimney defect) but had not gone any

further. This has been nullified by the CLA: NSW, s 46 (exercise of function or decision to exercise does not create duty). This provision also exists in the ACT: CLWA, s 114, Vic: WrA, s 85; Tas: CLA, s 43 and WA: CLA, s 5AA.

3. Highway authorities are a particular class of public authorities to whom special rules previously applied. In nuisance and negligence, a highway authority was liable only for a wrongful act (misfeasance), and not for the failure to act (non-feasance). Traditionally, highway authorities were regarded as immune from negligence with respect to omissions. In other words the fact that a road had not been repaired was not something that a highway authority could be held liable for. This meant that if a person was harmed because the highway authority was excavating a hole in the road they could be held to owe a duty of care to road users, but if the hole in the road had just developed over time, the highway authority was not responsible for any harm caused by it. Needless to say the distinction was not always clear and was regarded as somewhat artificial. This rule was rejected by the High Court in *Brodie v Singleton Shire Council* (2001) 206 CLR 512 and *Ghantous v Hawkesbury Shire Council* (2001) 206 CLR 512. It has been reinstated by the Civil Liability Acts in most jurisdictions.

PUBLIC AUTHORITIES' LIABILITY AND THE CIVIL LIABILITY LEGISLATION

The aims of the legislation

[11.45] So far we have considered the common law approach to the liability of public authorities. The Negligence Review Panel's (the Ipp Committee) recommendations in relation to public authorities were aimed at reducing the liability of public authorities by making them responsible for negligence only if their acts were so unreasonable that no reasonable public functionary could have made it (see [11.80] Note 1). They saw this as a defence to be used where appropriate, but they did not define the limits of this defence, preferring to leave that to the judiciary. The legislation as it was drafted, however, went further than the committee had suggested, although it drew on some of the recommendations, including the unreasonableness point. The Committee's formulation of the wording was picked up by most of the jurisdictions: see NSW: CLA, ss 42 – 45; Vic: WrA, ss 83 – 85; Qld: CLA, ss 35 – 37; WA: CLA, ss 5W – 5Z, 5AA; ACT: CLWA, ss 110 – 114; Tas: CLA, s 40(2)). The phrase "so unreasonable that ..." referred to above is intended to refer to the administrative law concept known as "Wednesbury unreasonableness". This comes from *Associated Provincial Picture Houses Ltd v Wednesbury Corporation* [1948] 1 AC 223. In that case a local authority had the power to permit Sunday opening of cinemas on certain conditions as it saw fit. It imposed a condition that no child under fifteen would be admitted to any showing at the cinema. The court refused to interfere on the basis that this was not so unreasonable as to amount to something no public authority could think proper. According to de Smith and Brazier in *Constitutional and Administrative Law* (6th ed, 1989, p 579) "[t]his seems to suggest that only a preposterous decision ('something overwhelming') could be successfully impugned on its merits".

However, many of the jurisdictions have used this wording, For example, Vic: WrA, s 84(2) provides:

> an act or omission of the public authority relating to a function conferred on the public authority specifically in its capacity as a public authority does not constitute a breach of

> statutory duty unless the act or omission was in the circumstances so unreasonable that no public authority having the functions of the authority in question could properly consider the act or omission to be a reasonable exercise of its functions.

Similar provisions exist in other jurisdictions: ACT: CLWA, s 111; Qld: CLA, s 36; Tas: CLA, s 40(2); Vic: WrA, s 84(2).

We have yet to see how the courts respond to these provisions which all refer to breach of statutory duty. It is not clear whether the provisions refer to the tort of breach of statutory duty which is discussed in Chapter 17 or to the significance of the breach of a statute in the tort of negligence. It seems likely to be the latter since breach of statutory duty is normally regarded as a strict liability tort. Many of the jurisdictions also have another provision using the *Wednesbury* formulation which does not mention breach of statutory duty. For example, NSW: CLA, s 43A provides for proceedings against public or other authorities for the exercise of special statutory powers (see also WA: CLA, s 5X and see Chapter 17 Statutory Duties). This is discussed further below.

The Ipp Committee suggested an express statement of the approach to public authorities should be as follows:

> A public functionary can be liable for damages for personal injury or death caused by the negligent exercise or non-exercise of a statutory public function only if the provisions and policy of the relevant statute are compatible with the existence of such liability. (Negligence Review Panel, *Review of the Law of Negligence, Final Report* (Commonwealth of Australia, Canberra, 2002), recommendation 41.)

This has been taken up by Victoria and Western Australia (Vic: WrA, s 84: WA: CLA, s 5Y) but different provisions have been enacted by New South Wales, Tasmania and the Australian Capital Territory (NSW: CLA, s 46; Tas: CLA, s 40; ACT: CLWA, s 110).

Despite the changes to the law made by the legislation it is still important to note that it was enacted on the basis of the background of the common law. It is not possible to approach the issue of liability of public authorities in negligence under the legislation without an understanding and continuing consideration of the common law authorities which we have reviewed.

Who or what is a public authority?

[11.50] The reform provisions vary across the jurisdictions. One matter which varies considerably is the class of bodies or people regarded as covered by the legislation. The broadest coverage is that of New South Wales which covers statutory authorities, governmental authorities and bodies having some sort of public function. New South Wales also has s 41(e1) which extends the definition of public or other authority to persons having "public official functions". This was enacted to extend the coverage to doctors exercising powers of detention under the *Mental Health Act 2007* (NSW). Queensland, the Australian Capital Territory, Tasmania, Western Australia and Victoria limit the protection to governmental bodies, although all the jurisdictions except Queensland allow the coverage to be extended by regulation. In New South Wales, for example, this extends the coverage of the protection to private schools.

Public functions and special statutory powers

[11.55] One of the difficulties with dealing with the notion of public authorities is that public power may be exercised by other bodies than public or governmental authorities. It is quite common for such power to be delegated to a private body or person. New South Wales has a unique provision which deals with such matters, and although it was rushed through Parliament in response to a particular case, it is an interesting provision. The case was *Presland v Hunter Area Health Service* [2003] NSWSC 754 in which a man having a severe psychotic episode was negligently released by a psychiatrist whereupon he went home and murdered his brother's fiancé. He later sued the psychiatrist for the time he spent as a forensic patient. He won at first instance, and although this was reversed in the Court of Appeal ((2005) 63 NSWLR 22) this was seen as an attempt to profit from his crime and the parliament passed s 43A NSW: CLA in response. It makes it impossible to sue a person exercising "special statutory powers" unless gross negligence can be established, thus reducing their standard of care. A person exercising "special statutory powers" clearly includes psychiatrists operating under the *Mental Health Act 2007*, but it also may include persons such as prison guards and others who meet the definition of exercising a "special statutory power" which is a power that people are not normally allowed to exercise unless they have specific statutory power to do so.

Section 43A was considered in *Precision Products (NSW) Ltd v Hawkesbury City Council* [2008] NSWCA 278. There the special statutory power purported to be exercised but had been exercised invalidly. Allsop P (with whom Beazley and McColl JJA agreed) said that it was not clear whether s 43A was an immunity, or whether it affects the duty of care [171]. He noted that to confine s 43A to validly exercised statutory powers would require the exercise of particular statutory interpretation rules such as the rule that common law rights should not be cut down unnecessarily and should be read jealously. However, if s 43A was to be seen as affecting purported exercise of powers then some other limiting factor might be needed, such as bona fide attempts etc as set out by Dixon J in *R v Hickman; ex parte Fox* (1945) 70 CLR 598. He also considered the *Wednesbury* unreasonableness test and suggested that such tests are also to be found in the law of company directors and other areas of private law. In the event he did not think that here there was an act so unreasonable that no public authority could consider it to be proper exercise of the power and therefore held that it did not fall within s 43A's proviso.

Road authorities

[11.60] The reforms in the new civil liability legislation also sought to reverse the effect of the decisions in *Brodie v Singleton Shire Council* (2001) 206 CLR 512; *Ghantous v Hawkesbury Shire Council* (2001) 206 CLR 512. See [11.40] Note 3. Specific provisions for highway authorities have been made in Western Australia, New South Wales, South Australia, Queensland; Tasmania, the Australian Capital Territory and Victoria: WA: CLA, s 5Z: NSW: CLA, s 45; SA: CLA, s 42; Qld: CLA, s 37; Tas: CLA, s 42; ACT: CLWA, s 113; *Road Management Act 2004*, s 102. See also [11.80] Note 2. Thus the immunity has been reinstated. The widest ranging version of road authority immunity is in South Australia. Only the Northern Territory has not reinstated the immunity.

Allocation of resources

[11.65] In *Brodie v Singleton Shire Council* (2001) 206 CLR 512, the High Court determined that although there was not to be an immunity for non-feasance according to the old rule for highway authorities, the question of the allocation of resources (which in many cases had been the substance of the policy/operation distinction in that budgetary allocation was regarded as policy) was to be determined not as a matter of immunity but was to be considered at the breach stage. Under the CLA the question of whether it is determined at duty or breach stage was removed. Allocation of resources was not to be justiciable, at least if it could be regarded as "general": NSW: CLA, s 42(b); ACT: CLWA, s 110; Qld: CLR, s 36(b); Tas: CLA, s 38(b); WA: CLA, s 5W(b). This was tested in *NSW v Ball* [2007] NSWCA 71 where a police officer who had been working in the child sexual abuse unit alleged that as a result of insufficient resources allocated to the unit (including not enough employees to share the work or to properly investigate and prosecute offenders) he suffered psychiatric harm. The NSW Court of Appeal struck out the case on the basis that it breached s 42, rejecting his argument that this was about a specific, not a general, allocation of resources. The case was settled before reaching the High Court.

Exercise of function or decision to exercise a function

[11.70] Many actions against public authorities arise because of a failure to do something, which may in some circumstances give rise to a duty of affirmative action. Usually in order to create a duty of affirmative action, the public authority will need to have been in a position of special knowledge or where it was clear that reliance would be placed on them, or that they had assumed responsibility in some way.

In *Pyrenees Shire Council v Day* (1998) 192 CLR 330, it was significant in the establishment of the duty of care that the Council had begun to act by giving a notice that the chimney was defective. They were then held to be negligent in not going further. The duty of care arose also because of the special position of control the Council had in the circumstances. Some of the jurisdictions have passed legislation to make it clear that the fact that a public authority has exercised a function or decided to exercise a function will not create a duty of care on its own: NSW: CLA, s 46–does not create a duty: ACT: CLWA, s 114; Tas: CLA, s 43; Vic: WrA, s 85; WA: CLA, s 5AA. It is not clear that this legislation actually achieves anything, as the questions to be answered will remain those above–was the public authority in a position of special knowledge or control or assumed responsibility?

Failure to exercise a regulatory function

[11.75] Three jurisdictions have enacted legislation making it clear that failure to exercise a regulatory function will not automatically give rise to a duty of care: NSW: CLA, s 44; ACT: CLWA, s 112; Tas: CLA, s 41. As Aronson notes, this legislation "is peculiar in a number of respects. First it is largely unnecessary ... The second peculiarity ... is its link between mandamus and negligence" (M Aronson, "Government Liability in Negligence" (2008) 32(1) MULR 44 at 75). The legislation appears to require that before an action can be brought for negligence, the plaintiff must be able to show that they could get an order of mandamus (order that the authority "exercise the function"). That would mean that merely getting a court to consider it or order reconsideration would not be enough; an order for action would be required. As Aronson notes, this would mean that the plaintiffs in both *Crimmins* and *Pyrenees* would have lost.

[11.80] **Notes&Questions**

1. The *Wednesbury* unreasonableness test is a public law concept that is being imported into the private law area of tort. What is the object of such legislation and how does it compare with the common law relating to public authorities you have considered thus far?

2. What is a highway authority? Traditionally a highway was any land (usually now a road) over which all members of the public may pass: Parrish and De Mauley, *Pratt and Mackenzie's Law of Highways* (21st ed, London, Butterworths, 1967, p 3). A highway authority is therefore someone having authority over such land. Legislation may be what gives a body authority over a highway in which case, they will be a highway authority. See *Leichhardt Municipal Council v Montgomery* (2007) 233 ALR 200 where the *Roads Act 1933* (NSW) was the relevant legislation.
3. Where a roads authority has failed to carry out road work, they may not be liable unless at the time of the failure they have actual knowledge of the particular risk which might give rise to harm. Where the plaintiff fell into a pothole half a metre wide and four or five inches (10-12 cm) deep at night in a Sydney street and was badly injured, this question arose. Where street sweepers who worked for the road authority had identified the hazard (and were supposed to report such hazards to their supervisors), did actual knowledge exist? At first instance in *Roman v North Sydney Council* [2007] HCATrans 405 it was held that it did, but this was overturned on appeal in *North Sydney v Roman* [2007] NSWCA 27. The matter was settled before the High Court could look at the issue. The majority in the Court of Appeal held that the actual knowledge had to be held in the mind of the officer in the council who had the authority to carry out the repairs.
4. For further reading on this area, see J Doyle and J Redwood, "The Common Law Liability of Public Authorities: The Interface Between Public and Private Law" (1999) 7 *Tort Law Review* 30; C Harlow, *State Liability* (Oxford University Press, Oxford, 2004); M Aronson, "Government Liability in Negligence" (2008) 32(1) MULR 44; GS Watson, "Section 43A of the Civil Liability Act 2002 (NSW): Public Law Styled Immunity for the Negligence of Public and Other Authorities" (2007) 15 *Torts Law Journal* 153.

OCCUPIERS' LIABILITY

[11.85] Well before *Donoghue v Stevenson* [1932] AC 562, occupiers of land were recognised as owing some duty of care to people who legally entered onto their land. The duty owed to the entrant depended on what category of entrant they were classified as; that is, whether that person was an invitee, licensee or trespasser. How the law worked is set out in the judgment of Dixon J in *Lipman v Clendinnen* (1932) 46 CLR 550 at 554-556. That approach to the liability of occupiers was ended in Australia in two ways. First, some legislatures passed legislation that occupiers' liability was to be dealt with in the same way as general negligence law (see [11.95] Note 1), and secondly, the High Court in the case next extracted, decided that the common law of negligence subsumed the common law of occupiers' liability.

Australian Safeway Stores v Zaluzna

[11.90] *Australian Safeway Stores Pty Ltd v Zaluzna* (1987) 162 CLR 479 High Court of Australia

(footnotes omitted)

[The facts are outlined in the majority judgment.]

MASON, WILSON, DEANE and DAWSON JJ: 481 On Saturday, 20 January 1979 towards midday the respondent entered what has been described as the "foyer area" of the appellant's supermarket at

Australian Safeway Stores v Zaluzna cont.

Mount Waverley in Victoria, intending to buy some cheese. It was a rainy day and in consequence the vinyl-tiled floor of the foyer area had become wet or moist. Unfortunately, before entering the area of the supermarket where the merchandise was displayed, the respondent slipped and fell heavily on the floor. … The learned trial judge … directed himself in accordance with the classic exposition of the occupier's duty to his invitee as laid down by Willes J in *Indermaur v Dames* (1866) LR 1 CP 274. … He dismissed the respondent's action. … The Full Court … ordered a new trial. …

The recent review of relevant authority undertaken by Deane J in *Hackshaw v Shaw* (1984) 155 CLR 614 at 642-663 and Mason J in *Papatonakis* (1985) 156 CLR 7 at 14-20 prepares the way for a more definitive statement on this aspect of the law in Australia. …

[Their Honours then referred to passages in High Court judgments suggesting that the "special duties" existing in the past may survive concurrently with the general duty supported by the judgment of Mason J and Deane J and continued:]

486 … Does a theory of concurrent general and special duties, giving rise as it does to complications that raise "some intricate and possibly confusing arguments" (the Judicial Committee in *Southern Portland Cements Ltd v Cooper* (1973) 129 CLR 295; [1974] AC 623 at 309 (CLR), 645 (AC)) serve any useful purpose as the law of negligence is now understood? Is there anything to be gained by striving to perpetuate a distinction between the static condition of the land and dynamic situations affecting the land as a basis for deciding whether the special duty is more appropriate to the circumstances than the general duty? The present case illustrates the neat issue that such a question can raise: on the one hand, the appellant argues that because the condition of the floor was caused by wet weather it was unrelated to any activity of the appellant and therefore the special duty supplied the relevant test; on the other hand, it was the activity of conducting a commercial operation on the premises that provided the context for the accident and what could be more dynamic than the constant movement of rain-soaked shoppers over the floor of a supermarket on a Saturday morning? If it was always the case that the formulations of an occupier's duty in specific terms contributed to the easy ascertainment of the law there would be a case for their retention, as Wilson J acknowledged in *Papatonakis* (1985) 156 CLR 7 at 23, but the pursuit of certainty in this way loses its attraction if its attainment depends on the resolution of difficult questions based on artificial distinctions. It seems to us that the utility of the theory of concurrent duties could be accepted only if a situation could arise in which it was possible to establish a cause of action in reliance on *Indermaur v Dames* (1866) LR 1 CP 274 which could not be pursued by reference to the general duty of care postulated in *Donoghue v Stevenson* [1932] AC 562. And yet case after case affirms, as the reviews to which we have referred demonstrate, that the special duties do not travel beyond the general law of negligence. They are no more than an expression of the general law in terms appropriate to the particular situation it was designed to address. …

… 488 … We think it is wholly consistent with the trend of recent decisions of this court touching the law of negligence, both in this area of an occupier's liability towards entrants on his land and in the areas which were the subject of consideration in *San Sebastian Pty Ltd v Minister Administering the Environmental Planning and Assessment Act 1979* (1986) 68 ALR 161 and *Cook v Cook* (1986) 61 ALJR 25; 68 ALR 353 to simplify the operation of the law to accord with the statement of Deane J in *Hackshaw v Shaw* (1984) 155 CLR 614 at 662-663:

> it is not necessary in an action of negligence against an occupier, to go through the procedure of considering whether either one or other or both of a special duty qua occupier and an ordinary duty of care was owed. All that is necessary is to determine whether, in all the relevant circumstances including the fact of the defendant's occupation of premises and the manner of the plaintiff's entry upon them, the defendant owed a duty of care under the ordinary principles of negligence to the plaintiff. A prerequisite of any such duty is that there be the necessary degree of proximity of relationship. The touchstone of its existence is that

Australian Safeway Stores v Zaluzna cont.

> there be reasonable foreseeability of a real risk of injury to the visitor or to the class of person of which the visitor is a member. The measure of the discharge of the duty is what a reasonable man would, in the circumstances, do by way of response to the foreseeable risk.

In the circumstances of the present case, the fact that the respondent was a lawful entrant upon the land of the appellant establishes a relationship between them which of itself suffices to give rise to a duty on the part of the appellant to take reasonable care to avoid a foreseeable risk of injury to the respondent. There must be a new trial to determine whether the appellant was in breach of that duty.

The appeal should be dismissed.

[Brennan J dissented.]

The question of the liability of an occupier in relation to actions taken by a third party was taken up in *Modbury Triangle Shopping Centre v Anzil* (2000) 205 CLR 254 extracted in Chapter 7 at [7.130].]

[11.95] **Notes&Questions**

1. Since the events which were the subject of the action in *Zaluzna* occurred before the introduction of the *Occupiers' Liability Act 1983* (Vic) there is no reference to it in the judgments in that case. Occupiers' liability legislation now exists in ACT: CLWA (ACT)s 168; SA: CLA (SA)ss 19 – 22; Vic: WrAPt IV; and *Occupiers' Liability Act 1985*, s 5.
2. Some of the jurisdictions exclude or limit liability if the conduct of the plaintiff was the conduct of an offence. This could include trespassers. See ACT: CLWAs 94; NSW: CLA, s 54; Qld: CLA, s 45; SA: CLA, s 43; Tas: CLA, s 6; NT: PICCA, s 10. Victoria's provision is slightly different in that it simply asks the court to consider either intoxication or illegal activity when it is determining breach of duty: Vic: WrA, s 14G.
3. In *Cole v South Tweed Heads Rugby Football Club Ltd* (2004) 207 ALR 52 the appellant had attended a breakfast at the respondent Club where free alcohol was provided and continued to drink by purchasing alcohol further into the afternoon. At 3 pm the club refused to serve her and at 5.30 pm asked her to leave and offered her a complimentary transfer bus or taxi. She refused the offer and left the club whereupon she was struck by a car as she walked along the edge of the highway about 100 metres from the club. The trial judge held the Club liable in negligence as to 40%, the driver 30% and Ms Cole was contributorily negligent as to 30% of the damage. The finding of negligence by the Club was struck down in the Court of Appeal. The High Court held, by a majority of 4:2 that the appeal of Ms Cole against the Court of Appeal's determination should be dismissed, there being no breach of the relevant duty of care. The Chief Justice held that there was no duty of care to protect the appellant from personal injury caused by excessive consumption of alcohol; Callinan J similarly thought there was no duty. Gummow and Hayne JJ did not discuss the question of duty but held there was no breach because of the club's offer to give her safe transport home. McHugh and Kirby JJ held there was a duty but dissented on the question of breach. McHugh J said (at [30-31]):

   > The common law has long recognised that the occupier of premises owes a duty to take reasonable care for the safety of those who enter the premises. That duty arises from the occupation of premises. Occupation carries with it a right of control over the premises

> and those who enter them. Unless an entrant has a proprietary right to be on the premises, the occupier can turn out or exclude any entrant–even an entrant who enters under a contractual right. Breach of such a contract will give an entrant a right to damages but not a right to stay on the premises.
>
> The duty of an occupier is not confined to protecting entrants against injury from static defects in the premises. It extends to the protection of injury from all the activities on the premises. Hence a licensed club's duty to its members and customers is not confined to taking reasonable care to protect them from injury arising out of the use of the premises and facilities of the club. It extends to protecting them from injury from activities carried on at the club including the sale or supply of food and beverages. In principle, the duty to protect members and customers from injury as a result of consuming beverages must extend to protecting them from all injuries resulting from the ingestion of beverages. It must extend to injury that is causally connected to ingesting beverages as well as to internal injury that is the result of deleterious material, carelessly added to the beverages.

See R Dixon and J Spinak, "Common Law Liability of Clubs for Injury to Intoxicated Patrons: *Cole v South Tweed Heads Rugby League Football Club Ltd*" (2004) 27(3) UNSWLJ 816; G Orr and G Dale, "Impaired Judgments? Alcohol Server Liability and "Personal Responsibility" after *Coles v South Tweed Heads Rugby League Football Club Ltd*" (2005) 13(2) *Torts Law Journal* 103.

4. What is the difference between the landlord's liability and an occupier's liability? Consider the situation in *Jones v Bartlett* (2000) 205 CLR 166 (extracted at [9.50]) as between the tenants of the house and their adult son who was injured on the premises? What duty did they owe him as occupiers of the premises? How different would that be if the person had come to their home for the first time?

5. The defendant held a garage sale at her home. To see the goods, people had to walk down the concrete driveway. The plaintiff did so and tripped on a piece of concrete sticking up about 10-12 mm from its neighbouring concrete. She was injured. There was no question but that a duty of care was owed by the occupier to the plaintiff. The main issue was the standard of care: *Neindorf v Junkovic* (2005) 222 ALR 631. See Chapter 12 Breach of Duty.

PROFESSIONALS

[11.100] The duty of care owed by professionals is generally not a distinct duty, but does raise some issues about the duty of care. The particular profession of a defendant may alter the kind of tests needing to be met to establish a duty of care. Professional advice raises the issues of negligent misstatement, which are canvassed in Chapter 10. The civil liability legislation has directed significant attention to issues relating to professionals, although the legislation does not define professional in most States. Queensland, Victoria and Tasmania give circular definitions ("a professional means a person practising a profession"; Qld: CLA, s 20; Vic: WrA, s 57; Tas: CLA, s 22 similar. Western Australia, however, focuses the duty here on health professionals and, in CLA, s 5PA gives a non-exclusive list of health professionals covered by the legislation. However, most of the issues concerning professionals turn on the standard of care and will be considered in Chapter 12 Breach of Duty.

Note also that most jurisdictions have Professional Standards Acts (PSA), which were passed after 2002: ACT: CLWA, Sch 4; *Professional Standards Act 2004* (NSW); *Professional Standards Act* (NT); *Professional Standards Act 2004* (Qld); *Professional Standards Act 2004*

(SA); *Professional Standards Act 2005* (Tas); *Professional Standards Act 2003* (Vic); *Professional Standards Act 1997* (WA). These Acts are expressly designed to limit liability of professionals in an occupational group. They do not apply to personal injury or death, fraud or bad faith but they do apply to pure economic loss.

Medical practitioners

[11.105] Where the defendant is a medical practitioner some different considerations arise, and this has been considered in some of the new Civil Liability Act regimes, in particular in relation to the duty to inform. There is no difficulty in establishing that a doctor owes a duty of care to a patient. This duty is a broad one "covering all the ways in which a doctor is called upon to exercise his skill and judgment" (*Sidaway v Governors of Bethlem Royal Hospital* [1985] AC 871 Lord Diplock at 893). Thus, it includes a duty to warn of risks or advise (*Rogers v Whitaker* (1992) 175 CLR 479). In *Rogers v Whitaker* (1992) 175 CLR 479, the scope of this duty was said to be based on the patient's view of whether the risk was material. By contrast, in the civil liability legislation, for example in New South Wales, the standard of care owed by professionals is limited to acting "in a manner that (at the time the service was provided) was widely accepted in Australia by peer professional opinion as competent professional practice" (NSW: CLA, s 5O). There is an exception if the court considers the opinion irrational (NSW: CLA, 5O(2)). However, the Act expressly states that this part of the Act does not apply to the duty to warn of risk of death of injury (NSW: CLA, s 5P). Other jurisdictions with equivalent or similar provisions are Queensland, Tasmania and Victoria (Qld: CLA s 22 (but note specific provision (s 21) about the standard of care for doctor's duty to warn); Tas: CLA, s 21 – 22 (as for Queensland); Vic: WrA, ss 59 – 60). Since the duty to warn is such a large part of the medical profession's duty these provisions are very significant. They are also examples of the crossover between duty and breach and are discussed in more detail in Chapter 12 Breach of Duty.

The duty is owed to the patient and generally not to a third party except in the rare circumstances of possible extreme danger to others caused by a patient. An example of this occurred where a general practitioner knew of his patient's HIV infection and that, because of this, he was endangering his partner. It was held that the doctor owed a duty to notify the partner: *BT v Oie* [1999] NSWSC 1082. See also *Harvey & 1 Ors v PD* [2004] NSWCA 97, where a paranoid schizophrenic had previously killed five people and it became clear that he was going to be released into the community, despite holding a continuing interest in guns and bombs. The defendant psychiatrist was held to have had a duty to make his patient's information known to protect the public (*W v Egdell* [1990] Ch 359; see also *Tarasoff v Regents of University of California* (1976) 55 P 2d 334). This duty should be distinguished from the non-delegable duty owed by a hospital to a patient. See Chapter 15 Concurrent Liability.

Because the civil liability legislation is focused on personal injury it has little to say about those professionals who may cause pure economic loss rather than personal injury (see Chapter 10).

Lawyers

[11.110] Lawyers were traditionally regarded as liable, if at all, for economic loss in contract only. This was a solicitor-only liability as clients could not contract with barristers and traditionally, barristers had immunity (discussed below at [11.120]). The question of whether a duty is owed in contract or tort or both is a significant one. It was held in *Astley v Austrust* (1999) 197 CLR 1 that the duty can be owed in both tort and contract and that the client of a solicitor, for example, may choose the most advantageous course of action. Furthermore, the duty solicitors owe has been extended beyond their contractual partners to third parties such as beneficiaries of wills: see *Hawkins v Clayton Utz* (1999) 78 ALR 69; *Ross v Caunters* [1980] Ch 297; *Watts v Public Trustee* [1980] WAR 97; *Hill v van Erp* (1997) 188 CLR 159 (see [10.50] Note 1); *White v Jones* [1995 2 AC 207. However, the High Court's emphasis in *Sullivan v Moody* (2001) 207 CLR 562 and *Perre v Apand* (1999) 198 CLR 180 that negligence should not be allowed to take over other areas of law may mean that these cases may not be followed.

As with medical practitioners, many of the issues relating to lawyers and other professionals in negligence concern breach of duty (see Chapter 12).

Where a matter could be regarded as an example of misleading and deceptive conduct, professionals such as lawyers might also be sued under ss 51A or 52 of the *Trade Practices Act 1974* (Cth). See, for example *RAIA Insurance Brokers Ltd v FAI General Insurance Co Ltd* (1983) 41 FCR 164 where insurance brokers had provided an appraisal of another insurance policy without a rational basis and *Qantas Airways Ltd v Cameron* (1996) 66 FCR 246 where an agent made an incorrect representation about which seat would be allocated to the client. In both cases, the defendants were found to have been engaged in misleading conduct.

Auditors

[11.115] The duty owed by auditors to prevent pure economic loss has been held to arise in a number of cases. For example, in the situation where the auditor certified negligently that a company was in a good financial position (their records showed a profit when in fact the company had made a loss), and in reliance on that certification, investors bought shares in the company which were not worth as much as the certification suggested, the auditors were held liable (*Caparo Industries Plc v Dickman* [1990] 2 AC 605). See *Esanda v Peat Marwick Hungerfords* (1997) 188 CLR 241, extracted at [10.20], for a similar Australian case and Chapter 10.

IMMUNE DEFENDANTS

[11.120] In Chapter 7 we discussed policy and the duty of care (at [7.165]) and considered some of the possible immunities which defendants, such as the police, may call on. Military personnel may also be immune in some circumstances. In *Shaw Savill & Albion Co Ltd v Commonwealth* (1940) 66 CLR 344 the High Court held that a naval vessel in the course of actual operations against the enemy owed no duty to private individuals. However this immunity does not apply in peacetime (*Parker v Commonwealth* (1965) 112 CLR 295; *Groves v Commonwealth* (1982) 56 ALJR 570; *Commonwealth v Connell* (1986) 5 NSWLR 218).

Some defendants clearly do have immunity from suit in negligence. These include judges for their actions while judging and the related immunity of advocates for their actions in court (*Windham v Clere* (1589) Cro Eliz 130; 78 ER 387; *Rajski v Powell* (1987) 11 NSWLR 522 and witnesses in court: *Jerom and Knight's case* (1588) 1 Leo 107; 74 ER 99; *Gibbons v Duffell* (1932) 47 CLR 520). This latter immunity has recently been abolished in both the United Kingdom (*Arthur JS Hall & Co v Simons* [2002] 1 AC 215) and New Zealand. The

Supreme Court of New Zealand considered the issue after the High Court of Australia decided in *D'Orta Ekanaike v Victoria Legal Aid* (2005) 223 CLR 1, that the immunity should remain. The New Zealand court were not convinced of the High Court's reasoning and decided unanimously that barrister's immunity should be abolished (*Chamberlains v Lai* [2006] NZSC 70). In *D'Orta Ekanaike* an applicant pleaded guilty at committal on the advice of the solicitor and barrister but then pleaded not guilty at the trial. His guilty plea was led in evidence at the trial and he was convicted. On appeal the verdict was set aside and a new trial was ordered where the evidence of the guilty plea was not admitted and he was acquitted. He sued Victoria Legal Aid and the barrister. The High Court, when the case reached it, held that the case could not be brought because barrister's immunity needed to be maintained. The argument of the court turned largely on the role of the principle of finality as part of the apparatus of the judiciary as the third arm of government. Gleeson CJ, Gummow, Hayne and Heydon JJ, in a joint judgment, observed:

> The question is not, as may be supposed, whether some special status should be accorded to advocates above that presently occupied by members of other professions. Comparisons made with other professions appear sometimes to proceed from an unstated premise that the law of negligence has been applied, or misapplied, too harshly against members of other professions, particularly in relation to factual findings about breach of duty, but that was not a matter argued in this Court and should, in any event, be put to one side. Nor does the question depend upon characterising the role which the advocate (a private practitioner) plays in the administration of justice as the performance of a public or governmental function.
>
> Rather, the central justification for the advocate's immunity is the principle that controversies, once resolved, are not to be reopened except in a few narrowly defined circumstances. This is a fundamental and pervading tenet of the judicial system, reflecting the role played by the judicial process in the government of society. If an exception to that tenet were to be created by abolishing that immunity, a peculiar type of re-litigation would arise. There would be re-litigation of a controversy (already determined) as a result of what had happened during, or in preparation for, the hearing that had been designed to quell that controversy. Moreover, it would be re-litigation of a skewed and limited kind. No argument was advanced to this Court urging the abolition of judicial or witness immunity. If those immunities remain, it follows that the re-litigation could not and would not examine the contribution of judge or witness to the events complained of, only the contribution of the advocate. An exception to the rule against the reopening of controversies would exist, but one of an inefficient and anomalous kind.

[11.125] **Notes&Questions**

1. Is the principle of finality a sufficient justification for the immunity of barristers and advocates from suit? See the discussion in *Chamberlains v Lai* [2006] NZSC 70.
2. In Chapter 7 we considered the question of public policy in the duty of care with respect to some other immune defendants. Which of these defendants' (eg, police, military etc) immunity is easiest to justify on a legal basis? On a policy basis?

RESCUERS, GOOD SAMARITANS AND VOLUNTEERS

[11.130] The common law protected rescuers from liability as a general rule (see Chapter 6) so that, unless one created the risk a person suffered from, there is no duty at common law to rescue a person. For instance, if one is walking along a river and sees a child drowning in the water, who could easily be rescued, there is no legal duty to do so, although the vast majority of people would regard this as a moral duty. The rule that there is no duty to rescue is connected to the unwillingness of the common law to recognise a duty of affirmative action. When a person did rescue another person, at common law there was a possibility that, if one commenced to rescue a person and made things worse, liability might arise. This led to some urban myths that doctors and nurses attending accidents were likely to be sued. Despite the fact that there is no evidence of any doctor or nurse in Australia being sued for first aid rendered at an accident scene, this is an area that appears to be perceived by medical practitioners as risky. The authors are not aware of any case law in Australia on the topic. In the United Kingdom it has been held that the doctor's duty in attending an emergency such as a road accident is no more than not to make the situation worse (*Capital and Counties plc v Hampshire County Council et al* [1997] 2 All ER 865). Similarly, there are few cases of volunteers being sued for injuries they cause, particularly outside the situation of office-holders in non-profit assocations (M McGregor-Lowndes and L Nguyen, "Volunteers and the New Tort Reform" (2005) 13(1) *Torts Law Journal* 41).

However, the 2002 reformers were concerned about these possibilities, and legislation aimed at "Good Samaritans" in general has recently been enacted in most jurisdictions although the Negligence Review Panel thought it was unnecessary. See ACT: CLWA, s 5; NSW: CLA, ss 56 – 57; NT: PICCA, s 8; *Law Reform Act 1995* (Qld), s 16 (medical practitioners and nurses only); SA: CLA, s 74; Tas: No relevant provision; Vic: WrA, s 31B; WA: CLA, s 5AD. A "Good Samaritan" is a person who voluntarily assists a person in an emergency. The provisions generally protect the person from liability in this situation unless the Good Samaritan caused the injury which occasioned the emergency in the first place or was intoxicated in some way at the time and failed to exercise reasonable care.

Volunteers' liability has also been limited in many jurisdictions where they have acted in good faith: *Commonwealth Volunteers Protection Act 2003* (Cth); ACT: CLWA, s 8; NSW: CLA, s 61; *Personal Injuries (Liability and Damages) Act* (NT), s 7; Qld: CLA, s 39; *Volunteers Protection Act 2001* (SA), s 4; Tas: CLA, s 47; Vic: WrA, s 37; *Volunteers (Protection from Liability) Act 2002* (WA), s 6. In most jurisdictions the liability is merely shifted to the organisation or to the State. However, the protection of the volunteer will not exist in certain circumstances, such as where they have not acted in good faith or where they are intoxicated or involved in criminal conduct, or acting outside the scope of the activity authorised by the organisation. Similarly the protection does not extend to defamation or discrimination, motor vehicle accidents or workers compensation. Jurisdictions differ so the relevant legislation should be consulted.

PARENTS AS DEFENDANTS

[11.135] The duty of care owed by a parent to a child is strictly limited. Professor Fleming observed, "[f]rom the outset, legal protection of the parental relationship was moulded by a one-sided concern for the parent's pecuniary interests" (JG Fleming, *The Law of Torts* (9th ed, LBC Information Services, Sydney, 1998), p 720). In Chapter 8 we considered aspects of the parent's duty to a child in relation to unborn children at [8.45]. Generally, parents owe no duty to a child in respect of feeding and clothing and "raising" (*Rogers v Rawlings* [1969] Qd R 262). However, they will owe a duty to drive carefully, even to a foetus (*Lynch v Lynch* (1991) 25 NSWLR 411), and a duty may arise where they create a situation of danger or increased risk for the child, such as where a father left his children in the car with matches and one of them was injured: *Dickinson v Dickinson* (1986) 3 SR WA 233; see also *Hahn v Conley*

(1971) 126 CLR 276 where a grandfather was held not to have a duty where his grandchild had called out to him from the other side of the road and he had answered, but not called her across the road.

Parents may also be vicariously liable for the acts of their children in some circumstances. See Chapter 15 Concurrent Liability.

Hahn v Conley

[11.140] *Hahn v Conley* [1971] 126 CLR 276 High Court of Australia

[A grandfather was talking to a neighbour when his granddaughter aged three, called out from across the road. It was not clear whether she called out to him or just generally, but he answered to indicate where he was, whereupon she crossed the road to him and was struck by a car and badly injured. At trial the defendant claimed an indemnity from the grandfather and the trial judge assessed him as 25% responsible for the damages. The major issue turned on the question of breach of duty, but the sections on the duty of care have been extracted here.]

BARWICK C.J: ...

9. The trial judge's finding of negligence on the part of the applicant was founded on his Honour's view that the applicant at the relevant time had assumed the charge and care of the plaintiff ...

15. There are at least three quite disparate bases selected by their Honours of the Supreme Court on which to place liability of the applicant towards the child. I emphasise "towards the child" because unless the child had a cause of action against the applicant for damages for her injuries, the respondent's claim to indemnity or contribution must fail. It is as a tortfeasor towards the child, and not as a tortfeasor towards himself, that the respondent claims against the applicant. (at 283)

16. The first of these bases about which I would wish to say something is that adopted by the Chief Justice, namely that the grandparents stood in loco parentis to the child during the weekend and that the child's parents, because of their parenthood would owe the child a legal obligation generally to take reasonable care to prevent her falling into danger. Consequently, for and during that weekend both grandparents owed the child that duty. (at 283)

17. I have examined the case law beginning with *Ash v Ash* (1696) Comb 357; Holt KB 701 90 ER 526 and 1287, which in my opinion is of no assistance in the present case, and ending with *Rogers v Rawlings* (1969) Qd R 262 .... One proposition which clearly emerges and which, in my opinion, is correct, is that, if there be a cause of action available to the child, the blood relationship of the defendant to the child will not constitute a bar to the maintenance by the child of the appropriate proceeding to enforce the cause of action. Whilst perhaps there is no clear decision of an appellate court in the United Kingdom, New Zealand or Australia to that effect, I think that the view for which there is most judicial support and the view which commends itself to me is that the moral duties of conscientious parenthood do not as such provide the child with any cause of action when they are not, or badly, performed or neglected. Further I think that the predominant judicial view to be extracted from those cases, and again a view which commends itself to me as correct is that, whilst in particular situations and because of their nature or elements, there will be a duty on the person into whose care the child has been placed and accepted to take reasonable care to protect the child against foreseeable danger, there is no general duty of care in that respect imposed by the law upon a parent simply because of the blood relationship. Also parents like strangers may become liable to the child if the child is led into danger by their actions. As a matter of principle, I find the view expressed by McCarthy J in *McCallion v Dodd* (1966) NZLR 710, at 729 acceptable. Though it may not provide a formula for solving all the problems which may arise out of parent-child relationships it does seem to me to afford a sound general approach. In the case of the parent, as in the case of a stranger it seems to me that the duty of care springs out of the particular situation: the extent and nature of the steps which it may be

Hahn v Conley cont.

necessary to take to discharge the duty may well be influenced by the fact of parenthood, though parenthood is not itself the source of the duty. … I turn then to consider whether a duty fell upon the grandfather because of the particular circumstances. In my opinion the grandfather owed no legal duty to the child to prevent her leaving the house at the time she apparently did so, even though the grandparents had assumed the place of her parents for the time being. Of course, they or one of them may have owed a duty to strangers likely to be caused injury by the wandering child. *Carmarthenshire County Council v Lewis* [1955] UKHL 2; (1955) AC 549.

But if so in particular circumstances, the child would not in my opinion necessarily have a cause of action against them or either of them. Did a situation arise in which an obligation to take care to protect the child against danger was imposed on the appellant? It is important to examine the developing events from the time the child cried out whilst near the rear of her uncle's house; the grandfather in my opinion then had no relevant legal duty towards her. However had he called her to come to him, he would have come under a duty to take reasonable care for her safety in relation to any danger to her which the crossing of the road would involve. That duty would spring in my opinion out of the fact that he beckoned her to him: or did something which he ought to have known would bring her to him. A stranger who did so could in my opinion in the same circumstances come under the same duty, if the child was likely to respond positively to his call. In the case of the applicant, this qualification is not necessary, in my opinion, because he was her grandfather. Whether or not there was then any relevant danger does not appear. There is no information as to the then state of traffic, if any, using the road in that vicinity. But, in any case, it is not clear on the evidence, and I doubt if there is really any evidence that the appellant did call the child to him. I think the predominant conclusion from the evidence is that the appellant's response to the child's cry was no more than a reassurance to her that she was not alone. The neighbour's description of the response as "natural in the circumstances" and the fact the appellant continued conversation with the neighbour - there being no suggestion of wantonness in the appellant's conduct - tend in that direction. There was therefore in my opinion no legal obligation imposed on the appellant by the situation which existed at the time of the child's cry or of the appellant's response: nor was there any relevant change in the situation until the child was seen by the appellant on the other side of the road opposite to where he then was. Accepting the trial judge's finding and the known presence of traffic then on the roadway, the appellant ought at that time to have realized the possibility of danger to the child should she attempt to cross the road. On his own statement he then contemplated crossing the road to her, no doubt as a means of protecting her. As the judge found, he had the opportunity to cross the road and to stop the child making any attempt to cross it. But did these facts impose a legal obligation upon him to go to her aid, so that upon his failure to do so with consequential damage to her, the child could have successfully sued him in tort? I think not. Whatever moral duty he may have had, and however imperative in good conscience, there was in my opinion no legal duty towards the child on which to base an action of negligence. (at 285)

19. It is said that the grandfather then assumed the charge and control of the child. How did he do so any more than did the neighbour who also saw the child and the traffic? I can see no basis for saying that he had. His blood relationship to her did not involve the conclusion that he had done so, though if there had been an ambiguous situation and material on which it could be held that the grandfather had then received the child into his care and control that blood relationship might have removed the ambiguity. (at 285)

20. It may be of course that when the grandfather saw the child opposite to him he ought to have realized that the child was intending to come towards him and that her crossing the road would have brought her into danger: and it may be that although he had not beckoned her to come to him at an earlier time and did not do so then, he might have been expected in good conscience to have gone to her, if as the trial judge found, there was opportunity for him to do so in order to prevent her entering

Hahn v Conley cont.

what might prove to be a field of danger. I leave on one side whether or not the road at that time ought to have been foreseen as dangerous to the child. But, in my opinion, neither the realization that she was intending to come to him nor that if she did so she might come to harm imposed a legal duty on the grandfather to go to her for breach of which the child could successfully sue the grandfather in tort for the whole of her injuries. To express this conclusion in the language chosen by the trial judge, by observing her on the opposite side of the road, and, if it be the fact, realizing both that she was intending to come to him and that that would bring her into danger the appellant had not taken her into his "care and control". Indeed it seems to me that the basis of the view that the appellant because of this situation was negligent is that his tort consisted in his not taking her into his care and control. In any case, in my opinion, where it is sought to make parents or blood relations liable to their children or relatives because of particular situations those who have to try the facts ought not to indulge in undue subtlety in order to create liability even in these days when the consequence of so many breaches of duty have been passed on by insurance to be borne by others. (at 286)

21. ... I am of opinion that the primary judge was in error in concluding that the applicant was in breach of any legal duty he owed the child to take reasonable care to protect her against danger. In my opinion, unless it could properly in this case be held that in substance the applicant called the child to come to him - and this was not held, nor in my opinion could it be - the applicant was not under any legal obligation to go to the assistance of the child or to take any positive steps to protect her from any danger that might be involved in crossing the road. (at 286) ...

WINDEYER J...

10. In the emphasis upon the element of duty it seemed to have been assumed that, if a duty of care existed, a breach of it was apparent. His Honour's finding that the appellant was negligent because he delayed "in taking up his responsibility" of "protecting" the child by "keeping her out of the path of traffic" seems to reflect propositions by counsel, based on dicta in judgments in other cases on different facts, that a person having a young child in his care has always an absolute obligation to prevent the child being on a highway unless accompanied by an adult. There is no such rule. A duty of care for a child is an obligation to take reasonable care in the existing circumstances. It is not an obligation to ensure the child's safety in any particular circumstances. In the present case a need, or duty, of care on the part of the appellant arose not from blood relationship or from his position in the household but from the particular situation. It was the relationship of "proximity", the facts of the occasion, which made the appellant's little granddaughter his "neighbour". Prominent among those facts was that he was not merely an onlooker, as for example was the man with whom he was conversing. He was known to the plaintiff as her grandfather and as the man who had called to her. He was aware of her presence and he knew she was aware of his. (at 294)

11. But this case is not one in which the concept of a duty of care needs to be considered as a separate element in an action of negligence. Negligence is not established by shewing that a duty of care existed, but by shewing a culpable carelessness in breach of that duty. Can it be said that the appellant was blameworthy for the accident? Did he fail to take precautions which he should have taken against a danger that he had foreseen or ought to have foreseen? His Honour found that he was not aware that the child was in danger until he saw her running towards him as the vehicle was approaching. The accident then happened because a vehicle was being negligently driven. There is no evidence that motor traffic on the road was so frequent that any crossing must have been hazardous. If the appellant had gone to the child when he first saw her, she would not have been hurt. When he decided to do so it was too late. But he is not to be said to be a tortfeasor simply because he did not prevent the accident. ...

Hahn v Conley cont.

[McTiernan J agreed with the Chief Justice and Windeyer J that the appeal should be allowed. Walsh and Menzies JJ disagreed on the question of breach and thought the appeal should be dismissed.]

EMPLOYERS, SCHOOLS, HOSPITALS

[11.145] Where an employee is injured at work he or she is generally entitled to workers' compensation and may have to choose between workers' compensation and damages in negligence. In negligence the general duty of employers to employees is a duty to provide them with a safe system of work. In *Wilson's and Clyde Coal Co Ltd v English* [1938] AC 57 at 78, Lord Wright classified this into three: "the provision of a competent staff of men, adequate material, and a proper system and effective supervision". This is now regarded as a single duty. This duty is a personal or non-delegable duty, so that the employer cannot merely declare that he or she has given the job to someone else: *Kondis v State Transport Authority* (1984) 154 CLR 672.

Non-delegable (or personal) duties also exist in some other situations where people are seen as particularly vulnerable. Thus, schools are regarded as owing a non-delegable duty to the children at the school: *Commonwealth v Introvigne* (1982) 150 CLR 258; and hospitals to their patients: *Allbrighton v RPAH* [1980] 2 NSWLR 542. See Chapter 15 Concurrent Liability which considers non-delegable duty and vicarious liability.

CONCLUSION

[11.150] This chapter concludes our survey of the approach to the duty of care taken by the courts. It is evident that the duty of care is not simple and where a case does not fit into a previous category of duty of care it can be extremely difficult to find an adequately principled way to determine whether the duty of care exists. The abstract nature of the duty of care and the policy issues, which necessarily occur when a "hard case" arises, make it very difficult. Clearly, the neighbour principle is the first step and at present, in Australia the courts proceed incrementally from this point, considering how salient factors arising in the case might be related to similar factors in previously recognised categories of duty of care. They also must consider policy in such a case.

However, the vast majority of cases that make their way into a solicitor's office fit into a previously defined category. It is absolutely clear, for example, that a motorist driving on the road owes a duty of care to other users of the road. In situations like this, the major issue being argued is whether or not the duty of care has been breached. The following chapters consider this issue and the consequences of any breach that may be found.

CHAPTER 12

Breach of Duty

INTRODUCTION

[12.05] To establish a breach of duty, the plaintiff must prove that the defendant's conduct fell below the required standard of care. Alderson B in *Blyth v Birmingham Waterworks Co* (1856) 11 Ex 781; 156 ER 1047 at 784 (EX 781) expressed the principle as follows:

> Negligence is the omission to do something which a reasonable man, guided upon those considerations which ordinarily regulate the conduct of human affairs, would do, or doing something which a prudent and reasonable man would not do.

The standard of care is determined by reference to the actions or omissions of a notional reasonable person (sometimes called the comparator) in the same circumstances as the defendant. The question of breach is then determined by comparing the defendant's actions in fact with those expected of the reasonable person. This involves consideration of the magnitude of the risk, the probability of its occurrence, and the burden of taking precautions to avoid the risk: *Wyong Shire Council v Shirt* (1980) 146 CLR 40 at 47-8 per Mason J. Section 48 of the *Wrongs Act 1958* (Vic), introduced as part of the civil liability reforms, reflects this notion of the reasonable person. The section mirrors the common law position, providing that:

> (1) A person is not negligent in failing to take precautions against a risk of harm unless … (c) in the circumstances, a reasonable person in the person's position would have taken those precautions.

There are comparable provisions in all jurisdictions except the Northern Territory: ACT: CLWA, s 4; NSW: CLA, s 5B; Qld: CLA, s 9(1); SA: CLA, s 32; Tas: CLA, s 11; Vic: WrA, s 48; WA: CLA, s 5B.

Notions of reasonableness vary over time and place and depend on the specific circumstances of each case. The majority judgement in *Bankstown Foundry Pty Ltd v Braistina* (1986) 160 CLR 301 (at 208-9 per Dixon CJ and Kitto J), an industrial accident case, illustrates this:

> It is unhelpful to attempt to arrive at conclusions about what changing standards of reasonable care require merely by comparing the decisions in different cases because no two cases can provide true comparability in circumstances …
>
> On the other hand, being a question of fact, it is undoubtedly true … that what reasonable care requires will vary with the advent of new methods and machines and with changing ideas of justice and increasing concern with safety in the community … What is considered to be reasonable in the circumstances of the case must be influenced by current community standards. In so far as legislative requirements touching industrial safety have become more demanding on employers, this must have its impact on community expectations of the reasonably prudent employer.

A decision that specific conduct in a given context constitutes a breach of duty does not create a precedent for other contexts, *Vairy v Wyong Shire Council* (2005) 223 CLR 422, per Gleeson CJ and Kirby J, and *Qualcast Wolverhampton Ltd v Haynes* [1959] AC 743. Breach is established once any degree of shortfall is proved.

GENERAL PRINCIPLES FOR ESTABLISHING BREACH OF DUTY

[12.10] The common law test for breach of duty in Australia was laid down by Mason J in *Wyong Shire Council v Shirt* (1980) 146 CLR 40 in these words:

> In deciding whether there has been a breach of the duty of care the tribunal of fact must first ask itself whether a reasonable man in the defendant's position would have foreseen that his conduct involved a risk of injury to the plaintiff or to a class of persons including the plaintiff. If the answer be in the affirmative, it is then for the tribunal of fact to determine what a reasonable man would do by way of response to the risk. The perception of the reasonable man's response calls for a consideration of the magnitude of the risk and the degree of the probability of its occurrence, along with the expense, difficulty and inconvenience of taking alleviating action and any other conflicting responsibilities which the defendant may have. (at 47-48)

In *NSW v Fahy* (2007) 232 CLR 486, the High Court emphasised that this remains the test for breach of duty. The civil liability legislation establishes a very similar test, with minor variations to this, although there is still some argument as to whether the test is exactly the same. The Queensland provision is extracted below. See also ACT: CLWA, s 43; NSW: CLA, s 5B; SA: CLA, s 32; Tas: CLA, s 11; Vic: WrA, s 48; WA: CLA, s 5B. There is no Northern Territory equivalent at present.

Civil Liability Act 2002 (Qld)

[12.15] *Civil Liability Act 2002* (Qld), s 9

9 General principles

(1) A person does not breach a duty to take precautions against a risk of harm unless:
   - (a) the risk was foreseeable (that is, it is a risk of which the person knew or ought reasonably to have known); and
   - (b) the risk was not insignificant; and
   - (c) in the circumstances, a reasonable person in the position of the person would have taken the precautions.

———— ꕥ ————

[12.20] The requirement, that the risk be "not insignificant", was intended to be a more stringent test than the common law position (Ipp Report, para 7.15) but most cases have treated it as the same as "not fanciful or far-fetched": *Doubleday v Kelly* [2005] NSWCA 151; *Drinkwater v Howart* [2005] NSWCA 222. The civil liability legislation has two main sections. The one above and a further section (extracted at [12.60]) which sets out what the court must take into account in deciding whether a reasonable person would have taken precautions against the risk of harm. In this chapter we examine breach using the structure now laid out in the civil liability legislation.

[12.25] **Note**

See also Negligence Review Panel, *Review of the Law of Negligence, Final Report*, (Commonwealth of Australia, Canberra, 2002) ("Ipp Report"), paras 7.5-7.19 Recommendation 28.

FORESEEABILITY OF HARM

[12.30] The concept of foreseeability operates in different ways at various stages in the proof of negligence, "progressively declin[ing] from the general to the particular" (*Minister Administering the Environmental Planning and Assessment Act 1979 v San Sebastian Pty Ltd* [1983] 2 NSWLR 268 at 295). In relation to duty, it is concerned with the foreseeability of the plaintiff; for breach, it relates to the risk of injury; and for remoteness, to the kind of damage or harm sustained by the plaintiff. In *Minister Administering the Environmental Planning and Assessment Act 1979 v San Sebastian Pty Ltd* [1983] 2 NSWLR 268 Glass JA said:

> The breach question requires proof that it was reasonably foreseeable as a possibility that the kind of carelessness charged against the defendant might cause damage of some kind to the plaintiff's person or property. Of course it must additionally be proved that a means of obviating that possibility was available and would have been adopted by a reasonable defendant. (at 295-6)

Wyong Shire Council v Shirt

[12.35] *Wyong Shire Council v Shirt* (1980) 146 CLR 40 High Court of Australia

(footnotes omitted)

[The plaintiff became a quadriplegic after striking his head on the bottom of a lake whilst water skiing. The water at that point was 3 feet 6 inches to 4 feet deep. The lake had been used for water skiing for some years despite its shallowness. Prior to the plaintiff's accident, the council had dredged deeper channels alongside a jetty, built by The Entrance Aquatic Club, to provide access for power boats involved in water skiing to the deeper parts of the lake. The plaintiff argued that he was misled into believing the lake was generally deep and safe for inexperienced skiers, by a nearby "Deep Water" sign, erected by a council engineer. The sign was one of three similar signs facing the jetty from the other side of the channel, intended to warn possible swimmers near the jetty of deep water in the channel. The water elsewhere in the vicinity was very shallow and in a number of places obviously so.

The plaintiff succeeded at first instance, the jury finding the council negligent in relation to the sign. A majority of the NSW Court of Appeal dismissed the council's appeal, Reynolds JA dissenting, and the defendant appealed to the High Court on the same issue. Two other defendants represented The Entrance Aquatic Club, whose alleged breach was failing to warn its members against possible misinterpretation of the sign. The trial judge had held that only the council owed Mr Shirt a duty of care. The Court of Appeal ordered a new trial against the club, holding that it too should have been found to owe a duty of care. The High Court (Wilson J dissenting) refused special leave to appeal against this order.]

MASON J: 44 The majority in the Court of Appeal thought that this question [of breach] should be answered in the affirmative when, as Glass JA put it: "allowance is made for the undemanding test of foreseeability" (1978) 1 NSWLR at p 641.

Glass JA described the test as "undemanding" because in his view in its application to breach of duty the test involves the defendant in liability for injury which, though foreseeable, is extremely unlikely and may be described as "only a remote possibility". His Honour specifically rejected the notion that the test denotes only events which are "likely to happen" or "not unlikely to happen". He relied on Lord Reid's observations in *Koufos v C Czarnikow Ltd* [1969] 1 AC 350, and comments made by the Judicial Committee in *The "Wagon Mound" (No 2)* [1967] 1 AC 617. But he made no reference to the opposing view expressed by Barwick CJ in *Caterson v Commissioner for Railways* (1973) 128 CLR 99 at 101-102, where the Chief Justice stated his preference for the "not unlikely to occur" formulation. ...

Notwithstanding [some] Australian support for a narrower version of the foreseeability doctrine as applied to breach of duty, this court would be well advised to accept that the law upon the point was

Wyong Shire Council v Shirt cont.

correctly stated and applied by the judicial committee in *The "Wagon Mound" (No 2)*. I say this not only because *The "Wagon Mound" (No 2)* was a unanimous decision given on appeal from the Supreme Court of New South Wales, but also because there are sound reasons for accepting it as a correct statement of the law.

In essence its correctness depends upon a recognition of the general proposition that foreseeability of the risk of injury and the likelihood of that risk occurring are two different things. I am of course referring to foreseeability in the context of breach of duty, the concept of foreseeability in connection with the existence of the duty of care involving a more generalised inquiry.

A risk of injury which is quite unlikely to occur, such as that which happened in *Bolton v Stone* (above) may nevertheless be plainly foreseeable. Consequently, when we speak of a risk of injury as being "foreseeable" we are not making any statement as to the probability or improbability of its occurrence, save that we are implicitly asserting that the risk is not one that is far-fetched or fanciful. Although it is true to say that in many cases the greater the degree of probability of the occurrence of the risk the more readily it will be perceived to be a risk, it certainly does not follow that a risk which is unlikely to occur is not foreseeable. ...

It was contended that the jury could not reasonably find that a reasonable man in McPhan's [the council engineer] circumstances would have foreseen that the message conveyed by the sign placed in the position in which it was fixed might lead to a risk of injury by inducing an inexperienced water skier unfamiliar with the area to ski in the water immediately beyond the sign in the mistaken belief that it was deep whereas in fact the depth was only 3 feet 6 inches.

Despite the force of Mr McHugh QC's argument I am not persuaded that a finding of breach of duty was beyond the jury's competence. A reasonable man might well have concluded that the sign was ambiguous and that it could be read as an indication that there was a zone of deep water beyond, rather than in front of, the sign. A reasonable man might also have concluded that a water skier, so reading the sign, might be induced to ski in that zone of water, mistakenly believing it to be deep. The possibility might also have occurred to a reasonable man that it would be unsafe for an inexperienced water skier to ski in water having a depth of 3 feet 6 inches and no more. He might well contemplate the possibility of a skier being projected into the water at a relatively high speed in consequence of a mishap and thereby sustaining injury in striking the bed of the lake.

As this is not an appeal against a finding of fact it is not for me to find that a reasonable man in McPhan's position would necessarily have foreseen the risk of injury. It is sufficient for me to say that the jury's conclusion that there was a foreseeable risk of injury was not unreasonable and that it was a conclusion which was open on the evidence. In saying this I am mindful that the foreseeability of the risk in the instant case is a question on which minds may well differ, as indeed they have done. It is not a question which a judge is necessarily better equipped to answer than a layman.

I would therefore dismiss the appeal.

[Stephen and Aickin JJ concurred in the reasoning and conclusion of Mason J. Murphy J concurred. Wilson J dissented. Appeal dismissed.]

Doubleday v Kelly

[12.40] *Doubleday v Kelly* [2005] NSWCA 151 NSW Court of Appeal

(footnotes omitted)

[The seven year old plaintiff was injured when she attempted to roller skate on a trampoline whilst staying at the defendants' house. She rolled backwards and fell off, sustaining a supra-condylar

Doubleday v Kelly cont.

fracture of the humerus (broken arm) and associated damage to the right medial nerve and brachial artery. She and the defendant's four year old daughter were unsupervised as they had gone outside to play early in the morning before the rest of the household was awake. In the District Court Blanch CJ found for the plaintiff. The defendant appealed to the Court of Appeal.]

BRYSON JA: [11] The actual events as they happened are not the circumstances to which consideration of foreseeability of risk of injury is applied; what is to be considered is foresight in more general terms of risk of injury to a child of seven if she were to use the trampoline without adult supervision: see *Chapman v Hearse* (1961) 106 CLR 112 at 120-121, *Mount Isa Mines Ltd v Pusey* (1970) 125 CLR 383 at 402, *Commonwealth of Australia v McLean* (1996) 41 NSWLR 389 at 403. The Trial Judge was correct to conclude that although, as his Honour said, "Obviously being on the trampoline with roller skates was a significant factor which led to the fall" there was a foreseeable risk of injury if the respondent were to use the trampoline at all without adult supervision. The fact that the respondent wore roller skates when she got on the trampoline is a bizarre complexity but not an important one; the risk that was foreseeable was that the child would not use the trampoline in a competent way and would injure herself by falling off, and that risk was realized.

Overall, the Trial Judge's observations mean, in my view, that it was found that a warning against using the trampoline was given to the respondent the previous night, but that this was not an adequate discharge of the duty of care ... An obvious and effective means of preventing small children from using the trampoline without supervision was to turn it over so that the jumping surface is on the ground, and to fold the legs up. A full articulation by his Honour was not necessary ...

In my opinion his Honour's conclusions were reached in accordance with the provisions of Pt 1A, including the general principles and other principles restated in ss 5B and 5C, and the general principles of causation in s 5D ...

[Young CJ in Equity, and Hunt AJA agreed with Bryson JA that the trial judge's finding of liability should be upheld. Some adjustment was made to the finding on damages.]

[12.45] **Notes&Questions**

1. Mason CJ says in *Shirt*: "I am mindful that the foreseeability of the risk in the instant case is a question on which minds may well differ, as indeed they have done. It is not a question which a judge is necessarily better equipped to answer than a layman". Do you agree with these comments? What function does the notion of foreseeability perform? Why do courts distinguish between foreseeability at the duty of care and breach stages?
2. In the context of the civil liability legislation, a "foreseeable" risk is a risk of which the defendant either knew or ought to have known. Particular or special knowledge of the risk of harm, such as the employer's knowledge in *Paris v Stepney Borough Council* [1951] AC 367 (see [12.120]) of the plaintiff's particular vulnerability to blindness because he was already blind in one eye, will be determinative of the foreseeability question. Where actual knowledge is not present, the defendant will be held to the standard of the reasonable person ("ought to have known").
3. In relation to nonfeasance by road authorities, the statutory test in most jurisdictions is actual knowledge, eg *Civil Liability Act 2002* (NSW), Pt 5 s 45. In *Roman v North Sydney Council* [2007] NSWCA 27, the NSW Court of Appeal held that such actual

knowledge had to be held by the person with the capacity to do something about it – in this case the person who could order someone to fix the pothole in the road. Constructive knowledge was not sufficient.

RESPONDING TO THE FORESEEABLE RISK

[12.50] Once the foreseeable risk is established the court must determine what the response of a reasonable person to the risk would be in the circumstances. The reasonable person test sets the standard of care, against which breach of duty is measured. Assessing what the reasonable person would have done in a given context is a far from value-neutral exercise, since it is a normative judgement which involves balancing competing interests. Reasonableness is always a question of determining the appropriate boundaries between individual and collective responsibility (via insurance and other loss spreading mechanisms) for injury and misfortune, and this is a question on which reasonable minds may well differ, ranging from requiring no action at all, to a requirement for a high level of precaution. In order to determine what the reasonable person's response would be the court is required to take into account a range of factors which we sometimes term the "calculus of negligence".

THE "CALCULUS" OF NEGLIGENCE

[12.55] As stated above, once foreseeability of "not fanciful or far-fetched" or "not insignificant" risk has been established, and it is apparent that reasonableness requires some response by the defendant, the balancing and weighing up of the various "considerations which ordinarily regulate the conduct of human affairs", is what ultimately determines the issue of breach. These considerations are what the reasonable person is expected to take into account in responding to a foreseeable risk. The balancing process is sometimes known as the "calculus of negligence", derived from the algebraic approach adopted in the American case of *United States v Carroll Towing Co.* 159 F 2d (1947. There, Learned Hand J described the level of care expected as "a function of three variables: (1) probability ... (2) the gravity of the resulting injury ... (3) the burden of adequate precautions". He later stated this approach in terms of an algebraic equation. The Australian decision of *Ryan v Fisher* (1976) 51 ALJR 125 has the same general effect. The High Court adopted a similar balancing approach in *Wyong Shire Council v Shirt* (1980) 146 CLR 40 (extracted above, [12.35]). These factors are now incorporated into the *Civil Liability Act 2002* (Qld), extracted below, and equivalent legislation, provisions of which are intended to reflect the common law position as stated in *Shirt*. See ACT: CLWA, s 43; NSW: CLA, s 5B; SA: CLA, s 32; Tas: CLA, s 11; Vic: WrA, s 48; WA: CLA, s 5B. There is no Northern Territory equivalent at present (see also, Ipp Report, paras 7.5-7.19, Recommendation 28).

Civil Liability Act 2002 (Qld)

[12.60] *Civil Liability Act 2002* (Qld), s 9(2)

9(2) In deciding whether a reasonable person would have taken precautions against a risk of harm, the court is to consider the following (among other relevant things)

(a) the probability that the harm would occur if care were not taken;

(b) the likely seriousness of the harm;

(c) the burden of taking precautions to avoid the risk of harm;

Civil Liability Act 2002 (Qld) cont.

(d) the social utility of the activity that creates the risk of harm.

[12.65] It is not clear whether the specific way the factors are set out in the civil liability legislation may have an unintended effect on the weighting of particular matters. While the list given is not exhaustive, referring to "among other relevant things", it may be that the four matters listed may come to be seen as more significant than other possible matters such as the level of knowledge existing at the time or the general circumstances applying at the time. The term "calculus" is unfortunate and misleading, see [12.90]. There is no formula or rule for deciding the weight to be given to each consideration, which will vary from case to case, depending on individual circumstances. As the decisions below illustrate, more than one factor is often emphasised, and it is somewhat arbitrary to categorise cases as illustrating one or the other. It must be emphasised that the question is always what the reasonable person would do in response to the circumstances.

Determining breach - the general approach

[12.70] The following cases are examples which show the court attempting to weigh up a range of different factors in order to determine whether the defendant has breached their duty of care. In other words, what the court is doing is trying to determine whether the defendant has acted like a reasonable person in the defendant's position. Certain matters of law are critical, such as the fact that foreseeability of harm must be assessed prospectively, that is, as circumstances were before the accident or wrong occurred.

Romeo v Conservation Commission

[12.75] *Romeo v Conservation Commission of the Northern Territory* (1998) 192 CLR 431 High Court of Australia

(footnotes partially omitted)

[The plaintiff failed at first instance, and again in the Supreme Court of the Northern Territory. She also failed in the High Court 5:2, with McHugh and Gaudron JJ dissenting. See also the extract at [8.25].]

KIRBY J:

Proper Approach and Issues

475 These proceedings therefore fall to be determined by the application of the tests accepted in *Nagle*. The way in which this Court approached the problem in *Nagle* provides a model for the way in which similar problems should be addressed in future cases where, as seems inevitable, claims by injured persons will be brought against local and other public authorities seeking damages in negligence ...

Breach of Duty

The conclusion that a duty of care is owed to a class of persons including the plaintiff, is not, of itself, determinative of the negligence of the defendant. The critical question in many cases is whether the plaintiff has proved that the duty has been breached in the circumstances of the case.

In *Wyong Shire Council v Shirt* [(1980) 146 CLR 40], Mason J expressed the test which is accepted in Australia for ascertaining whether a breach of a duty of care of the defined scope has occurred ... It

Romeo v Conservation Commission cont.

was not contested that this was the test to be applied in the present case. Thus, it is the reasonableness of a defendant's actions or inactions, when faced with the relevant risk, which is critical in determining whether a duty of care has been breached. The question whether the defendant has met the requisite standard of the reasonable person must be assessed on the facts of each case with reference to considerations such as those collected by Mason J in *Shirt*. These considerations provide a framework for determining which risks the defendant should guard against and which it can safely ignore.

Insufficient attention has been paid in some of the cases, and by some of the critics, to the practical considerations which must be "balanced out" before a breach of the duty of care may be found. It is here, in my view, that courts have both the authority and responsibility to introduce practical and sensible notions of reasonableness that will put a brake on the more extreme and unrealistic claims sometimes referred to by judicial and academic critics of this area of the law. Thus, under the consideration of the magnitude of the risk, an occupier would be entitled, in a proper case, to accept that the risk of a mishap such as occurred was so remote that "a reasonable man, careful of the safety of his neighbour, would think it right to neglect it" [*Overseas Tankship (UK) Ltd v The Miller Steamship Co Pty Ltd* [1967] 1 AC 617 at 642-643; cf *Inverell Municipal Council v Pennington* (1993) 82 LGERA 268 at 276 per Clarke JA]. It is quite wrong to read past authority as requiring that *any* reasonably foreseeable risk, however remote, must in *every* case be guarded against. Such an approach may result from the erroneous conflation of the three separate inquiries: duty, scope of duty and breach of duty. Although a reasonably forseeable risk may indeed give rise to a duty, it is the inquiry as to the scope of that duty in the circumstances and the response to the relevant risk by a reasonable person which dictates whether the risk must be guarded against to conform to legal obligations. Precautions need only be taken when that course is required by the standard of reasonableness [*Phillis v Daly* (1988) 15 NSWLR 65 at 73 per Mahoney JA]. Although it is true, as the appellant argued, that an occupier is not entitled to ignore safeguards against dangers because of the absence of past mishaps, it is equally true that years of experience without accidents may tend to confirm an occupier's assessment that the risks of harm were negligible.

As to the expense of taking alleviating action, it is increasingly recognised that courts must "bear in mind as one factor that resources available for the public service are limited and that the allocation of resources is a matter for" bodies accorded that function by law [*Knight v Home Office* [1990] 3 All ER 237 at 243 per Pill J; cf *Just v British Columbia* (1989) 64 DLR (4th) 689]. Demanding the expenditure of resources in one area (such as the fencing of promontories in natural reserves) necessarily diverts resources from other areas of equal or possibly greater priority [*Cekan v Haines* (1990) 21 NSWLR 296 at 314 per Mahoney JA; Dugdale, "Public Authority Liability: To What Standard?" (1994) 2 *Tort Law Review* 143 at 154-155]. Whilst this consideration does not expel the courts from the evaluation of what reasonableness requires in a particular case, it is undoubtedly a factor to be taken into account in making judgments which affect the operational priorities of a public authority and justify a finding that their priorities were wrong [*Swanson Estate v Canada* (1991) 80 DLR (4th) 741)] …

In the reference to "other conflicting responsibilities" regard may be had to considerations such as the preservation of the aesthetics of a natural environment [(*Phillis v Daly* (1988) 15 NSWLR 65 at 68 per Samuels JA)] and the avoidance of measures which would significantly alter the character of a natural setting at substantial cost and for an improvement in safety of negligible utility [(*South Australia v Wilmot* (1993) 62 SASR 562 at 569-570 per Cox J)].

When, therefore, the considerations mentioned by Mason J in *Shirt* are given their full measure, the conclusion in this case that no breach was shown on the part of the Commission must be upheld. The important distinction between this case and *Nagle* is that there the danger of the submerged rocks was hidden from the ordinary users of the Basin. Here, the danger of the elevation of the cliffs was perfectly obvious to any reasonable person.

Romeo v Conservation Commission cont.

In determining what risks the defendant was required by law to respond to, it is necessary to have regard to what acts the defendant may have reasonably anticipated in the circumstances. Given the prominence of the danger, past usage of the site and accident experience it was not reasonable to expect the defendant to anticipate the inadvertance of the plaintiff in this case. So far as her complaint about the clearing of the vegetation and its appearance as a path is concerned, that appearance would not have deceived her, according to the primary judge's findings, but for her alcohol affected state. It is true to say that the Commission, acting reasonably, would have to anticipate a variety of visitors, including children, the elderly, the shortsighted, the intoxicated and the exuberant. However, because the risk was obvious and because the natural condition of the cliffs was part of their attraction, the suggestion that the cliffs should have been enclosed by a barrier must be tested by the proposition that all equivalent sites for which the Commission was responsible would have to be so fenced. The proposition that such precautions were necessary to arrest the passage of an inattentive young woman affected by alcohol is simply not reasonable. The perceived magnitude of risk, the remote possibility that an accident would occur, the expense, difficulty and inconvenience of alleviating conduct and the other proper priorities of the Commission confirm the conclusion that breach of the Commission's duty of care to the appellant was not established. The Commission's failure to provide protection against the risk that occurred was not unreasonable. The decision of the Court of Appeal to that effect was correct. It should be confirmed.

The appeal should be dismissed.

McHUGH J: [Dissenting]

460 In my opinion, the appeal should be allowed and a verdict entered for the plaintiff …

So what did reasonable care require the Commission to do to protect the plaintiff from the reasonably foreseeable risk that she might fall from the cliff top? First, the Commission had to consider the magnitude of the risk. In this case, there was a grave risk of injury. Death and quadriplegia were among the reasonably foreseeable consequences of a fall from the cliff top. Second, the Commission had to consider the probability of the risk occurring. In this case, the probability of a fall was very low. No previous accident had been reported. Nevertheless, the risk was not negligible or so remote that a reasonable person would reject it as unworthy of consideration. It was not like the risk that a person standing in the street would be injured by a cricket ball, hit from a pitch 100 yards away over a fence 17 feet higher than the pitch, as in *Bolton v Stone* [[1951] AC 850]. There as Lord Radcliffe said [[1951] AC 850 at 869]:

> a reasonable man, taking account of the chances against an accident happening, would not have felt himself called upon either to abandon the use of the ground for cricket or to increase the height of his surrounding fences.

Here the chance of a person, intoxicated as the plaintiff was, inadvertently walking through the gap in the vegetation and over the cliff was a real one – sufficiently real to require consideration of what precautions should be taken to eliminate it. Indeed, once it is accepted that the risk of a fall was reasonably foreseeable, a reasonable person in the Commission's position was bound to consider what it "would do by way of response to the risk" [(*Shirt* (1980) 146 CLR 40 at 47]. As the Judicial Committee said in *Overseas Tankship (UK) Ltd v The Miller Steamship Co Pty Ltd* [[1967] 1 AC 617 at 642], a reasonable person would disregard a risk that was likely to happen even once in a very long period only "if he had some valid reason for doing so, eg, that it would involve considerable expense to eliminate the risk." Their Lordships went on to say [[1967] 1 AC 617 at 642-643]:

> In their Lordships' judgment *Bolton v Stone* [1951] AC 850 did not alter the general principle that a person must be regarded as negligent if he does not take steps to eliminate a risk which he knows or ought to know is a real risk and not a mere possibility which would never influence the mind of a reasonable man. What that decision did was to recognise and give

Romeo v Conservation Commission cont.

> effect to the qualification that it is justifiable not to take steps to eliminate a real risk if it is small and if the circumstances are such that a reasonable man, careful of the safety of his neighbour, would think it right to neglect it.

The risk in the present case was that a person, through inadvertence, might walk through the gap in the vegetation and step off the cliff. Given the likely consequences of a fall from the cliff top, no reasonable public authority, careful of the safety of the users of the Reserve, would think it right to neglect taking steps to eliminate that risk. Reasonable care required some sort of barrier to prevent that risk occurring if it could be done with little expense and without coming into conflict with other responsibilities which the Commission might have. A three strand wire fence is one precaution which would have eliminated the risk and which would have been relatively inexpensive to install. The learned trial judge believed that there was no certainty that a log fence closer to the cliff edge "would have avoided the plaintiff's mishap" [*Romeo* (1994) 123 FLR 71 at 83; 104 NTR 1 at 12]. It is probable, however, that his Honour had in mind the same low log fence that was situated within three or four metres of the cliff face. A three strand wire fence, on the other hand, would almost certainly have prevented the plaintiff's fall.

The Commission contended that, if it had to erect a wire fence at this spot, it would have to erect a fence along the rest of the coastline under its control (some eight kilometres). But that is not a necessary consequence of requiring the Commission to fence this particular area of the cliff face. The precautions which reasonable care requires always depend upon the particular nature of the risk and the likelihood of its occurrence.

Close to the cliff top from which the plaintiff fell was a car park. A great many people congregated in or near this car park from time to time, particularly at sunset. That they might stay on or come later at night was highly predictable, given the nature of the place, its views, the allurement of a graded but untarred road and carpark and a grass strip that was regularly cut by the Commission. As many as a thousand people were known to come to this area to watch the fireworks on "cracker night". Probably, only one other area along the coastline (where various facilities were provided) was likely to attract greater numbers at night. That being so, the carpark and its surrounds was an area where a fall from the cliff top was more likely to occur than at other parts of the coastline under the Commission's control.

In these circumstances, the Commission's failure to fence the cliff top at this point of the coastline was negligent. The appeal should be allowed and a verdict entered for the plaintiff. The matter should be remitted to the Supreme Court to determine the quantum of the plaintiff's damages and whether those damages should be reduced because of any contributory negligence on the plaintiff's part.

HAYNE J: 488 The fact that an accident has happened and injury has been sustained will often be the most eloquent demonstration that the possibility of its occurrence was not far-fetched or fanciful. Indeed, often it will be difficult, if not impossible, to demonstrate the contrary to a tribunal of fact. That is why it is of the first importance to bear steadily in mind that the duty is not that of an insurer but a duty to act reasonably.

What is reasonable must be judged in the light of *all* the circumstances. Usually the gravity of the injury that might be sustained, the likelihood of such an injury occurring and the difficulty and cost of averting the danger will loom large in that consideration. But it is not only those factors that may bear upon the question. In the case of a public authority which manages public lands, it may or may not be able to control entry on the land in the same way that a private owner may; it may have responsibility for an area of wilderness far removed from the nearest town or village or an area of carefully manicured park in the middle of a capital city; it may positively encourage, or at least know of, use of the land only by the fit and adventurous or by those of all ages and conditions. All of these matters may bear upon what the reasonable response of the authority may be to the fact that injury is reasonably foreseeable. Similarly, it may be necessary, in a particular case, to consider whether the danger was hidden or obvious, or to consider whether it could be avoided by the exercise of the degree of care ordinarily exercised by a member of the public, or to consider whether the danger is one created by the action of the authority or is naturally occurring. But all of these matters (and I am not to be taken as giving some exhaustive list) are no more than particular factors which *may* go towards judging what reasonable care on the part of a particular defendant required. In the end, that question, what is reasonable, is a question of fact to be judged in all the circumstances of the case [*Herrington v British Railways Board* [1971] 2 QB 107 at 120 per Salmon LJ cited with approval in *Hackshaw* (1984) 155 CLR 614 at 663 per Deane J]. …

The courts below have answered these questions in the negative and in my view no error is shown in those conclusions. They are, in the end, questions of fact and I see no error in their being resolved against the plaintiff in this case.

[Toohey and Gummow JJ, in a joint judgement (see [8.25]), reached a conclusion similar to that of Kirby and Hayne JJ. Brennan CJ dismissed the plaintiff's appeal on different grounds.]

Vairy v Wyong Shire Council

[12.80] *Vairy v Wyong Shire Council* (2005) 223 CLR 422 High Court of Australia

(footnotes partially omitted)

[This appeal was heard together with *Mulligan v Coffs Harbour City Council* (2005) 80 ALJR 43. Both cases were actions for damages for negligence brought by young men who suffered serious injury [tetraplegia and quadriplegia] in consequence of diving or plunging into water and striking their heads or necks on the sand below. Both plaintiffs sued public authorities, complaining of a failure to warn of the risk which materialised. In *Vairy* it was found that numerous other people had dived safely into the water on the day of the accident. A similar serious accident had occurred 15 years earlier at the same place, to the council's knowledge. Wyong Shire Council was responsible for 27 km of coastline along the New South Wales East Coast of Australia.

In each case, the trial judge accepted that the plaintiff was owed a duty to take reasonable care to protect him from unnecessary risk of physical harm. In *Vairy*, Bell J held that there had been a breach of that duty, although she reduced the damages substantially on account of contributory negligence. The NSW Court of Appeal found that the risk to Mr Vairy should have been obvious. The plaintiff appealed. The issues before the High Court were whether the council had a duty to warn of risks associated with diving from a rock platform and whether the council had a duty to prohibit diving from the rock platform. The appeal was dismissed 4:3, Gleeson CJ, Kirby and McHugh JJ dissenting].

HAYNE J: [415] The central issue in the appeal is whether the Council breached a duty of care it owed to the appellant by not erecting one or more signs warning against, or prohibiting, diving from the rock platform. Resolving that question, a question of fact, hinges critically upon recognising that what has come to be known as the "*Shirt* calculus" is not to be undertaken by looking back at what has in fact happened, but by looking forward from a time before the occurrence of the injury giving rise to the claim. The several questions described by Mason J in *Wyong Shire Council v Shirt* are to be asked and answered with that perspective. Thus, before the appellant was injured, would "a reasonable man in the [Council's] position … have foreseen that his conduct involved a risk of injury to the [appellant] or to a class of persons including the [appellant]"? [(1980) 146 CLR 40 at 47] that question is affirmative, "it is then for the tribunal of fact to determine what a reasonable man would do by way of response to the risk" [(1980) 146 CLR 40 at 47].

The inquiry into the causes of an accident is wholly retrospective. It seeks to identify what happened and why. The inquiry into breach, although made after the accident, must attempt to

Vairy v Wyong Shire Council cont.

answer what response a reasonable person, confronted with a foreseeable risk of injury, would have made to that risk. And one of the possible answers to that inquiry must be "nothing".

There are fundamental reasons why the inquiry cannot be confined to where the accident happened or how it happened. Chief among them is the prospective nature of the inquiry to be made about response to a foreseeable risk.

Look Forward or Look Back?

When a plaintiff sues for damages alleging personal injury has been caused by the defendant's negligence, the inquiry about breach of duty must attempt to identify the reasonable person's response to foresight of the risk of occurrence of the injury which the plaintiff suffered. That inquiry must attempt, after the event, to judge what the reasonable person *would* have done to avoid what is now known to have occurred. Although that judgment must be made after the event it must seek to identify what the response would have been by a person looking forward at the prospect of the risk of injury.

There may be more than one place where this risk of injury may come to pass. Because the inquiry is prospective there is no basis for assuming in such a case that the only risk to be considered is the risk that an injury will occur at one of the several, perhaps many, places where it could occur. *Romeo* was just such a case and so is this. In both cases there were many places to which the public had access and of which the Commission (in *Romeo*) and the Council (in this case) had the care, control and management. In *Romeo*, there were many places where a person could fall off a cliff; here, there were many places where a person could dive into water that was too shallow. Because the inquiry is prospective, all these possibilities must be considered. And it is only by looking *forward* from a time before the accident that due weight can be given to what Mason J referred [(1980) 146 CLR 40 at 47] to in *Shirt* as "consideration of the magnitude of the risk and the degree of the probability of its occurrence". It is only by looking *forward* that due account can be taken of "the expense, difficulty and inconvenience of taking alleviating action and any other conflicting responsibilities which the defendant may have" [(1980) 146 CLR 40 at 47-48].

If, instead of looking forward, the so-called *Shirt* calculus is undertaken looking back on what is known to have happened, the tort of negligence becomes separated from standards of reasonableness. It becomes separated because, in every case where the cost of taking alleviating action at the particular place where the plaintiff was injured is markedly less than the consequences of a risk coming to pass, it is well nigh inevitable that the defendant would be found to have acted without reasonable care if alleviating action was not taken. And this would be so no matter how diffuse the risk was – diffuse in the sense that its occurrence was improbable or, as in *Romeo*, diffuse in the sense that the place or places where it may come to pass could not be confined within reasonable bounds.

To approach the inquiry about breach in this prospective way is to apply long-established principle. [*Aiken v Kingborough Corporation* [(1939) 62 CLR 179 at 209]... *Shirt* is consistent with only that approach to the problem. And later decisions of the Court, notably *Romeo* [(1998) 192 CLR 431] and *Commissioner of Main Roads v Jones* [(2005) 79 ALJR 1104; 215 ALR 418], can be understood only in that way.

Before the appellant suffered his injury, a reasonable council would have recognised that there was a risk that a person diving or jumping off the rock platform would suffer catastrophic spinal injury if the water was too shallow. That this was foreseeable was amply demonstrated by the fact that, before the appellant suffered his injury, another man (Mr von Sanden) had sustained spinal injury when he dived off that rock platform. The occurrence of this accident was found to have been "common knowledge within the Council", but the Council took no steps to warn or prevent others diving from the rock platform. It may be that Mr von Sanden leapt off a point on the platform higher than the point from which the appellant dived. It matters not whether that is so. What matters is that it was reasonably foreseeable that a person entering the water from this point could suffer injury if the entry was head first and the water was too shallow.

[Hayne J went on to conclude that, although injury was foreseeable ...] It was not and could not be suggested that a reasonable council would have marked every point in its municipal district from which a person could enter a body of water, and warned against or prohibited diving from that point.

———— ☙❧ ————

[12.85] **Notes&Questions**

Romeo v Conservation Commission of the Northern Territory (1998) 192 CLR 431, in which the plaintiff failed, raised similar issues to those in *Nagle v Rottnest Island Board* in which the plaintiff succeeded. The view of what the reasonable response to the risk is clearly changed between those two cases. See P Vines, "Fault, Responsibility and Negligence in the High Court of Australia" (2000) 8(2) *Tort Law Review* 130-145.

Critique of the "calculus"

[12.90] In *Mulligan v Coffs Harbour City Council* (2005) 223 CLR 486, Gleeson CJ and Kirby J (at [2]) rejected the calculus notion, as follows (footnotes omitted):

> Reference is often made to the "*Wyong Shire Council v Shirt* calculus". In that case, Mason J referred to the way in which a tribunal of fact might determine what a reasonable person would do by way of response to a foreseeable risk. As he made clear, he was describing a process of factual judgment. He referred to such factors as the magnitude of the risk, the degree of probability of its occurrence, the expense, difficulty and inconvenience of taking alleviating action, and any other conflicting responsibilities of the defendant. These, he said, were matters to be balanced out in making a judgment about reasonableness. The later use of the word "calculus" to describe this passage is unfortunate. A calculus is a method of calculation. What is involved in the process to which Mason J was referring is not a calculation; it is a judgment. In *Ridge v Baldwin*, Lord Reid observed that "[t]he idea of negligence is ... insusceptible of exact definition". Moreover, depending upon what may be involved in the concept of conflicting responsibilities, in some contexts, of which the present is an example, to treat what was said in *Shirt* as an inflexible formula could produce a distinctly unreasonable result. Where the suggested alleviating action is putting up a single warning sign at a particular location in a public recreational area, the expense, difficulty and inconvenience involved may be made to appear negligible. The more important question may be why a public authority would choose to single out that particular spot, or that particular risk, as the subject of a warning. ... This Court recently said, in *Thompson v Woolworths (Qld) Pty Ltd* that reasonableness may require no response to a foreseeable risk, and pointed out that householders do not ordinarily place notices at their front doors warning entrants of all the dangers that await them if they fail to take reasonable care for their own safety. That observation was not the product of a calculus; it was simply a statement about community standards of reasonable behaviour.

Standards of Care in Negligence Law

[12.95] RW Wright, "The Standards of Care in Negligence Law" in DG Owen (ed), *Philosophical Foundations of Tort Law* (Clarendon Press, 1995), pp 249-265

(footnotes partially omitted)

II. The Unworkability of the Utilitarian "Hand Formula"

Negligence is generally described as behavior that creates unreasonable foreseeable risks of injury. Almost all jury instructions, the vast majority of judicial opinions, and many secondary sources do not provide any test or definition of what constitutes unreasonably risky behavior, other than an often circular reference to the "ordinary care" that would be exercised by the reasonable or prudent person in the same or similar circumstances.

Legal scholars are less reticent. There is an almost universal assumption among legal scholars that a person's conduct is deemed unreasonable, and hence negligent, if and only if the foreseeable risks created by such conduct exceed its expected social utility. This aggregate risk-utility test of reasonableness was most explicitly articulated in Judge Learned Hand's famous formula in *United States v Carroll Towing Co*: a person's conduct X is unreasonable only if P times L is greater than B, where P is the probability of an injury occurring, L is the magnitude of the injury, and B is the expected benefit of engaging in conduct X or, conversely, the expected burden or cost that would have to be borne to avoid engaging in conduct X.

The assumed prevalence of Hand's risk-utility formula as the operative test of reasonableness in negligence is deemed to be the strongest evidence of the utilitarian efficiency foundation of tort law. Under the utilitarian efficiency theory, conduct is efficient (hence reasonable and not negligent) if it maximizes the total sum of expected benefits minus costs; it does not matter who bears the costs and who gains the benefits. The Hand formula seems perfectly to reflect this view. However, there are insurmountable problems with the Hand formula even under the utilitarian efficiency theory ...

[F]rom the standpoint of utilitarian efficiency, the Hand formula must be abandoned. Negligence must be defined not as a failure to satisfy the Hand formula, but rather as a failure to adopt the efficient level of precaution ... Yet, as Hand himself noted, in practice it will be impossible to take into account more than a few options and their expected costs and benefits, and even for these options the expected costs and benefits generally cannot be estimated ...

III. Non-utilitarian Attempts to Justify the Hand Formula

Although the legal economists' aggregate risk-utility interpretation of negligence, especially as embodied in the Hand formula, is undermined by major theoretical and practical problems, almost all legal scholars, including those critical of the utilitarian efficiency theory, assume it is descriptively correct. Critics of utilitarian efficiency generally have attempted to construct non-utilitarian arguments to explain and justify the supposed use of the aggregate risk-utility formula in negligence and other tort cases. They rely explicitly or implicitly on the fundamental Kantian moral duty to respect the equal absolute moral worth of yourself and others as rational (human) beings. This duty is assumed to require that in all your actions you must weigh the interests of others equally with your own, which leads immediately and inevitably to the aggregate risk-utility conception of reasonableness and negligence.

For example, Ronald Dworkin, while not explicitly invoking Kant's (or any other) moral theory, attempts to explain the assumed use of the aggregate risk-utility formula in negligence and private nuisance cases by arguing that in such cases there are competing claims of "abstract right" (also more accurately described as mere "interests") which must be resolved by using the basic principle of "equal concern and respect" to "compromise" the competing claims so as to maximize the "collective utility" of the parties. Similarly, Ernest Weinrib, explicitly relying on Kantian moral theory, assumes that the categorical imperative, which requires one to act in accord with a maxim that one would adopt as an equal member of the "kingdom of ends", forbids any self-preference in conception or action. He argued, until recently, that this alleged requirement of complete impartiality of interest mandates an objective "comparison of interests" conception of reasonableness for both defendants and plaintiffs. Charles Fried also purports to find in Kantian morality a requirement of complete impartiality, which he at one time used not only to justify the aggregate risk-utility conception of negligence but also to construct a social risk pool from which persons supposedly can draw, within certain unclear limits, to expose others to minor or major risk.

These arguments, although meant to be non-utilitarian, are based directly on the utilitarian conception of equality, according to which treating people as equals simply means counting each person's interests equally while "maximizing the total satisfaction of interests" …

"Ethic of care" feminists such as Leslie Bender travel the same path as Dworkin, Weinrib, Fried, and Fletcher, although they seem unaware of the destination toward which they are traveling and might be shocked to learn of their traveling companions. Bender equates the reasonableness standard in negligence and, more generally, the liberal concepts of reason, autonomy, rights, equality, fairness, and justice with a "masculine" ethic of antisocial, self-interested, wealth-based, dehumanizing utilitarian calculation. She seeks to replace the reasonableness standard and its "masculine" ethic with a "feminine" ethic of care and concern for the needs and welfare of others, according to which a person in cases of both misfeasance (putting others at risk) and nonfeasance (failure to protect others from risks you did not create) should be held to a legal standard of "conscious care and concern of a responsible neighbor or social acquaintance for another under the same or similar circumstances".

Bender's "feminine" ethic of care might well be less caring than the complete impartiality requirement espoused by Dworkin, Weinrib, Fried, Fletcher, and the (mostly male) utilitarian efficiency theorists, according to which others' interests and welfare must always be treated as being equally as important as your own. Recognizing that "we all care differently for family and friends than we do for strangers" and that "we could not possibly have the energy to care about every person as we do our children or lovers", Bender prescribes varying levels of required care depending on the closeness of the relationship. Yet, given her rejection of the "masculine" notions of autonomy and self interest and her emphasis on the "feminine" ethic of care and concern for the needs and welfare of all others, it is not at all clear how she could justify such preferred treatment for one's family or friends (or oneself). Conversely, assuming a variable standard based on closeness of relationship, she seems unable to justify her proposed requirement that the concern appropriate for neighbors and acquaintances must also be afforded to strangers.

The proposed displacement of the "masculine" ethic of reason, autonomy, rights, equality, fairness, and justice by a "feminine" ethic of care and concern for others would seem to be, as feminists such as Catharine MacKinnon and Margaret Radin have argued, a trap for women-especially since, being a "feminine" rather than a "masculine" ethic, it apparently would only apply to women. In a recent article, Bender seems to acknowledge this problem. She now states that "reason has its place in tort law, but that reason is a richer and deeper concept than tort law has historically acknowledged", and she urges the usefulness of "the reason/care paradigm" in suggesting "reconceptualizations that make law more reflective of human experience and more responsive to concerns of justice".

IV. The Equal Freedom Standards of Care

… Tort law falls within the domain of corrective justice, although distributive justice considerations are interwoven in certain tort doctrines. Corrective justice aims at securing each person's existing stock of resources against conduct by others that would be inconsistent with the equal negative freedom of all. One's negative freedom – the freedom from unjustified interference with one's use of one's existing resources to pursue one's projects or life plan-will be completely undermined if one must always weigh

Standards of Care in Negligence Law cont.

the interests of all others equally with one's own when deciding how to deploy one's existing resources, as required by the utilitarian efficiency theory, the principle of "equal concern and respect" as interpreted by Dworkin and others, and Bender's feminist "ethic of care". Under these theories, no one is treated as a distinct person with one's own life to lead. Rather each "person" is merely a fungible addend in the calculation of some mystical aggregate social welfare. For any particular activity, it does not matter whom is being put at risk, by who, or for whose benefit; all that matters is the maximization of aggregate social welfare. This is the morally unattractive message and effect of the utilitarians' conception of reasonableness.

Under the Kantian-Aristotelian theory, which is based on the foundational norm of equal individual freedom rather than the maximization of aggregate social welfare, the respective weights to be given to an actor's interests and the interests of others who might be affected by that action will vary considerably depending on (among other factors) who is being put at risk, by whom, and for whose benefit. For example, given the Kantian requirement of treating others as ends rather than merely as means, it is impermissible to use someone as a mere means to your ends by exposing him (or his resources) to significant foreseeable unaccepted risks, regardless of how greatly the benefit to you might outweigh the risk to him …

It is the equal freedom conception of reasonableness, rather than the utilitarian efficiency conception, that is reflected in actual tort-law doctrines and decisions. Under the utilitarian-efficiency theory, it is as inefficient to be above the optimal level of care as to be below it: either form of divergence therefore should be considered negligent. However, consistent with the equal freedom theory, defendants and plaintiffs are only deemed negligent for being below the required level of care, not for being above it. Only when one is below the required level of care is there an impermissible interference with the rights of others (defendant's primary negligence) or a failure properly to respect one's own humanity (plaintiff's contributory negligence).

Moreover, although the utilitarian efficiency theory would apply the same aggregate risk-utility standard of care to plaintiffs and defendants in all situations, taking into account all risks and benefits to everyone, actual tort law–consistent with the equal freedom theory-applies quite different standards of care in different situations. This is evident for all three aspects of the standards of care: the risks taken into account, the perspectives applied, and the substantive criteria of reasonableness …

B. Perspective Applied (Objective or Subjective)

… Under Kant's moral theory, a subjective perspective would be required if the question were the moral *blameworthiness or merit* of the defendant's or plaintiff's conduct. But, when evaluating the defendant's conduct in a tort (rather than a criminal) action, that is not the relevant question (unless punitive damages are at issue). Instead, the relevant question is the defendant's moral *responsibility* for having adversely affected someone else's person or property. As such, the question is one of objective Right rather than subjective virtue … Thus, an objective standard of "legal fault" (moral *responsibility*), rather than a subjective standard of moral fault (blame), is required when considering legal responsibility for the adverse effects of a defendant's conduct on the person or property of others …

C. The Substantive Criteria of Reasonableness

Finally, different criteria of reasonableness are used in evaluating the alleged negligence of defendants and plaintiffs in different contexts. Contrary to what is commonly assumed, the courts rarely use the aggregate risk-utility formula or any other uniform definition of reason-ableness. Rather, different factors are taken into account and different weights are given to those factors depending on a number of considerations that are highly relevant under the equal-freedom theory but irrelevant under the utilitarian efficiency theory.

In an article published in 1915 that is often cited as presaging Judge Hand's formula, Henry Terry noted five factors that may be relevant, including [1] the probability and [2] the magnitude of any injury that might result from the conduct at issue and, in some cases, at least, [3] the probability and [4] the magnitude of the benefit expected to be attained by such conduct discounted by [5] the probability that the benefit would be attained in the absence of such conduct. In 1927, Warren Seavey warned against "assum[ing] that we can rely upon any formula in regard to 'balancing interests' to solve negligence cases", and he stated that the utility of the defendant's conduct usually is not considered or is weighted very low when the defendant for her own benefit puts another's property or especially person at risk, or intentionally interferes with the person or property of another. Judge Learned Hand himself, the author of the risk-utility formula, noted that the formula's factors

> are practically not susceptible of any quantitative estimate, and the second two [L and B] are generally not so, even theoretically. For this reason a solution always involves some preference, or choice between incommensurables, and it is consigned to a jury because their decision is thought most likely to accord with commonly accepted standards, real or fancied.

Similarly, after elaborating the usual academic aggregate risk-utility interpretation of reason-ableness, John Fleming warns:

> But negligence cannot be reduced to a purely economic equation … [I]n general, judicial opinions do not make much of the cost factor [of eliminating the risk], and for good reasons. For one thing, our legal tradition in torts has strong roots in an individualistic morality with its focus primarily on interpersonal equity rather than broader social policy … [T]he calculus of negligence includes some important noneconomic values, like health and life, freedom and privacy, which defy comparison with competing economic values. Negligence is not just a matter of calculating the point at which the cost of injury to victims (that is the damages payable) exceeds that of providing safety precautions. The reasonable man is by no means a caricature cold blooded, calculating Economic Man.

Very little scholarly attention has been paid to the criteria of reasonableness that are actually applied in different situations. In the remainder of this essay, I attempt to begin to fill this gap. The different situations will be distinguished primarily by who put whom at risk for whose benefit and by whether the person put at risk consented to such risk exposure. More specifically, I examine the standards of care in the following (nonexhaustive) contexts: (1) defendants' treating others as means, (2) defendants engaged in socially essential activities, (3) defendant occupiers' on-premises risks, (4) defendants' activities involving participatory plaintiffs, (5) paternalistic defendants, (6) plaintiffs' self-interested conduct, (7) plaintiffs' self-sacrificing conduct, and (8) defendants' failure to aid or rescue.

1. Defendants' Treating Others as Means: The first category, the "involuntary DPD" category, encompasses situations in which the defendant (D) put the plaintiff (P) at risk to benefit the defendant (D) or some third party, and the plaintiff did not seek to benefit directly from the defendant's risk-creating activity. Recently, a few scholars have noted that the actual test of negligence in such cases is not the utilitarians' aggregate risk-utility test but rather (consistent with the equal freedom theory) the defendant's creation of a significant, foreseeable, and unaccepted risk to the person or property of others. A risk is significant, and hence unreasonable unless accepted by the plaintiff, if it is a level of risk to which an ordinary person would be unwilling to be exposed without his consent.

The best known case of this type is the British House of Lords' decision in *Bolton v Stone*, in which the plaintiff, while standing in the road in front of her house, was seriously injured when she was struck by a ball that had been propelled by an "exceptional" hit out of the nearby cricket grounds over an intervening house and into the street. Each of the Law Lords assumed that the defendant cricket club would be liable in negligence if the risk were foreseeable and of a sufficiently high level, regardless of the utility of the defendant's conduct or the burden of avoiding creating the risk. Each lord concluded that the risk, although foreseeable, was not of a sufficiently high level to be deemed unreasonable as a matter of law, given the very low probabilities of a ball's being hit into the road and also hitting someone on the little-used residential side street. Lord Reid was the most explicit. He stated that in

Standards of Care in Negligence Law cont.

order to be negligent, a risk must not only be foreseeable but also be one that a reasonable person, "considering the matter from the point of view of safety", would consider "material" or "substantial":

> In considering that matter I think that it would be right to take into account not only how remote is the chance that a person might be struck but also how serious the consequences are likely to be if a person is struck; but I do not think that it would be right to take into account the difficulty of remedial measures. If cricket cannot be played on a ground without creating a substantial risk, then it should not be played there at all. ... I do not think that a reasonable man considering the matter from the point of view of safety would or should disregard any risk unless it is extremely small.

In a subsequent case, the Law Lords sitting as the Privy Council in a Commonwealth case on appeal from Australia, *The Wagon Mound (No 2)*, held that, even when the foreseeable risk is insubstantial (small), the defendant will still be held negligent if, but only if, the risk was "real" rather than "far-fetched" or "fantastic" and the defendant had no valid reason for failing to take steps to eliminate it. A valid reason could be "that it would involve considerable expense to eliminate the risk. [The defendant] would weigh the risk against the difficulty of eliminating it." *Bolton v Stone*, the court said, had involved such a real but insubstantial risk. But, the court reiterated, if the risk were real and substantial, it would be unreasonable not to take steps to eliminate it, regardless of the utility of the risk or the burden of eliminating it.

The *Wagon Mound (No 2)* is sometimes misread as abandoning *Bolton v Stone's* substantial risk criterion and replacing it with the risk-utility formula. But the Privy Council clearly states that the risk-utility formula, rather than being the universal test of defendants' negligence, is applicable only in those situations in which the risk ordinarily would be considered insubstantial. If the risk is substantial, the utility of the defendant's conduct is irrelevant. The risk-utility formula is used to expand the defendant's liability, to encompass situations in which the risk ordinarily would be deemed insubstantial but is nevertheless deemed unacceptable because it is real, rather than fantastic, and the cost of eliminating it would be similarly small (no precise quantitative balancing of risk and utility seems to be feasible, implied or justified even in these situations).

Although not usually employing language as explicit as Lord Reid's in *Bolton*, and despite sometimes employing balancing language, courts in the United States and elsewhere generally also find a defendant negligent if she created a foreseeable significant unaccepted risk of injury to the person or property of others. As we previously noted, jury instructions on a defendant's negligence rarely, if ever, refer to the aggregate risk-utility formula, focusing instead on the care expected of the reasonable ordinary or prudent person who acts with proper concern for the effects of her activity on the persons and property of others. Courts have upheld jury findings of negligence even though the jury has specifically found that the benefits "as a whole" of the defendant's conduct outweighed the risks. In a careful, documented study of all nineteenth century California and New Hampshire appellate court decisions on tort liability, Gary Schwartz reports:

> The factor of private profit was seen as a reason for being skeptical, rather than appreciative, of the propriety of risky activity engaged in by enterprise. In general, the New Hampshire and California Courts were reluctant to find that economic factors justified a defendant's risktaking. Neither Court even once held mere monetary costs rendered non-negligent a defendant's failure to adopt a particular safety precaution.

Defense lawyers carefully avoid making arguments to judges or jurors that seek to justify risks imposed on the plaintiff by allegedly offsetting enhancements of the defendant's utility. Defendants that are thought to have deliberately made such risk-utility decisions are often deemed by juries and judges not only to have been negligent, but also to have behaved so egregiously as to justify a hefty award of punitive damages, as occurred in the Ford Pinto and asbestos cases.

...

Probability of harm

[12.100] In *Bolton v Stone*, [1951] AC 850 an action was brought in negligence and nuisance by a woman who was struck on the head whilst standing outside her house, across the road from a cricket ground, by a cricket ball that had been hit for six (ie, out of the oval) from the ground. The ground had been in use since 1864, and the road was separated from the ground by a fence 17 feet above road level. The hit was described by a member of the defendant club as quite the biggest seen on that ground (90m), but evidence was adduced that on six to ten occasions cricket balls had been hit into the road in the past 30 years. The trial judge held that the plaintiff had failed to establish negligence. That decision was reversed by the Court of Appeal, but reinstated by the House of Lords somewhat controversially. Although Lord Radcliffe agreed "with regret" with the majority, he could "see nothing unfair in the appellants being required to compensate the respondent for the serious injury she received as a result of the sport that they have organised on their ground ... but the law of negligence is concerned less with what is fair than with what is culpable". Lord Reid said in the *Wagon Mound (No 2)* (at 642-643):

> What [*Bolton v Stone*] did was to recognise and give effect to the qualification that it is justifiable not to take steps to eliminate a real risk if it is small and if the circumstances are such that a reasonable man, careful of the safety of his neighbour, would think it right to neglect it.

RTA v Dederer

[12.105] *Roads and Traffic Authority of NSW v Dederer* (2007) 324 CLR 330 High Court of Australia (footnotes omitted)

[Mr Dederer, then aged 14, had often seen people jumping off a bridge in an estuary area which was very tidal. Where people jumped off there was a railing which had a slight ledge on top creating a platform on which people stood before jumping or diving off into the water. Apparently until Mr Dederer's dive no-one had been injured by such a dive or jump from the bridge. The bridge had been designed by the DMR (now the RTA). The bridge was completed in 1959 and was part of NSW Main Road No 111. Legislation directs the RTA to maintain the bridge, carry out roadwork. Work as a "roads authority" in relation to the bridge was shared with the local Council, but work of a capital nature was the responsibility of the RTA. The RTA carried out soundings of the river bed levels under the bridge every three months and knew that the riverbed levels continually altered. The Council conceded in evidence that it knew that people dived and jumped from the bridge, but the RTA, while it conceded that it knew of jumping, maintained that it had no notice of people diving from the bridge. There were signs on the bridge at each end saying "fishing and climbing prohibited" and Dederer acknowledged that he had seen and understood the "no diving" pictograms on the bridge. In 1992 a new Austroads Standard came into force requiring vertical rather than horizontal bars for bridge railings, but no modification of the bridge was carried out by the RTA, which had also been sent a message by the Council in 1993 about the problem of jumping into the channel. When Dederer dived in 1998 he had climbed onto the platform by using the horizontal bars as steps. He had been doing this the day before and seen many other people do so with no untoward effects. He climbed up,

RTA v Dederer cont.

listened for approaching boats and then dived. He hit the bottom and was made an incomplete paraplegic. Dederer argued that the RTA should have (1) provided the information on the signs that the danger was created by the shifting sands beneath the bridge; (2) modified the flat level railing so that it could not form a platform for diving or jumping and (3) it should have removed the horizontal railings and replaced them with vertical railings.

The trial judge found for Mr Dederer, agreeing that the RTA should have done the three things above, but reduced his damages by 25 per cent for contributory negligence. The Court of Appeal by majority agreed with the primary judge as to liability, but increased the amount of contributory negligence to 50 per cent. The RTA then appealed to the High Court. Dederer cross-appealed on the issue of contributory negligence.]

GUMMOW J: 337 In *Berrigan Shire Council v Ballerini*, Callaway JA remarked that "[t]he relationship between duty and breach in the law of negligence is causing more perplexity than it used to do". This appeal bears out the force of that statement.

The errors of which the appellant rightly complains, regarding both the reasons of the trial judge and those of the New South Wales Court of Appeal, did not turn on factual matters upon which reasonable minds might differ. Rather, they concerned the misapplication of basic and settled matters of legal principle. These principles may be restated shortly. First, the proper resolution of an action in negligence depends on the existence and scope of the relevant duty of care. Secondly, whatever its scope, a duty of care imposes an obligation to exercise reasonable care; it does not impose a duty to prevent potentially harmful conduct. Thirdly, the assessment of breach depends on the correct identification of the relevant risk of injury. Fourthly, breach must be assessed prospectively and not retrospectively. Fifthly, such an assessment of breach must be made in the manner described by Mason J in *Wyong Shire Council v Shirt*. ...344

... The appeal by the RTA to this Court should be allowed. ... the errors on the part of the majority of the Court of Appeal lay in fundamental matters of law: matters against which concurrent findings of fact are no insulation.

The scope of the RTA's duty of care

Although the existence of a duty of care owed by the RTA to Mr Dederer was not in dispute, two points must be made about the nature and extent of that obligation. First, duties of care are not owed in the abstract. Rather, they are obligations of a particular scope, and that scope may be more or less expansive depending on the relationship in question. Secondly, whatever their scope, all duties of care are to be discharged by the exercise of reasonable care. They do not impose a more stringent or onerous burden ...

The result of [*Brodie v Singleton Shire Council*] is that a road authority is obliged to exercise reasonable care so that the road is safe "for users exercising reasonable care for their own safety" [(2001) 206 CLR 512 at [163]]. The expression of the scope of the RTA's duty of care in those terms has long antecedents in the law relating to occupiers' liability. In *Indermaur v Dames* ... Willes J held that:

> We consider it settled law that [a visitor] using reasonable care on his part for his own safety, is entitled to expect that the occupier shall on his part use reasonable care to prevent damage from unusual danger.

The modern form of that principle has been frequently affirmed in recent times, both with regard to occupiers and roads authorities [he referred to *Romeo's case* and *Neindorf v Junkovic*]. Of course, the weight to be given to an expectation that potential plaintiffs will exercise reasonable care for their own safety is a general matter in the assessment of breach in every case (*Thompson v Woolworths (Qld) P/L*), but in the present case it was also a specific element contained, as a matter of law, in the scope of the RTA's duty of care ...

RTA v Dederer cont.

The RTA's duty of care was owed to all users of the bridge, whether or not they took ordinary care for their own safety; the RTA did not cease to owe Mr Dederer a duty of care merely because of his own voluntary and obviously dangerous conduct in diving from the bridge. However, the extent of the obligation owed by the RTA was that of a roads authority exercising reasonable care to see that the road is safe "for users exercising reasonable care for their own safety" (*Brodie*). The essential point is that the RTA did not owe a more stringent obligation towards careless road users as compared with careful ones. In each case, the same obligation of reasonable care was owed, and the extent of that obligation was to be measured against a duty whose scope took into account the exercise of reasonable care by road users themselves.

In the Court of Appeal, Ipp JA referred to and adopted remarks he made in the earlier case of *Edson v Roads and Traffic Authority*.in which the plaintiff and many others exercised an obvious disregard for their own safety when they crossed a busy highway on foot. After referring to the passage from *Brodie* set out above, his Honour remarked that:

> the factual underpinning of the proposition that a road authority is duty bound only to require a road to be safe not in all circumstances but for pedestrians exercising reasonable care for their own safety, was absent. Here, the RTA long knew that the pedestrians were not exercising reasonable care for their own safety and, in large numbers, were constantly not doing so. The RTA could not rely on residents in the vicinity of the path to look after themselves and to act with due care.

In the present case, his Honour concluded that "the 'factual underpinning' was also absent". This was in error, as the expectation of reasonable care was not merely a "factual underpinning", but rather a legal aspect of the scope of the duty owed by the RTA.

Reasonable care, not prevention

In simple and complicated cases alike, one thing is fundamental: while duties of care may vary in content or scope, they are all to be discharged by the exercise of *reasonable* care …

Such an obligation to exercise reasonable care must be contrasted with an obligation to prevent harm occurring to others. The former, not the latter, is the requirement of the law …

The RTA correctly complains that this orthodox approach was not applied at trial or in the Court of Appeal. The trial judge and the majority in the Court of Appeal each fixed on the failure of the "no diving" pictograms and "no climbing" signs to *prevent* diving or jumping from the bridge [and concluded that the RTA was unreasonable in ignoring this] …

The error in that approach lies in confusing the question of whether the RTA failed to prevent the risk-taking conduct with the separate question of whether it exercised reasonable care. If the RTA exercised reasonable care, it would not be liable even if the risk-taking conduct continued. If the contrary were true, then defendants would be liable in any case in which a plaintiff ignored a warning or prohibition sign and engaged in the conduct the subject of the warning. Whether or not other persons engaged in that conduct, such a defendant would *ipso facto* have failed to prevent at least the plaintiff from engaging in it. If this quasi-automatic form of liability represented the true state of the law, it would be startlingly at odds with the general proposition that liability in tort depends upon proof of fault through the intentional or negligent infliction of harm. More particularly, it would also be at odds with the decision in *Montgomery* that roads authorities owe only a duty to take reasonable care, and do not owe a more stringent or non-delegable duty.

The trial judge and the majority in the Court of Appeal impermissibly reasoned that if a warning is given, and if the conduct against which that warning is directed continues notwithstanding the warning, then the party who gave the warning is shown to have been negligent by reason of the warning having failed. Quite apart from its inconsistency with the scope of the RTA's duty of care, this reasoning erroneously short-circuits the inquiry into breach of duty that is required by *Shirt* …

RTA v Dederer cont.

Even reasonable warnings can "fail", but the question is always the reasonableness of the warning, not its failure. Ipp JA's statement… to the effect that a warning sign is "not an automatic, absolute and permanent panacea" was no substitute for a proper assessment of reasonableness.

….

The proper identification of the risk

… It is only through the correct identification of the risk that one can assess what a reasonable response to that risk would be. In this, too, the majority in the Court of Appeal erred.

In the Court of Appeal, the risk faced by Mr Dederer was characterised by the majority as being "serious spinal injury flowing from the act of diving off the bridge". That risk, it was said, was one created by the RTA through the erection of the bridge by its predecessor. However, such a characterisation of the risk obscured the true source of potential injury. This arose not from the state of the bridge itself, but rather from the risk of impact upon jumping into the potentially shallow water and shifting sands of the estuary. This mischaracterisation of the risk led to two consequent errors. First, the majority were distracted from a proper evaluation of the probability of that risk occurring. Secondly, they erroneously attributed to the RTA a greater control over the risk than it possessed.

The first error can be seen in Ipp JA's characterisation of the "startling frequency" of "large numbers" of people jumping and diving from the bridge; a practice that was "continuing unabated" notwithstanding the pictograms. Such a characterisation incorrectly focused attention on the frequency of an antecedent course of conduct, namely jumping and diving, and not on the probability of the risk of injury occurring as a result of that conduct, namely impact in shallow water. As Lord Porter observed in *Bolton v Stone*, "in order that the act may be negligent there must not only be a reasonable possibility of its happening but also of *injury being caused*" (emphasis added). In the present case, the frequency of jumping and diving was only startling if one ignored the fact that no-one was injured until Mr Dederer's unfortunate accident. Far from being a risk with a high probability of occurrence, the probability was in truth very low, and this fact was masked by the Court of Appeal's characterisation of the relevant risk.

Regarding the second error, by focusing on the RTA's role in constructing the bridge from which Mr Dederer dived, the majority in the Court of Appeal overlooked the limited nature of the RTA's control over the actual risk of injury faced by Mr Dederer.

… [W]hatever its role in creating the bridge the RTA did not control Mr Dederer's voluntary action in diving, and nor did it create or control the natural variations in the depth of the estuary beneath the bridge. .. Nor was it a case in which the "incentives" discerned by Ipp JA were ones created by the RTA. Rather, the risk arose because of the conjunction of the bridge's location and two factors outside the RTA's control: one human and the other environmental, namely Mr Dederer diving from the bridge and the natural variations of the estuary bed …

The proper assessment of breach

Having dealt with the relevant risk, it is appropriate to return to the inquiry into the assessment of breach. Whether reasonable care was exercised in the particular case is a question of fact going to the breach of any duty owed, not to the existence of that duty. In each case, the question of whether reasonable care was exercised is to be adjudged prospectively, and not by retrospectively asking whether the defendant's actions could have prevented the plaintiff's injury …

Each of these principles was misapplied by the trial judge and the majority in the Court of Appeal. As explained earlier in these reasons, their Honours erred by focusing in retrospect on the failure of the RTA to *prevent* Mr Dederer's dive, as opposed to asking what, in prospect, the exercise of reasonable care would require in response to a foreseeable risk of injury. The use of phrases such as "an accident waiting to happen" was redolent of a retrospective, not prospective, approach to the matter.

RTA v Dederer cont.

What, then, was the correct approach towards assessing breach? The particular trap into which the majority of the Court of Appeal fell was that warned against by Hayne J in *Vairy*:

> If, instead of looking forward, the so-called *Shirt* calculus is undertaken looking back on what is known to have happened, the tort of negligence becomes separated from standards of reasonableness. It becomes separated because, in every case where the cost of taking alleviating action at the particular place where the plaintiff was injured is markedly less than the consequences of a risk coming to pass, it is well nigh inevitable that the defendant would be found to have acted without reasonable care if alleviating action was not taken.

The relevant passage from the judgment of Mason J in *Shirt* should be set out yet again ...The continuing authority of this passage has recently been reaffirmed by this Court in *New South Wales v Fahy* (2007) 81 ALJR 102 ... What *Shirt* requires is a contextual and balanced assessment of the reasonable response to a foreseeable risk. Ultimately, the criterion is reasonableness, not some more stringent requirement of prevention.

Here, the risk of injury consequent upon jumping or diving from the bridge into water of variable depth was reasonably foreseeable. Indeed, the Court of Appeal correctly found, contrary to the trial judge, that the risk was one that was obvious even to a 14 year old boy, and it beggars belief that the RTA could not foresee the very conduct against which its signage warned. The RTA's evidentiary dispute about whether it did in fact know of the continued practice of diving is beside the point: reasonable foreseeability is to be determined objectively, and the present risk was plainly foreseeable on any objective standard.

The magnitude of the risk was self-evidently grave. Mr Dederer's partial paralysis is among the worst kinds of injuries imaginable. The probability of that injury occurring was, however, low. Despite the frequency of jumping and diving from the bridge, no-one was injured until Mr Dederer's unfortunate dive.

What, then, of the expense, difficulty and inconvenience of taking alleviating action? The erection of further warning signs would not have been expensive, but Mr Dederer provided no evidence that they would be reasonable. The installation of pool-type fencing and a triangular cap on the handrail would have been more expensive and intrusive. The estimate of the cost of the handrail modification was some $108,072, and it was accepted that the cost of new fencing would be around $150,000 but, again, the reasonableness of such measures is open to doubt.

...

The sign proposed by the trial judge was devised solely by his Honour and there was no evidence that such a sign would have been a reasonable response. The sign adopted by the Court of Appeal, a pictogram indicating "no diving, shallow water", scarcely seems reasonable in light of the trial judge's explicit finding that it would probably have been ignored as well... Mr Dederer admitted that he knew about the variable depth of the estuary and the moving sandbar. A warning sign would not have told him anything he did not already know.

The suggestion that it was negligent not to have installed "pool-type" fencing arose out of the 1992 Austroads Bridge Design Code, which recommended that bridges constructed after 1992 use such vertical balusters ... The Forster-Tuncurry bridge conformed to the applicable standards at the time of its construction. The matter was put to Mr Fogg, whose evidence was that he would be satisfied with the provision of a sign as an alternative to such "pool-type" fencing, and that such fencing was unlikely to deter a person of Mr Dederer's height who wished to dive from the bridge. The Council's Works Engineer and Asset Manager, Mr Keegan, also gave evidence that such fencing had not prevented people jumping from the nearby Bulahdelah bridge.

The suggestion of affixing a triangular cap to the handrail emerged only in the cross-examination of Mr Keegan.... Even if the cap made balancing more difficult, it might be doubted whether this would have impeded Mr Dederer's dive, especially as the risk and danger of diving were part of its attraction.

RTA v Dederer cont.

Returning, then, to the assessment of breach mandated by *Shirt*, it becomes apparent that the RTA did not breach its duty of care. Though grave, the risk faced by Mr Dederer was of a very low probability, and a reasonable response to that risk did not demand the measures suggested by him. Those measures lacked evidential support; were of doubtful utility; would have caused significant expense in the case of the modifications to the handrail and fencing; and were in some cases contrary to express findings of fact.

This was not a case in which the defendant had done nothing in response to a foreseeable risk. To the contrary, the RTA had erected signs warning of, and prohibiting, the very conduct engaged in by Mr Dederer. As this Court stated in *Nagle v Rottnest Island Authority*, a prohibition is "one form of notice – perhaps the most effective form of notice – warning of the danger of diving". In the circumstances, that was a reasonable response, and the law demands no more and no less....

...

KIRBY J: 371 [dissenting] ... An important aspect of the Court's reasoning in *Fahy*, both amongst those who were part of the majority and those who dissented, was an emphasis on the nuanced character of the approach explained in *Shirt*; the fact that the formula there stated is not mathematical in its application; and the fact that it permits a decision-maker, considering what a reasonable person would do by way of response to a foreseeable risk, to reach a conclusion that, in the particular circumstances of the case, it might indeed be that "nothing" or nothing more is required.

Like many decisions before it, *Fahy* emphasised that the formula in *Shirt* "does not focus only upon how the particular injury happened. It requires looking forward to identify what a reasonable person *would* have done, not backward to identify what would have avoided the injury".

...

Correct application of Shirt: The Court of Appeal majority considered the challenge to the primary judge's decision in favour of Mr Dederer, giving proper attention to the foregoing instruction. As well, the majority gave due consideration to later decisions of this Court concerning warning signs in the context of diving injuries. There is no indication that the majority overlooked the holdings of this Court on the approach to be taken to problems of the present kind. To the contrary, the relevant authorities were cited and accurately applied. ...

There is no indication in the majority reasons in the Court of Appeal that Ipp JA or Tobias JA overlooked any of the strictures against mechanistic reasoning or hindsight analysis contained in *Fahy* and in the other cases to which reference is made in their Honours' reasons. They could scarcely have fallen into such a basic error of reasoning in the light of the strongly expressed dissenting reasons of Handley JA.

There being no misapprehension or oversight of the applicable law, the question is whether the majority in the Court of Appeal nevertheless reached a conclusion on the breach of duty issue that indicates error and warrants the intervention of this Court.

Having identified the ambit of the RTA's duty of care and affirmed the primary judge's conclusion that the RTA knew of the continuing practice of children and young people jumping or diving off the bridge ... Ipp JA analysed, prospectively, what, armed with such knowledge, the RTA ought reasonably to have done. Into the equation, Ipp JA added the knowledge that the RTA had gathered over the years about the sand movements and variable depth of the river bed beneath the bridge ... [and the fact that the signs were useless] ... It is against this backdrop that Ipp JA addressed the reasonableness of the RTA's response to the clearly established risk to persons such as Mr Dederer. Correctly, his Honour rejected the suggestion that the RTA was excused from action simply because no significant injury had previously occurred ... The foregoing made it important that the RTA should respond to its demonstrated knowledge of the sources of the risk of which it was aware by taking accident prevention measures beyond mere reliance on signs, which can never be an "automatic, absolute and permanent panacea" for that purpose. Both Ipp JA (with whom Tobias JA agreed) and the primary judge concluded that reasonable steps involved the installation of a sign with a combination of symbols and words. The RTA's reliance alone on a sign of unexplained prohibition was inadequate ...

The use of such a verbal warning together with a symbol – especially if placed near where children and young people were frequently seen to be entering the water from the bridge – would have been a reasonable response, in terms of signage. Questions of resources would scarcely come into such a modification. What was needed was something more than the "least" response to the problem which the Council committee drew to the notice of the RTA ...

Ipp JA dealt in a convincing way with the lack of cogency of the excuse about the "availability of resources", with the justiciability of Mr Dederer's contentions and with the RTA's passing concentration on the need to upgrade the walkway and the suggested lack of resources available to it for that purpose....

More than signs needed: Given the fact that the existing signs were ineffective to deter or prevent children diving from the bridge, Ipp JA supported, apart from improved signage, the two further initiatives which the primary judge had held that the RTA should have taken ...

Three developments, noted in the evidence, lend strength to Ipp JA's conclusion. The first was the introduction of the new Bridge Design Code in 1992, of which the RTA was aware. The second was the opportunity provided in 1993 by the replacement of wire in the area of the horizontal railings which afforded such ease of access to the flat upper railing. The third was the growing familiarity of the Australian community with the special need to protect young people in the vicinity of water. If it was good enough to impose such an obligation on domestic pool owners, in all of their variety and with their many different means, it was not unreasonable, at least from the 1990s, to expect a similar sense of responsibility on the part of a public authority which had been alerted to the special dangers and risks to young persons in the use of a structure for which it was responsible. Clearly Ipp JA and Tobias JA so concluded. That conclusion was open to them.

[Gummow, Callinan and Heydon JJ thought the appeal should be allowed. Gleeson CJ and Kirby J thought the appeal should be dismissed. Note: The Council was joined late to these proceedings and for that reason was able to take advantage of the Recreational Activities provisions of the *Civil Liability Act 2002* (NSW). The Court of Appeal held that the Council was relieved from liability by the Act. See [12.205] Recreational activities below.]

[12.110] **Notes&Questions**

1. *Romeo v Conservation Commission* and *Bolton v Stone* [1951] AC 850 are both examples of serious injuries occurring in situations where the probability of the risk of injury eventuating was low, although the likely seriousness of any eventual injury was moderate to high. The plaintiff failed in both. Other cases in which the risk of injury has been held to be so small as to justify no precautions being taken include *Smith v BHP Co Ltd* (1957) 97 CLR 337; *Rae v BHP Co Ltd* (1957) 97 CLR 417; *Faufoulas v F G Strang Pty Ltd* (1970) 123 CLR 168. See also *Hoikkala v King* (1989) 9 MVR 293, and *Stewart v Connell* (1984) 2 MVR 239, quoted in *Winters v Davidson* (1989) 9 MVR 239 at 251. By contrast, in *Manley v Alexander* (2005) 80 ALJR 413 the defendant driver was held liable for running over the inebriated plaintiff despite the Court's view at [12] that "It may readily be accepted that the possibility that someone would be found lying on a roadway ... at 4am is properly to be described as remote".

2. As discussed above, probability cannot be judged in the light of the "hindsight bias", that is, the judgment must be made at a time prior to the plaintiff's accident, based on information available to the reasonable defendant at that time. Even the fact that another similar accident had occurred at the same place previously does not necessarily bear on the probability of the given accident occurring (see *Vairy v Wyong Shire Council* (2005) 223 CLR 422 at [12.80]) although it clearly affects the foreseeability of such an accident. The obviousness of the risk (see [12.185]) may affect the probability of its eventuating, as explained by Hayne J in *Vairy*: "The probability of occurrence of a risk that is not apparent on casual observation of a locality or of a set of circumstances may be higher than the probability of occurrence of a risk that is readily apparent to even the casual observer" (see [12.80]).

The gravity or likely seriousness of the harm

[12.115] The following extract, *Paris v Stepney Borough Council* [1951] AC 367, illustrates that, in situations where the defendant knows of some particular vulnerability to greater injury on the part of the plaintiff, the seriousness of the potential consequences elevates the level of care required by the defendant, notwithstanding that the probability of injury is the same for this individual as for all others.

Paris v Stepney Borough Council

[12.120] *Paris v Stepney Borough Council* [1951] AC 367 House of Lords

(footnotes partially omitted)

[The plaintiff was employed from 1942 as a fitter in the defendant's garage. The defendant employer knew he had the use of only one eye, having been partially blinded during an air raid. While he was using a hammer to remove a bolt on a vehicle, a chip of metal flew off and entered his good eye, injuring it so that he became almost totally blind. He alleged that the employer's failure to supply safety goggles constituted breach of duty. There was evidence that it was not the ordinary practice for employers to supply goggles to men employed in garages on the maintenance and repair of vehicles, and the Court of Appeal held there was no duty to do so (such a finding would not occur today). The trial judge's decision in favour of the plaintiff was reversed unanimously by the Court of Appeal, but he succeeded in the House of Lords 3:2].

LORD MACDERMOTT: 387 [The Court of Appeal's] decision appears to have been based on two conclusions – first, that on the evidence there was no duty on the respondents to provide goggles for the ordinary, two-eyed workman engaged on this work, and, secondly, that there was, therefore, no such duty on the respondents in respect of the appellant because, though the consequences for him were more serious, the risk of the accident occurring was no greater in his case than it was in the case of his two-eyed fellows. The proposition underlying this second conclusion is succinctly stated by Asquith LJ in a passage which, I believe, represented the unanimous opinion of the court ... "The disability can only be relevant to the stringency of the duty owed to the workman if it increases the risk to which the workman is exposed. A one-eyed man is no more likely to get a splinter or a chip in his eye than is a two-eyed man. The risk is no greater, but the damage is greater to a man using his only good eye than to a man using two good eyes. The *quantum* of damage, however, is one thing, and the scope of duty is another. The greater risk of injury is not the same thing as the risk of greater injury, and the first thing seems to me to be relevant here."

It is no less clear that the duty is owed to the workman as an individual and that it must be considered in relation to the facts of each particular case. Now, if the law is as stated by the Court of

Paris v Stepney Borough Council cont.

Appeal, it means that this duty of reasonable care can be discharged without regard to the gravity of the harm which is likely to fall on the workman concerned. Reasonable care is, indeed, to be taken in respect of risk that may cause injury, but the requisite degree of care is determinable irrespective of the likely consequences for the particular workman. In short, where the risk of an injury-producing event is the same for all, the standard of reasonable care is the same towards all, and the foreseeable extent of the resulting injury in any given case.

My Lords, this doctrine finds no support in authority, and is, in my opinion, entirely alien to the character of the relationship to which it has been applied by the Court of Appeal. For workman and employer alike such expressions as "risk," "danger" and "safety" would lose much of their everyday meaning if divorced from the results to life and limb. In this sphere they must surely, in the very nature of things, connote consequences as well as causes. If a bricklayer says that the risk is greater at the top of a building, he means that a slip there is more likely to bring him death or injury, and if he says that a particular form of scaffolding is dangerous or not safe, he means not merely that it may fall, but that those who use it may get hurt. What may happen to those engaged is no less important than how it may happen. It is the consequences that necessitate the precautions in this field. The habitual association of cause and effect in workshop and factory is, perhaps, nowhere more clearly recognised than in the nature of some of the safeguards in common use. Suitable goggles, for example, must be worn by those employed at grinding machines … Instances of this sort could be multiplied, but I think it is enough to say that the employer's duty to take reasonable care for the safety of his workmen is directed – and, I venture to add, obviously directed – to their welfare, and for that reason, if for no other, must be related to both the risk and the degree of the injury. If that is so, and if, as was very properly conceded, the duty is that owed to the individual and not to a class, it seems to me to follow that the known circumstance that a particular workman is likely to suffer a graver injury than his fellows from the happening of a given event is one which must be taken into consideration in assessing the nature of the employer's obligation to that workman.

For these reasons I am of opinion that the Court of Appeal was wrong and that Lynskey J was right regarding the relevance of the respondents' knowledge of the appellant's eye defect.

I incline to the view that it was the duty of the employers to [provide goggles]. The point, however, is a balanced one and I will proceed on the assumption that the Court of Appeal was right on this aspect of the case and that the respondents were not under any general obligation of this kind. So assuming, the question then arises whether the additional element, the fact that the respondents knew that the appellant was a one-eyed man, made it proper to arrive at a different conclusion regarding their duty to him. In my opinion, it did. Not merely was the risk of this sort of accident occurring to those engaged on this work known; it was also known that that risk was fraught with much graver consequence for the appellant than for his two-eyed companions. His chances of being blinded were appreciably greater and blindness is an affliction in a class by itself which reasonable men will want to keep from those who work for them if there are reasonable precautions which can be taken to that end. To my mind, whatever may be said of the respondents' duty to their two-eyed employees, there was ample evidence to sustain the view that they failed in their duty to the appellant. I would allow the appeal and restore the finding as to liability of the learned judge.

LORD NORMAND: 380 The test is what precautions would the ordinary, reasonable and prudent man take? The relevant considerations include all those facts which could affect the conduct of a reasonable and prudent man and his decision on the precautions to be taken. Would a reasonable and prudent man be influenced, not only by the greater or less probability of an accident occurring but also by the gravity of the consequences if an accident does occur? In *Mackintosh v Mackintosh* Lord Neaves … said (2 Macph (Ct of Sess) 1362):

> … it must be observed that in all cases the amount of care which a prudent man will take must vary infinitely according to circumstances. No prudent man in carrying a lighted candle

Paris v Stepney Borough Council cont.

> through a powder magazine would fail to take more care than if he was going through a damp cellar. The amount of care will be proportionate to the degree of risk run, and to the magnitude of the mischief that may be occasioned.

... The court's task of deciding what precautions a reasonable and prudent man would take in the circumstances of a particular case may not be easy. Nevertheless, the judgment of the reasonable and prudent man should be allowed its common every-day scope, and it should not be restrained from considering the foreseeable consequences of an accident and their seriousness for the person to whom the duty of care is owed. Such a restriction, if it might sometimes simplify the task of the judge or jury, would be an undue and artificial simplification of the problem to be solved. If the court were now to take the narrow view proposed by the respondents the cleavage between the legal conception of the precautions which a reasonable and prudent man would take and the precautions which reasonable and prudent men do in fact take would lessen the respect which the administration of justice ought to command. To guard against possible misunderstanding it may be well to add here that the seriousness of the injury or damage risked and the likelihood of its being in fact caused may not be the only relevant factors. For example, Asquith LJ in *Daborn v Bath Tramways Motor Co Ltd & Trevor Smithey*, pointed out that it is sometimes necessary to take account of the consequence of not assuming a risk. I am unable, therefore, to reject the conclusion arrived at by Lynskey J, on the ground on which the Court of Appeal proceeded, but that does not end the appeal. For there remains the question whether, assuming that the fact that the appellant was to the knowledge of the respondents a one-eyed man was a relevant circumstance, the judgment of Lynskey J was in accordance with the evidence. The kind of evidence necessary to establish neglect of a proper precaution was considered in *Morton v William Dixon* by Lord Dunedin, Lord President ... [who] said (1909 SC 809):

> Where the negligence of the employer consists of what I may call a fault of omission, I think it is absolutely necessary that the proof of that fault of omission should be one of two kinds, either – to show that the thing which he did not do was a thing which was commonly done by other persons in like circumstances or – to show that it was a thing which was so obviously wanted

The rule is stated with all the Lord President's trenchant lucidity. It contains an emphatic warning against a facile finding that a precaution is necessary when there is no proof that it is one taken by other persons in like circumstances, but it does not detract from the test of the conduct and judgment of the reasonable and prudent man. If there is proof that a precaution is usually observed by other persons, a reasonable and prudent man will follow the usual practice in the like circumstances. Failing such proof the test is whether the precaution is one which the reasonable and prudent man would think so obvious that it was folly to omit it.

In the present case, as I have already said, the balance of the evidence inclines heavily against the appellant on the question of the usual practice of others, but that evidence necessarily dealt with the normal case when the employee suffers from no special disablement. In the nature of things there could scarcely be proof of what was the usual precautions taken by other employers if the workmen had but one good eye. ... Even for a two-eyed man the risk of losing one eye is a very grievous risk, not to speak of the foreseeable possibility that both eyes might be simultaneously destroyed, or that the loss of one eye might have as a sequel the destruction of vision in the other. It may be said that, if it is obvious that goggles should have been supplied to a one-eyed workman, it is scarcely less obvious that they should have been supplied to all the workmen, and, therefore, that the judgment rests on unreal or insufficient distinction between the gravity of the risk run by a one-eyed man and the gravity of the risk run by a two-eyed man. I recognise that the argument has some force, but I do not assent to it. Blindness is so great a calamity that even the loss of one of two good eyes is not comparable, and the risk of blindness from sparks of metal is greater for a one-eyed man than for a two-eyed man, for it is less likely that both eyes should be damaged than that one eye should, and the loss of one eye is not necessarily or even usually followed by blindness in the other. What precautions were needed to protect two-eyed men, and whether it could properly be held, in the teeth of the evidence of the usual practice, that goggles should have been supplied for them, were not questions which the learned judge had necessarily to decide. Therefore, though there might have been advantages of lucidity and cogency if the precautions needed for the protection of the two-eyed men had first been considered and the increased risk of damage to which the one-eyed man is exposed had been expressly contrasted, I would allow the appeal and restore the judgment of Lynskey J.

[12.125] **Notes&Questions**

1. Lord Normand (at 381), in the majority in *Paris v Stepney Borough Council* [1951] AC 367, saw the question raised as: "Would a reasonable and prudent man be influenced, not only by the greater or less probability of an accident occurring, but also by the gravity of the consequences if an accident does occur?" In favour of an affirmative answer, he referred to the statement of Lord Neaves, in *Mackintosh v Mackintosh* (1864) 2 Macph (Ct of Sess) 1357 at 1362-1363, that "no prudent man in carrying a lighted candle through a powder magazine would fail to take more care than if he was going through a damp cellar". Thus, Lord Wright, in dealing with the risk of damage from gas escaping from a main in *Northwestern Utilities Ltd v London Guarantee & Accident Co Ltd* [1936] AC 108 at 126 said: "The degree of care which that duty involves must be proportioned to the degree of risk involved if the duty should not be fulfilled."
2. As some of the examples taken in *Paris v Stepney Borough Council* [1951] AC 367 indicate, the amount of harm which may be caused varies not only with the vulnerability of the plaintiff, but with the degree of danger arising out of the kind of agency with which the defendant is dealing. In *Thompson v Smiths Shiprepairers (North Shields) Ltd* [1984] QB 405, Mustill J pointed out that general damage to human hearing from the noise level in shipyards had come to be recognised in recent years and equipment to protect individual employees had become available. He therefore held the defendants liable to a number of plaintiff employees for failure to keep abreast of what was foreseeable and practicable to avoid in the light of scientific and industrial developments.

   In cases of dangerous chattels, the degree of danger in the situation goes to the question of what is required for the satisfaction of the standard of reasonable care. Thus, in *Adelaide Chemical & Fertilizer Co Ltd v Carlyle* (1940) 64 CLR 514, the High Court adopted this approach to the liability of a manufacturer of sulphuric acid, who had sent it out in brittle containers, and was held liable for the death of the plaintiff's husband caused by the container breaking when he was using it. Starke J said:

   > In my judgment, earthenware jars containing sulphuric acid do fall within the category of things dangerous in themselves because the acid if it escaped might put life or limb in peril, particularly the lives and limbs of those who handled them or used the acid. But still the law, in my judgment, does not impose a rule of strict and unqualified liability in the case of things dangerous in themselves. The degree of care that is required in the case of such things is that which is reasonable in the circumstances, that which a reasonably prudent man would exercise in the circumstances. A reasonably prudent man would, no doubt, in the cases of such things exercise a "keener foresight" or a

> "degree of diligence so stringent as to amount practically to a guarantee of safety" or "a high degree of care amounting in effect to an insurance against risk" or "the greatest care" or "consummate care". The duty is "more imperious" where things dangerous in themselves are being handled. (at 523)

This was echoed by the High Court in *Burnie Port Authority v General Jones Pty Ltd* (1994) 179 CLR 520:

> In the case of dangerous substances or activities, a reasonably prudent person would exercise a higher degree of care. Indeed, depending upon the magnitude of the danger, the standard of reasonable care may involve a degree of diligence so stringent as to amount practically to a guarantee of safety. (at 554)

3. Note that "practically a guarantee of safety" comes very close to the notion of strict liability. The High Court moved away from strict liability as the basis of liability in *Burnie Port Authority v General Jones* (1994) 179 CLR 520 when it decided that the old strict liability tort of *Rylands v Fletcher* (1868) LR 3 HL 330 had been subsumed into negligence (see [15.120]). However, an elevated standard of care is entirely consistent with a highly foreseeable risk of serious injury, such as the fire which destroyed the plaintiff's premises in *Burnie Port*. See also *New South Wales v Lepore; Samin v Queensland; Rich v Queensland* (2003) 212 CLR 511, Gleeson CJ at [33] and Gummow and Hayne JJ at [266] (see [15.130]).

4. Sometimes what is demanded in the way of reasonable care from the defendant is affected both by the fact that the defendant has been confronted with an especially vulnerable plaintiff and by the fact that there is an especially dangerous substance involved. In *Yachuk v Oliver Blais Co Ltd* [1949] AC 386 the defendant had supplied petrol to a nine year old boy, on the boy's deceitful statement that he wanted it for his mother "stuck down the road". In fact, it was used to make torches for a Red Indian game in which the plaintiff was injured. All the blame was attributed to the defendant without reduction for contributory negligence of the plaintiff. Lord Du Parcq, delivering the opinion of the Privy Council, said:

> To put a highly inflammable substance into the hands of a small boy is to subject him to temptation and the risk of injury, and this is no less true if the boy has resorted to deceit in order to overcome the supplier's scruples. The child's deceit can afford no excuse to the supplier when it is found that the story told was such as to arouse, rather than allay, suspicion in the mind of a reasonable man. In the circumstances, therefore, their Lordships think that McRuer JA was right in applying to this case the principle stated by Lord Denman CJ in *Lynch v Nurdin* (1841) 1 QB 30; 113 ER 1041 at 38 (QB): "The most blameable carelessness of this servant having tempted the child, he [the defendant] ought not to reproach the child with yielding to that temptation. He has been the real and only cause of the mischief. He has been deficient in ordinary care: the child, acting without prudence or thought, has, however, shown those qualities in as great a degree as he could be expected to possess them. His misconduct bears no proportion to that of the defendant which produced it". (at 394-395)

Burden of taking precautions

Woods v Multi-Sport Holdings

[12.130] *Woods v Multi-Sport Holdings Pty Ltd* High Court of Australia (2002) 208 CLR 460 (footnotes omitted)

[The plaintiff suffered serious injury, leading to 99 per cent blindness in one eye, during a game of indoor cricket organised by the defendant and played on its premises. Certain equipment was supplied, not including helmets or pads. Duty of care was conceded, the main issue being what steps the defendant ought reasonably to have taken to avoid the risk of injury. Particulars of negligence included failure to supply eye protection and failure to erect a sign warning of the dangers of the game. The High Court split 3:2, the majority finding for the defendant on breach of duty. Callinan J concurred with Gleeson CJ in a separate judgement, and Hayne JJ generally agreed. Kirby and McHugh JJ dissented. The case provides a good illustration of the balancing of the relevant factors and competing considerations, and illustrates conflicting approaches to expert evidence.]

GLEESON CJ: 465 This is a body contact sport, involving what Mr Lewis called "clashing". There is a good deal of diving by both fielders and batters, who throw themselves onto, and slide along, a synthetic carpet, as they seek to field the ball, or make runs, as the case may be. The prevalence of diving and sliding is significant in considering a suggestion that players should wear helmets with metal grills protruding some distance from their faces. So frequent are collisions, that there are rules which prescribe who has right of way. Because the game is played at a fast pace, in a confined space, there is not only a high risk of collision between players, there is also a danger of players being struck by the ball.

One of the medical witnesses called for the appellant gave evidence of a report he had prepared about eye injuries, and the possibility of protective measures, in indoor cricket. The trial judge summarised part of the report as follows:

> The report also notes that tests have indicated that eye protection where available for rac[qu]et sports is not able to withstand the impact of an indoor cricket ball. It is therefore considered that only full face cricket helmets would be adequate for eye protection in playing indoor cricket. It also notes that because of the proximity of players *every player* in an indoor cricket field would need to wear a full face batting helmet. (emphasis added)

Dr McAllister, who is head of the Ophthalmology Department of Royal Perth Hospital, said that most of the major eye injuries suffered in Western Australia as a result of trauma were referred to him. He estimated that over 10 years he would have seen approximately 20 significant eye injuries arising from accidents in indoor cricket. He did not attempt to distinguish between batsmen and fielders. The trial judge recorded that the witness "conceded that on the basis that there are approximately 12,500 people playing indoor cricket in Western Australia ... this was not a high percentage but ... his concern was that in his opinion the injuries were preventable". The significance of a figure of an average of two serious eye injuries per year in a population of 12,500 players was a matter for the trial judge to weigh.

The appellant, in his evidence, agreed that he was aware that in playing cricket, outdoors or indoors, either as a batsman or as a fielder, there was a risk of being struck in the head by a ball. French DCJ found that "he was well aware at the time that there was a risk of being hit with the ball". The same, of course, would have applied to the officers and employees of the respondent.

As Kitto J pointed out in *Rootes v Shelton* (1967) 116 CLR 383 at 387, people have taken pleasure in engaging in risky games since long before the law of negligence was formulated, and there is nothing new or mysterious about the application of the law to such conduct. But the sporting context may be of special significance in relation to a factual judgment that must be made.

Because the concept of foreseeability in the law of negligence has been taken to embrace risks which are quite unlikely to occur, and to mean only that a risk is not one that is far-fetched or fanciful,

Woods v Multi-Sport Holdings cont.

many of the cases which discuss the approach to be taken by a tribunal of fact in deciding whether there has been a breach of a duty of care speak in terms of balancing the magnitude of the risk with the cost or inconvenience of preventing it. But, as Mason J pointed out in *Wyong Shire Council v Shirt* (1980) 146 CLR 40 at 47, ultimately the question of fact is what a reasonable person, in the position of the defendant, would do by way of response to the risk.

In some cases, of which the present is an example, a court is not confronted with a risk that is quite unlikely to occur; it is dealing with an activity which carries with it the possibility of injury, including serious injury, in a number of different forms. The appellant was not a child, and he was not being compelled to play the game. He was an adult who chose, for his personal enjoyment, to play. That the activity is risky is plain to anyone who understands what it involves, including the respondent. The respondent carried on the business of providing facilities for persons such as the appellant to play the game. The question for the tribunal of fact was what reasonableness required by way of response from the respondent, having regard to the respects in which the respondent was alleged to have been negligent.

Where it is claimed that reasonableness requires one person to provide protection, or warning, to another, the relationship between the parties, and the context in which they entered into that relationship, may be significant. The relationship of control that exists between an employer and an employee, or of wardship that exists between a school authority and a pupil, may have practical consequences, as to what it is reasonable to expect by way of protection or warning, different from those which flow from the relationship between the proprietor of a sporting facility and an adult who voluntarily uses the facility for recreational purposes. I say "may", because it is ultimately a question of factual judgment, to be made in the light of all the circumstances of a particular case.

French DCJ ... was not prepared to conclude that it was reasonable to expect the respondent to provide players such as the appellant with a form of protective headgear in circumstances where none had been designed for the game, none was worn by players elsewhere, the rules of the game did not provide for such headgear, and the manner in which the game was played meant that there were considerations of convenience and safety that provided good reasons why such headgear was not worn. The respondent did not fail to provide the appellant with some item of protective equipment which was available on the market, and commonly used by indoor cricketers. The incidence of serious eye injuries, in the trial judge's view, was not such as to dictate that the respondent should have provided other than the standard equipment normally used by adult players of the sport. That was an assessment that was open as a matter of judgment. Decision-makers might respond differently to that part of the evidence, but French DCJ was the tribunal of fact, and the Full Court agreed with her. No sufficient reason has been shown for this Court to disagree with her assessment.

As to the matter of the warning, the trial judge dealt with the appellant's case as it was put to her. The case was that there should have been a warning of the dangers associated with indoor cricket and, in particular, the danger of serious eye injury. It is useful to reflect upon what exactly might have been the content of the warning. There was no reason to limit it to the risk of head injury, much less eye injury. There was one particular respect in which the type of eye injury suffered at indoor cricket can be different from the type suffered at outdoor cricket, but there were probably also a number of respects in which the risk of back injury, or concussion from collisions, might be different from the risks associated with outdoor cricket. The risk that, in the confined space in which the game was played, any player, batsman or fielder, might receive a severe blow to any part of the head, including the eye, was, the trial judge found, obvious, and well known to the appellant. It was argued that the appellant was not aware of the precise nature, and full extent, of the risk. But warnings of the kind here in question are not intended to address matters of precision. French DCJ concluded that the risk of a player being struck in the face by a cricket ball was so obvious that reasonableness did not require the respondent to warn players about it.

Woods v Multi-Sport Holdings cont.

The appeal should be dismissed with costs.

McHUGH J: [Dissenting] 475 In my opinion, Multi-Sport breached its duty in two respects: first, in not providing the appellant – Mr Michael Woods – with a protective helmet and second, in not warning him of the special risks of eye injury while playing indoor cricket. Accordingly, the appeal should be allowed and judgment entered in favour of Mr Woods.

Expert evidence established that squash and indoor cricket were responsible for the highest number of eye injuries in all sports in Western Australia. In a six month period in 1988-1989, ophthalmologists in Western Australia reported 38 injuries to a register of sport-related injury set up by a Save Sight Foundation. A test had also shown that any helmet that would protect against eye injury in outdoor cricket would provide sufficient protection for the playing of indoor cricket. Evidence also showed that the wearing of protective helmets and face guards in sports such as ice hockey and lacrosse had dramatically reduced the incidence of eye injury. The learned trial judge found that the cost of providing and maintaining outdoor helmets was not high enough to deter an indoor cricket centre from providing them.

According to the evidence of a witness, who was the owner of an indoor cricket centre and an experienced indoor cricket player, however, the protruding visor on the outdoor helmet posed an injury risk to other players. This evidence was effectively contradicted by Dr Anderson, an ophthalmologist expert in sport-related eye injuries. He had examined studies on the effect of wearing helmets. They had not shown any case anywhere in the world of another player being injured by the wearing of a helmet. He thought that the risk of injury to another player from the wearing of a helmet must be very small.

Upon these facts and this evidence, I am of the opinion that the respondent was in breach of the duty of care that it admittedly owed to Mr Woods. If a jury had tried the case, Multi-Sport could not have obtained a verdict as a matter of law. Multi-Sport knew or ought to have known of the risk of an eye injury. On the expert evidence, it was reasonably foreseeable that such an injury could occur. Those who organise activities for reward to themselves must keep abreast of publicly available or expert knowledge concerning the risks of injury in such activities. The duty of reasonable care demands nothing less. If Multi-Sport did not know of the risk of eye injury from indoor cricket, it ought to have known of it. There was also evidence that could support a finding that a protective helmet was available as a reasonably practicable means of avoiding the risk. The trial judge held that, if a helmet had been available, Mr Woods would have worn it.

As a matter of law, therefore, it was open to the trial judge to find as a fact that Multi-Sport had breached the duty of care that it admittedly owed to Mr Woods. And as a matter of fact, the trial judge, sitting as a juror, ought to have found that Multi-Sport had breached its duty. The gravity of the risk, the degree of probability of it occurring and the small cost of avoiding it combined to make it unreasonable for Multi-Sport to fail to eliminate the risk (*Wyong SC v Shirt* (1980) 146 CLR 40 at 47-48).

The appeal should be allowed.

Neindorf v Junkovic

[12.135] *Neindorf v Junkovic* (2005) 222 ALR 631 High Court of Australia

(footnotes partially omitted)

[The facts are adequately outlined within the judgment of Gleeson CJ.]

GLEESON CJ: [2] The respondent suffered injury when she tripped on an uneven surface in the driveway of the appellant's home while attending a garage sale, and fell …

Neindorf v Junkovic cont.

Ordinary dwelling houses contain many hazards which give rise to a real risk of injury. Most householders do not attempt to eliminate, or warn against, all such hazards ... Not all people live, or can afford to live, in premises that are completely free of hazards. In fact, nobody lives in premises that are risk-free. Concrete pathways crack. Unpaved surfaces become slippery, or uneven. Many objects in dwelling houses could be a cause of injury. People enter dwelling houses for a variety of purposes, and in many different circumstances. Entrants may have differing capacities to observe and appreciate risks, and to take care for their own safety. An ordinary kitchen might be reasonably safe for an adult, and hazardous to a small child. The expression "reasonable response in the circumstances" raises a question of normative judgment which has to grapple with all the practical problems that the law had earlier attempted to solve [by classifying entrants into categories for the purpose of determining an occupier's liability] ... The problems did not disappear. They now require consideration under a somewhat different rubric. The fundamental problem remains the extent to which it is reasonable to require occupiers to protect entrants from a risk of injury associated with the condition of the premises.

It is a matter upon which different views are legitimately open. When courts refer to "community values", they may create an impression that such values are reasonably clear, and readily discernible. Sometimes a judge might be attributing his or her personal values to the community with little empirical justification for a belief that those values are widely shared. Reasonableness, however, is not a matter of legal prescription. That was the fundamental weakness of the old approach to occupiers' liability. It was for the very purpose of avoiding that error that the new, more flexible, approach was adopted.

It has been many years since questions such as these were resolved in South Australia by juries. The jury system had the advantage of committing a judgment on reasonableness to the collective wisdom of a group of citizens chosen at random from the community. The divergence of judicial opinion in the present case upon what is essentially a question of the reasonableness of the behaviour of a householder probably reflects a diversity of opinion that would exist through the whole community. Such diversity is exposed when decisions are made by judges, who give reasons for their decisions, rather than by jurors, who simply deliver an inscrutable verdict.

In South Australia, the Parliament has intervened to an extent. Rather than rest with a standard of care at the level of generality expressed in *Hackshaw* [*Hackshaw v Shaw* (1984) 155 CLR 614)] and *Zaluzna* [*Australian Safeway Stores Pty Ltd v Zaluzna* (1987) 162 CLR 479] the South Australian Parliament, in Pt 1B of the *Wrongs Act 1936* (SA) (now Pt 4 of the *Civil Liability Act 1936* (SA)), gave directions to courts as to what was to be taken into account in determining the standard of care to be exercised by an occupier of premises. Section 17C(2) listed a series of matters, all of which go to questions of reasonable response to risk, and concluded by referring to "any other matter that the court thinks relevant". The matters listed in pars (a) to (g) of s 17C(2) included factors that, in one way or another, were taken into account in the old common law categories, but the inflexibility of the old approach was not revived. Section 17C(3) then provided:

> (3) The fact that an occupier has not taken any measures to eliminate, reduce or warn against a danger arising from the state or condition of premises does not necessarily show that the occupier has failed to exercise a reasonable standard of care.

That, from one point of view, is a statement of the obvious. If doing nothing about a hazard were of itself sufficient to constitute negligence, there would probably not be an occupier of land in South Australia who could pass that test. It is, however, a useful reminder to decision-makers. The kind of hazard involved in the present case illustrates why that is so. The hazard was an unevenness in the surface of land which could cause a person to trip and fall. There would be few, if any, suburban houses that do not contain hazards of that kind.

A similar reminder is to be found in par (g) of s 17C(2), which requires the court to take account of:

Neindorf v Junkovic cont.

(g) the extent *(if at all)* to which it would have been *reasonable* and practicable for the occupier to take measures to eliminate, reduce or warn against the danger. (emphasis added).

The response of most people to many hazards in and around their premises is to do nothing. The legislature has recognised, and has reminded courts, that, often, that may be a reasonable response. Whether, in any particular case, it is a reasonable response is not a matter of legal doctrine. It is not a question of law. It is a question that, historically, courts committed to juries as a question of fact. Judges will have their own opinions about reasonableness, but they are not opinions of law (cf *Woods v Multi-Sport Holdings Pty Ltd* (2002) 208 CLR 460 at 474 [44]-[45], 500 [127]).

In the Supreme Court of South Australia, two judges (Besanko J at first instance, and Doyle CJ in dissent on appeal) considered that the conduct of the appellant did not constitute a failure to take reasonable care for the safety of the respondent. The unevenness of the surface on which the respondent tripped was so ordinary, and so visible, that reasonableness did not require any action on the part of the occupier. Two judges (Nyland J and Gray J) came to a different view.

Like Hayne J and Callinan and Heydon JJ, and substantially for the reasons given by them, I agree with the conclusions reached by Besanko J and Doyle CJ.

I agree with the orders proposed by Hayne J.

KIRBY J: [Dissenting]

[18] This appeal concerns the law of negligence … Such disparity in judicial outcomes [referring to the differences of opinion at the various levels in the court hierarchy] in an otherwise unremarkable case suggests that legal doctrine in this field of law has become uncertain or unstable. In recent years, such uncertainty and instability has been introduced by changes in the basic rules applicable to negligence liability. Such changes are, in no small part, the product of legislation enacted in all Australian jurisdictions since 2001, designed to effect "tort law reform". But in part the changes have also come about as a result of decisions of this Court. Changing attitudes in this Court to the content of the common law of negligence have resulted in a discernible shift in the outcomes of negligence cases. According to Professors Skene and Luntz, "[t]he common law, as emanating from the High Court of Australia, was already moving to a much more restrictive attitude towards the tort of negligence." Now the shift has been accelerated by statute.

This trend was reflected in the rejection by this Court of the *Caparo* test (*Caparo Industries Plc v Dickman* [1990] 2 AC 605 at 617-618) for the establishment of a duty of care. That test is followed in most other jurisdictions of the common law; but not in Australia. One reason for rejecting *Caparo*, for the ascertainment of the existence (and hence the scope) of a duty of care in negligence, was said to be that it involves the courts too directly in addressing expressly questions of legal and social policy – matters that should be left to Parliament. Yet the shift in judicial outcomes in negligence cases plainly derives from a shift in legal policy, albeit one that is not usually spelt out by judges as *Caparo* would require.

Now, another case presents a defendant's attempt to have this Court alter course, this time from an approach expressed in 1982 (*Webb v South Australia* (1982) 56 ALJR 912; 43 ALR 465). Because this change of course would involve a departure from previous doctrine; undermine responsibility towards legal neighbours that lies at the heart of the modern tort of negligence; and weaken attention to accident prevention, I cannot agree with it.

In my view, the approach of the majority in the Full Court to the law of negligence was correct. This appeal should be dismissed. This Court should call a halt to the erosion of negligence liability and the substitution of indifference to those who are, in law, our neighbours. The erosion, and the indifference, has gone far enough. This appeal therefore involves important questions of legal principle and approach …

Neindorf v Junkovic cont.

As to the measures to eliminate, reduce or warn against the danger, no such measures were taken. None at all. To this day, the appellant simply asserts that the respondent was on her own; being obliged to look after herself.

If the statutory considerations "eliminate, reduce or warn" are taken into account, as an indication of what might be done in the attainment by occupiers of a reasonable standard of care, the measures that were available to the appellant were several. They were relatively obvious. And they were inexpensive. They included, as the magistrate pointed out, the placement of the table in a position straddling the fault in the concrete so as to prevent or diminish the need for members of the public to cross the fault line at its deepest point. They also included the placement of a painted line (or some other perhaps removable strip of identifying material) to highlight the gap in, and change of, the surface. Such markings are now quite common. They are extremely cheap to install. Alternatively, the simple expedient of placing a section of linoleum or a thick mat over the join of the concrete in front of the display table would have reduced the danger inherent in the uneven surface. A warning to elderly entrants to mind their step might have been given. Not one of these elementary and inexpensive precautions was taken.

Reasonableness of taking precautions: As to the extent to which it would have been reasonable and practicable to take such measures, the identified precautions are so modest, inexpensive and obvious that, if the appellant had given fractional attention to making her premises safe for potential entrants such as the respondent, it would not have been a large burden upon her. There is no objective evidence to indicate that any attention was given by her to the issue of accident prevention. The question for decision is therefore whether, within the Wrongs Act criteria and the general principles of the law of negligence that the Act reflects, this is the standard that we have reached in Australia in the exhibition of neighbourly care on the part of persons such as the appellant towards persons such as the respondent. I think not.

Conclusion: A Breach of the Duty of Care

Reasonableness of burden: This brings me to the essential reason that led Doyle CJ to his dissent in the Full Court. His Honour considered that to impose liability on the appellant would be unreasonable having regard to the modest character of the garage sale and the burden that would be involved in assigning a legal duty on suburban household occupiers of the kind propounded for the respondent.

I cannot agree with this conclusion. I consider that the approach of the majority in the Full Court is more consonant with this Court's past legal authority and approach. Whilst the common law of negligence is reflective of notions of reasonableness of outcome, the only safe way to judge particular cases is to approach them by reference to the relevant criteria. The approach of Doyle CJ (and of Besanko J) failed, in my respectful opinion, to pay due attention to three considerations of legal principle identified by Gray J in his reasons. These were first, the need to determine the case primarily by the application of the criteria expressed by Parliament in terms of the *Wrongs Act*. Secondly, to take into particular account the relationship of the parties, established in this case, because the appellant had invited the public at large to enter upon her premises and had an economic interest in their doing so. And thirdly, to consider the fact that apparently the appellant gave no thought whatever to accident prevention, which earlier decisions of this Court had repeatedly emphasised and required.

In his reasons, Gray J referred to the reasons of McHugh JA and myself in the New South Wales Court of Appeal in *Brady* (1986) 7 NSWLR 241. There, McHugh JA said [at 254-255]:

> Equally important in determining what reasonable care requires is the importance to the community of accident prevention. The High Court has recently stated that accident prevention is unquestionably one of the modern responsibilities of an employer: *McLean v Tedman (McLean* (1984) 155 CLR 306 at 313); *Bankstown Foundry Pty Ltd v Braistina (Braistina* (1986) 160 CLR 301 at 308-309) ... Likewise, accident prevention is one of the responsibilities

Neindorf v Junkovic cont.

> of those who for reward, direct or indirect, invite or permit members of the public to attend their premises. … A real risk of injury should be eliminated unless the cost of doing so is disproportionate to the risk.

Adhering to settled doctrine: This Court, if it pleases, can now turn its back on communitarian notions in the law, such as accident prevention. It can hold that the world, like ground surfaces, is not a level playing field [*Ghantous* at 639 [355] per Callinan J (dissenting)]. It can conclude that the common law imposes no relevant duty of care on householders who invite strangers and the public at large to enter their premises to do business there. It can subsume considerations logically applicable to the breach element into the duty of care. It can effectively restore contributory negligence to its former status as a complete defence to liability. However, the Court must be aware that so concluding involves an important change of legal policy. It involves rejection of earlier approaches of this Court and its exposition of the affirmative duties of occupiers (and others) to turn their minds to accident prevention (and hence to insurance).

To the extent that the Court turns away from the earlier principles, in my respectful view it endorses notions of selfishness that are the antithesis of the Atkinian concept of the legal duty that we all owe, in some circumstances, to each other as "neighbours". This is a moral notion, derived originally from Scripture, that has informed the core concept of the English law of negligence that we have inherited and developed in Australia. It is the notion that, in the past, encouraged care and attention for the safety of entrants on the part of those who invite others onto their premises. (It also encouraged such persons to procure insurance against risk). To the extent that these ideas are overthrown, and reversed, this Court diminishes consideration of accident prevention. (It also reduces the utility and necessity of insurance). From the point of view of legal policy, these are not directions in which I would willingly travel.

It is true that in *Thompson v Woolworths (Q'land) Pty Ltd* (2005) 79 ALJR 904 at 911 [36]; 214 ALR 452 at 460-461, five members of this Court, including myself, observed that there are "no risk-free dwelling houses" and that "[t]he community's standards of reasonable behaviour do not require householders to eliminate all risks from their premises, or to place a notice at the front door warning entrants of all the dangers that await them". I do not resile from these comments. In their generality, they remain true. It is not necessary to compile a list of every potential source of danger in and around the house and to install warnings at every possible point of entry to the land. Self-evidently, such a course could not be justified and would probably be futile. However, these comments do not address the risks of the present case which were beyond the ordinary, which were known or knowable to the householder and which were properly enlivened in her mind by her invitation to the public at large to come onto her premises to buy her goods …

Conclusion: What it is reasonable to expect of householders living in the citadel of their domestic premises, behind a closed gate that excludes the world at large, is different from what may reasonably be expected of those who invite the public to enter for desired economic advantage to the occupier. In the latter class of case it is not unreasonable to expect considerations of visitor safety (and in many cases insurance) to attract the occupier's attention. Had that been done in the present case, the precautions that should have been taken were obvious, inexpensive and comparatively trivial. The fact that the appellant did not take any measures at all to eliminate, reduce or warn against the danger did not necessarily show that she had failed to exercise a reasonable standard of care. But the fact that she invited the public at large and failed to attend to a known or knowable danger establishes breach of the appellant's duty of an applicable scope that results in legal liability in accordance with the principles of the law of negligence hitherto accepted by this Court.

Neindorf v Junkovic cont.

[The Appeal was allowed 4:1.]

[12.140] **Notes&Questions**

1. The question of deciding which precautions should have been adopted when there are conflicting possibilities was discussed in *Caledonian Collieries Ltd v Speirs* [1957] 97 CLR 202. There, the plaintiff's husband was killed when his car was struck by a line of runaway railway trucks on a level crossing. The High Court held by a majority of 4:1 that the damage was foreseeable, so what remained to be resolved was the question of how a reasonable person in the defendant's position would have acted as regards taking precautions. The factors considered were very similar to those subsequently laid down in *Wyong Shire Council v Shirt* (1980) 146 CLR 40 at 47-48 [12.35]. Much of the evidence was directed to establishing the relative merits of switch points, which were in place and did not cause derailment, and catch points, which the plaintiff argued should have been installed instead, and which would have derailed the trucks.

   The installation of catch-points would have caused little expense or difficulty. The defendant's case stressed the inconvenience, since long delays would have occurred whenever traffic either used the junction or passed over it, and the conflicting responsibilities, in the form of danger to traffic and persons at the point where trucks might be derailed at the catch-points. The majority judgment rejected the defendant's convenience argument largely on the basis of the sparseness of the traffic and its slowness at that point (at 223-225). On the alternative hazard argument the majority said (at 225):

   > there remained only the consideration that to cause a derailment of runaway trucks is a drastic measure to take in any circumstances. The trucks and the line, and perhaps other property as well, may be damaged, and there is a possibility, though perhaps hardly more, that someone may be injured. But when the danger to be guarded against is of the order of a level crossing collision, it may well be that drastic measures are within the limits of reasonable care. It was certainly a view upon which the jury might legitimately act that on a balance of considerations a reasonable man in the position of the appellant would not have allowed himself to be deterred by the dangers which a derailment might possibly involve from giving users of the level crossing the protection of catch-points.

   The considerations were differently balanced in the dissenting judgment of Webb J (at 228-229), who stressed the competing danger of derailing trucks, and held that the plaintiff had failed to discharge its onus of showing that such an "extreme measure" was a reasonable precaution.

2. See also *Romeo v Conservation Commission NT* ([12.75]), especially the judgment of Kirby J, in relation to resource implications and competing obligations of statutory authority defendants.

Social utility of the risk creating activity

E v Australian Red Cross Society

[12.145] *E v Australian Red Cross Society* (1991) 27 FCR 310 Federal Court of Australia

(footnotes partially omitted)

WILCOX J: 313 This case concerns one of the major health problems of our time: acquired immune deficiency syndrome (AIDS). It is a tragic case, of AIDS contracted by the recipient of a post-operative blood transfusion. Because of its contamination, the transfusion which saved the applicant's life in 1984 threatens now to shorten his life. [Forty two other similar cases were filed at the same time, alleging breaches of the *Trade Practices Act 1974* (Cth) and negligence.] ... Fundamental to each is the sufficiency of the steps taken by the respondents, especially the Society and the NSW Division, to protect the donated blood supply from HIV contamination. In particular, questions arise in each case as to the adequacy of the steps taken to screen donors – by such means as notices, questionnaires and interviews – and whether hepatitis B surrogate testing ought to have been adopted earlier or more widely ...

The respondents do not dispute that they each owed a duty of care to the applicant in connection with the transfused plasma. The question is whether any of them breached that duty. In that connection it is helpful to recall the words of Mason J (with whom Stephen and Aickin JJ agreed) in *Wyong Shire Council v Shirt* (1980) 146 CLR 40 at 47-48 [extracted at [12.35]].

There is no doubt that, in October 1984, a reasonable person in the position of the respondents would have foreseen the possibility of HIV infection from the transfusion supplied to the applicant. ... The whole debate about surrogate testing arose because of the participants' awareness of the risk of transfusion-infection, although they regarded the chance of infection in any particular case as extremely small ... Consequently, in the present case, the first question posed by Mason J [foreseeability] must be answered in the affirmative. The next task is the difficult one: to determine what a reasonable person would do by way of response to that risk. In that connection, it is salutary to recall the warning of Barwick CJ in *Maloney v Commissioner for Railways* (1978) 52 ALJR 292 at 292-293:

> It is easy to overlook the all important emphasis upon the word "reasonable" in the statement of the duty. Perfection or the use of increased knowledge or experience embraced in hindsight after the event should form no part of the components of what is reasonable in all the circumstances. That matter must be judged in prospect and not in retrospect. The likelihood of the incapacitating occurrence, the likely extent of the injuries which the occurrence may cause, the nature and extent of the burden of providing a safeguard against the occurrence and the practicability of the specific safeguard which would do so are all indispensable considerations in determining what ought reasonably to be done.

I turn now to the final ground of liability argued on behalf of the applicant: the failure of the first and second respondents to introduce, and the failure of the third respondent to insist upon, timely anti-HBc surrogate testing. ... [I]t is one thing to say that anti-HBc testing should have been investigated. It is another thing to say that the failure of the first and second respondents to introduce anti-HBc testing before August 1984 was a breach of their duties of care towards blood recipients. Before I could so conclude I would have to determine, upon the basis of the evidence before me, that "the magnitude of the risk and the degree of probability" of HIV blood-transfusion infection would outweigh "the expense, difficulty and inconvenience" of adopting an anti-HBc program: see Mason J in *Shirt*.

There is no question about the magnitude of the risk, for any particular blood recipient. As was appreciated at the time, any person who received blood infected by the agent now known as HIV, would be likely to contract an ultimately fatal disease. But there was considerable difficulty in predicting the chances of infection from a blood transfusion. ...

E v Australian Red Cross Society cont.

Even having regard to the limited, and erroneous, knowledge of the day, and although anti-HBc could only reduce, not eliminate, the risk, there was a case for its adoption ... But the case for adoption of the test had to be set against its disadvantages. The "magnet" factor is extremely difficult to assess ..., [it] cannot be excluded from consideration but I would not give it much weight ... Anti-HBc testing would, of course, have involved an additional financial cost ... [but] the financial cost of surrogate testing was not really an issue in the debate. The real cost would have been the wastage of useable blood.

There is not a lot of evidence about the ramifications for the blood supply of anti-HBc testing ... Sydney donations fell by 4,776 (2.45 per cent), as compared with the previous year. ... Expressed as a percentage, the 1983-1984 loss is not large. But that loss must be assessed in the context of ... "a constantly increasing demand for blood and blood components" ... Dr Archer believed that about 5 per cent of all blood donated in New South Wales would prove positive to an anti-HBc test. The reasonableness of this belief is not challenged ... So, a pre-August 1984 decision to introduce anti-HBc tests, and to discard positive donations, would have meant the likely loss of 5 per cent of all donations, on top of the 1.47 per cent already lost. How serious would that situation have been?

As Dr Baird commented in his evidence, blood is a "precious resource". Any inadequacy in the supply is a matter of major concern. If blood is not available for transfusion, operations will be postponed. Some postponements may cause mere inconvenience; others may lead to more serious consequences, even death. And of course, hospitals must have enough blood to cope with emergencies, especially accident cases; otherwise deaths will result. But how critical was the last 5 per cent of the supply? In practice, would the loss of a further 5 per cent of blood have caused any problem; and, if so, to what degree? Surprisingly, the evidence does not provide answers to these questions ... I think that I should interpret Dr Archer's general statements as an indication of his perception that any reduction in the available blood supply would have had serious practical effects.

Upon that basis, the problem for a person in the position of Dr Archer in, say, February 1984 would be to weigh the concern that contaminated blood will be received by the BTS, despite its appeals to high risk persons not to give blood, against the supply difficulties which would follow the introduction of anti-HBc testing. The Court could only uphold the applicant's claim that the first and second respondents were negligent in failing to introduce surrogate testing at that time if it were satisfied that a prudent person in the position of those respondents would have determined that the concern for contamination outweighed the difficulties which would ensue from reducing the blood supply. When the matter is stated in this way, it seems to me to be apparent that the claim cannot succeed ...

The claim that the first and second respondents ought to have decided to adopt anti-HBc surrogate testing earlier than August 1984 suffers from the handicap that it is opposed to the practice which predominated in the United States, the country with the greatest experience of AIDS cases. That handicap is formidable; but, as I have indicated, I would not be prepared to regard it as decisive. If I felt that, upon the evidence available to the Court, the only prudent course for persons in the position of the first and second respondents – in the light of their then knowledge – was to introduce anti-HBc, I would uphold the claim of breach of duty, whatever the American practice. But such a course would involve the Court in making the judgment, without any supporting expert evidence, that a prudent blood banker should have determined that it was better to accept the loss of 5 per cent of the blood supply rather than the mere risk of HIV contamination of the blood supply. Particularly in the absence of evidence as to the consequences of losing 5 per cent of the blood supply, I cannot make that judgment .... My findings against the applicant, in relation to each of the bases of liability argued on his behalf, require me to dismiss his application ...

In one sense, it is a cause of satisfaction to reach the conclusion that institutions with the respondents' reputations and history of service to the community have not been proved derelict in their duty towards the applicant. In another sense, the result gives me no satisfaction. During their

E v Australian Red Cross Society cont.

addresses, counsel for each of the respondents expressed the concern of their client about the future of the applicant. I am sure that, in so doing, they spoke also for themselves and their instructing solicitors. Nobody could have sat through this case without developing a deep sympathy for the applicant and his wife and an admiration for the stoical manner in which they have borne their affliction. No amount of money could compensate them for the injury they have suffered, but a monetary award would have made it easier for them to cope with the problems that lie ahead. However, I must decide the case according to law, and the evidence establishes no basis upon which the respondents may be required to pay damages.

Nonetheless, I cannot forebear the comment that this applicant, and any other people who are in a like position, have a strong moral claim upon the community for some financial assistance in coping with their illnesses. Upon the probabilities, the earlier introduction of anti-HBc surrogate testing would have led to the discarding of the donation which caused the applicant to become HIV infected. The only substantial argument against the earlier introduction of anti-HBc testing is that it would have led to the wasting of something like 5 per cent of all donations, most of which were in fact suitable for use. Although surrogate testing was not considered before August 1984, I must dismiss the claim because I am not satisfied that, had it been considered, a reasonable person in the position of the respondents would have decided to introduce anti-HBc testing at an earlier date. This is not because I doubt the foreseeability of HIV infection from a blood transfusion or that anti-HBc surrogate testing had a useful role to play in reducing the risk of such infection. The reason for my conclusion is the possibly serious effect on the blood supply. In the absence of that possibility, I would certainly hold the applicant entitled to recover damages.

But this is where the moral claim arises: to take into account the effect upon the blood supply is to say that a person in the position of the first and second respondents was entitled to give priority to the interests of all blood users – and everyone in the community is a potential blood user – over the interests of the relatively small number of individuals who might receive infected blood. To so say is to make the present applicant bear the burden of protecting the wider public interest. In some other areas of activity, in which individuals are sacrificed for the wider public good, the community recognises an obligation to provide some recompense; for example under war veterans' legislation. Perhaps the same attitude ought to be taken towards those people who contracted AIDS as a result of a blood transfusion or haemophilia treatment. I do not have in mind any extravagant [sic] award of money, but something to make up for the income which they have lost or will lose – after taking into account any social service entitlements – and their out-of-pocket expenses. I am aware that a fund has already been established but its adequacy is a matter of controversy. I say nothing about that matter. I merely express the hope that the extent of the benefits available to people in the position of the applicant will be reviewed in the light of these reasons. Apart from anything else, agreement upon a sufficient level of assistance might eliminate the need to determine most of the cases which remain pending in this Court and in other courts; whose litigation will divert into legal costs many millions of dollars which might better be spent on the victims of the problem.

The formal order of the Court will be that the application be dismissed with costs.

E v Australian Red Cross Society cont.

[On appeal, *E v Australian Red Cross Society* (1991) 31 FCR 299, the Full Court of the Federal Court unanimously dismissed the plaintiff's appeal, and the High Court refused leave to appeal: [1992] Leg Rep SL 2.]

[12.150] **Notes&Questions**

1. In *PQ v Australian Red Cross Society* [1992] 1 VR 19, with facts similar to *E v Australian Red Cross* (1991) 27 FCR 310, the defendant's case in part was based upon the argument that it was a charitable organisation with limited resources, partly staffed by volunteers. McGarvie J applied the Privy Council decision in *Goldman v Hargrave* [1967] 1 AC 645, holding that the court should not take the actual defendant's resources into account where the defendant's own activities had created the risk of injury. The standard of care to be applied was that of the reasonable person with adequate resources to perform the task concerned.
2. In *Watt v Hertfordshire County Council* [1954] 1 WLR 835 (CA) the plaintiff fireman was injured by a heavy lifting jack carried in the vehicle in which he was travelling to an accident involving a trapped woman. The jack slipped across the floor because there was no way of securing it in the emergency vehicle onto which it had been loaded while the vehicle equipped to carry it was properly on other service. The Court of Appeal held that the necessities, in the particular circumstances, of the fire service outweighed the risks to which the defendant subjected the plaintiff. Denning LJ said (at 838):

   > It is well settled that ... you must balance the risk against the measures necessary to eliminate the risk. ... you must [also] balance the risk against the end to be achieved. If this accident had occurred in a commercial enterprise without any emergency there could be no doubt that the servant would succeed. But the commercial end to make profit is very different from the human end to save life or limb. The saving of life or limb justifies taking considerable risk.

   Lord Denning went on to comment that there have never been wanting in England men of courage ready to take those risks, notably in the fire service. The risk was here not so great as to prohibit the attempt to save life.
3. Note, however, that the test to be applied in relation to emergency vehicles generally is still whether the defendant has exercised reasonable care in all the circumstances. So in *Patterson v McGinlay* (1991) 55 SASR 258, the driver of a police car was found to be guilty of contributory negligence in crossing an intersection against a red light, even though his lights were flashing and siren sounding. Similarly, in *Morgan v Pearson* (1979) 22 SASR 5, it was emphasised that there is no point in killing several people in the course of a journey designed to save the lives and property of others. See also *Johnstone v Woolmer* (1977) ACTR 6 at 9; *Marshall v Osmond* [1983] QB 1034 (CA); *Russell v Ridley* (1997) 25 MVR 142 (SA FC).

Time for assessing reasonableness

[12.155] In *E v Australian Red Cross Society* (1991) 27 FCR 310 (extracted at [12.145]), in which the plaintiff contracted AIDS after a post-operative blood transfusion, both Wilcox J at trial and the Full Court ((1991) 31 FCR 299) stressed the importance of judging reasonableness and breach in the context of the knowledge available to the reasonable man at the time, rather than deciding the issue with the use of hindsight. Wilcox J said (at 315):

> ... the date at which the particular applicants allegedly received the blood or blood product is an important matter. Most, if not all, claims relate to donations received during the years 1983, 1984 and 1985 ... During this period there was a steady growth in scientific knowledge about the virus and in awareness, both in scientific circles and amongst the public generally ... The danger of applying hindsight occurs in most litigation; but it is particularly pertinent to these cases. Since the relevant dates there has been a significant advance in the scientific understanding of AIDS, combined with massive publicity in the popular media. Everyone involved in this case has had constantly to remember the necessity of going back to the circumstances applicable at the time of the subject donation, as revealed by the evidence.

Does the breach of a statutory standard necessarily determine the breach of the duty in negligence?

[12.160] At first sight it may seem obvious that a person who has breached some statute must necessarily be regarded as in breach of their duty of care. However, this is not so. Consider the situation where a person has driven through a red light in breach of the Motor Traffic legislation of the relevant jurisdiction. They have clearly committed an offence under the legislation and may be liable to a fine or other penalty, but for the purposes of the law of negligence the question still remains, did the person in driving through the red light, act like a reasonable person in the circumstances or not? It is conceivable that the person was driving fast because they were driving away from a bushfire or there was some other reason to regard their behaviour as meeting the standard of care in negligence. Thus, although in many situations the breach of a statutory standard may also be the breach of the duty of care in negligence, such a breach of duty does not arise solely because of the breach of the statute: *Tucker v McCann* [1948] VLR 222.

INHERENT OR OBVIOUS RISK

Introduction

[12.165] The concepts of inherent and obvious risk have been part of the assessment of the standard of care throughout the history of negligence. However, with the advent of the civil liability legislation these concepts have developed a greater significance than they had before, because in some circumstances they will trigger a particular duty or prevent a duty from arising or reduce the standard of care.

Inherent risk

[12.170] Inherent risk is defined in the relevant civil liability acts as "a risk of something occurring that cannot be avoided by the exercise of reasonable care and skill". See NSW: CLA, s 5I; Qld: CLA, s 16; SA: CLA, s 39; Vic: WrA, s 55; WA: CLA, s 5E. There is no equivalent at present in the Australian Capital Territory, Northern Territory, or Tasmania. This is drawn from the High Court's decision in *Rootes v Shelton* (1967) 116 CLR 383. There, Barwick CJ said:

> No doubt there are risks inherent in the nature of water-skiing, which because they are inherent may be regarded as accepted by those who engage in the sport. The risk of a skier running into

> an obstruction which, because submerged or partially submerged ... is unlikely to be seen ... may well be regarded as inherent in the pastime ... But neither the possibility that the driver may fail to avoid, if practicable, or if not, to signal the presence of an ... obstruction is, in my opinion, a risk inherent in the sport. (at 385-6)

It is also consistent with the sense in which Kirby J used the term in *Woods v Multi-Sport Holdings Pty Ltd* (2002) 208 CLR 460 ([12.130]), as meaning risks that could not be avoided by the use of reasonable care and foresight. (Kirby J's dissent is not extracted at [12.130]). In *Woods v Multi-Sport Holdings Pty Ltd* (2002) 208 CLR 460, Gleeson CJ at 471 pointed out that at trial French DCJ had used the term "inherent risks" to refer to risks which are "by their nature obvious to persons participating in the sport". This is at odds with the statutory definitions.

Whether something is an inherent risk is a question of fact. No liability exists for the materialisation of an inherent risk, although the Civil Liability Act provisions, where enacted, do not operate to exclude liability in connection with a duty to warn of a risk, NSW: CLA, s 5I; Qld: CLA, s 16; SA: CLA, s 39; Vic: WrA, s 56; WA: CLA, s 5P. There is no equivalent at present in the Australian Capital Territory, Northern Territory, or Tasmania. The common law in England is similar, as illustrated in *Tomlinson v Congleton Borough Council* [2004] 1 AC 46 (HL). In this case the plaintiff ignored a prohibition on diving in a disused gravel pit and dived whilst standing thigh deep in water, injuring himself. The House of Lords rejected his argument that the local authority should have made it difficult for people to access the pool. Lord Hoffman said:

> it will be extremely rare for an occupier of land to be under a duty to prevent people from taking risks which are inherent in the activities they freely choose to undertake upon the land. If people want to climb mountains, go hang-gliding or swim or dive in ponds or lakes, that is their affair. (at [45])

Mulligan v Coffs Harbour CC

[12.175] *Mulligan v Coffs Harbour City Council* (2005) 80 ALJR 43 High Court of Australia (footnotes partially omitted)

[This appeal was heard together with *Vairy v Wyong Shire Council* (2005) 223 CLR 422. Both cases were actions for damages for negligence brought by young men who suffered serious injury [tetraplegia and quadriplegia] in consequence of diving or plunging into water and striking their heads or necks on the sand below. Both plaintiffs sued public authorities, complaining of a failure to warn of the risk that materialised.]

CALLINAN AND HEYDON JJ: [This extract quotes from the judgment of Tobias J in the New South Wales Court of Appeal. There, the court heard this matter together with Vairy: *Wyong Shire Council v Vairy* [2004] Aust Torts Reports 81-754 at 65,892-65,901 per Tobias J. Callinan and Heydon JJ described the facts of the case then proceeded to quote Tobias J as follows:]

> [72] An inherent danger is a danger (or risk) attaching to a condition or activity that cannot be removed by the exercise of due care. That is, by exposing oneself to a condition or activity involving an inherent danger one has thereby become subject to the possibility of the danger crystallising. For example, in *Prast*, Ipp J [*Prast v Town of Cottesloe* (2000) 22 WAR 474 at 482 [32]] explained that the risk of being dumped by a wave while bodysurfing was not only obvious, but also inherent .... Accordingly, even the exercise of reasonable care on the part of the surfer will not remove this danger. *Rogers* [*Rogers v Whitaker* (1992) 175 CLR 479] provides a further example, but from the perspective of a hidden danger. In that case the risk of surgery to one eye was found to carry with it the inherent danger of both the patient's eyes becoming subject to sympathetic ophthalmia and consequently blindness. This danger, while

inherent, would seem to have also been a hidden danger since a reasonable patient without specific medical knowledge would not, as at least a matter of commonsense, be aware of the danger. Hence the necessity for a warning.

Of particular concern in the context of the present case is the danger associated with diving into water of unknown depth. Generally speaking such a danger will be non-inherent where the depth of water is constant or stable; for example, in a swimming pool. By ascertaining either the depth of the water before diving or by the occupier giving a warning (or an indication of the depth) under such constant conditions, the danger (be it hidden or obvious) can be eliminated all together …

However, where the dive is to be undertaken in an environment where the depth of water is subject to change at short notice and without reasonable warning, then the danger (individual circumstances depending) will generally be an inherent danger. That is, under such conditions, the giving of a warning or the checking of the depth of the water prior to diving may not remove the risk. For instance, generally a dive into the sea will be subject to the surge, swell, tide and the continuous rise and fall of the waves. Further, the seabed itself may be undergoing change, sometimes at short notice, as sands are washed about as the sea's moods and tempers constantly fluctuate. In such cases, particular circumstances depending and irrespective of the danger being obvious or hidden, the danger will be inherent.

Obvious risk defined

[12.180] Common law principles have been modified by statute in some jurisdictions. In New South Wales, South Australia, Queensland, Tasmania, Victoria and Western Australia there is no duty to warn of an obvious risk. In various States, obvious risk is dealt with in relation to assumption of risk and again in relation to recreational activities. It does not appear in the legislation in the context of breach of duty, but is clearly relevant there, as well as in relation to duty of care, contributory negligence, and the defence of volenti not fit injuria (voluntary assumption of risk). The Victorian legislation is representative of the definition of "obvious risk" in other States, NSW: CLA, s 5F, SA: CLA, s 36; Tas: CLA, s 15; WA: CLA, s 5F. Note also that, subject to some exceptions, there is no proactive duty to warn of obvious risks, see NSW: CLA, s 5H; Qld: CLA, s 15; SA: CLA, s 38; Tas: CLA, s 17; WA: CLA, s 5O, the Victorian provision (Vic: WrA, s 50) is phrased differently. There is no equivalent at present in the Australian Capital Territory, Northern Territory, or Tasmania.

Wrongs Act 1958 (Vic)

[12.185] *Wrongs Act 1958* Vic, s 53

53 Meaning of obvious risk

(1) … an obvious risk to a person who suffers harm is a risk that, in the circumstances, would have been obvious to a reasonable person in the position of that person.

(2) Obvious risks include risks that are patent or a matter of common knowledge.

(3) A risk of something occurring can be an obvious risk even though it has a low probability of occurring.

(4) A risk can be an obvious risk even if the risk (or a condition or circumstance that gives rise to the risk) is not prominent, conspicuous or physically observable.

Wrongs Act 1958 (Vic) cont.

(5) To remove any doubt, it is declared that a risk from a thing, including a living thing, is not an obvious risk if the risk is created because of a failure on the part of a person to properly operate, maintain, replace, prepare or care for the thing, unless the failure itself is an obvious risk.

——— ꧁꧂ ———

[12.190] Recent decisions of the High Court have focused on two factors as being particularly important where public authorities are concerned. These are, first, the obviousness to the defendant or ordinariness of the risk, and secondly, the degree to which the risk which materialised was substantially different from similar or greater risks in other comparable locations under the defendant's control. *Vairy* [12.80] and *Mulligan* [12.175] illustrate both factors.

These views have also been applied in lower court decisions such as *Clarke v Coleambally Ski Club Inc* [2004] NSWCA 376 in which Ipp JA at [23]-[24] (Beazley JA agreeing) held that swinging on a rope over a river and attempting a backward somersault was "so obviously dangerous that no person, taking reasonable care for his or her safety, would do such a thing". Accordingly, the ski club that had effective control over the river was held not negligent in failing to remove the rope. In *Agar v Hyde* (2000) 201 CLR 552 at 600, Callinan J stated that places of recreation are not places to which people are compelled to resort, nor are they obliged to engage in physical activities once there.

Callinan and Heydon JJ commented in *Mulligan* [12.175] that "obviousness may be of such significance and importance ... as to be overwhelmingly so, and effectively conclusive in some cases". This may be contrasted with the view expressed by McHugh J in *Vairy v Wyong Shire Council* (2005) 223 CLR 422 [see [12.80] that "reference to a risk being 'obvious' cannot be used as a concept necessarily determinative of questions of breach of duty". McHugh J went further, saying "The obviousness of the risk goes to the issue of the plaintiff's contributory negligence, rarely to the discharge of the defendant's duty".

It is clear that the obvious nature of the danger is only one factor to be taken into account in determining whether reasonable care required the avoidance of that obvious danger, as explained in *Thompson v Woolworths (Q'land) Pty Ltd* (2005) 79 ALJR 904. In a joint judgement, Gleeson CJ, McHugh, Kirby, Hayne and Heydon JJ said (2005) 221 CLR 234 at [46] with whom Hayne J agreed at [162]:

> The obviousness of a risk, and the remoteness of the likelihood that other people will fail to observe and avoid it, are often factors relevant to a judgment about what reasonableness requires as a response. In the case of some risks, reasonableness may require no response. There are, for instance, no risk-free dwelling houses. The community's standards of reasonable behaviour do not require householders to eliminate all risks from their premises, or to place a notice at the front door warning entrants of all the dangers that await them if they fail to take care for their own safety. This is not a case about warnings. Even so, it may be noted that a conclusion, in a given case, that a warning is either necessary or sufficient, itself involves an assumption that those to whom the warning is addressed will take notice of it and will exercise care. The whole idea of warnings is that those who receive them will act carefully. There would be no purpose in issuing warnings unless it were reasonable to expect that people will modify their behaviour in response to warnings.
>
> The factual judgment involved in a decision about what is reasonably to be expected of a person who owes a duty of care to another involves an interplay of considerations. The weight to be given to any one of them is likely to vary according to circumstances. If the obviousness of a risk, and the reasonableness of an expectation that other people will take care for their own safety, were conclusive against liability in every case, there would be little room for a doctrine of

contributory negligence. On the other hand, if those considerations were irrelevant, community standards of reasonable behaviour would require radical alteration.

Neindorf v Junkovic

[12.195] *Neindorf v Junkovic* (2005) 222 ALR 631 High Court of Australia

(footnotes partially omitted)

[See facts, above at [12.135]. This judgment extract is important, because in it Kirby J explains how his dicta in *Romeo* [12.75] has been misunderstood and used elsewhere to support views that he does not hold.]

KIRBY J: [Dissenting]

Obviousness of the risk: [71] As the appellant pointed out, it is certainly true that passages appear in many judicial reasons to the effect that, in defining the standard of care in a particular case, it is appropriate to take into account whether the suggested risk is "obvious". In *Romeo* (1998) 192 CLR 431 at 478 [123], I wrote that "[w]here a risk is obvious to a person exercising reasonable care for his or her own safety, the notion that the occupier must warn the entrant about that risk is neither reasonable nor just." However, that statement was particular to the circumstances of that case. The case involved a manifestly dangerous cliff edge in a nature reserve with a large drop. The statement was qualified by the need of the occupier to take account of "the possibility of inadvertence or negligent conduct on the part of entrants". It could not constitute, and was not intended to constitute, a universal proposition of law, applicable whatever the facts and circumstances of a case (*Woods v Multi-Sport Holdings Pty Ltd* (2002) 208 CLR 460 at 474 [45]; 499-500 [127]). And it said nothing about precautions other than warnings – such as taking practical steps to prevent or reduce the risks of avoidable injury.

Based on a misunderstanding of *dicta* of the kind described in *Romeo*, the idea has spread through the courts of Australia that occupiers, with responsibilities for the safety of premises can totally ignore those responsibilities because of the alleged obviousness of the risk to entrants. In principle, that is not and cannot be the law (*Vairy v Wyong Shire Council* [2005] HCA 62 at [40]; contra *Tomlinson v Congleton Borough Council* [2004] 1 AC 46 at 85 [45]-[46]). In a sense, the obviousness of risk speaks chiefly to those who are in charge of the source of the risk and who have the opportunity, and prime responsibility, to reduce or eliminate it. The respondent had no entitlement to change the appellant's premises. She could not re-arrange the trestle table. Nor could she take steps so as to make the premises safer for members of the public, like herself, entering to do business there. In some circumstances, the more obvious the risk, the greater the responsibility of those with the relevant power to protect others from it (*Woods v Multi-Sport Holdings Pty Ltd* (2002) 208 CLR 460 at 500 [128]).

Entrants might (like the respondent in the present case) be momentarily distracted. The occupier will generally have more time and occasion to consider issues of risk and safety than short-term entrants. Further, a danger of placing so much emphasis on suggested obviousness is that, in a given case, it will distort proper consideration of a defence of contributory negligence (*Vairy v Wyong Shire Council* [2005] HCA 62 at [46], [162]). It will take that factor of alleged carelessness on the part of the plaintiff up into the negation of a breach of duty, instead of reaching it at the conclusion of conventional negligence analysis.

The mischief of this approach, which is spreading like wildfire through the courts of this land and must be arrested if proper negligence doctrine is to be restored, is that it can effectively revive the ancient common law position so that effectively, contributory negligence, of whatever proportion, becomes again a complete defence to an action framed in negligence and debars that action. That consequence would reverse the universal enactment of apportionment legislation. That legislation recognises that, in many cases, a plaintiff's inadvertence or momentary carelessness is much less

Neindorf v Junkovic cont.

significant in the responsibility for accidents than a defendant's indifferent neglect of considerations of accident prevention which are substantially the defendant's own obligation.

If I could expunge the quoted passage from my reasons in *Romeo*, I would gladly do so. I would take it out, not because it was incorrect as a factual observation in the context of that case but because it has been repeatedly deployed by courts as an excuse to exempt those with greater power, knowledge, control and responsibility over risks from a duty of care to those who are vulnerable, inattentive, distracted and more dependent. The present case is a good illustration. Most people do not normally walk, even on unfamiliar surfaces, looking constantly at their feet. The fact that there was a division in the slabs of concrete in the appellant's driveway was obvious. But the distinct unevenness in surface levels of the adjoining slabs may not have been obvious to a person, like the respondent, who had no warning of it and no reason to anticipate it. Especially if the respondent was distracted, as her accepted testimony said, the chances of overlooking the danger or "hazard" (as Doyle CJ described it) was great.

The appellant had the knowledge, the power and the economic interest to protect the public at large whom she had invited onto her property. In terms of fault, for failure to act in the circumstances, the responsibility fell mainly on the appellant. It is against risks of the kind that materialised that people such as the appellant can be expected to take precautions (and against the chance that they may fail, they can be expected normally to secure householders' insurance as thousands do).

The supposed Ghantous analogy: I would not deny that some of the statements of legal principle in Ghantous [*Ghantous v Hawkesbury City Council* (2001) 206 CLR 512] have application to injuries happening on private property. Nevertheless, Doyle CJ was clearly right in pointing to the significant factual differences between *Ghantous* and the present case. The relationship of the respondent to the appellant was much closer, more direct and with greater economic mutuality than was Mrs Ghantous' relationship with the local government authority. What might reasonably be expected of the repair and upkeep or precaution and warning in the context of a driveway and forecourt in confined suburban premises to which the public was invited could not reasonably be expected for the maintenance of all verges beside the entire network of a municipality's footpaths. This is precisely the consideration to which Pt 1B of the *Wrongs Act* was addressed and, in particular, the considerations mentioned in pars (a), (b) and (e) of s 17C(2).

A closer analogy to the present case than *Ghantous* is the decision of this Court in *Webb v South Australia* (1982) 56 ALJR 912; 43 ALR 465. Although that was an instance, like *Ghantous*, concerned with the liability of a public authority for the condition of the edge of a footpath and was decided by reference to the common law as it was understood before it was restated in *Brodie* and *Ghantous*, the issue concerned a "false kerb" to a footpath that was likely to present the risk of injury to a class of persons that included the plaintiff.

As in the present case, the defendant in *Webb* relied on the propositions that the intervening space, occasioned by the structure of the footpath, was "a very obvious feature" that was therefore not dangerous so that it deprived the plaintiff of a right to recovery. In this Court, these considerations proved persuasive for Wilson J and Dawson J who each dissented. They favoured affirming the conclusions of the trial judge and Full Court below. However, the majority of this Court (Mason, Brennan and Deane JJ) reached the opposite conclusion. They rejected the argument of "obviousness". It is instructive to recall what the majority said in *Webb*:

> This finding [below] seems to have been based on its obviousness and on the circumstance that in the seven years that elapsed since its construction there was no record of any previous accident. But obviousness and the absence of accident over this period does not mean that the construction presented no risk of injury. As the false kerb was adjacent to a bus stop there existed the distinct possibility that a pedestrian, because he was in a hurry to catch a bus or was intent on observing an approaching bus or because his attention was distracted for some

> other reason, would fail to take sufficient care to avoid injury to himself. The happening of the accident demonstrated, if demonstration was needed, that the construction had the potential to cause injury.
>
> Of course a pedestrian could avoid the possibility of injury by taking due care. However, the reasonable man does not assume that others will always take due care; he must recognize that there will be occasions when others are distracted by emergency or some other cause from giving sufficient attention to their own safety. It seems to us that the courts below gave undue emphasis to the circumstance that injury could be avoided by a pedestrian who took reasonable care for his own safety.

The present case is factually different in some respects, as is the way with negligence cases. There was no complaint about the original construction of the concrete slabs in the appellant's premises. Nevertheless, the issues of approach, the consideration of obviousness and the relevant place of contributory negligence in the sequence of the analysis of the legal responsibilities of the parties are all common to this appeal. The arguments of the appellant in this appeal harken back to the opinions of the dissenting judges in *Webb*. For my own part, I would adhere to the approach and reasoning of the majority in *Webb* for it correctly states the doctrine of the law of negligence which this Court has hitherto applied.

[12.200] **Notes&Questions**

1. The claimant was indoor rock climbing in the form of "bouldering" which is low level and done without ropes. There was no instruction given but outside the room (before entering) there were climbing rules which prohibited jumping from the walls. The floor was covered in 30cm-thick matting. The claimant saw another person jump off a wall to grab a high bar, and he did the same, but fell on his head and sustained severe spinal injuries. The English Court of Appeal held that as the risk was "plainly obvious", the defendant did not have to provide instruction for an activity which the claimant was voluntarily undertaking and denied liability: *Trustees of the Portsmouth Youth Activities Committee (a charity) v Poppleton* [2008] EWCA Civ 646.
2. Other cases where obvious risk was considered include: *Gillies v Saddington* [2004] NSWCA 110 (plaintiff slipped on steep wet driveway on defendant's property; defendant held not negligent in failing to provide alternative means of access such as steps); *Prast v Town of Cottesloe* (2000) 22 WAR 474 (WASC) (risk of being dumped and suffering serious spinal injury while bodysurfing both inherent (at 482) and obvious (at 483) to an experienced surfer, per Ipp J); *Enright v Coolum Resort Pty Ltd* [2002] QSC 394 (*Prast* followed; experienced swimmer swam too far out to sea at an unpatrolled beach and drowned; the risk was held to be an ordinary one associated with swimming in the sea); *Mountain Cattlemen's Association of Victoria Inc v Barron* [1998] 3 VR 302 at 308 (risk of horse slipping while approaching river bank to drink was obvious to an experienced rider); *Secretary to the Department of Natural Resources and Energy v Harper* (2000) 1 VR 133 at 148 (no obligation to warn since the risk of being injured by falling branches or trees is "endemic" or part and parcel of activities such as camping, walking and living outdoors in the Australian bush; authority entitled to rely on adults having knowledge of the possibility of falls in high winds).

RECREATIONAL ACTIVITIES UNDER THE CIVIL LIABILITY LEGISLATION

[12.205] In New South Wales, Queensland, Tasmania and Western Australia defendants are not liable for the materialisation of an obvious risk arising from a dangerous recreational activity, see NSW: CLA, s 5F; SA: CLA, ss 36 – 38; Vic: WrA, ss 53 – 54 and s 50; Tas: CLA, ss 15 – 17 and s 20; WA: CLA, ss 5F – 5I and ss 5N – 5O.

This is confined to negligence, so does not prevent liability arising, for example, from breach of statutory duty. The exclusion does not rely on any doctrine of volenti: NSW: CLA, Div 5; Qld: CLA, Div 4; Tas: CLA, Div 5; WA: CLA, Div 4. The Negligence Review Panel considered that its recommendations (para 4.17 Recommendation 32 (b)) would reverse *Nagle v Rottnest Island Authority* (1993) 177 CLR 423. These recommendations are incorporated into the legislation cited. The NSW:CLA introduces a (rebuttable) presumption of awareness of the risk of harm if it was an obvious risk, which constitutes a reversal of the common law onus of proof, see, NSW: CLAs 5G.

In *Dederer* (extracted at [12.105] above), the council was joined late to the action, and for that reason the new civil liability legislation on recreational activities applied to the Council. Dunford J at trial (*Dederer v RTA* [2005] NSWSC 185) held that the council was not protected by the legislation. He said:

> The Council however seeks to rely on the provisions of Part 1A of the *Civil Liability Act 2002* (the Act) on the ground that the plaintiff's action in diving off the bridge was a "dangerous recreational activity", as defined by s 5K, that the risk of harm was an "obvious" risk as defined by s 5F, that the plaintiff is therefore presumed to have been aware of the risk of harm: s 5G, and that accordingly, there was no proactive duty to warn of the risk: s 5H.
>
> I can accept for present purposes that the plaintiff was engaged in a "recreational activity" which was objectively a "dangerous recreational activity"; but I am not satisfied that it was an "obvious risk".
>
> Here the plaintiff was a 14 year old who had seen a large number of persons jumping and diving off the bridge over many years, without any apparent attempt by police or Council rangers to stop them and no known cases of injury. He may have been aware that sandbars shifted (if he thought of it) and know of the variable depth of the water, but from what he had observed and having regard to his age and lack of maturity, the fact that he knew vessels passed through the channel, he looked and saw the water was dark murky green and he could not see the bottom, all of which indicated to him that the water was deep, the risk of serious permanent physical injury would not have been obvious to him, even if it would have been obvious to a mature adult. Accordingly s 5H does not apply in the circumstances of this case, and neither does s 5L which also depends on an "obvious risk" as defined in s 5F. The Council also relies on s 5M which provides that there is no duty of care in respect of a recreational activity if the risk was the subject of a risk warning to the plaintiff, but for reasons already given, I do not consider that the signs which were displayed constituted a warning.

However in the Court of Appeal, Ipp, Handley and Tobias JJA held that the council was protected by the legislation, in that the plaintiff was engaged in a dangerous recreational activity and that the plaintiff was injured by the materialisation of an obvious risk; indeed they held that the risk would have been obvious even to a 14 year old boy.

The following case demonstrates the extent to which determining breach in this context has become a statutory interpretation activity.

Fallas v Mourlas

[12.210] *Fallas v Mourlas* (2006) 65 NSWLR 418, New South Wales Court of Appeal (footnotes omitted)

IPP JA: 420 Mr Alexander Con Fallas, the defendant below, accidentally shot his friend, Mr Con Mourlas, the plaintiff below, while hunting kangaroos by spotlight. Mr Mourlas was shot in the leg and sustained a comminuted fracture and other injuries. He sued Mr Fallas for the damages he had thereby incurred. At the trial, Mr Mourlas contended that Mr Fallas was liable to him in negligence for the damages he had thereby incurred. One of the grounds on which Mr Fallas denied liability was that he was entitled to immunity under s 5L of the *Civil Liability Act 2002* (NSW).

Quirk DCJ upheld Mr Mourlas's claim and found that Mr Fallas had been negligent. She rejected Mr Fallas's argument that Mr Mourlas had been guilty of contributory negligence. She held that s 5L did not assist Mr Fallas. Mr Fallas applied for leave to appeal against the verdict and judgment

Section 5L provides:

No liability for harm suffered from obvious risks of dangerous recreational activities

(1) A person (the defendant) is not liable in negligence for harm suffered by another person (the plaintiff) as a result of the materialisation of an obvious risk of a dangerous recreational activity engaged in by the plaintiff.

(2) This section applies whether or not the plaintiff was aware of the risk.

Certain of the expressions used in s 5L are defined in s 5K. Section 5K provides:

In this Division:

- dangerous recreational activity means a recreational activity that involves a significant risk of physical harm.
- obvious risk has the same meaning as it has in Division 4.
- recreational activity includes:
  (a) any sport (whether or not the sport is an organised activity), and
  (b) any pursuit or activity engaged in for enjoyment, relaxation or leisure, and
  (c) any pursuit or activity engaged in at a place (such as a beach, park or other public open space) where people ordinarily engage in sport or in any pursuit or activity for enjoyment, relaxation or leisure.

By s 5K, "obvious risk" in s 5L has the same meaning as it has in s 5F. Section 5F [the Victorian equivalent is extracted at [12.185].]

Quirk DCJ was not satisfied that the activity being undertaken at the time Mr Mourlas was shot was a "dangerous recreational activity" as defined by s 5K. Further, her Honour held that Mr Mourlas "did not suffer harm as a result of the materialisation of an obvious risk of a dangerous recreational activity". The argument on appeal concerned only whether her Honour was wrong in these two findings.

The deceptively simple wording of s 5K conceals difficult questions of construction. The difficulties concern not only the meaning of words and expressions but also the nature of the circumstances that that must be taken into account when determining the scope of the different risks and activities involved. On its face, s 5L concerns the materialisation of an obvious risk of a dangerous recreational activity engaged in by the plaintiff. These straightforward words carry with them complexities when regard is had to the definitions of "recreational activity", "dangerous recreational activity", and "obvious risk".

The "significance" of a risk

To assess whether a "recreational activity" is "dangerous", it is necessary to determine whether the recreational activity "involves a significant risk of physical harm" (s 5K).

Fallas v Mourlas cont.

In my reasons in *Falvo v Australian Oztag Sports Association* [2006] NSWCA 17 (with which Hunt AJA and Adams J agreed) I said (at [30]):

> In substance, it seems to me, that the expression constitutes one concept with the risk and the harm mutually informing each other. On this basis the "risk of physical harm" may be "significant" if the risk is low but the potential harm is catastrophic. The "risk of physical harm" may also be "significant" if the likelihood of both the occurrence and the harm is more than trivial. On the other hand, the "risk of physical harm" may not be "significant" if, despite the potentially catastrophic nature of the harm, the risk is very slight. It will be a matter of judgment in each individual case whether a particular recreational activity is "dangerous".

I agree with Basten JA that an objective test is required in determining whether in terms of s 5K a recreational activity is "dangerous".

But what does "significant" mean in s 5K? I think it is plain that it means more than trivial and does not import an "undemanding" test of foreseeability as laid down in *Wyong Shire Council v Shirt* (1980) 146 CLR 40.

The epithet "real" was suggested during the course of argument. But "real" can mean a risk that is not far-fetched or fanciful (*Wyong Shire Council v Shirt* at (48)) and "significant" means more than that.

On the other hand, it seems to me, a "significant risk" does not mean a risk that is likely to occur; that would assign to it too high a degree of probability. Had it been the legislature's intention to lay down an element for the application of s 5L involving the probability of harm occurring, different words would have been used.

In the present context, the word "significant" – coloured or informed as it is by the elements of both risk (which it expressly qualifies) and physical harm (which is indivisibly part of the expression under consideration) – is not susceptible to more precise definition.

Thus, I do not think it practicable or desirable to attempt to impose further definition on "significant", other than saying that the term lays down a standard lying somewhere between a trivial risk and a risk likely to materialise. Where the particular standard lies between these two extremes cannot be prescribed by any rule of thumb. Each individual case will have to depend on its particular circumstances and by having regard to the ordinary meaning of the term.

What evidence is relevant to prove the existence of a significant risk of physical harm?

The degree of likelihood of a risk occurring may be established in many ways. In *Seltsam Pty Ltd v McGuiness* (2000) 49 NSWLR 262 Spigelman CJ (at 278) referred to epidemiological evidence that suggested "some increase in risk"...

The Chief Justice was considering whether evidence of increased risk might be taken into account "for the purpose of drawing the inference that the particular exposure caused or materially contributed to the injury in the specific case". Nevertheless, his remarks indicate that epidemiological evidence may be relevant to establish the degree of risk involved in a given activity.

Expert opinion may be relevant to the degree or incidence of a risk, as might the application of logic, common sense or experience to the particular circumstances of the case.

But in the end, whatever the likely incidence of the risk, what has to be determined is more than that. The composite question is whether there is a significant risk of physical harm and that requires a ...

The differences between a "significant" risk and an "obvious" risk

A significant risk that converts a recreational activity into a dangerous recreational activity may be an entirely different risk from the risk (which may be obvious or not) that materialises...

Fallas v Mourlas cont.

...Take [an] example. Boxing is arguably a dangerous recreational activity on the ground that a boxer may be struck by a series of heavy blows to the head and body. But being punched in the kidneys after the bell has rung for the end of a round may not be the materialisation of a significant risk. It may, however, be the materialisation of an obvious risk, and a boxer who is so injured may be met with a s 5L defence if he sues his opponent.

Thus, s 5L may be held to apply where the significant risk (converting a recreational activity into a dangerous one) differs from the obvious risk that materialises. Accordingly, differences in the risks may occur not only by reason of the differences in meaning between the epithets "significant" and "obvious" but because the putative significant risks of physical harm stem from facts that differ from the facts that actually create the obvious risk that materialises.

Basten JA has expressed the opinion that "[f]or s 5L to be engaged, at least one of those [significant] risks must materialise [as an obvious risk] and result in harm suffered by the plaintiff". I respectfully disagree. In my view, there is nothing in s 5L that indicates that the obvious risk that materialises must be one of the significant risks that transforms a recreational activity into a dangerous recreational activity...

Different levels of generality or abstraction

In determining whether a recreational activity is dangerous, difficult questions arise in defining the scope of the recreational activity to which the expression "significant risk of physical harm" is to be applied. At what level of generality or abstraction is the scope to be ascertained?

"Recreational activity" is defined by s 5K in terms of very broad generalities. It comprises any sport, be it an organised activity or not (para (a)), any pursuit or activity engaged in for enjoyment, relaxation or leisure (para (b)) and even any pursuit or activity engaged in at a place where people ordinarily engage in sport or any pursuit or activity engaged in for enjoyment, relaxation or leisure (para (c))... [He held that]

in determining whether a recreational activity involves a significant risk of physical harm, regard is to be had only to the activities ordinarily involved in that particular recreational activity and not to the particular and limited activities undertaken in fact by the plaintiff. ...

...

There are, however, countervailing indications.

Factors such as time, place, competence, age, sobriety, equipment and even the weather may make dangerous a recreational activity which would not otherwise involve a risk of harm (and the converse may be the case). A cliff walk in daytime may be safe but at night it may be dangerous....[he gave other examples] ...

As the question whether a recreational activity may be dangerous will often depend on the particular circumstances, if such a determination does not take account of those circumstances it is likely to be unreliable, may be unfair and may give rise to injustice. ...

The unfairness may be particularly apparent where the recreational activity is generally regarded as having significant risks of physical harm, but the plaintiff, by limiting (perhaps deliberately) his or her participation in the activity, reduces those risks to a point where they are not significant risks of physical harm. In my view it would be unfair or unjust for such a plaintiff to have to face a s 5L defence. The same might be said of a plaintiff who is injured by the materialisation of an obvious risk that was not a significant risk of the activity concerned.

The higher level of generality approach may also give rise to unfairness to defendants. A recreational activity may generally not be regarded as having significant risks of physical harm, but the way in which a particular plaintiff engages in that activity may give rise to such risks. It would be unfair in those circumstances to deprive a defendant of the s 5K defence. ...

Fallas v Mourlas cont.

These potential situations of unfairness and injustice can be avoided if, for the purposes of s 5K, the scope of the recreational activity is determined by reference to the particular activities actually engaged in by the plaintiff at the relevant time. This would enable a decision to be made by reference to the actual circumstances giving rise to the harm, and not to a notional and artificial construct that bears little relationship to the reality of the case and to what actually occurred.

The matter is essentially one of statutory construction. In a case of clear ambiguity (as is the case with s 5K and s 5L), a construction that might result in potential unfairness and injustice should be avoided and a fair and just construction is to be preferred. There are no other policy factors involved. Deciding issues under s 5L by reference to all the circumstances that actually occurred may benefit a plaintiff in one case and a defendant in another.

Many of the provisions of the *Civil Liability Act* are modelled on the Recommendations of the Final Report by the panel appointed by the Commonwealth and State Governments to review the law of negligence (Second Reading Speech, *Hansard* 23 October 2002 at 5765). Sections 5K and 5L are based on Recommendations 11 and 12, although they differ materially from those Recommendations by not incorporating the element of voluntariness. Nevertheless, part of the reasoning expressed to be the rationale for Recommendations 11 and 12 applies to ss 5K and 5L. That is, a plaintiff who engages in a dangerous recreational activity in circumstances where the risks are obvious is to be regarded as having assumed those risks (see paras 4.20 to 4.24 of the Final Report).

In my view, the fulfillment of that rationale should be regarded as the purpose of the legislature in enacting ss 5K and 5L, and that rationale must inform the construction of ss 5K and 5L. Unless regard is had to the particular circumstances of each individual case, and this includes segmenting (where that is reasonably possible) the particular activities actually engaged in from the broader (and more general) activity of which it forms part, the rationale may often not be achieved. In my view, segmenting in this way would reasonably be possible where persons are engaged in a recreational activity that comprises sets of activities that, according to commonsense considerations, are distinguishable and separate from each other.

I would add this further consideration, which supports the conclusion that regard must be had to the particular activities engaged in by the plaintiff at the relevant time.... It is not possible, in my view, to provide a bright line distinction somewhere between the everyday general description of a recreational activity and the "particular activities engaged in by the plaintiff at the relevant time"...

If no practicable test for determining the scope of the activities exists, other than "the particular activities engaged in by the plaintiff at the relevant time", it is self-evident that the test so articulated must be regarded as the test intended. Otherwise uncertainty and confusion would be the result. No other test has been suggested.

Accordingly, in my view, the dangerousness (in terms of s 5L) of the recreational activity is to be determined by the activities engaged in by the plaintiff at the relevant time. All relevant circumstances that may bear on whether those activities were dangerous in the defined sense include relevant matters personal to the plaintiff and others of the kind I have mentioned.

The distinction between negligence and gross negligence

In cases where the obvious risk is of being harmed by the conduct of a person (and not by physical features of the locale or other natural phenomena), for s 5L to become relevant the obvious risk must at least be of negligent conduct. Without negligence there could be no cause of action and no liability. Section 5L therefore may involve a plaintiff in certain circumstances having to accept the risk of another person being negligent. This is consistent with the rationale of the legislation, to which I have previously referred.

Negligence comes in an infinite number of forms and the degrees of negligent conduct are infinite. The term "gross negligence" is nowadays not often used but courts from time to time still consider its

Fallas v Mourlas cont.

meaning and application: see for example *R v De'Zilwa* (2002) 5 VR 408, *R v Leusenkamp* (2003) 40 MVR 108, *Etna v Arif* [1999] VR 353 at 383, *Re Bendeich (No 2)* (1994) 53 FCR 422 at 427. It is sufficient, for the purposes of these reasons, to say that gross negligence is negligence to an extreme degree.

It goes without saying that in certain circumstances the risk of a person being negligent (and causing harm) might be obvious, but in the same circumstances the risk of a person being grossly negligent (and causing harm) might not be obvious. I think it also goes without saying that while a person might accept the risk of harm caused by another's negligent conduct, that person is less likely to accept the risk of a person being grossly negligent.

In my view, when considering whether there has been a materialisation of an obvious risk, a distinction may have to be drawn between a risk of negligent conduct on the part of another and conduct that is grossly negligent. In some circumstances, it may not be sufficient merely to ask whether the risk of harm caused by a person being negligent was obvious. If the conduct that caused the risk amounted to gross negligence, it would be necessary, in my opinion, to determine whether the risk of harm caused by gross negligence of the kind in question was obvious. Otherwise, if – for the purposes of s 5L – the "risk of negligence" is to be regarded as a descriptive catch-all for the risks of any kind of careless conduct, no matter how extreme, harm caused by grossly negligent conduct could be held to be an obvious risk where in fact such a risk was not obvious at all.

I would add that the question is not whether it was obvious that there was a risk that the very facts that did in fact materialise could materialise. Rather, it is whether there was an obvious risk that that kind of thing might materialise. That is consistent with the approach generally applicable to elements of the common law tort of negligence that in some respects are analogous.

The circumstances relating to the shooting

I now turn to the facts of the particular case…[he set out the facts including that the men had a few beers and then went shooting at about 10 pm. After some spotlighting, Mr Mourlas was sitting in the car alone and Mr Fallas returned to it. Mr M saw Mr F playing with the gun and made several entreaties to him to put it away or do it outside to which Mr F returned reassurances that he knew what he was doing. However at some stage the gun went off and Mr M was shot.

…

Was Mr Mourlas engaged in a dangerous recreational activity and was there a materialisation of an obvious risk? …

In my view, statistics relating to injury by gunshot would not be of much help in this case, nor would the statistics relating to accidental shootings on hunting expeditions. The unique circumstances render such statistics largely irrelevant. I agree with Basten JA that whether the group of men involved in the outing were competent, experienced, fresh or tired, sober or inebriated, and whether they were otherwise known to be careful and responsible, would be relevant to the issues that call for decision.

Senior counsel for Mr Fallas submitted to this Court that the activity engaged in by Mr Mourlas should be defined as "spotlighting" (that is hunting and shooting kangaroos at night with the aid of a spotlight). He repeated the submission that had been made on behalf of Mr Fallas at trial, namely, that the significant risk was that of being accidentally shot while spotlighting.

In my opinion, the activity that Mr Mourlas was engaged in was sitting in the vehicle, holding the spotlight for the shooters outside, on the basis that at various times one or more of the shooters might leave or enter the vehicle with firearms that might or might not be loaded. In my view that limited activity is distinguishable and separate from the other activities which fall under the general description of "shooting kangaroos by spotlight". The question, therefore, is whether there was a significant risk of physical harm in engaging in that particular limited activity.

Fallas v Mourlas cont.

The risks attendant on shooting kangaroos must depend on the circumstances. For example, if skilled and experienced hunters undertake the shooting, the risks might be relatively low. If the hunters are novices, the converse might be the case.

Mr Mourlas had no previous experience in shooting kangaroos. Mr Fallas told Mr Mourlas that he was the only one amongst the men who was a "licensed shooter". From the tenor of the evidence, generally, it seems that the men were not experienced at shooting. They were not country people for whom shooting kangaroos by spotlight might have been a familiar pastime.

The accident occurred at about 10.30 pm after the men, or some of them, had driven for some hours, had dinner, and some alcohol to drink. There would have been a measure of excitement from the shooting itself. Their alertness and ability to concentrate could not have been at an optimum level.

In my view, in these circumstances, there was a significant risk that one or other of the men, while leaving or entering or being in the vehicle as Mr Mourlas was operating the spotlight, might handle a loaded firearm in a negligent manner and cause someone in the vehicle to be shot. In other words, I am of the opinion that the recreational activity in which Mr Mourlas was engaged carried with it a significant risk of physical harm and, therefore, was a dangerous recreational activity within the meaning of s 5K.

I would answer the question whether Mr Mourlas was injured by the materialisation of an obvious risk in the negative.

Mr Mourlas asked Mr Fallas to make sure that there were [no] bullets in the gun but Mr Fallas merely reassured him that the gun was not loaded. Mr Falls later repeated that reassurance. Mr Mourlas told Mr Fallas more than once to "make sure it was safe". Mr Fallas did not take appropriate steps in this regard. Mr Mourlas told Mr Fallas not to come in to the vehicle with a loaded gun. Mr Fallas nevertheless did so. When he entered the vehicle, Mr Mourlas told Mr Fallas to take the gun outside. Mr Fallas did not. When he started to fiddle with the gun, Mr Mourlas told him to stop and to take the gun outside. Mr Fallas again did not comply. Mr Mourlas told him to "point it outside in the grass". Mr Fallas did not. This conduct comprised groundless reassurances and persistent failures to take steps to ensure that there would be no accident caused by the firearm, all in the face of earnest requests to be careful. The eventual shooting of the firearm was, in my view, gross negligence on the part of Mr Fallas.

Mr Fallas's replies to Mr Mourlas's questions, and his actions, had the effect of reassuring Mr Mourlas so that – in my view – there was no obvious risk to Mr Mourlas of being shot. This led to Mr Mourlas remaining in the vehicle and, immediately prior to being shot, looking to the left towards the other two men and away from Mr Fallas and the firearm.

In the circumstances, the correct question is whether in the particular circumstances the risk of Mr Mourlas being harmed by conduct as extreme as that of Mr Fallas (amounting to gross negligence) was obvious within the meaning of an obvious risk as defined by s 5K. I would answer this question in the negative.

I would dismiss the appeal with costs. ...

BASTEN JA: 436 ...

One might infer that the defendant, as a person in control of a handgun, was held to owe a duty of care to those in his proximity, in the manner in which he handled the gun. One may also infer that it was held to be a breach of that duty to allow the barrel of the gun to point towards another person, in circumstances where the gun had apparently jammed and the defendant was seeking to un-jam it. In those circumstances, there was a foreseeable risk that there might be a bullet in the gun and that it might discharge whilst being manipulated by the defendant.

On the basis that the plaintiff's version of the events was accepted, there appears to have been no dispute as to the liability of the defendant in negligence, if the matter were to be determined under

Fallas v Mourlas cont.

the general law. That may be inferred from the fact that her Honour did not consider it necessary to identify in express terms the nature of the duty owed by the defendant to the plaintiff, the foreseeability of the risk of injury, nor the conduct which constituted a breach of that duty. Rather, the dispute centred on the application of s 5L of the *Civil Liability Act 2002* (NSW) ("the Act"). Section 5L provides a defence to a claim "in negligence" which, if made out, will mean that the defendant is "not liable". In this section, the use of the preposition "in", rather than "for", suggests that the phrase "not liable in negligence" should be understood to refer to the tort of negligence and not merely a factual assertion of a "failure to exercise reasonable care and skill", which is the definition of "negligence" in s 5 of the Act.

It may be possible to dismiss a claim on the basis that s 5L applies, in which case the elements of the tort might not need to be identified in the usual way. However, where the section is found not to apply, the usual findings will need to be made, preferably in express terms.

[He noted that]the express purpose of the Act is to limit the recovery of damages in relation to negligence and it must be given effect in accordance with that purpose: see *Interpretation Act 1987* (NSW), s 33.....

The "activity"

The trial judge identified the activity by reference to the conduct of the plaintiff. That approach was correct. Section 5L refers to an activity "engaged in" by the person injured.... [O]nce the activity was identified as shooting kangaroo at night, and the relevant risk was identified as a wound caused by accidental discharge from a firearm, I do not think it is possible to characterise a person who merely drives, or who merely holds a spotlight, as not involved in the activity, because they are not involved in the actual shooting. To the extent that her Honour sought to draw such a distinction, in my view her reasoning was in error. If the only significant risk of the activity, which resulted in it being a "dangerous recreational activity" were a self-inflicted gunshot wound, the proper characterisation might be different. However, her Honour did not so limit the risks, nor would such a limitation have been reasonable in the circumstances. Whatever the precise definition of the risks, they must have included gunshot wounds caused to another by accidental discharge or other mishandling of a firearm. It follows, in my view, that the plaintiff was engaged in the recreational activity of shooting kangaroo at night.

By taking too limited a view of the activity in question, her Honour did not address the next issue which was to identify the risks involved in shooting kangaroo at night, and whether they constituted significant risks. Both parties joined in inviting this Court to determine the questions left unanswered at trial, if this Court were satisfied that the approach of the trial judge was erroneous....

...

"Dangerous recreational activity"

Section 5K defines "dangerous recreational activity" as a recreational activity which involves "a significant risk of physical harm". The natural reading of this definition is that what must be significant is either the "risk" or the "risk of physical harm". I would not read the word "significant" as requiring a particular level of physical harm. Nor, adopting a purposive approach, is there any reason to suppose that the legislature sought to exclude liability for serious physical harm, but not for insignificant physical harm. In my view the preferable approach is to treat that which is to be assessed as a "risk of physical harm". That will import a consideration of the seriousness of the harm which might occur. Thus, if, as in *Rogers v Whitaker* (discussed below) the harm is potentially catastrophic, a very low level of risk may be treated as "significant". On the other hand, where the harm is not serious at all, the risk may not be considered significant until it reaches a much higher level. This approach adequately reflects the concept of dangerousness, without imposing any separate and independent assessment of

Fallas v Mourlas cont.

the seriousness of the harm feared: c.f. *Falvo v Australian Oztag Sports Association* [2006] NSWCA 17 at [28]. For present purposes, it is sufficient to note that the physical harm in question was that resulting from being shot. There is no doubt that this form of harm fell comfortably within the concept of physical harm used in the definition of "dangerous recreational activity".

The real issue is the scope of the term "significant risk". On one view the concept of a "significant risk" is similar to that of "a material risk" used in other contexts in tort law. [He considered *Rogers v Whitaker*]

...

In the present statutory context the phrase "significant risk" is one which requires an objective test, not dependent upon the expectations of a person in a particular relationship with another, whether it be a drunken friend or a medical advisor. In relation to the definition of "obvious risk", s 5F(3) expressly provides that a risk may be obvious "even though it has a low probability of occurring". No doubt a low probability may nevertheless involve a significant risk, if it is not so low as to be "insignificant". As the joint judgment of Deane, Gaudron and McHugh JJ in *Malec v J C Hutton Pty Ltd* (1990) 169 CLR 638 at 643 stated, in relation to the assessment of damages for future or potential events:

> If the law is to take account of future or hypothetical events in assessing damages, it can only do so in terms of the degree of probability of those events occurring. The probability may be very high – 99.9% – or very low – 0.1%. But unless the chance is so low as to be regarded as speculative – say less than 1% – or so high as to be practically certain – say over 99% – the court will take that chance into account in assessing the damages.

In a separate judgment, Brennan and Dawson JJ in *Malec* noted that there are dangers in seeking to express probabilities as a percentage in determining what is speculative, or fanciful, or, on the other hand, certain. The same may be said in relation to determining whether a particular risk is "significant".

Section 5L of the Act does not in terms reinstate common law principles relating to the voluntary assumption of risk. Those principles required a careful consideration of the relationship between the plaintiff and the defendant and the extent to which the plaintiff had, by his or her voluntary conduct, assumed a level of risk. The Act, in contrast, creates a defence (by way of immunity from liability) generally with respect to dangerous recreational activities. As s 5L(2) expressly states, the section applies "whether or not the plaintiff was aware of the risk".

The fact that the plaintiff accepted that the risk of accidental injury existed, may mean that such a risk, very broadly defined, was "obvious". It does not follow that any activity using a firearm thereby qualifies as a "dangerous recreational activity". Some may have a very low risk of persons injuring each other. It may be that clay pigeon shooting falls into that category. What is less clear is whether hunting kangaroo at night falls into a different risk category. Such an activity may colloquially be described as "risky", especially if it is accompanied by undue consumption of alcohol. However, her Honour did not find that consumption of alcohol was a significant factor in the present events.

Common assumptions, in such circumstances, may form an inadequate basis for determining that a general law right to damages has been removed. The Court had no material before it to suggest how many shooting accidents occurred during kangaroo hunting at night in Australia in a year, or any other period of time. Assuming that the participants are not significantly affected by drugs or alcohol, it is difficult to infer that this recreational activity involved a significant risk of one participant being shot by another. What would be required for a shooting to occur would be not merely an accidental discharge of a gun, but the simultaneous pointing of the gun in the direction of another individual, whether accidentally or otherwise. Accidental discharges might perhaps be assumed to happen with a sufficient

Fallas v Mourlas cont.

frequency to constitute a significant risk during night hunting: the additional possibility of the gun being pointed towards a member of the hunting party, or sufficiently close to allow an injury by ricochet, may be too remote to be significant.

The approach to determining "significant risk" was not dealt with in detail at the trial, but one aspect, identified by the trial judge in her summary of the plaintiff's submissions set out at [126] above, was that some activities involved "inherent" risks. Thus, in motorcar racing or contact sports, the risk of injury caused by errors of judgment, which may be inevitable with human participants, may be significant. Other cases, such as use of firearms may fall into a different category. Modern small arms are highly accurate and do not explode, so that the only significant risks may arise from cases of incompetent or careless handling.

If that assessment be correct, it does not follow that activities involving firearms will not fall within s 5L; rather the risk would need to be assessed according to whether incompetence or carelessness on the part of the particular participants rises above the level of a fanciful suggestion and constitutes a significant risk. Which approach is correct may itself be a fact requiring evidence.

There are three ways of considering whether the risk of harm is significant. The first is to assume that any risk will be significant, because the results of it eventuating are likely to be catastrophic. The second is to look for statistics which might demonstrate whether accidental shootings on hunting expeditions occur with significant frequency, or whether they are so rare as to constitute an insignificant risk. The third approach is to look at the particular circumstances of the case and inquire whether the participants were competent and experienced users of firearms, whether they were fresh or tired, sober or inebriated and whether they were otherwise known to be careful and responsible people.

The first approach to hunting expeditions is to define them as inherently "dangerous" because injury by gunshot is potentially catastrophic. The factual assumption may well be justified: see for example, NSW Public Health Bulletin, Vol 10, No. 7, July 1999, Peters, Fitzsimmons and Nguyen *Firearm Injury and Death in NSW* at pp 74-79, which demonstrates that over five years between 1990 and 1994 almost one in two firearm accidents which resulted in death or hospitalisation, were fatal... But if the phrase "significant risk of physical harm" would not be satisfied by a miniscule risk, even of very serious harm, this approach would not reflect the statutory test. It also casts doubt on the usefulness of the plaintiff's concession in cross-examination that use of firearms was a dangerous activity.

The second approach was not proposed in the present case. There was no evidence as to whether accidental shootings were sufficiently common to constitute a significant risk...

According to the third approach, the defendant would have been entitled to rely upon circumstances specific to this case, such as the inexperience or state of inebriation of the participants. There was some (albeit limited) evidence before the trial judge in respect of those matters. However, the defendant does not appear to have run his case on that basis, nor was the Court's attention directed to evidence which would allow the significance of the risk to be assessed in this manner.

Given the way in which the parties ran their case, both at trial and on appeal, and in particular the way in which the defendant ran his case, in my view he failed to establish that there was a significant risk of injury occurring from the accidental discharge of a firearm whilst shooting kangaroo at night, in the circumstances in which the plaintiff was involved.

Was the risk which materialised an "obvious risk"?

... It may well be that a particular recreational activity is attended by a number of significant risks of physical harm. For s 5L to be engaged, at least one of those risks must materialise and result in the harm suffered by the plaintiff. Further, that risk must be an "obvious risk" within the meaning of s 5F of the Act. These two elements must, to an extent, be treated together.

Fallas v Mourlas cont.

At a general level, the words of these provisions are simple and readily understandable. However, difficulties arise in their application to specific circumstances. Thus, in the present case, different results were said to arise, depending on the level of particularity with which the relevant risk was identified. Section 5L(1) directs attention to that risk which has materialised, causing harm to the plaintiff, which must be an obvious risk. Section 5F(1) identifies the qualities of an "obvious risk" as being a risk that "in the circumstances" would have been obvious to a reasonable person "in the position of" the plaintiff.

Thus, if the risk which is said to have materialised is simply that of harm flowing from the accidental discharge of a gun, whilst pointed at the plaintiff, that risk was undoubtedly obvious to the plaintiff himself, and would have been obvious to any reasonable person in his position. On the other hand, if one takes into account the assurances given by the defendant that the gun was not loaded at the relevant time, the risk may not be obvious. These differences suggest that the application of s 5L(1) will depend upon the level of particularity at which "the circumstances" are identified and those aspects of "the position" of the plaintiff which are to be ascribed to the reasonable person, for the purposes of the definition in s 5F(1).

If the statutory defence were intended to apply in the same manner as the old common law principle of voluntary assumption of risk, one might need to determine the circumstances and the position of the plaintiff at a time when he had a reasonable opportunity to avoid the risk. Thus, if the first time at which the plaintiff could reasonably have realised that the defendant was behaving irresponsibly with the gun was a matter of seconds before it discharged, one might say that the risk was not obvious, because there was no realistic risk if the gun was not loaded and the defendant kept it pointing away from the plaintiff.

Section 5K defines "obvious risk", for the purposes of Division 5, "recreational activities" as having the same meaning as in Division 4, which deals with "assumption of risk". Division 4 has two operative provisions, the first of which requires that, in determining liability for negligence, the plaintiff is "presumed to have been aware of" an obvious risk of harm unless he or she proves the contrary: s 5G(1). The second operative provision relieves a person of an obligation to warn another of "an obvious risk to" that other person: s 5H(1). In relation to s 5G, it would seem that the state of awareness, and the hence the obviousness of the risk, must have existed at the time the risk materialised. However, in relation to s 5H, in practical terms, the obviousness of the risk should be capable of being assessed at the time the putative defendant might be required to take reasonable steps to warn of the risk, were it not obvious. In reality, it seems likely that s 5H(1) will operate as a retrospective release from a failure to warn, because the obviousness of the risk can only be assessed, for legal purposes, at the time it materialises. These considerations suggest that the nature of the risk should be identified by reference to the particular circumstances and the position of the plaintiff at the time the harm is suffered or, if it be different for the purposes of s 5L, when the risk materialises.

There remains a question as to the level of precision with which the risk is defined and the particularity of the circumstances which are taken into account. In that respect, s 5F causes a number of difficulties. For example, sub-s(4) provides that a risk can be obvious even if the condition or circumstance that gives rise to the risk "is not prominent, conspicuous or physically observable". In the present case, the risk involves two elements: the first is that the gun be loaded and the second that it be pointed towards the plaintiff. Furthermore, sub-s (3) states that a risk can be obvious "even though it has a low probability of occurring".

Reading s 5F as a whole, there must have been risk that there was a bullet in the pistol prior to its discharge, even though the defendant assured the plaintiff that there was not. The fact that the presence of the bullet was not physically observable by the plaintiff is not fatal to that conclusion. Similarly, there was, prior to the discharge of the gun, a risk that the defendant would point it at the plaintiff, even though that would be a careless act, done in contravention of standard rules for the handling of firearms. Although there was no evidence of it, the plaintiff might have believed that the defendant was experienced, careful and responsible in his handling of firearms. But even if he had, that would merely mean that the risk of an accidental pointing of the gun was probably low. It would remain an obvious risk.

It follows, in my view, that the risk which materialised, namely the accidental discharge of a firearm whilst pointed at the plaintiff, was "an obvious risk" whatever the knowledge, belief and circumstances which existed immediately prior to the discharge.

A risk "of" the dangerous recreational activity?

Assuming for present purposes that the relevant activity was shooting kangaroo at night and, at least in the conditions appertaining on the day in question, it was a "dangerous recreational activity" (contrary to the conclusion reached above) it would nevertheless be necessary to determine whether the risk which materialised was an obvious risk "of" that dangerous recreational activity.

On the approach adopted above it is not necessary to answer this question. Nevertheless, the reasoning of the trial judge shows that this question is closely related to the identification of the relevant activity.

In my view, there is at least doubt that the risk which materialised was such a risk. Those risks included risks of accidental or negligent discharge of a firearm in the course of shooting (or attempting to shoot - none appears to have been shot) kangaroos. The relevant risks would include a discharge caused by the movement of the vehicle whilst seeking, chasing or approaching animals; a discharge caused while entering or leaving the vehicle, a discharge caused whilst running to a position from which a shot might be fired or whilst aiming at an animal, especially if it were moving. However, other occasions on which discharge might occur might be too far removed from the activity to form part of it …

The answer to this question may depend on whether the defendant had "given up for the night" or was actively seeking to fix the gun, so that he could continue shooting. The evidence does not reveal any obvious answer to such a question …

… I am inclined to think that, whilst the risk of an accidental discharge of the gun, while sitting in a vehicle, may be of a different order to the risk of such an accident whilst participating in the shooting, that risk is nevertheless "obvious". On the other hand, the evidence to which the Court was taken left doubt that the risk which did materialise was a risk of the dangerous recreational activity…

This result may appear to turn on a technicality, but I do not think that it does. The risk of accidental discharge of a firearm, causing harm to a person, is far more likely to occur during a hunting activity at night. The more general risk of accidental discharge while manipulating a firearm which is thought to be unloaded, and thereby shooting a person may be far lower. Under the general law, care was taken to limit the defence of voluntary assumption of risk to those risks which the plaintiff should properly have been taken to have accepted, which may not have included the risk which materialised, causing harm. Thus, in *Beck v Mercantile Mutual Insurance Co Ltd*, a pillion passenger on a motorcycle was held to have accepted the risks flowing from the lack of a headlight, but was able to recover because he suffered injury as a result of the failure of the rider to keep on the correct side of the road. The fact that the statutory defence does not require subjective acceptance of risk by a plaintiff, does not mean that a broader effect should be given to the scope of the defence than the ordinary meaning of the language requires. The language is consistent with the approach adopted under the general law. Accordingly, it is necessary for the defendant to satisfy the Court that the risk which materialised was both a risk "of" a recreational activity, and that that recreational activity was dangerous because that risk was "significant". Although I would dismiss the appeal on another ground, in my view the defendant has failed to discharge either of these burdens.

Fallas v Mourlas cont.

Conclusion

I agree with Ipp JA that there are errors revealed in the approach adopted by the trial judge with respect to these questions and, for that reason, leave to appeal should be granted. However, the defendant has not persuaded me that the recreational activity in which the plaintiff was engaged on the night in question was a "dangerous recreational activity" for the purposes of s 5L of the Act. Accordingly that defence was not made out and I agree with Ipp JA that the appeal should be dismissed with costs.

[Tobias JA agreed with Ipp JA that this was a dangerous recreational activity and thought that the risk was dangerous. Thus he would have allowed the appeal.]

[12.215] **Notes&Questions**

1. In *Doubleday v Kelly* [2005] NSWCA 151, (see [12.40]), concerning a seven year old injured whilst attempting to roller skate on a trampoline, Bryson JA, after quoting NSW: CLA, s 5F (obvious risk) and 5L (obvious risks of dangerous recreational activities), said:

> Whether the respondent's injury was suffered as a result of the materialisation of an obvious risk requires reference by way of s 5K to subs 5F(1) and to whether the risk was "... a risk that, in the circumstances, would have been obvious to a reasonable person in the position of that person." It was contended: "... the full force of s 5L applies to children as though they were adults." It was the meaning of this contention that when addressing who is, for the purposes of s 5F(1) "a reasonable person in the position of (the respondent)," the fact that the respondent was a child of seven is not relevant, and the reference is to a generalised reasonable person. In my view this submission does not accord with the meaning of subs 5F(1), which requires consideration of the position of the person who suffers harm and whatever else is relevant to establishing that position. The characteristics of being a child of seven with no previous experience in the use of trampolines or roller skates, who chose to get up early in the morning and play unsupervised, is part of that position.
>
> The Trial Judge found ... that there are obvious dangers in respect of trampolines; this finding, in context, related to what is obvious to reasonable persons, not being young children ... [T]he Trial Judge found, after referring to s 5L, "We are talking here of a seven year old girl and in my view a reasonable seven year old would not regard the trampoline as an obvious risk." In my opinion the reference to "a reasonable person in the position of that person" in s 5F requires that this view be taken of s 5L. Upon the findings made by the Trial Judge neither Div 4 relating to assumption of risk nor Div 5 relating to recreational activities stands in the way of the respondent's recovering of damages.

2. The late Professor Fleming wrote the following in 1967 (J Fleming, "The Role of Negligence in Modern Tort Law" (1967) 53 *Virginia Law Review* 815 at 819-821):

> Negligence, with its familiar calculus of balancing to arrive at the requisite standard of care, is appropriate for those ordinary, commonplace activities with which the law was concerned during its formative period. It was the realm of conduct that juries, composed of people with ordinary experience, could adjudge. The balancing process, which weighed the risk threatened on the one hand against the utility of the proposed action on the other, assumed the existence of a broad consensus about values – social values by which the opposing pulls could be assessed. Typically, the cases involved the

> miscarriage of conduct that was safe enough if properly carried out. Rarely, if ever, was or is a negligence issue raised over the propriety of a whole enterprise, the expectation being that ordinarily it would be reasonably safe. Usually the issue was confined merely to the question whether the disappointment of that expectation was due to something done or omitted by the actor, but for which the activity would not have gone amiss. If it was, the accident must be attributed to negligence; if not, to pure mischance ...
>
> This image still fits well enough with familiar activities, especially leisure activities, that have not changed measurably over the years. It is, however, put under unbearable strain when applied to present-day industrial operations, the most fertile source of injuries in the production, distribution and consumption process. Two difficulties are most perplexing. First is the virtually insoluble problem of pitting a social against an economic judgment. A somewhat kindred, and all too familiar, difficulty is that encountered in so many professional negligence cases when a professional decision, like a doctor's or surgeon's, must be appraised for social adequacy ...
>
> Yet how is the predominance of the *legal* standard to be asserted when what is called in question is a deliberate decision based on complex economic criteria ? The conventional test ordains that, among the factors to be weighed against the gravity and imminence of the risk, are the utility of the defendant's conduct, as well as the cost and inconvenience of safety procedures, if any, that might have minimized or altogether eliminated the risk. Leaving aside altogether the difficulty of establishing the existence, yet alone the extra cost of such alternative devices (especially when they are not used by others engaged in the same line of endeavour), how is the jury to decide whether or not a managerial decision, choosing safety procedures that made the best *economic* sense, conformed to the legal standard of reasonable care? ...
>
> Is it at all possible, and if so in what meaningful sense, to test such a decision by the legal standard of "due care"? As already mentioned, we cultivate the pretense that the cost factor deserves consideration in that tally. Theoretically, there may be the distinction that, for purposes of the *managerial* decision, cost is considered in terms of economic efficiency, while for the legal test, cost must be weighed against the risk of injury ...
>
> In practice, however, these distinctions are likely to tax the ordinary jury beyond its capacity. What is here thrown in doubt is the ability of our traditional legal criteria to cope at all adequately with problems of this calibre.

Consider Professor Fleming's views in light of the cases and material studied in the first part of this chapter. How would the principles relating to breach of duty apply to, for example, the tobacco and alcohol industries? Alcohol is a leading cause of disease and is second only to tobacco as a preventable cause of drug-related morbidity and mortality. Overuse and abuse of alcohol and tobacco is a social and public health problem of major proportions in Australia, which has enormous cost implications for the health system, emergency services, policing and the criminal justice system, and society generally. Is the individualistic focus of negligence equipped to deal with such issues? Should negligence law be taking societal losses into account in its calculation of breach of duty?

We now turn to consider the standard against which the defendant's conduct is measured.

WHO IS THE REASONABLE PERSON?

[12.220] The defendant's conduct is measured by the standard of the "reasonable person" (formerly the "reasonable man") in the circumstances. The standard has been described variously as: the "man on the Clapham omnibus" (*McGuire v Western Morning News Co Ltd* [1903] 2 KB 100 at 109 per Collins MR); the "man on the Bondi tram" (*Papatonakis v*

Australian Telecommunications Commission (1985) 156 CLR 7 per Deane J at 36); the "reasonable man of ordinary intelligence and experience" (*Glasgow Corporation v Muir* [1943] AC 448 per Lord MacMillan at 457); and "the man who takes the magazines at home and in the evening pushes the lawn mower in his shirt sleeves" (*Hall v Brookland Auto Racing Club* [1933] 1 KB 205 per Greer LJ at 22).

Leon Green, in a seminal article ("The Negligence Issue" (1927) 37 Yale LJ 1029), explains the futility of any attempt to tailor negligence to the qualities of a particular individual or to particular situations. "The qualities of personality are ... numerous; their shadings are countless; the conduct of individuals incalculable at present in its variety; the possible combinations of these are literally infinite, as finite as space and time". In the face of such infinity, the law has developed a formula in which the particular qualities of the individual are ignored. The standard of care against the defendant's conduct is measured as the objective one of the reasonable person in the circumstances with no allowance for a defendant's individual idiosyncrasies (*Vaughan v Menlove* (1837) 3 Bing (NC) 468; 132 ER 490). The objective standard also extends to the defendant's finances. The test is that of a defendant with reasonable resources (*PQ v Australian Red Cross Society* [1992] VR 19, see [12.150] Note 1). Exceptions exist in relation to public authorities, see, for example NSW: CLA, s 42, duties to trespassers and in limited situations in nuisance, see [18.120] (*Stockwell v State of Victoria* [2001] VSC 497).

Atiyah points out:

> At the end of the day the judge has to say whether he thinks the defendant should have behaved in a certain way or not. It will be seen that this approach simply eliminates the personal element. The judge's decision is not dependent on whether the defendant could have personally foreseen the harm or could have avoided it. The defendant may be stupid, slow-witted, clumsy or accident prone; he may be disabled or sick; all this is irrelevant. The judge is saying what should have been done, not what could have been done, by this defendant. (PS Atiyah, Accidents, Compensation and the Law (3rd ed, CUP, Cambridge, 1980), p 57)

Mahoney P commented in *Bardsley v Batemans Bay Bowling Club Ltd* (unreported, New South Wales Court of Appeal, Mahoney P, 25 November 1996):

> As any experienced lawyer will know, what a reasonable person will do, or more accurately, is to be seen for this purpose to do, is measured by what, in the particular case, a judge will do. As Lord Radcliffe observed many years ago, the reasonable man is "an anthropomorphic conception of justice" in which what the reasonable person says is what the judge says. ... This means, of course, that what a defendant must do is what, as far as can be predicted, the judge who in due course tries the proceeding will determine that he should have done. What he has done in advance to safeguard the plaintiff will, in reality, be sufficient if his prediction is accurate.

Will the judge's assessment of what is reasonable reflect community values? It has been observed that until recent times the High Court of Australia was dominated by male appointees of British or Irish origins, principally from private schools and from the New South Wales or Victorian bar. It has not been representative of the general Australian community in any real sense, although in recent years there has been some limited progress (see A Reilly, "Cultural Diversity" in *Oxford Companion to the High Court of Australia*, (Oxford University Press, Melbourne, 2001), p 186).

This section explores the concept of the reasonable person considering the particular characteristics of gender, age, mental disability and skills.

Gender

Tort Law & the Feminist Critique of Reason

[12.225] J Conaghan, "Tort Law and the Feminist Critique of Reason" in A Bottomley (ed), *Feminist Perspectives on the Foundational Subjects of Law* (University of Kent, 1996), pp 51-58

(footnotes partially omitted)

The Feminist Critique of the Reasonable Man

It is commonly asserted that the standard of care in negligence is determined by recourse to the ubiquitous "reasonable man". He is said to originate in the early 19th century decision of *Vaughan v Menlove* which established that for purposes of determining negligence, the question was not whether or not a defendant had acted "bona fide and honestly to the best of his own judgment" but rather whether or not his conduct was that of "a man of ordinary prudence". Thus the emphasis of the court was on an objective standard to which all must conform rather than a subjective one which took account of individual human frailty.

Such a view has been confirmed by subsequent cases which have emphasised the abstract and "impersonal" nature of the standard being applied although it is also true that the reasonable man is not devoid of all characteristics which make him human: age, special skills and, in some instances, disability may all find their way into the fiction which the courts invoke. However, by and large, neither the personal characteristics nor the particular weaknesses of the defendant are considered when evaluating his behaviour and he may be liable even in circumstances where, in no moral sense, can he be said to be at fault.

However, despite his prestigious pedigree and briskly confident persona, the reasonable man is not without his critics. Even at his birth there was considerable disagreement as to his merits: defence counsel in *Vaughan* contended he established a standard "too uncertain to act upon". Moreover, in subsequent years judges and commentators have continued to acknowledge the uncertainty entailed in articulating a standard which, while purporting to be universal, nevertheless may produce considerable variety. As L MacMillan has forthrightly observed:

> It is still left to the judge to decide what in the circumstances of the particular case the reasonable man would have had in contemplation ... Here there is room for a diversity of view.

This has led some judges and commentators to conclude that the reasonable man is no more than a convenient legal fiction disguising the application of subjective judicial preferences and value judgments. He is merely one of a range of legal devices which operate to "obscure the policy content of judicial decision-making".

Thus, the reasonable man's claims to universality have long been questioned and recent feminist scrutiny has further compromised his reputation for impartiality. In particular, it is frequently asserted that his gender-specificity is not just a linguistic convention, whereby both sexes are denoted by reference to the masculine: the reasonable man is, in fact, male. It follows that the standard he expresses has a significant gender content.

Such a claim can be evidenced in a variety of ways. That judges and textbook writers invariably have a man, rather than a woman, in mind when they apply the test of reason-ableness is well illustrated by the images they invoke. Tort law is populated with references to "the man on the Clapham omnibus" (or, in Australia, the "Bondi tram"), "the man who takes the magazine at home and in the evening pushes the lawn mower in his shirt sleeves". The image of a man occupying the busy public realm by day and the leisure of domestic life in the evening may reflect the aspirations of the suburban middle-class male but it certainly does not capture the experience of women juggling duties between home and work.

Tort Law & the Feminist Critique of Reason cont.

The maleness of the reasonable man standard is further suggested by the absence of women, by and large, from his birth and subsequent upbringing. The reasonable man possesses an exclusively male parentage and even today, some 150 years after his birth, his continued sustenance remains in the hands of a predominantly male judiciary. In so far as the application of the reasonableness standard expresses, at least in part, the subjective preferences of particular judges, those preferences will inevitably be coloured by perceptions which derive from their sex (as well as class, race and other social characteristics) resulting (at least in some cases) in the application of an identifiably male standard to a female defendant. Lucinda Finley highlights the decision in *Tucker v Henniker*, where an appellate court expressly addressed the question of whether a teenage girl involved in an accident while driving her father's carriage should be held to the standard of reasonableness of "ordinary persons like herself" or whether she should be bound by the standard of "mankind" in general, that is the standard of competent and experienced carriage drivers, most of whom were male. The appellate court, not surprisingly, opted for the latter (anticipating the modern decision of *Nettleship v Weston* which coincidentally also involved a woman defendant) but, as Finley observes, the result of the decision in *Tucker* was to hold women to a standard which they were less likely to acquire by virtue of the social consequences which flowed from their sex, from which Finley concludes: "If women are unaccustomed to doing an activity, it would appear inherently unreasonable for them to attempt it." Similarly, Robyn Martyn points to the absurdity of a male judiciary assessing the reasonableness of Mrs Sayers' attempt to escape from a public toilet in *Sayers v Harlow UDC*.

> Three elderly judges were called upon to put themselves in the position of a woman, dressed in a tight skirt and high-heeled shoes, locked in a lavatory while her impatient husband waited for her at the bus stop.

The court's conclusion that Mrs Sayers was contributorily negligent in attempting to climb out of the lavatory cubicle is, Martyn argues, a prime example of the application of a male standard in circumstances where a reasonable woman might well have evaluated Mrs Sayers' conduct rather differently.

However, feminist scholars go further than simply highlighting the gender composition of the judiciary and its likely impact on the decision-making process. Feminists further assert that the legal attributes of the reasonable man – particularly his ability to detach himself from the specific circumstances of a situation and weigh up the costs and benefits of action without recourse to "emotional" or "sentimental" considerations – are male, in the sense that they rely upon characteristics conventionally attributed to, and applauded in, men and contrast with features typically associated with women, such as a lack of detachment, a passionate or emotional nature and a tendency to engage with aspects of a situation not necessarily relevant to rational calculation.

In what sense can it be said that the legal attributes of the reasonable man are male? Certainly it may be argued that such a gendered characterisation of reasonable behaviour bears some correspondence to popular perceptions of gender difference. Indeed it is a recognisable, if regrettable, feature of legal culture to associate men with certain "natural" qualities – reason and detachment, strength and courage – and to perceive women in terms of their opposites – emotion and sentiment, delicacy and timidity. This feature of legal culture is humorously captured by Sir Alan Herbert's depiction of women in his classic parody of the common law:

> There exist a class of beings illogical, impulsive, careless, irresponsible, extravagant, prejudiced and free for the most part from those worthy and repellent excellences which distinguish the Reasonable Man.

Herbert's picture presents women as emotional and frivolous beings, not capable of rational consideration of the weighty matters of importance which more appropriately preoccupy men. While widely acknowledged as a caricature, it retains its humour (and therefore its power) because it continues to draw on prevailing perceptions of gender difference in respect of rationality.

Tort Law & the Feminist Critique of Reason cont.

Historically, such perceptions of women's "irrationality" have been a source of their exclusion and disempowerment. Yet, perhaps surprisingly, feminist engagement with the question of women's rationality has not necessarily sought to deny the existence of gender differences in this context. Rather the strategy has been to challenge conventional understandings of what is rational (and therefore what is irrational) with a view to redefining rationality to include modes of analysis, forms of argument and approaches to decision-making typically deployed by women.

Such an approach derives in particular from Carol Gilligan's articulation of "a different voice" in the context of her empirical exploration of moral reasoning. Focusing on the limits of existing psychological evaluations of moral development (particularly the work of Kohlberg), Gilligan highlights and explores different approaches to the resolution of moral questions, at the same time revealing a significant gender dimension. In this respect, Gilligan points out that previous empirical work relied on observations of male rather than female children and she sets about re-examining conclusions about human development by exploring the differences between the way in which boys and girls approach and resolve moral dilemmas. Her results are controversial but strongly suggestive: they have been interpreted by many as evidence that women approach and resolve moral questions differently from men and that furthermore, "feminine" approaches to dispute resolution (Gilligan's "different voice") have been typically, but wrongly, characterised as naive and immature.

The content of Gilligan's different voice contrasts strongly with established assumptions about human moral development. While the implications of Kohlberg's work point mainly towards a developmental progression which culminates in the articulation and application of a "language of rights" to moral dilemmas, characterised by a tendency to invoke abstract principles or hierarchies of rights to resolve disputes, Gilligan's "voice" eschews a rights-based approach in favour of considerations which focus on the web of relationships which surround and connect the parties involved, and on modes of communication which might be deployed to resolve the conflict with minimal damage to, or disruption of, the relationships which bind the parties together.

Gilligan's argument is that such an approach, while traditionally devalued, is equally valid and no less "developed" than rights-based reasoning. The implications of her argument include the possibility that the bounds of reason, as traditionally conceived, have been drawn too narrowly.

Gilligan's work adds considerable weight to the feminist claim that the reasonable man is male (at least empirically). From Gilligan one can recognise that the standard implicit in the reasonable man test, with its emphasis on abstract cost benefit calculations, corresponds more closely with the "male" than the "female" voice in her work. This has led feminist torts scholar Leslie Bender to question the reliance of tort law on "algebraic formulations to [assess] behaviour"; to challenge the "language and value system [which] privileges economics and costs" and "dehumanizes people generally by valuing human life in largely monetary terms and, ultimately, to call for the rejection of a conception of justice as monetary compensation for harms (achieved through win/lose resolutions of rights conflicts)". Articulating what she claims as a feminist agenda for tort law, Bender concludes:

> We need … to help change the dominant ideology from individualist to interconnected. We need to shift from a right-based focus to a focus on both care and rights/justice, from power-over to empowering, from the prioritizing of the market and money to a priority of personal relationships, health, safety, and human dignity in deciding personal injury disputes.

For Bender, the identifying characteristics of the current standard of reasonableness invoked by tort law are an individualistic, rights-based focus and an emphasis on markets and money. It is a standard of efficiency, a classic expression of instrumental reason, concerned with ensuring the most efficient means to particular ends. However, the concept of instrumental rationality does not stand by itself. Inevitably it relies on certain underlying assumptions about human nature, typically expressed in terms of the physical separateness of individuals and/or the pursuit of individual self-interest. These are assumptions which feminist theory has challenged primarily on the grounds that they do not

Tort Law & the Feminist Critique of Reason cont.

correspond either materially or experientially with women's lives. Robin West, for example, has argued that "all our modern legal theory ... is essentially and irretrievably masculine" because it relies on "the separation thesis", that is, the assumption that human beings, whatever else they may be, are physically separate from each other:

> Women are not essentially, necessarily, inevitably, invariably, always and forever separate from other human beings: women, distinctively, are quite clearly "connected" to other human beings when pregnant ...

West goes on to argue that this "material fact" about women's lives, although it may result in a diversity in subjective experience, nevertheless evidences that the "human being" of legal and political theory is male rather than female. It follows that human nature (along with the characteristics attributed to it) is a social construct shaped and informed, inter alia, by gender-based assumptions. By challenging the understanding of human nature which instrumental rationality reflects and revealing its gendered content, feminist legal theory further evidences the masculinity of tort law's reasonable man.

The Maleness of the Reasonable Man: Different Interpretations

Feminist tort scholars have sought to demonstrate the claim that the reasonable man is male. However, there remains a fundamental ambiguity about the nature of this claim which continues to characterise the literature: what does it mean to assert that the reasonable man is male? It is important to distinguish the different levels at which this claim may operate. The claim may be, firstly, that the conception of reason which the reasonable man expresses is biologically male in the sense that only men possess the physical or intellectual attributes necessary to comply with it. Such a claim is rarely explicitly made although it is arguably implicit in judicial pronouncements such as Bradwell which rely on woman's "nature" to deny her capacity to engage in certain activities (such as practising law).

Secondly, the claim may be that the reasonable man expresses a standard which is socially male in the sense that men are more likely or more able to comply with it by virtue of their gender socialisation. Such a claim assumes that gender is a social construct and that many of the commonly perceived differences between men and women, in terms of ability or inclination, are socially rather than biologically based. This idea seems to inform much of the feminist exploration of case law, for example Finley's treatment of the *Tucker* case or Martyn's account of the decision in *Sayers*, discussed above. In both instances the writers highlight the different social roles assumed by, or allocated to, men and women and the corresponding differences in skills and/or perceptions which may result. It probably also underlies Bender's critique of the reasonable man and her rejection of the instrumental rationality which he articulates. In particular, Bender's reliance on Gilligan suggests her acceptance of the (empirical) claim that men and women tend to reason differently while at the same time she frequently appeals to perceived differences between men and women's social roles to explain and justify her rejection of the concept of legal responsibility which the reasonable man test entails:

> It is arguable that law's meaning of responsibility does not include interpersonal care-giving because that kind of work has been traditionally done by women, not by the men who created and developed tort law, nor by the men who ran the business world that created all these mass torts and personal injuries.

Thus Bender, Finley and others rely on differences between men and women's experiences in their efforts to identify the maleness of the reasonable man. Implicit in their claims is the assumption that experience can be identified and demarcated in terms of gender, an assumption which is increasingly controversial.

Thirdly, the claim that the reasonable man is male maybe made metaphorically rather than biologically or socially. Thus, for example, popular representations of rationality as "male" and "irrationality" as female may invoke a cultural understanding whereby "male" and "female" are deployed hierarchically, operating to include (male) or exclude (female), to approve (male) or disapprove (female), to render secure (male) or insecure (female). In this context gender functions symbolically, that is as a metaphor which carries particular meanings not necessarily biologically or socially derived. [60] Perhaps then the reasonable man is metaphorically male; that is, the attribution of maleness carries a particular cultural meaning which reinforces the legitimacy of the standard of care which he expresses and at the same time renders illegitimate alternative formulations. This is not a dimension which feminist tort scholars have sought to explore, yet it may be that the reasonable man is best understood in these terms, particularly given certain inherent weaknesses in socially-based claims. In any case it must be recognised that any evaluation of feminist responses to the perceived maleness of the reasonable man must be informed by an understanding of the basis of the perception under scrutiny. It does not appear that such an understanding is fully apparent in the literature to date. To what extent can it help to clarify the dilemma for feminists which the reasonable man creates?

[12.230] Notes&Questions

1. Do you agree with Keith J in *Rabidue v Osceola Refining Company* 805 F 2d 611 (1986) (below note 3) that a "reasonable woman" standard might well differ from that of a "reasonable man"? Would this apply in all types of cases, for example, motor vehicle accidents, or only certain categories of case? What about his notion of a "reasonable victim" standard? Would a variable standard promote a more just result, or a less just? Consider the position of both plaintiff and defendant.
2. See further, G Monti, "A Reasonable Woman Standard in Sexual Harassment Litigation" (1999) 19 Legal Stud 552; L Bender, "A Lawyer's Primer on Feminist Theory and Tort" (1988) 38 *Journal of Legal Education* 3, esp 20-25, 30-32; G Schwartz, "Feminist Approaches to Tort Law" (2001) 2 *Theoretical Inquiries in Law* 175.
3. In *Rabidue v Osceola Refining Company* 805 F.2d 611 1986 United States Court of Appeals for the 6th circuit (footnotes omitted), the plaintiff was dismissed from her position as office manager for a petrochemical company, and sued her employer for sexual discrimination and sexual harassment in the workplace, in violation of various statutory protections, including Title VII of the *Civil Rights Act 1964*. She was unsuccessful at trial and again on appeal. The case is not a negligence action, but the judgement of Keith J raises some relevant questions applicable to the determination of standard of care. Consider the views expressed below, in particular those contained in the dissenting opinion.

Delivering the majority judgment, Krupansky J described as "apt" the following statement from the trial judge, Judge Newblatt:

> Indeed, it cannot seriously be disputed that in some work environments, humor and language are rough hewn and vulgar. Sexual jokes, sexual conversations and girlie magazines may abound. Title VII was not meant to – or can – change this. It must never be forgotten that Title VII is the federal court mainstay in the struggle for equal employment opportunity for the female workers of America. But it is quite different to claim that Title VII was designed to bring about a magical transformation in the social mores of American workers.

Keith J dissented in part and (at 626) said the following:

Nor do I agree with the majority holding that a court considering hostile [workplace] environment claims should adopt the perspective of the reasonable person's reaction to a similar environment ... In my view, the reasonable person perspective fails to account for the wide divergence between most women's views of appropriate sexual conduct and those of men. *See* Comment, "Sexual Harassment Claims of Abusive Work Environment Under Title VII", 97 Harv L Rev 1449, 1451 (1984). As suggested by the Comment, I would have courts adopt the perspective of the reasonable victim which simultaneously allows courts to consider salient sociological differences as well as shield employers from the neurotic complainant ... Moreover, unless the outlook of the reasonable woman is adopted, the defendants as well as the courts are permitted to sustain ingrained notions of reasonable behaviour fashioned by the offenders, in this case, men.

... Nor can I agree with the majority's notion that the effect of pin-up posters and misogynous language in the workplace can have only a minimal effect on female employees and should not be deemed hostile or offensive "when considered in the context of a society that condones and publicly features and commercially exploits open displays of written and pictorial erotica at newsstands, on prime-time television, at the cinema and in other public places." ... "Society" in this scenario must primarily refer to the unenlightened; I hardly believe reasonable women condone the pervasive degradation and exploitation of female sexuality perpetuated in American culture. In fact, pervasive societal approval thereof and of other stereotypes stifles female potential and instils the debased sense of self worth which accompanies stigmatization. The presence of pin-ups and misogynous language in the workplace can only evoke and confirm the debilitating norms by which women are primarily and contemptuously valued as objects of male sexual fantasy. That some men would condone and wish to perpetuate such behavior is not surprising. However, the relevant inquiry at hand is what the reasonable woman would find offensive, not society, which at one point also condoned slavery. I conclude that sexual posters and anti-female language can seriously affect the psychological well being of the reasonable woman and interfere with her ability to perform her job.

Age – children

McHale v Watson

[12.235] *McHale v Watson* (1966) 115 CLR 199 High Court of Australia

(footnotes omitted)

[Barry Watson, aged 12, threw a piece of scrap metal or bolt, which he had sharpened at one end at a hardwood post expecting it to stick in the post. The dart either missed the post or hit it and glanced off and hit nine year old Susan McHale, who was standing near the post. Susan was blinded in one eye. She sued both Barry and his parents in negligence, and Barry in trespass. At trial Windeyer J found for both defendants. In relation to Barry, he applied the standard of care of an ordinary boy of 12. Susan appealed to the High Court against the decision in favour of Barry, on the issue of standard of care.]

McTIERNAN ACJ: 204 Windeyer J [the trial judge] said in his reasons for judgment:

It has been strongly urged for the plaintiff that, in considering whether Barry was negligent, I must judge what he did by the standard expected of a reasonable man, and that that standard is not graduated according to age. In one sense, of course, that is so; for the question whether conduct was negligent, in a legal sense, always depends on an objective standard. This has been generally recognized ever since Tindal CJ said in *Vaughan v Menlove*: "Instead of saying that the liability for negligence should be coextensive with the judgment of each individual, which would be as variable as the length of the foot of each individual, we ought rather to adhere to the rule which requires in all cases a regard to caution such as a man of ordinary prudence would observe". In *Glasgow Corporation v Muir* Lord Macmillan said: "The standard of foresight of the reasonable man is, in one sense, an impersonal test. It

McHale v Watson cont.

> eliminates the personal equation and is independent of the idiosyncrasies of the particular person whose conduct is in question. ... The reasonable man is presumed to be free both from over-apprehension and from over-confidence, but there is a sense in which the standard of care of the reasonable man involves in its application a subjective element. It is still left to the judge to decide what, in the circumstances of the particular case, the reasonable man would have had in contemplation, and what accordingly the party sought to be made liable ought to have foreseen". That is the question I have to determine. It is a question of fact, a jury question, not a question of law. I have not to determine it by regarding the facts of other cases, but by regarding all the circumstances of this case. I do not think that I am required to disregard altogether the fact that the defendant Barry Watson was at the time only twelve years old. In remembering that, I am not considering "the idiosyncrasies of the particular person". Childhood is not an idiosyncrasy. It may be that an adult, knowing of the resistant qualities of hardwood and of the uncertainty that a spike, not properly balanced as a dart, will stick into wood when thrown, would foresee that it might fail to do so and perhaps go off at a tangent. A person who knew, or might reasonably be expected to know that, might be held to be negligent if he were not more circumspect than was this infant defendant. But whatever the position would be if the facts were different, my conclusion on the facts of this case is that the injury to the plaintiff was not the result of a lack of foresight and appreciation of the risk that might reasonably have been expected, or of a want of reasonable care in aiming the dart. I find that Barry Watson was not negligent in the legal sense.

The appeal was argued on two main grounds: first that his Honour was in error in holding that the liability or degree of responsibility of the defendant Barry Watson or the standard of care to be exercised by him in any way differed from the liability degree of responsibility or standard of care which would have been proper had he been over the age of twenty-one years; and secondly that his Honour should have made a finding of negligence whether he applied the standard of the ordinary reasonable man or the standard (whatever it might be) appropriate to a twelve-year-old boy.

I do not agree with either of those grounds. In my opinion the passage which I have quoted from his Honour's judgment does not contain any misdirection in law and I see no reason for interfering with his conclusion. The crucial question is whether his Honour erred in saying that he could not disregard the fact that the defendant Barry Watson was twelve years old at the time of the accident and in order to answer that question it is necessary to determine by what standard of care the infant defendant should be judged. It is a well-established principle that an infant may be held liable for torts which are not ex contractu, but there is a paucity of judicial authority on the standard of care applicable to young children. Perhaps this lack of authority is due to the fact that young children are rarely worth suing and plaintiffs usually rely on making parents and guardians liable for the wrongful acts of their children and charges as was attempted in another case heard with the present and which Windeyer J dismissed.

There is ample authority for the proposition that in cases dealing with alleged contributory negligence on the part of young children they are expected to exercise the degree of care one would expect, not of the average reasonable man, but of a child of the same age and experience. No Australian or English decision was cited relating to the standard to be applied where a young child is sued in negligence ... Fleming, The Law of Torts (3rd ed, 1965), pp 117, 118 is to the same effect [that the standard is that of the reasonable child, and continues] "Some safeguard to the public is afforded by the obligation of parents and school authorities to observe reasonable care in the supervision of children under their control. Moreover, a minor who engages in dangerous adult activities, such as driving a car or handling industrial equipment, must conform to the standard of the reasonably prudent adult; his position being analogous to that of beginners who, as we have seen, are held to the objective standard" ...

In the present case we are concerned with a boy of the age of twelve years and two months. He was not, of course, a child of tender years. On the other hand, he was not grown up and, according to the

McHale v Watson cont.

evidence, he played as a child ... It cannot be laid down as an absolute proposition that a boy of twelve years of age can never be liable in negligence; nor that he would always be liable in the same manner as an adult in the case of that tort. The defendant's conduct in relation to this object which he threw, a useless piece of scrap metal, is symbolic of the tastes and simplicity of boyhood ... The evidence does not suggest that the defendant was other than a normal twelve-year-old-boy. His Honour considered that the defendant, being a boy of twelve years, did not have enough maturity of mind to foresee that the dart might glance off the post in the direction of Susan if he did not make it hit the post squarely, and that there was a possibility that he might not succeed in doing so. It seems to me that the present case comes down to a fine point, namely whether it was right for the trial judge to take into account Barry's age in considering whether he did foresee or ought to have foreseen that the so-called dart might not stick in the post but be deflected from it towards Susan who was in the area of danger in the event of such an occurrence. I think that there is no ground for disagreeing with the conclusion of Windeyer J on this question. The correctness of this decision depends upon the special circumstances of the case and it does not lay down any general principle that a young boy who cannot be classified as a grown-up person cannot be guilty of negligence in any circumstances.

I would dismiss the appeal.

KITTO J: 213 [A] defendant does not escape liability by proving that he is abnormal in some respect which reduces his capacity for foresight or prudence. The principle is of course applicable to a child. The standard of care being objective, it is no answer for him, any more than it is for an adult, to say that the harm he caused was due to his being abnormally slow-witted, quick-tempered, absent-minded or inexperienced. But it does not follow that he cannot rely in his defence upon a limitation upon the capacity for foresight or prudence, not as being personal to himself, but as being characteristic of humanity at his stage of development and in that sense normal. By doing so he appeals to a standard of ordinariness, to an objective and not a subjective standard. In regard to the things which pertain to foresight and prudence – experience, understanding of causes and effects, balance of judgment, thoughtfulness – it is absurd, indeed it is a misuse of language, to speak of normality in relation to persons of all ages taken together. In those things normality is, for children, something different from what normality is for adults; the very concept of normality is a concept of rising levels until "years of discretion" are attained. The law does not arbitrarily fix upon any particular age for this purpose, and tribunals of fact may well give effect to different views as to the age at which normal adult foresight and prudence are reasonably to be expected in relation to particular sets of circumstances. But up to that stage the normal capacity to exercise those two qualities necessarily means the capacity which is normal for a child of the relevant age; and it seems to me that it would be contrary to the fundamental principle that a person is liable for harm that he causes by falling short of an objective criterion of "propriety" in his conduct – propriety, that is to say, as determined by a comparison with the standard of care reasonably to be expected in the circumstances from the normal person – to hold that where a child's liability is in question the normal person to be considered is someone other than a child of corresponding age ...

I am therefore of opinion that the learned trial judge did not misdirect himself on the question of law. There remains the question of fact: did the respondent, in throwing the spike as he did though aware of the proximity of the appellant, do anything which a reasonable boy of his age would not have done in the circumstances – a boy, that is to say, who possessed and exercised such degree of foresight and prudence as is ordinarily to be expected of a boy of twelve, holding in his hand a sharpened spike and seeing the post of a tree-guard before him? On the findings which must be accepted, what the respondent did was the unpremeditated, impulsive act of a boy not yet of an age to have an adult's realization of the danger of edged tools or an adult's wariness in the handling of them. It is, I think, a matter for judicial notice that the ordinary boy of twelve suffers from a feeling that a piece of wood and a sharp instrument have a special affinity. To expect a boy of that age to consider

McHale v Watson cont.

before throwing the spike whether the timber was hard or soft, to weigh the chances of being able to make the spike stick in the post, and to foresee that it might glance off and hit the girl, would be, I think, to expect a degree of sense and circumspection which nature ordinarily withholds till life has become less rosy.

Sympathy with the injured girl is inevitable. One might almost wish that mediaeval thinking had led to a modern rule of absolute liability for harm caused. But it has not; and, in the absence of relevant statutory provision, children, like everyone else, must accept as they go about in society the risks from which ordinary care on the part of others will not suffice to save them. One such risk is that boys of twelve may behave as boys of twelve; and that, sometimes, is a risk indeed.

In my opinion the appeal should be dismissed.

MENZIES J: [dissenting] 219 [T]he acceptance of such a standard would require, in each case where there is an allegation that a child's negligence has caused damage to another, a determination of the age, intelligence and experience of the defendant himself as a prerequisite to ascertaining the duty of care to which he is subject by law. Furthermore, if a child's conduct is to be judged by a child's standards, presumably there should also be special standards of care applicable to other classes of persons having less capacity than the ordinary reasonably prudent man – eg the mentally defective or the senile …

It may, of course, be objected that the adoption of a hard-and-fast rule to be applied to all cases will sometimes produce what appears to be some hardship but, if so, it should also be recalled that hard cases make bad law. It is, moreover, necessary to observe that the law of negligence is primarily concerned with the circumstances under which a person who suffers damage may recover compensation, and there is no necessary connexion between legal liability to make compensation and moral culpability. Another objection to a standard rule is that it may appear ridiculous in determining liability to judge immaturity by maturity or, as it was put in argument, to put an old head upon young shoulders. Again the answer to such a criticism is that it was not without good reason that the law has adopted a general standard to determine liability for negligence and the application of a general standard to anyone who is himself either above or below the standard may produce a result that is open to criticism as ridiculous when judged by an irrelevant philosophy. Were the law to require from every person the exercise of all the skill of which he is capable to avoid harm to others, it would be a different law from the established law of negligence and it would be based upon a philosophy different from that underlying the present law. Whether or not it would be a better law is outside any question here relevant, but an attempt to use the results which would follow from the application of such a law, to test the reasonableness of what I understand the present law to require, appears to me to be misconceived.

My conclusion is, therefore, that as the duty of care which the respondent owed to the appellant was to take such care as an ordinary reasonable man would have taken in the circumstances, the appeal should succeed.

I would add that if, contrary to my opinion, the conduct of the respondent ought to be judged by the standard of a reasonable boy of the world rather than a reasonable man of the world, I would still conclude that the respondent had been negligent. It appears to me that no boy of twelve could reasonably think that he could hurl a nail into a post, and I have no doubt that the capacity of the respondent's missile to penetrate a piece of wood was less than that of an ordinary three-inch nail; it was blunt and lacked the weight of a head. Furthermore, in the face of the evidence I would not infer, as did his Honour, that the missile hit the post and was deflected. Upon the facts, I would conclude that a reasonable boy would not throw a three-inch piece of metal, head high, in the direction of another person.

I consider, therefore, that this appeal should be allowed and the action retried.

McHale v Watson cont.

[Owen J agreed with McTiernan and Kitto JJ]

Mental illness and disability

Carrier v Bonham

[12.240] *Carrier v Bonham* [2002] 1 Qd R 474 Queensland Court of Appeal

(footnotes omitted)

[Carrier was driving a bus when Bonham walked out in front of it. The driver braked but was unable to stop the bus before hitting Bonham. Bonham was injured. Carrier, suffered nervous shock and was unable to continue working as a bus driver. Bonham was a psychiatric patient with a long history of schizophrenia. He had escaped from the hospital where he was detained as he was intending to commit suicide. Evidence accepted by the trial judge was that Bonham would not have been aware that his conduct might cause injury to anyone on the bus. Bonham would not have had any concept that his actions might cause harm to anyone else.]

McPHERSON JA: [20] The appeal squarely raises the question whether a person of unsound mind is capable at common law of being legally liable in negligence for conduct by someone with the mental condition of Bonham that causes injury and loss to another ... [O]n the question of negligence, the learned judge decided that, being a person of unsound mind, Bonham was not liable for the injury inflicted on Carrier.

Essentially his Honour's reason for reaching that conclusion was that, for the purpose of the law of negligence, the legal position of a person of unsound mind ought to be equated with that of an infant; that Bonham was not capable of assessing the effect of his actions on someone else; and that his conduct was therefore not to be judged by the objective standard of the ordinary person. In respect of that conclusion, a notice of contention was filed by the plaintiff. Among the matters contested by the plaintiff on the appeal are his Honour's findings that:

(d) the first defendant's mental condition had an effect on the standard of care owed by him to the plaintiff;

(e) his mental condition had an effect on his liability in negligence; and

(g) his attempted suicide did not constitute a breach of his duty of care to the plaintiff ...

[Bonham] was, according to the evidence accepted by his Honour, actually unable to foresee that harm might result to the occupants of the bus, including the plaintiff Carrier, from his intentional act. ... In *Adamson v Motor Vehicle Insurance Trust* (1957) 58 WALR 56, Wolff SPJ held that the defendant, who like many of those considered in the reported cases, was schizophrenic, was liable for negligence in driving a car into a pedestrian who was crossing the road. The American and Canadian authorities are almost at one in holding persons liable for their tortious wrongs even though they may be suffering from unsoundness of mind ... [A]s observed by Wolff SPJ in *Adamson's* case, almost the only exception to this general trend of decided authority is *Buckley & Toronto Transportation Company v Smith Transport Limited* [1946] 4 DLR 721, where the Ontario Court of Appeal held a truck driver not liable because he was suffering from delusions which deprived him of the ability to understand his duty to take care and of his power to discharge it. Somewhat surprisingly, academic opinion seems, on the whole, to be the other way ...

What is in issue here is the significance of the defendant's mental incapacity to foresee that his actions might cause injury to someone else. Ever since the decision in *Vaughan v Menlove* (1837) 3 Bing (NC) 468; 132 ER 490, the established rule of our law has been that the standard for judging

Carrier v Bonham cont.

negligence is "the conduct of a man of ordinary prudence" (Tindal CJ, at 474). The decision is directly relevant here because the defendant who, against all advice, had risked spontaneous combustion in his hayrick, obtained a rule nisi for a new trial on the ground (at 471) that "he had acted bona fide to the best of his judgment; [and] if he had, he ought not to be responsible for the misfortune of not possessing the highest order of intelligence". It also appears from the report (at 472) that, a few years before, he had been successfully sued for burning weeds so near the boundary of his land as to set fire to and destroy his neighbour's wood. The point being made by the defendant there was that he was a man of reduced intelligence; but the rule nisi for a new trial was nevertheless discharged by the Common Pleas. The decision has been "generally recognised ever since" as having set an objective standard of conduct that is independent of the idiosyncrasies of particular individuals: *McHale v Watson* (1964) 111 CLR 384, 396-397 (Windeyer J).

What remains to be considered is the analogy sought to be drawn with the tortious liability of children. For Australia that question was settled in *McHale v Walson* (1966) 115 CLR 199, where the Full High Court, affirming the decision of Windeyer J, but with Menzies J dissenting, held that age was a relevant consideration which, in that instance resulted in the 12 year old male defendant being held not liable in tort to another child for his action in throwing a metal dart which glanced off a wooden post and struck her in the eye. In doing so, their Honours held that his conduct was to be judged, not in terms of the foresight and prudence of an ordinary person, but of the foresight and prudence of an ordinary boy of twelve. ...

The subsequent decision in *Cook v Cook* (1986) 162 CLR 376, which was concerned with the duty of care in a relationship that was special, did not, in my view, disturb that general conclusion but tends rather to confirm it. See the reasons of the majority at 162 CLR 376, 383. Sir Frank Kitto's rationalisation of the special category into which childhood foresight falls makes it, to my mind, clear that he would have regarded unsoundness of mind as an abnormality that did not attract special exemption from the ordinary standard of foresight and care expected of other people.

Indeed, it could hardly be otherwise. Unsoundness of mind is not a normal condition in most people, and it is not a stage of development through which all humanity is destined to pass. There is no such thing as a "normal" condition of unsound mind in those who suffer that affliction. It comes in different varieties and different shades or degrees. For that reason it would be impossible to devise a standard by which the tortious liability of such persons could be judged as a class. As Baron Bramwell once said, insanity is a misfortune and not a privilege. It attracts human sympathy but not, at least in the case of negligence, immunity under the law of civil wrongs.

In some of the discussions of the topic, there are appeals to the natural sentiment of sympathy for the wrongdoer and his family or dependants. Without invoking similar feelings for the victim and his family, it is relevant to mention the following point in the present case. Part at least of the reason why the defendant Bonham was able to escape from the hospital from which he absconded is that psychiatric practice no longer insists that persons in his condition be kept in strict custody. More humane methods of treatment now prevail, under which greater liberty of movement is, for their own perceived good, permitted to patients in this unhappy state. If in the process they take advantage of that liberty to venture, even if briefly, into "normal" society, it seems only proper that, in the event of their doing so, their conduct should be judged according to society's standards including the duty of exercising reasonable foresight and care for the safety of others. If that principle is not applied, then it is only a matter of time before there is reversion to the older and less humane practices of the past in the treatment of mental patients.

For these reasons I would, for the findings made by the learned trial judge, substitute findings that the first defendant's mental condition had no effect on the standard of care owed by him to the plaintiff, which, on the contrary, is to be judged by the standard of the ordinary and reasonable

Carrier v Bonham cont.

person, and that it did not diminish or reduce his liability in negligence to the plaintiff. This has the consequence that, as to liability, the appeal must be dismissed.

[The judgments of McMurdo P and Moynihan J agreeing with the outcome have been omitted.]

[12.245] **Questions**

What accounts for the difference in approach to child defendants, who are held to the standard of the reasonable child, and insane defendants, given that both may be incapable of achieving the level of care expected of the reasonable person? If the standard is truly objective, how do the courts justify a reduced standard for children?

Learners

Imbree v McNeilly; McNeilly v Imbree

[12.250] *Imbree v McNeilly; McNeilly v Imbree* (2008) 82 ALJR 1374; [2008] HCA 40 High Court of Australia

(footnotes omitted)

GUMMOW, HAYNE AND KIEFEL JJ: [25] The appellant (Paul Anthony Imbree) allowed the first respondent (Jesse McNeilly) to drive a four-wheel drive station wagon on Larapinta Drive in the Northern Territory, a gravel road between Kings Canyon and Hermannsburg. The first respondent was then aged 16 years and five months. As the appellant knew, the first respondent had little driving experience, he was not licensed to drive, and he did not hold any learner's permit. He lost control of the vehicle and the vehicle overturned. The appellant, then a front-seat passenger, was seriously injured.

What was the standard of care that the first respondent (the driver) owed the appellant (the passenger)? Was it, as this Court held in *Cook v Cook*, "that which is reasonably to be expected of an unqualified and inexperienced driver in the circumstances in which the pupil is placed"? Or was it, as the appellant submitted, the same objective standard of care as a licensed driver?

These reasons will show that the standard of care which the driver (the first respondent) owed the passenger (the appellant) was the same as any other person driving a motor vehicle - to take reasonable care to avoid injury to others. The standard thus invoked is the standard of the "reasonable driver". That standard is not to be further qualified, whether by reference to the holding of a licence to drive or by reference to the level of experience of the driver. *Cook v Cook* should no longer be followed.

[The judgment then referred to the detailed facts and then to the earlier proceedings in the Supreme Court of New South Wales and the subsequent appeal to the New South Wales Court of Appeal. It then turned to consider the decision in *Cook v Cook* and the influence of the proximity principle and continued:]

Cook v Cook concluded that:

> While the personal skill or characteristics of the individual driver are not directly relevant to a determination of the content or standard of the duty of care owed to a passenger, special and exceptional facts may so transform the relationship between driver and passenger that it would be unreal to regard the relevant relationship as being simply the ordinary one of driver and passenger and unreasonable to measure the standard of skill and care required of the driver by reference to the skill and care that are reasonably to be expected of an experienced and competent driver of that kind of vehicle.

Imbree v McNeilly; McNeilly v Imbree cont.

Thus, because "it would be to state a half-truth to say that the relationship was, if the pupil was driving, that of driver and passenger … the standard of care which arises from the relationship of pupil and instructor is that which is reasonably to be expected of an unqualified and inexperienced driver in the circumstances in which the pupil is placed" …

Reconsidering Cook v Cook

[45] In so far as the reasoning of the plurality in *Cook v Cook* depended upon the application of notions of proximity, it is reasoning that does not accord with subsequent decisions of this Court denying the utility of that concept as a determinant of duty. Subsequent development of legal doctrine denies the continued existence of the foundation upon which the reasoning of the plurality appears to have rested. This observation, however, does not conclude the issues that now arise. There are several reasons why that is so. First, the immediate question in this case concerns the content of the duty of care, not whether any duty of care should be found to exist. Secondly, it is to be noted that Brennan J arrived at substantially the same conclusion as the plurality about the content of the duty of care owed by a learner driver to the instructing or supervising driver, but expressly disclaimed reliance upon proximity. Thirdly, the reasoning of the plurality in *Cook v Cook*, which gave primacy in determining the content of the duty of care to identifying the relationship between the parties out of which the duty arose, reflected what had been said by Dixon J, in his dissenting reasons in *The Insurance Commissioner v Joyce*, more than 30 years before proximity was identified as a concept unifying at least some aspects of the law of negligence.

It follows, therefore, that simply to point to the frequency of reference to proximity in the plurality reasons in *Cook v Cook*, and couple that with the subsequent discarding of proximity as a tool for determining whether a defendant owes a duty of care, provides no sufficient basis for rejecting the principle that it established. It is necessary to look beyond the reliance on proximity reasoning.

The reasoning in *Cook v Cook*, of both the plurality and Brennan J, identified the factual consideration critical to the conclusion reached as being that the plaintiff *knew* that the driver was inexperienced. That is, what the plaintiff knew was held to affect the standard of care that the plaintiff could expect the learner driver to observe. Nonetheless, the standard of care was held to be an objective standard. That is, the relevant standard of care was identified not as what *this* plaintiff could reasonably have expected *this* defendant to have done or not done, but as what a particular class of defendants (within which this defendant fell) could reasonably be expected to do or not do. Thus, the plurality held that the standard of care in a particular case was not to be adjusted "by reference to the physical characteristics and expertise or the usual carefulness or otherwise of the *particular* driver" (emphasis added). Rather, it was held that:

> It is only when special and exceptional circumstances clearly transform the relationship between a particular driver and a particular passenger into a special or different class or category of relationship that the case will be one in which the duty of care owed by the particular driver to the particular passenger will be either expanded or confined by reference to the objective standard of skill or care which is reasonably to be expected of a driver to a passenger *in the category of a case where that special or different relationship exists*. (emphasis added)

The onus of establishing facts giving rise to such a special or different class or category was cast upon the party asserting it.

There have been various statements in this Court to the effect that in many well-settled areas of the law of negligence the existence of a duty of care and its content present no difficulty and that one such example concerns the responsibilities of a motorist on the highway to avoid causing injury to the person or property of another. The reference to "special and exceptional circumstances" in the passage from *Cook v Cook* set out above invites the question why the relevant legal relationship should

Imbree v McNeilly; McNeilly v Imbree cont.

be regarded as any more specific than that of driver and passenger. As Dias and Markesinis pointed out shortly after *Cook v Cook* was decided, the trend of English authority, including *Nettleship v Weston*, had been to eschew distinctions between categories of drivers of motor vehicles.

Further, the translation of the particular knowledge of a plaintiff into the identification of a separate category or class of relationship governed by a distinct and different duty of care encounters various difficulties. These are both doctrinal and practical.

The fundamental reason why *Cook v Cook* should no longer be treated as expressing any distinct principle in the law of negligence is that basic considerations of principle require a contrary conclusion. No different standard of care is to be applied in deciding whether a passenger supervising a learner driver has suffered damage a cause of which was the failure of the learner driver to act with reasonable care. ...

A reasonable learner driver?

[53] The basic considerations of principle may be stated as follows. First, the inquiry is about the applicable standard of care. Secondly, the standard to be applied is objective. It does not vary with the particular aptitude or temperament of the individual. Thirdly, it is, and must be, accepted that a learner driver owes all other road users a duty of care that requires the learner to meet the same standard of care as any other driver on the road. The learner may have to display "L-plates" for all other road users to see, but that learner will be held to the same standard of care as any other driver in fulfilling the learner's duty to take reasonable care to avoid injuring *other* road users. Fourthly, it was not suggested in argument, and there is nothing in *Cook v Cook* that would suggest, that a learner driver owes a lesser standard of care to any passenger in the vehicle *except* the licensed driver who sits in the adjoining seat. In particular, it was not suggested that any knowledge of another passenger that the driver was inexperienced affects the standard of care that the driver must observe to avoid injury to that other passenger.

Knowledge of inexperience can thus provide no sufficient foundation for applying different standards of care in deciding whether a learner driver is liable to one passenger rather than another, or in deciding whether that learner driver is liable to a person outside the car rather than one who was seated in the car, in the adjoining seat. The other passenger will ordinarily know that the driver is a learner driver; the road user outside the car can see the L-plates. Yet it is not disputed that the learner driver owes each of those persons a standard of care determined by reference to the reasonable driver.

To reject knowledge of inexperience as a sufficient basis upon which to found a different standard of care is to reject the only basis, other than proximity, for the decision in *Cook v Cook*. Yet rejection of knowledge as a basis for applying a different standard of care is required not only by the observation that knowledge of inexperience is held not to affect the standard of care owed to other passengers or other road users who observe a display of L-plates, but also by the essential requirement that the standard of care be objective and impersonal.

No matter whether the content of the standard of care is described as that of the "inexperienced driver of ordinary prudence" or the "unqualified and inexperienced driver (but with some knowledge of the controls of a motor vehicle) in the situation in which the [driver] was placed" there are evident practical difficulties in applying such a standard. ...Both statements of the standard would require the drawing of difficult distinctions between "inexperience" on the one hand and "prudence" on the other, or between a want of application of (as yet unlearned) skills and a want of reasonable care. And both forms of the statement of applicable standard leave unanswered the question whether the distinctions that are drawn are to be applied regardless of how long the person has been learning to drive and regardless of whether the driver has attained a standard (but not the age) at which a licence could be issued. That is, describing the relevant comparator as the reasonable "inexperienced" driver

Imbree v McNeilly; McNeilly v Imbree cont.

does not sufficiently identify the content of the standard that is intended to be conveyed by use of the word "inexperienced". In particular it leaves undefined what level of competence is to be assumed in such a driver.

Further, to describe the relevant comparator as "unqualified" points only to the absence of approved demonstration of adequate driving competence. Demonstration of relevant ability is beside the point. What is at issue is the definition of a standard of reasonable care, not any external recognition of attaining an ability to drive in accordance with that standard. And for like reasons, to describe the relevant comparator as a "licensed driver" diverts attention from the central inquiry: what would a reasonable driver do? Being authorised by the applicable law to drive unsupervised on a public road is neither a necessary nor a sufficient characteristic of the reasonable driver. Holding or not holding the relevant licence is irrelevant to the description or application of the relevant standard of care. The reasonable driver is to be identified by what such a driver would do or not do when driving, not by what authority a driver would need to have in order to drive lawfully.

Instructor or supervisor?

[59] One other possible footing for a conclusion that different standards of care are to be applied to a learner driver according to whether the person who suffered damage was the supervising driver, or was another passenger or other road user, should be examined. Both in *Cook v Cook*, and in the present case, the relationship between the parties was described by identifying the plaintiff as the "instructor" or "supervisor" of the defendant as a learner driver. What is meant in this context by "instructor" or "supervisor"?

Words like "instructor" or "supervisor" carry overtones of command or control. Those overtones may jar if they are heard in the context of a parent who has allowed a 16 year old child who holds a learner's permit to drive the family car. But whatever dissonance may stem from an unwillingness of the learner to respond to command or control, the parent, though licensed to drive the vehicle, may have no experience as a teacher, let alone experience in teaching another to drive a motor vehicle. This would suggest that the term "instructor" may not be apt. The expression "supervisor", however, is not wholly inapt, even in the case of the parent and a child who is not receptive to advice, let alone instruction. Use of the term "supervisor" reflects some important features of the legislative regulation of learning to drive a motor vehicle on public roads.

[The judgment then reviewed the Northern Territory statutory provisions relating to learner drivers and accompanying licensed drivers and concluded:]... [I]t is convenient, for present purposes, to proceed on the basis that the licensed driver who accompanies a learner driver is obliged at least to supervise the learner. ...

What is it about the relationship between supervisor and learner that would lead to the conclusion that the reasonable care which the learner must use to avoid damage to the supervisor is less than the reasonable care which the learner must show for the safety of others?

If the conclusion were to be based upon how the supervisor could influence (even direct) the learner driver, it would be based upon considerations that are more appropriately considered in connection with contributory negligence. If the supervisor *could* have influenced the outcome it may be that the supervisor failed to take reasonable care for his or her own safety. That is a matter which goes directly to questions of contributory negligence; it does not touch the question of the driver's negligence. And if the supervisor could *not* have influenced the outcome, what is the relevance of the supervisory role to the standard of care the learner should exercise in operating the vehicle?

No different standard of care

[69] The common law recognises many circumstances in which the standard of care expected of a person takes account of some matter that warrants identifying a class of persons or activities as

Imbree v McNeilly; McNeilly v Imbree cont.

required to exercise a standard of care different from, or more particular than, that of some wholly general and "objective community ideal". Chief among those circumstances is the profession of particular skill. A higher standard of care is applied in those cases. That standard may be described by reference to those who pursue a certain kind of occupation, like that of medical practitioner, or it may be stated, as a higher level of skill, by reference to a more specific class of occupation such as that of the specialist medical practitioner. At the other end of the spectrum, the standard of care expected of children is attenuated.

But what distinguishes the principle established in *Cook v Cook* from cases of the kind just mentioned is that *Cook v Cook* requires the application of a different standard of care to the one defendant in respect of the one incident yielding the same kind of damage to two different persons, according to whether the plaintiff was supervising the defendant's driving or not. In all other cases in which a different level of care is demanded, the relevant standard of care is applied uniformly. No distinction is drawn according to whether the plaintiff was in a position to supervise, even instruct, the defendant although, of course, if the plaintiff was in that position, a failure to supervise or instruct may be of great importance in deciding whether the plaintiff was contributorily negligent.

There is no warrant for the distinction that was drawn in *Cook v Cook*. *Cook v Cook* should no longer be followed in this respect.

... The plaintiff who was supervising the learner driver, the plaintiff who was another passenger in the vehicle, the plaintiff who was another road user are all entitled to expect that the learner driver will take reasonable care in operating the vehicle. The care that the learner should take is that of the reasonable driver.

The Insurance Commissioner v Joyce

[74] [The judgment then considered the High Court decision in *The Insurance Commissioner v Joyce*, see [16.20] and continued:] ...the doctrine of voluntary assumption of risk requires proof that "the plaintiff freely and voluntarily, with full knowledge of the nature and extent of the risk ... impliedly agreed to incur it". In the absence of some express exclusion of liability or notice of exculpation, demonstrating that a plaintiff both knew of a risk and voluntarily agreed to incur that risk will often be difficult. But if both conditions are satisfied, the plaintiff's claim against the defendant will fail. And the conclusion that a plaintiff voluntarily assumed the risk in question is readily seen as equivalent to concluding that the defendant owed that plaintiff *no* duty of care.

The conclusion that a defendant owed the plaintiff *no* duty of care is open in a case like *Joyce* if, as Latham CJ said, "[i]n the case of the drunken driver, *all* standards of care are ignored [because the] drunken driver cannot even be expected to act sensibly" (emphasis added). And as indicated earlier in these reasons, it is that same idea which would underpin a conclusion that the plaintiff voluntarily assumed the risk of being driven by a drunken driver.

But the analysis that has been made also reveals that a plaintiff's knowledge of the deficiencies of the defendant does not so readily lead to a conclusion of the kind reached in *Cook v Cook*: that the defendant does owe the plaintiff a duty of care, but that the standard of care to be met is less than the standard which otherwise would be expected.

Reference was made in *Cook v Cook* to the example cited by Latham CJ in *Joyce* of the person who gives a watch to a blacksmith for repair:

If a person deliberately agrees to allow a blacksmith to mend his watch, it may well be said that he agrees to accept a low standard of skill. But even in such a case, the blacksmith is bound to act sensibly, though he is not subject to the responsibilities of a skilled watchmaker.

The accuracy of the conclusion expressed may readily be accepted, if only because acting sensibly, the blacksmith should, perhaps, refuse to undertake the task. But the proposition is not one that provides a safe basis for extrapolation into a general proposition that the standard of care to be met varies according to the state of the plaintiff's knowledge of the defendant's ability to reach that standard.

A plaintiff's knowledge and the standard of care

[85] Actual knowledge of a defendant's inability to reach a standard of reasonable care may be a necessary, but it would not be a sufficient, step towards a conclusion about voluntary assumption of risk. And both what a plaintiff actually knows, and what that plaintiff ought reasonably to have known, will be relevant to an inquiry about contributory negligence. The answers to both questions (about what a plaintiff knew and what a plaintiff ought to have known) will bear upon whether the plaintiff failed to take reasonable care for his or her own safety.

Standing alone, however, a plaintiff's actual knowledge of good reasons to think that the defendant may not meet the standard of the reasonable person provides no sufficient or certain basis for concluding that some lesser yet objective standard of care should be applied. It provides no sufficient basis for that conclusion because there is an unarticulated middle step in reasoning from a plaintiff's knowledge that a defendant may not use reasonable care, to applying to the resolution of a claim for damages for negligence an objective, and thus generalised, standard of care which reduces the required standard of care by reference to some known attribute of the defendant. That middle step can be described in a number of different ways. Using the language of Dixon J in *Joyce*, it could be described as a step that defines or identifies the relevant "relations, juxtapositions, situations or conduct or activities" of or between the parties. Alternatively, it could be described as a step of identifying the relevant characteristics of the hypothesised reasonable actor whose conduct sets the standard of care that is being applied. It is not necessary to choose between those descriptions for they are not intended to be different in their operation. But without first identifying how that middle step is to be taken, the state of the plaintiff's actual knowledge of the defendant's deficiencies provides no certain basis for a conclusion about what is the relevant standard of care.

Joyce held that no relevant reasonable actor could be identified in that case because a drunken driver "cannot even be expected to act sensibly". By contrast, in *Cook v Cook*, the relevant reasonable actor was identified by the plurality as the "unqualified and inexperienced driver (but with some knowledge of the controls of a motor vehicle) in the situation in which the [driver] was placed when the [licensed driver] instructed her to turn left". As noted earlier, in his separate reasons Brennan J described the relevant reasonable actor as "an inexperienced driver of ordinary prudence".

The finding of negligence in the courts below

[88] Although this matter was decided at trial and on appeal to the Court of Appeal by application to the first respondent of too lax a standard of care, he was found not to have satisfied that standard. It follows that the appellant was entitled to succeed in his claim against both respondents. Had the correct standard of care been applied, the first respondent would have been held negligent.

It also follows that the respondents' application for special leave to appeal, to contend first, that the first respondent owed the appellant a standard of care less onerous than that of the reasonable driver, and secondly, that the appellant's claim should accordingly have been dismissed, should be refused.

[The judgment then considered the issue of the appellant's contributory negligence. It accepted that the appellant was contributorily negligent by failing to give the driver basic advice about driving on dirt roads and failing to instruct the driver to straddle observed debris on the road. Contributory negligence was held to be appropriately assessed by the trial judge at 30 per cent.

[The judgments of Gleeson CJ, Kirby and Crennan JJ agreeing with the outcome in the principal judgment have been omitted. Heydon J, although agreeing with the final result did not find it

Imbree v McNeilly; McNeilly v Imbree cont.

necessary to reconsider *Cook v Cook*. Note the second respondent was the owner of the motor vehicle.]

Professionals and those with special skills

[12.255] Notwithstanding the objective nature of the reasonable person standard, general conceptions such as "the man on the Bondi tram" have been developed and extended to include some characteristics or attributes of particular classes of defendant, which are grafted on to the basic standard of care. In *Overseas Tankship (UK) Ltd v The Miller Steamship Co Pty Ltd ("Wagon Mound" (No 2))* [1966] 2 All ER 709 (see [13.180] for example), the defendant was held vicariously liable for the actions of its employee, a ship's engineer. The Privy Council said:

> ... the only question is whether a reasonable man having the knowledge and experience to be expected of the chief engineer of the *Wagon Mound* would have known that there was a real risk ... In their lordships' view a properly qualified and alert chief engineer would have realised there was a real risk ... a vigilant ship's engineer would have noticed the discharge [of oil into the harbour] at an early stage. The findings show that he ought to have known.
>
> The reasonable person in this case possesses the knowledge, experience, qualifications and expertise of the specific class or type of defendant, that is ship's engineers in general, rather than the individual defendant. Similarly, in *Rogers v Whitaker* [12.260], in which the defendant was an ophthalmic surgeon, the High Court said: "The standard of reasonable care and skill required is that of the ordinary skilled person exercising and professing to have that special skill." (at 719-20)

In these situations the fact that the defendant possesses more than an average degree of skill due to the nature of his or her occupation and training raises the standard of care.

The common law standard of care to be applied to professionals is that of the reasonable skilled professional in the circumstances. In *Rogers v Whitaker* (1992) 175 CLR 479 (extracted below at [12.260]) for example, the standard employed was that of "an opthalmic surgeon specialising in corneal and anterior segment surgery". A similar approach has been adopted in relation to architects (*Voli v Inglewood Shire Council* (1963) 110 CLR 74 at 84 per Windeyer J), engineers (*Brickhill v Cooke* [1984] 3 NSWLR 396 at 398), solicitors (*Hawkins v Clayton* (1988) 164 CLR 539 at 580 per Deane J), accountants (*Henderson v Amadio* (1995) 62 FCR 1 at 135) and insurance brokers (*Lewis v Tressider Andrews Associates Pty Ltd* [1987] 2 Qd R 533 at 541-2). In the United Kingdom the Courts have adopted the professional standard known as the *Bolam* test derived from the case of *Bolam v Friern Hospital Management Committee* [1957] 1 WLR 582. It was described by Lord Scarman in *Sidaway v Governors of Bethlem Royal Hospital* [1985] AC 871 in the following terms:

> The *Bolam* principle may be formulated as a rule that a doctor is not negligent if he acts in accordance with a practice accepted at the time as proper by a responsible body of medical opinion even though other doctors adopt a different practice. In short, the law imposes the duty of care: but the standard of care is a matter of medical judgment. (at 881)

We now turn to consider the "professional standard" in the context of a duty to warn.

Rogers v Whitaker

[12.260] *Rogers v Whitaker* (1992) 175 CLR 479 High Court of Australia

(footnotes partially omitted)

[The appellant, Christopher Rogers, was an ophthalmic surgeon. The respondent, Maree Lynette Whitaker, was a patient of the appellant who became almost totally blind after Rogers had operated on her left eye. She had been blind in the left eye since the age of nine from an accident. There was no question that the surgeon conducted the operation with the required skill and care, and that his only possible negligence consisted in failing to warn the plaintiff of a one in 14,000 chance of a rare complication known as sympathetic opthalmia occurring in her good eye. According to the findings of the trial judge, the respondent had "incessantly" questioned the appellant as to the possible complications. She was, to the appellant's knowledge, keenly interested in the outcome of the suggested procedure, including the danger of unintended or accidental interference with her "good" left eye. On appeal by the defendant against the decision of the NSW Court of Appeal upholding the decision in the plaintiff's favour, the High Court unanimously dismissed the appeal.]

MASON CJ, BRENNAN, DAWSON, TOOHEY and McHUGH JJ: 483 ...

Breach of duty

The law imposes on a medical practitioner a duty to exercise reasonable care and skill in the provision of professional advice and treatment. That duty is a "single comprehensive duty covering all the ways in which a doctor is called upon to exercise his skill and judgment"; [*Sidaway v Board of Governors of Bethlem Royal Hospital* [1985] AC 871, per Lord Diplock at 893] it extends to the examination, diagnosis and treatment of the patient and the provision of information in an appropriate case ... It is of course necessary to give content to the duty in the given case.

The standard of reasonable care and skill required is that of the ordinary skilled person exercising and professing to have that special skill, [*Bolam v Friern Hospital Management Committee* [1957] 1 WLR 582 at 586] ... in this case the skill of an ophthalmic surgeon specialising in corneal and anterior segment surgery. As we have stated, the failure of the appellant to observe this standard, which the respondent successfully alleged before the primary judge, consisted of the appellant's failure to acquaint the respondent with the danger of sympathetic ophthalmia as a possible result of the surgical procedure to be carried out. The appellant's evidence was that "sympathetic ophthalmia was not something that came to my mind to mention to her".

The principal issue in this case relates to the scope and content of the appellant's duty of care: did the appellant's failure to advise and warn the respondent of the risks inherent in the operation constitute a breach of this duty? The appellant argues that this issue should be resolved by application of the so-called *Bolam* principle, derived from the direction given by McNair J to the jury in the case of *Bolam v Friern Hospital Management Committee* [[1957] 1 WLR 582]. In *Sidaway v Board of Governors of Bethlem Royal Hospital*, Lord Scarman stated the *Bolam* principle in these terms [[1985] AC 871 at 881]:

> The *Bolam* principle may be formulated as a rule that a doctor is not negligent if he acts in accordance with a practice accepted at the time as proper by a responsible body of medical opinion even though other doctors adopt a different practice. In short, the law imposes the duty of care: but the standard of care is a matter of medical judgment.

Before the primary judge there was evidence from a body of reputable medical practitioners that, in the circumstances of the present case, they would not have warned the respondent of the danger of sympathetic ophthalmia; there was also, however, evidence from similarly reputable medical practitioners that they would have given such a warning. The respondent, for her part, argues that the *Bolam* principle should not be applied if it entails courts deferring to the medical experts in medical negligence cases ...

Rogers v Whitaker cont.

The *Bolam* principle has invariably been applied in English courts ... In decisions outside the field of medical negligence, there are also statements consistent with an application of the *Bolam* principle ... At its basis lies the recognition that, in matters involving medical expertise, there is ample scope for genuine difference of opinion and that a practitioner is not negligent merely because his or her conclusion or procedure differs from that of other practitioners [see *Hunter v Hanley* [1955] SLT 213, per Lord President Clyde at 217]; a finding of negligence requires a finding that the defendant failed to exercise the ordinary skill of a doctor practising in the relevant field.

In *Sidaway*, the House of Lords considered whether the *Bolam* principle should be applied in cases of alleged negligence in providing information and advice relevant to medical treatment. The plaintiff underwent an operation on her spine designed to relieve her recurrent neck, shoulder and arm pain. The operation carried an inherent, material risk, assessed at between 1 and 2%, of damage to the spinal column and nerve roots. The risk eventuated and the plaintiff was severely disabled. She sued in negligence, alleging that the surgeon had failed to disclose or explain to her the risks involved in the operation. As the speeches in the House of Lords make clear, the action was destined to fail because there was no reliable evidence in support of the plaintiff's central pleading that the surgeon had given no advice or warning. Nevertheless, the majority of the court (Lord Scarman dissenting) held that the question whether an omission to warn a patient of inherent risks of proposed treatment constituted a breach of a doctor's duty of care was to be determined by applying the *Bolam* principle. However, the members of the majority took different views of the *Bolam* principle ...

One consequence of the application of the *Bolam* principle to cases involving the provision of advice or information is that, even if a patient asks a direct question about the possible risks or complications, the making of that inquiry would logically be of little or no significance; medical opinion determines whether the risk should or should not be disclosed and the express desire of a particular patient for information or advice does not alter that opinion or the legal significance of that opinion. The fact that the various majority opinions in *Sidaway*, [[1985] AC 871 at 895, 898, 902] for example, suggest that, over and above the opinion of a respectable body of medical practitioners, the questions of a patient should truthfully be answered (subject to the therapeutic privilege) indicates a shortcoming in the *Bolam* approach. The existence of the shortcoming suggests that an acceptable approach in point of principle should recognise and attach significance to the relevance of a patient's questions. Even if a court were satisfied that a reasonable person in the patient's position would be unlikely to attach significance to a particular risk, the fact that the patient asked questions revealing concern about the risk would make the doctor aware that *this patient* did in fact attach significance to the risk. Subject to the therapeutic privilege, the question would therefore require a truthful answer.

In Australia, it has been accepted that the standard of care to be observed by a person with some special skill or competence is that of the ordinary skilled person exercising and professing to have that special skill ... But, that standard is not determined solely or even primarily by reference to the practice followed or supported by a responsible body of opinion in the relevant profession or trade. ... Even in the sphere of diagnosis and treatment, the heartland of the skilled medical practitioner, the *Bolam* principle has not always been applied ... Further, and more importantly, particularly in the field of non-disclosure of risk and the provision of advice and information, the *Bolam* principle has been discarded and, instead, the courts have adopted ... the principle that, while evidence of acceptable medical practice is a useful guide for the courts, it is for the courts to adjudicate on what is the appropriate standard of care after giving weight to "the paramount consideration that a person is entitled to make his own decisions about his life" [*F v R* (1983) 33 SASR, at 193].

In *F v R*, [(1983) 33 SASR 189] which was decided by the Full Court of the Supreme Court of South Australia two years before *Sidaway* in the House of Lords, a woman who had become pregnant after an unsuccessful tubal ligation brought an action in negligence alleging failure by the medical practitioner

Rogers v Whitaker cont.

to warn her of the failure rate of the procedure. The failure rate was assessed at less than 1% for that particular form of sterilisation. The court refused to apply the *Bolam* principle. King CJ said: [(1983) 33 SASR 189 at 194].

> The ultimate question, however, is not whether the defendant's conduct accords with the practices of his profession or some part of it, but whether it conforms to the standard of reasonable care demanded by the law. That is a question for the court and the duty of deciding it cannot be delegated to any profession or group in the community.

King CJ considered [(1983) 33 SASR 189 at 192-3] that the amount of information or advice which a careful and responsible doctor would disclose depended upon a complex of factors: the nature of the matter to be disclosed; the nature of the treatment; the desire of the patient for information; the temperament and health of the patient; and the general surrounding circumstances. His Honour agreed with the following passage from the judgment of the Supreme Court of Canada in *Reibl v Hughes*: [(1980) 114 DLR (3d), at 13]

> To allow expert medical evidence to determine what risks are material and, hence, should be disclosed and, correlatively, what risks are not material is to hand over to the medical profession the entire question of the scope of the duty of disclosure, including the question whether there has been a breach of that duty. Expert medical evidence is, of course, relevant to findings as to the risks that reside in or are a result of recommended surgery or other treatment. It will also have a bearing on their materiality but this is not a question that is to be concluded on the basis of the expert medical evidence alone. The issue under consideration is a different issue from that involved where the question is whether the doctor carried out his professional activities by applicable professional standards. What is under consideration here is the patient's right to know what risks are involved in undergoing or forgoing certain surgery or other treatment.

The approach adopted by King CJ is similar to that subsequently taken by Lord Scarman in *Sidaway* and has been followed in subsequent cases … In our view, it is correct.

Acceptance of this approach does not entail an artificial division or itemisation of specific, individual duties, carved out of the overall duty of care. The duty of a medical practitioner to exercise reasonable care and skill in the provision of professional advice and treatment is a single comprehensive duty. However, the factors according to which a court determines whether a medical practitioner is in breach of the requisite standard of care will vary according to whether it is a case involving diagnosis, treatment or the provision of information or advice; the different cases raise varying difficulties which require consideration of different factors [*F v R* (1983) 33 SASR, at 191]. Examination of the nature of a doctor-patient relationship compels this conclusion. There is a fundamental difference between, on the one hand, diagnosis and treatment and, on the other hand, the provision of advice or information to a patient. In diagnosis and treatment, the patient's contribution is limited to the narration of symptoms and relevant history; the medical practitioner provides diagnosis and treatment according to his or her level of skill. However, except in cases of emergency or necessity, all medical treatment is preceded by the patient's choice to undergo it. In legal terms, the patient's consent to the treatment may be valid once he or she is informed in broad terms of the nature of the procedure which is intended [*Chatterton v Gerson* [1981] QB 432, at 443]. But the choice is, in reality, meaningless unless it is made on the basis of relevant information and advice. Because the choice to be made calls for a decision by the patient on information known to the medical practitioner but not to the patient, it would be illogical to hold that the amount of information to be provided by the medical practitioner can be determined from the perspective of the practitioner alone or, for that matter, of the medical profession. *Whether* a medical practitioner carries out a particular form of treatment in accordance with the appropriate standard of care is a question in the resolution of which responsible professional opinion will have an influential, often a decisive, role to play; *whether* the patient has been given all the relevant information to choose between undergoing and not undergoing the treatment is a question of a different order. Generally speaking, it is not a question the answer to which depends upon medical

Rogers v Whitaker cont.

standards or practices. Except in those cases where there is a particular danger that the provision of all relevant information will harm an unusually nervous, disturbed or volatile patient, no special medical skill is involved in disclosing the information, including the risks attending the proposed treatment … Rather, the skill is in communicating the relevant information to the patient in terms which are reasonably adequate for that purpose having regard to the patient's apprehended capacity to understand that information.

In this context, nothing is to be gained by reiterating the expressions used in American authorities, such as "the patient's right of self-determination" [see, eg, *Canterbury v Spence* (1972) 464 F 2d, at 784] or even the oft-used and somewhat amorphous phrase "informed consent". … Anglo-Australian law has rightly taken the view that an allegation that the risks inherent in a medical procedure have not been disclosed to the patient can only found an action in negligence and not in trespass; the consent necessary to negative the offence of battery is satisfied by the patient being advised in broad terms of the nature of the procedure to be performed [*Chatterton v Gerson* [1981] QB, at 443].

… We agree that the factors referred to in *F v R* by King CJ [(1983) 33 SASR, at 92-3] must all be considered by a medical practitioner in deciding whether to disclose or advise of some risk in a proposed procedure. The law should recognise that a doctor has a duty to warn a patient of a material risk inherent in the proposed treatment; a risk is material if, in the circumstances of the particular case, a reasonable person in the patient's position, if warned of the risk, would be likely to attach significance to it or if the medical practitioner is or should reasonably be aware that the particular patient, if warned of the risk, would be likely to attach significance to it. This duty is subject to the therapeutic privilege.

The appellant in this case was treating and advising a woman who was almost totally blind in one eye. As with all surgical procedures, the operation recommended by the appellant to the respondent involved various risks, such as retinal detachment and haemorrhage infection, both of which are more common than sympathetic ophthalmia, but sympathetic ophthalmia was the only danger whereby both eyes might be rendered sightless. Experts for both parties described it as a devastating disability, the appellant acknowledging that, except for death under anaesthetic, it was the worst possible outcome for the respondent. According to the findings of the trial judge, the respondent "incessantly" questioned the appellant as to, amongst other things, possible complications. She was, to the appellant's knowledge, keenly interested in the outcome of the suggested procedure, including the danger of unintended or accidental interference with her "good", left eye. On the day before the operation, the respondent asked the appellant whether something could be put over her good eye to ensure that nothing happened to it; an entry was made in the hospital notes to the effect that she was apprehensive that the wrong eye would be operated on. She did not, however, ask a specific question as to whether the operation on her right eye could affect her left eye.

The evidence established that there was a body of opinion in the medical profession at the time which considered that an inquiry should only have elicited a reply dealing with sympathetic ophthalmia if specifically directed to the possibility of the left eye being affected by the operation on the right eye. While the opinion that the respondent should have been told of the dangers of sympathetic ophthalmia only if she had been sufficiently learned to ask the precise question seems curious, it is unnecessary for us to examine it further, save to say that it demonstrates vividly the dangers of applying the *Bolam* principle in the area of advice and information. The respondent may not have asked the right question, yet she made clear her great concern that no injury should befall her one good eye. The trial judge was not satisfied that, if the respondent had expressed no desire for information, proper practice required that the respondent be warned of the relevant risk. But it could be argued, within the terms of the relevant principle as we have stated it, that the risk was material, in the sense that a reasonable person in the patient's position would be likely to attach significance to the risk, and thus required a warning. It would be reasonable for a person with one good eye to be concerned about the possibility of injury to it from a procedure which was elective. However, the respondent did not challenge on appeal that particular finding.

For these reasons, we would reject the appellant's argument on the issue of breach of duty ... we would dismiss the appeal.

[Gaudron J in a separate judgment also dismissed the appeal.]

[12.265] **Notes&Questions**

1. In *Rosenberg v Percival* (2001) 205 CLR 434 at 439, Gleeson CJ explained the effect of *Rogers* as follows:

   > The relevance of professional practice and opinion was not denied; what was denied was its conclusiveness. In many cases professional practice and opinion will be the primary, and in some cases it may be the only, basis upon which a court may reasonably act. But, in an action brought by a patient, the responsibility for deciding the content of the doctor's duty of care rests with the court, not with his or her professional colleagues.

2. In *Naxakis v Western General Hospital* (1999) 197 CLR 269 at 285-286 (per McHugh J), the High Court took the view that the decision in *Rogers* had rejected the *Bolam* principle as regards all aspects of a doctor's duty of care, not limited merely to diagnosis and treatment but also including the duty to warn of material risks.

3. In *Jones v Manchester Corp* [1952] 2 QB 852 the comparative inexperience of two house surgeons, who injected a powerful drug while a patient was under anaesthetic causing the patient's death, did not operate to reduce the ordinary standard of care expected of a properly qualified surgeon for the purposes of an action by the patient's representatives. However, when the question arose of the hospital's claim against the doctors for contribution, the Court then considered it relevant in fixing the proportions to be borne that the board had placed inexperienced practitioners in charge of the outpatients' department.

4. In *Wilsher v Essex Area Health Authority* [1987] QB 730, the English Court of Appeal considered the question of the standard of care to be expected of medical practitioners at various stages of their professional development. A junior doctor in a special baby care unit mistakenly inserted a catheter designed to measure arterial oxygen levels into a vein, instead of an artery, of the plaintiff premature baby. Both the junior doctor and the senior registrar realised there was something wrong and the senior registrar inserted another catheter instead, but repeated the mistake. After some 30 hours when the arteries had been supersaturated with oxygen by the treatment given, the second catheter was replaced by one placed in the artery, but for a period of weeks following the oxygen levels in the blood were still considered too high and the plaintiff developed a condition of the eyes causing near blindness. A likely cause was supersaturation of the blood with oxygen at some stage. It was held that a sufficient connection had been established between the negligence of the senior registrar in failing to appreciate

the incorrect positioning of the catheter, with X-ray means available to him, and the blindness, and the hospital was vicariously liable for that negligence. Mustill LJ said (at 751):

> To my mind, it would be a false step to subordinate the legitimate expectation of a patient that he will receive from each person concerned with this case a degree of skill appropriate to the task which he undertakes, to an understandable wish to minimise the psychological and financial pressures on hard-pressed young doctors ... the duty of care [relates] not to the individual, but to the post which he occupies. I would differentiate "post" from "rank" or "status". In a case such as the present, the standard is not just that of the averagely competent and well-informed junior houseman (or whatever the position of the doctor) but of such a person who fills a post in a unit offering a highly specialised service. But, even so, it must be recognised that different posts make different demands. If it is borne in mind that the structure of hospital medicine envisages that the lower ranks will be occupied by those of whom it would be wrong to expect too much, the risk of abuse by litigious patients can be mitigated, if not entirely eliminated.

In his Lordship's view, therefore, there is no single reasonable standard of skill to be expected of professional practitioners but the standard may vary with the position in an organisation. It was on this basis that he held that the junior houseman was entitled to rely on the skill of the senior registrar, and Glidewell LJ agreed (at 462), disagreeing with the disposition, as he saw it, of Browne-Wilkinson VC in the same case to apply a more lenient test to newly-qualified practitioners. The result was, however, reversed by the House of Lords on the separate issue of causation ([1988] AC 1074).

5. Various cases demonstrate that whether a person undertaking a skilled task will be expected to live up to the standard of care of a professional depends largely on the nature of the task and the context in which it is being performed. In *Philips v William Whitely Ltd* [1938] 1 All ER 566, a jeweller in a department store had pierced the plaintiff's ears, sterilising the piercing device with a flame, rather than using the more careful procedure which a surgeon would have adopted. The plaintiff's ears became infected and she developed an abscess. The court applied the standard of the reasonable jeweller rather than the reasonable surgeon. Similarly, in *Wells v Cooper* (1958) 2 Qd 265, the plaintiff was injured while trying to shut a door which had been repaired by the householder using the wrong size screws. The court held that the standard of care was that of the reasonably competent household carpenter, not a professional carpenter. This was particularly so because the task was "a trifling domestic replacement well within the competence of a householder accustomed to doing small carpentering jobs about his home". These examples both relate to ordinary persons performing fairly simple tasks. However, this is a matter of degree. Where the task requires special skill, as in *Papatonakis v Australian Telecommunications Commission* (1985) 156 CLR 7, the standard of care will be that of the reasonable person possessing that skill. In *Papatonakis*, a telephone linesman was killed when a cable, installed by an unskilled householder, gave way. Deane J (at 22) said: a "reasonably prudent occupier does not merely rely on his own judgement and skill in a situation where technical expertise which he does not possess is required."

[12.270] The test stated in *Rogers v Whitaker* (1992) 175 CLR 479 has been qualified by the civil liability legislation. *The Terms of Reference* paragraph (3(d)) for the Negligence Review Panel, required the Panel to "develop and evaluate options for a requirement that the standard of care in professional negligence matters (including medical negligence) accords with the generally accepted practice of the relevant profession at the time of the negligent act or omission". The Negligence Review Panel (*Review of the Law of Negligence, Final Report* (Commonwealth of Australia, Canberra, 2002), para 3.5) noted that there was a "significant body of opinion, especially among the medical profession, in favour of re-instating the *Bolam* rule in its original form" but went on to conclude that "it should not recommend the reintroduction of the *Bolam* rule in its original form but rather a modified version of that rule".

The civil liability legislation deals with the standard of care of professionals in four jurisdictions, NSW: CLA, s 5O; Qld: CLA, ss 21, 22; Tas: CLA, ss 21 – 22; Vic: WrA, ss 59 – 60. There are individual variations in the legislation. The Queensland provision is selected as broadly representative.

Civil Liability Act 2002 (Qld)

[12.275] *Civil Liability Act 2002* (QLD), s 22

Division 5

22

(1) A professional does not breach a duty arising from the provision of a professional service if it is established that the professional acted in a way that (at the time the service was provided) was widely accepted by peer professional opinion by a significant number of respected practitioners in the field as competent professional practice.

(2) However, peer professional opinion cannot be relied on for the purposes of this section if the court considers that the opinion is irrational or contrary to a written law.

(3) The fact that there are differing peer professional opinions widely accepted by a significant number of respected practitioners in the field concerning a matter does not prevent any 1 or more (or all) of the opinions being relied on for the purposes of this section.

(4) Peer professional opinion does not have to be universally accepted to be considered widely accepted.

[12.280] The civil liability legislation adopts a modified *Bolam* standard as the relevant standard of care to be applied in determining professional negligence cases. The modified standard does not apply where the professional has a duty to warn, such as in *Rogers v Whitaker* (1992) 175 CLR 479 itself, see NSW: CLA, s 5P. The statutory test avoids the extreme application of the *Bolam* test which, it has been suggested, would have required a court to find for the defendant where the defence relied on the evidence of a single expert witness as representing a responsible body of opinion. (The Negligence Review Panel, Review of the Law of Negligence, Final Report (Commonwealth of Australia, Canberra, 2002) para 3.7).

The provision applies only to persons engaged in a profession. What constitutes a profession is not defined in most jurisdictions but it would clearly extend to the legal and medical profession.

Despite the statutory heading "Standard of Care for Professionals", the New South Wales courts have held that the NSW: CLA, s 5O provides a *defence* to a negligence claim (*Dobler v Halvorsen* (2007) 70 NSWLR 151; [2007] NSWCA 335 at [59]-[60] per Ipp JA). The differing language in other jurisdictions does not necessarily require a similar finding. It was argued in *Vella v Permanent Mortgages Pty Ltd* [2008] NSWSC 505 at [547] that the New South Wales s 5O means that the standard of care is a matter for the profession, unless a practice is irrational. Hungerford J did not agree:

> The plaintiff still may present his or her case in exactly the same way as prior to s 5O. If there is no evidence called as to peer professional practice, then the court decides the matter in the same way as it always has decided the matter. However, if evidence is called, as the Court of Appeal notes usually by the defendant as to what is peer professional practice in Australia, then it may be that it is the profession that sets the standard. (at 548)

[12.285] **Notes&Questions**

1. The statutory *Bolam* standard applies unless it is "unreasonable" (Vic) or "irrational" (NSW and Qld). Would it be "unreasonable" or "irrational" if a substantial group of professionals continued practices despite unequivocal evidence that the practices were not only ineffective but in some cases dangerous? For some illustrations, see Australian Broadcasting Commission, Radio National, Health Report (15 January 2007).
2. Suppose a doctor has performed an operation according to a practice used by 30 per cent of Australian doctors; but there is evidence, that in no other country in the world, that this operation is performed in that way, and that it is clear that a great many more injuries are caused by the Australian method than the method used elsewhere. Will that satisfy the standard in Qld: CLA, s 22? The NSW: CLA, s 5O provides that there will not be liability in negligence ... "if it is established that the professional acted in a manner that (at the time the service was provided) was widely accepted in Australia by peer professional opinion as competent professional practice". Would the outcome be different in New South Wales?
3. When the relevant reasonable person is a public authority, the standard of care appears to drop. The legislation also reduces the liability of public authorities by making them responsible for negligence only if their acts or decisions were so unreasonable that no reasonable public functionary could have made them: ACT: CLWA, ss 110 – 114; NSW: CLA, ss 42 – 45; Qld: CLA, ss 35 – 37; Tas: CLA, s 40(2); Vic: WrA, ss 83 – 85; WA: CLA, ss 5W – 5Z, 5AA. Is this the same standard as that of the proviso to the *Bolam* principle discussed in Note 1?

PROOF OF NEGLIGENCE

Fact and law, onus and standard of proof

[12.290] The legal burden of proving negligence always rests with the plaintiff. The plaintiff must prove his or her case on the balance of probabilities. The question "what is the required standard of care" is a matter for the judge to determine. Whether that standard has been breached is a matter of fact for the tribunal of fact, that is, the jury or judge sitting without a jury. It is rare, nowadays, for negligence claims to be heard before a jury. The task of determining whether there has been negligence is not an easy one. There may be situations in which direct evidence is unavailable, such as a motor accident in which both drivers are killed and there are no witnesses. The action in such a case would be brought by the dependants of the deceased under legislation such as *Compensation to Relatives Act 1897* (NSW). Many cases deal with the question as to when there is sufficient evidence of negligence for the issue to be considered by the tribunal of fact. As explained in *Metropolitan Railway Co v Jackson* (1877) 3 App Cas 193 Lord Cairns at 197

> The judge has to say whether any facts have been established by evidence from which negligence may be reasonably inferred; the jurors have to say whether from those facts when submitted to them, negligence ought to be inferred.

The plaintiff may be able to rely on inferences drawn from circumstantial evidence, such as tyre skid marks and the position of vehicles. The inferences must be shown to be more probable than not in order to discharge the plaintiff's burden of proof. If the plaintiff fails to reach this threshold of establishing sufficient facts by the close of his or her evidence, a defence submission of "no case to answer" may be made. In some jurisdictions such a submission deprives the defence of the right to call evidence in the event that the submission is rejected. Alternatively, there may be an order of dismissal (non-suit) by the tribunal, or judgment entered for the defendant by direction of the court. In some situations plaintiffs may be able to invoke the maxim res ipsa loquitur (the thing speaks for itself), arguing that the mere fact that the accident happened raises an inference of the defendant's negligence.

Inference

[12.295] *Holloway v McFeeters* (1956) 94 CLR 470 continues to be a leading case on the question of sufficiency of evidence and inferences. The plaintiff sued in respect of the death of her husband killed by an unknown motorist. In an action against a defendant nominated by the pool of third party insurers, the plaintiff bore the burden of proving that the motorist was negligent and that the negligence caused her husband's death. The evidence was that the deceased's body lay in the middle of the road with injuries indicating that he had been run over, and tyre marks were traced from the body along the road for a distance of 42 feet. Where the tyre marks ended a heap of dirt was found, being the type which collects underneath the mudguard of a car. An excessive amount of alcohol was found in the deceased's body, but a neighbour testified that he had talked with the deceased as he passed along the road on the evening of the accident and the deceased was sober. At the trial damages were awarded by the jury, subject to a reduction for contributory negligence. Nevertheless the trial judge entered judgment for the defendant on the ground of insufficiency of evidence to go to the jury. The Full Court of the Supreme Court of Victoria allowed an appeal and directed judgment for the plaintiff. The defendant appealed to the High Court and the High Court dismissed the appeal by majority.

Dixon CJ, although dissenting on the facts, distinguished between conjecture and inference in what is a leading statement of principle:

> The state of facts which has been set out as the basis of the judgment of the Full Court is, of course, the product of inference. But ... the state of facts inferred itself leaves room for conflicting conjectures or hypotheses as to the cause of the accident. How came the deceased in the path of the approaching car? Did he move in front of it and into the range of vision suddenly? ... The conjecture that the driver must have been in fault in failing to see him in time to avoid him may be shrewd. But is it more than a conjecture? Before the plaintiff can succeed in such a case as this the circumstances must lead to a satisfactory inference, even though resting

> on a balance of probabilities, that the accident was caused by some negligence on the part of the driver. In the present case the true cause of the accident is in truth unknown. (at 476-77)

Dixon CJ went on to stress that where a situation may give rise to several hypotheses pointing in different directions, a particular hypothesis is not an inference. What is required is a foundation for positive inference on the basis of probable deduction, though it need not be an inference as to how precisely the accident occurred, provided that it is a reasonable conclusion that the accident in one way or another occurred through the negligence which has to be proved (at 477). The majority judges in *Holloway v McFeeters* (1956) 94 CLR 470 stressed the point mentioned by Dixon CJ that the inference need only be on the balance of probability, and considered that reasonable people could infer negligence on the balance of probabilities in the above circumstances left unexplained by any additional evidence. On the facts, they emphasised that the length of the skid pointed to excessive speed and that the evidentiary value of the fact that the driver took refuge in flight should not be overlooked (at 480-2).

Res ipsa loquitur

[12.300] The maxim res ipsa loquitur (the thing speaks for itself) represents a rule of evidence under which negligence may be inferred. The old English case of *Byrne v Boadle* (1863) 2 H & C 722; 159 ER 299 establishes that in some circumstances the mere occurrence of an accident is evidence of negligence, that is, proof of it is sufficient to provide evidence of negligence to go to the jury. In *Byrne* a barrel fell from an upper floor window of a flour dealer's premises, injuring the plaintiff. In *Scott v London & St Katherine's Docks Co*, (1865) 3 H & C 596; 159 ER 665, Erle CJ said in obiter:

> where the thing is shown to be under the management of the defendant or his servants, and the accident is such as in the ordinary course of things does not happen if those who have the management use proper care, it affords reasonable evidence, in the absence of explanation by the defendants, that the accident arose from want of care. (at 601; 667)

In both cases it was held that res ipsa applied. Although the above dictum seems to define the circumstances that will make a res ipsa loquitur case, this is deceptive. His Lordship is not saying that res ipsa applies in all cases where the agency of mischief is under control of the defendant. It must also be shown that the accident is one that does not happen if there has been proper care of the agency. And this is really no more than saying that the accident must be evidence of negligence. There is no general definition of *what* features of *what* accidents provide evidence of negligence by a person in the position of the defendant.

From the outset there was some suggestion that in some circumstances, the occurrence of an accident may not merely be evidence of negligence (presumption of fact), but will give rise to a presumption of law that negligence exists which needs some kind of rebuttal. This view has been firmly rejected in Australia. Kirby J's judgment in *Schellenberg v Tunnel Holdings Pty Ltd* (2000) 200 CLR 121, extracted below, provides a useful overview of the res ipsa loquitur principle in Australia.

Schellenberg v Tunnel Holdings

[12.305] *Schellenberg v Tunnel Holdings Pty Ltd* (2000) 200 CLR 121 High Court of Australia

(footnotes partially omitted)

GLEESON CJ and McHUGH J: 125 The principal question in this appeal is whether the plaintiff can rely on the doctrine of res ipsa loquitur to make out a case of negligence in circumstances where a

Schellenberg v Tunnel Holdings cont.

hose, carrying compressed air, which he was using in the course of employment, became loose and swung upwards striking him on the face. In our opinion, the doctrine of res ipsa loquitur did not apply, but, even if it did, its operation was spent once the trial judge found that the cause of the occurrence was the hose separating from a coupling to which it was attached. Once that finding was made, the question in the case was whether the plaintiff had proved that the separation was the result of the defendant's negligence. Because there was no evidence that established that the defendant was negligent in the assembly, inspection or maintenance of the hose and coupling, the Full Court of the Supreme Court of Western Australia was right to hold that the plaintiff's action failed …

KIRBY J: 153 … Nearly a century ago, in the first reported decision of this Court, it was recorded that the judgment under appeal was uncertain because it did not clearly appear whether the reasons below were based upon the maxim res ipsa loquitur. At that time, the maxim (or as it has variously been described, the "rule", "principle", "doctrine", "notion" or "method of inferring") had been propounded for nearly 40 years. But, although, in the intervening century, the maxim has been a frequent visitor to this Court, its application has continued to give rise to problems. The same has been true in other common law jurisdictions. The maxim has also occasioned much judicial and academic writing. A century after it was first propounded, such facts caused Windeyer J to remark that the one thing that can certainly be said of the "phrase" *res ipsa loquitur* is that "it has not been allowed to speak for itself"…

Dissatisfied with the defects of res ipsa loquitur, the Supreme Court of Canada recently declared, unanimously:

> Whatever value res ipsa loquitur may have once provided is gone. Various attempts to apply the so-called doctrine have been more confusing than helpful. Its use has been restricted to cases where the facts permitted an inference of negligence and there was no other reasonable explanation for the accident. Given its limited use it is somewhat meaningless to refer to that use as a doctrine of law.
>
> It would appear that the law would be better served if the maxim was treated as expired and no longer used as a separate component in negligence actions. After all, it was nothing more than an attempt to deal with circumstantial evidence. That evidence is more sensibly dealt with by the trier of fact, who should weigh the circumstantial evidence with the direct evidence, if any, to determine whether the plaintiff has established on a balance of probabilities a prima facie case of negligence against the defendant. Once the plaintiff has done so, the defendant must present evidence negating that of the plaintiff or necessarily the plaintiff will succeed.

In these proceedings this Court has been invited, if necessary, to follow the Canadian lead. …

The Ambit of an Employer's Liability in Negligence

[His honour considered the nature of the employer's non-delegable duty to the employee to take reasonable care for the safety of employees and continued:] … 159

[T]he burden of establishing a claim in negligence rests on the plaintiff throughout the proceedings. That burden requires the proof of a preponderance of evidence in favour of the plaintiff's case. This does not necessarily mean proof by direct evidence. The facts necessary to establish liability may be inferred from the proof of other facts. A plaintiff is not obliged to exclude all possibilities inconsistent with the defendant's liability. However, if at the end of the evidence the plaintiff has proved the negligence of someone but not identified the defendant as the person responsible (or has left it equally possible that some person other than the defendant was negligent or that some cause consistent with reasonable care brought about the plaintiff's damage) the claim must be dismissed.

Introduction of res ipsa: … [T]his Court has repeatedly emphasised… all that is involved in the maxim is a description of a "general method" of reasoning by which the decision-maker can infer "one

Schellenberg v Tunnel Holdings cont.

or more facts in issue from circumstances proved in evidence". In its origins, the maxim was offered as nothing more than a means by which a plaintiff could establish, by reasoning, the existence of "reasonable evidence of negligence".

But where the thing is shewn to be under the management of the defendant or his servants, and the accident is such as in the ordinary course of things does not happen if those who have the management use proper care, it affords reasonable evidence, in the absence of explanation by the defendants, that the accident arose from want of care.

Res Ipsa in Australian Courts

From its simple beginnings a number of propositions have been derived from the maxim res ipsa loquitur.

First, the plaintiff must show that the thing (*res*) which, without more, is said to indicate negligence was under the exclusive management and control of the defendant or someone for whom the defendant is responsible or whom it has a right to control. ...

Secondly, ... the... manner of reasoning the maxim describes does not... involve a shifting of the legal burden of proof from the plaintiff to the defendant, such that, unless the defendant establishes a want of any negligence on its part, it will be presumed to be liable. ... Thus, the maxim does not import a legal presumption having such effect. The defendant can remain silent and still succeed. If, in the particular case, the manner of reasoning described as res ipsa loquitur is applicable, it merely renders it *permissible* for the tribunal of fact to draw the inference which the plaintiff invites. It is not *obligatory*, as it would be if the maxim had the effect of creating a presumption which the defendant was obliged in law to rebut.

Thirdly, this does not mean that a failure on the part of a defendant to call evidence in a case where a plaintiff has invoked res ipsa loquitur is treated, in Australia (any more than elsewhere), as completely irrelevant. In some circumstances such an omission will have a telling forensic impact. From the earliest descriptions of the method of reasoning which res ipsa loquitur sanctions, reference has been made to the relevance of the "absence of explanation by the defendants". The practical necessities of an adversarial trial might, in at least some situations, effectively compel a defendant to attempt to show that the accident happened without negligence on its part.

It was in this sense, as a matter of forensic rather than legal necessity, that this Court was willing in *Mummery v Irvings Pty Ltd* to accept that "the defendant may, perhaps, be said, to carry an onus". However, the distinction between the *legal* burden (which remains throughout upon a plaintiff) and the *forensic* evidential burden of persuasion (which the state of the evidence may effectively impose upon a defendant) although elusive is important. The position consistently followed in this Court for more than half a century is that described by Barwick CJ in *Nominal Defendant v Haslbauer*:

> If then all the evidence as to the occurrence (if accepted) would itself support an inference of want of care on the defendant's part, it can properly be said that the defendant must negative that inference. ... [I]f he has given evidence as to the occurrence, which if accepted, and taken with the plaintiff's evidence, does not logically warrant an inference of his negligence, it is ... quite erroneous to say that none the less he must go further and show that the occurrence was without want of care on his part. So to conclude would be to reverse the onus, placing it on the defendant whereas in truth and unquestionably it remains throughout with the plaintiff.

...In Australia, the invocation of the maxim creates no presumption and shifts no burden of proof to the defendant. All that it does, when applicable, is to raise an inference of the existence of negligence. In days when jury trials of factual contests in civil causes were more common in Australia than they are today, the maxim was an occasional friend to a plaintiff to ensure that the plaintiff got to the jury. It did not, however, ensure a verdict from the jury in the plaintiff's favour. It still remained for the judge to

Schellenberg v Tunnel Holdings cont.

instruct the jury that the plaintiff bore the onus of proving the case on the balance of probabilities and for the jury to conclude whether they should draw the inference which the plaintiff invited.

Fourthly, there was for a time a belief that a plaintiff would lose any benefit of reliance on the maxim of res ipsa loquitur if an attempt were made to prove, by direct evidence, the *actual* cause of the injury giving rise to the proceedings. In Australia, this belief derived, understandably enough, from a remark in the reasons of the majority in *Mummery's Case*. The misunderstanding was corrected by this Court in *Anchor Products Ltd v Hedges*. In that decision the Court made it clear that the evidence might still give rise to an inference of negligence although a plaintiff has sought, but failed, to explain the specific cause as arising from the defendant's want of due care. For example, where a defendant drove his motor vehicle into the back of the plaintiff's vehicle the maxim would be given *prima facie* operation. However, when the defendant established explicitly that the cause of that action was an unexplained and unforeseen brake failure, the plaintiff could no longer rely on the maxim to prove negligence. If, as a result of evidence of a fact directly concerned with the cause of the incident, there is no room for inference, the method of reasoning which the maxim expresses was unavailing. The plaintiff would have to convince the court that the cause actually established betokened negligence on the defendant's part or, with some other fact, directly proved such negligence.

Res Ipsa is Unavailing in this Case

Assuming that the maxim res ipsa loquitur remains part of our law, I do not consider that it assisted the appellant in the circumstances of this case.

The difficulty lies not in respect of that element of the general exposition of the maxim which requires that the thing in question (in this case the grinder connected to the air hose supplying compressed air) should at all relevant times remain under the control of the respondent. During argument, it was faintly suggested that this was not the case here because the grinder was outside the control of the respondent and, for relevant purposes, was within the control of the appellant himself. Upon one view of the facts, this is undoubtedly true. But the "control" referred to in the authorities is not simply the physical possession of the thing in question. It is such control as imports responsibility for the event which has occurred. The duty resting on an employer to ensure that safe plant and equipment are provided to an employee cannot be deflected by asserting that it was the responsibility of others (including of the injured employee) to ensure that the plant and equipment in question were safe. For the purposes of the maxim, the "control" of the grinder and its component parts remained in the management of the respondent. The primary judge correctly so found.

... Instead, in this case, the difficulty of invoking the maxim of res ipsa loquitur arises from the requirement that the occurrence must be such that it would not have happened without negligence. This was not the present case. The air hose could have become disconnected from the coupling without any negligence on the part of the respondent. This would be so in a number of circumstances which are readily imaginable. They were in fact contemplated by the primary judge as a matter of "common sense". They would include:

1. That there was some latent defect in the hose not discoverable by external inspection (whether on the part of the appellant or of another employee of the respondent performing routine inspection on its behalf).
2. That there was some defect in the clamp used or in the coupling which was similarly not discoverable by prior inspection.
3. That the process of using the equipment, and the friction of the pressure involved, caused the hose clip to work itself loose in a way wholly unpredictable and insusceptible to discovery by prior inspection.

Schellenberg v Tunnel Holdings cont.

4. That the disconnection occurred as a result of a sudden, unexplained surge of air pressure, either from its source or as a result of the appellant's manoeuvring of the grinder in a particular way.
5. That even if the failure of the manager, Mr Mills, to give evidence of regular inspections of the equipment were deemed to carry some forensic weight, this would have to be judged in the context of a case in which the appellant (whilst making many other allegations of negligence) omitted to complain that his injuries were caused by the want of regular and timely inspection of the grinder and of its connection to the compressed air supply.

... In the end, therefore, there were various possibilities. All of them were "conjectural". This conclusion is not entirely surprising. The appellant's basic case was the one which he attempted, but failed, to prove against the respondent. As the record of the trial shows, the invocation of the maxim res ipsa loquitur was an afterthought. The first thoughts of those advising the appellant were correct. This was not a case where the maxim would avail the plaintiff. Air pressure hoses and their connection by specially designed couplings and clamps to grinders operated by hydraulic air pressure are not within the ordinary knowledge of tribunals of fact. They do not constitute simple implements with which the ordinary decision-maker (judge or jury) is familiar in daily life or which are so rudimentary that they may be readily understood. As the evidence revealed, it is a mistake to equate such equipment with garden hoses attached to domestic water taps. The peculiarities of the work equipment required explicit evidence. Such evidence was given. Once given, it left no real scope for the legitimate operation of informed inference. There was ample scope for speculation and conjecture. But this fell far short of establishing that the occurrence which happened would not have occurred in the absence of negligence on the part of the respondent. Equally consistent was the possibility that the defect was latent, the incident unpredictable and that any reasonable system of inspection and maintenance instituted by the employer would not have detected and predicted it.

Survival of the Res Ipsa Loquitur Maxim?

Faced with this conclusion, the appellant grasped at two possibilities which it is necessary to mention.

The first was an invitation that this Court should follow the lead of the Supreme Court of Canada, abolish the special exposition of res ipsa loquitur and substitute in its place an endorsement of the general principle that the trier of fact should weigh circumstantial evidence with direct evidence when judging whether, on the balance of probabilities, a prima facie case of negligence has been made out against the defendant.

There are various attractions in taking this course. This Court has emphasised many times, and for over 60 years, that the maxim res ipsa loquitur "should be regarded merely as an application of the general method of inferring one or more facts in issue from circumstances proved in evidence". In this respect, this Court has not been alone. Judges elsewhere have been at pains to deny to the maxim any "magic qualities". They have expressed exasperation at the suggestion that the maxim amounts to a "principle", or even worse, a doctrine of law. Lord Shaw of Dunfermline remarked nearly 80 years ago that if it "had not been in Latin, nobody would have called it a principle". Its invocation "is no substitute for reasonable investigation and discovery". Nor does it "relieve a plaintiff too uninquisitive to undertake available proof".

As these reasons demonstrate, despite the foregoing criticisms, in Australia as in other countries, the maxim has proved most resilient. Doubtless this is because its brevity expresses a vivid idea which may occasionally promise hope to a plaintiff who, through no fault of his or her own, is unable to establish exactly what caused the damage said to be the result of the defendant's want of care in respect of matters wholly or largely within the knowledge and control of the defendant.

An advantage of abolishing the maxim would be that it might release judicial minds from the encrustations of authority that have gathered around the maxim and its multitude of attempted

Schellenberg v Tunnel Holdings cont.

applications over the 130 years of its existence. But even if, in this case, res ipsa loquitur, as such, were overthrown and the facts analysed by reference solely to ascertaining the inferences available from the facts as found, this would make no difference. The position would remain the same. The attempts at specific explanations of the disengagement of the air hose and the grinder coupling would remain rejected. The possibility that the disengagement occurred for other reasons not alleged would still be, as the primary judge described them, "speculative". The question would come back to whether, in this context, the tribunal of fact was justified in inferring that it was more probable than not that the hose and coupling were insecurely fastened. That inference would remain just one of many possibilities. Selection of it as more probable than not would be as impermissible if no Latin maxim were invoked as it is if the established jurisprudence of res ipsa loquitur was applied.

Whilst, therefore, I am inclined to favour the conclusion reached by the Supreme Court of Canada, it is unnecessary to decide the point in this appeal. Nothing turns on it in this case. Where a maxim of the law has endured for so long, its resilience suggests a measure of utility that should restrain needless abolition. Perhaps res ipsa loquitur will continue to linger for a time as yet another indication of the attraction of lawyers to exotic labels. This case may have the merit of acting as a reminder of its limitations, the danger of treating it as a rule of law and the necessity to limit its use to that of an aid to logical reasoning by inference when considering whether the plaintiff has, or has not, established a cause of action in negligence.

CHAPTER 13

Damage: Causation and Remoteness

INTRODUCTION

Damage

[13.05] The plaintiff in a negligence claim must prove that the defendant's breach of duty is a cause of the plaintiff's harm or damage and that the defendant's negligence is a "proximate cause" of the harm or damage. The latter is usually referred to as the rule against remoteness of damage. Unlike the tort of trespass, the plaintiff must prove damage in order to recover. What constitutes "damage" for these purposes? Professor Fleming comments:

> What qualifies as actionable damage is a question of policy largely defined by the "duty rules" already considered ... The reason is that the concept is relative ... For example, while physical injury from external trauma is categorically included, liability for mental distress is more hedged ... Property damage is widely conceived, embracing any interference which diminishes

> the value of the object ... Pure economic loss ... is actionable only under controlled conditions. (*The Law of Torts* (9 th ed, Lawbook Co, Sydney), p 216))

Where there is merely a risk of harm, a plaintiff cannot recover until the harm has eventuated. This poses real difficulties where the plaintiff has been exposed to a toxic substance where the damage may occur decades later. There are two problems. The first is when does damage actually occur (see *Cartledge v Jopling* [1963] AC 758, Note 3 [16.210]) and the second, if damage has not yet occurred could a plaintiff recover for the costs of monitoring her or his condition?

In California in 1993, the Supreme Court handed down a landmark toxic tort decision in *Potter v Firestone Tire and Rubber Company*, 863 P 2d 795, 818 (Cal 1993). The case set the law for California on medical monitoring and fear of disease claims, and has been extremely influential. *Potter* concerned the contamination of drinking water by industrial solvents, cleaning fluids, oils and liquids from Firestone's tyre manufacturing plant, dumped into a municipal landfill. The plaintiffs were four residents whose private drinking wells were polluted. Two of the substances were known to be human carcinogens, and others were suspected carcinogens. At trial, Firestone was held liable for intentional infliction of emotional distress because of its "outrageous conduct" as well as negligence. The four plaintiffs were awarded $800,000 for their present fear of developing cancer in the future, $142,975 for the present value of future medical monitoring costs, as well as other sums for psychiatric illness and treatment costs, disruption of their lives, and punitive damages.

The Supreme Court held that the elements which must be proved in support of a fear of cancer claim are (slip Opinion 47-48):

> (1) as a result of the defendant's negligent breach of a duty owed to the plaintiff, the plaintiff is exposed to a toxic substance which threatens cancer; and 2) the plaintiff's fear stems from a knowledge, corroborated by reliable medical or scientific opinion, that it is more likely than not that the plaintiff would develop the cancer in the future due to toxic exposure. Under this rule a plaintiff must do more than simply establish knowledge of a toxic ingestion or exposure and a significant increased risk of cancer. The plaintiff must further show that based upon reliable medical or scientific opinion, the plaintiff harbors a serious fear that the toxic ingestion or exposure was of such magnitude and proportion as to likely result in the fear of cancer.

But this approach is not likely to find favour in either England or Australia. In the House of Lords in *Rothwell v Chemical and Insulating Company Ltd* [2008] 1 AC 281, the question was whether compensation was available for a plaintiff who had been negligently exposed to asbestos in the workplace, and had developed symptomless pleural plaques (fibrous thickening of the pleural membrane surrounding the lungs, indicating the presence of asbestos fibres, which could independently cause asbestosis or mesothelioma in the future). Lord Hoffman, expressing the view of the House, said "symptomless plaques are not compensatable damage. Neither do the risk of future illness or anxiety about the possibility of that risk materialising amount to damage for the purpose of creating a cause of action" (at [2]).

Statutory definition: Section 3 of the WA: CLA defines "harm" and is drafted similarly to provisions in other jurisdictions, see ACT: CLWA, s 40; NSW: CLA, s 5; Qld: CLA, Sch 2; SA: CLA, s 3; Vic: WrA, s 43. The Northern Territory and Tasmania have no similar provision and rely on the common law.

Civil Liability Act 2002 (WA)

[13.10] *Civil Liability Act 2002* (WA), s 3

3. Interpretation

In this Act, unless the contrary intention appears –

"harm" means harm of any kind, including the following –

(a) personal injury;

(b) damage to property;

(c) economic loss;

"personal injury" includes –

(a) death;

(b) pre-natal injury;

(c) impairment of a person's physical or mental condition; and

(d) disease ...

[13.15] The definitions of "harm" and "personal injury" are underpinned by common law notions of what is "damage" or harm for these purposes. Could compensable damage extend to loss of chance of a better outcome in medical cases? In *Gett v Tabet* [2009] NSWCA 76 (extracted at [13.145]) it was thought that it would not. Disease is recognised as personal injury. "Disease" would include occupationally caused diseases, for example, industrial deafness, mesothelioma, asbestosis, and brucellosis resulting from negligent exposure to toxic substances or sources of infection. The provisions are unlikely to extend the common law notions of what is relevant damage leaving no room for the innovative approach adopted in California in *Potter v Firestone Tire and Rubber Company* 863 P 2d 795, 818 (Cal 1993) to apply.

Causation and remoteness

[13.20] In *McGhee v National Coal Board* [1973] 1 WLR 1, Lord Reid stated:

> [I]t has often been said that the legal concept of causation is not based on logic or philosophy. It is based on the practical way in which the ordinary man's mind works in the every-day affairs of life. (at 5)

As will be made clear in this chapter, such an approach conceals important value laden choices. There is a constant tension between what are considered to be causation issues as distinct from remoteness of damage issues. Why should it matter? If causation is considered simply a matter of "common sense", as Mason J describes the test in *March v Stramare Ltd* (1991) 171 CLR 506 ([extracted at [13.30]), it does not involve explicit articulation of what values or policies are at play. This would then leave to remoteness of damage policy considerations on the reach of liability. The "common sense" causation test allows courts to avoid discussing the hard policy choices on the reach of liability.

Mason J's judgment in *March v Stramare Ltd* (1991) 171 CLR 506 (see [13.30] also makes it clear that the "foreseeability" test is not a test of causation. It is hard to reconcile this with the approach to questions of whether there is a new intervening cause, *novus actus interveniens*, see *Mahony v Kruschich* (extracted at [13.50]). How should *novus actus* cases be dealt with? Is the test of whether there is a novus actus, a test requiring some greater level of foresight and probability (Mason J in *March v Stramare* (1991) 171 CLR 506) or a matter of whether voluntary human action intervenes, or is a matter of excluding mere co-incidence (*Haber v Walker* [1963] VR 339 extracted at [13.45]). Why should "common sense" be utilised to obscure important policy choices in these cases?

The *Wagon Mound cases* ([13.175] and [13.180]) reject the directness test and establish foreseeability of the kind of harm as the test for remoteness of damage. The subsequent elaboration of the principles suggest that there may not be significant differences in application from the old directness test. A defendant may be held liable for unforeseeable damage: the *Wagon Mound cases* principles only require that the defendant be able to foresee the "kind of damage" not the actual damage. The incorporation of the egg-shell skull rule into the remoteness test can result in a defendant being liable for damage well beyond foreseeable damage.

The Statutory Test: The civil liability legislation explicitly deals with causation and remoteness of damage (the "scope of liability"). The Victorian provision is extracted here as an example. Similar, but not identical, provisions exist in all other jurisdictions except the Northern Territory: NSW: CLA, s 5D; Qld: CLA, s 11; Tas: CLA, s 13; Vic: WrA, s 51. See also, with minor variations: SA: CLA, s 34; WA: CLA, s 5C; ACT: CLWA, s 45. In Victoria, the general principles are set out in *Wrongs Act 1958* (VIC), s 51:

> (1) A determination that negligence caused particular harm comprises the following elements – (a) that the negligence was a necessary condition of the occurrence of the harm (factual causation); and (b) that it is appropriate for the scope of the negligent person's liability to extend to the harm so caused (scope of liability).

The statutory test reflects the common law, with some changes in emphasis. Paragraph (a) relates to factual causation and requires that the "negligence" must be a "necessary condition" of the harm. The Negligence Review Panel commented:

> [factual causation] is concerned with whether the negligent conduct in question played a part in bringing about the harm ... The long accepted basic test for answering this question is whether the conduct was a necessary condition of the harm, in the sense that the harm would not have occurred but for the conduct. (*Review of the Law of Negligence, Final Report* (Commonwealth of Australia, Canberra, 2002), para 7.26)

Paragraph (b) introduces the notion of "scope of liability" extending to the relevant harm. This clearly refers to remoteness of damage. Remoteness in itself is a matter of judgment and degree, influenced by policy. The section is similar to that proposed by the Negligence Review Panel:

> What is needed is a provision that will suggest to courts a suitable framework in which to resolve individual cases. Terms and phrases such as "effective cause", "foreseeability" and "commonsense causation" do not provide such a framework because they express a conclusion without explaining how that conclusion was reached. They discourage explicit considerations and articulation of reasons, for imposing or not imposing liability for the consequences of negligence, that are securely grounded in the circumstances of individual cases and address issues of personal responsibility. (at paras 7.47, 7.49)

The requirement that it is "appropriate" that the defendant's liability extend to the harm so caused will require the Courts to articulate and justify the value choices and policies which limit the defendant's liability. The section gives no guidance on how appropriateness should be determined, meaning that the settled common law principles for testing remoteness (those of reasonable foreseeability, discussed below) continue to apply.

The statutory provisions referred to above raise issues concerning the overlap between causation and remoteness of damage. The section gives pre-eminence to the "but for" (necessary condition) test. The cases extracted in the next section point to the problems in applying the "but for" test in a range of situations, particularly cases, where there are multiple causes, successive wrongdoers (*Baker v Willoughby* [1970] AC 467, extracted at [13.65]) and where there are intervening causes (*novus actus interveniens*). The civil liability legislation makes provision for "exceptional cases" which do not satisfy the "but for" (necessary condition) test, see [13.75]. In this situation the court is required to articulate and justify why the defendant should be liable. This appears to replicate the remoteness of damage (scope of liability) tests. Consider whether the provisions, in effect, adopt the reasoning of McHugh J in *March v Stramare* and reject Mason J's "common sense" approach.

CAUSATION

The common law

Necessary condition

[13.25] For something to be accepted in law as causal, it must normally be a necessary condition "causa sine qua non" for the loss. That is, the plaintiff must prove that the loss could not have occurred "but for" the defendant's negligence. It need not be the sole cause of the harm. The "but for" test is not without its limitations and critics, as the following passage from Justice McLachlin demonstrates:

> Tort law is about compensating those who are wrongfully injured. But even more fundamentally, it is about recognising and righting wrongful conduct by one person or a group of persons that harms others. If tort law becomes incapable of recognising important wrongs, and hence incapable of righting them, victims will be left with a sense of grievance and the public will be left with a feeling that justice is not what it should be. Some perceive that this may be occurring due to our rules of causation. In recent years, a conflation of factors have caused lawyers, scholars and courts to question anew whether the way tort law has traditionally defined the necessary relationship between tortious acts and injuries is the right way to define it, or at least the only way. This questioning has happened in the United States and in England and has surfaced in Australia. And it is happening in Canada. Why is this happening? Why are courts now asking questions that for decades, indeed centuries, did not pose themselves, or if they did, were of no great urgency? I would suggest that it is because too often the traditional "but-for", all-or-nothing, test denies recovery where our instinctive sense of justice-of what is the right result for the situation-tells us the victim should obtain some compensation. (Writing extra-judicially, B McLachlin, "Negligence Law-Proving the Connection", in Mullany and Linden (eds), Torts Tomorrow, A Tribute to John Fleming (LBC Information Services, Sydney, 1998), p 16, quoted in *Fairchild v Glenhaven* [2002] 1 WLR 1052. See also *March v Stramare* at [13.30].)

Barnett v Chelsea & Kensington Hospital Management Committee [1969] 1 QB 428 is a good illustration of the application of the "but for" test. There, the deceased had drunk some tea which was later found to be poisoned with arsenic. The deceased began vomiting and went to the hospital casualty department for treatment. The duty doctor refused to attend as he was unwell. The deceased attended another doctor but by this stage it was too late for effective treatment and the deceased died shortly thereafter. The trial judge found that although there was a negligent failure to treat, even if the doctor had come immediately and treated the deceased, this treatment would not have saved the deceased's life. The plaintiff (widow of the deceased) thus failed to discharge her burden of proving causation. As Neild J explained (at 433-4), the "[p]laintiff ... failed [because] ... had all care been taken, still the deceased must have died".

The following case is the leading common law authority on causation in Australia. This case needs to be read in conjunction with the civil liability legislation.

March v Stramare

[13.30] *March v E & M Stramare Pty Ltd* (1991) 171 CLR 506 High Court of Australia (footnotes omitted)

[The defendants parked a truck in the middle of a six-lane road outside a fruit and vegetable market in the early hours of the morning. Its parking and hazard lights were on and the street was moderately well lit. They had been using this method to unload the truck with a forklift for as long as the driver could remember. The plaintiff, who was speeding and affected by alcohol, was injured when his car collided with the truck. At trial the defendants and the plaintiff were both held to have been negligent, with a finding of 70 per cent contributory negligence against the plaintiff. On appeal, a majority of the Full Court of South Australia held that responsibility should be attributed solely to the plaintiff. The plaintiff appealed to the High Court. The Justices took differing views on the question of causation and the breadth of views indicates the complexity of the issue.]

MASON CJ: 508 Like McHugh J, I would allow this appeal but my reasons for taking this course are rather different from those stated by his Honour as I do not accept that the "but for" (*causa sine qua non*) test ever was or now should become the exclusive test of causation in negligence cases ...

Causation in the Context of Legal Responsibility

It has often been said that the legal concept of causation differs from philosophical and scientific notions of causation. That is because "questions of cause and consequence are not the same for law as for philosophy and science" ... In philosophy and science, the concept of causation has been developed in the context of explaining phenomena by reference to the relationship between conditions and occurrences. In law, on the other hand, problems of causation arise in the context of ascertaining or apportioning legal responsibility for a given occurrence. The law does not accept John Stuart Mill's definition of cause as the sum of the conditions which are jointly sufficient to produce it. Thus, at law, a person may be responsible for damage when his or her wrongful conduct is one of a number of conditions sufficient to produce that damage...

Causation and the Measure of Damages

Some of the confusion surrounding the legal concept of causation has been occasioned by the terminology employed in the various attempts which have been made over the years to express the principles governing the measure of damages recoverable in tort or contract.

Modern commentators take the view that these formulae ... conceal the making of value judgments or reliance on unexpressed policy reasons for refusing to allow liability to extend to the damage sustained in particular cases. The shortcomings of formulae of this kind were exposed in *Overseas Tankship (UK) Ltd v Morts Dock & Engineering Co Ltd (The Wagon Mound)*, ... and in *Overseas Tankship (UK) Ltd v Miller Steamship Co Pty ("The Wagon Mound [No 2]")*, where the criterion of reasonable foresight was applied so as to enable the plaintiffs to recover damages for the kind of loss as the reasonable man should have foreseen.

However, in *Chapman v Hearse*, this Court said, "the term 'reasonably foreseeable' is not, in itself, a test of 'causation'; it marks the limits beyond which a wrongdoer will not be held responsible for damage resulting from his wrongful act". More recently, in *Mahony v J Kruschich (Demolitions) Pty Ltd*, the Court said:

March v Stramare cont.

> A line marking the boundary of the damage for which a tortfeasor is liabl... be drawn either because the relevant injury is not reasonably foreseeab... chain of causation is broken by a *novus actus interveniens*: *M'Kew v Hollan... Cubitts*. But it must be possible to draw such a line clearly before a liability for... would not have occurred but for the wrongful act or omission of a tortfeasor ... reasonably foreseeable by him is treated as the result of a second tortfeasor's ne... alone: see *Chapman v Hearse*. Whether such a line can and should be drawn is very m... matter of fact and degree.

Just as *Chapman v Hearse* rejected reasonable foresight as a test of causation, so *M'Kew* and *Mahony* rejected it as an exclusive criterion of responsibility.

The Defence of Contributory Negligence

Another fertile source of confusion in the development of a coherent legal concept of causation has been the common law defence of contributory negligence. The existence of the defence, as well as the absence of any mechanism for apportionment of liability as between a plaintiff guilty of contributory negligence and a defendant and as between co-defendants who were concurrent tortfeasors, was a potent factor in inducing courts to embrace a view of causation which assigned occurrences to a single cause ...

The Effect of the Legislation Providing for Apportionment of Liability

The elimination of the defence of contributory negligence and the introduction by legislation (s 27a(3) of the *Wrongs Act 1936 (SA)*) providing for the apportionment between tortfeasors of damages in accordance with the degree of responsibility of the parties for the damage have meant that issues of causation could be approached afresh ...

[C]ourts are no longer as constrained as they were to find a single cause for a consequence and to adopt the "effective cause" formula. These days courts readily recognize that there are concurrent and successive causes of damage on the footing that liability will be apportioned as between the wrongdoers ...

So the end result of the apportionment legislation was to abolish ... the defence of contributory negligence.

Causation as a question of fact

The common law tradition is that what was the cause of a particular occurrence is a question of fact which "must be determined by applying common sense to the facts of each particular case" ...

It is beyond question that in many situations the question whether Y is a consequence of X is a question of fact. And, prior to the introduction of the legislation providing for apportionment of liability, the need to identify what was the "effective cause" of the relevant damage reinforced the notion that a question of causation was one of fact and, as such, to be resolved by the application of common sense.

Commentators subdivide the issue of causation in a given case into two questions: the question of causation in fact – to be determined by the application of the "but for" test – and the further question whether a defendant is in law responsible for damage which his or her negligence has played some part in producing: see, eg, Fleming, *Law of Torts*, 7th ed (1987), pp 172-173; Hart and Honore, *Causation in the Law*, 2nd ed (1985), p 110. It is said that, in determining this second question, considerations of policy have a prominent part to play, as do accepted value judgments: see Fleming, p 173. However, this approach to the issue of causation (a) places rather too much weight on the "but for" test to the exclusion of the "common sense" approach which the common law has always favoured; and (b) implies, or seems to imply, that value judgment has, or should have, no part to play in resolving causation as an issue of fact. As Dixon CJ, Fullagar and Kitto JJ remarked in *Fitzgerald v Penn*

... cont.

... s all ultimately a matter of common sense" and "[i]n truth the conception in question [ie, causation] is not susceptible of reduction to a satisfactory formula".

That said, the "but for" test, applied as a negative criterion of causation, has an important role to play in the resolution of the question. ... The commentators acknowledge that the "but for" test must be applied subject to certain qualifications. Thus, a factor which secures the presence of the plaintiff at the place where and at the time when he or she is injured is not causally connected with the injury, unless the risk of the accident occurring at that time was greater: see Hart and Honore, at p 122. As Windeyer J observed in *Faulkner v Keffalinos*:

> But for the first accident, the [plaintiff] might still have been employed by the [defendants], and therefore not where he was when the second accident happened: but lawyers must eschew this kind of "but for" or sine qua non reasoning about cause and consequence.

The "but for" test gives rise to a well-known difficulty in cases where there are two or more acts or events which would each be sufficient to bring about the plaintiff's injury. The application of the test "gives the result, contrary to common sense, that neither is a cause": *Winfield and Jolowicz on Tort*, 13th ed (1989), p 134. In truth, the application of the test proves to be either inadequate or troublesome in various situations in which there are multiple acts or events leading to the plaintiff's injury: see, eg, *Chapman v Hearse; Baker v Willoughby; McGhee v National Coal Board; M'Kew* ... The cases demonstrate the lesson of experience, namely, that the test, applied as an exclusive criterion of causation, yields unacceptable results and that the results which it yields must be tempered by the making of value judgments and the infusion of policy considerations...

Novus Actus Interveniens

In similar fashion, the "but for" test does not provide a satisfactory answer in those cases in which a superseding cause, described as a *novus actus interveniens*, is said to break the chain of causation which would otherwise have resulted from an earlier wrongful act. Many examples may be given of a negligent act by A which sets the scene for a deliberate wrongful act by B who, fortuitously and on the spur of the moment, irresponsibly does something which transforms the outcome of A's conduct into something of far greater consequence, a consequence not readily foreseeable by A In such a situation, A's act is not a cause of that consequence, though it was an essential condition of it. No doubt the explanation is that the voluntary intervention of B is, in the ultimate analysis, the true cause, A's act being no more than an antecedent condition not amounting to a cause. But this explanation is not a vindication of the adequacy of the "but for" test.

The facts of, and the decision in, *M'Kew* illustrate the same deficiency in the test. The plaintiff would not have sustained his ultimate injury but for the defendant's negligence causing the earlier injury to his left leg. His subsequent action in attempting to descend a steep staircase without a handrail in the normal manner and without adult assistance resulted in a severe fracture of his ankle. This action was adjudged to be unreasonable and to sever the chain of causation. The decision may be explained by reference to a value judgment that it would be unjust to hold the defendant legally responsible for an injury which, though it could be traced back to the defendant's wrongful conduct, was the immediate result of unreasonable action on the part of the plaintiff. But in truth the decision proceeded from a conclusion that the plaintiff's injury was the consequence of his independent and unreasonable action.

The fact that the intervening action is deliberate or voluntary does not necessarily mean that the plaintiff's injuries are not a consequence of the defendant's negligent conduct. In some situations a defendant may come under a duty of care not to expose the plaintiff to a risk of injury arising from deliberate or voluntary conduct or even to guard against that risk: see *Chomentowski v Red Garter Restaurant Ltd*. To deny recovery in these situations because the intervening action is deliberate or voluntary would be to deprive the duty of any content.

March v Stramare cont.

> It has been said that the fact that the intervening action was foreseeable does not mean that the negligent defendant is liable for damage which results from the intervening action: see *Chapman v Hearse; M'Kew; Caterson v Commissioner of Railways.* But it is otherwise if the intervening action was in the ordinary course of things the very kind of thing likely to happen as a result of the defendant's negligence...

As a matter of both logic and common sense, it makes no sense to regard the negligence of the plaintiff or a third party as a superseding cause or *novus actus interveniens* when the defendant's wrongful conduct has generated the very risk of injury resulting from the negligence of the plaintiff or a third party and that injury occurs in the ordinary course of things. In such a situation, the defendant's negligence satisfies the "but for" test and is properly to be regarded as a cause of the consequence because there is no reason in common sense, logic or policy for refusing to so regard it.

Conclusion

Viewed in this light, the respondents' negligence was a cause of the accident and of the appellant's injuries. The second respondent's wrongful act in parking the truck in the middle of the road created a situation of danger, the risk being that a careless driver would act in the way that the appellant acted. The purpose of imposing the common law duty on the second respondent was to protect motorists from the very risk of injury that befell the appellant. In these circumstances, the respondents' negligence was a continuing cause of the accident. The chain of causation was not broken by a novus actus. Nor was it terminated because the risk of injury was not foreseeable; on the contrary, it was plainly foreseeable.

In the result I would allow the appeal ...

McHUGH J: 529 The adaptation of [John Stuart] Mill's theory holds that every necessary member of the set of conditions or relations which is sufficient to produce the relevant damage is a cause of that damage: *International Encyclopedia of Comparative Law*, vol XI, (1983), Ch 7, p 27; Prosser, *Law of Torts*, 4th ed (1971), p 237; Fleming, *Law of Torts*, 7th ed (1987), p 173; *Nader v Urban Transit Authority of (NSW)*. Hence, for the purposes of the common law, a person may be causally responsible for damage even though his or her act or omission was one only of the conditions or relations sufficient to produce the damage. This is the basis of the "but for" test of causation which, apart from some exceptional cases, most writers and judges agree is the threshold test for determining whether a particular act or omission qualifies as a cause of the damage sustained. If the damage would have occurred notwithstanding the negligent act or omission, the act or omission is not a cause of the damage and there is no legal liability for it: *Duyvelshaff v Cathcart & Ritchie Ltd.*

However ... a powerful school of opinion asserts that the fact that a person's act or omission was a necessary condition of the occurrence of the damage is not itself sufficient to make that act or omission a legal cause of the damage. This school of opinion asserts that, to be a legal cause of damage, the act or omission charged must not only have been a *sine qua non* of its occurrence, but it must also have been a cause according to "common sense principles" ...

The view that the notion of "cause" in everyday speech and for legal purposes means more than a necessary condition or causa sine qua non also has the powerful support of Hart and Honore in the influential textbook, *Causation in the Law*, 2nd ed (1985) ...

Whatever label is given to such a rule – "common sense principles", "foreseeability", "novus actus interveniens", "effective cause", "real and efficient cause", "direct cause", "proximate cause" and so on – the reality is that such a limiting rule is the product of a policy choice that legal liability is not to attach to an act or omission which is outside the scope of that rule even though the act or omission was a necessary precondition of the occurrence of damage to the plaintiff. That is to say, such a rule is concerned only with the question whether a person should be held responsible for an act or omission which ex hypothesi was necessarily one of the sum of conditions or relations which produced the damage.

March v Stramare cont.

That a policy choice is involved in the use of some rules which limit liability for wrongful acts and omissions is obvious. Thus, the rule that a defendant is only legally liable for damage "of such a kind as the reasonable man should have foreseen" (*Overseas Tankship (UK) Ltd v Morts Dock & Engineering Co Ltd (The Wagon Mound)* [94]) is clearly a rule of policy. The rule that a defendant is not liable for damage which has been brought about by an overwhelming supervening event ("a novus actus interveniens") is also a rule of policy despite the use of metaphors such as "snapping the causal chain" to explain it. It may be less obvious, but it is still true, that the other labels to which I have referred are also the products of policy choices …

[T]he use of commonsense notions of causation and the use of expressions such as those to which Taylor J referred require the application of a policy choice, for they allow the tribunal of fact to determine legal liability on broad grounds of moral responsibility for the damage which has occurred …

[R]eflection on the matter has persuaded me that, if the "but for" test is applied in a "practical commonsense way", it enables the tribunal of fact, consciously or unconsciously, to give effect to value judgments concerning responsibility for the damage. If the "but for" test is applied in that way, it gives the tribunal an unfettered discretion to ignore a condition or relation which was in fact a precondition of the occurrence of the damage.

Moreover, it is doubtful whether there is any consistent commonsense notion of what constitutes a "cause" …

Indeed, I suspect that what commonsense would not see as a cause in a non-litigious context will frequently be seen as a cause, according to commonsense notions, in a litigious context…

[N]ow that contributory negligence is no longer an absolute bar, why should the courts continue to sanction the use of formulas which allow tribunals of fact, under the guise of using commonsense, to determine legal responsibility by applying their own idiosyncratic values? Directions to use commonsense notions of causation to find the "proximate", "real", "efficient" or "substantial" cause of an occurrence are invitations to use subjective, unexpressed and undefined extra-legal values to determine legal liability. To hold a person liable for damage resulting from a set of conditions or relations simply because his or her wrongful act or omission was a necessary condition of the occurrence of that damage would be an unacceptable extension of the boundaries of legal liability in some cases. But this truth does not justify the use of vague rules which permit liability to be determined by subjective, unexpressed and undefined values …

[T]he preferable course is to use the causa sine qua non test as the exclusive test of causation. One obvious exception to this rule must be the unusual case where the damage is the result of the simultaneous operation of two or more separate and independent events each of which was sufficient to cause the damage. None of the various tests of causation suggested by courts and writers, however, is satisfactory in dealing with this exceptional case …

In general, however, the "but for" test should be seen as the test of legal causation. Any other rule limiting responsibility for damage caused by a wrongful act or omission should be recognized as a policy-based rule concerned with remoteness of damage and not causation …

Remoteness of Damage and Causation

Once it is recognised that foreseeability is not the exclusive test of remoteness and that policy-based rules, disguised as causation principles, are also being used to limit responsibility for occasioning damage, the rationalization of the rules concerning remoteness of damage requires an approach which incorporates the issue of foreseeability but also enables other policy factors to be articulated and examined.

One such approach, and the one I favour, is the "scope of the risk" test … [which] enables relevant policy factors to be articulated and justified in a way which is not possible when responsibility is limited

March v Stramare cont.

by reference to commonsense notions of causation or to more specific criteria such as "novus actus interveniens", "sole cause" or "real cause", all of which conceal unexpressed value judgments'.

[McHugh J held the defendants liable on the basis that the plaintiff's injury was within the scope of the risk created by their negligence. The judgments of Gaudron, Deane, Toohey JJs agreeing with the outcome have been omitted. The plaintiff succeeded on the appeal, and the trial judge's decision on apportionment was upheld.]

[13.35] **Notes&Questions**

1. Do you agree with McHugh J's approach in the extract above? Can legal ideas of causation be divorced from normative questions about who "should" be liable? Should they be?
2. Mason CJ in *March v Stramare* referred to the limitations of the "but for" test:

   > the "but for" test must be applied subject to certain qualifications. Thus, a factor which secures the presence of the plaintiff at the place where and at the time when he or she is injured is not causally connected with the injury, unless the risk of the accident occurring at that time was greater.

   Such factors are known as necessary pre-conditions, that is, the damage could not have occurred without their existence, but the law recognises that these are not causes. The example given by Deane J in *March* illustrates this:

   > the mere fact that something constitutes an essential condition (in the "but for" sense) of an occurrence does not mean that, for the purposes of ascribing responsibility or fault, it is properly to be seen as a "cause" of that occurrence as a matter of either ordinary language or common sense. Thus, it could not, as a matter of ordinary language, be said that the fact that a person had a head was a "cause" of his being decapitated by a negligently wielded sword notwithstanding that possession of a head is an essential precondition of decapitation.

3. Is the statutory test outlined in [13.20] closer to Mason CJ, or to McHugh J's preferred views of causation?

Novus actus interveniens

[13.37] The following cases illustrate the difficulties frequently encountered in determining whether a given event constitutes a novus actus interveniens (new intervening cause).

Chapman v Hearse

[13.40] *Chapman v Hearse* High Court of Australia (1961) 106 CLR 112 High Court of Australia (footnotes omitted)

[A car negligently driven by Chapman collided with the rear of another vehicle driven by Emery. Chapman was thrown out onto the road, and Emery's vehicle was overturned. It was dark and wet and visibility was poor. Several people stopped to assist, including Dr Cherry. Dr Cherry was standing or stooping near the centre of the road attending to Chapman when he was negligently run down and killed by another car driven by Hearse. An action was brought against Hearse on behalf of Dr Cherry's wife and children pursuant to the *Wrongs Act 1936-1956* (SA). Hearse joined Chapman as a third party. The trial judge found that Hearse was negligent and held that Chapman was liable to make a contribution of one-fourth of the damages awarded. Chapman appealed. The High Court affirmed the decision of the Supreme Court of South Australia (Full Court), upholding the trial judge's verdict and apportionment. This case is important on issues of duty of care, foreseeability, causation and remoteness. The extract below deals with causation and novus actus interveniens.]

DIXON CJ, KITTO, TAYLOR, MENZIES AND WINDEYER JJ: 122 [T]he question whether, as the learned Chief Justice decided, Chapman's negligence was in the proved circumstances of the case a cause of Dr Cherry's death … must now be considered. At the outset, however, it should be said that the approach to this question in the course of argument was, with some resulting confusion, overlaid by a discussion of the decision of the Judicial Committee in *Overseas Tankship (UK) Ltd v Morts Dock & Engineering Co Ltd (The Wagon Mound)* [36] . In effect, the argument of the respondent proceeded upon the basis that if the ultimate damage was "reasonably foreseeable" that circumstance would conclude this aspect of the matter against the appellant. But what this argument overlooks is that when the question is whether damage ought to be attributed to one of several "causes" there is no occasion to consider reasonable foreseeability on the part of the particular wrongdoer unless and until it appears that the negligent act or omission alleged has, in fact, caused the damage complained of. As we understand the term "reasonably foreseeable" is not, in itself, a test of "causation"; it marks the limits beyond which a wrongdoer will not be held responsible for damage resulting from his wrongful act. This distinction is of some importance in cases such as the present where there have been successive acts of negligence and where it is sought to establish, notwithstanding the fact that the ultimate consequence might have been reasonably foreseeable at the time of the earlier act of negligence, that the later negligent act was the sole cause of the damage complained of. This, of course, is what Chapman seeks to do in the present case. Dealing with this aspect as an independent matter he concedes the foreseeability of some event such as that which actually happened, but asserts that as a matter of practical fact, Dr Cherry's death was caused solely by Hearse's negligent driving. It was, it is said, a case of *novus actus interveniens*, or that, otherwise, Hearse's negligent driving operated to break the chain of causation between the original negligent act and Dr Cherry's death. Whether this was so or not must, we think, be very much a matter of circumstance and degree …

[Chapman] insists that the fact that Hearse's later act was wrongful operated to break the chain of causation between his negligence and Dr Cherry's death. Why this should be so, however, does not clearly emerge but as far as we can see the submission rests solely upon the general proposition that there should not be imputed to a wrongdoer, as a reasonable man, foreseeability of subsequent intervening conduct which is, itself, wrongful … [O]n principle, it is impossible to exclude from the realm of reasonable foresight subsequent intervening acts merely on the ground that those acts, when examined, are found to be wrongful. Indeed, that view is necessarily implicit in a multitude of street accident cases where passengers or pedestrians have sought damages. Of course, "where a clear line can be drawn the subsequent negligence is the only one to look to" (*The Volute* [43]) but in the general run of cases of the type with which we are dealing no such clear line can be drawn … It is, we think, beyond doubt that once it be established that reasonable foreseeability is the criterion for measuring the extent of liability for damage the test must take into account all foreseeable intervening conduct whether it be wrongful or otherwise.… When these objections of the appellant are disposed of there remains little upon which it may be urged that his negligence was not a cause of Dr Cherry's death. There can, we think, be no doubt that Dr Cherry's presence in the roadway was, immediately, the result of Chapman's negligent driving and if any support for this conclusion should be thought to be necessary ample can be found in the analogous so-called "rescue cases". The degree of risk which his presence in the roadway entailed depended, of course, on the circumstances as they in fact existed and the circumstances were, in fact, such that the risk of injury from passing traffic was real and substantial and not, as would have been the case if the accident had happened in broad daylight, remote and fanciful. Perhaps, some confirmation for the proposition that the risk was substantial may be found in the fact that within a minute or two, or even less, Dr Cherry was run down by a driver

Chapman v Hearse cont.

whose vision of the roadway must have been impeded to a great extent by the prevailing conditions. In these circumstances, we have no doubt that Chapman's negligence must be regarded as a cause of Dr Cherry's death and since, for the reasons which we have given, some casualty of that character was within the realm of reasonable foreseeability the judgment against Chapman should stand.

Haber v Walker

[13.45] *Haber v Walker* [1963] VR 339 Full Court of the Supreme Court of Victoria

(footnotes omitted)

[The plaintiff's husband was injured in a motor vehicle accident that resulted from the defendant's negligence. He suffered severe brain damage and developed gross mental depression and an outlook of hopelessness as to his future. In hospital he made one attempt on his life and the following year he committed suicide by hanging himself. His widow sued the negligent driver on behalf of herself and their eight children for his death under s 16 of the *Wrongs Act 1958* (Vic). The jury found that the accident was caused by the defendant's negligence and that the husband's death was caused by the accident, but that the suicide of the husband was not something that the defendant could reasonably be expected to have foreseen. Judgment having been entered for the plaintiff, the defendant appealed. The negligent driver argued in part that the suicide represented a novus actus interveniens, that is, it was a voluntary act that severed the chain of causation between the death and the driver's negligence.]

LOWE J: 348 In the present action, s 16 of the *Wrongs Act* requires that the plaintiff establish that the deceased's death was caused by some act, neglect or default of the defendant. The fact then which the plaintiff must establish is that the deceased's death by suicide was so caused. It is obvious that several 349 difficulties must be overcome before this conclusion can be reached. The death occurred almost 18 months from the injury by the collision and it was immediately brought about by the deceased's own act. Was the chain of causation from the injury unbroken and was it the proximate cause of the death? …

I should like to say something as to what may break the chain of causation between the injury suffered by the deceased and his death. To hold that the conscious act even of a sane person necessarily breaks the chain of causation is inconsistent with the decision of the High Court in *Chapman v Hearse* (1962) 106 CLR 112; [1962] ALR 379. Whether there is a novus actus is, as the Court said, "very much a matter of circumstance and degree" and (I add for myself) this is a question of fact. But it would seem clear on principle if the act relied on is not the conscious act of a sane person it does not break the chain …

SMITH J: 354 I agree with the conclusions reached by [Lowe J]. [His honour referred to the question of whether foreseeability was relevant to the construction of the statutory provision and to the earlier High Court decision in *Chapman v Hearse* and continued:

The High Court in *Chapman v Hearse* (1962) 106 CLR 112; [1962] ALR 379,… lays down that "the term 'reasonably foreseeable' is not, in itself, a test of causation", but "marks the limits beyond which a wrongdoer will not be held responsible for damage resulting from the wrongful act". Furthermore, it is there stated that "when the question is whether damage ought to be attributed to one of several 'causes' there is no occasion to consider reasonable foreseeability on the part of the particular wrongdoer unless and until it appears that the negligent act or omission alleged has, in fact, caused the damage complained of" (see at 122).

… [T]the Court [in *Chapman*] quoted and adopted a statement to the effect that an intervening negligent act of a third person will not break a chain of causation if the original wrongdoer should have realized that a third person might so act. But clearly that particular negative proposition does not involve making reasonable forseeability "in itself a test of causation". The proposition is, in my view, perfectly consistent with, and indeed may be regarded as an application of, the general principles of causation which I shall hereafter be attempting to state. To put the matter in summary form, the intervening act of negligence is not sufficient to break the chain of causation because the fact that the wrongdoer should have realized that such a thing might occur involves that it was not so unlikely as to amount to a coincidence; and by hypothesis it is not a fully voluntary act in the sense of one which produced intended consequences ...

... The legal principles governing questions of causation are in some respects unsettled. It is, of course, clearly established that the ideas of causation with which the law is concerned when attributing responsibility for harm suffered are not those of the philosophers or the scientists but are those of the plain man, guided by common-sense considerations....:. But the statements to this effect that are to be found in the cases are not uncommonly accompanied by observations suggesting that common-sense considerations do not provide clear principles for the solution of problems of causation...: I venture to think that, at least in its main principles, the legal doctrine of causation based on common-sense considerations has now been made reasonably clear.... Confining attention to what is relevant to the present case the main principles, I consider, are these. In the first place a wrongful act or omission cannot ordinarily be held to have been a cause of subsequent harm unless that harm would not have occurred without the act or omission having previously occurred with such of its incidents as rendered it wrongful. Exceptions to this first principle are narrowly confined. Secondly, where the requirements of this first principle are satisfied, the act or omission is to be regarded as a cause of the harm unless there intervenes between the act or omission and the harm an occurrence which is necessary for the production of the harm and is sufficient in law to sever the causal connexion. And, finally, the intervening occurrence, if it is to be sufficient to sever the connexion, must ordinarily be either– (a) human action that is properly to be regarded as voluntary, or (b) a casually independent event the conjunction of which with the wrongful act or omission is by ordinary standards so extremely unlikely as to be termed a coincidence ...'

[The Court held that since the deceased's suicide was not voluntary there was no novus actus interveniens and the claim was entitled to succeed.]

Mahony v Kruschich Demolitions

[13.50] *Mahony v J Kruschich Demolitions* (1985) 156 CLR 522 High Court of Australia

(footnotes omitted)

[The plaintiff, Branko Glogovic, made a claim against his employer (Kruschich) for injuries sustained when he was employed on the demolition of a power house. He alleged that his injuries required significant medical treatment over a period of five years. The employer claimed contribution from one of the treating medical practitioners, Dr Mahony, arguing that Dr Mahony's negligence "caused or contributed to the continuing injuries and incapacities alleged by the plaintiff". Kruschich claimed a complete indemnity against Dr Mahony, or, alternatively, contribution pursuant to s 5(1)(c) of the *Law Reform (Miscellaneous Provisions) Act 1946* (NSW).]

GIBBS CJ, MASON, WILSON, BRENNAN AND DAWSON JJ: 528 A negligent tortfeasor does not always avoid liability for the consequences of a plaintiff's subsequent injury, even if the subsequent injury is tortiously inflicted. It depends on whether or not the subsequent tort and its consequences are themselves properly to be regarded as foreseeable consequences of the first tortfeasor's negligence. A line marking the boundary of the damage for which a tortfeasor is liable in negligence may be drawn

Mahony v Kruschich Demolitions cont.

either because the relevant injury is not reasonably foreseeable or because the chain of causation is broken by a novus actus interveniens: *M'Kew v Holland & Hannen & Cubitts*, at 25. But it must be possible to draw such a line clearly before a liability for damage that would not have occurred but for the wrongful act or omission of a tortfeasor and that is reasonably foreseeable by him is treated as the result of a second tortfeasor's negligence alone: see *Chapman v Hearse*, at 124-125. Whether such a line can and should be drawn is very much a matter of fact and degree ...

Where it is not possible to draw a clear line, the first tortfeasor may be liable in negligence for a subsequent injury and its consequences although the act or omission of another tortfeasor is the more immediate cause of that injury: cf *Lothian v Rickards*, per Griffith CJ. Thus Gibbs J in *Dillingham* accepted the suggestion that if a pedestrian were run over by two drivers consecutively, and both were negligent, the injuries caused by the negligence of the second driver would be damage for which both drivers are liable if those injuries were also the foreseeable consequence of the first driver's negligence.

In particular circumstances, minds may differ as to whether a subsequent injury was foreseeable or whether it is too remote to be regarded as a consequence for which an earlier tortfeasor may be held liable. When an injury is exacerbated by medical treatment, however, the exacerbation may easily be regarded as a foreseeable consequence for which the first tortfeasor is liable. Provided the plaintiff acts reasonably in seeking or accepting the treatment, negligence in the administration of the treatment need not be regarded as a novus actus interveniens which relieves the first tortfeasor of liability for the plaintiff's subsequent condition. The original injury can be regarded as carrying some risk that medical treatment might be negligently given: see *Beavis v Apthorpe*, at 858; *Moore v AGC (Insurances) Ltd*, at 394; *Lawrie v Meggitt*, at 8; *Price v Milawski*, at 141-142; *Katzman v Yaeck*. It may be the very kind of thing which is likely to happen as a result of the first tortfeasor's negligence: cf per Lord Reid in *Dorset Yacht Co v Home Office*, at 1030. That approach is consistent with the view taken in workers' compensation cases that the total condition of a worker whose compensable injury is exacerbated by medical treatment, reasonably undertaken to alleviate that injury, is to be attributed to the accident (see *Lindeman Ltd v Colvin*, at 321, per Dixon J; *Migge v Wormald Bros Industries Ltd*, at 48, per Mason JA; on appeal), although medical negligence or inefficiency can be held to amount to a new cause of incapacity in some circumstances: *Rothwell v Caverswall Stone Co*, at 365...However, in the ordinary case where efficient medical services are available to an injured plaintiff, the original injury does not carry the risk of medical treatment or advice that is "inexcusably bad" (*Martin v Isbard*, at 56), or "completely outside the bounds of what any reputable medical practitioner might prescribe" (*Lawrie v Meggitt*) or "so obviously unnecessary or improper that it is in the nature of a gratuitous aggravation of the injury" (*South Australian Stevedoring Co Ltd v Holbertson*, at 264) or "extravagant from the point of view of medical practice or hospital routine": Hart and Honore, *Causation in the Law* (1959), p 169. In such a case, it is proper to regard the exacerbation of a plaintiff's condition as resulting solely from the grossly negligent medical treatment or advice, and the fact that the plaintiff acted reasonably in seeking and accepting the treatment or in following the advice will not make the original tortfeasor liable for that exacerbation.

The appeal should be dismissed.

——— ꙮ ———

[13.55] **Notes&Questions**

1. In *McKew v Holland Hannen and Cubitts (Scotland) Ltd* [1969] 3 All ER 1621, the claimant injured his leg at work as a result of the employer's negligence. Some time later he was injured again when his leg gave way as he was about to walk down some stairs. Trying to save himself, he jumped down to the lower landing and injured his

ankle. The House of Lords held that the chain of causation had been severed by the claimant's decision to go down a steep stairway with no handrail without seeking help, knowing that his leg had previously given way in similar circumstances. Is this conceptually different from *Haber*? Why?

2. In *Medlin v State Government Insurance Commission* (1995) 182 CLR 1, Medlin, a university professor made a "voluntary" decision to retire early. He had been involved in a serious car accident five years beforehand and experienced ongoing pain. In order to decide the plaintiff's claim for loss of earnings during the early retirement period, the court had to determine whether the decision to retire was causally related to the negligence of the driver in the accident. Deane, Dawson and Toohey JJ (at 183) said:

> Two or more distinct causes, without any one of which the particular damage would not have been sustained, can each satisfy the law of negligence's common sense test of causation ... In some cases it may be potentially misleading to pose the question of causation in terms of whether an intervening act or decision has interrupted or broken a chain of causation which would otherwise have existed ... for example [where] the negligent act or omission was itself the direct or indirect contributing cause of the intervening act or decision.

3. In *State Rail Authority of NSW v Wiegold* (1991) 26 NSWLR 500 the plaintiff suffered serious injuries as a consequence of his employer's negligence. Following the accident, and after his employer had wrongfully cut off his workers' compensation payments, but prior to the trial, Wiegold was convicted of cultivating Indian hemp. He served nine months in prison. The trial judge, McInerney J, found that the "plaintiff was induced into this criminal enterprise by his impecuniosity which resulted from the accident ... Whilst it was not a direct result of the accident, one can say that but for the accident he would not have been involved." He therefore assessed Wiegold's economic loss from the accident on the basis that if he had not had the accident he would still have been employed by State Rail. On appeal to the (the NSW Court of Appeal, the majority (Samuels JA, with whom Handley JA agreed) (at 517) said:

> the question of causation [was determined] by application of the undemanding "but for" test. Following *March* ... this is an incorrect approach. Causation is as much a normative question as it is a factual one. It seems to me that the application of the "but for" test, tempered by considerations of public policy, lead to the result that the respondent's crime cannot be said to have been caused by the appellant's negligence.(p 13) ... To my mind a defendant should not be held responsible for the losses a plaintiff sustains that result from a rational and voluntary decision to engage in criminal activity. Such losses, to echo the words of *Chapman*, fall outside the limits for which the wrongdoer should be held responsible.

Do you agree with this view? Would the outcome be different if an accident victim became a heroin user to overcome incapacitating pain but had so far been fortunate not to be prosecuted? (*Grey v Simpson* (unreported, New South Wales Court of Appeal, 3 April 1978, the plaintiff recovered damages for heroin addiction). How would the civil liability legislation deal with this situation?

4. In sharp contrast to the *Wiegold* decision (Note 3 above), in *Meah v McCreamer* [1985] 1 All ER 367, the plaintiff sustained brain damage in a car accident caused by the defendant's negligence. He committed a series of brutal rapes two years later. Woolf J held that the dis-inhibiting effects of the brain injury entitled the

plaintiff to recover damages for the life imprisonment imposed upon him. Where should the line be drawn? Will criminality of the plaintiff's conduct always mean that as a matter of policy there is no recovery for the consequences of that criminal conduct? Should this be regarded a issue more properly regarded as a question of remoteness of damage where policy considerations can more explicitly be brought into consideration?

5. In *Hunter Area Health Service & Anor v Presland* [2005] NSWCA 33, the plaintiff sued the defendants for negligently failing to detain him under the *Mental Health Act 1990* (NSW). He was brought into hospital in a psychotic state, and shortly after his release, killed his brother's fiancée. At trial (*Presland v Hunter Area Health Service* [2003] NSWSC 754) he was found not guilty of murder on the grounds of mental illness and was detained for a period in a psychiatric hospital. On his release he sued for the distress and economic loss resulting from the killing and the imprisonment. Sheller JA acknowledged that: "public policy must loom large in a court's consideration of whether the plaintiff should be compensated ... the nature of the harm suffered by the plaintiff points as a matter of commonsense against the existence of a legal responsibility in the defendants". Santow JA said: "in terms of the normative aspects of causation, it would be unjust to render the appellants as defendants legally responsible for a non-physical injury traced back to unlawful but not criminal conduct. This is because it is excused but not justified by the law on the ground of ... insanity. It nonetheless constituted wholly unreasonable action on the respondent's part". Spigelman CJ, dissenting, said: "Where a person has been held not to be criminally responsible for his actions on the grounds of insanity, the common law should not deny that person the right to a remedy as a plaintiff and the acts which would otherwise constitute a crime do not break the causal chain."
   What are the competing policy considerations operating in *State Rail Authority of NSW v Wiegold* (1991) 26 NSWLR 500, *Meah v McCreamer* [1985] 1 All ER 367, *Grey v Simpson* (unreported, New South Wales Court of Appeal, 3 April 1978, the plaintiff recovered damages for heroin addiction), and *Presland v Hunter Area Health Service* [2003] NSWSC 754? Do you think the law has adequately weighed those considerations in the outcomes of the cases? Compare the treatment of these situations in the civil liability legislation.

Multiple sufficient causes

[13.60] Multiple sufficient causes exist where there are two or more events, each of which is sufficient to cause the harm. Mason CJ in *March v Stramare* said (at [21]):

> The "but for" test gives rise to a well-known difficulty in cases where there are two or more acts or events which would each be sufficient to bring about the plaintiff's injury. The application of the test "gives the result, contrary to common sense, that neither is a cause". In truth, the application of the test proves to be either inadequate or troublesome in various situations in which there are multiple acts or events leading to the plaintiff's injury.

The Negligence Review Panel (at para 7.26) agreed that harm that is attributable to more than one sufficient condition, could not be accommodated within the "but for" test. The Panel made no recommendations on this because "the law has devised rules for resolving such cases in ways that are generally considered to be satisfactory and fair". Thus, common law principles, as discussed below, continue to apply where there are multiple causal events.

In *Snell v Farrell* (1990) 72 DLR (4th) 289 (Can) at 294 (quoted in *Fairchild v Glenhaven* [2003] 1 AC 32, [13.105]), Sopinka J, delivering the judgment of the Supreme Court of Canada, said:

> The traditional approach to causation has come under attack in a number of cases in which there is concern that due to the complexities of proof, the probable victim of tortious conduct will be deprived of relief. This concern is strongest in circumstances in which, on the basis of some percentage of statistical probability, the plaintiff is the likely victim of the combined tortious conduct of a number of defendants, but cannot prove causation against a specific defendant or defendants on the basis of particularized evidence in accordance with traditional principles. The challenge to the traditional approach has manifested itself in cases dealing with non-traumatic injuries such as man-made diseases resulting from the widespread diffusion of chemical products, including product liability cases in which a product which can cause injury is widely manufactured and marketed by a large number of corporations.

Sometimes the problem facing the plaintiff is that the plaintiff is unable to prove on the balance of probabilities which one of several potential defendants caused the plaintiff's harm. In the Canadian case of *Cook v Lewis* [1951] SCR 830, the plaintiff was accidentally shot whilst hunting. It was found at trial that each of the two defendants had been negligent in firing his gun in the direction of the plaintiff without making sure that it was safe to do so, but the jury had been unable to decide which gun had fired the single shot that struck the plaintiff. By majority the Supreme Court of Canada held that as the jury could not decide between two negligent plaintiffs, both should be held liable. The Canadian court in *Cook* had followed a decision of the Supreme Court of California in *Summers v Tice* 199 P 1 (1948), involving a similar hunting accident. The *Summers* court had shifted the burden of proof to each defendant to show that it was not his bullet which struck the plaintiff. In the event that neither could do so, both would be held jointly and severally liable. Consider what may be problematic with this approach as a matter of principle. Is the approach justified? Why? What are the alternatives?

Another solution to this problem was the concept of "market share liability" developed by the Supreme Court of California in *Sindell v Abbott Laboratories* 26 Cal 3d 588 (1980). It was an extension of the "alternative liability theory" of causation devised in *Summers v Tice* 199 P 1 (1948). This case, and many others following it, concerned a synthetic hormone known as diethylstilboestrol or DES, marketed to pregnant women to control miscarriage. Over several decades a clear correlation emerged between women who took the drug during pregnancy, and a high incidence of a rare form of cancer of the reproductive tract in their adult daughters. As the drug had been made and marketed generically by over 200 manufacturers, the plaintiffs were in the unusual position of being able to prove breach of duty and causation and injury, but not being able to identify which of the 200 potential defendants' drug had caused their cancer. Market share liability solved this problem for plaintiffs. It meant that "[e]ach defendant will be held liable for the proportion of the judgment represented by its share of the market unless it demonstrates that it could not have made the product which caused the plaintiff's injuries" (at 612). See E Handsley, "Market Share Liability and the Nature of Causation in Tort" (1993) 1(1) *Torts Law Journal* 24.

Difficult causation issues also arise where a plaintiff suffers successive injuries each of which is capable of causing the plaintiff's damage.

Successive causes

Baker v Willoughby

[13.65] *Baker v Willoughby* [1970] AC 467 House of Lords

(footnotes omitted)

[The appellant (plaintiff) was injured in a car accident caused by the defendant's negligence. The accident caused a serious injury to his left leg and ankle. This caused some loss of earning capacity, pain and suffering and loss of amenities; the appellant's stiff leg reduced the appellant's ability to move freely. Three years later the appellant whilst at work was shot in the left leg by a robber. The appellant's injured leg had to be amputated.]

LORD REID: 490 ...There is no doubt that it is proper to lead evidence at the trial as to any events or developments between the date of the accident and the date of the trial which are relevant for the proper assessment of damages ... And it is always proper to take account of developments with regard to the injuries which were caused by the defendant's tort; those developments may show that any assessment of damages that might have been made shortly after the accident can now be seen to be either too small or too large. The question here is how far it is proper to take into account the effects of a second injury which was in no way connected with the first. ...

The appellant argues that the loss which he suffered from the car accident has not been diminished by his second injury. He still suffers from reduced capacity to earn although these may have been to some extent increased. And he will still suffer these losses for as long as he would have done because it is not said that the second injury curtailed his expectation of life. The respondent on the other hand argues that the second injury removed the very limb from which the earlier disability had stemmed, and that therefore no loss suffered thereafter can be attributed to the respondent's negligence. He says that the second injury submerged or obliterated the effect of the first and that all loss thereafter must be attributed to the second injury. The trial judge rejected this argument which he said was more ingenious than attractive. But it was accepted by the Court of Appeal.

The respondent's argument was succinctly put to your Lordships by his counsel. He could not run before the second injury; he cannot run now. But the cause is now quite different. The former cause was an injured leg but now he has no leg and the former cause can no longer operate. His counsel was inclined to agree that if the first injury had caused some neurosis or other mental disability, that disability might be regarded as still flowing from the first accident; even if it had been increased by the second accident the respondent might still have to pay for that part which he caused. I agree with that and I think that any distinction between a neurosis and a physical injury depends on a wrong view of what is the proper subject for compensation. A man is not compensated for the physical injury; he is compensated for the loss which he suffers as a result of that injury. His loss is not in having a stiff leg; it is in his inability to lead a full life, his inability to enjoy those amenities which depend on freedom of movement and his inability to earn as much as he used to earn or could have earned if there had been no accident. In this case the second injury did not diminish any of these. So why should it be regarded as having obliterated or superseded them? [Lord Reid discussed some related cases, including the following.]

493 [I]n *Performance Cars Ltd v Abraham* [1962] 1 QB 33 ... a Rolls Royce Silver Cloud sustained two slight collisions, each damaging a similar area of the vehicle.: Repairing the damage caused by the first collision also repaired the damage done by the second. The plaintiff was unable to enforce a judgment obtained against the person responsible for the first collision. He then sued the second tortfeasor. His action failed, since the second wrongdoer had damaged a car which was already damaged, causing no additional loss to the plaintiff. The plaintiff, who had been the victim of two negligent crashes causing damage to his property, thus ended up with no compensation, and both defendants escaped having to pay damages ...

Baker v Willoughby cont.

These cases exemplify the general rule that a wrongdoer must take the plaintiff (or his property) as he finds him; that may be to his advantage or disadvantage. In the present case the robber is not responsible or liable for the damage caused by the respondent; he would only have to pay for additional loss to the appellant by reason of his now having an artificial limb instead of a stiff leg.

It is argued – if a man's death before the trial reduces the damages why do injuries which he has received before the trial not also reduce the damages? I think that it depends on the nature and result of the later injuries. Suppose that but for the first injuries the plaintiff could have looked forward to 20 years of working life and that the injuries inflicted by the defendant reduced his earning capacity. Then but for the later injuries the plaintiff would have recovered for loss of earning capacity during 20 years. And then suppose that later injuries were such that at the date of the trial his expectation of life had been reduced to two years. Then he could not claim for 20 years of loss of earning capacity because in fact he will only suffer loss of earning capacity for two years. Thereafter he will be dead and the defendant could not be required to pay for a loss which it is now clear that the plaintiff will in fact never suffer. But that is not this case; here the appellant will continue to suffer from the disabilities caused by the car accident for as long as he would have done if his leg had never been shot and amputated … .

Finally, I must advert to the pain suffered and to be suffered by the appellant as a result of the car accident. If the result of the amputation was that the appellant suffered no more pain thereafter, then he could not claim for pain after the amputation which he would never suffer. [There was no evidence of this].... So in these circumstances we can neglect this matter.

I would allow the appeal …

LORD PEARSON: 495 [The respondent's argument] is formidable. But it must not be allowed to succeed, because it produces manifest injustice. The supervening event has not made the appellant less lame nor less disabled nor less deprived of amenities. It has not shortened the period over which he will be suffering. It has made him more lame, more disabled, more deprived of amenities. He should not have less damages through being worse off than might have been expected.

The nature of the injustice becomes apparent if the supervening event is treated as a tort (as indeed it was) and if one envisages the appellant suing the robbers who shot him. They would be entitled, as the saying is, to "take the plaintiff as they find him". They have not injured and disabled a previously fit and able-bodied man. They have only made an already lame and disabled man more lame and more disabled …

I think a solution of the theoretical problem can be found in cases such as this by taking a comprehensive and unitary view of the damage caused by the original accident. Itemisation of the damages by dividing them into heads and sub-heads is often convenient, but is not essential. In the end judgment is given for a single lump sum of damages and not for a total of items set out under heads and sub-heads. The original accident caused what may be called a "devaluation" of the plaintiff, in the sense that it produced a general reduction of his capacity to do things, to earn money and to enjoy life. For that devaluation the original tortfeasor should be and remain responsible to the full extent, unless before the assessment of the damages something has happened which either diminishes the devaluation (eg, if there is an unexpected recovery from some of the adverse effects of

Baker v Willoughby cont.

the accident) or by shortening the expectation of life diminishes the period over which the plaintiff will suffer from the devaluation. If the supervening event is a tort, the second tortfeasor should be responsible for the additional devaluation caused by him.

Jobling v Associated Dairies

[13.70] *Jobling v Associated Dairies Ltd* [1982] AC 794 House of Lords

(footnotes omitted)

LORD KEITH OF KINKEL: 801 In January 1973 the appellant, in the course of his employment with the respondents and as a result of their negligence, suffered an injury to his back in the shape of a slipped disc. This had the effect of incapacitating him for any but light work. In September 1976 the appellant was found to be suffering from a condition known as cervical myelopathy, unrelated to the accident, which by the time his claim came to trial, in March 1979, had resulted in a total incapacity for work. According to an agreed medical report, there were no discernible signs or symptoms of myelopathy at the date of the accident in 1973.

In that state of affairs the question arose whether the respondents were liable to pay damages for loss of earnings on the basis of a partial incapacity continuing throughout the period which, in the absence of the myelopathy, would have represented the balance of the appellant's normal working life, or whether their liability was limited to loss of earnings up to the time when the myelopathy resulted in total incapacity....[His Lordship then referred to the decision in *Baker v Willoughby* and continued:]

A notable feature of the speeches in *Baker v Willoughby* is the absence of any consideration of the possible implications of what may be termed the "vicissitudes" principle. The leading exposition of this principle is to be found in the judgment of Brett LJ in *Phillips v London and South Western Railway Co* (1879) 5 CPD 280 at 291:

> if no accident had happened, nevertheless many circumstances might have happened to prevent the plaintiff from earning his previous income; he may be disabled by illness, he is subject to the ordinary accidents and vicissitudes of life; and if all these circumstances of which no evidence can be given are looked at, it will be impossible to exactly estimate them; yet if the jury wholly pass them over they will go wrong, because these accidents and vicissitudes ought to be taken into account. It is true that the chances of life cannot be accurately calculated, but the judge must tell the jury to consider them in order that they may give a fair and reasonable compensation.

This principle is to be applied in conjunction with the rule that the court will not speculate when it knows, so that when an event within its scope has actually happened prior to the trial date, that event will fall to be taken into account in the assessment of damages ...

It is implicit in ... [*Baker v Willoughby*] that the scope of the "vicissitudes" principle is limited to supervening events of such a nature as either to reduce the disabilities resulting from the accident or else to shorten the period during which they will be suffered. I am of opinion that failure to consider or even advert to this implication weakens the authority of the ratio decidendi of the case, and must lead to the conclusion that in its full breadth it is not acceptable. The assessment of damages for personal injuries involves a process of restitutio in integrum. The object is to place the injured plaintiff in as good a position as he would have been in but for the accident. He is not to be placed in a better position. The process involves a comparison between the plaintiff's circumstances as regards capacity to enjoy the amenities of life and to earn a living as they would have been if the accident had not occurred and his actual circumstances in those respects following the accident. In considering how matters might have been expected to turn out if there had been no accident, the "vicissitudes" principle says that it is right to take into account events, such as illness, which not uncommonly occur in the ordinary course of human life. If such events are not taken into account, the damages may be greater than are required to compensate the plaintiff for the effects of the accident, and that result would be unfair to the defendant. Counsel for the appellant sought to draw a distinction between the case where the plaintiff, at the time of the tortious injury, is already suffering from a latent undetected condition which later develops into a disabling illness and the case where the inception of the illness occurs wholly at a later date. In the former case, so it was maintained, the illness would properly fall to be taken into account in diminution of damages, on the principle that the tortfeasor takes his victim as he finds him, but in the latter case it would not. There is no trace of the suggested distinction in any of the authorities, and in my opinion it is unsound and apt to lead to great practical difficulties ...

I am therefore of opinion that the majority in *Baker v Willoughby* were mistaken in approaching the problems common to the case of a supervening tortious act and to that of supervening illness wholly from the point of view of causation. While it is logically correct to say that in both cases the original tort and the supervening event may be concurrent causes of incapacity, that does not necessarily, in my view, provide the correct solution. In the case of supervening illness, it is appropriate to keep in view that this is one of the ordinary vicissitudes of life, and when one is comparing the situation resulting from the accident with the situation, had there been no accident, to recognise that the illness would have overtaken the plaintiff in any event, so that it cannot be disregarded in arriving at proper compensation, and no more than proper compensation.

Additional considerations come into play when dealing with the problems arising where the plaintiff has suffered injuries from two or more successive and independent tortious acts. In that situation it is necessary to secure that the plaintiff is fully compensated for the aggregate effects of all his injuries. As Lord Pearson noted in *Baker v Willoughby* [1969] 3 All ER 1528 at 1535, [1970] AC 467 at 495 it would clearly be unjust to reduce the damages awarded for the first tort because of the occurrence of the second tort, damages for which are to be assessed on the basis that the plaintiff is already partially incapacitated. I do not consider it necessary to formulate any precise juristic basis for dealing with this situation differently from the case of supervening illness. It might be said that a supervening tort is not one of the ordinary vicissitudes of life, or that it is too remote a possibility to be taken into account, or that it can properly be disregarded because it carries its own remedy. None of these formulations, however, is entirely satisfactory. The fact remains that the principle of full compensation requires that a just and practical solution should be found. In the event that damages against two successive tortfeasors fall to be assessed at the same time, it would be highly unreasonable if the aggregate of both awards were less than the total loss suffered by the plaintiff. The computation should start from an assessment of that total loss. The award against the second tortfeasor cannot in fairness to him fail to recognise that the plaintiff whom he injured was already to some extent incapacitated. In order that the plaintiff may be fully compensated, it becomes necessary to deduct the award so calculated from the assessment of the plaintiff's total loss and award the balance against the first tortfeasor. If that be a correct approach, it follows that, in proceedings against the first tortfeasor alone, the occurrence of the second tort cannot be successfully relied on by the defendant as reducing the damages which he must pay. That, in substance, was the result of the decision in *Baker v Willoughby*, where the supervening event was a tortious act, and to that extent the decision was, in my view, correct.

Before leaving the case, it is right to face up to the fact that, if a non-tortious supervening event is to have the effect of reducing damages but a subsequent tortious act is not, there may in some cases be difficulty in ascertaining whether the event in question is or is not of a tortious character, particularly in the absence of the alleged tortfeasor. Possible questions of contributory negligence may cause additional complications. Such difficulties are real, but are not sufficient, in my view, to warrant the

Jobling v Associated Dairies cont.

conclusion that the distinction between tortious and non-tortious supervening events should not be accepted. The court must simply do its best to arrive at a just assessment of damages in a pragmatical way in the light of the whole circumstances of the case.

My Lords, for these reasons I would dismiss the appeal.

LORD WILBERFORCE: ... 1. Causation arguments. The unsatisfactory character of these is demonstrated by the case of *Baker v Willoughby* [1969] 3 All ER 1528, [1970] AC 467...

In the present case, and in other industrial injury cases, there seems to me no justification for disregarding the fact that the injured man's employer is insured (indeed since 1972 compulsorily insured) against liability to his employees. The state has decided, in other words, on a spreading of risk. There seems to me no more justification for disregarding the fact that the plaintiff (presumably; we have not been told otherwise), is entitled to sickness and invalidity benefit in respect of his myelopathy, the amount of which may depend on his contribution record, which in turn may have been affected by his accident. So we have no means of knowing whether the plaintiff would be over-compensated if he were, in addition, to receive the assessed damages from his employer, or whether he would be under-compensated if left to his benefit. It is not easy to accept a solution by which a partially incapacitated man becomes worse off in terms of damages and benefit through a greater degree of incapacity. Many other ingredients, of weight in either direction, may enter into individual cases. Without any satisfaction I draw from this the conclusion that no general, logical or universally fair rules can be stated which will cover, in a manner consistent with justice, cases of supervening events, whether due to tortious, partially tortious, non-culpable or wholly accidental events. The courts can only deal with each case as best they can in a manner so as to provide just and sufficient but not excessive compensation, taking all factors into account. I think that this is what *Baker v Willoughby* did, and indeed that Lord Pearson reached his decision in this way; the rationalisation of the decision, as to which I at least have doubts, need and should not be applied to other cases. In the present case the Court of Appeal reached the unanswerable conclusion that to apply *Baker v Willoughby* to the facts of the present case would produce an unjust result, and I am willing to accept the corollary that justice, so far as it can be perceived, lies the other way and that the supervening myelopathy should not be disregarded. If rationalisation is needed, I am willing to accept the "vicissitudes" argument as the best available. I should be more firmly convinced of the merits of the conclusion if the whole pattern of benefits had been considered, in however general a way. The result of the present case may be lacking in precision and rational justification, but so long as we are content to live in a mansion of so many different architectures this is inevitable.

I would dismiss the appeal ... .

[Lords Russell and Bridge delivered similar speeches to Lord Keith; Lord Edmund-Davies also dismissed the appeal, distinguishing *Baker* on the facts.]

"Exceptional cases"

[13.75] The civil liability legislation in all jurisdictions, except the Northern Territory and Tasmania, contains a provision dealing specifically with the complex issue of multiple causes. Provisions are drafted differently across the jurisdictions. Qld: CLA, s 11(2); WA: CLA, s 5C(2); Vic: WrA, s 51(2); ACT: CLWA, s 45(2); SA: CLA, 34(2)

The New South Wales provision is extracted as an example.

Civil Liability Act 2002 (NSW)

[13.80] *Civil Liability Act 2002* (NSW), s 5D(2)

s 5D(2) In determining in an exceptional case, in accordance with established principles, whether negligence that cannot be established as a necessary condition of the occurrence of harm should be accepted as establishing factual causation, the court is to consider (amongst other relevant things) whether or not and why responsibility for the harm should be imposed on the negligent party.

[13.85] This provision concedes that in certain circumstances a breach of duty may be considered causal even if it cannot be proved to be a necessary condition of the injury. It refers to "established principles" of common law as the method for determining causation in these exceptional cases. The section introduces explicitly normative factors ("whether or not and why") into the determination of factual causation. We now turn to consider those "exceptional cases".

Material cause and cumulative causation

[13.90] Cumulative causes are independent acts, none of which is alone sufficient to produce the injury but which combine to do so. *Medlin v State Government Insurance Commission* (1995) 182 CLR 1 (see [13.55] Note 2) is an example of a causal breach of duty by the negligent driver leading the plaintiff to make his decision to take early retirement. The two factors in conjunction led to the plaintiff's loss of income during that period. Many industrial disease cases feature cumulative causes, since plaintiffs may have been exposed to toxic or injurious substances by more than one employer over a long period. In cases involving mesothelioma and asbestosis arising from exposure to asbestos, for example, causation is problematic because the disease mechanism is not well understood. The issue in such cases is whether the result is to be determined by the normal operation of burden of proof rules, whereby the plaintiff would fail because the plaintiff is unable to discharge the burden of proving causation, or whether the manifest injustice of such a result justifies adapting the rules of causation to assist plaintiffs. The test developed in *Bonnington Castings v Wardlaw* [1956] AC 613 discussed in both *McGhee*, and *Fairchild* (extracted below at [13.95] and [13.105] respectively), requires each act to have "caused or materially contributed to" the injury, and overcomes some of the difficulty. Where there is more than one defendant, each will be jointly and severally liable, meaning each is liable for the totality of the plaintiff's injury (although the plaintiff cannot recover more than 100 per cent overall). In asbestos cases, the courts have accepted that where a plaintiff has been negligently exposed to asbestos by an employer and where that exposure is a material cause of the disease, then that employer will be liable for the loss. For example, in *Wallaby Grip (BAE) Pty Ltd (in Liq) v Macleay Area Health Service* (1998) 17 NSWCCR 355, it was held that one or more defendants could be held liable if it had been proved that each had negligently exposed the plaintiff to a risk of contracting a fatal disease.

McGhee takes the *Bonnington* test a step further, requiring only that the breach of duty "materially increases the *risk* of injury". The legal burden of proving causation remains with the plaintiff throughout the case, but the evidentiary burden may shift, in the sense that where the plaintiff has proved a breach of duty by the defendant and can establish that the breach increased the risk of injury, and that the risk eventuated, the defendant will be held liable in the absence of proof of an alternative cause. The House of Lords has considered and reinterpreted

McGhee in several cases, notably *Wilsher v Essex Area Health Authority* [1988] AC 1074 and *Fairchild v Glenhaven* [2003] 1 AC 32 (see [13.105]). The approach in the following extract, *McGhee v National Coal Board* [1973] 1 WLR 1, has found support in the High Court in a number of cases. For example, in *Chappel v Hart* (1998) 195 CLR 232, (the facts of which are set out at [13.125]),the judgments of Gaudron, (238) McHugh (244), Gummow (257) and Kirby JJ (273) accept that a defendant will be taken to have materially contributed to an injury if the defendant's negligence results in an increased risk to the plaintiff and that risk eventuates.

Material increase in risk

McGhee v National Coal Board

[13.95] *McGhee v National Coal Board* [1972] 3 All ER 1008 House of Lords

(footnotes omitted)

LORD REID: 1010 My Lords, the appellant was employed for many years by the respondents as a labourer at their Prestongrange brickworks. His normal work was emptying pipe kilns. On 30th March 1967 (a Thursday) he was sent to empty brick kilns. Working conditions there were much hotter and dustier than in the pipe kilns. On Sunday, 2nd April, he felt extensive irritation of his skin. He continued to work on the Monday and Tuesday and then went to his doctor who put him off work and later sent him to a skin specialist. He was found to be suffering from dermatitis. He sued the respondents for damages alleging breaches on their part of common law duties to him …

[The employer's arguments based on denial of duty and non occupational character of the dermatitis having been rejected] … the respondents' defence in the Inner House and before your Lordships has taken the unusual form that breach of duty [to provide showers] is admitted, and that it is admitted that the disease is attributable to the work which the appellant performed in the brick kiln, but that it has not been proved that failure to carry out the admitted duty caused the onset of the disease.

The medical witnesses are in substantial agreement. Dermatitis can be caused, and this dermatitis was caused, by repeated minute abrasion of the outer horny layer of the skin followed by some injury to or change in the underlying cells, the precise nature of which has not yet been discovered by medical science … .

It has always been the law that a pursuer succeeds if he can show that fault of the defender caused or materially contributed to his injury. There may have been two separate causes but it is enough if one of the causes arose from fault of the defender. The pursuer does not have to prove that this cause would of itself have been enough to cause him injury. That is well illustrated by the decision of this House in *Bonnington Castings Ltd v Wardlaw* [[1956] 1 All ER 615, [1956] AC 613]. There the pursuer's disease was caused by an accumulation of noxious dust in his lungs. The dust which he had inhaled over a period came from two sources. The defenders were not responsible for one source but they could and ought to have prevented the other. The dust from the latter source was not in itself sufficient to cause the disease but the pursuer succeeded because it made a material contribution to his injury. The respondents seek to distinguish *Wardlaw's* case n1 by arguing that then it was proved that every particle of dust inhaled played its part in causing the onset of the disease whereas in this case it is not proved that every minor abrasion played its part.

In the present case the evidence does not show – perhaps no one knows – just how dermatitis of this type begins. It suggests to me that there are two possible ways. It may be that an accumulation of minor abrasions of the horny layer of skin is a necessary precondition for the onset of the disease. Or it

McGhee v National Coal Board cont.

may be that the disease starts at one particular abrasion and then spreads, so that multiplication of abrasions merely increases the number of places where the disease can start and in that way increases the risk of its occurrence.

I am inclined to think that the evidence points to the former view. But in a field where so little appears to be known with certainty I could not say that that is proved. If it were then this case would be indistinguishable from *Wardlaw's* case [[1956] 1 All ER 615, [1956] AC 613]. But I think that in cases like this we must take a broader view of causation. The medical evidence is to the effect that the fact that the man had to cycle home caked with grime and sweat added materially to the risk that this disease might develop. It does not and could not explain just why that is so. But experience shows that it is so. Plainly that must be because what happens while the man remains unwashed can have a causative effect, although just how the cause operates is uncertain. I cannot accept the view expressed in the Inner House that once the man left the brick kiln he left behind the causes which made him liable to develop dermatitis. That seems to me quite inconsistent with a proper interpretation of the medical evidence. Nor can I accept the distinction drawn by the Lord Ordinary between materially increasing the risk that the disease will occur and making a material contribution to its occurrence.

There may be some logical ground for such a distinction where our knowledge of all the material factors is complete. But it has often been said that the legal concept of causation is not based on logic or philosophy. It is based on the practical way in which the ordinary man's mind works in the every-day affairs of life. From a broad and practical viewpoint I can see no substantial difference between saying that what the respondents did materially increased the risk of injury to the appellant and saying that what the respondents did made a material contribution to his injury.

I would therefore allow this appeal.

LORD WILBERFORCE: ... It was not enough for the appellant to establish a duty or a breach of it. To succeed in his claim he had to satisfy the court that a causal connection existed between the default and the disease complained of, i e according to the formula normally used, that the breach of duty caused or materially contributed to the injury. Here two difficulties arose. In the first place, little is known as to the exact causes of dermatitis. The experts could say that it tends to be caused by a breakdown of the layer of heavy skin covering the nerve ends provoked by friction caused by dust, but had to admit that they knew little of the quantity of dust or the time of exposure necessary to cause a critical change. Secondly, there could be little doubt that the appellant's dermatitis resulted from a combination, or accumulation, of two causes: exposure to dust while working in hot conditions in the kiln and the subsequent omission to wash thoroughly before leaving the place of work; the second of these, but not the first, was, on the findings, attributable to the fault of the respondents. The appellant's expert was unable to attribute the injury to the second of these causes for he could not say that if the appellant had been able to wash off the dust by showers he would not have contracted the disease. He could not do more than say that the failure to provide showers materially increased the chance, or risk, that dermatitis might set in.

My Lords, I agree with the judge below to the extent that merely to show that a breach of duty increases the risk of harm is not, in abstracto, enough to enable the pursuer to succeed. He might, on this basis, still be met by successful defences. Thus, it was open to the respondents, while admitting, or being unable to contest that their failure had increased the risk, to prove, if they could, as they tried to do, that the appellant's dermatitis was "non-occupational".

But the question remains whether a pursuer must necessarily fail if, after he has shown a breach of duty, involving an increase of risk of disease, he cannot positively prove that this increase of risk caused or materially contributed to the disease while his employers cannot positively prove the contrary. In this intermediate case there is an appearance of logic in the view that the pursuer, on whom the onus lies, should fail – a logic which dictated the judgments below. The question is whether we should be

McGhee v National Coal Board cont.

satisfied in factual situations like the present, with this logical approach. In my opinion, there are further considerations of importance. First, it is a sound principle that where a person has, by breach of duty of care, created a risk, and injury occurs within the area of that risk, the loss should be borne by him unless he shows that it had some other cause. Secondly, from the evidential point of view, one may ask, why should a man who is able to show that his employer should have taken certain precautions, because without them there is a risk, or an added risk, of injury or disease, and who in fact sustains exactly that injury or disease, have to assume the burden of proving more: namely, that it was the addition to the risk, caused by the breach of duty, which caused or materially contributed to the injury? In many cases of which the present is typical, this is impossible to prove, just because honest medical opinion cannot segregate the causes of an illness between compound causes. And if one asks which of the parties, the workman or the employers should suffer from this inherent evidential difficulty, the answer as a matter in policy or justice should be that it is the creator of the risk who, ex hypothesi, must be taken to have foreseen the possibility of damage, who should bear its consequences.

There are analogies in this field of industrial disease. In cases concerned with pneumoconiosis, the courts faced with a similar, although not identical, evidential gap, have bridged it by having regard to the risk situation of the pursuer ... [Discussion of *Bonnington Castings* and various other dust disease cases followed] ...

The present factual situation has its differences: the default here consisted not in adding a material quantity to the accumulation of injurious particles but by failure to take a step which materially increased the risk that the dust already present would cause injury. And I must say that, at least in the present case, to bridge the evidential gap by inference seems to me something of a fiction, since it was precisely this inference which the medical expert declined to make. But I find in the cases quoted an analogy which suggests the conclusion that, in the absence of proof that the culpable condition had, in the result, no effect, the employers should be liable for an injury, squarely within the risk which they created and that they, not the pursuer, should suffer the consequence of the impossibility, foreseeably inherent in the nature of his injury, of segregating the precise consequence of their default.

I would allow this appeal.

[13.100] **Notes&Questions**

1. Since *McGhee* was decided in 1972 the House of Lords has re-visited the question in three key cases: *Hotson v East Berkshire Area Health Authority* [1987] AC 750, extracted at [13.120]; *Wilsher v Essex Area Health Authority* [1988] AC 1074; and *Fairchild v Glenhaven Funeral Services Ltd* [2003] 1 AC 32. In both *Hotson* and *Wilsher*, the House reversed awards in favour of the claimant because of the plaintiff's failure to prove causation, demonstrating a desire to confine and/or curtail *McGhee*. *Fairchild* is extracted below.
2. In *Wilsher v Essex Area Health Authority* [1987] QB 730 (CA), the English Court of Appeal extended the *McGhee* principle by finding for the infant plaintiff in circumstances where the defendant's negligence had materially increased an existing risk of injury of blindness (RLF) but was only one of a number of possible causes of the injury. The decision was overturned on appeal to the House of Lords [1988] AC 1074. The subsequent House of Lords decision in *Fairchild* [Lord Bingham of Cornhill at

[22]] accepted the views of the dissenting judgment of Browne-Wilkinson V-C in the Court of Appeal in *Wilsher* as setting out the correct approach. Browne-Wilkinson V-C said:

> To apply the principle in *McGhee v National Coal Board* to the present case would constitute an extension of that principle. In *McGhee* ... There was only one possible agent which could have caused the dermatitis, viz brick dust, and there was no doubt that the dermatitis from which he suffered was caused by that brick dust. In the present case the question is different. There are a number of different agents which could have caused the RLF. ... The defendants failed to take reasonable precautions to prevent one of the possible causative agents (eg excess oxygen) from causing RLF. But no one can tell in this case whether excess oxygen did or did not cause or contribute to the RLF suffered by the plaintiff. The plaintiff's RLF may have been caused by some completely different agent or agents, eg hypercarbia, intraventricular haemorrhage, apnoea or patent ductus arteriosus. In addition to oxygen, each of those conditions has been implicated as a possible cause of RLF. This baby suffered from each of those conditions at various times in the first two months of his life. There is no satisfactory evidence that excess oxygen is more likely than any of those other four candidates to have caused RLF in this baby. To my mind, the occurrence of RLF following a failure to take a necessary precaution to prevent excess oxygen causing RLF provides no evidence and raises no presumption that it was excess oxygen rather than one or more of the four other possible agents which caused or contributed to RLF in this case. The position, to my mind, is wholly different from that in McGhee ... In such a case, I can see the common sense, if not the logic, of holding that, in the absence of any other evidence, the failure to take the precaution caused or contributed to the dermatitis. To the extent that certain members of the House of Lords decided the question on inferences from evidence or presumptions, I do not consider that the present case falls within their reasoning. A failure to take preventive measures against one out of five possible causes is no evidence as to which of those five caused the injury.

The House of Lords reversed the Court of Appeal awards in favour of the claimant in both *Hotson* (see [13.120]) and *Wilsher*. They made it plain in *Wilsher* that *McGhee* was not to be taken as having established a rule that the burden of proof shifts to defendants in such cases.

Causation in conditions of uncertainty

Fairchild v Glenhaven

[13.105] *Fairchild v Glenhaven Funeral Services Ltd* [2003] 1 AC 32 House of Lords

(footnotes omitted)

[Three plaintiffs contracted mesothelioma after being exposed to asbestos by successive employers. The deficiencies in medical understanding of the disease process are summarised at the start of the extract. The plaintiffs lost at trial and again in the Court of Appeal, based on their inability to prove causation. The House of Lords unanimously allowed the appeal, constructing a narrowly confined exception to the normal rules of causation. Liability was imposed for conduct by the employers which materially increased the risk of disease, consistent with its earlier decision in *McGhee v National Coal Board*, see [13.95].]

LORD BINGHAM OF CORNHILL: [2] The essential question underlying the appeals may be accurately expressed in this way. If (1) C was employed at different times and for differing periods by both A and B, and (2) A and B were both subject to a duty to take reasonable care or to take all practicable measures to prevent C inhaling asbestos dust because of the known risk that asbestos dust (if inhaled) might cause a mesothelioma, and (3) both A and B were in breach of that duty in relation

Fairchild v Glenhaven cont.

to C during the periods of C's employment by each of them with the result that during both periods C inhaled excessive quantities of asbestos dust, and (4) C is found to be suffering from a mesothelioma, and (5) any cause of C's mesothelioma other than the inhalation of asbestos dust at work can be effectively discounted, but (6) C cannot (because of the current limits of human science) prove, on the balance of probabilities, that his mesothelioma was the result of his inhaling asbestos dust during his employment by A or during his employment by B or during his employment by A and B taken together, is C entitled to recover damages against either A or B or against both A and B? To this question (not formulated in these terms) the Court of Appeal (Brooke, Latham and Kay LJJ), in a reserved judgment of the court ([2001] EWCA Civ 1881, [2002] 1 WLR 1052), gave a negative answer. It did so because, applying the conventional "but for" test of tortious liability, it could not be held that C had proved against A that his mesothelioma would probably not have occurred but for the breach of duty by A, nor against B that his mesothelioma would probably not have occurred but for the breach of duty by B, nor against A and B that his mesothelioma would probably not have occurred but for the breach of duty by both A and B together. So C failed against both A and B. The crucial issue on appeal is whether, in the special circumstances of such a case, principle, authority or policy requires or justifies a modified approach to proof of causation ...

[7] From about the 1960s, it became widely known that exposure to asbestos dust and fibres could give rise not only to asbestosis and other pulmonary diseases, but also to the risk of developing a mesothelioma. This is a malignant tumour, usually of the pleura, sometimes of the peritoneum. In the absence of occupational exposure to asbestos dust it is a very rare tumour indeed, afflicting no more than about one person in a million per year. But the incidence of the tumour among those occupationally exposed to asbestos dust is about 1,000 times greater than in the general population, and there are some 1,500 cases reported annually. It is a condition which may be latent for many years, usually for 30-40 years or more; development of the condition may take as short a period as ten years, but it is thought that that is the period which elapses between the mutation of the first cell and the manifestation of symptoms of the condition. It is invariably fatal, and death usually occurs within one to two years of the condition being diagnosed. The mechanism by which a normal mesothelial cell is transformed into a mesothelioma cell is not known ... It is not known what level of exposure to asbestos dust and fibre can be tolerated without significant risk of developing a mesothelioma, but it is known that those living in urban environments (although without occupational exposure) inhale large numbers of asbestos fibres without developing a mesothelioma. It is accepted that the risk of developing a mesothelioma increases in proportion to the quantity of asbestos dust and fibres inhaled: the greater the quantity of dust and fibre inhaled, the greater the risk. But the condition may be caused by a single fibre, or a few fibres, or many fibres: medical opinion holds none of these possibilities to be more probable than any other, and the condition once caused is not aggravated by further exposure ... It is on this rock of uncertainty, reflecting the point to which medical science has so far advanced, that the three claims were rejected by the Court of Appeal and by two of the three trial judges.

Principle

...[8] In a personal injury action based on negligence or breach of statutory duty the claimant seeks to establish a breach by the defendant of a duty owed to the claimant, which has caused him damage. For the purposes of analysis, and for the purpose of pleading, proving and resolving the claim, lawyers find it convenient to break the claim into its constituent elements: the duty, the breach, the damage and the causal connection between the breach and the damage. In the generality of personal injury actions, it is of course true that the claimant is required to discharge the burden of showing that the breach of which he complains caused the damage for which he claims and to do so by showing that but for the breach he would not have suffered the damage.

Fairchild v Glenhaven cont.

[9] The issue in these appeals does not concern the general validity and applicability of that requirement, which is not in question, but is whether in special circumstances such as those in these cases there should be any variation or relaxation of it. The overall object of tort law is to define cases in which the law may justly hold one party liable to compensate another. Are these such cases? A and B owed C a duty to protect C against a risk of a particular and very serious kind. They failed to perform that duty. As a result the risk eventuated and C suffered the very harm against which it was the duty of A and B to protect him. Had there been only one tortfeasor, C would have been entitled to recover, but because the duty owed to him was broken by two tortfeasors and not only one, he is held to be entitled to recover against neither, because of his inability to prove what is scientifically unprovable. If the mechanical application of generally accepted rules leads to such a result, there must be room to question the appropriateness of such an approach in such a case.

[10] In *March v E & M H Stramare Pty Ltd* (1991) 171 CLR 506 at 508, Mason CJ, sitting in the High Court of Australia, did not "accept that the 'but for' (causa sine qua non) test ever was or now should become the exclusive test of causation in negligence cases" ...

[12] [His Lordship then referred to recent authority that the Court is not required to adopt a mechanical approach to causation issues and continued:] ...

[13] I do not therefore consider that the House is acting contrary to principle in reviewing the applicability of the conventional test of causation to cases such as the present. Indeed, it would seem to me contrary to principle to insist on application of a rule which appeared, if it did, to yield unfair results ...

Authority

[14] [There followed a detailed discussion of *Bonnington Castings Ltd v Wardlaw*, along with many other similar cases, and an exhaustive review of *McGhee*] ...

[21] This detailed review of *McGhee's* case permits certain conclusions to be drawn. First, the House was deciding a question of law. Lord Reid expressly said so. The other opinions, save perhaps that of Lord Kilbrandon, cannot be read as decisions of fact or as orthodox applications of settled law. Secondly, the question of law was whether, on the facts of the case as found, a pursuer who could not show that the defender's breach had probably caused the damage of which he complained could nonetheless succeed. Thirdly, it was not open to the House to draw a factual inference that the breach probably had caused the damage: such an inference was expressly contradicted by the medical experts on both sides; and once that evidence had been given the crux of the argument before the Lord Ordinary and the First Division and the House was whether, since the pursuer could not prove that the breach had probably made a material contribution to his contracting dermatitis, it was enough to show that the breach had increased the risk of his contracting it. Fourthly, it was expressly held by three members of the House ([1972] 3 All ER 1008 at 1011, 1014, 1018, [1973] 1 WLR 1 at 5, 8, 12-13 per Lord Reid, Lord Simon and Lord Salmon respectively) that in the circumstances no distinction was to be drawn between making a material contribution to causing the disease and materially increasing the risk of the pursuer contracting it. Thus the proposition expressly rejected by the Lord Ordinary, the Lord President and Lord Migdale was expressly accepted by a majority of the House and must be taken to represent the ratio of the decision, closely tied though it was to the special facts on which it was based. Fifthly, recognising that the pursuer faced an insuperable problem of proof if the orthodox test of causation was applied, but regarding the case as one in which justice demanded a remedy for the pursuer, a majority of the House adapted the orthodox test to meet the particular case ...

[A discussion of *Wilsher v Essex* followed, see [13.100] Note 2.] It is plain, in my respectful opinion, that the House was right to allow the defendants' appeal in *Wilsher*'s case, for the reasons which the Vice-Chancellor had given and which the House approved. It is one thing to treat an increase of risk as

Fairchild v Glenhaven cont.

equivalent to the making of a material contribution where a single noxious agent is involved, but quite another where any one of a number of noxious agents may equally probably have caused the damage. The decision of the Court of Appeal did indeed involve an extension of the *McGhee* principle, as Mustill LJ recognised ([1986] 3 All ER 801 at 829, [1987] QB 730 at 771-772) ...

[30] Cases decided in the High Court of Australia do not disclose a clear ratio on which the appellants were able to rely before the House, although they drew attention to dicta which were helpful to them. For example, in *Chappel v Hart* (1998) 195 CLR 232 at 244 (para 27) McHugh J said, in a passage reminiscent of *McGhee's* case, although without referring to that case:

> Before the defendant will be held responsible for the plaintiff's injury, the plaintiff must prove that the defendant's conduct materially contributed to the plaintiff suffering that injury. In the absence of a statute or undertaking to the contrary, therefore, it would seem logical to hold a person causally liable for a wrongful act or omission only when it increases the risk of injury to another person. If a wrongful act or omission results in an increased risk of injury to the plaintiff and that risk eventuates, the defendant's conduct has materially contributed to the injury that the plaintiff suffers whether or not other factors also contributed to that injury occurring. If, however, the defendant's conduct does not increase the risk of injury to the plaintiff, the defendant cannot be said to have materially contributed to the injury suffered by the plaintiff. That being so, whether the claim is in contract or tort, the fact that the risk eventuated at a particular time or place by reason of the conduct of the defendant does not itself materially contribute to the plaintiff's injury unless the fact of that particular time or place increased the risk of the injury occurring.

In that case McHugh J dissented on the facts but in *Naxakis v Western General Hospital* (1999) 197 CLR 269 both Gaudron J (at 279 (para 31)) and Callinan J (at 312 (para 127)) quoted what he had said with approval. In Canada, Sopinka J, speaking for the Supreme Court in *Snell v Farrell* (1990) 72 DLR (4th) 289 at 299 said:

> I have examined the alternatives arising out of the *McGhee* case. They were that the plaintiff simply prove that the defendant created a risk that the injury which occurred would occur. Or, what amounts to the same thing, that the defendant has the burden of disproving causation. If I were convinced that defendants who have a substantial connection to the injury were escaping liability because plaintiffs cannot prove causation under currently applied principles, I would not hesitate to adopt one of these alternatives. In my opinion, however, properly applied, the principles relating to causation are adequate to the task. Adoption of either of the proposed alternatives would have the effect of compensating plaintiffs where a substantial connection between the injury and the defendant's conduct is absent. Reversing the burden of proof may be justified where two defendants negligently fire in the direction of the plaintiff and then by their tortious conduct destroy the means of proof at his disposal. In such a case it is clear that the injury was not caused by neutral conduct. It is quite a different matter to compensate a plaintiff by reversing the burden of proof for an injury that may very well be due to factors unconnected to the defendant and not the fault of anyone.

[31] There is a small but important body of authority on the problem of attribution in mesothelioma cases where the plaintiff has been exposed to asbestos during employment by more than one employer. *Bendix Mintex Pty Ltd v Barnes* (1997) 42 NSWLR 307 was such a case. A majority of the Court of Appeal of New South Wales held against the plaintiff on the causation issue, relying on Wilsher's case among much other authority. Stein JA dissented, citing with approval the following passage from the judgment of King CJ in *Birkholtz v -RJ Gilbertson Pty Ltd* (1985) 38 SASR 121 at 130:

> ... the law's view of causation is less concerned with logical and philosophical considerations than with the need to produce a just result to the parties involved. Where a defendant is under a legal duty to take precautions to protect the plaintiff from the risk of contracting disease, and, by omitting those precautions he substantially increases the risk of the plaintiff

> contracting that disease, the law treats that increase in risk as a sufficient basis, in the absence of evidence showing how the infection occurred, for an inference that the omission of the precautions materially contributed to the contracting of the disease. Justice requires such an approach to the problem of causation and it is the approach which was taken by the House of Lords in *McGhee v National Coal Board*.

The majority decision in the *Bendix* case was followed in *Wallaby Grip (BAE) Pty Ltd v Macleay Area Health Service* (1998) 17 NSWCCR 355. A different result was reached in *EM Baldwin & Son Pty Ltd v Plane* (1999) Aust Torts Reports 81-499, but on different medical evidence. A different view of the law was also expressed in *Rutherford v Owens-Illinois Inc* (1997) 67 Cal Rptr 2d 16. In a judgment with which the Chief Justice and all save one member of the Supreme Court of California concurred, Baxter J observed (at 19):

> Proof of causation in such cases will always present inherent practical difficulties, given the long latency period of asbestos-related disease, and the occupational settings that commonly exposed the worker to multiple forms and brands of asbestos products with varying degrees of toxicity. In general, however, no insuperable barriers prevent an asbestos-related cancer plaintiff from demonstrating that exposure to the defendant's asbestos products was, in reasonable medical probability, a substantial factor in causing or contributing to his risk of developing cancer. We conclude that plaintiffs are required to prove no more than this. In particular, they need not prove with medical exactitude that fibers from a particular defendant's asbestos-containing products were those, or among those, that actually began the cellular process of malignancy.

[32] This survey shows, as would be expected, that though the problem underlying cases such as the present is universal the response to it is not. Hence the plethora of decisions given in different factual contexts. Hence also the intensity of academic discussion, exemplified by the articles of the late Professor Fleming (*Probabilistic Causation in Tort Law* 68 *Canadian Bar Review*, No 4, December 1989, 661) and Professor Robertson ("The Common Sense of Cause in Fact" (1996-1997) 75 *Tex L Rev* 1765) … But it appears that in most of the jurisdictions considered the problem of attribution would not, on facts such as those of the present cases, be a fatal objection to a plaintiff's claim. Whether by treating an increase in risk as equivalent to a material contribution, or by putting a burden on the defendant, or by enlarging the ordinary approach to acting in concert, or on more general grounds influenced by policy considerations, most jurisdictions would, it seems, afford a remedy to the plaintiff. Development of the law in this country cannot of course depend on a head-count of decisions and codes adopted in other countries around the world, often against a background of different rules and traditions. The law must be developed coherently, in accordance with principle, so as to serve, even-handedly, the ends of justice. If, however, a decision is given in this country which offends one's basic sense of justice, and if consideration of international sources suggests that a different and more acceptable decision would be given in most other jurisdictions, whatever their legal tradition, this must prompt anxious review of the decision in question. In a shrinking world (in which the employees of asbestos companies may work for those companies in any one or more of several countries) there must be some virtue in uniformity of outcome whatever the diversity of approach in reaching that outcome.

Policy

[33] The present appeals raise an obvious and inescapable clash of policy considerations. On the one hand are the considerations powerfully put by the Court of Appeal ([2002] 1 WLR 1052 at [103]) which considered the claimants' argument to be not only illogical but:

> also susceptible of unjust results. It may impose liability for the whole of an insidious disease on an employer with whom the claimant was employed for quite a short time in a long working life, when the claimant is wholly unable to prove on the balance of probabilities that that period of employment had any causative relationship with the inception of the disease. This is far too weighty an edifice to build on the slender foundations of *McGhee v National*

Fairchild v Glenhaven cont.

> *Coal Board*, and Lord Bridge has told us in *Wilsher v Essex Area Health Authority* that McGhee established no new principle of law at all. If we were to accede to the claimants' arguments, we would be distorting the law to accommodate the exigencies of a very hard case. We would be yielding to a contention that all those who have suffered injury after being exposed to a risk of that injury from which someone else should have protected them should be able to recover compensation even when they are quite unable to prove who was the culprit. In a quite different context Lord Steyn has recently said in [*White v Chief Constable of the South Yorkshire Police* [1999] 1 All ER 1 at 30, [1999] 2 AC 455 at 491] that our tort system sometimes results in imperfect justice, but it is the best the common law can do.

The Court of Appeal had in mind that in each of the cases (*Wardlaw's*, *Nicholson's*, *Gardiner's* and *McGhee's* cases) ... there was only one employer involved. Thus there was a risk that the defendant might be held liable for acts for which he should not be held legally liable but no risk that he would be held liable for damage which (whether legally liable or not) he had not caused. The crux of cases such as the present, if the appellants' argument is upheld, is that an employer may be held liable for damage he has not caused. The risk is the greater where all the employers potentially liable are not before the court. This is so on the facts of each of the three appeals before the House, and is always likely to be so given the long latency of this condition and the likelihood that some employers potentially liable will have gone out of business or disappeared during that period. It can properly be said to be unjust to impose liability on a party who has not been shown, even on a balance of probabilities, to have caused the damage complained of. On the other hand, there is a strong policy argument in favour of compensating those who have suffered grave harm, at the expense of their employers who owed them a duty to protect them against that very harm and failed to do so, when the harm can only have been caused by breach of that duty and when science does not permit the victim accurately to attribute, as between several employers, the precise responsibility for the harm he has suffered. I am of opinion that such injustice as may be involved in imposing liability on a duty-breaking employer in these circumstances is heavily outweighed by the injustice of denying redress to a victim. Were the law otherwise, an employer exposing his employee to asbestos dust could obtain complete immunity against mesothelioma (but not asbestosis) claims by employing only those who had previously been exposed to excessive quantities of asbestos dust. Such a result would reflect no credit on the law. It seems to me, as it did to Lord Wilberforce in *McGhee's* case [1972] 3 All ER 1008 at 1013, [1973] 1 WLR 1 at 7, that:

> the employers should be liable for an injury, squarely within the risk which they created and that they, not the pursuer, should suffer the consequence of the impossibility, foreseeably inherent in the nature of his injury, of segregating the precise consequence of their default.

Conclusion

[34] To the question posed in [2], above, I would answer that where conditions (1)-(6) are satisfied C is entitled to recover against both A and B. That conclusion is in my opinion consistent with principle, and also with authority (properly understood). Where those conditions are satisfied, it seems to me just and in accordance with common sense to treat the conduct of A and B in exposing C to a risk to which he should not have been exposed as making a material contribution to the contracting by C of a condition against which it was the duty of A and B to protect him. I consider that this conclusion is fortified by the wider jurisprudence reviewed above. Policy considerations weigh in favour of such a conclusion. It is a conclusion which follows even if either A or B is not before the court. It was not suggested in argument that C's entitlement against either A or B should be for any sum less than the full compensation to which C is entitled, although A and B could of course seek contribution against each other or any other employer liable in respect of the same damage in the ordinary way. No argument on apportionment was addressed to the House. I would in conclusion emphasise that my opinion is directed to cases in which each of the conditions specified in (1)-(6) of [2], above is satisfied and to no other case. It would be unrealistic to suppose that the principle here affirmed will not over

time be the subject of incremental and analogical development. Cases seeking to develop the principle must be decided when and as they arise. For the present, I think it unwise to decide more than is necessary to resolve these three appeals which, for all the foregoing reasons, I concluded should be allowed.

[35] For reasons given above, I cannot accept the view (considered in the opinion of my noble and learned friend Lord Hutton) that the decision in *McGhee's* case was based on the drawing of a factual inference. Nor, in my opinion, was the decision based on the drawing of a legal inference. Whether, in certain limited and specific circumstances, a legal inference is drawn or a different legal approach is taken to the proof of causation, may not make very much practical difference. But Lord Wilberforce, in one of the passages of his opinion in *McGhee's* case quoted in [20], above, wisely deprecated resort to fictions and it seems to me preferable, in the interests of transparency, that the courts' response to the special problem presented by cases such as these should be stated explicitly. I prefer to recognise that the ordinary approach to proof of causation is varied than to resort to the drawing of legal inferences inconsistent with the proven facts.

[13.110] **Notes&Questions**

1. The Negligence Review Panel endorsed the "material contribution to harm" and the "material contribution to risk" principles saying:

> ... in certain circumstances it may be appropriate to "bridge the evidentiary gap" by allowing proof that negligent conduct materially contributed to harm or the risk of harm to satisfy the requirement of proof of factual causation ... this would be considered to be fair and reasonable. The decisions in *Bonnington Castings* and *Fairchild* support this conclusion, as does the practice of the New South Wales Dust Disease Tribunal ... The major difficulty ... is to define those cases in which the normal requirements of proof of causation should be relaxed. ... this is a normative issue that depends ultimately on a value judgment about how the costs of injuries and death should be allocated. The Panel believes that detailed criteria for determining this issue should be left for common law development. (*Review of the Law of Negligence, Final Report* (Commonwealth of Australia, Canberra, 2002), paras 7.31-7.33)

2. Cases of occupational exposure to asbestos are normally dealt with in New South Wales in the Dust Diseases Tribunal. The principles to be applied in asbestos cases were discussed and summarised in eight points in *Wallaby Grip (BAE) Pty Ltd (in Liq) v Macleay Area Health Service* (1998) 17 NSWCCR 355 (CA). It was held inter alia that one or more defendants may be liable if each had negligently exposed the plaintiff to a risk of contracting a fatal disease. Where more than one defendant was involved, liability was established if their several acts caused or materially contributed to the onset of mesothelioma. A material increase in the risk of injury by a defendant is not legally equated with a material contribution to the injury. However, a court might infer causation in some circumstances on proof of material increase in the risk by the defendant. The Negligence Review Panel expressly approved these principles.
3. For an analysis of *Fairchild* see J Stapleton, "Lords A'leaping Evidentiary Gaps" (2002) 10 *Torts Law Journal* 276. The High Court has yet to explicitly follow *Fairchild* although there is dicta supporting this approach, see [13.90].

Loss of chance

[13.115] The following cases illustrate the difficulties caused in loss of chance cases. Many concern breaches of a duty to warn, where the loss complained of is loss of a chance to take a different course of action or achieve a better outcome. A loss of chance such as a lost opportunity to sue for an injury because the case has become statute barred (*Bennett v Minister for Community Welfare* (1992) 176 CLR 408) or lost commercial opportunity (*Sellars v Adelaide Petroleum NL* (1994) 179 CLR 332) is treated as loss of an asset that has value. The position is different with regard to loss of a chance of a better medical outcome flowing from a medical practitioner's negligent delay in diagnosis or failure to warn. The critical question is whether loss of chance could be accepted as a compensable type of harm. The plaintiff in *Hotson* inevitably lost because, in view of the trial judge's findings, he was unable to meet the requirement of proving causation on the balance of probabilities (more than 50/50). Had the case been decided on loss of chance, the plaintiff would have succeeded on the evidence in proving harm, and the issue would then have been the quantification of his lost chance (that is, assessment of damages). The significance of this is that proof of injury leading to a finding of liability must meet the "balance of probabilities" standard. *Hotson* was the first significant English case to consider the issue of loss of chance in tort.

Hotson v East Berkshire Area Health

[13.120] *Hotson v East Berkshire Area Health Authority* [1987] 1 AC 750 House of Lords

(footnotes omitted)

[The plaintiff, a 13 year old boy, fell 12 feet (3.66m) from a tree and fractured his left hip. The hospital failed to diagnose the fracture for five days and he suffered an avascular necrosis with the certainty of osteoarthritis developing. The Health Authority admitted the hospital had been negligent but argued that there was a 75 per cent chance that the osteoarthritis would have developed even if the fracture had been correctly treated. With prompt diagnosis, there would have been a 25 per cent chance of avoiding the necrosis and future osteoarthritis. The trial judge and Court of Appeal (unanimously) assessed damages for the loss of the 25 per cent chance of full recovery. This was overturned on appeal, the House of Lords holding that the claimant must prove on the balance of probabilities that the negligent delay materially contributed to the osteoarthritis and necrosis. The case is extracted as to whether there could be recovery for loss of a chance of a better outcome.]

LORD BRIDGE OF HARWICH: 782 Your Lordships were invited to approach the appeal more broadly [than causation] and to decide whether, in a claim for damages for personal injury, it can ever be appropriate, where the cause of the injury is unascertainable and all the plaintiff can show is a statistical chance which is less than even that, but for the defendant's breach of duty, he would not have suffered the injury, to award him a proportionate fraction of the full damages appropriate to compensate for the injury as the measure of damages for the lost chance.

There is a superficially attractive analogy between the principle applied in such cases as *Chaplin v Hicks* [1911] 2 KB 786, [1911-13] All ER Rep 224 (award of damages for breach of contract assessed by reference to the lost chance of securing valuable employment if the contract had been performed) and *Kitchen v Royal Air Forces Association* [1958] 2 All ER 241, [1958] 1 WLR 563 (damages for solicitors' negligence assessed by reference to the lost chance of prosecuting a successful civil action) and the principle of awarding damages for the lost chance of avoiding personal injury or, in medical negligence cases, for the lost chance of a better medical result which might have been achieved by prompt diagnosis and correct treatment. I think there are formidable difficulties in the way of accepting the analogy. But I do not see this appeal as a suitable occasion for reaching a settled conclusion as to whether the analogy can ever be applied.

Hotson v East Berkshire Area Health cont.

As I have said, there was in this case an inescapable issue of causation first to be resolved. But if the plaintiff had proved on a balance of probabilities that the authority's negligent failure to diagnose and treat his injury promptly had materially contributed to the development of avascular necrosis, I know of no principle of English law which would have entitled the authority to a discount from the full measure of damage to reflect the chance that, even given prompt treatment, avascular necrosis might well still have developed. The decisions of this House in *Bonnington Castings Ltd v Wardlaw* [1956] 1 All ER 615, [1956] AC 613 and *McGhee v National Coal Board* [1972] 3 All ER 1008, [1973] 1 WLR 1 give no support to such a view.

I would allow the appeal to the extent of reducing the damages awarded to the plaintiff by £ 11,500 and the amount of any interest on that sum which is included in the award ...

LORD MACKAY OF CLASHFERN: 783 My Lords, I have had the advantage of reading in draft the speeches prepared by my noble and learned friends Lord Bridge and Lord Ackner. I agree with them that this appeal should be allowed for the reasons which they have given ...

When counsel for the plaintiff was invited to say what he meant by a chance he said that in relation to the facts of this case as found by the judge what was meant by a chance was that if 100 people had suffered the same injury as the plaintiff 75 of them would have developed avascular necrosis of the whole femoral head and 25 would not. This, he said, was an asset possessed by the plaintiff when he arrived at the authority's hospital on 26 April 1977. It was this asset which counsel submits the plaintiff lost in consequence of the negligent failure of the authority to diagnose his injury properly until 1 May 1977.

...

In the circumstances of this case the probable effect of delay in treatment was determined by the state of facts existing when the plaintiff was first presented to the hospital. It is not, in my opinion, correct to say that on arrival at the hospital he had a 25 per cent chance of recovery. If insufficient blood vessels were left intact by the fall he had no prospect of avoiding complete avascular necrosis whereas if sufficient blood vessels were left intact on the judge's findings no further damage to the blood supply would have resulted if he had been given immediate treatment, and he would not have suffered the avascular necrosis.

As I have said, the fundamental question of fact to be answered in this case related to a point in time before the negligent failure to treat began. It must, therefore, be a matter of past fact. It did not raise any question of what might have been the situation in a hypothetical state of facts. To this problem the words of Lord Diplock in *Mallett v McMonagle* [1969] 2 All ER 178 at 191, [1970] AC 166 at 176 apply:

> In determining what did happen in the past a court decides on the balance of probabilities. Anything that is more probable than not it treats as certain.

In this respect this case is the same, in principle, as any other in which the state of facts existing before alleged negligence came into play has to be determined ...

On the other hand, I consider that it would be unwise in the present case to lay it down as a rule that a plaintiff could never succeed by proving loss of a chance in a medical negligence case. In *McGhee v National Coal Board* [1972] 3 All ER 1008, [1973] 1 WLR 1 this House held that where it was proved that the failure to provide washing facilities for the pursuer at the end of his shift had materially increased the risk that he would contract dermatitis it was proper to hold that the failure to provide such facilities was a cause to a material extent of his contracting dermatitis and thus entitled him to damages from his employers ... Material increase of the risk of contraction of dermatitis is equivalent to material decrease in the chance of escaping dermatitis ...

I think it unwise to do more than say that unless and until this House departs from the decision in *McGhee* your Lordships cannot affirm the proposition that in no circumstances can evidence of loss of

Hotson v East Berkshire Area Health cont.

a chance resulting from the breach of a duty of care found a successful claim of damages, although there was no suggestion that the House regarded such a chance as an asset in any sense.

Chappel v Hart

[13.125] *Chappel v Hart* (1998) 195 CLR 232 High Court of Australia

(footnotes omitted)

[The plaintiff suffered from a deteriorating condition of the throat, which would have eventually caused her to lose her voice if left untreated. During an operation to correct the condition her oesophagus was perforated. Infection set in and she lost her voice. As the risk of perforation was inherent in this type of surgery it was held that the operation was performed with "skill and care" and not negligently. The case then turned on failure to warn. The defendant doctor argued that there was no causal connection between his failure to warn of the risk of this complication and the plaintiff's damage, and that the plaintiff's loss was a loss of chance. Such a chance was valueless in the circumstances, he argued, since the loss of voice would have occurred eventually without the operation. Alternatively, the infection was a novus actus interveniens.]

KIRBY J: 274 *Valuing a lost chance*: A further way in which, in some circumstances, the difficulties of causation for a plaintiff are alleviated is by treating the plaintiff's loss as a "loss of a chance". In cases in which this approach is permissible, it may allow evaluation of the plaintiff's loss in terms of comparing the chances of suffering harm (given the breach which has occurred) against those that would have existed (if the breach is hypothesised away). In *CES v Superclinics (Aust)* Pty Ltd I indicated my attraction to this approach as a more rational and just way of calculating damages caused by established medical negligence. It is clearly laid down by the authority of this Court that, in some circumstances, a plaintiff may recover the value of a loss of a chance caused by a wrongdoer's act or omission. The approach also has some judicial support in the context of medical negligence in England, Canada and the United States. A number of commentators favour this approach because of the failure of orthodox reasoning to do justice to some patients' losses and because it invites a more empirical calculation of loss, with the use of statistics which might offer outcomes that are more accurate and fair to all concerned. On the other hand, the weight of judicial opinion in England and Canada and some academic writing appears to be critical of the application of the loss of a chance theory to cases of medical negligence. In part this is because, where medical negligence is alleged, "destiny ... [has] taken its course", arguably making an analysis by reference to chance inappropriate or unnecessary in the view of the critics of this approach. Alternatively, the loss of a chance calculation has been criticised on the ground that it would discard commonsense, undermine the plaintiff's onus of proving the case and submit the law to the "paralysis" of statistical abstractions ...

HAYNE J: 288 [Dissenting] ... I deal first with the contention that the failure to warn deprived the respondent of a chance to seek better treatment.

I do not think it necessary or appropriate to analyse this case as one of loss of a chance. There are several reasons why that is so.

First, the case was not put in this way at trial. The damage which the respondent alleged that she had suffered was the physical damage to her voice and the economic consequences of that damage. She did not seek to make any loss of chance case at trial.

Secondly, the chance which it is now said that the respondent lost is the chance to engage a better doctor. She said in evidence that she "would have wanted the most experienced person, with a record and reputation in the field". But it was never part of the respondent's case that the appellant should have told her to seek a better doctor; it was never suggested that there had been some negligent failure by the appellant to refer the respondent to another doctor. Moreover, it is important to bear steadily in mind that it was not said that the appellant had performed the procedure negligently. Thus it was never suggested that she was deprived of the opportunity to have the procedure performed properly – only that had she been advised of the risks to her voice she (of her own volition) would have sought out the "most experienced" practitioner in the field.

I do not consider that the appellant should be held responsible for the loss of that chance. No doubt it may be said that the failure to warn led to this result – in the sense that "but for" the negligent failure to advise, the respondent would have pursued the course that she described in her evidence – but why should the law provide for compensation for loss of that chance and what is it that she lost?

The law of negligence is intended to compensate those who are injured as a result of departures from standards of reasonable care. It is not intended to compensate those who have received reasonable care but who may not have had the best available care. To hold that the appellant's failure to warn the respondent of the risks of the operation caused her to lose the chance of the best available care would depart from that fundamental premise of the law of negligence.

Further, what is it that is lost when it is said that the respondent lost a chance of better treatment? It is said that by going to the best doctor in the field she could have reduced the chance of an adverse outcome of the operation. She could not, however, have eliminated those risks. How then is this alteration in the size of the risks to be measured and how is the loss of it to be compensated?

Leaving aside whatever may have been the difficulty of assembling evidence that bore upon the point (and those difficulties may have been very large) what kind of enquiry would have to be undertaken? Presumably the comparison to be made would be a comparison between the risks if the procedure was carried out by the appellant and the risks if the best available doctor carried it out. But how would that be measured? Any observer of skilled professionals at work knows that some are better than others but it is equally obvious that the performance of even the best is subject to variation. Is the comparison to be made a comparison with the best performer doing his or her best work? But how is that to be demonstrated? It is often enough difficult to identify what *reasonable* care requires; proof of what would be the *best* available care would be harder. And why should the law of negligence concern itself with more than what reasonable conduct would require?

Further, the risks of which we are speaking are risks that are very small. If the risk of disaster is assessed as being (say) one in 100 if the procedure is performed by the appellant but one in 200 if performed by another, what use is to be made of that data? If we are to speak in the language of loss of chance, has the respondent lost the chance of a 99.5 per cent chance of successful operation in return for a 99 per cent chance? Has she, that is, lost a 0.5 per cent chance of success? What is that worth? (The point is all the sharper if the comparison is between a one in 10,000 and a one in 20,000 chance.) Or is the relevant conclusion that the chances of disaster could have been halved?

Whichever description of the change in the risks is adopted, how does one assess the value of the chance that has been lost? It was suggested in the course of argument that it is reflected in the assessment of damages by discounting the damages otherwise allowed. But that invites attention to what are those damages that are to be discounted – is it, as the argument appeared to assume, the damages attributable to the physical consequences which the respondent suffered? That could be so only if the physical consequences which the respondent suffered were caused by the appellant's negligence.

All of these considerations point to the conclusion that the loss of chance analysis is flawed and should not be adopted. I therefore need not (and do not) express any view on the difficult questions that arise where a plaintiff claims damages for negligence, as opposed to contract, and contends that the damage suffered is the loss of a chance ...

Chappel v Hart cont.

The respondent did not establish that she had suffered damage as a result of the appellant's negligence. The claim having been framed in breach of contract and breach having been established, she is, of course, entitled to nominal damages but, in my view, to no more. I would allow the appeal.

[The court held in favour of the plaintiff with Gaudron, Gummow and Kirby JJ in the majority. Gaudron and Kirby JJ based their reasoning on an analysis of the risk, whereas Gummow J based his conclusion on the failure to warn.]

[13.130] **Notes&Questions**

1. In *Rogers v Whitaker* (1992) 175 CLR 479, the operation performed on the plaintiff was elective, whereas in *Chappel v Hart* (1998) 195 CLR 232 the plaintiff would have been forced to have the surgery at some time. Why is this significant?
2. The extracts above from *Chappel* demonstrate the High Court's acceptance of loss of chance as a real and actionable loss. Consider the views expressed in *Chappel* by McHugh JJ below ([13.165]), where the case is again extracted in relation to failure to warn. What additional factors need to be established for loss of chance in failure to warn cases?
   If the foreseeable risk to Mrs Hart was the loss of an opportunity to undergo surgery at the hands of a more experienced surgeon, the duty would have been a duty to inform her that there were more experienced surgeons practising in the field (see Gaudron J at 239).
   No part of the relationship between the plaintiff and the defendant involved her being given the opportunity to seek a higher standard of care or better treatment from another surgeon or an opportunity to have the procedure carried out without perforation of the oesophagus (see McHugh J at 252).

Naxakis v Western General Hospital

[13.135] *Naxakis v Western General Hospital* (1999) 197 CLR 269 High Court of Australia

(footnotes omitted)

[The plaintiff, a 12 year old boy, was hit on the head with a vinyl schoolbag at school. He collapsed and was taken to hospital, where he was diagnosed as suffering from traumatic haemorrhage. He remained in hospital for nine days. Two days after his discharge he collapsed again. On this occasion an angiogram was performed, which revealed that the plaintiff had suffered from an aneurysmal bleed not traumatic haemorrhage. He sustained severe injuries from a burst aneurysm.]

GAUDRON J:

Loss of a Chance

277 It was contended for the appellant that, even if the evidence did not permit of a finding that, if an angiogram had been undertaken, surgery would have been performed in time to prevent the aneurysm from bursting, there was evidence upon which the jury could conclude that the appellant had lost a valuable chance, namely, the chance of successful surgery. In the view that I take of the evidence in this case, it is not strictly necessary to consider that further argument. However, as there must be a rehearing, it is appropriate that I express my view on the notion that, in a case such as the present, damages are recoverable for the loss of a chance.

Naxakis v Western General Hospital cont.

It is well settled that, where breach of contract results in the loss of a promised chance, that is an actual loss for which damages will be awarded "by reference to the degree of probabilities, or possibilities, inherent in the plaintiff's succeeding had the plaintiff been given the chance which the contract promised." So, too, damages may be recovered for a commercial opportunity that is lost in consequence of a breach of contract. And it was held in *Sellars v Adelaide Petroleum NL* [(1994) 179 CLR 332 at 348] that the loss of a commercial opportunity is "loss or damage" for the purposes of s 82(1) of the *Trade Practices Act 1974* (Cth). Moreover, there is no reason in principle why loss of a chance or commercial opportunity should not constitute damage for the purposes of the law of tort where no other loss is involved. However, different considerations apply where, as here, the risk eventuates and physical injury ensues.

In cases involving the failure to diagnose or treat a pre-existing condition, there is no philosophical or logical difficulty in viewing the loss sustained as the loss of a chance to undergo treatment which may have prevented some or all of the injuries or disabilities sustained. Indeed, in such cases, philosophical or logical analysis would lead to the conclusion that characterisation of the loss as the loss of a chance is strictly correct. It would also lead to the conclusion that the all or nothing approach involved in allowing damages for the actual harm suffered on the basis that it was more likely than not that the harm would have been prevented by proper treatment is, at best, rough justice.

It has been suggested that to allow compensation for the loss of chance would alleviate problems associated with proof of causation. There is, in my view, a tendency to exaggerate the difficulties associated with proof of causation, even in medical negligence cases. For the purposes of the allocation of legal responsibility, "[i]f a wrongful act or omission results in an increased risk of injury to the plaintiff and that risk eventuates, the defendant's conduct has materially contributed to the injury that the plaintiff suffers whether or not other factors also contributed to that injury occurring." And in that situation, the trier of fact – in this case, a jury – is entitled to conclude that the act or omission caused the injury in question unless the defendant establishes that the conduct had no effect at all or that the risk would have eventuated and resulted in the damage in question in any event.

The notion that, in cases of failure to diagnose or treat an existing condition, the loss suffered by the plaintiff is the loss of chance, rather than the injury or physical disability that eventuates, is essentially different from the approach that is traditionally adopted. On the traditional approach, the plaintiff must establish on the balance of probabilities that the failure caused the injury or disability suffered, whereas the lost chance approach predicates that he or she must establish only that it resulted in the loss of a chance that was of some value. As already indicated, it has been suggested that the lost chance approach avoids problems of proof of causation. However, it may be that if damages were to be awarded for the loss of a chance, the difficulties associated with proof of causation would simply reappear as difficulties in establishing the value of the chance in question.

Moreover, the lost chance approach is not one that necessarily works to the benefit of the individual plaintiff. If damages were to be awarded for the chance lost, rather than the actual injuries or disabilities suffered, consistency would require that damages be assessed according to the value of the chance, not the injury or disability. Thus, a chance which is 51 per cent or greater but less than 100 percent, must result in an award of damages less than would be the case if damages were awarded for the injury or disability which eventuates.

Additionally, the lost chance approach cannot easily be applied in conjunction with the traditional balance of probabilities approach. As already indicated, the lost chance approach requires proof that a valuable chance has been lost. A chance would have no value if the defendant could establish, on the balance of probabilities, that the pre-existing condition would have resulted in the injury or disability in question in any event. Thus, if proof on the balance of probabilities were also retained, damages for loss of a chance would be awarded only in those cases where the plaintiff cannot establish, on the

Naxakis v Western General Hospital cont.

balance of probabilities, that the risk would not have eventuated and the defendant cannot establish that it would. There is, thus, limited practical significance for an approach which allows for loss of a chance if the traditional approach is also retained.

There is a further difficulty in allowing damages for the loss of a chance in a case such as the present. Assessment of the value of the chance must depend either on speculation or statistical analysis. And in the case of statistics, there is the difficulty that a statistical chance is not the same as a personal chance. Thus, as was pointed out by Croom-Johnson LJ in *Hotson v East Berkshire Area Health Authority*:

> If it is proved statistically that 25 per cent of the population have a chance of recovery from a certain injury and 75 per cent do not, it does not mean that someone who suffers that injury and who does not recover from it has lost a 25 per cent chance. He may have lost nothing at all. What he has to do is prove that he was one of the 25 per cent and that his loss was caused by the defendant's negligence.

And as his Lordship also pointed out, if a plaintiff establishes that he was one of the 25 per cent who would have recovered if properly treated, his or her loss is not merely the loss of a chance, but the injury or disability that eventuated.

Finally, where the risk inherent in a pre-existing but undiagnosed or untreated condition eventuates, there is not simply the loss of a chance. Rather, the "factors bound up in the earlier chance have already played themselves out" and all that is in issue are past events "for which the cause is uncertain". At least, their cause is uncertain if philosophical or scientific notions are employed. However, that does not mean that their cause is uncertain in law. For the purpose of assigning legal responsibility, philosophical and scientific notions are put aside in favour of a common sense approach which allows that "breach of duty coupled with an [event] of the kind that might thereby be caused is enough to justify an inference, in the absence of any sufficient reason to the contrary, that in fact the [event] did occur owing to the act or omission amounting to the breach". For that reason, I am of the view that the notion that, in a case such as the present, a plaintiff can recover damages on the basis that what has been lost is a chance of successful treatment must be rejected.

CALLINAN J: 312 On the evidence here the jury were entitled to hold that the failure, the treating doctor's omission either to undertake an angiogram or the failure to give any consideration to the undertaking of it, materially contributed to the appellant's condition. They would also be entitled to take an alternative view that the second respondent's conduct, although it might not be possible to say (on the balance of probabilities) that it definitely materially contributed to the plaintiff's final condition, at least caused him to lose a valuable chance (the value of which it was for them to assess) of avoiding being in the condition that he now finds himself. There is still, in my opinion, room for the operation of the loss of chance rule (particularly in cases involving the practice of what is even today said to be an art rather than a scientific skill), enabling a plaintiff to recover damages to be equated with, and reduced to the value of the chance he or she has lost, rather than the damages which would be appropriate if it has been proved on the balance of probabilities that the plaintiff's condition owes itself to the defendant's acts or omissions.

It must be acknowledged that this approach is not without its difficulties. If the chance that has been lost is a 51 per cent or greater chance, why should not the plaintiff be taken to have proved his or her case on the balance of probabilities? I think that in such a situation, the plaintiff has, and should recover his or her damages in full. *Rogers v Whitaker* is, in one sense, such a case. The Court there accepted on the balance of probabilities, that the plaintiff would not have had the operation to which she submitted, and which caused the problems for her that it did, if she had been warned of the risk that the Court thought material there. Perhaps the plaintiff's damages there might have been reduced, and indeed significantly so, if what had been established there, was that she might not have had, as opposed to, would not have had the operation.

[13.140] **Notes and Questions**

1. The House of Lords confronted these issues in *Gregg v Scott* [2005] UKHL 2, [2005] 2 AC 176 in which a general practitioner had misdiagnosed a cancerous lump in the claimant's armpit as benign, and negligently failed to order routine follow-up tests. The resulting nine-month delay in obtaining treatment caused the claimant's prospects of a cure to diminish from 42 per cent at the date of consultation to 25 per cent at trial. His chances of surviving the cancer had always been less than 50/50. Judge Inglis found that prompt treatment would probably have prevented the cancer spreading and made high-dose chemotherapy unnecessary, at least initially. He also found, however, that a better long-term outcome was never a probability. The case raised issues of causation, loss of chance and proportionate damages. The claim was dismissed at trial, based on the binding authority of *Hotson v East Berkshire Health Authority* [1987] AC 750. The claimant lost his appeals to the Court of Appeal and the House of Lords, although both courts split.

   The majority in *Gregg* thought that allowing the claim would constitute a "radical departure from precedent". It would, it was held, mean abandoning the limits laid down in *Fairchild* and generalising the rule to allow damages in all cases in which the defendant *may* have caused an injury, and has increased the likelihood of injury (Lord Hoffman at [84]-[85]). In Lord Hoffman's view (at [90]), "[a] wholesale adoption of possible rather than probable causation as the criterion of liability would be so radical a change in our law as to amount to a legislative act. It would have enormous consequences for insurance companies and the National Health Service."

   In his dissenting judgment, however, Lord Nicholls said [at 2-5]:

   > This is the type of case under consideration. A patient is suffering from cancer. His prospects are uncertain. He has a 45 per cent chance of recovery. Unfortunately his doctor negligently misdiagnoses his condition as benign. So the necessary treatment is delayed for months. As a result the patient's prospects of recovery become nil or almost nil. Has the patient a claim for damages against the doctor? No, the House was told. The patient could recover damages if his initial prospects of recovery had been more than 50 per cent. But because they were less than 50 per cent he can recover nothing.
   >
   > This surely cannot be the state of the law today. It would be irrational and indefensible. The loss of a 45 per cent prospect of recovery is just as much a real loss for a patient as the loss of a 55 per cent prospect of recovery. In both cases the doctor was in breach of his duty to his patient. In both cases the patient was worse off. He lost something of importance and value. But, it is said, in one case the patient has a remedy, in the other he does not.
   >
   > This would make no sort of sense. It would mean that in the 45 per cent case the doctor's duty would be hollow. The duty would be empty of content. For the reasons which follow I reject this suggested distinction. The common law does not compel courts to proceed in such an unreal fashion. I would hold that a patient has a right to a remedy as much where his prospects of recovery were less than 50-50 as where they exceeded 50-50.

   See P Watson, "Medical Negligence: loss of a chance, causation and proportionate damages: *Gregg v Scott*" (2005) 70 *Precedent* 47.

Gett v Tabet

[13.145] *Gett v Tabet* (2009) 254 ALR 504

[On 14 January 1991, Reema Tabet, aged six years, was diagnosed with a brain tumour. After suffering a seizure she was given a CT scan and an EEG. Following her diagnosis, she underwent an operation to remove the tumour. She suffered irreversible brain damage, partly as a result of events on 14 January, partly from the tumour, and partly from the operative procedure and other treatment (not said to be in any way negligently performed). Tabet sued Dr Gett, a specialist paediatrician, for negligence, alleging that had the CT scan been conducted on either 11 or 13 January, she would have had a better medical outcome. At trial, Studdert J found that Gett had breached his duty of care by failing to order the CT scan on 13 January, but that he was not negligent prior to that time. Studdert J found that Tabet had lost a chance of a better medical outcome, assessed at 40%, of avoiding a 25% brain damage.

Gett appealed and Tabet cross-appealed. Key issues raised were the legitimacy of loss of a chance of a better medical outcome as a basis for awarding damages in personal injury; causation; and the correctness of *Rufo v Hosking* [2004] NSWCA 391; 61 NSWLR 678. The decision of the NSW Court of Appeal was unanimous.]

ALLSOP P; BEAZLEY JA; BASTEN JA: [329] … [I]t is clear that the principle identified in *Fairchild* was designed to address a problem of insufficient scientific knowledge to identify the precise causative factor in a known past event (the contraction of mesothelioma). That is, on any view, different from the problem with respect to a hypothetical assessment of an event which, because of negligent failure to diagnose, did not take place …

The law does not equate the situation where the defendant had materially increased the risk of injury with one where he had materially contributed to the injury …

[332] The history of claims for a loss of a chance in Australia has an uncertain foundation. The uncertainty arises in part from the narrow dividing line between matters going to causation (to be determined on the balance of probabilities) and matters involving the assessment of loss in hypothetical circumstances.

[334] … Causation, including the place of any "but for" analysis therein, has always been held to be required to be proved on the balance of probabilities. In the resolution of many causation questions in the law of negligence, the process of fact finding, including the drawing of inferences, will involve the consideration of the assessment of a chain of circumstances with a factual postulate (the careless conduct of the defendant) removed. That does not mean, however, that this aspect of the resolution of causation is evaluated otherwise than on the balance of probabilities. *Malec* provides no support for the resolution of any hypothetical element in causation on a loss of a chance basis by an increased risk short of a conclusion on the balance of probabilities…

[336] In recent times the uncertain foundation of claims for loss of a chance is reflected in an extrapolation of two cases involving loss of a commercial advantage or benefit: *Commonwealth v Amann Aviation Pty Ltd* (*Amann Aviation*) and *Sellars.*

[337] The first, *Amann Aviation*, involved a consideration of heads of damage flowing from a breach of contract and a loss of an opportunity to secure a renewal of the contract when it would have expired, absent unlawful termination. The second, *Sellars*, concerned the loss of a commercial advantage or opportunity resulting from misleading conduct in contravention of s 52(1) of the *Trade Practices Act 1974* (Cth). Such a loss was held to be loss or damage suffered by a person for the purposes of a claim under s 82(1) of that Act. In such cases, the need to prove reliance upon the misleading conduct involved the plaintiff proving that he or she would, but for the inducement of the misrepresentation, have taken up an alternative commercial opportunity. The next step is to place a value on the lost opportunity …

Gett v Tabet cont.

[338] … *Sellars* has been seen (wrongly in our view) as permitting the development by analogy of recovery for loss of a chance in medical negligence claims …

[The Court of Appeal then discussed *Malec v Hutton* and *Sellars*, and considered various dicta on loss of chance, in *CES v Superclinics (Australia) Pty Ltd (CES), Chappel v Hart*, and *Naxakis*, all medical negligence cases, and continued:]

[359] As subsequent authorities have recognised, conflicting dicta in the High Court provide no guidance to intermediate courts of appeal, let alone trial judges, as to how to approach such an issue. Nevertheless, recognition that such a course [extension of loss of chance to personal injury] would be a departure from the traditional approach and that it involves significant issues of policy should discourage both trial judges and intermediate courts of appeal from adopting such an approach, absent further guidance …

[360] The earliest reported Australian case in which damages were expressly awarded for harm identified as a loss of a chance of a better medical outcome appears to have been *Gavalas v Singh* (2001) 3 VR 404; [2001] VSCA 23 (*Gavalas*). That case also involved a failure to diagnose a brain tumour. The negligence, as found by the trial judge, resulted in a delay of some 10 weeks. Damages were awarded by the trial judge on the basis of a prolongation of intractable headaches and left-sided weakness during that period. There was, accordingly, no dispute that the tort was established. The question was whether the trial judge had failed to allow some further amount for the loss of a chance of a more successful removal of the tumour when the diagnosis should have been made. The primary opinion in the Court of Appeal was delivered by Smith AJA (Ormiston and Callaway JJA agreeing). Smith AJA noted debate as to whether damages for a lost opportunity were available in tort, noting "judicial support for the two extreme positions but no binding authority denying the entitlement to compensation for such a loss in all cases": at [37]. His Honour continued, at [38]:

> [38] …there is a strong case for saying that lost opportunity should be recognised by the law as a head of damage and compensated because it enables a plaintiff to obtain compensation in circumstances where negligence has deprived that plaintiff of a real chance or opportunity while at the same time avoiding the potentially unreasonable result of excessive compensation or no compensation despite the negligence of the defendant…

(4) Reconsidering "loss of a chance" as a form of harm

[In *Rufo v Hosking* Hodgson JA and Santow JA accepted loss of chance as] … consistent with the principles established in *Malec* and *Sellars* to say that it is enough if the plaintiff proves, on the balance of probabilities, that he or she has been deprived of a valuable chance.

[366] To say that such an approach is consistent with *Malec* and *Sellars* is not to justify its adoption. Indeed, it is, with respect, to ignore the distinction between causation of loss and assessment of proven loss, established in *Malec* and the fact that "different considerations apply" in respect of medical negligence, as compared with the circumstances in *Sellars*, as noted by Gaudron J in *Naxakis* at [29]. Further, once one views the harm (and its assessment) by reference to the materialised physical harm or debility, the role of increased risk in the analysis becomes clear.

[The court discussed *State of New South Wales v Burton* [2006] NSWCA 12 and *Barker v Corus*] [370] To the extent that these authorities suggest that a chance of avoiding or diminishing the severity of a disease or injury is sufficient harm to satisfy the requirements of the tort of negligence, that is a step having potentially far-reaching consequences. For example, in what cases will it apply? Will it limit recovery in cases where the plaintiff establishes a loss to a degree of probability between 50% and, say, 90%? Perhaps because the issues have not previously been fully debated (such a claim was not pleaded in *Gavalas*, its availability was conceded in *Rufo*, which was followed without its validity being questioned in *Burton*) these issues have not been adequately addressed. As the UK courts have all recognised, they involve issues of high policy affecting the scope and operation of the most dominant

Gett v Tabet cont.

aspect of tort law. A statement that "[n]o advanced system of law could deny recovery where late diagnosis, in breach of duty to the patient, appreciably reduces the prospects of success of an operation" (*Gavalas* at [15]) does not provide reasoned support for a major new direction in negligence…

[374] … cases such as *Sellars* provide no basis to undermine the existing orthodoxy in the law of recovery of damages for personal injury as a result of negligence. To the contrary, the reiteration in *Sellars* of the statements of general principle as to proof of causation were contradictory to any permission to extend loss of a chance outside the realm of loss of a commercial opportunity.

[375] In case of physical harm or injury, the damage can generally be seen to be the physical injury, debility, pain, bodily or mental harm or deterioration and consequences thereof. The court awards damages for that harm and its consequences. This occurs when the breach of duty is proven on the balance of probabilities to have caused the damage. Despite the different expression of the loss of an opportunity or chance, the damages in such a case are still formulated by reference to the harm that has materialised. This can be seen in *Rufo* itself and the approach of the trial judge in the present case. The damages awarded in the present case were for the physical harm suffered, but calculated, not on the basis of full recovery consequent upon causation having been proved on the balance of probabilities, but rather on a lesser scale commensurate with the increased risk caused by the breach of duty. This was consistent with the part played in the reasons of Hodgson JA in *Rufo* at [3] of the increase in risk (see [306] above). The "opportunity" that was lost was to have a better outcome without negligence, the value of the lost opportunity being assessed as the percentage risk or chance of the harm that did occur. So, here, 25% of the whole debility was caused by the seizure and deterioration on 14 January. The respondent did not prove on the balance of probabilities that that damage was caused by the breach of duty on 13 January. Rather, it is said that because of the breach of duty on 13 January the respondent lost the opportunity of a better medical outcome (measured by the avoidance of the damage on 14 January) assessed at 40%. This is to say no more than that the assessed likelihood of the damage is 40%, so that the respondent has "lost the opportunity" of a better outcome (the harm not occurring) calculated accordingly. Yet, one thing is plain: the respondent was awarded damages not for the harm of suffering the increased risk, but by reference to the physical harm and debility suffered, which, ex hypothesi, had not been shown to have been caused by the breach of duty.

[376] It is to be recalled that causation, in this context, incorporates the notion of material contribution: *Bonnington Castings Ltd v Wardlaw* [1956] AC 613; [1956] 1 All ER 615; and *Chappel* at [25] (per McHugh J).

[377] Once one appreciates that the so-called loss of an opportunity in this field is in fact the increased risk of harm (short of proof on the balance of probabilities) there is an essential conflict between the concept of damages for loss of a chance and the authorities discussed by Ipp JA in *Flounders v Millar*, in particular *Bendix*; and see now *Royal* at [25] (per Gummow, Hayne and Heydon JJ) and [135]-[144] (per Kiefel J). Though the debate in such cases as *Bendix; Wallaby Grip E M Baldwin v Plane*; and *Seltsam v McGuinness* has generally been discussed (as M W Campbell AJA did in *Rufo* at [413]-[446]) in the context of causation and material contribution, once one appreciates the true character of loss of a chance in medical negligence cases as damages for increased risk of harm, one needs to confront and depart from cases such as *Bendix*. No such attempt was made in *Gavalas* or *Rufo*. Nor is there any warrant for this course to be taken.

(5) Gavalas and Rufo not followed

[378] Somewhat paradoxically, factors favouring caution generally may favour a departure from existing authority in particular circumstances, one of which arises in this case. Recovery for loss of a chance was accepted in *Rufo* for the first time in this Court without clear support from High Court

Gett v Tabet cont.

authority; although its adoption was by no means inadvertent, it was not opposed by any party to those proceedings. *Rufo* was followed, but not challenged, in *Burton*. In neither case were the full ramifications of such a development analysed. Accordingly, it is appropriate to consider whether it was a development which this Court would now take if *Rufo* and *Burton* had not preceded this case and, if it would not, whether it should now depart from that authority. At the second stage of that analysis, it is appropriate to ask not merely whether the step taken in *Rufo* was plainly wrong, but also whether the step having been taken, the authority should properly be followed. The fact of consent may diminish the justification for adhering to a precedent held to be erroneous in principle.

[379] There was no licence to be found for the course taken in *Rufo* in the dicta of single justices of the High Court: Callinan J in *Naxakis* at [127]-[130] and Kirby J in *Chappel* at [93], contra Gaudron J in *Naxakis* at [20]-[36], and Gleeson CJ in *Naxakis* at [5] expressing no opinion. *Sellars* stands as authority for the proposition that deprivation of a commercial opportunity or advantage is compensable harm in contract, tort and under the *Trade Practices Act*, its value to be assessed on the basis of possibilities as an hypothetical circumstance; but the general standard of proof will govern the issue of causation of loss, properly identified.

[380] The arguments in favour of permitting damages for loss of a chance cannot, in circumstances where the approach conflicts with conventional authority, be justified on the basis that there is no express superior court authority inconsistent with the proposed approach. Nor can the approach be preferred on the basis that it avoids the potential injustice which may flow from a bright line drawn in accordance with the balance of probabilities. Such a rationalisation would have operation well beyond the scope of the proposed new principle.

[381] It is for the High Court, and only the High Court, to reformulate the law of torts to permit recovery for physical injury not shown to be caused or contributed to by a negligent party, but which negligence has deprived the victim of the possibility (but not the probability) of a better outcome. Such an approach would not readily be limited to medical negligence cases, but would potentially revolutionise the law of recovery for personal injury. It would do so by reference to an assessment of increased risk of harm, verbally reformulated into loss of a chance or opportunity in order to equate it with the recognition in *Sellars* and like cases of the existence in commerce of a coherent notion of loss of a right or chance of financial benefit. No doubt the limits of the "commercial" or financial opportunity or advantage dealt with in *Sellars* will be a matter of future debate: see the discussion in *Gregg* at 232 (Baroness Hale of Richmond). In our view, its limits (unless expanded by the High Court) must fall short of a proposition which revolutionises the proof of causation of injury or (by redefining what is "harm") in personal injury cases.

[382] Our view is supported by final courts of appeal; in the UK see *Wilsher v Essex Area Health Authority* [1988] AC 1074; *Fairchild Hotson v East Berskshire Area Health Authority Gregg* and *Barker*; and in Canada, see *Laferriere*.

[383] A further matter to be considered is that there is now a statutory definition in the *Civil Liability Act* which implicitly does not include a risk of physical or mental injury. Part 1A of the *Civil Liability Act* applies to "any claim for damages for harm resulting from negligence, regardless of whether the claim is brought in tort, in contract under statute or otherwise": s 5A(1). Various terms used in this provision are defined in s 5:

5 Definitions

In this Part:

"harm" means harm of any kind, including the following:

(a) personal injury or death,

(b) damage to property,

(c) economic loss.

Gett v Tabet cont.

"negligence" means failure to exercise reasonable care and skill.
"personal injury" includes:
(a) pre-natal injury, and
(b) impairment of a person's physical or mental condition, and
(c) disease.

[384] General principles are then stated by reference to "a risk of harm": ss 5B, 5C, 5F-5I, 5L, 5M and 5R. None of these provisions expressly excludes the identification of harm as loss of an opportunity, but the inclusion of such a concept is at best awkward. For example, to speak in the terms of s 5B(2)(c), of "the burden of taking precautions to avoid the risk of harm", is readily understandable in the context of harm as physical injury, but is at best obscure and semantically inappropriate, if the phrase "loss of an opportunity of a better outcome" is substituted for the word "harm".

[385] On the alternative approach, if provision of damages for the loss of a chance of a better outcome involves a new concept of causation, that construction would not be consonant with the principles relating to causation set out in ss 5D and 5E of the *Civil Liability Act*. In particular, s 5E requires that the plaintiff always bears the onus of proving, on the balance of probabilities, any fact relevant to the issue of causation.

[386] Any change to the common law of negligence is a change to the common law (or general law) of Australia. Therefore, the form of one statute in one State may not be seen as adequate either for the analogical development of the common law ... or for restriction on any change ...

[388] Though this point was not the subject of argument on the appeal, it might be thought that it would be inappropriate for the general law to develop a concept of harm which departed from the assumptions underlying a tolerably uniform statutory definition of harm.

[389] For the above reasons and as summarised below, we consider the approach adopted in *Rufo* and *Gavalas* to have involved a departure from conventional principles. There were no compelling reasons to adopt that approach and to do so was, in all the circumstances in our respectful view, plainly wrong, in the sense discussed above. In summary, we would not follow *Rufo* and *Gavalas* for the following reasons. First, the doctrine espoused formed part of no recognised stream of authority. Second, the doctrine espoused was not consistent with or permitted by *Sellars*. To the contrary, it fell outside the expression of principle as to commercial advantages and opportunities in *Sellars*, which otherwise stated orthodoxy of proof of causation. Third, the setting of the law of torts on a new path of proof of causation, whether for medical negligence cases or torts generally, based on creation of risk and policy for fair recompense for loss is (and was in 2001 and 2004) a matter of high policy for the High Court. Fourth, in neither *Gavalas* nor *Rufo* were the difficulties and complexities of the application of the doctrine considered ... Other difficulties and complexities arise at the point of assessing the accrual of any cause of action for limitation purposes. Fifth, no clear limitations have been formulated for the application of the new doctrine. No logical distinction limits its development to personal injury caused by medical negligence. Sixth, the doctrine can be seen to be inconsistent with conventional authority, now reflected in the *Civil Liability Acts*, as to the nature of harm required to justify a finding of negligence. Seventh, the general principle that a causal connection between the tortious conduct and the plaintiff's injury must be established on the balance of probability is now expressly enacted in the *Civil Liability Acts*. Eighth, there is no evidence that insurance companies or members of the public have adapted their personal or commercial relations in reliance upon these authorities ...

Failure to warn

[13.150] As we saw above (at [13.80]), NSW: CLA, s 5D(2) and its equivalents (Vic: WrA, s 51(2); Qld: CLA, 11(2); SA: CLA, s 34(2); WA: CLA, s 5C(2); Tas: CLA, s 13(2); ACT:

CLWA, s 45(2)) deals with exceptional cases, that is, those in which the suggested cause cannot be established as a necessary condition. NSW: CLA, s 5D(3), (4) relate specifically to exceptional cases in which the breach of duty is a failure to warn.

Civil Liability Act 2002 (NSW)

[13.155] *Civil Liability Act 2002* (NSW), ss 5D(3), 5E

s 5D (3) If it is relevant to the determination of factual causation to determine what the person who suffered harm would have done if the negligent person had not been negligent:

(a) the matter is to be determined subjectively in the light of all relevant circumstances, subject to paragraph (b), and

(b) any statement made by the person after suffering the harm about what he or she would have done is inadmissible except to the extent (if any) that the statement is against his or her interest.

(4) For the purpose of determining the scope of liability, the court is to consider (amongst other relevant things) whether or not and why responsibility for the harm should be imposed on the negligent party.

5E Onus of proof

In determining liability for negligence, the plaintiff always bears the onus of proving, on the balance of probabilities, any fact relevant to the issue of causation.

[13.160] *Rogers v Whitaker* (1992) 175 CLR 479 was the first High Court decision in which a duty to warn was accepted. There, the plaintiff succeeded in an action against the opthalmic surgeon who had operated on her blind eye, partly for cosmetic reasons and partly in an attempt to restore her sight. Although the operation was performed competently and without negligence, the patient was blinded in her good eye by a rare complication known as sympathetic opthalmia, leaving her almost totally blind. The surgeon had not warned her of the 1 in 14,000 risk of this complication occurring, despite her repeated requests for information and reassurance. Mason CJ, Dawson, Brennan, Toohey and McHugh JJ accepted that had Mrs Whitaker been warned of the risk, she would not have agreed to the operation, taking into account the fact that she had led a normal life until this point despite the childhood injury to her eye, and her continual requests for information. This is a critical issue in failure to warn cases, as it goes directly to the proof of causation of the damage. If the plaintiff, despite having been warned, would not have acted differently, then the failure to warn cannot have caused the injury. This issue arises frequently in medical negligence cases, but also in other types of negligent advice situations. In *Rosenberg v Percival* (2001) 205 CLR 434 the High Court accepted that the appropriate test for determining whether the plaintiff would have proceeded with the surgery if appropriately warned of the risk, is the subjective test. McHugh J said "a court asks whether *this patient* would have undertaken the surgery ... It is not decisive that a reasonable person would or would not have undertaken the surgery ... If the tribunal of fact ... accepts the evidence of the patient as to what he or she would have done, then, subject to appellate review as to the correctness of that finding, that is the end of the matter".

The NSW: CLA, s 5D(3) adopts the common law test by providing that the test for establishing what the plaintiff would have done if warned is a subjective one. This is in keeping with *Rogers v Whitaker* (1992) 175 CLR 479 and other common law decisions, although at odds with some overseas jurisdictions. In a move to avoid self-serving statements, and in a departure from the common law, s 5D(3)(b) was added. This renders inadmissible any self-serving statement made after suffering the injury concerning what the plaintiff would have done if warned.

Chappel v Hart

[13.165] *Chappel v Hart* (1998) 195 CLR 232 High Court of Australia

(footnotes omitted)

[The facts are outlined in the extract at [13.125].]

McHUGH J: 245 [I]f the defendant negligently fails to warn the plaintiff that a particular route is subject to landslides, no causal connection will exist between the failure to warn and subsequent injury from a landslide if every other available route carried the same degree of risk of injury from a landslide. In such a case, the injury suffered is simply an inherent risk in the course of action pursued by the plaintiff. Although the negligence of the defendant has resulted in the plaintiff being in the place where and at the time when the landslide occurred, that negligence is to be regarded as merely one of the set of conditions that combined to produce the injury. Because the negligent failure of the defendant to give a warning did not increase the risk of injury to the plaintiff, the defendant should not incur liability for the plaintiff's injury.

On the other hand, if there were alternative routes involving a lesser risk of landslide and the plaintiff would probably have taken one of them, if given a warning, the defendant's failure to warn would be causally connected with the plaintiff's injury. That is because the failure to warn deflected the plaintiff from taking a safer course and increased the chance that he or she would suffer injury. By doing so, the defendant has materially contributed to the occurrence of that injury. The case is a fortiori if the plaintiff, on being warned, would have abandoned the journey.

Furthermore, a defendant is not causally liable, and therefore legally responsible, for wrongful acts or omissions if those acts or omissions would not have caused the plaintiff to alter his or her course of action. Australian law has adopted a subjective theory of causation in determining whether the failure to warn would have avoided the injury suffered. The inquiry as to what the plaintiff would have done if warned is necessarily hypothetical. But if the evidence suggests that the acts or omissions of the defendant would have made no difference to the plaintiff's course of action, the defendant has not caused the harm which the plaintiff has suffered.

Moreover, even when the defendant's wrongful act or omission has exposed the plaintiff to a risk to which the plaintiff would not have been exposed but for that act or omission, the correct conclusion may nevertheless be that no causal connection exists between the negligence and the injury suffered. Thus, in *Central of Georgia Railway Co v Price*, a railway company was held not liable for injury sustained as the result of a lamp exploding in a hotel where the plaintiff had to stay as the result of the company negligently taking her beyond her destination. The risk of such an event occurring in that hotel on that particular night was so insignificant and therefore so abnormal as to be fairly described as a coincidence, rather than an event causally connected to the defendant's negligence.

The foregoing observations lead me to the following conclusions concerning whether a causal connection exists between a defendant's failure to warn of a risk of injury and the subsequent suffering of injury by the plaintiff as a result of the risk eventuating: (1) a causal connection will exist between the failure and the injury if it is probable that the plaintiff would have acted on the warning and desisted from pursuing the type of activity or course of conduct involved; (2) no causal connection will exist if the plaintiff would have persisted with the same course of action in comparable circumstances even if a warning had been given; (3) no causal connection will exist if every alternative means of achieving the plaintiff's goal gave rise to an equal or greater probability of the same risk of injury and

Chappel v Hart cont.

the plaintiff would probably have attempted to achieve that goal notwithstanding the warning; (4) no causal connection will exist where the plaintiff suffered injury at some other place or some other time unless the change of place or time increased the risk of injury; (5) no causal connection will exist if the eventuation of the risk is so statistically improbable as not to be fairly attributable to the defendant's omission; (6) the onus of proving that the failure to warn was causally connected with the plaintiff's harm lies on the plaintiff. However, once the plaintiff proves that the defendant breached a duty to warn of a risk and that the risk eventuated and caused harm to the plaintiff, the plaintiff has made out a prima facie case of causal connection. An evidentiary onus then rests on the defendant to point to other evidence suggesting that no causal connection exists. Examples of such evidence are: evidence which indicates that the plaintiff would not have acted on the warning because of lack of choice or personal inclination; evidence that no alternative course of action would have eliminated or reduced the risk of injury. Once the defendant points to such evidence, the onus lies on the plaintiff to prove that in all the circumstances a causal connection existed between the failure to warn and the injury suffered by the plaintiff.

Upon the unusual facts of the present case – they are set out in detail in other judgments – the defendant in my opinion can escape liability only if the proper conclusion is that the plaintiff did not prove that the defendant's failure to warn resulted in her consenting to a procedure that involved a higher risk of injury than would have been the case if the procedure had been carried out by another surgeon.

REMOTENESS OF DAMAGE

Introduction

[13.170] This section deals with remoteness of damage. Civil liability legislation refers to the "scope of liability" extending to the relevant harm: NSW: CLA, s 5D(1)(b); ACT: CLWA, s 45(1); Qld: CLA, s 11(1); SA: CLA, 34(1); Vic: WrA, s 51(1); WA: CLA, s 5C(1). This clearly encompasses remoteness of damage issues. Remoteness in itself is a matter of judgment and degree, being heavily influenced by policy. It marks the boundary beyond which it would be unjust to hold the defendant liable. Section 5D(4) of the NSW: CLA recognises this in the requirement that: "For the purpose of determining the scope of liability, the court is to consider ... whether or not and why responsibility for the harm should be imposed". See also ACT: CLWA, s 45(3); Qld: CLA, s 11(3); SA: CLA, 34(3); Vic: WrA, s 51(3); WA: CLA, s 5C(3). This does not alter the common law, although it requires policy considerations to be more clearly articulated.

Until the 1960s, the common law applied the "direct consequences" test of remoteness, that is, defendants were held responsible for all the direct consequences flowing from their breach of duty. This test was laid down in *Re Polemis & Furness, Withy and Co Ltd* [1921] 3 KB 560. In that case a ship was totally destroyed by fire while being unloaded in Casablanca. It was found as a fact by arbitrators that the fire was caused when local stevedores employed by the charterers of the ship dislodged a heavy plank which fell into the hold. The hold contained leaking petrol drums, and a spark from the impact ignited petrol vapour in the hold. The arbitrators found that the fall of the plank was caused by the stevedores' negligence, but that "the causing of the spark could not reasonably have been anticipated from the falling of the board, though some damage to the ship might reasonably have been anticipated." The Court of Appeal held the defendants liable for the destruction of the ship, being a direct consequence of the falling plank. The decision was controversial at the time, and the subject of criticism by judges trying to apply it subsequently. The glaring discrepancy between the degree of fault and the extent of the liability is apparent. The Privy Council finally disapproved it in *Overseas Tankship (UK) Ltd v Morts Dock & Engineering Co Ltd* [1961] 1 AC 388, substituting in its place the foreseeability test.

Foreseeability of damage

The Wagon Mound (No 1)

[13.175] *Overseas Tankship (UK) Ltd v Morts Dock & Engineering Co Ltd (The "Wagon Mound" (No 1))* [1961] 1 AC 388 Privy Council

(footnotes omitted)

[This case and *Wagon Mound (No 2)* which follows it (see [13.180]) arise from facts that occurred in 1951. The defendants (OT), charterers of the *Wagon Mound,* are the same in both cases, but there are two separate plaintiffs. Both cases were brought in negligence and nuisance, although the nuisance claim in *Wagon Mound (No 1)* was ultimately not pursued. The ship *Wagon Mound* was taking on furnace oil at the Caltex wharf in Balmain, Sydney. The defendants' employees negligently allowed a large amount of oil to spill into Sydney Harbour, which spread over much of the bay and under the plaintiff's wharf (Sheerlegs wharf), fouling the slipways. A ship called the *Corrimal* was being refitted at Sheerlegs wharf. When the plaintiff's manager arrived next morning and saw the oil, he gave instructions that no welding was to be done on the *Corrimal.* He rang the manager at the Caltex wharf who came round to Sheerlegs wharf and assured him it was safe to resume welding. The plaintiffs did so, and work continued until the next day when the oil caught fire, severely damaging the ship and wharf. The flashpoint of this type of oil was very high, meaning it could not normally be set alight while spread on a large body of cold water. More than six years later, Kinsella J in the Supreme Court found that the fire had been started by some molten metal falling onto a floating piece of rag or cotton waste, which had acted as a wick. Kinsella J found that damage to the wharf from fouling was foreseeable, but the defendant "did not know, and could not reasonably be expected to have known, that it was capable of being set on fire when spread on water". Applying the direct consequences test from *Re Polemis,* he held the defendants liable for the burning of the wharf. The defendants' appeal was unsuccessful in the Full Court. Manning J felt bound to apply *Re Polemis,* notwithstanding his strongly expressed views about the unworkability of the test. The defendant appealed to the Privy Council, which at that time was the final appellate court for Australia.]

VISCOUT SIMONDS: 422 Enough has been said to show that the authority of *Polemis* has been severely shaken, though lip-service has from time to time been paid to it. In their Lordships' opinion, it should no longer be regarded as good law. It is not probable that many cases will for that reason have a different result, though it is hoped that the law will be thereby simplified, and that, in some cases at least, palpable injustice will be avoided. For it does not seem consonant with current ideas of justice or morality that, for an act of negligence, however slight or venial, which results in some trivial foreseeable damage, the actor should be liable for all consequences, however unforeseeable and however grave, so long as they can be said to be "direct". It is a principle of civil liability, subject only to qualifications which have no present relevance, that a man must be considered to be responsible for the probable consequences of his act. To demand more of him is too harsh a rule, to demand less is to ignore that civilised order requires the observance of a minimum standard of behaviour. This concept, applied to the slowly developing law of negligence, has led to a great variety of expressions which can, as it appears to their Lordships, be harmonised with little difficulty with the single exception of the so-called rule in *Polemis.* For, if it is asked why a man should be responsible for the natural or necessary

The Wagon Mound (No 1) cont.

or probable consequences of his act (or any other similar description of them), the answer is that it is not because they are natural or necessary or probable, but because, since they have this quality, it is judged, by the standard of the reasonable man, that he ought to have foreseen them. Thus it is that, over and over again, it has happened that, in different judgments in the same case and sometimes in a single judgment, liability for a consequence has been imposed on the ground that it was reasonably foreseeable, or alternatively on the ground that it was natural or necessary or probable. The two grounds have been treated as conterminous, and so they largely are. But, where they are not, the question arises to which the wrong answer was given in *Polemis*. For, if some limitation must be imposed on the consequences for which the negligent actor is to be held responsible – and all are agreed that some limitation there must be – why should that test (reasonable foreseeability) be rejected which, since he is judged by what the reasonable man ought to foresee, corresponds with the common conscience of mankind, and a test (the "direct" consequence) be substituted which leads to nowhere but the never ending and insoluble problems of causation. "The lawyer" said Sir Frederick Pollock "cannot afford to adventure himself with philosophers in the logical and metaphysical controversies that beset the idea of cause."

Yet this is just what he has most unfortunately done and must continue to do if the rule in *Polemis* is to prevail. A conspicuous example occurs when the actor seeks to escape liability on the ground that the "chain of causation" is broken by a "nova causa" or "novus actus interveniens."

It is, no doubt, proper when considering tortious liability for negligence to analyse its elements and to say that the plaintiff must prove a duty owed to him by the defendant, a breach of that duty by the defendant, and consequent damage. But there can be no liability until the damage has been done. It is not the act but the consequences on which tortious liability is founded. Just as (as it has been said) there is no such thing as negligence in the air, so there is no such thing as liability in the air. Suppose an action brought by A for damage caused by the carelessness (a neutral word) of B, for example a fire caused by the careless spillage of oil. It may, of course, become relevant to know what duty B owed to A, but the only liability that is in question is the liability for damage by fire. It is vain to isolate the liability from its context and to say that B is or is not liable, and then to ask for what damage he is liable. For his liability is in respect of that damage and no other. If, as admittedly it is, B's liability (culpability) depends on the reasonable foreseeability of the consequent damage, how is that to be determined except by the foreseeability of the damage which in fact happened–the damage in suit? And, if that damage is unforeseeable so as to displace liability at large, how can the liability be restored so as to make compensation payable? … We have come back to the plain common sense stated by Lord Russell of Killowen in *Hay (or Bourhill) v Young*. As Denning LJ said in *King v Phillips* ([1953] 1 All ER at 623; [1953] 1 QB at 441) "… there can be no doubt since *Hay (or Bourhill) v Young* that the test of *liability for shock* is foreseeability of *injury by shock*." Their Lordships substitute the word "fire" for "shock" and indorse this statement of the law.

Their Lordships conclude this part of the case with some general observations. They have been concerned primarily to displace the proposition that unforeseeability is irrelevant if damage is "direct." In doing so, they have inevitably insisted that the essential factor in determining liability is whether the damage is of such a kind as the reasonable man should have foreseen. This accords with the general view thus stated by Lord Atkin in *M'Alister (or Donoghue) v Stevenson* ([1932] All ER Rep at 11; [1932] AC at 580): "The liability for negligence, whether you style it such or treat it as in other systems as a species of 'culpa,' is no doubt based upon a general public sentiment of moral wrongdoing for which the offender must pay."

It is a departure from this sovereign principle if liability is made to depend solely on the damage being the "direct" or "natural" consequence of the precedent act. Who knows or can be assumed to know all the processes of nature? But if it would be wrong that a man should be held liable for damage unpredictable by a reasonable man because it was "direct" or "natural", equally it would be wrong

The Wagon Mound (No 1) cont.

that he should escape liability, however "indirect" the damage, if he foresaw or could reasonably foresee the intervening events which led to its being done; cf *Woods v Duncan* ([1946] AC at 442). Thus foreseeability becomes the effective test. In reasserting this principle, their Lordships conceive that they do not depart from, but follow and develop, the law of negligence as laid down by Alderson B, in *Blyth v Birmingham Waterworks Co* ...

Their Lordships will humbly advise Her Majesty that this appeal should be allowed and the respondents' action so far as it related to damage caused by the negligence of the appellants be dismissed with costs but that the action so far as it related to damage caused by nuisance should be remitted to the full court to be dealt with as that court may think fit. The respondents must pay the costs of the appellants of this appeal and in the courts below.

Appeal allowed.

The Wagon Mound (No 2)

[13.180] *Overseas Tankship (UK) Ltd v Miller Steamship Co Pty Ltd (The "Wagon Mound" (No 2))* [1967] 1 AC 617 Privy Council

[The plaintiffs in *Wagon Mound* (No 2) were the owners of the ships *Corrimal* and *Audrey D*, moored at Sheerlegs wharf when the fire broke out. This was an appeal from the Supreme Court of New South Wales.]

LORD REID: 640 It is now necessary to turn to the respondents' submission that the trial judge was wrong in holding that damage from fire was not reasonably foreseeable. In *Wagon Mound (No 1)* ([1961] 1 All ER at 407; [1961] AC at 413), the finding on which the Board proceeded was that of the trial judge: "... [the appellants] did not know and could not reasonably be expected to have known that [the oil] was capable of being set afire when spread on water."

In the present case the evidence led was substantially different from the evidence led in *Wagon Mound (No 1)* and the findings of Walsh J are significantly different. That is not due to there having been any failure by the plaintiffs in *Wagon Mound (No 1)* in preparing and presenting their case. The plaintiffs there were no doubt embarrassed by a difficulty which does not affect the present plaintiffs. The outbreak of the fire was consequent on the act of the manager of the plaintiffs in *Wagon Mound (No 1)* in resuming oxy-acetylene welding and cutting while the wharf was surrounded by this oil. So if the plaintiffs in the former case had set out to prove that it was foreseeable by the engineers of the Wagon Mound that this oil could be set alight, they might have had difficulty in parrying the reply that then this must also have been foreseeable by their manager. Then there would have been contributory negligence and at that time contributory negligence was a complete defence in New South Wales.

The crucial finding of Walsh J ([1963] 1 Lloyd's Rep at 426) in this case is in finding (v): that the damage was "not reasonably foreseeable by those for whose acts the defendant would be responsible". That is not a primary finding of fact but an inference from the other findings, and it is clear from the learned judge's judgment that in drawing this inference he was to a large extent influenced by his view of the law. The vital parts of the findings of fact which have already been set out in full are (i) that the officers of the Wagon Mound "would regard furnace oil as very difficult to ignite on water" – not that they would regard this as impossible: (ii) that their experience would probably have been "that this had very rarely happened" – not that they would never have heard of a case where it had happened, and (iii) that they would have regarded it as a "possibility, but one which could become an actuality only in very exceptional circumstances" – not, as in *Wagon Mound (No 1)*, that they could not reasonably be expected to have known that this oil was capable of being set afire

The Wagon Mound (No 2) cont.

when spread on water. The question which must now be determined is whether these differences between the findings in the two cases do or do not lead to different results in law.

In *Wagon Mound (No 1)* the Board were not concerned with degrees of foreseeability because the finding was that the fire was not foreseeable at all. So Viscount Simonds ([1961] 1 All ER at 415; [1961] AC at p 426) had no cause to amplify the statement that the "essential factor in determining liability is whether the damage is of such a kind as the reasonable man should have foreseen". Here the findings show, however, that some risk of fire would have been present to the mind of a reasonable man in the shoes of the ship's chief engineer. So the first question must be what is the precise meaning to be attached in this context to the words "foreseeable" and "reasonably foreseeable".

Before *Bolton v Stone* the cases had fallen into two classes: (i) those where, before the event, the risk of its happening would have been regarded as unreal either because the event would have been thought to be physically impossible or because the possibility of its happening would have been regarded as so fantastic or far-fetched that no reasonable man would have paid any attention to it – "a mere possibility which would never occur to the mind of a reasonable man" (per Lord Dunedin in *Fardon v Harcourt-Rivington* ([1932] All ER Rep 81 at 83) – or (ii) those where there was a real and substantial risk or chance that something like the event which happens might occur and then the reasonable man would have taken the steps necessary to eliminate the risk.

Bolton v Stone posed a new problem … The House of Lords held that the risk [of a cricket ball hit out of the ground striking somebody] was so small that in the circumstances a reasonable man would have been justified in disregarding it and taking no steps to eliminate it.

It does not follow that, no matter what the circumstances may be, it is justifiable to neglect a risk of such a small magnitude. A reasonable man would only neglect such a risk if he had some valid reason for doing so: eg, that it would involve considerable expense to eliminate the risk. He would weigh the risk against the difficulty of eliminating it. If the activity which caused the injury to Miss Stone had been an unlawful activity there can be little doubt but that *Bolton v Stone* would have been decided differently. In their lordships' judgment *Bolton v Stone* did not alter the general principle that a person must be regarded as negligent if he does not take steps to eliminate a risk which he knows or ought to know is a real risk and not a mere possibility which would never influence the mind of a reasonable man. What that decision did was to recognise and give effect to the qualification that it is justifiable not to take steps to eliminate a real risk if it is small and if the circumstances are such that a reasonable man, careful of the safety of his neighbour, would think it right to neglect it.

In the present case there was no justification whatever for discharging the oil into Sydney Harbour. Not only was it an offence to do so, but also it involved considerable loss financially. If the ship's engineer had thought about the matter there could have been no question of balancing the advantages and disadvantages. From every point of view it was both his duty and his interest to stop the discharge immediately.

…

In their lordships' view a properly qualified and alert chief engineer would have realised there was a real risk here, and they do not understand Walsh J to deny that; but he appears to have held that, if a real risk can properly be described as remote, it must then be held to be not reasonably foreseeable. That is a possible interpretation of some of the authorities; but this is still an open question and on principle their lordships cannot accept this view. If a real risk is one which would occur to the mind of a reasonable man in the position of the defendant's servant and which he would not brush aside as far-fetched, and if the criterion is to be what that reasonable man would have done in the circumstances, then surely he would not neglect such a risk if action to eliminate it presented no difficulty, involved no disadvantage and required no expense.

In the present case the evidence shows that the discharge of so much oil on to the water must have taken a considerable time, and a vigilant ship's engineer would have noticed the discharge at an early

The Wagon Mound (No 2) cont.

stage. The findings show that he ought to have known that it is possible to ignite this kind of oil on water, and that the ship's engineer probably ought to have known that this had in fact happened before. The most that can be said to justify inaction is that he would have known that this could only happen in very exceptional circumstances; but that does not mean that a reasonable man would dismiss such risk from his mind and do nothing when it was so easy to prevent it. If it is clear that the reasonable man would have realised or foreseen and prevented the risk, then it must follow that the appellants are liable in damages… Taking a rather different view of the law from that of the learned judge, their lordships must hold that the respondents are entitled to succeed on this issue....

Appeal and cross-appeal allowed.

—— ঌ৫ ——

[13.185] **Notes&Questions**

A contemporaneous account and photographs of the *Wagon Mound* fire can be found in "Firemen Fight Harbour Fire" Daily Telegraph, 2 November 1951, p 3. In the *Wagon Mound cases*, the Privy Council considered the foreseeability test to be far more favourable (and fairer) to defendants than the direct consequences test. Consider whether, in the light of the decisions next extracted, any sharp distinctions that may have existed between the old "directness" test and the foreseeability test have now been eroded.

Kind of injury and manner of its occurrence

Hughes v Lord Advocate

[13.190] *Hughes v Lord Advocate* [1963] AC 837 House of Lords

(footnotes omitted)

[An eight year old boy was severely burned as the result of the explosion of a paraffin lamp which was one of several left at night surrounding an unguarded open manhole in the street. Further facts are set out in the judgments.]

LORD REID: 845 My Lords, I have had an opportunity of reading the speech which my noble and learned friend Lord Guest is about to deliver. I agree with him that this appeal should be allowed and I shall only add some general observations. I am satisfied that the Post Office workmen were in fault in leaving this open manhole unattended and it is clear that if they had done as they ought to have done this accident would not have happened. It cannot be said that they owed no duty to the appellant. But it has been held that the appellant cannot recover damages.

It was argued that the appellant cannot recover because the damage which he suffered was of a kind which was not foreseeable. That was not the ground of judgment of the First Division or of the Lord Ordinary and the facts proved do not, in my judgment, support that argument. The appellant's injuries were mainly caused by burns, and it cannot be said that injuries from burns were unforeseeable. As a warning to traffic the workmen had set lighted red lamps round the tent which covered the manhole, and if boys did enter the dark tent it was very likely that they would take one of these lamps with them. If the lamp fell and broke it was not at all unlikely that the boy would be burned and the burns might well be serious. No doubt it was not to be expected that the injuries would be as serious as those which the appellant in fact sustained. But a defender is liable, although the damage may be a good deal greater in extent than was foreseeable. He can only escape liability if the damage can be regarded as differing in kind from what was foreseeable.

Hughes v Lord Advocate cont.

So we have (first) a duty owed by the workmen, (secondly) the fact that if they had done as they ought to have done there would have been no accident, and (thirdly) the fact that the injuries suffered by the appellant, though perhaps different in degree, did not differ in kind from injuries which might have resulted from an accident of a foreseeable nature. The ground on which this case has been decided against the appellant is that the accident was of an unforeseeable type. Of course the pursuer has to prove that the defender's fault caused the accident and there could be a case where the intrusion of a new and unexpected factor could be regarded as the cause of the accident rather than the fault of the defender. But that is not this case. The cause of this accident was a known source of danger, the lamp, but it behaved in an unpredictable way. The explanation of the accident which has been accepted, and which I would not seek to question, is that, when the lamp fell down the manhole and was broken, some paraffin escaped, and enough was vaporized to create an explosive mixture which was detonated by the naked light of the lamp. The experts agree that no one would have expected that to happen: it was so unlikely as to be unforeseeable. The explosion caused the boy to fall into the manhole: whether his injuries were directly caused by the explosion or aggravated by fire which started in the manhole is not at all clear. The essential step in the respondent's argument is that the explosion was the real cause of the injuries and that the explosion was unforeseeable.

The only authority cited to us from which the respondent can derive any assistance is *Glasgow Corpn v Muir* and I shall examine that case ... [discussion omitted]. If that means that the mere fact that the way in which the accident happened could not be anticipated is enough to exclude liability although there was a breach of duty and that breach of duty in fact caused damage of a kind that could have been anticipated, then I am afraid that I cannot agree with Lord Thankerton ... This accident was caused by a known source of danger, but caused in a way which could not have been foreseen, and in my judgment that affords no defence. I would therefore allow the appeal ...

LORD PEARCE: 857 My Lords, I agree with the opinion of my noble and learned friend, Lord Guest.

The dangerous allurement was left unguarded in a public highway in the heart of Edinburgh. It was for the respondent to show by evidence that, although this was a public street, the presence of children there was so little to be expected that a reasonable man might leave the allurement unguarded. But in my opinion their evidence fell short of that, and the Lord Ordinary rightly so decided.

The defenders are therefore liable for all the foreseeable consequences of their neglect. When an accident is of a different type and kind from anything that a defender could have foreseen he is not liable for it (see *The Wagon Mound*). But to demand too great precision in the test of foreseeability would be unfair to the pursuer since the facets of misadventure are innumerable (see *Miller v South of Scotland Electricity Board; Harvey v Singer Manufacturing Co, Ltd*). In the case of an allurement to children it is particularly hard to foresee with precision the exact shape of the disaster that will arise. The allurement in this case was the combination of a red paraffin lamp, a ladder, a partially closed tent, and a cavernous hole within it, a setting well-fitted to inspire some juvenile adventure that might end in calamity. The obvious risks were burning and conflagration and a fall. All these in fact occurred, but unexpectedly the mishandled lamp instead of causing an ordinary conflagration produced a violent explosion. Did the explosion create an accident and damage of a different type from the misadventure and damage that could be foreseen? In my judgment it did not. The accident was but a variant of the foreseeable. It was, to quote the words of Denning LJ, in *Roe v Ministry of Health* "within the risk created by the negligence." No unforeseeable extraneous, initial occurrence fired the train. The children's entry into the tent with the ladder, the descent into the hole, the mishandling of the lamp, were all foreseeable. The greater part of the path to injury had thus been trodden, and the mishandled lamp was quite likely at that stage to spill and cause a conflagration. Instead, by some curious chance of combustion, it exploded and no conflagration occurred, it would seem, until after the explosion. There was thus an unexpected manifestation of the apprehended physical dangers. But it would be, I

Hughes v Lord Advocate cont.

think, too narrow a view to hold that those who created the risk of fire are excused from the liability for the damage by fire, because it came by way of explosive combustion. The resulting damage, though severe, was not greater than or different in kind from that which might have been produced had the lamp spilled and produced a more normal conflagration in the hole.

I would therefore allow the appeal.

[13.195] **Notes&Questions**

The *Wagon Mound* principles have the effect that even if the particular injury is not foreseeable, the plaintiff will be able to recover if the harm comes within a more general kind of damage that is foreseeable. In *Mt Isa Mines v Pusey* (1970) 125 CLR 383, the plaintiff, an employee working in a powerhouse, went to the assistance of a workmate who was electrocuted and very badly burned in an accident. The plaintiff suffered schizophrenia as a consequence. Whilst it was foreseeable that the plaintiff might have suffered some form of nervous shock as a consequence of witnessing the horrific accident, the specific condition, schizophrenia, was not foreseeable. The High Court held, on appeal, that the plaintiff was entitled to recover damages for nervous shock on the basis that it was sufficient if the particular condition came within a class or kind of injury that could be foreseen. Walsh J said (at 413):

> In the application of this principle there may be difficulty in some cases in determining whether damage for which an action is brought and damage which was foreseeable are the same "kind" of damage. But in the present case there are two reasons which appear to me to justify the conclusion reached by Skerman J. The first is that it is not a condition of liability that either the precise character of the damage or the extent of it should have been foreseen. It is necessary only that the damage suffered should not be different in kind from that which was foreseeable: see *Hughes v Lord Advocate and Chapman v Hearse*. The second reason is that in *The "Wagon Mound" [No 1]* express approval was given to the statement of Denning LJ in *King v Phillips* that "there can be no doubt since *Bourhill v Young* that the test of liability for shock is foreseeability of injury by shock". Thus injury by shock is treated as a distinct "kind" or class of damage for the purposes of the general principle enunciated in *The "Wagon Mound" [No 1]* that liability depends upon the foreseeability of the kind of damage for which the defendant is sued.

Jolley v Sutton LBC

[13.200] *Jolley v Sutton London Borough Council* [2000] 3 All ER 409 House of Lords

(footnotes omitted)

[This statement of the facts is taken from the judgment of Lord Steyn: "In the grounds of a block of council flats owned and occupied by the London Borough of Sutton, Justin Jolley, then a schoolboy aged 14, sustained serious spinal injuries in an accident. It arose when a small, abandoned cabin cruiser, which had been left lying in the grounds of the block of flats, fell on Justin as he lay underneath it while attempting to repair and paint it. As a result he is now a paraplegic. He claimed damages in tort from the council." On appeal to the House of Lords.]

LORD HOFFMANN: It is also agreed that the plaintiff must show that the injury which he suffered fell within the scope of the council's duty and that in cases of physical injury, the scope of the duty is determined by whether or not the injury fell within a description which could be said to have been reasonably foreseeable....[T]he present law is that unless the injury is of a description which was reasonably foreseeable, it is (according to taste) "outside the scope of the duty" or "too remote".

It is also agreed that what must have been foreseen is not the precise injury which occurred but injury of a given description. The foreseeability is not as to the particulars but the genus. And the description is formulated by reference to the nature of the risk which ought to have been foreseen. So, in *Hughes v Lord Advocate* [1963] 1 All ER 705, [1963] AC 837 the foreseeable risk was that a child would be injured by falling in the hole or being burned by a lamp or by a combination of both. The House of Lords decided that the injury which actually materialised fell within this description, notwithstanding that it involved an unanticipated explosion of the lamp and consequent injuries of unexpected severity ... I can see no inconsistency between anything said in *The Wagon Mound (No 1)* and the speech of Lord Reid in *Hughes'* case. The two cases were dealing with altogether different questions. In the former, it was agreed that damage by burning was not damage of a description which could reasonably be said to have been foreseeable. The plaintiffs argued that they were nevertheless entitled to recover by the two-stage process I have described. It was this argument which was rejected. Hughes's case starts from the principle accepted in The *Wagon Mound (No 1)* and is concerned with whether the injury which happened was of a description which was reasonably foreseeable.

The short point in the present appeal is therefore whether the judge was right in saying in general terms that the risk was that children would "meddle with the boat at the risk of some physical injury" ([1998] 1 Lloyd's Rep 433 at 439) or whether the Court of Appeal were right in saying that the only foreseeable risk was of "children who were drawn to the boat climbing upon it and being injured by the rotten planking giving way beneath them": see [1998] 3 All ER 559 at 568, [1998] 1 WLR 1546 at 1555 per Roch LJ. Was the wider risk, which would include within its description the accident which actually happened, reasonably foreseeable?

My Lords, although this is in end the question of fact, the courts are not without guidance. "Reasonably foreseeable" is not a fixed point on the scale of probability. As Lord Reid explained in *The Wagon Mound (No 2), Overseas Tankship (UK) Ltd v Miller Steamship Co Pty Ltd* [1966] 2 All ER 709 at 718, [1967] 1 AC 617 at 642 other factors have to be considered in deciding whether a given probability of injury generates a duty to take steps to eliminate the risk. In that case, the matters which the Privy Council took into account were whether avoiding the risk would have involved the defendant in undue cost or required him to abstain from some otherwise reasonable activity. In *Bolton v Stone* [1951] 1 All ER 1078, [1951] AC 850 there was a foreseeable risk that someone might one day be hit by a cricket ball but avoiding this risk would have required the club to incur very large expense or stop playing cricket. The House of Lords decided that the risk was not such that a reasonable man should have taken either of these steps to eliminate it. On the other hand, in *The Wagon Mound (No 2)*, the risk was caused by the fact that the defendant's ship had, without any need or excuse, discharged oil into Sydney Harbour. The risk of the oil catching fire would have been regarded as extremely small. But, said Lord Reid:

> It does not follow that, no matter what the circumstances may be, it is justifiable to neglect a risk of such a small magnitude. A reasonable man would only neglect such a risk if he had some valid reason for doing so: eg, that it would involve considerable expense to eliminate the risk. He would weigh the risk against the difficulty of eliminating it. (See [1966] 2 All ER 709 at 718, [1967] 1 AC 617 at 642.)

[T]he concession by the council is of significance. The council admit that they should have removed the boat. True, they make this concession solely on the ground that there was a risk that children would suffer minor injuries if the rotten planking gave way beneath them. But the concession shows that if there were a wider risk, the council would have had to incur no additional expense to eliminate it. They would only have had to do what they admit they should have done anyway. On the principle

Jolley v Sutton LBC cont.

as stated by Lord Reid, the wider risk would also fall within the scope of the council's duty unless it was different in kind from that which should have been foreseen (like the fire and pollution risks in *The Wagon Mound (No 1)*) and either wholly unforeseeable (as the fire risk was assumed to be in *The Wagon Mound (No 1)*) or so remote that it could be "brushed aside as far-fetched": see *The Wagon Mound (No 2)* [1966] 2 All ER 709 at 719, [1967] 1 AC 617 at 643 per Lord Reid.

I agree ... that one cannot so describe the risk that children coming upon an abandoned boat and trailer would suffer injury in some way other than by falling through the planks.......

In the Court of Appeal, Lord Woolf MR ([1998] 3 All ER 559 at 566, [1998] 1 WLR 1546 at 1553) observed that there seemed to be no case of which counsel were aware "where want of care on the part of a defendant was established but a plaintiff, who was a child, has failed to succeed because the circumstances of the accident were not foreseeable". I would suggest that this is for a combination of three reasons: first, because a finding or admission of want of care on the part of the defendant establishes that it would have cost the defendant no more trouble to avoid the injury which happened than he should in any case have taken; secondly, because in such circumstances the defendants will be liable for the materialisation of even relatively small risks of a different kind, and thirdly, because it has been repeatedly said in cases about children that their ingenuity in finding unexpected ways of doing mischief to themselves and others should never be underestimated. For these reasons, I think that the judge's broad description of the risk as being that children would "meddle with the boat at the risk of some physical injury" was the correct one to adopt on the facts of this case. The actual injury fell within that description and I would therefore allow the appeal.

Extent of damage and the eggshell skull rule

[13.205] The foreseeability test laid down in *Wagon Mound* only requires that the defendant foresee injury of the same kind as sustained by the plaintiff in relation to the initial injury. As *Hughes v Lord Advocate* [1963] AC 837 demonstrated, any subsequent injuries flowing from that initial one need not be foreseen. This is significant in relation to the rule that defendants must take their victims as they find them, otherwise known as the eggshell skull rule. The application of the rule is demonstrated in the cases below. Kennedy J in *Dulieu v White & Sons* [1901] 2 KB 669 (at 679) explained it as follows:

> If a man is negligently run over or otherwise negligently injured in his body, it is no answer to the sufferer's claim for damages that he would have suffered less injury, or no injury at all, if he had not had an unusually thin skull or an unusually weak heart.

Stephenson v Waite Tileman Ltd

[13.210] *Stephenson v Waite Tileman Limited* [1973] 1 NZLR 152 Court of Appeal of New Zealand (footnotes omitted)

RICHMOND J: The central issue in this appeal is the correct application of the decision of the Privy Council in *Overseas Tankship (UK) Ltd v Morts Dock & Engineering Co Ltd (The Wagon Mound No 1)* [1961] AC 388; [1961] 1 All ER 404, to actions for damages for bodily injury.

The appellant was employed by the respondent as a steeplejack. On 15 March 1965 he was engaged in the course of his employment in resetting the wire rope system of a crane. The evidence showed that the particular wire rope which required attention by the appellant was very rusty and was starting to de-strand itself and producing little sprags, that is to say little sections of main strands which had broken off and, due to tension, had sprung out and thus were capable of inflicting a scratch

Stephenson v Waite Tileman Ltd cont.

or wound on anyone required to handle the rope. While the appellant was working on the rope it suddenly sprang free from a sheave and struck the appellant's right hand, cutting it or slashing it on the back. It seems that the appellant thereupon washed the cut in cold water and covered it with a plaster, but within a day or two his hand began to swell, he became feverish, fell ill and went to bed. He was admitted to hospital and although his swelling and feverish condition subsided after a fairly short time, he developed symptoms of a very serious and debilitating kind which have persisted ever since. He is unable to concentrate, suffers from headaches and loss of balance and is scarcely able to look after himself. He walks with the aid of a stick. The learned trial Judge described his physical condition at the time of the trial as pitiful. [The jury found that the cut was the cause of the plaintiff's disability, but that such disability was not of a kind reasonably foreseeable by the defendant. The plaintiff succeeded and general damages were assessed at the full amount claimed, namely $35,000, but with a finding of 60 per cent contributory negligence against him for failing to wear protective gloves.]

... The obvious starting point is a consideration of the decisions in *The Wagon Mound* itself and in the only other cases of the highest authority, namely *Hughes v Lord Advocate* ... and *The Wagon Mound (No 2)* ... As a result of the three cases it is now quite clear that the rule of foreseeability of damage is concerned only with foreseeability of a real risk of injury of a kind (or class or character) which embraces the actual damage in suit. Although the broad basis of the rule is that it would be unjust to hold a wrongdoer liable for damage of a kind which he could not reasonably foresee, nevertheless the rule accepts the position that there are many matters of detail which nobody could predict but for which the wrongdoer nevertheless remains liable. These details may occur either in an unforeseeable concatenation of circumstances which lead up to the occurrence of damage of the foreseeable kind or they may consist of unpredictable details going to the extent or severity of the damage ...

One of the obvious questions to ask [after *Wagon Mound* (No 1)] was, "What would become of the 'eggshell skull' cases?" So far as I have been able to ascertain, nobody seriously felt that the long standing principle that a wrongdoer should take his victim as he found him should be altered ... The difficulty has been rather to find a satisfactory theoretical basis whereby to reconcile such cases with the principle of foreseeability of damage ... [lengthy discussion of precedents omitted]

The result of this lengthy review of the authorities is to disclose the existence of a very strong body of judicial opinion both in England and in Commonwealth jurisdictions in favour of the view that the eggshell skull rule remains part of our law notwithstanding the decision in *The Wagon Mound (No 1)*. As already indicated, I accept that view myself and for reasons which I have endeavoured to express I am also satisfied that similar principles must be applied to cases where a foreseeable kind of physical injury gives rise to some new risk or state of susceptibility in the victim. I have also found it helpful to consider the various fact situations which have arisen in the reported cases while endeavouring to arrive at some general principle which may be fairly and properly applied. I now summarise my conclusions:

1 In cases of damage by physical injury to the person the principles imposing liability for consequences flowing from the pre-existing special susceptibility of the victim and/or from new risk or susceptibility created by the initial injury remain part of our law.

2 In such cases the question of foreseeability should be limited to the initial injury. The tribunal of fact must decide whether that injury is of a kind, type or character which the defendant ought reasonably to have foreseen as a real risk.

3 If the plaintiff establishes that the initial injury was within a reason-ably foreseeable kind, type or character of injury, then the necessary link between the ultimate consequences of the initial injury and the negligence of the defendant can be forged simply as one of cause and effect – in other words by establishing an adequate relationship of cause and effect between the initial injury and the ultimate consequence.

Stephenson v Waite Tileman Ltd cont.

If I am correct in the foregoing conclusions then juries will be left to deal with the question of foreseeability in an area which is readily comprehensible and in which the test of the ordinary reasonable man can be applied in an atmosphere of reality. They will not have to decide the ability of the ordinary man to foresee the risks of "kinds" of harm resulting from a "sub-compartmentalisation" of secondary consequences of an initial injury. Nor will it be necessary to decide whether a doctor driving a motor car is to be made liable for a greater field of injury than would the ordinary layman in similar circumstances. I remain very conscious of the fact, however, that only the Judicial Committee can give a final answer to this difficult but very practical problem.

In the present case it is accepted by Mr Casey that the initial injury to the appellant was of a kind which was reasonably foreseeable by the respondent... On any view the case is one of special susceptibility on the part of the respondent (that is, to the particular infection which entered the wound, or to functional disorder) or else is one of a normal reaction on the part of the appellant to a new risk created by the initial injury (that is, the risk of infection or the risk of functional disorder). It may be a mixture of both. However that may be it follows from what I have said earlier in this judgment that the issue as to foreseeability of ultimate consequences should not have been put to the jury in the circumstances of this case. The appeal should in my opinion be allowed and judgment entered for the appellant in accordance with the other findings of the jury.

[Turner J and Richmond J agreed with Macarthur JJ]

[13.215] **Notes&Questions**

1. Among the many authorities reviewed by Richmond J in *Stephenson* was *Smith v Leech Brain & Co Ltd* [1962] 2 QB 405, which was the first English case after *Wagon Mound* to consider the eggshell skull rule. His Honour said (at 163):

> In that case a galvaniser employed by the defendants was exposed in the ordinary course of his work to a foreseeable risk of receiving a burn from molten metal unless adequately protected. As a result of the failure of the defendants to provide such protection he was struck on the lower lip by a piece of molten metal, causing a burn. The burn was the promoting agent of cancer which developed at the site of the burn, and from which he died some three years later. The cancer developed in tissues which already had a pre-malignant condition. Lord Parker (at 414; 1161) expressed himself as satisfied that the Judicial Committee in *The Wagon Mound* case did not have the thin skull cases in mind. "The test is not whether these employers could reasonably have foreseen that a burn would cause cancer and that he would die. The question is whether these employers could reasonably foresee the type of injury he suffered, namely, the burn. What, in the particular case, is the amount of damage which he suffers as a result of that burn, depends upon the characteristics and constitution of the victim."
>
> It is of importance to note that Lord Parker regarded the kind of damage which had to be foreseeable as a burn from molten metal. He regarded the effects of that burn on the latent susceptibility of the deceased workman to cancer as going only to the extent of the damage and regarded it as irrelevant that those effects might be unforeseeable ... The decision in *Smith v Leech Brain & Co Ltd* appears to have remained unchallenged ever since.

2. In *Nader v Urban Transit Authority of NSW* (1985) 2 NSWLR 501 the plaintiff was a 10 year old boy who struck his head on a bus stop pole while alighting from a slowly moving bus. He developed a rare psychological condition known as Ganser Syndrome. Nothing in his physical or psychological make up could be

proved to pre-dispose him to this condition. The defendant argued that his illness resulted from his family's response to the accident. The accident was held by the majority (Samuels JA and McHugh JA) to have been a legal cause of the reaction because it materially contributed to the onset and continuation of the condition. McHugh J discussed the eggshell skull rule.

> The rule of the "eggshell skull cases" should not be confined to the physical or constitutional characteristics of the particular individual. When a defendant takes a plaintiff as he finds him, he does not take him as a naked human being divorced from his environment. Clearly enough taking the plaintiff as you find him involves taking him in at least his social and earning capacity setting. ... I think that the defendant must take the plaintiff with all his weaknesses, beliefs and reactions as well as his capacities and attributes, physical, social and economic. If the result of an accident is that a ten year old boy reacts to his parents' concern over his injuries and develops an hysterical condition, no reason of justice, morality or entrenched principle appears to me to prevent his recovery of compensation. Not everyone has shared Lord Simond's view that it is not consonant with current ideas of justice and morality that a defendant should be liable for all the consequences of a trivial act of negligence so long as they are direct ([1961] AC 388 at 422). In *Siwek v Lambourn* [1964] VR 337 at 339 Dean J observed that the "subsequent erosion of *The Wagon Mound* would appear to have been dictated by a consideration opposed to that quoted, namely, that it is just that the wrongdoer rather than his victim, should bear the loss occasioned by the wrong". Justice to the defendant is fulfilled by the requirement that the plaintiff must belong to the class of persons whom the defendant can reasonably foresee may be injured by his carelessness and by the requirement of a causal connection between the negligence and the plaintiff's condition ...

The Court of Appeal held that the damage which the plaintiff suffered, namely the Ganser Syndrome, was damage of a kind which was reasonably foreseeable.

3. In *Kavanagh v Akhtar* (1998) 45 NSWLR 588 the respondent (plaintiff) was seriously injured due to the appellant's (defendant) negligence. The plaintiff was an Indian Muslim woman. The injury caused her significant discomfort with caring and brushing of her long hair. Contrary to her husband's cultural and religious beliefs she cut her long hair without first consulting her husband. She believed, wrongly, that her husband would not object. Her husband's reactions were extreme. She was subject to insult, loss of assistance in the household, his refusal of sexual relations with her; and her husband sleeping with other women. It effectively caused a break up of the marriage. The plaintiff suffered a serious psychiatric illness as a consequence. The NSW Court of Appeal held that the plaintiff was entitled to recover damages for the psychiatric Illness. Mason P said:

> The principle that a tortfeasor takes the victim as he or she is found is not absolute and unqualified. However, I see no reason why the appellant should not take the respondent in the family and cultural setting that she lived (cf *Nader* at 537). Equality before the law puts a heavy onus on the person who would argue that the "unusual" reaction of an injured plaintiff should be disregarded because a minority religious or cultural situation may not have been foreseeable (cf generally Calabresi, *Ideals, Beliefs, Attitudes and the Law* (1985)). Whether or not the husband's response (with its consequences) was consistent with his marital obligations (and I am not inferring a judgment either way), the unchallenged evidence showed that it was a direct response to the hair-cutting.

Evidence was accepted that the husband's reaction would have been a "well-known" reaction in the Islamic community even if not foreseeable to a Burwood shopkeeper. Mason P concluded:

> [T]he respondent's psychiatric injuries were foreseeable and the award of general damages should have taken them into account. It was perfectly foreseeable that a severe and continuing shoulder injury would affect a plaintiff's capacity to attend to matters of personal hygiene and adornment, particularly in a context where she was a home maker. And it was equally foreseeable that this would put strain on marital relations, as it certainly did in the months prior to the hair cutting incident. That such strain might lead to a severe breakdown of that marital relationship with extreme psychiatric consequences for a vulnerable plaintiff was also foreseeable. The fact that the breakdown occurred in consequence of a *perhaps* unforeseeable step taken by the respondent (cutting her hair) or the *perhaps* unforeseeable reaction of her husband is irrelevant in the light of cases such as *Hughes* and *Nader*, so long as psychiatric injury is itself regarded as a foreseeable consequence of the physical injury inflicted on the respondent...

Priestley and Handley JJA agreed with Mason P.

CHAPTER 14

Damages

INTRODUCTION

[14.05] The assessment of damages for personal injury and death are discussed in this chapter.

McGregor on Damages defines damages as:

> pecuniary compensation, obtainable by success in an action, for a wrong which is either a tort or a breach of contract, the compensation being in the form of a lump sum which is awarded unconditionally and is generally but not necessarily expressed in [the local] currency. (16 th ed, Sweet & Maxwell, London, 1997), [1])

"Personal injury" can be inflicted in many ways, overlapping different areas of law, notably torts, contracts and criminal law. The measure of damages in contract is similar in many respects to tort, but there are significant differences. It should be assumed that the principles of compensation discussed in this chapter apply to personal injury caused by negligence. For this type of injury, the civil liability legislation makes it immaterial whether the case is pleaded in tort, contract, pursuant to statute or any other cause of action: eg, NSW: CLA, s 11A; Vic: WrA, s 28C(3). The principles and rules governing damages derive from a mixture of common law and statute. Key statutes in all jurisdictions include motor accidents, workers compensation, and criminal injuries legislation–all of which fall outside the scope of this chapter. The civil liability Acts of each State and Territory are the principal statutes that will be considered in Chapter 14.

Compensatory damages

[14.10] Compensation is the reparation of a wrong by provision of a sum of money (damages) awarded by a court and it is the focus of this chapter. Losses arising from personal injury will normally be both financial and personal, and the award of damages must take both into account. Clearly, the value of personal losses, such as pain and suffering, loss of enjoyment of life, and diminished life expectancy, cannot be calculated in monetary terms. How then can a figure be arrived at? This is examined under "non economic loss" at [14.215]. Courts do attempt to calculate monetary losses, and in relation to specific past losses, such as expenditure or lost income to the date of the trial, this can be done with a high degree of accuracy. In relation to future losses, such as loss of income and the costs of upkeep for an injured person, because of the "once and for all" rule (see [14.40]) assumptions need to be made concerning the injured person's life had the tort not been committed (for purposes of comparison), as well as in relation to his or her future post-tort. This is fraught with difficulty.

Exemplary, punitive and aggravated damages

[14.15] Punishment and deterrence are the purposes of exemplary damages. Both functions are most commonly associated with the criminal law. Their presence in tort reflects the shared historical origins of the two branches of law. Exemplary damages, also known as punitive, vindictive, or retributory damages, have been recognised in tort since at least the 18th century. As Lord Justice Pratt said in *Wilkes v Wood* (1763) Lofft 1 at 18-19; 98 ER 489:

> a jury have it in their power to give damages for more than the injury received. Damages are designed not only as a satisfaction to the injured person, but likewise as a punishment to the guilty, to deter from any such proceeding for the future, and as a proof of the detestation of the jury to the action itself.

In *Cotogno v Lamb* (1986) 5 NSWLR 559 at 586-587, McHugh JA justified awards of exemplary damages in the following way:

> [The award] acts as an example to all those in the community who might engage in wrongdoing ...The sanctions of the criminal law are not always sufficient to protect the weak and the disadvantaged against the oppressive conduct of the powerful and the wealthy. .. exemplary damages also serves another useful social purpose: it helps to remove the sense of grievance which the plaintiff feels...

Exemplary damages are the exception rather than the rule in civil settings, and depend upon the ability of the award to fulfil its purpose (*Gray v Motor Accidents Commission* (1998) 196 CLR 1), as well as the presence of such egregious conduct on the part of the defendant that it ought not to go unpunished: *Lamb v Cotogno* (1987) 164 CLR 1; *Whitfield v De Lauret & Co Ltd* (1920) 29 CLR 71 at 77 per Knox CJ. The usual requirement is "contumelious wrongdoing in conscious disregard of [the plaintiff's] rights" (*Whitfield*, at 77). "Conscious" has been interpreted as deliberate, intentional, or reckless, and is thus not restricted to intentional torts. Unlike a fine in criminal law, which goes to the benefit of the state, exemplary damages are a "windfall" to plaintiffs in the sense that they constitute sums over and above those needed to restore the plaintiff to his or her pre-tort position, representing a departure from the compensation principle. Exemplary damages have been awarded at common law in Australia for a range of torts, including defamation, assault, negligence, nuisance, trespass to land, trespass to chattels, conversion, detinue, deceit, misfeasance in public office, false imprisonment, and others.

Lord Hoffman outlined some of the differences between exemplary damages and criminal punishment in *W v W* [1999] 2 NZLR 1 at [6] (PC), a case dealing with sexual abuse:

> The procedure is ... radically different and so is the standard of proof. A prosecution is generally speaking initiated and controlled by the state. A civil action is initiated and controlled by the victim. Thus the prosecution of an action for exemplary damages enables the victim publicly to vindicate his or her version of events and inflict punishment, even revenge, in ways which a criminal prosecution may not satisfy. Punishment takes the form of damages which go to the victim rather than imprisonment or a fine which can afford her only a more indirect satisfaction. Allowing the victim to pursue such a claim may have a therapeutic value which mitigates the effects of the offence.

Questions of double jeopardy can arise where the conduct is both criminal and tortious. The High Court has made it plain that exemplary damages may not be awarded if the defendant has already suffered "substantial" punishment in criminal proceedings for substantially the same conduct: *Gray v Motor Accidents Commission* (1998) 196 CLR 1; see also *Daniels v Thompson, J v Bell, W v W, H v P* (conjoined appeals) [1998] 3 NZLR 22 (CA) (a majority of the NZ Court of Appeal decided that either conviction or acquittal in prior criminal proceedings prevented subsequent recovery of exemplary damages). What constitutes "substantial" punishment was left open, although there was support for the view that imprisonment would always qualify. Disquiet about punishment as an appropriate function of tort law has been frequently voiced, not least because of the absence of criminal safeguards such as the higher standard of proof (beyond reasonable doubt). Criticism has been particularly marked in relation to defamation. The House of Lords severely circumscribed exemplary damages in the leading case of *Rookes v Barnard* [1964] AC 1129, but the High Court declined to follow suit (*Uren v John Fairfax & Sons Ltd* (1966) 117 CLR 118; *Australian Consolidated Press Ltd v Uren* (1966) 117 CLR 185). Legislatures too, have exhibited mixed reactions to exemplary damages, with those in New South Wales, Queensland and the Northern Territory prohibiting them under civil liability legislation: NSW: CLA, s 21; Qld: CLA, s 52; *Personal Injuries (Liabilities and Damages) Act 2003* (NT), s 19. Uniform defamation laws, adopted in Australia in 2006, also prohibit awards of exemplary damages (eg, *Defamation Act 2005* (NSW) s 37).

In the United States, punitive damages (as they are called there) frequently exceed compensatory damages and can be enormous, whereas in Australia and the United Kingdom more modest sums are awarded. For example, in *Lamb v Cotogno* (1987) 164 CLR 1, the plaintiff was awarded $5000 exemplary damages in 1979 by the New South Wales Supreme Court, out of a total award of $203,570. Compare this with the United States case of *Henley v Phillip Morris Inc* 113 Cal Rptr 2d 494 (2001) (US), in which a plaintiff who began smoking in the 1960s at the age of 15 sued the tobacco giant for her lung cancer, seeking compensatory damages and $15 million in punitive damages. At trial in 1999 the jury returned a verdict for the plaintiff, awarding $1.5 million in compensatory damages and $50 million in punitive damages. This was affirmed in 2001, but has since been reviewed (9 Cal Rptr 3d 29 (2004) (US)). See also *Engle v RJ Reynolds Tobacco Co*, No 94-08273 CA 22 (Dade County Circuit Court, Florida) (2000) (US).

Aggravated damages are considered to be compensatory, and are directed at restoration or appeasement of the plaintiff's dignity. They are frequently difficult to distinguish from exemplary damages. In *Uren v John Fairfax & Sons Pty Ltd* (1966) 117 CLR 118 at 149, Windeyer J explained the purpose of aggravated damages as being "to compensate the plaintiff when the harm done to him by a wrongful act was aggravated by the manner in which the act was done". In *New South Wales v Ibbett* (2006) 229 CLR 638 at [31], the High Court described aggravated damages as "a form of general damages, given by way of compensation for injury to the plaintiff, which may be intangible, resulting from the circumstances and manner of the wrongdoing". Awards of aggravated damages are usually restricted to torts which are actionable per se, without proof of damage, such as trespass to person, land, or goods, conspiracy, defamation, malicious falsehood, intimidation, and deceit. Since the passage of the civil liability legislation, awards of exemplary, punitive and aggravated damages have been precluded for personal injury or death arising from negligence in some Australian jurisdictions: NSW: CLA, s 21; NT: *Personal Injuries (Liabilities and Damages) Act 2003*, s 19; Qld: CLA, s 52 (but note these damages are allowed if damage caused by unlawful intentional act or unlawful sexual assault). No such restrictions have been enacted in the other jurisdictions.

Nominal and contemptuous damages

[14.20] Nominal damages are small sums awarded in recognition that a plaintiff's rights have been invaded in a technical sense, but no damage has been sustained. This may occur in breach of contract, for example, or trespass. Nominal damages cannot be awarded in negligence, because damage is the gist of the action, and personal injury always constitutes damage. For example, *Wilton v Commonwealth of Australia* (1990) 12 MVR 243 (NSW CA); *Sivas v GIO (NSW)* (1990) 12 MVR 272 (NSW CA); *Victorian Railways Commissioners v Hennings* (1917) 22 CLR 482. Contemptuous damages are very trivial sums which reflect the jury's belief that the claim should not have been brought (eg, the jury award of a farthing in *Shallue v Long Tunnel Gold Mine* (1994) 10 VLR (L) 56 (FC)). *Wynbergen v Hoyts Corporation* (1997) 72 ALJR 65, in which the plaintiff recovered against his employer for personal injury (slipping on a wet floor) but was awarded only the cost of the initial GP's visit in damages, is another example.

BASIC PRINCIPLES IN COMPENSATORY DAMAGES AWARDS

[14.25] This section examines the basic assumptions and principles underlying compensation in tort for personal injury, and contrasts them with alternative approaches to compensation adopted in social security and workers' compensation schemes. The assumptions derive from the common law, and have not been altered in any substantial way by legislation. Gibbs CJ and Wilson J in *Todorovic v Waller* (1981) 150 CLR 402 at 412, summarised them as follows:

> Certain fundamental principles are so well established that it is unnecessary to cite authorities in support of them. In the first place, a plaintiff who has been injured by the negligence of the defendant should be awarded such a sum of money as will, as nearly as possible, put him in the position as if he had not sustained the injuries. Secondly, damages for one cause of action must be recovered once and forever, and (in the absence of any statutory exception) must be awarded as a lump sum; the court cannot order a defendant to make periodic payments to the plaintiff. Thirdly, the court has no concern with the manner in which the plaintiff uses the sum awarded to him; the plaintiff is free to do what he likes with it. Fourthly, the burden lies on the plaintiff to prove the injury or loss for which he seeks damages.

Fault

[14.30] The element of fault is central in almost all torts, supplying the legal and moral justification for a transfer of resources from the defendant to the plaintiff by way of damages. As Lord Atkin said in *Donoghue v Stevenson* [1932] AC 562 at 580, "the law is based upon the general public sentiment of moral wrongdoing for which the offender must pay". Supporters of the fault principle argue that it is in accordance with community expectations and acts to deter dangerous conduct, as well as fulfilling a corrective justice function: see, eg, New South Wales Law Reform Commission, Report on a Transport Accident Scheme for NSW (LRC 43/1, 1984), ch 3.

Restitutio in integrum or the compensatory principle

[14.35] At common law, it has long been accepted that the primary principle underlying damages is restitutio in integrum, that is, plaintiffs are entitled to be restored to the position they would have been in but for the defendant's wrongdoing. Tort damages are intended to provide "fair" rather than "perfect" compensation for the plaintiff's loss (*Lee Transport Co Ltd v Watson* (1940) 64 CLR 1 discussed below in *Sharman v Evans* (1977) 138 CLR 563 at 586 per Gibbs CJ and Stephen J, see [14.100]). In *Livingstone v Rawyards Coal Co* (1880) 5 App Cas 25 at 39, Lord Blackburn referred to:

> [the] general rule that, where any injury is to be compensated by damages, in settling the sum of money to be given for reparation of damages you should as nearly as possible get at that sum of money which will put the party who has been injured, or who has suffered, in the same position as he would have been in if he had not sustained the wrong for which he is now getting his compensation or reparation.

This means that a plaintiff who earned $500,000 per annum before the accident and who can no longer work will have his or her damages calculated on the basis of a $500,000 loss per annum. A low skilled worker earning $25,000 per annum before the accident and who can no longer work will have damages assessed on the basis of a $25,000 loss per annum. Because of its individualised focus the common law system has been seen as the "Rolls Royce" of compensation systems, premised on corrective justice notions. Precise justice in this context is seen as being as important in determining the quantum of damages as it is at the liability stage.

The "once and for all" rule

[14.40] In actions for negligence the cause of action arises when the damage is suffered. At common law the plaintiff recovers a single lump sum payment intended to compensate for all past and future losses relating to the action. In *Murphy v Stone-Wallwork (Charlton) Ltd* [1969] 1 WLR 1023 at 1027, Lord Pearce said:

> Our courts have adopted the principle that damages are assessed at the trial once and for all. If later the plaintiff suffers greater loss from an accident than was anticipated at the trial, he cannot come back for more. Nor can the defendant come back if the loss is less than was anticipated. Thus, the assessment of damages for the future is necessarily compounded of prophecy and calculation. The court must do the best it can to reach what seems to be the right figure on a reasonable balance of the probabilities, avoiding undue optimism and undue pessimism.

(See also *Todorovic v Waller* (1981) 150 CLR 402 at 412 per Gibbs CJ and Wilson J.) According to one judge, what the court is being asked to do in this process is "to assess the unassessable, to pronounce on the unpronounceable, to judge the unjudgeable" (*Mundy v Government Insurance Office of New South Wales*, unreported, NSW SC, Spender AJ, 5 June 1995, BC9504763. The case concerned a three year old child who had suffered catastrophic physical and mental injuries). The inability to re-open assessments can give rise to serious hardship for injured plaintiffs, as well as to unmerited windfalls for their estates in the event of earlier than anticipated death. The evidence suggests that in the most serious cases plaintiffs are frequently under compensated (NSWLRC, Report on a Transport Accident Scheme for NSW (LRC 43/1, 1984), ch 3). In some Australian jurisdictions modifications of the "once and for all" rule have been adopted or recommended in relation to certain types of action: *Motor Accidents Act 1988* (NSW), s 81; *Supreme Court Act 1935* (SA), s 30B; *Motor Vehicle (Third Party Insurance) Act 1943* (WA), s 16(4); *Transport Accident Act 1986* (Vic), ss 44 – 45, 47 – 51. Although legislation in Western Australia (*Motor Vehicle (Third Party Insurance) Act 1943* (WA), s 16(4)) and South Australia (*Supreme Court Act 1935* (SA), s 30b) has long permitted the courts to make orders for periodic payments, these powers are rarely used. Note: the WA provision is limited to personal injury claims caused by or arising out of the use of a motor vehicle. There is provision under the *Workers' Compensation Act 1987* (NSW), s 151Q for the periodic payment of future economic losses, known as structured settlements. The civil liability legislation in all jurisdictions (except South Australia) provides for structured settlements by consent of the parties, but these are the exception not the norm: see also ACT: CLWA, s 106; NT: *Personal Injuries (Liabilities and Damages) Act 2003*, s 31; NSW: CLA, Pt 2, Div 7, ss 22 – 26; Qld: CLA, s 65; Tas: CLA, Pt 5; Vic: WrA, ss 28M, 28N; WA: CLA, s 15. For example, s 22 of the NSW: CLA makes provision for periodic payments, funded by an annuity or similar method. Section 23 states that the "purpose ... is to enable the court to give the parties ... a reasonable opportunity to negotiate a structured settlement". Section 23(3) – (5) deals with structured awards for "persons in need of protection" pursuant to the *Protected Estates Act 1983* (NSW). There are other statutory exceptions to the once and for all rule. For example, Pt 5 of the *Supreme Court Act 1970* (NSW) allows the court to make interim payments in any case for damages, and the District Court has the same power under s 58 of the *District Court Act 1973* (NSW). Provisional damages are available before the Dust Diseases tribunal. The *Motor Accidents Act 1988* (NSW) (as amended by *Motor Accidents (Amendment) Act 1989* (NSW)) provides that both parties in transport related personal injury claims may consent to a structured settlement for periodic payments of damages for future economic loss, medical expenses and home care services. This is most likely to occur with plaintiffs who have sustained catastrophic injury and will be in need of institutional care (see M Tilbury, M Noone, B Kercher, Remedies Commentary and Materials (4 th ed, Lawbook Co, 2004), p 73).

In *Murphy v Stone-Wallwork* [1969] 1 WLR 1023 at 1027-1028, Lord Pearce went on to say that although periodic payments, and a right of recourse whenever circumstances change might seem an attractive solution to the difficulties imposed by once and for all assessment, they too have serious drawbacks, such as the unending possibility of litigation. Finality in judgments was seen as an important principle. See the confirmation by Lord Scarman in *Lim Poh Choo v Camden & Islington Health Area Authority* [1980] AC 174 at 182-183.

Damages awarded unconditionally

[14.45] As we will see in *Todorovic v Waller* (1981) 150 CLR 402 (see [14.60]), "the court has no concern with the manner in which the plaintiff uses the sum awarded to him… [he] is free to do what he likes with it".

[14.50] **Notes&Questions**

1. Given that plaintiffs' damages are reduced for contributory negligence, can the fault principle be reconciled with the restitutio in integrum principle? What role would contributory negligence play in a needs based system of compensation?
2. How convincing are the fault and deterrence arguments in light of insurance?
3. What would happen if a plaintiff squandered all of his or her damages on, say, gambling? What should happen?

A system in need of reform?

[14.55] Many commentators, both judicial and academic, have criticised the tort system of compensation, as discussed in the opening chapter of this book. Professor Patrick Atiyah has been a strong critic, arguing that by definition many deserving victims of accidents are precluded from recovering compensation at all, simply because they are unable to prove fault, whereas others with identical injuries who can prove fault may recover large sums. As approximately 55 per cent of injuries requiring hospital treatment occur in the home, this is undeniable. For more information on accident statistics see Australian Institute of Health and Welfare (AIHW), Australian Hospital Statistics, 1999-2000 (AIHW, Health Services Series No 17, 2001), Table 9.6. See also Chapter 1 of this book.)

Atiyah says:

> the system is about as fair as a lottery. In fact it is not too much to say that it is a lottery, a lottery by law. It is almost a matter of chance whether you can obtain damages for disabilities

> and injuries; it is almost a matter of chance who will pay them, it is almost a matter of chance how much you will get. (PS Atiyah, The Damages Lottery (Oxford: Hart Publishing, 1997), p 143)

Atiyah attacks what he calls "stretching" the law, that is, judicial extension of the boundaries of the system in favour of plaintiffs for reasons of sympathy, and he criticises the restitutio in integrum basis of compensation. He says (at 33):

> The basic problem is that those who are compensated with damages are a tiny minority of all victims of accidents and disabilities, and the more we squeeze into this category, the less money is likely to be available for the great majority of victims. It is rather as though, faced with a hundred homeless people living on the street, we picked out one or two and lodged them in the Ritz at our expense. If we stretch things a little more ... perhaps we could afford to help one or two more of the homeless and put them in the Ritz too. But we shall then find that the bill from the Ritz is so large that we shall have little or nothing to spend on the remaining 96 sleeping on the street. So stretching things here will actually have made things worse.

This is, of course, the other side of the "Rolls Royce" coin. Sugarman argues that the "moral cost of inconsistent treatment of equals" is higher in restitution systems of compensation (SD Sugarman, "Tort Reform Through Damages Law Reform: An American Perspective" (2005) 27 Sydney Law Rev 507). This of course begs the question whether it is fairer (more equal) to treat like with like, or all alike. Using the tort system of compensation to impose social levelling only upon a randomly selected group of accident victims in an otherwise unequal society, would be regarded by many as very unjust. Other comments seeing "stretching" as an issue have been made by, eg, Thomas J in *Lisle v Brice* (2001) 34 MVR 206 (Qld CA) at [4]-[5]. Other models exist and have been briefly discussed in Chapter 1.

Todorovic v Waller

[14.60] *Todorovic v Waller* (1981) 150 CLR 402 High Court of Australia

(footnotes omitted)

[Two cases were heard together in the High Court, *Todorovic v Waller* on appeal from the Court of Appeal of New South Wales, and *Jetson v Hankin*, brought from the Full Court of the Supreme Court of Victoria. Both concerned plaintiffs in their thirties who had suffered brain damage rendering them unemployable or virtually so. The award in *Jetson* was reduced by 90% for contributory negligence.]

MURPHY J: 453 Despite the paucity of statistics on extent of injuries and costs, it is clear that the direct social costs of industrial and road accidents greatly exceed the national defence budget. The problem is aggravated in financial terms because the advancement of medical science makes it possible to keep alive for many years persons who previously would have died soon after accidents; the costs of doing so are enormous. With the present death and injury rates, awards based on full restitution may be an unacceptable burden upon the community, particularly upon vehicle owners and industrial concerns, through the insurance system.

One way to reduce the burden is to transfer some or all of the social costs to the injured persons and their dependants. This has been the preferred judicial method, achieved (a) by unjustifiable discount rates (reaching even 8 per cent) applied to earnings and expected medical expenses which the courts pretend will not increase with inflation (b) by ignoring general increases in wages due not to inflation, but to increases in productivity, (c) by miserable awards for pain and suffering for catastrophic injuries, and perhaps the worst (d) by declining to implement the direction in compensation to relatives legislation to award damages proportioned to the injury (see *Jacobs v Varley* (1976) 50 ALJR 519). For many years, but especially after *Arthur Robinson (Grafton) Pty Ltd v Carter* (1968) 122 CLR 649; *Chulcough v Holley* (1968) 41 ALJR 336 and up to *Pennant Hills Restaurants Pty Ltd*

Todorovic v Waller cont.

v Barrell Insurances Pty Ltd (1981) 145 CLR 625, in serious personal injury cases the social function of the courts has been to depress damages. This has transferred much of the cost of serious road or industrial accidents (which would otherwise be borne by insurance companies and ultimately the public) to the injured person. The principle of restitution has been theory, not practice. Defendant's insurers often appealed, upon the ground of excessiveness, against awards which, in my opinion, were inadequate, and sometimes succeeded (as in *Sharman v Evan* (1977) 138 CLR 563); sometimes not (as in *Kaufmann v Van Rymenant* (1975) 49 ALJR 227).

A second way to reduce the burden is to transfer some or all of it to the social welfare system. A third is to reduce the accidents.

Lim Poh Choo v Camden

[14.65] *Lim Poh Choo v Camden* [1980] AC 174 House of Lords

(footnotes omitted)

[The facts are stated by Lord Scarman.]

LORD SCARMAN: 182 My Lords, on 28 February 1973 Dr Lim Poh Choo, a senior psychiatric registrar employed in the national health service, was admitted to a national health service hospital for a minor operation ... When, following on the operation, she was in the recovery room, she suffered a cardiac arrest. It was the result of the negligence of some person for whom the area health authority is vicariously responsible. The consequences for Dr Lim have been disastrous. Before 1 March 1973 Dr Lim, who was then 36 years old, had a career ahead of her in her chosen speciality of psychiatric medicine. She was described by one who knew her and her work as a "remarkably intelligent doctor". She is now the wreck of a human being, suffering from extensive and irremediable brain damage, which has left her only intermittently, and then barely, sentient and totally dependent on others.

... shortly before trial, the defendants admitted liability. The one issue at trial was, therefore, the question of damages. But its complexities are such that it occupied the trial judge for the best part of five days, the Court of Appeal six days, and your Lordships' House five days.

It cannot be said that any of the time judicially spent on these protracted proceedings has been unnecessary. The question, therefore, arises whether the state of the law which gives rise to such complexities is sound. Lord Denning MR in the Court of Appeal declared that a radical reappraisal of the law is needed. I agree. But I part company with him on ways and means. Lord Denning MR believes it can be done by the judges, whereas I would suggest to your Lordships that such a reappraisal calls for social, financial, economic and administrative decisions which only the legislature can take. The perplexities of the present case, following on the publication of the report of the Royal Commission on Civil Liability and Compensation for Personal Injury the ("Pearson report"), emphasise the need for reform of the law.

The course of the litigation illustrates, with devastating clarity, the insuperable problems implicit in a system of compensation for personal injuries which (unless the parties agree otherwise) can yield only a lump sum assessed by the court at the time of judgment. Sooner or later, and too often later rather than sooner, if the parties do not settle, a court (once liability is admitted or proved) has to make an award of damages. The award, which covers past, present and future injury and loss, must, under our law, be of a lump sum assessed at the conclusion of the legal process. The award is final; it is not susceptible to review as the future unfolds, substituting fact for estimate. Knowledge of the future

Lim Poh Choo v Camden cont.

being denied to mankind, so much of the award as is to be attributed to future loss and suffering (in many cases the major part of the award) will almost surely be wrong. There is really only one certainty: the future will prove the award to be either too high or too low.

—— ∞ ——

[14.70] **Notes**

For a fascinating account of many of the older English decisions see Lord Denning, What Next in the Law (Butterworths, London, 1982), Part 4 Personal Injuries, especially chs 5-9. Chapter 6 Living Death is Lord Denning's account of *Lim Poh Choo v Camden* [1980] AC 174.

"Tort reform" and the civil liability legislation

[14.75] All Australian jurisdictions have introduced legislative tort reform, based on the recommendations of the Negligence Review Panel in 2002 (Review of the Law of Negligence, Final Report (Commonwealth of Australia, Canberra, 2002): ACT: CLWA; NSW: CLA; Qld: CLA; SA: CLA; Tas: CLA; Vic: WrA; WA: CLA.

The legislation does not function as a code, which means the common law is still relevant and it must be applied in conjunction with the statutes. The legislation relates to issues of liability, as we have seen in previous chapters, but is also very significant regarding damages. Whether legislative tort reform has in fact achieved reform, and how one might define and measure reform, is *the* key issue in personal injuries compensation post-2002. Consider some questions: What is meant by reform? Who has benefited by tort reform? Who has lost? What are the justice and equity dimensions of the changes? Why have they been introduced? What evidence is there to support allegations of a "blame and claim" culture or "Santa Claus judges" prior to 2002? Have costs of insurance declined post 2002 (one of the major arguments in support of tort reform)? As you work through the principles governing assessment in the next sections, keep these questions in mind. The law of damages is just as much about who should be compensated and why (which are both normative questions relating to justice), as it is about the rules governing how compensation is assessed.

Despite the criticisms of the common law outlined above, the recommendations contained in the Ipp report (Negligence Review Panel, Review of the Law of Negligence, Final Report, (Commonwealth of Australia, Canberra, 2002) accepted the basic philosophical premises of the common law, including fault and restitutio. In most jurisdictions the common law rules relating to assessment of damages for personal injuries have been substantially modified by legislation, both before and as a result of "tort reform". This occurred first in relation to workplace accidents and motor vehicle accidents, the two most litigated sources of personal injury. It has now been extended more generally to personal injuries caused by negligence through civil liability legislation. Most States have legislated to limit compensation for injuries for the purpose of reducing costs, rather than on the principled basis suggested in the Ipp Report. Many of the "reforms" introduced depart from the Ipp Recommendations, and most jurisdictions only selectively adopted the recommendations: see D Butler, "A Comparison of the Adoption of the Ipp Report Recommendations and Other Personal Injuries Liability Reforms" (2005) 13 *Torts Law Journal* 203; EW Wright, "National trends in Personal Injury Litigation: Before and After "Ipp"" (2006) 14(3) *Torts Law Journal* 233.

ASSESSMENT OF DAMAGES

Date of assessment

[14.80] The normal rule at common law is that a plaintiff's entitlement to damages arises when the cause of action is complete. In negligence, the cause of action is complete when the harm is sustained. An exception to this rule is made for personal injury, wrongful birth and wrongful death actions. For these, the date of assessment is the date of trial commencement.

This is fairer to plaintiffs in a once and for all system, especially where there are long delays in coming to trial, since it allows the court to take account of known factors such as inflation and changes in wages. In *Johnson v Perez* (1988) 166 CLR 351, a construction worker instructed his solicitors to sue three separate employers for injuries sustained at work over a five year period. The claims were eventually struck out for want of prosecution. Perez sued the solicitors for negligently allowing the claims to fail. In addition, he claimed psychological injury arising from the workplace injuries, aggravated by the solicitor's negligence. One of the issues considered was whether the date for assessment of damages was the original hearing date (assuming the solicitors had not been negligent), the later date when the causes of action were struck out, or the date of making the eventual award. The Supreme Court of Queensland and the Full Court on appeal both assessed damages as at the date of the award.

Another reason for allowing the later date to prevail is greater accuracy in determining the personal circumstances of the plaintiff. As Uthwatt J said in *In re Bradberry* [1943] Ch 35 at 45, "facts are to be preferred to prophecies". *Baker v Willoughby* [1970] AC 467 (HL) illustrates the complications which can arise. There, the plaintiff was injured in the leg in a car accident, with a prognosis of lasting disability. Prior to the motor vehicle case coming to trial, he was shot in the same leg during a robbery at his workplace, and his leg had to be amputated. The trial judge held that no account was to be taken of the shooting and amputation in the assessment of damages for the motor vehicle accident. See discussion of this case, and *Jobling v Associated Dairies* [1982] AC 794 which reviewed it, at [13.75]

On appeal, Lord Reid pointed out (at 490-91) that:

> There is no doubt that it is proper to lead evidence at the trial as to any events or developments between the date of the accident and the date of the trial which are relevant for the proper assessment of damages ... And it is always proper to take account of developments with regard to the injuries which were caused by the defendant's tort: those developments may show that any assessment of damages that might have been made shortly after the accident can now be seen to be either too small or too large.

In relation to a plaintiff's medical prognosis, the Privy Council said in *Thompson v Faraonio* (1979) 24 ALR 1 at 7:

> [A]ctual improvement or deterioration in the medical condition of the injured person is taken into account and it would be carrying theory to absurd lengths if such medical history had to be disregarded in favour of prognosis made immediately after the accident.

The principle of preferring facts also applies in wrongful death claims. Latham CJ in this context, taking into account the re-marriage of the plaintiff, said in *Willis v The Commonwealth* (1946) 73 CLR 105 at 109, that "where actual facts are known, speculation as to the probability of those facts occurring is surely an unnecessary second-best". For a discussion on re-marriage, see *De Sales v Ingrilli* (2002) 212 CLR 338, discussed below at [14.305].

Other examples of factors which can be taken into account include increases in wage rates for the plaintiff's or deceased's occupation (*The Swynfleet* (1948) 81 Lloyd's Lists Reps 116), death of the plaintiff from an independent cause, imprisonment of the plaintiff, the birth of children (*Sullivan v Gordon* [1999] 47 NSWLR 319, see [14.185]-[14.190]) and evidence of subsequent injuries (*Baker v Willoughby* [1970] AC 467 (HL) [13.65]).

Recoverable heads of loss

[14.85] Australian courts no longer take a global approach to the assessment of damages, instead preferring to itemise the award under various headings or "heads of loss", to avoid double counting and omission. Windeyer J identified the general areas of loss in *Teubner v Humble* (1963) 108 CLR 491 at 505-6, saying:

> Broadly speaking there are, it seems to me, three ways in which a personal injury can give rise to damage. First, it may destroy or diminish, permanently or for a time, an existing capacity, mental or physical. Secondly, it may create needs that would not otherwise exist. Thirdly, it may produce physical pain and suffering.

The High Court expanded on this in *CSR Ltd v Eddy* (2005) 226 CLR 1 at [28]-[31] per Gleeson CJ, Gummow and Heydon JJ:

> [Plaintiffs] are seen as able to recover three types of loss. The first covers non pecuniary losses such as pain and suffering, disfigurement, loss of limbs or organs, loss of the senses - sight, taste, hearing, smell and touch; and loss of the capacity to engage in hobbies, sport, work, marriage and child-bearing. Damages can be recovered in respect of these losses even if no actual financial loss is caused and even if the damage caused by them cannot be measured in money
>
> The second type of loss is loss of earning capacity both before the trial and after it... those damages are awardable only to the extent that the loss has been or may be productive of financial loss...
>
> The third type of recoverable loss is actual financial loss, for example, ambulance charges; charges for medical, hospital and professional nursing services; travel and accommodation expenses incurred in obtaining those services; the costs of rehabilitation needs, special clothing and special equipment; the costs of modifying houses; the costs of fund management; and the costs of professionally supplied home maintenance services.

The common law separates losses into two categories, special and general damages. In older cases the term special (specifiable) damages refers to medical and associated costs and loss of earnings up to the date of trial (or settlement). The plaintiff could recover as special damages those medical costs which had been paid or where there was an existing legal obligation to pay. In contrast to general damages, special damages can be calculated or estimated with some accuracy.

General damages on the other hand, are, of their very nature, incapable of mathematical calculation. They are "at large" in the sense that a judge or jury has, in serious cases, a wide discretion in assessing them. Also, general damages may be assessed not with reference to any limited period, but with reference to an indefinite time. General damages include those awarded for "pain and suffering", and such damages are assessable for past, present and future pain and suffering.

In more modern usage, the term "special damages" tends to be loosely equated with economic loss, both past and future. The civil liability Acts of New South Wales, Queensland, Victoria and Western Australia adopt a similar approach, but use the language of "economic loss" and "non economic loss (general damages)": NSW: CLA, Pt 2 (Personal Injury Damages), ss 12 – 15A (economic loss), ss 3B, 11A (non-economic loss), see also ss 16 – 17A. Part 2 does not apply to intentional torts, any form of sexual misconduct, dust diseases, injury or death resulting from smoking or use of tobacco, workers compensation claims, and compensation for victims of crime, discrimination claims, and sporting injuries. See Qld: CLA, Ch 3 Pt 3 (no use of non-economic, but to similar effect); Vic: WrA, Pt VB; WA: CLA, Pt 2 (pecuniary and non-pecuniary). Other jurisdictions are silent on economic loss but contain provisions concerning non-economic loss: ACT: CLWA, s 139F; NT: *Personal Injuries (Liabilities and Damages) Act 2003*, Pt 4 Div 2; SA: CLA, Pt 8; Tas: CLA, Pt 7. The structure and terminology employed in this chapter mirror that of the New South Wales legislation.

DAMAGES FOR ECONOMIC LOSS

Past out of pocket expenses

[14.90] All reasonable medical treatments and expenses relating to the injury are recoverable upon proof of payment or liability to pay by the plaintiff. This is normally straight-forward. Medical expenses are both a new need arising from the defendant's negligence, and mitigation by the plaintiff. Past expenses are recoverable under either analysis. The decision in *British Westinghouse Electric & Manufacturing Co Ltd v Underground Electric Railways Co of London Ltd* [1912] AC 673 established that plaintiffs in all types of actions have a duty to mitigate, or minimise, their losses. Where the loss is personal injury, mitigation requires acceptance of reasonable medical or other treatment. This is considered further below at [14.270].

Loss of earning capacity

[14.95] The two main heads of economic loss are loss of earning capacity and new economic needs created by the injury. Young plaintiffs who are permanently incapacitated as regarding work, but who may still have a long life expectancy, can expect to be awarded very considerable sums under these two heads. Loss of earning capacity refers to income that the plaintiff would have earned but now cannot earn as a result of injury, both past (between the date of the injury and the trial) and future. The distinction between loss of wages and loss of earning capacity is significant, as explained by Barwick CJ in *Cullen v Trappell* (1980) 146 CLR 1 at 7-8:

> In the first place, the replacement of the capacity to earn money by damages was, by the very statement of the problem, not an exercise in replacing the wages which were currently being earned or which might be expected to be earned by the injured person ... The problem is to value the capital asset of the injured person, namely, his capacity to earn money. Whilst it is true what that capital asset by its exercise may produce in the form of money will quite properly be an element and perhaps in some cases a dominant element in that valuation, the exercise is not in my opinion, one in which it is sought merely to replace the wages themselves.

See also *Arthur Robinson (Grafton) Pty Ltd v Carter* (1968) 122 CLR 649, at 658; *Paff v Speed* (1961) 105 CLR 549 at 566 per Windeyer J; *Husher v Husher* (1999) 197 CLR 138 at 143; *Medlin v State Government Insurance Commission* (1995) 182 CLR 1 at 4 per Deane, Dawson, Toohey and Gaudron JJ.

The distinction is particularly significant for plaintiffs who are unemployed or under-employed at the date of the accident, for example, part time or casual workers, students, children, and unpaid domestic carers. An analogy can be drawn with residential property available for lease. The dwelling is the capital asset, which has value even if temporarily untenanted. The income is the rent produced when that asset is put to work (leased). The amount of rent able to be achieved helps set the market value of the property, but is not the only factor. In *Atlas Tiles Ltd v Briers* (1978) 144 CLR 202 at 210, Barwick CJ said:

> Some have thought the distinction I have drawn between loss of earnings and loss of earning capacity is illusory or insubstantial. But, in my opinion, it is real and radical. A capacity to earn which is not being exercised nor presently intended to be exercised has a value which can be estimated, though no current earnings are available to demonstrate its worth even with approximation. Again, the plaintiff may have been currently employed in an industry which, for some reason or other, was doomed to extinction or in a capacity which technology was likely to render redundant. Yet retrained, other and more remunerative employment may be available. Earning capacity may produce, not merely earnings, but a satisfactory way of life which, being denied or destroyed, may need to be reflected in the value of the capacity.

Damages for future economic loss depend on the extent to which a plaintiff is able to prove his or her full capacity would have been exercised in the future, and the level of income that could have been expected. Foreseeability has no part to play in determining economic loss. As Scrutton LJ pointed out in *The Arpad* [1934] P 189 (CA) at 202-3:

> [If] you negligently run down a shabby looking man in the street and he … turn[s] out to be a millionaire engaged in a very profitable business which the accident disables him from carrying on … [y]ou have to pay damages resulting from the circumstances of which you have no notice. You have to pay the actual loss to the man.

This is what is meant by the eggshell skull rule, or taking your victim as you find him or her. If a plaintiff has a solid history of stable employment in a particular occupation, loss of capacity will normally be valued by reference to his or her usual salary or wages. *Mann v Ellbourn* (1974) 8 SASR 298 decided, however, that a loss of capacity to earn which is not fully exploited is not to be compensated on the basis of full exploitation. Similarly, in *Leschke v Jeffs* [1955] QWN 67, approved in *Faulkner v Keffalinos* (1970) 45 ALJR 80 at 85 per Windeyer J, the plaintiff was not compensated for loss of earning capacity for the ten year period he spent in jail. The earnings taken into account are the net after tax sums the plaintiff would have earned without the injury, reduced by expenses and outgoings necessarily associated with producing that income. That the calculations must be based on net income was decided by the High Court in *Cullen v Trappell* (1980) 146 CLR 1 and *Atlas Tiles Ltd v Briers* (1978) 144 CLR 202. Deduction of expenses is discussed in the next extract from *Sharman v Evans* (1977) 138 CLR 563.

Economic loss must be calculated by:

> reference to the actual loss of wages which occurs up to the time of the trial and which can be more or less precisely ascertained and then, having regard to the plaintiff's proved condition at the time of trial, to attempt some assessment of his future loss. (*Graham v Baker* (1961) 106 CLR 340 at 347)

Sharman v Evans (1977) 138 CLR 563 is an important case which demonstrates many aspects of damages assessment, so will be revisited several times in this chapter. The facts are set out in detail in this extract only. The sum originally awarded to Ms Evans, $300,000, was a record at the time and was subsequently reduced by the High Court. The New South Wales record is currently $16,347,477.91 million, awarded in *Palmer v Roads and Traffic Authority of NSW* [2001] NSWSC 846 for tetraplegia resulting from a motor vehicle accident.

Sharman v Evans

[14.100] *Sharman v Evans* (1977) 138 CLR 563 High Court of Australia

(footnotes omitted)

[The facts are outlined in the judgment of Gibbs and Stephen JJ.]

GIBBS AND STEPHEN JJ: 569 The defendant, Dennis Sharman, appeals against the dismissal, by a majority of the New South Wales Court of Appeal, of his appeal from a verdict for $300,547.50 in favour of the plaintiff, June Marilyn Evans.

Miss Evans, then aged 20, was injured in a motor car accident in December 1971. She suffered very serious injuries including brain stem damage; she was unconscious for almost a month and is now a quadriplegic. This condition, disastrous enough in itself, is in her case aggravated by trauma-caused epilepsy, by unusually severe impairment to her respiratory function as a consequence of the brain injury and by an almost total loss of the ability to speak because of the injury to the larynx. She is fully aware of her plight.

By the time of the trial, in November 1973, Miss Evans had undergone a great number of operations and had endured much pain; her condition had become stabilised …

Before the accident the prospects for Miss Evans' future were bright; she was a healthy, out-going and intelligent girl who was trained for and was experienced in secretarial work; by taking two jobs in her home State of Western Australia she had saved enough money to undertake a two-year full-time course as a resident student at the Commonwealth Bible College in Brisbane. At the time of the accident, she had just completed her first year there, coming dux of her year. She had an understanding with a young man, a fellow student, that they would marry in due course. After the accident their engagement was announced and but for her ultimate decision that she could not permit him to take as his wife a quadriplegic she would by the time of the trial have been married to him; he has a good position and a secure future in the Department of Civil Aviation. Had she resumed her secretarial work after finishing her two-year college course she could have earned at least $70 per week net. …

A variety of difficulties, both of principle and of fact, surround the assessment of damages in this case. They stem from at least three distinct sources: the great increase in the cost of future nursing care should the plaintiff be cared for at home rather than in hospital; a variety of problems involved in assessing compensation for the plaintiff's loss of future earning capacity and, finally, the doubts as to the plaintiff's present life expectancy.

That the learned trial judge should have engaged in a close scrutiny of each head of detriment was, we think, inevitable; that in doing so he should seek to evaluate that detriment in money terms was a necessary consequence of the fact that it is only by recourse to those terms that the plaintiff can be compensated for the wrong done to her. Criticism was directed both to this separate examination of the conventional heads of damage and also to the ascertainment of a sum appropriate as a starting point for compensation under a particular head of damages, followed by a process of discounting or deduction from it. We regard this criticism as misconceived; so long as courts are careful to avoid the risk, inherent in such a procedure, of compensating twice over for the one detriment there seems no better way of applying processes of reasoning and the realistic and methodical evaluation of probabilities to the task of assessing compensation. In cases of any complexity any other approach is open to serious objection, especially in times of rapid inflation. In such times what Salmon LJ described in *Fletcher v Autocar & Transporters Ltd* [1968] 2 QB 322 at 362 as the "uncertain role" of instinct, and what this Court has described as a "general awareness", a knowledge of "current general ideas of fairness and moderation" (*Planet Fisheries Pty Ltd v La Rosa* (1968) 119 CLR 118 at 125), while still of use in determining, as a matter of first impression, the general level of appropriateness of an award, tends to become blurred by the constant shift of money values. Moreover where the assessment of damages is undertaken by a judge sitting without a jury it is, we think, most desirable that the process of assessment should be described in the reasons for judgment. As was pointed out by Sachs LJ in *George v Pinnock* [1973] 1 All ER 926 at 934, it is only by the setting out in a judgment of the main components of an award of damages, or at least of the approach taken to each component, that the parties may obtain a proper insight into the process of assessment and an adequate opportunity of seeking the correction of error on appeal. In the particular circumstances of this case Sheppard J found himself unable to assign anything like precise money sums to the different heads of damages; he did however very clearly explain his approach to each head of damages, a course which has lightened the task of appellate courts ...

We turn next to the question of compensation for lost earning capacity and in particular to an examination of the deductions which should be made in assessing that compensation. In doing so we leave aside, for the present, the question of compensation for loss of earning capacity during the years by which the plaintiff's life expectancy has been shortened, the "lost years".

Both principle and authority (*Skelton v Collins* (1966) 115 CLR 94) establish that where, as here, there is included in the award of damages for future nursing and medical care the plaintiff's entire cost of future board and lodging there will be overcompensation if damages for loss of earning capacity are awarded in full without regard for the fact that the plaintiff is already to receive as compensation the cost of her future board and lodging, a cost which but for her injuries she would otherwise have to meet out of future earnings. If the true concept be that it is lost earning capacity to the extent to which it is likely to be exercised in the future, rather than loss of future earnings, that is to be compensated it may seem inelegant to speak of deducting from damages for that lost capacity an amount for some saving in outgoings. It would better accord with principle if the savings in board and lodging could be isolated from, and excluded from the damages to be awarded in respect of, hospital expenses. However so long as the true nature of the adjustment is understood no harm is done by making an appropriate deduction from the damages for lost earning capacity. What is to be avoided is double compensation and, as is apparent from what was said by their Lordships in *Shearman v Folland* [1950] 2 KB 43, it is not a question of estimating the plaintiff's likely future costs for board and lodging and treating them as an outgoing which the consequences of the defendant's tortious act have now spared her from making; that is a notion which is as distasteful as it is misconceived. Rather is it a matter of her already having been compensated for future board and lodging as a component of hospital expenses, so that to disregard this and award the full sum for lost earning capacity, part of which would be used to provide the very item of board and lodging already compensated for, would be to award compensation twice over. Accordingly some no doubt fairly arbitrary proportion of the present value of future hospital expenses regarded as attributable to board and lodging must be taken and deducted from the present value of lost earning capacity; it will be quite irrelevant how expensively or how frugally the plaintiff might in fact have lived had she not been injured.

Although it is only the cost of board and lodging which, unless subject to deduction in this way, will lead to actual double compensation there are other items which require consideration as possible deductions when assessing damages for loss of earning capacity. This is because, quite apart from double compensation, that is, the payment twice over in respect of one and the same item of loss, it is also necessary to avoid compensating for gross rather than for net losses. This becomes of particular importance not only when assessing compensation for ordinary loss of earning capacity but also when that process of assessment must be undertaken in the context of a plaintiff's "lost years", his life expectancy having been reduced as a result of the injuries he has received.

Again we ignore for the moment the question of "lost years". Where, as here, a plaintiff suffers a total loss of earning capacity he will not normally continue to incur all of the outgoings necessary for the realization of that capacity which would have been incurred had his capacity been unaffected; items such as the cost of clothing suitable to his particular employment and of transportation to and

Sharman v Evans cont.

from work provide examples, no doubt there are others. Compensation for loss of earning capacity is paid only because it is or may be productive of financial loss (*Graham v Baker* (1961) 106 CLR 340) and to compensate for total loss of earning capacity without making allowance for the cessation of these outgoings is to compensate for a gross loss when it is only the net loss that is in fact suffered.

On the other hand there are other types of saved expenditure upon which a defendant cannot rely in diminution of damages. It is now well established that no reduction is to be made, when awarding damages for loss of earning capacity, for the cost of maintaining oneself and one's dependants unless an element of double compensation would otherwise intrude, as in the case of hospitalization as a non-fee paying patient or where the cost of future hospital expenses is also awarded and necessarily includes, as in the present case, the patient's board and lodging...

The present plaintiff is now denied many of the opportunities for pleasure-giving expenditure, as distinct from what may be regarded as expenditure on maintenance, which our society affords. Are the savings in expenditure, thus involuntarily thrust upon her by reason of the state to which her injuries have reduced her, to have the effect of reducing the damages awarded for her loss of earning capacity? We think not. They may be left out of reckoning, they neither produce double compensation nor compensate for gross rather than net loss. Indeed to treat them as items going to reduce damages is unjustifiably to assume that because pre-accident avenues of expenditure are now foreclosed to a plaintiff the necessary consequence is a corresponding non-expenditure ...

As to "lost years", the plaintiff is to be compensated in respect of lost earning capacity during those years by which her life expectancy has been shortened, at least to the extent that they are years when she would otherwise have been earning income (*Skelton v Collins*). But, unlike the thirty years of her actual post-accident life expectancy, no outgoings whatever will be involved in respect of that period since it is assumed that the plaintiff will then be dead. What adjustments are, then, to be made on that account in assessing damages for loss of earning capacity in respect of those lost years? This is not a question giving rise to considerations of double compensation; the only element involving any possibility of double compensation, the component of board and lodging contained in the award of future hospital expenses, will have ceased to operate by the time that the "lost years" are reached. It is rather a question of confining an award of damages to no more than compensation, ensuring that the plaintiff is merely compensated for loss and is not positively enriched, at the defendant's expense, by the damages awarded.

It is well established in Australia that there should be taken into account in reduction of damages for the lost earning capacity of "lost years" at least the amount that the plaintiff would have expended on his own maintenance during those lost years: *Skelton v Collins*, per Taylor J (at 121-2) ... [A detailed discussion followed regarding whether deductions in the "lost years" should include not only moneys which would have been spent by the deceased in the maintenance of himself, but also moneys which would have been spent by him in the maintenance of dependants. Their honours continued.] We share the difficulty felt by Sheppard J and have concluded that, properly regarded, *Skelton v Collins* does not require that anything, other than the cost of a plaintiff's own maintenance, should go in reduction of damages for lost earning capacity for "lost years" ...

... [I]t would, we think, be wrong to treat *Skelton v Collins* as any authority for the proposition that only surplus income, in effect savings, are to be taken into account in assessing economic loss in the "lost years". It is well enough to take into account in reduction of damages the likely expenditure on the plaintiff's own maintenance and this for the reason stated by Sheppard J in *Jackson v Stothard* [1973] 1 NSWLR 292. As Jolowicz observed in a note in the Cambridge Law Journal (1960), at 163, "a dead man has no personal expenses", hence there should be a deduction of "the plaintiff's personal living expenses"...

There remains one future aspect of the assessment of damages for loss of earning capacity. Loss must depend upon the likelihood that there would have been a future exercise of that earning capacity, but what of a female plaintiff likely to marry and who may cease to exercise her earning capacity on, or at some time after, marriage? Despite recent changes in patterns of employment of married women this remains a not unusual situation, the woman in effect exchanging the exercise of her earning capacity for such financial security as her marriage may provide. The measure of the one of course bears no necessary relationship to the other and the whole situation must be full of critical uncertainties such as whether the plaintiff marries, the extent if any of her employment after marriage, the success of that marriage and the extent to which it in fact provides her with economic security. Perhaps the only relatively certain factor will be her pre-injury possession of earning capacity and this in itself may be sufficient reason, absent any clear evidence pointing in a contrary direction, for the adoption of the expedient course of simply disregarding the prospect of marriage as a relevant factor in the assessment of such a plaintiff's future economic loss; this course at least recognises the plaintiff's retention of capacity, which would have been available to her for exercise, in case of need, despite her marriage.

... Having made these general observations concerning the award of damages in a case such as the present it remains only to look more specifically at the damages in fact awarded. The total award is said to be the largest yet made for personal injuries in Australia, although it is modest indeed compared with that in the very recent case of a young Canadian quadriplegic, *Thornton v Board of School Trustees* (1975) 57 DLR (3d) 438. The award includes two components with a stated money value or range: the cost of nursing and medical attention, a "figure of the order of $150,000 to $175,000", and the amount for loss of expectation of life, $6,000. Each we regard on the approach we would adopt as excessive for reasons already stated; the former we would assess as of the order of $128,000, made up, in round figures, of 103,000 for hospital expenses, $15,500 for medical and physiotherapy services and $10,000 for special beds and the like, the latter at not more than $2,000. To these two must be added the sum of $20,000 which we have assessed in respect of the cost of constant nursing attention and transportation during periodic visits to the world outside the hospital ward.

The learned trial judge specified no precise amounts for lost earning capacity or for pain, suffering and loss of the amenities of life. The former will, in the case of the thirty years of life expectancy, necessarily be considerable, representing as it does a loss of earning capacity the exercise of which would have produced net earnings of $70 per week over those years. There must, however, be brought to account the minor expenses, such as fares and special clothing, which would have been incurred in earning that income, also some allowance for sickness, early death, a measure of unemployment and the like. In all we would deduct $2 per week, a figure which is necessarily arbitrary, in respect of these matters. In addition some allowance, again an arbitrary one, must also be made because of the inclusion in the hospital costs of the element of board and lodging. To take about twelve per cent of these hospital costs, say $16 per week, may not be inappropriate; that this percentage represents much less than actual costs of board and lodging is to be accounted for by the surprisingly low total charges, of only $20 per day, made for the all-inclusive hospital services, due perhaps to some element of government subsidy. The present value, on six per cent tables, of, say $52 per week, being $70 – ($16 + $2), is about $38,500 and an award somewhere in the range of $34,000 to $43,000 could not be regarded as erroneous. For the twenty-four lost years quite different considerations apply both because of the need to take into account maintenance "saved" and because for part at least of that period the plaintiff, if regarded as having a working life, would have ceased to work or, if regarded as enjoying the security provided by her likely husband, would be the wife or widow of a retired breadwinner. To award more than a quite small sum for the present value of this long deferred and greatly to be discounted loss of earning capacity would be wrong; to take these "lost years" into account it is enough to increase the above range to one of from $37,000 to $45,000. Reviewing all these sums they come to a minimum total of $187,000 and to a maximum total of $195,000 ...

Sharman v Evans cont.

We conclude, therefore, that the amount awarded cannot stand. It is necessary therefore for us to determine what was a proper amount. We make this determination wholly on the basis of the findings of fact made by the trial judge. It must, however, be made clear that, while the process which we have followed of analysing the separate maximum amounts possible under the various heads of damage will be of assistance in a re-assessment, they cannot of themselves lead to a conclusion on the amount proper to be substituted. In all the circumstances we are of the opinion that a proper amount is $270,547.50.

We would accordingly allow this appeal and substitute for the present award an amount of $270,547.50.

[14.105] **Notes&Questions**

1. In the area of damages for lost earning capacity, the House of Lords followed the lead given by the Australian High Court in cases like *Skelton v Collins* (1966) 115 CLR 94, and *Sharman v Evans* (1977) 138 CLR 563. The English landmark case in this respect is *Pickett v British Rail Engineering Ltd* (1980) AC 136.

   The English case was unlike the leading Australian cases so far discussed in that the plaintiff died before the hearing of the appeal. Since the action had been taken as far as judgment by the plaintiff while alive, the principles of assessment of damage discussed are those applicable to a living plaintiff, and not those applicable to an action by an estate.

   The House of Lords followed the Australian cases in holding, first, that an injured plaintiff was entitled to recover damages for loss of earnings during the lost years and, secondly, that those damages should be computed after the deduction of the plaintiff's probable living expenses during that period. These holdings involved overruling *Harris v Brights Asphalt Contractors Ltd* [1953] 1 QB 617 and *Oliver v Ashman* [1962] 2 QB 210. The suggestion that dicta in *Benham v Gambling* [1941] AC 157 at 167 meant that damages for the lost years must be wholly confined to the conventional sum for loss of expectation of life, was rejected, as it had been in *Skelton v Collins* (1966) 115 CLR 94. Lord Wilberforce said ([1980] AC 136 at 149):

   > Is he [the plaintiff] not entitled to say, at one moment I am a man with existing capability to earn well for 14 years: the next moment I can only earn less well for one year? And why should he be compensated only for the immediate reduction in his earnings and not for the loss of the whole period for which he has been deprived of his ability to earn them? To the argument that "they are of no value because you will not be there to enjoy them" can he not reply: "yes they are: what is of value to me is not only my opportunity to spend them enjoyably, but to use such part of them as I do not need for my dependants, or for other persons or causes which I wish to support. If I cannot do this, I have been deprived of something on which a value-a present value-can be placed"?

   Lord Wilberforce added (at 150) that in the case of a young child, as in *Benham v Gambling* [1941] AC 157, neither present nor future earnings could enter into the matter; in the case of adolescents just embarking on the process of earning, the value would be real but the assessment probably small.

2. Where a plaintiff is partially incapacitated for work, issues arise as to the value of any residual capacity. If a plaintiff is able to find other employment at a reduced salary, the current income will be set off (deducted) from the former higher income over the relevant period in order to establish the amount of loss. The assessment of future economic loss takes into account factors which may affect earning, such as promotions, overtime, sickness, and child rearing responsibilities (see the discussion of discounting at [14.140]). In *GMH Ltd v Whetstone* (1988) 50 SASR 199, the Full Court of South Australia refused to treat the assessment of pre-trial loss of earning capacity as a purely arithmetical exercise. There, the plaintiff had periods of unemployment caused by his injuries. In the periods he was employed his earnings were higher than the amount he would have received had he continued in his old job. It was held that the plaintiff's loss was not to be assessed by simply working out what the plaintiff would have earned had he continued in employment and then deducting sums actually earned within that period. The plaintiff was entitled to be compensated for periods of unemployment. Loss of income is calculated on a net of tax basis, (see the discussion of taxation at [14.285]). Loss of entitlements may also be factored into the loss, as the next case demonstrates.

Loss of entitlements

[14.110] Entitlements such as sick pay, holiday pay, pensions, and superannuation may be relevant to determining a plaintiff's economic loss, as *Graham v Baker* (1961) 106 CLR 340 demonstrates below.

Graham v Baker

[14.115] *Graham v Baker* (1961) 106 CLR 340 High Court of Australia

(footnotes omitted)

[The plaintiff was compulsorily retired from his job as a fire station officer because of injuries caused by the defendant's negligence. Before the retirement he received 178 days' "sick pay" from his employer. The trial judge excluded evidence of the sick pay so that the plaintiff obtained damages for loss of wages or earning capacity during this 178 day period. This was upheld by the Full Court of the Supreme Court of New South Wales. The defendant appealed to the High Court.]

DIXON CJ, KITTO and TAYLOR JJ: 346 So far the matter has been discussed as if the right of a plaintiff whose earning capacity has been diminished by the defendant's negligence is concerned with two separate matters, that is, loss of wages up to the time of trial and an estimated future loss because of his diminished earning capacity. It is, we think, necessary to point out that this is not so. A plaintiff's right of action is complete at the time when his injuries are sustained and if it were possible in the ordinary course of things to obtain an assessment of his damages immediately it would be necessary to make an assessment of the probable economic loss which would result from his injuries. But for at least two obvious reasons it has been found convenient to assess an injured plaintiff's loss by reference to the actual loss of wages which occurs up to the time of trial and which can be more or less precisely ascertained and then, having regard to the plaintiffs proved condition at the time of trial, to attempt some assessment of his future loss. We mention this matter because it has been suggested that since an injured plaintiff is entitled to recover damages for the impairment of his earning capacity, the fact that a totally incapacitated plaintiff has, during the period of his incapacity, received his ordinary wages is not a matter to be taken into consideration. To be more precise, however, an injured plaintiff recovers

Graham v Baker cont.

not merely because his earning capacity has been diminished but because the diminution of his earning capacity is or may be productive of financial loss. And if, notwithstanding such impairment, both his contract of employment and his right to ordinary wages continue, how can it be said that his impairment has resulted in any loss so far as his earning capacity is concerned? ...

In the present case the sick leave credit or entitlement is not such that it can be converted into cash if the employee does not otherwise find it necessary to avail himself of it. It is the measure, no more and no less, of the employee's right to receive ordinary pay notwithstanding his absence on sick leave. If received pursuant to such a right it is, in our view, impossible to say that, *pro tanto*, there has been any loss of wages ...

Needless to say, such [sick leave] payments are quite different in character from ex gratia payments made or advanced either unconditionally or conditionally on repayment at some future date or so that they will be repayable upon a contingency. Nor do they share the same character as payments made to an employee pursuant to some provident or social welfare scheme ...

For these reasons the appeal should, we think, be allowed and, since the parties are not in agreement that we should dispose of the appeal by reducing the verdict by the amount involved, there must be a new trial on the issue of damages. But before parting with the case it is desirable to point out that, in an appropriate case, the extinguishment or diminution of sick leave credits of the character in question here may, notwithstanding the view we have expressed, result in some damage. As Windeyer J said in *Paff v Speed* (1961) 105 CLR 549 at 566: "A plaintiff entitled to be paid by his employer (whether the payments be called sick pay is immaterial) while incapacitated, and who when he recovered returned to work in his old position, may nevertheless have suffered some compensable loss by his absence. If, for example, he was by the terms of his employment permitted only a certain number of days sick leave on pay during the year, he would incur some loss if those days were used up in an absence caused by the defendant." In other words, he may incur a loss because he may face the possibility of being sick in future from extraneous causes at his own expense so far as wages are concerned ...

Appeal allowed.

[14.120] **Notes&Questions**

1. The principle applied to sick pay received under the conditions of the employment, was applied to award make up payments in *Evans v Port of Brisbane Authority* (1992) Aust Torts Reports 81-169, and holiday pay in *Bosche v Liebe* [1976] VR 265. Some allowance is made for loss of holiday pay credits (same case) and for loss of sick leave credits: *Loughman v Kurzyp* [1977] Tas SR 132. On the other hand, voluntary payments by an employer, as distinct from those paid under the conditions of the employment, are not deductible. See *Allev v Minister of Works* (1974) 9 SASR 306; *Cunningham v Harrison* [1973] 1 QB 943; *Volpato v Zachorv* (1971) SASR 166 Cf *Hobbelen v Nunn* [1965] Qd R105, *Koremans v Sweeney* [1966] QWN 46 and *Evans v Port of Brisbane Authority* (1992) Aust Torts Reports 81-169.

2. In New South Wales and Queensland, the civil liability legislation contains provisions regarding damages and superannuation. The maximum that may be awarded for economic loss due to the loss of employer superannuation contributions is the minimum employer contribution required by law: NSW: CLA, s 15C; Qld: CLA, s 56. The New South Wales Court of Appeal in *Najdovski v Crnojlovic* [2008] NSWCA 175

interpreted s 15C as providing for a cap on awards for superannuation entitlements of nine per cent of net earnings. There are no equivalent provisions in other jurisdictions

3. The civil liability legislation contains provisions that cap damages for past or future economic loss. Under the legislation, no person's loss may exceed 3 times the amount of average weekly earnings in the relevant jurisdiction at the date of the award: ACT: CLWA, s 98; NSW: CLA, s 12; NT: *Personal Injuries (Liabilities and Damages) Act 2003*, s 20; Qld: CLA, s 54; Tas: CLA, s 26; Vic: WrA, s 28F(2); WA: CLA, s 11. There is no South Australian provision. This applies to both past and future economic loss, as well as claims by dependants for loss of financial support flowing from the death of a breadwinner. Are these provisions consistent with the restitutio in integrum principle discussed above at [14.35]? Consider whether the provisions constitute an erosion of the restitutio principle, depressing awards at the top end of the income scale. Dependants' claims are made pursuant to the *Compensation to Relatives Act 1897* (NSW), based on the English *Fatal Accidents Act 1846* (UK) (*Lord Campbell's Act*). This has equivalents in all Australian jurisdictions, and is considered below, at [14.290], dealing with Wrongful Death.

4. Section 13 of the NSW: CLA and NT: *Personal Injuries (Liabilities and Damages) Act 2003*, s 21, require a court to determine what the plaintiff's most likely future circumstances would have been if the tort had not been committed, and to award damages for future economic loss based only on those circumstances. Then the court must determine the percentage possibility that the plaintiff's most likely future circumstances might have occurred anyway, and adjust the award accordingly. This is consistent with the common law position laid down by the High Court in *Malec v JC Hutton Pty Ltd* (1990) 169 CLR 638 (extracted at [14.130]) which continues to apply in other jurisdictions that do not contain this provision.

Certainty and proof of loss

[14.125] How can a court determine what may happen in the future? Or what might have happened to the plaintiff had the tort not been committed?

For past losses, such as loss of income, the normal civil standard of proof applies. The plaintiff's future losses, needs, and prognosis are far more difficult to establish with sufficient certainty, as is loss of chance. As we saw in Chapter 13, Causation, Remoteness and Harm, loss of chance is sometimes treated as an aspect of causation, sometimes as a type of harm, (both relevant to liability), and sometimes as a question of assessment of damages. Where it is treated as an assessment issue, proof does not have to reach the balance of probabilities standard, for reasons explained in the next extract.

Malec v JC Hutton Pty Ltd

[14.130] *Malec v JC Hutton Pty Ltd* (1990) 169 CLR 638 High Court of Australia

(footnotes omitted)

[The plaintiff was employed as a labourer in a meatworks from 1972 to 1980. He contracted brucellosis, which is a disease carried by animals. Brucellosis may lead to degeneration of the spine; it may also lead to depression. In the Supreme Court of Queensland, Kelly SPJ, in awarding damages of $19,468.54, found that the disease had been contracted between 1975 and 1977 as a result of the company's negligence, it being equally probable that the plaintiff's supervening neurotic condition

Malec v JC Hutton Pty Ltd cont.

was "precipitated by brucellosis" or attributable to other unrelated circumstances. The trial judge also found that by June 1983 acute brucellosis was no longer present, but that since May 1982 the plaintiff had suffered from a degenerative spinal condition. He was not satisfied that this resulted from the brucellosis. Matthews and Ambrose JJ in the Full Court concluded that the plaintiff's personality might have led to a similar neurotic condition irrespective of brucellosis. They refused damages for economic loss after May 1982 but increased the award to $36,928.47, on the basis that the neurotic condition was induced by the brucellosis. Carter J, in dissent, declined to limit economic loss to the pre-May 1982 period, and considered that damages should have been assessed in part at $148,277.63 and an inquiry should have been ordered to assess a further award. Malec appealed to the High Court.]

BRENNAN AND DAWSON JJ: 639 We are in agreement with the judgment of Deane, Gaudron and McHugh JJ and with the order that they propose, subject to some brief observations. The judgment of the majority in the Full Court seems to us to overlook the difference between the fact that the plaintiff had not been working for some time before the trial and an evaluation of the plaintiff's earning capacity which was destroyed in consequence of the defendant's negligence. The fact that the plaintiff did not work is a matter of history, and facts of that kind are ascertained for the purposes of civil litigation on the balance of probabilities: if the court attains the required degree of satisfaction as to the occurrence of an historical fact, that fact is accepted as having occurred. By contrast, earning capacity can be assessed only upon the hypothesis that the plaintiff had not been tortiously injured: what would he have been able to earn if he had not been tortiously injured? To answer that question, the court must speculate to some extent. As the hypothesis is false – for the plaintiff has been injured – the ascertainment of earning capacity involves an evaluation of possibilities, not establishing a fact as a matter of history. Hypothetical situations of the past are analogous to future possibilities: in one case the court must form an estimate of the likelihood that the hypothetical situation would have occurred, in the other the court must form an estimate of the likelihood that the possibility will occur. Both are to be distinguished from events which are alleged to have actually occurred in the past. Lord Diplock said in *Mallett v McMonagle*:

> The role of the court in making an assessment of damages which depends upon its view as to what will be and what would have been is to be contrasted with its ordinary function in civil actions of determining what was. In determining what did happen in the past a court decides on the balance of probabilities. Anything that is more probable than not it treats as certain. But in assessing damages which depend upon its view as to what will happen in the future or would have happened in the future if something had not happened in the past, the court must make an estimate as to what are the chances that a particular thing will or would have happened and reflect those chances, whether they are more or less than even, in the amount of damages which it awards.

In assessing the plaintiff's earning capacity in the present case, what had to be evaluated was the prospect that the deteriorating back condition would have precluded him from engaging in gainful employment had he not contracted brucellosis. An evaluation of that prospect had to be made. To make a finding on the balance of probabilities as though the prospect were something that had occurred in the past was to misconceive the process of evaluation.

Although we agree with the general thrust of the reasoning on this point in the judgment of Deane, Gaudron and McHugh JJ, we think it undesirable for damages to be assessed on the footing of an evaluation expressed as a percentage. Damages need not be assessed by first determining an award on the footing that the hypothetical situation would have occurred and then discounting the award by a selected percentage. Damages founded on hypothetical evaluations defy precise calculation. We should add that we would not favour the use of the term "probability" to describe the possibility of occurrence of a situation when the possibility is minimal.

Subject to these observations, we agree in the order as formulated in their Honours' reasons for judgment.

Malec v JC Hutton Pty Ltd cont.

DEANE, GAUDRON AND McHUGH JJ:

Assessing Damages for Future or Potential Events

642 When liability has been established and a common law court has to assess damages, its approach to events that allegedly would have occurred, but cannot now occur, or that allegedly might occur, is different from its approach to events which allegedly have occurred. A common law court determines on the balance of probabilities whether an event has occurred. If the probability of the event having occurred is greater than it not having occurred, the occurrence of the event is treated as certain; if the probability of it having occurred is less than it not having occurred, it is treated as not having occurred. Hence, in respect of events which have or have not occurred, damages are assessed on an all or nothing approach. But in the case of an event which it is alleged would or would not have occurred, or might or might not yet occur, the approach of the court is different. The future may be predicted and the hypothetical may be conjectured. But questions as to the future or hypothetical effect of physical injury or degeneration are not commonly susceptible of scientific demonstration or proof. If the law is to take account of future or hypothetical events in assessing damages, it can only do so in terms of the degree of probability of those events occurring. The probability may be very high – 99.9 per cent – or very low – 0.1 per cent. But unless the chance is so low as to be regarded as speculative – say less than 1 per cent – or so high as to be practically certain – say over 99 per cent – the court will take that chance into account in assessing the damages. Where proof is necessarily unattainable, it would be unfair to treat as certain a prediction which has a 51 per cent probability of occurring, but to ignore altogether a prediction which has a 49 per cent probability of occurring. Thus, the court assesses the degree of probability that an event would have occurred, or might occur, and adjusts its award of damages to reflect the degree of probability. The adjustment may increase or decrease the amount of damages otherwise to be awarded. See *Mallett v McMonagle*; *Davies v Taylor*; *McIntosh v Williams*. The approach is the same whether it is alleged that the event would have occurred before or might occur after the assessment of damages takes place.

The Assessment of Damages in the Present Case

... True it is that the plaintiff developed a neurotic condition as the result of contracting brucellosis... It by no means follows from what occurred as the result of his contracting brucellosis that there is an overwhelming likelihood that another event or other events would have precipitated a similar neurotic condition. First, there was a substantial chance that, even if the plaintiff's back had made him unemployable, he would have gone through life without suffering from a neurotic condition similar to his present condition. Secondly, in determining the chance that unemployability as the result of his back condition would have precipitated a similar neurotic condition, it is necessary to bear in mind that more than one probability is involved. There is the degree of probability that the plaintiff would have become unemployable in any event as the result of his back condition and there is the degree of probability that the happening of that occurrence would have precipitated a neurotic condition. When those probabilities are combined, the chance that the plaintiff would develop a neurotic condition decreases exponentially. If, for example, and only by way of illustration, there was a 75 per cent probability of his becoming unemployable by reason of his back condition even if he had not contracted brucellosis and a 75 per cent chance that that unemployability would have caused a similar neurotic condition, there was only a 56.25 per cent chance (75 per cent × 75 per cent) that, if he had not contracted brucellosis, he would have developed a similar neurotic condition.

Whatever the precise chance that the plaintiff would have developed a similar neurotic condition, the majority in the Full Court erred in refusing to award him any damages for the care and attention given to him by his wife and for the neurotic condition from which he presently suffers. The plaintiff is entitled to damages for pain and suffering on the basis that his neurotic condition is the direct result of the defendant's negligence. Those damages must be reduced, however, to take account of the chance

Malec v JC Hutton Pty Ltd cont.

that factors, unconnected with the defendant's negligence, might have brought about the onset of a similar neurotic condition. Likewise, the plaintiff is entitled to compensation for the care and attention provided by his wife. Again that award must be reduced to take account of the chance that factors, unconnected with the defendant's negligence, would have necessitated similar care and attention.

The appeal must be allowed.

[Appeal allowed and case remitted to the Supreme Court of Queensland for assessment of damages in accordance with the findings of Carter J in the Full Court and the judgment of the High Court.]

[14.135] **Notes&Questions**

1. Loss of chance was discussed in Chapter 13, in the context of whether it should properly be treated as an issue of causation, harm, or of damages [13.120]. The choice has significant implications for the standard of proof. Kirby J said in *Chappel v Hart* (1998) 195 CLR 232:

> *Valuing a lost chance*: In cases in which ... [loss of chance] is permissible, it may allow evaluation of the plaintiff's loss in terms of comparing the chances of suffering harm (given the breach which has occurred) against those that would have existed (if the breach is hypothesised away). In *CES v Superclinics (Aust) Pty Ltd* I indicated my attraction to this approach as a more rational and just way of calculating damages caused by established medical negligence. It is clearly laid down by the authority of this Court that, in some circumstances, a plaintiff may recover the value of a loss of a chance caused by a wrongdoer's act or omission.

In *Gregg v Scott* [2005] 2 WLR 268, a claimant whose prospects of recovering from cancer were always less than 50 per cent, had his prospects reduced even further by the defendant's failure to diagnose the illness. Should such a claimant be entitled to recover a proportion of the damages he would have received if he had been able to prove the doctor negligently caused his premature death? The plaintiff bears the onus of proving causation on the balance of probabilities. Where the injury is reduction in life expectancy, the likelihood of a cure must have exceeded 50-50 prior to the negligence, otherwise no loss is proved and no damages are recoverable. See, for example, *Malec v Hutton; Mallett v McMonagle* [1970] AC 166. Where past fact rather than future hypothetical is concerned, "[a] happening in the past either occurred or it did not ... [and] no discount is made for the possibility that it did not" (*Gregg v Scott* [2005] 2 WLR 268 per Lord Nicholls at [9]).

2. It is crucial in this context to distinguish between issues of causation, harm, and onus of proof on the one hand (which are relevant to liability), and certainty as to quantum of future loss on the other (which is relevant to damages). Once the liability threshold has been reached by proof of past facts, the likelihood of a given future contingency or hypothetical event occurring is reflected in the damages; that is, the notional full sum will be discounted by the percentage chance of that future contingency eventuating.

In *Gregg v Scott* [2005] 2 WLR 268, Baroness Hale discussed (at [225], [226]) the implications for awards of damages of accepting loss of chance as personal injury.

The "real problem" the case raised was whether personal injury law "should never be about outcomes but only about chances"? Would proportionate recovery "cut both ways"? It is accepted that loss of chance must be equated with a similarly discounted damages award, but would it also follow that a loss of outcome (cure) proved on the balance of probabilities should be discounted by the amount its proof falls short of 100 per cent? If the two approaches are viewed as alternatives, the defendant will always be liable where breach of duty is established, on a "heads you lose everything, tails I win something" basis. Baroness Hale rejected this as "a case of two steps forward, three steps back", concluding "not without regret" that its introduction "would cause far more problems in the general run of personal injury claims than the policy benefits are worth." Both Lords Nicholls and Hope, who found for the claimant, appear to have favoured proportionate deductions. Proportionate damages for personal injury would be a radical departure from principle, and contrary to the overriding tort goal of restitutio in integrum compensation. See P Watson, "Loss of a Chance, Causation and Proportionate Damages: *Gregg v Scott*" (2005) 70 *Precedent* 47; J Stapleton, "Loss of the Chance of Cure from Cancer" (2005) 68 MLR 996.

The issue of how to characterise a loss of chance, and in particular whether it is relevant to liability or to damages arose again in *Gett v Tabet* [2009] NSWCA 76, [13.145] a medical negligence case. The NSW Court of Appeal referred to the "narrow dividing line between matters going to causation (to be determined on the balance of probabilities) and matters involving the assessment of loss in hypothetical circumstances" (at [332]) going to quantification of the damages. The Court stressed that what was said in *Malec* [14.130] about proportionate compensation concerns the assessment of damages, and does not apply to liability issues such as causation (see Chapter 13).

Discounting for vicissitudes or contingencies in assessing loss of earning capacity

[14.140] There are two types of discounting and it is important not to confuse them. At common law the plaintiff's damages for loss of earning capacity must be discounted for contingencies or vicissitudes. This is what is referred to in some jurisdictions as adjusting the award. Section 13 of the NSW: CLA and NT: *Personal Injuries (Liabilities and Damages) Act 2003*, s 21, require a court to determine what the plaintiff's most likely future circumstances would have been if the tort had not been committed, and to award damages for future economic loss based only on those circumstances. The court must then determine the percentage possibility that the plaintiff's most likely future circumstances might have occurred anyway, and adjust the award accordingly. This is arguably consistent with the common law position laid down by the High Court in *Malec v JC Hutton Pty Ltd* (1990) 169 CLR 638 (see [14.130]), and is clearly intended to incorporate the common law "vicissitudes" discount into the civil liability legislation. For discussion of the New South Wales section, see *Macarthur Districts Motorcycle Sportsman Inc v Ardizzone* [2004] NSWCA 145, below, at [14.155]. The second type (present value discount) is covered in NSW: CLA, s 14, discussed at [14.195].

Discounting for vicissitudes simply means allowing in the award for the ups and downs of everyday life. Personal factors such as prospects of promotion, future educational opportunity, likelihood of unemployment or imprisonment, period of working life remaining, likelihood of child rearing responsibilities, prospects of improvement or deterioration in physical or mental health, pecuniary benefit to be obtained from future marriage, and others, are all taken into account. The adjustment is made on the basis of evidence about this particular plaintiff and his or her individual prospects, therefore there can be no fixed percentage rate for this discount. The High Court has pointed out on several occasions that "[a]ll contingencies are not adverse: all vicissitudes are not harmful... Why count the buffets and ignore the rewards of fortune?" (Eg *Bresatz v Przibilla* (1962) 108 CLR 541 (Windeyer J, at 544). Yet a 15 percent discount is regarded as usual in New South Wales. The next two cases indicate how this process works. Note the dramatic difference between the discount rates applied by the various courts in *Wynn* (ranging from 5% to 28% to 12.5%). What is the significance of this for the plaintiff?

Wynn v NSW Insurance Ministerial Corp

[14.145] *Wynn v NSW Insurance Ministerial Corporation* (1995) 184 CLR 485 High Court of Australia

(footnotes omitted)

[The plaintiff was injured in a motor vehicle accident in 1986. She was awarded $990,547.30 damages in the District Court by Kirkham J. The award took into account the fact that she had been injured in another motor vehicle accident in 1972. As a result of the earlier accident she had undergone surgery to stabilise a fracture and dislocation in her spine. The defendant appealed, limited to the question of damages. The Court of Appeal (Clarke, Handley and Sheller JJA) reduced the assessment for future economic loss from $705,980 to $411,350 and reduced the total sum awarded to $678,334.70. Part of the reduction was based on saved outgoings for child care and domestic assistance that would have been necessary had the plaintiff continued to work. The plaintiff appealed to the High Court.]

DAWSON, TOOHEY, GAUDRON AND GUMMOW JJ:

The Appellant, Her Circumstances, Employment History and Prospects

492 The appellant commenced work with American Express in 1981. She was hard-working and ambitious, intent upon making a career with the company and hoping, one day, to become a vice-president. She was promoted to a managerial position in 1985 and, following further promotion, was made manager of authorisations in 1986. She continued with her work for some little time after the accident and was promoted in October 1987 to the position of Director of Customer Services, one step below vice-president. Her work as Director of Customer Services involved long hours, many of them at a computer. In 1992, the position attracted a salary package of $75,556 net per year or $1,453 net per week.

The 1986 accident undid the positive effects of the surgical fusion carried out in 1974 and brought about a serious aggravation of the injury sustained by the appellant in 1972. Her symptoms progressed and began seriously to interfere with her work. She found it necessary to cease work with American Express in 1988 and, apart from one period of casual employment with that organisation, has since worked only part-time in the family business. This is run by her husband, whom she married in 1990, and her brother.

The Trial Judge's Calculation of Damages for Future Economic Loss

The trial judge found that, but for the aggravation of her earlier injury, the appellant "would have worked within the American Express organisation at least until the age of sixty years". In reaching that conclusion, his Honour found that it was not very probable that, having worked her way to the position of Director of Customer Services, she would retire by reason of marriage or motherhood.

Wynn v NSW Insurance Ministerial Corp cont.

The appellant's net weekly loss as at the date of hearing was assessed at $1,013. This figure was reached by deducting $440 for present earning capacity from the then net weekly salary package of $1,453 for Director of Customer Services. Calculation of that loss until the age of sixty (23.75 years) in accordance with Sch 3 to the *Motor Vehicles (Third Party Insurance) Amendment Act 1984* (NSW) produced an amount of $743,137. That sum was then discounted by 5 per cent to take account of contingencies or what are commonly called "the vicissitudes of life", resulting in the sum of $705,980 for future economic loss.

In deciding on a discount of 5 per cent for contingencies, the trial judge made allowance for the possibility that, had she remained in employment with American Express, the appellant might have taken maternity leave but considered that, except for ordinary transient illnesses, her work would not otherwise have been interrupted. In particular, his Honour considered that, although her 1972 injury would have produced symptoms by the time she was fifty-five, it would not have prevented her continuing in employment until the age of sixty. His Honour balanced against the possible need to take maternity leave the prospect that the appellant might have been promoted to a vice-presidential position.

The Approach of the Court of Appeal

In the Court of Appeal, Handley JA (with whom Clarke and Sheller JJA agreed) considered that the calculation of future economic loss should be reduced by amounts to allow for superannuation contributions and the cost of child care and domestic help... So far as concerns child care and domestic help, a deduction of $125 per week was made for the whole of what would have been the appellant's working life. In the result, future economic loss was assessed at $571,320.34 before allowing for contingencies.

The Court of Appeal held that there should be a discount of 28 per cent for contingencies, of which 8 per cent was for two years' absence from the workforce to have two children. The balance of the discount was for the prospect that the appellant "would at some stage [choose] or [be] forced to accept a less demanding job" because she "would be unable or unwilling to remain in her job which placed such heavy demands on her time, energy and health and the love and patience of her husband"...

So far as concerns the prospect of reduced participation in the workforce, there is nothing in the evidence to suggest that the appellant was any less able than any other career oriented person, whether male or female, to successfully combine a demanding career and family responsibilities. Rather, the evidence of her rapid promotion within the American Express organisation, her ambition to advance further and her desire to remain in the paid workforce, when considered in the light of the practice of American Express to promote from within the organisation, clearly justified the trial judge in forming the view that there was a prospect of her further advancement. As will later appear, the trial judge was correct to treat this as a positive factor to be taken into account in allowing for contingencies.

So far as maternity leave is concerned, the appellant gave evidence that, for her first child at least, she would have wished to take twelve months' maternity leave if she had continued to work with American Express. Even if allowance is made for two years' unpaid maternity leave for two children – calculated by the Court of Appeal as 8 per cent of net loss after deduction for child care and domestic help – there is no reason to think that it was not adequately reflected in the trial judge's balancing exercise which, after allowing for the possibility of promotion and increased earnings, resulted in a discount of 5 per cent.

The position with respect to the deduction of child care expenses for the purpose of calculating net loss is, perhaps, not so clear. It is well settled that "[c]ompensation for loss of earning capacity is paid

Wynn v NSW Insurance Ministerial Corp cont.

only because it is or may be productive of financial loss". Thus, it has been said that "outgoings necessary for the realisation of that capacity", such as transport costs, tools and equipment, must be deducted.

There is simply no basis for treating domestic help as necessary for the realisation of earning capacity and, to the extent that the Court of Appeal thought otherwise, it was clearly wrong... There are, however, circumstances in which the cost of caring for very young children may properly be seen as an "essential prerequisite" to the earning of income and, in this sense, as an outgoing "necessary for the realisation of [earning] capacity". However, outgoings which are deducted for the purpose of calculating economic loss are those which are necessarily incurred in or in connection with the employment or undertaking by which earning capacity is realised, not those which are incurred, even as a "necessary prerequisite", merely to provide an opportunity to realise that capacity. In a sense, child care can be regarded as an opportunity cost. But even that mistakes its true nature.

Child care is a cost that may be incurred by men or women. It may be incurred whether or not the child's mother is in the paid workforce. On the other hand, not all women in the paid workforce incur a cost for the care of their young children... These considerations lead to the conclusion that the cost of child care is simply one of various costs associated with having children. And as such, the cost is properly characterised for the purpose of calculating economic loss, as it is for the purposes of taxation law, as essentially private or domestic in character. So characterised, it is no more to be deducted when calculating loss of earning capacity than are other items of expenditure for personal amenity...

The Respondent's Argument in this Court

The argument for the respondent in this Court was that allowance should have been made for the possibility that the appellant's 1972 injury would have prevented her working in a high level managerial position until age sixty even if the 1986 accident had not occurred... As it was developed in this Court, the argument was that, overall, the appropriate discount was 38 per cent, resulting, after allowance for superannuation contributions, in a verdict in the sum allowed by the Court of Appeal. More precisely, it was argued that no allowance should be made for the prospect of advancement and that 38 per cent fairly represents the possibility that the appellant would have taken unpaid maternity leave and the further possibility that her previous neck injury would have prevented her continued employment until age sixty.

It is necessary to say something as to contingencies or "vicissitudes". Calculation of future economic loss must take account of the various possibilities which might otherwise have affected earning capacity. The principle and the relevant considerations were identified by Barwick CJ in *Arthur Robinson (Grafton) Pty Ltd v Carter ...*

It is to be remembered that a discount for contingencies or "vicissitudes" is to take account of matters which might otherwise adversely affect earning capacity and as Professor Luntz notes, death apart, "sickness, accident, unemployment and industrial disputes are the four major contingencies which expose employees to the risk of loss of income". Positive considerations which might have resulted in advancement and increased earnings are also to be taken into account for, as Windeyer J pointed out in *Bresatz v Przibilla*, "[a]ll 'contingencies' are not adverse: all 'vicissitudes' are not harmful". Finally, contingencies are to be considered in terms of their likely impact on the earning capacity of the person who has been injured, not by reference to the workforce generally. Even so, the practice in New South Wales is to proceed on the basis that a 15 per cent discount is generally appropriate, subject to adjustment up or down to take account of the plaintiff's particular circumstances.

Leaving aside the appellant's previous neck injury and the possibility that she might have taken unpaid maternity leave, there was little, if anything, in her circumstances to suggest that her earning capacity was at risk from any of the four major items which Professor Luntz has identified as detrimentally affecting earning capacity. She was in good health, fit and energetic; she was employed in a position which would not seem to involve exposure to accident or disease; and as an employee in a managerial position with American Express, she would not seem to have been at particular risk of redundancy or the possibility of being involved in industrial disputes.

As already indicated, there was evidence upon which the trial judge might properly form the view that, had the accident not occurred, there was a prospect that the appellant would have been further promoted within American Express. The argument of the respondent to the contrary must be rejected. All that had to be established was "a real possibility" of promotion. The evidence clearly permitted an inference to that effect. And once that inference was drawn by the trial judge, it was necessary for the prospect of advancement to be taken into account and balanced against the need to take maternity leave. If they were the only personal considerations to be taken into account, it could not be said that, in the circumstances of this case, a discount of 5 per cent was inappropriate.

However, the evidence clearly established that, following the injury in 1972 and notwithstanding the bone graft carried out in 1974, the appellant's spine was susceptible to further injury and was likely to suffer degenerative changes. If there was a chance that the 1972 injury would have reduced the appellant's ability to work in any event, that chance had to be assessed and allowed for in the calculation of future economic loss. Unless allowed for in that way, the defendant would be held responsible for loss which was not causally related to the injury suffered in 1986.

It is necessary to say something of susceptibility to further injury. It is not permissible in assessing the chance that an earlier injury may have resulted in impaired earning capacity to have regard to the possibility of further tortious injury. That possibility must be disregarded because, in the event of further injury, damages would be assessed, as in this case, by allowing for any pre-condition resulting in or having the possibility of resulting in impaired earning capacity. Only by disregarding the possibility of further tortious injury does the law ensure full compensation…

…[T]he evidence clearly established the possibility of degenerative changes [to the spine]. The trial judge's finding, on the probabilities, that the changes would have produced symptoms at age fifty-five but would not have prevented continued employment until age sixty did not eliminate the possibility that symptoms might have occurred earlier, resulting in reduced earnings or in early retirement. This and the possibility of non-tortious injury should have been allowed for in determining the appropriate discount for contingencies.

As Brennan and Dawson JJ pointed out in *Malec v J C Hutton Pty Ltd*, "[d]amages founded on hypothetical evaluations defy precise calculation". The discount to be allowed for the possibility that the appellant's previous injury might have resulted in her impaired earning capacity can at best be a matter of impression. Having regard to the better than average result of the surgical fusion carried out in 1974 and the diminishing nature of the risk of further injury, the discount should not be great. In our view, the appropriate discount for maternity leave and the possible effects of the condition brought about by the 1972 accident, balanced against the prospect of further advancement, is $12\,^1/_2$ per cent.

Conclusion

The appeal should be allowed in part. Paragraphs 1 and 3 of the order of the Court of Appeal should be set aside and in lieu thereof there should be judgment for the appellant in accordance with these

Wynn v NSW Insurance Ministerial Corp cont.

reasons. The appellant should have her costs at first instance and 85 per cent of her costs in the Court of Appeal and in this Court ...

[14.150] **Note**

In *Gett v Tabet* [2009] NSWCA 76, the plaintiff's claim included loss of pecuniary benefits that might have been expected to accrue on marriage. The female plaintiff was six years old at the time of the alleged medical negligence. After reviewing the authorities, the Court upheld the approach taken at trial. There, Studdert J concluded that it would not be appropriate to make a discrete allowance as a separate head of damages for loss of marriage benefits. Instead he included that loss in the allowance for vicissitudes in relation to the claim for loss of earning capacity. Discounting for re-marriage prospects in the context of a dependant's claim under Lord Campbell's Act is discussed in *De Sales v Ingrilli* (2002) 212 CLR 338 at [14.305].

Macarthur Districts Motorcycle Sportsman v Ardizzone

[14.155] *Macarthur Districts Motorcycle Sportsman Inc v Ardizzone* [2004] NSWCA 145 New South Wales Court of Appeal

(footnotes omitted)

[The facts are taken from the judgment of Bryson J in the Supreme Court [18]]:

On 15 August 2003 the learned Trial Judge awarded the plaintiff, now the respondent, damages of $242,000 for personal injuries sustained on 6 April 1997 while he was participating in a motor cross race at a motor cross track at Appin. The track and the event were controlled by the first appellant Macarthur Districts Motor Cycle Sportsmen Inc (hereinafter the Club) ... The respondent ... was 12 years of age when injured. He already had much experience riding in motor cross events over about five years. He attended the Appin track in the care of his father and in the company of other family members and friends... According to the respondent's evidence, which was accepted by the Trial Judge, the respondent was proceeding along a straight when he came to a jump, rode over the jump and fell on the far side. He was then struck by a following motorcycle and suffered severe injuries. ... the issue came down to whether or not there were sufficient marshals.

HODGSON JA: [2] I wish to make some ... comments concerning s 13 of the *Civil Liability Act 2002*, which is in the following terms:

13 Future economic loss – claimant's prospects and adjustments

(1) A court cannot make an award of damages for future economic loss unless the claimant first satisfies the court that the assumptions about future earning capacity or other events on which the award is to be based accord with the claimant's most likely future circumstances but for the injury.

(2) When a court determines the amount of any such award of damages for future economic loss it is required to adjust the amount of damages for future economic loss that would have been sustained on those assumptions by reference to the percentage possibility that the events might have occurred but for the injury.

(3) If the court makes an award for future economic loss, it is required to state the assumptions on which the award was based and the relevant percentage by which damages were adjusted.

Macarthur Districts Motorcycle Sportsman v Ardizzone cont.

Thus, s 13(1) and s 13(3) require identification and statement by the court of "assumptions about future earning capacity or other events on which the award [of damages for future economic loss] is to be based"; and s 13(1) requires satisfaction that these assumptions "accord with the claimant's most likely future circumstances but for the injury."

Then, s 13(2) requires an adjustment of the "amount of damages for future economic loss that would have been sustained on those assumptions" by reference to the "percentage possibility that the events might have occurred but for the injury"; and s 13(3) requires the court to state "the relevant percentage by which damages were adjusted."

In general terms, the "assumptions" referred to in s 13(1) and s 13(3) are the views about what the future economic situation of the plaintiff would have been but for the injury, with which the court compares the future economic situation of the plaintiff resulting from the injury, as it is understood to be. Normally, these views will be expressed in terms of a capacity to earn a certain amount net per week as from the date of hearing until an estimated retiring date, perhaps with adjustments for promotion or other possible circumstances which could be anticipated as affecting earning capacity.

In my opinion, the provisions in s 13(2) and s 13(3) concerning a "percentage" are meant to be a statutory implementation of the practice of making a deduction in relation to future economic loss for "vicissitudes", for which 15 percent is the percentage conventionally adopted in most cases.

However, the precise formulation of these provisions raises some problems.

In the first place, there is at least theoretically some tension between the requirements of s 13 and what the High Court of Australia said in *Malec v JC Hutton Pty Ltd* (1990) 169 CLR 638 at 643 about assessing damages, namely, that in respect of hypothetical and future events, the court assesses the degree of probability that an event would have occurred, or might occur, and adjusts the award of damages to reflect that degree of probability. This could be understood as suggesting that the court should not base its award on the "most likely future circumstances" but rather should base it on probability weightings of a range of alternative possibilities.

That matter was considered with some care in *Norris v Blake (No 2)* (1997) 41 NSWLR 49 where it was concluded that the proper approach in that case was to assess what it was most likely the plaintiff would have earned during the rest of his working life, and then adjust this for contingencies. So far, this would appear generally in accord with s 13. But in *Blake*, at 73, it was expressly noted that the contingencies included the possibility that the plaintiff might have done far better; and that is a matter to which s 13 appears to make no reference.

Subject to what I say later about "buffer" awards, it seems that the *Blake* approach has in fact been adopted in most personal injury cases, as a practical way to give effect to the *Malec* principle; and s 13 may be regarded as making it mandatory to do this. However, and this leads to the second major problem with s 13, the wording of s 13(2) is not entirely apt to the purpose of requiring an appropriate adjustment for vicissitudes or contingencies.

At first blush, "the events" referred to in s 13(2) would seem to be the events (including those relating to future earning capacity) on which the award is to based, which according to s 13(1) have been considered most likely but for the injury. "Most likely" here does not mean more likely than not, but more likely than any other possible scenario; and the "percentage possibility that such events might have occurred but for the accident" could be any percentage at all, depending on the number and respective probabilities of alternative scenarios. To adjust the damages according to this percentage possibility would make no sense at all.

In my opinion, having regard to the apparent purpose of the section, "the events" in s 13(2) must be those corresponding to the future economic situation of the plaintiff as it is understood to be resulting from the injury, not those corresponding to his future situation but for the injury. (I note this has much the same effect as reading s 13(2) as if "the events" were those referred to in s 13(1), but

Macarthur Districts Motorcycle Sportsman v Ardizzone cont.

reading the last seven words of s 13(2) as if they were "might not have happened even if the injury had not occurred"). Even this has the difficulty that the percentage possibility that those events (that is, all those events, not just some of them) might have occurred even if the injury had not occurred would be vanishingly small. The vicissitudes that are normally allowed for are a multitude of possibilities that, even without the injury, could have in various ways prevented the plaintiff from completely achieving the economic situation considered most likely.

The usual allowance of 15 percent is not on the basis that there is a 15 percent possibility that even without the injury, the plaintiff would not have achieved the most likely economic situation, but on the basis that this is a reasonable discount having regard to a myriad of possibilities each of which could have meant that the plaintiff fell short of this situation to various degrees. In my opinion, despite problems with the literal wording of s 13(2), it should be read as having this effect.

There is the additional difficulty that s 13(2) does not seem to deal with the situation, contemplated in *Blake*, where there is a significant chance that the plaintiff's economic circumstances but for the accident might have been far better than the most likely circumstances. In that case, there was a moderate but not negligible chance that the plaintiff might have become a "superstar" earning huge amounts of money. It may be that, consistently with a purposive interpretation of s 13(2), positive vicissitudes can be taken into account in reaching the appropriate figure for adjustment, and perhaps even completely balance out negative vicissitudes. However, at present I am doubtful that s 13 would permit an upward adjustment if positive vicissitudes were considered to outweigh negative vicissitudes. It is not necessary to determine that question in this case.

One final problem with s 13 is whether it permits an award for future economic loss in the nature of what is called a "buffer". In some personal injury cases, the court has taken the view that the plaintiff should be compensated, not for any ongoing difference between the most likely economic situation but for the accident and the actual future economic situation as it is understood to be, but rather for the chance that the plaintiff will be disadvantaged in the future because of the injury. It is a possible view of s 13 that it precludes this approach.

In the present case, the primary judge referred to a cushion or buffer, but went on to assess future economic loss on the basis of the figure of $100 per week. In my opinion, this, together with the other matters referred to in paragraphs [67]-[68] of the primary judge's judgment, was an adequate indication of assumptions on which the award was to be based, including the assumption that the plaintiff's future earning capacity but for the accident was $100 a week net greater than his reduced future earning capacity; and an adequate indication that these assumptions accorded with the plaintiff's most likely future circumstances but for the injury. The allowance of 20 per cent for vicissitudes sufficiently complied with s 13(2) and s 13(3). Thus this was not strictly a buffer award, and it is not necessary in this case to decide if s 13 precludes such awards.

I would conclude by suggesting that Parliament reconsider the wording of s 13. It appears deficient in three respects:

1. Its wording is inapt to its manifest purpose of providing for the usual "vicissitudes" deduction.
2. It may not allow for positive vicissitudes.
3. It may not allow for "buffer" awards, which on *Malec* principles are most appropriate in some cases.

New economic needs created: past and future care costs

[14.160] Entitlement under this head of loss used to be regarded as dependent upon the plaintiff having incurred expense or liability to meet expenses. Since the decision in *Griffiths v*

Kirkemeyer (1977) 139 CLR 161 (this is extracted at [14.170] below), it has been clear that the creation of a need is the foundation, rather than any obligation to pay for satisfaction of that need. Expenses included under this head include medical, hospital, nursing, physiotherapy, and ongoing care costs.

Sharman v Evans

[14.165] *Sharman v Evans* (1977) 138 CLR 563 High Court of Australia (footnote omitted)

[See [14.100] for a detailed description of the facts.]

GIBBS AND STEPHEN JJ: 574 In view of the attack made upon various aspects of his Honour's assessment of damages it is appropriate to examine the various heads of damage which presented themselves for assessment so as to appreciate and deal with the various criticisms raised by the appellant. First are those costs which the plaintiff will be obliged to incur in consequence of her injuries, principally although not exclusively, the cost of nursing and medical care. It is clear that she will require such care for the rest of her life. It can be provided either in a hospital in Perth devoted to the care of persons incapacitated as she is or, at very much greater cost, in her own home. The plaintiff would much prefer the latter but the question is whether the defendant should be required to make compensation upon this much more expensive basis. The learned trial judge's award of damages contemplated that the plaintiff, while spending the greater part of her life in hospital, would spend some part of it being cared for at home.

Where the plaintiff is to be cared for in the future will not only directly affect the extent of nursing and medical expenses which are to be compensated for; it will also bear upon the extent of her loss of the amenities and enjoyment of life, a lifetime substantially spent in hospital will greatly aggravate that loss. In our view the medical evidence in this case does not justify the conclusion that the defendant should be required to compensate for future nursing and medical expenses on any basis other than that the plaintiff's future will be one substantially spent in hospital.

The appropriate criterion must be that such expenses as the plaintiff may reasonably incur should be recoverable from the defendant; as Barwick CJ put it in *Arthur Robinson (Grafton) Pty Ltd v Carter* "The question here is not what are the ideal requirements but what are the reasonable requirements of the respondent", and see *Chulcough v Holley*, per Windeyer J. The touchstone of reasonableness in the case of the cost of providing nursing and medical care for the plaintiff in the future is, no doubt, cost matched against health benefits to the plaintiff. If cost is very great and benefits to health slight or speculative the cost-involving treatment will clearly be unreasonable, the more so if there is available an alternative and relatively inexpensive mode of treatment, affording equal or only slightly lesser benefits. When the factors are more evenly balanced no intuitive answer presents itself and the real difficulty of attempting to weigh against each other two incomparables, financial cost against relative health benefits to the plaintiff, becomes manifest. The present case is however one which does to our minds allow of a definite answer; it is a case of alternatives in which the difference in relative costs is great whereas the benefit to the plaintiff of the more expensive alternative is entirely one of amenity, in no way involving physical or mental well-being. This may be demonstrated from the evidence.

Assuming, for convenience of comparison, a life expectancy of twenty years, the future expenses of the plaintiff if confined to hospital would be of the order of a present value, computed on six per cent tables, of $108,500, inclusive of nursing, medical and physiotherapy services and cost of special beds etc. The provision to her of like services at her mother's home over that period would amount to a present value of about $390,000, to which would have to be added a weekly cost for medicaments etc of about $23 per week and a capital cost of some $11,750 for suitable alterations to her mother's home; moreover this is exclusive of the cost of food and of the cost of providing another home should her mother die during the period and the present home cease to be available to the plaintiff. The

Sharman v Evans cont.

benefit to the plaintiff of being cared for at home rather than in hospital is not any benefit to her health but rather to her future enjoyment of life which would be enhanced by a home atmosphere; her life would not thereby be prolonged nor would her physical condition be at all improved; indeed she would be somewhat more at risk physically at home than in hospital. There is no evidence suggesting any likely psychiatric benefits, probable though these might appear to the layman.

In these circumstances the future cost of reasonable nursing and medical attention must, we think, be assessed on the basis of a lifetime substantially spent in hospital. We have, to date, for convenience of comparison, quoted costs based upon a post-accident life expectancy of twenty years. Assuming a lifetime of hospital care, devoid of the extra risks involved in nursing care at home, the medical evidence suggests that this is too conservative an estimate. His Honour, without specifically nominating any precise period as that selected by him as appropriate, clearly contemplated that if the plaintiff spent part of her life at home something in excess of twenty years was nevertheless an appropriate assumption as to life expectancy. For the purpose of our present examination of the award, and since we would regard the plaintiff's future as one involving permanent hospitalization in conditions of maximum nursing and medical care, we adopt thirty years as the appropriate period. For that period the present value, on six per cent tables, of the cost of hospital care, medical and physiotherapy treatment and the provision of a special bed and the like will amount to about $128,000.

There is another item of future expense which must enter into the assessment process. Because we conclude that the defendant should not be required to compensate the plaintiff on any basis other than that of a lifetime in hospital it follows that the plaintiff's loss of the enjoyment and amenities of life will be the greater. She must be regarded as wholly deprived of the everyday pleasures of living in the environment of her own home. Instead she will be exposed to a lifetime of institutional life. Not only must this be reflected in the damages to be awarded under the conventional head of pain, suffering and the loss of enjoyment and amenities of life. In the present case it is also appropriate to reflect rather more positively one particular aspect of this situation of permanent hospitalization. The effect of the latter upon the plaintiff can clearly be somewhat mitigated if she is able to vary the monotony of the hospital ward by occasional day visits to her home and by other outings, possibly even by occasional weekends away from hospital. The medical evidence discloses that these would be possible provided that constant nursing attention was provided. Applying again the criterion of reasonableness but now weighing the expense of such attention against the clear benefits in amenity and enjoyment of life that such breaks in a lifetime in hospital would provide we are in no doubt that the plaintiff is entitled to compensation for the cost of such outings. That their cost will be high is apparent from the data as to nursing costs already referred to, to which must be added transportation either by ambulance or by chauffeur-driven car. If enjoyed as frequently as, say, once every few weeks over thirty years that cost would not be overstated by the adoption of a present value figure of about $20,000. We accordingly adopt that sum as a second item of future cost to be compensated for by the defendant.

In dealing in this way with these two items of future expenditure we have departed in principle from the method of assessment adopted by the learned trial judge but have endeavoured to reflect, as do his reasons for judgment, the need for damages to be more liberal than they would be were the plaintiff to be restricted to recovery only of the present value of the cost of thirty years of hospitalization. Our approach conduces, we believe, to clarity of analysis while emphasizing the extent to which damages for loss of amenity must interact with other heads of damages, including that concerned with the defraying of future expenditure reasonably incurred by the plaintiff and attributable to her injuries.

Gratuitous attendant care services

Griffiths v Kerkemeyer

[14.170] *Griffiths v Kerkemeyer* (1977) 139 CLR 161 High Court of Australia

(footnotes omitted)

[The respondent in the current appeal suffered severe injuries and became quadriplegic as a result of a road accident occasioned by the appellant's negligence. From the judgment of Mason J (at 181): "The respondent recovered judgment on 10th December 1975 in the sum of $249,736, representing damages and interest, in the Supreme Court of South Australia (Bright J). The judgment was for $221,936 damages and $27,800 interest. The appellant's case is that the damages awarded were excessive, and there is a cross-appeal on the ground that the damages awarded were inadequate."]

GIBBS J: 163 It is common in cases where a plaintiff has been injured for some member of his family, or a devoted friend, to perform for him services that have been rendered necessary by his injuries. Sometimes the relative or friend provides care of a kind that would otherwise have to be provided in a hospital or nursing home, or by a paid nurse or team of nurses working in the plaintiff's home. Sometimes the service provided is of a domestic nature – for example the relative or friend does housework that the injured plaintiff is unable to do. In some cases the relative or friend suffers financial loss by providing the service–he may have to give up his employment or forego wages that would otherwise have been earned. In other cases the relative or friend may assume a heavy physical and emotional burden but may not suffer actual financial loss, either because he has no outside employment or because it is possible to perform the services in his spare time. These situations are of an everyday character but the law governing the right of the injured plaintiff to recover the cost or value of the services has been uncertain, and the decisions conflicting ...

However in my opinion this Court should not abandon the principle that a plaintiff whose injuries have created a need for hospital or nursing services cannot recover damages in respect of that need (except of course for loss of amenities or pain and suffering) unless the satisfaction of the need is or may be productive of financial loss. However it should no longer be held that the fact that the services have been and will be provided gratuitously is conclusive of this question. The matter should, as it were, be viewed in two stages. First, is it reasonably necessary to provide the services, and would it be reasonably necessary to do so at a cost? If so, the fulfilment of the need is likely to be productive of financial loss. Next, is the character of the benefit which the plaintiff receives by the gratuitous provision of the services such that it ought to be brought into account in relief of the wrongdoer? If not, the damages are recoverable ...

Where necessary services have been provided gratuitously by a relative or friend, it should now, as a general rule, be held that the value of the services so provided should not reduce the damages payable to the plaintiff. Notwithstanding that Lord Reid, in the passage cited from *Parry v Cleaver* equated public with private benevolence, I consider that if the hospital, medical and nursing services provided by the state are such that the plaintiff has been and will be supplied with all the services that he reasonably requires at no charge to himself, the case will, as a general rule, be one in which the wrongdoer should have the benefit of that circumstance. There appear to me to be strong grounds of

Griffiths v Kerkemeyer cont.

policy which distinguish services which the state makes available for all persons, or for all in a certain category, on the one hand, from services provided as a result of a sacrifice made by a relative or friend of the plaintiff, on the other hand … .

STEPHEN J: … [T]he charitable friend or relative is a peculiarly inappropriate person to be saddled with any ultimate loss, being inherently unlikely to have any capacity to serve as an efficient loss distributor. Accordingly a result which allows the injured person to recover damages in respect of the provider's services, so that he may be in a position to reimburse the provider, is a desirable policy goal; the wrongdoer, likely to carry liability insurance, will prove a much better loss distributor.

… the plaintiff should, I think, be regarded as beneficially entitled to the judgment he obtains without question of the imposition of any trust in respect of some part of his damages in favour of one who has rendered, or may in the future render, gratuitous services to him.

[14.175] **Notes&Questions**

1. Is there a conflict between the principles expressed in *Griffiths v Kerkemeyer* (1977) 139 CLR 161 and *Graham v Baker* (1961) 106 CLR 340?

2. Damages awarded for care and attention rendered gratuitously must be reduced to take account of the chance that factors, unconnected with the defendant's negligence, would have necessitated similar care and attention: *Malec v Hutton* (1990) 169 CLR 638 (discussed at [14.130]). See also the discussion on discounting at [14.140].

3. Awards for gratuitous care costs (*Griffiths v Kerkemeyer* (1977) 139 CLR 161 "damages") are controversial. Compare the following two judicial views, first, that of Callinan J in *Grincelis v House* (2000) 201 CLR 321 at [51]:

> Experience recalls to mind the incredulous expressions of delight of plaintiffs, and of disbelieving dismay of defendants, on being told that damages for gratuitous care and services at common law are available, and that there is no legal obligation in this country for them to be paid to the gratuitous carer and provider of services.

Contrast this with the view of Kirby J in *Hodges v Frost* (1984) 53 ALR 373 (Fed Ct of A, at 379-80):

> [I]n terms of public policy, it is at least arguable that the law of damages should encourage the provision of non-institutional care by acknowledging some entitlement to compensation in respect of gratuitous services benevolently offered by relatives and friends. Such services may prove to be more efficacious and certainly more congenial than paid services in respect of which there would be no dispute as to recovery. They may be available during longer hours. Encouraging such facilities may actually minimise the liability of defendants. A rule against such compensation could have a tendency to force injured persons to secure more expensive, less convenient, less readily available and less congenial paid services.

Which of these views do you find more persuasive? Why?

4. In *Van Gervan v Fenton* (1992) 175 CLR 327 the issue was the appropriate valuation of the *Griffiths v Kerkemeyer* (1977) 139 CLR 161 component of an award. Mason CJ, Toohey and McHugh JJ said (at 333):

> Once it is recognized that it is the need for the services which gives the plaintiff the right to an award of damages, it follows that the damages which he or she receives are not

determined by reference to the actual cost to the plaintiff of having them provided or by reference to the income forgone by the provider of the services. As Stephen J pointed out in *Griffiths* ..., the principle laid down in *Donnelly* "is concerned not with what outlays of money the plaintiff will in fact incur as a consequence of his injuries but with the objective monetary 'value' of his loss". Because the market cost of services is ordinarily the reasonable and objective value of the need for those services, the market cost, as a general rule, is the amount which the defendant must pay as damages ... [I]n some cases the market cost may be too high to be the reasonable value of the services ... but the case will be rare indeed where the income forgone by the care provider is ever an appropriate guide to the fair value of the services required by the injured person ...

... there are sound policy reasons why the law should reject the income lost by the provider as the criterion for measuring the plaintiff's loss. First, fairness to the provider as well as to the plaintiff requires that the plaintiff should have the ability to pay the provider a sum equivalent to what the provider would earn if he or she was supplying those services in the marketplace. It does not seem reasonable that the defendant's liability to pay damages should be reduced at the indirect expense of the provider by invoking notions of marital or family obligation to provide the services free of charge or at less than market rates ... Moreover, a plaintiff should be entitled to arrange his or her affairs in the way in which that person pleases and should not be constrained by monetary considerations from dispensing with gratuitous services and obtaining outside services if they are desired. Indeed, the relationship between the provider and the plaintiff may continue to exist in some cases only because outside help is able to be obtained.

Secondly, since there is no binding agreement with the provider to continue to provide the services, the Court would have to make a finding as to whether the care would continue to be provided and, if so, for how long ... It is true that any assessment of damages may be falsified by the occurrence of what the courts have called "the vicissitudes of life". But the common law should seek to reduce, where possible, the uncertainty involved in the assessment of damages. The use of the market cost criterion enables the plaintiff to be properly compensated by the award of a reasonable sum whether or not the gratuitous care provider continues to provide that care.

Restrictions on awards for gratuitous attendant care

[14.180] In 2002, *Griffiths v Kerkemeyer* (1977) 139 CLR 161 awards for care given by family members, on average, comprised 25 per cent of damages awards over $500,000 (Negligence Review Panel, Review of the Law of Negligence, Final Report (Commonwealth of Australia, Canberra, 2002) at para 13.73). The Negligence Review Panel (at para 13.75) recommended some limits be placed on recovery of these damages, because "claims ... about ... need for gratuitous services are easy to make and difficult to refute". Most States have enacted legislation to restrict *Griffiths v Kerkemeyer* (1977) 139 CLR 161 damages awards, in their workers' compensation and motor accidents legislation, as well as in the civil liability legislation. In some jurisdictions, compensation for gratuitous services may also be restricted by only allowing damages for the work of certain family members providing services: SA: CLA, s 59(1)(a)(b) (parent, spouse or child of the injured person); WA: CLA, s 12(1) and *Motor Vehicle (Third Party Insurance) Act 1943*, s 3 (motor vehicle accidents) (a member of the same household or family of the injured person). In the ACT: CLWA there are no restrictions, but note that the provisions also apply to motor vehicle accident claims and although claims under the *Workers Compensation Act 1951* (ACT) are excluded, it has been assumed that the provisions apply to common law claims for workplace injuries; this is under review. Tasmanian legislation which appeared to abolish these claims (*Common Law (Miscellaneous Actions) Act 1986* (Tas), s 5) has been read restrictively: see *Southern Regional*

Health Board v Grimsey [1998] 8 Tas R 166; *Crockett v Roberts* [2002] 11 Tas R 393. The CLA provisions impose a cap on gratuitous care, which does not apply in relation to paid care. It introduces a threshold of a minimum requirement for care of six hours per week for a minimum period of six months. The rate payable is not to exceed average weekly earnings. No recovery may be had for services that would have been provided irrespective of the plaintiff's injury, and there must be a "reasonable" need for the services: NSW: CLA, s 15; NT: *Personal Injuries (Liabilities and Damages) Act 2003*, s 23; Qld: CLA, s 59; Tas: CLA, s 28B; Vic: WrA, s 28IA; WA: CLA, s 12 (but note differences in this provision "not less than 40 hours per week"). See also ACT: CLWA, s 100 and SA: CLA, s 58 which are less restrictive. For a discussion of the correct interpretation of s 15 of the *Civil Liability Act 2002* (NSW) see *Woolworths v Lawlor* [2004] NSWCA 209 ..

Damages for loss of capacity to provide domestic services to others

[14.185] Another issue arising out of *Griffiths v Kerkemeyer* (1977) 139 CLR 161 is whether the plaintiff can recover damages for domestic services which he or she would normally perform, but is now unable to perform, throwing extra obligations on other family members. The question is whether such a loss is compensable as an extension of the *Griffiths v Kerkemeyer* (1977) 139 CLR 161 principle, since arguably it is distinguishable from *Griffiths* because the need is that of the third party rather than the plaintiff. In *Sullivan v Gordon* (1999) 47 NSWLR 319, the New South Wales Court of Appeal allowed recovery for future child care that the plaintiff was unable to provide. The plaintiff was 15 at the time of the accident. Years later she had two children that she was unable to care for because of her injuries. It was held that she was entitled to recover damages for the value of the services that the family provided in the care of her children. Although there is some variation State to State, the trend of recent decisions had been to allow recovery prior to the High Court's 2005 decision in *CSR v Eddy* (2005) 80 ALJR 59 overturning such awards. See also *Easther v Amaca Pty Ltd* [2001] WASC 328; *CSR v Thompson* (2003) 59 NSWLR 77; *Sturch v Willmot* [1997] 2 Qd R 310. Note, in Queensland, this claim is now limited to services within the injured person's household, see Qld: CLA, s 59(3) and contrast *Weinert v Schmidt* (2002) 84 SASR 307. *CSR* itself was reversed by statute in New South Wales in the following year. See Notes 2 and 3 below. Consider the relationship between *Sullivan v Gordon* [1999] 47 NSWLR 319 and *Griffiths v Kerkemeyer* (1977) 139 CLR 161 damages, and whether the position adopted by the High Court or the New South Wales Parliament is preferable.

[14.190] **Notes&Questions**

1. The decision in *Sullivan v Gordon* (1999) 47 NSWLR 319 (CA) allowed an injured plaintiff to claim compensation for the inability to provide services to the family. It provides compensation for some of the losses that at common law would have been recoverable in a separate action by a husband, as an action for loss of consortium. At common law in an action for loss of consortium, a husband would have been able to bring a separate claim for loss of society, companionship and services as well as medical costs resulting from injury to his wife. The action for loss of consortium would have covered the inability to look after the home and family as well as loss of social and sexual companionship. This was one of the very rare instances where one person could bring an action for damages resulting from injuries suffered by another. (The other

principal exception is an action by a dependant for the death of a parent, spouse or child.) The action for loss of consortium was based on the long outdated concept that a husband had an action for interference with his proprietary interest in his wife's services. In the Australian Capital Territory, New South Wales, Tasmania and Western Australia, the husband's action for loss of consortium has been abolished: ACT: CLWA, s 218; NSW: *Law Reform (Marital Consortium) Act 1984*; Tas: *Common Law (Miscellaneous Actions) Act 1986*, s 3; WA: *Law Reform (Miscellaneous Provisions) Act 1941* (note the repeal occurred prior to the 2003 amendments which replaced the repealing section, s 3). The *Sullivan v Gordon* [1999] 47 NSWLR 319 head of damages will cover some of these losses. It allows the injured plaintiff to recover damages for the inability to look after the family. Other elements of consortium such as loss of social and sexual companionship would be recoverable by the injured spouse in her claim for loss of enjoyment of life. The husband's separate action for loss of consortium survives in the other States. In Queensland and South Australia it has been extended to claims by wives for loss of consortium of their husbands. At common law, the action was available only to a husband: *Best v Fox* [1952] AC 716. In Queensland and South Australia and the Northern Territory the action is also available to a wife: *Law Reform Act 1995* (Qld), s 13; Qld: CLA, s 58 (limits on recovery of damages for loss of consortium); SA: CLA, s 65; *Compensation (Fatal Injuries) Ordinance* (NT), s 10(3)(c). In those jurisdictions, some adjustments need to be made if the injured spouse is allowed to claim damages for the inability to provide services to other family members and a separate claim for loss of consortium is brought by the spouse, otherwise the defendant would be paying twice for the same loss: see *CSR Ltd v Thompson* (2003) 59 NSWLR 77 dealing with the South Australian provision. Note also Qld: CLA, s 58 (no claim unless the injured person has died or general damages for the injured person assessed at $30,000 or more; damages for loss of services not to exceed three times average weekly earnings).

2. *Sullivan v Gordon* [1999] 47 NSWLR 319 was overruled by the High Court in *CSR v Eddy* (2005) 80 ALJR 59, which concerned a 61 year old plaintiff who had contracted mesothelioma from workplace exposure to asbestos. He was awarded damages by O'Meally J in the Dust Diseases Tribunal, in part for his loss of ability to assist his wife with domestic and garden chores. On appeal from the New South Wales Court of Appeal, the High Court set aside the judgment in favour of the plaintiff, saying that to allow *Sullivan v Gordon* [1999] 47 NSWLR 319 damages is to "create an indirect avenue of compensation to the persons no longer supplied" with services. Reference was made in the judgment to the "controversial" status of *Griffiths v Kerkemeyer* (1977) 139 CLR 161, "as evidenced by the number of legislative reversals or qualifications of it". There is also judicial dissatisfaction with it. It "can produce very large awards, some think disproportionately large" (*CSR v Eddy* (2005) 80 ALJR 59 Gleeson CJ, Gummow and Heydon JJ at [26]). This is consistent with the recent judicial trend of depressing awards at the expense of plaintiffs, in line with the clearly expressed legislative view embodied in the civil liability legislation. The Court concluded in *CSR v Eddy* (2005) 80 ALJR 59 (at [66]) that:

> The [plaintiff's] arguments ...are not necessarily to be rejected for flaws in the policy reasoning... they are to be rejected because they rest on policy reasoning which it is more appropriate for legislatures to weigh than courts.

3. *Sullivan v Gordon* [1999] 47 NSWLR 319 damages were re-instated in New South Wales after *CSR v Eddy* (2005) 80 ALJR 59 by insertion of new provisions in the NSW: CLA, ss 15A and 15B. Section 15A relates to damages for gratuitous attendant care services for dust-related conditions. Section 15B relates to "assisted care" whether or not provided gratuitously, defined to include respite care, care of dependants including spouses, de facto spouses, children, a wide range of extended family members, and unborn children at the time the claim arises. This is a significantly more generous class of care recipients than in *Sullivan v Gordon* [1999] 47 NSWLR 319. In relation to services previously provided gratuitously by the plaintiff, the claimant must have provided the services to those dependants before the injury, and the dependants must be incapable of performing the services themselves "by reason of their age or physical or mental incapacity". There must be a "reasonable expectation" that the services would have been provided for a minimum of six hours per week for six months, in line with s 15, and would have been reasonably needed for that period. Double recovery will not be permitted where a dependant has recovered for that loss of capacity independently. Damages must not exceed the *Griffiths v Kerkemeyer* (1977) 139 CLR 161 rate regardless of the number of hours involved. In determining the value of any gratuitous domestic services, the court must take into account the extent of the claimant's capacity to provide the services before the injury; the extent to which provision of the services would have also benefited other persons in respect of whom damages could not be awarded; and the vicissitudes or contingencies of life for which allowance is ordinarily made in the assessment of damages.

Present value discounting

[14.195] It is recognised at common law that receiving damages in a lump sum now for loss of earning capacity and care costs extending well into the future confers a benefit on the plaintiff. This is because under normal circumstances a plaintiff earns his or her salary or wages on a periodic basis, and for all but the very well off, consumes a large portion of the amount received on sustenance and upkeep costs week to week. Any surplus can be saved and invested to produce additional income, but for most people this is a small proportion of the total. The "once and for all" rule results in plaintiffs having much larger sums of capital available for investment. Present value discounting adjusts for this, as well as for factors such as taxation, and movements in wages and prices. Note that the damages to be discounted under this section include sums awarded for all future special damages, that is, future economic loss, future out of pocket expenses, and future care costs including any allowance for gratuitous care (the *Griffiths v Kerkemeyer* (1977) 139 CLR 161 component). Present value discounting is not applicable to general damages (non economic loss), nor to sums awarded in respect of past losses. A uniform percentage discount is applied to all plaintiffs, both at common law and pursuant to statute. The present value discount is equivalent to negative compound interest, as contrasted with "vicissitudes" discounts, which are equivalent to negative simple interest. The present value discount must be calculated first, then that discounted sum is discounted again by the percentage allowed for contingencies. The judgment of Stephen J in *Todorovic v Waller* (1981) 150 CLR 402, is regarded as the classic statement of principle in this area. It was endorsed by the House of Lords in *Wells v Wells* [1999] 1 AC 345. The discount rate is now mandated by legislation. For an example of the calculations, illustrating the substantial inroads made on damages by discounting, particularly in relation to longer term injuries, see Note 3, [14.200].

[14.200] **Notes&Questions**

1. It has been said that *Todorovic v Waller* (1981) 150 CLR402, which established a discount rate of 3%:

   > was a victory for judicial compromise, grudging consensus and unstated policy: Gibbs and Wilson JJ preferred 4 per cent, Mason J 2 per cent [and Stephen and Murphy JJ preferred nil per cent]. Three per cent therefore met the bill not as a matter of truth but of mere convenience. The decision has totally failed to quiet disagreement within the practising profession, on the Bench and amongst the legal academic community ... [some ask] whether a negative discount might not be more in line with the aim of restitutio in integrum. (M Tilbury, M Noone, B Kercher, Remedies: Commentary and Materials (4 th ed, Thomson Lawbook Co, 2004, p 370)).

2. The common law discount rate of 3 per cent has been varied upwards by legislation in all States and Territories except the Australian Capital Territory. In New South Wales, the Northern Territory, Queensland, South Australia, Tasmania and Victoria the rate is now 5 per cent: see NSW: CLA, s 14; NT: *Personal Injuries (Liabilities and Damages) Act 2003*, s 22; Qld: CLA, s 57; SA: *Wrongs Act 1936*, s 24; Tas: CLA, s 28A; Vic: WrA, s 281. In Western Australia it is 6 per cent,: WA: *Law Reform (Miscellaneous Provisions) Act 1941*, s 5. The 5 per cent rate in New South Wales is consistent with that provided for in motor accidents and workers' compensation legislation. Do you think this increase in the common law rate is justified on principle? Since the effect of increasing the discount rate is to reduce the damages paid to plaintiffs, is it justified on any other grounds? Is it consistent with the compensation principle (restitutio in integrum)?

3. The example below demonstrates the significant effect discounting has on damages awards, especially over the medium to long term. It assumes a future economic loss figure of $500 per week, and calculates the discount based on inability to work for one year, and then 20 years. Actuarial tables are used to calculate the present value (compound) discount, and to ascertain the appropriate "multiplier". Tables are not relevant for the vicissitudes discount.
   Example
   Present value discount
   $500 per week loss for one year
   Not discounted = $500 x 52 weeks = $ 26,000
   Discounted at 3% = $500 x 51.4 = $ 25,700
   Discounted at 5% = $500 x 50.9 = $ 25,450
   $500 per week loss for 20 years
   No discount = $500 wk x 52 wks x 20 yrs = $ 520,000 (multiplier = 52 x 20 ie 1040)
   Discounted at 3% = $500 x multiplier of 788.0 = $ 394,000 (use actuarial tables)
   Discounted at 5% = $500 x multiplier of 666.3 = $ 333,150 (use actuarial tables)

Vicissitudes discount

[14.205] Once the present value discount has been calculated, that sum will be discounted again for vicissitudes. (Remember that the present value discount is performed on all future special damages.) As we saw in *Wynn v NSW Insurance Ministerial Corporation* (1995) 184 CLR 485, vicissitudes discounting requires the court to arrive at a figure representing this particular plaintiff's individual circumstances and prospects. It is also necessary to discount past special damages (between date of injury and date of trial) for vicissitudes, based on the individual plaintiff's employment history and other factors. General damages are exempt from both types of discount. Assuming a typical vicissitudes discount of 15 per cent, the present value (discounted) sum must be multiplied by 85 per cent. In the example above, the figure of $500 per week over 20 years, discounted by 5 per cent, yielded a lump sum of $333,150. After discounting for vicissitudes ($333,150 x 85% = $283,177), the remaining lump sum is $283,177. In this example, beginning with an undiscounted lump sum of $520,000, and applying the statutory rate of present value discount, plus a standard vicissitudes discount, the plaintiff's damages were reduced by almost 50 per cent.

Collateral source rule

[14.210] It is common for injured plaintiffs to receive benefits associated with the injury from sources other than the defendant. Examples include social security payments such as sickness and unemployment benefits, insurance pay-outs, employment-related payments and benefits like sick pay, statutory compensation such as workers' compensation, superannuation payments, hospital or pharmaceutical benefits, and gifts. The issue here is whether such benefits should be set off against the plaintiff's damages, that is, should damages be reduced by the amount of the collateral benefit, to avoid over-compensating the plaintiff? This area is marked by a lack of consistency, and a tendency by the courts to adopt a benefit by benefit approach, prompting one judge to comment that "[i]n this field logic is conspicuous by its absence" (*Browning v War Office* [1963] 1 QB 750 (CA) at 762 per Donovan LJ). In *National Insurance Co of New Zealand Ltd v Espagne* (1961) 105 CLR 569, however, the High Court laid down two tests for collateral benefits. First, the court should consider the essential nature of the benefit (for example, is it in the nature of wages, pension, social security or other). Secondly, the court should look to the intention behind the benefit. Was it conferred upon the plaintiff with the intention that the plaintiff should enjoy it in addition to any damages flowing from the defendant? This is somewhat analogous to the reasoning in *Griffiths v Kerkemeyer* (1977) 139 CLR 161 claims, where the gratuitous services provided by the family members are not applied to reduce the defendant's obligation to pay proper compensation.

Section 15C of the NSW: CLA, discussed above, deals with damages for loss of superannuation. See also Qld: CLA, s 56. Apart from this, the rules are contained in the various statutes relating to that type of benefit, such as the *Social Security Act 1991* (Cth). Following the decision in *Redding v Lee; Evans v Muller* (1982) 151 CLR 117, in which it was decided that invalid pensions were not to be taken into account but that unemployment benefits should be set off, the *Social Security Act 1947* (Cth) was amended so that sickness benefits, invalid pensions and unemployment benefits would all be governed by the same rules. Between 1987 and 1991 all social security payments were required to be set off, that is, deducted from awards. Payments made under the *Social Security Act 1991* (Cth) are recouped in part or full in accordance with the legislative formula, rather than being set off. Future benefits that would be referable to the period already provided for in the lump sum award are precluded. Similarly, the costs of medical treatment via Medicare are recouped by the Health Insurance Commission (HIC) from damages awards, pursuant to the *Health and Other Services Compensation Act 1995* (Cth). Workers' compensation benefits are repayable where a common law damages award is made subsequently.

The common law rule is that gifts are not to be taken into account in assessing damages, irrespective of whether the gift comes from a public or private source. Similarly, benefits payable under insurance policies are not set off, since the plaintiff has had the foresight and prudence to provide for him or her self in this way, and has "purchased" that benefit through the payment of premiums. The rule on accident insurance was laid down in *Bradburn v Great Western Railway Co* (1874) LR 10 Exch 1. Benefits which derive from the employment, such as sick pay, must be set off against loss of earning capacity, as discussed above in *Graham v Baker* (1961) 106 CLR 340 [14.115]. *Graham* dealt with sick pay received as part of a plaintiff's ordinary wages, but the position is less clear where such payments are made voluntarily by an employer rather than as of right. In *Jones v Gleeson* [1966] ALR 235 the High Court held that employment pensions payable to injured workers unable to return to work should not be taken into account in reduction of damages, and the House of Lords reached a similar decision in *Parry v Cleaver* [1970] AC 1. See also *Smoker v London Fire and Civil Defence Authority* [1991] 2 AC 502.

DAMAGES FOR NON-ECONOMIC LOSS: GENERAL DAMAGES

[14.215] The civil liability legislation does not uniformly define "non economic loss", however, there is consistency on key aspects of the definition including pain and suffering, loss of amenities of life, loss of expectation of life, and disfigurement (in some jurisdictions). The ACT: CLWA does not contain a general definition, but see s 99(4). See NSW: CLA, s 3; NT: *Personal Injuries (Liabilities and Damages) Act 2003*, s 18; SA: CLA, s 3; Tas: CLA, s 3 (loss of enjoyment of life, curtailment of life expectancy, and bodily or mental harm also included); Vic: WrA, 28B; WA: CLA, s 9(4)(a). The legislation in each jurisdiction should be consulted where detail is required on this point. These provisions are consistent with the common law. The following case is a leading authority on allowable items in the determination of general damages.

Skelton v Collins

[14.220] *Skelton v Collins* (1966) 115 CLR 94 High Court of Australia

(footnotes omitted)

[The 19 year old plaintiff suffered severe brain damage as a result of the defendant's negligence and was likely to remain unconscious in hospital until his death, expected within 6 months from the date of the trial. Damages were assessed by the trial judge on these assumptions. The trial judge awarded the plaintiff lost wages (with a minor deduction) up to the date of trial, future hospital costs for the six month period to the plaintiff's anticipated death and future loss of earning capacity for the six month period from the date of trial to the plaintiff's anticipated death. To this was added the sum of £1,500 in general damages. The total sum was reduced by 25% for the plaintiff's contributory negligence. The plaintiff appealed to the High Court on the ground that the damages awarded were inadequate.]

KITTO J: [His Honour agreed with Taylor J's judgment on the question of damages for economic loss, and continued:] ... What I have to say will relate to the challenge that has been made to trial judge's allowance of £1,500 under the head of general damages. He allowed nothing for pain and

Skelton v Collins cont.

suffering, either physical or mental; and in this he was plainly right, for the plaintiff was rendered unconscious by the collision, had remained unconscious ever since, and, as his Honour found, would never regain consciousness.

There were only two forms of loss for which the £1,500 could have been intended as compensation, namely those which are often described, conveniently if not very happily, as a loss of expectation of life and a loss of amenity during his reduced life span. Each is a matter properly to be taken into account in assessing damages, but judicial opinion as to the way in which the task of allowing for them should be approached has not been unanimous. Obviously each may have a subjective as well as an objective aspect: the plaintiff may not only have sustained the loss itself but may also have to bear a sense of his loss. But the differences of opinion which are to be found in the judgments, in England at least, are not as to whether the objective aspect is to be concentrated upon to the exclusion of the subjective; it is simply as to the manner in which each is to be separately allowed for. [His Honour considered the English authorities

In *Benham v Gambling* [1941] AC 157 the injured person was a child of two and a half. He was unconscious from the moment of the accident until his death, which occurred later on the same day ... The sole question was how much should be allowed as compensation for the objective element, the loss of such chance as the child had had, immediately before the accident, of living longer than he did. Should that chance be treated as having been worth much or little, when a judge or jury is trying to find an appropriate sum to award as fair compensation for the loss ... [The Lord Chancellor in *Benham v Gambling*] ... said that damages which would be proper for a disabling injury may well be much greater than for deprivation of life (at 168). His Lordship was not, I think, saying anything so trite as that the fixing of a sum of money as compensation for what cannot be bought and sold is difficult because of the different natures of the things that are being weighed against one another. What I understand him to be pointing to as the fact which brings in its train a special consequence for a tribunal assessing damages is that, since none can form any opinion as to what would have been the experience through which the victim would have lived if he had not suffered the injury, that which has to be measured against money is not only different from money but cannot itself be known and therefore cannot be measured at all. For this reason it is simply impossible to select any substantial figure as compensation for the loss of years of living (as distinguished from the mental distress due to realisation of the loss) and feel any degree of satisfaction with it as fair compensation ...

Twenty years later, there came before the Court of Appeal the case of *Wise v Kaye* [1962] 1 QB 638. It resembled the present case in that the plaintiff, having been rendered permanently unconscious by the accident, had never had any knowledge of her condition. Her expectation of life had been reduced. The trial judge awarded her £400 for loss of expectation of life and £15,000 for general damages, as well as other sums for items of economic loss. He awarded nothing for pain and suffering, for there had been none and could be none. Accordingly the £400 must have been awarded simply for the objective fact that her life had been shortened, and the £15,000 must have been awarded for the objective fact that she had lost, though she did not know it, the whole of the very good chance she would have had of keeping her faculties during the remaining years of her existence. The defendants contended that the £400 represented a correct application of *Benham v Gambling* and therefore could not be challenged, but that the £15,000 was excessive and should be reduced to a fraction of that amount by virtue of the considerations which had led to the decision in *Benham v Gambling*. The argument was, in effect, that the plaintiffs loss in respect of the remaining years of her life, like her loss in respect of the years which the accident had cut off from her existence, was simply a loss of experiences capable of yielding a general balance of happiness, and that for want of further information about it an award of so substantial an amount as £15,000 must necessarily be erroneous as purporting to be what it could not be-an amount fixed in exercise of a real judgment and based upon a sense of appropriateness and proportion ...

Skelton v Collins cont.

Sellers and Upjohn LJJ held, in effect, that it was a loss of all the plaintiffs' faculties, and that since a loss of some faculties only must have called for a substantial award of damages a loss of all must call for a still larger award.

Diplock LJ who dissented, held that the loss to be compensated for was the whole enjoyment of life from the time of the accident to the time when the plaintiff would have died if the accident had not happened; and as that meant a balance of pleasure over pain a small amount only should have been awarded by analogy with *Benham v Gambling*. …

I do not find myself able to put aside *Benham v Gambling* as affording no guidance for such a case as the present. It treated of life not as a state of being, a mere physical phenomenon, but as a thing to be lived and lived consciously. Thus, what was meant by every reference to loss of expectation of life was, in truth, loss of the possibility of conscious experience. The whole burden of the Lord Chancellor's speech was the legal impropriety of attempting to place any but the most modest figure on a human being's capacity to experience the varied quality of life; and I cannot bring myself to say that although the law sees the impropriety where a person has died it does not see it where he has lost all capacity for thought and feeling.

I turn now to the later case in the House of Lords, *H West & Sons Ltd v Shephard* [1964] AC 326 where four of their Lordships interpreted *Benham v Gambling* as saying nothing of value for any case save that where the person injured has lost his life. … Needless to say, I have earnestly and respectfully attended to the speeches of those of their Lordships who formed the majority of the House, but I venture to comment upon one passage only. Lord Morris said (at 349): "An unconscious person will be spared pain and suffering and will not experience the mental anguish which may result from knowledge of what has in life been lost from knowledge that life has been shortened. The fact of unconsciousness is therefore relevant in respect of and will eliminate those heads or elements of damage which can only exist by being felt or thought or experienced. The fact of unconsciousness does not, however, eliminate the actuality of the deprivations of the ordinary experiences and amenities of life which may be the inevitable result of some physical injury." What is here said of the fact of unconsciousness may be said with equal truth of the fact of death; but in relation both to death and to unconsciousness surely it is true that what ought to affect the quantum of damages is not the actuality of the deprivations but their value: what would "the ordinary experiences and amenities of life" (in the future) have added up to, if the plaintiff had not been cut off from them? The trouble is not just that the assessment of compensation is difficult; it is that there is simply no way of forming any reliable idea, any "confident estimate" ([1941] AC 157 at 167) as to what the thing would have been like for which the compensation is to be assessed; and therefore an award so substantial as necessarily to imply that the judge (or jury) has in fact formed such an idea must be unsupportable. This is true, it seems to me, whether the injured person is physically dead or only dead to all experience. …

His Honour was in a difficult position. … The figure which he finally adopted to cover both the loss of expectation of life and the loss of enjoyment of life during the period of continuing existence was £1,500. Having regard to currency equivalents and changes in the value of money I am not able to say that by adopting this figure his Honour failed to give due effect to the principle of *Benham v Gambling*, and I would therefore not disturb it. …

TAYLOR J: 107 In the present case two main complaints are made. The first is that general damages for the plaintiffs injuries, excluding those assessed for physical pain and suffering, should have been assessed without regard to the fact that he had remained unconscious since the accident. They should, it is said, have been assessed on what has, somewhat unhappily, been called an "objective" basis. The second is that in assessing damages for the plaintiffs lost earning capacity regard should have been had to the probable period of the plaintiffs working life immediately before he sustained his injuries and not merely to the period of life which remained to him after that event … .

Skelton v Collins cont.

[I]n assessing damages for a loss of the amenities of life resulting from the physical destruction or impairment of some part of the body, I find it impossible to ignore, or to regard merely as a minimal factor, what has been referred to as the subjective element. The expression "loss of the amenities of life" is a loose expression but as a head of damages in personal injury cases it is intended to denote a loss of the capacity of the injured person consciously to enjoy life to the full as, apart from his injury, he might have done. It may be said, of course, that a person who is completely incapacitated as a result of his injuries suffers such a loss whether or not his injuries are of such a character to render him insensible to his loss. But, in my view, a proper assessment can be made only upon a comparison of the condition which has been substituted for the victim's previously existing capacity to enjoy life and where the mind is, as it were, willing and the body incapable there is, in my view, a much higher degree of loss than where the victim is completely insensible to his lost capacity. Perhaps, in other words, it may be said that a person who is obliged for the rest of his life to live with his incapacity, fully conscious of the limitations which it imposes upon his enjoyment of life, is entitled to greater compensation than one who, although deprived of his former capacity is spared, by insensibility, from the realisation of his loss and the trials and tribulations consequent upon it. In the result I am left with a firm view that the plaintiff's general damages in this case were assessed on a proper basis. This conviction coupled with the fact that a body of authority inconsistent with the decision of the majority in *West's* case has grown up in this country and the fact that there was a remarkable diversity of opinion in that case induces me to say that we ought not to follow it. Accordingly, I would reject the appellant's first contention.

The further question arises whether in assessing damages for the destroyed earning capacity of the appellant it was proper to have regard only to the period of life which remained to him after receipt of his injuries. *Oliver v Ashman* [1962] 2 QB 210 is, of course, an authority for the course which his Honour took. …

The decision was based upon observations made in the House of Lords in *Rose v Ford* (above) and in *Benham v Gambling* (above) and it becomes necessary to consider precisely what it was that these cases decided. In the earlier case two questions arose. First of all there was the question whether the decision of the Court of Appeal in *Flint v Lovell* [1935] 1 KB 354 that a living plaintiff could recover damages for the diminution of his expectation of life was sound, and secondly, the question arose whether damages under this head could be recovered in an action by the personal representative of a deceased person pursuant to the *Law Reform (Miscellaneous Provisions) Act*. The House of Lords decided both questions in favour of the plaintiff. It may not be to the point to notice that the decision in *Flint v Lovell* did not introduce a novel doctrine into the law as is shown by the observations of Lord Wright in *Rose v Ford* (above at 848) though, no doubt, it gave the clearest authority to the principle which it enunciated. I observe that the same principle had been followed in New South Wales almost without question: *Bruce v Rutherford* (1885) 1 WN (NSW) 102. But it is of importance to notice that in *Flint v Lovell* there was no claim for damages for the diminution of the plaintiffs earning capacity; the plaintiff was 70 years of age when the trial took place, special damages had been agreed at £400 and there was no suggestion of any economic loss by reason of a resultant diminution of the plaintiff's earning capacity. Nor was there any suggestion that the head of damage which the decision recognised should be regarded as a substitute for, or, as embracing, economic loss of that character. In *Rose v Ford*, in the action brought pursuant to the *Law Reform (Miscellaneous Provisions) Act*, there was, again, no claim for any such loss. The claim which had been made related to: (1) the deceased's pain and suffering; (2) the loss of her leg; and (3) the shortening of her expectation of life. In the House of Lords only the last item was in question. This claim had been rejected in the Court of Appeal but all of the members of that court had agreed that if damages for loss of expectation of life could be recovered the appropriate award under this head was £1,000. In the result the House of Lords held that *Flint v Lovell* had been correctly decided, that, therefore, in her lifetime the deceased had vested in her a right to recover damages for her loss of expectation of life, that the right survived to her legal personal representative

Skelton v Collins cont.

and their Lordships increased the amount of the award by £1,000. In doing so their Lordships, it seems to me, treated this head of damages as completely independent of any other legitimate head of damages and were not concerned and did not concern themselves with any question of loss resulting from a diminished or lost earning capacity. *Benham v Gambling* (above) was decided some three and a half years later and this case was concerned with an action commenced by the administrator of a child who had died shortly after having been injured by the negligence of the defendant. It was said that since the decision in *Rose v Ford* the amounts that had been awarded as damages for a diminished expectancy of life had varied enormously and the decision represents an attempt to set a standard by "indicating the main considerations to be borne in mind in assessing damages under this head" in the hope that "the views of this House, expressed in dealing with the present appeal, may help to set a lower standard of measurement than has hitherto prevailed for what is in fact incapable of being measured in coin of the realm with any approach to real accuracy". In the result the decision gave rise to the rule (said by Lord Reid in *West's* case to be "a rule of law") that a conventional sum only should be awarded for the loss of a measure of prospective happiness. But again the House of Lords was not concerned with any question of economic loss resulting from a destroyed earning capacity.

However, in *Oliver v Ashman* the Court of Appeal took the view that the question before it had been concluded by observations made in *Benham v Gambling* ...

I need scarcely mention the anomaly that would arise if is taken to have been correctly decided. An incapacitated plaintiff whose life expectation has not been diminished would be entitled to the full measure of the economic loss arising from his lost or diminished capacity. But an incapacitated plaintiff whose life expectancy has been diminished would not. Yet the recovery by him of damages that does not take into account his full economic loss will operate to prevent his dependants, in the event of his death, from recovering damages under the Fatal Accidents Act. However if he dies without having sued for damages his dependants will be entitled to recover damages assessed upon a consideration of what his economic prospects would have been had he survived for the full period of his pre-accident expectancy.

For the reasons I have given I find myself forced to the conclusion that the recognition which has been accorded to the right of an injured plaintiff to recover damages for "the loss of a measure of prospective happiness" in no way operates to displace or destroy his right to recover damages for economic loss resulting from his diminished earning capacity. Accordingly in my view damages in the present case should have been assessed under this head having regard to the plaintiffs pre-accident expectancy and not only to the expectancy of life remaining to him after the receipt of his injuries. Any assessment should, of course, take into account the vicissitudes and uncertainties of life and also the fact that if the plaintiff had survived for the full period it would have been necessary for him to maintain himself out of his earnings and, no doubt, his expenditure on his own maintenance would have increased as his earnings increased.

In considering what he called the plaintiffs economic loss the learned trial judge in the present case did not have regard to the plaintiffs pre-accident expectancy of life and he assessed an amount of £1,500 for general damages which I take to be the amount which he considered an appropriate award to compensate the plaintiff both for his loss of amenities of life during the period of life remaining to him after the accident and also for his diminished expectancy of life. In making this assessment he proceeded "on the basis that in assessing damages for personal injuries beyond economic loss the primary, although not the sole, ground for awarding damages is to be for what the plaintiff consciously suffers". Assuming, for the moment, that £500 of this amount was in effect a *Benham v Gambling* award merely for loss of expectancy of life, the question is whether the sum of £1,000 is manifestly inadequate to compensate him on an objective basis for his injuries and his loss of the amenities of life during the residue of his life. In the circumstances I am not disposed to think that it is and, accordingly, that we should not interfere. So far as his economic loss is concerned the material

Skelton v Collins cont.

before us indicates that the plaintiff at the time of the injury was earning approximately £13 a week, that at the age of 21 he would probably have earned something in excess of £20 a week and that by the time he attained the age of 30 his salary would have been, had it not been for the accident, some £2,000 or £2,500 per annum. In those circumstances it seems to me that on a balance of what his future income and expenditure on maintenance would have been the economic loss resulting from his destroyed earning capacity should not be rated highly. Particularly is this so when account is taken of the uncertainties and vicissitudes of life. Under this head of damages I would assess the sum of £2,000 as reasonable compensation ...

[The concurring judgments of Windeyer and Owen JJ and the dissenting judgment of Menzies J have been omitted.]

[14.225] Notes

In *Skelton v Collins* (1966) 115 CLR 94, the plaintiff was only expected to live a short time after the trial, so there was not a great deal of importance to be attached, in money terms, either to what should determine the reasonableness of the award for future expenses while he remained alive, or to the precise calculation of the items of loss of wages after the trial until his death. Both these matters were extensively considered in the next case, because of the different circumstances. Although in *Skelton v Collins* (1966) 115 CLR 94 the award for loss of earnings during the "lost years" (the period of normal life expectancy now lost to the plaintiff) was very important, the court concentrated on establishing the plaintiff's entitlement to this item, rather than focusing on the principles applying to its calculation. This last issue was discussed in *Sharman v Evans* (1977) 138 CLR 563.

Sharman v Evans

[14.230] *Sharman v Evans* (1977) 138 CLR 563 High Court of Australia

(footnotes omitted)

[The facts are stated at [14.100].]

GIBBS AND STEPHEN JJ: ... 584 The last two heads of damages which call for particular mention are those conventionally described as pain, suffering and loss of the enjoyment and amenities of life and damages for shortening of life expectancy. As to the latter it bears no relationship to lost earning capacity during "lost years" but is rather the loss of a measure of prospective happiness (*Skelton v Collins*, per Taylor J); it is not compensation for "the mental distress due to the realization of the loss" (per Kitto J). That forms instead a part of the general damages for pain and suffering: compare Windeyer J In the present case a figure "of the order of" $6,000 was allowed for this item in reliance upon the views expressed by Windeyer J in *Skelton v Collins*. If it be correct that compensation under this head is not to take into account the anguish of mind which any appreciation of the loss may cause, that being compensated for under another head, then Windeyer J's suggested maximum figure of $6,000, which reflected this very factor, may be thought to have been excessive at the time and to depart from the general standard of the "conventional sum" which the courts have quite arbitrarily fixed upon ever since *Benham v Gambling*. The amount awarded may properly take into account a fall in the value of money *(Yorkshire Electricity Board v Naylor*) but is to be no more than a quite conventional sum, very moderate in amount. In our view, despite the fall in the value of money, $6,000 departs from previous notions of what is appropriate under this curious and unsatisfactory

Sharman v Evans cont.

head of damages. We would have thought that the sum of $2,000 is about the amount now appropriate as the conventional award under this head.

It remains only to say something about damages for loss of the enjoyment and amenities of life. It is in this field that there exists the need to recall what has often been said about fairness, moderation and the undesirability of striving to provide an injured plaintiff with "perfect" compensation. The warning against attempting perfectly to compensate means, we think, in the case of pecuniary loss, no more than the need to make allowance for contingencies, for the vicissitudes of life, compensating for probable rather than for merely speculative detriments. But when a non-pecuniary detriment is in question the injunction against "perfect" compensation means rather more. It cannot refer to the exclusion of all question of punishment of the wrongdoer; the word "compensation" standing on its own would be sufficient to do this; rather is it designed to remind that the maiming of a plaintiff and its consequences cannot wholly be made good by an award of damages and that the recognition of this fact is to be no occasion for any instinctive response that no amount is too large to atone for the plaintiff's suffering. Such a response will be unfair to the defendant and may be of little advantage to the plaintiff; many consequences of injury are not capable of remedy by the receipt of damages, particularly those of the most personal character – the loss of the opportunity of a fulfilling marriage, of parenthood, of sexual satisfaction, of the realization of ambitions. It is very much at these detriments that the warning against any attempt at "perfect" compensation must be aimed. The authorities also require, as does good sense, that to the extent that damages awarded under other heads produce freedom from economic uncertainty and the availability of funds for pleasurable activities, the less will be the loss to be compensated under this head. This will be of particular relevance when a considerable sum is assessed for lost earning capacity ...

There remains the question of damages for pain and suffering and the loss of the enjoyment and amenities of life. As to the last item in this category we need say very little, what has already been said of the plaintiff's present state (not least her constant hospitalization) and a comparison between it and her former prospects of a happy and rewarding life is enough to establish entitlement to substantial damages under this head. Although she is a quadriplegic, the very numerous operations and other treatments which have been necessary, and in particular those involving her larynx, an area in which she retains full feeling, have caused her long periods of great pain and discomfort. She has suffered and will continue to suffer pain for the rest of her life in her left shoulder, another of her few remaining sensory areas. In addition there is her mental suffering, including the anguish which knowledge that her life expectancy has been substantially reduced must entail. Proper allowance must of course be made for such of the remaining pleasures life as money can now afford her. There is no doubt that, as we have already pointed out, her lot can be made much more enjoyable by the expenditure of money and will be materially improved by her financial ability to enjoy periodic outings from hospital. There nevertheless remains a great area for the award of damages under this head.

The learned trial judge awarded a total of $275,000 for general damages, or $80,000 more than what we would regard as the maximum for heads of damage other than pain, suffering and loss of the amenities of life ... Pain and suffering and loss of the amenities of life is a head of damages which is peculiarly difficult to assess but when full compensation has been determined in respect of all other heads of damages, it appears to us that an additional sum of $80,000 exceeds what could properly be awarded under this last head.

[14.235] **Notes&Questions**

1. Decisions in the House of Lords on damages for loss of amenities have diverged from the position adopted in Australia. In *Lim Poh Choo v Camden & Islington Area Health*

Authority [1980] AC 174, for example, the plaintiff suffered irreparable brain damage as a result of the defendant's negligence, leaving her barely sentient [14.65]. For practical purposes, therefore, her position in this respect was indistinguishable from that of the plaintiff in the Australian case of *Skelton v Collins* (1966) 115 CLR 94 [14.220].

However, whereas *Skelton v Collins* (1966) 115 CLR 94 disapproved *Wise v Kaye* [1962] 1 QB 638 and *H West & Son Ltd v Shephard* [1964] AC 326, the House of Lords in *Lim Poh Choo v Camden & Islington Area Health Authority* [1980] AC 174, adhered to these earlier Court of Appeal and House of Lords cases. Lord Scarman delivered the principal judgment in the House with which the other law Lords agreed. His Lordship said (at 188-189) that he thought it would be wrong now to reverse by judicial decision the rules that: (1) the fact of unconsciousness does not eliminate the actuality of the deprivation of the ordinary experiences and amenities of life; and (2) that, if damages are awarded on a correct basis, it is of no concern to the court to consider any question as to the use that will be thereafter made of the money awarded. The reversal of *West's case*, when the decision in it had been taken in 1963, would cause widespread injustice.

Thus, in England, the position continues to be that total deprivation of sensitivity can be expected to inflate the damages for loss of amenities, whereas in Australia it will deflate them because of the absence of the plaintiff's consciousness of the loss. This applies even where the plaintiff retains some consciousness if there is reduced consciousness of the loss suffered: *Dundas v Harbour Motors Pty Ltd* (1988) Aust Torts Reports 80-161.

2. Awards for pain and suffering can only be made where the loss is subjectively experienced. For example, where pain and suffering is consciously experienced even by an infant several months old (nine years at the time of judgment) substantial awards under this head may be made: *Del Ponte v Del Ponte* (1987) 11 NSWLR 498 (CA).

Thresholds on general damages

[14.240] The civil liability legislation in various jurisdictions imposes a threshold on general damages. In some jurisdictions, the threshold is a stated figure (indexed) and in others it is determined by a formula: ACT: CLWA, s 139F(1) ($250,000); NSW: CLA, s 16 ($350,000); NT: *Personal Injuries (Liabilities and Damages) Act 2003*, s 27(a) ($350,000); Qld: CLA (no provision); SA: CLA (no provision); Tas: CLA, s 27 (formula); Vic: WrA, s 28G ($371,380); WA: CLA, Pt 2 Div 2 (formula). Indexation occurs according to separate provisions: ACT: CLWA, s 139F(4); NSW: CLA, s 17; NT: *Personal Injuries (Liabilities and Damages) Act 2003*, s 28; Qld: CLA, s 62; SA: CLA, s 52; Tas: CLA, s 27; Vic: WrA, s 28H; WA: CLA, Pt 2 Div 2. In New South Wales, Queensland and South Australia, the legislation employs a sliding scale. For example, the New South Wales provision restricts claims falling below 32 per cent of "a most extreme case" to less than full compensation, in accordance with the table contained in subs (3). A sliding scale is employed so that at 15 per cent of a most extreme case only 1 per cent of the maximum set by the legislation may be awarded. The proportion increases with the severity of the loss, equalling the loss when it reaches 33 per cent. For example, at 20 per cent of a most extreme case, 3.5 per cent of the maximum may be awarded, at 25 per cent of a most extreme case 6.5 per cent may be awarded, but at 32 per cent of a most extreme case, 30 per cent may be awarded: NSW: CLA, s 16(3); Qld: CLA, s 62 (sliding scale); SA: CLA, s 52 (sliding scale).

Subsection (1) provides that: "No damages may be awarded for non-economic loss unless the severity of the non–economic loss is at least 15 per cent of a most extreme case". This is known as a threshold. The phrase has been adopted in a number of statutory schemes to limit recovery for general damages, eg, *Workers' Compensation Act 1987* (NSW), s 67; *Motor Accidents Act 1988* (NSW), s 79 and 79A. *Southgate v Waterford* (1990) 21 NSWLR 427, extracted below at [14.245], examines the relationship between common law principles of assessment and the statutorily mandated limits on recovery. *Southgate* discusses the meaning of "a most extreme case" as contained in s 79 of the *Motor Accidents Act 1988* (NSW). Courts have emphasised that "a" most extreme case is conceptually different from "the" most extreme case. In *Matthews v Dean* [1990] Aust Torts Reports 81-037 at 68,014, for example, Grove J said:

> ... No doubt Parliament recognised that comparisons of the extent of bodily injury must be odious by the choice of language "A most extreme case" which avoids any requirement to apply the superlative by imagining *the* most extreme case and put that at the top of some grisly table of catastrophes.

This passage was endorsed in *Southgate*, the New South Wales Court of Appeal noting that although opinions on what constitutes "a most extreme case" will vary, quadriplegia certainly fulfilled the requirement. In *Dell v Dalton* (1991) 23 NSWLR 528, at 533, Handley JA, delivering the judgment of the New South Wales Court of Appeal, said that the word "most" is synonymous with "very" (as in the expressions "you are most welcome", or "this is a most unfortunate occurrence") and did not mean "in the greatest quantity, amount, measure, degree or number". His Honour continued: "In my opinion the definition of non-economic loss and the bench mark in s 79(3) do not enact a statutory table of maims which reduces all human beings to some common denominator and requires the impact of particular injuries on a given individual to be ignored. The terms of s 79(3) provide for a class of 'most extreme' cases the members of which will be entitled to an award of the maximum amount. It is not to be expected that the members of that class will have identical or nearly identical injuries or that their pre-injury situations will have been practically the same. ... The use of the indefinite article in the subsection ... provides for the creation of a class of most extreme' cases which necessarily means that the cases may be different, and some may be worse than others" (quoted in D Villa, *Annotated Civil Laibility Act 2002 (NSW)* (Lawbook Co, 2004), p 149).

Southgate v Waterford

[14.245] *Southgate v Waterford* (1990) 21 NSWLR 427 New South Wales Court of Appeal (footnotes omitted)

[The facts are immaterial for the purposes of this extract.]

THE COURT: [Gleeson CJ, Kirby P and Meagher JA] 429 This appeal raises a short but important point of statutory construction. The statutory provisions concerned are principally those of s 79 of the *Motor Accidents Act 1988* (the Act). The point raised is the approach that is to be taken in calculating the amount which may be recovered under the Act for non-economic loss as a component of damages ...

Calculation of the Non-economic Loss:

Section 79, as it stood at the relevant time provided:

Southgate v Waterford cont.

> 79. (2) The amount of damages to be awarded for non-economic loss shall be a proportion, determined according to the severity of the non-economic loss, of the maximum amount which may be awarded.
>
> (3) The maximum amount which may be awarded for non-economic loss is $180,000, but the maximum amount shall be awarded only in a most extreme case.
>
> (4) If the amount of non-economic loss is assessed to be $15,000 or less, no damages for non-economic loss shall be awarded …

… According to the appellant, s 79(2) and s. 79(3) merely fix the maximum which may be recovered for non-economic loss. Subject to the maximum, the amount to be recovered is to be calculated in accordance with ordinary common law principles developed for the ascertainment of general damages …

The appellant supported her interpretation of s 79 by reference both to the terms of the Act and to its legislative history. Reference was also made to the Second Reading Speech by which the Attorney-General introduced the Bill into Parliament which later became the Act.

The appellant acknowledged that the purpose of the Act was to reintroduce damages for motor accidents in a controlled way. Relevantly, it was admitted that the controls included the statutory designation of "the maximum amount which may be awarded" for "non-economic loss" by the combined operation of s 79(2) and s 79(3). The appellant further acknowledged that it was necessary to give the word "proportion" in s 79(2) work to do. According to her argument, the result of fixing the amount of damages for non-economic loss in accordance with established common law principles would ordinarily be to produce an award for that purpose which, in the result, represented a "proportion … of the maximum amount which may be awarded", viz. $180,000. The "proportion" was, according to this argument, the resulting ratio which existed between the damages awarded on ordinary common law principles and the maximum amount recoverable as fixed by Parliament in s 79(3) …

It is a legitimate approach to statutory construction to consider any inconvenient, arbitrary or apparently irrational consequences which flow from a particular construction. This is because courts will not readily attribute to Parliament an intention to achieve such consequences, if an alternative construction is available which avoids them. In the present case, the appellant suggested that no criteria would exist by reference to which judges and others assessing the amount of damages to be awarded for non-economic loss could apportion a particular case "according to the severity" of such loss in comparison to a notional loss for which, "in a most extreme case", a maximum of $180,000 could be awarded. The appellant argued that the process would be wholly unscientific, idiosyncratic and arbitrary. Views would inescapably differ as to what "a most extreme case" was. Where a particular case should be placed on the scale in relation to such "a most extreme case" would depend on a lottery, determined by nothing more than the impressionistic, unscientific guesswork of the particular decision-maker referred to his or her scale of values, usually unexpressed or unexpressable.

This point was illustrated during argument by reference to the present case. If the approach taken in it were to be sanctioned, how, the appellant asked, was the trial judge's specification of the appellant's case "as being one-sixth that of a most extreme case" to be justified? Did it mean that if the appellant had suffered six times her proved level of pain, suffering, loss of amenities etc., that she would have recovered $180,000? How was the one-sixth determined? If an injured quadriplegic were taken as "a most extreme case" was a scale fixed by reference to such a person's non-economic loss? How could damages of different kinds, to different people, over different periods be scaled in such a way? …

Southgate v Waterford cont.

The criticisms of s 79(2) of the Act are understandable. There is no gainsaying the difficulty which will face a judge, in a particular case, in awarding an amount of damages for non-economic loss as "a proportion" of a notional "most extreme case" and in a ratio to the allowance of $180,000 for such a case. ...

The provisions in s 79 of the Act have no exact parallel in this State or other jurisdictions. However, they are not entirely novel. Assessment of compensation proportionate to injury has long been provided under workers' compensation legislation ...

In the United States of America, as a result of the rise of jury awards of damages for non-economic loss, as well as punitive damages, legislation has more recently been enacted in a number of States to place a limit on the amount which could be recovered. In 1987, it was recorded that monetary caps on non-economic damages were provided by legislation in forty-two States ... Such limits are necessarily arbitrary. They are justified upon the basis that fixing a maximum recovery is preferable to abolition of the right to such damages altogether, as occurred under the *Transport Accidents Compensation Act 1987*. The major stimulus to legislation of this kind in the United States arose from the difficulty of securing affordable insurance against the very high risks of liability.

To address the foregoing problem, various statutory options are available. They range from the comprehensive scheme adopted under the *Accidents Compensation Act 1972* (NZ) and that proposed by the New South Wales Law Reform Commission in its report (Accidents Compensation LRC 43) of 1984 on that subject to the provision of a "cap" on damages for non-economic loss, as enacted by s 79 of the Act. When such a "cap" is provided by statute, a choice must be made for the award of compensation in a particular case ...

Courts have for many years been engaged in the unscientific task of awarding damages for non-economic loss, that is, for pain and suffering, loss of the amenities of life, loss of expectation of life, disfigurement, etc. The theoretical bases of such awards of damages were always controversial: see AI Ogus, "Damages for Lost Amenities: For a Foot, a Feeling or a Function?" (1972) 35 Mod L Rev 1 at 12; *Skelton v Collins* (1966) 115 CLR 94 at 130-131. Attempts to introduce a more normative approach, as by comparison of apparently like cases in some systematic way have been rejected: see *Planet Fisheries Pty Ltd v La Rosa* (1968) 119 CLR 118 at 125; *Hirsch v Bennett* [1969] SASR 493 at 497 and *Moran v McMahon* (1985) 3 NSWLR 700 at 724, 726 ... [Note, this process of comparison involves what is known as a tariff, or usual sum in the circumstances, determined by reference to awards in other cases. Section 17A CLA 2002 (NSW) endorses a comparative approach, providing that "a court may refer to earlier decisions of that or other courts for the purpose of establishing the appropriate award".]

The key word in s 79(2) which presents the fatal obstacle to the appellant's contention is "proportion". It is the duty of the court to award damages for non-economic loss only as "a proportion ... of the maximum amount which may be awarded". Dictionary meanings make it clear that this word imports a "comparative relation between things or magnitudes as to size, quantity, number, etc.; a ratio ... a proper relation between things or parts ... a portion or part in its relation to the whole": see the Macquarie Dictionary (Revised ed) (1985) at 1362 ...

The court, which may not award damages except in accordance with that section, is therefore enjoined to look for the relationship between the "amount of damages to be awarded for non-economic loss" and the maximum amount which may be awarded, viz. (relevantly) $180,000. The harmony or symmetry which is imported by the word would not be achieved if the relationship between the amount of damages awarded by reference to common law principle and the maximum were the accidental one established in the way the appellant urged. Adopting a construction of s 79(2) of the Act by which the maximum could be reached by the application of common law principles, although the case was not one properly described as "a most extreme case", conflicts with the obvious way in which the first three subsections of s 79 are intended to operate together. Accordingly, as a plain matter of statutory construction, the argument of the appellant cannot be accepted ...

Southgate v Waterford cont.

As the purpose of the statute, derived from its language, is abundantly clear, it must be given effect whatever views the court may have about its policy or the difficulty of applying it in a particular case. Such difficulty falls far short of the capricious or irrational operation which the appellant urged. It is clear that one reason which lay behind the fixing of a "cap" on the recovery of damages for non-economic loss was an estimation of what the community could afford. The provision so determined was to be increased regularly. When this is seen as a purpose of the legislature, the procedure adopted by s 79(2) and s 79(3) is far from irrational or capricious. Arguably, it is perfectly rational and justifiable as providing equity between injured persons claiming such damages in circumstances where the maximum amount recoverable is limited.

It is true that it will be difficult to assign a particular case to its appropriate slot in the scale between a nil recovery and $180,000. But it will be no more difficult than the task required under [various apportionment statutes]. Nor is the unscientific nature of the exercise, or its lack of clear norms for the judicial activity involved, any different in kind from the assignment of money sums for the intangibles of general damages which the statutory provisions replace.

... clearly, because the task in hand is that of awarding damages for "non-economic loss", it is appropriate for the trial judge to consider and make findings on those elements in the evidence which are relevant to such loss. This will require the judge to consider and make findings on the evidence relevant to those heads of damage formerly considered in the award of general damages. Then it is necessary for the judge to conceive "a most extreme case". Only for such a case may the maximum amount provided by s 79(3) be awarded. The use of the indefinite article "a" has already been noted. Opinions of what constitute "a most extreme case" will doubtless vary. But clearly quadriplegia would fall into that class. The amount to be awarded must then be apportioned somewhere between nil and $180,000; but in a ratio which the judge fixes keeping in mind the fact that the cap of a statutory maximum is retained for "a most extreme case" ...

The only criterion for the apportionment prescribed is the comparison of the severity of the non-economic loss, as disclosed by the evidence, suffered by the injured person in the case before the judge and that suffered in "a most extreme case". The statutory maximum may only be awarded in the latter case. The judge must then assign the case as found somewhere along the resulting scale.

Once the proportion is fixed, as required by s 79(2) the calculation of the award for non-economic loss is a mathematical task by relating that proportion to the statutory maximum fixed by s 79(3) ...

It is likely that, over time, experience will develop in assigning cases on the scale, just as earlier it did in the apportionment required for contributory negligence. But each case will necessarily depend upon its own facts. At least in the first instance, the determination of the "proportion" is committed by law to the trial judge. He or she has the outside parameters which are fixed by the legislation. The task of determining the "proportion" which follows may not be scientific or normative; but it is not wholly at large. A wide measure of discretion has always existed in fixing damages for non-economic loss. All that this legislation does is to require that the damages under this head be fixed in harmony with the fact that Parliament has determined that a maximum will be laid down, varied from time to time and reserved for "a most extreme case".

[14.250] **Notes&Questions**

1. In *Dell v Dalton* (1991) 23 NSWLR 528, Handley JA (at 531) stated that the four heads of non-economic loss set out in the *Motor Accidents Act 1988* (NSW), s 68 must be read disjunctively so that loss falling within any category can constitute compensable non-economic loss. His Honour added that it is not necessary that a plaintiff, in order

to qualify as "a most extreme case", be able to show extreme loss within all four categories. Thus, a quadriplegic or paraplegic who suffers a small or insignificant loss of expectation of life may still qualify for the maximum amount. His Honour continued:

> On the other hand a plaintiff who continues to experience extreme pain and suffering may find release in premature death. In such a case a diminished life expectancy may actually reduce the overall non-economic loss. The facts in *Skelton v Collins* (1966) 115 CLR 94 [extracted at [14.220]] ... provides a graphic illustration of the fact that extreme loss in two of the categories can mitigate rather than aggravate the injured person's overall non-economic loss. Such a plaintiff would not constitute a most extreme case. ...

2. The process of determining the percentage of a most extreme case under the civil liability legislation is illustrated in the next case.

Woolworths v Lawlor

[14.255] *Woolworths v Lawlor* [2004] NSWCA 209 New South Wales Court of Appeal (footnotes omitted)

[The facts are briefly contained within the judgment of Beazley JA.]

BEAZLEY JA: [The 56 year old plaintiff] ... [4] claimed damages for injuries sustained by her on 19 September 2001 when she fell due to the malfunction of a moving walkway in the Marketplace Shopping Centre, Wagga Wagga ... Liability was admitted at trial and the matter proceeded before Sidis DCJ for assessment of damages only, which fell to be assessed under the *Civil Liability Act 2002* [NSW]. Her Honour awarded damages in the sum of $219,536.60. The appellants appeal against two components of the award of damage: first, against the award of non-economic loss which her Honour assessed at 30% of a most extreme case ...

There is no dispute as to the nature and extent of the respondent's injuries. The only question is whether, having regard to the injuries sustained, those two components of the damages award were excessive ...

The trial judge found that as a result of the accident the respondent had suffered aggravations of pre-existing degenerative conditions in both her neck and her lower back which had left her "with continuing symptoms of some significance" ...

Her Honour accepted that as a result, the respondent needed to resort frequently to anti-inflammatory and pain-killing medication ... [and] suffered a significant interference with her amenity of life to the extent that "her active and fulfilling life has now ceased" with the exception of the respondent's participation in Wagga Wagga's Sister City Programme. It also appears that her Honour accepted that for a period after the accident the respondent was depressed, and that whilst she might have had a predisposition to stress or depression that predisposition "was not assisted by the current incident".

Although the respondent had suffered a major interference in her general amenity of life, she had been able to return to work and as the respondent was on leave at the time of the incident, she had suffered no loss of income as a result of her injuries.

Award of non-economic loss

[10] In making the award of non-economic loss, her Honour said:

> The principles of the decision in *Reece v Reece* (1994) 19 MVR 103 were not raised in argument, although I have taken into account the plaintiff's age in assessing her injuries and ongoing disabilities at thirty per cent of a most extreme case.

Woolworths v Lawlor cont.

Reece's case was an appeal involving a 64 year old female plaintiff who was injured in a motor vehicle accident. She suffered extensive injuries and was left with disabilities which were such that she had lost much of the efficient use of her right wrist, including the right thumb and two fingers. She was also affected by pain and weakness which affected her ability to carry out the myriad of daily tasks that are carried out with the dominant hand. The plaintiff also had an injury to her left thumb and partial loss of the efficient use of the left wrist. It was likely that she would suffer degenerative and arthritic changes. She too, like the respondent in this case had, pre-accident, led an active personal life which was substantially impaired as a result of the on-going effects of her injuries. The trial judge awarded damages for non-economic loss, assessed at one third of a most serious case.

Handley JA, with whom Clarke and Sheller JJA agreed, held that a finding of 33?% of a most extreme case represented *"a wholly disproportionate assessment of the … plaintiff's loss"*. His Honour continued:

The difficulty, in my opinion, with his Honour's assessment is to reconcile it with the assessment that might properly be made in the case of a much younger woman, say thirty, who before her injury had a similar range of interests and hobbies but had young children to help bring up and who of course, faced a much longer period during which she would experience the pain, the disabilities and the progression of her condition.

His Honour held that if that hypothetical comparison was made, it was not possible to support the trial judge's finding that the plaintiff should be assessed as being one-third of a most extreme case. The Court substituted an assessment of twenty-two and one-half percent of a most extreme case.

This case, of course, differed in a significant respect from *Reece* in that there was a substantial age difference between the respective plaintiffs. In *Reece,* the plaintiff was 64 years old at the time of accident. In this case the plaintiff was 56 years old. The life expectancy of each thus differed markedly. Mrs. Reece's life expectancy was, at the date of trial, 18 years, the accident having occurred 2 years previously. In this case, the Court was informed by senior counsel for the respondent that the respondent's life expectancy was 28.58 years. … this Court would have been entitled to have regard to the life tables itself in considering the matter. But in any event, the respondent's life expectancy can be ascertained from the Schedule of Damages which were handed to her Honour by the parties for the purpose of calculating the judgment sum …

The injuries suffered by the plaintiffs in the two cases were quite different, although both were serious. The seriousness of the injuries and their on-going effect were matters to be assessed in each case, having regard to the plaintiff's personal circumstances. In this case, the injuries were aggravation injuries to the respondent's spine from her neck down to her coccyx. Those injuries had the effect on the respondent and impact upon her lifestyle as found by her Honour. It is necessary for the appellants, in order for the trial judge's assessment of non-economic loss to be disturbed, to demonstrate appealable error. The assessment of general damages is an evaluative process in respect of which minds may reasonably differ. Senior counsel for the appellants termed it an impressionistic process, although that terminology may not accurately reflect the process of judicial evaluation involved. Senior counsel submitted however, that the purpose of the *Civil Liability Act 2002* was to achieve moderation in verdicts and that an assessment in the order of fifteen to twenty percent of a most extreme case would more than adequately have compensated the respondent for the injuries which she sustained.

In my opinion an assessment in that order would be too low. The plaintiff has significant on-going pain on a daily basis, she requires on-going medication and she has had a significant interference with nearly all aspects of her personal life. Her life expectancy is almost another thirty years and there was no medical evidence to the effect that her condition was likely to improve. Looked at another way, her life expectancy is such that she still has about a third of her life to live. In my opinion, the appellants have failed to demonstrate that her Honour's assessment is excessive given the type and expected duration of the respondent's injuries. Accordingly I would dismiss this ground of appeal.

———— ꟿ ————

Interest on damages

[14.260] Interest on damages was not available at common law, but is provided for by statute in all jurisdictions: *Supreme Court Act 1933* (ACT), s 69; *Supreme Court Act 1970* (NSW), s 94; *District Court Act 1973* (NSW), s 83A(1); *Supreme Court Act* (NT), s 84; *Supreme Court Act 1995* (Qld), s 47; *Supreme Court Act 1935* (SA), s 30C; *Supreme Court Civil Procedure Act 1932* (Tas), s 34; *Supreme Court Act 1986* (Vic), ss 58 – 60; *Supreme Court Act 1935* (WA), s 32. The civil liability legislation in New South Wales, Queensland and Victoria operates to limit and regulate the award of interest: NSW: CLA, s 18(1); Qld: CLA, s 55(1); Vic: WrA, s 60(1). All jurisdictions except Tasmania prohibit the awarding of compound interest. As an example of the legislation providing for interest, the *Supreme Court Act 1970* (NSW) provides in s 94 that:

> (1) In any proceedings for the recovery of money (including any debt or damages ...) the Court may order that there shall be included, in the sum for which judgment is given, interest at such rate as it thinks fit on the whole or any part of the money for the whole or any part of the period between the date when the cause of action arose and the date when the judgment takes effect.

The purpose of interest is compensatory, as explained by Barwick CJ in *Ruby v Marsh*: (1975) 132 CLR 642 at 652

> [T]he successful plaintiff, who by the verdict has been turned into an investor ... ought in justice to be placed in the position he would have been had the amount of the verdict been paid to him at the date of the commencement of the action ... [Also] the power to award interest on the verdict from the date of the writ is to provide a discouragement to defendants, who in the greater number of actions are insured, from delaying settlement of the claim or an early conclusion of proceedings so as to have over a longer period of time the profitable use of the money.

Section 18(1) of the NSW: CLA prohibits the awarding of interest on damages for non-economic loss. It also precludes interest being awarded on the *Griffiths v Kerkemeyer Griffiths v Kerkemeyer* (1977) 139 CLR 161 component of an award (damages for gratuitous attendant care) and on *Sullivan v Gordon* [1999] 47 NSWLR 319 damages (relating to plaintiff's capacity to provide gratuitous services to dependants): see [14.185], [14.190]. These provisions reverse the common law. Section 18(1) has no effect on sums awarded for commercially provided care. Apart from these restrictions, interest is payable in accordance with normal principles, preserving the court's discretion discussed above in relation to *Supreme Court Act 1970* (NSW), s 94. It is clear, however, that since the decision in *Hungerfords v Walker* (1990) 171 CLR 125, awards of pre-judgment interest may be made independently of statute. In that case the plaintiffs sued their accountants for damages for loss of use of money paid as a result of negligence or breach of contract. The negligence had resulted in overpayment of tax, which could not be recovered from the tax office. The High Court allowed interest on the money, based on common law principles of remoteness and foreseeability and the decision in *Hadley v Baxendale* (1854) 9 Ex 341; 156 ER 145, which deals with remoteness of damage in contract. The Federal Full Court applied *Hungerfords* to a personal injury claim in *Commonwealth v Chessell* (1991) 30 FCR 154 at 185-187.

QUALIFICATIONS TO THE COMPENSATORY PRINCIPLE

[14.265] Various factors make inroads upon the compensatory principle. These include the rules relating to causation, certainty, contributory negligence, remoteness, the duty to mitigate, collateral benefits, and taxation. Many of these have been discussed elsewhere in this book in relation to liability; certainty has been dealt with above (see *Malec v Hutton* [14.130]), and contributory negligence and apportionment were discussed in Chapter 16. The factors meriting further discussion here are mitigation and taxation.

Mitigation

[14.270] The decision in *British Westinghouse Electric & Manufacturing Co Ltd v Underground Electric Railways Co of London Ltd* [1912] AC 673 established that plaintiffs owe a duty to defendants to take reasonable steps to mitigate, or minimise, their losses. Viscount Haldane LC said (at 689):

> This first principle [restitutio in integrum] is qualified by a second, which imposes on a plaintiff the duty of taking all reasonable steps to mitigate the loss consequent on the breach [of contract], and debars him from claiming any part of the damage which is due to his neglect to take such steps. The second principle does not impose on the plaintiff an obligation to take any step which a reasonable and prudent man would not ordinarily take ... [the assessor of damages must] look at what actually happened, and ... balance loss and gain.

Although *British Westinghouse* concerned breach of contract, it has been widely applied in personal injury cases. As explained by Viscount Haldane, the consequence of a failure to mitigate is reduction of damages. In the context of personal injury, failure to mitigate often arises in relation to a plaintiff's refusal of medical treatment. The next case examines what constitutes a reasonable or unreasonable refusal to undergo treatment.

Glavonjic v Foster

[14.275] *Glavonjic v Foster* [1979] VR 536 Supreme Court of Victoria

(footnotes omitted)

[The facts are stated within the judgment of Gobbo J.]

GOBBO J: 536 This is a claim for damages by the plaintiff against the two defendants arising out of a collision on 28 July 1976. On that date the plaintiff was on his way to work at the Carlton and United Brewery when he was struck by a motor car, was rendered unconscious for some 15 minutes and taken to hospital. The matter proceeded before me as an assessment.

[After considering the history of the claim and the approach that should be adopted in connection with the presence of a medical condition of a pre-existing nature, which would have disabled the plaintiff even if the accident had not occurred, his Honour proceeded.] The next matter that needs to be considered is the question of refusal of the plaintiff to undergo brain surgery in October 1976. This raises squarely the question of the plaintiff's duty to mitigate his damages. It was submitted there is no doubt that if a medical operation might have alleviated the plaintiff's condition and it was reasonable for him to undergo it, then the damages are to be assessed on the basis that he did undergo it. At the same time it is clear that since the onus is on the defendant to prove that the plaintiff's subsisting injuries were capable of alleviation the defendant must show how and to what extent this would have occurred had the operation been undertaken. In the present case I am satisfied that the defendant proved how and, in general terms, to what extent the loss could have been diminished had the plaintiff undergone the surgical procedure in October 1976. It was said, however, that it was

Glavonjic v Foster cont.

reasonable for the plaintiff in the circumstances to refuse the operation and that accordingly he should not have his damages cut down on the basis that his operation would have successfully shortened the effect of the accident. …

The question of unreasonable refusal to undergo surgical treatment has frequently arisen in workers' compensation cases, both in England and, as already indicated, in Australia. In *Steele v Robert George Co Ltd* [1942] AC 497; [1942] 1 All ER 443, the House of Lords decided that the question whether a worker is unreasonable in refusing to undergo a surgical operation is a question of fact to be decided by the judge of fact on the evidence…

…Lord Wright seems to me to include a sympathetic estimate of the workman's personality as being relevant.

I have come to the view that it is consistent with the views of the House of Lords that the test of reasonableness is one to be achieved by considering what a reasonable man would have done assuming he was faced by all the circumstances of the case as they presented themselves to the plaintiff. Though one might properly exclude the peculiar reservations of a neurotic person, it is appropriate to take into consideration a mental condition such as an anxiety state where that was itself related to the injuries and was caused or contributed to by the accident in question. Again, it is proper in my opinion to take into account whether the plaintiff was made to understand what was the choice before him. It can hardly be said that a plaintiff unreasonably refused medical treatment if, for example, there was not available to him an adequate interpreter where that was necessary for that particular plaintiff.

In the present case there was a substantial amount of material relied upon to support the reasonableness of the refusal by the plaintiff. In the first place the plaintiff pointed to the failure of the operation on his right hand some few months before the accident. He had there been assured in strong terms that there would be a successful result of the operation but none the less he was left with a permanent deformity of his finger. In addition to this he further relied upon the fact that his de facto wife had had a long series of operations for various conditions and that some of these operations had been unsuccessful and had lead to further treatment and hospitalization. It was also said on his behalf that brain surgery was notoriously a type of surgery where the risks of failure were all the more serious because there was no redressing the situation. It was graphically put by the plaintiff himself that he only had one brain and in effect if there was a failure, there was not much that could be done about giving him another one.

It was also put on behalf of the plaintiff that the plaintiff's anxiety condition and depression in October 1976 had to be taken into account in explanation of his decision at that stage not to submit to surgery. The final matters that may be legitimate to take into account were the plaintiff's relatively poor education, his unfamiliarity with institutions different from those of his own country, his very limited command of English and the fact that the advice he has received from the doctors, was, on the face of it not unanimous in terms of the percentage degree of success that was to be expected from this type of surgical procedure. It may be said that it was scarcely conducive to confidence that the plaintiff had been sent home after the accident upon the basis that there was little wrong with him and it was not until some two months later that the clot on his brain had been discovered… I am of the view that if the matter is to be judged entirely objectively without regard to the plaintiff's knowledge, circumstances and mental condition, refusal of the operation was not a reasonable one. I am of the opinion however that upon analysis of the authorities I am not constrained to apply such a strict and technical test. It seems to me more appropriate to have regard to the circumstances of the plaintiff. That is not to say that one simply applies a subjective test and considers whether the plaintiff thought it was reasonable for him to refuse surgery. It is however appropriate to adopt a test that asks whether a reasonable man in the circumstances as they existed for the plaintiff and subject to the various factors such as difficulty of understanding and the plaintiff's medical history and condition that

Glavonjic v Foster cont.

affected the plaintiff, would have refused treatment. In my opinion, applying the broader test, I am of the view that the defendants have not discharged the onus which is upon them of showing that it was unreasonable of the plaintiff to refuse the surgery proposed.

[14.280] **Notes&Questions**

1. Since *Glavonjic v Foster* [1979] VR 536 courts have tended to adopt a more sympathetic approach to subjective factors: see, for example, *Karabatsos v Plastex Industries Pty Ltd* [1981] VR 675 (FC); *Lorca v Holts' Corrosion Control Pty Ltd* [1981] Qd R 261 (FC). Gobbo J, in *Glavonjic*, referred to an "intervening position", based on a mixture of subjective and objective factors. Should this be the general rule?
2. As we saw in Chapter 13, Damage: Causation and Remoteness defendants are required to take their victims as they find them (the eggshell skull rule). Does this mean that a Jehovah's Witness would be justified in refusing a blood transfusion? What about a plaintiff who believed in alternative medicine such as acupuncture and iridology? Or faith healing?

Taxation

[14.285] Awards of damages for personal injury are treated as capital, therefore exempt from income tax. The distinction between loss of earning capacity (an asset) and loss of earnings (income) is significant in relation to taxation. In *Atlas Tiles v Briers* (1978) 144 CLR 202 (at 220) Gibbs J said:

> I have already expressed the opinion that in Australia an award of damages for personal injury is not taxable ... I adhere to that view. Indeed so far as I am aware it has never been seriously challenged. The Commissioner does not attempt to assess tax on awards of damages for personal injuries. He is never likely to do so while the law remains as it is.

The facts of *Atlas* turned on a differential tax rate between the plaintiff's income if he had remained in his employment, and the damages he received for wrongful dismissal. Tax on damages at that time was assessed at 5 per cent, a lower rate than for income tax. The trial judge held that the defendant should pay the full pre-tax amount in damages. The majority in the High Court considered that to ignore the effect of the tax rate differential amounted to abandonment of the compensatory principle. In dissent, Stephen J reasoned that the damages needed to be adjusted to eliminate the benefit that the plaintiff would obtain from the tax rate differential, since without adjustment the plaintiff would recover more than he had lost. The High Court later endorsed the dissenting views of Stephen and Gibbs JJ in *Cullen v Trappell* (1980) 146 CLR 1, deciding by a narrow majority of 4:3 that damages for loss of earning capacity must be calculated on a net/net basis, that is, net income in relation to both past and future losses. This has been the position in the United Kingdom since *British Transport Commission v Gourley* [1956] AC 185, but the opposite applies in Canada, New Zealand, and most of the United States. Neither position is self evident; assessing the losses on a net basis deprives the taxation commissioner of tax, to the benefit of the defendant, whereas assessing damages on a pre-tax basis inflates insurance costs. Both impact on the community at large. Personal injury damages are specifically exempted from capital gains tax by s 160ZB(1) of the *Income Tax Assessment Act 1936* (Cth).

Past and future care expenses including gratuitous care will be assessed on a pre-tax (cost) basis, since the plaintiff will have to pay the gross cost, leaving tax to be paid by the recipient. The benefit obtained by having the capital in advance as a lump sum is adjusted for in the present value discount: (see discounting [14.195], especially *Todorovic v Waller* (1981) 150 CLR 402 [14.195]-[14.200]]). Income produced by investing the capital is taxable. Whether the interest components of the award are taxable was considered in *Whitaker v Commissioner of Taxation (Cth)* (1998) 98 ATC 2. The taxpayer in that case was the plaintiff in *Rogers v Whitaker* (1992) 175 CLR 479, who had been blinded in her good eye after an operation on her blind eye, by the occurrence of a rare complication which the defendant ophthalmologist had failed to warn her about. The interest on her damages in *Rogers* was subsequently assessed for tax by the taxation commissioner, which she challenged in *Whitaker v Commissioner*. The Full Federal Court held that pre-judgment interest (in respect of past losses to the date of trial) was not income but capital. Interest awarded in this context was compensation for not having received the award at the time of the injury (when the cause of action arose), which is distinguishable from interest awarded in a commercial context. The latter, such as interest on loans or bank deposits, is taxable as income. After the decision in *Whitaker* the *Income Tax Assessment Act* (Cth) was amended so that post judgment interest (on future losses) from the 1992/93 year is also tax free for personal injury awards.

WRONGFUL DEATH

Survival of actions to the estate

[14.290] Pursuant to the *Law Reform (Miscellaneous Provisions) Act 1944* (NSW) and its equivalents in other States, the estate of a person killed, whether wrongfully or not, retains any cause of action the deceased would have had if alive. See [8.185ff] and for other jurisdictions the following statutes: *Law Reform (Miscellaneous Provisions) Act 1955* (ACT); *Law Reform (Miscellaneous Provisions) Act 1956* (NT); *Law Reform (Miscellaneous Provisions) Act 1941* (WA); *Succession Act 1981* (Qld); *Survival of Causes of Action Act 1940* (SA); *Administration and Probate Act 1935* (Tas); *Administration and Probate Act 1958* (Vic). The estate cannot claim for any loss which the deceased could not have recovered, including any reduction for contributory negligence. Some entitlements attaching to the deceased do not pass to the estate. Examples include post-death loss of earning capacity, that is, loss of capacity during the "lost years" (discussed in *Sharman v Evans* (1977) 138 CLR 563 above at [14.100]) This was recoverable after the High Court's decision in *Fitch v Hyde-Cates* (1982) 150 CLR 482, but was abolished by legislation in all jurisdictions. Exemplary damages cannot be recovered in survival actions, and, in all states except Tasmania, defamation actions die with the deceased. The duty to mitigate attaches to the estate in so far as this is possible. Damages for non-economic loss or general damages for "pain and suffering", "any bodily or mental harm", and "curtailment of expectation of life" are excluded in jurisdictions other than New South Wales, Victoria, Northern Territory and Australian Capital Territory. Harold Luntz explains that "the unedifying spectacle of accelerated death-bed hearings [in dust disease cases] led to further amendments in New South Wales and Victoria to preserve the damages for non-pecuniary loss in such cases" (H Luntz, *Assessment of Damages for Personal Injury and Death* (4th ed, LexisNexis Butterworths, 2002), p 479): See *Dust Diseases Tribunal Act 1989* (NSW), s 12B (operation is preserved by *Law Reform (Miscellaneous Provisions) Act 1944* (NSW), s 2(7)); *Administration and Probate Act 1958* (Vic), s 29. These and other restrictions mean that damages are generally limited to: recovery of lost earning capacity to the date of death; medical expenses and the value of gratuitous services rendered prior to death; and funeral expenses. Damages that are awarded to the estate are in most cases set off against dependants' claims pursuant to Lord Campbell's Act, to avoid double recovery.

Dependants' claims: Lord Campbell's Act

[14.295] The *Fatal Accidents Act 1846* (UK) (*Lord Campbell's Act*) has been replicated in all Australian jurisdictions: *Compensation to Relatives Act 1897* (NSW); *Compensation (Fatal Injures) Act 1968* (ACT); *Wrongs Act 1958* (Vic); *Wrongs Act 1936* (SA); *Fatal Accidents Act 1959* (WA); *Compensation (Fatal Injuries) Act* (NT); *Common Law Practice Act 1867-1981* (Qld). The basic provisions have remained fairly uniform, with amendments in various jurisdictions relating to persons for whose benefit the action may be brought, deduction of benefits received, and the time within which the action must be commenced. The *Compensation to Relatives Act 1897* (NSW) is typical, but the detail may vary in other jurisdictions. Section 3(1) gives dependants a cause of action when the death of a breadwinner is caused by a "wrongful act, neglect, or default" which would have allowed the deceased to sue if he or she had been injured rather than killed. The defendant in that action then becomes liable to the dependants, including for payment of funeral expenses in New South Wales, but not in all jurisdictions. Section 3(3)(a) provides that insurance held by the deceased is irrelevant, since the benefit of insurance must go to the person paying the premiums or his family, not to the wrongdoer. A single action will be taken by the legal personal representative of the deceased on behalf of all dependants falling within the class of specified relatives. These are defined in s 4 and s 7(1) to include spouses, de facto spouses, parents, siblings, half siblings, children, step children, and grandchildren. Ex-spouses are excluded, even where there is an entitlement to maintenance. The court will apportion the sum recovered according to the loss suffered by each dependant.

Part 1A, Div 8 of the *Civil Liability Act 2002* (NSW) provides that any contributory negligence of the deceased applies against his or her dependants. Section 5T(1) provides that in Compensation to Relatives claims "the court is entitled to have regard to the contributory negligence of the deceased person" and NSW: CLAs 5T(2) states that s 13 of the *Law Reform (Miscellaneous Provisions) Act 1965* (NSW) "does not apply so as to prevent the reduction of damages by the contributory negligence of a deceased person in respect of a claim for damages brought under the *Compensation to Relatives Act 1897*". As we have seen (see [16.140]), civil liability legislation may allow damages to be reduced by up to 100 per cent for contributory negligence.

It is clearly established that damages are recoverable only for expectations of financial support, not for losses in the nature of general damages, that is, grief or other non financial loss. The highest amounts will normally be recovered by the youngest child or a wholly dependent spouse.

Courts in recent years have taken a more generous approach to the interpretation of "financial loss". For example, in *Nguyen v Nguyen* (1990) 169 CLR 245, the plaintiffs (husband and children of the deceased) claimed for "loss of the deceased's domestic capacity being the value of services such as child care, cooking, washing, ironing and cleaning". The High Court accepted that there "is no reason why 'services' in this context should be given an unduly narrow construction, as if the wife were no more than a housekeeper" but stressed that "compensation [for lost gratuitous domestic services] should not be confused with the actual cost to the bereaved husband [of] providing substitute services" (per Dawson, Toohey, McHugh JJ, [263]).

Compensation would be payable even where it appeared that those services had not been and were not likely to be replaced by hired help. Any such compensation must be reasonable or "proportioned" to the injury, and cannot simply be equated with actual lost services. This is because "the ultimate burden of liability to pay damages under a *Lord Campbell's Act* action will ordinarily be cast upon the community generally through the direct and indirect cost of insurance premiums [so assessment must occur] by reference to current local standards and values". For example, loss of the services of a full or part time daily housekeeper will not be included at that level for an adult dependant, unless "some special need can be identified, such as infant children, old age, injury, infirmity, or the unusual demands of a particular occupation" (*Nguyen*, Deane J at 258).

The effect of remarriage on damages under the Act is discussed in the next extract, and was also considered in *Nguyen*. Justices Dawson, Toohey and McHugh (at 266) explained that where services are likely to be replaced as a result of re-marriage, "the reasonable prospect of that remarriage will serve to reduce the compensation... not because the plaintiff's need for the services will then be satisfied, but because the plaintiff's loss is thereby directly reduced. The prospect of remarriage has always been regarded under *Lord Campbell's Act* as providing a gain to the husband in the form of revival of the capacity to marry".

Discount for re-marriage

[14.300] In making an assessment of pecuniary loss pursuant to Lord Campbell's Act, courts are necessarily engaged in attempting to determine what would have happened if the deceased had not been killed, including contingencies or vicissitudes. In addition, factors which might affect the financial circumstances of his or her family in the future need to be taken into account. The process is similar to that for normal personal injury calculations, with many of the same difficulties. The next case considers the issue of whether a discount for a widow's prospects of remarriage (and assumed financial benefit) should be made.

De Sales v Ingrilli

[14.305] *De Sales v Ingrilli* (2002) 212 CLR 338 High Court of Australia

(footnotes omitted)

[The plaintiff's husband was killed in an accident in 1990 on the property of the defendant. Negligence was found against the defendant, with contributory negligence on the part of the husband. The plaintiff was 27 at the time. There were two children of the marriage. The deceased was a practising accountant and tax agent. The plaintiff had not remarried at the time of trial in 1999. In the period since her husband's death, she had been involved in one relationship of limited duration, in which marriage was never contemplated. The trial judge made no deduction for the general "vicissitudes of life", but applied a discount of five per cent to the appellant's damages to reflect the chance of the appellant obtaining financial benefit from remarriage ("the remarriage discount"). There was an appeal, and cross-appeal, to the Full Court of the Supreme Court of Western Australia, including in relation to the remarriage discount. By majority (Wallwork J dissenting) the Full Court allowed the defendant's appeal. Miller J, with whom Parker J agreed, found that the discount applied by the trial judge was "very slight", and that "for a woman of the appellant's age and credentials a 20 per cent deduction would be appropriate." The overall deduction made in relation to the appellant's

De Sales v Ingrilli cont.

damages was 20 per cent for the possibility of remarriage and five per cent for general contingencies. The general contingencies applied also in the case of the children. The plaintiff appealed to the High Court.]

GAUDRON, GUMMOW AND HAYNE JJ: 356 The issue in this appeal is whether, in assessing damages to be allowed in an action brought on behalf of a surviving spouse (or de facto spouse) and children under the *Fatal Accidents Act 1959* (WA) ("the *Fatal Accidents Act*") in respect of the wrongful death of the partner and parent, the prima facie value of what is lost should be reduced for the contingency that the surviving partner will remarry …

Society has changed markedly since *Lord Campbell's Act* was first enacted. The *Fatal Accidents Act*, unlike its predecessor, deals not only with surviving spouses but with survivors of de facto relationships. Very great changes occurred during the last half of the twentieth century in the nature and durability of family relationships, in the labour market, and in the expectations that individual members of society have for themselves and about others – economically, socially, domestically, culturally, emotionally. Even if once it were the case, no longer can a court make any assumption about the role that an individual can be expected to play in the family or in the economy. Yet it is assumptions of conformity to some unstated norm which underpin the making of a "discount for remarriage".

To assess the pecuniary loss that the death has caused the relatives, it is necessary to take account of what may have happened in the future had the death not occurred and, as well, to take account of what may happen to the relatives in the future even though the death has occurred. These predictions, about the "vicissitudes of life", are "very much a matter of speculation". It follows that the pecuniary loss that has resulted from death cannot be calculated with accuracy. The best that can be done is to assess a sum which will, *as far as the limits implicit in the task will permit*, represent the value of that loss, assessed at the date of judgment.

Some calculations, which will assist in assessing the value of the loss, can be made. The amount of financial benefit being provided by the deceased to the relatives, immediately before death, can be demonstrated. The present value of that stream of income, if it were to continue into the future, can be calculated (although choosing the appropriate discount rate and the length of time for which the stream is to be assumed to continue will affect the result).

How is account then to be taken of life's uncertainties? Had the deceased not died as he or she did, who is to say how long a life the deceased would have led? What would have happened? Would the deceased have continued to earn at the level being earned before death? Or would death, incapacitating illness or financial calamity (in one form or another) have intervened? If it had, would any of the survivors have then contributed to the financial well-being of the family? Even if there were no disaster (physical, financial or other) would the financial contribution made by the surviving spouse or de facto spouse, have changed anyway? And if action is brought on behalf of a surviving spouse, or de facto spouse, can it be assumed that the relationship would have endured? Will the surviving spouse remarry after the date of judgment, or form some continuing relationship which will have some financial consequence for any of those for whose benefit the action is brought? All these, and more, are possibilities that may have to be reflected in any assessment of the present value of the economic loss suffered by all of the relatives as a result of the deceased's death, not just a surviving spouse. Because the assessment requires estimation and judgment rather than calculation, seldom, if ever, will it be right to express the result as if it were correct to the nearest dollar. That falsely asserts a degree of accuracy in the assessment that is impossible. All that can be done is to select a percentage or lump sum to allow for the estimated value of those possibilities which may or may not have eventuated if the deceased had lived and those which may or may not eventuate in the future.

Of course, in doing that, it is necessary to take due account of the fact that what is sought is a sum for damages that will represent, at the date of judgment, the *present* value of the benefits which would

De Sales v Ingrilli cont.

have been received over time. In assessing those damages, it would be wrong to think that reducing the period during which the benefits will be received from (say) 20 years to 15 years would reduce the amount of damages to be awarded by 25 per cent. The reduction thus effected would be much less than 25 per cent. Conversely, and confining attention to the period of future receipts, to make a deduction of (say) five per cent from the amount that is calculated as the present value of benefits to be received over 20 years is not to assume that the period of benefits that is being considered is reduced from 20 years to 19. It would assume that the benefits would cease much earlier than the end of the nineteenth year. And, of course, a deduction from the present value may reflect not only a reduction in the future period that is being taken to account, it may reflect a reduction in the amount that it is expected will be received. Fixing when that reduction occurs affects the calculation of present value. If it is assumed that the reduction will occur early in the period, the effect on present value is large. If it is assumed that it will occur late in the period, the effect is small.

Statistics may throw some light on some of the questions we have mentioned. They may tell their reader what is the average life expectancy of a person of a certain age. They may reveal how frequent is remarriage among people of a certain age. But great care must be exercised in their use. What are the characteristics reflected in the statistics? Are those relevant to the present inquiry? Why can it be assumed that the individual will conform to the average? To apply a statistical average to an individual case assumes that the case has all the characteristics which, blended together, create the statistic.

The judgment of Windeyer J in *Parker v The Commonwealth* indicates that his Honour was alive to these considerations. Windeyer J observed:

> I was told by the actuary who gave evidence that about one-third of the women who become widows at the age of forty remarry at some time. This piece of information seems to me interesting but not very helpful. So much depends upon matters peculiar to the person and her circumstances, on various factors both emotional and material.

The range of possibilities that lie before those for whose benefit a claim is made under legislation modelled on *Lord Campbell's Act* is very wide. The financial consequences of some may be to the advantage of the surviving relatives, others may be to their disadvantage. Why should one of those possibilities (remarriage, or the formation of some other continuing relationship) be considered separately from all others? To consider it separately assumes that it is a contingency whose likelihood of occurrence can be separately assessed with reasonable accuracy, and that the financial consequences of its occurrence will, more probably than not, tend in one direction (financial advantage) rather than the other.

Both those assumptions may be flawed. Seldom, if ever, will a court be able to make any useful prediction about whether, or when, one human being will form a close emotional attachment with another. Statistics may provide some basis for saying, in some cases, that it is more probable than not that, at some time over (say) the next 20 years a surviving spouse will form a new relationship. The younger the survivor, the more likely may that be to occur. But, in very many cases, statistics will provide little useful guidance about the time by which it is more probable than not that it will occur. Again, perhaps, the younger the survivor, the easier it may be to fix some outer limit to the time by which the probabilities are that it will occur, but even that would be a hazardous prediction. And it is never assisted by fastening upon some superficial characteristics labelled as "appearance", "personality", "credentials" or the like and having the judge or jury base on those characteristics some estimate of "marriageability".

Even if these difficulties of predicting that a surviving spouse will form some new continuing relationship were to be surmounted, the financial consequences of its occurrence are even less predictable. Who is to say that the new relationship will endure, and that, if it endures, it will provide financial advantage to the person who is now the surviving spouse? And if it is a financially beneficial relationship at its outset, who is to say what events will intervene thereafter? Will the new spouse or

De Sales v Ingrilli cont.

partner suffer some catastrophe and the person who is now the surviving spouse then have to care and provide for the new partner, the children of the first union, any children brought by the new partner to the new union, and any children born of the new union? Who can say?

It is these last points about the financial consequences of a new relationship which are of critical importance. They deny the validity of looking separately at some "discount for remarriage" over and above whatever discount is made for the "vicissitudes of life". Among those vicissitudes are all the hazards and benefits that may befall a person or, where the claim is made for a surviving spouse, may befall a couple during life. Any new union, which is formed after the termination of the union which underlies a claim made pursuant to a wrongful death statute modelled on *Lord Campbell's Act*, is as exposed to precisely the same kinds of hazard and danger as was the earlier union. It, too, may end in death, separation or divorce. The financial advantages and disadvantages to one partner will change throughout the continuance of the union as the careers and ambitions of the partners change both with and against their will. Those, who today are receiving income from personal exertion, may, tomorrow, cease doing so for any number of reasons. Those who are employed may have the employment terminated. Those who are self-employed may fall ill, or the venture in which they are engaged may fail. Those who receive income from investments may invest unwisely or unprofitably. Those who are now not employed outside the house may later forge a new career either because they want to or because they feel they should or must do so. And so the examples can be multiplied. Yet if these possibilities are taken to account in assessing the vicissitudes to which the former union was subject (and they must) to ignore them when considering a new union, by assuming that the new union would be destined to survive and prosper, would be to shut one's eyes to reality.

It is, therefore, wrong to treat the prospect of remarriage or the prospect of forming some new continuing relationship as a separate item for which some identified discount must be made from whatever calculation is made of the present value of future benefits that would have flowed from the deceased to the relatives. Even if the prospects that a surviving spouse would remarry or enter a new continuing relationship could be assessed (and there will be few cases where that would be possible), predicting when that would occur is impossible, and predicting some likely outer limit of time by which it would probably have occurred is only slightly less difficult. But most importantly, it cannot be assumed that any new union will be, or will remain, of financial advantage to any of those for whose benefit the action is brought. That being so, some financially advantageous marriage or relationship must be treated as only one of many possible paths that the future may hold. It is wrong to single it out for special and separate allowance. That others in the past have had damages reduced on this account is not reason enough to continue the error.

Nor can the prospect of remarrying or forming a new relationship properly be seen as a matter which, under the general heading of "the vicissitudes of life", enlarges the discount which otherwise must be made from the present value of the benefits which the deceased was providing at death. The assessment of that discount is not easy. It must reflect not only the fact that the future may have been better than the past but also the fact that it may not. It is wrong to fasten upon *one* of the myriad possible paths that life may take and say that, on account of *that* possibility, it is right to enlarge the discount that must be made. The discount can be assessed only as a single sum which reflects *all* of the possibilities.

That is not to say that, if there is evidence at trial that a new relationship has been formed, account may not be taken of evidence revealing whether that brings with it financial advantage or disadvantage. It would be wrong to adopt the rule followed in some American jurisdictions [See, for example, *Davis v Guarnieri* 15 NE 350 (1887) (US); *McFarland v Illinois Central Railroad Co* 127 So 2d 183 (1961) (US); *Reynolds v Willis* 209 A 2d 760 (1965) (US); *Cherrigan v City and County of San Francisco* 262 Cal App 2d 643 (1968) (US); *Dubil v Labate* 245 A 2d 177 (1968) (US); *Seaboard Coast Line Railroad Co v Hill* 250 So 2d 311 (1971), cert discharged 270 So 2d 359 (1972) (US). See also PC

De Sales v Ingrilli cont.

Kober, "The Case of the "Wife After Death": Reflections on the Admissibility of Evidence of Remarriage Under the Massachusetts Wrongful Death Statute" (1980) 15 *New England Law Review* 227.] and require the tribunal of fact to assess the damages without that evidence. If the relationship is reflected in marriage, or if there is relevant legislation creating rights between de facto partners, the property rights of the partners will no doubt loom large in that assessment. Likewise, if there is evidence that a surviving spouse (or de facto spouse) intends, at the time of trial, to establish such a relationship with an identified person, account may be taken of evidence of the probable financial consequences of that relationship. In each case, however, it would be wrong to assume that the financial consequences revealed in evidence will inevitably continue.

Ordinarily, such cases apart, no separate allowance should be made for the possibility, even probability, that a new relationship will be formed. That is because it cannot be said, even on the balance of probabilities, whether, having regard to the whole of the period which must be considered, that relationship would be to the financial advantage or disadvantage of those relatives of the deceased for whose benefit the action is brought. If the period to be considered is very long (as would be the case where the surviving relatives are young) the range of possibilities that must be considered is very large. By contrast, if the period is short (where the surviving relatives are older) the possibilities of death, illness, loss of employment and the like are all the higher. No doubt, as was said more than 70 years ago in the United States District Court:

> If we should enter upon an inquiry as to the relative merits of the new husband as a provider, coupled with his age, employment, condition of health, and other incidental elements concerning him, unavoidably we should embark upon a realm of speculation and be led into a sea of impossible calculations.

But the critical point is not that the inquiry is hard, it is that it is an inquiry which does not lead to a useful answer. In the end, all that can be said is that the future is uncertain. The value of what is lost as a result of the wrongful death must strike a balance of all the gains and losses that have been and may thereafter be suffered. There is no basis for fastening upon some to the exclusion of others …

The appeal should be allowed to the extent necessary to set aside order 2 of the Orders of the Full Court made on 1 December 2000.

PUBLIC POLICY AND DAMAGES: WRONGFUL BIRTH AND WRONGFUL LIFE

[14.310] The point emphasised throughout this chapter, that compensation for personal injury involves major normative choices about who *should* be compensated and in what circumstances, is most starkly revealed in actions known as wrongful birth and wrongful life. The chapter therefore concludes with consideration of the most recent of these cases in Australia.

The choices of judges occur in a societal context, reflecting views about responsibility and communitarian approaches versus individualistic approaches to treatment of the injured. Legal "rules" cannot be divorced from the values and assumptions that underpin them. In both wrongful birth and wrongful life actions, plaintiffs seek damages arising from the negligence of a doctor or health care provider which allows a child to be born who would otherwise have been aborted or not conceived. In wrongful birth, the claim is brought by the parent(s) of an unintended child, whose conception often results from a surgical sterilisation negligently performed by the defendant. This is what occurred in *Cattanach v Melchior* (2003)

215 CLR 1 (extracted below). Wrongful birth cases differ from wrongful life in that they may, but do not necessarily, involve impaired or handicapped children.

Wrongful life actions are always brought by a disabled child in his or her own right. The essence of such claims is that the child would have been aborted, but because of the doctor's failure to warn the parents about the disability, that child is now condemned to a life of suffering with associated expense. The child's disability stems from disease or genetic factors, and is not caused by the defendant. Very few jurisdictions, none of which is in Australia, have recognised wrongful life as a cause of action, and therefore the issue of damages has not been explored in depth (see in Australia, *Harriton v Stephens* (2006) 226 CLR 52; *Waller v James; Waller v Hoolihan* (2006) 226 CLR 136; in the United Kingdom, *McKay v Essex Area Health Authority* [1982] 1 QB 1166. It has also been rejected in 23 states in the United States). In the few successful wrongful life cases in the United States (*Curlender v Bio-Science Labs* 106 Cal App 3d 811 (1980) (US); *Turpin v Sortini* 643 P 2d 954 (1982) (US); *Procanik v Cillo*, NJ 339; 478 A 2d 755 (1997) (US); *Harbeson v Parke-Davis* 98 Wn 2d 460, 656 P 2d 483 (1983) (US)) damages have been awarded only for extraordinary medical and other expenses associated with or arising from the disability. In no case has an award for general damages, that is, pain and suffering and loss of amenity, been allowed. Similarly, no cases have allowed damages for future rearing costs. The additional claim for loss of income put in *Waller v James* is not normally even attempted.

Wrongful birth is well established as a cause of action, but the appropriate measure of damages is contentious. Wrongful birth plaintiffs generally seek damages for the mother for pain and discomfort experienced during the pregnancy or birth, plus related out of pocket expenses, economic loss, and, sometimes, nervous shock. The controversy centres on whether damages for the upkeep costs of the child can be awarded, particularly where the child is not disabled. In *Veivers v Connolly* [1995] 2 Qd R 326, the mother of a severely handicapped child born as a result of negligence recovered costs associated with past and future care of the child, covering a period of thirty years. In *CES v Superclinics (Australia) Pty Ltd* (1995) 38 NSWLR 47, the plaintiff mother lost the opportunity to terminate her pregnancy lawfully because of repeated failure by the defendants to diagnose her pregnancy. The child in this case was not disabled. The New South Wales Court of Appeal allowed her claim in a split decision. Damages did not include the costs of raising the child, because it was said that the child could have been adopted. Kirby A-CJ would have allowed costs of raising the child, Priestley JA took the middle view based on the possibility of adoption, and Meagher JA considered the cause should fail.

The inconsistency of allowing recovery in wrongful birth but denying upkeep costs was pointed out by three of the majority judges in *Cattanach v Melchior* (2003) 215 CLR 1. The negligent defendants bore the onus of proving "some legitimate basis recognised in the law for providing an immunity from a head of damages for personal injury well recognised at law", which they were unable to do. Hayne J, whilst denying the parents' claim in relation to their healthy child, suggested that in the case of a disabled child with special needs, the parents "could seek to demonstrate the costs incurred in meeting those needs without in any way denying or diminishing the benefits of being parent to the child".

English courts have decided a number of wrongful birth cases at a high level, including *Udale v Bloomsbury Area Health Authority* [1983] 1 WLR 1098, *Emeh v Kensington & Chelsea & Westminster Area Health Authority* [1985] QB 1012, and *Thake v Maurice* [1986] QB 644. Both *Emeh* and *Thake* were overruled by the House of Lords in *Macfarlane v Tayside*

Health Board (Scotland) [2000] 2 AC 59. The mother's claim for pain and discomfort associated with the pregnancy and delivery of a healthy child was allowed in *Macfarlane*, but not the parents' joint claim for costs of the child's upbringing. Lord Steyne said that considerations of distributive justice precluded acceptance of the claim, whilst Lord Clyde felt that the parents' joint claim went beyond restitution for the wrong. In *Parkinson v St James & Seacroft University Hospital* [2001] 3 All ER 97, decided after *Macfarlane*, the plaintiff was allowed to recover some costs of raising a disabled child, limited to extra expenses associated with the child's disability. In both *Groom v Selby* [2001] EWCA 1522 and *Rees v Darlington Hospital NHS Trust* [2002] EWCA Civ 88, the plaintiff recovered additional costs referable to the difference between bringing up a healthy child and a disabled child. Availability of upkeep costs was the sole issue in the High Court in *Cattanach v Melchior* (2003) 215 CLR 1. The Queensland Court of Appeal had decided that the parents were entitled to recover the reasonable costs of raising a healthy child, contrary to the decision of the House of Lords in *Macfarlane*. The majority in *Cattanach v Melchior* (2003) 215 CLR 1 decided the parents' loss was based on personal injury, rejecting the categorisation of the damage as pure economic loss, a categorisation adopted by both the Queensland Court of Appeal and the House of Lords in *Macfarlane*.

Cattanach v Melchior

[14.315] *Cattanach v Melchior* (2003) 215 CLR 1 High Court of Australia

(footnotes omitted)

[The duty of care aspects of the case are extracted at [8.50].]

[Ms Melchior was awarded damages at trial for pain and suffering and loss of amenities, loss of earnings and *Griffiths v Kerkemeyer* damages totalling $103,672. Her husband was awarded $3000 for loss of consortium. The couple also received a joint award of $20,353 for past costs of raising their son Jordan, and $105,249 for his future upkeep costs until the age of 18. The Queensland Court of Appeal dismissed the defendant doctor's appeal, and he appealed to the High Court solely on the issue of upkeep damages. The order of judgments has been altered to aid the flow of reasoning.]

MCHUGH AND GUMMOW JJ: ...

... The statement of relevant legal principle by Dixon J also shows why it is an error to think that awarding damages for the cost of raising a child inevitably requires the courts to balance the "monetary value of the child" against the cost of maintaining the child. In assessing damages, it is impermissible in principle to balance the benefits to one legal interest against the loss occasioned to a separate legal interest. The benefits received from the birth of a child are not legally relevant to the head of damage that compensates for the cost of maintaining the child. A different case would be presented if the mother claimed damages for "loss of enjoyment of life" as the result of raising the child. If such a head of damage were allowable, it would be correct to set off against the claim all the benefits derived from having the child. But the head of damages that is relevant in the present case is the financial damage that the parents will suffer as the result of their legal responsibility to raise the child. The benefits to be enjoyed as a result of having the child are not related to that head of damage. The coal miner, forced to retire because of injury, does not get less damages for loss of earning capacity because he is now free to sit in the sun each day reading his favourite newspaper. Likewise, the award of damages to the parents for their future financial expenditure is not to be reduced by the enjoyment that they will or may obtain from the birth of the child.

Logically, those persons like Lord Millett who would deny the cost of maintaining the child because of what they see as the immeasurable benefits gained from the birth of the child must deny the right of

Cattanach v Melchior cont.

action itself. If the immeasurability of those benefits denies damages for the cost of maintaining the child, there must also be denied recovery for the hospital and medical costs of the birth and for the attendant pain and suffering associated with the birth. Yet, illogically as it seems to us, those persons permit the action and allow damages to be recovered in respect of these two heads of damage.

The appeal should be dismissed with costs.

GLEESON CJ: [Dissenting] ... 10 ...

The next matter to be considered is what was earlier described as the selectivity of the respondents' approach to the incidents of the parent-child relationship created in consequence of the negligence of which they complain. The object of an award of damages in a case such as the present is not to punish a wrongdoer; it is to restore the plaintiffs, as nearly as possible as can be done by an award of financial compensation, to the position in which they would have been but for the wrongdoing. It is to effect "reasonable restitution for the wrong done". Is that object achieved by the award of damages made in favour of the respondents at trial? They have a loving relationship with a healthy child. It does not involve any special financial or other responsibilities that might exist if, for example, the child had an unusual and financially burdensome need for care. The financial obligations which the respondents have incurred, legal and moral, are of the same order as those involved in any ordinary parent-child relationship. They must feed the child. Of course, he remains their child. Does reasonable restitution involve obliging Dr Cattanach to pay for the food? The Christmas and birthday presents, for which they claimed and were awarded damages, will presumably be received with gratitude, and perhaps, at some future time, reciprocated. Does reasonable restitution require Dr Cattanach to pay for them? The entertainment they will provide the child will, no doubt, be enjoyed. Should Dr Cattanach have to pay for it? Some of those items would be unremarkable in a claim, in the Family Court, by one parent against another, for child maintenance. But when they appear in a schedule of damages in tort, they prompt questions as to the nature of the entire claim. When Mr and Mrs Melchior have spent the money itemised in their claim on food, clothing, education, maintenance and entertainment, what will they have to show for it? An adult son. No allowance has been, or can be, made for that ...

One of the grounds upon which "wrongful life" claims by children have been rejected is the impossibility of making a rational or fair assessment of damages. A similar difficulty is encountered in awarding damages for loss of expectation of life. The indeterminate nature of the financial consequences, beneficial and detrimental, of the parent-child relationship has already been noted. In deciding whether, in the contemplation of the law, the creation of that relationship is actionable damage, it is material to note that it is unlikely that the parties to the relationship, or the community, would regard it as being primarily financial in nature. It is a human relationship, regarded by domestic law and by international standards as fundamental to society. To seek to assign an economic value to the relationship, either positive or negative, in the ordinary case, is neither reasonable nor possible....

...

[The appeal was dismissed 4:3, with the majority formed by McHugh, Gummow, Kirby and Callinan JJ. Hayne and Heydon JJ dissented along with Gleeson CJ.]

[14.320] **Notes&Questions**

1. Shortly after this decision, the civil liability Acts were amended in New South Wales, Queensland and South Australia (see [8.65]). Section 71(1) in New South Wales (which is representative) provides that in such claims:

   the court cannot award damages for economic loss for:

a) the costs associated with rearing or maintaining the child that the claimant has incurred now or will incur in the future, or

b) any loss of earnings by the claimant while the claimant rears or maintains the child (2) Subsection (1) (a) does not preclude the recovery of any additional costs associated with rearing or maintaining a child who suffers from a disability that arise by reason of the disability.

The damages awarded in the principal case are therefore no longer available in New South Wales, Queensland, and South Australia, but remain available at common law elsewhere.

2. In the principal case, McHugh and Gummow JJ refused to make the distinction made in subs (2) quoted in Note 1, saying: "The differential treatment of the worth of the lives of those with ill health or disabilities has been a mark of the societies and political regimes we least admire". Which is the better view? Why?

3. Kirby J, in his dissent in the principal case, examined the various options available to courts. In relation to the first option, which results in no damages for the birth of a healthy child and which now represents the statutory position in three States, see the extract of his judgment at [8.50].

   Does the comment from Kirby J explain the addition of s 71? Do you agree with Kirby J's analysis? In discussing the different roles of the courts and Parliament, His Honour said (at 53) that judges "have the responsibility of expressing, refining and applying the common law in new circumstances in ways that are logically reasoned and shown to be a consistent development of past decisional law" and are not permitted to make decisions based on personal morality or belief, "concealed in an inarticulate premise dressed up, and described, as legal principle or policy". Do you agree?

4. Kirby J, in *Harriton v Stephens* (2006) 226 CLR 52 (extracted at [8.160], discussed and endorsed comments made by Mason P in the Court of Appeal (*Harriton v Stephens* (2004) 59 NSWLR 694 at 722-23), concerning New South Wales, ss 70 and 71. President Mason pointed out that s 70 of the NSW: CLA provides that the restriction on wrongful birth actions contained in s 71 "does not apply to any claim for damages by a child in civil proceedings for personal injury ... sustained by the child prenatally". Justice Kirby continued: "Therefore, so far as New South Wales is concerned, Parliament has left this particular question [of wrongful life damages] to the Courts" (*Harriton v Stephens* (2006) 226 CLR 52 at [142]). It is clear that at least part of the legislative intention in s 71 (and its equivalents) is to preserve the existing common law rights of the unborn to sue in negligence once they are "born alive" for injuries sustained in utero, for example, in car accidents or by medical negligence: see *Watt v Rama* [1972] VR 353; *X and Y (by her tutor X) v Pal* (1991) 23 NSW LR 26; *Burton v Islington Health Authority* [1993] QB 204. As long as the injury in wrongful life is categorised as personal injury rather than pure economic loss, the section also catches wrongful life claims, thus leaving the issue of upkeep costs open in New South Wales.

   Justice Kirby (dissenting) concluded (at [154]-[155]) in *Harriton v Stephens* (2006) 226 CLR 52 that:

> legislatures in Australia would ultimately have the last word. But just as parliaments have their functions in our governance and law-making, so have the courts. The courts develop the common law in a principled way. They give reasons for what they do. They constantly strive for the attainment of consistency with established legal principles as well as justice in the individual case ... that approach favours the provision of damages to the [plaintiff] whose life of profound suffering and costly care is a direct result of the agreed negligence of the [defendant]. ... The question is who should pay for the suffering, loss and damages that flow from the [defendant's] carelessness. ... The ordinary principles of negligence law sustain a decision in the [plaintiff's] favour. None of the propounded reasons of legal principle or legal policy suggests a different outcome.

Do you agree?

5. The majority in *Cattanach v Melchior* (2003) 215 CLR 1 decided the parents' loss was based on personal injury. In *Harriton v Stephens* (2006) 226 CLR 52, in the New South Wales Court of Appeal, Mason P also classified that case as a claim for damages for personal injury, avoiding the concerns about indeterminacy and remoteness that arise in regard to pure economic loss. Mason P referred (at [67]) to the different categorisations of the problem in various jurisdictions. These ranged from:

> strict logic, viewing the outcome as an inexorable consequence of applying ostensibly neutral and universal principles of tort law ... [to] recogniz[ing] the influence of policy. Some see the issue in terms of causation, others in terms of recoverable damages, others in terms of identifying the proper plaintiff to receive the damages. Many authorities talk in terms of a duty of care, although ... some deny duty because of fundamental problems in assessing damages and/or problems in describing the nature of the injury inflicted.

The "strict legalism" of cases such as *Becker v Schwartz* 413 NTS 2d 895, 900-1 (1978) (US) was contrasted with those in which "policy factors ... peep out", such as *McKay v Essex* [1982] 1 QB 1166. Of the different categorisations Mason P suggests, which do you think is the most coherent? In framing your answer, consider the material you have read in this chapter regarding the importance of policy within this area of tort law.

CHAPTER 15

Concurrent Liability

INTRODUCTION

Benefits of concurrent liability

[15.05] Multiple defendants can be liable in tort for the same injury or damage. This is usually described as concurrent liability. Where this exists, the plaintiff can choose to sue one or more of the defendants in a single action or a series of actions. At common law only one action could be brought if the defendants were characterised as joint tortfeasors; such as where an employer was liable for an employee's torts committed within the course of employment. The employee committed the tort but both employer and employee were jointly liable. This has now been reversed by statute. Now the position is that more than one action may be brought, but there are restrictions on recovery of damages and costs in subsequent actions. See [15.195] and ACT: CLWA, s 20(1)(2); *Law Reform (Miscellaneous Provisions) Act 1946* (NSW), s 5(1)(a)(b); *Law Reform (Miscellaneous Provisions) Act* (NT), s 12(2)(3); *Law Reform Act 1995* (Qld), s 6(a)(b); *Law Reform (Contributory Negligence and Apportionment* *of Liability) Act 2001* (SA), s 5; *Wrongs Act 1954* (Tas), s 3(1)(a)(b); Vic: WrA, ss 23B(1), 24AA, 24AB; *Law Reform (Contributory Negligence and Tortfeasors' Contribution) Act 1947* (WA), s 7(1)(a)(b).

It is usually more efficient and cheaper for the plaintiff to sue all relevant defendants in a single action. At common law, a plaintiff could recover the whole of the damage (solidary liability) against one of the concurrently liable defendants even if that defendant had been only a minor contributor to the plaintiff's injuries or damage. This gives significant protection to litigants against the risk that one of the defendants may be unable to pay compensation.

Statutory amendments in most jurisdictions provide for each wrongdoer to be liable for their proportionate share (proportionate liability) for negligently caused property damage and economic loss, see [15.185]. A defendant tortfeasor who is only partially responsible can claim contribution from another tortfeasor who is liable to the plaintiff, see [15.175]. In some States, contribution may be claimed where a defendant is liable on some basis other than tort, see [15.160].

Concurrent tortfeasors

[15.10] Concurrent liability seems obvious when both defendants have been guilty of independent torts that cause the plaintiff's damage. A typical illustration is where a pedestrian is injured as a consequence of a two-car collision caused by the negligence of both drivers. Both drivers are liable for all the pedestrian's injuries although, as we will see, there are mechanisms allowing contribution between the defendants. This is only one of the ways in which more than one defendant might be liable for the same damage. This section gives a brief introduction to the situations that may give rise to concurrent liability in tort for the same damage:

- where tortious conduct occurs during a joint enterprise;
- liability for the tortious conduct of an employee within the course of employment (vicarious liability);
- where there are special duties to ensure that others take due care (non-delegable duties); and
- where there are multiple torts causing the same damage

Joint enterprise

[15.15] Concurrent liability provides a mechanism for attributing liability for tortious wrongdoing to persons engaged in a joint enterprise or common design. In *Brooke v Bool* [1928] 2 KB 578, a landlord and a passerby investigated a gas leak in a tenant's shop. The landlord and then the passerby inspected the gas pipe with a lighted match; this caused an explosion. The landlord was held liable for the passerby's negligence. One of the grounds for finding the landlord liable was that "the act which was the immediate cause of the explosion was their joint act done in pursuance of a concerted purpose" (Salter J at 585).

Vicarious liability

[15.20] Concurrent liability can impose legal responsibility on an otherwise blameless defendant for the tortious conduct of another. Typical of this responsibility is an employer's liability for the tortious conduct of an employee committed during the course of employment–this is termed vicarious liability. This may seem surprising when the dominant theory of tort liability is individual responsibility and when strict liability has largely given way to liability based on negligence. However, in this area the broader policies of deterrence, compensation and loss distribution are dominant. See [15.35] for further consideration of this.

Non-delegable duties

[15.25] In some situations a defendant may be liable for the tortious conduct of a person who is not an employee but is an independent contractor. A defendant may be held concurrently liable with the wrongdoer where a plaintiff at special risk is negligently injured by another–particularly in cases where the plaintiff is vulnerable and the defendant has the capacity to exercise some control. These are known as non-delegable duties. If the duty is non-delegable, a defendant has a duty not only to act carefully itself (a direct duty), but also a duty to ensure that others delegated the task take reasonable care for the protection of the plaintiff. For example, an employer has a non-delegable duty to provide a safe working place for its employees. If a cleaning contractor (not an employee) in the course of her or his duties negligently creates a hazardous condition at the workplace which causes injury to an employee, both the employer and the cleaning contractor are liable (*Wilsons & Clyde Coal Co v English* [1938] AC 57). The nature of this liability, and how it is distinguished from vicarious liability, is examined by the High Court in *State of New South Wales v Lepore* (2003) 212 CLR 511, extracted below at [15.130].

Individual torts causing the same damage

[15.30] Concurrent liability may also exist where several defendants commit individual torts injuring the plaintiff. A preliminary question is: which of the several actors actually caused injury to the plaintiff? And then, did each actor cause separate, identifiable damage? If the damage caused by each wrongdoer is separately identifiable, the wrongdoer is liable for the damage caused by that wrongdoer. But where the tortious conduct of more than one person has caused the damage, and it is not feasible to attribute particular damage to a particular defendant, at common law all defendants are liable for the same damage. So in the initial example given of a pedestrian injured as a consequence of a collision between two vehicles, this is a case where the independent negligent acts of both drivers cause the same damage to the pedestrian; both defendants are concurrently liable for the whole of the pedestrian's damage. This does not mean that the plaintiff recovers double damages but gives the plaintiff the option of obtaining damages against the defendant with the most resources or a defendant who is insured against the loss. We will see later there is provision for claims for contribution between the defendants, see [15.150]. The civil liability reforms introduced a different rule which applies where the damage caused is property damage or economic loss. In that case each defendant is liable proportionately to the harm for which that defendant was responsible, see discussion [15.185].

This chapter examines the two key areas where concurrently liability arises, vicarious liability and non-delegable duties. We turn first to examine vicarious liability in more detail.

LIABILITY FOR THE CONDUCT OF OTHERS – VICARIOUS LIABILITY

Introduction

[15.35] The typical case of vicarious liability is the liability of an employer for a tort committed by an employee within the course of employment: the conduct must be that of an employee and the tortious wrongdoing must be within the course of employment. Professor Fleming summarises the policy reasons that underpin the existence of vicarious liability as follows (footnotes omitted):

> Most important of these is the belief that a person who employs others to advance (the employer's) own economic interest should in fairness be placed under a corresponding liability for losses incurred in the course of the enterprise; that the master is a more promising source of recompense than his servant who is apt to be a man of straw without insurance; and that the rule promotes wide distribution of tort losses, the employer being a most suitable channel for passing them on through liability insurance and higher prices. The principle gains additional support for its admonitory value in accident prevention. In the first place, deterrent pressures are most effectively brought to bear on larger units like employers who are in a strategic position to reduce accidents by efficient organisation and supervision of their staff. Secondly, the fact that employees are, as a rule, not worth suing because they are rarely financially responsible, removes from them the spectre of tort liability as a deterrent of wrongful conduct. By holding the master liable, the law furnishes an incentive to discipline servants guilty of wrongdoing .... (JG Fleming, The Law of Torts (9th ed, LBC Information Services, Sydney, 1998), p 410.)

This section examines cases where an employer is liable for the conduct of an employee acting within the course of employment. The cases extracted explore the policy questions underpinning vicarious liability and the nature of the relationships that give rise to this form of strict liability. These policies shed light on how courts approach the traditional requirements for liability. First, is there a requisite relationship that imposes responsibility for the conduct of others? Secondly, is there a sufficiently close relationship between the wrongful conduct causing injury and what the person was employed to do: that is, was the conduct within the course of employment?

Relationships giving rise to vicarious liability

[15.40] An employer is liable for the tortious conduct of an employee within the course of employment. But who is an employee? The "control test" was the classical test for deciding whether a person is an employee (often referred to in judgments as a servant). The greater the degree of control exercised over the person, the more likely that the person is an employee. This reasoning suggests that where the employer is able to exercise control they are also in a position to minimise risks and reduce accidents. In its crudest form, the test states that a person is an employee if the employer can tell the person not only what to do but how to do it. This test is useful when the employer has the relevant expertise, but it is unhelpful for professional and skilled employees, such as trapeze artists (*Zuijs v Wirth Bros Pty Ltd* (1955) 93 CLR 561) and hospital professionals (*Albrighton v Royal Prince Alfred Hospital* [1980] 2 NSWLR 542). The test has been modified by emphasising the *right* to exercise control where possible; this would include such things as working hours, use of equipment and so on. The question is whether "ultimate authority over (the person) resided in the employer so that [the person] was subject to the [employer]'s order and directions" (*Humberstone v Northern Timber Mills* (1949) 79 CLR 389 at 404-405). Whilst the control test is likely to be the most influential in deciding status, other factors are also relevant in making the determination. These include, hours of work, the right to hire and fire, payment of wages, deductions for taxation, the provision of equipment, dress codes and so on. In *Stevens v Brodribb Sawmilling Co Pty Ltd* (1986) 160 CLR 16 at 24 Mason J concluded that:

> the existence of control, whilst significant, is not the sole criterion by which to gauge whether a relationship is one of employment. The approach of this court has been to regard it merely as one of a number of indicia which must be considered in the determination of that question ... Other relevant matters include, but are not limited to, the mode of remuneration, the provision and maintenance of equipment, the obligation to work, the hours of work and provision of holidays, the deduction of income tax and the delegation of work by the putative employee.

Conversely, where workers determine their own hours, provide their own equipment, are able to delegate the job to someone else and where payment is made on completion of the job, these factors point to the person being an independent contractor rather than an employee. The older cases distinguished between a contract for services and a contract of service. An independent contractor contracts to provide services in much the same way as a plumber goes to a domestic home to fix the hot water. In contrast, an employee provides ongoing service and is subject to the directions and control of the employer.

Courts continue to have difficulties in determining whether an employment contract exists. An alternative approach looked more broadly at the place of the person in question within the organizational structure. Denning LJ suggested that "the test of being a servant does not rest nowadays on submission to orders. It depends on whether the person is part and parcel of the organisation" (*Bank Voor Handel en Scheepvaart NV v Slatford* [1953] 1 QB 248 at 295). In a later case, *Stevenson, Jordan and Harrison Ltd v McDonald and Evans* [1952] 1 TLR 101 at 110, Denning LJ also commented:

> One feature which seems to run through the instances is that, under a contract of service, a man is employed as part of the business, and his work is done as an integral part of the business; whereas, under a contract for services, his work, although done for the business, is not integrated into it but is only accessory to it.

This test has not made the task any easier and the Australian courts have largely not utilised it (see *Stevens v Brodribb Sawmilling Co Pty Ltd* (1986) 160 CLR 16 Mason J at 27-28). Sometimes the issue is whether the parties intended a legal relationship at all. This may be in doubt within family relationships and, perhaps, spiritual relationships as well. There is no automatic presumption that these relationships cannot give rise to contractual responsibilities (*Ermogenous v Greek Orthodox Community of SA Inc* (2002) 209 CLR 95 at [26]).

The relationship of parent and child does not itself give rise to vicarious liability. A parent of course can be liable for the parent's own negligence, for example, in failing to properly supervise a child. Exceptionally in the Northern Territory, Pt VIIIA of the *Law Reform (Miscellaneous Provisions) Act* (NT), inserted in 1991, makes a parent of a child jointly and severally liable with the child for damage done intentionally to property by the child up to an amount of $5,000. The Northern Territory legislation also provides that a community organisation is liable for the conduct of a volunteer as if the volunteer were an employee of the organisation (*Personal Injuries (Liabilities and Damages) Act* (NT), s 7(3)(b).

In cases on the margins, the task is not easy, as the following decision in *Hollis v Vabu* (2001) 207 CLR 21 illustrates.

Who is an employee?

Hollis v Vabu

[15.45] *Hollis v Vabu* (2001) 207 CLR 21 High Court of Australia
(footnotes partially omitted)

[Hollis was injured when struck by an unidentified cyclist on the footpath. The cyclist was wearing a jacket with the words "Crisis Couriers" on it. Crisis Couriers was owned and operated by Vabu. Individual couriers filled out a 3 page contract titled Contract for Service. It contained an inventory sheet relating to radio equipment and uniforms and a checklist for equipment. It provided that the Company did not pay hospital bills but required the courier to report any accidents. It required the courier to wear the company uniform at all times and to be neat and tidy. Drivers were responsible for loss or damage to goods and insurance was deducted from their pay. The company retained ownership of equipment and uniforms which had to be returned on termination of the contract. Losses or damage to equipment was to be paid for by the courier. Vabu did not make payments for annual or sick leave nor were superannuation deductions made for the couriers. Although the trial judge found on the facts, that the cyclist was an employee, he felt obliged to follow the decision of the New South Wales Court of Appeal in earlier proceedings which held that Vabu's couriers were not employees but independent contractors for taxation purposes. On appeal to the High Court from a decision of the New South Wales Court of Appeal dismissing the plaintiff's claim:]

GLEESON CJ, GAUDRON, GUMMOW KIRBY AND HAYNE JJ:

[Their Honours distinguished the earlier Court of Appeal decision in *Vabu v Federal Commissioner of Taxation* (1996) 33 ATR 537 that held that the couriers were independent contractors, on the ground that the evidence there concerned motor cycle and motor vehicle couriers and not bicycle couriers. The judgment then referred to the terms of the contract between the couriers and Vabu and continued:]

Vicarious liability

36 … It has long been accepted, as a general rule, that an employer is vicariously liable for the tortious acts of an employee but that a principal is not liable for the tortious acts of an independent contractor. That general rule was not challenged in this appeal. … 37 The tokens – "employer", "employee", "principal" and "independent contractor" – which provide the currency in this field of discourse have survived for a very long time and have been adapted to very different social conditions. As was pointed out in *Scott v Davis* (2000) 74 ALJR 1410 at 1452, vicarious liability derived originally from mediaeval notions of headship of a household, including wives and servants; their status in law was absorbed into that of the master. … 38

In *Colonial Mutual Life Assurance Society Ltd v Producers and Citizens Co-operative Assurance Co of Australia Ltd* (1931) 46 CLR 41, Dixon J explained the dichotomy between the relationships of employer and employee, and principal and independent contractor, in a passage 39 which has frequently been referred to in this Court. His Honour explained (at 48) that, in the case of an independent contractor:

> [t]he work, although done at [the principal's] request and for his benefit, is considered as the independent function of the person who undertakes it, and not as something which the person obtaining the benefit does by his representative standing in his place and, therefore, identified with him for the purpose of liability arising in the course of its performance. The independent contractor carries out his work, not as a representative but as a principal.

This statement merits close attention. It indicates that employees and independent contractors perform work for the benefit of their employers and principals respectively. Thus, by itself, the circumstance that the business enterprise of a party said to be an employer is benefited by the

Hollis v Vabu cont.

activities of the person in question cannot be a sufficient indication that this person is an employee. However, Dixon J fixed upon the absence of representation and of identification with the alleged employer as indicative of a relationship of principal and independent contractor. These notions later were expressed positively by Windeyer J in *Marshall v Whittaker's Building Supply Co* (1963) 109 CLR 210 at 217. His Honour said that the distinction between an employee and an independent contractor is "rooted fundamentally in the difference between a person who serves his employer in his, the employer's, business, and a person who carries on a trade or business of his own". In *Northern Sandblasting*, McHugh J said (at 36):

> The rationale for excluding liability for independent contractors is that the work which the contractor has agreed to do is not done as the representative of the employer.

In *Bazley v Curry* [1999] 2 SCR 534 at 552-555, the Supreme Court of Canada saw two fundamental or major concerns as underlying the imposition of vicarious liability. The first is the provision of a just and practical remedy for the harm suffered as a result of the wrongs committed in the course of the conduct of the defendant's enterprise. The second is the deterrence of future harm, by the incentive given to employers to reduce the risk of accident, even where there has been no negligence in the legal sense in the particular case giving rise to the claim.

40 In general, under contemporary Australian conditions, the conduct by the defendant of an enterprise in which persons are identified as representing that enterprise should carry an obligation to third persons to bear the cost of injury or damage to them which may fairly be said to be characteristic of the conduct of that enterprise. In delivering the judgment of the Supreme Court of Canada in *Bazley v Curry* [1999] 2 SCR 534, McLachlin J said of such cases that "the employer's enterprise [has] created the risk that produced the tortious act" and the employer must bear responsibility for it. McLachlin J termed this risk "enterprise risk" and said that "where the employee's conduct is closely tied to a risk that the employer's enterprise has placed in the community, the employer may justly be held vicariously liable for the employee's wrong". Earlier, in *Ira S Bushey & Sons, Inc v United States* 398 F 2d 167 at 171 (1968), Judge Friendly had said that the doctrine of *respondeat superior* rests:

> in a deeply rooted sentiment that a business enterprise cannot justly disclaim responsibility for accidents which may fairly be said to be characteristic of its activities

.

"Control"

These notions also influence the meaning to be given today to "control" as a discrimen between employees and independent contractors. In *Stevens v Brodribb Sawmilling Co Pty Ltd* (1986) 160 CLR 16, the Court was adjusting the notion of "control" to circumstances of contemporary life and, in doing so, continued the developments in *Zuijs v Wirth Brothers Pty Ltd* (1955) 93 CLR 561 and *Humberstone v Northern Timber Mills* (1949) 79 CLR 389. In *Humberstone*, Dixon J observed that the regulation of industrial conditions and other statutes had made more difficult of application the classic test, whether the contract placed the supposed employee subject to the command of the employer. Moreover, as has been pointed out (by Glass, McHugh and Douglas, *The Liability of Employers in Damages for Personal Injury*, 2nd ed (1979) at 72-73):

> The control test was the product of a predominantly agricultural society. It was first devised in an age untroubled by the complexities of a modern industrial society placing its accent on the division of functions and extreme specialisation. At the time when the courts first formulated the distinction between employees and independent contractors by reference to the test of control, an employer could be expected to know as much about the job as his employee. 41 Moreover, the employer would usually work with the employee and the test of control and supervision was then a real one to distinguish between the employee and the independent contractor. With the invention and growth of the limited liability company and

Hollis v Vabu cont.

> the great advances of science and technology, the conditions which gave rise to the control test largely disappeared. Moreover, with the advent into industry of professional men and other occupations performing services which by their nature could not be subject to supervision, the distinction between employees and independent contractors often seemed a vague one.

It was against that background that in *Brodribb* Mason J said that, whilst these criticisms might readily be acknowledged:

> the common law has been sufficiently flexible to adapt to changing social conditions by shifting the emphasis in the control test from the actual exercise of control to the right to exercise it, "so far as there is scope for it", even if it be "only in incidental or collateral matters": *Zuijs v Wirth Brothers Pty Ltd* (1955) 93 CLR 561 at 571. Furthermore, control is not now regarded as the only relevant factor. Rather it is the totality of the relationship between the parties which must be considered.

So it is that, in the present case, guidance for the outcome is provided by various matters which are expressive of the fundamental concerns underlying the doctrine of vicarious liability. These include, but are not confined to, what now is considered "control".

The facts of this case

... In classifying the bicycle couriers as independent contractors, the Court of Appeal fell into error in making too much of the circumstances that the bicycle couriers owned their own bicycles, bore the expenses of running them and supplied many of their own accessories. Viewed as a practical matter, the bicycle couriers were not running their own business or enterprise, nor did they have independence in the conduct of their operations. A different conclusion might, for example, be appropriate where the investment in capital equipment was more significant, and greater skill and training 42 were required to operate it. The case does not deal with situations of that character. The concern here is with the bicycle couriers engaged on Vabu's business. A consideration of the nature of their engagement, as evidenced by the documents to which reference has been made and by the work practices imposed by Vabu, indicates that they were employees.

First, these couriers were not providing skilled labour or labour which required special qualifications. A bicycle courier is unable to make an independent career as a free-lancer or to generate any "goodwill" as a bicycle courier. The notion that the couriers somehow were running their own enterprise is intuitively unsound, and denied by the facts disclosed in the record.

Secondly, the evidence shows that the couriers had little control over the manner of performing their work. They were required to be at work by 9.00 am and were assigned in a work roster according to the order in which they signed on. If they signed on after this time, they would not necessarily work on their normal "channel". Couriers were not able to refuse work. It was stated in Document 590 that "ANY DRIVER WHO DOES SO WILL NO LONGER WORK FOR THIS FIRM." The evidence does not disclose whether the couriers were able to delegate any of their tasks or whether they could have worked for another courier operator in addition to Vabu during the day. It may be thought unlikely that the couriers would have been permitted by Vabu to engage in either activity.

Thirdly, the facts show that couriers were presented to the public and to those using the courier service as emanations of Vabu. They were to wear uniforms bearing Vabu's logo..... 43

Fourthly, there is the matter of deterrence. Reference has been made to the findings of fact in this case respecting the knowledge of Vabu as to the dangers to pedestrians presented by its bicycle couriers and the failure to adopt effective means for the personal identification of those couriers by the public. One of the major policy considerations said by the Supreme Court of Canada in *Bazley v Curry* [1999] 2 SCR 534 to support vicarious liability was deterrence of future harm. ...

Fifthly, Vabu superintended the couriers' finances: Vabu produced pay summaries and couriers were required to dispute errors by 6.00 pm Friday of the same week. "Unjustified or unsubstantiated" claims

Hollis v Vabu cont.

for additional charges, such as due to waiting time, wrong address or excess weight, could result in total deduction of that particular job payment. There was no scope for the couriers to bargain for the rate of their remuneration. Evidence in chief was given by Vabu's fleet administrator that the rate of remuneration to the bicycle couriers had remained unchanged between 1994 and 1998. Vabu was authorised to [44] hold for six weeks the last week's pay of a courier against any overcharges, unpaid cash jobs or outstanding insurance claims. Final cheques would not be processed until all of Vabu's property had been returned. Failure to return Vabu's equipment, including the uniforms, or the return of damaged equipment or unwashed uniforms resulted in replacement or washing costs being deducted from this amount. Vabu undertook the provision of insurance for the couriers and deducted the amounts from their wages and, as discussed above, passed on an excess to all bicycle couriers and did not pay medical or hospital costs. The method of payment, per delivery and not per time period engaged, is a natural means to remunerate employees whose sole duty is to perform deliveries, not least for ease of calculation and to provide an incentive more efficiently to make deliveries.

Moreover, Vabu stipulated in Document 590 that "[n]o annual leave will be considered for the period November to Christmas Eve, nor for the week prior to Easter. Leave requests will be considered in accordance with other applications and should be submitted to the manager in writing at least 14 days prior." This suggests that their engagement by Vabu left the couriers with limited scope for the pursuit of any real business enterprise on their own account.

Sixthly, the situation in respect of tools and equipment also favours, if anything, a finding that the bicycle couriers were employees. Apart from providing bicycles and being responsible for the cost of repairs, couriers were required to bear the cost of replacing or repairing any equipment of Vabu that was lost or damaged, including radios and uniforms. Although a more beneficent employer might have provided bicycles for its employees and undertaken the cost of their repairs, there is nothing contrary to a relationship of employment in the fact that employees were here required to do so. This is all the more so because the capital outlay was relatively small and because bicycles are not tools that are inherently capable of use only for courier work but provide a means of personal transport or even a means of recreation out of work time. The fact that the couriers were responsible for their own bicycles reflects only that they were in a situation of employment more favourable than not to the employer; it does not indicate the existence of a relationship of independent contractor and principal.

Finally, and as a corollary to the second point mentioned above, this is not a case where there was only the right to exercise control in incidental or collateral matters. Rather, there was considerable scope for the actual exercise of control. Vabu's whole business consisted of the delivery of documents and parcels by means of couriers. Vabu retained control of the allocation and direction of the [45] various deliveries. The couriers had little latitude. Their work was allocated by Vabu's fleet controller. They were to deliver goods in the manner in which Vabu directed. In this way, Vabu's business involved the marshalling and direction of the labour of the couriers, whose efforts comprised the very essence of the public manifestation of Vabu's business. It was not the case that the couriers supplemented or performed part of the work undertaken by Vabu or aided from time to time; rather, as the two documents relating to work practices suggest, to its customers they *were* Vabu and effectively performed all of Vabu's operations in the outside world. It would be unrealistic to describe the couriers other than as employees ... [46]

Conclusion

The relationship between Vabu and the bicycle courier who struck down Mr Hollis was that of employer and employee. Vabu thus was vicariously liable for the consequences of the courier's negligent performance of his work.

It is unnecessary in the light of the above to address the submissions as to non-delegability of the duty of care.

Hollis v Vabu cont.

The appeal should be allowed with costs. ...

McHUGH J: 47 In my opinion, Vabu is liable because the courier was an agent of Vabu – but not an independent contractor – and was acting as Vabu's representative in carrying out a contractual obligation of Vabu.

I am not in favour of extending the classical tests or their application to make the couriers employees of Vabu. To do so would be likely to unsettle many established business arrangements and have far-reaching consequences for industrial relations, for workers' compensation law, for working conditions, for the obligations of employers to make superannuation contributions and group tax deductions and for the payment of annual and long service leave and taxes such as payroll tax. ... 51

In *Colonial Mutual Life Assurance Society Ltd v Producers and Citizens Co-operative Assurance Co of Australia Ltd* (1931) 46 CLR 41 ("*CML*"), this Court held that a principal may be liable for the careless conduct of an agent causing damage to a third party even if the agent is not an employee. The principal will be liable when the conduct occurs while the agent is carrying out a task for the benefit of the principal as his or her representative. In my view, it is the agency principle recognised by this Court in *CML* that provides the appropriate solution for this important case. Applying that principle, the courier was an agent for whose negligence Vabu was responsible. ... 53

Changing social conditions and new work practices

The practice of employers contracting out work that, in former times was done by their employees is nowadays a common practice. ... 54 If the law of vicarious liability is to remain relevant in the contemporary world, it needs to be developed and applied in a way that will accommodate the changing nature of employment relationships. But any such developments or applications must be done consistently with the principles that have shaped the development of vicarious liability and the rationales of those principles. They should also be done in a way that has the least impact on the settled expectations of employers and those with whom they contract.

[McHugh J held that Vabu was liable because the courier acted as its agent. This promoted policies of effective compensation, fairness and deterrence.]

[15.50] **Notes&Questions**

1. Sometimes there is uncertainty about who is the relevant employer at the time the tortious conduct was committed. For example, owners of plant or equipment, such as bulldozers or cranes, may be reluctant to hire out equipment without a qualified operator. In these circumstances, it is the person hiring the equipment that may give directions as to what is to be done. Does this make the hirer the temporary employer pro hac vice ("for the time being") and vicariously liable for negligent operation of the equipment? Mostly not in the case of skilled employees, because the plant owner will usually retain the right to control how the equipment is to be used, see *Mersey Docks & Harbour Board v Coggins and Griffith (Liverpool) Ltd* [1947] AC 1.

2. The judgment of McHugh J in *Vabu* suggests that employment is too narrow a basis for the imposition of vicarious liability. The traditional full-time employment relationship with one employer over an extended period has given way to high levels of casual and part-time employment, significant levels of outsourcing of work and the creation of independent contractor relationships instead of employment relationships. It is

common to obtain labour and expertise through a third party or agency.

One such arrangement occurs with labour-only hire contracts. The workforce is employed by an agency and hired out for periods of time as needed. This provides the hirer with flexibility and frees up the hirer from the normal run of employment administration such as long service, holiday and other leave, superannuation and issues relating to termination and redundancy. If the hirer can direct the worker, not only what is to be done but how it is to be done, does this make the business hiring the labour an employer for purposes of vicarious liability? Who should bear the ultimate responsibility? Is loss distribution and accident reduction better served by making the agency vicariously liable rather then the hirer? Where the worker is an employee, the authorities show a preference for finding that the agency is the employer rather than the client so that the agency is vicariously liable rather than the hirer, see as an example, *Deutz Australia Pty Ltd v Skilled Engineering Ltd* [2001] VSC 194 (forklift driver). For critical comment on changing employment practices, see A Stewart, "Redefining Employment? Meeting the Challenge of Contract and Agency Labour" (2002) 15 AJLL 10.

Liability for agents and independent contractors

[15.55] In *Sweeney v Boylan Nominees* (2006) 226 CLR 161 (extracted below), the High Court confirms the general principle that a principal is not vicariously liable for the wrongdoing of an independent contractor. The Court rejects attempts to extend vicarious liability for the wrongful conduct of persons described loosely as "agents" who act for a principal's benefit or advantage. For the purposes of vicarious liability, "agency" is given a very restricted meaning consistent with the general principles of vicarious liability stated by the famous jurist Pollock: where a principal conducts a business and for that purpose engages staff, the principal is liable for the way in which the principal's business is conducted. There must be a close connection between the principal's business and the contractor's conduct. The solicitation of insurance proposals by an insurance agent in *Colonial Mutual Life Assurance Society Ltd v Producers and Citizens Co-operative Assurance Co of Australia Ltd* (1931) 46 CLR 41 is cited as a clear example of this liability. *Sweeney v Boylan Nominees* (2006) 226 CLR 161 is yet another illustration of the High Court's retreat from the expansion of liability despite the clear advantages and the plaintiff's expectation of being able to sue the equipment owner for its defective condition.

Sweeney v Boylan Nominees

[15.60] *Sweeney v Boylan Nominees Pty Ltd* (2006) 226 CLR 161 High Court of Australia

(footnotes omitted)

[The plaintiff (appellant) went to a service station to buy some milk. When she opened the refrigerator door it fell off and injured her when it hit her on the head. She sued the owner of the refrigeration equipment (Boylan Nominees) who was obliged to maintain and service the refrigerator. The key issue was the liability of Boylan Nominees (the respondent) for the negligence of a refrigeration mechanic engaged by it to undertake repairs. Neither the mechanic nor his company had been sued by the plaintiff. In the District Court the trial judge found that the mechanic was Boylan's employee and was negligent and the company vicariously liable. On appeal to the Court of Appeal it was found that the mechanic was not an employee and the respondent not vicariously liable. On appeal to the High Court the respondent was held not to be liable.]

Sweeney v Boylan Nominees cont.

GLEESON CJ, GUMMOW, HAYNE, HEYDON, CRENNAN JJ: [Their Honours first noted that there was no satisfactory rationale for vicarious liability and continued:] 167 ...

Nonetheless, as the decisions in *Scott*, *Hollis* and *Lepore* show, there are some basic propositions that can be identified as central to this body of law. For present purposes, there are two to which it will be necessary to give principal attention. First, there is the distinction between employees (for whose conduct the employer will generally be vicariously liable) and independent contractors (for whose conduct the person engaging the contractor will generally not be vicariously liable). Secondly, there is the importance which is attached to the course of employment. ...

Whatever may be the justification for the doctrine, it is necessary always to recall that much more often than not, questions of vicarious liability fall to be considered in a context where one person has engaged another (for whose conduct the first is said to be vicariously liable) to do something that is of advantage to, and for the purposes of, that first person. Yet it is clear that the bare fact that the second person's actions were intended to benefit the first or were undertaken to advance some purpose of the first person does not suffice to demonstrate that the first is vicariously liable for the conduct of the second. The whole of the law that has developed on the distinction between employees and independent contractors denies that benefit or advantage to the one will suffice to establish vicarious liability for the conduct of the second. But there is an important, albeit distracting, consequence that follows from the observation that the first person seeks to gain benefit or advantage from engaging the second to perform a task. It is that the relationship is one which invites the application of terms like "representative", "delegate" or "agent". The use of those or other similar expressions must not be permitted to obscure the need to examine what exactly are the relationships between the various actors.

168 In the present case, the appellant's contention that the respondent was vicariously liable for the negligence of the mechanic fastened upon a number of statements found in the reasons for judgment of Dixon J in *Colonial Mutual Life Assurance Society Ltd v Producers and Citizens Co-operative Assurance Co of Australia Ltd* (1931) 46 CLR 41. ... 169

In *Colonial Mutual Life* the person, for whose statements the appellant was sought to be made vicariously liable, had been engaged by the appellant to canvass for proposals for life insurance. The statements which it was alleged that he made, and which were slanderous of the respondent company, had been uttered in the course of his attempting to induce persons to make proposals for life insurance by the appellant. He was not a servant of the appellant company. Yet it was held that the appellant was vicariously liable for his statements because he made them in acting as the company's agent.

In soliciting proposals, the person who made the slanderous statements was acting in right of the company and with its authority. He had express authority to canvass for the making of contractual offers to his principal. Although he had no authority from his principal to accept any offers that were made, "the Company in confiding to his judgment, within the limits of relevance and of reasonableness, the choice of inducements and arguments, authorized him on its behalf to address to prospective proponents such observations as appeared to him appropriate". "[T]he very service to be performed consist[ed] in standing in [the principal's] place and assuming to act in [its] right and not in an independent capacity" (emphasis added) in a transaction with others. He acted in right of the principal, and not in an independent capacity, because he acted in execution of his authority to canvass for offers to contract with his principal.

In *Colonial Mutual Life*, Dixon J said that the rule imposing liability upon a master for the wrongs of a servant committed in the course of employment was (then) commonly regarded as part of the law of agency. And ...Dixon J emphasised the difficulties that attend the use of the word "agent". Rather than being used with a single and fixed meaning...words like "agent", "representative", "for", "on behalf

Sweeney v Boylan Nominees cont.

of", are often used in this context as statements of conclusion that mark the limits to which vicarious liability is extended. But when used in that way, they are statements of conclusion that do not necessarily proceed from an articulated underlying principle that identifies why there should be vicarious liability in one case but not another.

170 ... [T]he conclusion reached in *Colonial Mutual Life* fits entirely within the explanation of vicarious liability identified by Pollock and reflected in the subsequent decisions of this Court culminating in *Scott, Hollis* and *Lepore.*

Colonial Mutual Life establishes that if an independent contractor is engaged to solicit the bringing about of legal relations between the principal who engages the contractor and third parties, the principal will be held liable for slanders uttered to persuade the third party to make an agreement with the principal. It is a conclusion that depends directly upon the identification of the independent contractor as the principal's agent (properly so called) and the recognition that the conduct of which complaint is made was conduct undertaken in the course of, and for the purpose of, executing that agency.

Pollock identified the element common to cases of vicarious liability as being that "a man has for his own convenience brought about or maintained some state of things which in the ordinary course of nature 171 may work mischief to his neighbours". Pollock further concluded that where an employer conducted a business, and for that purpose employed staff, the employer brought about a state of things in which, if care was not taken, mischief would be done. But the liability to be imposed on the employer was liability for the way in which the business (that is, the employer's business) was conducted. Conduct of the business and the employee's actions in the course of employment in that business were the only state of things which the employer created and for which the employer would be responsible. Thus for Pollock, course of employment was not a limitation or an otherwise more general liability of the employer; it was a necessary element of the definition of the extent of liability.

The conclusion reached in *Colonial Mutual Life* ... stands wholly within the bounds of the explanations proffered by Pollock for the liability of a master for the tortious acts of a servant. It stands within those bounds because of the closeness of the connection between the principal's business and the conduct of the independent contractor for which it is sought to make the principal liable. The relevant connection is established by the combination of the engagement of the contractor as the agent of the principal to bring about legal relations between the principal and third parties, and the slander being uttered in the course of attempting to induce a third party to enter legal relations with the principal.

Now it may also well be that, as pointed out in *Lepore,* cases of the deliberate misdoings of a servant, like *Lloyd v Grace, Smith & Co* [1912] AC 716, are also to be understood as informed by notions of course of employment. It is not necessary to explore that question further here, beyond noting that, as was also pointed out in *Lepore,* such cases may yield to simpler analysis revealing the employer's direct rather than vicarious liability for what has occurred.

But the wider proposition that underpinned the argument of the appellant in this case, that if A "represents" B, B is vicariously liable for the conduct of A, is a proposition of such generality that it goes well beyond the bounds set by notions of control (with old, and now imperfect analogies of servitude) or set by notions of course of employment.

These bounds should not now be redrawn in the manner asserted by the appellant. Hitherto the distinction between independent contractors and employees has been critical to the definition of the ambit of 172 vicarious liability. The view, sometimes expressed, that the distinction should be abandoned in favour of a wider principle, has not commanded the assent of a majority of this Court.

In *Scott,* the majority of the Court rejected the contention that the owner of an aircraft was vicariously liable for the negligence of the pilot of that aircraft if the pilot operated the aircraft with the owner's consent and for a purpose in which the owner had some concern. The argument that "a new species of actor, one who is not an employee, nor an independent contractor, but an 'agent' in a non-technical sense" should be identified as relevant to determining vicarious liability, was rejected.

In *Hollis*, the Court amplified the application of the distinction between independent contractors and employees to take account of differing ways in which some particular enterprises are now conducted. As was said in the joint reasons:

> In general, under contemporary Australian conditions, the conduct by the defendant of an enterprise in which persons are identified as representing that enterprise should carry an obligation to third persons to bear the cost of injury or damage to them which may fairly be said to be characteristic of the conduct of that enterprise.

But neither in *Scott* nor in *Hollis*, nor earlier in *Colonial Mutual Life*, was there established the principle that A is vicariously liable for the conduct of B if B "represents" A (in the sense of B acting for the benefit or advantage of A). On the contrary, *Scott* rejected contentions that, at their roots, were no different from those advanced in this case under the rubric of "representation" rather than, as in *Scott*, under the rubric "agency". As was said in *Scott* of the word "agent", to use the word "representative" is to begin but not to end the inquiry. ...

[The judgment then referred to the facts in *Hollis* and held that the mechanic was not an employee and continued:] 173 ...

Whatever may be the logical and doctrinal imperfections and difficulties in the origins of the law relating to vicarious liability, the two central conceptions of distinguishing between independent contractors and employees and attaching determinative significance to course of employment are now too deeply rooted to be pulled out. And without discarding at least the first and perhaps even the second, the appellant's claim against the respondent must fail. The mechanic was an independent contractor. He did what he did for the benefit of the respondent and in attempted discharge of its contractual obligations. But he did what he did not as an employee of the respondent but as a principal pursuing his own business or as an employee of his own company pursuing its business.

The conclusion that the mechanic was an independent contractor is determinative of the issue that arises in the appeal. The appeal must be dismissed with costs.

[The dissenting judgment of Kirby J has been omitted. His honour held that the respondent was vicariously liable for the conduct of its agent. His honour also remarked on the failure by the defendant to disclose until trial that the contractor was not an employee as "the vestigial relics of ambush trial".]

[15.65] In addition to the circumstances set out in *Sweeney* (above), a defendant can be liable for the tortious conduct of a person who is not an employee if the defendant is personally (as distinct from vicariously) responsible for that wrongdoing. That is, if the defendant instigates the tortious conduct, authorises (see *AF Textile Printers Pty Ltd v Thalut Nominees Pty Ltd* [2007] VSC 73), ratifies (see *Brockway v Pando* [2000] WASCA 192), or adopts the wrongful conduct, the defendant will be personally responsible. This will also apply between a principal and an agent, for example (*Gaunt v Hille* [2007] FCA 2017). An employer can also be liable for the conduct of another who is not an employee where there is a non-delegable duty, see below [15.115]. Motor vehicle legislation has special provisions relating to personal injury or death arising out of the use of a motor vehicle. The required third party statutory insurance applies to the driver of a motor vehicle even if the driver is unauthorised or a thief, see, for example, *Motor Accidents Compensation Act 1999* (NSW), s 10.

The following section deals with the requirement for vicarious liability that the tortious conduct is "in the course of employment".

In the course of employment

[15.70] An employer is liable only for what might be considered "business risks" related to the enterprise. The tortious conduct must be "in the course of employment". When will the relevant conduct have a sufficiently close connection with the "employment" so as to make the "employer" liable? What role should policy have in making this determination? Will it be sufficient that the enterprise creates a risk that the wrongful conduct might occur? These issues are addressed in the High Court decision in *New South Wales v Lepore* (2003) 212 CLR 511, extracted at [15.100].

Before turning to the cases, it is useful to give a brief outline of the application of the "course of employment" test.

Negligent performance of the employment

[15.75] The High Court's decision in *New South Wales v Lepore* (2003) 212 CLR 511 [15.100] concerned intentional wrongdoing. The Court found Salmond's traditional test for determining whether conduct is within the course of employment unhelpful. Salmond's traditional formulation is that the employer is liable if the conduct is authorised or a "wrongful and unauthorised mode" of doing an authorised act. Although the Salmond test is more easily applied where negligence is involved, the reasoning adopted by the High Court in *Lepore* will influence how courts determine whether an employee's negligence is within the course of employment.

Under the Salmond test, an employer is vicariously liable for the negligent performance of required work even if in breach of workplace rules or directives. In *Limpus v London General Omnibus Co* (1962) 1 H & C 526 the employer was held liable where bus drivers disobeyed the order that they were not to obstruct or race rival buses in order to obtain customers. Even a prohibition from undertaking certain tasks or from performing them in a particular manner will not necessarily take the negligence outside the course of employment especially in a case where the employer benefits from the conduct. In *Rose v Plenty* [1976] 1 WLR 141, milkmen were prohibited from getting children to help deliver the milk. The employer was held liable to a child negligently injured by the milkman during deliveries; having a helper was an unauthorised way of carrying out the job.

If vicarious liability imposes liability for normal business risks, the relevant risks are those related to the particular employment. Where the employee who is employed in a particular capacity independently (or contrary to directions) undertakes work not within that capacity, the employer would not normally be liable. For example, an employer would not be liable for the conduct of a bus ticket collector who drives the bus (*Beard v London General Omnibus Co* [1900] 2 QB 530).The result may well be different if the employer knew that the ticket collectors assisted by turning around the bus whilst waiting for the driver or if there were a sudden emergency in which the driver was incapacitated.

Criminal conduct during the employment

[15.80] The judgments in *New South Wales v Lepore* (2003) 212 CLR 511, concerning the sexual abuse of children by teachers, explore the limits of vicarious liability for an employee's intentional and criminal conduct. An employer should not be liable simply because the employment offers an opportunity for wrongdoing. Nor, according to the majority in *New South Wales v Lepore* (2003) 212 CLR 511, is it sufficient that the employment creates a risk that this wrongdoing may occur. Three judges take a narrow view of vicarious liability. For Gummow and Hayne JJ, the relevant conduct must be either done in the intended performance of the employee's job or "done in the apparent execution of authority actually, or ostensibly, given to the employee by the employer". Excessive chastisement of a student by a teacher on school premises might fit within the first category, but not the second; the sexual abuse of a student would not fit within either category. Callinan J held that intentional criminal misconduct is outside the scope of a teacher's duties. Other judgments leave open the possibility that the employer might be vicariously liable for the teachers' intentional and criminal conduct. Gleeson CJ thought a teacher's responsibilities may involve "an undertaking of personal protection, and a relationship of such power and intimacy, that sexual abuse may properly be regarded as sufficiently connected with their duties to give rise to vicarious liability". Kirby J preferred a broader analysis adopted in English and Canadian decisions. His Honour was of the view that in determining whether there was a sufficient connection with the enterprise, it was relevant that the conduct occurred in school time and on school property. In the case of vulnerable and immature children, the risk might be regarded as inherent in the enterprise such that it would be just and reasonable that the employer should be vicariously liable.

Conduct outside the employment

[15.85] Where the conduct is outside the employment, employees are said to be on a frolic of their own (*Joel v Morison* (1834) 6 Car & P 502, Parke B at 503). This issue frequently arises when an employee on a road trip detours for some private purpose. Despite some earlier contrary authority, this should not be judged too rigidly, employees on long road trips need to make comfort stops, eat lunch and so on (*Harvey v R G O'Dell* [1958] 2 QB 78, contrast *Crook v Derbyshire Stone* [1956] 2 All ER 447). It is clearly a frolic where employees quit work early, fill in time at the café and have an accident on the way back to work to clock out (*Hilton v Thomas Burton (Rhodes) Ltd* [1961] 1 All ER 74).

Independent discretion or statutory authority

[15.90] At common law, an employer is not liable where the employee exercises some independent discretion or authority at common law or under statute, such as a police officer exercising an independent discretion to effect an arrest (*Enever v R* (1906) 4 CLR 97). Similarly, in *Oceanic Crest Shipping Co v Pilbara Harbour Services Pty Ltd* (1986) 160 CLR 626, an employer was held not liable for the negligence of its employee, a ship's pilot, as the employee's negligence had arisen in the exercise of an independent function pursuant to an appointment by the Governor to provide compulsory pilotage services. Nor would the Commonwealth be vicariously liable for the conduct of its Directors of Native Affairs and Welfare in the exercise of an independent statutory discretion for the removal of Aboriginal children (*Cubillo v Commonwealth* (2000) 103 FCR 1 and on appeal (2001) 112 FCR 455 at [1116-1123] (FCR)). In New South Wales, the general principle has been statutorily modified and in some other jurisdictions modified in relation to police officers. See the *Law Reform (Vicarious Liability) Act 1983* (NSW) and note the special provisions for torts committed by police officers: *State of NSW v Eade* [2006] NSWSC 84; *New South Wales v Ibbett* (2006) 229

CLR 638; *Crown Proceedings Act 1958* (Vic), s 23(1)(b); *Police Service Administration Act 1990* (Qld), s 10.5; *Police Regulation Act 1898* (Tas), s 52.

Employee's liability

[15.95] The vicarious liability of the employer does not absolve the employee from liability. At common law, both employer and employee are liable as concurrent (joint) tortfeasors. The teachers in *New South Wales v Lepore* (2003) 212 CLR 511 were personally liable for the assaults (batteries) and although sued together with the employer, they took no active part in the proceedings. It is rare, but not unknown, for a plaintiff to seek payment of damages from an employee. For example, a negligent employee remained liable after the claim against the employer was settled for less than the full amount of damages: *Baxter v Obacelo Pty Ltd* (2001) 205 CLR 635.

The most usual course is for the plaintiff to look to the employer for payment of damages. At common law, a blameless employer could, in theory, recover these damages from the employee. Legislative amendments have been made to this rule in a number of States. In those States, and in the absence of serious and wilful misconduct, the employer (or the employer's insurer) is not permitted to recover the damages paid from the employee, see [15.175]. However, the teachers in *Lepore* would not have been protected because their actions amounted to serious and wilful misconduct.

New South Wales v Lepore

[15.100] *New South Wales v Lepore; Samin v Queensland; Rich v Queensland* (2003) 212 CLR 511 High Court of Australia

(footnotes partially omitted)

[Three cases came on appeal to the High Court. Two appeals from the Queensland Court of Appeal, *Samin* and *Rich*, involved sexual assaults on school children by teachers during school hours on school premises. The Queensland Court of Appeal held that the State of Queensland, was not liable for breach of a non-delegable duty of care towards the children. The New South Wales Court of Appeal came to the opposite conclusion in *Lepore*, where a seven-year-old child was assaulted in a school storeroom. It was accepted in all three cases, that there had been no negligence by the School authorities. This case extract deals with vicarious liability, see [15.130] for a further extract on non-delegable duties.]

GLEESON CJ: 522 If a teacher employed by a school authority sexually abuses a pupil, is the school authority liable in damages to the pupil? ...

One potentially important matter is fault on the part of the school authority. The legal responsibilities of such an authority include a duty to take reasonable care for the safety of pupils. There may be cases in which sexual abuse is related to a failure to take such care. A school authority may have been negligent in employing a particular person, or in failing to make adequate arrangements for supervision of staff, or in failing to respond appropriately to complaints of previous misconduct, or in some other respect that can be identified as a cause of the harm to the pupil. The relationship between school authority and pupil is one of the exceptional relationships which give rise to a duty in one party to take reasonable care to protect the other from the wrongful behaviour of third parties even if such behaviour is criminal. Breach of that duty, and consequent harm, will result in liability for damages for negligence.

We are not presently concerned with such a case. Our concern is with the more difficult problem of liability in the absence of such fault. ... 523 ...

New South Wales v Lepore cont.

The plaintiffs' claims

In the first matter, the first respondent sued the appellant (the State of New South Wales) and the second respondent (the teacher) in the District Court of New South Wales. The events complained of occurred in 1978, when the first respondent, then aged seven, was attending a State primary school. He alleged that he was assaulted by the second respondent. The assaults were said to have occurred in the context of supposed misbehaviour by the first respondent, 524 and the imposition of corporal punishment for such misbehaviour. On a number of occasions, the first respondent, after being accused of misbehaviour, was sent to a storeroom, told to remove his clothing, smacked, and then touched indecently. On some occasions, other boys would be present, also ostensibly being punished.

Neither at first instance, nor in the Court of Appeal, was the case against the appellant put on the basis of vicarious liability. There may have been an arguable case based on vicarious liability, even on a narrow view of the potential scope of such liability. Chastisement of a pupil is within the course of a teacher's employment (*Ryan v Fildes* [1938] 3 All ER 517). On the account given by the first respondent, the inappropriate conduct seems to have taken place in the context of punishment for misbehaviour. However, no such argument was advanced, and the factual findings necessary for the purpose of considering such an argument were not made. ...

The second and third matters both arose out of the conduct of a teacher (the third respondent) at a one-teacher State primary school in rural Queensland. In each case, the appellant was a young girl attending the school. At the relevant times (between 1963 and 1965) the appellants were aged between seven and ten. The third respondent has taken no part in the proceedings. He was sentenced to a lengthy term of imprisonment. Each appellant alleged serious acts of sexual assault by the third respondent. Those acts, as particularised in the Statement of Claim, occurred, at school, during school hours, and in a classroom or adjoining rooms. Because no evidence has been taken, the full circumstances of the alleged assaults are not apparent. For example, it is not clear whether the third respondent's behaviour allegedly occurred in front of other pupils, or how he came to be in intimate physical contact with the appellants. ...

[The section of the judgment dealing with non-delegable duties is extracted at [15.130].] ... 535 ...

Vicarious liability

An employer is vicariously liable for a tort committed by an employee in the course of his or her employment. The limiting or controlling concept, course of employment, is sometimes referred to as scope of employment. Its aspects are functional, as well as geographical and temporal. Not everything that an employee does at work, or during working hours, is sufficiently connected with the duties and responsibilities of the employee to be regarded as within the scope of the employment. And the fact that wrongdoing occurs away from the workplace, or outside normal working hours, is not conclusive against liability.

It is clear that if the wrongful act of an employee has been authorised by the employer, the employer will be liable. The difficulty relates to unauthorised acts. The best known formulation of the test to be applied is that in Salmond, *Law of Torts* in the first edition in 1907, and in later editions: an employer is liable even for unauthorised acts if they are so connected with authorised acts that they may be regarded as modes – although improper modes – of doing them, but the employer is not responsible if the unauthorised and wrongful act is not so connected with the authorised act as to be a mode of doing it, but is an independent act. ... 536 ...

A major development in the law occurred with the decision of the House of Lords in 1912 in *Lloyd v Grace, Smith & Co* [1912] AC 716. Until then, vicarious liability of an employer for the unauthorised fraud of an employee had been confined to conduct that was engaged in for the benefit of the

New South Wales v Lepore cont.

employer. In that case, the managing clerk of a firm of solicitors defrauded a client of the firm. His employer was held liable to the client. The claim was based both on contract and tort. It was dealt with in that manner. ... 537 ...

If the solicitors' clerk had assaulted the client, or stolen money from her purse, a different result would have followed. In neither of those cases would the clerk have been undertaking duties imposed on him by the nature of his employer's business and the nature of his employment. His act would have been an "independent" act, of which no more could be said than that the employment created the opportunity for the wrongdoing. In *Deatons Pty Ltd v Flew* (1949) 79 CLR 370 at 381, Dixon J explained the decision as concerning "one of those wrongful acts done for the servant's own benefit for which the master is liable when they are acts to which the ostensible performance of his master's work gives occasion or which are committed under cover of the authority the servant is held out as possessing or of the position in which he is placed as a representative of his master". It is the nature of that which the employee is employed to do on behalf of the employer that determines whether the wrongdoing is within the scope of the employment.

An act of negligence may be easy to characterise as an unauthorised mode of performing an authorised act. An act of intentional, criminal wrongdoing, solely for the benefit of the employee, may be easy to characterise as an independent act; but it is not necessarily so, and there are many examples of cases where such conduct has been found to be in the course of employment ... 538 ...

The leading Australian authority on the subject of vicarious responsibility for an assault by an employee is *Deatons Pty Ltd v Flew* (1949) 79 CLR 370. ... The plaintiff sued a hotel barmaid and her employer in trespass. The barmaid had thrown the contents of a glass of beer, and then the glass itself, into his face. He lost an eye. There was conflicting evidence as to what led up to the incident. The plaintiff's version was that he simply asked to speak to the publican, and the next thing he remembered was that he woke up in the eye hospital. There was other evidence that he was drunk and aggressive, and that he had quarrelled with the barmaid, striking her and calling her names. The jury found against both defendants. ... 539 ...

The employer ... appealed to this Court, contending, successfully, that it was entitled ... to a verdict by direction. The Court considered that, on either version of the facts, the employer was not vicariously liable for the trespass: on the plaintiff's version what the barmaid did was a gratuitous, unprovoked act; the only alternative view open was that it was an act of personal retribution. Either way, it was not incidental to the work she was employed to do. It was emphasised that it was not the duty of the barmaid to keep order in the bar. There were other people to do that. Her job was merely to serve drinks. Her conduct was not an excessive method of maintaining order. It was "a spontaneous act of retributive justice".

... [T]he outcome turned upon application of the Salmond test. The test serves well in many cases, but it has its limitations. As has frequently been observed, the answer to a question whether certain conduct is an improper mode of performing an authorised act may depend upon the level of generality at which the authorised act is identified. If, on the facts, it had been possible to treat maintaining order in the bar as one of the barmaid's responsibilities, and if, on the facts, it had been open to regard her conduct as an inappropriate response to disorder, then the jury could properly have held the employer liable in trespass. However, the barmaid's only responsibility was to serve drinks, and throwing a glass of beer at a customer could not be regarded as an improper method of doing that. The level of generality at which it is proper to describe the nature of an employee's duties ought not to be pitched so high as to pre-empt the issue. The fact that an employer owes a common law duty of care to an injured person does not mean that it is appropriate to describe the employment duties of all the employees as including taking care of the person. (at 382 per Dixon J).

When the specific responsibilities of an employer relate in some way to the protection of person or property, and an intentional wrongful act causes harm to person or property, then the specific

New South Wales v Lepore cont.

responsibilities of a particular employee may require close examination 540. The defendants in *Morris v C W Martin & Sons Ltd* [1966] 1 QB 716 were sub-bailees for reward of the article [a fur stole] stolen by their employee, and had a duty to protect it from theft. The employee was the person in charge of the article. The defendants in *Lloyd v Grace, Smith & Co* [1912] AC 716 were fiduciaries. The clerk was the person who was managing the relevant transaction. Although the hotel proprietor in *Deatons Pty Ltd v Flew* (1949) 79 CLR 370 owed a duty of care to customers at its premises, the barmaid's responsibilities were not protective. Stealing a fur stole is not an improper method of cleaning it, but as the employer was a bailee, with custodial responsibility, and it put the goods in charge of a particular employee, then it was proper to regard that responsibility as devolving upon the employee. The theft was so connected with the custodial responsibilities of the employee as to be regarded as in the course of employment; not because it was in furtherance of the employee's responsibilities, but because the nature of his responsibilities extended to custody of the fur as well as cleaning it.

It is the element of protection involved in the relationship between school authority and pupil that has given rise to difficulty in defining the circumstances in which an assault by a teacher upon a pupil will result in vicarious liability on the part of a school authority. The problem is complicated by the variety of circumstances in which pupil and teacher may have contact, the differing responsibilities of teachers, and the differing relationships that may exist between a teacher and a pupil. Some teachers may be employed simply to teach; and their level of responsibility for anything other than the educational needs of pupils may be relatively low. Others may be charged with responsibilities that involve them in intimate contact with children, and require concern for personal welfare and development. The ages of school children range from infancy to early adulthood. Although attendance at school is compulsory for children between certain ages, many secondary school students remain at school for several years after it has ceased to be obligatory.

Where acts of physical violence are concerned, the nature and seriousness of the criminal act may be relevant to a judgment as to whether it is to be regarded as a personal, independent act of the perpetrator, or whether it is within the scope of employment. A security guard at business premises who removes a person with unnecessary force may be acting in the course of employment. On the other hand, as Jordan CJ pointed out in *Deatons Pty Ltd v Flew* (1949) 79 CLR 370, extreme and unnecessary violence, perhaps combined with other factors, such as personal animosity towards the victim, might lead to a conclusion that what is involved is an act of purely personal vindictiveness. Sexual abuse, which is so obviously inconsistent with the responsibilities of anyone involved with the instruction and care of children, in former times would readily have been regarded as conduct of a personal and independent nature, unlikely ever to be treated as within the course of employment. Yet such conduct might take different forms. An opportunistic act of serious and 541 random violence might be different, in terms of its connection with employment, from improper touching by a person whose duties involve intimate contact with another. In recent years, in most common law jurisdictions, courts have had to deal with a variety of situations involving sexual abuse by employees.

In 1999, the Supreme Court of Canada dealt consecutively with two such cases. The judgments were handed down on the same day. The first case was *Bazley v Curry* [1999] 2 SCR 534. A non-profit organization, which operated residential care facilities for the treatment of emotionally troubled children, required its employees to perform parental duties, ranging from general supervision to intimate functions like bathing and tucking in at bedtime. It employed a man who was a paedophile. He sexually abused a child. The question was whether the organization was vicariously liable for his wrongdoing. That question was answered in the affirmative.

McLachlin J, who delivered the judgment of the Court, examined the considerations of policy underlying the concept of vicarious liability, and said (at 557):

> Underlying the cases holding employers vicariously liable for the unauthorized acts of employees is the idea that employers may justly be held liable where the act falls within the

New South Wales v Lepore cont.

> ambit of the risk that the employer's enterprise creates or exacerbates. Similarly, the policy purposes underlying the imposition of vicarious liability on employers are served only where the wrong is so connected with the employment that it can be said that the employer has introduced the risk of the wrong (and is thereby fairly and usefully charged with its management and minimization). The question in each case is whether there is a connection or nexus between the employment enterprise and that wrong that justifies imposition of vicarious liability on the employer for the wrong, in terms of fair allocation of the consequences of the risk and/or deterrence.

Later, McLachlin J elaborated her views on the concept of sufficiency of connection, saying (at 559):

> The fundamental question is whether the wrongful act is *sufficiently related* to conduct authorized by the employer to justify the imposition of vicarious liability. Vicarious liability is generally appropriate where there is a significant connection between the *creation or enhancement of a risk* and the wrong that accrues therefrom, even if unrelated to the employer's desires.

(emphasis in original)

Factors to be taken into account, relevant to sexual abuse, were said 542 to include the opportunity for abuse afforded to the employee, relationships of power and intimacy, and the vulnerability of potential victims. The focus of the test for vicarious liability for an employee's sexual abuse was said to be "whether the employer's enterprise and empowerment of the employee materially increased the risk of the sexual assault and hence the harm".

Jacobi v Griffiths [1999] 2 SCR 570, which was decided on the same day as *Bazley*, concerned the vicarious liability of a non-profit organization, which operated a recreational club for children, for sexual assaults upon two children by one of the club's employees. The employee was a program director, whose job was to organize after-school recreational activities. He cultivated an intimate association with the two victims, and assaulted them at his home. It was held that the club was not liable. ...

Dealing with the consideration that a sexual assault is almost never conduct that could advance the purposes of the employer's enterprise, Binnie J [speaking for the majority] observed that, whilst that was not conclusive, it could not be dismissed as insignificant. It was a factor relevant to the sufficiency of the connection between the criminal acts and the employment. He then examined cases concerning the nature of an employer's enterprise, and inherent and foreseeable risks, pointing out that a combination of power and intimacy can create a strong connection between the enterprise and sexual assault ...

Turning to considerations of policy, Binnie J said (at 610-617) that *Bazley* proceeded upon the theory of "enterprise risk" as the rationale of vicarious liability, the employer being responsible because "it introduced the seeds of the potential problem into the community, or aggravated the risks that were already there, but only if its enterprise *materially* increased the risk of the harm that happened" (emphasis in original). *Bazley* was distinguished as a case where the 543 sexual abuse occurred in a special environment that involved intimate private control, and quasi-parental relationship and power. In *Jacobi*, on the other hand, the club offered group recreational activities in the presence of volunteers and other members. Those activities were not of such a kind as to create a relationship of power and intimacy; they merely provided the offender with an opportunity to meet children. The children were free to come and go as they pleased; and they returned to their mother at night. There was no close connection between the employee's duties and his wrongful acts. ...

The concept of enterprise risk, and material increase of risk, has been influential in the North American cases. As a test for determining whether conduct is in the course of employment, as distinct from an explanation of the willingness of the law to impose vicarious liability, it has not been taken up in Australia, or, it appears, the United Kingdom. However, in Australia, and in the United Kingdom, as in Canada and the United States, the sufficiency of the connection 544 between employment and wrongdoing to warrant vicarious responsibility is examined by reference to the course or scope of employment. In practice, in most cases, the considerations that would justify a conclusion as to whether an enterprise materially increases the risk of an employee's offending would also bear upon an examination of the nature of the employee's responsibilities, which are regarded as central in Australia. In *Deatons Pty Ltd v Flew* (1949) 79 CLR 370, for example, the fact that it was no part of the barmaid's responsibilities to keep order in the bar was important. If that had been part of her duties, then presumably there would have been an increased risk that any violent propensities on her part could result in harm to customers. In argument in the present cases, the Solicitor-General for Queensland pointed out that providing schools for children, and making attendance compulsory, does not increase the risk that they will be sexually abused; it probably reduces it. Much would depend on what they might otherwise be doing. That, however, is not the comparison that the Supreme Court of Canada was making. Attention was directed to the nature of the services being provided to the victims, and to whether those services were of a kind that increased the danger of abuse from an employee with criminal propensities. …

It cannot be said that the risk of sexual abuse ought to be regarded as an incident of the conduct of most schools, or that the ordinary responsibilities of teachers are such that sexual assaults on pupils would normally be regarded as conduct (albeit serious misconduct) within the scope of employment. However, there are some circumstances in which teachers, or persons associated with school children, have responsibilities of a kind that involve an undertaking of personal protection, and a relationship of such power and intimacy, that sexual abuse may properly be regarded as sufficiently connected with their duties to give rise to vicarious liability in their employers.

A recent decision of the House of Lords, *Lister v Hesley Hall Ltd* [2002] 1 AC 215 concerned a school, operated as a commercial enterprise, mainly for children with emotional and behavioural difficulties. Boarding facilities were provided for some of the pupils. A warden was in charge of the boarding annex. He and his wife, for most of the time, were in sole charge. The annex was intended to be a home, not a mere extension of the school environment, and the warden had many of the responsibilities of a parent. He sexually abused some of the pupils. The question was whether his employer was vicariously liable for his assaults. The House of Lords answered that question in the affirmative. … 546 …

I do not accept that the decisions in *Bazley*, *Jacobi*, and *Lister* suggest that, in Canada and England, in most cases where a teacher has sexually abused a pupil, the wrong will be found to have occurred within the scope of the teacher's employment. However, they demonstrate that, in those jurisdictions, as in Australia, one cannot dismiss the possibility of a school authority's vicarious liability for sexual abuse merely by pointing out that it constitutes serious misconduct on the part of a teacher.

It is necessary now to turn to the cases before the Court. …547 …

The case of Lepore

The fact-finding at the first hearing was so deficient that it is not possible to form a clear view as to the strength of such a case. However, the maintenance of discipline is clearly within the employment responsibilities of the teacher, and much, perhaps all, of the alleged misconduct appears to have taken place in the context of administering punishment for supposed misbehaviour. It may be possible that some or all of it could properly be regarded as excessive chastisement, for which a school authority would be vicariously liable. The relatively minor criminal charges laid against the teacher, and the modest penalties imposed, may be consistent with this view of the matter. Whether excessive or inappropriate chastisement results from the sadistic tendency of a teacher, or a desire for sexual gratification, or both, it is conduct in the course of employment, for which a school authority is vicariously liable. If, on the other hand, some or all of the conduct of the teacher was found to be so

New South Wales v Lepore cont.

different from anything that could be regarded as punishment that it could not properly be seen as other than merely sexually predatory behaviour, then, in relation to such conduct, the plaintiff would have no case based on vicarious liability. There appears to have been nothing about the duties or responsibilities of the teacher that involved him in a relationship with his pupils of such a kind as would justify a conclusion that such activity was in the course of his employment.

The proceedings at first instance comprehensively miscarried. There should be a new trial on all issues although, as will appear from the above, the argument based on non-delegable duty should no longer be treated as open, and the only potential basis for a case of vicarious liability depends upon finding that the relevant conduct amounted to excessive or inappropriate chastisement. ... 548 ...

The cases of Samin and Rich

The Court of Appeal of Queensland was correct to reject the only case advanced in argument before it, which was a case of strict and absolute liability based on non-delegable duty.

However, the plaintiffs now seek also to make out a case of vicarious liability. Unless such a case is unarguable, then they should have an opportunity to do so. The Court of Appeal gave them unqualified leave to deliver a further Statement of Claim.

All that this Court knows about the alleged facts is what appears in the proposed Amended Statement of Claim, which has been summarised earlier. One thing we do not have, that would be of importance to a claim of vicarious liability, is evidence as to the nature of the functions and responsibilities of the teacher at a one-teacher school in rural Queensland in 1965. Nor does the pleading provide a clear picture of the facts and circumstances of the alleged assaults. This is consistent with the approach that has so far been taken by the plaintiffs' lawyers, which has been that it is only necessary to show that the plaintiffs were sexually assaulted, at school, by a teacher. That is not sufficient to make the State vicariously liable. How much more is necessary?

For the reasons given earlier, in order to make the State of Queensland vicariously liable for the teacher's sexual assaults, it would be necessary for the plaintiffs to show that his responsibilities to female pupils of the age of the plaintiffs at the time, placed him in a position of such power and intimacy that his conduct towards them could fairly be regarded as so closely connected with his responsibilities as to be in the course of his employment. That would involve making findings both as to his powers and responsibilities, and as to the nature of his conduct. It would not be enough that his position provided him with the opportunity to gratify his sexual desires, and that he took advantage of that opportunity.

The appeals should be dismissed.

GUMMOW AND HAYNE JJ: 582

[Their Honours referred to the evidence and the judgments leading up to the current appeals and the current unsatisfactory explanations for vicarious liability. Their Honours then referred to Pollock's views concerning vicarious liability and continued.]

The common element which Pollock identified ... was "that a man has for his own convenience brought about or maintained some state of things which in the ordinary course of nature may work mischief to his neighbours". Accordingly, where an employer conducted a business, and for that purpose employed staff, the employer brought about a state of things in which, if care was not taken, mischief would be done. It was, he concluded, right to hold the employer responsible for loss sustained as a result of acts done in the course of that venture. But the liability to be imposed on the employer was liability for the way in which the business was conducted. Accordingly, the employer should be held responsible only for negligence which occurred *in the course of* the servant's employment. Conduct of the business (and the employee's actions in the course of employment in that business) were the only state of things which the employer created and for which the employer should be held responsible. "Course of employment" was, in Pollock's view, not some limitation to an otherwise more general liability of an employer; it was a necessary element of the definition of the extent of the liability.

[Their Honours then referred to the Canadian cases and continued:] … 586 …

As the differing outcomes in *Bazley* and *Jacobi* reveal, the considerations described by McLachlin J in *Bazley* give no bright line test for deciding whether vicarious liability is to be found. The question was approached in the Supreme Court of Canada as one of policy – *should* vicarious liability be found? And no doubt it was the same kind of question which Lord Steyn answered in *Lister* by saying that it was "fair and just" to hold the employer liable.

We would accept that an important element in considering the underlying policy questions in cases such as the present is the nature and extent (the "sufficiency") of the relationship between the employee's authorised conduct and the wrongful act or, as was said in *Dubai Aluminium*, "the closeness of the connection" between the employment relationship and the wrongful act. But adopting either of these tests simply restates, in other words, the problem presented by the concept of "course of employment".

[Their Honours rejected the risk analysis adopted in the Canadian cases. Their Honours then turned to the "course of employment" and intentional torts making reference to cases including *Morris v Martin* (cited above) and Dixon J's judgment in *Deatons v Flew* (1949) 79 CLR 370 on the circumstances where vicarious liability would exist and continued:] … 591 …

The answer given by Dixon J (at 381), in *Deatons*, was that the barmaid's action was not

> a negligent or improper act, due to error or ill judgment, but done in the supposed furtherance of the master's interests. Nor [was] it one of those wrongful acts done for the servant's own benefit for which the master is liable when they are acts to which the ostensible performance of his master's work gives occasion or which are committed under cover of the authority the servant is held out as possessing or of the position in which he is placed as a representative of his master (see *Lloyd v Grace, Smith & Co* [1912] AC 716; *Uxbridge Permanent Benefit Building Society v Pickard* [1939] 2 KB 248).

It may be doubted that what Dixon J said was intended to describe exhaustively all the circumstances which would attract vicarious liability. The statement was made in connection with a claim that an employer was vicariously liable for an *intentional* tort. Nonetheless, there are two elements revealed by what his Honour said that are important for present purposes. First, vicarious liability may exist if the wrongful act is done in *intended pursuit* of the employer's interests or in *intended performance* of the contract of employment. Secondly, 592 vicarious liability may be imposed where the wrongful act is done in *ostensible pursuit* of the employer's business or in the *apparent execution of authority* which the employer holds out the employee as having.

What unites those elements is the identification of what the employee is actually employed to do or is held out by the employer as being employed to do. It is the identification of what the employee was actually employed to do and held out as being employed to do that is central to any inquiry about course of employment. Sometimes light may be shed on that central question by looking at a subsidiary question of who stood to benefit from the employee's conduct. But that inquiry must not be permitted to divert attention from the more basic question we have identified. That is why, in *Lloyd*, Lord Macnaghten (at 732) rejected the proposition that actual or intended benefit to the employer was a necessary condition of vicarious liability. Rather, in *Lloyd*, the determinative finding was, as we have noted earlier, that the fraudulent clerk was authorised by his employer to act for the firm in a class of matters including the conveyancing transactions which Emily Lloyd instructed him to effect. At trial Scrutton J had found that it was within the scope of the clerk's employment to advise clients like

New South Wales v Lepore cont.

Mrs Lloyd who came to the firm to sell property "as to the best legal way to do it, and the necessary documents to execute" ([1911] 2 KB 489 at 494). The fraud was held to have been committed in the course of that employment.

By contrast, in *Deatons*, the barmaid who threw the glass did so in retaliation for a blow and an insult, not in self-defence and not in any way in the supposed furtherance of the employer's interests (whether in keeping order in the bar or otherwise). Nor, unlike *Lloyd*, was it a case where the act done was one to which the ostensible performance of the employer's work gave occasion, or which was committed under cover of the authority the employee was held out as possessing, or of the position in which the employee was placed as representative of the employer.

Many cases in which it is sought to hold an employer vicariously liable for the intentional tort of an employee can be determined by reference to the first of these elements. The act of which complaint is made can be seen to have been done in the intended performance of the task which the employee was employed to perform. Cases of excessive punishment by a teacher may fall within this category. So too will many cases where a store detective wrongfully arrests 593 and detains a person or in that process assaults them. No doubt the examples could be multiplied.

That kind of analysis is not available in cases of fraud. The commission of a fraud can seldom be said to have been in the intended performance of the employee's duties. In those cases, however, it will often be the case that what was done by the employee was done in the apparent execution of authority actually, or ostensibly, given to the employee by the employer. ... Very often, however, such cases will yield to simpler analysis. The employer may be in direct breach of an obligation owed to the person who has been defrauded. That obligation may arise from a contract between the employer and the person who has been defrauded: a contract which can be seen as having been made by the fraudster on behalf of the employer. Or the obligation may be proprietary in nature as will often be the case where money or other property is to be held in trust for the person defrauded.

Other direct obligations may be relevant. In *Morris*, there had been a bailment of goods. It was for the employer to demonstrate that its inability to return them in good order was not due to fault on its part. It may be doubted that it could have done so. ...

In his note in the *Law Quarterly Review* about *Lloyd* Pollock pointed out that the solicitor was bound to attend to his client's work personally or if he delegated it, to supervise that work. That being so, the solicitor was in breach of his contract of retainer by not supervising the work of the fraudulent clerk. Emily Lloyd could, therefore, have recovered on that basis. Moreover, having held out the clerk as authorised to act on his behalf, it may be that the solicitor was estopped from denying that what was done was authorised. That was the preferred basis upon which, in *Lloyd*, Vaughan Williams LJ had placed his dissenting judgment in the Court of Appeal.

It may be, therefore, that extending vicarious liability to cases where the intentional conduct of which complaint is made was done in ostensible pursuit of the employer's business, or in the apparent execution of authority which the employer held out the employee as having, was an unnecessary extension of the concept of course of employment. It may also be that the content of concepts of ostensible pursuit and apparent execution of ostensible authority depends upon, or at least runs parallel with, whether a simpler basis of liability can be identified in the fashion of the examples given. Those are questions which may require further consideration in cases which raise the issue.

594 For present purposes, it is enough to conclude that when an employer is alleged to be vicariously liable for the intentional tort of an employee, recovery against the employer on that basis should not be extended beyond the two kinds of case identified by Dixon J in *Deatons*: first, where the conduct of which complaint is made was done in the intended pursuit of the employer's interests or in the intended performance of the contract of employment or, secondly, where the conduct of which

complaint is made was done in the ostensible pursuit of the employer's business or the apparent execution of the authority which the employer held out the employee as having.

The present cases

The deliberate sexual assault on a pupil is not some unintended by-product of performance of the teacher's task, no matter whether that task requires some intimate contact with the child or not. It is a predatory abuse of the teacher's authority in deliberate breach of a core element of the contract of employment. Unlike the dishonest clerk in *Lloyd,* or the dishonest employee in *Morris,* the teacher has no actual or apparent authority to do any of the things that constitute the wrong. In *Lloyd,* the clerk had, and was held out as having, authority to act in conveying the property which Emily Lloyd had and which he took to his own use; in *Morris,* the employee had authority to receive the garment that he stole. When a teacher sexually assaults a pupil, the teacher has not the slightest semblance of proper authority to touch the pupil in that way. …

The wrongful acts of the teacher in these cases were not done in the intended pursuit of the interests of the State in conducting the particular school or the education system more generally. They were not done in intended performance of the contract of employment. Nor were 595 they done in the ostensible pursuit of the interests of the State in conducting the school or the education system. Though the acts were, no doubt, done in abuse of the teacher's authority over the appellants, they were not done in the *apparent* execution of any authority he had. He had no authority to assault the appellants. What was done was not in the guise of any conduct in which a teacher might be thought to be authorised to engage.

If the present pleadings reveal no arguable cause of action, leave to replead to allege vicarious liability of the State should have been refused.

[The extract omits the judgments of Gaudron J holding that an employer may be estopped from denying that the employee was acting within the course of employment where there was a close connection between what the employee was authorised to do and the harmful conduct. Kirby J thought that the previous Australian decisions had adopted too narrow a view of vicarious liability and preferred the approach adopted in the Canadian decisions: "There is no reason why the common law of Australia should be less protective of the legal entitlements of child victims of sexual assault on the part of teachers and carers than is the common law of England an Canada". McHugh J found it unnecessary to consider the issue of vicarious liability. His Honour found that there could be liability based on a non-delegable duty of care. The judgment of Callinan J has also been omitted. His Honour held that there was no vicarious liability because intentional criminal misconduct is outside the scope of a teacher's duties.

The decision of the High Court did not finalise the claims. The issue of whether the defendants were vicariously liable awaited final determination in the lower courts. A further extract of the case dealing with the issue of whether a non-delegable duty could be owed is found at [15.130].]

[15.105] **Notes&Questions**

1. A bouncer at a nightclub ejects a boisterous patron. The patron returns the next night and threatens to punch the bouncer. The bouncer responds by stabbing the patron. Is the bouncer's employer vicariously liable? See *Mattis v Pollock* [2003] 1 WLR 2158 (yes). There are numerous decisions holding an employer liable for assaults committed by security guards and bouncers. It seems that very little is required to find that the conduct is in the course of employment even if there were some level of personal

animosity involved, see *Ryan v Ann St Holdings P/L* [2006] QCA 217; *Sprod v Public Relations Oriented Security Pty Ltd* [2007] NSWCA 319 (special leave to appeal to the High Court was refused). This approach moves closer to the risk basis of liability referred to in *Lepore.*

2. A customer abuses and makes extremely offensive comments to a bar attendant. In an early example of "glassing", the bar attendant throws a glass of beer at the customer who is injured. Is the employer vicariously liable? Will it make any difference if the bar attendant intentionally or accidentally threw the glass at the customer? What if the bar attendant also has responsibility for conduct in the bar? Do you think that the High Court in *Deatons v Flew* (1949) 79 CLR 370 (cited extensively in *Lepore*) took too narrow a view of liability in that case? Might this have been coloured by evidence in *Deatons* that Opal Pearl Ruby Barlow (the bar attendant) was "a wicked girl"? Would it make any difference if the employer knew that the bar attendant had on previous occasions thrown glasses at customers?

3. In *Ffrench v Sestili* [2007] SASC 241 the defendant's employee was the plaintiff's personal carer. The plaintiff was a quadriplegic and dependent upon her carer for virtually all her everyday needs. The relationship was one of "extreme trust, reliance, and confidence". The carer's duties were personal care, home help and shopping if needed. The plaintiff did not always have cash on hand for shopping, could not operate an ATM machine and was restricted in her ability to go shopping. It was accepted that the carer would handle money and payments for shopping. The plaintiff provided her carer with her credit card and her PIN number for a small account used for everyday purposes. On return from shopping, the carer usually returned the credit card and accounted for payments by producing the receipts. The carer did not return the credit card and gave various excuses as to why the credit card could not be returned. The carer withdrew a total of $33,350 from the plaintiff's account. A small amount came from the small everyday account with a larger sum from funds transferred from another deposit account which had a separate pin number that had not been disclosed to the carer. It was not proved how the carer got the details and PIN of the deposit account. The carer spent the money on gambling and was later convicted of larceny. Was the carer's employer liable? (yes) How would you apply the tests from the case extracted to come to a conclusion? Would a direction not to use the client's credit card or use the client's confidential information affect the outcome?

4. Where the wrongful conduct of the employee is "an intentional act that is done with intention to cause injury", the civil liability legislation does not apply to the claim against an employer who is vicariously liable, see *State of NSW v Ibbett* (2005) 65 NSWLR 168 (appeal to HC on different grounds, (2006) 229 CLR 638), see [3.180] Note 2.

The requirement of tortious wrongdoing

[15.110] Vicarious liability renders the employer liable for the employee's tortious conduct within the course of employment. If the employee's conduct is not tortious, the employer is not vicariously liable. This is known as the servant's tort theory – the master is liable for the *tort* committed by the servant, (*New South Wales v Ibbett* (2006) 229 CLR 638 at [6]). Occasionally, this orthodoxy has been tested. Could an employer avoid liability if a negligent employee was not liable because of some personal immunity? This inconvenient outcome is avoided if the employer's liability is characterised as a personal rather than vicarious liability:

> The master's liability, when it exists, is not a liability substituted for that of the servant. It exists ... not because the servant is liable, but because of what the servant has done. It is a separate and independent liability, resulting from attributing to the master the conduct of the servant, with all its objective qualities, but not with the quality of wrongfulness which, in an action against the servant, it may be held to have because of considerations personal to the servant. The master "is to answer for the act as if it were his own" ... per Kitto J, *Darling Island Stevedoring v Long* (1958) 97 CLR 36 at 61 per Kitto J.

Using this approach the employer in *Broom v Morgan* [1953] 1 QB 597 was held liable for an employee's negligence even though the employee could not have been liable because at that time the plaintiff husband could not have sued his negligent employee wife. This immunity has been reversed by statute, (see *Family Law Act 1975* (Cth), s 119). Conversely, an employer was not vicariously liable for breach of a statutory duty imposed directly on an employee and not on the employer: *Darling Island Stevedoring & Lighterage Co v Long* (1957) 97 CLR 36. In New South Wales this is amended by the *Law Reform (Vicarious Liability) Act 1983* (NSW), ss 7, 8. The most recent authority generally reaffirms the principle that if the employee is not tortiously liable then the employer is not liable: see *Bell v The State of WA* [2004] WASCA 205 (statutory immunity of employee); *The Finance Brokers Supervisory Board v Van Stokkum* [2006] WAQSCA 97; *Commonwealth of Australia v Griffiths* [2007] NSWCA 370 (witness immunity). Note also *Law Reform (Vicarious Liability) Act 1983* (NSW), s 9B, *New South Wales v Ibbett* (2006) 229 CLR 638. In New South Wales, s 3C of the CLA avoids the potential to argue this issue by providing that if the CLA Act limits or excludes tortious liability of a person, this also operates to limit or exclude the vicarious liability of another person for that tort. Apart from CLA liability, there is further provision in New South Wales that where a statute provides a statutory exemption or limitation of liability, that exemption is to be disregarded in determining whether an employer is vicariously liable, *Law Reform (Vicarious Liability) Act 1983* (NSW) s 10. See for example *Ambulance Service NSW v Worley* [2006] NSWCA 102 where the statutory protection of an ambulance officer did not prevent potential for vicarious liability for the employer.

Vicarious liability imposes liability on "employers" for tortious wrongdoing in the course of employment. If its purpose is to impose upon the "employer" normal business risks, should the employer's liability extend to wrongful conduct that does not give rise to a torts claim against the employee?

NON-DELEGABLE DUTIES

[15.115] The previous section on vicarious liability concerned the liability of an "employer" for the tortious conduct of an employee acting within the course of employment. Non-delegable duties are another area where a blameless defendant may be liable for the negligence of another. This is quite different from those cases where a defendant is liable for its own negligence in failing to take reasonable care to guard against the tortious conduct of another, (direct liability).

As the reader will see from the cases below, non-delegable duties are at once broader and narrower than vicarious liability. Unlike vicarious liability, non-delegable duties may result in a defendant being liable for the negligence of an independent contractor and perhaps even the conduct of an agent or employee acting outside the scope of the employment. What is also apparent from *New South Wales v Lepore* (2003) 212 CLR 511 (below [15.130]) is that a non-delegable duty, unlike vicarious liability, does not extend to make the "employer" liable for intentional wrongdoing. In *Leichhardt Municipal Council v Montgomery* (2007) 230 CLR 22, Kirby J at [94], [95]. outlined the supposed advantages of the non-delegability principle in relation to an accident on the footpath caused by the Council's independent contractor: a plaintiff need not be concerned about the contracting and other arrangements entered into by the Council; the Council as roads authority is in a superior position to see that care is taken and to secure a contractual indemnity from the contractor if third parties are injured. A plaintiff is therefore protected if the contractor is not adequately insured, giving greater assurance of recovery if negligence is found. But Kirby J did not find these arguments particularly convincing. A contractor is normally in as good a position as the Council to insure and compensate an injured plaintiff and deterrence is of doubtful value where the negligent conduct is that of an independent contractor (at [112], [113]). Kirby J at [98] was of the view that Courts should be reluctant to create exceptional cases where there is liability for the negligence of independent contractors or contractors' employees:

> The general rule is that the principal is not liable for the wrongs done by an independent contractor or its employees. It is not easy to see why an exception should be specifically carved out allowing the person injured to recover from a roads authority in addition to the normal rights that the person enjoys against the independent contractor posited as the effective cause of the wrong. In particular, it is difficult to see why the general policy of the law that the economic cost of the wrong should be borne by the legal entity immediately responsible for it should not be enforced in this case given the strong reasons for economic principle and social policy that lie behind that rule.

The cases extracted examine the circumstances in which the Courts will find that there is a non-delegable duty which could make a defendant liable for the negligence of an independent contractor. The first of these, *Burnie Port Authority v General Jones Pty Ltd* (1994) 179 CLR 520 High Court of Australia, is important for its rejection of the former rule in *Rylands v Fletcher* (1898) LR 3 HL 330. The *Rylands v Fletcher* (1898) LR 3 HL 330 principle imposed strict liability on an occupier of land who brought onto (or kept on) the land something dangerous which would cause serious risks to others if it should escape from the property. The rule applied only where there was a "special use bringing with it increased danger to others" (*Rickards v Lothian* [1913] AC 263 at 280 per Lord Moulton) and only if there was an escape onto other property. Although lack of negligence was not a defence, the range of defences available left little scope for it to operate as a tort of strict liability. The circumstances which might have attracted the former rule may now give rise to a non-delegable duty of care.

Burnie Port Authority v General Jones P/L

[15.120] *Burnie Port Authority v General Jones Pty Ltd* (1994) 179 CLR 520 High Court of Australia

(footnotes partially omitted)

[Burnie Port Authority's building was destroyed by a huge fire. Frozen vegetables stored in the building were ruined. The vegetables were owned by General Jones Pty Ltd, the plaintiff. General Jones Pty Ltd occupied cool rooms and offices in the building. The Authority occupied the rest of the building. The fire was caused when welding caused nearby cardboard boxes containing insulating material (Isolite EPS) to catch alight. The insulation material when alight burnt with "extraordinary ferocity". Independent contractors (W & S) were employed by the defendant Authority to provide additional refrigeration for extensions to the building; they were found to be negligent. The insulation

Burnie Port Authority v General Jones P/L cont.

material was stacked in cardboard boxes in a roof void occupied by the Authority and close to the area where welding would occur. General Jones sued both the independent contractor and the Port Authority.

The Full Court of Tasmania had held that the Port Authority was liable to General Jones under the *Rylands v Fletcher* (1898) LR 3 HL 330 principle. Under this principle a defendant is strictly liable for the escape of a dangerous substance without the need to prove fault, if it brings on to land, collects or keeps there anything that "is likely to do mischief" if it escapes. The defendant is liable for the natural consequences of its escape. The principle applies only if there is a non-natural user of land, that is, a special use bringing with it increased danger to others. On appeal to the High Court:]

MASON, CJ, DEANE, DAWSON, TOOHEY AND GAUDRON JJ: 528 In this Court, General has argued that it is entitled to maintain the judgment in its favour on each of three distinct grounds, namely, (i) the ignis suus principle; (ii) *Rylands v Fletcher* (1898) LR 3 HL 330 liability; and (iii) ordinary (or *Donoghue v Stevenson* [1932] AC 562) negligence. A fourth ground, ordinary nuisance, was raised in General's written outline of argument but was abandoned in the course of oral argument. ...

[The majority held that there are no special liability rules applying to fire and that the principle in *Rylands v Fletcher* (1898) LR 3 HL 330 should no longer be considered a separate basis of liability but should be regarded as being absorbed into the tort of negligence and continued:]

The "non-delegable" duty

550 ...It has long been recognized that there are certain categories of case in which a duty to take reasonable care to avoid a foreseeable risk of injury to another will not be discharged merely by the employment of a qualified and ostensibly competent independent contractor. In those categories of case, the nature of the relationship of proximity gives rise to a duty of care of a special and "more stringent" kind, namely a "duty to ensure that reasonable care is taken". Put differently, the requirement of reasonable care in those categories of case extends to seeing that care is taken. One of the classic statements of the scope of such a duty of care remains that of Lord Blackburn in *Hughes v Percival* (1883) 8 App Cas 443:

> that duty went as far as to require [the defendant] to see that reasonable skill and care were exercised in those operations ... If such a duty was cast upon the defendant he could not get rid of responsibility by delegating the performance of it to a third person. He was at liberty to employ such a third person to fulfil the duty which the law cast on himself ... but the defendant still remained subject to that duty, and liable for the consequences if it was not fulfilled.

In *Kondis v State Transport Authority* (1984) 154 CLR 672, in a judgment with which Deane J and Dawson J agreed, Mason J identified some of the principal categories of case in which the duty to take reasonable care under the ordinary law of negligence is non-delegable in that sense: adjoining owners of land in relation to work threatening support or common walls; master and servant in relation to a safe system of work; hospital and patient; school authority and pupil; and (arguably), occupier and invitee. In most, though conceivably not all, of such categories of case, the common "element in the relationship 551 between the parties which generates [the] special responsibility or duty to see that care is taken" is that "the person on whom [the duty] is imposed has undertaken the care, supervision or control of the person or property of another or is so placed in relation to that person or his property as to assume a particular responsibility for his or its safety, in circumstances where the person affected might reasonably expect that due care will be exercised". It will be convenient to refer to that common element as "the central element of control". Viewed from the perspective of the person to whom the duty is owed, the relationship of proximity giving rise to the non-delegable duty of care in such cases is marked by special dependence or vulnerability on the part of that person.

The relationship of proximity which exists, for the purposes of ordinary negligence, between a plaintiff and a defendant in circumstances which would prima facie attract the rule in *Rylands v Fletcher*

Burnie Port Authority v General Jones P/L cont.

(1898) LR 3 HL 330 is characterized by such a central element of control and by such special dependence and vulnerability. One party to that relationship is a person who is in control of premises and who has taken advantage of that control to introduce thereon or to retain therein a dangerous substance or to undertake thereon a dangerous activity or to allow another person to do one of those things. The other party to that relationship is a person, outside the premises and without control over what occurs therein, whose person or property is thereby exposed to a foreseeable risk of danger. In such a case, the person outside the premises is obviously in a position of special vulnerability and dependence. He or she is specially vulnerable to danger if reasonable precautions are not taken in relation to what is done on the premises. He or she is specially dependent upon the person in control of the premises to ensure that such reasonable precautions are in fact taken. Commonly, he or she will have neither the right nor the opportunity to exercise control over, or even to have foreknowledge of, what is done or allowed by the other party within the premises. Conversely, the person who introduces (or allows another to introduce) the dangerous substance or undertakes (or allows another to undertake) the dangerous activity on premises which he or she controls is "so placed in 552 relation to [the other] person or his property as to assume a particular responsibility for his or its safety".

It follows that the relationship of proximity which exists in the category of case into which *Rylands v Fletcher* (1898) LR 3 HL 330 circumstances fall contains the central element of control which generates, in other categories of case, a special "personal" or "non-delegable" duty of care under the ordinary law of negligence. Reasoning by analogy suggests, but does not compel, a conclusion that that common element gives rise to such a duty of care in the first-mentioned category of case. There are considerations of fairness which support that conclusion, namely, that it is the person in control who has authorized or allowed the situation of foreseeable potential danger to be imposed on the other person by authorizing or allowing the dangerous use of the premises and who is likely to be in a position to insist upon the exercise of reasonable care. It is also supported by considerations of utility: "the practical advantage of being conveniently workable, of supplying a spur to effective care in the choice of contractors, and in pointing the victim to a defendant who is easily discoverable and probably financially responsible". The weight of authority confirms that the duty in that category of case is a non-delegable one ...

The degree of care

Where a duty of care arises under the ordinary law of negligence, the standard of care exacted is that which is reasonable in the circumstances. It has been emphasized in many cases that the degree of care under that standard necessarily varies with the risk involved and that the risk involved includes both the magnitude of the risk of an accident happening and the seriousness of the potential damage if an accident should occur. Even where a dangerous substance or a dangerous activity of a kind which might attract the rule in *Rylands v Fletcher* (1898) LR 3 HL 330 is involved, the standard of care remains "that which is reasonable in the circumstances, that which a reasonably prudent man would exercise in the circumstances". In the case of such substances or activities, however, a reasonably prudent person would exercise a higher degree of care. Indeed, depending upon the magnitude of the danger, the standard of "reasonable care" may involve "a degree of diligence so stringent as to amount practically to a guarantee of safety". 555

Conclusion

Once it is appreciated that the special relationship of proximity which exists in circumstances which would attract the rule in *Rylands v Fletcher* (1898) LR 3 HL 330 gives rise to a non-delegable duty of care and that the dangerousness of the substance or activity involved in such circumstances will heighten the degree of care which is reasonable, it becomes apparent, subject to one qualification,

Burnie Port Authority v General Jones P/L cont.

that the stage has been reached where it is highly unlikely that liability will not exist under the principles of ordinary negligence in any case where liability would exist under the rule in *Rylands v Fletcher* (1898) LR 3 HL 330. ...

The qualification ... is that there may remain cases in which it is preferable to see a defendant's liability in a *Rylands v Fletcher* (1898) LR 3 HL 330 situation as lying in nuisance (or even trespass) and not in negligence. It follows that the main consideration favouring preservation of the rule in *Rylands v Fletcher* (1898) LR 3 HL 330, namely, that the rule imposes liability in cases where it would not otherwise exist, lacks practical substance. In these circumstances, and subject only to the above-mentioned possible qualification in relation to liability in nuisance, the rule in *Rylands v Fletcher* (1898) LR 3 HL 330, with all its difficulties, uncertainties, qualifications and exceptions, should now be seen, for the purposes of the common law of this country, as absorbed by the principles of ordinary negligence. Under those principles, a person who takes advantage of his or her control of premises to introduce a dangerous substance, to carry on a dangerous activity, or to allow another to do one of 557 those things, owes a duty of reasonable care to avoid a reasonably foreseeable risk of injury or damage to the person or property of another. In a case where the person or property of the other person is lawfully in a place outside the premises that duty of care both varies in degree according to the magnitude of the risk involved and extends to ensuring that such care is taken. It is unnecessary for the purposes of the present case to express a concluded view on the question whether the duty of care owed, in such circumstances, to a lawful visitor on the premises is likewise a non-delegable one. The ordinary processes of legal reasoning by analogy, induction and deduction would prima facie indicate that it is. Like Windeyer J in *Benning v Wong* (1969) 122 CLR 249, we have added the qualifications "lawfully" and "lawful" to reserve the position of, rather than to exclude, the unlawful plaintiff.

The present case

... The critical question for the purposes of applying the principles of ordinary negligence to the circumstances of the present case is whether the Authority took advantage of its occupation and control of the premises to allow its independent 558 contractor to introduce or retain a dangerous substance or to engage in a dangerous activity on the premises. The starting point for answering that question must be a consideration of what relevantly constitutes a dangerous substance or activity.

In the context of the ordinary law of negligence, the character of "dangerous" is not confined to those classes of things, such as poison, a loaded gun or explosives, which are "inherently dangerous" or "dangerous in themselves". This point was made by Lord Atkin in *Donoghue v Stevenson* [1932] AC 562:

> I do not find it necessary to discuss at length the cases dealing with duties where the thing is dangerous, or, in the narrower category, belongs to a class of things which are dangerous in themselves. I regard the distinction as an unnatural one so far as it is used to serve as a logical differentiation by which to distinguish the existence or non-existence of a legal right. In this respect I agree with what was said by Scrutton LJ in *Hodge & Sons v Anglo-American Oil Co*, a case which was ultimately decided on a question of fact. "Personally, I do not understand the difference between a thing dangerous in itself, as poison, and a thing not dangerous as a class, but by negligent construction dangerous as a particular thing. The latter, if anything, seems the more dangerous of the two; it is a wolf in sheep's clothing instead of an obvious wolf." The nature of the thing may very well call for different degrees of care, and the person dealing with it may well contemplate persons as being within the sphere of his duty to take care who would not be sufficiently proximate with less dangerous goods; so that not only the degree of care but the range of persons to whom a duty is owed may be extended. But they all illustrate the general principle.

The fact that a particular substance or a particular activity can be seen to be "inherently" or "of itself" likely to do serious injury or cause serious damage will, of course, ordinarily make characterization as

Burnie Port Authority v General Jones P/L cont.

"dangerous" more readily apparent. That fact does not, however, provide a criterion of what is and what is not dangerous for the purpose of determining whether the duty of a person in occupation or control of premises to take care to avoid injury or damage outside the premises is or is not a delegable one. It suffices for that purpose that the combined effect of the magnitude of the foreseeable risk of an accident happening and the magnitude of the foreseeable potential injury or damage if an accident does occur is such that an ordinary person acting reasonably would 559 consider it necessary to exercise special care or to take special precautions in relation to it.

Similarly, a substance or activity entrusted to an independent contractor or other agent may be relevantly dangerous notwithstanding that foreseeable injury or danger will arise only in the event of what is commonly described as "collateral" negligence. If X engages an independent contractor to separately move two chemicals, which will cause a major explosion if they come into contact with one another, into separate storage areas, there may be no real risk of injury or damage at all if the independent contractor does what he or she is engaged to do. The activity is, however, obviously fraught with danger unless special precautions are taken to ensure that the independent contractor does not, through "collateral" negligence, transport the two chemicals together and in a way which causes contact between them. As Professor Thayer correctly pointed out, "collateral" is used in this context as a "most conveniently question-begging adjective" which, so far as it points to a definite conception, does no more than "indicate a distinction according to the definiteness of the danger inherent and visible in the nature of the undertaking".

In the present case, the particular qualities of EPS made the stacked cardboard containers of Isolite in the roof area of the Authority's premises a dangerous substance in the sense that, if one of the cardboard containers were accidentally set alight, an uncontrollable conflagration would almost inevitably result. Clearly, the introduction of more than twenty of those cardboard containers called for special precautions to be taken to avoid any risk of that happening. A fortiori, the carrying out of welding activities in the premises within which the cardboard containers of Isolite were stacked was itself a dangerous activity in that it was reasonably foreseeable that, unless special precautions were taken, sparks or molten metal might fall upon one of the containers and set the cardboard alight.

... It suffices for present purposes that the Authority engaged and authorized its independent contractor to 560 carry out work within its premises which required both the introduction of such large quantities of EPS to the premises and the carrying out of extensive welding work within the premises. [Their Honours then referred to the evidence that the Authority knew that the isolite was in cardboard containers and stored in the roof area.]...

In these circumstances, the overall work which the independent contractor was engaged to carry out on the premises was a dangerous activity in that it involved a real and foreseeable risk of a serious conflagration unless special precautions were taken to avoid the risk of serious fire. It was obvious that, in the event of any serious fire on the premises, General's frozen vegetables would almost certainly be damaged or destroyed. In these circumstances, the Authority, as occupier of those parts of the premises into which it required and allowed the Isolite to be introduced and the welding work to be carried out, owed to General a duty of care which was non-delegable in the sense we have explained, that is to say, which extended to ensuring that its independent contractor took reasonable care to prevent the Isolite being set alight as a result of the welding activities. It is now common ground that W & S did not take such reasonable care.

It follows that the Authority was liable to General pursuant to the ordinary principles of negligence for the damage which General sustained. The appeal must be dismissed.

MCHUGH J: [Dissenting]

[I]n recent years, Law Reform Commissions and equivalent bodies have advocated the enactment of strict liability rules in various areas of social activity which involve the use of substances likely to cause great harm if they escape. Clearly, the investigations of those bodies have not revealed the superiority of the negligence action to an action based on a prima facie rule of strict liability. With great respect to those who hold the contrary view, much more evidence, analysis and argument than was put before this Court in this case is needed before the Court can properly determine whether the rule in *Rylands v Fletcher* (1898) LR 3 HL 330 should be banished from the books. In the meantime, we should continue to apply the established rule.

[His Honour held that General Jones failed under the *Rylands v Fletcher* (1898) LR 3 HL 330 principle as there was no non-natural user of land. Nor was the Port Authority liable for the negligence of the independent contractor. The dissenting judgment of Brennan J finding for the Burnie Port Authority on similar grounds to that of McHugh J has been omitted.]

[15.125] **Notes&Questions**

1. The former *Rylands v Fletcher* (1898) LR 3 HL 330 principle has been largely, but not comprehensively, subsumed under the tort of negligence: see [7.110]. Nuisance and trespass continue to play a role in the escape of dangerous substances, see Chapter 18 and Chapter 4. In United Kingdom, the *Rylands v Fletcher* (1898) LR 3 HL 330 principle is regarded as an extension of the law of nuisance, see *Cambridge Water Co v Eastern Counties Leather Plc* [1994] 2 AC 264; *Transco plc v Stockport Metropolitan Borough Council* [2004] 2 AC 1.
2. It is apparent that the High Court is reluctant to extend non-delegable duties beyond the *Kondis v State Transport Authority* (1984) 154 CLR 672 categories referred to in *Burnie* [15.120]. A majority of the High Court in *Northern Sandblasting Pty Ltd v Harris* (1997) 188 CLR 313 thought that a landlord's duty to the tenant's family on the leased property was not a non-delegable duty; this was confirmed by *Jones v Bartlett* (2000) 205 CLR 166 [9.50]. Unless the relevant statute imposes a non-delegable duty, a statutory road authority does not have a non-delegable duty in relation to work done on a highway or public road on behalf of a statutory road authority: *Leichhardt Municipal Council v Montgomery* (2007) 230 CLR 220 and see analysis Witting, "*Leichhardt Municipal Council v Montgomery*: Non-Delegable Duties and Roads Authorities" (2008) 32 MULR 332.
3. What are the limits of the non-delegability principle established in the principal case? If the notions of control, dependence and vulnerability are the principal markers for the existence of a duty of care, what then distinguishes non-delegable duties from ordinary duties of care? One suggestion not commanding universal agreement is that there are two elements: substantial risk and an assumption of a particular responsibility towards the claimant. Kirby J in *Leichhardt Municipal Council v Montgomery* (2007) 230 CLR 220 adopted this view taken from Murphy, "Juridical Foundations of Common Law Non-Delegable Duties" in Neyers, Chamberlain and Pitel (eds), *Emerging Issues In Tort Law* (Hart Publishing, Oxford, 2007). The debate on the question continues, see Murphy, "The Liability Bases of Common Law Non-Delegable Duties–A Reply to Christian Witting" (2007) 30 *University of New South Wales Law Journal* 86, 99 and Witting "Breach of the Non-Delegable Duty: Defending Limited Strict Liability in Tort" (2006) 29 UNSWLJ 33.

4. How far should the *Burnie case* extend? Should it be limited to those situations which have been characterised as involving extra hazardous risks such as those that might have attracted the former *Rylands v Fletcher* (1898) LR 3 HL 330 principle? There are a growing number of first instance decisions applying *Burnie* to situations which would not have qualified as being extra hazardous. The cases suggest disquiet by State Courts about the shedding of risk by outsourcing basic operations to contractors where there are obvious dangers to vulnerable third parties. For some examples, see *AF Textile Printers Pty Ltd v Thalut Nominees Pty Ltd* [2007] VSC 73 at [72] (liability for a contractor using a high pressure water hose on an asbestos roof causing significant water damage to factory beneath); *Twentieth Super Pac Nominees Pty Ltd v Australian Rail Track Corporation Ltd* [2006] VSC 253 at [266] (derailment, railway track owner has a non-delegable duty to the train operator to keep the track in good repair); *McLean v Meech* [2005] VSCA 305 (non-delegable duty of occupier of land for escape of horses onto the road); *Mendrecki v Doan & Pham* [2006] SADC 140 (occupier, home owner non-delegable duty to contractor installing air conditioning where the ceiling joist gave way). There is some doubt whether the liberal application of *Burnie* will survive. This is due to the reluctance of the High Court in *Leichhardt Municipal Council v Montgomery* (2007) 230 CLR 22 to extend the categories of non-delegable duties and the reaffirmation of the general principle that the actual wrongdoer should bear the liability. See *Transfield Services (Australia) v Hall* [2008] NSWCA 29.

5. The Negligence Review Panel, *Review of the Law of Negligence, Final Report* (Commonwealth of Australia, Canberra, 2002), recommended that liability for non-delegable duties be treated in the same fashion as vicarious liability. The reasoning of the committee was:

> 11.10 ... Although the precise nature of non-delegable duty is a matter of controversy and uncertainty, one thing is clear: a non-delegable duty is not a duty to take reasonable care. For this reason, liability for breach of a non-delegable duty will not fall within the terms of the provision contained in our overarching Recommendation 2 (For limitation of damages in personal injury claims resulting from negligence, see Chapter 15).
>
> 11.11 ... [Non-delegable duties] are typically not thought of as a form of strict liability. It is often said, for instance, that although a non-delegable duty is not a duty of care, it is a duty "to see that care is taken". The implication of this statement is that there are steps (typically not specified) that can be taken to discharge a non-delegable duty. By contrast, there is nothing that an employer can do to prevent being subject to vicarious liability for the negligence of its employees. ... The only way of avoiding vicarious liability is not to be an employer.

Do the judgments of the High Court in *New South Wales v Lepore* (extracted below) agree with this approach?

6. In New South Wales, Victoria and Western Australia, the Ipp Report recommendations have been enacted in legislation: NSW: CLA, s 5Q; Vic: WrA, s 61; WA: CLA, s 5Q and compare Tas: CLA, s 3C. There is no special provision in the Australian Capital Territory, Northern Territory or South Australia. The New South Wales, Victorian and Western Australian Acts direct that liability is to be determined "as if the liability were the vicarious liability of the defendant for the negligence of the person in connection with the performance of the work or task". The section restricts the conduct for which the employer is liable by

requiring the conduct to be "within the course of employment". These amendments implementing the *Ipp Report* predated the decision in *Lepore.*

New South Wales v Lepore

[15.130] *New South Wales v Lepore; Samin v Queensland; Rich v Queensland* (2003) 212 CLR 511 High Court of Australia

[The facts of the case and the extract of the judgment dealing with vicarious liability may be found at [15.100].]

GLEESON CJ: 527

The non-delegable duty of care

For more than a century, courts have described certain common law duties of care as "non-delegable" or "personal". The purpose and effect of such a characterisation of a duty of care is not always entirely clear. However, in a number of cases, members of this Court have so described the duty owed by a school authority to its pupils.

In *Dalton v Angus* (1881) 6 App Cas 740 at 829, Lord Blackburn referred to the inability of a person subject to a certain kind of responsibility to 528 "escape from the responsibility attaching on him of seeing that duty performed by delegating it to a contractor". His Lordship's reference to a responsibility of "seeing" a duty performed has echoes in later judicial statements. The concept was taken up in relation to the duty of an employer to take reasonable care for the safety of a workman. In *Wilsons and Clyde Coal Co v English* [1938] AC 57 at 84, Lord Wright described the duty as "personal", and said that it required the provision of competent staff, adequate material, and a proper system of effective supervision. Lord Thankerton (at 73) said that such duties "cannot be delegated", explaining that "the master cannot divest himself of responsibility by entrusting their performance to others". It would, perhaps, have been more accurate to say that the duties cannot be discharged by delegation. At all events, to describe a duty of care as "personal" or "non-delegable", in the sense that the person subject to the duty has a responsibility either to perform the duty, or to see it performed, and cannot discharge that responsibility by entrusting its performance to another, conveys a reasonably clear idea; but it addresses the nature of the duty, rather than its content.

This point was made in relation to another class of case in which resort was had to the concept of a personal or non-delegable duty: cases concerning the relationship between hospital and patient. Cases of that kind caused difficulty for the application of the principle of vicarious liability because of the variety of professional skills and arrangements that may be involved in a hospital organization. In *Gold v Essex County Council* [1942] 2 KB 293 at 301-302, Lord Greene MR, referring to the duty of care undertaken by a hospital, said:

> Apart from any express term governing the relationship of the parties, the extent of the obligation which one person assumes towards another is to be inferred from the circumstances of the case. This is true whether the relationship be contractual (as in the case of a nursing home conducted for profit) or non-contractual (as in the case of a hospital which gives free treatment). In the former case there is, of course, a remedy in contract, while in the latter the only remedy is in tort, but in each case the first task is to discover the extent of the obligation assumed by the person whom it is sought to make liable. Once this is discovered, it follows of necessity that the person accused of a breach of the obligation cannot escape liability because he has employed another person, whether a servant or agent, to discharge it on his behalf, and this is equally true whether or not the obligation involves the use of skill. It is also true that, if the obligation is undertaken by a corporation, or a body of trustees or governors, they cannot escape liability for its breach, any more 529 than can an individual, and it is no answer to say that the obligation is one which on the face of it they could never perform themselves. Nor can it make any difference that the obligation is assumed

New South Wales v Lepore cont.

> gratuitously by a person, body or corporation which does not act for profit ... Once the extent of the obligation is determined the ordinary principles of liability for the acts of servants or agents must be applied.

His Lordship's insistence that the first step is to identify the extent of the obligation that arises out of a particular relationship, whether contractual or non-contractual, is important. In the context of employment, for example, a duty to take reasonable care for the safety of workers cannot be discharged by delegation; but delegation does not transform it into a duty to keep workers free from all harm. A duty to see that reasonable care is taken for the safety of workers is different from a duty to preserve them from harm. Some confusion may result from describing it as a duty to "ensure" that reasonable care is taken for the safety of workers, which may give rise to the misconception that the responsibility of an employer is absolute.

Because the hospital cases were treated by Mason J (of this Court), in *The Commonwealth v Introvigne* (1982) 150 CLR 258 at 270, as analogous, it is useful to note the state of the Australian law in relation to the duties owed by hospitals to patients at about the time *Introvigne* was decided. This appears from the decision of the Court of Appeal of New South Wales in *Albrighton v Royal Prince Alfred Hospital* [1980] 2 NSWLR 542, which was decided two years before *Introvigne*. Reynolds JA, with whom Hope JA and Hutley JA agreed, said that the concept that a hospital fulfils its duty of care to persons treated in it by selecting and appointing competent medical staff had been discarded. Referring to an argument that the hospital was in breach of a duty which it owed to the plaintiff, and of which it could not divest itself by delegation, he said that the precise content of the responsibility assumed by a hospital might vary with individual cases, and had to be determined by reference to the particular facts. It is significant that the duty of care is personal or non-delegable; but it is always necessary to ascertain its content.

The case of *Introvigne* raised an unusual problem. The plaintiff, a schoolboy aged 15, attended the Woden Valley High School in the Australian Capital Territory. One morning before class, he and some friends entertained themselves by swinging on a flagpole in the school grounds. As a result of their exertions, the truck of the flagpole became detached, and fell on the plaintiff's head. He was injured. ... 530 ... [T]he plaintiff obtained leave to amend his Statement of Claim by alleging negligence on the part of the teachers. In particular, he alleged that the acting principal failed to arrange for adequate supervision in the school grounds. The plaintiff claimed that the Commonwealth was liable as a result of that failure. However, the Commonwealth was not the employer of the acting principal, or the other teachers. They were all employees of the New South Wales Department of Education which, at the relevant time, operated the Woden Valley High School on behalf of the Commonwealth pursuant to an inter-governmental arrangement. It was too late for the plaintiff to sue the State of New South Wales. The trial judge found no negligence. That finding was reversed on appeal. The factual issue is presently irrelevant. What was significant for future cases was the basis on which the Court attributed responsibility to the Commonwealth for the negligence of the teachers.

Mason J, with whom Gibbs CJ agreed, ... rested his decision on the ground that "[t]he duty ... imposed on a school authority is akin to that owed by a hospital to its patient". In *Gold*, it had been held that the liability of a hospital arises out of an obligation to use reasonable care in treatment, the performance of which cannot be delegated to someone else. This is a "personal" duty. It is more stringent than a duty to take reasonable care; it is a duty to ensure that reasonable care is taken. The reason for its imposition in the case of schools is the immaturity and inexperience of pupils, and their need for protection. This gives rise to a special responsibility akin to that of a hospital for its patients.

Having regard to the existing authorities on personal or non-delegable duties, and in the light of what he said in later cases, it is clear that Mason J intended to make no distinction between a duty to ensure that reasonable care is taken and a duty to see that reasonable care is taken. It also seems clear that the increased stringency to which he was referring lay, not in the extent of the responsibility undertaken (reasonable care for the safety of the pupils), but in the inability to discharge that responsibility by delegating the task of providing care to a third party or third parties. ... 531 ...

What was decided in *Introvigne* was that, even though it may have been doubtful that the Commonwealth was vicariously liable for the negligent failure of the teachers to provide adequate supervision, (the doubt arising from the inter-governmental arrangement), nevertheless the Commonwealth was under a duty to provide reasonable supervision; it could not discharge that duty by arranging for the State of New South Wales to conduct the school; it had a responsibility to see that adequate supervision was provided; and the absence of adequate supervision meant that it had not fulfilled its responsibility and was in breach of its duty of care. That produced the same practical result as would have followed if the Commonwealth had employed the teachers ...

The failure to take care of the plaintiff which resulted in the Commonwealth's liability in *Introvigne* was a negligent omission on the part of the teachers at the school, acting in the course of their ordinary duties. The hospital cases, which were treated by Mason J as analogous, similarly involved negligence. A responsibility to take reasonable care for the safety of another, or a responsibility to see that reasonable care is taken for the safety of another, is substantially different from an obligation to prevent any kind of harm. Furthermore, although deliberately and criminally inflicting injury on another person 532 involves a failure to take care of that person, it involves more. If a member of a hospital's staff with homicidal propensities were to attack and injure a patient, in circumstances where there was no fault on the part of the hospital authorities, or any other person for whose acts or omissions the hospital was vicariously responsible, the common law should not determine the question of the hospital's liability to the patient on the footing that the staff member had neglected to take reasonable care of the patient. It should face up to the fact that the staff member had criminally assaulted the patient, and address the problem of the circumstances in which an employer may be vicariously liable for the criminal acts of an employee. Intentional wrongdoing, especially intentional criminality, introduces a factor of legal relevance beyond a mere failure to take care. Homicide, rape, and theft are all acts that are inconsistent with care of person or property, but to characterise them as failure to take care, for the purpose of assigning tortious responsibility to a third party, would be to evade an issue.

As will appear, courts of the highest authority in England and Canada, and courts in other common law jurisdictions, have analysed the problem of the liability of a school authority for sexual abuse of pupils by teachers in terms of vicarious liability. If the argument based on non-delegable duty, said to be supported by *Introvigne*, is correct, their efforts have been misdirected, and the conclusions they have reached have unduly restricted liability. If the proposition accepted in the Court of Appeal of New South Wales is correct, and represents the law in Australia, then the liability of school authorities in this country extends beyond that which has been accepted in other common law jurisdictions. Moreover, in this country, where a relationship of employer and employee exists, if the duty of care owed to a victim by the employer can be characterised as personal, or non-delegable, then the potential responsibility of an employer for the intentional and criminal conduct of an employee extends beyond that which flows from the principles governing vicarious liability. It is unconstrained by considerations about whether the employee was acting in the course of his or her employment. It is enough that the victim has been injured by an employee on an occasion when the employer's duty of care covered the victim. The employer's duty to take care, or to see that reasonable care is taken, has been transformed into an absolute duty to prevent harm by the employee. It is similar to the duty owed by the owners of animals known to have vicious propensities. ... 533

The proposition that, because a school authority's duty of care to a pupil is non-delegable, the authority is liable for any injury, accidental or intentional, inflicted at school upon a pupil by a teacher, is too broad, and the responsibility with which it fixes school authorities is too demanding.

New South Wales v Lepore cont.

In *Kondis v State Transport Authority* (1984) 154 CLR 672 at 684-687, a case concerning an employer's duty to provide a safe system of work, Mason J developed what he had earlier said in *Introvigne*. He said that, when we look at the classes of case in which the existence of a non-delegable duty has been recognized, it appears that there is some element in the relationship between the parties that makes it appropriate to impose a duty to ensure that reasonable care and skill is taken for the safety of another's person or property. He went on (at 687):

> The element in the relationship between the parties which generates a special responsibility or duty to see that care is taken may be found in one or more of several circumstances. The hospital undertakes the care, supervision and control of patients who are in special need of care. The school authority undertakes like special responsibilities in relation to the children whom it accepts into its care. If the invitor be subject to a special duty, it is because he assumes a particular responsibility in relation to the safety of his premises and the safety of his invitee by inviting him to enter them. 534 And in *Meyers v Easton* (1878) 4 VLR 283 the undertaking of the landlord to renew the roof of the house was seen as impliedly carrying with it an undertaking to exercise reasonable care to prevent damage to the tenant's property. In these situations the special duty arises because the person on whom it is imposed has undertaken the care, supervision or control of the person or property of another or is so placed in relation to that person or his property as to assume a particular responsibility for his or its safety, in circumstances where the person affected might reasonably expect that due care will be exercised.

In cases where the care of children, or other vulnerable people, is involved, it is difficult to see what kind of relationship would not give rise to a non-delegable duty of care. It is clearly not limited to the relationship between school authority and pupil. A day-care centre for children whose parents work outside the home would be another obvious example. The members or directors of the club, which provided recreational facilities for children, considered by the Supreme Court of Canada in *Jacobi v Griffiths* [1999] 2 SCR 570, presumably owed a non-delegable duty of care to the children who were sexually assaulted by the club's employee. It would be wrong to assume that the persons or entities potentially subject to this form of tortious liability have "deep pockets", or could obtain, at reasonable rates, insurance cover to indemnify them in respect of the consequences of criminal acts of their employees or independent contractors. Whether the organization providing care is public or private, commercial or charitable, large or small, religious or secular, well-funded or mendicant, its potential no-fault tortious liability will be extensive. Furthermore, if deterrence of criminal behaviour is regarded as a reason for imposing tortious liability upon innocent parties, three things need to be remembered. First, the problem only arises where there has been no fault, and therefore no failure to exercise reasonable care to prevent foreseeable criminal behaviour on the part of the employee. Secondly, it is primarily the function of the criminal law, and the criminal justice system, to deal with matters of crime and punishment. (Most Australian jurisdictions also have statutory schemes for compensating victims of crime.) Thirdly, by hypothesis, the sanctions provided by the criminal law have failed to deter the employee who has committed the crime.

There is a further difficulty with the proposition under consideration. If a pupil is injured by the criminal act of another pupil, or of a stranger, then the possible liability of the school authority is determined by asking whether some act or omission of the school authority, or of some person for whose conduct it is vicariously 535 responsible, was a cause of the harm suffered by the pupil. Why is a different question asked when the injury results from the criminal act of a teacher?

There is no reason, either in principle or in authority, to treat the existence of a non-delegable duty of care as having the consequences held by the New South Wales Court of Appeal. ...

New South Wales v Lepore cont.

The orthodox method of analysing the problem is that adopted by the House of Lords and the Supreme Court of Canada. On the assumption that there has been no fault on the part of the school authority, the question to be addressed is whether the authority is vicariously liable for the wrongdoing of its employee. ...562 ...

MCHUGH J:

In my opinion a State education authority owes a duty to a pupil to take reasonable care to prevent harm to the pupil. The duty cannot be delegated. If, as is invariably the case, the State delegates the performance of the duty to a teacher, the State is liable if the teacher fails to take reasonable care to prevent harm to the pupil. The State is liable even if the teacher intentionally harms the pupil. The State cannot avoid liability by establishing that the teacher intentionally caused the harm even if the conduct of the teacher constitutes a criminal offence. It is the State's duty to protect the pupil, and the conduct of the teacher constitutes a breach of the State's own duty. ... Vicarious liability arises for the purposes of tort law when the law makes a person – usually an employer – liable for another person's breach of duty. In a non-delegable duty case, however, the liability is direct – not vicarious. The wrongful act is a breach of the duty owed by the person who cannot delegate the duty ... 608 ...

KIRBY J:

[T]he non-delegable nature of the duty was not designed ... to expand the *content* of the duty imposed upon the superior party to the relationship, so as to enlarge that duty into one of strict liability or insurance. It was simply a device to bring home liability in instances that would otherwise have fallen outside the recognised categories of vicarious liability. ...

[His honour went on to hold that since the teachers were employees in respect of whom the employer could be vicariously liable, non-delegable duties could not be considered.]

[The judgments of Gummow, Hayne and Callinan JJ taking a similar approach to that of Gleeson CJ on the issue of non-delegable duties have been omitted. Gaudron J agreed that a non-delegable duty is a duty of reasonable care to avoid foreseeable harm in the provision of a safe school environment.]

[15.135] **Notes&Questions**

1. The majority in *New South Wales v Lepore* held that a non-delegable duty is a duty of reasonable care and does not extend to intentional wrongdoing. As the earlier extract of this case demonstrates, this does not prevent an employer being vicariously liable (see [15.100]), or directly liable for its own negligence. See for example, *Roman Catholic Episcopal Corporation of St Georges v John Doe* [2004] 1 SCR 436 (Canada) (failure to act where known abuse of children by parish priest). Litigation is limited in its ability to provide for the needs of survivors of institutional abuse, see Law Commission of Canada, *Restoring Dignity: Responding to Child Abuse in Canadian Institutions* (Minister of Public Works and Government Services, Ottawa, 2000). See also P Vines, "*New South Wales v Lepore; Samin v Queensland; Rich v Queensland; Schools Responsibility for Sexual Assault: Non-delegable Duty and Vicarious Liability*" (2003) 27 MULR 612.

2. In relation to existing categories of non-delegable duties, would a non-delegable duty extend to a child enrolled in a tae kwon do class as analogous to a relationship between a school and its pupils? *Fitzgerald v Hill* [2008] QCA 283 (yes). Do you agree? Is the relationship between detainees at the Baxter detention centre analogous to the

relationship between a hospital and patient and a goaler and a prisoner? *S v Secretary, Dept of Immigration & Multicultural & Indigenous Affairs* [2005] FCA 549 (yes).

3. If a duty is non-delegable, the principal may be liable for the negligent conduct of its independent contractor. But can it make the defendant liable for a person who is not in any sense a delegate? For example, could a school be liable for a pupil's injury caused by a trespasser's negligence on school premises during school hours where the school authority is not negligent? If, on one view, the imposition of a non-delegable duty may make the employer liable for the conduct of an employee outside the course of employment, why is the position of a stranger different? Note that in relation to liability affected by the civil liability legislation, liability is to be determined "as if the liability were the vicarious liability of the defendant for the negligence of the person in connection with the performance of the work or task" (see [15.125] Note 6 above).

CONCURRENT LIABILITY – APPORTIONING RESPONSIBILITY BETWEEN WRONGDOERS

[15.140] The earlier sections of this chapter have considered the liability of concurrent tortfeasors towards an injured plaintiff. We will now consider the mechanisms for apportioning responsibility between these tortfeasors.

Review of the Law of Negligence

[15.145] Negligence Review Panel, *Review of the Law of Negligence, Final Report* (Commonwealth of Australia, Canberra, 2002)

12. Proportionate liability

12.1 After careful consideration, we have come to the firm view that personal injury law should not be reformed by the introduction of a system of proportionate liability ...

12.2 Multiple wrongdoers are "severally liable". This means that each can be held liable for the full amount of any damages awarded to the plaintiff, and the plaintiff is entitled to seek to recover the full amount of those damages from any of the people held liable. Of course, the plaintiff can only recover once, but is free to get as much of the total amount due as it is possible to get from any of the persons held liable. This maximises the plaintiff's chance of full recovery. If, for instance, there were two wrongdoers and one of them is solvent and the other is insolvent, the plaintiff is entitled to recover the full amount of the damages from the solvent wrongdoer. This phenomenon is sometimes referred to as "solidary liability" (as opposed to "proportionate liability").

12.3 The basic justification for solidary liability is that because the wrongful conduct of each of the wrongdoers was a necessary condition of the harm suffered by the plaintiff, it should not be open to any of the wrongdoers to resist – as against the plaintiff – the imposition of liability for the whole of the harm suffered.

12.4 Any and every one of a number of multiple wrongdoers is entitled to recover "contribution" from the others towards any amounts paid to the plaintiff. Under the statutes dealing with contribution, the court has a very wide discretion to "apportion" the liability between the various wrongdoers in such proportions as the court thinks just. The most important practical consequence of solidary liability is that the risk that one or more of the multiple wrongdoers will not be available to be sued or will not be able to pay the damages awarded, rests on the other wrongdoers rather than on the plaintiff. The justification for this is that as between the various wrongdoers and an innocent plaintiff, it is unfair that the risk that one or more of the wrongdoers will be unavailable to be sued or will be insolvent should rest on the plaintiff. This reasoning explains suggestions made from time to time that the rule of solidary liability should be reformed, but only in cases where the plaintiff was contributorily negligent.

12.5 Contrasted with solidary liability is proportionate liability. Under a regime of proportionate liability, liability for the harm caused (jointly or concurrently) by the multiple wrongdoers is divided (or "apportioned") between them according to their respective shares of responsibility. A plaintiff can recover from any particular wrongdoer only the proportion of the total damages awarded for which that wrongdoer is held liable, assessed by reference to the wrongdoer's comparative degree of responsibility (defined in terms of some statutory criterion or criteria). The main practical effect of proportionate liability is that the risk that one or more of the multiple wrongdoers will be unavailable to be sued, or will be insolvent, rests on the person who suffers the harm.

Law reform, academic and legislative opinions regarding the issue

12.6 Many law reform bodies, both in Australia and overseas, have considered the question of whether solidary liability should be replaced by a system of proportionate liability. Some have concluded that in cases of pure economic loss, that is, loss not consequent upon personal injury or death, proportionate liability should be introduced. ... The strong weight of academic opinion is ... that solidary liability is preferable to proportionate liability in cases of personal injury or death.

12.7 This preponderance of opinion is reflected in legislation. There is no statutory enactment in Australia that provides for proportionate liability in cases involving personal injury or death. There are certain statutory provisions in the States and Territories that establish a system of proportionate liability, but none apply to claims for personal injury or death.

The problem with proportionate liability

12.14 In the Panel's view, although no significant practical problems would arise as a result of the introduction of a system of proportionate liability in relation to negligently-caused personal injury or death, there is a major problem of principle that weighs conclusively against any proposal for such a system.

12.15 Under a system of proportionate liability, the plaintiff bears the risk that one of a number of multiple wrongdoers will be impecunious or unavailable to be sued. If there are two wrongdoers, D1 and D2, each of whom is 50 per cent responsible for the same harm, and D2 is impecunious or unavailable to be sued, under a system of proportionate liability the plaintiff will only recover 50 per cent of their loss (from D1). This is so regardless of whether the plaintiff was also in any way at fault. In the result, a person who is harmed by two people may be worse off than a person who is harmed by one. Conversely, a person who negligently causes harm to another will be better off merely because someone else also caused the person harm. This is difficult to justify.

12.16 For this reason, the Panel is firmly of the view that it should make no recommendation to replace joint and several liability with proportionate liability.

Recommendation 44

In relation to claims for negligently-caused personal injury and death, the doctrine of solidary liability should be retained and not replaced with a system of proportionate liability.

———— ꙮ ————

Contribution claims

Statutory claim for contribution

[15.150] At common law, a concurrent tortfeasor was liable for all of the plaintiff's damages (solidary liability) even if that tortfeasor was only a small contributor to the plaintiff's harm;

as a general rule a concurrent tortfeasor could not obtain any contribution from the other wrongdoer (*Merryweather v Nixon* (1879) 101 ER 1337) but an innocent agent acting on the principal's instructions could recover from the principal, see *Adamson v Jarvis* (1827) 130 ER 693. Exceptionally, at common law a blameless employer held vicariously liable could, in theory, recover from a negligent employee all damages paid to an injured plaintiff; the employee was regarded as being in breach of the employee's contractual or tortious duty to carry out the employment with reasonable care (*Lister v Romford Ice & Cold Storage Co* [1957] AC 555). Some jurisdictions have restricted the employer's right to recover an indemnity or contribution, see [15.175]. Uniform legislation introduced in the 1940s and 1950s in Australia allowed "tortfeasors liable" to make claims against "tortfeasors who were liable or would if sued be liable". The current provisions are ACT: CLWA, Pt 2.5; *Law Reform (Miscellaneous Provisions) Act* (NT), Pt IV; *Law Reform (Miscellaneous Provisions) Act 1946* (NSW), ss 5(1)(c), 5(2); *Law Reform Act 1995* (Qld), Pt 3; *Law Reform (Contributory Negligence and Apportionment of Liability) Act 2001* (SA); *Wrongs Act 1954* (Tas), s 3; *Law Reform (Contributory Negligence and Tortfeasors' Contribution) Act 1947* (WA). Note the very different Victorian provisions In Pt IV of the Victorian WrA. Typical of the provisions is the New South Wales sections set out below.

Law Reform (Miscellaneous Provisions) Act 1946 (NSW)

[15.155] *Law Reform (Miscellaneous Provisions) Act 1946* (NSW), 5(1)(c), 2

s 5(1)(c) Any tortfeasor in respect of that damage may recover contribution from any other tortfeasor who is, or would if sued have been liable in respect of the same damage, whether as a joint tortfeasor or otherwise, so, however, that no person shall be entitled to recover contribution under this section from any person entitled to be indemnified by him in respect of the liability in respect of which the contribution is sought.

s 5(2) In any proceedings for contribution under this section the amount of contribution recoverable from any person shall be such as may be found by the court to be just and equitable having regard to the extent of that person's responsibility for the damage and the court shall have power to exempt any person from liability to make contribution or to direct that the contribution to be recovered from any person shall amount to a complete indemnity.

Who may make a claim for contribution?

[15.160] *Is it limited to tortfeasors?* Under the original legislation, contribution was allowed only between tortfeasors liable for the same damage. This is still the case in New South Wales, Northern Territory and Western Australia: *Law Reform (Miscellaneous Provisions) Act* (NT), s 12(4); *Law Reform (Miscellaneous Provisions) Act 1946* (NSW), s 5; *Law Reform (Contributory Negligence and Tortfeasors' Contribution) Act 1947* (WA), s 7. In these jurisdictions, if contribution is limited to tortfeasors, this can give rise to perverse effects where a plaintiff chooses to sue the defendant guilty of tortious conduct not in tort but on some other cause of action. There is authority that, if the defendant would have been liable in tort had the plaintiff chosen to sue in tort, the defendant may still qualify as a "tortfeasor" for purposes of the contribution provisions: see *AWA v Daniels* (1992) 7 ACSR 759. Both parties must be "tortfeasors" in relation to the "same damage".

The other States have adopted differing solutions to these problems. In the Australian Capital Territory and Queensland, contribution claims can only be made where there is either tortious liability, to which the defence of contributory negligence would apply (see [16.115] Note 4), or where there is a co-extensive concurrent contractual duty to take reasonable care: ACT: CLWA, s 19 "wrong"; Qld: *Law Reform Act 1995* (Qld), s 5 "wrong". Compare this with the wider South Australian and Tasmanian provisions that extend to torts liability, breach of a contractual duty of care or liability for damages for breach of statute: *Law Reform (Contributory Negligence and Apportionment of Liability) Act 2001* (SA), s 4(1); Tas: CLA, s 2 "wrongful act". Victorian legislation allows contribution claims whatever the legal basis of liability: Vic: WrA, s 23A "tort, breach of contract, breach of trust or otherwise". This would allow even a breach of Fair Trading Act legislation to qualify (*Alexander v Perpetual Trustees WA Ltd* (2004) 216 CLR 109; *BHPB Freight Pty Ltd v Cosco Oceania Chartering Pty Ltd (No 2)* [2008] FCA 1656).

Proportionate liability cases: In claims for negligently caused property damage or economic loss, contribution claims are not needed because of proportionate liability legislation in most jurisdictions, see [15.185]. Under this legislation, concurrent wrongdoers are liable only for that proportion of the harm for which they are responsible. Where that legislation is excluded or does not apply, the contribution provisions may apply: compare Qld: CLA, s 32H.

Claimant "liable": The claimant for contribution must be a person "liable in respect of that damage". In *Bitumen and Oil Refineries (Aust) Ltd v Commission for Government Transport* (1955) 92 CLR 200 at 212-213, the High Court held that a tortfeasor who had been sued and held liable in judgment qualified as "liable" (see Vic: WrA, s 23(5)). Whilst a court must accept the judgment as conclusive as to the existence and amount of the contribution claimant's liability, this does not prevent the Court from examining whether the claim for contribution is excessive:

> The court, however, is required to find what is just and equitable as an amount of contribution having regard to the extent of the responsibility for the damage of the tortfeasor against whom the claim is made. There does not seem to be any valid reason why that tortfeasor may not say to the tortfeasor making the claim, if he has improvidently agreed to pay too large an amount or by unreasonable or negligent conduct in litigation has incurred or submitted to an excessive verdict, that the excess is due to his fault and not to that of the tortfeasor resisting the claim. It would be a matter for the court to consider under the heading of "just and equitable."

Note the special provisions in Vic: WrA, s 24(2B) and *Law Reform (Contributory Negligence and Apportionment of Liability) Act 2001* (SA), s 6(8), See also *Singleton v Freehill Hollingdale & Page* [2000] SASC 278.

A claimant who has settled the case without proceeding to judgment can also claim contribution. In *Stott v West Yorkshire Road Car Co Ltd* [1971] 2 QB 651 the English Court of Appeal held that a claimant would qualify as "liable" if the claimant was "responsible in law" (and see *Brambles Australia Limited v British & American Tobacco Australia Services Limited; Re Mowbray* [2005] NSWDDT 8). The contribution provision applied even if the claim had been settled without admission of liability provided that the existence of such liability was established in the contribution proceedings themselves. If the settlement is unreasonable or excessive this is relevant to the quantum of contribution recoverable and both Victoria and Tasmania have specific provisions dealing with this issue: Vic: WrA, ss 23B(4)(6), 24(2B); *Wrongs Act 1954* (Tas), s 3(1)(d).

Parties subject to contribution

[15.165] Under the standard provision, claims for contribution can be made against a tortfeasor "who is, or would if sued be liable in respect of the same damage". Note the

Victorian legislation is not limited to tortfeasors). The provision extracted above at [15.155] contemplates two classes of defendants subject to contribution claims:

> The defendant tortfeasor must be one (i) "who is ... liable in respect of the same damage" or (ii) would if sued have been, liable in respect of the same damage'.
>
> Only those who satisfy (i) or (ii) are amenable to a claim for contribution. Further, those who have been sued to judgment, whatever its outcome, do not fall within (ii) (*James Hardie v Seltsam Pty Ltd* (1998) 196 CLR 53 Gaudron and Gummow JJ at 66-67).

Limitation periods and contribution

[15.170] Difficulties arise where the claim for contribution is made at a time when the injured plaintiff would no longer be able to sue the wrongdoer because the limitation period had expired. In *Brambles Constructions Pty Ltd v Helmers* (1966) 114 CLR 213, an employee sued the employer for negligence causing work injuries. This claim was brought within the limitation period, which was then six years. During the course of the proceedings, but more than six years after the employee was injured, the employer claimed contribution from a third party. If the injured employee had sued the third party directly at the time contribution was claimed, the claim would have been dismissed as being out of time. Nevertheless, this did not prevent a contribution claim:

> The effect of s 5(1)(c) [NSW]... is that a tortfeasor ... may ... recover contribution from any other tortfeasor who, not having been sued by the injured party, had he been sued would have been found to have caused or contributed to the same damage by a tortious act. ... [T]here is no need whatever to specify any point of time as at which the expression "if sued" should be applied. It can be read "if sued at any time" which, of course, does not import a temporal element into the section. (*Brambles Constructions Pty Ltd v Helmers* per Barwick CJ at 219)

In some States specific provision is made for this circumstance, see SA: CLA, s 6(8)(d); Tas: CLA, s 3(1)(c); VIC: WrA s 23B(3). Most States also set out specific limitation periods which apply to commencement of contribution claims: *Limitation Act 1985* (ACT), s 21; *Limitation Act 1969* (NSW), s 26; *Limitation Act* (NT), s 24; *Limitation of Actions Act 1974* (Qld), s 40; SA: CLA, s 6(4); VIC: WrA, s 24(4)(5) compare *Limitation Act 1974* (Tas), s 7.

Indemnity and contribution

[15.175] The legislation also provides that no person is entitled to claim contribution from any person entitled to be indemnified by the person claiming contribution (compare Vic: WrA, s 23B(1))and note the specific provisions relating to indemnity in *Law Reform (Contributory Negligence and Tortfeasors' Contribution) Act 1947* (WA), s 7.

At common law an employer held vicariously liable for an employee's negligence was, in theory, entitled to recover from the employee the full amount of damages paid. However, if the employer has been guilty of independent negligence it would not amount to a complete indemnity (*Jones v Manchester Corporation* [1952] 2 QB 852). This was because an employee has a duty to carry out the employment with due care; a breach of this duty gives rise to liability in contract or tort, *Lister v Romford Ice & Cold Storage* [1957] AC 555 and see *Rowell v Alexander Mackie College of Advanced Education* (1988) 1 Qd R 404; *AR Griffiths & Sons P/L v Richards* [2000] 1 Qd R 116; *Toomey v Scolaro's Concrete Constructions Pty Ltd* (No 3) [2001] VSC 477.

In some States this rule has been reversed to protect the employee from indemnity claims by the employer: *Law Reform (Miscellaneous Provisions) Act* (NT), s 22A; NSW and SA expressly prevent contribution claims as well, *Employees Liability Act 1991* (NSW), s 3(1);

Law Reform (Contributory Negligence and Apportionment of Liability) Act 2001 (SA), s 6(9)(c). Actions against employees for an indemnity were often brought by the employer's insurer who was entitled to bring any claims the employer could have brought to recoup the insured loss (known as the right of subrogation). Section 66 of the *Insurance Contracts Act 1984* (Cth) now withdraws the insurer's right of subrogation unless the conduct of the employee constituted serious or wilful misconduct.

The general statutory protection is lost if the employee has been guilty of serious and wilful misconduct: *Employees Liability Act 1991* (NSW), s 5; *Law Reform (Miscellaneous Provisions) Act* (NT), s 22A(2); *Law Reform (Contributory Negligence and Apportionment of Liability) Act 2001* (SA), s 6(9)(c) (contribution claims); SA: CLA, s 59 (see also *Sheridan International Pty Ltd v Brooks* [2005] NSWSC 140; *State of NSW v Eade* [2006] NSWSC 84). This legislation does not, however, prevent an injured plaintiff suing the employee directly and recovering damages. At common law an employee is not protected against liability simply because the wrong is committed within the course of employment. In some States the employer is required to indemnify the employee against such claims: *Employees Liability Act 1991* (NSW), s 3(1)(b); *Law Reform (Miscellaneous Provisions) Act* (NT), s 22A(1); SA: CLA, s 59(1). However, note the employer's limited duty to provide insurance to employees in Tasmania, *Workers Rehabilitation and Compensation Act 1988* (Tas), s 97.

Amount of contribution

[15.180] The amount of contribution should be assessed as just and equitable having regard to the extent of that person's responsibility for the damage. The court can exempt a party from liability to pay contribution or order a complete indemnity: ACT: CLWA, s 21(2); NSW: CLA, s 5(2); NT: PICCA, s 13; Qld: *Law Reform Act 1995* (Qld), s 7; SA: CLA, s 6(5), 6(7); Tas: CLA, s 3(2); Vic: WrA, s 24(2); WA: CLA, s 7(2).

In *Podrebersek v Australian Iron & Steel Pty Ltd* (1985) 59 ALJR 492 at 494, the High Court said:

> The making of an apportionment as between a plaintiff and a defendant of their respective shares in the responsibility for the damage involves a comparison both of culpability i.e. of the degree of departure from the standard of care of the reasonable man ... and of the relative importance of the acts of the parties in causing the damage. ... It is the whole conduct of each negligent party in relation to the circumstances of the accident which must be subjected to comparative examination.

This parallels the test used in determining a plaintiff's contributory negligence [16.65], for example, the negligence of a pedestrian in not looking properly before crossing the road might involve less culpability than that of a speeding driver: see *Pennington v Norris* (1956) 96 CLR 10 and [16.125]. In circumstances where the defendant bears the entire responsibility, the claimant will be entitled to 100% contribution (*Pantalone v Alaouie* (1989) 18 NSWLR 119). This applies, for example, where the plaintiff's liability is a statutory, absolute liability and the defendant is wholly at fault (*Sherras v Van der Maat* [1989] 1 Qd R 114). Where the liability is vicarious and the employee has been completely at fault, subject to legislative provisions referred to above [15.175], the employer will be entitled to a complete indemnity from the employee.

PROPORTIONATE LIABILITY

Exception to solidary liability

[15.185] In most jurisdictions proportionate liability applies to negligently caused property damage and economic loss: *Trade Practices Act 1974* (Cth), Pt VIA; ACT: CLWA, Ch 7A; NSW: CLA, Pt 4; *Proportionate Liability Act 2005* (NT); Qld: CLA, Pt 2; *The Law Reform (Contributory Negligence and Apportionment of Liability)(Proportionate Liability) Amendment Act 2005* (SA); *Civil Liability Amendment (Proportionate Liability) Act 2005* (Tas); Vic: WrA, Pt IVAA; WA: CLA 2002, Pt 1F. Note that the legislation in Queensland and South Australian may apply only to concurrent wrongdoers not joint tortfeasors (such as employer/employee), see Qld: CLA, s 30(1); SA: CLA, ss 3(2), 8(3); and see T Carver, "Proportionate Liability: Reviewing the National Approach" (2005) (2) *Australian Civil Liability* 55. Proportionate liability does not apply to personal injury claims: Cth: *Trade Practices Act 1974* (Cth), s 87CB; ACT: CLWA, s 107B(3); NT: *Proportionate Liability Act 2005* (NT), s 4(3); NSW: CLA, s 34(1); Qld: CLA, s 28(3); SA: *The Law Reform (Contributory Negligence and Apportionment of Liability)(Proportionate Liability) Amendment Act 2005* (SA), s 3(2)(a); Tas: *Civil Liability Amendment (Proportionate Liability) Act 2005* (Tas), s 43A(1); Vic: WrA, s 24AG; WA: CLA, s 5AI(1).

Proportionate liability is an exception to the rule that a concurrent tortfeasor is liable for all of the plaintiff's damage (solidary liability). Where proportionate liability applies, wrongdoers are liable only for that proportion of the harm for which they are responsible. This means that the plaintiff bears the risk that one or more of the concurrent wrongdoers may not be able to pay their share of the damages. If liability is apportioned D1:70% and D2:30%. D2 will not be liable for more than 30% even if the plaintiff is not able to recover any funds from D1 because of insolvency. Whilst big business will always run these risks, are these risks ones which should be borne by an ordinary domestic consumer? Such an approach is at odds with the philosophy of consumer protection in legislation and decisions such as *Bryan v Maloney* (1995) 182 CLR 609 (see Chapter 9) protecting domestic consumers. It also makes the classification of the type of harm very important. It should be noted here that Queensland, the Australian Capital Territory and the Northern Territory have exempted "consumer claims": Qld: CLA, s 28(3)(b); ACT: CLWA, ss 107B(3), 107C; *Proportionate Liability Act 2005* (NT), s 4(3).

Types of claims covered

[15.190] Proportionate liability legislation applies to negligently caused economic loss and property damage claims: ACT: CLWA, s 107B(3); NT: *Proportionate Liability Act 2005* (NT), s 4(3)(a); NSW: CLA, s 34(1); Qld: CLA, s 28; SA: *The Law Reform (Contributory Negligence and Apportionment of Liability)(Proportionate Liability) Amendment Act 2005* (SA), s 3(2)(a); Tas: *Civil Liability Amendment (Proportionate Liability) Act 2005* (Tas), s 43A; Vic: WrA, s 24AF; WA: CLA, s 5AJ. Proportionate liability legislation applies only when a claim which comes within its provisions has been proven and established (*Reinhold v NSW Lottery Corporation (No 2)* [2008] NSWSC 187 followed by *Godfrey Spowers (Vic) Pty Ltd v Lincole Scott Australia Pty Ltd* [2008] VSCA 208, claim for contribution available where a claim had been settled without judgment being given). Proportionate liability legislation also applies to claims for property damage or economic loss for "misleading or deceptive conduct" under Fair Trading legislation or the *Trade Practices Act 1974*: Cth: *Trade Practices Act 1974* (Cth), s 87CB(1); NT: *Proportionate Liability Act 2005* (NT), s 4(2)(b); Qld: CLA, s 28(2); Tas: *Civil Liability Amendment (Proportionate Liability) Act 2005* (Tas), s 43A; WA: CLA, s 5AI(1)(b); Vic: WrA, s 24AF (see also *BHPB Freight Pty Ltd v Cosco Oceania Chartering Pty Ltd (No 2)* [2008] FCA 1656 dealing with the Victorian provisions).

Apportionable claims (other than those involving "misleading or deceptive conduct"), must arise "from a failure to take reasonable care". Unlike claims for contribution which in some states are limited to claims between tortfeasors (*Reinhold v New South Wales Lotteries Corporation (No 2)* [2008] NSWSC 187 at [6],[7]), proportionate liability is not limited to torts claims but is variously expressed to cover negligence whether in "contract, tort, or otherwise": ACT: CLWA, s 107B(2)(a); NT: *Proportionate Liability Act 2005* (NT), s 4(2)(a); SA: *The Law Reform (Contributory Negligence and Apportionment of Liability)(Proportionate Liability) Amendment Act 2005* (SA), s 3; Tas: *Civil Liability Amendment (Proportionate Liability) Act 2005* (Tas), s 43A(1); Vic: WrA, s 24AF; WA: CLA, s 5AI(1) (but compare NSW: CLA, s 5A negligence). New South Wales, Victoria and Northern Territory also specifically refer to statute in the provision. Queensland refers to "breach of duty of care" only (CLA, s 28(1)(a)).

Intentional torts, torts or statutory liability based on some form of strict liability, such as manufacturers liability under Part VA of the *Trade Practices Act 1974* (Cth) (see Chapter 9), are not covered. Similarly breach of contractual terms, such as merchantability or fitness for purpose under Sale of Goods Acts or the *Trade Practices Act 1974*, may fall outside the provisions (*BHPB Freight Pty Ltd v Cosco Oceania Chartering Pty Ltd (No 2)* [2008] FCA 1656, breach of warranty of authority not within the Victorian provisions). Liability in equity on the basis of a breach of a fiduciary duty might also be outside the legislative reach.

In relation to claims for breach of contract, there is authority that proportionate liability is not limited to cases where there is a contractual duty of care co-extensive with the ordinary tort duty of care. So that "a claim may properly be regarded as one 'arising from a failure to take reasonable care' if, at the end of the trial, the evidence warrants a finding to that effect and regardless of the absence of 'any plea of negligence' or a 'failure to take reasonable care'" (*Reinhold v New South Wales Lotteries Corporation (No 2)* [2008] NSWSC 187 at [30] following *Dartberg Pty Ltd v Wealthcare Financial Planning Pty Ltd* [2007] FCA 1216 at [30]). But note *BHPB Freight Pty Ltd v Cosco Oceania Chartering Pty Ltd (No 2)* [2008] FCA 1656 at [9] where a breach of warranty of authority was held not to be within the Victorian provisions. Note also Qld: CLA, s 28(1) "breach of duty of care", SA: CLA, s 4(1)(b). The *Reinhold* decision opens up argument that even in cases of strict liability, if, in fact, there has been negligence which causes loss, then proportionate liability applies. It would have the curious consequence that a non-negligent defendant held liable for breach of contract is worse off than a negligent defendant in relation to the same breach; proportionate liability applies to the latter but not the former.

An apportionable claim can be based on more than one cause of action. The legislation defines an apportionable claim where there are "proceedings in respect of the same loss or damage even if the claim for the loss or damage is based on more than one cause of action (whether or not of the same or a different kind)": Cth: *Trade Practices Act 1974* (Cth), s 87CB(2); NSW: CLA, s 34(1A); Tas: *Civil Liability Amendment (Proportionate Liability) Act 2005* (Tas), s 43A(9); WA: CLA, s 5AJ(4). Note the differing provisions in Qld: CLA, s 28(2) and Vic: WrA, s 24AF(2) Note also the definition of concurrent wrongdoer as "a person who is one of two or more persons whose act or omission, caused independently of each other or jointly, the damage or loss that is the subject of the claim": NSW: CLA, s 34(2); Tas: *Civil Liability Amendment (Proportionate Liability) Act 2005* (Tas), s 43A(2); Vic: WrA, s 24AH(1); WA: CLA, s 5AI. Contrast Qld: CLA, s 30(1) and SA: *The Law Reform (Contributory Negligence and Apportionment of Liability)(Proportionate Liability) Amendment Act 2005* (SA), s 8(3).

The benefit of proportionate liability does not apply to intended or fraudulent property damage or economic loss, so a fraudulent wrongdoer is liable for the whole of the damage. Moral blameworthiness deprives defendants of the protection of proportionate liability and withdrawing the protection is effectively punitive: Cth: *Trade Practices Act 1974* (Cth), s 87CC; ACT: CLWA, ss 107B(2)(a), 107E; NT: *Proportionate Liability Act 2005* (NT), ss 4(2)(a), 7; NSW: CLA, ss 34A(1), 3B; Qld: CLA, ss 32D, 32E; SA: *The Law Reform (Contributory Negligence and Apportionment of Liability)(Proportionate Liability) Amendment Act 2005* (SA), s 3(2)(a), 3(2)(c); Tas: *Civil Liability Amendment (Proportionate Liability) Act 2005* (Tas), s 43A(5); Vic: WrA, ss 24AM, 24AF(1)(a) (reasonable care); WA: CLA, s 5AJA.

Verdict shopping

[15.195] Legislation discourages plaintiffs from verdict shopping, that is, bringing more than one action against a series of defendants in the hope of obtaining higher damages in the later claim. Usually, the judgment sum in the first action provides the maximum sum recoverable and costs of any subsequent claim may not be recoverable: ACT: CLWA, s 20(2); *Law Reform (Miscellaneous Provisions) Act 1946* (NSW), s 5(1)(b); *Law Reform (Miscellaneous Provisions) Act* (NT), s 12(3); *Law Reform Act 1995* (Qld), s 6(b); *Law Reform (Contributory Negligence and Apportionment of Liability) Act 2001* (SA), s 5(2), 5(3); *Wrongs Act 1954* (Tas), s 3(1)(b); *Law Reform (Contributory Negligence and Tortfeasors' Contribution) Act 1947* (WA), s 7(1)(b). Note the differing Victorian provision, Vic: WrA, s 24AB. Proportionate liability is not subject to the same restrictions.. For example, a plaintiff may obtain a judgment against a wrongdoer for 20% of the plaintiff's damage. This does not prevent the plaintiff later suing another wrongdoer not sued in the first action and recover damages in excess of the 20% awarded against the wrongdoer in the first action. This is subject to the safeguard that the plaintiff cannot recover compensation in excess of the plaintiff's loss or damage: Cth: *Trade Practices Act 1974* (Cth), s 87CG; ACT: CLWA, s 107I; NSW: CLA, s 37; NT: *Proportionate Liability Act 2005* (NT), s 16; Qld: CLA, s 32B; Tas: CLA, s 43E; Vic: WrA, s 24AK and see *McAskell v Cavendish Properties Ltd* [2008] VSC 97; WA: CLA, s 5AM. Note the differing SA provision, *The Law Reform (Contributory Negligence and Apportionment of Liability)(Proportionate Liability) Amendment Act 2005* (SA), ss 5(4)(b), 11.

Procedure

[15.200] Under the standard provision relating to proportionate liability, the court assesses each defendant wrongdoer's responsibility for the plaintiff's damage according to what is just and equitable: Cth: *Trade Practices Act 1974* (Cth), s 87CD(3)(4); ACT: CLWA, ss 107F, 107D(2); NSW: CLA, s 35(1)(3)(4); NT: *Proportionate Liability Act 2005* (NT), ss 10, 13; Qld: CLA, s 35(3); Tas: *Civil Liability Amendment (Proportionate Liability) Act 2005* (Tas), s 43B; Vic: WrA, s 24AI; WA: CLA, s 5AK (and see Sudweeks, "What Proportionate Liability Means for Defendants" (2005) 2(8) Aust Civil Liability 97); *Yates v Mobile Marine Repairs*

Pty Ltd [2007] NSWSC 1463 at [93]-[94]; *Vella v Permanent Mortgages Pty Ltd* [2008] NSWSC 505, apportionment where there is fraud).

Each defendant is liable to the plaintiff for that proportionate share only. With the exception of Victoria, (Vic: WrA, s 24AI) the court can take into account the responsibility of any concurrent wrongdoer whether or not that person is a party to the proceedings. The plaintiff's contributory negligence is deducted before the relevant proportions are worked out. This legislation, together with Professional Standards legislation (see Chapter 12), gives significant protection to professional groups anxious to limit their liability for economic loss. A defendant held liable for a proportionate share cannot be the subject of a contribution or indemnity claim. See Cth: *Trade Practices Act 1974* (Cth), s 87CF; ACT: CLWA, s 107H; NT: *Proportionate Liability Act 2005* (NT), s 15; NSW: CLA, s 36; Qld: CLA, s 32A; Tas: *Civil Liability Amendment (Proportionate Liability) Act 2005* (Tas), s 43C; Vic: WrA, s 24AJ; WA: CLA, s 5AL. Compare SA: *The Law Reform (Contributory Negligence and Apportionment of Liability)(Proportionate Liability) Amendment Act 2005* (SA), s 9. Note Queensland and Victoria preserve the right to claim contribution from non-parties: Qld: CLA, s 32H, Vic: WrA, s 24AO. The Victorian provisions were considered in *Godfrey Spowers (Victoria) Pty Ltd v Lincolne Scott Australia Pty Ltd* [2008] VSCA 208 (effect of settlement of apportionable claims); *BHPB Freight Pty Ltd v Cosco Oceania Chartering Pty Ltd (No 2)* [2008] FCA 1656. Indemnity agreements continue to be enforceable in some States: NSW: CLA, s 3A(2)(3); NT: *Proportionate Liability Act 2005* (NT), s 15; Tas: *Civil Liability Amendment (Proportionate Liability) Act 2005* (Tas), s 43C(2); WA: CLA, ss 4A, 5AL(2) contrast Qld: CLA, ss 7(3), 32A, 32H.

Where proportionate liability exists, there is no advantage to the plaintiff to select a particular defendant and not sue others if the conduct of non-parties can be taken into account. The defendant must give the plaintiff notice of other concurrent wrongdoers or risk additional costs being awarded to the plaintiff: Cth: *Trade Practices Act 1974* (Cth), s 87CE; ACT: CLWA, s 107G; NSW: CLA, s 35A; NT: *Proportionate Liability Act 2005* (NT), s 12; Qld: CLA, s 32; SA: *The Law Reform (Contributory Negligence and Apportionment of Liability)(Proportionate Liability) Amendment Act 2005* (SA), s 10; Tas: CLA, s 43D; WA: CLA, s 5AKA; Vic: no provision. A defendant can always seek to have other wrongdoers joined as defendants in the proceedings. Queensland specifically preserves the defendant's right to claim contribution from some-one else in relation to an apportionable claim, s 32H. This aside, in most jurisdictions, selecting a particular defendant to sue will not benefit the plaintiff as the defendant's comparative responsibility takes into account the negligent conduct of other wrongdoers. In Victoria, the proportionate liability provisions apply only to those who are joined in the proceedings unless the other wrongdoer is deceased or a company that has been wound up: Vic: WrA, s 24AI.

CHAPTER 16

Defences to Torts of Negligence

INTRODUCTION

[16.05] In an action for negligence, the plaintiff's claims can be defeated or, in the case of contributory negligence, damages reduced by the defendant proving a relevant defence. The key defences available to a defendant are:

- the plaintiff's pre-existing knowledge about the defendant's incapacity or pre-existing knowledge of the risk associated with the state of affairs that gave rise to the negligence (known by the maxim volenti non fit injuria, or simply volens);
- the plaintiff's failure to take reasonable care of his or her own safety (contributory negligence);
- the plaintiff's unlawful conduct;
- the plaintiff's delay in initiating proceedings (statute of limitations).

The characterisation of these issues as "defences" is procedurally very important. It means the defendant must plead these matters by filing a defence that raises these matters and produce evidence to prove those matters on the balance of probabilities. This is not the case if all the defendant wishes to do is to challenge the plaintiff's case; the defendant might argue and bring evidence that there is no breach of duty, because it had done all that could reasonably be done to avoid the harm, or that the negligence did not cause the plaintiff's damage. Here, all the defendant need do is to cast sufficient doubt on the plaintiff's case to allow a finding that the plaintiff has not proven negligence on the balance of probabilities. Where the defendant raises a defence, the converse is true and the defendant bears the onus of proving the defence. For example, the defendant may argue as a defence that the plaintiff was contributorily negligent. If the plaintiff brings sufficient evidence showing that reasonable care had been taken for his or her own safety, the defendant will be unable to prove contributory negligence on the balance of probabilities. The defence will then fail. Alternatively, a plaintiff might give no evidence on issues going to the defence in the hope that the defendant will not be able to prove the defence on the balance of probabilities.

This chapter will focus on the principal defences to a claim in negligence. It does not include reference to the defence of statutory authority nor to special defences such as that available to good Samaritans under the civil liability legislation as to which see: ACT: CLWA, s 5; NSW: CLA, ss 56 – 58; *Personal Injuries (Liabilities and Damages) Act* (NT), s 8; *Law Reform Act 1995* (Qld), ss 15 – 16; SA: CLA, s 74; Vic: WrA, s 31B; WA: CLA, ss 5AB, 5AD, 5AE and [11.130] It does not consider special "defences" available under the civil liability legislation. The "defence" of compliance with widely accepted competent professional practice is referred to at [12.275]. The first of the defences concerns assumption of risk.

VOLENTI NON FIT INJURIA – ASSUMPTION OF RISK

[16.10] A plaintiff who takes the risk of injury upon him or herself has no claim and cannot recover any damages. This is captured in the latin phrase *volenti non fit injuria (volens)*, which means where there is consent there is no injury. The reason for this rule is eloquently expressed by Lord Hobhouse in his dissenting judgment in *Reeves v Commissioner of Police* [2001] 1 AC 360, where the House of Lords held that the police could be liable for failing to take reasonable measures to prevent a sane prisoner from committing suicide:

> First there is the fundamental principle of human autonomy. Where a natural person is not under any disability, that person has a right to choose his own fate. He is constrained in so far as his choice may affect others, society or the body politic. But, so far as he himself alone is concerned, he is entitled to choose. The choice to commit suicide is such a choice. A corollary of this principle is, subject to the important qualification to which I will refer, the principle that a person may not complain of the consequences of his own choices. This both reflects coherent legal principle and conforms to the accepted use of the word "cause:" the person's choice becomes, so far as he is concerned, the cause. The autonomy of the individual human confers the right and the responsibility.
>
> To qualify as an autonomous choice, the choice made must be free and unconstrained – ie voluntary, deliberate and informed. If the plaintiff is under a disability, either through lack of mental capacity or lack or excess of age, the plaintiff will lack autonomy and will not have made a free and unconstrained choice. Child plaintiffs come into this category. Both as a matter of causation and the attribution of responsibility, their conduct does not (without more) remove the responsibility of the defendant or transfer the responsibility to the child plaintiff ... Similarly, plaintiffs suffering from a temporary or a more serious loss of mental capacity ... will not have made the requisite free and unconstrained choice. Where the plaintiff's lack of mental capacity has been caused by the defendant's breach of duty, the entitlement to recover is all the stronger. On the same basis choices made under constraint of circumstances, such as those made by rescuers or persons placed in immediate danger, will not carry with them the

> consequence that the choice was the sole cause of the subsequent injury to the plaintiff nor will it result in his bearing the sole responsibility for his injury ... The same applies if the plaintiff's choice was vitiated by misinformation or lack of information. In the context of employment, the question of the reality of the employee's assent and his acceptance of risk has been the subject of many decisions; perhaps the most illuminating discussion for present purposes is to be found in *Imperial Chemical Industries Ltd v Shatwell* [1965] AC 656, particularly per Lord Hodson, at pp. 680-681, where he stresses that the plaintiff's conduct cannot be described as voluntary unless he truly had a free choice. These qualifications are fundamental and are the basis of the decisions where a plaintiff has been held entitled still to sue notwithstanding his having made a choice which led to the event of which he complains.

The majority held that the deceased's conduct in committing suicide could qualify as contributory negligence and damages were reduced by 50% (compare *AMP v RTA & Anor* [2001] Aust Torts Reports 81-619 NSWCA 186 where suicide was held to break chain of causation).

The passage above sets out the key elements required for volens. The first requirement is actual knowledge. This requirement is affected by the civil liability legislation see [16.50]. At common law, this is a subjective test–it is what the plaintiff actually knew at the relevant time. So, in *Scanlon v American Cigarette Company (Overseas) Pty Ltd (No 3)* [1987] VR 289, 291, it was insufficient for a cigarette manufacturer to allege that a user ought to have known of the harmful character of the product as a basis for raising the volenti defence. The plaintiff must also have acted voluntarily and with full appreciation of the risk involved. In *Avram v Gusakoski* [2006] WASCA 16, the passenger did not act voluntarily when the passenger had little time to consider alternatives when confronted with a drunken, aggressive and intimidating driver. It is these further elements that almost invariably result in the defence not applying. It is difficult to find a modern case in which the defence has denied the plaintiff's claim. Defendants continue to plead the defence and courts continue to hold that it does not apply, usually on the ground that the plaintiff did not fully appreciate the risk. So a plaintiff who employed an ex-prisoner knowing that he had been gaoled for assault was not volens to the risk of being shot (*Monie v Commonwealth of Australia* [2007] NSWCA 230) nor was a plaintiff volens who knew that the footpath might be slippery which added to the risk of falling over (*Randwick City Council v Muzic* [2006] NSWCA 66). The defence is most usually argued in personal injury claims but can equally apply to other damage. For example, *Honeychurch Management Pty Ltd v Deloitte Touche Tohmatsu* [2005] TASSC 13.

Volenti non fit injuria was, for a time, successfully used to defeat actions by rescuers against defendants whose negligence had created the danger which made the rescue attempt necessary. This practice was brought to an end by the English Court of Appeal decision in *Haynes v Harwood* [1934] 2 KB 240. Roche LJ in that case suggested that the facts of the case fell outside the maxim of volenti non fit injuria on the grounds that the rescuer/plaintiff had not chosen or consented to the risk in the sense required by the maxim (see [16.25]).This was relied upon by way of analogy in *Hirst v Nominal Defendant* [2005] QCA 65 where a policeman was injured whilst pursuing an unidentified vehicle being driven at high speed and dangerously. Keane JA commented (at [24]):

> In the rescue cases, a rescuer, responding to the call of a moral duty to help those in danger, voluntarily exposes himself or herself to a dangerous situation. In my view, the position of a policeman responding to the call of a legal duty to prevent unlawful conduct on the highway and to protect the safety of those making lawful use of it, must afford a stronger illustration of this point than the rescue cases. In such a case, the "free choice" of the police officer as to his

> conduct is constrained by the twin circumstances of his legal duties as a police officer, and the occurrence of the unlawful conduct which it is his or her duty to prevent.

For further reading on these elements see McDonald, "Legislative Intervention in the Law of Negligence" (2005) 27 Syd Law Review at 468-471

Volens and its relationship to other elements of negligence

[16.15] There are very few instances where the defence of volens successfully defeats the plaintiff's claim. Many of the cases in this area are probably better characterised as cases where there has been no negligence (that is, no breach of duty), because the harm could not have been avoided by the use of due care. For example, where an employee consents to inherent risks in the employment, inherent risks are those risks that cannot be avoided by due care and skill. This definition is also adopted in civil liability legislation, see [16.60] Note 6. But this amounts to no more than saying that where the employer has not been negligent there is no breach of duty. Therefore, what initially appears to be a volens case is frequently disposed of as a breach of duty question. This is apparent in the sporting injuries cases referred to below [16.40].

Similarly, what might appear to be a case of volens may be resolved by reference to the scope of the defendant's duty. The nature of the defendant's duty towards the plaintiff can preclude consideration of volenti. For example, if the defendant's duty is to take reasonable measures to prevent a prisoner from harming himself, the defence of volens will not apply to a claim for damages arising out of the prisoner's suicide: *Reeves v Commissioner of Police* [2001] 1 AC 360 (see [16.10]). Conversely, absent special knowledge, the defendant's duty may be to make an environment safe for ordinary anticipated usage. Consequently, the NSW State Rail Authority owed no duty to a 15 year old who squeezed himself out a train window in order to spray graffiti on the roof of the train (*Rundle v State Rail Authority of NSW* [2002] NSWCA 354). The court considered the question to be the nature of the duty, not volens.

We turn now to look at some of the key areas where the defence of volens has assumed importance. The problem of the passenger accepting a lift with an incapacitated drunken driver has been the most common situation where the defence of volens has been raised.

Volens: assuming the risk – the drunken driver and passenger

[16.20] In *Insurance Commissioner v Joyce* (1948) 77 CLR 39 the High Court thought that where a person knowingly accepts a lift in a vehicle being driven by an obviously drunken driver, the passenger's claim may fail on any of the three following grounds: the passenger consented to the risk of injury (volens), or the relevant standard of care was not that of a reasonably prudent driver but one whereby the passenger could not expect the driver to drive carefully at all (no breach of duty) or that the passenger by accepting the lift failed to take due care of her or his own safety, contributory negligence. At the time *Joyce's case* was decided contributory negligence was a complete defence so it was not important which of the three approaches were adopted. Subsequent changes to the law have reduced the importance of these defences in relation to drunken drivers and their passengers. A plaintiff's contributory negligence results in a reduction of damages rather than barring a claim [16.105]; some jurisdictions have introduced special statutory provisions to deal with defendants who are affected by alcohol [16.140] Notes 7, 8, and the High Court in *Imbree v McNeilly* (2008) 82 ALJR 1374 [12.250] rejected the view that a standard of care could be modified in the case of a learner driver and supervising driver. Even before the *Imbree* case, courts in recent times had been reluctant to characterise the issue as one that could be resolved by reference to the standard of care (see *Radford v Ward* (1990) ATR 81-064; *Wills v Bell* [2002] QCA 419). The reason is that, unlike the defence of volens, a modified standard of care approach does not give the courts leeway to decide that although the plaintiff knew of the risk, the risk was not fully appreciated so that the defence of volens failed.

Although older authorities frequently applied the defence of volens to deny a plaintiff's claim (see, eg, *Roggenkamp v Bennett* (1950) 80 CLR 292) in recent times courts have been quick to find that the defence of volens does not apply because the plaintiff either did not know of the risk or did not fully appreciate the risk. This might occur because, for example, the plaintiff did not fully realise that the driver could not drive safely, or that the plaintiff was not sufficiently sober to comprehend the driver's incompetence. For instance, a 16 year old thought that the driver was drunk but ok to drive, *Suncorp Insurance & Finance v Blakeney* (1993) 18 MVR 361; *McPherson v Whitfield* [1995] QCA 62. The failure to appreciate that the driver could not drive safely could, however, give rise to contributory negligence because the passenger ought to have known of the risk (*Joslyn v Berryman* (2003) 214 CLR 552; *McPherson v Whitfield* [1995] QCA 62, however compare a rare case where there was no contributory negligence, *AAMI Ltd v Hain* [2008] NSWCA 46 where there was no reason to suspect that the driver may have been drinking to excess). The modern day judicial reluctance to apply the defence of volens reflects an implicit view that an absolute barrier to recovery is unfair where the defendant is backed by compulsory statutory insurance in motor vehicle and work accidents, whether this is acknowledged explicitly by the courts or not. The goal of deterrence, if it is achievable, is sufficiently served by reduction of the plaintiff's damages in the defence of contributory negligence.

[16.25] **Notes&Questions**

1. At common law, the plaintiff must voluntarily undertake the risk. Should the volens defence apply in the following situations? The plaintiff's partner is drunk and aggressive and refuses to let the plaintiff drive back to their home. Would it be relevant that the plaintiff is the owner of the vehicle or that it would cost $200 to get a cab home? The plaintiff has been injured and requires immediate medical attention, the only choice is to get a drunken party goer to drive the plaintiff to the nearest medical centre? Are these situations where the plaintiff has a legal or moral claim to remain in the vehicle or did not have a real choice in the situation? In *Insurance Commissioner v Joyce* (1948) 77 CLR 39, Dixon J said (at 58), in relation to a passenger accepting a lift from a drunken driver:

   > If he has no real or practical choice he does not voluntarily consent. ... It is to be borne in mind also that if the passenger has a legal or moral claim to his place in the car, the improper conduct of the driver in reducing by intoxication his competence to discharge his functions will not put the passenger in the dilemma of either relinquishing his claim or consenting to take the consequences of the risk. A legal claim must, no doubt, arise as an incident, either of property or of contract, but a moral claim might form an incident of domestic relationship or arise from fortuitous circumstances.

2. What risks does the plaintiff consent to in accepting a lift from a drunken driver? Is it any risk resulting from the driving? What if the driver deliberately starts driving on the wrong side of the road at high speed or playing chicken with other

vehicles? Can a passenger expect a drunken driver to be careful at all? *Insurance Commissioner v Joyce* (1948) 77 CLR 39, Latham CJ (no) at 46:

> In the case of the drunken driver, all standards of care are ignored. The drunken driver cannot even be expected to act sensibly. The other person simply "chances it". Accordingly, the case may be described as involving a dispensation from all standards of care.

This contrasts with situations not involving drunk drivers. Generally it is not sufficient that the plaintiff knew that there might have been some risk of injury. At *common law* the defendant must show that the plaintiff consented to the particular risk that caused injury. In *Oran Park v Fleissig* [2002] NSWCA 371, the plaintiff knew that go-karting was risky and although it was obvious for all to see that there was no padding against the racing track concrete wall, there was no evidence that the plaintiff actually knew this. Einstein J [at 104] found that the defendant was not volens to the risk posed by the lack of padding on the concrete wall: "The plaintiff must be shown to have fully appreciated the nature and extent of the risk and not merely the existence of a danger". In *Gent-Diver v Neville* [1953] QSR 1, the plaintiff was riding pillion on the defendant's motor cycle when it collided with a car travelling in the opposite direction. The collision occurred at night after the headlight of the motor cycle had ceased working. At the commencement of the journey the plaintiff was aware of the defective condition of the light. On the application of the defence of volenti, Townley J said (at 8) that whilst the plaintiff accepted the risks arising out of the failure of the headlight, he did not accept the risk "as to the whole field of possible negligent acts". In particular, the plaintiff did not accept the risk that the defendant would not keep a proper look out for oncoming vehicles. The decisions suggest that courts are quick to find that the risk to which the plaintiff consented was different to the rise that arose. See, for example, *Martin v Howard* [1983] Tas R 188 holding that a plaintiff clinging to the boot of a car did not consent to the defendant driving off at speed; *Kent v Scattini* [1961] WAR 74 where it was held that occupants of vehicles spraying each other with water pistols did not consent to fast and negligent driving. This issue is affected by the civil liability legislation. Under that legislation, where the risk is obvious (see [16.50]) it is presumed that the plaintiff was aware of that risk unless the plaintiff proves otherwise, on the balance of probabilities.

3. In New South Wales and Queensland, in personal injury claims arising out of the use of a motor vehicle, circumstances attracting the defence of volens are now to be treated as contributory negligence cases, see [16.60] Note 7. See also *Motor Accidents Act 1988* (NSW), s 76; *Motor Accidents Compensation Act 1999* (NSW), s 140 and note NSW: CLA, s 3B(2)(a); Qld: CLA, s 48 and see SA: CLA, s 47(4), 47(6). There are other general provisions not limited to motor vehicle accidents in the ACT (CLWA, s 96(5)) replacing the defence of volens with deemed contributory negligence where the injured plaintiff relies upon the skill of an intoxicated person. The issue of intoxication and the impact of civil liability legislation is discussed [16.140] Notes 7 and 8.

Employee injuries

[16.30] Workplace injuries are another illustration of courts' unwillingness to apply the volens defence. An employee on the job may not be in a position to complain or take steps to avoid the risk of injury (*Smith v Charles Baker* [1891] AC 325). It is even more difficult to prove volens in relation to an employee than it is motor vehicle cases. In this respect Australia has followed the English approach (see as illustrations, *Bowater v Rowley Regis Corp* [1944] KB 476, where an employee did not consent to risk even if he knew that the work horse was unruly, and *Corbett v Toll Stevedoring Pty Ltd & Ors* [2007] NSWSC 656). It is not enough that the employee knows of the risk; the employee has to, in effect, agree to waive her or his right to sue the employer (Walsh JA appears to have acknowledged this in *Sara v Government Insurance Office of New South Wales* (1969) 89 WN (Pt I) (NSW) 203 at 207). This is now the accepted view.

In *Bowater v Rowley Regis Corp* [1944] KB 476 at 479, Scott LJ observed:

> a man cannot be said to be truly "willing" unless he is in a position to choose freely, and freedom of choice predicates, not only full knowledge of the circumstances on which the exercise of choice is conditioned, so that he may be able to choose wisely, but the absence from his mind of any feeling of constraint so that nothing shall interfere with the freedom of his will. Without purporting to lay down any rule of universal application, I venture to doubt the maxim can very often apply in circumstances of an injury to a servant by the negligence of his master.

The principle also applies where the employee is injured in the course of employment by someone other than the employer, see *Burnett v British Waterways Board* [1973] 1 WLR 700. In *Patrick Stevedores (No 1) Pty Limited v Vaughan* [2002] NSWCA 275 volens did not apply where an employee attending work during a strike suffered nervous shock brought on by aggressive picketing and intimidation at the employer's premises.

Suppose that the injured employee was not only aware of the dangerous situation but had been instrumental in creating the danger. Would this be sufficient to persuade a court to apply the defence to an employee? The House of Lords in *Imperial Chemical Industries Ltd v Shatwell* [1965] AC 656 thought that it would. There, the plaintiff and his brother were using explosives. The employer had directed (and the relevant statutory regulations provided) that detonators were only to be tested from a shelter. The plaintiff and his brother disregarded this and both were seriously injured. The statutory responsibility was imposed directly on the employees and not on the employer and there was no independent fault on the part of the employer. Could the plaintiff argue that because his brother was also in breach of the statutory regulations, the employer should be vicariously liable for his brother's breach of statutory duty? The House of Lords held that the plaintiff could not recover against his employer. This is regarded as a very exceptional case where the defence of volens might prevent a plaintiff employee's claim. The special features of the case were: that the statutory duty was imposed on the employees and not on the employer; both brothers were equal actors in the situation and there was a deliberate breach of statutory regulations by the two brothers (in relation to vicarious liability for breach of a statutory duty imposed on the employee, see [17.80] Note 2). The regulations were subsequently amended by imposing duties directly on the employer. This explains why it is difficult to find any subsequent cases where the courts have applied the *Shatwell case* and accepted the volens defence in relation to an employee.

[16.35] **Notes&Questions**

1. An employee is said to be "volens" (that is, to have accepted) risks that are inherent in the employment. In *Smith v Baker* [1891] AC 325, Lord Watson said (at 356):

   > There are many kinds of work in which danger is necessarily inherent, where precautions such as would ensure safety to the workman are either impossible, or would only be attainable at an expense altogether incommensurate with the end to be accomplished. In all such cases the workman must rely upon his own nerve and skill; and, in the absence of express stipulation to the contrary, the risk is held to be with him and not with the employer.

   This approach might be more properly characterised as a case where the defendant has not been negligent as there was no breach of duty.

2. New South Wales is the only state to legislatively provide that the defence of volens does not apply to claims to which the *Workers Compensation Act 1987* (NSW) applies. Section 151O of the *Workers Compensation Act 1987* provides:

   > The defence of volenti non fit injuria is not available in an action for the award of damages but, where that defence would otherwise have been available, the amount of any damage is to be reduced to such extent as is just and equitable on the presumption that the injured or deceased person was negligent in failing to take sufficient care for his or her own safety.

   The defence of contributory negligence and its application to employee injuries is discussed below.

3. In most jurisdictions, the civil liability legislation does not apply to claims governed by workers compensation legislation, see [16.85].

Sporting events and recreational activities

[16.40] Sporting events and recreational activities provide a quite different context within which the defence of volens is said to operate. In this section the position at common law is first discussed followed by discussion of the impact of civil liability reforms. Whilst employees may be in a special position, this cannot be said of participants or spectators at sporting events. Participants and spectators are taken to have consented to risks inherent in the sport. Diplock LJ observed in *Wooldridge v Sumner* [1963] 2 QB 43 at 68, that where no negligence is proved the plaintiff "takes the risk" because there is no breach of the duty owed to him or her by the other participant. "He does not take the risk by virtue of the doctrine expressed or obscured by the maxim volenti non fit injuria." *Wooldridge v Sumner* [1963] 2 QB 43 was a case of an experienced horseman who lost control of the horse he was riding in a hunting competition at a horse show. He had galloped the horse so fast around a corner that it left the course and plunged down a line of shrubs where the plaintiff, a photographer, was standing. The plaintiff took fright and in his efforts to save a spectator from danger fell into the path of the horse, was knocked down and seriously injured. In an action by the plaintiff against the owner of the horse, the English Court of Appeal reversed the trial judge's finding of negligence (at 67):

> A reasonable spectator attending voluntarily to witness any game or competition knows and presumably desires that a reasonable participant will concentrate his attention upon winning, and if the game or competition is a fast-moving one, will have to exercise his judgment and attempt to exert his skill in what, in the analogous context of contributory negligence is

> sometimes called "the agony of the moment". If the participant does so concentrate his attention and consequently does exercise his judgment and attempt to exert his skill in circumstances of this kind which are inherent in the game or competition in which he is taking part, the question whether any mistake he makes amounts to a breach of duty to take reasonable care must take account of those circumstances.

The tendency to describe a participant or spectator in sporting events as volens to the risks inherent in the game has encouraged the use of the maxim volenti non fit injuria in circumstances in which, as Diplock LJ points out, it has no place. To say that a person is volens to certain sporting injuries, not caused by negligence, is no different from saying that a person using the highways is volens to accidents not caused by negligence. In both cases the injured party has undertaken an activity which, in its own way, is fraught with danger and in which, it is generally known, injury may be caused without negligence on the part of anyone. In the end the question that has to be asked is, in the words of Kitto J in *Rootes v Shelton* (1967) 116 CLR 383 at 390: "was the defendant's conduct which caused the injury to the plaintiff reasonable in all the circumstances?" See also *Ollier v Magnetic Island Country Club* [2004] Aust Torts Reports 81-273 (special leave to HC refused) where a golfer on the fairway was struck by a golf ball. There was no volens to the defendant's negligence in the failure to keep a proper look out.

In relation to spectators, often the defendant is not the player or participant but the occupier of the premises on which the sport is being played. See, for example, *Hall v Brooklands Auto Racing Club* [1933] 1 KB 205; *Murray v Harringay Arena Ltd* [1951] 2 KB 52; and *Paltidis v The State Council of the Young Men's Christian Association of Victoria Inc* [2006] VSCA 122. The plaintiff's complaint may be the failure of the defendant, as occupier of the premises, to take sufficient precautions for the protection of spectators, not at any negligent act on the field of play (*White v Blackmore* [1972] 2 QB 651 at 673).

Where risks are obvious to a reasonable observer, a plaintiff is more likely to fail because the defendant has not breached its duty of care rather than under the volens defence. A spate of High Court decisions, all concerning diving accidents, take this approach: see *Roads and Traffic Authority of NSW v Dederer* (2007) 324 CLR 330 [12.105] and Chapter 12, Breach of Duty. In *Woods v Multisport Holdings* (2002) 208 CLR 460 [12.130] an indoor cricketer was struck in the eye by a cricket ball. It was held that there was no negligence by the defendant owner and operator of the facility. The defendant neither had a duty to warn of the obvious risk nor to provide protective helmets. Whereas a 12 year old motor cycle rider was held able to recover when the organisers of a race failed to provide sufficient track marshals to prevent the rider who had fallen from being run over by other riders (*Macarthur Districts Motor Cycle Sportsmen Inc v Ardizzone* (2004) 41 MVR 235; [2004] NSWCA 145). If the defendant has been negligent, the plaintiff might avoid the volens defence by showing that the risk was not fully appreciated. In *Moore v Woodforth* [2003] Aust Torts Reports 81-686 the plaintiff was injured by a motor-boat whilst diving in channel known to be used by motor boats. It was held that the defence of volens did not apply because the plaintiff did not fully appreciate the risk.

Volens and the civil liability legislation

Review of the Law of Negligence

[16.45] Negligence Review Panel, *Review of the Law of Negligence, Final Report* (Commonwealth of Australia, Canberra, 2002)

(footnotes partially omitted)

8.29 Making it easier to establish the defence of assumption of risk would obviously promote objectives underlying the Terms of Reference ... The Panel's opinion is that there are two ways in which the law could be changed that might encourage greater use by courts of the defence of assumption of risk.

8.30 The first would be to reverse the burden of proof on the issue of awareness of risk in relation to obvious risks as defined ... This could be done by a provision to the effect that for the purposes of the defence of assumption of risk, it would be presumed that the person against whom the defence is pleaded was actually aware of an obvious risk unless that person could prove, on the balance of probabilities, that he or she was actually not aware of the risk.

8.31 The second possible change would be to provide that for the purposes of the defence of assumption of risk, the test of whether a person was aware of a risk is whether he or she was aware of a risk of the type or kind of risk and not of its precise nature, extent or manner of occurrence.

8.32 The Panel recommends provisions embodying these principles. We would not recommend any provision dealing with the issue of voluntariness. Whether or not a risk was taken voluntarily is ultimately an evaluative question about which it would be difficult to make general provision.

Recommendation 30: The Proposed Act should embody the following principles: For the purposes of the defence of assumption of risk:

- Where the risk in question was obvious, the person against whom the defence is pleaded (the plaintiff) is presumed to have been actually aware of the risk unless the plaintiff proves on the balance of probabilities that he or she was not actually aware of the risk.
- An obvious risk is a risk that, in the circumstances, would have been obvious to a reasonable person in the plaintiff's position. Obvious risks include risks that are patent or matters of common knowledge. A risk may be obvious even though it is of low probability.
- The test of whether a person was aware of a risk is whether he or she was aware of the type or kind of risk, not its precise nature, extent or manner of occurrence.

Civil Liability Act 2002 (WA)

[16.50] *Civil Liability Act 2002* (WA), s 5F(1) – (4)

5F (1) For the purposes of this Division, an obvious risk to a person who suffers harm is a risk that, in the circumstances would have been obvious to a reasonable person in the position of that person;

(2) Obvious risks include risks that are patent or a matter of common knowledge

(3) A risk of something occurring can be an obvious risk even though it has a low probability of occurring

(4) A risk can be an obvious risk even if the risk (or a condition or circumstance that gives rise to the risk) is not prominent conspicuous or physically observable

[16.55] The New South Wales provision is in the same terms. Queensland and Victoria are similar, but add (Qld: CLA, s 13; Vic: WrA, s 53(5)):

(5) To remove any doubt, it is declared that a risk from a thing, including a living thing, is not an obvious risk if the risk is created because of a failure on the part of a person to properly operate, maintain, replace, prepare or care for the thing, unless the failure itself is an obvious risk.

And Tasmania adds (Tas: CLA, s 20(5):

(5) A risk is not an obvious risk merely because a warning about the risk has been given.

The South Australian provision CLA, s 36 mirrors subsections (1) to (3) of the NSW provisions. The Australian Capital Territory has no equivalent provision.

[16.60] **Notes&Questions**

1. *Obvious risks and defences:* The Ipp recommendations have been enacted in most jurisdictions, although with some variation. Four States specifically refer to the defence of assumption of risk in the context of obvious risks: Qld: CLA, s 14; SA: CLA, s 37; Tas: CLA, s 16; Vic: WrA, s 54. The Victorian provision, Vic: WrA, s 56, reverses the onus of proof where the issue is one of breach of duty and the plaintiff relies on failure to give a warning or information. Others, such as NSW: CLA, s 5G and WA: CLA, s 5N, are cast more broadly and do not refer to assumption of risk (volens) except under the heading "Assumption of Risk". The New South Wales sections have been read restrictively so that they are relevant only to defences, *Angel v Hawkesbury City Council* [2008] NSWCA 130 at [83]. We have noted earlier that under the general law, volens is very rarely effective to prevent recovery as most often a defendant has not breached its duty of care, see *Roads and Traffic Authority of NSW v Dederer* (2007) 324 CLR 330 [12.105] and Chapter 12 Breach of Duty.

2. *Obvious risks and the plaintiff's knowledge:* Under the legislation the plaintiff is presumed to know about obvious risks: ACT: CLWA, Sch 13, s 3.1 (equine activities); NSW: CLA, s 5F; Qld: CLA, s 13; WA: CLA, s 5F; Tas: CLA, s 15; SA: CLA, s 36. Compare Vic: WrA, s 54(2) excepting professional or health services or damages claims "in respect of risks associated with work done by one person for another". Note the special provisions relating to a failure to property maintain etc in Vic: WrA, s 53(5) and Qld: CLA, s 13. The risk is obvious if it would have been obvious "to a reasonable person in the position of that person". It is sufficient if the plaintiff has knowledge "of the type or kind of risk, even if the person is not aware of the precise nature, extent or manner of occurrence of the risk". These provisions substantially modify the common law principles relating to volens. *At common law* a plaintiff could argue that he or she was not aware of the particular risk or did not fully appreciate the risk; this is a subjective test of what the plaintiff actually knew and understood. Under the civil liability legislation, knowledge is assessed objectively taking into account the plaintiff's knowledge and experience in the particular circumstances.

   The plaintiff, a 19 year old, has seen many young people diving from the wharf. He knows that diving into shallow water can be dangerous. But the water looks deep and when he tests its depth by treading water, he can't touch the bottom. He dives off a bollard on the wharf some 2-3 metres above the water. He suffers serious spinal injuries when his head strikes the bottom. There has been a finding that the Council was in breach of its duty of care. Is the risk obvious? (Yes) *Jaber v Rockdale City Council* [2008] NSWCA 98 at [39]. Pedestrians know that footpaths can be uneven. Is the risk obvious where the raised lip of a concrete slab is obscured by shade? Is this a "particular circumstance" that is to be taken into account in ascertaining obviousness? (Yes) *Angel v Hawkesbury City Council* [2008] NSWCA 130 at [64]. In relation to children, the test is that of a reasonable child of that age. Diving nine metres off a bridge into water where there was a "no diving" sign would be an obvious risk to a reasonable 14 year old even if many had dived off safely before, *Great Lakes Shire Council v Dederer* [2006] NSWCA 101. The plaintiff also failed at common law against the Roads and Traffic Authority, see *Roads & Traffic Authority of NSW v Dederer* (2007) 324 CLR 330, see [12.105]. But the risk of injury might not be obvious to a seven year old jumping on a trampoline with her roller skates on, *Doubleday v Kelly* [2005] NSWCA 151 (extracted at [12.40]). The statutory provisions relating to obvious risks are relevant to the defence of volens. The statutory provisions are also important under the civil liability legislation because there is no duty to warn of obvious risks, see Chapter 12 Breach of Duty.

3. *Assuming the risk:* Knowledge is only one element of volens. So even if the risk is an "obvious risk" the common law requirement that the plaintiff voluntarily undertake the risk, except to the extent it is specifically amended, continues to apply(Victoria specifically preserves the common law, Vic: WrA, ss 47A, 54(3), compare SA: CLA, s 37(3)). This gives scope to the courts to ameliorate the harsh consequences of the defence of volens (as amended by CLA) by finding that the plaintiff did not agree to accept the risk. In *Carey v Lake Macquarie City Council* [2007] NSWCA 4, McLelland J, after dealing with obvious risks under the CLA, thought that a cyclist riding at speed along a path in the dark without a light was not volens to the risk that he might collide with unlit bollards in the middle of the path despite knowing that there were bollards on the path. The cyclist had simply not thought about the risk of injury.

> A genuine belief that the risk would not materialise will negative the defence, but a positive belief that the risk would materialise is not required to make the defence out...
>
> The question is not simply whether the plaintiff freely and voluntarily decided to embark upon a course of conduct that involved a risk of which he or she was aware. There must also be some conscious advertence to the possibility that the known risk might eventuate, and a decision to proceed with the conduct regardless. It is not enough that the plaintiff knows of the physical factors or circumstances that constitute the risk and exposes him or herself to them, although proof of this will in many cases be sufficient to support an inference that the plaintiff voluntarily assumed the risk (at [84],[107]).

Other members of the Court of Appeal found it unnecessary to deal with the defence of volens but all found that the plaintiff had been contributorily negligent and his damages should be reduced by 50%. The approach taken allows a court to avoid dismissing the plaintiff's claim in the face of a defendant's negligence but to acknowledge the plaintiff's lack of care by finding substantial contributory negligence. See M Lunney, "Personal responsibility and the "new" volenti" (2005) 13 Tort L Rev 76; J Keeler, "Personal Responsibility and the Reforms Recommended by the Ipp Report: Time Future Contained in Time Past" (2006) 14 TLJ 48.

4. *Recreational activities:* Plaintiffs engaging in recreational activities will be affected by the provisions relating to obvious risks: NSW: CLA, s 5J(2); Qld: CLA, s 17(2); Tas: CLA, s 18(2); WA: CLA, s 5G(2). Where the risk is obvious

within the meaning of the statutory provisions, the defendant has no duty to warn the plaintiff of obvious risks; a plaintiff will fail if the only negligence alleged is a failure to warn, *Jaber v Rockdale City Council* [2008] NSWCA 98 at [32]. Note also the provision that there is no duty of care in relation to recreational activities where a risk warning has been given even if the person injured did not receive the warning or understand it: NSW: CLA, s 5M; WA: CLA, 5I. Note also the provision allowing contractual limitation of liability for negligence in relation to recreational activities, NSW: CLA, s 5N; *Lormine v Zuereb* [2006] NSWCA 200; SA: *Recreational Services (Limitation of Liability) Act 2002* (SA): Vic: *Fair Trading Act 1999* (Vic), s 32N; Cth: *Trade Practices Act 1974* (Cth), s 68B.

5. *Dangerous recreational activities:* In some States the legislation makes further provision in relation to dangerous recreational activities: see NSW: CLA, ss 5K, 5L; Qld: CLA, ss 17 – 19; Tas: CLA, s 20; WA: CLA, s 5H. A plaintiff who engages in dangerous recreational activities has no claim for injuries resulting from the materialisation of an obvious risk; knowledge is not relevant to this provision. This defence prevents recovery in circumstances where the defence of volens would not. So a plaintiff cannot argue that there was no subjective knowledge of the particular risk that eventuated nor that the risk was not fully appreciated. A dangerous recreational activity is a recreational activity that involves "a significant risk of physical harm": NSW: CLA, s 5K; Qld: CLA, s 19; Tas: CLA, s 20 WA: CLA, s 5H. In *Jaber v Rockdale City Council* [2008] NSWCA 98 (referred to in Note 2, special leave to appeal to the High Court refused), the NSW Court of Appeal accepted that the meaning of a dangerous recreational activity is informed both by the risk of occurrence and the seriousness of the potential harm. The risk must be more than trivial but need not be likely. It qualifies as dangerous if there is a real risk of catastrophic spinal injury from diving into shallow water of unknown depth. The actual circumstances in which the injury occurred are relevant to whether it is a dangerous activity. It was relevant that the 19 year old had observed others diving off the wharf but not from the particular bollard nor in the direction that the plaintiff dived. It did not cease to qualify as a dangerous recreational activity because the plaintiff had mistakenly thought that the water was deep enough, (at [42], [54]). It was held that the plaintiff was not entitled to recover, see Tobias JA at [50]-[55], with the other members of the Court of Appeal concurring. In recent times plaintiffs in diving accidents have been particularly unsuccessful in claims against Councils and Roads Traffic authorities. Plaintiffs have fared better in other situations: see the NSW Court of Appeal in *Lormine Pty Ltd v Xuereb* [2006] NSWCA 200 at [33] (whale watching on a boat); *Smith v Perese* [2006] NSWSC 228 (spearfishing in an appropriately signed netted area for spearfishing not a dangerous recreational activity).

Would shooting kangaroos by spotlight at night constitute a dangerous recreational activity? What if the risk that eventuates is not one that arises from the particular danger but from something else, such as where the plaintiff is shot by the negligence of the defendant waving the gun around whilst trying to unjam it? Would it make any difference that at the time the plaintiff was in the vehicle, he had asked the defendant to take care, not to point the gun in his direction and not to bring the gun into the vehicle? The injured plaintiff in *Fallas v Mourlas* [2006] NSWCA 32 was held entitled to succeed in those circumstances (see [12.210]). Where the risk involved relates to the physical environment such as diving into shallow water, the Courts focus on whether there is an obvious risk of physical injury. But where the risks relate to the conduct of others as in *Fallas*, the focus is upon whether it was an "obvious risk" that the defendant may be negligent. Should it be so?

There are no comparable provisions in Victoria, the Northern Territory or the Australian Capital Territory. Note also *Recreational Services (Limitation of Liability) Act 2002* (SA). See generally, Dietrich, "Liability for Personal Injuries Arising from Recreational Services: The Interaction of Contract, Tort, State Legislation and the *Trade Practices Act* and the Resultant Mess" (2003) 11 TLJ 16.

6. *Materialisation of inherent risks*: The legislation also provides that a defendant is not liable for the materialisation of an inherent risk unless there is a duty to warn of that risk. An inherent risk is one "that can not be avoided by the exercise of due care and skill": NSW: CLA, s 5I; Qld: CLA, s 16; SA: CLA, s 39; WA: CLA, s 5P; Vic: WrA, s 55 (omits "and skill"). This does no more than declare the position at common law. At common law, a plaintiff was taken to have consented to the risk if the risk was one that could not be avoided by due care and skill. As we have noted earlier at [16.15], this is a case where there is no breach of duty and no liability. If in NSW, CLA, s 5I is a defence, which appears to be the view of the NSW Court of Appeal in *Lormine Pty Ltd v Xuereb* [2006] NSWCA 200 at [35], [36] (boat swamped by a large wave injuring P, not an inherent risk of whale watching on a boat), then the defendant is required to prove the harm could not have been avoided by using due care and skill. This is at odds with the common law position that it is up to the plaintiff to prove lack of due care and skill amounting to a breach of duty. At common law a defendant could be liable for the materialisation of an inherent risk, if there were a duty to warn of the risk and no warning was given. *Rogers v Whitaker* (1992) 175 CLR 479 (duty to warn of risk of blindness from medical procedure) is such an example. In most jurisdictions, defendants are relieved of the duty to warn of obvious risks unless there is a request for advice, a written legal requirement to warn or there is a risk of death or personal injury from a professional service, see NSW: CLA, s 5H; Qld: CLA, s 15; SA: CLA, s 38; Tas: CLA, s 17; WA: CLA, s 5O.

7. In some jurisdictions motor vehicle accidents are given separate treatment. In New South Wales and Queensland, in personal injury claims arising out of the use of a motor vehicle, circumstances attracting the defence of volens are now to be treated as contributory negligence cases (Qld: CLA, s 48). In New South Wales, the defence of volens continues to apply to car racing unless the person is a minor or under a disability: *Motor Accidents Act 1988* (NSW), s 76; *Motor Accidents Compensation Act 1999* (NSW), s 140. In New South Wales, the provisions relating to obvious risks apply to motor vehicle accidents: NSW: CLA, s 3B(2)(a). There are more general provisions not limited to motor vehicle accidents in South Australia (SA: CLA, s 47(4), 47(6)) and the Australian Capital Territory (ACT:

CLWA, s 96(5)) replacing the defence of volens with deemed contributory negligence where the injured plaintiff relies upon the skill of an intoxicated person.

CONTRIBUTORY NEGLIGENCE

Introduction

[16.65] At common law, a plaintiff guilty of contributory negligence was not entitled to any damages; that is, contributory negligence was a complete defence. Exceptionally a plaintiff might still be subject to the common law rule in cases like the *Voyager cases* where the events occurred prior to apportionment legislation, see *Ackland v Commonwealth of Australia* [2007] NSWCA 250. Courts found ways to avoid this harsh result where the plaintiff's negligence was insignificant in comparison to that of the defendant. These measures became unnecessary with the enactment of contributory negligence (apportionment) legislation in Australia: ACT: CLWA, ss 41, 101, 102; *Law Reform (Miscellaneous Provisions) Act* (NT), s 16(1); *Law Reform Act 1995* (Qld), s 10(1); *Law Reform (Contributory Negligence and Apportionment of Liability) Act 2001* (SA), ss 3, 4, 7; *Wrongs Act 1954* (Tas), s 2 ("wrongful act"), s 4(1); *Law Reform (Contributory Negligence and Tortfeasors' Contribution) Act 1947* (WA), s 4(1). Under this legislation, where the plaintiff has been guilty of contributory negligence, the plaintiff's damages are to be reduced to the extent that is just and equitable having regard to the plaintiff's share in the responsibility for the damage, see below [16.105].

At common law, it is a question of fact in the individual case whether the defendant's conduct amounts to contributory negligence. This has been modified in some situations where legislation deems certain conduct to constitute contributory negligence with special provisions applying to intoxicated drivers and their passengers (see [16.140] Notes 7 and 8). As the issue of contributory negligence is a question of fact, this imposes serious constraints on the ability of a court on appeal to interfere with the initial assessment of contributory negligence. In *Podrebersek v Australian Iron and Steel Pty Ltd* (1985) 59 ALJR 492 at 493-494 the High Court commented:

> A finding on a question of apportionment is a finding upon a "question, not of principle or of positive findings of fact or law, but of proportion, of balance and relative emphasis, and of weighing different considerations. It involves an individual choice or discretion, as to which there may well be differences of opinion by different minds" ... Such a finding, if made by a judge, is not lightly reviewed. The task of an appellant is even more difficult when the apportionment is made by a jury.

Under the general law, the defence of contributory negligence is available if the following requirements are satisfied:

(1) the plaintiff failed to take reasonable care for his or her own safety or for the protection of the plaintiff's interests;

(2) this negligence was a cause of the plaintiff's harm;

(3) the harm that eventuated was within the risk created by the plaintiff's conduct.

The contributory negligence standard – the general law

[16.70] Against what standard is the plaintiff's conduct judged in deciding whether the conduct amounts to contributory negligence? It is not surprising that at common law a plaintiff's conduct was judged with greater leniency given that contributory negligence was a complete defence at common law. As you read this section, you should consider whether this leniency should continue when courts can simply reduce the plaintiff's damages for contributory negligence. This question is affected by civil liability legislation (see [16.140] Note 1).

Agony of the moment

[16.75] At common law, the plaintiff might not be guilty of contributory negligence if in response to a defendant's negligence, the plaintiff acted in the "agony of the moment" and was injured. For example, if the plaintiff broke a leg jumping off a wall to get out of the way of a runaway truck, when the plaintiff might have adopted an alternative course of action involving less risk. Or where a passenger released a seatbelt when a car was about to hit a pole on the passenger side of the vehicle (see *Avram v Gusakoski* [2006] WASCA 16 and also *Jones v Boyce* (1816) 1 Stark 493; 171 ER 540). In *Caterson v Commissioner for Railways* (1973) 128 CLR 99, the plaintiff was held not to be contributory negligent when he jumped off a train that was leaving a remote country platform. No warning was given that the train was about to depart, the next station was 80 miles away and the plaintiff's son was left on the platform. The High Court held that the plaintiff had not been guilty of contributory negligence. The question whether the plaintiff's action in taking the risk was unreasonable was to be answered by weighing the degree of inconvenience to which he was to be subjected against the risk taken to escape from it. On that test the jury was not bound to find that the plaintiff's injuries had been contributed to by any negligence on his part. Is such a lenient approach still warranted? It is clear that mere inconvenience or discomfort is not sufficient to absolve the plaintiff from contributory negligence. Consequently, a prudent pedestrian would walk on the side of the road when it was dark and had been raining even if the road edge is rough, wet and slippery rather than risk being hit by a vehicle on the road (see *Purcell v Watson* (1979) 26 ALR 235; *Anikin v Sierra* [2004] 211 ALR 621; *Consolidated Broken Hill Ltd v Edwards* [2005] NSWCA 380).

Anticipating the negligence of others

[16.80] A plaintiff may be contributorily negligent for failing to anticipate the possible negligence of others. Lord du Parcq, in *Grant v Sun Shipping Co Ltd* [1948] AC 549 at 567, expressed the opinion: "a prudent man will guard against the possible negligence of others when experience shows such negligence to be common". Road users might be negligent in failing to anticipate that other road users may be negligent. Lord Uthwatt observed in *London Passenger Transport v Upson* [1949] AC 155 at 173 that it is common experience that road users do not behave with reasonable care: "A driver is not, of course, bound to anticipate folly in all its forms but he is not, in my opinion, entitled to put out of consideration the teachings of experience as to the form those follies commonly take". Such observations do not exclude some cases in which a plaintiff has been held to have acted reasonably in assuming that another road user would exercise care at least to the extent of observing basic rules of the road, for example stopping at a red light (*Hopwood Homes Ltd v Kennerdine* [1975] RTR 82 (UK CA); *McCutcheon v Grimmond (No 2)* (1986) 40 SASR 487), or assuming that a car will give way to the right as required by road rules (*Cooper v Bech (No 2)* (1975) 12 SASR 151; *Bradbury v Henshall* (1987) 5 MVR 248, but compare *Sibley v Kais* (1967) 118 CLR 424).

For other illustrations, see *Tea Tree Gully v Doyle* (1986) 4 MVR 63; *Cocks* (1979) 53 ALJR 591; *Dos Santos v Morris Painting & Décorating* [2006] NSWC

A lenient approach

[16.85] At common law it is said that the standard applied to the plaintiff is more subjective, thus making allowance for personal idiosyncrasies which have no place in the traditional objective standard of the ordinary and reasonable person. Support for this view can be found in the judgment of Menzies J in *McHale v Watson* (1966) 115 CLR 199 at 223-225. In accordance with the normal negligence rule, allowance is made for children. There are, however, cases where children have been held guilty of contributory negligence by failing to show the care expected of children of like age and experience: see *Bullock v Miller* (1987) 5 MVR 55; *Guerin v Rossiter* (1984) 37 SASR 312; *Berzins v Lulic* (1986) 41 SASR 306; *Bye v Bates* (1989) 51 SASR 67 (6 1/2 year old child). It is certainly true that in actions against employers, the conduct of plaintiff employees has been measured by a comparatively generous standard which makes allowance for momentary lapses of attention in the performance of prolonged repetitive work in distracting conditions. Where the civil liability legislation applies this more generous approach cannot apply, see [16.140] Note 1. In *Commissioner for Railways (Qld) v Ruprecht* (1979) 142 CLR 563 at 567-568, Gibbs J said:

> in deciding whether the respondent was guilty of contributory negligence, one may consider, as part of all the circumstances, such things as inattention born of familiarity and repetition, and the man's preoccupation with the matter in hand, with a view to deciding "whether any of these things caused some temporary inadvertence to danger, some lapse of attention, some taking of risk or other departure from the highest degree of circumspection, excusable in the circumstances because not incompatible with the conduct of a prudent and reasonable man": *Sungravure Pty Ltd v Meani* (1964) 110 CLR 24 at 37 per Windeyer J.

Courts may be reluctant to find contributory negligence by an employee where the employer's negligence consists in the setting up of an unsafe system of work and the alleged contributory negligence of the employee manifests in acquiescence to the system or even participation in executing the system. In *State Rail Authority of New South Wales v Wiegold* (1991) Aust Torts Reports 81-148 NSWCA, an employee was injured in a fall caused by a defective torch supplied by the employer. The employees had complained about the torches. Samuels JA held that there was no contributory negligence. In *Czatyrko v Edith Cowan University* [2005] 79 ALJR 839, an employee sued his employer for injuries sustained when he stepped backwards and fell. The plaintiff had assumed that the platform behind him abutted and was level with the tray of the truck he was loading. The platform had been lowered without his knowledge and without warning. On the question whether the plaintiff was contributorily negligent in failing to look behind him before stepping back, the High Court in a joint judgment said (at [18]):

> In the present case, the [plaintiff] appellant did no doubt omit to take a simple precaution of looking to see whether the platform was raised before stepping on to it, and this omission was a cause of his injuries. But in acting as he did, the appellant did not disobey any direction or warning from the respondent. No directions or warnings of any kind were given by the respondent in relation to the use of the platform. Furthermore, [the employees] ... were under pressure from their supervisor to complete the job promptly. The work was repetitive. In all of these circumstances it presented a fertile field for inadvertence. The onus of proving contributory negligence lay upon the [defendant] respondent. This it failed to do in this case. The appellant's attempt to step on to the platform in the mistaken belief that it was still raised, and in an effort to finish loading the truck, was the product of nothing more than "mere

> inadvertence, inattention or misjudgement". It was not a remote risk that the appellant might step back without looking behind him. His actions were neither deliberate, intentional, nor in disregard of a direction or order from the respondent. No finding of contributory negligence should have been made.

However, this does not mean that the conduct of a worker will never constitute contributory negligence. Some recent decisions suggest a more robust view where the worker has acted contrary to instructions and adopted a different system of work. For example, *Moller v Trollope Silverwood and Beck Pty Ltd* [2004] VSCA 22 where an experienced tradesman's unsafe use of a ladder in a confined space resulted in a finding of 40% contributorily negligence, or *South v James Loughran & Sons Pty Ltd & Ors* [2003] TASSC 59 (4 July 2003) where a gap in walk-way was known to employer and employee–the employee was found 30% contributory negligence. However, the contributory negligence of an independent contractor may be higher in the same circumstances: see *Thompson v Woolworths (Q'land) Pty Ltd* [2005] 214 ALR 452, where a back injury sustained in moving heavy bins and compare it with *Liftronic Pty Ltd v Unver* (2001) 179 ALR 321 (the court refused to interfere on appeal with jury verdict of 60% contributory negligence).

The standard by which the plaintiff's conduct is to be judged is affected by civil liability legislation (see [16.140] Note 1). Common law claims against employers are governed by workers compensation legislation and may be excluded from some or all of the civil liability legislation; ACT: CLWA, ss 41, 93(2); NSW: CLA, s 3B(1)(f), *New South Wales v Ball* [2007] NSWCA 71; NT: PICCA, s 4(3)(b); Qld: CLA, s 5; SA: CLA, s 4(4); Tas: CLA, s 3B(3)(4); Vic: WrA, s 45; WA: CLA, s 3A, item 3. If the general civil liability principles are excluded, courts may continue to exercise a generous approach in assessing whether an injured plaintiff's conduct constitutes contributory negligence.

Statutory safety requirements

[16.90] Where a particular safety requirement is mandated by legislation, breach of a rule creating an offence is generally held to be evidence of negligence, but not conclusive evidence. The weight to be attached to breach of the regulation will vary with the circumstances. Legislation creating offences in relation to seat belts and special restraining devices–for example, in relation to children–has been progressively tightened and the weight to be attached to breach has grown correspondingly in the course of judicial decision. Quite apart from statutorily mandated contributory negligence for failure to wear an available seatbelt, the community standard is such that failure to wear an available seat belt that would have reduced injury is almost invariably contributory negligence. For rare instances when it was not, see *Hooker v Farquhar* [1995] 21 MVR 468 (QSC) (plaintiff asleep on the back seat not anticipating that car would be driven); *Avram v Gusakoski* [2006] WASCA 16 (passenger releases seatbelt when car about to hit a pole on the passenger side of the vehicle).

Special statutory provisions apply for failure to wear a seat belt or a protective helmet as required by regulations. Subject to some qualifications especially for minors, that failure is presumed to be contributory negligence with the defendant bearing the onus of proof that the plaintiff was not wearing a seat belt: *Motor Accidents Compensation Act 1999* (NSW), s 138(2)(c)(d); *Petracho v Griffiths* [2007] NSWCA 302; *Civil Law (Wrongs) Act 2002* (ACT), s 97; SA: CLA, s 49. Differences in the provisions require noting.

Community standards

[16.95] Where a particular precaution is not mandated by statute, community standards will be relevant to determining whether the failure to adopt that precaution amounts to contributory negligence. In *Kirk v Nominal Defendant* [1984] 1 Qd R 592, the Full Court of the Supreme Court of Queensland held that it was not contributory negligence to ride pillion on a motor cycle without wearing jeans or other tough protective clothing. In the first place it was held that the evidence did not demonstrate that tough clothing would have prevented the injury. Secondly, it was not thought that the social consciousness of those who rode motor cycles in our community had reached a stage where it is recognised that it shows a lack of due care if one fails to wear tough clothing. It was different with seat belts.

Causation

[16.100] Some causal connection between the plaintiff's negligence and the damage must be established. To illustrate in *Gent-Diver v Neville* [1953] QSR 1 (see [16.25] Note 2), the risk voluntarily accepted, namely a defective headlight, was not a cause of the accident (failure to keep a proper lookout). For this reason the volenti defence failed and so to did the defence of contributory negligence. The plaintiff's contributory negligence need not be a cause of the accident, it is sufficient if the conduct aggravated the plaintiff's injuries. The issue arose in *Froom v Butcher* [1976] 1 QB 286 when the Court of Appeal considered whether failure to wear a seat belt could be contributory negligence. Lord Denning MR said:

> The question is not what the cause of the accident was. It is rather what was the cause of the damage. In most accidents on the road the bad driving, which causes the accident, also causes the ensuing damage. But in seat belt cases the cause of the accident is one thing. The cause of the damage is another. The *accident* is caused by the bad driving. The *damage* is caused in part by the bad driving of the defendant, and in part by the failure of the plaintiff to wear a seat belt. If the plaintiff was to blame in not wearing a seat belt, the damage is in part the result of his own fault. He must bear some share in the responsibility for the damage: and his damages fall to be reduced to such extent as the court thinks just and equitable.

On the question of how far damages should be reduced, Lord Denning, MR said:

> Sometimes the evidence will show that the failure made no difference. The damage could have been the same, even if a seat belt had been worn. In such case the damages should not be reduced at all. At other times the evidence will show that the failure made all the difference. The damage would have been prevented altogether if a seat belt had been worn. In such cases I would suggest that the damages should be reduced by 25%. But often enough the evidence will only show that the failure made a considerable difference. Some injuries to the head, for instance, would have been a good deal less severe if a seat belt had been worn, but there would still have been some injury to the head. In such cases I would suggest that the damages attributable to the failure to wear a seat belt should be reduced by 15%.

The other familiar situation where contributory negligence is frequently argued is the position of a passenger accepting a lift with a drunken driver. In such cases the plaintiff contributes to his or her harm–just by being in the vehicle when he or she should not have been, but the plaintiff's presence may have nothing to do with the accident itself. See *MacKenzie v The Nominal Defendant* [2005] NSWCA 180 [16.145] as an illustration.

Apportionment legislation

[16.105] At common law a plaintiff's contributory negligence was a complete defence to the claim. In 1945 in the United Kingdom, legislation was passed which provided that contributory negligence no longer barred the plaintiff's claim but operated to reduce the plaintiff's damages: *Law Reform (Contributory Negligence) Act 1945* (UK). In all jurisdictions with which this casebook is concerned, the English legislative model was substantially, though not exactly, followed. In recent times the Australian legislation has been amended as a consequence of the High Court's decision in *Astley v Austrust Ltd* (1999) 197 CLR 1 (extracted at [16.170]). There the High Court held that contributory negligence was not a defence to a claim based on contract. This was despite the fact that if the plaintiff had instead sued in the tort of negligence, which the plaintiff could have done, the plaintiff's contributory negligence would have reduced damages recoverable. This would allow a plaintiff to avoid the reduction of damages by reason of the plaintiff's contributory negligence by suing on the contract. This reluctance to allow contributory negligence to apply beyond the confines of the tort of negligence has been confirmed in relation to damages claims under the *Trade Practices Act 1974* (Cth) (*Henville v Walker* (2001) 206 CLR 459; *I & L Securities Pty Ltd v HTW Valuers (Brisbane) Pty Ltd* (2002) 192 ALR 1) and in relation to equitable claims (*Pilmer v Duke Group Ltd (in liq)* (2001) 207 CLR 165). The *Trade Practices Act 1974* has subsequently been amended to allow apportionment for breaches of s 52 (misleading or deceptive conduct). In response to *Astley v Austrust Ltd* (1999) 197 CLR 1, all jurisdictions have amended the apportionment legislation to allow the defence of contributory negligence where the defendant's contractual duty of care is the same as the defendant's liability in the tort of negligence independently of the existence of any contract. The New South Wales provision, contained in the *Law Reform Miscellaneous Provisions Act 1965* is set out below.

Law Reform Miscellaneous Provisions Act 1965

[16.110] *Law Reform Miscellaneous Provisions Act 1965* (NSW), ss 8, 9(1)

s 8 wrong means an act or omission that:

(a) gives rise to a liability in tort in respect of which a defence of contributory negligence is available at common law, or

(b) amounts to a breach of a contractual duty of care that is concurrent and co-extensive with a duty of care in tort.

s 9(1) If a person (the claimant) suffers damage as the result partly of the claimant's failure to take reasonable care (contributory negligence) and partly of the wrong of any other person:

(a) a claim in respect of the damage is not defeated by reason of the contributory negligence of the claimant, and

(b) the damages recoverable in respect of the wrong are to be reduced to such extent as the court thinks just and equitable having regard to the claimant's share in the responsibility for the damage.

[16.115] **Notes&Questions**

1. Similar provisions exist in most jurisdictions: ACT: CLWA, ss 41, 101, 102; *Law Reform (Miscellaneous Provisions) Act 1956* (NT), s 16(1); *Law Reform Act 1995* (Qld), s 10(1); *Law Reform (Contributory Negligence and Apportionment of Liability) Act 2001* (SA), ss 3, 4, 7; *Wrongs Act 1954* (Tas), s 2 ("wrongful act"), s 4(1); *Wrongs Act 1958* (Vic) ss 25, 26; *Law Reform (Contributory Negligence and Tortfeasors'*

Contribution) Act 1947 (WA), s 4(1).

In New South Wales, the *Workers Compensation Act 1987* (NSW) applies the apportionment principles to claims governed by the Workers Compensation legislation: s 151N(4) including actions for breach of statutory duty, s 151N(3), see Chapter 17. However, the damages are not to be reduced below what the worker might have obtained by way of workers' compensation if his or her compensation could have been commuted to a lump sum (s 151N(2)), see also *Law Reform (Miscellaneous Provisions) Act 1965* (NSW), s 10.

2. The apportionment legislation raises the question whether devices used to avoid the harsh effects of the common law rule that contributory negligence was an absolute defence can still apply. One such rule was known as the "last opportunity rule". In a complicated and contorted history, the rule was restated by the High Court in *Alford v Magee* (1952) 85 CLR 437 at 461:

> [M]ost probably the fundamental idea behind all the cases ... is that there are cases in which there is so substantial a difference between the positions of the plaintiff and the position of the defendant at the material time that (although the accident could not have happened if the plaintiff's conduct had not been negligent) it would not be fair or reasonable to regard the plaintiff as in any real sense the author of his own harm. This position may arise because the defendant had, *and the plaintiff had not*, a real opportunity, of which a "reasonable man" would have available himself, of "avoiding the mischief" ... It may arise because the defendant's negligent conduct is substantially later in point of time than the plaintiff's negligent conduct, and a reasonably behaving defendant would have seen its effect and avoided its "consequences" ... It may arise because the defendant had an advantage over the plaintiff, in that he was "master of the situation", but chose to run a risk ... It may arise because the defendant had such an advantage over the plaintiff that he ought to have been "master of the situation" but unreasonably failed to take advantage of his superior position ....

Except for limited provision in Western Australia (*Law Reform (Contributory Negligence and Tortfeasors' Contribution) Act 1947* (WA), s 4 and *Aird v Grantham* [1998] WASCA 254), the Australian States and Territories have followed the English example in making no reference in their apportionment legislation to the last opportunity rule and it has been left to the courts to say whether the doctrine is finally buried. It seems now to be accepted by the High Court that the last opportunity rule has been abolished by statute; the apportionment statute now prescribes what is to be done in cases of comparative fault: *Chapman v Hearse* (1961) 106 CLR 112; *March v E & M H Stramare Pty Ltd* (1991) 171 CLR 506 Mason CJ at 513.

Independently of the "last opportunity rule", there may still be cases where the plaintiff's negligent conduct is no longer a relevant cause of her or his harm.

3. The definition of "wrong" in the legislation (see above, [16.110]) refers to liability in tort in respect of which the defence of contributory negligence was available at common law: see ACT: CLWA, s 101; NSW: *Law Reform (Miscellaneous Provisions) Act 1965* (NSW), s 8; NT: *Law Reform (Miscellaneous Provisions) Act 1956* (NT), s 15; Qld: *Law Reform Act 1995* (Qld), s 5; SA: *Law Reform (Contributory Negligence and Apportionment of Liability) Act 2001* (SA), s 4; Tas: *Wrongs Act 1954* (Tas), s 2 ("wrongful act"); Vic: *Wrongs Act 1958* (Vic), s 25; WA: *Law Reform (Contributory Negligence and Tortfeasors'*

Contribution) Act 1947 (WA), s 3A. Subject to concurrent contractual duties, the apportionment provisions do not apply if the *defendant* is not liable in tort; the opening phrase, "liability in tort" refers to the defendant's liability. So, if the defendant is exclusively liable in contract or in equity, the defence of contributory negligence is not available. This reluctance to allow contributory negligence to apply beyond the confines of the tort of negligence has been confirmed in relation to damages claims under the *Trade Practices Act 1974* (Cth) (*Henville v Walker* (2001) 206 CLR 459; *I & L Securities Pty Ltd v HTW Valuers (Brisbane) Pty Ltd* (2002) 210 CLR 109) and in relation to equitable claims (*Pilmer v Duke Group Ltd (in liq)* (2001) 207 CLR 165). The *Trade Practices Act 1974* (Cth), s 82(1B) now provides that in relation to economic loss or damage to property caused by contravention of s 52 (misleading or deceptive conduct), damages may be reduced to the extent just and equitable having regard to the claimant's share in the responsibility for the loss or damage.

4. There is the additional requirement that the defence applies only if contributory negligence would have been a defence at common law. It was not a defence to claims in the tort of deceit (*Standard Chartered Bank v Pakistan National Shipping Corp (No 2)* [2002] 2 All ER (Comm) 931) nor in relation to intentional torts, see Chapter 6 Defences to Intentional Torts.

5. The *plaintiff's conduct* need not involve a breach of duty to some-one else. It is sufficient if it is a failure to take reasonable care for the plaintiff's own safety such as a failure to wear an available seat belt. Nor does the plaintiff's conduct need to be negligent. A plaintiff's intentional wrongdoing can be the subject of apportionment. In *Adams by her next friend O'Grady v State of New South Wales* [2008] NSWSC 1257 at [131]-[133] the Plaintiff stabbed a teacher. The plaintiff alleged that the defendant was negligent in allowing the plaintiff access to a knife. It was held that even if the plaintiff was able to show a duty of care, which it could not, the plaintiff's conduct could be regarded as 100% contributory negligence.

6. A further question, described either as causation or remoteness, is whether the harm actually suffered must be within the risk which the plaintiff as a reasonable person should have guarded against; that is, is it the type of harm which he or she might have anticipated. In *Jones v Livox Quarries Ltd* [1952] 2 QB 608, the question was whether a worker riding on the back of a truck, rather like a footman on a carriage, was guilty of contributory negligence when another vehicle collided with the back of the vehicle. The most usual risk would have been that he might have fallen off or got tangled up with the machinery. Denning LJ said (at 626):

> if the plaintiff, whilst he was riding on the towbar, had been hit in the eye by a shot from a negligent sportsman, I should have thought that the plaintiff's negligence would in no way be a cause of his injury. It would only be the circumstances in which the cause operated. It would only be part of the history. But I cannot say that in the present case. The man's negligence here was so much mixed up with his injury that it cannot be dismissed as mere history. His dangerous position on the vehicle was one of the causes of his damage.

[16.120] Just as introduction of the apportionment legislation has enabled the courts to more easily accept the causal relevance of the plaintiff's negligence, so also it may affect the standard applied to the plaintiff's conduct. Professor Fleming, referring to the doctrine of the "agony of the moment", suggests that it is questionable "whether the courts will continue to display quite the same indulgence" (JG Fleming, *The Law of Torts* (9th ed, LBC Information Services, Sydney, 1998), p 319). Like the last opportunity rule, the "agony of the moment" doctrine was a means of enabling the plaintiff to recover although his or her conduct was clearly a departure from the standard of reasonable care.

The typical apportionment provision requires the court to reduce the plaintiff's damages as the court thinks just and equitable having regard to the claimant's share in the responsibility for the damage. The following case deals with how an actual apportionment is to be made.

Pennington v Norris

[16.125] *Pennington v Norris* (1956) 96 CLR 10 High Court of Australia

(footnotes omitted)

[Plaintiff was knocked down and severely injured by a car driven by the defendant (respondent). The High Court judgment is extracted on the question whether the Tasmanian trial judge's reduction of the damages by 50% on the ground of plaintiff's contributory negligence was correct.]

THE COURT: 15 It is clear that the Act intends to give a very wide discretion to the judge or jury entrusted with the original task of making the apportionment. Much latitude must be allowed to the original tribunal in arriving at a judgment as to what is just and equitable. It is to be expected, therefore, that cases will be rare in which the apportionment made can be successfully challenged: see *British Fame (Owners) v Macgregor (Owners)* [1943] AC 197; *Ingram v United Automobile Service Ltd* [1943] KB 612. But, giving full weight to these considerations in the present case, we are unable to avoid the conclusion that, in apportioning the responsibility equally, his Honour must have overlooked certain features of the case, and that the amount by which he reduced the assessed damages cannot really be supported.

The only guide which the statute provides is that it requires regard to be had to "the claimant's share in the responsibility for the damage". As to the effect of this see generally an article by Mr Douglas Payne, "Reduction of Damages for Contributory Negligence" (1955) 18 Mod LR 344. What has to be done is to arrive at a "just and equitable" apportionment as between the plaintiff and the defendant of the "responsibility" for the damage. It seems clear that this must of necessity involve a comparison of culpability. By "culpability" we do not mean moral blameworthiness but degree of departure from the standard of care of the reasonable man. To institute a comparison in respect of blameworthiness in such a case as the present seems more or less impracticable, because, while the defendant's negligence is a breach of duty owed to other persons and therefore blameworthy, the plaintiff's "contributory" negligence is not a breach of any duty at all, and it is difficult to impute "moral" blame to one who is careless merely of his own safety.

Here, in our opinion, the negligence of the defendant was in high degree more culpable, more gross, than that of the plaintiff. The plaintiff's conduct was ex hypothesi careless and unreasonable but, after all, it was the sort of thing that is very commonly done: he simply did not look when a reasonably careful man would have looked. We think too that in this case the very fact that his conduct did not endanger the defendant or anybody else is a material consideration. The defendant's position was entirely different. The learned judge found only that he was negligent in not keeping a proper lookout, but there were several other important elements in the case, as Mr Wright pointed out. We think, indeed, that the equal allocation of responsibility by his Honour must have proceeded from an overlooking of these elements. The first matter is his speed. It could not on the evidence have been found to be less than 30 miles per hour. Again, there was a large number of people in the vicinity–the defendant himself says that he noticed "quite a number of people about". The hotels, of which there were three in the immediate vicinity, had closed a very short time previously. It was a misty night, and the road was wet. Visibility must have been impaired by these factors, and it was further impaired by mistiness on the inside and outside of the windscreen. To drive at 30 miles per hour in a town at night under these circumstances seems to us to have been to do an obviously dangerous thing, and to have amounted to negligence of far greater culpability than anything that can possibly be attributed to the plaintiff.

Having regard to these factors, and to all the circumstances of the case, we are of opinion that a fair and reasonable allocation of the responsibility for the damage done is to attribute it, as to 80 per cent to the defendant and, as to 20% to the plaintiff. The appeal should be allowed, and the judgment of the Supreme Court of Tasmania varied so as to give effect to this apportionment.

[16.130] **Notes&Questions**

1. The standard provision requires a court to assess contributory negligence and reduce damages "to such extent as the court thinks just and equitable having regard to the claimant's share in the responsibility for the damage", see above. In what has become the authoritative statement on the correct approach to be adopted, the High Court in *Podrebersek v Australian Iron and Steel Pty Ltd* (1985) 59 ALJR 492 at 494 said:

   > The making of an apportionment as between a plaintiff and a defendant of their respective shares in the responsibility for the damage involves a comparison both of culpability, ie of the degree of departure from the standard of care of the reasonable man (*Pennington v Norris* (1956) 96 CLR 10 at 16) and of the relative importance of the acts of the parties in causing the damage: *Stapley v Gypsum Mines Ltd* [1953] AC 663 at 692; *Smith v McIntyre* [1958] Tas SR 36 at 42-49 and *Broadhurst v Millman* [1976] VR 208 at 219, and cases there cited. It is the whole conduct of each negligent party in relation to the circumstances of the accident which must be subjected to comparative examination. The significance of the various elements involved in such an examination will vary from case to case; for example, the circumstances of some cases may be such that a comparison of the relative importance of the acts of the parties in causing the damage will be of little, if any, importance.

   Would failure to keep a look out for obstructions whilst walking and talking on a mobile phone be contributory negligent? *Skulander v Willoughby City Council* [2007] NSWCA 116 (yes–50% contributory negligent).

2. The New South Wales provision relating to motor vehicle accidents directs the court to reduce damages "by such percentage as the court thinks just and equitable *in the circumstances of the case*" (italics added), *Motor Accidents Compensation Act 1999* (NSW), s 138(3). Kirby J (at 133) in *Joslyn v Berryman* (2003) 214 CLR 552 thought this had the effect that contributory negligence was to be determined only by reference to what was just and equitable. Hayne J (at 157) thought the standard approach in *Podrebersek v Australian Iron and Steel Pty Ltd* (1985) 59 ALJR 492 (cited above) should apply. Hayne J's view was adopted by the NSW Court of Appeal in *Mackenzie v The Nominal Defendant* [2005] NSWCA 180 extracted below at [16.145].

3. Special statutory provisions deeming contributory negligence and setting out defined percentages for contributory negligence ap alcohol impaired plaintiffs, motor vehicle accidents and passe driven by intoxicated drivers (see [16.140] Notes 7 and 8).

Contributory negligence and the civil liability legislation

Review of the Law of Negligence

[16.135] Negligence Review Panel, *Review of the Law of Negligence, Final Report*, (Commonwealth of Australia, Canberra, 2002)

(footnotes partially omitted)

Contributory negligence

The same standard of care

8.10 In the opinion of the Panel, there is in the Australian community today a widely-held expectation that, in general, people will take as much care for themselves as they expect others to take for them. This is an application of the fundamental idea that people should take responsibility for their own lives and safety, and it provides powerful support for the principle that the standard of care for negligence and contributory negligence should be the same.

8.11 Leading textbook writers have asserted that in practice, the standard of care applied to contributory negligence is lower than that applied to negligence despite the fact that, in theory, the standard should be the same. There is a perception (which may reflect the reality) that many lower courts are more indulgent to plaintiffs than to defendants. ... This may result, for example, in motorists being required to keep a better lookout than pedestrians. In the Panel's view, this approach should not be supported. ...

8.13 In the view of the Panel, a legislative statement setting out the approach to be followed in dealing with the issue of contributory negligence, emphasising that contributory negligence is to be measured against an objective standard of reasonable conduct, stating that the standard of care applicable to negligence and contributory negligence is the same, and establishing the negligence calculus as a suitable basis for considering contributory negligence, could discourage the tendency of courts to be overly indulgent to plaintiffs when apportioning damages for contributory negligence. ...

Assumption of risk and 100 per cent contributory negligence

8.20 [T]he Apportionment Legislation gives the court a very wide discretion to reduce the damages payable to a plaintiff who has been contributorily negligent. ... The only guidance the Apportionment Legislation gives to courts is that the reduction should be such as the court considers "just and equitable".

8.21 In exercising this discretion, courts have reduced a plaintiff's damages by as much as 90 per cent (*Podrebersek v Australia Iron and Steel Pty Limited* (1985) 59 ALR 492). However, the High Court has held that a reduction of 100 per cent is not permissible (*Wynbergen v Hoyts Corporation Pty Limited* (1997) 149 ALR 25). The basis of this decision is that an apportionment of 100 per cent contributory negligence amounts to a finding that the plaintiff was wholly responsible for the damage suffered, whereas the Apportionment Legislation operates on the premise that the plaintiff suffered damage partly as a result of his or her own fault and partly of the fault of another person (per Hayne J at 29-30). In one case, a reduction of the plaintiff's damages by 95 per cent was overturned on appeal on the basis that such a large reduction amounted, in effect, to a holding that the plaintiff was entirely to blame (*Civic v Glastonbury Steel Fabrications Pty Limited* (1985) Aust Torts Reports 80-746). The view has been expressed that the reasons given by the High Court for not permitting a reduction in ages of 100 per cent would preclude a reduction of any more than 90 per cent because a duction of any greater amount would necessarily mean that the defendant's fault was so negligible that it should be ignored (*Kelly v Carroll* [2002] NSWCA 9, [37] per Heydon JA).

8.22 Despite these decisions, the Panel's view is that a provision that a court is entitled to reduce a contributorily negligent plaintiff's damages by 100 per cent would be a desirable reform of the law of negligence. Our reason rests on our understanding of the relationship between the defences of contributory negligence and voluntary assumption of risk in the light of Terms of Reference 1(f) and 3(b).

8.23 Voluntary assumption of risk is a complete defence in the sense that it provides the basis for denying the plaintiff any damages at all. A person will be held to have voluntarily assumed a risk only if they were actually aware of the precise risk in question and freely accepted that risk. Since the introduction of the defence of contributory negligence, the defence of voluntary assumption of risk has become more or less defunct. This is because any conduct that could amount to voluntary assumption of risk would also amount to contributory negligence. Courts prefer the defence of contributory negligence because it enables them to apportion damages between the parties, thus allowing the plaintiff to recover something, even in cases where the plaintiff bears a very significant share of responsibility for the harm suffered. ...

8.25 Our view is that while the cases in which it will be appropriate to reduce the damages payable to a contributorily negligent plaintiff by more than 90 per cent will be very rare, there may be cases in which such an outcome would be appropriate in terms of the statutory instruction to reduce the damages to such an extent as the court considers "just and equitable". The sort of case we have in mind is where the risk created by the defendant is patently obvious and could have been avoided by the exercise of reasonable care on the part of the plaintiff. ...

8.26 Such a provision might also give a signal to judges in the ordinary run of cases that it is appropriate to hold plaintiffs responsible for their own negligence on the same basis as defendants are held responsible for theirs.

8.27 Accordingly, the Panel recommends that the Proposed Act provide that under the Apportionment Legislation, a court is entitled to reduce a plaintiff's damages by 100 per cent where the court considers that it is just and equitable to do so.

[16.140] **Notes&Questions**

1. *The contributory negligence standard:* Turning first to the contributory negligence standard. The Ipp Report recommendation that the standard of care for contributory negligence should be the same as the standard applying to negligence has been adopted in most States. The standard applicable is that of a reasonable person in the position of that person having regard to what the person knew or ought to have known at the time: NSW: CLA, s 5R; Qld: CLA, s 23; Tas: CLA, s 23; Vic: WrA, s 62; WA: CLA, s 5K; compare SA: CLA, ss 44, 3 ("contributory negligence"). The Australian Capital Territory and the Northern Territory have no similar provision.
2. *Leniency towards plaintiffs:* The Ipp Committee said that a more lenient approach to plaintiffs had resulted in motorists being required to keep a better lookout than pedestrians. In the Panel's view, this approach should not be supported. For an example of what appears to be a lenient approach despite NSW: CLA, s 5R, see *Pollard v Baulderstone Hornibrook Engineering Pty Ltd* [2008] NSWCA 99 a truck driver was

held not to be contributorily negligent where he was cleaning the tyres of his vehicle on a muddy site and stepped back without looking and was injured. How would a Court now deal with *Pennington v Norris* (1956) 96 CLR 10 [16.125]? See *Hathaway v Thorpe* [2006] NSWCA 163 following *Pennington* on the basis that a motor vehicle driver although unable to see a cyclist until the last moment is in a superior position to a cyclist in dark clothing on a bike without a headlight–contributory negligence assessed at 30%.

3. *Plaintiff's duty to care for own safety:* In *Consolidated Broken Hill Ltd v Edwards* [2005] NSWCA 380, Ipp J, in delivering the judgment of the Court of Appeal, at [68] quoted from the judgments of Callinan and Heydon JJ in *Vairy v Wyong Shire Council* [2005] 80 ALJR 1 at [220] in relation to contributory negligence to the effect:

> it is not right to say, without qualification, that the difference between the duties of an injured plaintiff, and those of a tortfeasor, is that the former owes absolutely no duties to others including the defendant, while the latter owes duties to all of his "neighbours". The "duty" to take reasonable care for his own safety that a plaintiff has is not simply a nakedly self-interested one, but one of enlightened self-interest which should not disregard the burden, by way of social security and other obligations that a civilized and democratic society will assume towards him if he is injured. In short the duty that he owes is not just to look out for himself, but not to act in a way which may put him at risk, in the knowledge that society may come under obligations of various kinds to him if the risk is realized.

Ipp J commented [at 69] that these remarks are consistent with the *Civil Liability* legislation provisions referred to in Note 1 above.

4. *The reasonable person in the position of that person:* The standard of care required is that of a reasonable person in "the position of that person" and contributory negligence is determined on the basis of what the person knew or ought to have known, see statutory references in Note 1, above. In *Doubleday v Kelly* [2005] NSWCA 151, a seven year old girl, was injured on a trampoline. She had been warned not to get onto the trampoline, but had got onto it with her roller skates on. The trial judge refused to find contributory negligence. On appeal to the Court of Appeal, the court rejected the argument that the statute required the court to ignore the fact that the plaintiff was a seven year old child. Bryson JA remarked that that would require a radical departure from the common law and that was not the intention of the section. In the circumstances, a seven year old may have limited perception of the dangers and the finding by the trial judge that her conduct was not contributorily negligent should be upheld (at [26]). Nor was the risk to be regarded as an obvious risk in relation to a seven year old child for the purposes of the legislation (at [29]). Similarly a 12 year old might not perceive that there was a risk of falling through a roof by sitting on the roof skylight, *Waverley Council v Ferreira* [2005] NSWCA 418. But an 11 year old could be expected to have sufficient road sense not to run across the road when drivers would not have had time to observe him, *Kain v Mobbs* [2008] NSWSC 383.

5. *Contributory negligence may be 100%*: In some States under the civil liability reforms, contributory negligence may be assessed at 100%: NSW: CLA, s 5S; Qld: CLA, s 24; Vic: WrA, s 63; ACT: CLWA, s 47; compare Tas: CLA, s 4(1)

("up to 100%"). The effect of this provision is referred to in *Mackenzie v The Nominal Defendant* [2005] NSWCA 180 [16.145] and *Adams by her next friend O'Grady v State of New South Wales* [2008] NSWSC 1257 (100% contributory negligence). In other jurisdictions, South Australia and the Northern Territory, the High Court decision in *Wynbergen v Hoyts Corporation* (1997) 149 ALR 25, referred to in the Ipp Report para 8.21 (above), continues to apply. The High Court rejected the argument that contributory negligence can be assessed at 100%. In *Reeves v Commissioner of Police* [2000] 1 AC 360, Lord Hoffman in the House of Lords commented on the lower court's assessment of contributory negligence at 100%. This was a case where the police had been held negligent for failure to prevent a sane prisoner from committing suicide. His Lordship said that 100% contributory negligence:

> gives no weight at all to the policy of the law in imposing a duty of care upon the police. It is another different way of saying that the police should not have owed [the deceased prisoner] a duty of care. The law of torts is not just a matter of simple morality but contains many strands of policy, not all of them consistent with each other, which reflect the complexity of life. An apportionment of responsibility "as the court thinks just and equitable" will sometimes require a balancing of different goals.

6. *Actions by dependants*: Contributory negligence by a deceased person may operate to reduce damages in a statutory action for damages brought by dependants. In New South Wales, earlier legislation providing that a deceased's contributory negligence was not a defence (*Law Reform (Miscellaneous Provisions) Act 1965* (NSW), s 13) has gradually been abrogated: *Motor Accidents Compensation Act 1999* (NSW), s 139 (motor vehicle accidents); *Workers Compensation Act 1987* (NSW), s 151N(5) (injuries to workers); NSW: CLA, s 5T. Victoria has a general provision that a deceased's contributory negligence is not a defence to the statutory action for damages brought by dependants, nor are damages reduced by reason of the deceased's contributory negligence: Vic: WrA, s 26(4)): There is also a protective provision in the Australian Capital Territory that contributory negligence is not a defence if death results from negligence: ACT: CLWA, s 27 (compare s 104 CLWA). In other States the contributory negligence of a deceased is a defence and will operate to reduce damages recoverable by dependants: *Law Reform (Miscellaneous Provisions) Act* (NT), s 17(2); *Compensation (Fatal Injuries) Act* (NT), s 11; *Law Reform Act 1995* (Qld), s 10(5); SA: CLA, s 45; *Law Reform (Contributory Negligence and Apportionment of Liability) Act 2001* (SA), s 7(4); *Wrongs Act 1954* (Tas), s 4(4); *Law Reform (Contributory Negligence and Tortfeasors' Contribution) Act 1947* (WA), s 4(2).

7. *Motor vehicle accidents:* Motor vehicle accidents are given separate treatment in some states. Special statutory provisions apply to motor vehicle accidents involving drug and alcohol impaired drivers and their passengers and intoxicated plaintiffs. In New South Wales the *Motor Accidents Compensation Act 1999* (NSW), which predates the civil liability legislation, largely continues to apply. See *Motor Accidents Compensation Act 1999* (NSW), s 138 (deemed contributory negligence for driver or deceased with drug or alcohol convictions where drugs or alcohol a contributing factor); s 138(2)(b) (adult passengers in vehicles driven by

alcohol or drug impaired drivers deemed to be contributorily negligent plaintiff was aware or ought to have been aware of the impairment, see [16.14.], NSW: CLA, s 49 (effect of intoxication on duty and standard of care) applies to motor vehicle accidents to the extent that there is any inconsistency with the motor accidents legislation. The provisions relating to contributory negligence also apply to motor vehicle accidents, NSW: CLA, s 3B(2)(a). The interaction between the *Motor Accidents Compensation Act 1999* (NSW) contributory negligence provisions and the *Civil Liability Act 2002* are dealt with in *Mackenzie v The Nominal Defendant* [2005] NSWCA 180 [16.145].

With some variation there are also deemed contributory negligence provisions in civil liability legislation in Queensland (Qld: CLA, ss 47 – 49), South Australia (SA: CLA, ss 46 – 50) and ACT (ACT: CLWA, ss 95 – 96). These provisions apply generally where there is reliance on the care and skill of an intoxicated person and are not limited to motor vehicle accidents. Tasmania and Western Australia have no special provision for passengers: Tas: CLA, s 5; WA: CLA, s 5L.

Queensland and South Australia make additional special provision for intoxicated drivers and their passengers in motor accidents with a deemed minimum rate of 50% contributory negligence: Qld: CLA, ss 47, 48, 49; SA: CLA, ss 46, 47, 48. In Victoria the common law applies (Vic: WrA, ss 14F, 14G), but there are exclusions in relation to the transport accidents no fault scheme: *Transport Accident Act 1986* (Vic), ss 39 – 41. The *Personal Injuries (Liabilities and Damages) Act* (NT), does not apply to motor vehicle accidents, *Personal Injuries (Liabilities and Damages) Act*s 4(3)).

The effect of failure to wear seatbelts or protective helmets is referred to above at [16.90]. What legal policies are served by imposing special punitive rates on intoxicated drivers and their passengers? Is this likely to deter drink driving any more than criminal penalties?

8. *Intoxicated plaintiffs:* Civil liability legislation makes specific provision for intoxicated plaintiffs. The relevance of intoxication to a duty of care or the standard of care owed is discussed at Chapter 12. We are here concerned with a plaintiff's intoxication and the defence of contributory negligence. In most States the civil liability legislation applies generally to personal injury claims including motor accidents but excludes claims under workers compensation legislation. In the Australian Capital Territory, Queensland, South Australia and Tasmania, the civil liability provisions apply to both motor vehicle accidents as well as other claims. In the Northern Territory, s 4(3)(a) of the *Personal Injuries (Liability and Damages) Act* (NT) excludes "a claim for benefits ... within ... the *Motor Accidents Compensation Act 1999*".

New South Wales is exceptional in having special rules for motor accidents, which have been set out above in Note 7. In other cases, at the most extreme and punitive is the general New South Wales provision in CLA, s 50 barring an intoxicated plaintiff's claim if the plaintiff's (or deceased person's) capacity to exercise care and skill was impaired by self induced intoxication unless the harm would have been likely without the intoxication. Even if unlikely, contributory negligence (set at a minimum 25%) applies unless the intoxication did not contribute in any way to "the cause of the death, injury or damage". In *Russell v*

Edwards [2006] NSWCA 19, a drunken 16 year old at a birthday party was seriously injured when he dived into the swimming pool. He was denied recovery even though there may have been a negligent failure to appropriately supervise. Note the broad definition of "intoxication" in NSW: CLA, s 48.

More moderate provisions apply in other States, which have either opted for deemed minimum contributory negligence or left the extent of contributory negligence up to the court to decide. The Northern Territory (*Personal Injuries (Liabilities and Damages) Act* (NT), ss 14 – 17), Queensland, (CLA, s 47) and South Australia (CLA, s 47) do not bar the claim but deem contributory negligence set at a minimum of 25% (Qld & SA–50% minimum rate for motor vehicle accidents, see above). The Australian Capital Territory, Tasmanian and Western Australian provisions dealing with intoxicated plaintiffs are less strict with a rebuttable presumption of contributory negligence and flexibility for the court to determine the extent of contributory negligence: ACT: CLWA, ss 95, 96; Tas: CLA, s 5; WA: CLA, s 5L. The Tasmanian provisions apply to motor vehicle accidents (Tas: CLA, ss 3B, 4A and 16 (obvious risks)).

The legislation (other than in New South Wales) also deems contributory negligence when another relies on the care and skill of an intoxicated person in circumstances where the plaintiff was aware or ought to have been aware that the other person was intoxicated. The presumption can be rebutted if it is shown, on the balance of probabilities, that the intoxication did not contribute to the breach of duty, or that the injured person could not reasonably be expected to have avoided the risk that caused the injury. Contributory negligence is a deemed to be a minimum of 25% (50% for motor vehicle accidents in Qld and SA): *Personal Injuries (Liabilities and Damages) Act* (NT), ss 15 – 17; Qld: CLA, s 48, 49; SA: CLA, s 47. The Negligence Review Panel (at 8.16-8.19), thought the setting of a minimum for contributory negligence was undesirable as it fettered the Court's ability to respond to an infinite variety of situations and assumed that it was possible to predicate in advance that certain types of conduct amounted to contributory negligence.

The case next extract looks at the impact of the civil liability legislation on the determination of contributory negligence in a drink driving situation.

Mackenzie v The Nominal Defendant

[16.145] *Mackenzie v The Nominal Defendant* [2005] NSWCA 180 NSW Court of Appeal

(footnotes omitted)

[Mackenzie was a pillion passenger on a motor bike driven by Brown. Both were severely injured when the bike ran off the road. Mackenzie sued Brown for damages for negligent driving. Both had been binge drinking over several days and there was evidence that both of them were extremely drunk. The motor bike, a Harley Davidson, was owned by Mackenzie and was unregistered and uninsured. Mackenzie knew that Brown never had a licence, no experience with riding a large bike and thought Brown "immature and irresponsible" and gave evidence that he would not be "in his right mind" to let Brown ride his motor bike. Despite an earlier refusal, Mackenzie invited Brown to ride his bike. Mackenzie went into the house and got the keys, helmets and footwear for them both. He then unlocked the bike and a padlocked gate to get the bike out for the ride. Mackenzie argued that he was so inebriated that he was not capable of making a rational assessment of Brown's ability to ride the

Mackenzie v The Nominal Defendant cont.

motor bike. The trial judge found that Mackenzie retained sufficient capacity to be aware of Brown's inexperience and drunkenness and that Brown was incapable of managing the bike at the time he rode on the bike. The trial judge found that, in the circumstances, Mackenzie's conduct was such that he should be found 100% contributorily negligent. The plaintiff appealed. Three of the issues before the NSW Court of Appeal were: (1) whether the trial judge had been in error in using an objective standard for contributory negligence and apportionment and (2) whether the judge had been in error in not considering the whole conduct of the parties in the entire incident and (3) whether the apportionment of 100% contributory negligence was justified.]

GILES JA: 47 [His honour set out the statutory provision requiring a finding of contributory negligence where the plaintiff was a voluntary passenger in or on a vehicle driven by a drug or alcohol impaired driver, *Motor Accidents Compensation Act 1999* (NSW), s 138. His honour continued:]

48 Within its scope, this supplements and modifies the common law. The statutory direction to find contributory negligence does not exclude any other ground on which a finding of contributory negligence may be made, see s 138(6). Prior to such a direction a passenger who should have been aware of the driver's intoxication, including a passenger who had allowed himself to become intoxicated so as to be unable to appreciate the driver's condition, could be found to have been contributorily negligent: *Insurance Commissioner v Joyce* (1948) 77 CLR 397; *Mendola v Warren* (1993) 19 MVR 385; *Williams v Government Insurance Office (NSW)* (1995) 21 MVR 148. Such a passenger could be found to have been contributorily negligent if the driver's condition was not intoxication but, for example, inexperience, whereby accompanying him as passenger was failure to take reasonable care for his own safety.

49 Section 138(2)(b) does not require that the reason for the passenger's unawareness of the driver's intoxication was the passenger's own intoxication. Nor, if that was the reason for the passenger's unawareness, does s 138(2)(b) cease to apply. It is enough that the passenger ought to have been aware of the driver's impaired ability.

50 In *Joslyn v Berryman* (2003) 214 CLR 552 an intoxicated passenger was injured in an accident caused by the driver's intoxication. It was held that the passenger was a voluntary passenger and, by force of s 74(2)(b) of the *Motor Accidents Act 1988* ("the MA Act"), the predecessor to s 138(2)(b) of the MAC Act, had been contributorily negligent, because a reasonable man in his position would have known that the driver's ability to drive the motor vehicle was impaired by her consumption of alcohol. McHugh J in particular discussed contributory negligence at common law, under which the passenger had also been contributorily negligent because a reasonable man in his position would have known of the driver's intoxicated condition and also of her inexperience and that the vehicle was defective. The reasonable man did not have the intoxicated passenger's impaired capacity to know that the driver was intoxicated or inexperienced and that the vehicle was defective, or to appreciate that by becoming a passenger he was exposing himself to a risk of injury.

51 The question in *Joslyn v Berryman* (2003) 214 CLR 552 was the extent of the circumstances to which regard was had in determining what the passenger ought to have known. The passenger and the driver had earlier consumed much alcohol, to the point where the driver was "staggering drunk". Their journey began with the passenger as driver. His companion remonstrated with him, whereupon he said she should drive and she took over as driver. It was found that at that time the driver was not showing objective signs of intoxication. The trial judge held that there was contributory negligence and reduced the passenger's damages by 25 per cent. In the Court of Appeal, where the common law was applied without reference to s 74 of the MA Act, it was held that the relevant circumstances were confined to what the passenger knew or ought to have known at the time his companion began to drive, and that contributory negligence had not been established. In the High Court it was held that this was incorrect. It was held that, whether at common law or under s 74, in determining whether the

Mackenzie v The Nominal Defendant cont.

passenger ought to have been aware that the driver's ability was impaired by alcohol regard should be had to the events of the preceding hours, so that a reasonable man in the passenger's position would have known that the driver was probably still affected by alcohol.

52 The *Civil Liability Act 2002* ("the CL Act") applied to this case, ss 5R and 5S providing –

5R Standard of contributory negligence

(1) The principles that are applicable in determining whether a person has been negligent also apply in determining whether the person who suffered harm has been contributorily negligent in failing to take precautions against the risk of that harm.

(2) For that purpose:

(a) the standard of care required of the person who suffered harm is that of a reasonable person in the position of that person, and

(b) the matter is to be determined on the basis of what that person knew or ought to have known at the time.

5S Contributory negligence can defeat claim

In determining the extent of a reduction in damages by reason of contributory negligence, a court may determine a reduction of 100% if the court thinks it just and equitable to do so, with the result that the claim for damages is defeated.

53 Section 5R did not diminish the authority of *Joslyn v Berryman* (2003) 214 CLR 552. Section 5S addressed in one respect the consequences of contributory negligence.

54 By s 138(3) of the MAC Act, the damages are to be reduced "by such percentage as the court thinks just and equitable in the circumstances of the case". The wording differs from that in the long-standing general provision in s 10(1) of the *Law Reform (Miscellaneous Provisions) Act 1965* ("the LR Act"), and from that in the replacement s 9(1) of the LR Act since 2000 (but applicable to earlier wrongs). [His honour then referred to ss 9, 10 of that legislation and the principles set out In *Podrebersek v Australian Iron & Steel Pty Ltd* (1985) 59 ALJR 492 see [[16.130] Note 1] and continued:]

59 This replaces references to fault with references to failure to take reasonable care and to a "wrong", but continues to refer to regard to the claimant's share in the responsibility for the damage. The last mentioned words are omitted from s 138(3) of the MAC Act. The equivalent omission from s 74(3) of the MA Act was noted in *Nicholson v Nicholson* (1994) 35 NSWLR 308. The statutory direction concerned failure to wear a seat belt. It was held that, if the failure had not contributed at all to the passenger's injury, it could be just and equitable to reduce his damages by a percentage of nil; as Mahoney JA put it (at 332), it was consistent with the provision to find the passenger guilty of contributory negligence but refuse to reduce his damages. His Honour pointed out that s 74 called for a finding of contributory negligence where perhaps at common law a finding could not be made, and surmised (at 333-4) that the formula in s 74(3) was used to enable the Court to decline to reduce the damages where there was "no contribution by the deemed negligence".

60 In *Joslyn v Berryman* (2003) 214 CLR 552 at [133] Kirby J thought that the more limited formula wrought a change and "leaves wholly at large the reduction for contributory negligence, made by reference to nothing more than what 'the court thinks just and equitable'". His Honour did not more directly indicate whether or not the approach in *Podrebersek v Australian Iron & Steel Pty Ltd* (1985) 59 ALJR 492 no longer held good. Hayne J at [157], on the other hand, said that s 74(3) of the MA Act required that the process described in *Podrebersek v Australian Iron & Steel Pty Ltd* (1985) 59 ALJR 492 be undertaken.

61 Section 5S of the CL Act overcame the decision in *Wynbergen v Hoyts Corporation Pty Ltd* (1997) 149 ALR 25 …

62 It may be that the omission from the s 74(3) and s 138(3) formulae of "having regard to the claimant's share in the responsibility for the damage" was a corollary to this legislative change, by

Mackenzie v The Nominal Defendant cont.

removal of express reference to shared responsibility in order better to accommodate 100 per cent contribution. Whatever the explanation, it is difficult to see that the approach described in *Podrebersek v Australian Iron & Steel Pty Ltd* (1985) 59 ALJR 492 has fallen away. Particularly is that so when the reduction required by s 138(3) is when a finding of contributory negligence directed by s 138(2) has been made, but contributory negligence may be found at common law where the passenger should have been aware of the driver's intoxication and where the passenger should have been aware of, for example, the driver's inexperience. There could hardly be overlapping different processes of determining a reduction in damages, with different outcomes.

63 What is just and equitable must be determined in a principled way, and as Priestley JA observed (in a judgment dissenting in the result) in *Bradshaw v Wallis* (CA, 1 April 1996, unreported), "[t]o comply with s 74(3) requires the court to arrive at a percentage which inevitably involves as part of the process some kind of comparison between the balance to be attached (in this case) to the driver and the plaintiff". In the comparison, the degree of departure from the standard of care of the reasonable man and the relative importance of the acts of the parties in causing the damage will call for attention. In the present case, neither the appellant nor the respondent suggested that the approach described in *Podrebersek v Australian Iron & Steel Pty Ltd* (1985) 59 ALJR 492 was inappropriate. ...

The questions on appeal

... 79 The contentions came down to –

(a) error in fact-finding, in accepting Mr Brown's evidence of the events at the appellant's house before they set out on the motor cycle;

(b) error in law, in determining what was just and equitable on an objective standard of a reasonable person in the position of the appellant without regard to the appellant's intoxicated condition; and

(c) appellable error in assessment of what was just and equitable, going beyond the error in (b), in failing to have regard to the whole of the conduct of the appellant and Mr Brown including that appellant's intoxication made him incapable of knowing that Mr Brown was unlicensed, inexperienced and intoxicated.

80 There was particular overlap in the submissions as to contentions (b) and (c), and the distinction between them was not clearly drawn. Buried within the submissions was the more limited contention –

(d) appellable error in assessment of what was just and equitable, in failing to have regard to the effect of the appellant's intoxication, short of incapacity, on his acting as described in the judge's [167] with the knowledge of the matters in his [168].

Contention (a): error in fact finding

[Giles JA found no error in the fact finding by the trial judge as to the circumstances leading up to the accident, and continued:]

Contention (b): error in law

87 The appellant accepted that the judge had correctly stated the process for apportionment in accordance with *Podrebersek v Australian Iron & Steel Pty Ltd* (1985) 59 ALJR 492, but submitted that he had misapplied the process. He submitted that, while an objective test is applied when finding contributory negligence, that is not so at the separate and next stage of determining what percentage reduction is just and equitable, when a subjective test is applied. It was said that the judge had erred in applying an objective standard to the appellant's conduct when making the comparison of culpability and causal potency.

88 While the terms are convenient, it can be misleading to refer to an objective test and a subjective test, and to draw a sharp line between them. In determining contributory negligence there must be regard to the circumstances of the plaintiff whose conduct is in question, because the ordinary reasonable man is engaged in the person's conduct. Under s 5R of the CL Act, the standard of care required of the person who suffered harm is "that of a reasonable person in the position of that person", and contributory negligence is determined subjectively so far as it is to be determined "on the basis of what that person knew or ought to have known at the time" (emphasis added). Section 138(2)(b) of the MAC Act refers to impaired driving ability of which the injured person "was aware, or ought to have been aware" (emphasis added). Further, referring to a wholesale objective test or subjective test overlooks that in determining what percentage reduction is just and equitable there may be reference to the subjective (the plaintiff's conduct) and the objective (the reasonable man's conduct).

89 What did the judge do by way of applying an objective standard to the appellant's conduct? When that is understood, he did not err in the manner suggested.

90 I have described the basis for the judge's assessment of 100 per cent contributory negligence. He did not attribute to the appellant, when the appellant allowed Mr Brown to ride the motor cycle with himself as pillion passenger, the reasonable man's capacity to understand what he was doing. The judge found that, despite his intoxication, the appellant had that capacity. He did not attribute to the appellant the reasonable man's knowledge of the matters [Brown's lack of licence, inexperience, immaturity, intoxication]. ... He found that, despite his intoxication, the appellant had that knowledge. Only [later] ... did the judge refer to what a reasonable person in the position of the appellant ought to have known, namely, that Mr Brown was so incapable of riding the motor cycle that it was inevitable that the accident would occur.

91 So far as the judge did this, he was not in error. The reasonable man's knowledge attributed to the appellant was knowledge of a conclusion, from the appellant's knowledge of Mr Brown's inability safely to ride the motor cycle. It was the contributory negligence itself, the appellant's falling short of the standard of care of a reasonable man. Where the defendant has been negligent and the plaintiff has been contributorily negligent, each of them having in his conduct fallen short of the standard of care of the reasonable man, that each has so departed is a necessary foundation for any process affecting the plaintiff's recovery. It does not matter whether the process is an assessment of what is just and equitable, without more, or is an assessment of what is just and equitable with added reference to the plaintiff's share in the responsibility for the damage. There can not be jettisoned that each of them failed to take due care, in the case of the defendant for the plaintiff's safety and in the case of the plaintiff for his own safety; it is the starting-point for the process.

92 The appellant submitted that the judge erroneously imported s 5R(2) of the CL Act into determining what was just and equitable, because he had regard to that provision ... when he rejected the submission that an objective test was confined to whether the appellant was guilty of contributory negligence. ... The dicta of Macrossan CJ in *McPherson v Whitfield* [1995] QCA 62 on which the appellant relied ... were to the effect that there may not be contributory negligence at all if the passenger became intoxicated at a time when travelling as a passenger could not be foreseen. It is difficult to see that this has survived s 138(2)(b) of the MAC Act. The judge correctly considered that the contributory negligence itself, ascertained in accordance with s 5R(2), remained for his determination of what was just and equitable.

93 When arriving at his assessment of 100 percent contributory negligence, the judge proceeded upon his findings as to the appellant's conduct and his actual knowledge. He did not exclude from his consideration that the appellant was intoxicated, or the circumstances in which he came to be intoxicated. His attention was drawn to those matters in the appellant's submission ... and he did not reject them as irrelevant. Rather, given his findings as to the appellant's conduct and knowledge, he

Mackenzie v The Nominal Defendant cont.

did not think they took the case out of a worst situation of contributory negligence. The appellant's complaint should not have been that the judge applied an objective test in determining a just and equitable percentage reduction, but that his subjective basis in the appellant's conduct and knowledge was flawed because not tempered by regard to whether in acting as he did, and with the knowledge found, the appellant's intoxication caused him to act impulsively and without full consideration of what might occur.

Contention (c): whole conduct and incapacity

94 The appellant submitted that the judge had misapplied the process described in *Podrebersek v Australian Iron & Steel Pty Ltd* (1985) 59 ALJR 492 because he had failed adequately to take account of Mr Brown's role in the accident or of the whole of the conduct of the appellant and Mr Brown in relation to the accident. He said that the only reference to Mr Brown's conduct in assessing the just and equitable reduction … referred to Mr Brown's negligence [but] it did not refer to the fact that Mr Brown was unlicensed and inexperienced, was intoxicated, and had agitated for a ride on the motor cycle. He put forward a number of matters as to the appellant's conduct which he said fell for consideration, in substance that the appellant would normally not have let Mr Brown ride the motor cycle, and only did so, and went with him as pillion passenger, because he was incapable, as a result of his drinking at a time when riding the motor cycle was not in contemplation, of knowing that Mr Brown was unlicensed and inexperienced and was grossly impaired in his ability to ride the motor cycle.

95 It is fanciful to regard the judge as having failed to take into account that Mr Brown was unlicensed, inexperienced and intoxicated. They were the stuff of Mr Brown's negligence. When the judge said that the appellant put Mr Brown in the driver's seat, that necessarily involved regard to the conduct of Mr Brown, together with that of the appellant, from Mr Brown's agitation for a ride …

96 Nor did the judge fail to take into account the appellant's drinking and any resultant incapacity in knowing that Mr Brown was unlicensed, inexperienced and intoxicated. The appellant's case was pitched at the level of incapacity. To repeat, the judge's attention was drawn to the appellant's intoxication and the circumstances in which he came to be intoxicated in the appellant's submission … a submission that the appellant had lost the capacity to judge whether or not Mr Brown had lost the capacity to ride safely. He considered that the appellant's conduct, with the knowledge he found the appellant had despite his intoxication, was nonetheless a worst case situation, where the appellant's departure from the standard of care of a reasonable man and the importance of his conduct in the occurrence of the accident when compared with Mr Brown's departure and conduct were such that 100 per cent reduction was just and equitable.

Contention (d): effect of intoxication short of incapacity

97 The appellant submitted that the judge's assessment of what was just and equitable was plainly unjust and unreasonable, and so appellably erroneous. He said that it could not be just and reasonable "for a drunk driver to walk away effectively blameless … so that the passenger, who was also drunk, is deemed to be solely responsible and wholly to blame". …

98 [His honour then referred to *Podrebersek v Australian Iron & Steel Pty Ltd* (1985) 59 ALJR 492 on the role of a Court on appeal on a question of apportionment (the passage is quoted at [16.60]) and continued:]

99 On the judge's basis for his assessment of 100 per cent contribution, I do not think it can be held that the judge's exercise of discretion miscarried. It is not correct to say that the intoxicated Mr Brown walked away blameless and the intoxicated appellant was deemed to be wholly to blame. As the Panel pointed out in *Review of the Law of Negligence*, September 2002, it remained that Mr Brown was at fault and the appellant was also at fault. As between them, the appellant would be judged wholly

Mackenzie v The Nominal Defendant cont.

responsible, but because the law required such a judgment as a matter of legal responsibility. If the intoxicated appellant, knowing despite his intoxication that Mr Brown was unlicensed, inexperienced and wholly unfit to be allowed to ride the motor cycle, and was severely intoxicated, invited Mr Brown to ride the motor cycle and joined him as pillion passenger, the judge's determination was open to him.

100 The appellant called in aid the assessment of responsibility made by Cooper J in *Morton v Knight* [1990] 2 Qd R 419. The passenger had drunk beer and whisky to the stage that he was "paralytic" and "a mess". He met the driver by chance, and was offered a lift home. Cooper J held that the passenger was contributorily negligent in becoming a passenger in a car driven by the obviously intoxicated driver, and that it did not matter that his own intoxication precluded him from knowing the driver's condition and appreciating the risk. His Honour went on (at 430) –

> In determining the relative culpability of the plaintiff and the defendant, I am satisfied that by far the greater culpability rests with the defendant. The defendant was in charge of the motor vehicle, his actions had the greatest potential to cause injury to the plaintiff, he was aware that the plaintiff was very intoxicated and impaired in his capacity to make decisions in his own interest and the defendant's intoxication caused or contributed to his negligent driving. The plaintiff for his part did not go out on a drinking spree with the defendant and did nothing to encourage the defendant to become as intoxicated and impaired in his driving as I have found him to be. That is, the contributory negligence had no "causative potency" (see *Davies v Swan Motor Co.* [1949] 2 KB 291, 326) in the negligent conduct of the defendant or the accident. The negligence of the plaintiff was passive, and lay in placing himself in a position of danger within the car. In all the circumstances, I find that the conduct of the plaintiff in getting into and remaining in the motor vehicle on its journey contributed to the extent of 20 per cent of the injuries which he suffered.

101 The facts were very different from those of the present case. The appellant was in charge of the motor cycle; his negligent conduct was in no sense passive. The assessment was, with respect, remarkably low. In reconsidering the reduction of the passenger's damages in *Berryman v Joslyn* (2003) 214 CLR 552 a reduction of 60 per cent was found, and in *Williams v Government Insurance Office (NSW)* (1995) 21 MVR 148 a reduction of 80 per cent was upheld. The cases turn on their own facts. I have gone to a number of other cases of intoxicated passengers of intoxicated drivers, and the assessments vary widely. It is necessary to make an assessment on the facts of this case.

102 In my opinion, the only occasion for questioning the judge's determination is that he did not take into account that the conduct of the appellant in putting Mr Brown in the driver's seat, with the knowledge found, was affected by his own intoxication so as to be impulsive and without full consideration of what might occur …

103 [Giles JA referred to the evidence that Mackenzie's intoxication was such that he was not likely to have sufficient insight or capacity to understand the consequences of permitting Brown to drive the bike and continued:]

104 In my opinion it was relevant. [His honour then referred to the decision in *Talbot-Butt v Holloway* (1990) 12 MVR 70 involving an intoxicated pedestrian who was injured when she ran across the road in front of a car]. …

108 Just as the pedestrian's intoxication could be taken into account, because it was one of the facts in the case and could ameliorate her culpability and the causal potency of her contributory negligence, so can the appellant's intoxication be taken into account as part of the circumstances in which the appellant put Mr Brown in the driver's seat. His conduct was that of a man who, in his intoxicated condition, acted impulsively and without full consideration of what might occur. I do not think that anything in s 138(2) of the MAC Act or s 5R of the CL Act has displaced the reasoning of

Mackenzie v The Nominal Defendant cont.

Clarke JA, with which Kirby P must have agreed. It should be noted that in *Nicholson v Nicholson* (1994) 35 NSWLR 308 a finding of contributory negligence as directed by s 74(2) of the MA Act did not compel a just and equitable reduction.

109 The judge appears to have regarded the appellant as having engaged in a deliberate act of negligence. No doubt because the appellant's case was pitched at the level of incapacity, he appears not to have addressed the lesser case within it. In my opinion, to this extent appealable error has been shown.

110 In many cases, the plaintiff's intoxication will not ameliorate his culpability or the causal potency of his contributory negligence. The further enquiry must be into the circumstances in which the plaintiff became intoxicated. A plaintiff who goes on a drinking spree with the driver, contemplating from the beginning that he will be a passenger in a vehicle driven by the driver, will only add to his departure from the standard of care of the reasonable man. A plaintiff who becomes intoxicated when being the passenger of an intoxicated driver is not in contemplation can say that his departure from the standard of care of the reasonable man is not complete, and perhaps that his conduct was less important in causing the damage. Although in a different context, such an enquiry underlies the dicta of Macrossan CJ in *McPherson v Whitfield* [1995] QCA 62 and of Lee J at 484-5 in the same case.

111 In the present case ... the appellant let himself get into a thoroughly intoxicated condition which, on any consideration before he did so, would have been seen as inimical to any rational and well thought out decision, whether as to riding the motor cycle or anything else. Deliberate drinking to the point of severe intoxication exposed him to acting impulsively and without full consideration of what might occur, which happened to occur in relation to riding the motor cycle. The departure from the standard of care of the reasonable man at this point can not be ignored in the degree of departure in putting Mr Brown in the driver's seat.

112 I do not think the justice and equity of the reduction in damages is, in these circumstances, significantly moved in the appellant's favour. He did put Mr Brown in the driver's seat, knowing that he was unlicensed, inexperienced and intoxicated; and acting irrationally and without well thought out decision was to be expected when he began and maintained his drinking. In my opinion, the just and equitable reduction in all the circumstances is 80 per cent.

[Stein AJA and Gzell J concurred.]

Contributory negligence of others

[16.150] As a general rule, the contributory negligence of others does not affect a plaintiff's claim unless the plaintiff would have been vicariously or directly liable for that other person's conduct (*Mills v Armstrong (The "Bernina")* (1883) 13 AC 1). Consider an example: there is a collision between two negligently driven vehicles, one of which is being driven by an employee for work purposes. If the employer sued the other driver for damage to the employer's vehicle, the employer's damages would be reduced to the extent of the employee's negligence; the employer is said to be "identified" with the employee's negligence. This is the case even though the wording of most apportionment legislation refers to the *claimant's* contributory negligence (see *William A Jay & Sons v JS Veevers Ltd* [1946] 1 All ER 646). In some jurisdictions "fault" of a person is defined to include fault for which that person is vicariously responsible: *Law Reform (Miscellaneous Provisions) Act 1956* (NT), s 15(2); *Wrongs Act 1954* (Tas), s 4(7); *Law Reform (Contributory Negligence and Tortfeasors' Contribution) Act 1947* (WA), s 3 ("plaintiff", query whether the same result occurs in Western Australia); compare *Law Reform*

(Contributory Negligence and Apportionment of Liability) Act 2001 (SA), s 7(4) where a claim by employer against a negligent third party for damage to the employer's vehicle driven by a negligent employee is not deemed to be a claim for derivative harm as defined, *Law Reform (Contributory Negligence and Tortfeasors' Contribution) Act 1947* (WA)s 3. Professor Fleming remarks that the:

> doctrine of identification is difficult to harmonise with the philosophy of individualism which shrinks from holding an innocent person responsible for the fault of another. Like the parent defence of contributory negligence, it was a stratagem of the early 19th century to ease the load of vulnerable tortfeasors. (JG Fleming, *The Law of Torts* (9th ed, LBC Information Services, Sydney, 1998), p 323.)

Professor Fleming also notes that the doctrine of identification never went so far at common law to prevent the employer suing the employee directly for the employee's negligence (p 323, note 156). In some States employees are protected against such claims by the employer, see Chapter 15 Concurrent Liability.

Claims arising out of injuries to family members

[16.155] There are exceptional situations where a plaintiff may be able to claim damages for losses to the plaintiff resulting from injuries to a spouse or a family member. One such action is the action for loss of consortium by a husband where his wife was tortiously injured by the defendant. At common law, the plaintiff husband's claim was not affected by the contributory negligence of his wife (*Curran v Young* (1965) 112 CLR 99). In most States this is no longer of any importance as the action by a husband for loss of consortium of his wife has been abolished. In the Australian Capital Territory, New South Wales, Tasmania, Victoria and Western Australia, the action for loss of consortium has been abolished: ACT: CLWA, s 218; *Law Reform (Marital Consortium) Act 1984* (NSW); *Common Law (Miscellaneous Actions) Act 1986* (Tas), s 3; see *Civil Liability Amendment Bill 2005* (Tas); *Civil Law (Wrongs) Act 2002* (Vic), s 218; *Law Reform (Miscellaneous Provisions) Act 1941* (WA) (note the repeal occurred prior to the 2003 amendments which replaced the repealing section, s 3). The action is still available in Queensland and South Australia who have extended the claim to wives: *Law Reform Act 1995* (Qld), s 13; *Civil Liability Act 1936* (SA), s 65. There are also some general provisions in the Australian Capital Territory, South Australia and the Northern Territory which attribute the contributory negligence of another to the plaintiff. This occurs where the plaintiff's damage is suffered as a result of injury or damage to that other person: *Law Reform (Contributory Negligence and Apportionment of Liability) Act 2001* (SA), s 7(4) (see illustrations in s 3 definition of "derivative harm"); ACT: CLWA, s 104; *Law Reform (Miscellaneous Provisions) Act 1956* (NT), s 18. The issue may also arise in relation to the statutory action by dependant relatives where the deceased has been contributorily negligent (see [16.140] Note 6).

Nervous shock in New South Wales

[16.160] *Civil Liability Act 2002* (NSW), s 30(3) is an exceptional provision applying only in New South Wales. This provides that in claims for nervous shock, damages can be reduced by reference to the contributory negligence of the victim. In New South Wales, in areas where the civil liability legislation does not apply, the contributory negligence of the victim might not be attributed to the plaintiff. In *Scala v Mammolitti* (1965) 114 CLR 153, Windeyer J in dealing with an action for nervous shock under Pt III of the *Law Reform (Miscellaneous Provisions) Act 1944* (NSW) suggested that the contributory negligence of the person "killed, injured or put in peril" would not affect the claim by the member of the family who suffered nervous shock. This Act continues to operate in cases excluded by NSW: CLA, s 3B. The Australian Capital Territory and Northern Territory provisions (ACT: CLWA, s 104; *Law Reform (Miscellaneous Provisions) Act* (NT), s 15(2)) referred to at [16.155] refer to "damage" rather than "injury" suggesting that they do not cover nervous shock. The South Australian provision (*Law Reform (Contributory Negligence and Apportionment of Liability) Act 2001* (SA), s 7(4)) specifically excludes nervous shock resulting from personal injury or death from its definition of "derivative harm". Why should the NSW provision apply only to nervous shock? Does it suggest that "nervous shock" is regarded as less debilitating than a broken leg or that there is continuing doubt on the authenticity of some claims or is it simply a cost reduction measure?

Contributory negligence and breach of contract

[16.165] A plaintiff may be able to frame the damages action in either tort or contract. Of immediate concern to the plaintiff and of special relevance to this chapter is whether by exercising a choice in favour of contract, the plaintiff could, at common law, deprive the defendant of the defence of contributory negligence, thus controlling the allocation of loss between the plaintiff and the defendant. The High Court, in *Astley v Austrust Ltd* (1999) 197 CLR 1 (extracted below), addressed this question and also the issue whether a plaintiff can be guilty of contributory negligence where the defendant's duty is to protect the plaintiff against that type of harm. Although most jurisdictions have legislated to reverse the decision, it remains important for those instances not covered by the legislation.

Astley v Austrust Ltd

[16.170] *Astley v Austrust Ltd* (1999) 197 CLR 1 High Court

(footnotes omitted)

GLEESON CJ, MCHUGH, GUMMOW AND HAYNE JJ: 5 ... Two important questions arise for determination in this appeal. The first is whether a plaintiff can be guilty of contributory negligence where the defendant has contractually agreed to protect the plaintiff from the very loss or damage which the plaintiff has suffered as the result of the defendant's breach of duty. The second is whether an award of damages for breach of contract may be reduced under apportionment of liability legislation, such as s 27A of the *Wrongs Act 1936* (SA), because of contributory negligence on the part of the plaintiff where the defendant is liable concurrently in tort and contract for breach of a duty of care.

6 The appeal is brought against an order of the Full Court of the Supreme Court of South Australia. That order set aside the finding of a trial judge in the Supreme Court who had held that the respondent had been guilty of contributory negligence in failing to protect its property and that the damages it was entitled to in actions for breach of contract and negligence should be reduced by 50 per cent. In our opinion, the Full Court erred in finding that the respondent was not guilty of contributory negligence. However, the respondent sued in contract as well as in tort. It was entitled to recover for the whole of the damage that it suffered because damages awarded pursuant to a claim in contract cannot be reduced by reason of conduct that constitutes contributory negligence for the purposes of the Wrongs Act. The history, text and purpose of the Wrongs Act make it clear that that Act was not intended to apply to claims for breach of contract. ...

Contributory negligence at common law

14 ... There is no rule that apportionment legislation does not operate in respect of the contributory negligence of a plaintiff where the defendant, in breach of its duty, has failed to protect the plaintiff

Astley v Austrust Ltd cont.

from damage in respect of the very event which gave rise to the defendant's employment. A plaintiff may be guilty of contributory negligence, therefore, even if the "very purpose" of the duty owed by the defendant is to protect the plaintiff's property. Thus, a plaintiff who carelessly leaves valuables lying about may be guilty of contributory negligence, calling for apportionment of loss, even if the defendant was employed to protect the plaintiff's valuables.

A finding of contributory negligence turns on a factual investigation of whether the plaintiff contributed to his or her own loss by failing to take reasonable care of his or her person or property. What is reasonable care depends on the circumstances of the case. In many cases, it may be proper for a plaintiff to rely on the defendant to perform its duty. But there is no absolute rule. The duties and responsibilities of the defendant are a variable factor in determining whether contributory negligence exists and, if so, to what degree. In some cases, the nature of the duty owed may exculpate the plaintiff from a claim of contributory negligence; in other cases the nature of that duty may reduce the plaintiff's share of responsibility for the damage suffered; and in yet other cases the nature of the duty may not prevent a finding that the plaintiff failed to take reasonable care for the safety of his or her person or property. Contributory negligence focuses on the conduct of the plaintiff. The duty owed by the defendant, although relevant, is one only of the many factors that must be weighed in determining whether the plaintiff has so conducted itself that it failed to take reasonable care for the safety of its person or property.

Courts, including this Court, accept that contributory negligence can be made out in non-contractual situations, notwithstanding that the 15 defendant was under a duty to protect people in the class of which the plaintiff was a member.

... The important question in this case is whether the contributory negligence of the plaintiff also requires the apportionment of damages between the plaintiff and the defendant where the plaintiff has sued in contract in circumstances where he or she has, or could have, sued in tort.

Section 27A of the Wrongs Act

Section 27A of the *Wrongs Act 1936* relevantly provides:

> (1) In this section – ... "fault" means negligence, breach of statutory duty or other act or omission which gives rise to a liability in tort or would, apart from this Act, give rise to the defence of contributory negligence.
>
> (2) Every reference in this section to the fault of a person shall be deemed to include a reference to a fault for which that person is vicariously responsible and in a case where the claim arises out of the death of a person, a fault of the deceased shall be deemed to be a fault of the claimant.
>
> (3) Where any person suffers damage as the result partly of his own fault and partly of the fault of any other person or persons, a claim in respect of that damage shall not be defeated by reason of the fault of the person suffering the damage, but the damages recoverable in respect thereof shall be reduced to such extent as the court thinks just and equitable having regard to the claimant's share in the responsibility for the damage ... 18

Section 27A(3), which provides the apportionment mechanism, is the key provision. Its operation is conditioned on the term "fault" which appears twice in the opening statement in the sub-section. Apportionment applies 19 where "any person suffers damage as the result partly of his own fault and partly of the fault of any other person or persons". When first used in s 27A(3), the "fault" is that of the plaintiff and the term "fault" identifies "negligence, breach of statutory duty or other act or omission" which would, apart from the *Wrongs Act 1936*, "give rise to the defence of contributory negligence". The defence of contributory negligence was available in an action for damages in tort; as will appear, it was not available as a defence in contract. When used for the second time in s 27A(3), the "fault" is that of the defendant and the term "fault" identifies the "negligence, breach of statutory duty or other act or omission which gives rise to a liability in tort" ...

Astley v Austrust Ltd cont.

Nothing in s 27A(3) suggests that "fault" – in either of its uses in s 27A(3) – includes rights and obligations arising from a breach of contract. Nor is there anything in the ordinary and natural meaning of the section that can be said to assume or by necessary implication authorise the apportionment of damages in claims for breach of contract. On its face, s 27A deals only with actions in tort. ...

Concurrent liability

[The High Court reviewed the decisions on the concurrent liability of professionals and continued:]

22 ... The implied term of reasonable care in a contract of professional services arises by operation of law. It is one of those terms that the law attaches as an incident of contracts of that class. It is part of the consideration that the promisor pays in return for the express or implied agreement of the promisee to pay for the services of the person giving the promise. Unlike the duty of care arising under the law of tort, the promisee in contract always gives consideration for the implied term. And it is a term that the parties can, and often do, bargain away or limit as they choose. Rather than ask why the law should imply such a term in a contract for professional services, it might be more appropriate to ask why should the law of negligence have any say at all in regulating the relationship of the parties to the contract? The contract defines the relationship of the parties. Statute, criminal law and public policy apart, there is no reason why the contract should not declare completely and exclusively what are the legal rights and obligations of the parties in relation to their contractual dealings. The [23] proposition that, in the absence of express agreement, tort and not contract regulates the duty of care owed by a professional person to a person hiring the professional services is inconsistent with the historical evolution of professional duties of care which, until recently, could be the subject of action only in contract. Moreover, the conceptual and practical differences between the two causes of action remain of "considerable importance". The two causes of action have different elements, different limitation periods, different tests for remoteness of damage and, as will appear, different apportionment rules.

The theoretical foundations for actions in tort and contract are quite separate. Long before the imperial march of modern negligence law began, contracts of service carried an implied term that they would be performed with reasonable care and skill. Persons who give consideration for the provision of services expect that those services will be provided with due care and skill. Reliance on an implied term giving effect to that expectation should not be defeated by the recognition of a parallel and concurrent obligation under the law of negligence. The evolution of the law of negligence has broadened the responsibility of professional persons and requires them to take reasonable care and skill even in situations where a contractual relationship cannot be established. But given the differing requirements and advantages of each cause of action, there is no justification in recognising the tortious duty to the exclusion of the contractual duty. ... [24]

The case law

Judicial exposition of the construction of apportionment legislation has largely turned on the meaning of "fault" as defined in that legislation and the extent to which the history and purpose of the legislation should colour that construction. The phrase "negligence, breach of statutory duty or other act or omission" governs the balance of the definition which is introduced by "which" and has two limbs. The first is "gives rise to a liability in tort" and the second is "would, apart from this Act, give rise to the defence of contributory negligence". However, the cases diverge over whether the word "negligence" is disconnected from the balance of the definition, so that there may be "fault" by reason of "negligence" which need not be tortious. Another view of the legislation is that it applies to claims for breach of contract because contributory negligence always constituted a possible defence to an action for damages for breach of contract. This position was advanced by Professor Glanville Williams in his influential book, *Joint Torts and Contributory Negligence*.

Astley v Austrust Ltd cont.

Two further considerations are evident in some of the cases. First, there appears to be an implied view that the principle of apportionment in the legislation is paramount and that it should apply in all cases where there is a breach of both a tortious and contractual duty of care. Second, there is an assumption that an implied duty of care within a contract is identical to a duty of care under the law of negligence and that the same rule should apply to both duties irrespective of how the action is pleaded.

[The Court then reviewed the authorities and continued:] 31 …

In our opinion, those decisions which have applied apportionment legislation, based on the *Law Reform (Contributory Negligence) Act 1945* (UK), to breaches of contract are wrong and should not be followed in this country. The interpretation of the legislation adopted by those courts which have applied the legislation to contract claims is strained, to say the least. It relies principally, if not exclusively, on the use of the term "negligence" in the definition of "fault". It ignores not only the context of that term in the definition itself but also the context provided by the various equivalents of s 27A(3) which is the principal substantive provision of the legislation. It also ignores the mischief which the legislation was intended to remedy.

The construction of s 27A

… [S]o far as issues of statutory construction go, on any fair reading of the apportionment legislation against the background of the mischief it was intended to remedy, it is clear to the point of near certainty that the legislation does not and was never intended to apply to contractual claims. … [The Court then analysed in detail the terms of s 27A and concluded:]

On any view of the matter, apportionment legislation was intended to give plaintiffs a cause of action which they did not have because of their contributory negligence. … 36 …

Policy considerations

It seems likely that those judges who have held that apportionment legislation applies to contract claims have regarded the contrary view as either anomalous or unfair or both. But when the nature of an action for breach of a contractual term to take reasonable care and the nature of an action in tort for breach of a general law duty of care are examined, it is by no means evident that there is anything anomalous or unfair in a plaintiff who sues in contract being outside the scope of the apportionment legislation. Tort obligations are imposed on the parties; contractual obligations are voluntarily assumed. In *Simonius v Vischer* Samuels JA noted that "the first count founds upon a duty imposed by the relationship in which the parties stood, and the second upon a duty imposed by their agreement". In *Henderson*, Lord Goff of Chieveley emphasised the will of the parties as the factor which supported different results in contract and tort:

> The result may be untidy; but, given that the tortious duty is imposed by the general law, and the contractual duty is attributable to the will of the parties, I do not find it objectionable that the claimant may be entitled to take advantage of the remedy which is most advantageous to him.

In contract, the plaintiff gives consideration, often very substantial 37 consideration, for the defendant's promise to take reasonable care. The terms of the contract allocate responsibility for the risks of the parties' enterprise including the risk that the damage suffered by one party may arise partly from the failure of that party to take reasonable care for the safety of that person's property or person. Ordinarily, that risk is borne by the party whose breach of contract is causally connected to the damage. Rarely do contracts apportion responsibility for damage on the basis of the respective fault of the parties. Commercial people in particular prefer the certainty of fixed rules to the vagueness of concepts such as "just and equitable". That is why it is commonplace for contracts to contain provisions regulating liability for breach of a duty to take reasonable care, whether by excluding liability altogether or limiting it in some other way.

Astley v Austrust Ltd cont.

Absent some contractual stipulation to the contrary, there is no reason of justice or sound legal policy which should prevent the plaintiff in a case such as the present recovering for all the damage that is causally connected to the defendant's breach even if the plaintiff's conduct has contributed to the damage which he or she has suffered. By its own voluntary act, the defendant has accepted an obligation to take reasonable care and, subject to remoteness rules, to pay damages for any loss or damage flowing from a breach of that obligation. If the defendant wishes to reduce its liability in a situation where the plaintiff's own conduct contributes to the damage suffered, it is open to the defendant to make a bargain with the plaintiff to achieve that end. Of course, the result of such a bargain may be that the defendant will have to take a reduced consideration for its promise to take reasonable care. But the bargain will be the product of the parties' voluntary agreement to subject themselves to their respective obligations.

In an action in tort, however, the duty of the defendant to take reasonable care and the obligation of the plaintiff to take reasonable care for his or her own safety or interests are imposed on the parties by law. Absent a contractual stipulation varying the rights of the parties, it is the general law that defines their rights and liabilities. It is one thing to apportion the liability for damage between a person who has been able to obtain the gratuitous services of a defendant where the negligence of each has contributed to the plaintiff's loss. It is another matter altogether to reduce the damages otherwise payable to a plaintiff who may have paid a very large sum to the defendant for a promise of reasonable care merely because the plaintiff's own conduct has also contributed to the suffering of the relevant damage.

Perhaps the apportionment statute should be imposed on parties to a contract where damages are payable for breach of a contractual duty of care. If it should, and we express no view about it, it will have to be done by amendment to that legislation. If courts are to give effect to the will of the legislature, it is not possible to do so having regard to the terms of apportionment legislation, based on the United Kingdom legislation of 1945, and the evil that it was designed to remedy. 38

Conclusion

For the above reasons, a construction applying the apportionment legislation to contract cases is contrary to the text, history and purpose of the legislation ...

[The judgment of Callinan J has been omitted.]

[16.175] **Notes&Questions**

1. In *Forsikringsaktieselskapet Vesta v Butcher* [1986] 2 All ER 488, Hobhouse J distinguished three types of situations which he considered called for consideration of the application of the *Law Reform (Contributory Negligence) Act 1945* (UK) when there was a contract involved (at 508):

   [a] Where the defendant's liability arises from some contractual provision which does not depend on negligence on the part of the defendant.

   [b] Where the defendant's liability arises from a contractual obligation which is expressed in terms of taking care (or its equivalent) but does not correspond to a common law duty to take care which would exist in the given case independently of contract.

   [c] Where the defendant's liability in contract is the same as his liability in the tort of negligence independently of the existence of any contract.

2. All jurisdictions have enacted legislation effectively reversing the decision in *Astley* where there is a concurrent and co-extensive duty of care in tort, the equivalent of Hobhouse J's third category of case: ACT: CLWA, ss 101, 102; *Law Reform (Miscellaneous Provisions) Amendment Act* (NT), ss 15, 16; *Law Reform (Miscellaneous Provisions) Act 1965* (NSW), s 8; *Law Reform Act 1995* (Qld), ss 5, 6; *Law Reform (Contributory Negligence and Apportionment of Liability) Act 2001* (SA), s 4; *Wrongs Act 1954* (Tas), ss 2 (wrongful act), 4; Vic: WrA, ss 25, 26; *Law Reform (Contributory Negligence and Tortfeasors' Contribution) Act 1947* (WA), s 3A. The Australian Capital Territory, New South Wales, Queensland and Victorian provisions apportion damages where damage is suffered as a result "partly of the wrong of any other person". "Wrong" is defined to mean

   > an act or omission that:
   >
   > (a) gives rise to a liability in tort in respect of which a defence of contributory negligence is available at common law, or
   >
   > (b) amounts to a breach of a contractual duty of care that is *concurrent and co extensive* with a duty of care in tort (emphasis added).

3. In relation to the first category of case mentioned by Hobhouse J, where the defendant's contractual liability does not depend on negligence, a plaintiff's negligence would not reduce damages recoverable, *Banque Keyser Ullmann SA v Skandia (UK) Insurance Co Ltd* [1990] QB 665, Steyn J (at 720-721) (breach of a contractual duty of utmost good faith in relation to an insurance contract).
4. In the second category referred to by Hobhouse J, the contractual duty is not co-extensive with a tortious duty of care. The amending legislation applies only where the contractual duty is concurrent and co-extensive. If it is not, the decision in *Astley* continues to apply.

ILLEGALITY

Plaintiff's unlawful conduct

[16.180] In a long stream of cases the High Court and State courts have considered the effect of illegality on a plaintiff's claim. The High Court last considered the issue in *Gala v Preston* (1991) 172 CLR 243.

Gala v Preston

[16.185] *Gala v Preston* (1991) 172 CLR 243 High Court of Australia

(footnotes omitted)

The relevant text of this case has been extracted at [7.170].

[16.190]

Notes&Questions

1. The decision in *Gala v Preston* (1991) 172 CLR 243 must now be reviewed in the light of the High Court's rejection of proximity as an overarching test of duty (see

Chapter 7) and the rejection of modified standards of care in *Cook v Cook* (1986) 162 CLR 376 (see *Imbree v McNeilly* (2008) 82 ALJR 1374 [12.250]). If illegality is relevant to the nature of the relationship between the parties and whether a duty of care is owed, illegality is not then a matter of defence, but of duty. For a recent illustration of the application of what might constitute "salient features" in a case involving a stolen vehicle, see *Miller v Miller* [2008] WADC 46.

2. In *Gala v Preston* (1991) 172 CLR 243, both the plaintiff and the defendant were engaged in an illegal enterprise. What is the position where the plaintiff is involved in some illegal conduct but not the defendant? There may be circumstances where a duty of care is owed to the plaintiff but some element of the plaintiff's claim is affected by illegality. For example, a plaintiff could not recover future loss of earnings if all the plaintiff's earnings were from theft: *Mills v Baitis* [1968] VR 583 at 590 per Gowans J, *Sami v Roads Corporation* [2008] VSC 377 at [142]-[146] (no recovery of losses because the sale of reshelled motor cars without a motor car traders licence was illegal).

3. Consider the following situation: A 35 year old crane driver is seriously injured due to his employer's negligence. The crane driver has epilepsy, which is well controlled by daily medication with no fits for over 15 years and an 80% probability of no further fits. In order to keep his job, the crane driver lies about his epilepsy and his medication in the twice-yearly medical examinations. He would not have been employed if his epilepsy were known to the employer as the safety of other workers could be put at risk. The deceit amounted to a criminal offence punishable by five years imprisonment. Should the crane driver be able to claim for loss of future earnings? Consider how the various rationales for refusing recovery might apply: deterring illegal conduct; a plaintiff cannot rely on an illegal act in order to recover; a plaintiff cannot benefit from an illegal act; recovery would condone the illegal conduct. How would you decide? What factors would you take into account in making this decision? What would be the outcome under civil liability legislation, referred to below? Compare *Hewison v Meridian Shipping PTE* [2002] All ER (D) 146 disallowing the claim for future loss of earnings.

4. In the United Kingdom, the Law Commission proposed that the law be reformed by giving the court discretion to bar a claim if the claim arises from, or is connected to, a plaintiff's unlawful act. The suggested factors that should be taken into account are: the seriousness of the illegality, the knowledge and intention of the plaintiff; deterrence; whether denying relief would further the legal purpose of the breached law; whether denial would be proportionate to the unlawful conduct and the degree of connection between the illegal act and the circumstances of the claim (The Law Commission (UK), *The Illegality Defence in Tort* (Consultation Paper No 160), paras 6.21- 6.45). Is such an approach preferable to that adopted by the High Court in *Gala v Preston* (1991) 172 CLR 243?

Unlawful conduct and the civil liability legislation

[16.195] In all States except Western Australia, the position is now affected by civil liability legislation. See ACT: CLWA, s 94; NSW: CLA, s 54; NT: PICCA, s 10; Qld: CLA, s 45; SA: CLA, s 43; Tas: CLA, s 6. The Victorian provision preserves the common law but requires the court to take into consideration illegality in determining whether there has been a breach of duty, Vic: WrA, ss 14B, 14G.

There is considerable variability to the qualifications on the inability to sue. For example, the Queensland CLA, s 45 provides, in part,

> 45 Criminals not to be awarded damages
>
> (1) A person does not incur civil liability if the court is satisfied on the balance of probabilities that–
>
> (a) the breach of duty from which civil liability would arise, apart from this section, happened while the person who suffered harm was engaged in conduct that is an indictable offence; and
>
> (b) the person's conduct contributed materially to the risk of the harm.
>
> (2) Despite subsection (1), the court may award damages in a particular case if satisfied that in the circumstances of the case, subsection (1) would operate harshly and unjustly.

The provisions reflect the sense of public outrage in the event that criminals might be able to sue for injuries received whilst executing a crime. See the illustrations from the United Kingdom, Australia and New Zealand referred to in H Luntz, "The Australian Picture" [2006] VUW L Rev 40. Note also the additional punitive measures in *Civil Liability Amendment (Offender Damages Trust Fund) Act 2005* (NSW); *Civil Liability Amendment (Offender Damages) Act 2005* (NSW). Do these provisions go too far? Reference has already been made to other areas that may involve criminal conduct, such as intoxicated plaintiffs (see [16.140] Notes 7 and 8), and where the plaintiff acts in self-defence, see Chapter 6 Defences to Intentional Torts.

The New South Wales provisions seem particularly punitive. NSW: CLA, s 54A relating to serious offences committed by mentally ill plaintiffs, was introduced to overcome the decision in *Presland v Hunter Area Health Service* [2003] NSWSC 754 (plaintiff who murdered whilst criminally insane recovered damages for incarceration and detention in a mental health facility). This decision was subsequently overruled by the Court of Appeal: *Hunter Area Health Service v Presland* [2005] NSWCA 33. For a recent application of the NSW provisions, see *Presidential Security Services of Aust Pty Ltd v Brilley* [2008] NSWCA 204. For a critical review of the policy grounds for denying a claim and the effect of civil liability provisions in each jurisdiction, see J Goudkamp, "A Revival of the Doctrine of Attainder? The Statutory Illegality Defences to Liability in Tort" (2007) Syd LR 18; G Watson, "Civil claims and civil death: "Offender damages" and the *Civil Liability Act 2002* (NSW)" (2008) 16 TLJ 81.

LIMITATION PERIODS

[16.200] Failure by the plaintiff to commence a claim "in time" is a good defence to the plaintiff's claim with the onus on the defendant to prove that the claim is out of time: *Pullen v Gutteridge Haskin & Davey Pty Ltd* [1993] 1 VR 27, at 72-73, 76; *Cigna Insurance Asia Pacific Ltd v Packer* [2000] WASC 415; *Sherson & Associates Pty Ltd v Bailey* [2000] NSWCA 275. A limitation period sets a period of time within which the plaintiff must commence court proceedings to make a claim. The plaintiff commences proceedings by filing a statement of claim or issuing a summons. The limitation period does not require that a trial, if there is one, occurs within the period. In some circumstances there may be provision to extend the limitation period for personal injury claims but this may be an expensive and difficult exercise. See *Limitation Act 1985* (ACT), s 36; *Limitation Act 1969* (NSW), s 58 (pre 6/12/2002), ss 62A – 62F (on or after 6/12/2002); *Limitation Act* (NT), s 44; *Limitation of Actions Act 1974* (Qld), s 31; *Limitation of Actions Act 1936* (SA), s 48; *Limitations Act 1974* (Tas), ss 5(3), 5A(3)(b); *Limitation of Actions Act 1958* (Vic), ss 23A, 27K – 27M; *Limitation*

Act 2005 (WA), ss 11, 38(1) and see *Queensland v Stephenson* (2006) 80 ALJR 923. This section gives a very brief account of the law relating to limitation periods. The Negligence Review Panel considered the issue of limitation periods and made a number of recommendations in relation to personal injury claims. The Report provides a useful summary of the tension between the needs of plaintiffs to obtain compensation and the defendants and their insurers to obtain finality.

Review of the Law of Negligence

[16.205] Negligence Review Panel, *Review of the Law of Negligence, Final Report,* (Commonwealth of Australia, Canberra, 2002), Ch 6 Limitation of Actions

(footnotes omitted)

Limitation periods provide a time limit for the bringing of legal proceedings. They should not be seen as arbitrary cut-off points unrelated to the demands of justice or the general welfare of society. They represent the legislature's judgment that the welfare of society is best served by causes of action being litigated within a limited time, notwithstanding that their enforcement may result in good causes of action being defeated.

It has been said that there are four broad rationales for the enactment of limitation periods. These are: As time goes by relevant evidence is likely to be lost. It is oppressive to a defendant to allow an action to be brought long after the circumstances that gave rise to it occurred. It is desirable for people to be able to arrange their affairs and utilise their resources on the basis that claims can no longer be made against them after a certain time. The public interest requires that disputes be settled as quickly as possible ...

Limitation period issues

When evaluating an appropriate limitation system, consideration needs to be given to the following issues: The date when the limitation period commences to run; The length of the limitation period; Whether there should be an ultimate bar to commencing proceedings (a "long-stop" provision); Whether the court should have discretion to extend the limitation period and, if so, on what basis; and Whether the limitation period should be suspended, particularly for minors and incapacitated persons.

The date when the limitation period should commence

There are four principal options in regard to the date from which the limitation period should run, namely: The date of the event(s) that resulted in the personal injury or death; the date of the accrual of the cause of action; the date when damage occurred; and the date of discoverability.

Whichever option is adopted, it will need to cater for many different kinds of damage. Different considerations arise depending upon whether damage is suffered in consequence of an accident that causes trauma or whether it is suffered in consequence of the contraction of a disease. In the case of an accident, the damage is usually (but not always) suffered immediately or soon after the accident. However, there are cases, such as those involving certain kinds of post-traumatic stress disorder, where the damage can manifest itself many years after an accident. In the case of a disease (such as mesothelioma, for instance), damage may also manifest itself many years after negligent conduct. Damage may occur progressively, with the result that a plaintiff may only realise after many years of being subjected to wrongful conduct that significant damage has been sustained (for example, in the case of industrial deafness). There are some kinds of damage which manifest themselves late and which are not capable of ready classification. An example is the delayed psychological effect of sexual or other physical abuse.

The date from which the limitation period commences should deal fairly with all these various kinds of damage ...

Review of the Law of Negligence cont.

The date of discoverability

The date of discoverability is the Panel's preferred option. The date of discoverability means the date on which the plaintiff knew, or ought to have known, that personal injury or death: had occurred; and was attributable to negligent conduct of the defendant; and in the case of personal injury, was sufficiently significant to warrant bringing proceedings …

The long-stop provision and the discretionary power to extend

We now turn to the difficulties that may be caused by adoption of the date of discoverability as the date for commencement of the limitation period. … [T]he date of discoverability is not a fixed date, capable of ready determination. In cases where damage manifests itself long after the event, or in a form difficult to detect, the date of discoverability could extend interminably into the future. … the date of discoverability is potentially unfair to defendants. The unfairness arises because, in cases where the date of discoverability may not occur until many years after the damage-causing event, witnesses may die or be difficult to find, memory may be impaired and records may be lost. In that event, the defendants could be hampered in the preparation of their defence and the fairness of the trial may be prejudiced.

Cases of the kind that lead to delay sufficiently long as to result, potentially, in an unfair trial are likely to be relatively few in number (although important in themselves). In the Panel's view, these cases could fairly be dealt with by what is termed an "ultimate bar" or "long-stop provision", coupled with a discretionary power on the part of the court, exercisable at any time, to extend the long-stop period.

The purpose of a long-stop period is to fix a date on which an action will become statute-barred, irrespective of whether the date of discoverability has occurred. In other words, under the proposed system, a claim will become statute-barred on the expiry of the limitation period or the long-stop period, whichever is the earlier.

In the Panel's view, the long-stop period should run from the date on which the allegedly negligent conduct took place. …

The Panel has concluded that the period should be 12 years from the date the allegedly negligent conduct occurred. In our view, this strikes a reasonable balance between the need to cater for cases in which damage manifests itself late and the need to ensure a fair trial. The Panel is aware that in some cases, damage will not manifest itself until after the expiry of the 12-year period. But plaintiffs who suffer such damage will be protected by the discretion to extend the long-stop period …

The Panel has previously noted that it is desirable to avoid providing for a discretionary extension of the limitation period. When it comes to the long-stop period, however, justice requires a discretionary power to extend in order to provide fairly for cases (including cases of diseases with a long latency period) in which damage is not discoverable until after the expiry of the long-stop period.

The long-stop coupled with the discretion to extend also caters for the legitimate interests of defendants. It does this by requiring a plaintiff who wishes to commence an action after the expiry of the long-stop period to seek the permission of the court. At this point the court is able to take account of the defendant's interest in securing a fair trial of the claim. …

Review of the Law of Negligence cont.

A prospective plaintiff should be entitled to apply at any time before the expiry of 3 years after the date of discoverability for an extension of the long-stop period. The court should have the power to extend the long-stop period to the expiry of that 3-year period. ...

[16.210] **Notes&Questions**

1. The Commonwealth, New South Wales, Tasmania and Victoria have implemented these recommendations in conjunction with civil liability reforms relating to personal injury claims: Cth: *Trade Practices Act 1974* (Cth), ss 87F, 87G (smoking or tobacco related claims are excluded, s 87F(1A)); *Limitation Act 1969* (NSW), Pt 2 Div 6 (acts or omissions occurring on or after Dec 6, 2002 but not motor accidents, s 50A(3)); *Limitation Act 1974* (Tas), ss 2(1) ("discoverability"), 5A (actions accruing after Jan 1, 2005); *Limitation of Actions Act 1958* (Vic), Pt 11A (acts or omissions occurring on or after 21 May 2003, does not apply to transport accidents, claims under the *Accident Compensation Act 1985*, workers compensation claims, dust diseases or tobacco products or smoking claims, s 27B). Some States have special legislative provisions applying to motor vehicle and public transport accidents, claims governed by workers compensation legislation and latent diseases. See for example *Dust Diseases Tribunal Act 1989* (NSW), s 12A (no limitation period applying to dust diseases). In relation to "discoverability", see *Baker-Morrison v State of New South Wales* [2009] NSWCA 35; *Spandideas v Vellar* [2008] VSC 198 leave to appeal refused [2008] VSCA 138.
   There are special provisions relating to minors or persons with incapacity (Cth: *Trade Practices Act 1974* (Cth), s 87G(4) (5); NSW: *Limitation Act 1969* (NSW), ss 50E, 50F; Tas: *Limitation Act 1974* (Tas), ss 26, 27; Vic: *Limitations of Actions Act 1958* (Vic), ss 27E, 27I, 27J) survival actions and claims by dependant relatives (Cth: *Trade Practices Act 1974* (Cth), s 87G(6); NSW: *Limitation Act 1969* (NSW), ss 50C(2), 50C(3), 50D(4); Tas: *Limitation Act 1974* (Tas), s 5A(4)(6); Vic: *Limitation of Actions Act 1958* (Vic), ss 27B(3), 27F(4), 27G, 27H).
   Independent of the limitation provisions, some jurisdictions require notice of a claim to given within a prescribed period before a claim may be made. ACT: CLWA, Ch 5 Personal Injuries Claims; Qld: *Personal Injuries Proceedings Act 2002* (Qld). In relation to motor vehicle accidents in NSW, see *Motor Accidents Compensation Act 1999* (NSW), Ch 4. Note also *Limitation of Actions Act 1936* (SA), s 48.
2. Children and persons with mental incapacity are a special case. Traditionally, limitation periods were suspended during periods of mental incapacity. The time started to run only when the person was no longer incapacitated. At common law, children are free of legal incapacity when they attain majority, 18 years. With the usual limitation period of three years for personal injury, this allowed a claim to be made until age 21 years. The potential for a very long period before claims could be settled adversely affected insurance, particularly in relation to public liability claims and claims against obstetricians. The Negligence Review Panel accepted the view that "society can reasonably expect parents and guardians, and those who care for incapacitated persons, to take necessary steps on behalf of their charges to initiate claims within the time limits imposed on the rest of the community" (at para 6.46). The

consequence is that in New South Wales, Tasmania, and Victoria, if a child under 18 has a parent, guardian or is a protected person, the limitation period is not suspended but runs from the time the cause of action is discoverable by the person responsible for the child as parent/guardian, or as a protected person's guardian. Conversely, time will not run during periods in which the victim is not a "protected person" or does not have a relevant parent or guardian. (NSW: *Limitation Act 1969* (NSW), ss 50F, s 61D (irrational decision not to sue)); Tas: *Limitation Act 1974* (Tas), s 26(6); Vic: *Limitation of Actions Act 1958* (Vic), s 27J; compare WA: *Limitation Act 2005*, ss 30 – 32). In these States an exception is made if a child is injured by a parent/guardian or close associate of a parent or guardian, in which case time begins to run from the age of 25. The period runs from the time the victim turns 25 or the later time of actual discovery with a long stop period of 12 years from the time the victim turns 25 years: NSW: *Limitation Act 1969* (NSW), s 50E; Vic: *Limitation of Actions Act 1958* (Vic), s 27I; compare Tas: ss 5A, 26(7) (8); and WA: *Limitation Act 2005*, s 33 (action ceases at age 25 years). See Mathews, "Post-Ipp Special Limitation Periods for Cases of Injury to a Child by a Parent or Close Associate: New Jurisdictional Gulfs" (2004) 12 TLJ 239. These provisions may be especially important in sexual abuse cases. Such abuse is secretive, with little in the way of independent evidence and often in a family or institutional context in which a child is particularly vulnerable. The victim's fear of the perpetrator, shame and fear of disbelief make it unsurprising that these claims often emerge later in adulthood. At the extreme end, see *McDonnell v Congregation of Christian Brothers Trustees* [2003] UKHL 63 (plaintiff aged 61 years at time of claim). A random sample of other cases shows the ages of the plaintiffs when they instituted claims arising from sexual abuse as children: *Hodges v Northampton County Council* [2004] EWCA Civ 526 (31 years); *Carter v Corporation of the Sisters of Mercy of the Diocese of Rockhampton & Ors* [2001] QCA 335 (38 yrs); *NF v State of Queensland* [2005] QCA 110 (49 years); *Hopkins v State of Queensland* [2004] QDC 21 (28 years); *Tusyn v State of Tasmania* [2004] TASSC 50 (52 years); *Eijkman v Magann* [2005] NSWCA 358 (32 years).

Do these legislative reforms achieve an appropriate balance between the needs of insurers and the protection of the most vulnerable within our community, children and those suffering incapacity? See L Sarmas, "Mixed Messages on Sexual Assault and the Statute of Limitations; *Stingel v Clark*, The Ipp Reforms and the argument for Change" (2008) 32(2) MULR 609.

3. The relevant limitation period runs from the time the cause of action accrues. That is, the period starts to run from the time the cause of action is complete. In the tort of negligence, damage is the gist of the action so that the cause of action is not complete until the plaintiff suffers the required damage. We have already referred to some problematic cases where it might not be clear when or whether relevant damage has been sustained, see Chapter 14. The Ipp Report (above) alludes to the circumstance whereby the plaintiff did not bring proceedings in time because the plaintiff was not aware that damage had occurred. This has proved particularly difficult with progressive diseases resulting from continuing exposure to harmful substances. There are two issues: (a) when does damage occur? (dealt with in Chapter 14); and (b) will the time run even if the plaintiff did not know nor could reasonably be expected to know that

damage had occurred? In *Cartledge v Jopling* [1963] AC 758, the House of Lords held that time began to run when material damage occurred even if unknown to the plaintiff. Lord Pearce said, at 772:

> In my opinion, it is impossible to hold that a man who has no knowledge of the secret onset of pneumoconiosis and suffers no present inconvenience from it cannot have suffered any actionable harm. So to hold might possibly, on the wording of the Fatal Accidents Act, deprive of all remedy a widow whose husband dies of pneumoconiosis without having any knowledge of symptom of the disease. And it would be wrong to deny a right of action to a plaintiff who can prove by X-ray photographs that his lungs are damaged but cannot prove any symptom or present physical inconvenience. Nor can his knowledge of the state of his lungs be the deciding factor. It would be impossible to hold that while the X-ray photographs are being taken he cannot yet have suffered any damage to his body, but that immediately the result of them is told to him, he has from that moment suffered damage ... It is a question of fact in each case whether a man has suffered material damage by any physical changes to his body. Evidence that those changes are not felt by him and may never be felt tells in favour of the damage coming within the principle of de minimis non curat lex. On the other hand, evidence that in usual exertion or at the onslaught of disease he may suffer from his hidden impairment tells in favour of the damage being substantial. There is no legal principle that lack of knowledge in the plaintiff must reduce the damage to nothing or make it minimal.

The principle in *Cartledge v Jopling* [1963] AC 758 continues to apply unless the statute starts the limitation period running from the time of discoverability. In most jurisdictions the discoverability rule applies to personal injuries claims, see Note 1 above. Victoria had such a provision predating the civil liability reforms (*Limitation of Actions Act 1958* (Vic), s 5(1A), *Stingel v Clark* (2006) 80 ALJR 1339). See WA: *Limitation Act 2005*, ss 55, 56, ACT: *Limitation Act 1985*, s 16B (actions on or after July 1, 2003).

4. Amendments to Limitation Acts following the Ipp Report affect only personal injury claims. Unless the relevant statute expressly allows the period to run from the date of discoverability, the limitation period will run from the date damage occurs whether or not it was discoverable. Subject to the individual State and Territory statutory provisions, the principle in *Cartledge v Jopling* [1963] AC 758 also applies to property damage. In some jurisdictions there is separate statutory provision for building damage caused by latent defects in building construction, see next note.

5. Economic loss cases pose particular difficulties. The first step is to identify what the relevant interest is that is infringed and then when measurable economic loss was sustained. The principal judgment in the High Court in *Commonwealth v Cornwell* (2007) 229 CLR 519 concerned the application of *Limitation Act 1985* (ACT), s 11 to economic losses. The relevant part of the section provided:

> an action on any cause of action is not maintainable if brought after the expiration of a limitation period of 6 years running from the date on which the cause of action first accrues to the plaintiff...

The Court adopted the view that no gloss was to be put on the statutory text. It endorsed the views of the High Court in an earlier decision declaring at [6] that:

> The Court rejected the proposition that, at least in the case of claims in negligence for economic loss, time does not run until the plaintiff discovers or could on reasonably inquiry have discovered that damage was sustained.

This means that the limitation period expires when some measurable damage occurs and this may be before the plaintiff could have discovered or was aware of the loss. A mere contingent loss which may never eventuate is not sufficient. The NSW Court of Appeal in *Christie v Purves* (2007) 69 ATR 155, Ipp JA at [40], (Beazley and Campbell JJA concurring) stated the general rule as follows:

> For economic loss (as with other forms of damage) to be sustained, there has to be some actual, measurable damage that is beyond what can be regarded as negligible. While prospective loss, alone, is not enough, a cause of action of negligence will accrue when the plaintiff first suffers any actual damage of the kind described. The cause of action will then be regarded as having accrued, even if some of the plaintiff's damages are prospective. The plaintiff may then claim for the actual damages that have been incurred and should quantify and claim for the prospective damages (such as, for example, future loss of profits). This, for example, is what occurred in *Perre v Apand Pty Limited* [1999] HCA 36; (1999) 198 CLR 180. These propositions are well-established and are manifest from *Commonwealth v Cornwell* (at 152 to 153, [16] to [18]), *Wardley Australia Limited v Western Australia* [1992] HCA 55; (1992) 175 CLR 514 (at 530 to 531) ... (other citations omitted).

6. The High Court in *Commonwealth v Cornwell* (2007) 229 CLR 519 (noted above) did not comment upon what is regarded as the accepted position in Australia in relation to latent building defects giving rise to economic loss, see [9.30]. It has generally been accepted that in latent defect cases, economic losses may not have been sustained until the defect becomes known or manifest (see *Pullen v Gutteridge Haskins & Davey Pty Ltd* [1993] 1 VR 27; *Sherson & Associates Pty Ltd v Bailey* [2000] NSWCA 275). Until then, the latent defect is unlikely to cause economic loss either by way of a need for remedial work or for loss of value on sale.

New South Wales, South Australia, Victoria, the Australian Capital Territory and the Northern Territory, restrict the exposure of the building industry to long periods of potential liability by setting special limitation rules applying to building defects. The legislation sets a final 10 year limitation period with the commencement of the period related to the completion of building work/occupation certificate: *Building Act 2004* (ACT), s 142 (10 years from certificate of completion or last inspection or first occupation or use); *Environmental Planning & Assessment Act 1979* (NSW), s 109ZK (10 years from final occupation certificate issued); *Development Act 1993* (SA), s 73 (the period runs from date of completion of building work); *Building Act 1993* (Vic), ss 134, 134A (plumbing works period runs from the date of occupancy permit or if the permit is not issued, the certificate of final inspection); *Building Act* (NT), s 160 (10 years from occupancy permit). ACT: *Limitation Act 1985*, s 40 (extension of time for latent damage to property and economic loss with a long stop period of 15 years from the date of the relevant act or omission). Note the special statutory warranties applying to the construction of dwellings and other buildings: *Building Act 2004* (ACT) Part VI; *Home Building Act 1989* (NSW), ss 18A – 18G, Part VI; *Building Services Authority Act 1991* (Qld), ss 68 – 71; *Building Work Contractors Act 1995* (SA), ss 32 – 35; *Housing Indemnity Act 1992* (Tas); *House*

Contracts Guarantee Act 1987 (Vic); *Domestic Building Contracts Act 1995* (Vic); *Home Building Contracts Act 1991* (WA).

7. In relation to other forms of economic loss, one typical type of claim is for financial loss flowing from a solicitor's failure to bring proceedings within the limitation period. Ipp JA, delivering the judgment of the NSW Court of Appeal in *Cheney & Wilson v Duncan* [2001] NSWCA 197, summarised the relevant principles:

> Generally, where, through the negligence of solicitors, a client's cause of action becomes statute barred, the client's right of action in negligence against those solicitors accrues at the time the action becomes statute barred, and damages are to be assessed at that time... There is no "general overriding qualification" to the effect that a limitation period does not begin to run "until the stage is reached when the plaintiff discovers, or could on any reasonable inquiry have discovered, that the loss has been sustained": *Wardley* at 540 per Deane J; *Hawkins v Clayton* at 561 to 562 per Brennan J, at 587 to 588 per Deane J, at 599 to 601 per Gaudron J; (other citations omitted). In *Hawkins v Clayton* Deane J expressed the opinion that the general rule as to when a cause of action accrues might be subject to qualification in some special circumstances....
>
> The essence of the exception as so enunciated is that it applies when the very act of negligence that inflicts the injury also has the effect of precluding the bringing of an action for damages. There must be a coincidence between the negligent conduct and the conduct that conceals from the plaintiff that he or she has a cause of action.
>
> The practical operation of the exception so propounded is best seen from the unusual circumstances of *Hawkins v Clayton* itself. In that case the wrongful action that inflicted the injury was the negligent failure of the defendant firm of solicitors to inform the plaintiff of the existence and contents of the testatrix's last will. Injury was inflicted by reason of that negligent failure, because, in consequence, a tenant could not be found for the property of the estate (and other damage was suffered, as well). But, at the same time as causing the injury, the defendant's negligence concealed from the plaintiff the existence of the cause of action.

PART 4: STRICT LIABILITY

PART 4

CHAPTER 17

Statutory Duties

INTRODUCTION

[17.05] A torts action for damages may be available for breach of a duty imposed by statute. This may be surprising when the statute says nothing about awarding damages for a statutory breach. For example, a workers safety statute might require an employer to provide a safety guard to protect employees working with dangerous machinery. It may also provide that breach of that duty would result in a fine. In these circumstances, courts have allowed an injured worker to bring an action in tort for damages for breach of this statutory duty. Statutes rarely state an intention to give a private remedy for damages for breach, however, consumer protection legislation is an exception, see *Trade Practices Act 1974* (Cth), s 82(1) and the Fair Trading Acts in the various States.

The action for breach of statutory duty is very different to the action for negligence. The statute may impose strict liability, see [17.95]; defences to breach of statutory duty may be more restricted than at common law (see [17.140]) and there is the suggestion that rules for remoteness of damage do not apply once a breach of statute is shown to have caused the plaintiff's harm, see [17.125]. A plaintiff might succeed in an action for breach of statutory duty where a claim in negligence might fail: the plaintiff's claim is for breach of a duty imposed by statute, not negligence. In *Darling Island Stevedoring & Lighterage Co Ltd v Long* (1957) 97 CLR 36 an action was brought against an employer for negligence and had failed; this did not prevent a separate claim being brought for breach of statutory duty, see [17.75]. Even if an action for breach of statutory duty is not available, statutory breach provides evidence that the defendant has been negligent, *Tucker v McCann* [1948] VLR 222.

The Australian courts have adopted the English position that the action for breach of statutory duty is a separate tort quite distinct from the tort of negligence.

In order to succeed in a tort action for breach of statutory duty, a plaintiff must show that:

1. Parliament intended to give a private right of action for damages for breach of a statutory duty imposed on the defendant;
2. the defendant was in breach of that statutory duty;
3. the plaintiff is within the class of persons protected by the statute;
4. the injury or damage is within scope of statutory protection; and
5. the plaintiff's damage was caused by the breach

There must be an express statutory duty, so if no express statutory duty was imposed on the Director as Guardian of Aboriginal Children, no action for breach of statutory duty was available, *Cubillo v Commonwealth* (2000) 103 FCR 1 (appeal dismissed without reference to this issue, (2001) 112 FCR 455). Actions for breach of statutory duties have been common for duties involving workers safety, but exceptional in other areas, *Crimmins v Stevedoring Industry Finance Committee* (1999) 200 CLR 1 per Gummow J at 58. One explanation is that in the 19 th century an employee's ability to recover compensation for work injuries was very difficult because of the defences of volenti, contributory negligence and common employment. An action for statutory breach was one method of avoiding these difficulties. In the first modern action for breach of statutory duty, *Groves v Wimborne* [1898] 2 QB 402, it was held that an injured employee was entitled to recover damages against the employer for breach of a statutory duty imposed by the *Factory and Workshop Act 1878* (UK), s 5(4), to maintain fencing for dangerous machinery. Vaughan Williams, LJ (at 415-416) said that:

> where a statute provides for the performance by certain persons of a particular duty, and someone belonging to a class of persons for whose benefit and protection the statute imposes the duty is injured by failure to perform it, prima facie, and, if there be nothing to the contrary, an action by the person so injured will lie against the person who has failed to perform the duty.

But breach of statute by itself is not sufficient (see *Atkinson v Newcastle Waterworks Co* (1877) 2 Exch D 441–no action was available against a private waterworks company for failure to provide water at pressures as required by statute). Subsequent decisions have insisted that no action is available unless it can be shown that parliament intended that statutory breach should give rise to a private right of action for damages. Both English and Australian courts have repeatedly justified using the presumption of statutory intent to determine whether an action for breach of statutory duty exists. In what has become a classic statement, Dixon J in *O'Connor v SP Bray Ltd* (1937) 56 CLR 464 at 477-478 said:

> [A]n interpretation of the statute, according to ordinary canons of construction, will rarely yield a necessary implication positively giving a civil remedy. As an examination of the decided cases will show an intention to give, or not to give, a private right has more often than not been ascribed to the legislature as a result of presumptions or by reference to matters governing the policy of the provision rather than the meaning of the instrument. Sometimes it almost appears that a complexion is given to the statute upon very general considerations without either the authority of any general rule of law or the application of any definite rule of construction.

This approach provided a flexible vehicle for often unexpressed policy preferences. In the case of public utilities, the test was used to exclude liability in order to protect utilities against unreasonable burdens that would otherwise result if claims were available for any breach of a statutory duty, see PD Finn, "A Road Not Taken: The Boyce Plaintiff and Lord Cairns' Act" (1983) 57 ALJ 493. Prosser observed:

> Much ingenuity has been expended in the effort to explain why criminal legislation should result in a rule for civil liability ... Many courts have, however, purported to "find" in the statute a supposed "implied", "constructive", or "presumed" intent to provide for tort liability. In the ordinary case this is pure fiction concocted for the purposes. The obvious conclusion can only be that when the legislators said nothing about it, they either did not have the civil suit in mind at all, or deliberately omitted to provide for it.
>
> Perhaps the most satisfactory explanation is that the courts are seeking, by something in the nature of judicial legislation, to further the ultimate policy for the protection of individuals which they find underlying the statute, and which they believe the legislature must have had in mind. (Prosser, *Law of Torts* (4 th ed, 1971), pp 191-192.)

The views of Dixon J, and Prosser quoted above, contrast with those of Kitto J in the principal Australian decision *Sovar v Henry Lane Pty Ltd* (1967) 116 CLR 397 at 405:

> [T]he question whether a contravention of a statutory requirement of the kind in question here is actionable at the suit of a person injured thereby is one of statutory interpretation. The intention that such a private right shall exist is not ... conjured up by judges to give effect to their own ideas of policy and then "imputed" to the legislature. The legitimate endeavour of the courts is to determine what inference really arises, on a balance of considerations, from the nature, scope and terms of the statute, including the nature of the evil against which it is directed, the nature of the conduct prescribed, the pre-existing state of the law, and, generally, the whole range of circumstances relevant upon a question of statutory interpretation.

DETERMINING WHETHER A CAUSE OF ACTION ARISES

Presumptions of statutory intention

[17.10] Despite what Prosser has called the fiction of statutory intent, the plaintiff is nevertheless called upon to show that the legislature intended that there be a private right of action for damages for breach. Judges, such as Kitto J in *Sovar v Lane* (1967) 116 CLR 397, see this as essentially a matter of statutory construction. Older authorities developed presumptions to decide whether there was a legislative intention to grant a civil remedy for breach. Some presumptions favoured finding a duty, others did not, depending on the statutory circumstances. Ultimately, the various presumptions are not particularly helpful in determining legislative intent. Despite this, courts continue to quote them and for this reason we will briefly explain each presumption in turn by reference to the nature of the statutory circumstances.

Statute contains no penalty for breach

[17.15] It was presumed that where there was no penalty for breach of a statute, a person who had been injured by the breach of that statute had a right to recover damages unless it could be established by considering the Act as a whole, that no such right was intended to be given. Without this presumption the statute was a mere "pious aspiration" (*Cutler v Wandsworth Stadium Ltd* [1949] AC 398 per Lord Simonds at 407). The stream of cases dealing with welfare statutes suggests the demise of this as a general principle, see below [17.45].

Penalty imposed by statute

[17.20] There was a different presumption where a penalty was imposed. According to the view derived from Lord Tenterden CJ in *Doe d Murray, Bishop of Rochester v Bridges* (1831) 1 B & Ad 847; 109 ER 1001 at 859 (B & Ad), where an Act creates an obligation, and enforces the performance in a specified manner, such as by the imposition of criminal penalties, that performance cannot be enforced in any other manner. But this presumption has not prevented the courts finding an appropriate legislative intention when dealing with industrial safety statutes. It is also clear that the existence of alternative remedies in the statute itself has not always been fatal to a plaintiff's claim. In the case establishing the action in its modern form, *Groves v Wimborne* [1898] 2 QB 402, the plaintiff's claim was made out despite a provision in the *Factory and Workshop Act 1878* (UK), s 82, which allowed the Secretary of State to direct that the penalty or part of it shall be applied for the benefit of the person injured or his or her family. But, as with other presumptions, there are invariably exceptions that support Prosser's argument that legislative intent is a fictitious concoction.

Adequate alternative remedies

[17.25] An action might be refused if there are adequate alternative remedies (*Phillips v Britannia Hygienic Laundry Co Ltd* [1923] 1 KB 539 at 842 per Atkin LJ). In *Dennis v Brownlee* (1963) 63 SR (NSW) 719, the Full Court of the Supreme Court of New South Wales refused to find an action for breach of statutory duty for breach of certain local government ordinances requiring safety precautions to be taken in the course of road repairs. General tort remedies were adequate.

This principle did not prevent claims by injured workers for breach of statutory duty under industrial safety statutes, despite the existence of negligence claims against the employer for injuries sustained in the course of employment. Today, it is rare for plaintiffs not to have some sort of public law remedy through, for example, administrative appeals tribunals, ombudsman's offices or various complaints procedures. However, unless the statute expressly provides otherwise, these avenues of redress do not normally provide compensatory damages to the plaintiff (see *Park Ho v Minister for Immigration & Ethics Affairs* (1989) 88 ALR 517 in relation to the *Administrative Decisions (Judicial Review) Act 1977* (Cth)). This explains why plaintiffs might sue for breach of statutory duty rather than pursue public law remedies.

In recent times, the courts have dismissed claims by prisoners for breach of statutory duties on the ground that other remedies are available. In *Olotu v Home Office* [1997] 1 WLR 328, the Crown breached its statutory duty to bring the plaintiff before the court within a defined time. It was held that no action for damages was available; the plaintiff could have sought bail or brought public law proceedings. Similarly no action was available where, in breach of statute, an accused was not allowed access to a solicitor; all the more reason to deny the claim when the plaintiff had not suffered any tangible damage (*Cullen v Chief Constable of the Royal Ulster Constabulary* [2004] 2 All ER 237 (HL)).

Duty for the benefit of a limited class

[17.30] Where the statutory duty was enacted for the benefit of the public rather than for the protection of a defined class, parliament was presumed not to have intended to grant a private right of action. Thus, industrial regulations enacted for the protection of a limited class, such as factory workers, can give rise to actions for breach of statutory duty; whereas traffic regulations whose concern is highway users and therefore the general public do not (*Phillips v*

Britannia Hygienic Laundry Co Ltd [1923] 1 KB 539 at 840 per Banks LJ). A similar argument is relevant to deciding whether a power to act can give rise to a duty, see *Graham Barclay Oysters Pty Ltd v Ryan* (2002) 211 CLR 540, and Chapter 11 Duty–Special Defendants.

Categories unlikely to give rise to actions

Political decisions and priorities

[17.35] Presumptions aside, some general observations can be made about the categories of cases where courts are unlikely to find the requisite statutory intention. It is no surprise that many of the reasons for refusing a claim were encountered in deciding whether a public authority owed a duty of care (see Chapter 11 Duty–Special Defendants). First, in the absence of clear statutory language, courts will not allow actions which require an evaluation of what are really political decisions, those that involve policy making or quasi-legislative functions (see [11.10]). These might, for example, involve setting political priorities for government, the allocation of resources and balancing of competing societal demands. It is not the role of the courts in damages claims to review these functions or "second guess" these decisions.

General duties

[17.40] Courts have often rejected claims where duties are expressed in broad general terms rather than imposing specific duties. For example, in relation to road traffic, a duty for "each local authority (to) prepare and carry out a programme of measures designed to promote road safety" (*Gorringe v Calderdale Metropolitan Borough Council* [2004] 1 WLR 1057 at [18]-[20] per Lord Hoffman), or a duty that "Australia Post shall, as far as practicable, perform its functions in a manner consistent with sound commercial practice" (*Kirkup v Commonwealth of Australia* [2001] FCA 1243).

Broadly expressed duties may be aspirational in character and not intended to give rise to private actions for breach. In *Roots v Oentory Pty Ltd* [1983] 2 Qd R 745, a code of conduct for real estate agents was held not to give rise to an action.

Health, education and welfare duties

[17.45] Wade (in *Administrative Law* (6th ed, 1988), p 750) suggests that general duties imposed on public authorities for the benefit of the general public in the areas of health, education and welfare are not intended to be enforceable by damages claims brought by individuals. To do so would impose unreasonable burdens on government, particularly because the statutory duty may be couched in absolute terms, that is, breach may occur without negligence or fault, see [17.95]. For examples of these cases, see *X v Bedfordshire County Council* [1995] 2 AC 633 (health); *Cubillo v Commonwealth* [2000] FCA 1084, at [1183] (welfare) (appeal dismissed on different grounds (2000) Aust Torts Reports 81-578; *Williams v Minister, Aboriginal Rights Act 1983* (1999) Aust Torts Reports 81-526 (welfare).

In *X v Bedfordshire County Council* [1995] 2 AC 633 at 731-732, Lord Browne-Wilkinson said:

> Although regulatory or welfare legislation affecting a particular area of activity does in fact provide protection to those individuals particularly affected by that activity, the legislation is not to be treated as being passed for the benefit of those individuals but for the benefit of society in general ... The cases where a private right of action for breach of statutory duty have been held to arise are all cases in which the statutory duty has been very limited and specific as opposed to general administrative functions imposed on public bodies and involving the exercise of administrative discretions.

On the issue of whether an action was available for breach of a statutory duty concerned with child protection, Lord Browne-Wilkinson also observed (at 747):

> [T]he Acts in question are all concerned to establish an administrative system designed to promote the social welfare of the community. The welfare sector involved is one of peculiar sensitivity, involving very difficult decisions how to strike the balance between protecting the child from immediate feared harm and disrupting the relationship between the child and its parents. Decisions often have to be taken on the basis of inadequate and disputed facts. In my judgment in such a context it would require exceptionally clear statutory language to show a parliamentary intention that those responsible for carrying out these difficult functions should be liable in damage if, on subsequent investigation with the benefit of hindsight, it was shown that they had reached an erroneous conclusion and therefore failed to discharge their statutory duties.

Plaintiffs have not had any greater success in negligence claims, see *Sullivan v Moody* (2001) 207 CLR 562 at [7.120].

In *O'Rourke v Camden London Borough Council* [1998] AC 188, the House of Lords held that a breach of a statutory duty to provide housing did not give rise to an action for damages for breach of statutory duty. Lord Hoffman (other Lords agreeing) said at 193:

> [T]he Act is a scheme of social welfare, intended to confer benefits at the public expense on grounds of public policy. Public money is spent on housing the homeless not merely for the private benefit of people who find themselves homeless but on grounds of general public interest: because, for example, proper housing means that people will be less likely to suffer illness, turn to crime or require the attention of other social services. The expenditure interacts with expenditure on other public services such as education, the National Health Service and even the police. It is not simply a private matter between the claimant and the housing authority.

There is general acceptance that in the absence of very clear statutory language, welfare legislation is unlikely to give rise to actions for breach of statutory duty. Even in those areas concerned with statutory protection of individual liberty, there has been no success with actions for breach of statutory duty. A statutory provision giving prisoners a right of access to a lawyer does not give rise to an action despite the Act's long title that it was intended "to confer ... rights on persons detained". Lord Millet in *Cullen v Chief Constable of the Royal Ulster Constabulary* [2004] 2 All ER 237 at [67], said that the right was,

> a quasi-constitutional right of fundamental importance in a free society–indeed its existence may be said to be one of the tests of a free society–and like habeas corpus and the right to a fair trial it is available to everyone. It is for the benefit of the public at large. We can all of us, the innocent as well as the guilty, sleep more securely in our beds for the knowledge that we cannot be detained any moment at the hands of the state and denied access to a lawyer.

Similarly in *Chan v Minister for Immigration* (1991) 103 ALR 499 where there was no cause of action for breach of the *Migration Act 1958* (Cth), s 38, which required the Minister to bring a proposed deportee before a magistrate or other prescribed authority within 48 hours of arrest and thereafter as provided for.

In Australia, in a series of cases concerning the Aboriginal "stolen generations", welfare legislation has been held not to give rise to actions for breach of statutory duties. In *Williams v Minister, Aboriginal Rights Act 1983* (1999) Aust Torts Reports 81-526 at [681], Abadee J held that there was no action for breach of statutory duties imposed by the *Aborigines Protection Act 1909* (NSW); the purpose of the Acts was for the "orderly settlement and supervision of Aborigines for their benefit and for the benefit of the community under control of a public authority established under the Act". There was no intention to grant a private right of action for statutory breach. The plaintiff had alleged that the Act imposed duties to provide for the plaintiff's "'custody, maintenance and education'; and (b) to exercise a general supervision and care over all matters affecting her interests and welfare and to protect her against injustice, imposition and fraud." An appeal to the Court of Appeal was dismissed without reference to breach of statutory duty issue, see (2000) Aust Torts Reports 81-578. The authorities indicate that even if the statute appears to be enacted to protect a restricted class, it is rare for courts to find that an action for breach of statutory duty is available.

The *Liquor Ordinance 1975* (ACT), s 79 provided that the holder of a licence or permit under the Ordinance shall not sell or supply liquor to a person in respect of whom there are reasonable grounds for believing that he or she is intoxicated. In *Chordas v Bryant (Wellington) Pty Ltd* (1988) 20 FCR 91, the Full Federal Court held that such a provision did not give rise to an action for breach of statutory duty against the hotel keeper by a bar patron who was assaulted by an intoxicated customer. The Ordinance was enacted in the general public interest not for the protection of others who might be injured by an intoxicated person. See also *Soutter v P & O Resorts P/L* [1998] QCA 5. More recent authority has not relied on actions for breach of statutory duty in this context, see *Cole v South Tweed Heads Rugby League Football Club* (2004) 217 CLR 469, and see also *Foroughi v Star City Pty Ltd* [2007] FCA 1503 (where no action was available for breach of statutory duty by a gambler against the casino).

Investigatory, regulatory and administrative functions

[17.50] The policy reasons for excluding a duty of care in relation to a statutory authority (see Chapter 11 Duty–Special Defendants) apply with greater force to an action for breach of a statutory duty which may impose strict liability. There is reluctance to allow actions for breach of statutory duties in relation to government bodies or officials exercising investigative powers (*Nathan Wortley v Health Care Complaints Commission* [2003] NSWSC 61), regulatory functions (failure to exercise a regulatory function, see [11.45]), or carrying out administrative duties (*Scott v Secretary, Department of Social Security* [2000] FCA 1241, duties under social security legislation). Similarly, duties to ensure timely performance and administrative efficiency are unlikely to give rise to actions (*R v Deputy Governor of Parkhurst* [1991] 3 WLR 340 (HL), a prisoner does not have an action for breach of prison rules which were concerned with management, treatment and control of prisoners and regulatory in character). Otherwise, it is argued, these bodies become excessively cautious and defensive with scarce resources being diverted to protect against claims. As a recent example, see *Hunter Area Health Service v Presland* [2005] NSWCA 33 and see the critical evaluation of this argument in B Markesinis et al *Tortious Liability of Statutory Bodies* (Hart Press, Oxford, 1999), pp 80-81. In *Calveley v Chief Constable of the Merseyside Police* [1989] 2 WLR 624, one of the issues was whether a police officer had an action for breach of a statutory duty imposed by the *Police (Discipline) Regulations 1977* (UK). Regulation 7 required the officer investigating a complaint to give appropriate notice to the person the subject of investigation as soon as practicable. Lord Bridge, other members of the House agreeing, accepted that the duty was imposed for the benefit of the police officer subject to investigation. His Lordship said at 629-630:

> the duty is imposed as a procedural step to protect the position of the officer subject to investigation in relation to any proceedings which may be brought against him. ... If ... the delay in giving notice ... coupled with other factors causes irremediable prejudice to the officer in disciplinary proceedings which result in his conviction of an offence against the discipline

> code, he has his remedy by way of judicial review to quash that conviction and nullify its consequences. The proposition that the legislature should have intended to give a cause of action in contemplation of the remoter economic consequences of any delay in giving notice ... is really too fanciful to call for serious consideration.

In *Chan v Minister for Immigration* (1991) 103 ALR 499, one of the issues was whether an action was available for breach of the *Migration Act 1958* (Cth), s 38 which required the Minister to bring a proposed deportee before a magistrate or other prescribed authority within 48 hours of arrest and thereafter as provided for. Einfeld J found that no action was available on this basis. His Honour said (at 508)"there is a need to balance the protection of liberty and due process with the need for public officials to carry out their obligations honestly and in good faith free from the fear of actions for damages, either against themselves or their employers who would normally be vicariously liable."

Accountability of public bodies

[17.55] Much of the recent litigation concerning actions for breach of statutory duty has involved the intersection between public and private law. In particular, courts have considered whether statutory duties imposed on government, government officers or instrumentalities can give rise to claims for damages for breach. As noted above, these attempts have, on the whole, been unsuccessful. Nevertheless, courts in the United Kingdom have been increasingly prepared to hold government accountable through actions in negligence. The policy reasons for withholding claims, even in sensitive areas such as where there is negligence in failing to prevent sexual abuse, now seem much less compelling, at least, where the claim is in negligence rather than the separate action for breach of statutory duty. In *W v Essex County Council* [2001] 2 AC 592, a claim was allowed by parents for sexual abuse of their children brought against the authority for placing a known sexual abuser in their home. There has been a refusal to strike out claims against government in *Barrett v Enfield London Borough Council* [2001] 2 AC 550 in relation to foster care and in *Phelps v Hillingdon London Borough Council* [2001] AC 619 in relation to a child's education. But the line was drawn in *JD v East Berkshire Community Health NHS Trust* [2005] UKHL 23, holding that there was no duty to parents for negligently misdiagnosed child abuse. The Australian judicial and legislative approach is more conservative, see *Sullivan v Moody* (2001) 207 CLR 562, *SB v State of NSW* [2004] VSC 514 (reviewing the authorities) with civil liability legislation limiting the exposure of government, its instrumentalities and public authorities for negligence, see Chapter 11 Duty–Special Defendants.

In comparison, it is remarkable that French law has not been inhibited by policy reasons regarded as compelling in common law decisions. In French law compensating citizens "for the damages suffered because of administrative activities can never be a wrong use of public money; on the contrary, it may even be seen as the best possible use of public money when it is viewed as serving the principle of equality by avoiding a result that means that people who have randomly been affected by administrative action remain without compensation"; moreover, liability in French law is regarded as a method of holding the administration accountable and as an adjunct to existing judicial review.

Restrictions on claims

[17.60] Traditionally, the action for breach of statutory duty has had its most prolific application in actions by injured workers for breaches of industrial safety legislation. The curtailment of common law actions by employees against employers significantly limits the extent to which injured employees can recover damages against the employer, see Chapter 14 Damages. Additionally, occupational health and safety legislation has, in some States, limited the availability of the action for breach of statutory duty based on that legislation. The legislative pattern has been to set general performance standards for occupational health and safety. For example, in New South Wales, the *Occupational Health and Safety Act 2000* (NSW), s 8(1), requires that every "employer shall ensure the health, safety and welfare at work of all the employees of the employer". See also *Occupational Health, Safety and Welfare Act 1986* (SA), s 19(1); *Occupational Health and Safety Act 2004* (Vic), s 21(1); the *Industrial Safety, Health and Welfare Act 1977* (Tas), s 32; compare the *Occupational Safety and Health Act 1984* (WA), s 19(1). These more generalised standards reflect the philosophy, encompassed in the influential Robens Report, from the United Kingdom, that detailed safety standards should be left to voluntary codes of practice developed within the industry concerned rather than to legally enforceable regulations (Great Britain, Committee on Safety and Health at Work (Lord Robens-Chair), *Safety and Health at Work: Report of the Committee 1970-72* (Cmnd 5034, London, HMSO, 1972). Under current legislation, either WorkCover, Occupational Health and Safety Commissions (and similar bodies), or the relevant Minister, are given power to develop and declare standards and codes of practice.

In New South Wales, Victoria, Western Australia and at the federal level, the legislation provides that a person shall not be liable in any civil or criminal proceedings because the person has failed to observe any provision of any approved industry code of practice: *Occupational Health and Safety (Commonwealth Employment) Act 1991* (Cth), s 70(8); *Occupational Health and Safety Act 2000* (NSW), s 46(2); *Occupational Health and Safety Act 2004* (Vic), s 150; *Occupational Safety and Health Act 1984* (WA), s 57(7). Contrast *Occupational Health, Safety and Welfare Act 1986* (SA), s 6(2). This prevents any action for breach of statutory duty based directly and exclusively on breach of industry codes of practice or compliance codes. In New South Wales, Victoria and at the federal level, common law actions for breach of statutory duty involving general performance duties imposed by the Occupational Health and Safety Acts are specifically excluded: *Occupational Health and Safety (Commonwealth Employment) Act 1991* (Cth), s 79; *Occupational Health and Safety Act 2000* (NSW), s 32; *Occupational Health and Safety Act 2004* (Vic), s 34. This exclusion does not affect breaches of duties imposed by regulations which are still actionable: *Occupational Health and Safety Act 2000* (NSW), s 32(2); *Occupational Health and Safety Act 2004* (Vic), s 34(c). The Australian Capital Territory and the Northern Territory provisions exclude actions for breach of statutory duties imposed by the OH&S Act and regulations, *Occupational Health and Safety Act 1989* (ACT), s 223, *Edwards v Woolworths Ltd* [2009]ACTSC 4; *Workplace Health & Safety Act* (NT), s 67. Actions are available for breach under the Queensland provisions (*Calvert v Mayne Nickless Ltd (No 1)* [2005] QCA 263).

Civil liability legislation

[17.65] The civil liability legislation, in dealing with the liability of public and other authorities (see Chapter 11 Duty–Special Defendants), makes reference to actions for breach of statutory duty. A typical provision is NSW: CLA, s 43(2) which provides:

> an act or omission of the authority does not constitute *a breach of statutory duty* unless the act or omission was in the circumstances so unreasonable that no authority having the functions of

> the authority in question could properly consider the act or omission to be a reasonable exercise of its function.

(italics inserted)

The Australian Capital Territory, Queensland, Tasmania and Victoria have similar legislative provisions: ACT: CLWA, s 111; Qld: CLA, s 36; Tas: CLA, s 40(2); Vic: WrA, s 84(2) (note the exclusion of absolute statutory duties in s 84(4)). But despite the reference to actions for *breach of statutory duty*, it is difficult to envisage how the section can apply to actions for breach of statutory duty unless the statute sets a negligence standard for breach, see [17.105]. This is because unreasonableness is not relevant to actions for breach of statutory duty. A statutory "duty" is by its nature mandatory not discretionary. Unreasonableness could be relevant if there were discretionary elements related to the exercise of the statutory duty. In *X v Bedfordshire* [1995] 2 AC 633, at 736, Lord Wilkinson referred to discretion to the extent and methods by which a duty is to be performed; or where the duty arises only when certain preconditions requiring exercise of discretion have been met, see P Cane, "Ultra Vires Breach of Statutory Duty" (1981) *Public Law* 11 at 18-19, suggesting that some "duties" are in reality "powers"; or possibly if the statutory duty is cast in very broad language permitting the authority to exercise discretion in determining how the statutory outcome is to be met.

Could the section have a broader operation? For example, if a public authority has an absolute statutory duty to assist people in need of care but it does not have sufficient funds to provide that care, it might not be unreasonable to refuse to provide it. It should be remembered that the civil liability legislation does not apply to employee claims against employers (see [17.135]) which are almost the exclusive domain for the action for breach of statutory duty. Consequently, there is very little scope for this provision to apply. There may be scope to apply s 43 (and its equivalents in other states) where breach of statutory duty is relied upon as evidence of negligence in a negligence claim, see [17.85]. A different view is taken by Aronson (M Aronson, "Government Liability in Negligence" (2008) 32(1) MULR 44) who accepts that the provision can substitute a modified and reduced standard of care for breach.

There is an additional provision which may apply to actions for breach of statutory duty. Failure to exercise a function to prohibit or regulate an activity cannot be the basis of civil liability unless the plaintiff could have brought public law proceedings forcing the authority to take action: NSW: CLA, s 44 and see Brennan CJ in *Pyrenees Shire Council v Day* (1998) 192 CLR 330 at 347-348. In *Fatouros v Randwick CC* [2006] NSWSC 483, Council approval of a dangerous open stairway was held unreasonable and in breach of NSW: CLA, ss 43, 44.

THE NATURE OF THE ACTION FOR BREACH OF STATUTORY DUTY

[17.70] We now turn to consider some illustrations of the general principles referred to earlier in this chapter. The following extract takes up three issues: first, the question upon whom is the statutory duty imposed, secondly, whether breach of regulations can give rise to actions for breach of statutory duty and, thirdly, whether an employer can be vicariously liable for breach of a statutory duty imposed directly on the employee.

Darling Island Stevedoring v Long

[17.75] *Darling Island Stevedoring Co Ltd v Long* (1956-7) 97 CLR 36 High Court of Australia (footnotes omitted)

[The facts are outlined in the judgments below.]

Darling Island Stevedoring v Long cont.

WILLIAMS J: 43 This is an appeal by leave from an order of the Full Supreme Court of New South Wales that judgment on demurrer be entered for the plaintiff. The appellant which is a stevedoring company is the defendant in an action in which the plaintiff, who is a wharf labourer, is suing it for £10,000 damages alleging in the sole count in the declaration that he was employed by the defendant to load and unload a ship in the port of Sydney, that these operations were carried on under a supervisor or foreman representing the defendant, and that the defendant was required by the *Navigation (Loading and Unloading) Regulations* where any hatch beam was left in place, before loading or unloading work began, securely to fasten it at each end by means of stout bolts, with nuts attached, or other suitable fastenings provided for the purpose of preventing, and in such manner as to prevent, its accidental displacement yet the defendant failed to do so whereby the hatch beam became displaced and the plaintiff was injured. ...

...[T]he points of law argued before their Honours were as follows: whether reg 31 of the *Navigation (Loading and Unloading) Regulations* creates a civil right of action; if it does, whether such an action can be brought only against the person on whom the obligation is expressly imposed by the regulation, that is to say the person-in-charge, or against what other persons; whether "person-in-charge" in the regulation includes only the person actually in control of the loading or unloading, in this case the supervisor or foreman, or whether it also includes the employer of the person-in-charge; and if it does not, whether the employer is nevertheless liable for a breach of the regulation committed by its servant, the supervisor or foreman, in the course of his employment. ... 46 The power under which the *Navigation (Loading and Unloading) Regulations* were made is contained in s 425 of the *Navigation Act 1912-1953* (Cth). This section provides that:

> The 47 Governor-General may make regulations not inconsistent with this Act, prescribing all matters which by this Act are required or permitted to be prescribed or which are necessary or convenient to be prescribed for carrying out or giving effect to this Act or for the conduct of any business under this Act, and in particular prescribing matters providing for and in relation to.

(Then follow fifteen paragraphs.) These paragraphs include: "(*c*) the protection of the health and the security from injury of persons engaged in the loading or unloading of ships;" and "(*h*) the fixing of penalties for breaches of the regulations, but so that no prescribed period of imprisonment shall exceed three months, and no pecuniary penalty shall exceed One hundred pounds". Regulation 4 of the *Navigation (Loading and Unloading) Regulations* provides *inter alia* that, unless the contrary intention appears, a "person-in-charge", in relation to the loading or unloading of any ship, means any person directly or indirectly in control of the persons actually engaged in the process of loading or unloading that ship. *Navigation (Loading and Unloading) Regulations*Regulation 31 on which the present action is founded provides: "(1) Before any loading or unloading work is begun at a hatch on any vessel to which these Regulations apply, all hatch beams shall be removed, unless the hatch is of such size as to permit of the work being carried out without any danger to the workers in the hold from a load striking against any beam left in place. (2) If the cargo is to be loaded or unloaded through more than one hatch and it is necessary to remove the hatch beams, the beams from the topmost hatch shall be removed first, and the beams from upper hatches shall be removed before those from lower hatches. (3.) Where any hatch beam is left in place it shall, before loading or unloading work begins, be securely fastened at each end by means of stout bolts, with nuts attached, or other suitable fastenings provided for the purpose of preventing, and in such manner as to prevent, its accidental displacement. Penalty, on the person in charge: One hundred pounds." *Navigation (Loading and Unloading) Regulations*Regulation 53 provides that: "When loading or unloading operations on a ship are being carried out – (*a*) under a supervisor or foreman as person-in-charge representing a stevedoring firm; or (*b*) under a responsible officer of the ship as person-in-charge, the person-in-charge shall be responsible for appropriate measures being taken for the protection against accident of

Darling Island Stevedoring v Long cont.

any person employed on or about the ship, and for the effectiveness of the cargo gear for those operations." *Navigation (Loading and Unloading) Regulations*Regulation 55 provides that: "(1) Any person who commits a breach of, or fails to comply with, any of these regulations shall be guilty of an offence. Penalty: Except where otherwise provided, Fifty pounds. (2) 48 Except where a duty or obligation is laid by a regulation upon some other person (in which case the penalty for breach of the regulation shall be upon that person), the master, owner and agent of the ship shall be jointly and severally liable to penalty in respect of any breach of the requirements of the regulation which occurs in relation to the loading or unloading of the ship."

The plaintiff had already sued the defendant for negligence at common law in respect of the same accident and in this action the regulations were tendered as evidence of negligence but the jury found a verdict for the defendant. An appeal to the Full Supreme Court of New South Wales was dismissed: *Long v Darling Island Stevedoring & Lighterage Co Ltd* (1956) 56 SR (NSW) 387. The present action is therefore an attempt to relitigate very much the same facts to prove a separate cause of action, the advantage accruing to the plaintiff being that if he succeeds in establishing that the defendant is liable for a breach of a duty imposed by *Navigation (Loading and Unloading) Regulations*reg 31 the defendant will be deprived of the defence of contributory negligence assuming that the *Statutory Duties (Contributory Negligence) Act 1945* (NSW) applies to duties imposed by regulations made under a statute as well as to duties imposed by the statute itself and also applies to duties imposed by a law of the Commonwealth. The courageous submission which is really on the threshold of the appeal was made by Sir *Garfield Barwick* that in the case of a statute such as the *Navigation Act 1912-1953* a power to make regulations such as that Act contains should not be construed as a delegation by Parliament of a power to enforce those regulations by any means other than the means provided by the power itself – in this case by the power to prescribe a period of imprisonment not exceeding three months or a pecuniary penalty not exceeding £100. It should not therefore be construed as a power to make a regulation prescribing specific precautions to be taken before loading or unloading ships for the safety of those engaged in these operations which gives rise to a civil right correlative to the duty for the breach of which the person on whom the duty is imposed is liable to punishment. The correlative right has been found to exist in numerous regulations made under statutes in the United Kingdom but it was sought to distinguish these regulations made under the *Navigation Act 1912-1953* because the Imperial statutes themselves prescribed the punishment for breach of the regulations whereas in the *Navigation Act 1912-1953* this prescription, within limits, is delegated to the Governor-General in Council. It was contended that where the statute itself prescribes 49 the punishment it is easy to ascribe to Parliament an implied intention to authorise the delegate to create a correlative civil right but the same intention should not be attributed to Parliament where, instead of prescribing the penalty itself, it authorises its delegate to prescribe the penalty. In this case it should not be implied that Parliament intended to authorise its delegate to make regulations that could be enforced except by the prescribed means.

But it is impossible to see how the circumstance that in one case the criminal sanction is created by Parliament itself whereas in the other it is created by its delegate can produce such a distinction. The question in each case, whether the duty is created by a statute or by a regulation made under the authority of a statute, is whether the duty appears to be created for the individual benefit of all such persons as can bring themselves within its scope or only for the benefit of the State and is of such a kind that the injury likely to be sustained by such individuals from its breach is of such a character that it could be made the subject matter of an action for damages at common law. The principle is now clearly established that where a statute is passed requiring an employer to take specific precautions for the protection of his employees, although the statute only provides for a prosecution for breach, the statute creates an individual civil right of action in the class of persons for whose protection it is passed so that any one of them who is injured by the breach can sue the employer in an action for damages at

Darling Island Stevedoring v Long cont.

common law. The principle is stated in felicitous terms in the passage in the judgment of Dixon J, as the Chief Justice then was, which is reported in *O'Connor v SP Bray Ltd* (1937) 56 CLR 464: "Whatever wider rule may ultimately be deduced, I think it may be said that a provision prescribing a specific precaution for the safety of others in a matter where the person upon whom the duty laid is, under the general law of negligence, bound to exercise due care, the duty will give rise to a correlative private right, unless from the nature of the provision or from the scope of the legislation of which it forms a part a contrary intention appears. The effect of such a provision is to define specifically what must be done in furtherance of the general duty to protect the safety of those affected by the operations carried on". It is impossible to limit this principle to duties created by statutes. It must apply equally to regulations made under the authority of statutes where the delegate is authorised to make regulations relating to such a subject matter. The regulation if valid must create the same correlative civil right as the same provision in the statute would create unless the delegate is expressly 50 confined by the statute to making regulations which can only be enforced in a particular manner. The duty could then be enforced in that manner and in no other manner. In the present case s 425 of the *Navigation Act 1912-1953* authorises the Governor-General in Council to fix penalties for breaches of the regulations. This does not indicate at all that Parliament intended that the regulations should be enforced in this and in no other manner. The indications are to the contrary. The power to fix penalties is simply one of a number of specific powers delegated to the Governor-General in Council. A regulation that is authorised by the general power to make regulations for carrying out or giving effect to the Act or by any of the powers to make regulations relating to specific subject matters would be a valid regulation although the power to fix a penalty for the breach was not exercised at all and the breach of the duty could be punished only as a misdemeanour at common law. Section 425 specifically authorises the Governor-General in Council to make regulations in relation to the protection of the health and the security from injury of persons engaged in the loading or unloading of ships and a law of this character whether contained in a statute or in a regulation made under the authority of a statute is the very kind of law which is likely to give rise to such a correlative civil right.

Regulation 31 of the *Navigation (Loading and Unloading) Regulations* imposes a penalty of £100 for breach of duty on the person-in-charge. ... The supervisor or foreman could clearly be prosecuted for a breach of the duty imposed by the regulation. The question is whether the duty is also imposed upon the defendant by the regulation. The definition of "person-in-charge" includes any person indirectly in control of the persons actually engaged in the process of loading or unloading a ship. ... The definition of "person-in-charge" seems to be quite inapt to make such a person include the employer of the person actually in control of the work. ... Regulation 31 relates to certain simple but very important precautions that must be taken before loading or unloading begins. They are precautions which fall aptly to be observed by the person actually on the spot and in control of the operations. There is no sufficient indication of intention in the regulations as a whole or in particular in reg 31 that duties imposed upon the person in charge should be imposed upon any person except the person actually in control of the work of loading or unloading the ship. This was the unanimous conclusion of their Honours in the Supreme Court and with that conclusion we should agree.

The final question is whether the appellant can be sued at common law for breach of the statutory obligation placed upon its supervisor or foreman but not upon it by reg 31 because it is the employer of the supervisor or foreman. ... If the defendant can be sued it must be because an employer is responsible for statutory wrongs committed by his servant in the course of his employment. In this case reg 31 provides that the supervisor or foreman of a stevedore shall see that certain precautions are taken before the work of loading or unloading a ship begins. It was contended that this is a statutory duty imposed upon the supervisor or foreman in the course of his employment and that the employer is vicariously liable for breach of such a duty by his employee. But the vicarious liability of an employer for the acts and omissions of his servant in the course of his employment is a liability at common law.

Darling Island Stevedoring v Long cont.

If the omission of the supervisor or foreman to take the precautions before loading or unloading a ship prescribed by reg 31 would be a breach of the duty of care that the supervisor or foreman owed those engaged in loading or unloading the ship at common law the stevedore could be sued at common law because he would be vicariously responsible for this breach of duty. But the employer could not be made liable for the breach by his servant of a duty imposed by a statute or regulation on the servant and not on the employer. To make the employer liable in such a case would be to enlarge the scope and operation of the statute or regulation. Where a statute or regulation creates a civil right of action it can be enforced in an action for damages at common law. But it is the statute or regulation that creates the civil right and not the common law. It is the common law that supplies the remedy. It is only in this respect and to this extent that such a duty can be said to become part of the common law. ... The civil right does not originate in the common law at all. It is necessary to go to reg 31 in order to ascertain the nature and extent of the duty and the persons who are bound to perform it. The duty created by that regulation is imposed not on the stevedore but on his supervisor or foreman. The stevedore is not included within its scope and to hold that the stevedore could be responsible for a breach of the regulation by the supervisor or foreman simply because the latter is in the employment of the former would give the regulation an operation not justified by its provisions. The regulation, as has been said, is a regulation of the kind apt to create a correlative civil right and such a right was probably created by it. But this right would be correlative with the criminal liability and punishment for breach of the duty is not imposed on the defendant but on its supervisor or foreman. Any correlative civil liability for breach of the duty 53 created by the regulation must therefore also be confined to the supervisor or foreman. It would seem to be quite inconsistent with principle to hold that an employer upon whom no personal liability is imposed by a statute or regulation can be sued for a breach of that duty simply because it is committed by an employee in the course of his employment. The statute or regulation can, if Parliament or its duly authorised delegate sees fit, impose a personal duty on the employer and he is then bound to see that the duty is performed. If the statute or regulation creates a correlative civil right the employer is personally liable if any person whom the law was intended to benefit suffers injury from the failure to perform the duty whether it is the employer himself who fails to do so or his servant or even an independent contractor. But where the employer is only vicariously liable for the acts and omissions of his servant in the course of his employment, the employer could only be liable for the breach by his servant of a statutory duty laid on the servant alone if he was sued at common law and that breach was evidence of the negligence of the servant at common law.

For these reasons the appeal should be allowed.

[Webb, Fullagar, Kitto and Taylor JJ delivered judgments concurring in general with the judgment of Williams J.]

[17.80] **Notes&Questions**

1. *Stoneman v Lyons* (1975) 133 CLR 550 considered the effect of reg 1604 of the *Uniform Building Regulations* (Vic), made under the *Local Government Act 1958* (Vic) ss 925, 926 which provided that:

   > (a)(i) where excavation or demolition is to be made in proximity to an existing building, the walls of such building shall be shored and/or underpinned and/or protected as may be necessary to ensure stability.

   The High Court, by majority, held that the regulation imposed a duty only on the builder not the landowner for whom the building work was being done. There was therefore no action for breach of statutory duty against the defendant landowner. Contrast statutes variously imposing duties on "the building owner" (*Anderson v Mackellar County Council* (1968) 69 SR NSW 444) or "the person causing the excavation to be made" (*Pantalone v Alaouie* (1989) 18 NSWLR 119), or where an action is available for breach of a statutory condition for development consent (*Piling v Prynew, Nemeth v Prynew* [2008] NSWSC 118). These are rare instances where an action for breach of statutory duty has been held to be available in a case not involving workers' safety.

2. In New South Wales, the *Law Reform (Vicarious Liability) Act 1983* (NSW), s 7 reverses the effect of the *Darling Island Stevedoring v Long* (1956-7) 97 CLR 36 on the issue of vicarious liability. Contrary to the views of the High Court in *Darling Island Stevedoring*, recent English authority now suggests that an employer can be vicariously liable for breach of a statutory duty imposed on an employee provided the conduct has a sufficiently close connection to the employment and there is nothing in the statute which negatives vicarious liability. In *Majrowski v Guy's & St Thomas's NHS Trust* [2005] IRLR 340 the Court of Appeal held that an employer could be vicariously liable for the harassment of an employee by his supervisor in breach of the *Protection from Harassment Act 1997* (UK). Auld LJ (with whom other members of the Court concurred) agreed that "from a policy point of view it is hard to find one good reason why the action for breach of statutory duty should constitute a solitary exception to the otherwise universal principle of the law that a master is vicariously liable for the torts of his servant committed in the course of his employment" (at [34]).

3. Breach of an award clause, created under the authority of the *Industrial Relations Act 1988* (Cth), that dismissal of an employee "shall not be harsh, unjust or unreasonable" does not give rise to an action for breach of statutory duty. In *Byrne v Australian Airlines Ltd* (1995) 185 CLR 410, the High Court held that the purpose of the industrial legislation was to promote industrial harmony and co-operation with provision for prevention and settlement of industrial disputes by conciliation and arbitration. It disclosed no intention to give a civil action for its breach nor did it disclose an intention that an award should be so enforceable. Other provisions of the Act (ss 178, 179, 356) which allowed recovery of payments due under an award, or payment of penalty for breach, pointed against availability. There was the further difficulty alluded to by McHugh and Gummow JJ (at 462) that the claimant sought to enforce an award as the basis of an action for breach of statutory duty:

> The question ... is whether the statute gives power to create by regulation duties enforceable by action at the suit of a person injured by breach thereof. If the statute does not expressly confer on the Executive a power by regulation to create an action for damages at the suit of any person injured by breach of the substantive provisions of the regulations, it must be difficult to construe the statute and the delegated legislation as impliedly bringing about that result. This must be so ... where the silent statute operates upon an Award made by an arbitral body established by statute.

Statutory breach and negligence

[17.85] Assume that whilst you are driving on the road, another vehicle drives through a red light and crashes into your car. Running a red light would be a breach of motor traffic regulations. Breaches of traffic regulations do not give rise to actions for breach of statutory duty (see below). But running a red light in breach of motor traffic regulations may be evidence that the driver has been negligent for the purposes of the tort of negligence. It is not conclusive as the driver might not have been negligent. For example, the vehicle might have been shunted through the red light by another speeding vehicle. Statutory breach does not automatically mean that the defendant has been negligent, particularly in cases involving motor traffic regulations, *Tucker v McCann* [1948] VLR 222 see [12.160]. In *Abela v Giew* (1965) 65 SR (NSW) 485, at 490-491, the Full Court confirmed the accepted position that traffic regulations do not give rise to a private right of action for breach:

> The scope of this legislation indicates ... that its purpose is the control and regulation of traffic by way of securing a measure of order which will promote its free movement, and in the interest of safety, these ends being sought to be secured by appropriate penal sanctions; it is not the conferment of private rights of action upon injured individuals. Duties are not merely imposed upon one class of persons for securing the safety of another class of persons. The whole scheme of legislation is one of mutual and reciprocal obligations imposed upon all who engage in traffic for the benefit and safety of all others so engaged as well as for their own benefit and safety. These have to be applied to an infinite number and variety of constantly and rapidly changing situations as between two vehicles or as between a vehicle and a pedestrian. In these circumstances the prescription of pre-appointed regulatory measures cannot be regarded as more than an attempt to secure in the general interest that order will obtain and that safety will be preserved. It cannot be regarded as an attempt to provide in advance a solution for every claim for damages which one person may make against another arising out of any of the variety of situations that may arise.

ESTABLISHING A BREACH

The scope of statutory protection

[17.90] Once it has been established that the relevant statutory provisions can give rise to an action for breach of statutory duty, and that the statutory provision was directed to the protection of a particular class, the plaintiff must show membership of that class. The damage suffered by the plaintiff must also be within the risk contemplated by the statute. These requirements can act to impose some limits on liability and act as a type of remoteness of damage rule (JG Fleming, *The Law of Torts* (9 th ed, Law Book Co, Sydney, 1998), p 147, note 227).

A fireman attending a fire in a building cannot rely on safety regulations concerning electricity switches passed for the benefit of persons employed in a building (*Hartley v Mayoh & Co* [1954] 1 QB 383), nor can a sub-contractor necessarily rely on building regulations passed for the protection of a "person employed" (*Herbert v Harold Shaw Ltd* [1959] 2 QB 138). In *Millington v Wilkie Plumbing Services* [2005] NSWCA 45, Ipp JA stated that the protected class should exclude "employees whose actions have put the employer in breach, where nothing done or omitted by the employer itself has contributed to the breach". Performers, but not record companies, are the protected class under the *Dramatic and Musical Performers' Protection Act 1958* (UK) (*RCA Corp v Pollard* [1983] Ch 135; *Rickless v United Artists Corp* [1988] QB 40; *CBS Songs Ltd v Amstrad Consumer Electronics Plc* [1988] 1 Ch 61, affirmed on appeal on different grounds, [1988] AC 1013 (HL)).

In a similar way the plaintiff must prove that the damage suffered was within the risk at which the statute is directed. One popular illustration of the requirement is found in *Gorris v Scott* (1874) 9 Ex D 125. In that case the plaintiff claimed for the loss of sheep that had been swept overboard while being shipped by the defendant. The plaintiff alleged a breach of an order under the *Contagious Diseases (Animals) Act 1869* (UK) requiring pens of specified size to be supplied on deck to accommodate the sheep. It was held that even if the supply of such pens would have prevented the sheep being washed overboard, no action for breach of statutory duty could be based on provisions that aimed, not at protection from perils of the sea, but prevention of the spread of disease. In *Far North Queensland Electricity Board v Masterwood P/L* [1998] QCA 431 at [8] per McPherson JA a statutorily required warning sign for water vessels was not intended for the protection of aircraft. Similarly, the provisions of the *Local Government Ordinances* (NSW), Pt 31, "Excavation, Earthwork and Retaining Walls" are directed to the prevention of the collapse of the walls of an excavation rather than the protection of adjoining land (*Kebewar Pty Ltd v Harkin* (1987) 9 NSWLR 738). Issues relating to the scope of statutory protection have also arisen in dealing with the liability of statutory authorities for damage resulting from the exercise or failure to exercise statutory powers. In *Sutherland Shire Council v Heyman* (1985) 157 CLR 424, Deane J held, at 509, that "the protection of the owner of land from the mere economic loss which might be sustained by reason of a defect in a building erected upon his or her land is no part of the purpose for which the relevant legislative powers and functions were conferred upon the council". A spate of English cases in dealing with liability of statutory authorities have held that it is no part of the purpose of the statutory provisions being considered to protect the plaintiff against economic loss. The cases suggest a general reluctance to find that protection against economic loss is within the purview of the statutory provisions. See as one of a number of cases, *Murphy v Brentwood Borough Council* [1991] 1 AC 398.

If the kind of damage that occurred is within the contemplation of the statute there is authority, certainly in the case of safety statutes, that no further remoteness of damage rule is to be applied that might require the damage to be of a foreseeable kind, see [17.125] (*Grant v National Coal Board* [1956] AC 649; *Littler v GL Moore (Contractors) Ltd* [1967] 1 WLR 1241; compare *McGovern v British Steel Corp* [1986] ICR 608 (below, [17.120] Note 5)). But the construction of the statute may itself provide the court with a means of introducing a limitation on the manner in which the injury must occur for liability to arise. In *Mummery v Irvings Pty Ltd* (1956) 96 CLR 99, the High Court held that the fencing statute did not impose an obligation to guard against dangerous materials being ejected from the machine while in motion.

The statutory standard

Galashiels Gas Co v O'Donnell

[17.95] *Galashiels Gas Co Ltd v O'Donnell* [1949] AC 275, House of Lords (footnotes omitted).

[The deceased was employed in the defendants' gas works. He was using a lift for work purposes when an electricity failure prevented the automatic brake on the lift from working. As a result the lift rose above the floor where the deceased had left it and when he returned he stepped into the empty shaft and fell to the bottom. Subsequent investigation by engineers found no explanation for the failure, which had never occurred before. The *Factories Act 1937* (UK), s 22(1) required every hoist or lift to be "properly maintained". "Maintained" was defined in s 152(1) as "maintained in an efficient state, in efficient working order, and in good repair".]

LORD MORTON

[His Lordship referred to the definition of "maintained" in s 152(1) and continued:]

Galashiels Gas Co v O'Donnell cont.

I think there can be no doubt that this subsection imposes a continuous obligation on the [defendants] ... Equally there can be no doubt ... that the brake of the lift in question was not in efficient working order at the time when the accident happened, though it would appear to have worked efficiently during the periods before and after the accident.

The contention of the [plaintiff] ... is that she has established a breach of statutory duty ... by proving that the brake was not in efficient working order at that time. If this contention is sound, the appeal must fail ...

The [defendants] contend that no breach of statutory duty has been proved. They contend that their statutory duty is to take such active steps as will ensure that the lift is in efficient working order, and that the [plaintiff] cannot succeed unless she can point to some particular step which the [defendants] omitted to take and which would have prevented the accident. They say truly that the [plaintiff] cannot point to any such step and failed to prove any specific cause for the failure of the brake to operate.

[His Lordship then referred to the judgment in the lower court and approved the statement that there was an "absolute and continuing obligation...which is not discharged if at any time their lift mechanism, in this case the brake, is not maintained in an efficient state, in efficient working order, and in good repair." His Lordship continued:] The words of the sub-section are imperative "shall be properly maintained" and I can find nothing in the context or in the general intention of the Act, read as a whole, which would lead your Lordships to infer any qualification upon that absolute obligation ... [T]he sub-section, so read, imposes a heavy burden upon employers, but the object of this group of sections is to protect the workman ... [T]he subsection must have been so worded in order to relieve the injured workman from the burden of proving that there was some particular step which the employers could have taken and did not take. This would often be a difficult matter, more especially if the cause of the failure of the mechanism to operate could not be ascertained. The statute renders the task of the injured workman easier by saying, "You need only prove that the mechanism failed to work efficiently and this failure caused the accident."

[Lords Normand, Macdermott and Reid agreed.]

[17.100] **Notes&Questions**

1. The *Galashiels case* demonstrates that the action for breach of statutory duty can have some obvious advantages over an action for negligence. The statutory standard may be more specific, onerous and without any need to prove fault. Additionally, once the duty is shown to have been imposed on the defendant, liability cannot be escaped by showing that the conduct constituting the breach was the act of another, *Lochgelly Iron & Coal Co v M'Mullan* [1934] AC 1. A statutory duty is, if unqualified in its terms, non-delegable. The defence of common employment (now abrogated by statute) did not apply in an action for breach of a statutory duty imposed on the employer, see *Groves v Wimborne* [1898] 2 QB 402.
2. In *Doval v Anka Builders Pty Ltd*, (1992) Aust Torts Reports 81-174, the New South Wales Court of Appeal held, by majority, that there was a breach of a duty to maintain sufficient and suitable lighting when as a result of an unexplained power blackout, the plaintiff stumbled in the dark and was injured. Clarke JA, Handley JA concurring, said (at 81-174):

> "maintain" indicates that the obligation is not complied with simply by the provision of a system–there must at all times either be adequate natural light or a system which is operative while persons are engaged in the relevant building work. If this means that compliance with the sub-regulation requires a back-up system so be it.

Contrast *Austral Bronze Co Pty Ltd v Ajaka* (1970) 44 ALJR 52 where the High Court placed a qualified interpretation on the words "all floors ... shall be of sound construction and properly maintained", from s 34(a) of the *Factories, Shops and Industries Act 1962* (NSW). Section 4(1) of the Act defined "maintained" to mean "maintained in good order, condition and repair and in an efficient state". The plaintiff was employed in the defendant's factory. He was injured when he slipped on a grease or oil slick on the factory floor. There was no evidence as to how the oil or grease came to be on the floor or how long it had been there. Barwick CJ (with whom Kitto, Menzies, Owen and Walsh JJ agreed) could not accept a construction of the section that placed the defendants in breach of it in the circumstances.

3. In the *Galashiels case* extracted above, the Court held that the defendants were strictly liable without any need to prove fault. However, courts have been astute in finding in the statutory language qualifications to a seemingly absolute standard and in particular, introducing some element of foreseeability. In *Dunlop Rubber Australia Ltd v Buckley*, (1952) 87 CLR 313 at 320, Dixon CJ, in determining whether there was a breach of the duty to "securely fence all dangerous parts ... of machinery" within the meaning of *Factories, Shops & Industries Act 1912* (NSW), s 33, adopted the view that machinery will be dangerous if it is such that it may reasonably be foreseen to be a source of injury to people who may be in the vicinity, taking them with all the ordinary infirmities to which human nature can be prone. A similar view was adopted by the High Court in *Dairy Farmers Co-op v Azar* (1990) 170 CLR 293 in relation to the duty to fence dangerous machines under the *Factories, Shops and Industries Act 1962* (NSW), s 27(1). In *Andriolo v G & G Constructions Pty Ltd* (1989) Aust Torts Reports 80-235, the *Scaffolding and Lifts Ordinance 1957* (ACT) required "safe" means of access to every workplace. In line with numerous English authorities it was held that access would not be safe if it was a possible cause of injury to a worker acting in a way in which a worker can reasonably be expected to act.

4. Statutory duties may also be moderated by finding that the defendant must have some level of knowledge for liability. A duty not to "permit or allow" certain conduct presupposes some level of knowledge. In *Waugh v Kippen*, (1986) 60 ALJR 250, the *Factories and Shops Act 1960* (Qld) provided that an adult male employee "shall not be permitted or allowed to ... carry by hand any object so heavy as to be likely to cause risk of injury". Unknown to the employers the plaintiff had existing back trouble. The High Court, in the majority judgment, said the words "permitted or allowed" presupposed awareness, actual or constructive on the part of the employer, that the employee was moving by hand an object so heavy as to be likely to cause risk of injury to him. It would be unreasonable to construe the clause as imposing an obligation on the employer to protect the employee from a risk of injury of which the employer neither knew

nor ought to have known. The phrase "likely to cause risk of injury" required a real or not remote chance or possibility regardless of whether it was less or more than 50 per cent.

5. It is common for statutory provisions to impose duties where it is "reasonably practicable". This must be assessed in the light of current knowledge (*McDonald v Girkaid Pty Ltd* (2004) Aust Torts Reports 81-768), and permits cost and other elements to be brought into balance in determining what is reasonable (*Holmes v R E Spence* (1993) 5 VIR 119). It is doubtful whether this imposes more onerous duties than an ordinary duty of care. A duty on a designer to "ensure" the safety of a designed structure "so far as is reasonably practicable" applies only "to matters which are within the power of the designer to perform or check" and there will be no breach of this duty if the construction does not comply with the design (*Slivak v Lurgi (Australia) Pty Ltd* (2001) 205 CLR 304).

6. A statutory duty to "take all practicable steps" can be the basis of an action for breach of statutory duty even though it does not prescribe particular conduct. In *Slivak v Lurgi (Australia) Pty Ltd* (2001) 205 CLR 304, an action for breach of statutory duty was available for breach of the *Occupational Health, Safety and Welfare Act 1986* (SA), s 24(2)(a) which provided "where any structure is to be erected in the course of any work–(a) the person who designs the structure must ensure so far as is reasonably practicable that the structure is designed so that the persons who are required to erect it are, in doing so, safe from injury and risks to health". This contrasts with the decision in *McDonald v Girkaid Pty Ltd* [2004] NSWCA 297. There, the *Dangerous Good Regulation 1978* (NSW), reg 19(g) imposed an absolute prohibition on any act which may cause fire and prohibited all acts that were "not reasonably necessary for purposes of, or properly incidental to, the keeping ... of dangerous goods". McColl J (other members of the NSW Court of Appeal agreeing) distinguished the *Slivak case* and said (at [177]): "It prescribes the end but not the means. It does not identify any specific precaution or measure ... It is a blanket prohibition on doing the act in question ... the absence of identification of specific precautions means that reg 19(g) should not be construed as conferring a correlative private cause of action".

Negligence as the statutory standard

[17.105] If the statute, or regulations, impose a qualified standard which approximates the negligence standard, are there any benefits to be gained from proceeding in an action for breach of statutory duty rather then proceeding in negligence?

Unless excluded by statute, there is authority in South Australia and Queensland that a generalised duty to "ensure so far as is reasonably practicable that the employee is, while at work, safe from injury and risks to health" can form the basis of an action for breach of statutory duty: *Occupational Health, Safety and Welfare Act 1986*, (SA) s 19(1), *Crisa v John Shearer* (1981) 27 SASR 422, *Slivak v Lurgi* (2001) 205 CLR 304; *Workplace Health and Safety Act 1995* (Tas), s 9(4), *Coote v A R and G R Padgett Pty Ltd* (2004) Aust Torts Reports 81-758; *Occupational Health & Safety Act 1995* (Qld), s 28(1)(3), *Schiliro v Peppercorn Childcare Centres Pty Ltd* [2001] 1 Qd R 518, compare *Wilkinson v BP Australia Pty Ltd* [2008] QSC 171 at [22]-[25]. Other states specifically exclude actions for breach of statutory duty based on general duties under the legislation, see [17.60]. Where the statutory standard approximates the negligence standard, there may be advantages in bringing an action for breach of statutory duty: defences may be more limited in an action for breach of statutory duty, see [17.140] and there are dicta that remoteness of damage rules may not apply to actions for breach of statutory duty, see [17.125]. But unless the statute provides otherwise, there is no advantage on the onus of proof issue; the suggestion that the onus of proof may shift to the defendant to show that there is no "reasonably practicable" alternative has been rejected (*Slivak v Lurgi (Australia) Pty Ltd* (2001) 205 CLR 304; *Chugg v Pacific Dunlop Ltd* (1990) 170 CLR 249). It is otherwise if the statute specifically makes proof that there is no reasonably practicable alternative a matter of defence, see *Workplace Health & Safety Act 1995* (Qld), s 37. A more liberal common law regime may apply to actions for breach of statutory duty involving employees than negligence actions covered by civil liability legislation (see D Villa, *Annotated Civil Liability Act 2002* (Thomson Lawbook Co., Sydney, 2004), p 74).

Causation

[17.110] The plaintiff must prove that the injury complained of was caused by the statutory breach upon which the plaintiff's action is based. The usual rule applies that the causal connection must be proved on the balance of probabilities, see Chapter 13. Particular difficulties arise if the circumstances giving rise to the statutory breach create a risk which cannot be quantified or if the risk that can be quantified by statistical evidence is below the level of probability. These issues are raised in an earlier chapter, see Chapter 13. Professor Fleming remarks, "in practice at least an *inference* of causality is easily drawn when the accident is one which the statutory duty was designed to prevent" (JG Fleming, *The Law of Torts* (9th ed, Law Book Co, Sydney, 1998), p 567) and see *Quigley v Commonwealth* (1981) 55 ALJR 579 at 584. Breach of a statutory duty to ensure that a machine operator holds the requisite licence or competency may be a cause of a plaintiff's injuries when an unlicensed operator negligently operates the machine (see *John Pfeiffer Pty Ltd v Canny* (1981) 148 CLR 218). Could a failure to carry out a required risk assessment be a cause of an injured plaintiff's injuries? A recent decision suggests it could (*Griffith v Vauxhall Motors Ltd* [2004] EWCA Civ 412 (CA). See also *Power v Snowy Mountains Authority* [1957] SR (NSW) 9).

Despite an employer's breach of statutory duty, an employee might be held to have caused her or his own harm so as to defeat the employee's action for breach of statutory duty. This may occur only in the clearest of cases where the injured plaintiff 's conduct put the defendant in breach of the statutory duty so that the plaintiff can be regarded as exclusively responsible for the breach of statutory duty. Older authorities may have described this as a question of whether the plaintiff's conduct was the sole cause of the plaintiff's harm. As the extract which follows demonstrates, it might now be characterised a case where the statute is so interpreted that the protected class excludes an injured plaintiff in those circumstances (Fleming (p 574) regards it as a formal defence). In either case the plaintiff will have no claim. Would it be preferable to allow the plaintiff's claim for breach of statutory duty but reduce the plaintiff's damages under the defence of contributory negligence? The issue was canvassed in dicta in the High Court in the extract below and in *Millington v Wilkie Plumbing Services* [2005] NSWCA 45 [17.120] Note 2.

Andar Transport v Brambles

[17.115] *Andar Transport Pty Ltd v Brambles Ltd* (2004) 217 CLR 424 High Court of Australia

[The High Court considered whether an employer (Andar Transport) could be liable to an employee (Wail) for failure to provide a safe system of work when Wail, the employee, was one of the employer's two directors and shareholders and ran the day to day operations for the employer. The employer argued that by analogy with the action for breach of statutory duty, the employee should be taken to have caused his own harm.]

GLEESON CJ, McHUGH, GUMMOW, HAYNE AND HEYDON JJ: 440 The submissions of Andar seek to derive support from decisions given in litigation concerning statutory obligations imposed upon employer and employee alike. One example is the decision of Pearson J in *Ginty v Belmont Building Supplies Ltd* [1959] 1 All ER 414. In that case, the plaintiff employee was injured as a result of failing to use boards to support his weight when working on an asbestos roof. He had been instructed to use the boards by his employer and had been supplied with them. His failure to follow his employer's instructions amounted to a breach of the *Building (Safety, Health and Welfare) Regulations 441 1948* on the part of both himself and his employer. In such circumstances, Pearson J held that the plaintiff was unable to recover damages from the employer for breach of statutory duty. His Lordship observed (at 423-424):

> [T]he important and fundamental question in a case like this is not whether there was a delegation, but simply the usual question: *Whose fault was it?* … If the answer to that question is that in substance and reality *the accident was solely due to the fault of the plaintiff*, so that he was the sole author of his own wrong, he is disentitled to recover. But that has to be applied to the particular case and it is not necessarily conclusive for the employer to show that it was a wrongful act of the employee plaintiff which caused the accident. … One has to inquire whether the fault of the employer under the statutory regulations consists of, and is co-extensive with, the wrongful act of the employee. If there is some fault on the part of the employer which goes beyond or is independent of the wrongful act of the employee, and was a cause of the accident, the employer has some liability.

(emphasis added)

441 … Various rationales have been posited in order to justify the propositions outlined by Pearson J and subsequently developed in *Ross* and *Boyle*. For Pearson J himself, as for the House of Lords in the two later cases, the issue was best seen as one of causation; hence the requirement propounded by Pearson J that the plaintiff will be unsuccessful where the accident was "solely due" to the plaintiff's own conduct.

The reasoning evident in *Ginty, Ross* and *Boyle* suffers from fundamental infirmities. In *March v Stramare (E & M H) Pty Ltd* (1991) 171 CLR 506, Mason CJ (at 511) ascribed the historical concern with the identification of a "sole" or "effective" cause to the existence of the absolute defence of contributory negligence at common law and the absence of any mechanism for the apportionment of liability between plaintiff and defendant. In the joint judgment in *Astley v Austrust Ltd* [(1999) 197 CLR 1], reference 442 was made to the course of authority culminating in *Davies v Adelaide Chemical and Fertilizer Co Ltd* (1946) 74 CLR 541. This established that a plaintiff could be guilty of contributory negligence and the defendant have a good defence even though the plaintiff was injured as a result of a breach of a statutory duty whose very purpose was to prevent that type of injury by placing the defendant under a duty to protect people in the class of which the plaintiff was a member.

However, since the displacement of the absolute defence by the statutory apportionment of damages between those at fault in accordance with the degree of their individual responsibility, a different situation has applied. In *March*, Mason CJ (at 512) concluded that "the courts are no longer as constrained as they were to find a single cause for a consequence". The propositions contained in *Ginty*, and developed in *Ross* and *Boyle Boyle v Kodak Ltd* [1969] 1 WLR 661, would, if adopted, mark a

Andar Transport v Brambles cont.

significant exception to that circumstance. To the extent that the reasoning in *Ginty* and cognate decisions was adopted in this Court in *Nicol v Allyacht Spars Pty Ltd* (1987) 163 CLR 611, it should now be emphasised that that reasoning has since been undermined by that in *March* which fixed upon the removal of that "fertile source of confusion" in the common law, the defence of contributory negligence, for "the development of a coherent legal concept of causation". The reasoning in *Ginty* should no longer be accepted. Further, the reasoning of Dawson J in his dissenting judgment in *Nicol* should be preferred.

Moreover, the reliance on principles of causation evident in *Ginty* and its successors may more accurately be viewed as a means of masking the introduction of an extraneous policy judgment as to the circumstances in which an employee should be permitted to recover against an employer who has contravened an obligation imposed by statute. That causation has, in truth, only a small role to play is demonstrated by the principle that an employee can recover damages from an employer for breach of a statutory duty notwithstanding that the "sole cause" of the plaintiff's injury is a breach of the same duty committed by a fellow employee. Perhaps with this objection in mind, attempts have been made to present the reasoning of Pearson J as an aspect of the proper construction of the relevant statutory obligation. The necessary tension that results from such an approach is evident in the judgment of Mason J in *Buckman (H C) & Son Pty Ltd v Flanagan* (1974) 133 CLR 422. There, his Honour observed (at 442): 443

> The language in which the principle has been expressed, notably that of Lord Reid in *Boyle's Case*, tends perhaps to suggest that it is a rule invented by the courts as a proposition of the general law superimposed upon statutory provisions which impose a duty and create a cause of action in favour of private individuals. I would not wish to quarrel with these observations so long as it is understood that the formulation of the principle is not unconnected with the construction of the relevant statutory provisions. Were it otherwise I should feel some difficulty in its application in New South Wales in face of s 2(1) of the *Statutory Duties (Contributory Negligence) Act* [1945 (NSW)] [Now repealed, see [17.155 Note 3] which provides that contributory negligence shall not be a defence to an action for damages for personal injury founded on a breach of a statutory duty imposed on the defendant for the benefit of a class of persons of which the plaintiff was a member.

The liability incurred by employers on breach of statutory obligations of the kind considered in cases such as *Ginty* is, ordinarily, strict. In such circumstances, caution should be exercised before implying limitations on the right of an employee to recover for breach of that obligation. Especially is this the case where Parliament has provided a mechanism for the apportionment of responsibility between employee and employer.

It may certainly be accepted that, in the absence of an express provision conferring a cause of action upon employees for breach of their employers' obligation, courts have recognised the plaintiff's right by implication and as an exercise in statutory interpretation. However, that process does not in turn permit the development of a limitation which cannot legitimately be inferred from the nature, scope and terms of the legislation in question. These implications are, as Kitto J put it in *Sovar v Henry Lane Pty Ltd* (1967) 116 CLR 397 at 405, not to be "conjured up by judges to give effect to their own ideas of policy". There must be read with these qualifications in mind statements to the effect of those in *Nicol* that "[t]he courts, having created the liability, are able to confine it" and that "the approach [in *Ginty*] to the question of an employer's escape from liability for breach of statutory duty may be applied with equal validity to the question of an employer's escape from liability for breach of a common law duty".

[17.120] **Notes&Questions**

1. For a discussion critical of the decision, see Glasbeek, "The Legal Pulverisation of Social Issues" (2005) 13 TLJ 217. Would the High Court's reasoning require reconsideration of the decision in *Sherman v Nymboida Collieries Pty Ltd* (1963) 109 CLR 580 (not subject to comment by the High Court in *Andar*)? There, a mine deputy employee was charged with the responsibility to check whether ventilation in the mine was adequate. In breach of his statutory responsibilities, there was evidence that the employee opened his safety lamp and attempted to light it with his cigarette lighter. There had been a build up of methane caused by inadequate ventilation in breach of the employer's statutory obligations. There was an explosion which killed the employee. It was held that no action was available for the employer's breach of statutory duty as "the act of the deceased was the real and effective cause of his death". Should this be sufficient to relieve the employer of responsibility? If not, when could an employee's conduct be such as to make the employee the cause of her or his own harm? In this context, consider the next note.

2. In *Millington v Wilkie Plumbing Services* [2005] NSWCA 45, Ipp J in the NSW Court of Appeal, after referring to the High Court's decision in *Andar* (above), said:

> For my part I found the proposition advanced on the appellant's behalf, in regard to damages for breach of statutory duty, impossible to accept. The appellant's argument was that an employer is liable to an employee for damages in circumstances where:
>
> (a) The employee was injured by performing an act which the employer expressly instructed him not to do.
>
> (b) By performing that act contrary to his employer's express instructions, the employee caused the employer to breach of statutory duty.
>
> (c) Apart from the employee's own conduct in disobeying the instructions, nothing done or omitted to be done by the employer, or any person for whom it is vicariously liable, brought about the employer's breach of statutory duty.
>
> (d) By performing the act in question, the employee, himself, breached his statutory duty.
>
> (e) As the employee was alone at the ladder at the time, there was nothing the employer could have done to stop him from disobeying his instructions.
>
> In *Brancato v Australian Telecommunications Commission* (1986) 7 NSWLR 30 Mahoney JA (at 36) said that to impose liability for damages in circumstances such as the present would do nothing to help in the achievement of the purpose of the statute that is breached and would invite those to whom the statute was directed "to see the result as ridiculous or", as [Lord Reid in *Boyle v Kodak Ltd* [1969] 1 WLR 661 at 665] said, "absurd". I would add the epithet, "grossly unfair". ...
>
> When this approach is applied to the construction of regs 73 and 80(6) the result, in my view, is inevitable. It could not have been intended by the legislature that an

> employee would be able to recover damages from an employer in the circumstances in question. Such a result would be so improbable that the regulations should be construed to exclude from the class of persons for whose benefit the statutory duties thereunder were imposed, the class described by Hodgson JA as "employees whose actions have put the employer in breach, where nothing done or omitted by the employer itself has contributed to the breach".

Do you agree with Ipp J? If another employee had been injured would the employer have been liable to that employee for a breach of statutory duty? Special leave to appeal to the High Court was refused.

3. In *Texcrete Pty Ltd v Khavin* [2003] NSWCA 337, the New South Wales Court of Appeal considered whether the plaintiff could recover for an occupier's breach of a statutory duty to fence a dangerous machine when the guard was removed in order to allow the plaintiff to test and adjust the machine. It was argued that the plaintiff caused his own injuries by proceeding to test the machine when the guard was removed. The Court of Appeal rejected this argument. The machine's design did not allow safe testing and better design would have given alternative methods of carrying out the testing. The occupier's removal of the guard implicitly invited the plaintiff to test with the guard removed. Santow JA (with whom other members of the Court agreed) said at [45]: "[I]f even careless and inattentive workers must be secured from danger, a fortiori [with stronger reason] a prudent, alert and skilled operative who commits an error of judgment encouraged by the pre-existing unfenced state of the machine by reason of the removal of the guard, and here under the exigency of having to perform his task, should be able to invoke that duty." The plaintiff's damages might, however, be reduced for his contributory negligence, see [17.155].

4. The High Court in *Andar* (at [49-50]) agreed with the dissenting observation of Mason JA in *Shedlizki v Bronte Bakery Pty Ltd* (1970) 72 SR NSW 378. There the plaintiff was the managing director and principal shareholder of the defendant "one man" company. He was injured when he failed to guard a machine which constituted a breach of duty by the company. The majority held that the plaintiff was solely to blame for his injury and could not recover. Mason JA dissenting said (at 386) that "it matters not that the plaintiff had control or the capacity to control the defendant's activities, for the principle that a corporation is a legal entity distinct from the corporators applies with equal force to a company which is a 'one man' company."

5. In *McGovern v British Steel Corp* [1986] ICR 608, the Court of Appeal held that a plaintiff injured whilst trying to remove an obstruction was entitled to damages for breach of a regulation requiring walkways to be kept free of obstructions. Neill LJ, on the issue of causation, said (at 624):

> In my view the "but for" test provides a useful starting point for the purpose of examining the issue of causation but it is an inadequate criterion by which to determine liability. A more detailed analysis is required.
>
> From an examination of the authorities I would venture to suggest that where a breach of statutory duty has been established in a case such as the present the issue of causation should be approached on the following lines. (1) It is first necessary to identify the relevant breach of statutory duty and the injury which it is alleged was

> caused by that breach. (2) The next step is to trace the events which form the links between the breach and the injury. (3) These events may, as in the present case, involve the intervention of some human action either by the plaintiff or by a third party. It will then be necessary to examine: (a) whether the intervention was a natural and probable consequence of the breach; and (b) if so, whether the conduct of the intervener was nevertheless such as to break the chain of causation. Thus the intervener may have acted foolishly or otherwise in such a manner that his or her act rather than the breach was the cause of the injury: see, eg, *Norris v W Moss & Sons Ltd* [1954] 1 WLR 346. (4) The onus of proving the necessary causal connection rests on the plaintiff; it is not enough for the plaintiff merely to prove that there was a breach of duty which *may* have caused his or her injury. (5) The question of causation is to be decided by applying common sense to the facts of the particular case, and not by applying some logical or scientific theory of causation: see *Stapley v Gypsum Mines Ltd* [1953] AC 663 at 681 per Lord Reid.

Damage

Remoteness of damage?

[17.125] If the kind of damage which occurred is within the contemplation of the statute, there is authority that, in the case of safety statutes at any rate, there is no further remoteness of damage rule to be applied which requires that the damage must be of a foreseeable kind. *Grant v National Coal Board* [1956] AC 649; *Littler v G L Moore (Contractors) Ltd* [1967] 1 WLR 1241; compare *McGovern v British Steel Corp* [1986] ICR 608 (above, [17.120] Note 5). In *Millard v Serck Tubes Ltd* [1969] 1 WLR 211, the Court of Appeal rejected the contention that where a machine formed a rope from waste material and dragged the operator into it, this rendered the damage too remote from the employer's breach of statutory duty to fence. As noted earlier, construction of the statute may itself provide the court with a means of introducing a limitation on the manner in which the injury must occur for liability to arise, see [17.90].

Actual damage

[17.130] Does the plaintiff have to prove actual damage in an action for breach of statutory duty? In *Cullen v Chief Constable of the Royal Ulster Constabulary* [2004] 2 All ER 237, a majority in the House of Lords were of the view that if the plaintiff suffered no injury or damage and judicial review would have been a satisfactory remedy, this indicated that no action lay for breach of statutory duty; nominal damages should not be awarded for breach of a statutory duty. If an action is available, there is authority that aggravated damages might be awarded for breach of statutory duty (*Collings Constructions Co Pty Ltd v ACCC* (1998) 43 NSWLR 131). This may be affected by limitations on recovery of aggravated damages under civil liability legislation, see for example NSW: CLA, s 21.

DEFENCES

[17.135] Actions for breach of statutory duties may be affected by some sections of the civil liability legislation: ACT: CLWA, ss 92 ("claim"), 93; Vic: WrA, ss 43 ("negligence"), 44; WA: CLA ss 5A(1) ("fault"), 5A(2), 5R, 6(2). The impact of this legislation on defences is referred to at [16.50]-[16.55]. If the injury is one to which the Workers Compensation legislation applies, in some States that injury claim is excluded from the operation of the civil liability legislation but may be subject to its own restrictions on recovery of common law damages:

NSW: CLA, s 3B: ACT: CLWA, s 93 (Part 7 does not apply to claims under *Workers Compensation Act 1951* (ACT)); Qld: CLA, s 5; Vic: WrA, s 45(1)(c) (excluding claims under the *Workers Compensation Act 1958* (Vic)); WA: CLA, s 3A(1).

Volenti non fit injuria

Wheeler v New Merton Board Mills

[17.140] *Wheeler v New Merton Board Mills* [1933] 2 KB 669 Court of Appeal

SCRUTTON LJ: 687 A boy of 18 years of age at the time of the accident was employed as what is called a "shavings boy" in a factory. There is a machine which cuts cardboard, and in doing so makes shavings, and some of the shavings fall about the floor, and some of the shavings stick in the knives in the machine and it is desirable to have them cleared out. The machinery can easily be stopped by a lever, and the boy knew within a week of his employment that it could be stopped by a lever, but he says the foreman never told him to stop it. However, he knew it could be stopped by a lever, and he went on for three months taking shavings out of the knives while the machine was working, and by good luck he did so for three months without having his fingers cut off, but at last the evil day came when he lost his hand and fingers. He thereupon sued his employers for damages, saying in effect: "There is a statutory obligation on you to fence this dangerous machine; I have been injured by your not fencing this dangerous machine. I am a private person who has been injured by your breach of a public obligation; I claim damages," and certain questions were left to the jury.

[His Lordship noted, with some surprise, that the question of contributory negligence had not been argued. He accepted the jury findings that the machine was dangerous and the plaintiff undertook the work knowing the danger and accepting the risk, and continued:]

Then I am confronted with this problem. If there is a breach of the statute in that a dangerous machine is not fenced, is it a defence for the employer to say that the plaintiff, the workman, took the risk? I will use the exact words of the jury: "Did the plaintiff undertake the work knowing the danger and taking the risk? Answer: Yes." Is that good defence for the employer? Now, the immediate authority we have to consider in relation to that is a case which was tried 50 years ago, the case of *Baddeley v Granville (Earl)* (1887) 19 QBD 423, which was followed 11 years later by the case of *Groves v Wimborne (Lord)* [1898] 2 QB 402, where Vaughan Williams LJ said this [at 415]: "It cannot be doubted that, where a statute provides for the performance by certain persons of a particular duty, and someone belonging to a class of person for whose benefit and protection the statute imposes the duty is injured by failure to perform it, prima facie, and, if there be nothing to the contrary, an action by the person so injured will lie against the person who has so failed to perform the duty." Vaughan Williams LJ goes on at a later stage of the judgment to say that one of the matters that excuse the employer from the charge that he has not performed his statutory duty is that there was contributory negligence on the part of the plaintiff. ... Vaughan Williams LJ does say that contributory negligence would be a defence, I do not find that he says that volenti proved by itself would be a defence. When we turn to *Baddeley's case* (1887) 19 QBD 423, which Talbot J said he was bound by, the question is, are we prepared to overrule a case which has stood for 50 years, and has no doubt been the basis of many transactions? The facts in *Baddeley v Granville (Earl)* (1887) 19 QBD 423 were these: Rules made under the *Coal Mines Regulation Act 1872*, required the banksman to be constantly present at the pit's mouth when men were going up and down the shaft. In that particular mine for years that rule had been broken; it was the regular practice that no banksman should be present during the night when the men went up and down the shaft. The man who was killed, the husband of the plaintiff, was aware of the fact that there was no banksman, but he continued going up and down the shaft, and when he was going up the shaft one night a boy of 14 years of age called out an order to the engineman which, being acted on, resulted in the plaintiff's husband being killed. The question in *Baddeley's case*

Wheeler v New Merton Board Mills cont.

undoubtedly was: Is it a defence to an action against the employer for an injury arising from the breach of a statutory duty on the part of the employer to say that the man who was killed knew all about it, and in *Baddeley's case* the Divisional Court held that it was not a good defence. I confess I should have been happier if I had understood why they did so, because I cannot make out from Wills J's judgment whether he was deciding the case on the ground that it is contrary to public policy that where there is a statutory obligation on the employer the workman should contract out of it, or whether he was deciding the case on some ground which I do not understand. He does not hold as a matter of law that the agreement would be legal as being against public policy. But though I do not understand the ground upon which the case proceeded, it is a case which has stood for 50 years, and it fits in with the decision in *Groves v Wimborne (Lord)* [1898] 2 QB 402, and though I am not satisfied with the way in which the case has been tried, I am satisfied that it is now too late to interfere with the decision in *Baddeley's case* (1887) 19 QBD 423, which has stood in the books for 50 years, and that disposes of the case.

[Greer and Slesser LJJ delivered concurring judgments, both stressing the inexpediency of overruling a decision which had been acted on for 46 years. Slesser LJ concluded his judgment thus:]

I would only add this. Mr Cave has asked us to say why it is (asking the question rhetorically) that in the case of contributory negligence it has been decided that the defence will lie notwithstanding that there has been a breach of the statute. The difference seems to me to be this, that where contributory negligence is found, that is a finding that the essential cause of the accident is the negligence of the plaintiff himself, and therefore he fails for that reason. That is not the case either in common employment or where the doctrine of volenti non fit injuria is set up. I agree with what has been said by Mr Fox-Andrews as to the distinction, because in one case there is a further intervening cause that is the negligence of the plaintiff, which does not arise in the case of volenti non fit injuria or common employment.

[17.145] **Notes&Questions**

1. The views of Slesser LJ on the distinction between the defences of volens and contributory negligence are not consistent with judicial approaches on issues of causation (see Chapter 13). Is public policy the better rationale for disallowing volens as a defence?
2. The principal case extracted establishes the common law position that the defence of volenti does not apply to claims for breach of statutory duty. This appears to be now confirmed in New South Wales, at least with reference to workers covered by the *Workers Compensation Act 1987* (NSW), s 151O which provides that the defence of volenti non fit injuria "is not available in an action for the award of damages but, where that defence would otherwise have been available, the amount of any damages is to be reduced to such extent as is just and equitable on the presumption that the injured or deceased person was negligent in failing to take sufficient care for his or her own safety".
3. The principle established in *Wheeler's case* is qualified by the decision in *Imperial Chemical Industries Ltd v Shatwell* [1965] AC 656, see [16.30]. See also dicta in *Andar Transport Pty Ltd v Brambles Ltd* (2004) 217 CLR 424 [17.115].

——— ꙮ ———

Contributory negligence

Piro v Foster

[17.150] *Piro v Foster* (1943) 68 CLR 313 High Court of Australia

Piro v Foster cont.

LATHAM CJ: 318 Appeal from a judgment of the Supreme Court of South Australia for the defendant in an action in which the plaintiff, a boy of 14 years of age, claimed damages from the respondent, his employer ...

The boy was engaged at a machine which pressed and ironed sheepskins from which the wool had been removed. He worked on one side of the machine, placing the skins in position while the machine was at rest, and another workman, known as the "operator", who worked on the other side of the machine, put the machine in motion. When the machine was working a strip upon which a sheepskin rested was pressed by a heavy roller up against the bottom of a heavy plate. In this way irregularities in the surface were ironed out and a smooth, or, if desired, a patterned, surface was produced upon the skin. The plaintiff had been clearly and adequately warned, the learned judge found, not to put his fingers into the machine, but to feed the skin into the machine and to leave all straightening and smoothing of the skin to the operator. If these instructions had been obeyed the plaintiff could not have been injured. In fact he 319 put his left hand into the machine to straighten out a sheepskin. The operator, having no reason to suppose that the plaintiff's hand was in the machine, put the roller into operation, and the plaintiff's fingers were caught and seriously injured. Upon these facts the plaintiff was found guilty of contributory negligence and accordingly failed in his action for negligence.

The *Industrial Code 1920-1926* (SA), s 321, provides that the occupier of a factory shall securely fence or safeguard all dangerous parts of the machinery therein. The learned judge found that the machine was a dangerous machine and had not been fenced or safeguarded. This finding had not been challenged and there was clearly evidence to support it. If the machine had been safeguarded the plaintiff could not have been injured in the way in which he was injured. The *Industrial Code 1920-1926* is plainly a statute designed for the protection of persons working with such machinery as that to which s 321 applies and it had not been disputed that, in accordance with well-known principles, the injury which the plaintiff suffered gave him a cause of action: see *Groves v Wimborne (Lord)* [1898] 2 QB 402; *Phillips v. Britannia Hygienic Laundry Co Ltd* [1923] 1 KB 539 and the cases mentioned in *Lochgelly Iron & Coal Co Ltd v M'Mullan* [1934] AC 1 at 8. ... 321 ...

The decisions in *Caswell's case* [1940] AC 152 and *Lewis v Denye* [1940] AC 921 are clear that contributory negligence is a defence in a case where the plaintiff bases his action for damages upon personal injury suffered by him in consequence of a breach of a statutory duty by the defendant, that duty having been imposed for the purpose of protecting members of a class of which the plaintiff is one from the kind of injury which he has suffered. Such an action may be regarded from two points of view–either as an action for negligence, the breach of statutory duty being evidence, possibly conclusive evidence, of negligence, or as a common law action for a breach of statutory duty in which it is irrelevant to inquire whether such breach amounts to negligence on the part of the defendant or not. A statement of the former method of approach may be found in *Lochgelly's case* [1934] AC 1 at 9, 23. On the other hand, in *Watkins v Naval Colliery Co (1897) Ltd* [1912] AC 693 at 702, 703 Lord Haldane adopted the other view, which also commended itself to this court in *Bourke v Butterfield & Lewis Ltd* (1926) 38 CLR 540: see also per Lord Wright in *Caswell's case* [1940] AC 152 at 177, 178. It is not, however, necessary to determine whether such an action is technically an action for negligence or a common law action for a breach of statutory duty independent of negligence, because upon either view it should now be held by this court that contributory negligence on the part of the plaintiff is a defence to such an action.

There remains for consideration the contention of the appellant that the learned trial judge wrongfully found contributing negligence on the part of the plaintiff in the present case ... 322 ...

There is no dispute as to the facts in the present case. The action of the plaintiff in straightening the skin was a natural action not found to have been deliberately done in defiance of warning. The learned judge expressly said that, if the plaintiff had not been adequately warned not to put his hand under the plate, he might well have said, having regard to the circumstances, that what he did was the result of "mere heedlessness or inadvertence or, at the worst, of carelessness" – which would not have amounted, in the circumstances, to contributory negligence. Accordingly, if it had not been for the warnings given to the plaintiff, the learned judge would have held that what the plaintiff did was mere heedlessness or inadvertence or, at the worst, "carelessness". Similar words are to be found in *Caswell's case* [1940] AC 152 at 176 where Lord Wright speaking of contributory negligence in such a case as this, says that it is a question of degree and that "the jury have to draw the line where mere thoughtlessness or inadvertence or forgetfulness ceases and where negligence begins". The question here is whether an inference of contributory negligence should be drawn from facts which are not in doubt. In such a case an appellate court is in as good a position to decide the question as the judge at the trial: *Powell v Streatham Manor Nursing Home* [1935] AC 243. The question is one of facts, depending upon the circumstances of each case.

If there had been a finding that what the plaintiff did was a deliberate act whereby in defiance of known danger he invited or consciously took the risk of injury, that finding would have justified an inference of contributory negligence. But there is no such finding. I read the reasons for the judgment of the learned judge as stating that, though the plaintiff had been warned not to put his hand 323 into the machine, he inadvertently, without thinking on the particular occasion of the warning or of the danger involved, did put his hand into it. If the machine had been properly guarded he could not have put his hand into it. The statute was designed to protect the plaintiff and other persons using dangerous machines from just this kind of injury resulting from inadvertence or forgetfulness. This, to use the words of Goddard LJ in *Hutchinson v London & North Eastern Railway Co* [1942] 1 KB 481 at 488 is a case "where the contributory negligence alleged was the very thing which the statutory duty of the employer was designed to prevent". In my opinion an employer cannot safeguard himself against the civil liability imposed upon him by the statute by saying to his employees in effect: "This machine ought to be fenced; it is not fenced; therefore you must be very careful in using it" and by repeating this warning from time to time. If such warnings were held to be decisive in determining whether or not contributory negligence was established the policy of protective statutes, in so far as they involve a civil liability for damages, could readily be defeated and destroyed. The fact that such warning was given is a circumstance to be taken into account but it is not, in my opinion, in itself decisive upon the question of contributory negligence. The inadvertence of the plaintiff remained inadvertence notwithstanding the warning, and in all the circumstances of this particular case, the finding of contributory negligence cannot, in my opinion, be supported upon the evidence.

On this ground, in my opinion, the appeal should be allowed and the judgment for the defendant should be set aside. All the relevant facts have been determined by the learned trial judge and there is no reason why the parties should be put to the expense of a new trial upon any issue other than that of damage. In my opinion, therefore, the case should be remitted to the trial judge for the purpose of assessing damages upon the plaintiff's claim for damages for negligence and giving judgment accordingly.

Piro v Foster cont.

[Rich, Starke, McTiernan and Williams JJ delivered separate judgments concurring in the conclusion that contributory negligence was a defence, but Rich and Williams JJ dissented from the rest of the court on the issue of fact.]

[17.155] **Notes&Questions**

1. In *Davies v Adelaide Chemical & Fertilizer Co Ltd* (1946) 74 CLR 541, the High Court confirmed that a plaintiff could be contributorily negligent even if the legislative duty was enacted for the very purpose of protecting the plaintiff. Latham CJ warned, however, (at 545):

   > the statutes are intended to prevent accidents happening through carelessness and they should not be so construed and applied as to deprive of remedy a person within their protection whenever there is any carelessness on his part which helps to bring about this injury.

   In *Kakouris v Gibbs Burge & Co Pty Ltd* [1970] VR 502, the Full Court of the Supreme Court of Victoria held that these remarks could not be taken to mean that mere carelessness could not amount to contributory negligence for the purposes of such an action and that some wilful act going beyond mere forgetfulness or inadvertence was required. The question is one of fact and the correct test is whether the plaintiff workman had failed to take such reasonable care for his own safety as could be expected from an ordinary workman in all the circumstances.

2. Where there is a statutory duty imposed for the protection of workers and the worker has been guilty of momentary inattention to the task, courts are likely to be more forgiving in judging whether the workers conduct amounts to contributory negligence, see [16.85]. In *Kenyon v Barry Bros Specialised Services Pty Ltd* [2001] VSCA 3, the Supreme Court of Victoria Court of Appeal held that a jury finding that the employee was 85% contributorily negligent should be set aside. There, an employee was engaged in unblocking a large suction hose that was blocked with sand. The method employed was to lift up the large and very heavy hose and thump it down on the ground to remove the blockage. This was done to the knowledge of the plaintiff's immediate supervisor. The plaintiff employee suffered back injury in lifting the heavy hose. The method adopted was "likely to cause injury". Winneke P (other members of the Court agreeing) said (at [16]):

   > [A] finding of 85 per cent responsibility … was not … reasonably open to the jury. Once the jury had concluded that [the defendant] was in breach of its common law duty not to unreasonably expose the employee to unnecessary risk of injury, and was also in breach of its statutory duty imposed by the manual handling regulations, by employing a system of lifting heavy hoses and throwing them to the ground, I cannot accept that it was then open to them to find that the [plaintiff] was more than five times more responsible for his injury than was the [employer] simply because he employed the tolerated system so provided with excessive zeal and enthusiasm; or failed to choose a less strenuous and, on the evidence, less effective or less favoured method.

The English Court of Appeal also demonstrates a reluctance to find contributory negligence in cases of breach of statutory duty. In *Cooper v Carillion PLC* [2003] EWCA Civ 1811, Keene LJ said (at [13]), other members of the Court agreeing:

> [I]t is ... well established ... that an employee is normally entitled to assume that his employer has complied with his statutory duties ... Where there has been such a breach of statutory duty by the employer ... it is important to ensure that the statutory requirement placed on the employer is not emasculated by too great a willingness on the part of the courts to find that the employee has been guilty of contributory negligence. It is very easy for a judge with the advantage of hindsight to identify some act on the part of the employee which would have avoided the accident occurring. That in itself does not demonstrate negligence on the part of the employee. As Lord Tucker put it in *Staveley Iron & Chemical Co Ltd v Jones* [1956] AC 627, [1956] 1 All ER 403 at 648, one must avoid treating every risky act by an employee due to familiarity with the work or some inattention resulting from noise or strain as contributory negligence. ... To impose too strict a standard of care on the workman would defeat the object of the statutory requirement.

3. Apportionment legislation applies to reduce damages for the plaintiff's contributory negligence. The legislation applies to "wrongs" defined to include actions for breach of statutory duty: ACT: CLWA, s 101; *Law Reform (Miscellaneous Provisions) Act* (NT), s 15; *Workers Compensation Act 1987* (NSW), s 151N(3); *Law Reform (Miscellaneous Provisions) Act 1965* (NSW), s 8 ("wrong" would include breach of statutory duty as it is "a liability in tort in respect of which a defence of contributory negligence is available at common Law"); similarly *Law Reform Act 1995* (Qld), s 5; *Law Reform (Contributory Negligence and Apportionment of Liability) Act 2001* (SA), ss 3, 4(c) ("fault"); *Wrongs Act 1954* (Tas), s 2 ("wrongful act"); *Law Reform (Contributory Negligence and Tortfeasors' Contribution) Act 1947* (WA), s 3 ("negligence"). In New South Wales it is only after 2002 that contributory negligence is a defence to claims for breach of statutory duty. The *Statutory Duties (Contributory Negligence) Act 1945* (contributory negligence not a defence to breach of statutory duty) was repealed by the *Civil Liability Amendment (Personal Responsibility) Act 2003* (NSW) (see also *Booksan Pty Ltd & ors v Wehbe & Ors* [2006] NSWCA 3; *Transfield Construction v Peers* [2008] NSWCA 215. It was previously reversed in relation to employee claims against the employer by the *Workers Compensation Act 1987* (NSW), s 151M(3)). In the Australian Capital Territory there is a special provision preventing reduction of damages for contributory negligence causing personal injury where the wrong was a breach of statutory duty. ACT: CLWA, s 102(2).

4. Under the civil liability legislation, the plaintiff's negligence is to be adjudged by the same standards as a defendant's negligence, see [16.140] Note 1]. These provisions may be excluded in relation to claims by employees against their employer, see [17.135].

Plaintiff's unlawful conduct

[17.160] In *Progress and Properties Ltd v Craft* (1976) 135 CLR 651 one question for the High Court to decide was the application of the defence of complicity in a joint illegal enterprise to a claim for breach of statutory duty as distinct from a claim in negligence. Jacobs J, with whose judgment the majority agreed, said (at 669):

> I do not think that the fact that the law declines to impose a duty of care towards a person engaged in a joint illegal enterprise in respect of that enterprise can be applied in a case where the illegality, if it be assumed to be so, is one which arises from the breach of specific statutory duties of care for the safety of one of the participants. The reason for the law declining to raise a duty of care towards a joint participant in an illegal enterprise in respect of the manner in which that enterprise may be carried out is wholly inapplicable to the circumstances of regulations designed to enforce a high specific duty to ensure the safety of that participant.

In *Gala v Preston* (1991) 172 CLR 243, see [7.170], the principal judgment referred to *Progress and Properties* and commented:

> [I]n cases of illegality arising from infringement of statutory provisions which are designed to promote safety, e.g. traffic laws and industrial safety regulations, there is no reason why illegality of that kind should negate the existence of a duty of care.

The issue of illegality is affected by the civil liability legislation, see [16.195]).

CIVIL LIABILITY LEGISLATION

[17.165] Civil liability legislation may apply to actions for breach of statutory duty was well as actions in negligence. In some jurisdictions the legislation does not apply to claims by employees against their employers, see ([17.135]). Predominantly, actions for breach of statutory duty are available to employees for breach of safety statutes, so that it will be a fairly rare case where the civil liability legislation applies to these actions. Where the CLA provisions have not been excluded, the legislation will generally apply to actions for breach of statutory duty as it does to negligence. Apart from the negligence provisions and mental harm, other parts of the Act such as personal injuries damages, apply more broadly and are not limited to negligence, see as examples, NSW: CLA, s 11A (personal injury damages), Vic: WrA, s 28C (personal injury damages) and see *Booksan Pty Ltd. Jaymay Constructions Pty Ltd v Wehbe & Ors* [2006] NSWCA 3 at [167]. This is subject to the qualification that those parts of the CLA provisions dealing with negligence, will not apply where the action for breach of statutory duty involves strict liability. The CLA negligence provisions, as well as the limitations on claims for mental harm, apply to any claim for "damages for harm resulting from *negligence*, regardless of whether the claim is brought in tort, in contract, under statute or otherwise" (italics inserted) see as illustrations: NSW: CLA, ss 5A, 28; Vic: WrA, ss 44, 68 and see *Shipley v Masu Financial Management Pty Ltd* [2008] NSWSC 252 at [74]-[76]. We have already mentioned the operation of the CLA provisions in relation to public authorities (see Chapter 11 Duty–Special Defendants) and contributory negligence (see [16.135]).

CHAPTER 18

Nuisance

INTRODUCTION

[18.05] The two torts that constitute nuisance are public nuisance and private nuisance. Private nuisance concerns a nuisance to the private rights of an individual and public nuisance to those interests that are shared by the public, that is, public rights.

PUBLIC NUISANCE

Introduction

[18.10] Public nuisance is "an unlawful act or omission ... which ... endangers the lives, safety, health, property or comfort of the public or by which the public are obstructed in the exercise or enjoyment of any right common to all" (*Kent v Johnson* (1973) 21 FLR 177 at 203-204). To establish a prima facie case of public nuisance, a private individual will have to prove (1) title to sue, (2) the interference is with a public right and (3) that the defendant's interference is substantial and unreasonable.

Title to sue

[18.15] Since public nuisance involves an interference with public rights, a private individual is usually precluded from instituting an action in respect of the interference. The appropriate entity to bring suit for infringement of public rights is the Attorney-General as he or she represents the public. This prevents multiplicity of actions based on trivial complaints by members of the public.

A private individual is able to initiate proceedings for a public nuisance if he or she can prove that they have suffered "special" or "particular" damage; damage over and above that which is suffered by the rest of the public. The circumstances that satisfy special or particular damage are considered in the following extract.

Walsh v Ervin

[18.20] *Walsh v Ervin* [1952] VLR 361 Supreme Court of Victoria

(footnotes omitted)

[The plaintiff and defendant were farmers; their properties were divided by a highway. The defendant ploughed and planted crops on a section of the highway reducing its surface to one-third. The defendant also erected gates at various points along the ploughed section. For more than three years the plaintiff was prevented from entering his land by motor vehicle at any point along the fenced off area. When moving his sheep between two paddocks he had to use the main road which involved a substantial loss of time, as well asl with the inconvenience of the gates. The plaintiff sued the defendant in public nuisance.]

SHOLL J: 368 As the general principle is usually stated, an individual cannot sue alone for relief in respect of a nuisance to a public highway unless he has sustained some particular damage, in the sense of some substantial injury, direct and not merely consequential, beyond that suffered by the public generally.

...

What, then, is particular damage? For injury occasioned by the nuisance to his person, his life, his servant, or his chattels, an individual can plainly sue–*Fowler v Sanders* (1617) Cro Jac 446 [79 ER 382]; Com Dig, Action upon the Case for a Nuisance (C) (5th ed, 1822), Vol I, p 421. Whether loss of custom due to the nuisance is enough was for long the subject of controversy–see Halsbury's Laws of England (2nd ed), Vol 16, 366 and note (r), I should myself have thought it sufficient since the decisions in *Lyons, Sons & Co v Gulliver* [1914] 1 Ch 631, and *Blundy, Clark & Co Ltd v London & North Eastern Railway Co* [1931] 2 KB 334. Depreciation of the actual value of property by reducing or cutting off the approach to it is sufficient–see the numerous cases, including compensation decisions, cited in Halsbury's Laws of England (2nd ed), Vol 16, 365-366, and notes (m) and (n). Must any other injury, to be sufficient, involve, as Mr Jones contended, actual pecuniary loss, in the sense in which we speak of "special damage" in, for example, a negligence action? I think not. In my opinion, delay and inconvenience of a substantial character, direct and not merely consequential, so long as not merely similar in nature and extent to that in fact suffered by the rest of the public, may amount to sufficient damages, particular to the individual plaintiff, notwithstanding that, in another sense, it is "general" and not "special" damage to him. In such a case there is no more reason for denying compensation for such injury, as a particular injury, than there would be for denying the right to general damages for pain and suffering if the plaintiff fell over the obstruction in the highway and broke his leg, thus suffering particular damage, but happened to be a retired pensioner who was treated *gratis* in a public hospital, and so suffered no "special" damage.

... In *Smith v Wilson* [1903] 2 IR 45, which contains the fullest discussion of the point in any reported case I have seen, four judges of the King's Bench Division in Ireland had to determine whether the plaintiff, a small farmer, could recover individual damages on the ground that, by reason of the obstruction of a highway, he was ... deprived of his ordinary route to his market; loss of time in

Walsh v Ervin cont.

working a farm, and occasional expenditure on car hire, ... and the plaintiff's damage was different in kind from that of the mere passer-by. Gibson J ... stated his view as follows (at 76):

> Mere inconvenience, as in *Winterbottom v [Lord] Derby*, may not be enough; but where premises are prejudicially affected by a direct near approach being permanently stopped, and replaced by a circuitous and longer way, or where business will be impeded, or additional expense may be probably necessary in consequence of the change, direct damage may be inferred.

See also Lord O'Brien LCJ (at 80) to similar effect. Kenny J (at 54) dissented on the ground, principally, that there was no evidence that the time lost by the plaintiff was of any pecuniary value whatsoever, and that if the plaintiff could sue, so could every wayfarer.

I respectfully think the view of the majority in that case is common sense, and good law. I do not think it depends on the necessity of inferring actual pecuniary loss, any more than *Chichester v Lethbridge* (1738) Willes 71 [125 ER 1061] the observations in *Vanderpant's case*, or the statement of the Full Court in *Harvey v Shire of St Arnaud* (1879) 5 VLR (L) 312. It is peculiarly applicable, and accordingly I willingly apply it, to the case of a government road in this country, dividing large pastoral and farming holdings, and useful to, and used by, practically nobody but the owners of those adjoining holdings. It would, in my judgment, seem to any Australian countryman the negation of common sense to say that a person using a public government road as this plaintiff used it would not suffer peculiar prejudice by its being closed, or rendered more difficult of use. So long as the delay and inconvenience is substantial, it can in my opinion make no difference that the way is not wholly closed, if it is effectively rendered unavailable for important purposes of the plaintiff, even though it be not possible to infer actual pecuniary loss by him. After all, to apply the view of the Irish Court in such a case has the merit of resolving the controversies of 300-400 years by reverting to the simple tests of Fitzherbert J – "greater hurt, or inconvenience, than every man had", and "especial hurt".

In my opinion, the law is too narrowly stated in Winfield on Torts (2nd ed), 480-481, and Clerk & Lindsell on Torts (8th ed), 358-359; and also in Halsbury's Laws of England (2nd ed), Vol 16, 366, insofar as that passage is limited to "pecuniary" loss.

...

The conclusions of law which I have above stated on this branch of the case may now be summarised.

(1) An individual person or corporation cannot sue in his or its own name in respect of a nuisance to a public highway, except for "particular damage" occasioned to him or it thereby.

(2) "Particular damage" is not limited to "special damage" (in the sense of actual pecuniary loss).

(3) It may consist of proved general damage, for example, inconvenience and delay–as in the present case–Provided that it is substantial, that it is direct and not consequential, and that it is appreciably greater in degree than any suffered by the general public.

(4) Since such particular damage must be thus proved, it follows that mere nominal damages cannot be recovered, since there is no presumption of particular damage.

(5) But I see no reason why exemplary damages might not in a proper case be awarded ...

ꕥ

[18.25] **Notes&Questions**

1. The decision in *Walsh v Ervin* [1952] VLR 361 has been criticised as contrary to the principle that the plaintiff must suffer harm, not only different in degree, but different in kind from that of the rest of the public. Arguably, if a plaintiff suffers harm to a much greater degree than the rest of the public, this makes the plaintiff's damage different in kind to the rest of the public.
2. As noted in the extracted case, special damage may be established in different ways, for example: if the plaintiff is able to show that as a result of the public nuisance he or she has suffered personal injury, property damage, pecuniary loss or additional trouble and expense: *Fowler v Sanders* (1617) Cro Jac 446; 79 ER 382 (horseman fell over logs in highway); *Castle v St Augustine's Links Ltd* (1922) 38 TLR 615 (golf balls smashed the windscreen of the plaintiff's taxi which was on the highway); *Taylor v City of Perth* (1988) Aust Torts Reports 80-191 (the plaintiff lost custom due to the defendant's obstruction of the highway).
3. In *Ball v Consolidated Rutile Ltd* [1991] 1 Qd R 524, no special damage was held to be sustained by professional fishermen whose livelihood was affected when a mining company's activities caused earth and slurry to enter prawn fishing grounds depleting the prawn population. The fishermen did not suffer damage above and beyond other members of the public given that the watercourse was open to all members of the public to fish. In *Wallace v Powell* [2000] NSWC 406, Hodgson CJ found that the plaintiff had not suffered particular damage as a result of the construction of buildings on a highway which infringed access to a tract of land he intended to subdivide and sell. He was able to access the property along an alternative route without inconvenience and until such time as he was in a position to subdivide and develop the land there was insufficient damage.

Interference with a public right

[18.30] To sue in public nuisance the court must be satisfied that the interference is with a "public right". In *Attorney-General v PYA Quarries Ltd* [1957] 2 QB 169 at 170 Lord Denning described a public nuisance as "a nuisance which is so widespread in its range or so indiscriminate in its effect that it would not be reasonable to expect one person to take proceedings on his own responsibility to put a stop to it, but that it should be taken on the responsibility of the community at large". The extent to which the public is affected is therefore a central consideration in determining whether the defendant's act interferes with a public right.

In *R v Clifford* [1980] 1 NSWLR 314, the New South Wales Court of Criminal Appeal highlighted the considerations involved in determining whether the interference has a wide enough effect to be regarded as a public nuisance. Four prisoners had climbed onto a prison roof and remained there for approximately 14 hours. Under s 23(1) of the *Prisons Act 1952* (NSW), acts of nuisance by prisoners constituted an offence against prison discipline. Was it a public nuisance? Reynolds JA (other members of the Court agreeing) said (at 318):

A public nuisance has been defined as being (for relevant purposes) an act not warranted by law, if the effect is to endanger the life, health, property, morals or comfort of the public. The public in this context includes a class of persons who come within the sphere or neighbourhood of its operation. A public nuisance can exist or be created, as the Act contemplates, in a gaol, notwithstanding the limited access thereto, just as much as it can be created in, eg, a cricket ground to which the public is not admitted except upon payment of a fee. In both cases there can exist a class of persons who are affected. Whether, in a particular case, the number of persons is sufficient to constitute a class is a question of fact. Even if there is such a class capable of being affected, the question still remains as to whether the conduct complained of was capable of being described as the commission of a nuisance.

[18.35] **Notes&Questions**

1. *R v Clifford* [1980] 1 NSWLR 314 clearly states that the number of persons that are required to be affected for an interference to constitute a public nuisance will depend upon the circumstances of each case. In *Walsh v Ervin* [1952] VLR 361 (extracted [18.20]) the road which was obstructed by the defendant served only one or two properties; could it be argued that this was too small an interference to constitute a public nuisance? Not according to Lord Denning (in the *PYA case* at 191), it may be sufficient that anyone wishing to use the road would be obstructed even though only one or two property owners use the road.
2. In the case of *R v Madden* [1933] Ch 298, a bomb hoax was received by telephone. The police and the security office on the premises were contacted and a thorough search was then undertaken by eight security officers. The search was called off after one hour when it was discovered that it was a hoax. The Court of Appeal held that as the bomb hoax did not affect a considerable number of persons or a section of the public as distinct from individual persons, it was not a public nuisance. Compare the case of *R v Shorrock* [1994] QB 279, which did constitute a public nuisance. The appellant had granted a licence to use his field over a weekend for an "acid house party". Between 3000 and 5,000 people attended. 275 telephone complaints were made in respect of extensive noise caused by the music and public address system.
3. The High Court in *Brodie v Singleton Shire Council* (2001) 206 CLR 512 determined that actions can no longer be brought in nuisance against public authorities in respect of the construction, maintenance and repair of public roads, including bridges, culverts and footpaths. Nuisance in this area has been absorbed by the law of negligence. See Chapter 11 Special Defendants "Public Authorities" at [11.40] Note 3.

Interference must be substantial and unreasonable

[18.40] The interference with the public right must be substantial and unreasonable for it to constitute a public nuisance. In the modern world, inconveniences and annoyances must be expected. They are part of everyday life and cannot constitute grounds for instituting action. Business and commerce must be permitted to effectively operate. On this basis, in the absence of negligence, a danger created in the highway as a result of ordinary use by traffic is not a public nuisance. See *Maitland v Raisbeck* [1944] 1 KB 689 at 691-692, in which the tail light of the defendant's car was defective, leading to a collision. The Court concluded that if this was classed as a nuisance "it would seem that every driver of a vehicle on the road would be turned into an insurer in respect of latent defects in his machine." Likewise, temporary obstructions to the use of the highway or to the enjoyment of adjoining premises will not give rise to liability in public nuisance where the obstruction is reasonable in quantum and duration. In *Harper v Haden* [1933] Ch 298, the UK Court of Appeal refused to uphold an injunction awarded to a shopkeeper who complained of scaffolding and boarding erected in front of his shop by the defendants for the purpose of conducting building operations on their upper floor premises. The defendants had erected only what was necessary and reasonable for the conduct of the works. In comparison, the assembly of crowds or queues of people seeking to do business with the defendant who obstruct the use of the highway may constitute nuisance if the crowd is attracted by something done by a defendant which is *not* necessary for the bona fide carrying on of the defendant's trade. Consequently in *R v Carlile* (1834) 6 C & P 636; 172 ER 1397, the defendant was held liable in public nuisance when a crowd of people gathered to watch the burning of a libellous effigy. If however the business is carried on in suitable premises and in a normal and proper manner and there are no reasonable means by which the business could prevent the interference, there will be no nuisance (*Silservice Pty Ltd v Supreme Bread Pty Ltd* (1950) 50 SR (NSW) 127 Roper CJ at 129).

PRIVATE NUISANCE

Introduction

[18.45] Private nuisance arose out of action on the case and protects a person's right to use and enjoyment of their land. As a consequence, a nuisance may be caused by an indirect, as well as a direct act whereas a trespass to land can only result from a direct interference. Unlike trespass to land, private nuisance offers protection in respect of interferences that are intangible as well as tangible. Consequently, intangible invasions such as noise, smell, and offensive sights have been found to constitute a private nuisance, as well as tangible invasions such as fire, leaves, tree roots, flood and dust.

Title to sue

[18.50] As the tort of private nuisance is concerned with protecting the plaintiff's right to use and enjoyment of land only a person with rights in or over property has standing to sue. For example, the individual must be an owner or tenant of the property who is in actual possession of the property and who has the right to exclusive possession (*Hunter v Canary Wharf Ltd* [1997] AC 655, *Stockwell v State of Victoria* [2001] VSC 497 at [248] (extracted at [18.120])). An owner, however, will not be entitled to sue if he or she only has a reversionary interest in the land, for example, the owner who has leased his or her premises to a tenant, unless the nuisance is of sufficiently permanent character so as to damage his or her reversion, for example permanent devaluation of the property (*Hunter v Canary Wharf Ltd* [1997] AC 655, at 688). As the right to exclusive possession is necessary, immediate family members who do not possess that right will not have standing. So, in *Oldham v Lawson (No 1)* [1976] VR 654, in which the plaintiffs, husband and wife, sued for nuisance, it was held that the husband, who was a mere licencee, had no title to sue but the wife as owner did have title to sue. Since *Oldham v Lawson (No 1)* [1976] VR 654 there have been decisions which have permitted immediate family members who reside in the premises but do not have the right to exclusive possession to sue (*Khorasandjian v Bush* [1993] QB 727 (CA), a daughter living in her parents' house was permitted to sue in respect of an ex-boyfriend's harassing phone calls; *Motherwell v Motherwell* (1976) 73 DLR (3d) 62 (Alta App Div), a wife who occupied the matrimonial home was found to have sufficient interest to sue). These cases, however, are no longer considered to be authoritative on the basis that it would transform private nuisance from a tort against the land to one against the person (*Khorasandjian v Bush* [1993] QB 727 (CA), was expressly overruled upon this issue by the House of Lords in *Hunter v Canary Wharf Pty Ltd* [1997] AC 655).

Nature of the interests protected

[18.55] Private nuisance is concerned with preventing an interference with the use and enjoyment of land or some right connected with land. The interference with an individual's right to use and enjoyment of their land may consist of:

1. a disturbance of the comfort, health and convenience caused, for example, through dust, smell and noise (certain interferences such as to privacy, light and views are not protected see [18.75] Note 3) ; or
2. material physical damage such as caused for example through flooding, fire and vibrations.

Interference with the enjoyment of the land

[18.60] Just as in public nuisance, the law of private nuisance holds that modern society must make some allowance for the actions of neighbours (*Kennaway v Thompson* [1981] QB 88 at 94, a process of "give and take"). A balance must be struck between the defendant's right to use property on the one hand and the plaintiff's right to enjoy their property on the other, with legal intervention warranted only when an interference goes beyond what others in the vicinity should be expected to bear. Therefore the interference must be of a substantial and unreasonable nature to qualify as private nuisance.

Substantial and unreasonable interference

[18.65] In determining whether a defendant's act is a substantial and unreasonable interference with the use and enjoyment of land, the court will seek to balance the give and take of the relationship. The court weighs the nature and circumstances of the defendant's activity and the character of the resulting interference against the plaintiff's interests. The following case considers the assessment of these competing interests.

Munro v Southern Dairies

[18.70] *Munro v Southern Dairies Ltd* [1955] VLR 332 Supreme Court of Victoria

(footnotes omitted)

SHOLL J: 332 In this case, the plaintiff, who has at all material times been the owner and occupier of a house and land at 23 Willis Street, Hampton, sues the defendant, which is an incorporated company carrying on the business of a milk distributor, for an injunction and/or damages. The plaintiff's cause of action set out in his statement of claim is founded on nuisance, and in substance he alleges that since in or about the year 1952, his quiet enjoyment of his premises had been interfered with by reason of noise, smell and flies, occasioned by the keeping of horses on that part of the defendant's premises which abuts on Willis Street. …

[Nuisance] is defined in one of the textbooks as "An unlawful interference with a person's use or enjoyment of land, or of some right over, or in connection with it", but that definition of itself is so wide that it is necessary to add to it and qualify it in order to set out clearly what it is that will constitute

Munro v Southern Dairies cont.

an actionable private nuisance of the kind here complained of. In the first place, there must be a substantial degree of interference with the comfort and convenience of the occupier who complains of a private nuisance, or with some other aspect of the use or enjoyment of his land. The interference must be so substantial as to cause damage to him. On that matter I may refer to what is said in *Winfield on Torts* (2nd ed), 482. Dealing with the subject of interference, the learned author says:

> The forms of this are innumerable. Noise, smells, pollution of air or water, are the most usual instances, but there are many others. The two main heads are injury to property and interference with personal comfort. The escape of fumes which kill vegetation and cattle is an illustration of the first, and excessive tolling of church bells of the second. But whatever be the type, it does not follow that any harm constitutes a nuisance. The whole law on the subject really represents a balancing of conflicting interests. Some noise, some smell, some vibration, every one must endure in any modern town, otherwise modern life would be impossible.

And later he continues:

> Where the interference is with personal comfort, it is not necessary in order to establish a nuisance that any injury to health should be shown. It is enough that there is a material interference with the physical comfort of human existence reckoned "not merely according to elegant or dainty modes and habits of living, but according to plain and sober and simple notions among the English people".

The last phrase, of course, is a quotation from the well known judgment of Knight-Bruce V-C, as he then was in *Walter v Selfe* (1851) 4 De G & Sm 315 at 322 [64 ER 849 at 851]. I think Mr Jacobs was right in his submission that the loss of even one night's sleep may amount to such a substantial interference with personal comfort as to constitute a nuisance, and I adopt with respect what was said by Sir Wilfred Greene MR in a case to which Mr Jacobs referred me, *Andrae v Selfridge & Co Ltd* [1937] 3 All ER 255 at 261. Speaking there of interference with rest caused by the defendant's working of cranes, his Lordship said:

> There were other occasions on which it conducted noisy operations at night. I do not propose to go through them. There are a number of letters of complaint, and those complaints were either attempted to be explained away or they were remedied. But that the complaints were substantial complaints I, for one, am satisfied, and I certainly protest against the idea that, if persons, for their own profit and convenience, choose to destroy even one night's rest of their neighbours, they are doing something which is excusable. To say that the loss of one or two nights' rest is one of those trivial matters in respect of which the law will take no notice appears to me to be quite a misconception, and, if it be a misconception existing in the minds of those who conduct these operations, the sooner it is removed the better.

I have already said something in the remarks I have just made about the standard of comfort which a land owner is entitled to expect. The test which the law applies is not the test of an abnormal sensitiveness. A man is not entitled to relief merely because he may happen to be unduly sensitive to noise or smell or any other form of interference with his property. Nevertheless a man who lives next door to premises from which some interference emanates may get relief when another man some distance away will fail to obtain it. That, after all, is only commonsense, because the degree of interference may and frequently does vary with the distance of the plaintiff's premises from the source of the interference. A good deal of evidence was led in the present case to show that the defendant's use of the premises was in accordance with accepted standards, and evidence was called from an inspector of the Department of Agriculture and from the Senior Health Inspector of the City of Sandringham on that point. That evidence was, of course, relevant insofar as it tended to negative the facts alleged by the plaintiff and his witnesses, but it was irrelevant, in my opinion, insofar as it was relied on, if it was relied on, for the purposes of the submission that reasonable use of the premises was

Munro v Southern Dairies cont.

sufficient to negative nuisance. On that point there are a number of authorities. I need, I think, refer only to three. In *Broder v Saillard* (1876) 2 Ch D 692 at 700-702, Sir George Jessel MR was dealing with a case in which a nuisance of noise from a stable was complained of, among other things, and (at 700-701) he said:

> I come now to the second branch of the case – the noise. It is very hard on the defendant, who is a gentleman with three horses in his stable, and whose horses do not appear to make more than the ordinary noise that horses do, if he is not to be allowed to keep his horses in his stable. On the other hand, it is very hard on the plaintiffs if they cannot sleep at night, and cannot enjoy their house, because the noise from the stables is so great as seriously to interfere with their rest and comfort. The question is, on which side the law inclines? If there were no authority on the question I should have felt no difficulty about it, because I take it the law is this, that a man is entitled to the comfortable enjoyment of his dwelling-house. If his neighbour makes such a noise as to interfere with the ordinary use and enjoyment of his dwelling-house, so as to cause serious annoyance and disturbance, the occupier of the dwelling-house is entitled to be protected from it. It is no answer to say that the defendant is only making a reasonable use of his property, because there are many trades and many occupations which are not only reasonable, but necessary to be followed, and which still cannot be allowed to be followed in the proximity of dwelling-houses, so as to interfere with the comfort of their inhabitants. I suppose a blacksmith's trade is as necessary as most trades in this kingdom; or I might take instances of many noisy and offensive trades, some of which are absolutely necessary, and some of which, no doubt, may not only be reasonably followed, but to which it is absolutely and indispensably necessary for the welfare of mankind that some houses and some pieces of land should be devoted; therefore I think that is not the test. If a stable is built, as this stable is, not as stables usually are, at some distance from dwelling-houses, but next to the wall of the plaintiff's dwelling-house, in such a position that the noise would actually prevent the neighbours sleeping, and would frighten them out of their sleep, and would prevent their ordinary and comfortable enjoyment of their dwelling-house, all I can say is, that is not a proper place to keep horses in, although the horses may be ordinarily quiet.

At 702 his Lordship added: "The test, therefore, is whether the stables are unluckily so situated as that the noise from the horses, not being uncommon horses in any way materially disturbs the comfort of the plaintiff's dwelling-house, and prevents the people sleeping at night."

....

In the same way, it has been held that the mere fact that a business may be so carried on as to be useful to the public, or even important from the point of view of public benefit, is insufficient to justify what otherwise would be a nuisance. On that I need only to make a brief reference to a case cited during the argument before me, *Shelfer v City of London Electric Lighting Co* [1895] 1 Ch 287. The relevant passage is in the judgment of Lindley LJ (at 315-316). His Lordship said:

> The court has always protested against the notion that it ought to allow a wrong to continue simply because the wrongdoer is able and willing to pay for the injury he may inflict. Neither has the circumstance that the wrongdoer is in some sense a public benefactor (for example, a gas or water company or a sewer authority) ever been considered a sufficient reason for refusing to protect by injunction an individual whose rights are being persistently infringed. Expropriation, even for a money consideration, is only justifiable when Parliament has sanctioned it. Courts of Justice are not like Parliament, which considers whether proposed works will be so beneficial to the public as to justify exceptional legislation, and the deprivation of people of their rights with or without compensation.

In one paragraph of the defence reference was made to the carrying on of the stabling of horses in their present position on the Willis Street property, since the year 1934 or thereabouts. I do not think that Mr Frederico in his final address really advanced the contention that it was a defence to show that

Munro v Southern Dairies cont.

the plaintiff had in any sense "come to the nuisance", as the common phrase is, and it is sufficient to refer to the authorities collected in *Winfield on Torts* (2nd ed), 511-512, to show that the mere fact that a plaintiff can in a sense be said to have "come to a nuisance" is not of itself a defence. The locality, however, is of importance and, as Professor Winfield observes (p 512): "If a man chooses to make his home in the heart of a coal-field or in a manufacturing district, he can expect no more freedom from the discomfort usually associated with such a place than any other resident can."

In the present case it is, of course, material to consider the general nature of the locality of Willis Street, Hampton, and particularly whether the discomfort or inconvenience of which the plaintiff now complains is so characteristic of the general neighbourhood that he ought not to be heard to complain of what other people are accustomed habitually to put up with. Evidence was also led before me as to the general nature of the retail milk distribution trade in Melbourne and the economic necessity for the use of horses for milk delivery in this city. I allowed that evidence, though I had some doubt as to its true relevance. I allowed it because I thought it was necessary to consider an allegation of nuisance against the social background of the time, and there is some authority for the view that the operations of a trade in a locality where it is essential cannot be complained of. Even if that proposition, however, can be maintained to its full extent, which I greatly doubt, it can extend only to what can be shown to be essential and unavoidable in the particular locality. I therefore take into account only within the limits stated the evidence given as to the necessity for horse delivery. …

I am satisfied … that horse delivery is still, and is for some time likely to be, the most suitable and economical method of retail milk delivery in the particular conditions of the Melbourne industry, and that suburban stables are quite common, and for the most part, at all events, occasion no great trouble. But that is not to say that delivery by electric or motor vehicles may not be on the way in this city, and it seems to me that the general improvement in living and social standards in this country, which is a very estimable matter in itself, is likely to cause a necessary acceleration in that process, which milk distributors would be wise to recognise. Though one must judge a question of nuisance in the social and local setting in which it is complained of, changes in the organisation of industry must necessarily follow changes in social conditions. I have now referred to all the witnesses called in this lengthy hearing, and I am in a position to state my conclusions of fact and of law in the light of the legal principles which I enunciated earlier. In my judgment, there has been caused by the defendant's keeping of horses on its Willis Street premises a substantial nuisance of noise, smell and manure and urine, and flies, to the plaintiff, as occupier of the premises at 23 Willis Street, from at least the latter part of 1952 onwards. Though there has recently been some improvements as regards smell and flies, there is still, in my judgment, what amounts to a substantial and actionable nuisance. I do not say that it is occasioned daily, but when the prevailing wind is south-westerly, and the nuisance is continuous in the sense that more often than not the plaintiff must be getting smell and noise. The flies, I think, are probably seasonal, and are troublesome in the hot weather. The nuisance has not been cured since the issue of the writ. With regard to the evidence about the stables, proper management probably could avoid smell and flies sufficiently to constitute a nuisance, if stables were built; but I am not satisfied that on their past record the persons responsible for the conduct of the dairy would avoid the creation of such a nuisance. I say that, not because I think it has any relevance to the question whether the defendant company should or should not proceed to erect stables, but because of the application which was made to me to refuse an injunction in this case, upon the basis of an undertaking by the defendant company to erect stables. That must be a matter resting in the court's discretion, and since I am not satisfied that those responsible for the conduct of this dairy up to the present time would be likely to conduct stables in such a way as to avoid a nuisance of smell or flies, I decline to entertain the suggestion made by Mr Frederico. I decline to entertain it also for the further reason that I am not satisfied that, even if stables were erected, and whoever ran the dairy, a nuisance of noise would be avoided, especially since it is proposed to have more horses there, and since that would involve more

Munro v Southern Dairies cont.

handling of horses and carts, and, doubtless, of milk. Nor am I satisfied, if it be material, that the proposed stables are an essential and unavoidable incident of the conduct of the defendant's business in that locality. In the result, I think there has been a serious nuisance which has gone on too long in disregard of the defendant's neighbours, and their comfort and convenience. I think definitely it is not a case for an award of damages only. There has been a clear invasion of a legal right of the plaintiffs, and an injunction must go. For reasons already stated it is not a case where I would consider refusing an injunction upon the giving of undertakings. In my judgment there should be an injunction to restrain the defendant, by its directors, servants and agents, from causing or committing on the premises at Grenville Street and Willis Street, Hampton, on which it conducts its business, any nuisance (whether by way of smell, noise or flies) to the plaintiff as owner and occupier of premises at 23 Willis Street, Hampton, by the having or keeping of horses on or near the defendant's said premises.

[His Honour then considered the question of damages.]

Judgment for the plaintiff.

[18.75] **Notes&Questions**

1. The interference must be "material" or "substantial" to constitute a nuisance. What is the standard by which this is measured? By the standard of the ordinary person and "not merely according to elegant or dainty modes and habits of living ..." per Bruce V-C, in *Walter v Selfe* (1851) 4 De G & Sm 315 at 322 (64 ER 849 at 851) as quoted in the extracted case. Accordingly, if the plaintiff or their activities are abnormally sensitive, he or she will not be entitled to relief unless able to establish the interference would constitute a nuisance to the ordinary person. Consequently, in *Clarey v The Principal and Counsel of the Women's' College* (1953) 90 CLR 170, the plaintiff's claim of nuisance was unsuccessful and the actions of the students were found to be reasonable. The defendant occupied part of a house and the remainder was occupied by students. The plaintiff had claimed that the noise of the students walking about, scrapping chairs, taking baths, laughing and preparing for bed constituted a nuisance.

2. The factors considered by Scholl J in the principal case as relevant to the "give and take" equation include: the duration of the interference; the frequency of the interference; the extent of the interference, the time of the interference and the locality of the interference.

   As the Court points out, the fact that an interference is temporary does not mean it is not substantial. The courts have often said with respect to noise that the loss of one night's sleep is a substantial interference. However, as a general rule, a temporary interference will usually not qualify as nuisance.

   The time of day may therefore be important in assessing what is a reasonable interference. In *McKenzie v Powley* [1916] SALR 1, the plaintiff's house was next door to a Salvation Army Hall where services began at 7am on Sunday mornings. It was held that the noise of clapping, and shouting "Hallelujah" at that time of morning constituted an unreasonable interference with the plaintiff's enjoyment and use of the house.

The nature and the character of the locality is also taken into account in determining what the plaintiff should be expected to bear; the more exclusively a locality is devoted to one thing the more likely a different activity will be unsuitable. What if the plaintiff moves to a locality where an activity has been carried on for some time, for example, builds a house next to a golf course and balls are continually hit into the plaintiff's backyard; should this preclude any complaint? No. This issue is discussed in detail at [18.135]-[18.140].

3. Subject to the interference being substantial and unreasonable, the courts have found both tangible invasions, such as fire, leaves, tree roots, flood and dust, and intangible invasions, such as smell, noise and offensive sights, to constitute private nuisances. In comparison, certain invasions have been found not to qualify as private nuisance by their very nature. A landowner does not have a right to natural light (*Tapling v Jones* (1854) 11 HLC 290) or to a view from his or her property (*Kent v Johnson* (1973) 21 FLR 177 at 212-213: construction of a multipurpose telecommunications tower on Black Mountain held not to be a nuisance), nor to unhindered television reception (*Hunter v Canary Wharf* [1997] AC 655; compare *Nor-Video Services v Ontario Hydro* (1978) 84 DLR (3d) 221 (Can)). Nor does an interference whereby others can see into another's property constitute a nuisance (*Victoria Park Racing v Taylor* (1937) 58 CLR 479).

For what reason are courts unwilling to find that these types of invasions, even if substantial, are private nuisances? The interferences with respect of view, light and air have occurred as a result of the building a structure upon land and the common law does not prevent someone from building upon their own land, See *Hunter v Canary Wharf Ltd* [1997] AC 655. It is otherwise if something emanates from a neighbour's land, see for example *Thompson-Schwab v Costaki* [1956] 1 WLR 151 in which the court determined that the view of prostitutes bringing clientele they solicited in a nearby street to premises located next to the plaintiffs' residences was a private nuisance. Compare, however, the Western Australian case of *Pioneer Concrete (WA) Pty Ltd v Elwood* [2005] WASCA 48, in which the Court of Appeal refused to strike out an action for "visual pollution", stating that the issue was arguable. (See also the lower court decision of *Elwood v Pioneer Concrete (WA) Pty Ltd* [2002] WASC 32 in which the same conclusion was reached.)

4. The nature of nuisance, both private and public, overlaps with issues of environmental protection, for example, in relation to noise pollution (*McKenzie v Powley* [1916] SALR 1 Note 2 above), pollution of water ways (*Van Son v Forestry Commission of New South Wales* (1995) 86 LGERA 108), and of land (*In re Corby Group Litigation* [2009] 2 WLR 609 (discussed at [18.175] Note 1)). It has therefore been argued that nuisance may be utilised as a vehicle for environmental protection. Success in this area has been limited, however, due principally to the restrictive standing requirements of both private [18.50] and public nuisance [18.15]-[18.25]. Courts have also argued that this is an area better regulated by the legislature, which mirrors Goff LJ's conclusion in *Cambridge Water Co Ltd v Eastern Collieries Plc* [1994]1 All ER 53 at 75: "given that so much well-informed and carefully structured legislation is now being put in place for this purpose, there is less need for the courts to develop a common law principle to achieve the same end and indeed it may well be undesirable that they should do so".

Legislation exists in all Australian jurisdictions with the purpose of promoting use and protection of the environment: See for example *Environmental Protection Act 1997* (ACT); *Environmental Planning and Assessment Act 1979* (NSW); *Environmental Assessment Act* (NT); *Environmental Protection Act 1994* (Qld); *Environment Protection Act 1993* (SA); *Environmental Management & Pollution Act 1994* (Tas); *Environment Protection Act 1970* (Vic); *Environment Protection Act 1986* (WA). For further discussion see R Lyster, Z Lipman and N Franklin, Environmental and Planning Law in New South Wales (Federation Press, 2007) at pp 2-5.

Assessment of the defendant's activity

[18.80] The defendant's actions and the utility or usefulness of the defendant's conduct are considerations in assessing the give and take. This is considered in the following case.

Hollywood Silver Fox Farm v Emmett

[18.85] *Hollywood Silver Fox Farm v Emmett* [1936] 2 KB 468 King's Bench Division

(footnotes omitted)

[The plaintiffs bred silver foxes on land adjoining that of the defendant. The plaintiff erected a prominent advertising sign which the defendant requested be removed because he feared it would be detrimental to the development of his building estate. When the plaintiffs refused to remove it the defendant threatened the plaintiff's managing director that during the breeding season he would shoot with black powder upon his own land as near as possible to the breeding pens, so that the plaintiffs would not raise a single cub. He carried out this threat and the shooting greatly alarmed the vixens and thereby reduced the number of cubs reared.]

MACNAGHTEN J: 472 This action, which was tried before me without a jury, was brought by the plaintiffs, Hollywood Silver Fox Farms Ltd, to recover damages for nuisance by noise and for an injunction. It raises once again the question, which was debated in the case of *Allen v Flood* [1898] AC 1 whether the decision of the Court of King's Bench in the famous duck decoy case, *Keeble v Hickeringill* (1706) 11 Mod 74; 103 ER 1127 was well-founded.

[After stating the facts as set out above, his Lordship continued.]

In these circumstances the decision of the Court of King's Bench in *Keeble v Hickeringill* (1706) 11 Mod 74; 103 ER 1127, if it be well-founded, is a clear authority that the defendant has committed an actionable wrong. In that case the plaintiff, the owner of a duck decoy, brought an action against the defendant for shooting at and disturbing the ducks in his decoy. The jury found a verdict for the plaintiff and the question whether the action was maintainable was argued before the Full Court.

During the argument there was some question whether the defendant had actually trespassed on the plaintiff's land, and according to the report in 11 Mod (at 74) Lord Holt said: "But suppose the defendant had shot in his own ground, if he had occasion to shoot, it would have been one thing; but to shoot on purpose to damage the plaintiff is another thing and a wrong."

The court decided that the action was maintainable and judgment was entered for the plaintiffs.

Mr Roche, who put the case for the defendant extremely well, submitted that the defendant was entitled to shoot on his own land, and that even if his conduct was malicious he had not committed any actionable wrong. In support of his argument, Mr Roche relied mainly on the decision of the House of Lords in the case of *Bradford Corp v Pickles* [1895] AC 587. In that case the Corporation of Bradford sought to restrain Mr Pickles from sinking a shaft on land which belonged to him because, according to their view, his object in sinking the shaft was to draw away from their land water which

Hollywood Silver Fox Farm v Emmett cont.

would otherwise come into their reservoirs. Mr Pickles, they said, was acting maliciously, his sole object being to do harm to the Corporation. The House of Lords decided once and for all that in such a case the motive of the defendant is immaterial.

In the case of *Allen v Flood* [1898] AC 1 at 124, Lord Herschell, commenting on the decision in *Bradford Corp v Pickles* [1895] AC 587, said: "It has recently been held in this House, in the case of *Bradford Corp v Pickles* [1895] AC 587, that acts done by the defendant upon his own land were not actionable when they were within his legal rights, even though his motive were to prejudice his neighbour. The language of the noble and learned Lords was distinct." The Lord Chancellor said: "This is not a case where the state of mind of the person doing the act can affect the right. If it was a lawful act, however ill the motive might be, he had a right to do it. If it was an unlawful act, however good the motive might be, he would have no right to do it. The statement was confined to the class of cases then before the House; but I apprehend that what was said is not applicable only to rights of property, but is equally applicable to the exercise by an individual of his other rights."

Mr Roche argued that in the present case the defendant had not committed any nuisance at all in the legal sense of the term, and he referred to the case of *Robinson v Kilvert* (1889) 41 Ch D 88. … Mr Roche submitted that the keeping of a silver fox farm is not an ordinary use of land, and that the shooting would have caused no alarm to the animals which are usually to be found on farms in Kent or done them any harm.

Apart from the case of *Keeble v Hickeringill* (1706) 11 Mod 74 at 130; 11 East 574 n; 3 Salk 9; Holt 14 [103 ER 1127] there is authority for the view that in an action for nuisance by noise the intention of the person making the noise must be considered. In the case of *Gaunt v Fynney* (1872) LR 8 Ch App 8 at 12, Lord Selborne, delivering the judgment of the court, said: "A nuisance by noise (supposing malice to be out of the question) is emphatically a question of degree." The parenthetical statement, "supposing malice to be out of the question", clearly indicated that his Lordship thought that in the case of an alleged nuisance by noise where the noise was made maliciously different considerations would apply from those applicable where the defendant had in the words of Lord Holt "occasion" to make the noise. In *Christie v Davey* [1893] 1 Ch 316 at 326 the plaintiffs, Mr and Mrs Christie, and the defendant lived side by side in semi-detached houses in Brixton. Mrs Christie was a teacher of music, and her family were also musical, and throughout the day sounds of music pervaded their house and were heard in the house of their neighbour. The defendant did not like the music that he heard, and by way of retaliation he took to making noises himself, beating trays and rapping on the wall. The action came on for trial before North J, who delivered judgment in favour of the plaintiffs and granted an injunction restraining the defendant from causing or permitting any sounds or noises in his house so as to vex or annoy the plaintiffs or the occupiers of their house. In the course of his judgment, he said (at 326) after dealing with the facts as he found them, "The result is that I think I am bound to interfere for the protection of the plaintiffs. In my opinion the noises which were made in the defendant's house were not of a legitimate kind. They were what, to use the language of Lord Selborne in *Gaunt v Fynney* (1872) LR 8 Ch App 8, 'ought to be regarded as excessive and unreasonable'. I am satisfied that they were made deliberately and maliciously for the purpose of annoying the plaintiffs." Then come the significant words: "If what has taken place had occurred between two sets of persons both perfectly innocent, I should have taken an entirely different view of the case. But I am persuaded that what was done by the defendant was done only for the purpose of annoyance, and in my opinion it was not a legitimate use of the defendant's house to use it for the purpose of vexing and annoying his neighbours."

The case of *Ibottson v Peat* (1865) 3 H & C 644 [159 ER 684] affords an exact precedent for the statement of claim in this action. Mr Ibottson was a landowner in the parish of Brampton, in Derbyshire, and his land adjoined a grouse moor belonging to the Duke of Rutland. Mr Ibottson, for the purpose of inducing the grouse on the Duke of Rutland's moor to come on to his own land, put

Hollywood Silver Fox Farm v Emmett cont.

down corn and thereby lured and enticed the grouse to come away from the Duke's land. The defendant, Peat, was it appears, a gamekeeper in the employ of the Duke of Rutland, and, in order to prevent Mr Ibottson from getting any benefit from such unneighbourly conduct, he let off fireworks, rockets, and bombs as near as he could get to Mr Ibottson's land for the purpose of frightening away the grouse which had been attracted by the corn. In answer to the declaration in that case the defendant set up as a plea that he was justified in letting off the rockets and bombs because of the improper conduct of the plaintiff in luring away the Duke's grouse. The question for the consideration of the court was whether that was a good plea, and it was held to be bad.

The cases to which I have referred were decided before the decision of the House of Lords in *Bradford Corp v Pickles* [1895] AC 587; and the question therefore arises whether those cases must now be considered as overruled. It is to be observed that in *Allen v Flood* [1898] AC 1 at 101 Lord Watson discussed fully the case of *Keeble v Hickeringill* (1706) 11 Mod 74; 11 East 474 *n*; 3 Salk 9; Holt 14 [103 ER 1127] and said with reference to that case: "No proprietor has an absolute right to create noises upon his own land, because any right which the law gives him is qualified by the condition that it must not be exercised to the nuisance of his neighbours or of the public. If he violates that condition he commits a legal wrong, and if he does so intentionally he is guilty of a malicious wrong, in its strict sense."

In my opinion the decision of the House of Lords in *Bradford Corp v Pickles* [1895] AC 587 has no bearing on such cases as this. I therefore think that the plaintiff is entitled to maintain this action. I think also that in the circumstances an injunction should be granted restraining the defendant from committing a nuisance by the discharge of firearms or the making of other loud noises in the vicinity of the Hollywood Silver Fox Farm during the breeding season – namely, between 1 January and 15 June – so as to alarm or disturb the foxes kept by the plaintiffs at the said farm, or otherwise to injure the plaintiff company.

Judgment for plaintiffs.

[18.90] **Notes&Questions**

1. The motives behind the defendant's acts may have a direct bearing upon the give and take of the relationship. Compare the principal case with *Rattray v Daniels* (1959) 17 DLR (2d) 134 (Can) in which the defendant used a bulldozer to clear land adjacent to the plaintiff's property knowing that the plaintiff's minks were sensitive to noise and that the noise would cause the mother minks to kill their young. The defendant had stopped initial clearing of his land when he learnt of the problem, but resumed it at a later date. The Court found that his actions were not a nuisance as they were not done maliciously, and it was impossible for the defendant to complete the clearing and levelling of the land because the only time of the year during which the bulldozer was available happened to coincide with the mink breeding season.

   In *Stoakes v Brydges* [1958] QWN 5, the defendant believed himself injured by noise made by servants of the plaintiff's company (a milk vendor). In retaliation he took to dialling the plaintiff's telephone number in the middle of the night. The court issued a perpetual injunction. Compare this, however, with the case of *Fraser v Booth* (1949) 50 SR (NSW) 113. There, the defendant's retaliatory measures took the form of noise-making, hosing and the throwing of firecrackers. Except for the use of firecrackers, these behaviours were found not to be actionable: the noises "were made under the stress of annoyance from an existing nuisance in the hope of alleviating that annoyance, or having it alleviated by the person responsible for it. They cannot be regarded as merely malicious and spiteful acts done simply to cause damage to the defendant".

2. The utility of the defendant's activities is a relevant consideration. In *Munro v Southern Dairies Ltd* [1955] VLR 332 (extracted [18.70]) Scholl J reached the conclusion that the delivery of retail milk by way of horse was and still would be for some time the most suitable and economical method of retail delivery. On the facts of the case the utility of the defendant's activity was not enough to overcome the nuisance created by the keeping of the horses. More recently in *Cohen v City of Perth* [2000] WASC 306 the defendant city council's collection of garbage on a nightly basis under the plaintiff's apartment was found to constitute a nuisance even though the apartment was located in a downtown area in which several restaurants were located and daily garbage collection a necessity.

3. The Court will also consider whether there were steps that could be taken by the defendant to minimise the nuisance. See *Rattray v Daniels* (1959) 17 DLR (2d) 134 (Can) (above Note 1); *Munro v South Dairies* [1955] VLR 332 (extracted [18.70]) in which the possibility of building stables to minimise the nuisance was considered and *Campbelltown Golf Club Ltd v Winton* [1998] NSWCA 257(discussed at [8.125] Note 3) in which the NSW Court of Appeal considered that the nuisance caused by the barrage of golf balls onto the plaintiff's land could be minimized by the re-siting of the direction of the hole and/or by the use of appropriate screens.

Material physical damage

[18.95] Whilst private nuisance does not require that the plaintiff suffer actual physical damage, if the plaintiff's property has been physically damaged, will this damage be sufficient to constitute a nuisance? Yes subject to the physical damage being of sufficient degree. In *Halsey v Esso Petroleum Co Ltd* [1961] 1 WLR 683, the plaintiff, who lived in a residential area opposite the oil depot, alleged that acid smuts emitted from the depot's chimneys had stained and damaged washing hung out to dry and the paintwork on the plaintiff's car. The court (at 691) concluded that "liability for nuisance by harmful deposits could be established by proving damage by the deposits to the property in question, provided of course that the injury was not merely trivial". *Corbett v Pallas* [1995] Aust Torts Reports 62,236 (Qld Ct App) is an example of physical damage adjudged to be of sufficient degree. The plaintiff's premises suffered material damage from flooding as a result of the defendant's construction of a swimming pool without installation of appropriate drainage for sub-surface water.

In coming to the decision above, the court in *Halsey* (at 691) refuted the suggestion that negligence was a prerequisite to physical damage sounding a cause of action in private nuisance. In addition, the court found that there was no need to take into account other factors such as locality, the physical damage being sufficient to qualify as substantial and unreasonable interference without the necessity of addressing these factors.

Who can be sued?

[18.100] Liability for the tort of private nuisance is determined by reference to the distinction between misfeasance and nonfeasance. A person who creates a nuisance by an act of misfeasance is strictly liable. In contrast, where the nuisance arises by nonfeasance, liability generally depends upon proof of fault on the part of the occupier. Exceptionally, where the nuisance arises from failure to repair a structure, liability may exist in the absence of any fault, (*Cartwright v McLaine* (1979) 143 CLR 549 at 566 per Gibbs J). Therefore, a person can be sued for nuisance in three ways: if they are the creator of the nuisance; if they authorise the nuisance; or if they adopt or continue the nuisance.

Creator of the nuisance

[18.105] It is not necessary that the defendant be the occupier of land to be liable for a nuisance. It is sufficient the defendant has created the nuisance. For example, an excavator was found to be liable in *Pantalone v Alaouie* (1989) 18 NSWLR 119 and the picketing of the plaintiff's premises was found to be a nuisance in *Animal Liberation (Vic) Inc v Gasser* [1991] 1 VR 51. The creator of a nuisance is strictly liable for the nuisance that he or she creates. This is so even if the person is no longer in occupation of the land from which the nuisance emanates, provided that they have created it. In *Roswell v Prior* (1701) 12 Mod 635; 88 ER 1570, a tenant for a term of years erected a house on the leased premises which stopped "ancient lights" to premises in the occupation of the plaintiff. Under property law in England, an owner of land for 20 years or longer was entitled to maintain the level of natural lighting ("ancient lights") which he or she had enjoyed during this period of time. Another, therefore, could not obstruct this right to light (a right to light does not exist in Australia). The plaintiff brought proceedings in nuisance for the interference with his right and obtained damages. The defendant then leased the property to a third party. The plaintiff brought another action in nuisance against the defendant for the continuance of the nuisance. It was held that the defendant as creator of the nuisance remained liable.

Authorisation of the nuisance

[18.110] If an occupier permits others to undertake activities that constitute a nuisance, then the occupier is also liable for the nuisance created by that individual. Consequently, in *De Jager v Payneham & Magill Lodges Hall Inc*, (1984) 36 SASR 498, the defendant owner-occupier of a hall, which was hired out for functions, was liable for the excessive noise levels created by those who hired the hall. Even though the defendant made all reasonable efforts to stop the noise and even installed a noise regulator on the amplification equipment, which the hirers neutralised, the defendant was still found to have authorised the nuisance. Liability was imposed upon the basis that if one hires out property for a particular purpose, which involves a special danger of nuisance, they are liable for the nuisance created by the hirer. See also *R v Shorrock* [1994] QB 279 discussed at [18.35] Note 2.

Compare this, with the case of *Peden Pty Ltd v Bortolazzo* [2006] QCA 350 in which the appellant brought an action against the respondent as landlord of tenants who were creating a nuisance through excessive noise, repeated smoke (through burning off), excessive barking of a dog and unruly and drunken behaviour at all hours of the day and night. There was evidence that the landlord was aware at least of these complaints. The court relied upon well established precedent to determine that the respondent landlord was not liable for the tenants' nuisance unless she had authorised it, and given that the terms of the tenancy expressly prohibited the creation of a nuisance, this was not the case.

Continuer or adopter of the nuisance

[18.115] A defendant who does not create the nuisance, but who continues or adopts the nuisance, can be liable for that nuisance. The next case discusses an example of an occupier being considered as "continuing" a nuisance.

Stockwell v Victoria

[18.120] *Stockwell v State of Victoria* [2001] VSC 497 Supreme Court of Victoria

(footnotes omitted)

GILLARD J: 231 The plaintiff alleges that the defendant State, as owner and occupier of the Reference Area and/or surrounding Crown land, permitted wild dogs to occupy the said areas and permitted them to leave the areas, move onto his top paddocks and kill or severely injure his property, namely, his sheep. The alleged nuisance has its genesis in wild dogs moving onto land owned and occupied by the State, without any human intervention, and the wild dogs which are not owned, controlled or managed by the State or its employees, move onto the plaintiff's property and cause a nuisance. In those circumstances, the question is why should the State, as owner and occupier of the surrounding land, be under any obligation to protect the plaintiff's property rather than the plaintiff protecting his own personal interests against the intrusion of the marauding dogs, which cause him damage?

232 The old law did not oblige the land owner on whose land the problem arose from, what might be described as, natural causes to do anything, but the modern law has recognised such an obligation upon the land owner, in certain circumstances.

233 The modern law can be traced from *Sedleigh-Denfield v O'Callaghan* [1940] AC 880; 56 TLR 887; [1940] 3 All ER 349, *Goldman v Hargrave* (1966) 115 CLR 458, in the Privy Council, [1967] 1 AC 645 and *Leakey v National Trust for Places of Historic Interest* (1980) QB 485. All these cases recognised a liability in a land owner for damage caused to an adjoining land owner by reason of things which occurred on his land, even though they occurred as a result of natural causes or the actions of a trespasser. In the *Sedleigh-Denfield case*, water escaped onto the plaintiff's land from the defendant's land because a trespasser had installed a pipe, and the occupier was held liable for failing to take reasonable means to eradicate the nuisance, after he had knowledge of its existence. The House of Lords held that the knowledge of a responsible servant was the knowledge of the occupier.

234 In the *Goldman case*, a gum tree was set on fire during a storm and the occupier took some steps to extinguish the fire, but they were inadequate. The fire was whipped up by the weather and travelled across to the adjoining land owner, who suffered damage. The High Court and the Privy Council held the occupier liable.

235 In *Leakey's case*, the defendant's land had a large mound of soil and rubble on it, and over the years, soil and rubble fell onto the plaintiff's land due to natural weathering and the nature of the soil. The defendant was well aware of the instability of the land. After the dry summer of 1976, a crack opened up in the mound. The defendant refused to do anything about it, and some weeks later a large quantity of earth and tree stumps fell on the plaintiff's land. It was the contention of the defendant that because it was not responsible for the mound and secondly, the natural movement of the land was the cause of the fall of soil, it was not liable. The Court of Appeal held that it was.

236 The principles established in those cases have been applied in a number of cases in England since 1980.

237 The modern law can be summarised as follows. Where a nuisance has been created by the actions or omissions of a trespasser, or by some other means, without the actions, omissions, authority

Stockwell v Victoria cont.

or permission of the occupier of land, the occupier is liable if he has knowledge or ought to know of the existence of the nuisance, it is foreseeable that damage could occur, and he fails to comply with a measured duty of care to abate the nuisance.

238 In *Goldman case* in the Privy Council, the Judicial Committee held that there was a general duty of care upon occupiers in relation to hazards occurring on their land, whether natural or man made. Lord Wilberforce, at 662, described the duty as "a measured duty of care by occupiers to remove or reduce hazards to their neighbours".

239 However, the duty is different to the normal duty of care which rests upon a person to take reasonable care in the particular circumstances. This measured duty of care takes into account the resources of the land owner, the gravity of the nuisance, and the ability of the land owner to eradicate it.

240 Lord Wilberforce, at 663, described the scope of the duty. In the later case of *Leakey*, McGaw J dealt with the scope of the duty.

241 In my opinion, the plaintiff, in order to prove his case in nuisance against the State, has to establish the following elements–

(i) That the plaintiff is a person in actual possession of the land affected, either as a freeholder or tenant of the land in question or as a licensee with exclusive possession of the land – see *Hunter v Canary Wharf Ltd* [1997] AC 655, at 688.

242 The plaintiff was, at all relevant times, the registered proprietor of the top paddocks, and has the necessary interest in the property to bring this proceeding. No argument was addressed to the contrary.

(ii) That the activity which causes the damage to the plaintiff's enjoyment of his land, is a nuisance, ie interferes with the enjoyment of his rights in his land.

(iii) That the activity which constitutes the nuisance by the defendant occupier was created by the defendant occupier or was created by the actions or omissions of another or by natural causes and with knowledge of its existence or circumstances where he ought to have known of its existence, suffers the nuisance to continue.

243 In *Sedleigh-Denfield v O'Callaghan* [1940] AC 880; 56 TLR 887; [1940] 3 All ER 349, supra, the defendant's servant was aware of the existence of the trap and the defendant occupier was held liable for failing to take reasonable steps to stop the nuisance escaping to the next door neighbour, despite the fact that the nuisance was created by the actions of a trespasser, for which the occupier would not be vicariously liable. In *Goldman v Hargrave* (1967) 1 AC 645, the principle was extended to a hazard caused on the defendant's land by the operation of nature. There is no difference in principle between the creation of a nuisance by first, the occupier, secondly, a trespasser, or thirdly, the forces of nature, if the defendant knew or ought to have known of the existence of the nuisance.

(iv) Once a defendant occupier knows or is presumed to know of the hazards on his land and if as a reasonable man he could foresee that the defect or condition if not remedied may cause damage to his neighbour's land, a measured duty of care arises.

244 As I have said, the concept of the "measured duty of care" was stated by Lord Wilberforce in *Goldman's case*, who described it as follows–

> So far it has been possible to consider the existence of a duty, in general terms. But the matter cannot be left there without some definition of the scope of his duty. How far does it go? What is the standard of the effort required? What is the position as regards expenditure? It is not enough to say merely that these must be reasonable, since what is reasonable to one man may be very unreasonable, and indeed ruinous, to another: the law must take account of the fact that the occupier on whom the duty is cast has, ex hypothesi, had this hazard thrust upon him through no seeking or fault of his own. ... *One may say in general terms that the*

Stockwell v Victoria cont.

> *existence of a duty must be based upon knowledge of the hazard, ability to foresee the consequences of not checking or removing it, and the ability to abate it.* (at 663) (emphasis added)

245 In *Leakey v National Trust for Places of Historic Interest* (1980) QB 485, Megaw LJ, after considering the authorities, said, concerning the scope of the duty, at 524–

> The duty is the duty to do that which is reasonable in all the circumstances, and no more than that, if anything, is reasonable, to prevent or minimise the known risk of damage or injury to one's neighbour or to his property. The considerations with which the law is familiar are all to be taken into account in deciding whether there has been a breach of duty, and if so, what that breach is, and whether it is causative of the damage in respect of which the claim is made. Thus, there will fall to be considered the extent of the risk; what, so far as reasonable can be foreseen, are the chances that anything untoward will happen or that any damage will be caused? What is to be foreseen as to the possible extent of the damage if the risk becomes a reality? Is it practicable to prevent, or to minimise, the happening of any damage? If it is practical, how simple or how difficult are the measures which could be taken, how much and how lengthy work do they involve, and what is a probable cost of such works? Was there sufficient time for preventative action to have been taken, by persons acting reasonably in relation to the known risk, between the time when it became known to, or should have been realised by, the defendant, and the time when the damage occurred? Factors such as these, so far as they apply in a particular case, fall to be weighed in deciding whether the defendant's duty of care requires, or required him, to do anything, and if so, what.

246 It is clear from what his Lordship said that there are a number of factors that need to be taken into account.

247 The relevant considerations stated by both Lord Wilberforce and Megaw LJ are not an exhaustive list of relevant considerations. Nevertheless, they give a good guide to determining what the measured duty of care demanded in the circumstances.

(v) That the plaintiff suffered damage as a result of the nuisance.

(vi) That the failure to prevent or minimise the nuisance, was a cause of the plaintiff's injury or damage.

(vii) That an employee, agent or independent contractor of the State, acting in the course and scope of his employment or engagement, was guilty of the wrongdoing, and if sued personally by the plaintiff would have been liable.

248 This added element comes about because the plaintiff is suing the Crown.

249 The modern law of nuisance in cases where the defendant does not create the nuisance is very similar to the modern law of negligence. Indeed, many cases of nuisance also involve liability in common law negligence. In *Goldman's case*, two of the judges in the High Court found against the defendant occupier in nuisance and negligence, Windeyer J held the defendant liable in negligence, and the Privy Council decided the case in negligence but made it quite clear that the case could also have been decided in nuisance. At 656, Lord Wilberforce said –

> As this board has recently explained in the *Wagon Mound No 2*, the tort of nuisance, uncertain in its boundary, may comprise a wide variety of situations, in some of which negligence plays no part, in others of which it is decisive. The present case is one where liability, if it exists, rests upon negligence and nothing else; whether it falls within or overlaps the boundaries of nuisance is a question of classification which need not here be resolved. …

342 The authorities support the conclusion that the presence of animals ferae naturae on land can be cause of a private nuisance and make the land owner liable. But the basis for liability was some fault on the part of the land holder.

Stockwell v Victoria cont.

343 Fault by a land holder in respect of the commission of a nuisance was essential – see *Torette House Pty Ltd v Berkman* (1939) 62 CLR 637 at 659 per Dixon J. If these were operations on the land which produced the nuisance, the plaintiff was more likely to succeed.

344 The law has moved on since 1939 and in the following year, the important case of *Sedleigh-Denfield v O'Callaghan* [1940] AC 880; 56 TLR 887; [1940] 3 All ER 349 was decided. But in addition, in this State, from 1949, Parliament imposed a duty on all land occupiers, including the Crown and a Minister of the Crown, to take reasonable action to destroy and suppress all vermin on their land.

345 Given the old law which, in my view, imposed liability where the animals came onto land and caused damage because of the extraordinary non-natural or unreasonable action on the part of the adjoining land holder, coupled with the obligations imposed by the *Vermin and Noxious Weeds Act 1958* (and the new regime under the *Catchment and Land Protection Act 1994*) on land holders, no land holder in this State can defend any claim brought against him in nuisance and negligence, on the ground that the animals concerned were ferae naturae and he had no control over them.

346 No longer could an owner-occupier, up to 15 December 1994, sit back and do nothing in respect to animals ferae naturae which were on his land. It is not open to the State to defend this proceeding on the basis that it had no obligation to control wild dogs on its land because they were always there, and were not owned or controlled by it.

347 The question is, did the State's employees know, or should they have known, of the nuisance that interfered with the plaintiff's enjoyment of his top paddocks, and did they permit its existence? In my opinion, the evidence of knowledge is all one way. ...

372 In my opinion, the relevant employees, from 1 July 1989 through to 1996, knew of the extent of the risk, could reasonably foresee the likelihood of damage to the plaintiff's stock, but, in my view, failed to take reasonable steps to prevent or minimise the happening of the damage. It would not have been difficult to lay traps within the Reference Area, it would not have been difficult to increase the poison bait programmes around the area and also involve programmes within the area. To attempt to capture dogs around the edges of the area was inadequate. A programme should have been established to eradicate or minimise the number of wild dogs within the area itself. This reasonable preventative action was not taken and, in my opinion, the probabilities are that if it had, the problem could have been substantially minimised to the point of eradicating the dogs in the vicinity.

[18.125] **Notes&Questions**

1. As Gillard J states, "[t]he modern law can be traced from *Sedleigh-Denfield v O'Callaghan*, *Goldman v Hargrave* (1966) 115 CLR 458, in the Privy Council, [1967] 1 AC 645 and *Leakey v National Trust for Places of Historic Interest* (1980) QB 485." A person will be liable if he or she adopts or continues a nuisance that has been created by another or by a natural occurrence. A person will be taken to have adopted or continued a nuisance if he or she had knowledge or should have had knowledge of the nuisance and did not take reasonable steps to abate it. As *Stockwell v State of Victoria* [2001] VSC 497 discusses, the general principle applies whether the hazard is natural or man-made and can include the actions of a trespasser.

   There has been debate, however, as to whether the principle applies to the escape of water from the defendant's land. It has been generally accepted that a proprietor of land will not be liable merely because surface water flows naturally from the proprietor's land on to lower land: *Elston v Dore* (1983) 57 ALJR 83. English authority, however, suggests that even in the case of surface water there may at least be a duty to abate, or if this is too expensive to permit the neighbour whose property is at risk, to do so, Megaw LJ (at 526-527) in *Leakey's case*.

2. The principal case also discusses the fact that a "measured duty" arises once the defendant becomes aware of the nuisance, and this is limited to taking "reasonable steps" to abate the nuisance. What are reasonable steps in the circumstances? A list of factors (though not exhaustive) are discussed by Megaw J (at 524) in *Leakey v National Trust for Places of Historic Interest* (1980) QB 485, extracted in the principal case, that assist in making this assessment. In *Owners Strata Plan 4085 v Mallone* [2006] NSWSC 1381, the plaintiff sued the defendant in respect of rocks falling onto the plaintiffs' property (flats) from a cliff face on the defendant's land. The person who quarried the area prior to subdivision created the nuisance. However the defendant was aware of the falling rocks and as such had to take reasonable steps to abate. The cost of stabilising the rock wall was approximately $85,000. Given that the defendant was a widowed pensioner who lacked the financial means to effect the repairs, and that the plaintiffs were made up of a number of owners of flats who could better absorb the burden, the defendant was not required to bear the entire cost, however she was to contribute and to allow reasonable access to her property and permit reasonable disturbance for the repair to be effected.

3. For other examples in an urban setting, see *Campbelltown Gold Club Ltd v Winton* [1998] NSWSC 257 and *Challen v McLeod Country Golf Club* [2004] QCA 358. Both cases are similar in that they involved, over a period of years, a large number of golf balls being hit onto the plaintiff's' land. In the case of *Challen*, at least 526 golf balls landed in the plaintiff's property in a period of one year. The balls were hit by players who had the permission of the golf course to use the golf course's facilities. Some, not all, of the balls caused damage, for example, broken tiles and windows and on one occasion a ball hit the plaintiff. As MacPherson JA stated (at[2]) "[i]f an occupier of land permits a nuisance to be conducted on its land of which it knows or ought to know, it becomes liable for that nuisance and its potentially harmful consequences to others from the time at which it acquired that knowledge or ought to have done so."

4. If the defendant is not the creator of the nuisance, is not aware of it, and is not required to have been aware it, he or she will not be liable. For example, in *Montana Hotels Pty Ltd v Fasson Pty Ltd* (1986) 69 ALR 258, water was found in the cellar of the plaintiff's hotel. It was traced to a faulty down pipe on the newly built building next door, which had been leased by the defendant. The defendant was not liable as he had not created the nuisance nor did he know or have the means of knowing that there was a fault in the down pipe before the water was discovered. See also *Sutherland Shire Council v Becker* [2006] NSWCA 344 in which the court determined that the Council had no reason to be aware that its drainage pipes were leaking causing saturation of neighbouring land and resultant land slippage. Inspection of the pipes from an operational perspective was conducted upon complaint and whilst aware of slippage of land between two properties, there was no indication that this was caused by water seepage from the council's pipelines.

5. *Stockwell* involved the nuisance of feral dogs entering the plaintiff's property. What if a domestic dog bites a person or an elephant escapes from handlers at the circus and tramples a child? At common law, the *scienter* rule operates in respect of the responsibility of owners and keepers for the acts of their animals. It is a form of strict liability. The rule proceeds upon the basis of the classification of the animal; that is the circumstances that lead to liability will depend upon whether the animal is classified as *ferae naturare* (wild) or as *mansuetae naturarae* (domesticated). If the animal is wild, for example a chimpanzee or a tiger, strict liability is imposed and it does not matter that the keeper of the animal took all possible precautions to stop the injury occurring. If the animal is domesticated, for example a dog or a cat, liability will only be imposed if the keeper had knowledge of the vicious propensity of the particular animal, for example the predisposition of their dog to bite. The ability to sue based on the scienter rule in the Australian Capital Territory, New South Wales and South Australia has been abolished: ACT: CLWA, s 214; *Animals Act 1977* (NSW), s 7(2)(a), *Wrongs Act 1936* (SA), s 18. Actions in these jurisdictions can still be instituted in negligence, nuisance and trespass in respect of the acts of animals.

   Legislation has been passed in all jurisdictions governing the control of dogs. The legislation generally makes it unnecessary to prove a previous vicious propensity of which the owner had actual knowledge. The standard approach is that the owner is deemed to be strictly liable for any injury caused by the dog. Most obviously this includes dog bites but has also been extended to include injury to motorists caused by straying dogs. See *Domestic Animals Act 2000* (ACT), *Companion Animals Act 1998* (NSW); *Law Reform (Miscellaneous Provisions) Act* (NT), *Dog and Cat Management Act 1995* (SA); *Dog Control Act 2000* (Tas); *Domestic (Feral and Nuisance Act) 1994* (Vic); *Dog Act 1976* (WA). The Queensland legislation does not impose liability and preserves the common law actions: *Animal Management (Cats and Dogs) Act 2008* (Qld).

DEFENCES

[18.130] A defendant may be able to continue with the interference objected to, if he or she is able to establish one of the following defences: prescription, conduct or consent of the plaintiff or statutory authorisation and possibly contributory negligence. The most commonly used of these defences, the conduct and consent of the plaintiff and statutory authorisation, will form the basis of the discussion that follows. It is important, though, that the reader has a general understanding of prescription and the role, if any, of contributory negligence. Prescription occurs where the nuisance has been carried on openly, continuously and as of right for at least 20 years; this continuous use can give rise to an easement in favour of the benefitting land *Sturges v Bridgman* (1879) 11 Ch D 852. There may be difficulties in enforcing these easements over Torrens title land, see P Butt, Land Law (5th ed, Lawbook Co, 2006), p 780. It is also possible that contributory negligence may be an available defence, however, arguably only where nuisance has been created as a result of the defendant's negligent actions: *Mitchell v Tsiros (No 2)* [1982] VR 301; *White v Humphries* (1984) 1 MVR 426 (WA FC); *Stockwell v State of Victoria* [2001] VSC 497 (extracted [18.120]) and *Volman t/as Volman Engineering v Lobb* [2005] NSWCA 348. If, like highway cases, all actions for nuisance based upon the negligent conduct of the defendant are now subsumed within negligence, contributory negligence will no longer be a defence in an action for nuisance.

Conduct or consent of the plaintiff

[18.135] The provision of express consent by a plaintiff will nullify the alleged nuisance. Toleration of the nuisance, however, is not evidence of the plaintiff's implied consent. Upon the same basis it is no defence to state that the plaintiff "came to the nuisance" and therefore cannot complain, nor that by the act of coming to the nuisance the plaintiff has impliedly consented to it. The reasons for this rule were discussed in *Sturges v Bridgman* (1879) 11 Ch D 852. In this case the defendant occupied a store and carried on the business of a confectioner. For this purpose he used the rear of the house as a kitchen and for over 20 years he had used two large mortars for grinding. The plaintiff, a physician, occupied the adjoining property, which previously had a garden at the rear until a recent extension. The garden had been separated from the defendant's premises by a wall and this wall now was a mutual wall between the defendant's kitchen and the plaintiff's new consulting room. The noise from the mortars seriously inconvenienced the plaintiff's use of his new consulting room. The court dealt with the argument of whether or not coming to a nuisance should preclude the ability to sue for nuisance concluding that public interest necessitated that coming to a nuisance was no answer:

> It would be on the one hand in a very high degree unreasonable and undesirable that there should be a right of action for acts which are not in the present condition of the adjoining land, and possibly never will be any annoyance or inconvenience to either its owner or occupier; and it would be on the other hand in an equally degree unjust, and, from a public point of view, inexpedient that the use and value of the adjoining land should, for all time and under all circumstances, be restricted and diminished by reason of the continuance of acts incapable of physical interruption, and which the law gives no power to prevent. Individual cases of hardship may occur in the strict carrying out of the principle upon which we found our judgment, but the negation of the principle would lead even more to individual hardship, and would at the same time produce a prejudicial effect upon the development of land for residential purposes. ((1879) 11 Ch D 852 at 865)

[18.140] **Notes&Questions**

1. This rule has been affirmed in Australia in *Campbelltown Golf Club Ltd v Winton* [1998] NSWSC 257 and *Challen v McLeod Country Golf Club* [2004] QCA 358 (discussed at [8.125] Note 3). In both cases It was no answer to the plaintiff's claim that the golf courses had been in existence before the plaintiff's moved to their homes. In *Proprietors Strata Plan 14198 v Cowell* (1989) 24 NSWLR 478, the court held that it was no defence to the plaintiff's claim for damage caused by tree roots that the tree's roots had encroached upon the plaintiff's property prior to the building of the units nor that the units had been erected close to the boundary and that this had contributed to the problem. Compare these cases with the dissenting judgment of Lord Denning in *Miller v Jackson* [1977] QB 966, in which his Lordship concluded that the homeowners who bought a newly built house next to a cricket ground that had been in existence for 70 years should be expected to live with the nuisance. Who do you think has the better argument?
2. Upon the same basis it has been held that it is no defence to a nuisance that the activity in question will benefit the public: see *York Bros (Trading) Pty Ltd v Commissioner of Main Roads* [1983] 1 NSWLR 391 at 395-397 (discussed at [18.145]). See also comments to this effect in *Munro v Southern Dairies* (extracted [18.70]).

Statutory authorisation

[18.145] It is a defence to an action for nuisance that the legislature authorised the commission of the nuisance. It is a fundamental principle of statutory interpretation that legislation does not override common law rights unless there is clear language to this effect. Therefore it will not, in itself, be sufficient for an activity in general to be authorised by statute, rather the act which creates the nuisance must either be expressly or impliedly authorised or the nuisance must be a necessary incident of the authorised activity. This is a matter of statutory construction. In the case of *Allen v Gulf Oil Refining Company* [1981] 2 WLR 188 the statute authorised the compulsory acquisition of land for the purpose of constructing and operating an oil refinery. An action in nuisance was brought in respect of the smell, noise and vibrations caused by the operation of the refinery. The House of Lords found that whilst the statute did not expressly confer authority to commit the alleged nuisances, if it was the case that the nuisances arose as part of the inevitable result of operating a refinery, then power to construct and operate the refinery must, by necessary implication, include authority to commit the nuisances. If it were otherwise there would have been no point in authorising the construction of the refinery.

When an activity is authorised by legislation, the defence will nevertheless not be successful if the activity which is authorised could have reasonably been performed without the commission of nuisance, for example, by adopting one of several methods of performing a specific task. Similarly, if the creation of the nuisance was as a result of the exercise of want of reasonable care, that is, negligence in performing the authorised activity, the fact that the activity was authorised by statute will not relieve the defendant from liability. The defendant bears the onus of proving that the activity, though it may be authorised by legislation, could not have reasonably been performed without the commission of the nuisance. The defendant was unable to do this in *York Bros (Trading) Pty Ltd v Commissioner of Main Roads* [1983] 1 NSWLR 391. The defendant road authority had built a road bridge across a navigable river obstructing its flow. The authority unsuccessfully argued that it had power pursuant to statute to build and maintain roads and bridges. It was held that the defendant could have reasonably built the bridge in a different way, or in a different place, without causing a nuisance. The general authorisation of the construction of a bridge did not provide a defence. However, in *Nalder v Commissioner for Railways* [1983] 1 Qd R 620, the court held that due to the unreasonable expense that would be incurred in building the railway line in another location, the nuisance was authorised by the statute in question.

REMEDIES

Three remedies are available in the case of nuisance: damages; an injunction; or an abatement of the nuisance.

Damages

Test of Remoteness

Before a plaintiff is able to recover damages in respect of an action for nuisance, the test of remoteness, as applied to cases of negligence, is applied to both the nuisance and the resultant injury.

"Wagon Mound" (No 2)

[18.160] *Overseas Tankship (UK) Ltd v Miller Steamship Co Pty Ltd ("Wagon Mound" (No 2))* [1967] 1 AC 617 Privy Council

[This was an appeal from the Supreme Court of New South Wales. The facts are outlined at [13.175]-[13.180].

LORD REID: 639 The next argument was that at all events the measure of damages is the same throughout the law of tort. But there are many special features in various kinds of tort, and again their Lordships do not find it necessary to make the extensive investigations which would be required before reaching a conclusion on this matter.

Comparing nuisance with negligence the main argument for the respondent was that in negligence foreseeability is an essential element in determining liability and therefore it is logical that foreseeability should also be an essential element in determining the amount of damages: but negligence is not an essential element in determining liability for nuisance and therefore it is illogical to bring in foreseeability when determining the amount of damages. It is quite true that negligence is not an essential element in nuisance. Nuisance is a term used to cover a wide variety of tortious acts or omissions and in many negligence in the narrow sense is not essential. An occupier may incur liability for the emission of noxious fumes or noise although he has used the utmost care in building and using his premises. The amount of fumes or noise which he can lawfully emit is a question of degree and he or his advisers may have miscalculated what can be justified. Or he may deliberately obstruct the highway adjoining his premises to a greater degree than is permissible, hoping that no one will object. On the other hand the emission of fumes or noise or the obstruction of the adjoining highway may often be the result of pure negligence on his part: there are many cases (for example, *Dollman v Hillman* [1941] 1 All ER 355 (CA)) where precisely the same facts will establish liability both in nuisance and in negligence. And although negligence may not be necessary, fault of some kind is almost always necessary and fault generally involves foreseeability, for example, in cases like *Sedleigh-Denfield v O'Callaghan* [1940] AC 880; 56 TLR 887; [1940] 3 All ER 349 the fault is in failing to abate the nuisance of the existence of which the defender is or ought to be aware as likely to cause damage to his neighbour. (Their Lordships express no opinion about cases like *Wringe v Cohen* [1940] 1 KB 229; [1939] 4 All ER 241; 56 TLR 101 (CA), on which neither counsel relied.) The present case is one of creating a danger to persons or property in navigable waters (equivalent to a highway) and there it is admitted that fault is essential – in this case the negligent discharge of the oil.

> But how are we to determine whether a state of affairs in or near a highway is a danger? This depends, I think, on whether injury may reasonably be foreseen. If you take all the cases in the books, you will find that if the state of affairs is such that injury may reasonably be anticipated to persons using the highway it is public nuisance: per Lord Denning MR in *Morton v Wheeler* (unreported, CA, 31 January 1956).

So in the class of nuisance which includes this case foreseeability is an essential element in determining liability.

It could not be right to discriminate between different cases of nuisance so as to make foreseeability a necessary element in determining damages in those cases where it is a necessary element in determining liability, but not in others. So the choice is between it being a necessary element in all cases of nuisance or in none. In their Lordships' judgment the similarities between nuisance and other forms of tort to which *The "Wagon Mound" (No 1)* [1961] AC 388 applies far outweigh any differences,

"Wagon Mound" (No 2) cont.

and they must therefore hold that the judgment appealed from is wrong on this branch of the case. It is not sufficient that the injury suffered by the respondents' vessels was the direct result of the nuisance if that injury was in the relevant sense unforeseeable.

[18.165] **Notes&Questions**

As far as assessment of damages is concerned a defendant will, upon the basis of the test of remoteness of damage, only be liable for that damage which was reasonably foreseeable. Consequently, if the defendant creates a nuisance and in doing so causes material damage to the plaintiff's property, the defendant will not be liable if the damage could not have been reasonably foreseen. This was the case in *Savage v Fairclough* [2000] Env LR 183 (CA) in which a pig farmer had sought the advice of an agronomist in respect of the use of pig manure and inorganic fertilizers on his fields. The spreading of the fertilizers accorded with what was regarded as good farming practice at the time. Nitrates from the fertilizers in fact resulted in contamination of the local water supply. The English Court of Appeal concluded that based on the advice of the agronomist and good farming practice at the time, the defendant could not have foreseen the contamination of the water.

Assessment of damages

Quantum of damages will depend upon the type of damage suffered. Damages may therefore be awarded to compensate for physical damage to property as well as for financial loss such as diminution in the value of the property and loss of trade. If the claim of nuisance is based solely upon interference with the plaintiff's interest in use and enjoyment of his or her property, the court will award an amount of damages for the subjective experience of the plaintiff. Damages will be assessed for both past and future damage caused by the nuisance. However, if the nuisance is likely to continue, the plaintiff may seek an injunction, either in addition to or in substitution of damages, and if successful the award of damages will be limited to the past nuisance.

In *Bone v Seale* [1975] 1 WLR 797, the plaintiffs were awarded substantial damages for loss of amenity caused by smells emanating from the defendant's pig farm over a period of 12½ years. The nuisance caused no diminution in value of the properties. On appeal to the Court of Appeal on the quantum of damages, Stephenson LJ (Scarman and Ormrod LJJ agreeing) said (at 803):

> It is difficult to find an analogy to damages for interference with the enjoyment of property. … Is it possible to equate loss of sense of smell as a result of the negligence of a defendant motor driver with having to put up with positive smells as a result of a nuisance created by a negligent neighbour? There is, as it seems to me, some parallel between the loss of amenity which is caused by personal injury and the loss of amenity which is caused by a nuisance of this kind. If a parallel is drawn between those two losses, it is at once confirmed that this figure is much too high. It is the kind of figure that would only be given for a serious and permanent loss of amenity as the result of a very serious injury, perhaps in the case of a young person. Here we have to remember that the loss of amenity which has to be quantified in pounds and pence extends over a long period–a period of twelve and a half years–but it must not take account of any future loss.

[18.175] **Notes&Questions**

1. The English Court of Appeal recently dealt with the issue of whether personal injury damages are recoverable in public nuisance, concluding that they can be awarded. In the case of *In re Corby Group Litigation* [2009] 2 WLR 609, 18 individuals who were born with deformities sued the city council in negligence and public nuisance. They claimed that their deformities resulted from their mothers' exposure whilst pregnant to toxic materials that the Council allowed to escape from land that that they were reclaiming and decontaminating. Authority also exists in Australia allowing the recovery for personal injury damages as a result of a public nuisance: see *Cartwright v McLain & Long Pty Ltd* (1979) 143 CLR 549 (pedestrian slipped on oil on a footpath that had escaped from a disused service station site), *Volman t/as Volman Engineering v Lobb* [2005] NSWCA 348 (plaintiff slipped on a mud covered footpath caused by construction on the defendant's land). However, the ability to award personal injury damages in a case of public nuisance was not in issue in either case.
2. In respect of private nuisance however, English authority is that personal injury damages cannot be recovered as private nuisance protects the right in or enjoyment of the land and the more appropriate action for personal injury damages is negligence: see *Hunter v Canary Wharf Ltd* [1997] AC 655; *Transco v Stockport Metropolitan Borough Council* [2004] 2 AC 1. In comparison there is dicta to the effect that personal injury damages may be recoverable in Australia. Windeyer J in *Benning v Wong* (1969) 122 CLR 249, at 318 stating, "[i]n nuisance [the] claim would not only be for an injurious affection of his land diminishing the value of his interest in it ... I see no reason why ... damages should not extend to any personal harm the nuisance has there caused him." For further discussion of this issue refer to Davies, "Private Nuisance, Fault and Personal Injuries" (1990) 20 WAL Rev 129.
3. If personal injuries damages are awarded, will the Civil Liability Acts apply to the award? Generally, limitations on damages awards under the legislation will apply unless excluded, for example, unless it can be proven that the nuisance was committed with intent to cause injury: see [3.180] Notes 2and 5.

INJUNCTION

In determining whether to issue an injunction in respect of a successful nuisance action, the issue which courts face is whether damages will suffice to compensate the injury caused by the nuisance. If damages will suffice an injunction will not be granted.

Interlocutory injunction

Prior to trial the plaintiff may seek an interlocutory injunction to restrain the continuing nuisance until the matter can be resolved. To gain an interlocutory injunction, the plaintiff must satisfy the court, pursuant to principles of equity, that there is "a serious question to be tried" (that is, the defendant's conduct likely constitutes a nuisance) and that it is, on the "balance of convenience", proper to restrain the defendant until that question is determined at trial *Australian Coarse Grains Pool Pty Ltd v Barley Marketing Boards* (1985) 157 CLR 605. A court will not grant an injunction if the interference is regarded as trivial or temporary and in these circumstances damages will be the appropriate award.

Permanent injunction

At the trial, providing the plaintiff is successful and the nuisance is continuing, the court may grant a permanent injunction. In order for a permanent injunction to be issued, the court will need to be satisfied that a nuisance exists, that the nuisance is a substantial interference and that the nuisance is likely to recur or continue.

Where a nuisance has not yet occurred but is threatened, a quia timet injunction maybe granted to prevent the nuisance ever taking place. For example, in *Miller v Shoalhaven Shire Council* (1957) 2 LGRA 46, a quia timet injunction was issued to prevent the construction of a public urinal and in *York Bros (Trading) Pty Ltd v Commissioner of Main Roads* [1983] 1 NSWLR 391 (discussed at [18.145]), a quia timet injunction was issued to prevent the construction of a bridge which would if built have interfered with the water flow. This type of injunction will not be granted unless the nuisance is imminent or highly likely to occur and damages would not suffice. It should be noted that authority does exist that a quia timet injunction may be granted in circumstances which do not involve an imminent harm or that it is highly likely: *Barbagallo v J & F Catelan Pty Ltd* [1986] 1 Qd R 245. However, authority after this case seriously questions its correctness, see for example *Wherry v KB Hutcherson Pty Ltd* [1987] Aust Torts Reports 80-107 (SC NSW); *Taylor v City of Perth* [1988] Aust Torts Reports 80-191 (FC WA) (when dealing with an interlocutory injunction).

Abatement or self-help

[18.195] A person whose land is interfered with or is threatened with interference, can take steps to help him or herself by abating the interference; that is, by removal of the offending interference (for example, by cutting encroaching branches or roots of trees).

In exercising abatement the plaintiff should exercise a method that is reasonable in the given circumstances (see *Richter v Risby* [1987] Tas R 36, where the removal of an environmental protestor by force was found not to constitute reasonable abatement). This may involve taking steps upon his or her own land, or it can include entering the land of the defendant to abate the nuisance. However, entry upon another's land to abate a nuisance will only be adjudged as reasonable if there are strong reasons, and notice of entry will be required (*Lemmon v Webb* [1895] AC 1 at 8; *Trajan v Ware* [1957] VR 200), unless it is a situation of imminent danger to life or health (*Jones v Williams* (1843) 11 M & W 176 at 1821; 152 ER 764).

The general rule is that the costs of abatement are not recoverable (*Barbagallo v J & F Catelan* [1986] 1 Qd R 245; *Young v Wheeler* (1987) Aust Torts Reports 80-126), but if the situation is that the action was taken to mitigate the plaintiff's damages, then he or she will be able to recover the cost of abatement as part of reasonable mitigation (*Proprietors of Strata Plan No 14198 v Cowell* (1991) ATR 81-083).

If an individual chooses to exercise the privilege of abatement, he or she is exercising an alternative to legal proceedings. That is, the plaintiff will not be able to institute proceedings except in respect of damage that has occurred prior to the abatement (*Young v Wheeler* [1987] Aust Torts Reports 80-126 (NSWSC); *Richmond City Council v Scantelbury* [1991] 2 VR 38). The converse is also true: where an individual institutes proceedings in respect to a nuisance he or she is unable to exercise the privilege of abatement (*Burton v Winters* [1993] 1 WLR 1077 (CA)). The failure to abate does not affect any right to seek damages or an injunction (*Lawlor v Johnson* [1905] VLR 714).

Finally, it should be noted that prudence is advocated in the exercise of this remedy. In *Trajan v Ware* [1957] VR 200 (citing *Lagan Navigation Co v Lambeg Bleaching, Dyeing & Finishing Co Ltd* [1927] AC 226 at 244-245) the Victorian Supreme Court cautioned against the use of this self-help mechanism:

> The law does not favour the remedy of abatement in preference to legal action ... and requires strong reason to justify it when it involves entering upon the land of another.

INDEX

D

O

P

R